THE MACMILLAN

GW00792115

SMALL CRAFT

ALMANAC
2000

EDITORS

Basil D'Oliveira, Brian Goulder & Edward Lee-Elliott

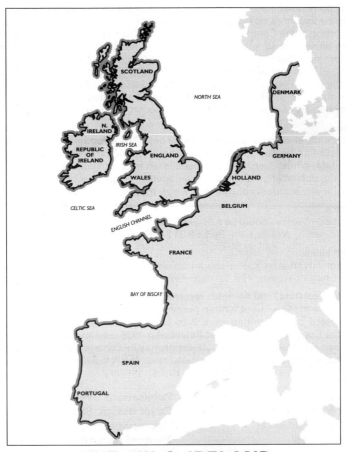

THE UK & IRELAND
DENMARK TO GIBRALTAR

THE
MACMILLAN·REEDS
SMALL CRAFT
ALMANAC
2000

Editors: Basil D'Oliveira, Brian Goulder & Edward Lee-Elliott

The Editors would like to thank the many individuals and official bodies who have kindly provided essential information and much advice in the preparation of this Almanac. They include the UK Hydrographic Office, Trinity House, Northern Lighthouse Board, Irish Lights, HM Nautical Almanac Office, HM Stationery Office, HM Customs, Meteorological Office, Proudman Oceanographic Laboratory, British Telecom, BBC and IBA, Maritime and Coastguard Agency, RNLI, Port of London Authority, Associated British Ports, countless Harbour Masters, and the many individuals who have so generously helped, advised and assisted.

The tidal predictions have been computed by the Proudman Oceanographic Laboratory. Copyright reserved. Tidal curves, streams and secondary port data are Crown Copyright and are reproduced with the permission of the Controller of HM Stationery Office and the Hydrographer of the Navy. Sun and moon phases are supplied by HM Nautical Almanac Office and the Particle Physics and Astronomy Research Council. Copyright reserved. Data contained in the Lights, Radio and Weather sections is largely drawn from *Admiralty Lists of Lights* and *Admiralty Lists of Radio Signals* with the permission of the Controller of HM Stationery Office and the Hydrographer of the Navy. **Warning:** The UK Hydrographic Office has not verified the reproduced data and does not accept any liability for the accuracy of reproduction or any modifications made thereafter.

Important note

This Almanac is intended as an aid to navigation only. The information contained within should not solely be relied on for navigational use, rather it should be used in conjunction with official hydrographic data. Whilst every care has been taken in compiling the information contained in this Almanac, the publishers, editors and their agents accept no responsibility for any errors or omissions, or for any accidents or mishaps which may arise from its use.

Correspondence

Letters on nautical matters should be addressed to: The Editors, Macmillan Reeds Almanacs, 41 Arbor Lane, Winnersh, Wokingham, Berks RG11 5JE

Advertisement sales

Enquiries about advertising space should be addressed to: Communications Management International, Chiltern House, 120 Eskdale Avenue, Chesham, Buckinghamshire HP5 3BD

Production control: Chris Stevens

Cartography & production: Jamie Russell, Chris Stevens, Garold West

Advertisement sales:

Sales manager: Elizabeth Tildesley

Sales co-ordinator: Anne Bailey

Production: Ian Garner

Publications director: Martyn Gunn

Cover design: Slatter-Anderson

Cover photography: Detlef Jens

Nautical Data Limited, Dudley House, 12 North Street, Emsworth, Hampshire, PO10 7DQ, UK *Tel:* +44 (0)1243 377977 *Fax:* +44 (0)1243 379136 www.nauticaldata.com

CONTENTS

DISTANCES BETWEEN STRATEGIC PORTS

Distances given are the shortest practicable deep-water sea routes whilst abiding by inshore traffic zone regulations

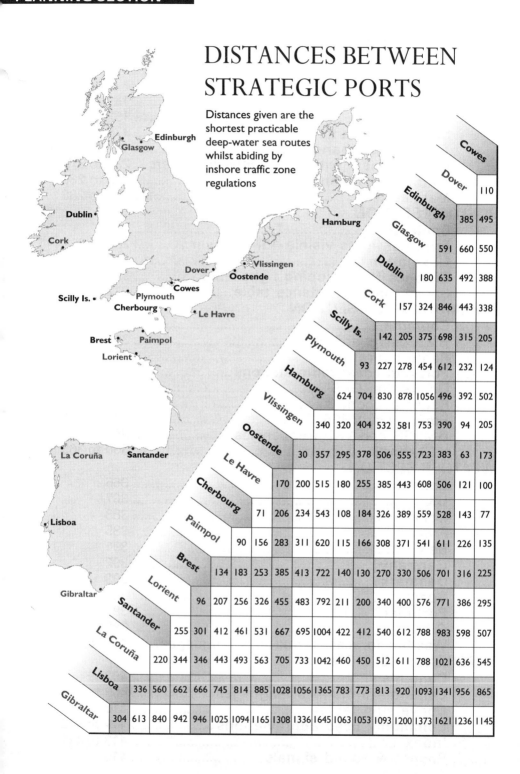

From \ To	Lisboa	La Coruña	Santander	Lorient	Brest	Paimpol	Cherbourg	Le Havre	Oostende	Vlissingen	Hamburg	Plymouth	Scilly Is.	Cork	Dublin	Glasgow	Edinburgh	Dover	Cowes
Dover																			110
Edinburgh																		385	495
Glasgow																	591	660	550
Dublin																180	635	492	388
Cork															157	324	846	443	338
Scilly Is.														142	205	375	698	315	205
Plymouth													93	227	278	454	612	232	124
Hamburg												624	704	830	878	1056	496	392	502
Vlissingen											340	320	404	532	581	753	390	94	205
Oostende										30	357	295	378	506	555	723	383	63	173
Le Havre									170	200	515	180	255	385	443	608	506	121	100
Cherbourg								71	206	234	543	108	184	326	389	559	528	143	77
Paimpol							90	156	283	311	620	115	166	308	371	541	611	226	135
Brest						134	183	253	385	413	722	140	130	270	330	506	701	316	225
Lorient					96	207	256	326	455	483	792	211	200	340	400	576	771	386	295
Santander				255	301	412	461	531	667	695	1004	422	412	540	612	788	983	598	507
La Coruña			220	344	346	443	493	563	705	733	1042	460	450	512	611	788	1021	636	545
Lisboa		336	560	662	666	745	814	885	1028	1056	1365	783	773	813	920	1093	1341	956	865
Gibraltar	304	613	840	942	946	1025	1094	1165	1308	1336	1645	1063	1053	1093	1200	1373	1621	1236	1145

PLANNING SECTION

CONTENTS

TIDAL NOTES

The tidal data herein is supplied by The Proudman Oceanographic Laboratory whose work is accepted as authoritative. Please note that heights and times of tides can be considerably affected by barometric pressure and prevailing winds.

When there are two low waters, *eg* Portland, the time shown is for the first. Where there are two high waters, *eg* Southampton, the time shown is for the first. However, for Rotterdam the low water time shown is the mean of the two low waters.

WAYPOINT WARNING

Always check on an Admiralty chart before navigating between two waypoints to make sure that the track is safe. The tracks shown in dotted lines on the Area Planners pass close to dangers. If a strong wind puts a waypoint on a lee shore it is prudent to create a new waypoint to weather.

Check the actual location of the waypoint, eg No 27 is 1M east of Poole Fairway Buoy, not at the buoy itself. Note that floating marks can shift on the tide up to three times the depth of the water.

SMALL CRAFT ALMANAC STANDARD PORTS

Defined positions of height predictions:

Aberdeen	57°09'·00N	02°05'·00W
Antwerpen	51°21'·00N	04°14'·00E
Avonmouth	51°31'·00N	02°43'·00W
Belfast	54°36'·00N	05°55'·00W
Bremerhaven	53°32'·00N	08°35'·00E
Brest	48°23'·00N	04°30'·00W
Calais	50°58'·00N	01°51'·00E
Cherbourg	49°39'·00N	01°37'·00W
Cobh	51°50'·00N	08°18'·00W
Cuxhaven	53°52'·00N	08°43'·00E
Dieppe	49°56'·00N	01°05'·00E
Dover	51°07'·00N	01°19'·00E
Dublin	53°21'·00N	06°13'·00W
Dunkerque	51°03'·00N	02°22'·00E
Esbjerg	55°29'·00N	08°28'·00E
Galway	53°16'·00N	09°03'·00W
Gibraltar	36°08'·00N	05°21'·00W
Greenock	55°58'·00N	04°49'·00W
Harwich	51°57'·00N	01°17'·00E
Helgoland	54°11'·00N	07°54'·00E
Hoek van Holland	51°59'·00N	04°07'·00E
Holyhead	53°19'·00N	04°37'·00W
Immingham	53°38'·00N	00°11'·00W
Isles of Scilly	49°55'·00N	06°19'·00W
Le Havre	49°29'·00N	00°06'·00E
Leith	55°59'·00N	03°11'·00W
Lerwick	60°09·00'N	01°08·00'W
Lisboa	38°42'·00N	09°08'·00W
Liverpool	53°25'·00N	03°00'·00W
London Bridge	51°30'·00N	00°05'·00W
Londonderry	55°00'·00N	07°19'·00W
Lowestoft	52°28'·00N	01°45'·00E
Margate	51°24'·00N	01°23'·00E
Milford Haven	51°42'·00N	05°03'·00W
Oban	56°25'·00N	05°29'·00W
Plymouth	50°22'·00N	04°11'·00W
Pointe de Grave	45°34'·00N	01°04'·00W
Poole	50°42'·00N	01°59'·00W
Portland	50°34'·00N	02°26'·00W
Portsmouth	50°48'·00N	01°07'·00W
River Tees	54°38'·00N	01°09'·00W
River Tyne	55°00'·00N	01°26'·00W
Rosyth	56°01'·00N	03°27'·00W
Rotterdam	51°55'·00N	04°30'·00E
St Helier - Jersey	49°11'·00N	02°07'·00W
St Malo	48°38'·00N	02°02'·00W
Sheerness	51°27'·00N	00°45'·00E
Shoreham	50°50'·00N	00°15'·00W
Southampton	50°54'·00N	01°24'·00W
Swansea	51°37'·00N	03°55'·00W
Ullapool	57°54'·00N	05°09'·00W
Vlissingen (*Flushing*)	51°27'·00N	03°36'·00E
Walton on Naze	51°51'·00N	01°16'·00E
Wick	58°26'·00N	03°05'·00W

DISTANCE TO HORIZON TABLE

feet	metres	distance NM	feet	metres	distance NM
1	0.31	1.1	41	12.51	7.3
3	0.92	2.0	43	13.12	7.5
5	1.53	2.6	45	13.73	7.7
7	2.14	3.0	47	14.34	7.8
9	2.75	3.4	49	14.95	8.0
11	3.36	3.8	51	15.56	8.2
13	3.97	4.1	53	16.17	8.3
15	4.58	4.4	55	16.78	8.5
17	5.19	4.7	57	17.39	8.6
19	5.80	5.0	59	18.00	8.8
21	6.41	5.2	61	18.61	8.9
23	7.02	5.5	63	19.22	9.1
25	7.63	5.7	65	19.83	9.2
27	8.24	5.9	67	20.44	9.4
29	8.85	6.2	69	21.05	9.5
31	9.46	6.4	71	21.66	9.6
33	10.07	6.6	73	22.27	9.8
35	10.68	6.8	75	22.88	9.9
37	11.29	7.0	77	23.49	10.0
39	11.90	7.1	79	24.10	10.2

SOUTH COAST OF ENGLAND Time Zone UT

St Mary's * Plymouth * Dartmouth * Portland * Poole * Southampton * Portsmouth * Shoreham * Dover

TIDE TABLES JANUARY 2000

ST MARY'S, SCILLY Time m	PLYMOUTH Time m	DARTMOUTH Time m	PORTLAND Time m	POOLE Time m	SOUTHAMPTON Time m	PORTSMOUTH Time m	SHOREHAM Time m	DOVER Time m	Day
0026 4.4	0115 4.4	0130 3.9	0208 1.4	0002 1.1	0709 3.9	0008 1.7	0049 1.7	0136 2.1	1 SA
0652 2.0	0727 2.2	0717 2.0	0715 0.9	0837 1.8	1234 1.7	0732 4.1	0654 5.2	0648 5.6	
1255 4.5	1337 4.5	1351 4.0	1405 1.5	1243 1.1	1938 3.7	1250 1.8	1327 1.7	1413 1.9	
1929 1.8	2003 2.0	1956 1.8	1951 0.7	2043 1.6		2001 3.8	1934 4.9	1932 5.4	
0130 4.5	0224 4.6	0238 4.1	0311 1.5	0107 1.1	0103 1.7	0115 1.7	0153 1.7	0242 2.0	2 SU
0754 1.9	0832 2.0	0826 1.9	0823 0.8	0845 1.8	0806 3.9	0827 4.2	0756 5.2	0753 5.7	
1355 4.6	1445 4.6	1500 4.1	1510 1.5	1339 1.1	1334 1.6	1349 1.7	1427 1.6	1516 1.8	
2023 1.7	2100 1.8	2059 1.7	2045 0.6	2045 1.7	2034 3.8	2057 3.9	2033 5.0	2030 5.6	
0224 4.8	0321 4.8	0337 4.2	0403 1.6	0159 1.0	0159 1.6	0209 1.6	0250 1.6	0342 1.9	3 M
0846 1.7	0927 1.8	0924 1.7	0917 0.7	0845 1.8	0853 4.0	0915 4.2	0850 5.3	0848 5.8	
1445 4.8	1540 4.8	1559 4.2	1606 1.6	1425 1.0	1425 1.4	1437 1.5	1518 1.4	1609 1.6	
2109 1.5	2151 1.6	2152 1.5	2133 0.5	2046 1.8	2121 4.0	2142 4.1	2123 5.2	2118 5.8	
0309 5.0	0407 5.0	0427 4.4	0448 1.7	0244 1.0	0248 1.4	0256 1.5	0339 1.4	0432 1.7	4 TU
0931 1.5	1014 1.6	1015 1.5	1004 0.6	0847 1.9	0932 4.1	0957 4.3	0938 5.5	0935 6.0	
1528 5.0	1626 5.0	1648 4.4	1657 1.6	1507 1.0	1510 1.2	1520 1.3	1602 1.2	1654 1.5	
2151 1.4	2234 1.4	2238 1.4	2217 0.4	2052 1.8	2159 4.1	2223 4.2	2207 5.5	2200 6.0	
0348 5.2	0448 5.2	0512 4.6	0531 1.9	0324 0.9	0328 1.2	0338 1.3	0421 1.3	0514 1.5	5 W
1011 1.4	1057 1.4	1059 1.3	1047 0.5	0855 1.9	1007 4.2	1033 4.4	1019 5.7	1016 6.1	
1606 5.1	1706 5.1	1731 4.5	1743 1.7	1546 0.8	1547 1.0	1600 1.2	1641 1.1	1733 1.4	
2228 1.3	2315 1.3	2318 1.2	2300 0.4	2105 1.9	2235 4.2	2300 4.3	2246 5.7	2239 6.2	
0425 5.3	0525 5.3	0549 4.7	0613 1.9	0402 0.9	0406 1.1	0417 1.3	0457 1.2	0552 1.3	6 TH ●
1048 1.2	1137 1.2	1138 1.2	1129 0.4	0910 2.0	1040 4.3	1109 4.5	1056 5.8	1054 6.2	
1642 5.2	1745 5.2	1810 4.6	1827 1.8	1621 0.8	1622 0.9	1636 1.1	1715 1.0	1809 1.3	
2303 1.2	2354 1.2	2355 1.2	2340 0.3	2129 2.0	2309 4.3	2337 4.4	2322 5.8	2314 6.3	
0500 5.4	0601 5.4	0626 4.8	0653 2.0	0438 0.8	0440 1.0	0453 1.2	0531 1.1	0628 1.2	7 F
1123 1.2	1216 1.1	1215 1.1	1208 0.4	0934 2.0	1112 4.4	1143 4.5	1129 5.9	1128 6.3	
1716 5.2	1822 5.2	1847 4.6	1909 1.8	1655 0.7	1656 0.7	1710 1.0	1748 1.0	1844 1.2	
2337 1.2				2204 2.0	2343 4.4		2355 5.9	2348 6.4	
0533 5.4	0032 1.1	0029 1.1	0019 0.3	0511 0.8	0515 0.9	0013 4.5	0604 1.2	0704 1.1	8 SA
1157 1.1	0637 5.4	0659 4.8	0731 2.0	1007 2.0	1146 4.4	0526 1.2	1201 5.9	1200 6.3	
1748 5.2	1254 1.1	1250 1.0	1245 0.3	1728 0.7	1731 0.7	1216 4.5	1821 1.0	1918 1.2	
	1857 5.1	1921 4.6	1948 1.8	2248 2.0		1743 1.0			
0012 1.2	0109 1.1	0104 1.1	0055 0.3	0545 0.8	0016 4.4	0048 4.5	0028 5.9	0021 6.4	9 SU
0606 5.4	0711 5.4	0732 4.8	0806 2.0	1048 2.0	0550 0.9	0559 1.2	0637 1.2	0739 1.1	
1232 1.1	1330 1.1	1325 1.0	1320 0.3	1802 0.7	1219 4.4	1248 4.5	1235 5.9	1232 6.2	
1822 5.2	1931 5.1	1953 4.6	2023 1.8	2339 2.0	1804 0.7	1816 1.0	1855 1.0	1952 1.2	
0045 1.2	0144 1.2	0139 1.1	0128 0.3	0620 0.8	0049 4.3	0121 4.5	0101 5.9	0054 6.4	10 M
0640 5.4	0743 5.3	0806 4.8	0839 1.9	1139 2.0	0625 0.9	0633 1.2	0713 1.2	0815 1.2	
1307 1.2	1406 1.2	1400 1.1	1351 0.3	1837 0.7	1252 4.3	1321 4.5	1311 5.8	1304 6.2	
1857 5.2	2002 5.0	2026 4.5	2056 1.7		1839 0.7	1850 1.0	1931 1.0	2027 1.2	
0121 1.3	0218 1.3	0212 1.2	0157 0.4	0036 1.9	0124 4.3	0154 4.4	0135 5.8	0126 6.3	11 TU
0716 5.3	0814 5.2	0839 4.8	0910 1.8	0655 0.8	0701 1.0	0707 1.2	0750 1.2	0849 1.2	
1344 1.3	1439 1.3	1436 1.2	1421 0.3	1242 1.9	1330 4.3	1357 4.4	1348 5.7	1339 6.1	
1933 5.1	2032 4.9	2100 4.4	2128 1.7	1915 0.8	1914 0.8	1926 1.1	2009 1.0	2100 1.3	
0159 1.4	0251 1.4	0248 1.3	0227 0.4	0147 1.9	0203 4.2	0231 4.4	0211 5.8	0200 6.3	12 W
0755 5.2	0845 5.1	0913 4.6	0940 1.7	0734 0.9	0739 1.0	0745 1.3	0830 1.2	0925 1.4	
1424 1.4	1514 1.4	1513 1.3	1454 0.4	1359 1.9	1410 4.2	1437 4.3	1428 5.6	1416 6.0	
2015 4.9	2104 4.8	2137 4.3	2202 1.6	1955 0.8	1953 1.0	2005 1.2	2049 1.1	2137 1.5	
0241 1.5	0327 1.6	0325 1.5	0300 0.5	0313 1.9	0247 4.2	0314 4.3	0251 5.7	0239 6.2	13 TH
0839 5.1	0918 5.0	0950 4.5	1013 1.6	0820 0.9	0821 1.3	0829 1.4	0913 1.2	1003 1.5	
1509 1.5	1553 1.6	1553 1.5	1534 0.4	1533 1.8	1457 4.0	1524 4.2	1513 5.5	1502 5.9	
2102 4.8	2142 4.7	2217 4.2	2242 1.5	2043 0.9	2035 1.2	2051 1.3	2133 1.2	2218 1.7	
0330 1.7	0409 1.7	0408 1.7	0343 0.5	0452 1.9	0339 4.1	0405 4.3	0337 5.5	0327 6.1	14 F
0931 4.9	1000 4.9	1032 4.3	1054 1.6	0914 1.0	0910 1.4	0921 1.6	1003 1.3	1048 1.6	
1603 1.6	1640 1.7	1639 1.6	1627 0.4	1719 1.8	1555 3.9	1620 4.1	1603 5.3	1559 5.8	
2200 4.6	2233 4.6	2306 4.1	2335 1.5	2142 0.9	2130 1.4	2148 1.4	2226 1.3	2309 1.8	
0430 1.8	0503 1.9	0502 1.8	0442 0.6	0633 1.8	0440 4.0	0506 4.2	0435 5.3	0427 5.9	15 SA
1033 4.8	1057 4.7	1127 4.2	1154 1.5	1022 1.1	1013 1.6	1027 1.6	1105 1.4	1145 1.8	
1709 1.7	1741 1.8	1739 1.7	1738 0.5	1902 1.7	1704 3.9	1727 4.0	1707 5.1	1706 5.7	
2311 4.6	2342 4.5			2255 1.0	2240 1.6	2300 1.5	2334 1.4		

● ● Time: UT. For British Summer Time (shaded) March 26th to October 29th ADD ONE HOUR ● ●

JANUARY 2000 TIDE TABLES

•• Time: UT. For British Summer Time (shaded) March 26th to October 29TH ADD ONE HOUR ••

	ST MARY'S SCILLY		PLYMOUTH		DARTMOUTH		PORTLAND		POOLE		SOUTHAMPTON		PORTSMOUTH		SHOREHAM		DOVER	
	Time	m	Time	m	Time	m	Time	m	Time	m	Time	m	Time	m	Time	m	Time	m
16 SU	0545	1.8	0612	2.0	0012	4.0	0045	1.4	0754	1.8	0551	4.0	0615	4.2	0545	5.2	0013	1.9
	1148	4.8	1215	4.7	0611	1.9	0603	0.7	1140	1.0	1127	1.6	1145	1.6	1219	1.4	0536	5.9
	1824	1.7	1854	1.8	1241	4.2	1314	1.5	2013	1.7	1820	3.9	1840	4.0	1822	5.1	1256	1.8
					1852	1.7	1858	0.5			2357	1.6					1818	5.7
17 M	0029	4.7	0108	4.6	0134	4.1	0209	1.5	0009	1.0	0702	4.1	0015	1.5	0051	1.4	0130	1.9
	0701	1.7	0733	1.8	0731	1.8	0730	0.7	0835	1.9	1242	1.4	0725	4.3	0700	5.3	0648	5.9
	1303	4.9	1342	4.7	1408	4.2	1442	1.5	1248	1.0	1934	4.0	1255	1.5	1336	1.3	1413	1.7
	1935	1.5	2014	1.6	2012	1.6	2015	0.5	2042	1.8			1957	4.1	1938	5.4	1930	5.8
18 TU	0139	4.9	0226	4.8	0252	4.3	0330	1.7	0115	0.9	0113	1.4	0123	1.4	0204	1.2	0248	1.7
	0810	1.4	0851	1.5	0848	0.6	0845	1.9	0805	4.2	0835	4.4	0811	5.6	0757	6.1		
	1410	5.1	1459	4.9	1527	4.4	1603	1.7	1349	0.8	1351	1.2	1359	1.2	1445	1.1	1527	1.4
	2039	1.2	2127	1.3	2126	1.3	2122	0.4	2045	1.9	2038	4.2	2106	4.3	2046	5.7	2036	6.1
19 W	0241	5.3	0335	5.1	0404	4.6	0440	1.8	0216	0.8	0220	1.1	0227	1.2	0310	1.0	0359	1.4
	0912	1.1	1001	1.2	1002	1.2	0953	0.5	0845	2.0	0900	4.4	0933	4.6	0913	5.9	0900	6.3
	1509	5.4	1609	5.1	1636	4.7	1713	1.8	1447	0.7	1453	0.8	1459	1.0	1545	0.8	1635	1.2
	2136	0.9	2232	1.0	2234	1.0	2221	0.3	2048	2.0	2133	4.4	2203	4.6	2147	6.0	2136	6.4
20 TH ○	0336	5.6	0439	5.3	0505	4.9	0542	2.0	0311	0.7	0320	0.8	0324	1.0	0409	0.8	0502	1.1
	1008	0.8	1103	0.8	1105	0.8	1050	0.3	0852	2.1	0951	4.5	1023	4.7	1010	6.2	0957	6.6
	1602	5.6	1712	5.3	1737	4.8	1815	2.0	1539	0.5	1549	0.5	1553	0.7	1641	0.7	1737	1.0
	2230	0.7	2330	0.7	2332	0.7	2314	0.2	2102	2.1	2224	4.6	2252	4.7	2243	6.3	2230	6.7
21 F	0426	5.8	0537	5.5	0602	5.1	0638	2.2	0402	0.6	0416	0.6	0417	0.8	0501	0.7	0600	0.8
	1100	1.4	1159	0.5	1202	0.5	1142	0.2	0910	2.2	1040	4.6	1109	4.8	1102	6.4	1050	6.7
	1651	5.8	1811	5.3	1831	5.0	1910	2.1	1628	0.4	1641	0.3	1643	0.5	1731	0.6	1835	0.8
	2319	0.6							2131	2.2	2313	4.7	2339	4.8	2334	6.4	2320	6.8
22 SA	0514	6.0	0023	0.6	0026	0.5	0003	0.1	0451	0.5	0507	0.4	0506	0.6	0550	0.8	0654	0.7
	1149	0.4	0631	5.6	0651	5.2	0729	2.3	0944	2.2	1127	4.7	1154	4.9	1150	6.5	1140	6.8
	1739	5.8	1251	0.4	1253	0.4	1230	0.1	1714	0.4	1731	0.2	1729	0.4	1818	0.7	1928	0.7
			1903	5.4	1921	5.0	2000	2.2	2219	2.2								
23 SU	0007	0.5	0112	0.5	0112	0.4	0048	0.1	0536	0.5	0001	4.7	0026	4.8	0024	6.5	0007	6.9
	0600	6.0	0720	5.7	0736	5.3	0815	2.3	1036	2.2	0556	0.4	0551	0.6	0637	0.8	0745	0.6
	1236	0.4	1338	0.4	1339	0.3	1315	0.1	1759	0.4	1215	4.6	1239	4.8	1237	6.4	1228	6.8
	1823	5.7	1950	5.3	2005	5.0	2045	2.1	2326	2.1	1817	0.2	1813	0.4	1903	0.7	2015	0.7
24 M	0051	0.6	0157	0.5	0157	0.4	0130	0.1	0620	0.5	0048	4.7	0113	4.8	0109	6.5	0052	6.9
	0644	5.9	0803	5.6	0820	5.2	0857	2.3	1140	2.1	0640	0.4	0633	0.7	0723	0.8	0832	0.6
	1321	0.6	1421	0.5	1420	0.4	1357	0.1	1842	0.5	1301	4.6	1322	4.7	1322	6.3	1313	6.6
	1906	5.5	2031	5.2	2046	4.8	2124	2.0			1900	0.3	1855	0.5	1946	0.7	2058	0.8
25 TU	0134	0.8	0237	0.7	0237	0.6	0211	0.2	0047	2.1	0135	4.6	0200	4.7	0151	6.4	0134	6.8
	0727	5.7	0842	5.4	0900	5.0	0935	2.1	0703	0.6	0722	0.6	0715	0.8	0806	0.9	0915	0.7
	1403	0.8	1500	0.8	1459	0.7	1439	0.2	1259	2.0	1346	4.4	1406	4.6	1407	6.1	1356	6.4
	1948	5.3	2108	5.1	2126	4.6	2201	1.9	1926	0.6	1940	0.5	1937	0.7	2029	0.8	2136	1.0
26 W	0216	1.0	0315	1.0	0313	0.9	0250	0.3	0221	2.0	0221	4.4	0248	4.5	0232	6.2	0215	6.6
	0809	5.4	0917	5.2	0938	4.8	1009	2.0	0749	0.7	0800	0.8	0759	1.0	0849	1.0	0954	0.9
	1445	1.1	1537	1.1	1536	1.0	1518	0.3	1429	1.9	1435	4.2	1452	4.4	1450	5.8	1439	6.2
	2032	5.0	2141	4.8	2203	4.4	2234	1.7	2012	0.7	2018	0.8	2021	0.9	2110	0.9	2210	1.3
27 TH	0258	1.3	0349	1.4	0348	1.2	0327	0.4	0406	1.9	0310	4.2	0341	4.4	0310	5.9	0258	6.3
	0853	5.0	0949	5.0	1012	4.5	1039	1.8	0837	0.9	0839	1.1	0845	1.3	0933	1.2	1033	1.3
	1529	1.5	1612	1.5	1611	1.3	1557	0.4	1614	1.8	1525	4.0	1545	4.1	1531	5.5	1524	5.9
	2118	4.7	2215	4.6	2237	4.1	2307	1.5	2101	0.8	2058	1.1	2108	1.2	2153	1.2	2245	1.6
28 F	0345	1.7	0425	1.8	0425	1.6	0406	0.6	0546	1.8	0401	4.0	0436	4.2	0353	5.6	0346	6.0
	0942	4.7	1025	4.7	1046	4.2	1109	1.6	0930	1.0	0923	1.4	0936	1.6	1021	1.5	1113	1.6
	1619	1.8	1651	1.8	1652	1.7	1639	0.5	1806	1.7	1622	3.8	1648	3.9	1621	5.1	1618	5.6
	2214	4.4	2257	4.4	2317	3.9	2345	1.4	2156	1.0	2147	1.5	2202	1.6	2245	1.5	2325	2.0
29 SA	0442	2.0	0510	2.1	0509	1.9	0452	0.7	0709	1.7	0500	3.8	0532	4.0	0446	5.2	0443	5.7
	1043	4.4	1115	4.5	1130	4.0	1147	1.4	1034	1.1	1019	1.7	1039	1.8	1119	1.8	1202	1.9
	1722	2.0	1745	2.1	1742	1.9	1730	0.6	1937	1.6	1728	3.6	1757	3.7	1722	4.8	1723	5.3
	2326	4.2	2358	4.3					2307	1.1	2249	1.8	2312	1.8	2350	1.8		
30 SU	0554	2.1	0616	2.3	0012	3.8	0039	1.3	0808	1.7	0605	3.7	0633	3.9	0552	4.9	0021	2.2
	1201	4.2	1225	4.3	0611	2.1	0557	0.8	1157	1.2	1127	1.9	1203	1.9	1231	1.9	0554	5.4
	1837	2.1	1857	2.2	1234	3.8	1242	1.3	2029	1.5	1842	3.6	1909	3.6	1837	4.6	1304	2.1
					1852	2.0	1839	0.7									1840	5.2
31 M	0045	4.2	0115	4.3	0123	3.8	0153	1.3	0029	1.2	0003	2.0	0036	1.9	0104	2.0	0134	2.3
	0710	2.1	0736	2.3	0731	2.1	0727	0.8	0839	1.6	0714	3.7	0741	3.8	0707	4.8	0710	5.3
	1318	4.3	1348	4.4	1353	3.8	1400	1.3	1310	1.2	1242	1.9	1318	1.9	1343	1.9	1420	2.2
	1947	2.0	2013	2.1	2010	2.0	1956	0.7	2044	1.5	1954	3.6	2022	3.7	1953	4.7	1953	5.3

SOUTH COAST OF ENGLAND Time Zone UT

St Mary's * Plymouth * Dartmouth * Portland * Poole * Southampton * Portsmouth * Shoreham * Dover

TIDE TABLES FEBRUARY 2000

ST MARY'S, SCILLY Time m	PLYMOUTH Time m	DARTMOUTH Time m	PORTLAND Time m	POOLE Time m	SOUTHAMPTON Time m	PORTSMOUTH Time m	SHOREHAM Time m	DOVER Time m	
0154 4.4	0233 4.5	0241 3.9	0310 1.4	0133 1.2	0115 1.9	0142 1.8	0215 1.9	0257 2.2	**1 TU**
0815 2.0	0847 2.1	0845 2.0	0845 0.7	0845 1.7	0813 3.8	0843 3.9	0816 4.9	0818 5.4	
1421 4.4	1503 4.5	1516 3.9	1523 1.3	1402 1.1	1349 1.7	1413 1.7	1446 1.8	1531 2.0	
2043 1.8	2116 1.9	2116 1.8	2100 0.6	2045 1.6	2053 3.8	2121 3.9	2056 4.9	2052 5.5	
0247 4.7	0335 4.8	0352 4.1	0412 1.6	0223 1.1	0216 1.7	0235 1.7	0312 1.7	0401 1.9	**2 W**
0908 1.7	0945 1.8	0945 1.7	0940 0.6	0845 1.7	0904 3.9	0933 4.0	0915 5.2	0913 5.7	
1509 4.7	1601 4.7	1623 4.1	1629 1.5	1446 1.0	1443 1.5	1458 1.5	1537 1.5	1626 1.7	
2129 1.6	2209 1.6	2209 1.6	2151 0.5	2048 1.8	2139 4.0	2206 4.1	2148 5.3	2139 5.8	
0330 4.9	0424 5.0	0447 4.4	0503 1.7	0305 1.0	0305 1.4	0318 1.5	0358 1.5	0451 1.6	**3 TH**
0951 1.5	1034 1.5	1035 1.4	1027 0.5	0850 1.8	0945 4.1	1013 4.2	1002 5.5	0958 5.9	
1550 4.9	1648 4.9	1713 4.3	1724 1.6	1524 0.9	1528 1.2	1538 1.3	1620 1.2	1712 1.5	
2209 1.3	2254 1.4	2255 1.3	2238 0.4	2058 1.9	2218 4.1	2243 4.3	2229 5.6	2219 6.0	
0408 5.2	0506 5.2	0530 4.6	0551 1.9	0343 0.9	0347 1.2	0357 1.3	0438 1.3	0534 1.3	**4 F**
1030 1.2	1119 1.3	1118 1.2	1109 0.4	0900 1.9	1022 4.2	1048 4.3	1040 5.7	1035 6.0	
1626 5.1	1729 5.0	1755 4.5	1814 1.7	1600 0.8	1606 0.9	1615 1.1	1657 0.9	1752 1.3	
2245 1.2	2337 1.2	2337 1.1	2321 0.3	2116 1.9	2254 4.3	2318 4.4	2306 5.8	2254 6.2	
0442 5.3	0545 5.3	0610 4.7	0637 2.0	0417 0.8	0424 0.9	0432 1.2	0513 1.1	0613 1.2	**5 SA**
1106 1.1	1200 1.1	1158 1.0	1148 0.3	0918 2.0	1057 4.3	1121 4.4	1114 5.9	1108 6.2	
1659 5.2	1806 5.1	1833 4.6	1900 1.8	1635 0.7	1641 0.7	1650 0.9	1731 0.9	1830 1.1	●
2321 1.0				2141 2.0	2327 4.4	2351 4.5	2340 5.9	2327 6.4	
0515 5.5	0017 1.1	0015 1.0	0002 0.2	0451 0.7	0500 0.8	0506 1.0	0546 1.0	0651 1.0	**6 SU**
1140 0.9	0621 5.4	0645 4.8	0719 2.0	0944 2.0	1130 4.4	1154 4.5	1145 6.0	1140 6.3	
1731 5.3	1239 1.0	1236 0.9	1227 0.2	1709 0.6	1716 0.6	1724 0.8	1805 0.9	1906 1.0	
2355 0.9	1841 5.2	1906 4.6	1940 1.9	2217 2.0					
0548 5.6	0054 0.9	0051 0.9	0040 0.2	0525 0.7	0000 4.4	0024 4.5	0012 6.0	0000 6.5	**7 M**
1214 0.9	0654 5.4	0719 4.9	0758 2.1	1020 2.0	0536 0.7	0540 0.9	0620 1.0	0727 1.0	
1803 5.4	1316 0.9	1312 0.8	1303 0.2	1744 0.6	1203 4.5	1227 4.5	1219 6.0	1212 6.4	
	1914 5.2	1939 4.7	2017 1.9	2301 2.0	1752 0.5	1758 0.8	1839 0.8	1940 1.0	
0029 0.9	0130 0.9	0128 0.8	0116 0.1	0601 0.7	0032 4.5	0057 4.5	0045 6.1	0033 6.5	**8 TU**
0621 5.6	0727 5.5	0752 4.9	0833 2.0	1108 2.0	0612 0.6	0615 0.9	0655 0.9	0802 0.9	
1249 0.8	1351 0.8	1349 0.8	1337 0.1	1819 0.6	1235 4.5	1302 4.6	1256 6.0	1246 6.4	
1837 5.6	1945 5.2	2012 4.7	2050 1.9	2357 2.0	1826 0.5	1832 0.8	1915 0.7	2012 1.0	
0104 0.9	0203 0.9	0202 0.8	0148 0.2	0636 0.7	0104 4.5	0132 4.5	0119 6.1	0106 6.6	**9 W**
0657 5.6	0759 5.4	0826 4.9	0905 2.0	1209 2.0	0646 0.7	0649 0.9	0732 0.8	0835 0.9	
1324 0.9	1424 0.9	1423 0.8	1409 0.2	1855 0.6	1309 4.4	1339 4.5	1334 6.0	1321 6.4	
1912 5.3	2017 5.2	2046 4.7	2121 1.8		1900 0.6	1907 0.8	1952 0.7	2044 1.0	
0140 1.0	0236 1.0	0237 0.9	0219 0.2	0104 2.0	0138 4.4	0209 4.5	0152 6.1	0140 6.5	**10 TH**
0734 5.5	0830 5.3	0900 4.8	0935 1.8	0715 0.7	0721 0.7	0726 1.0	0809 0.8	0907 1.0	
1402 1.0	1457 1.0	1457 0.9	1442 0.2	1322 2.0	1347 4.3	1418 4.5	1410 5.9	1357 6.3	
1951 5.2	2049 5.1	2120 4.5	2150 1.7	1933 0.6	1932 0.7	1944 0.9	2029 0.7	2118 1.2	
0219 1.2	0309 1.2	0311 1.1	0251 0.3	0225 2.0	0217 4.4	0250 4.5	0228 5.9	0216 6.4	**11 F**
0815 5.3	0904 5.2	0936 4.7	1006 1.7	0756 0.8	0756 0.9	0806 1.1	0849 0.9	0942 1.2	
1443 1.2	1532 1.2	1533 1.2	1518 0.3	1451 1.9	1431 4.2	1503 4.4	1448 5.8	1438 6.2	
2035 5.0	2124 4.9	2157 4.4	2223 1.6	2017 0.7	2010 1.0	2026 1.0	2108 0.9	2155 1.3	
0303 1.4	0347 1.4	0348 1.3	0327 0.4	0357 1.9	0304 4.2	0336 4.4	0308 5.7	0259 6.3	**12 SA**
0901 5.1	0940 5.0	1013 4.4	1040 1.6	0844 0.8	0838 1.2	0852 1.2	0934 1.1	1021 1.4	
1531 1.4	1613 1.5	1613 1.4	1601 0.4	1631 1.8	1524 4.1	1554 4.2	1533 5.5	1528 6.0	
2126 4.8	2206 4.7	2237 4.2	2303 1.5	2110 0.8	2057 1.3	2117 1.2	2156 1.1	2239 1.6	
0358 1.6	0434 1.7	0434 1.6	0415 0.5	0541 1.9	0402 4.1	0433 4.3	0400 5.4	0354 6.1	**13 SU**
0959 4.8	1028 4.7	1058 4.2	1126 1.5	0946 0.9	0934 1.5	0952 1.4	1031 1.3	1111 1.6	
1633 1.7	1706 1.7	1705 1.6	1700 0.5	1820 1.8	1631 3.9	1657 4.1	1631 5.2	1632 5.8	
2232 4.6	2306 4.6	2333 4.0		2219 1.0	2203 1.6	2224 1.5	2301 1.4	2337 1.8	
0509 1.8	0536 1.9	0536 1.8	0001 1.5	0717 1.8	0513 4.0	0539 4.1	0509 5.1	0503 5.9	**14 M**
1114 4.6	1142 4.6	1207 4.0	0524 0.6	1106 1.0	1049 1.6	1111 1.6	1146 1.5	1218 1.8	
1751 1.8	1816 1.8	1815 1.8	1236 1.4	1951 1.7	1752 3.9	1812 4.0	1752 5.0	1747 5.6	
2357 4.5			1821 0.6	2343 1.0	2327 1.7	2348 1.6			
0636 1.8	0032 4.5	0056 4.0	0122 1.4	0823 1.8	0633 4.0	0657 4.1	0024 1.5	0054 1.9	**15 TU**
1241 4.6	0700 1.9	0659 1.8	0700 0.7	1226 1.0	1216 1.6	1233 1.5	0635 5.1	0621 5.7	
1915 1.7	1317 4.5	1340 4.0	1412 1.4	2039 1.7	1917 4.0	1942 4.0	1313 1.6	1342 1.8	
	1946 1.8	1944 1.8	1954 0.6				1922 5.2	1910 5.6	

● ● Time: UT. For British Summer Time (shaded) March 26th to October 29th ADD ONE HOUR ● ●

FEBRUARY 2000 TIDE TABLES

•• Time: UT. For British Summer Time (shaded) March 26th to October 29TH ADD ONE HOUR ••

Day	ST MARY'S, SCILLY Time	m	PLYMOUTH Time	m	DARTMOUTH Time	m	PORTLAND Time	m	POOLE Time	m	SOUTHAMPTON Time	m	PORTSMOUTH Time	m	SHOREHAM Time	m	DOVER Time	m
16 W	0122	4.7	0201	4.6	0227	4.1	0259	1.5	0059	1.0	0054	1.6	0107	1.5	0150	1.4	0224	1.8
	0757	1.5	0831	1.7	0830	1.6	0835	0.6	0844	1.8	0748	4.1	0820	4.2	0757	5.3	0744	5.8
	1359	4.8	1445	4.7	1512	4.2	1551	1.5	1336	0.9	1336	1.3	1345	1.4	1432	1.3	1510	1.6
	2027	1.4	2111	1.5	2110	1.5	2112	0.5	2045	1.8	2029	4.2	2100	4.2	2039	5.5	2028	5.9
17 TH	0230	5.0	0322	4.9	0347	4.4	0424	1.7	0207	0.9	0211	1.3	0218	1.3	0301	1.2	0345	1.5
	0903	1.1	0948	1.3	0951	1.2	0948	0.5	0845	1.9	0850	4.3	0923	4.4	0907	5.7	0855	6.1
	1501	5.1	1605	4.9	1629	4.5	1708	1.7	1437	0.7	1442	0.9	1449	1.1	1537	1.0	1625	1.3
	2128	1.0	2221	1.1	2222	1.1	2213	0.4	2047	2.0	2126	4.4	2155	4.5	2143	5.9	2130	6.2
18 F	0327	5.4	0433	5.2	0455	4.8	0531	1.9	0304	0.7	0313	0.9	0317	1.0	0401	0.9	0453	1.1
	1000	0.8	1053	0.9	1055	0.8	1045	0.3	0849	2.0	0942	4.4	1012	4.6	1004	6.1	0954	6.4
	1554	5.4	1709	5.1	1730	4.7	1809	1.9	1529	0.6	1539	0.6	1543	0.8	1631	0.7	1731	1.0
	2221	0.7	2320	0.8	2320	0.7	2305	0.2	2058	2.1	2216	4.6	2242	4.6	2237	6.2	2222	6.5
19 SA O	0416	5.7	0531	5.4	0551	5.0	0627	2.1	0353	0.6	0406	0.6	0407	0.8	0452	0.7	0553	0.8
	1051	0.5	1149	0.5	1151	0.5	1133	0.2	0903	2.1	1029	4.5	1056	4.7	1053	6.3	1044	6.6
	1640	5.6	1804	5.3	1820	4.9	1901	2.0	1615	0.4	1630	0.3	1630	0.5	1720	0.6	1830	0.8
	2308	0.5					2351	0.1	2120	2.1	2301	4.7	2325	4.7	2324	6.4	2309	6.8
20 SU	0501	5.9	0012	0.5	0013	0.4	0717	2.3	0437	0.5	0454	0.4	0452	0.6	0539	0.7	0647	0.6
	1136	0.3	0621	5.6	0637	5.2	1218	0.0	0931	2.1	1114	4.6	1139	4.7	1137	6.4	1130	6.7
	1723	5.7	1238	0.3	1239	0.2	1947	2.1	1658	0.4	1715	0.2	1713	0.4	1804	0.5	1920	0.7
	2351	0.4	1850	5.4	1905	5.0			2158	2.1	2345	4.7					2351	6.9
21 M	0543	6.0	0057	0.4	0058	0.3	0034	0.0	0518	0.4	0539	0.3	0008	4.7	0007	6.5	0734	0.5
	1218	0.3	0704	5.6	0721	5.2	0800	2.3	1012	2.1	1159	4.6	0533	0.5	0621	0.6	1213	6.7
	1803	5.7	1321	0.3	1321	0.2	1300	-0.0	1740	0.4	1759	0.1	1220	4.7	1220	6.4	2002	0.6
			1930	5.4	1945	5.0	2027	2.1	2251	2.1			1754	0.4	1845	0.5		
22 TU	0032	0.4	0139	0.4	0138	0.3	0115	-0.0	0559	0.5	0028	4.7	0050	4.7	0049	6.5	0032	6.9
	0622	5.9	0742	5.6	0800	5.2	0839	2.3	1105	2.1	0619	0.3	0613	0.5	0703	0.7	0815	0.5
	1257	0.5	1400	0.4	1400	0.3	1339	-0.0	1820	0.4	1240	4.6	1300	4.7	1301	6.3	1253	6.6
	1842	5.6	2004	5.3	2023	4.9	2103	2.1	2355	2.1	1837	0.2	1833	0.4	1925	0.5	2037	0.7
23 W	0109	0.6	0215	0.6	0213	0.4	0153	0.0	0638	0.5	0108	4.6	0131	4.6	0126	6.4	0110	6.8
	0700	5.7	0815	5.5	0837	5.0	0912	2.2	1211	2.0	0656	0.4	0651	0.6	0741	0.7	0852	0.6
	1333	0.7	1434	0.7	1434	0.5	1417	0.0	1859	0.5	1320	4.4	1340	4.5	1340	6.2	1330	6.5
	1919	5.4	2034	5.2	2057	4.7	2133	1.9			1913	0.4	1911	0.6	2000	0.6	2107	0.9
24 TH	0146	0.8	0246	0.9	0247	0.7	0227	0.1	0110	2.0	0147	4.5	0212	4.5	0158	6.2	0148	6.7
	0738	5.4	0844	5.3	0910	4.8	0939	2.0	0719	0.6	0728	0.6	0730	0.8	0817	0.8	0924	0.8
	1409	1.0	1504	1.0	1504	0.8	1451	0.1	1328	1.9	1401	4.3	1421	4.4	1417	5.9	1407	6.3
	1956	5.1	2102	5.0	2127	4.5	2159	1.8	1939	0.6	1943	0.7	1949	0.8	2036	0.8	2133	1.2
25 F	0221	1.2	0314	1.2	0316	1.0	0300	0.3	0233	1.9	0228	4.3	0254	4.4	0230	6.0	0225	6.4
	0815	5.1	0911	5.1	0937	4.5	1003	1.8	0759	0.8	0758	0.9	0809	1.1	0852	1.0	0954	1.1
	1445	1.4	1530	1.4	1533	1.2	1521	0.3	1457	1.8	1444	4.0	1506	4.2	1451	5.6	1446	6.0
	2035	4.8	2130	4.8	2154	4.2	2223	1.6	2020	0.8	2015	1.1	2029	1.1	2112	1.1	2200	1.5
26 SA	0259	1.5	0341	1.6	0344	1.4	0330	0.4	0402	1.8	0311	4.0	0339	4.2	0304	5.6	0306	6.1
	0856	4.7	0942	4.8	1003	4.2	1027	1.5	0843	0.9	0833	1.3	0851	1.4	0931	1.3	1025	1.5
	1524	1.7	1600	1.8	1602	1.6	1548	0.4	1635	1.7	1531	3.8	1556	3.9	1529	5.2	1530	5.7
	2121	4.6	2206	4.6	2224	4.0	2250	1.4	2105	1.0	2053	1.5	2112	1.5	2154	1.5	2232	1.8
27 SU	0345	1.9	0415	2.0	0418	1.8	0400	0.6	0538	1.7	0400	3.8	0431	4.0	0348	5.1	0354	5.7
	0945	4.3	1025	4.5	1037	3.9	1054	1.4	0934	1.1	0916	1.7	0940	1.7	1020	1.7	1103	1.9
	1616	2.0	1639	2.1	1641	1.9	1616	0.6	1829	1.5	1627	3.6	1703	3.7	1621	4.7	1626	5.3
	2221	4.1	2300	4.4	2312	3.8	2327	1.3	2205	1.2	2146	1.9	2210	1.8	2251	1.9	2318	2.2
28 M	0448	2.2	0508	2.3	0505	2.1	0443	0.7	0711	1.6	0458	3.6	0534	3.7	0451	4.7	0458	5.3
	1057	4.0	1130	4.3	1136	3.7	1136	1.2	1052	1.2	1019	1.9	1057	2.0	1127	2.1	1157	2.2
	1733	2.2	1744	2.3	1737	2.2	1705	0.7	1956	1.5	1740	3.5	1817	3.5	1737	4.5	1742	5.0
	2350	4.0							2346	1.3	2259	2.1	2351	2.1				
29 TU	0616	2.3	0013	4.3	0020	3.7	0027	1.3	0816	1.5	0610	3.6	0645	3.6	0009	2.2	0023	2.4
	1234	4.0	0631	2.4	0622	2.3	0615	0.8	1235	1.2	1141	2.0	1242	2.0	0613	4.5	0624	5.0
	1902	2.2	1254	4.2	1256	3.6	1248	1.2	2038	1.5	1905	3.5	1936	3.5	1250	2.2	1309	2.4
			1917	2.4	1910	2.3	1848	0.7							1908	4.5	1911	5.0

SOUTH COAST OF ENGLAND Time Zone UT

St Mary's * Plymouth * Dartmouth * Portland * Poole * Southampton * Portsmouth * Shoreham * Dover

TIDE TABLES MARCH 2000

ST MARY'S, SCILLY (Time m)	PLYMOUTH (Time m)	DARTMOUTH (Time m)	PORTLAND (Time m)	POOLE (Time m)	SOUTHAMPTON (Time m)	PORTSMOUTH (Time m)	SHOREHAM (Time m)	DOVER (Time m)	Day
0117 4.1 0739 2.1 1352 4.1 2012 2.1	0139 4.3 0804 2.3 1423 4.3 2040 2.2	0141 3.7 0802 2.2 1427 3.6 2038 2.1	0204 1.3 0814 0.7 1439 1.2 2026 0.7	0111 1.3 0842 1.5 1336 1.2 2045 1.6	0026 2.1 0726 3.6 1305 1.9 2020 3.7	0119 2.0 0800 3.6 1345 1.8 2048 3.7	0132 2.2 0739 4.6 1408 2.0 2025 4.7	0155 2.4 0747 5.1 1442 2.3 2021 5.3	**1 W**
0219 4.4 0840 1.8 1446 4.4 2103 1.7	0257 4.6 0915 2.0 1533 4.6 2142 1.9	0307 3.9 0913 1.8 1552 3.9 2139 1.7	0333 1.4 0918 0.6 1607 1.3 2127 0.6	0202 1.2 0845 1.6 1422 1.0 2046 1.7	0142 1.9 0831 3.8 1413 1.6 2114 3.9	0213 1.8 0903 3.8 1433 1.6 2140 4.0	0240 2.0 0848 4.9 1507 1.7 2122 5.1	0327 2.1 0849 5.4 1554 1.9 2114 5.6	**2 TH**
0306 4.7 0926 1.5 1527 4.7 2145 1.4	0354 4.8 1010 1.6 1624 4.8 2232 1.5	0415 4.2 1008 1.5 1648 4.2 2230 1.4	0436 1.6 1004 0.5 1707 1.5 2215 0.4	0243 1.0 0846 1.7 1459 0.9 2051 1.8	0239 1.5 0919 3.9 1503 1.2 2155 4.1	0255 1.6 0948 4.0 1512 1.3 2219 4.2	0331 1.6 0939 5.3 1553 1.4 2206 5.5	0425 1.7 0936 5.7 1646 1.6 2154 5.9	**3 F**
0344 5.0 1006 1.2 1602 5.0 2222 1.1	0441 5.1 1057 1.3 1706 5.0 2316 1.2	0505 4.5 1054 1.2 1733 4.4 2312 1.1	0528 1.8 1045 0.3 1758 1.7 2258 0.3	0318 0.9 0852 1.8 1534 0.7 2102 1.9	0323 1.2 0958 4.1 1543 0.9 2231 4.2	0332 1.3 1024 4.2 1548 1.1 2253 4.4	0412 1.3 1018 5.7 1631 1.1 2243 5.8	0512 1.3 1012 5.9 1730 1.3 2229 6.2	**4 SA**
0418 5.3 1042 0.9 1635 5.2 2257 0.9	0521 5.3 1139 1.0 1743 5.1 2357 1.0	0548 4.7 1137 0.9 1812 4.6 2354 0.8	0617 1.9 1125 0.2 1844 1.8 2340 0.2	0352 0.8 0904 1.9 1608 0.6 2120 2.0	0403 0.9 1035 4.3 1620 0.6 2304 4.4	0406 1.1 1057 4.4 1623 0.8 2324 4.5	0448 1.0 1051 5.9 1706 0.8 2315 6.0	0554 1.1 1042 6.2 1812 1.1 2301 6.4	**5 SU** ●
0451 5.5 1116 0.7 1707 5.4 2333 0.7	0557 5.4 1218 0.8 1818 5.3	0624 4.8 1216 0.7 1847 4.7	0701 2.1 1203 0.1 1925 2.0	0426 0.6 0923 2.0 1643 0.5 2146 2.0	0439 0.7 1109 4.4 1657 0.5 2336 4.5	0441 0.9 1129 4.5 1658 0.7 2356 4.5	0522 0.8 1124 6.1 1742 0.7 2348 6.1	0634 0.9 1114 6.4 1850 0.9 2334 6.6	**6 M**
0524 5.7 1151 0.6 1740 5.5	0034 0.7 0633 5.5 1255 0.6 1852 5.4	0033 0.7 0659 4.9 1254 0.5 1921 4.8	0019 0.1 0742 2.1 1241 0.0 2003 2.0	0501 0.6 0953 2.0 1719 0.5 2224 2.0	0516 0.5 1142 4.5 1733 0.4	0516 0.7 1203 4.6 1734 0.6	0557 0.7 1158 6.2 1818 0.6	0712 0.8 1148 6.5 1924 0.8	**7 TU**
0008 0.6 0559 5.8 1227 0.6 1815 5.6	0110 0.6 0707 5.6 1330 0.6 1926 5.4	0111 0.5 0734 5.0 1332 0.5 1953 4.9	0056 0.0 0818 2.1 1317 -0.0 2036 2.0	0536 0.5 1037 2.1 1755 0.5 2318 2.1	0007 4.6 0553 0.4 1214 4.6 1809 0.3	0030 4.6 0551 0.6 1240 4.6 1809 0.5	0022 6.2 0634 0.6 1236 6.2 1855 0.5	0008 6.7 0746 0.7 1223 6.6 1956 0.8	**8 W**
0044 0.6 0634 5.7 1303 0.6 1851 5.5	0145 0.6 0742 5.6 1405 0.6 2000 5.4	0148 0.5 0809 5.0 1406 0.5 2027 4.8	0131 0.0 0851 2.1 1351 0.0 2106 1.9	0613 0.5 1135 2.1 1832 0.5	0040 4.6 0629 0.4 1248 4.5 1842 0.4	0108 4.6 0627 0.6 1319 4.6 1845 0.6	0058 6.3 0712 0.5 1314 6.3 1932 0.5	0042 6.7 0817 0.7 1259 6.6 2026 0.8	**9 TH**
0121 0.7 0712 5.6 1341 0.8 1930 5.4	0218 0.7 0816 5.5 1438 0.8 2035 5.3	0222 0.6 0843 4.9 1441 0.7 2103 4.7	0203 0.1 0923 2.0 1425 0.1 2136 1.8	0024 2.1 0653 0.5 1247 2.0 1911 0.5	0114 4.6 0703 0.5 1327 4.6 1916 0.5	0147 4.6 0705 0.7 1400 4.6 1923 0.7	0133 6.3 0750 0.5 1352 6.2 2009 0.6	0118 6.7 0848 0.8 1336 6.5 2059 0.9	**10 F**
0200 0.9 0753 5.4 1421 1.0 2012 5.1	0253 0.9 0851 5.3 1513 1.0 2110 5.1	0254 0.8 0920 4.7 1516 1.0 2139 4.5	0236 0.1 0954 1.8 1500 0.2 2206 1.7	0141 2.0 0734 0.6 1415 2.0 1955 0.7	0153 4.5 0737 0.7 1411 4.3 1952 0.8	0228 4.6 0745 0.8 1445 4.4 2005 0.8	0207 6.1 0829 0.7 1429 5.9 2048 0.8	0154 6.6 0922 0.9 1418 6.3 2136 1.1	**11 SA**
0244 1.2 0839 5.1 1509 1.3 2103 4.8	0330 1.2 0929 5.0 1552 1.4 2151 4.8	0330 1.1 0959 4.5 1553 1.3 2219 4.3	0312 0.3 1028 1.7 1541 0.3 2244 1.6	0313 2.0 0821 0.7 1558 1.9 2047 0.8	0240 4.3 0816 1.0 1505 4.2 2038 1.2	0314 4.4 0830 1.1 1537 4.3 2055 1.2	0246 5.8 0911 1.0 1512 5.6 2135 1.1	0238 6.4 1001 1.2 1508 6.1 2220 1.4	**12 SU**
0337 1.5 0936 4.7 1609 1.6 2208 4.5	0415 1.6 1016 4.7 1643 1.7 2248 4.6	0414 1.6 1043 4.2 1642 1.6 2312 4.1	0357 0.4 1112 1.5 1636 0.5 2336 1.5	0457 1.8 0921 0.9 1753 1.8 2157 1.0	0336 4.2 0910 1.3 1613 4.0 2143 1.5	0408 4.2 0928 1.3 1640 4.1 2203 1.5	0336 5.6 1007 1.3 1611 5.2 2240 1.5	0333 6.1 1049 1.5 1611 5.8 2317 1.7	**13 M**
0451 1.7 1053 4.4 1731 1.8 2338 4.4	0516 1.8 1131 4.4 1754 2.0	0515 1.7 1151 3.9 1753 1.9	0506 0.6 1218 1.4 1802 0.6	0646 1.7 1043 1.0 1942 1.7 2329 1.1	0448 4.0 1027 1.6 1738 3.9 2312 1.7	0515 4.0 1048 1.5 1802 4.0 2334 1.7	0447 5.0 1124 1.6 1737 5.0	0444 5.8 1157 1.8 1730 5.5	**14 TU**
0624 1.8 1230 4.4 1903 1.7	0014 4.5 0643 1.9 1310 4.4 1932 2.0	0034 3.9 0642 1.8 1329 3.9 1930 1.9	0055 1.4 0653 0.7 1401 1.4 1944 0.6	0815 1.7 1212 1.0 2039 1.7	0615 3.9 1200 1.6 1910 4.0	0643 3.9 1218 1.6 1939 4.0	0008 1.7 0621 4.9 1218 1.6 1915 5.1	0036 1.9 0611 5.5 1327 2.0 1902 5.5	**15 W**

● ● Time: UT. For British Summer Time (shaded) March 26th to October 29th ADD ONE HOUR ● ●

MARCH 2000 TIDE TABLES

•• Time: UT. For British Summer Time (shaded) March 26th to October 29TH ADD ONE HOUR ••

	ST MARY'S, SCILLY		PLYMOUTH		DARTMOUTH		PORTLAND		POOLE		SOUTHAMPTON		PORTSMOUTH		SHOREHAM		DOVER	
	Time	m	Time	m	Time	m	Time	m	Time	m	Time	m	Time	m	Time	m	Time	m
16 TH	0111	4.5	0148	4.6	0211	4.1	0239	1.5	0053	1.1	0046	1.6	0101	1.6	0141	1.5	0213	1.8
	0749	1.5	0821	1.7	0820	1.6	0833	0.6	0844	1.7	0737	4.0	0812	4.0	0751	5.2	0742	5.7
	1351	4.6	1445	4.6	1505	4.1	1550	1.5	1327	0.9	1325	1.3	1336	1.4	1422	1.4	1502	1.7
	2018	1.4	2100	1.6	2059	1.6	2103	0.6	2045	1.8	2023	4.2	2053	4.2	2035	5.5	2022	5.8
17 F	0221	4.9	0317	4.8	0335	4.4	0412	1.7	0201	0.9	0202	1.3	0212	1.4	0254	1.2	0337	1.4
	0855	1.1	0938	1.3	0939	1.2	0941	0.5	0845	1.8	0842	4.2	0913	4.2	0901	5.5	0854	6.0
	1452	5.0	1602	4.9	1619	4.4	1702	1.7	1427	0.8	1433	0.9	1439	1.1	1527	1.0	1618	1.4
	2117	1.0	2209	1.2	2209	1.1	2202	0.4	2046	2.0	2118	4.4	2145	4.4	2135	5.9	2121	6.2
18 SA	0315	5.3	0424	5.1	0441	4.7	0517	1.9	0253	0.7	0302	0.9	0306	1.1	0351	0.9	0444	1.0
	0948	0.8	1040	0.9	1041	0.8	1033	0.3	0847	1.9	0933	4.3	0959	4.4	0955	5.9	0948	6.3
	1541	5.3	1700	5.0	1717	4.7	1757	1.9	1515	0.6	1526	0.6	1528	0.8	1617	0.8	1722	1.0
	2206	0.7	2306	0.8	2306	0.7	2251	0.3	2053	2.0	2204	4.5	2227	4.6	2224	6.2	2209	6.5
19 SU O	0401	5.6	0518	5.4	0534	4.9	0611	2.1	0338	0.6	0351	0.6	0352	0.8	0440	0.7	0542	0.8
	1035	0.5	1133	0.6	1134	0.4	1118	0.1	0857	2.0	1017	4.5	1040	4.6	1039	6.2	1034	6.5
	1624	5.5	1748	5.3	1803	4.8	1845	2.0	1557	0.5	1613	0.3	1612	0.5	1703	0.6	1817	0.8
	2251	0.5	2354	0.6	2355	0.4	2334	0.1	2109	2.1	2245	4.6	2306	4.7	2307	6.4	2251	6.7
20 M	0442	5.8	0603	5.5	0619	5.1	0657	2.2	0418	0.5	0435	0.4	0433	0.6	0522	0.6	0633	0.6
	1116	0.4	1218	0.4	1219	0.3	1200	-0.0	0917	2.1	1059	4.5	1120	4.6	1120	6.3	1115	6.6
	1703	5.6	1828	5.4	1844	4.9	1927	2.1	1638	0.4	1655	0.2	1653	0.4	1743	0.5	1902	0.7
	2330	0.4							2137	2.1	2325	4.7	2346	4.7	2346	6.4	2331	6.8
21 TU	0521	5.8	0037	0.4	0037	0.3	0015	0.0	0457	0.4	0515	0.3	0512	0.5	0600	0.6	0715	0.5
	1154	0.4	0641	5.5	0658	5.1	0738	2.3	0948	2.1	1138	4.6	1158	4.6	1158	6.3	1153	6.6
	1739	5.6	1258	0.4	1258	0.2	1239	-0.1	1716	0.4	1734	0.2	1731	0.4	1821	0.5	1938	0.7
			1902	5.4	1921	4.9	2004	2.2	2217	2.1								
22 W	0008	0.4	0114	0.5	0114	0.3	0054	-0.0	0535	0.4	0002	4.7	0024	4.6	0021	6.4	0009	6.8
	0557	5.7	0714	5.5	0735	5.1	0814	2.2	1032	2.0	0553	0.3	0550	0.5	0637	0.6	0751	0.5
	1229	0.5	1333	0.5	1334	0.3	1317	-0.1	1753	0.4	1216	4.5	1236	4.6	1236	6.2	1229	6.6
	1815	5.5	1933	5.4	1955	4.9	2036	2.1	2308	2.0	1810	0.3	1807	0.5	1856	0.5	2008	0.7
23 TH	0042	0.6	0146	0.6	0148	0.4	0131	-0.0	0611	0.5	0039	4.6	0102	4.6	0054	6.3	0045	6.8
	0633	5.6	0744	5.4	0809	4.9	0844	2.1	1129	2.0	0625	0.4	0625	0.6	0711	0.6	0823	0.6
	1303	0.7	1403	0.7	1403	0.5	1351	-0.0	1829	0.5	1252	4.4	1315	4.5	1310	6.1	1303	6.5
	1849	5.4	2000	5.3	2026	4.8	2103	2.0			1842	0.5	1842	0.6	1929	0.6	2033	0.9
24 F	0115	0.8	0215	0.9	0216	0.6	0205	0.1	0009	2.0	0113	4.4	0139	4.5	0124	6.2	0119	6.6
	0706	5.3	0812	5.3	0839	4.7	0909	1.9	0647	0.6	0654	0.6	0700	0.6	0743	0.7	0851	0.8
	1334	1.0	1430	1.0	1432	0.8	1421	0.1	1235	1.9	1329	4.3	1353	4.4	1342	5.9	1336	6.3
	1923	5.1	2027	5.1	2053	4.6	2125	1.8	1905	0.6	1909	0.7	1917	0.8	2000	0.8	2058	1.1
25 SA	0148	1.1	0240	1.2	0243	0.9	0234	0.2	0116	1.9	0149	4.2	0215	4.4	0153	5.9	0154	6.4
	0741	5.0	0840	5.1	0904	4.5	0930	1.7	0724	0.7	0721	0.9	0735	1.0	0814	0.9	0918	1.1
	1406	1.3	1454	1.4	1456	1.1	1445	0.3	1349	1.8	1407	4.1	1432	4.2	1413	5.6	1411	6.1
	1958	4.8	2056	5.0	2117	4.4	2146	1.7	1941	0.8	1936	1.1	1951	1.1	2033	1.1	2124	1.4
26 SU	0221	1.4	0306	1.5	0309	1.3	0258	0.4	0229	1.8	0225	4.0	0252	4.2	0223	5.6	0229	6.1
	0817	4.7	0911	4.8	0929	4.2	0953	1.5	0759	0.8	0749	1.2	0809	1.2	0850	1.3	0947	1.4
	1440	1.6	1520	1.7	1521	1.5	1503	0.4	1513	1.7	1450	3.9	1514	4.0	1448	5.2	1448	5.8
	2038	4.5	2130	4.7	2143	4.1	2209	1.5	2019	1.0	2009	1.5	2028	1.5	2112	1.6	2156	1.7
27 M	0301	1.8	0337	1.9	0337	1.6	0319	0.5	0347	1.7	0309	3.8	0331	3.9	0302	5.1	0309	5.7
	0900	4.3	0950	4.6	0957	3.9	1018	1.4	0840	1.0	0828	1.5	0848	1.5	0931	1.7	1021	1.9
	1524	2.0	1555	2.1	1553	1.8	1519	0.5	1657	1.6	1541	3.7	1608	3.7	1534	4.8	1535	5.4
	2128	4.2	2215	4.5	2223	3.9	2239	1.4	2105	1.2	2057	1.8	2112	1.8	2203	2.0	2238	2.0
28 TU	0354	2.1	0423	2.2	0417	2.0	0351	0.6	0528	1.5	0403	3.7	0425	3.7	0358	4.6	0405	5.2
	0959	4.0	1048	4.3	1049	3.6	1056	1.2	0936	1.2	0923	1.9	0942	1.9	1030	2.1	1106	2.2
	1628	2.2	1649	2.4	1639	2.2	1551	0.6	1909	1.5	1648	3.5	1732	3.6	1644	4.5	1642	5.1
	2246	4.0	2321	4.3	2327	3.7	2326	1.3	2237	1.3	2206	2.1	2242	2.1	2314	2.3	2335	2.3
29 W	0515	2.3	0534	2.4	0521	2.2	0502	0.7	0730	1.4	0513	3.5	0550	3.5	0518	4.4	0530	4.9
	1136	3.8	1208	4.2	1211	3.5	1200	1.1	1146	1.3	1044	2.0	1151	2.0	1152	2.3	1213	2.4
	1805	2.3	1813	2.5	1757	2.4	1715	0.8	2016	1.4	1815	3.5	1845	3.5	1816	4.4	1816	4.9
											2336	2.1						
30 TH	0026	4.0	0044	4.3	0051	3.6	0051	1.3	0042	1.3	0635	3.5	0049	2.1	0043	2.4	0054	2.5
	0651	2.2	0712	2.4	0703	2.3	0733	0.7	0828	1.4	1216	1.9	0708	3.4	0652	4.4	0706	4.9
	1310	4.0	1338	4.2	1340	3.5	1351	1.2	1301	1.2	1937	3.6	1309	1.9	1319	2.2	1339	2.4
	1929	2.1	1954	2.4	1946	2.2	1948	0.8	2042	1.5			2000	3.7	1943	4.7	1939	5.1
31 F	0139	4.2	0207	4.5	0216	3.8	0242	1.4	0134	1.2	0101	1.9	0143	1.9	0159	2.1	0235	2.2
	0800	1.9	0836	2.1	0834	1.9	0847	0.6	0844	1.5	0749	3.7	0820	3.6	0810	4.7	0814	5.2
	1410	4.2	1453	4.5	1507	3.8	1539	1.3	1347	1.1	1334	1.6	1357	1.7	1425	1.9	1508	2.1
	2027	1.8	2106	2.0	2101	1.9	2057	0.6	2045	1.7	2038	3.8	2102	3.9	2045	5.1	2037	5.5

SOUTH COAST OF ENGLAND Time Zone UT

St Mary's * Plymouth * Dartmouth * Portland * Poole * Southampton * Portsmouth * Shoreham * Dover

TIDE TABLES APRIL 2000

1 SA

Port				
ST MARY'S, SCILLY	0230 4.6	0851 1.5	1454 4.6	2112 1.4
PLYMOUTH	0314 4.7	0936 1.7	1548 4.7	2200 1.6
DARTMOUTH	0331 4.1	0931 1.5	1611 4.1	2154 1.5
PORTLAND	0400 1.6	0933 0.5	1642 1.5	2146 0.5
POOLE	0213 1.1	0845 1.6	1426 0.9	2046 1.8
SOUTHAMPTON	0204 1.6	0845 3.8	1428 1.3	2121 4.0
PORTSMOUTH	0224 1.6	0914 3.9	1438 1.4	2147 4.2
SHOREHAM	0254 1.7	0904 5.2	1515 1.5	2131 5.5
DOVER	0347 1.8	0902 5.6	1609 1.7	2120 5.8

2 SU

Port				
ST MARY'S, SCILLY	0310 4.9	0933 1.2	1530 4.9	2151 1.1
PLYMOUTH	0405 5.0	1026 1.3	1633 5.0	2246 1.3
DARTMOUTH	0427 4.4	1020 1.2	1659 4.4	2242 1.1
PORTLAND	0457 1.8	1015 0.3	1733 1.7	2230 0.3
POOLE	0247 0.9	0847 1.8	1502 0.8	2052 1.9
SOUTHAMPTON	0252 1.2	0928 4.1	1511 0.9	2159 4.2
PORTSMOUTH	0300 1.3	0954 4.1	1515 1.1	2222 4.2
SHOREHAM	0337 1.3	0944 5.6	1556 1.1	2209 5.8
DOVER	0439 1.4	0939 5.9	1659 1.3	2156 6.2

3 M

Port				
ST MARY'S, SCILLY	0347 5.3	1010 0.8	1605 5.3	2229 0.8
PLYMOUTH	0448 5.2	1109 1.0	1712 5.2	2329 0.9
DARTMOUTH	0514 4.6	1105 0.8	1740 4.6	2326 0.8
PORTLAND	0548 1.9	1055 0.2	1818 1.9	2312 0.2
POOLE	0321 0.7	0853 1.9	1537 0.6	2103 2.0
SOUTHAMPTON	0333 0.8	1005 4.2	1550 0.6	2233 4.4
PORTSMOUTH	0335 1.0	1028 4.3	1551 0.8	2254 4.5
SHOREHAM	0415 0.9	1020 5.9	1635 0.8	2243 6.1
DOVER	0525 1.1	1011 6.2	1745 1.0	2229 6.4

4 TU ●

Port				
ST MARY'S, SCILLY	0422 5.5	1048 0.6	1639 5.5	2306 0.6
PLYMOUTH	0527 5.4	1151 0.7	1750 5.4	
DARTMOUTH	0556 4.8	1149 0.6	1819 4.8	
PORTLAND	0634 2.1	1135 0.0	1900 2.0	2353 0.1
POOLE	0357 0.6	0906 2.0	1614 0.5	2122 2.0
SOUTHAMPTON	0411 0.6	1041 4.4	1629 0.4	2306 4.6
PORTSMOUTH	0412 0.8	1102 4.5	1629 0.6	2327 4.6
SHOREHAM	0453 0.7	1054 6.1	1713 0.6	2318 6.2
DOVER	0609 0.8	1044 6.4	1826 0.9	2303 6.6

5 W

Port				
ST MARY'S, SCILLY	0457 5.7	1125 0.4	1715 5.7	2344 0.4
PLYMOUTH	0009 0.7	0606 5.6	1230 0.5	1827 5.5
DARTMOUTH	0009 0.5	0634 5.0	1230 0.4	1855 4.9
PORTLAND	0717 2.2	1214 -0.0	1939 2.1	
POOLE	0434 0.5	0931 2.0	1652 0.4	2154 2.1
SOUTHAMPTON	0450 0.4	1117 4.5	1708 0.3	2340 4.7
PORTSMOUTH	0449 0.6	1139 4.6	1707 0.4	
SHOREHAM	0531 0.5	1133 6.3	1751 0.5	2356 6.4
DOVER	0648 0.7	1120 6.6	1903 0.7	2339 6.8

6 TH

Port				
ST MARY'S, SCILLY	0534 5.8	1203 0.4	1751 5.7	
PLYMOUTH	0047 0.5	0644 5.7	1307 0.4	1904 5.6
DARTMOUTH	0050 0.4	0712 5.1	1310 0.3	1931 5.0
PORTLAND	0031 -0.0	0756 2.2	1252 -0.1	2015 2.1
POOLE	0512 0.4	1009 2.1	1730 0.4	2241 2.1
SOUTHAMPTON	0530 0.3	1152 4.6	1747 0.3	
PORTSMOUTH	0004 4.7	0527 0.4	1218 4.7	1745 0.4
SHOREHAM	0611 0.5	1213 6.3	1831 0.5	
DOVER	0724 0.6	1158 6.7	1936 0.7	

7 F

Port				
ST MARY'S, SCILLY	0022 0.4	0612 5.8	1242 0.5	1830 5.7
PLYMOUTH	0124 0.4	0723 5.7	1344 0.5	1942 5.6
DARTMOUTH	0128 0.4	0749 5.1	1348 0.4	2009 5.0
PORTLAND	0109 -0.0	0833 2.1	1330 -0.0	2048 2.1
POOLE	0552 0.4	1105 2.1	1810 0.4	2345 2.1
SOUTHAMPTON	0014 4.7	0609 0.3	1229 4.6	1825 0.3
PORTSMOUTH	0043 4.7	0606 0.5	1300 4.7	1824 0.5
SHOREHAM	0034 6.4	0650 0.5	1255 6.4	1910 0.5
DOVER	0017 6.9	0757 0.6	1238 6.7	2008 0.7

8 SA

Port				
ST MARY'S, SCILLY	0102 0.5	0653 5.7	1321 0.7	1911 5.5
PLYMOUTH	0201 0.5	0802 5.5	1425 0.6	2021 5.4
DARTMOUTH	0205 0.5	0827 5.0	1425 0.6	2045 4.9
PORTLAND	0145 0.0	0907 2.0	1406 0.1	2120 2.0
POOLE	0632 0.5	1220 2.1	1853 0.5	
SOUTHAMPTON	0051 4.6	0645 0.3	1310 4.5	1901 0.5
PORTSMOUTH	0125 4.7	0645 0.6	1345 4.6	1905 0.7
SHOREHAM	0113 6.4	0732 0.5	1336 6.3	1950 0.6
DOVER	0057 6.8	0830 0.7	1320 6.6	2043 0.8

9 SU

Port				
ST MARY'S, SCILLY	0144 0.8	0736 5.4	1405 0.9	1956 5.2
PLYMOUTH	0238 0.8	0842 5.3	1457 1.0	2100 5.2
DARTMOUTH	0243 0.7	0907 4.8	1500 0.9	2125 4.7
PORTLAND	0221 0.1	0942 1.9	1445 0.2	2154 1.8
POOLE	0104 2.1	0716 0.6	1351 2.0	1939 0.7
SOUTHAMPTON	0134 4.5	0723 0.5	1358 4.4	1940 0.8
PORTSMOUTH	0209 4.6	0727 0.7	1433 4.5	1949 0.9
SHOREHAM	0151 6.2	0812 0.7	1417 6.0	2032 0.9
DOVER	0138 6.7	0906 0.8	1405 6.4	2123 1.0

10 M

Port				
ST MARY'S, SCILLY	0231 1.1	0825 5.0	1454 1.3	2048 4.9
PLYMOUTH	0318 1.1	0926 4.9	1539 1.4	2145 4.9
DARTMOUTH	0321 1.0	0949 4.4	1540 1.3	2206 4.4
PORTLAND	0302 0.3	1020 1.7	1528 0.4	2233 1.7
POOLE	0237 2.0	0806 0.7	1539 1.9	2034 0.8
SOUTHAMPTON	0222 4.4	0804 0.9	1455 4.2	2029 1.2
PORTSMOUTH	0256 4.5	0815 1.0	1527 4.3	2042 1.3
SHOREHAM	0233 5.9	0858 1.0	1504 5.7	2124 1.2
DOVER	0226 6.4	0948 1.2	1458 6.1	2209 1.3

11 TU

Port				
ST MARY'S, SCILLY	0328 1.4	0924 4.6	1557 1.6	2157 4.5
PLYMOUTH	0406 1.5	1021 4.6	1632 1.8	2246 4.7
DARTMOUTH	0406 1.4	1039 4.1	1631 1.6	2302 4.2
PORTLAND	0352 0.4	1108 1.5	1627 0.6	2326 1.6
POOLE	0426 1.8	0908 0.9	1745 1.8	2147 1.0
SOUTHAMPTON	0322 4.1	0900 1.2	1606 4.0	2137 1.5
PORTSMOUTH	0351 4.2	0915 1.3	1635 4.1	2153 1.6
SHOREHAM	0326 5.4	0954 1.4	1606 5.3	2232 1.6
DOVER	0324 6.0	1039 1.5	1603 5.8	2309 1.6

12 W

Port				
ST MARY'S, SCILLY	0444 1.7	1045 4.3	1721 1.8	2327 4.4
PLYMOUTH	0509 1.8	1139 4.4	1746 2.0	
DARTMOUTH	0508 1.7	1150 3.9	1743 1.9	
PORTLAND	0508 0.6	1218 1.4	1756 0.7	
POOLE	0626 1.7	1031 1.0	1944 1.7	2321 1.1
SOUTHAMPTON	0437 3.9	1016 1.5	1733 3.9	2305 1.7
PORTSMOUTH	0501 4.0	1036 1.5	1804 4.0	2326 1.7
SHOREHAM	0438 5.0	1112 1.6	1733 5.1	
DOVER	0439 5.7	1150 1.9	1722 5.6	

13 TH

Port				
ST MARY'S, SCILLY	0615 1.7	1220 4.3	1851 1.7	
PLYMOUTH	0009 4.5	0639 1.9	1310 4.4	1924 2.0
DARTMOUTH	0023 4.0	0635 1.8	1323 3.9	1916 1.8
PORTLAND	0044 1.5	0653 0.7	1403 1.4	1933 0.7
POOLE	0810 1.6	1159 1.0	2037 1.7	
SOUTHAMPTON	0604 3.9	1147 1.5	1901 4.0	
PORTSMOUTH	0636 3.9	1205 1.5	1931 4.1	
SHOREHAM	0001 1.7	0612 4.9	1245 1.6	1906 5.2
DOVER	0030 1.8	0611 5.5	1323 1.9	1853 5.6

14 F

Port				
ST MARY'S, SCILLY	0057 4.5	0736 1.4	1337 4.5	2003 1.4
PLYMOUTH	0140 4.6	0810 1.7	1439 4.6	2045 1.7
DARTMOUTH	0156 4.1	0806 1.5	1451 4.1	2041 1.5
PORTLAND	0226 1.5	0821 0.6	1540 1.5	2048 0.6
POOLE	0044 1.1	0842 1.7	1313 0.9	2045 1.8
SOUTHAMPTON	0034 1.5	0728 3.9	1309 1.3	2011 4.2
PORTSMOUTH	0051 1.6	0800 3.9	1321 1.4	2039 4.2
SHOREHAM	0130 1.6	0742 5.1	1406 1.4	2021 5.5
DOVER	0205 1.7	0739 5.7	1451 1.7	2007 5.8

15 SA

Port				
ST MARY'S, SCILLY	0204 4.8	0838 1.1	1434 4.9	2059 1.1
PLYMOUTH	0303 4.8	0921 1.3	1548 4.8	2151 1.3
DARTMOUTH	0316 4.4	0920 1.1	1602 4.4	2148 1.1
PORTLAND	0351 1.7	0924 0.4	1644 1.7	2143 0.5
POOLE	0147 0.9	0845 1.8	1408 0.8	2045 1.9
SOUTHAMPTON	0147 1.2	0830 4.1	1414 0.9	2103 4.4
PORTSMOUTH	0157 1.4	0859 4.1	1419 1.1	2127 4.4
SHOREHAM	0240 1.3	0849 5.4	1508 1.1	2118 5.8
DOVER	0324 1.3	0844 5.9	1603 1.4	2103 6.1

• • Time: UT. For British Summer Time (shaded) March 26th to October 29th ADD ONE HOUR • •

APRIL 2000 TIDE TABLES

•• Time: UT. For British Summer Time (shaded) March 26th to October 29TH ADD ONE HOUR ••

	ST MARY'S, SCILLY		PLYMOUTH		DARTMOUTH		PORTLAND		POOLE		SOUTHAMPTON		PORTSMOUTH		SHOREHAM		DOVER	
	Time	m	Time	m	Time	m	Time	m	Time	m	Time	m	Time	m	Time	m	Time	m
16 SU	0256	5.2	0406	5.1	0419	4.6	0454	1.9	0235	0.7	0243	0.9	0247	1.1	0334	1.0	0428	1.0
	0928	0.8	1019	1.0	1019	0.8	1012	0.3	0846	1.9	0919	4.3	0942	4.3	0940	5.8	0934	6.2
	1521	5.2	1640	5.1	1655	4.6	1735	1.9	1454	0.6	1505	0.7	1507	0.9	1558	0.8	1703	1.1
	2146	0.8	2244	0.9	2244	0.8	2230	0.3	2049	2.0	2146	4.5	2207	4.5	2204	6.1	2148	6.4
17 M	0340	5.4	0456	5.3	0512	4.8	0545	2.0	0317	0.6	0329	0.6	0331	0.8	0420	0.8	0523	0.8
	1012	0.6	1109	0.7	1109	0.6	1054	0.2	0851	1.9	1001	4.4	1021	4.4	1021	6.0	1015	6.4
	1601	5.4	1723	5.3	1738	4.8	1820	2.0	1536	0.5	1549	0.5	1550	0.7	1641	0.6	1753	0.9
	2228	0.6	2330	0.7	2330	0.6	2312	0.2	2059	2.0	2224	4.6	2245	4.6	2243	6.3	2229	6.6
18 TU O	0420	5.5	0536	5.4	0555	4.9	0630	2.1	0357	0.5	0409	0.5	0412	0.6	0501	0.6	0609	0.7
	1051	0.5	1151	0.6	1154	0.4	1135	0.1	0905	2.0	1040	4.5	1059	4.5	1057	6.1	1053	6.5
	1638	5.4	1759	5.4	1817	4.8	1900	2.1	1615	0.5	1629	0.4	1630	0.5	1719	0.6	1833	0.8
	2306	0.6					2352	0.1	2118	2.0	2300	4.5	2322	4.6	2319	6.3	2307	6.7
19 W	0457	5.6	0010	0.6	0011	0.5	0711	2.2	0434	0.5	0448	0.4	0449	0.6	0536	0.6	0648	0.7
	1127	0.6	0612	5.4	0631	4.9	1214	0.0	0929	2.0	1116	4.5	1136	4.5	1134	6.1	1128	6.5
	1713	5.5	1228	0.6	1230	0.4	1936	2.1	1651	0.5	1705	0.4	1706	0.5	1755	0.6	1906	0.8
	2342	0.6	1830	5.4	1852	4.9			2148	2.0	2335	4.5	2358	4.6	2352	6.3	2344	6.7
20 TH	0531	5.5	0045	0.7	0046	0.6	0031	0.1	0510	0.5	0523	0.4	0525	0.6	0610	0.6	0721	0.7
	1200	0.7	0642	5.4	0706	4.9	0745	2.1	1005	2.0	1153	4.4	1214	4.5	1209	6.1	1203	6.5
	1748	5.4	1301	0.7	1304	0.5	1251	0.0	1727	0.5	1740	0.5	1742	0.6	1828	0.6	1934	0.8
			1900	5.4	1925	4.8	2006	2.1	2229	2.0								
21 F	0015	0.7	0115	0.8	0118	0.6	0108	0.1	0546	0.5	0009	4.5	0034	4.5	0023	6.2	0020	6.6
	0605	5.4	0713	5.4	0739	4.8	0814	2.0	1054	1.9	0554	0.5	0600	0.7	0642	0.7	0751	0.7
	1233	0.9	1330	0.8	1334	0.7	1324	0.1	1801	0.5	1226	4.4	1252	4.4	1243	6.0	1238	6.4
	1821	5.3	1929	5.4	1955	4.8	2032	2.0	2319	2.0	1810	0.6	1815	0.8	1859	0.8	2001	0.9
22 SA	0047	0.9	0145	1.0	0146	0.7	0142	0.1	0620	0.6	0040	4.4	0109	4.5	0052	6.1	0054	6.5
	0639	5.2	0743	5.3	0810	4.7	0839	1.9	1154	1.9	0622	0.6	0633	0.8	0712	0.8	0819	0.9
	1303	1.1	1357	1.1	1400	0.9	1354	0.2	1835	0.7	1300	4.2	1330	4.3	1315	5.8	1311	6.3
	1854	5.1	1959	5.2	2023	4.6	2054	1.9			1837	0.9	1848	1.0	1929	1.0	2029	1.0
23 SU	0119	1.1	0212	1.2	0212	1.0	0211	0.2	0018	1.9	0113	4.2	0144	4.4	0121	5.8	0126	6.3
	0712	4.9	0815	5.1	0837	4.4	0903	1.7	0652	0.7	0648	0.8	0704	1.0	0743	1.0	0847	1.1
	1335	1.3	1424	1.4	1423	1.2	1415	0.3	1303	1.8	1336	4.1	1408	4.2	1345	5.6	1343	6.1
	1929	4.9	2030	5.1	2049	4.5	2117	1.7	1908	0.8	1904	1.1	1920	1.2	2002	1.3	2058	1.3
24 M	0153	1.4	0240	1.5	0240	1.3	0233	0.4	0120	1.8	0150	4.0	0217	4.2	0151	5.5	0157	6.0
	0747	4.7	0847	4.8	0903	4.2	0927	1.6	0725	0.8	0717	1.1	0736	1.2	0816	1.3	0917	1.4
	1409	1.6	1452	1.7	1449	1.5	1429	0.4	1417	1.7	1418	3.9	1446	4.1	1420	5.3	1417	5.9
	2007	4.6	2102	4.8	2115	4.2	2140	1.6	1944	1.0	1938	1.4	1954	1.5	2040	1.6	2131	1.6
25 TU	0230	1.7	0312	1.8	0309	1.6	0252	0.5	0229	1.7	0231	3.9	0252	4.0	0230	5.1	0234	5.7
	0827	4.6	0924	4.6	0933	3.9	0956	1.4	0801	0.9	0755	1.4	0811	1.4	0856	1.6	0951	1.8
	1449	1.9	1526	2.0	1521	1.8	1444	0.5	1547	1.6	1508	3.7	1531	3.9	1503	5.0	1459	5.6
	2053	4.3	2141	4.6	2149	4.0	2207	1.5	2025	1.1	2024	1.7	2034	1.8	2127	2.0	2211	1.9
26 W	0318	1.9	0354	2.1	0347	1.8	0321	0.6	0357	1.6	0322	3.7	0336	3.7	0320	4.7	0324	5.3
	0919	4.1	1011	4.3	1016	3.7	1033	1.3	0847	1.1	0847	1.7	0855	1.7	0948	2.0	1035	2.1
	1544	2.1	1613	2.3	1604	2.0	1513	0.6	1804	1.5	1610	3.6	1647	3.7	1604	4.7	1557	5.3
	2156	4.0	2233	4.4	2242	3.8	2248	1.4	2129	1.3	2129	2.0	2135	2.1	2229	2.3	2301	2.2
27 TH	0424	2.1	0454	2.3	0441	2.1	0417	0.7	0601	1.4	0427	3.6	0445	3.5	0430	4.5	0439	5.0
	1036	3.9	1118	4.2	1128	3.5	1132	1.2	1018	1.2	0959	1.9	1023	1.9	1056	2.2	1133	2.3
	1705	2.2	1722	2.5	1708	2.3	1615	0.8	1940	1.5	1728	3.5	1800	3.6	1724	4.6	1716	5.1
	2323	4.0	2346	4.4			2357	1.3	2346	1.3	2251	2.0	2352	2.1	2349	2.3		
28 F	0552	2.1	0615	2.3	0000	3.7	0630	0.7	0755	1.4	0545	3.5	0616	3.5	0556	4.4	0009	2.3
	1210	3.9	1242	4.2	0600	2.2	1306	1.2	1206	1.2	1125	1.8	1212	1.9	1220	2.2	0609	4.9
	1833	2.1	1851	2.4	1252	3.5	1855	0.8	2028	1.6	1848	3.6	1908	3.7	1848	4.7	1246	2.4
					1838	2.3											1841	5.2
29 SA	0044	4.2	0108	4.4	0122	3.8	0140	1.4	0048	1.2	0013	1.9	0055	1.9	0106	2.1	0133	2.2
	0709	1.9	0741	2.1	0734	2.0	0757	0.6	0836	1.5	0702	3.6	0728	3.6	0717	4.7	0722	5.2
	1321	4.2	1359	4.4	1412	3.7	1454	1.3	1301	1.1	1243	1.6	1309	1.7	1332	1.9	1409	2.2
	1939	1.8	2013	2.2	2005	2.0	2017	0.7	2044	1.7	1951	3.8	2013	3.9	1955	5.1	1946	5.4
30 SU	0143	4.5	0220	4.7	0237	4.0	0312	1.5	0130	1.1	0119	1.5	0139	1.7	0207	1.7	0254	1.9
	0806	1.6	0849	1.8	0842	1.6	0851	0.5	0845	1.6	0802	3.8	0830	3.8	0817	5.1	0815	5.5
	1411	4.5	1500	4.7	1520	4.1	1604	1.5	1344	0.9	1343	1.3	1354	1.4	1428	1.5	1521	1.8
	2030	1.5	2115	1.8	2109	1.6	2111	0.5	2045	1.8	2039	4.0	2106	4.1	2046	5.5	2036	5.8

SOUTH COAST OF ENGLAND Time Zone UT

St Mary's * Plymouth * Dartmouth * Portland * Poole * Southampton * Portsmouth * Shoreham * Dover

TIDE TABLES   MAY 2000

ST MARY'S SCILLY	PLYMOUTH	DARTMOUTH	PORTLAND	POOLE	SOUTHAMPTON	PORTSMOUTH	SHOREHAM	DOVER	Day
Time m	Time m	Time m	Time m	Time m	Time m	Time m	Time m	Time m	
0230 4.9	0318 4.9	0339 4.3	0418 1.7	0209 0.9	0211 1.2	0220 1.4	0256 1.3	0355 1.4	1 M
0852 1.2	0945 1.4	0938 1.2	0937 0.3	0845 1.7	0850 4.0	0918 4.1	0903 5.5	0857 5.9	
1453 4.9	1551 5.0	1615 4.4	1657 1.7	1424 0.8	1430 1.0	1436 1.1	1516 1.1	1618 1.4	
2115 1.1	2208 1.4	2202 1.2	2157 0.4	2046 1.9	2120 4.2	2146 4.4	2128 5.8	2116 6.2	
0311 5.2	0408 5.2	0433 4.6	0512 1.9	0247 0.7	0255 0.8	0300 1.0	0339 0.9	0448 1.1	2 TU
0935 0.9	1033 1.0	1030 0.9	1021 0.2	0847 1.9	0931 4.2	0957 4.3	0942 5.8	0935 6.2	
1531 5.3	1636 5.2	1704 4.7	1745 1.9	1505 0.6	1513 0.7	1518 0.8	1559 0.8	1709 1.1	
2156 0.8	2256 1.0	2254 0.8	2241 0.2	2051 2.0	2157 4.4	2221 4.5	2207 6.1	2154 6.5	
0351 5.5	0454 5.4	0521 4.8	0603 2.0	0326 0.6	0338 0.6	0340 0.7	0422 0.7	0536 0.9	3 W
1016 0.6	1118 0.5	1118 0.6	1103 0.1	0855 2.0	1010 4.4	1034 4.5	1022 6.1	1012 6.5	
1610 5.6	1718 5.4	1748 4.9	1830 2.1	1545 0.5	1556 0.5	1559 0.6	1642 0.6	1754 0.9	
2237 0.6	2340 0.7	2341 0.6	2324 0.1	2104 2.1	2233 4.6	2258 4.7	2248 6.3	2232 6.7	
0430 5.8	0537 5.6	0606 5.0	0649 2.1	0406 0.4	0421 0.4	0421 0.5	0504 0.5	0620 0.7	4 TH ●
1057 0.4	1202 0.5	1204 0.4	1145 0.0	0913 2.0	1049 4.5	1114 4.6	1105 6.3	1053 6.7	
1649 5.7	1800 5.6	1830 5.0	1912 2.2	1626 0.4	1640 0.4	1641 0.4	1725 0.5	1836 0.8	
2319 0.4				2130 2.1	2312 4.7	2338 4.8	2329 6.4	2312 6.9	
0511 5.9	0023 0.5	0026 0.4	0006 0.1	0448 0.4	0505 0.3	0503 0.4	0547 0.5	0700 0.6	5 F
1139 0.4	0621 5.6	0650 5.1	0733 2.2	0947 2.1	1130 4.6	1157 4.7	1152 6.4	1135 6.8	
1730 5.8	1243 0.4	1247 0.3	1227 -0.0	1709 0.4	1724 0.3	1724 0.4	1808 0.6	1914 0.7	
	1842 5.7	1911 5.1	1952 2.2	2213 2.2	2351 4.7			2354 6.9	
0002 0.4	0104 0.5	0110 0.3	0047 0.0	0531 0.4	0548 0.2	0021 4.8	0012 6.4	0737 0.6	6 SA
0553 5.8	0705 5.6	0731 5.1	0814 2.2	1042 2.1	1213 4.6	0546 0.4	0632 0.5	1221 6.8	
1222 0.5	1324 0.5	1329 0.4	1309 0.0	1752 0.4	1808 0.4	1244 4.7	1239 6.4	1951 0.6	
1812 5.7	1925 5.6	1950 5.1	2030 2.2	2315 2.1		1806 0.5	1852 0.7		
0047 0.5	0145 0.5	0152 0.4	0128 0.1	0616 0.4	0032 4.6	0106 4.8	0055 6.4	0039 6.8	7 SU
0637 5.6	0750 5.6	0813 4.9	0854 2.1	1159 2.1	0630 0.3	0630 0.5	0716 0.7	0815 0.6	
1307 0.7	1406 0.7	1409 0.6	1350 0.1	1838 0.4	1259 4.5	1333 4.7	1324 6.3	1309 6.7	
1857 5.6	2009 5.5	2032 5.0	2107 2.1		1851 0.5	1851 0.7	1937 0.8	2032 0.7	
0133 0.7	0228 0.7	0233 0.6	0211 0.2	0031 2.1	0119 4.5	0151 4.6	0139 6.2	0128 6.7	8 M
0724 5.4	0837 5.2	0857 4.7	0934 1.9	0703 0.5	0712 0.5	0715 0.7	0802 0.8	0856 0.8	
1354 0.9	1450 0.9	1450 0.9	1433 0.3	1333 2.0	1351 4.4	1424 4.6	1412 6.1	1400 6.5	
1946 5.3	2055 5.3	2113 4.8	2145 2.0	1928 0.7	1936 0.8	1939 1.0	2025 1.0	2116 0.8	
0225 1.0	0313 1.0	0316 0.9	0257 0.3	0207 2.0	0211 4.3	0241 4.5	0227 5.9	0222 6.4	9 TU
0818 5.0	0929 4.9	0945 4.5	1018 1.8	0756 0.7	0759 0.7	0806 0.9	0851 1.1	0942 1.1	
1448 1.3	1534 1.3	1536 1.2	1522 0.4	1533 1.9	1452 4.3	1524 4.4	1504 5.8	1454 6.2	
2042 5.0	2145 5.0	2201 4.5	2229 1.8	2027 0.9	2029 1.1	2035 1.3	2120 1.3	2207 1.2	
0325 1.3	0404 1.4	0405 1.3	0354 0.5	0400 1.8	0313 4.1	0338 4.2	0322 5.5	0324 6.1	10 W
0919 4.7	1028 4.7	1039 4.2	1111 1.6	0859 0.8	0855 1.0	0906 1.2	0950 1.3	1038 1.5	
1551 1.5	1629 1.7	1628 1.5	1623 0.6	1755 1.8	1603 4.1	1641 4.2	1606 5.5	1556 6.0	
2150 4.7	2247 4.8	2258 4.3	2324 1.7	2138 1.0	2134 1.4	2144 1.5	2227 1.5	2309 1.4	
0437 1.5	0508 1.7	0504 1.5	0508 0.6	0615 1.7	0426 3.9	0454 4.0	0431 5.1	0436 5.8	11 TH
1036 4.4	1139 4.5	1147 4.0	1221 1.5	1015 0.9	1006 1.3	1020 1.4	1101 1.5	1148 1.7	
1708 1.7	1740 1.9	1735 1.8	1742 0.7	1939 1.8	1723 4.0	1759 4.1	1723 5.3	1709 5.7	
2312 4.5				2301 1.1	2252 1.5	2306 1.6	2347 1.7		
0557 1.6	0000 4.7	0012 4.2	0037 1.6	0801 1.7	0550 3.9	0624 3.9	0556 5.0	0025 1.6	12 F
1159 4.4	0627 1.8	0621 1.6	0636 0.6	1135 1.0	1128 1.3	1140 1.5	1223 1.6	0600 5.6	
1828 1.7	1257 4.5	1308 4.0	1351 1.5	2030 1.8	1842 4.1	1913 4.2	1846 5.3	1311 1.8	
	1904 1.9	1853 1.8	1909 0.7					1830 5.7	
0032 4.6	0120 4.7	0133 4.2	0203 1.6	0018 1.0	0012 1.5	0024 1.6	0109 1.6	0148 1.5	13 SA
0711 1.4	0746 1.6	0741 1.5	0754 0.6	0839 1.7	0707 3.9	0739 3.9	0718 5.0	0718 5.7	
1311 4.5	1415 4.6	1425 4.1	1512 1.6	1246 0.9	1243 1.2	1253 1.4	1339 1.5	1428 1.7	
1936 1.5	2019 1.7	2010 1.5	2021 0.7	2044 1.9	1948 4.2	2016 4.3	1955 5.5	1940 5.9	
0137 4.8	0236 4.8	0248 4.4	0321 1.7	0121 0.9	0120 1.2	0130 1.4	0216 1.4	0300 1.3	14 SU
0812 1.2	0851 1.2	0851 1.2	0854 0.5	0845 1.7	0810 4.0	0836 4.1	0823 5.3	0820 5.9	
1408 4.8	1519 4.9	1531 4.4	1613 1.7	1342 0.8	1346 1.0	1352 1.2	1440 1.2	1534 1.4	
2033 1.2	2121 1.4	2116 1.3	2116 0.6	2045 1.9	2041 4.3	2104 4.4	2050 5.7	2036 6.1	
0230 5.0	0337 5.0	0350 4.5	0421 1.8	0210 0.8	0216 1.0	0221 1.2	0310 1.1	0401 1.1	15 M
0901 1.0	0950 1.2	0949 1.0	0942 0.4	0845 1.8	0900 4.2	0921 4.2	0914 5.5	0909 6.1	
1454 5.0	1609 5.1	1626 4.5	1704 1.8	1429 0.7	1437 0.9	1441 1.0	1529 1.0	1631 1.3	
2120 1.0	2215 1.2	2212 1.0	2203 0.5	2046 2.0	2123 4.4	2144 4.4	2136 5.9	2122 6.3	

● ● Time: UT. For British Summer Time (shaded) March 26th to October 29th ADD ONE HOUR ● ●

MAY 2000 TIDE TABLES

•• Time: UT. For British Summer Time (shaded) March 26th to October 29TH ADD ONE HOUR ••

	ST MARY'S, SCILLY Time	m	PLYMOUTH Time	m	DARTMOUTH Time	m	PORTLAND Time	m	POOLE Time	m	SOUTHAMPTON Time	m	PORTSMOUTH Time	m	SHOREHAM Time	m	DOVER Time	m
16 TU	0315	5.2	0425	5.1	0441	4.6	0513	1.9	0253	0.7	0302	0.8	0306	1.0	0355	0.9	0454	1.0
	0945	0.9	1038	1.0	1040	0.8	1024	0.3	0847	1.9	0942	4.3	1000	4.3	0956	5.7	0951	6.2
	1536	5.2	1651	5.2	1710	4.6	1748	1.9	1511	0.6	1521	0.7	1524	0.9	1614	0.8	1720	1.1
	2202	0.9	2300	1.0	2259	0.9	2245	0.4	2051	2.0	2201	4.4	2221	4.5	2216	6.0	2203	6.4
17 W	0354	5.3	0506	5.2	0526	4.7	0559	1.9	0334	0.6	0342	0.7	0348	0.8	0435	0.8	0539	0.9
	1024	0.8	1119	0.9	1122	0.8	1105	0.2	0857	1.9	1020	4.3	1039	4.3	1035	5.8	1028	6.3
	1613	5.3	1727	5.3	1748	4.7	1828	2.0	1551	0.6	1600	0.7	1605	0.8	1652	0.8	1800	1.1
	2240	0.8	2339	0.9	2341	0.8	2327	0.3	2104	2.0	2236	4.4	2258	4.5	2252	6.1	2242	6.5
18 TH O	0432	5.3	0540	5.3	0603	4.7	0639	2.0	0411	0.6	0418	0.6	0426	0.7	0512	0.7	0617	0.9
	1100	0.8	1156	0.9	1159	0.7	1145	0.2	0915	1.9	1056	4.3	1117	4.4	1111	5.9	1105	6.4
	1649	5.4	1759	5.4	1821	4.8	1904	2.1	1628	0.6	1636	0.7	1643	0.8	1728	0.8	1833	1.0
	2316	0.8							2127	2.0	2309	4.4	2334	4.5	2326	6.1	2321	6.5
19 F	0507	5.3	0014	0.9	0016	0.8	0006	0.2	0448	0.6	0452	0.6	0503	0.7	0545	0.8	0649	0.9
	1134	0.9	0613	5.3	0638	4.7	0715	2.0	0945	1.9	1130	4.3	1155	4.4	1147	5.9	1141	6.4
	1724	5.3	1230	0.9	1233	0.8	1223	0.2	1704	0.6	1709	0.7	1719	0.9	1801	0.9	1903	1.0
	2351	0.9	1830	5.4	1855	4.8	1936	2.1	2200	2.0	2341	4.4			2357	6.0	2357	6.5
20 SA	0542	5.2	0046	1.0	0049	0.8	0045	0.2	0522	0.6	0523	0.6	0010	4.5	0616	0.8	0720	0.9
	1206	1.0	0645	5.3	0712	4.7	0745	1.9	1030	1.9	1204	4.3	0537	0.8	1221	5.8	1217	6.4
	1758	5.3	1301	1.0	1303	0.9	1258	0.2	1739	0.7	1740	0.8	1235	4.4	1833	1.0	1933	1.0
			1902	5.4	1925	4.8	2003	2.0	2245	1.9			1753	1.0				
21 SU	0024	1.0	0118	1.1	0119	0.9	0121	0.2	0555	0.7	0012	4.3	0046	4.4	0028	5.9	0033	6.3
	0615	5.1	0719	5.2	0745	4.6	0814	1.8	1127	1.9	0552	0.7	0609	0.9	0647	1.0	0751	1.0
	1239	1.2	1332	1.2	1331	1.0	1329	0.3	1811	0.8	1238	4.2	1314	4.3	1254	5.7	1251	6.3
	1832	5.1	1934	5.3	1958	4.7	2030	1.9	2337	1.9	1810	1.0	1825	1.1	1906	1.2	2005	1.1
22 M	0057	1.2	0150	1.3	0148	1.0	0151	0.3	0628	0.7	0045	4.2	0120	4.3	0058	5.7	0106	6.2
	0649	4.9	0754	5.0	0815	4.4	0842	1.7	1233	1.8	0622	0.9	0641	1.0	0719	1.1	0821	1.2
	1312	1.4	1402	1.4	1359	1.2	1354	0.4	1844	0.9	1315	4.1	1352	4.2	1327	5.6	1324	6.2
	1907	5.0	2007	5.1	2026	4.5	2055	1.8			1842	1.1	1857	1.3	1940	1.4	2038	1.2
23 TU	0131	1.4	0221	1.5	0218	1.2	0218	0.4	0033	1.8	0122	4.1	0152	4.2	0130	5.5	0137	5.9
	0725	4.7	0827	4.8	0845	4.2	0910	1.6	0700	0.8	0654	1.0	0712	1.2	0753	1.3	0854	1.4
	1346	1.5	1433	1.7	1427	1.4	1412	0.5	1343	1.8	1355	4.0	1429	4.1	1402	5.4	1357	6.0
	1945	4.8	2039	5.0	2056	4.4	2121	1.7	1919	1.0	1918	1.4	1930	1.5	2017	1.6	2112	1.5
24 W	0209	1.6	0256	1.7	0249	1.5	0239	0.5	0139	1.7	0203	3.9	0227	4.0	0208	5.2	0212	5.7
	0804	4.5	0901	4.6	0917	4.0	0941	1.5	0737	0.9	0733	1.3	0748	1.3	0833	1.5	0929	1.6
	1426	1.7	1508	1.9	1500	1.7	1430	0.6	1503	1.7	1442	3.8	1509	4.0	1443	5.2	1436	5.8
	2027	4.6	2113	4.8	2129	4.2	2150	1.6	2000	1.1	2002	1.6	2010	1.7	2101	1.8	2151	1.7
25 TH	0253	1.7	0335	1.9	0328	1.7	0306	0.5	0301	1.6	0252	3.8	0308	3.9	0255	4.9	0255	5.5
	0851	4.3	0940	4.5	0956	3.8	1018	1.4	0821	1.0	0820	1.5	0830	1.5	0919	1.8	1009	1.9
	1515	1.9	1550	2.1	1541	1.9	1500	0.6	1642	1.7	1538	3.7	1600	3.9	1534	5.0	1524	5.6
	2120	4.4	2156	4.6	2212	4.0	2226	1.5	2054	1.2	2059	1.8	2101	1.8	2155	2.0	2236	1.9
26 F	0348	1.9	0424	2.1	0414	1.9	0354	0.6	0444	1.6	0349	3.7	0401	3.7	0352	4.7	0356	5.2
	0950	4.1	1031	4.4	1052	3.7	1110	1.3	0921	1.1	0921	1.6	0928	1.7	1015	1.9	1100	2.1
	1618	2.1	1645	2.3	1637	2.1	1554	0.7	1842	1.6	1644	3.7	1712	3.8	1637	4.9	1627	5.4
	2227	4.3	2252	4.6	2312	3.9	2321	1.4	2217	1.2	2208	1.8	2222	2.0	2259	2.1	2333	2.0
27 SA	0457	2.0	0527	2.2	0516	2.0	0518	0.6	0646	1.5	0458	3.6	0515	3.6	0503	4.6	0510	5.2
	1105	4.1	1139	4.3	1201	3.7	1224	1.3	1053	1.1	1034	1.7	1058	1.8	1122	2.0	1203	2.2
	1733	2.0	1755	2.3	1746	2.1	1742	0.8	1957	1.6	1755	3.7	1818	3.9	1749	4.9	1739	5.4
	2342	4.3							2343	1.2	2321	1.8	2348	1.9				
28 SU	0611	1.8	0004	4.5	0026	3.9	0045	1.4	0808	1.5	0610	3.6	0633	3.7	0010	2.0	0042	2.0
	1220	4.3	0640	2.1	0631	1.9	0653	0.6	1204	1.1	1146	1.6	1210	1.7	0616	4.7	0621	5.3
	1845	1.9	1257	4.4	1316	3.8	1354	1.4	2033	1.7	1859	3.9	1920	4.0	1234	1.8	1315	2.1
			1912	2.2	1905	2.0	1921	0.7							1858	5.1	1848	5.5
29 M	0049	4.5	0120	4.7	0140	4.0	0216	1.5	0039	1.1	0029	1.5	0046	1.7	0115	1.7	0157	1.8
	0715	1.6	0753	1.8	0746	1.7	0800	0.5	0838	1.6	0714	3.8	0738	3.8	0721	5.0	0722	5.6
	1321	4.6	1406	4.7	1426	4.0	1514	1.5	1257	1.0	1251	1.4	1305	1.5	1338	1.5	1428	1.8
	1944	1.6	2024	1.9	2017	1.7	2026	0.6	2044	1.8	1953	4.0	2017	4.2	1955	5.4	1945	5.8
30 TU	0145	4.8	0227	4.9	0248	4.3	0332	1.6	0127	0.9	0125	1.2	0136	1.4	0212	1.3	0306	1.5
	0809	1.3	0857	1.5	0851	1.3	0854	0.4	0845	1.7	0808	4.0	0834	4.0	0816	5.4	0813	5.9
	1412	4.9	1504	4.9	1528	4.3	1615	1.7	1345	0.8	1346	1.1	1355	1.2	1433	1.2	1532	1.5
	2036	1.2	2125	1.5	2120	1.3	2119	0.5	2045	1.9	2039	4.2	2105	4.3	2047	5.7	2033	6.2
31 W	0234	5.2	0325	5.1	0350	4.5	0434	1.8	0213	0.7	0216	0.9	0224	1.1	0303	1.0	0406	1.2
	0859	0.9	0954	1.2	0949	1.0	0944	0.2	0845	1.9	0856	4.2	0922	4.3	0904	5.7	0859	6.2
	1458	5.2	1557	5.2	1625	4.6	1709	1.9	1431	0.7	1435	0.9	1443	0.9	1524	0.9	1629	1.2
	2124	0.9	2220	1.1	2217	0.9	2209	0.3	2046	2.0	2121	4.4	2148	4.5	2133	6.0	2118	6.5

SOUTH COAST OF ENGLAND Time Zone UT
St Mary's * Plymouth * Dartmouth * Portland * Poole * Southampton * Portsmouth * Shoreham * Dover
TIDE TABLES JUNE 2000

Day	ST MARY'S SCILLY Time	m	PLYMOUTH Time	m	DARTMOUTH Time	m	PORTLAND Time	m	POOLE Time	m	SOUTHAMPTON Time	m	PORTSMOUTH Time	m	SHOREHAM Time	m	DOVER Time	m
1 TH	0320	5.5	0418	5.3	0447	4.7	0530	1.9	0257	0.6	0304	0.7	0310	0.8	0353	0.7	0500	1.0
	0946	0.7	1046	0.9	1045	0.7	1033	0.1	0849	2.0	0942	4.3	1007	4.4	0953	6.0	0944	6.5
	1542	5.5	1647	5.4	1716	4.9	1800	2.1	1517	0.5	1525	0.6	1531	0.7	1614	0.7	1721	1.0
	2211	0.7	2311	0.8	2312	0.7	2256	0.2	2054	2.1	2203	4.5	2230	4.7	2219	6.2	2203	6.7
2 F ●	0406	5.7	0510	5.5	0538	4.9	0622	2.1	0343	0.5	0353	0.5	0357	0.5	0441	0.6	0550	0.8
	1033	0.6	1136	0.7	1138	0.5	1120	0.1	0902	2.0	1026	4.5	1053	4.6	1043	6.3	1030	6.7
	1627	5.7	1736	5.6	1805	5.0	1847	2.2	1603	0.5	1615	0.5	1618	0.6	1702	0.7	1810	0.8
	2258	0.5					2343	0.1	2114	2.1	2246	4.6	2315	4.8	2306	6.4	2249	6.8
3 SA	0451	5.8	0000	0.6	0004	0.5	0712	2.1	0429	0.4	0442	0.3	0444	0.4	0529	0.6	0637	0.7
	1120	0.5	0600	5.5	0629	5.0	1206	0.1	0932	2.1	1112	4.5	1140	4.7	1134	6.3	1118	6.8
	1712	5.8	1223	0.5	1227	0.4	1933	2.2	1651	0.4	1704	0.4	1706	0.5	1751	0.7	1856	0.7
	2347	0.4	1824	5.7	1851	5.1			2151	2.2	2330	4.6			2354	6.4	2337	6.9
4 SU	0538	5.8	0047	0.5	0053	0.4	0030	0.1	0515	0.4	0530	0.2	0001	4.8	0617	0.7	0722	0.6
	1207	0.5	0651	5.5	0718	5.0	0759	2.1	1024	2.1	1200	4.6	0530	0.4	1226	6.3	1209	6.8
	1759	5.8	1309	0.5	1314	0.4	1253	0.1	1739	0.5	1753	0.4	1230	4.7	1838	0.8	1941	0.6
			1912	5.7	1935	5.1	2017	2.2	2248	2.1			1753	0.6				
5 M	0036	0.5	0134	0.5	0139	0.4	0116	0.1	0604	0.4	0017	4.6	0048	4.8	0042	6.4	0028	6.8
	0627	5.6	0743	5.4	0805	4.9	0845	2.1	1139	2.1	0619	0.3	0618	0.5	0706	0.8	0807	0.7
	1256	0.7	1355	0.7	1400	0.6	1339	0.2	1828	0.6	1251	4.5	1321	4.7	1317	6.3	1301	6.7
	1848	5.7	2001	5.6	2022	5.1	2100	2.2			1842	0.5	1841	0.7	1927	1.0	2027	0.7
6 TU	0127	0.6	0221	0.6	0225	0.6	0204	0.2	0004	2.1	0108	4.5	0136	4.7	0132	6.2	0123	6.7
	0717	5.4	0835	5.2	0852	4.8	0930	2.0	0654	0.5	0705	0.4	0706	0.6	0756	0.9	0854	0.8
	1347	0.9	1442	0.9	1444	0.8	1426	0.3	1318	2.1	1345	4.5	1416	4.6	1409	6.2	1353	6.6
	1939	5.4	2051	5.4	2109	4.9	2143	2.1	1919	0.7	1931	0.7	1930	0.9	2019	1.1	2115	0.8
7 W	0219	0.9	0309	0.9	0311	0.8	0254	0.3	0139	2.0	0201	4.3	0227	4.5	0222	6.0	0219	6.4
	0809	5.1	0928	5.0	0940	4.5	1018	1.9	0747	0.6	0754	0.6	0757	0.7	0846	1.1	0943	1.0
	1440	1.1	1530	1.2	1530	1.1	1515	0.4	1533	2.0	1445	4.3	1524	4.5	1501	6.0	1445	6.4
	2034	5.0	2142	5.2	2156	4.7	2229	1.9	2015	0.8	2024	1.0	2024	1.2	2114	1.3	2206	1.0
8 TH	0316	1.1	0400	1.2	0400	1.1	0348	0.4	0333	1.9	0302	4.2	0324	4.3	0317	5.7	0317	6.2
	0908	4.8	1022	4.8	1033	4.3	1109	1.7	0843	0.7	0847	0.8	0851	1.0	0941	1.2	1037	1.3
	1538	1.4	1622	1.5	1620	1.3	1610	0.6	1753	1.9	1550	4.2	1640	4.4	1557	5.7	1541	6.2
	2135	4.9	2237	5.0	2249	4.5	2321	1.8	2117	0.9	2122	1.2	2124	1.4	2214	1.4	2304	1.2
9 F	0419	1.3	0457	1.5	0452	1.3	0348	0.5	0551	1.8	0409	4.0	0439	4.0	0417	5.3	0420	5.9
	1013	4.6	1121	4.6	1132	4.1	1209	1.6	0948	0.8	0948	1.1	0954	1.3	1042	1.4	1138	1.6
	1644	1.5	1722	1.7	1715	1.6	1715	0.7	1919	1.9	1701	4.1	1741	4.3	1700	5.5	1643	6.0
	2243	4.7	2337	4.8	2350	4.3			2227	1.0	2228	1.4	2232	1.5	2323	1.5		
10 SA	0527	1.5	0601	1.6	0553	1.5	0020	1.7	0737	1.7	0523	3.9	0557	4.0	0527	5.1	0009	1.4
	1124	4.5	1225	4.6	1238	4.0	0601	0.6	1058	0.9	1056	1.2	1103	1.4	1151	1.5	0530	5.7
	1754	1.6	1831	1.9	1821	1.7	1317	1.5	2014	1.8	1812	4.1	1842	4.2	1809	5.4	1245	1.7
	2356	4.6					1827	0.7	2341	1.0	2338	1.4	2346	1.6			1753	5.8
11 SU	0636	1.5	0045	4.7	0058	4.2	0127	1.6	0827	1.7	0638	3.9	0706	3.9	0035	1.6	0118	1.5
	1234	4.5	0710	1.7	0702	1.5	0712	0.6	1209	1.0	1207	1.3	1215	1.5	0641	5.0	0642	5.7
	1901	1.6	1334	4.6	1346	4.1	1429	1.6	2039	1.8	1917	4.1	1942	4.2	1301	1.5	1352	1.7
			1940	1.8	1931	1.6	1939	0.7							1915	5.4	1901	5.8
12 M	0103	4.7	0156	4.7	0209	4.2	0237	1.6	0047	1.0	0044	1.4	0054	1.5	0141	1.6	0224	1.4
	0737	1.4	0815	1.6	0809	1.4	0814	0.5	0843	1.7	0742	3.9	0806	4.0	0746	5.0	0744	5.7
	1335	4.6	1439	4.7	1451	4.2	1532	1.6	1310	0.9	1309	1.3	1318	1.4	1404	1.4	1456	1.6
	2000	1.5	2044	1.7	2037	1.5	2040	0.7	2045	1.9	2012	4.2	2033	4.3	2013	5.5	2001	5.9
13 TU	0200	4.8	0259	4.8	0312	4.3	0340	1.6	0141	0.9	0141	1.2	0151	1.4	0238	1.4	0326	1.4
	0830	1.3	0912	1.5	0910	1.3	0906	0.5	0845	1.7	0837	4.0	0857	4.0	0842	5.2	0837	5.8
	1426	4.8	1533	4.9	1547	4.3	1626	1.7	1401	0.9	1405	1.2	1412	1.3	1459	1.3	1554	1.5
	2051	1.3	2139	1.5	2135	1.3	2131	0.6	2045	1.9	2057	4.2	2118	4.3	2104	5.6	2052	6.0
14 W	0248	4.9	0351	4.9	0408	4.4	0435	1.7	0228	0.8	0231	1.1	0240	1.2	0327	1.2	0421	1.3
	0916	1.2	1002	1.4	1003	1.2	0951	0.4	0846	1.8	0921	4.1	0941	4.1	0929	5.4	0923	6.0
	1510	5.0	1621	5.1	1636	4.4	1712	1.8	1447	0.8	1451	1.1	1459	1.2	1546	1.2	1645	1.4
	2136	1.2	2226	1.4	2227	1.2	2218	0.5	2047	1.9	2136	4.3	2158	4.3	2149	5.7	2138	6.2
15 TH	0331	5.0	0434	5.0	0455	4.4	0524	1.7	0311	0.7	0314	1.0	0324	1.1	0410	1.1	0507	1.2
	0957	1.1	1046	1.3	1049	1.1	1034	0.4	0851	1.8	1000	4.2	1021	4.2	1012	5.5	1005	6.1
	1551	5.1	1657	5.2	1717	4.5	1754	1.9	1528	0.8	1533	1.0	1542	1.1	1629	1.1	1727	1.3
			2308	1.3	2309	1.1	2300	0.4	2056	1.9	2212	4.3	2236	4.4	2228	5.8	2220	6.3

● ● Time: UT. For British Summer Time (shaded) March 26th to October 29th ADD ONE HOUR ● ●

JUNE 2000 TIDE TABLES

•• Time: UT. For British Summer Time (shaded) March 26th to October 29TH ADD ONE HOUR ••

Date	ST MARY'S, SCILLY Time	m	PLYMOUTH Time	m	DARTMOUTH Time	m	PORTLAND Time	m	POOLE Time	m	SOUTHAMPTON Time	m	PORTSMOUTH Time	m	SHOREHAM Time	m	DOVER Time	m
16 F O	0411	5.1	0512	5.1	0535	4.5	0607	1.8	0350	0.7	0352	0.8	0404	1.0	0449	1.0	0547	1.2
	1036	1.1	1125	1.2	1129	1.1	1116	0.3	0905	1.9	1036	4.2	1100	4.3	1052	5.6	1044	6.2
	1628	5.2	1732	5.3	1755	4.6	1833	2.0	1607	0.7	1610	1.0	1622	1.1	1707	1.1	1803	1.2
	2254	1.1	2345	1.2	2349	1.0	2342	0.4	2113	1.9	2244	4.3	2313	4.4	2306	5.8	2300	6.3
17 SA	0448	5.1	0548	5.2	0613	4.5	0646	1.8	0427	0.7	0427	0.8	0442	0.9	0524	1.0	0621	1.2
	1112	1.1	1202	1.2	1205	1.0	1157	0.3	0931	1.9	1112	4.2	1139	4.3	1130	5.7	1121	6.3
	1705	5.2	1806	5.3	1830	4.7	1909	2.0	1645	0.7	1645	0.9	1700	1.1	1741	1.1	1838	1.1
	2330	1.1							2140	1.9	2317	4.3	2350	4.4	2338	5.9	2338	6.3
18 SU	0523	5.1	0022	1.1	0023	1.0	0023	0.3	0503	0.7	0500	0.7	0518	0.9	0557	1.0	0654	1.1
	1146	1.2	0624	5.2	0650	4.5	0722	1.8	1011	1.9	1147	4.2	1219	4.3	1205	5.7	1158	6.3
	1739	5.2	1238	1.2	1237	1.0	1235	0.3	1721	0.8	1718	1.0	1736	1.1	1814	1.2	1912	1.1
			1839	5.4	1904	4.7	1942	2.0	2219	1.9	2350	4.3						
19 M	0005	1.1	0058	1.2	0057	1.0	0101	0.3	0539	0.7	0532	0.8	0026	4.4	0010	5.8	0015	6.2
	0557	5.0	0700	5.1	0725	4.5	0756	1.8	1102	1.9	1221	4.2	0553	1.0	0629	1.1	0727	1.1
	1220	1.2	1312	1.3	1310	1.1	1311	0.3	1755	0.8	1751	1.0	1258	4.3	1240	5.7	1234	6.3
	1814	5.2	1914	5.3	1936	4.7	2013	1.9	2305	1.9			1809	1.2	1848	1.3	1945	1.1
20 TU	0039	1.2	0133	1.3	0129	1.1	0136	0.3	0610	0.7	0024	4.2	0100	4.3	0042	5.7	0048	6.1
	0632	4.9	0734	5.0	0759	4.4	0827	1.7	1204	1.9	0605	0.8	0624	1.0	0702	1.2	0800	1.2
	1254	1.3	1346	1.4	1341	1.2	1342	0.4	1828	0.9	1257	4.1	1336	4.3	1314	5.6	1308	6.2
	1849	5.1	1947	5.2	2009	4.6	2042	1.9	2357	1.8	1826	1.1	1841	1.3	1922	1.4	2021	1.2
21 W	0114	1.3	0207	1.4	0201	1.2	0206	0.4	0644	0.8	0059	4.1	0132	4.2	0116	5.6	0121	6.0
	0706	4.8	0808	4.9	0832	4.3	0900	1.7	1306	1.8	0639	0.9	0657	1.1	0738	1.3	0835	1.3
	1329	1.4	1419	1.5	1413	1.3	1407	0.4	1902	0.9	1335	4.1	1410	4.2	1348	5.5	1341	6.1
	1925	5.0	2019	5.1	2042	4.5	2112	1.8			1902	1.2	1914	1.4	2000	1.5	2057	1.3
22 TH	0151	1.4	0242	1.5	0236	1.3	0232	0.4	0059	1.8	0139	4.0	0206	4.2	0153	5.4	0154	5.9
	0743	4.7	0840	4.8	0904	4.2	0932	1.6	0719	0.8	0716	1.1	0730	1.2	0816	1.4	0910	1.4
	1407	1.6	1453	1.7	1447	1.5	1430	0.5	1415	1.8	1418	4.0	1445	4.2	1426	5.4	1415	6.0
	2005	4.8	2052	5.0	2115	4.4	2142	1.7	1941	1.0	1943	1.3	1951	1.5	2040	1.6	2134	1.5
23 F	0231	1.5	0318	1.7	0313	1.5	0259	0.4	0213	1.7	0223	3.9	0244	4.1	0235	5.2	0232	5.7
	0825	4.6	0915	4.7	0940	4.0	1007	1.5	0759	0.9	0757	1.2	0809	1.3	0855	1.5	0948	1.6
	1450	1.7	1531	1.8	1525	1.6	1459	0.6	1535	1.8	1505	3.9	1525	4.1	1507	5.3	1455	5.9
	2050	4.7	2128	4.9	2152	4.2	2215	1.6	2027	1.0	2030	1.5	2035	1.6	2125	1.6	2214	1.6
24 SA	0318	1.7	0400	1.8	0354	1.6	0336	0.5	0345	1.7	0315	3.8	0330	4.0	0321	5.0	0318	5.6
	0913	4.5	0955	4.6	1023	3.9	1049	1.4	0848	1.0	0847	1.4	0856	1.4	0941	1.6	1031	1.8
	1541	1.8	1616	2.0	1610	1.6	1542	0.6	1714	1.7	1600	3.9	1617	4.0	1556	5.2	1545	5.8
	2143	4.6	2213	4.8	2237	4.1	2257	1.5	2121	1.1	2125	1.6	2128	1.7	2216	1.7	2301	1.8
25 SU	0412	1.7	0449	1.9	0444	1.7	0432	0.5	0529	1.6	0413	3.8	0426	3.9	0415	4.9	0418	5.5
	1012	4.4	1048	4.5	1114	3.9	1144	1.4	0949	1.0	0945	1.5	0955	1.6	1036	1.7	1124	1.9
	1642	1.9	1712	2.1	1706	1.9	1646	0.7	1853	1.7	1703	3.9	1720	4.0	1655	5.1	1644	5.7
	2246	4.5	2310	4.7	2333	4.0	2359	1.4	2234	1.1	2230	1.7	2239	1.7	2317	1.7	2358	1.8
26 M	0518	1.7	0549	1.9	0543	1.8	0546	0.5	0711	1.6	0520	3.7	0534	3.8	0518	4.9	0524	5.5
	1121	4.4	1155	4.5	1220	3.9	1256	1.4	1104	1.0	1052	1.5	1109	1.6	1141	1.7	1226	2.0
	1751	1.8	1818	2.1	1814	1.9	1812	0.7	2001	1.8	1807	3.9	1824	4.1	1800	5.1	1750	5.7
	2355	4.6							2347	1.1	2337	1.6	2353	1.6				
27 TU	0626	1.6	0023	4.7	0044	4.1	0119	1.4	0815	1.6	0629	3.8	0643	3.9	0024	1.6	0105	1.8
	1231	4.6	0659	1.9	0653	1.7	0703	0.5	1212	1.0	1200	1.5	1218	1.5	0626	5.0	0629	5.6
	1859	1.6	1310	4.6	1334	4.0	1416	1.5	2034	1.8	1907	4.1	1924	4.2	1249	1.6	1336	1.9
			1932	1.9	1928	1.7	1933	0.6							1906	5.3	1854	5.9
28 W	0102	4.8	0138	4.8	0201	4.2	0243	1.5	0047	0.9	0041	1.4	0054	1.4	0131	1.4	0216	1.6
	0729	1.4	0810	1.6	0805	1.5	0811	0.4	0841	1.7	0731	3.9	0749	4.0	0731	5.2	0730	5.9
	1333	4.8	1419	4.9	1444	4.3	1531	1.6	1310	0.9	1306	1.3	1318	1.3	1355	1.3	1447	1.7
	2000	1.4	2044	1.6	2041	1.5	2040	0.5	2045	1.9	2001	4.2	2024	4.3	2008	5.5	1954	6.1
29 TH	0201	5.1	0246	5.0	0312	4.4	0357	1.7	0141	0.8	0141	1.1	0151	1.2	0233	1.2	0324	1.4
	0827	1.2	0917	1.4	0913	1.2	0912	0.3	0845	1.8	0827	4.1	0850	4.2	0833	5.5	0827	6.1
	1429	5.2	1521	5.1	1549	4.5	1635	1.8	1403	0.8	1404	1.1	1414	1.1	1455	1.1	1553	1.4
	2057	1.2	2148	1.3	2147	1.1	2139	0.4	2045	2.0	2052	4.4	2118	4.5	2105	5.8	2049	6.4
30 F	0255	5.3	0349	5.2	0418	4.6	0502	1.8	0233	0.7	0237	0.8	0245	0.9	0330	0.9	0427	1.1
	0921	0.9	1018	1.1	1016	0.9	1008	0.3	0846	1.9	0918	4.3	0945	4.4	0931	5.9	0921	6.4
	1521	5.4	1620	5.3	1649	4.8	1733	2.0	1456	0.6	1501	0.8	1509	0.9	1553	0.9	1654	1.1
	2151	0.8	2247	0.9	2248	0.8	2236	0.3	2049	2.1	2140	4.5	2209	4.6	2159	6.1	2142	6.6

SOUTH COAST OF ENGLAND Time Zone UT

St Mary's * Plymouth * Dartmouth * Portland * Poole * Southampton * Portsmouth * Shoreham * Dover

TIDE TABLES JULY 2000

ST MARY'S, SCILLY Time m	PLYMOUTH Time m	DARTMOUTH Time m	PORTLAND Time m	POOLE Time m	SOUTHAMPTON Time m	PORTSMOUTH Time m	SHOREHAM Time m	DOVER Time m	
0347 5.5	0449 5.3	0519 4.8	0602 2.0	0324 0.5	0331 0.6	0338 0.7	0424 0.8	0525 0.9	**1 SA**
1014 0.7	1114 0.8	1116 0.7	1102 0.2	0856 2.0	1009 4.4	1037 4.6	1027 6.1	1015 6.6	
1611 5.7	1716 5.5	1745 5.0	1827 2.1	1548 0.6	1556 0.6	1602 0.7	1645 0.8	1750 0.9	
2243 0.6	2342 0.7	2347 0.6	2328 0.2	2104 2.1	2226 4.6	2257 4.8	2250 6.3	2234 6.8	
0438 5.7	0547 5.4	0614 4.9	0657 2.1	0414 0.4	0424 0.4	0429 0.5	0516 0.8	0621 0.8	**2 SU**
1105 0.6	1207 0.7	1211 0.5	1153 0.1	0922 2.1	1059 4.5	1127 4.7	1123 6.3	1107 6.8	●
1700 5.8	1810 5.6	1836 5.1	1919 2.2	1638 0.5	1650 0.5	1653 0.6	1738 0.9	1842 0.7	
2335 0.5				2136 2.2	2315 4.6	2345 4.8	2342 6.4	2327 6.8	
0527 5.7	0035 0.5	0039 0.4	0019 0.2	0503 0.4	0516 0.3	0518 0.4	0608 0.8	0713 0.7	**3 M**
1156 0.6	0643 5.4	0706 4.9	0750 2.1	1008 2.1	1150 4.6	1217 4.8	1216 6.4	1159 6.8	
1749 5.9	1258 0.6	1303 0.5	1242 0.1	1727 0.5	1743 0.5	1742 0.6	1829 0.8	1933 0.6	
	1903 5.7	1925 5.2	2008 2.3	2228 2.1					
0027 0.4	0125 0.5	0129 0.3	0109 0.1	0552 0.4	0004 4.6	0033 4.8	0031 6.4	0020 6.8	**4 TU**
0616 5.7	0737 5.4	0756 4.9	0839 2.1	1119 2.1	0607 0.2	0606 0.4	0658 0.8	0803 0.7	
1246 0.6	1347 0.6	1350 0.5	1329 0.1	1816 0.5	1241 4.6	1309 4.8	1309 6.4	1251 6.8	
1838 5.8	1954 5.6	2012 5.2	2054 2.3	2339 2.1	1833 0.5	1830 0.7	1920 1.0	2023 0.6	
0117 0.5	0214 0.5	0216 0.4	0157 0.1	0641 0.4	0054 4.5	0121 4.7	0122 6.3	0114 6.7	**5 W**
0705 5.5	0827 5.3	0843 4.8	0925 2.1	1253 2.1	0656 0.3	0654 0.5	0746 0.9	0852 0.7	
1335 0.7	1433 0.8	1436 0.6	1415 0.2	1905 0.6	1333 4.6	1403 4.7	1400 6.3	1340 6.7	
1927 5.6	2042 5.5	2059 5.0	2139 2.2		1922 0.6	1917 0.8	2010 1.0	2112 0.6	
0206 0.7	0300 0.7	0300 0.6	0244 0.2	0104 2.0	0147 4.4	0209 4.5	0212 6.1	0206 6.5	**6 TH**
0754 5.3	0915 5.1	0930 4.7	1009 1.9	0729 0.5	0743 0.4	0740 0.7	0835 0.9	0939 0.9	
1424 0.9	1518 1.0	1518 0.8	1500 0.3	1555 2.0	1428 4.5	1535 4.6	1448 6.2	1427 6.6	
2017 5.4	2128 5.3	2145 4.8	2221 2.0	1955 0.7	2010 0.8	2005 1.0	2100 1.1	2200 0.9	
0257 0.9	0346 1.0	0344 0.8	0332 0.3	0251 1.9	0242 4.2	0303 4.4	0301 5.8	0257 6.3	**7 F**
0845 5.0	1001 4.9	1016 4.4	1054 1.8	0820 0.6	0829 0.7	0829 0.9	0924 1.0	1026 1.2	
1515 1.2	1604 1.3	1602 1.1	1547 0.4	1726 2.0	1524 4.3	1624 4.5	1535 6.0	1515 6.4	
2109 5.1	2214 5.1	2229 4.6	2304 1.9	2048 0.8	2059 1.0	2056 1.2	2152 1.2	2249 1.0	
0349 1.2	0433 1.3	0430 1.1	0422 0.4	0454 1.8	0341 4.0	0406 4.2	0352 5.5	0349 6.0	**8 SA**
0939 4.7	1048 4.8	1103 4.2	1139 1.6	0914 0.8	0920 1.0	0921 1.1	1014 1.2	1114 1.4	
1609 1.4	1651 1.6	1648 1.4	1637 0.6	1838 1.9	1626 4.2	1709 4.3	1626 5.7	1608 6.1	
2206 4.8	2301 4.9	2317 4.3	2349 1.7	2147 1.0	2153 1.3	2153 1.4	2247 1.4	2341 1.3	
0447 1.5	0523 1.7	0518 1.4	0518 0.5	0648 1.7	0447 3.9	0516 4.0	0448 5.2	0447 5.7	**9 SU**
1041 4.5	1139 4.6	1156 4.0	1231 1.5	1016 0.9	1018 1.2	1021 1.4	1112 1.5	1206 1.7	
1712 1.6	1746 1.9	1739 1.6	1736 0.7	1940 1.8	1731 4.0	1800 4.2	1723 5.4	1708 5.9	
2312 4.6	2356 4.7			2255 1.0	2254 1.5	2300 1.6	2351 1.6		
0551 1.7	0621 1.9	0011 4.1	0040 1.6	0800 1.6	0558 3.8	0622 3.9	0550 4.9	0037 1.5	**10 M**
1149 4.4	1239 4.5	0614 1.6	0619 0.6	1125 1.0	1122 1.5	1130 1.6	1216 1.7	0551 5.6	
1818 1.8	1851 2.0	1254 3.9	1332 1.5	2023 1.8	1838 4.0	1857 4.1	1826 5.2	1304 1.9	
		1841 1.8	1845 0.8		2359 1.6			1815 5.7	
0021 4.5	0101 4.6	0115 4.0	0140 1.5	0009 1.1	0708 3.8	0015 1.7	0058 1.7	0139 1.7	**11 TU**
0656 1.7	0726 2.0	0719 1.7	0724 0.6	0836 1.6	1228 1.6	0728 3.8	0700 4.8	0700 5.5	
1257 4.3	1346 4.6	1358 4.0	1439 1.5	1235 1.0	1938 4.0	1242 1.6	1324 1.8	1409 2.0	
1924 1.7	1957 2.0	1951 1.8	1957 0.8	2042 1.8		1957 4.1	1931 5.1	1923 5.7	
0127 4.5	0212 4.6	0223 4.0	0248 1.4	0113 1.0	0104 1.5	0121 1.6	0201 1.7	0245 1.7	**12 W**
0756 1.7	0830 1.9	0826 1.7	0825 0.6	0845 1.6	0810 3.8	0830 3.8	0805 4.8	0803 5.6	
1357 4.6	1451 4.7	1505 4.1	1542 1.5	1335 1.0	1331 1.6	1344 1.6	1426 1.7	1515 1.9	
2022 1.6	2100 1.9	2056 1.7	2100 0.7	2045 1.8	2029 4.0	2051 4.1	2031 5.2	2024 5.8	
0224 4.6	0315 4.7	0330 4.1	0353 1.5	0204 1.0	0200 1.4	0215 1.5	0258 1.6	0345 1.7	**13 TH**
0848 1.6	0927 1.7	0926 1.5	0918 0.6	0845 1.7	0900 3.9	0922 4.0	0901 5.0	0857 5.7	
1448 4.8	1545 4.9	1601 4.2	1635 1.6	1424 1.0	1424 1.5	1436 1.5	1521 1.6	1612 1.7	
2112 1.5	2154 1.7	2154 1.5	2152 0.6	2045 1.8	2113 4.1	2136 4.2	2123 5.3	2116 5.9	
0312 4.7	0407 4.9	0426 4.2	0448 1.5	0250 0.9	0249 1.3	0303 1.3	0346 1.4	0438 1.5	**14 F**
0934 1.4	1016 1.6	1017 1.4	1006 0.5	0848 1.8	0944 4.0	1006 4.1	0952 5.3	0944 5.9	
1531 5.0	1630 5.1	1649 4.4	1721 1.6	1509 0.9	1510 1.3	1522 1.4	1607 1.4	1700 1.5	
2156 1.3	2241 1.5	2242 1.3	2238 0.5	2050 1.8	2150 4.2	2216 4.2	2210 5.5	2202 6.0	
0354 4.9	0451 5.0	0514 4.3	0538 1.6	0331 0.8	0331 1.1	0345 1.2	0429 1.3	0521 1.4	**15 SA**
1015 1.3	1100 1.4	1103 1.3	1051 0.4	0859 1.8	1022 4.1	1045 4.2	1036 5.5	1025 6.1	
1611 5.1	1710 5.2	1731 4.5	1806 1.9	1550 0.8	1550 1.2	1604 1.3	1648 1.3	1742 1.4	
2236 1.2	2324 1.3	2325 1.2	2321 0.4	2102 1.9	2225 4.2	2253 4.3	2249 5.7	2242 6.1	

● ● Time: UT. For British Summer Time (shaded) March 26th to October 29th ADD ONE HOUR ● ●

JULY 2000 TIDE TABLES

•• Time: UT. For British Summer Time (shaded) March 26th to October 29TH ADD ONE HOUR ••

	ST MARY'S, SCILLY		PLYMOUTH		DARTMOUTH		PORTLAND		POOLE		SOUTHAMPTON		PORTSMOUTH		SHOREHAM		DOVER	
	Time	m	Time	m	Time	m	Time	m	Time	m	Time	m	Time	m	Time	m	Time	m
16 SU O	0431	5.0	0530	5.1	0556	4.4	0624	1.7	0409	0.7	0408	0.9	0424	1.0	0507	1.1	0600	1.3
	1052	1.2	1142	1.3	1142	1.2	1133	0.4	0918	1.9	1057	4.2	1122	4.3	1115	5.6	1103	6.3
	1648	5.2	1746	5.3	1810	4.6	1847	1.9	1627	0.8	1626	1.1	1642	1.2	1724	1.3	1819	1.2
	2312	1.1							2123	1.9	2259	4.2	2329	4.4	2323	5.8	2320	6.2
17 M	0506	5.1	0004	1.2	0004	1.1	0002	0.4	0446	0.7	0442	0.8	0501	1.0	0540	1.1	0635	1.3
	1128	1.2	0607	5.1	0633	4.4	0706	1.8	0950	1.9	1132	4.2	1200	4.2	1151	5.7	1139	6.4
	1722	5.3	1220	1.3	1219	1.1	1215	0.3	1703	0.8	1700	1.0	1718	1.2	1758	1.3	1854	1.2
	2347	1.1	1821	5.4	1845	4.7	1926	2.0	2154	1.9	2332	4.3			2356	5.8	2355	6.2
18 TU	0540	5.1	0042	1.2	0040	1.0	0041	0.3	0521	0.7	0517	0.7	0004	4.4	0614	1.1	0709	1.2
	1202	1.2	0642	5.1	0709	4.5	0744	1.8	1032	1.9	1206	4.3	0536	1.0	1225	5.8	1214	6.4
	1756	5.3	1257	1.2	1253	1.1	1253	0.3	1736	0.8	1736	0.9	1236	4.4	1832	1.3	1930	1.1
			1855	5.4	1921	4.7	2001	2.0	2234	1.9			1751	1.2				
19 W	0021	1.1	0118	1.2	0114	1.0	0118	0.3	0554	0.7	0006	4.3	0038	4.4	0027	5.8	0029	6.2
	0613	5.1	0716	5.1	0742	4.5	0819	1.8	1124	1.9	0551	0.7	0608	1.0	0648	1.1	0744	1.2
	1236	1.2	1331	1.2	1326	1.1	1327	0.3	1809	0.8	1239	4.3	1312	4.4	1258	5.8	1248	6.4
	1830	5.3	1928	5.4	1953	4.7	2035	1.9	2321	1.9	1812	0.9	1823	1.2	1906	1.3	2006	1.1
20 TH	0055	1.1	0152	1.2	0149	1.0	0150	0.3	0626	0.7	0041	4.2	0110	4.4	0102	5.7	0101	6.2
	0646	5.0	0748	5.1	0816	4.4	0851	1.8	1218	1.9	0626	0.8	0639	1.0	0722	1.1	0818	1.2
	1310	1.2	1404	1.3	1401	1.1	1357	0.3	1842	0.8	1313	4.2	1344	4.4	1331	5.7	1320	6.3
	1904	5.2	2000	5.3	2027	4.7	2106	1.9			1847	1.0	1855	1.2	1941	1.2	2041	1.1
21 F	0130	1.2	0226	1.3	0222	1.1	0219	0.3	0016	1.9	0116	4.2	0143	4.3	0136	5.6	0133	6.1
	0721	5.0	0820	5.0	0849	4.4	0923	1.7	0700	0.7	0700	0.8	0712	1.0	0758	1.1	0853	1.3
	1346	1.3	1437	1.4	1434	1.2	1424	0.3	1320	1.9	1350	4.2	1417	4.3	1405	5.7	1352	6.3
	1940	5.1	2033	5.2	2100	4.6	2136	1.8	1919	0.8	1923	1.1	1930	1.2	2018	1.2	2116	1.2
22 SA	0207	1.3	0300	1.4	0256	1.2	0246	0.3	0126	1.9	0155	4.1	0220	4.3	0213	5.5	0206	6.0
	0758	4.9	0853	4.9	0923	4.3	0954	1.6	0736	0.8	0735	1.0	0747	1.1	0833	1.2	0927	1.4
	1425	1.4	1512	1.5	1509	1.3	1450	0.4	1433	1.9	1431	4.1	1454	4.3	1440	5.6	1426	6.2
	2021	5.0	2106	5.1	2134	4.4	2206	1.7	1958	0.9	2002	1.2	2008	1.3	2056	1.3	2152	1.4
23 SU	0248	1.4	0336	1.6	0333	1.4	0318	0.4	0249	1.8	0239	4.0	0302	4.2	0251	5.4	0245	5.9
	0841	4.8	0927	4.8	0959	4.2	1028	1.5	0818	0.8	0815	1.2	0827	1.2	0913	1.3	1005	1.5
	1509	1.6	1550	1.7	1547	1.5	1524	0.5	1602	1.8	1518	4.1	1539	4.2	1520	5.5	1506	6.1
	2106	4.8	2143	5.0	2212	4.3	2240	1.6	2045	0.9	2048	1.4	2053	1.4	2140	1.4	2231	1.5
24 M	0335	1.5	0416	1.7	0414	1.5	0400	0.4	0426	1.8	0332	3.9	0351	4.1	0335	5.2	0333	5.8
	0931	4.6	1010	4.7	1040	4.0	1109	1.5	0908	0.9	0903	1.4	0915	1.3	0959	1.4	1048	1.7
	1601	1.7	1636	1.9	1634	1.7	1611	0.5	1740	1.8	1614	4.0	1632	4.2	1609	5.3	1558	6.0
	2202	4.7	2229	4.8	2256	4.2	2325	1.5	2144	1.0	2143	1.6	2150	1.5	2235	1.5	2318	1.7
25 TU	0433	1.7	0507	1.8	0504	1.6	0457	0.5	0612	1.7	0435	3.8	0452	4.0	0429	5.0	0434	5.7
	1033	4.5	1106	4.6	1133	4.0	1206	1.4	1013	1.0	1006	1.5	1018	1.5	1057	1.6	1142	1.9
	1706	1.8	1734	2.0	1732	1.8	1718	0.6	1911	1.8	1719	4.0	1734	4.2	1712	5.1	1701	5.9
	2309	4.6	2333	4.7	2357	4.1			2259	1.0	2251	1.6	2304	1.6	2340	1.6		
26 W	0542	1.7	0612	1.9	0608	1.7	0031	1.4	0741	1.7	0548	3.8	0601	4.0	0539	5.0	0019	1.8
	1147	4.5	1221	4.6	1247	4.0	0613	0.5	1131	1.0	1119	1.6	1136	1.5	1210	1.6	0543	5.7
	1821	1.7	1848	2.0	1845	1.8	1322	1.4	2014	1.8	1828	4.0	1841	4.2	1826	5.1	1251	1.9
							1843	0.7									1812	5.9
27 TH	0025	4.7	0057	4.7	0119	4.1	0157	1.5	0013	1.0	0005	1.5	0019	1.5	0055	1.6	0132	1.8
	0655	1.6	0729	1.8	0727	1.6	0735	0.5	0831	1.7	0702	3.9	0715	4.0	0657	5.1	0656	5.8
	1302	4.7	1341	4.8	1408	4.2	1448	1.5	1241	1.0	1235	1.5	1248	1.5	1326	1.5	1409	1.8
	1933	1.5	2009	1.8	2007	1.6	2009	0.6	2041	1.8	1933	4.1	1952	4.2	1940	5.3	1924	6.0
28 F	0136	4.9	0217	4.8	0243	4.2	0327	1.6	0117	0.9	0117	1.3	0125	1.3	0209	1.4	0250	1.6
	0803	1.4	0848	1.6	0845	1.4	0850	0.5	0845	1.8	0808	4.1	0830	4.2	0811	5.4	0806	6.0
	1408	5.0	1454	5.0	1524	4.4	1607	1.7	1344	0.9	1345	1.3	1354	1.3	1437	1.3	1527	1.6
	2039	1.2	2124	1.5	2124	1.3	2124	0.5	2045	1.9	2031	4.3	2100	4.4	2047	5.7	2031	6.2
29 SA	0239	5.1	0330	5.0	0359	4.5	0444	1.7	0216	0.7	0221	1.0	0227	1.1	0315	1.1	0403	1.3
	0905	1.1	0957	1.3	0956	1.1	0955	0.4	0845	1.9	0906	4.3	0934	4.4	0917	5.7	0910	6.3
	1506	5.3	1602	5.3	1630	4.7	1715	1.9	1443	0.8	1448	1.0	1455	1.1	1540	1.1	1635	1.2
	2138	0.9	2230	1.1	2233	0.9	2226	0.4	2047	2.0	2124	4.4	2155	4.6	2146	6.0	2131	6.4
30 SU	0336	5.4	0438	5.2	0506	4.7	0550	1.9	0312	0.6	0319	0.7	0325	0.8	0413	0.9	0509	1.1
	1001	0.8	1100	1.0	1101	0.8	1052	0.2	0853	2.0	0958	4.4	1027	4.6	1017	6.1	1006	6.6
	1559	5.6	1704	5.5	1731	5.0	1815	2.1	1537	0.6	1546	0.7	1551	0.9	1637	0.9	1736	0.9
	2233	0.6	2330	0.7	2334	0.6	2321	0.2	2058	2.1	2213	4.5	2244	4.7	2240	6.3	2226	6.7
31 M	0427	5.6	0539	5.4	0605	4.9	0648	2.0	0403	0.5	0414	0.4	0418	0.5	0507	0.8	0610	0.9
	1054	0.6	1156	0.7	1159	0.6	1143	0.1	0914	2.1	1049	4.6	1115	4.7	1113	6.3	1058	6.8
	1649	5.8	1800	5.6	1824	5.2	1909	2.3	1627	0.5	1640	0.5	1642	0.7	1728	0.9	1833	0.7
	2324	0.4							2124	2.2	2302	4.6	2330	4.8	2330	6.4	2318	6.8

SOUTH COAST OF ENGLAND Time Zone UT

St Mary's * Plymouth * Dartmouth * Portland * Poole * Southampton * Portsmouth * Shoreham * Dover

TIDE TABLES AUGUST 2000

ST MARY'S, SCILLY Time	m	PLYMOUTH Time	m	DARTMOUTH Time	m	PORTLAND Time	m	POOLE Time	m	SOUTHAMPTON Time	m	PORTSMOUTH Time	m	SHOREHAM Time	m	DOVER Time	m		
0515	5.7	0024	0.5	0027	0.3	0011	0.1	0451	0.4	0505	0.2	0506	0.4	0557	0.8	0706	0.7	**1**	**TU**
1144	0.5	0635	5.5	0657	5.0	0741	2.1	0953	2.2	1137	4.7	1203	4.8	1205	6.4	1148	6.9		
1736	5.9	1248	0.5	1250	0.4	1231	0.1	1714	0.5	1731	0.4	1729	0.6	1819	0.9	1926	0.5		●
		1853	5.7	1914	5.2	1958	2.4	2207	2.2	2350	4.6								
0013	0.3	0115	0.4	0117	0.2	0058	0.1	0538	0.4	0555	0.2	0016	4.8	0019	6.4	0009	6.8	**2**	**W**
0602	5.7	0725	5.5	0743	5.0	0828	2.2	1052	2.1	1226	4.7	0552	0.4	0645	0.8	0758	0.7		
1231	0.5	1335	0.5	1338	0.3	1315	0.1	1759	0.5	1820	0.4	1251	4.8	1254	6.5	1235	6.9		
1822	5.9	1940	5.7	2000	5.2	2043	2.4	2308	2.1			1813	0.6	1907	0.9	2015	0.5		
0100	0.4	0200	0.4	0202	0.2	0143	0.0	0622	0.4	0038	4.6	0102	4.7	0106	6.4	0058	6.7	**3**	**TH**
0646	5.6	0810	5.4	0829	4.9	0911	2.1	1211	2.1	0641	0.2	0635	0.4	0731	0.8	0844	0.7		
1316	0.6	1419	0.6	1419	0.4	1358	0.1	1844	0.6	1313	4.7	1340	4.7	1340	6.4	1319	6.9		
1906	5.8	2024	5.6	2043	5.1	2124	2.3			1905	0.5	1857	0.7	1952	0.9	2101	0.5		
0144	0.6	0243	0.6	0243	0.4	0226	0.1	0024	2.0	0125	4.5	0147	4.6	0152	6.2	0143	6.6	**4**	**F**
0730	5.4	0851	5.3	0910	4.8	0951	2.0	0706	0.5	0724	0.3	0718	0.6	0815	0.8	0924	0.8		
1400	0.8	1459	0.9	1459	0.6	1439	0.2	1347	2.1	1401	4.5	1431	4.6	1422	6.3	1401	6.7		
1951	5.5	2104	5.5	2123	4.9	2202	2.1	1928	0.6	1946	0.6	1939	0.9	2037	0.9	2142	0.7		
0227	0.9	0322	0.9	0321	0.7	0308	0.2	0153	2.0	0214	4.3	0234	4.4	0235	6.0	0226	6.3	**5**	**SA**
0814	5.2	0930	5.1	0949	4.5	1027	1.9	0750	0.6	0804	0.6	0800	0.8	0857	0.9	1001	1.1		
1444	1.1	1536	1.2	1536	0.96	1518	0.3	1539	2.0	1451	4.4	1527	4.5	1501	6.1	1443	6.5		
2036	5.2	2141	5.2	2201	4.6	2236	1.9	2015	0.8	2027	0.9	2024	1.1	2120	1.1	2222	1.0		
0312	1.2	0359	1.3	0358	1.1	0348	0.3	0337	1.8	0306	4.1	0326	4.2	0316	5.7	0310	6.1	**6**	**SU**
0900	4.9	1006	4.9	1026	4.3	1102	1.7	0838	0.8	0845	0.9	0846	1.1	0939	1.1	1037	1.4		
1530	1.4	1613	1.6	1611	1.3	1558	0.5	1715	1.9	1543	4.1	1618	4.4	1543	5.8	1529	6.2		
2124	4.8	2217	4.9	2236	4.3	2310	1.7	2106	0.9	2110	1.2	2113	1.4	2206	1.4	2303	1.4		
0400	1.6	0437	1.7	0437	1.4	0430	0.5	0531	1.7	0404	3.9	0427	4.0	0401	5.3	0400	5.8	**7**	**M**
0953	4.6	1045	4.7	1103	4.0	1139	1.5	0931	0.9	0933	1.3	0937	1.4	1026	1.5	1116	1.8		
1624	1.7	1655	2.0	1653	1.7	1642	0.6	1839	1.8	1642	3.9	1710	4.2	1630	5.3	1622	5.9		
2221	4.5	2300	4.6	2316	4.0	2347	1.5	2207	1.1	2202	1.6	2212	1.7	2259	1.7	2348	1.7		
0458	1.9	0523	2.1	0521	1.8	0518	0.6	0712	1.6	0509	3.7	0535	3.8	0455	4.9	0459	5.5	**8**	**TU**
1058	4.3	1136	4.5	1153	3.9	1227	1.4	1036	1.1	1031	1.7	1041	1.7	1125	1.8	1206	2.1		
1730	2.0	1751	2.3	1747	1.9	1741	0.8	1948	1.7	1746	3.8	1808	4.0	1730	5.0	1727	5.6		
2335	4.2							2324	1.2	2308	1.8	2329	1.8						
0609	2.0	0001	4.5	0011	3.8	0035	1.4	0816	1.5	0625	3.6	0645	3.7	0005	2.0	0045	2.0	**9**	**W**
1216	4.3	0627	2.3	0622	2.0	0622	0.7	1158	1.2	1143	1.9	1204	1.9	0607	4.6	0612	5.3		
1845	2.0	1246	4.5	1256	3.8	1333	1.4	2030	1.6	1855	3.8	1913	3.9	1238	2.1	1312	2.3		
		1906	2.4	1900	2.1	1907	0.8							1844	4.8	1844	5.4		
0054	4.2	0121	4.4	0126	3.7	0145	1.3	0044	1.2	0022	1.9	0051	1.8	0119	2.1	0155	2.1	**10**	**TH**
0721	2.0	0744	2.3	0741	2.0	0741	0.7	0842	1.5	0739	3.7	0759	3.7	0725	4.6	0729	5.3		
1328	4.4	1406	4.6	1413	3.9	1453	1.4	1312	1.2	1256	1.9	1320	1.6	1351	2.1	1433	2.2		
1954	1.9	2023	2.2	2020	2.0	2034	0.8	2044	1.6	1958	3.8	2020	3.9	1958	4.8	1957	5.5		
0201	4.3	0242	4.5	0250	3.8	0312	1.3	0143	1.1	0131	1.8	0153	1.7	0226	2.0	0310	2.1	**11**	**F**
0823	1.8	0854	2.1	0853	1.9	0849	0.7	0845	1.6	0840	3.8	0901	3.8	0834	4.8	0833	5.5		
1426	4.6	1514	4.8	1527	4.1	1600	1.5	1407	1.1	1400	1.8	1418	1.7	1455	2.0	1545	2.0		
2051	1.7	2127	2.0	2126	1.7	2133	0.7	2045	1.7	2049	3.9	2114	4.0	2101	5.0	2057	5.6		
0254	4.5	0345	4.8	0402	4.0	0421	1.4	0230	1.0	0228	1.5	0242	1.5	0322	1.7	0411	1.8	**12**	**SA**
0912	1.6	0952	1.8	0952	1.6	0942	0.6	0846	1.7	0928	3.9	0948	4.0	0932	5.1	0924	5.8		
1513	4.8	1606	5.0	1626	4.3	1653	1.7	1451	1.0	1451	1.6	1504	1.6	1546	1.7	1638	1.7		
2136	1.5	2220	1.7	2219	1.5	2218	0.6	2047	1.8	2131	4.0	2156	4.1	2152	5.3	2145	5.9		
0336	4.8	0433	5.0	0455	4.2	0516	1.5	0311	0.9	0314	1.2	0324	1.3	0409	1.5	0500	1.6	**13**	**SU**
0954	1.4	1041	1.6	1041	1.4	1028	0.5	0853	1.8	1007	4.1	1027	4.2	1018	5.4	1006	6.1		
1553	5.0	1650	5.2	1713	4.5	1741	1.8	1531	0.9	1533	1.3	1545	1.4	1628	1.5	1722	1.4		
2215	1.3	2306	1.4	2305	1.2	2300	0.5	2054	1.9	2208	4.2	2232	4.3	2233	5.6	2225	6.0		
0413	5.0	0513	5.1	0538	4.4	0605	1.7	0349	0.8	0352	1.0	0403	1.1	0447	1.3	0541	1.4	**14**	**M**
1032	1.2	1124	1.4	1122	1.2	1111	0.4	0906	1.9	1042	4.2	1101	4.4	1058	5.7	1043	6.3		
1628	5.2	1727	5.4	1753	4.6	1826	1.9	1606	0.8	1609	1.1	1621	1.2	1705	1.3	1802	1.3		
2251	1.1	2346	1.2	2345	1.1	2339	0.4	2109	1.9	2243	4.3	2306	4.4	2307	5.8	2300	6.2		
0447	5.1	0549	5.2	0617	4.5	0650	1.8	0424	0.7	0427	0.8	0439	1.0	0521	1.1	0618	1.3	**15**	**TU**
1107	1.1	1203	1.2	1201	1.1	1151	0.3	0929	2.0	1114	4.3	1136	4.4	1132	5.8	1117	6.4		
1701	5.3	1802	5.4	1829	4.7	1908	2.0	1641	0.8	1645	0.9	1656	1.1	1738	1.2	1832	1.3		
2326	1.0							2131	2.0	2315	4.3	2339	4.4	2336	5.9	2332	6.3		

● ● Time: UT. For British Summer Time (shaded) March 26th to October 29th ADD ONE HOUR ● ●

AUGUST 2000 TIDE TABLES

•• Time: UT. For British Summer Time (shaded) March 26th to October 29TH ADD ONE HOUR ••

	ST MARY'S, SCILLY		PLYMOUTH		DARTMOUTH		PORTLAND		POOLE		SOUTHAMPTON		PORTSMOUTH		SHOREHAM		DOVER	
	Time	m	Time	m	Time	m	Time	m	Time	m	Time	m	Time	m	Time	m	Time	m
16 W	0518	5.2	0024	1.1	0022	0.9	0018	0.3	0457	0.6	0501	0.7	0512	0.9	0555	1.0	0654	1.2
	1141	1.0	0623	5.2	0651	4.6	0730	2.0	0959	2.0	1146	4.4	1209	4.5	1203	5.9	1150	6.5
	1733	5.4	1239	1.1	1237	0.9	1230	0.2	1713	0.7	1719	0.8	1728	1.0	1811	1.1	1915	1.0
	2359	0.9	1836	5.5	1904	4.8	1947	2.1	2203	2.0	2347	4.4						
17 TH	0550	5.3	0100	1.0	0058	0.8	0054	0.2	0530	0.6	0535	0.6	0012	4.5	0007	5.9	0003	6.3
	1215	1.0	0655	5.3	0725	4.6	0806	1.9	1040	2.0	1217	4.4	0545	0.8	0627	1.0	0728	1.1
	1806	5.5	1313	1.1	1311	0.9	1306	0.2	1746	0.7	1754	0.8	1242	4.5	1235	5.9	1222	6.5
			1909	5.5	1936	4.8	2021	2.0	2244	2.0			1800	1.0	1844	1.0	1950	1.0
18 F	0033	0.9	0133	1.0	0132	0.8	0127	0.2	0602	0.6	0019	4.4	0045	4.5	0041	5.9	0035	6.4
	0621	5.3	0727	5.3	0758	4.6	0839	1.9	1129	2.0	0609	0.6	0616	0.8	0702	0.9	0801	1.1
	1248	1.0	1346	1.1	1346	0.9	1339	0.2	1819	0.7	1248	4.4	1315	4.5	1307	6.0	1254	6.5
	1839	5.4	1941	5.5	2010	4.8	2054	2.0	2337	2.0	1829	0.8	1832	1.0	1918	1.0	2024	1.0
19 SA	0106	0.9	0206	1.1	0205	0.9	0158	0.2	0635	0.6	0051	4.4	0120	4.5	0114	5.9	0106	6.3
	0655	5.3	0800	5.3	0829	4.6	0909	1.8	1227	2.0	0641	0.6	0648	0.8	0735	0.9	0833	1.1
	1323	1.1	1418	1.1	1418	0.9	1406	0.2	1854	0.7	1320	4.4	1349	4.5	1339	6.0	1324	6.5
	1915	5.4	2014	5.4	2043	4.8	2124	1.9			1903	0.8	1906	1.0	1953	0.9	2056	1.1
20 SU	0142	1.0	0239	1.2	0239	1.0	0227	0.2	0042	1.9	0127	4.3	0157	4.4	0149	5.9	0139	6.3
	0731	5.2	0832	5.2	0903	4.5	0938	1.7	0710	0.7	0713	0.8	0722	0.9	0810	0.9	0905	1.2
	1400	1.2	1451	1.3	1450	1.1	1433	0.3	1337	2.0	1358	4.3	1426	4.5	1412	5.9	1356	6.4
	1952	5.2	2046	5.3	2116	4.6	2153	1.8	1931	0.8	1937	1.0	1942	1.1	2030	1.0	2128	1.2
21 M	0220	1.2	0312	1.4	0311	1.2	0257	0.3	0159	1.9	0209	4.2	0237	4.3	0223	5.7	0215	6.2
	0811	5.0	0905	5.0	0937	4.4	1007	1.6	0750	0.7	0748	1.0	0800	1.0	0846	1.1	0939	1.4
	1440	1.4	1525	1.5	1525	1.3	1503	0.3	1501	1.9	1441	4.2	1508	4.4	1449	5.7	1433	6.3
	2036	5.0	2119	5.1	2150	4.4	2224	1.6	2015	0.8	2016	1.2	2024	1.2	2110	1.2	2203	1.4
22 TU	0303	1.4	0348	1.6	0347	1.4	0333	0.4	0335	1.8	0258	4.1	0325	4.2	0303	5.5	0259	6.0
	0857	4.8	0941	4.9	1013	4.2	1042	1.6	0837	0.8	0831	1.3	0845	1.2	0928	1.3	1018	1.6
	1530	1.6	1606	1.8	1605	1.6	1543	0.5	1641	1.9	1534	4.1	1559	4.3	1534	5.4	1521	6.1
	2127	4.8	2158	4.9	2229	4.2	2302	1.5	2108	0.9	2106	1.5	2115	1.4	2159	1.4	2247	1.6
23 W	0357	1.6	0433	1.8	0432	1.6	0421	0.5	0526	1.8	0359	3.9	0424	4.1	0353	5.2	0357	5.8
	0956	4.6	1030	4.7	1100	4.1	1130	1.5	0937	1.0	0931	1.6	0943	1.5	1025	1.6	1109	1.9
	1633	1.8	1700	2.0	1659	1.8	1641	0.6	1825	1.8	1640	4.0	1700	4.2	1636	5.1	1625	5.9
	2235	4.6	2259	4.7	2327	4.0			2220	1.0	2216	1.7	2225	1.6	2307	1.7	2345	1.9
24 TH	0508	1.8	0535	2.0	0535	1.8	0000	1.4	0711	1.7	0517	3.8	0534	4.0	0506	5.0	0509	5.6
	1113	4.5	1145	4.6	1212	4.0	0535	0.6	1058	1.1	1051	1.8	1103	1.7	1140	1.8	1218	2.0
	1755	1.8	1815	2.1	1815	1.9	1242	1.4	1951	1.8	1758	4.0	1812	4.1	1756	5.0	1743	5.7
							1812	0.7	2347	1.1	2340	1.7	2353	1.6				
25 F	0000	4.5	0031	4.6	0055	3.9	0130	1.4	0824	1.7	0645	3.9	0658	4.0	0030	1.7	0102	2.0
	0633	1.8	0700	2.1	0658	1.9	0715	0.6	1224	1.1	1220	1.7	1230	1.7	0636	5.0	0633	5.6
	1241	4.6	1316	4.7	1344	4.1	1417	1.5	2038	1.8	1916	4.1	1938	4.1	1308	1.7	1344	2.0
	1919	1.6	1949	2.0	1948	1.8	2000	0.7							1923	5.2	1909	5.8
26 SA	0124	4.7	0203	4.7	0229	4.1	0313	1.5	0103	1.0	0103	1.5	0111	1.5	0155	1.6	0231	1.8
	0750	1.5	0832	1.8	0829	1.7	0842	0.6	0845	1.8	0800	4.1	0827	4.2	0801	5.3	0758	5.8
	1356	4.9	1440	4.9	1509	4.4	1549	1.7	1336	1.0	1339	1.4	1345	1.5	1427	1.5	1512	1.7
	2030	1.3	2112	1.6	2113	1.4	2121	0.6	2045	1.9	2020	4.2	2052	4.3	2038	5.5	2027	6.0
27 SU	0231	5.0	0327	4.9	0352	4.4	0438	1.7	0208	0.8	0214	1.1	0219	1.2	0305	1.3	0351	1.5
	0855	1.2	0946	1.4	0947	1.3	0949	0.5	0845	1.9	0859	4.3	0930	4.4	0911	5.7	0905	6.2
	1457	5.3	1554	5.2	1619	4.7	1702	1.9	1437	0.8	1443	1.1	1449	1.2	1532	1.2	1623	1.3
	2129	0.9	2221	1.1	2222	1.0	2221	0.4	2046	2.0	2115	4.4	2146	4.5	2138	5.9	2129	6.4
28 M	0327	5.3	0435	5.2	0459	4.7	0543	1.9	0303	0.6	0312	0.7	0316	0.9	0404	1.0	0500	1.2
	0951	0.8	1049	1.0	1051	0.9	1043	0.3	0851	2.1	0950	4.5	1018	4.7	1009	6.1	0959	6.6
	1548	5.6	1657	5.5	1720	5.0	1802	2.1	1528	0.7	1538	0.7	1542	0.9	1628	0.9	1724	0.9
	2221	0.5	2319	0.7	2322	0.6	2312	0.2	2054	2.1	2203	4.5	2232	4.7	2229	6.2	2221	6.6
29 TU	0415	5.6	0532	5.4	0553	4.9	0638	2.1	0352	0.5	0402	0.4	0406	0.6	0455	0.8	0601	0.9
	1041	0.6	1145	0.7	1147	0.6	1131	0.2	0906	2.2	1036	4.7	1102	4.8	1059	6.4	1046	6.8
	1635	5.9	1749	5.7	1812	5.2	1854	2.3	1614	0.5	1628	0.5	1629	0.7	1716	0.8	1822	0.7
	2309	0.3					2358	0.1	2114	2.2	2249	4.6	2315	4.8	2316	6.4	2308	6.8
30 W	0500	5.8	0012	0.5	0015	0.3	0727	2.2	0436	0.4	0451	0.2	0451	0.4	0542	0.7	0657	0.8
	1127	0.4	0621	5.5	0641	5.0	1215	0.1	0936	2.2	1120	4.8	1145	4.8	1146	6.5	1130	7.0
	1718	6.0	1233	0.5	1234	0.3	1941	2.4	1657	0.5	1715	0.4	1712	0.5	1802	0.7	1914	0.5
	2354	0.3	1837	5.8	1857	5.3			2147	2.2	2334	4.6	2357	4.8	2359	6.5	2353	6.8
31 TH ●	0542	5.8	0058	0.3	0100	0.2	0042	0.0	0518	0.4	0537	0.1	0533	0.3	0625	0.7	0743	0.7
	1210	0.4	0706	5.6	0725	5.1	0810	2.3	1021	2.2	1204	4.8	1228	4.8	1230	6.5	1213	7.0
	1800	6.0	1318	0.5	1318	0.3	1257	0.0	1739	0.5	1759	0.3	1753	0.5	1846	0.7	1959	0.5
			1920	5.8	1939	5.3	2023	2.4	2236	2.1								

SOUTH COAST OF ENGLAND Time Zone UT
St Mary's * Plymouth * Dartmouth * Portland * Poole * Southampton * Portsmouth * Shoreham * Dover

TIDE TABLES SEPTEMBER 2000

ST MARY'S, SCILLY		PLYMOUTH		DARTMOUTH		PORTLAND		POOLE		SOUTHAMPTON		PORTSMOUTH		SHOREHAM		DOVER		Day
Time	m	Time	m	Time	m	Time	m	Time	m	Time	m	Time	m	Time	m	Time	m	
0036	0.3	0140	0.4	0142	0.2	0123	0.0	0558	0.4	0017	4.6	0039	4.7	0042	6.4	0035	6.8	1 F
0621	5.7	0745	5.5	0805	5.0	0848	2.2	1122	2.1	0619	0.2	0612	0.4	0707	0.7	0823	0.7	
1251	0.5	1357	0.6	1357	0.4	1336	0.0	1819	0.5	1246	4.7	1311	4.8	1311	6.5	1253	6.9	
1841	5.8	1958	5.7	2019	5.2	2100	2.3	2339	2.1	1840	0.4	1832	0.6	1927	0.8	2039	0.5	
0115	0.6	0218	0.6	0219	0.4	0201	0.0	0638	0.5	0100	4.5	0121	4.6	0123	6.3	0114	6.6	2 SA
0700	5.5	0821	5.4	0843	4.8	0923	2.1	1235	2.1	0658	0.3	0651	0.6	0746	0.7	0857	0.9	
1330	0.7	1432	0.8	1433	0.6	1414	0.1	1859	0.6	1329	4.6	1353	4.7	1348	6.4	1331	6.8	
1920	5.5	2033	5.5	2055	4.9	2133	2.1			1917	0.6	1911	0.8	2006	0.8	2115	0.7	
0153	0.9	0251	1.0	0252	0.7	0237	0.2	0053	2.0	0143	4.4	0203	4.5	0201	6.1	0151	6.4	3 SU
0739	5.3	0852	5.2	0915	4.6	0954	1.9	0719	0.6	0732	0.6	0730	0.8	0823	0.9	0927	1.1	
1409	1.1	1504	1.2	1504	0.9	1448	0.3	1357	2.0	1411	4.4	1436	4.5	1422	6.1	1409	6.6	
2000	5.1	2103	5.2	2127	4.6	2202	1.9	1941	0.7	1950	0.9	1951	1.0	2042	1.0	2148	1.1	
0230	1.3	0321	1.4	0323	1.1	0310	0.3	0221	1.9	0228	4.1	0248	4.3	0237	5.7	0230	6.1	4 M
0820	4.9	0922	5.0	0945	4.4	1021	1.7	0800	0.8	0806	1.0	0810	1.1	0900	1.1	0956	1.5	
1449	1.4	1533	1.6	1534	1.4	1521	0.4	1527	1.9	1457	4.1	1521	4.3	1457	5.8	1450	6.3	
2042	4.8	2134	4.9	2154	4.3	2227	1.7	2024	0.9	2025	1.2	2033	1.3	2121	1.3	2220	1.5	
0312	1.6	0351	1.8	0353	1.5	0339	0.5	0402	1.7	0319	3.9	0339	4.0	0314	5.3	0314	5.8	5 TU
0906	4.6	0955	4.8	1015	4.1	1048	1.5	0846	1.0	0844	1.4	0854	1.5	0941	1.5	1027	1.8	
1535	1.8	1606	2.0	1607	1.7	1552	0.6	1706	1.8	1547	3.9	1613	4.1	1537	5.3	1537	5.9	
2131	4.4	2211	4.6	2226	4.0	2254	1.4	2114	1.1	2108	1.6	2121	1.7	2207	1.7	2257	1.9	
0402	2.0	0426	2.2	0428	1.9	0408	0.7	0608	1.6	0418	3.7	0449	3.8	0403	4.9	0408	5.5	6 W
1005	4.3	1042	4.5	1056	3.9	1121	1.4	0942	1.2	0936	1.9	0948	1.8	1035	2.0	1109	2.2	
1637	2.1	1653	2.4	1653	2.1	1633	0.8	1849	1.6	1648	3.7	1717	3.9	1635	4.8	1639	5.4	
2242	4.1	2309	4.4	2317	3.7	2331	1.3	2226	1.2	2210	2.0	2231	2.0	2310	2.1	2346	2.3	
0515	2.2	0523	2.5	0521	2.2	0450	0.8	0743	1.5	0533	3.5	0603	3.6	0513	4.5	0521	5.2	7 TH
1129	4.1	1151	4.4	1201	3.7	1215	1.3	1117	1.3	1050	2.1	1122	2.1	1148	2.3	1211	2.5	
1801	2.2	1810	2.6	1804	2.3	1806	0.9	2004	1.5	1801	3.6	1827	3.7	1755	4.6	1804	5.1	
										2333	2.1							
0018	4.0	0036	4.3	0037	3.6	0039	1.2	0017	1.3	0700	3.5	0023	2.1	0031	2.3	0056	2.5	8 F
0642	2.3	0654	2.6	0648	2.3	0639	0.9	0833	1.5	1216	2.2	0719	3.6	0643	4.5	0651	5.1	
1256	4.2	1319	4.4	1323	3.8	1348	1.3	1253	1.3	1919	3.6	1301	2.1	1313	2.4	1341	2.5	
1924	2.1	1948	2.5	1945	2.2	2018	0.8	2039	1.5			1942	3.7	1922	4.6	1932	5.2	
0137	4.1	0209	4.4	0213	3.7	0234	1.2	0121	1.2	0058	2.0	0130	1.9	0151	2.2	0227	2.4	9 SA
0754	2.1	0825	2.4	0822	2.2	0822	0.8	0845	1.6	0813	3.7	0832	3.8	0804	4.7	0806	5.4	
1400	4.4	1440	4.7	1451	3.9	1521	1.5	1349	1.2	1333	2.0	1359	1.9	1424	2.2	1514	2.2	
2025	1.8	2103	2.1	2101	1.9	2116	0.7	2045	1.6	2022	3.8	2046	3.8	2034	4.8	2038	5.4	
0232	4.4	0319	4.7	0337	3.9	0401	1.4	0208	1.1	0204	1.7	0219	1.7	0253	2.0	0342	2.1	10 SU
0848	1.8	0929	2.1	0926	1.8	0918	0.7	0845	1.7	0906	3.9	0925	4.0	0906	5.1	0901	5.7	
1448	4.7	1539	5.0	1557	4.2	1622	1.6	1431	1.1	1430	1.7	1443	1.7	1519	1.9	1613	1.8	
2111	1.5	2157	1.8	2155	1.6	2156	0.6	2045	1.7	2110	3.9	2132	4.0	2129	5.2	2127	5.8	
0314	4.7	0409	5.0	0433	4.2	0456	1.5	0247	0.9	0253	1.4	0300	1.4	0341	1.6	0433	1.7	11 M
0930	1.5	1018	1.7	1015	1.5	1003	0.5	0848	1.8	0946	4.1	1003	4.2	0953	5.4	0943	6.0	
1528	5.0	1624	5.2	1648	4.5	1712	1.8	1508	0.9	1512	1.3	1521	1.4	1602	1.5	1658	1.5	
2150	1.3	2242	1.5	2241	1.3	2233	0.4	2049	1.8	2147	4.1	2208	4.2	2209	5.6	2204	6.0	
0349	5.0	0450	5.1	0516	4.4	0543	1.7	0322	0.8	0332	1.0	0336	1.2	0420	1.3	0516	1.5	12 TU
1007	1.2	1100	1.4	1058	1.2	1045	0.4	0856	1.9	1019	4.2	1037	4.4	1029	5.7	1018	6.3	
1603	5.3	1703	5.4	1728	4.7	1759	2.0	1541	0.8	1549	1.0	1555	1.2	1638	1.3	1739	1.2	
2225	1.2	2324	1.2	2320	1.0	2311	0.3	2057	1.9	2222	4.3	2241	4.4	2241	5.8	2235	6.2	
0421	5.2	0526	5.3	0553	4.6	0627	1.9	0356	0.7	0405	0.8	0411	1.0	0454	1.1	0556	1.2	13 W
1042	1.0	1139	1.2	1138	1.0	1125	0.3	0910	2.0	1050	4.4	1109	4.5	1103	5.9	1050	6.5	O
1635	5.5	1738	5.5	1806	4.8	1842	2.1	1613	0.7	1623	0.8	1628	1.0	1711	1.0	1818	1.1	
2259	0.8			2359	0.8	2348	0.2	2113	2.0	2253	4.4	2314	4.5	2310	6.0	2304	6.4	
0452	5.4	0001	1.0	0629	4.7	0708	2.0	0429	0.6	0439	0.6	0444	0.8	0527	0.9	0633	1.1	14 TH
1115	1.0	0559	5.4	1216	1.0	1203	0.2	0933	2.0	1120	4.5	1141	4.6	1134	6.1	1121	6.6	
1707	5.6	1216	1.0	1841	4.9	1923	2.1	1645	0.7	1658	0.7	1700	0.9	1744	0.9	1854	1.0	
2332	0.7	1812	5.6					2137	2.0	2325	4.5	2346	4.6	2341	6.1	2334	6.5	
0523	5.5	0036	0.9	0036	0.7	0024	0.1	0502	0.6	0514	0.5	0517	0.7	0601	0.8	0708	1.0	15 F
1149	0.8	0632	5.5	0701	4.8	0745	2.0	1004	2.0	1151	4.6	1213	4.6	1206	6.1	1152	6.7	
1739	5.7	1251	0.9	1251	0.7	1240	0.1	1718	0.6	1734	0.6	1733	0.8	1818	0.8	1930	0.9	
		1846	5.7	1915	5.0	2000	2.1	2213	2.1	2356	4.5							

● ● Time: UT. For British Summer Time (shaded) March 26th to October 29th ADD ONE HOUR ● ●

SEPTEMBER 2000 TIDE TABLES

•• Time: UT. For British Summer Time (shaded) March 26th to October 29TH ADD ONE HOUR ••

Day	ST MARY'S SCILLY Time	m	PLYMOUTH Time	m	DARTMOUTH Time	m	PORTLAND Time	m	POOLE Time	m	SOUTHAMPTON Time	m	PORTSMOUTH Time	m	SHOREHAM Time	m	DOVER Time	m
16 SA	0006	0.7	0111	0.8	0111	0.7	0059	0.1	0535	0.5	0548	0.5	0550	0.7	0015	6.1	0006	6.6
	0555	5.6	0706	5.5	0734	4.8	0818	2.0	1047	2.1	1221	4.6	1247	4.6	0635	0.8	0740	1.0
	1224	0.8	1324	0.9	1326	0.7	1313	0.1	1753	0.6	1809	0.6	1807	0.8	1239	6.2	1224	6.7
	1813	5.7	1920	5.7	1949	5.0	2033	2.1	2301	2.1					1853	0.8	2002	0.9
17 SU	0040	0.8	0144	0.9	0146	0.7	0132	0.1	0610	0.6	0028	4.5	0057	4.6	0050	6.1	0039	6.6
	0629	5.5	0739	5.5	0807	4.8	0849	2.0	1142	2.1	0622	0.5	0624	0.7	0710	0.8	0811	1.0
	1259	0.9	1357	1.0	1400	0.8	1344	0.2	1829	0.6	1253	4.6	1323	4.6	1313	6.2	1255	6.7
	1849	5.6	1954	5.6	2023	4.9	2105	2.0			1842	0.6	1842	0.8	1929	0.8	2033	1.0
18 M	0116	0.9	0216	1.0	0218	0.8	0202	0.2	0002	2.0	0104	4.4	0135	4.6	0125	6.1	0112	6.5
	0706	5.4	0812	5.4	0842	4.7	0918	1.9	0646	0.6	0654	0.6	0659	0.8	0745	0.8	0842	1.1
	1336	1.0	1430	1.2	1433	1.0	1413	0.3	1249	2.0	1329	4.5	1401	4.6	1346	6.1	1329	6.6
	1927	5.4	2028	5.4	2057	4.7	2136	1.9	1906	0.7	1915	0.8	1918	1.0	2005	0.9	2104	1.1
19 TU	0155	1.1	0249	1.2	0250	1.1	0233	0.3	0122	2.0	0145	4.3	0218	4.5	0200	5.9	0150	6.4
	0746	5.2	0846	5.2	0915	4.6	0946	1.8	0726	0.7	0728	0.9	0737	1.0	0822	1.0	0916	1.3
	1418	1.3	1505	1.4	1506	1.3	1445	0.4	1413	2.0	1412	4.3	1444	4.5	1423	5.8	1407	6.4
	2011	5.1	2101	5.1	2134	4.5	2207	1.7	1950	0.8	1952	1.1	2000	1.1	2046	1.1	2139	1.4
20 W	0239	1.4	0325	1.6	0327	1.4	0308	0.4	0257	1.9	0235	4.2	0306	4.3	0241	5.6	0234	6.1
	0833	5.0	0921	5.0	0953	4.4	1020	1.7	0813	0.9	0810	1.3	0822	1.3	0905	1.3	0957	1.6
	1508	1.5	1546	1.7	1546	1.6	1524	0.5	1553	1.9	1505	4.2	1534	4.3	1510	5.5	1456	6.2
	2103	4.8	2141	4.8	2215	4.2	2247	1.6	2043	0.9	2042	1.4	2051	1.4	2136	1.4	2223	1.7
21 TH	0333	1.7	0410	1.9	0410	1.7	0354	0.6	0454	1.8	0338	4.0	0406	4.2	0334	5.3	0333	5.9
	0932	4.7	1009	2.0	1040	4.1	1106	1.6	0913	1.0	0910	1.6	0920	1.6	1004	1.6	1048	1.9
	1614	1.8	1640	2.0	1641	1.9	1621	0.7	1748	1.8	1612	4.0	1637	4.1	1613	5.1	1603	5.8
	2214	4.5	2246	4.6	2316	4.0	2348	1.4	2155	1.1	2153	1.7	2201	1.7	2244	1.7	2323	2.0
22 F	0448	1.9	0513	2.2	0514	2.0	0512	0.7	0656	1.7	0502	3.8	0522	4.0	0450	5.0	0450	5.6
	1054	4.5	1129	4.6	1156	4.0	1218	1.5	1042	1.2	1036	1.9	1047	1.9	1125	1.9	1200	2.1
	1744	1.9	1800	2.2	1800	2.0	1810	0.8	1939	1.7	1738	3.9	1759	4.0	1740	4.9	1731	5.6
	2349	4.4							2334	1.1	2325	1.7	2339	1.8				
23 SA	0621	1.9	0027	4.5	0051	3.9	0124	1.4	0825	1.7	0637	3.9	0701	4.0	0015	1.8	0048	2.1
	1230	4.6	0647	2.3	0645	2.1	0712	0.8	1220	1.2	1212	1.8	1226	1.9	0629	5.0	0625	5.5
	1912	1.6	1306	4.6	1333	4.1	1359	1.5	2038	1.7	1905	4.0	1936	4.0	1300	1.8	1334	2.0
			1942	2.0	1942	1.9	2005	0.7							1915	5.1	1910	5.6
24 SU	0118	4.6	0206	4.6	0227	4.2	0316	1.5	0056	1.0	0056	1.5	0104	1.6	0145	1.6	0224	2.0
	0742	1.6	0824	2.0	0822	1.8	0839	0.7	0845	1.8	0756	4.1	0824	4.2	0755	5.4	0754	5.8
	1347	4.9	1438	4.9	1500	4.4	1536	1.7	1333	1.0	1333	1.5	1342	1.6	1420	1.5	1503	1.6
	2022	1.2	2105	1.6	2105	1.4	2118	0.6	2045	1.9	2014	4.2	2047	4.3	2031	5.5	2028	6.0
25 M	0222	5.0	0328	5.0	0347	4.4	0433	1.7	0201	0.9	0206	1.1	0211	1.3	0255	1.3	0343	1.6
	0845	1.2	0936	1.5	0937	1.3	0939	0.5	0845	2.0	0852	4.4	0921	4.5	0901	5.8	0857	6.2
	1445	5.3	1550	5.3	1610	4.8	1646	1.9	1429	0.9	1435	1.1	1441	1.3	1523	1.2	1612	1.2
	2118	0.8	2209	1.1	2210	0.9	2210	0.4	2045	2.0	2107	4.4	2136	4.5	2129	5.9	2125	6.3
26 TU	0314	5.3	0428	5.3	0448	4.8	0531	1.9	0250	0.7	0301	0.7	0303	1.0	0350	0.9	0448	1.2
	0937	0.9	1036	1.0	1037	0.9	1029	0.4	0848	2.1	0938	4.6	1005	4.7	0954	6.2	0946	6.6
	1533	5.6	1645	5.6	1705	5.1	1743	2.1	1515	0.7	1526	0.7	1529	0.9	1614	0.9	1712	0.9
	2206	0.5	2305	0.7	2306	0.6	2255	0.2	2050	2.1	2151	4.5	2217	4.7	2215	6.2	2211	6.6
27 W	0358	5.6	0518	5.5	0537	5.0	0621	2.1	0335	0.5	0348	0.4	0349	0.7	0438	0.7	0547	1.0
	1024	0.6	1128	0.7	1129	0.6	1113	0.2	0859	2.2	1020	4.7	1045	4.8	1040	6.4	1029	6.8
	1617	5.9	1733	5.7	1753	5.2	1833	2.3	1557	0.5	1611	0.5	1612	0.7	1700	0.7	1806	0.7
	2249	0.4	2353	0.5	2355	0.4	2338	0.1	2104	2.1	2233	4.6	2257	4.8	2257	6.4	2252	6.8
28 TH	0439	5.8	0601	5.6	0620	5.1	0705	2.2	0416	0.4	0432	0.2	0431	0.5	0521	0.6	0636	0.8
	1106	0.4	1213	0.6	1215	0.4	1154	0.1	0920	2.2	1101	4.8	1124	4.9	1122	6.5	1109	6.9
	1657	6.0	1815	5.8	1836	5.3	1917	2.4	1637	0.5	1654	0.5	1652	0.6	1741	0.6	1853	0.6
	2330	0.3							2129	2.1	2314	4.7	2337	4.8	2336	6.4	2331	6.8
29 F	0518	5.8	0036	0.5	0037	0.3	0018	0.0	0456	0.4	0514	0.2	0511	0.4	0601	0.6	0718	0.8
	1146	0.4	0639	5.6	0659	5.1	0745	2.3	0953	2.2	1140	4.8	1203	4.8	1200	6.5	1148	7.0
	1736	5.9	1254	0.5	1254	0.4	1234	0.1	1715	0.5	1734	0.3	1730	0.6	1821	0.7	1933	0.6
			1853	5.8	1915	5.2	1957	2.4	2207	2.1	2355	4.6						
30 SA ●	0008	0.5	0114	0.5	0115	0.3	0057	0.0	0533	0.4	0554	0.3	0016	4.7	0015	6.3	0008	6.8
	0554	5.7	0715	5.6	0736	5.1	0821	2.2	1040	2.1	1218	4.7	0548	0.5	0639	0.6	0752	0.8
	1224	0.6	1330	0.7	1331	0.5	1312	0.1	1752	0.5	1811	0.4	1242	4.8	1238	6.4	1225	6.9
	1812	5.7	1928	5.7	1952	5.1	2031	2.2	2258	2.1			1806	0.7	1856	0.6	2009	0.7

SOUTH COAST OF ENGLAND Time Zone UT
St Mary's * Plymouth * Dartmouth * Portland * Poole * Southampton * Portsmouth * Shoreham * Dover

TIDE TABLES OCTOBER 2000

ST MARY'S, SCILLY Time m	PLYMOUTH Time m	DARTMOUTH Time m	PORTLAND Time m	POOLE Time m	SOUTHAMPTON Time m	PORTSMOUTH Time m	SHOREHAM Time m	DOVER Time m	
0044 0.7	0148 0.8	0150 0.5	0132 0.1	0610 0.5	0033 4.5	0055 4.6	0052 6.2	0044 6.6	**1 SU**
0631 5.6	0747 5.5	0810 4.9	0851 2.1	1137 2.1	0628 0.5	0624 0.7	0713 0.8	0822 1.0	
1300 5.4	1402 0.9	1402 0.7	1347 0.2	1830 0.6	1255 4.6	1320 4.7	1312 6.3	1300 6.8	
1849 5.4	2000 5.5	2025 4.9	2100 2.1		1843 0.6	1843 0.8	1931 0.8	2040 0.9	
0118 1.0	0218 1.1	0219 0.8	0204 0.2	0001 2.0	0112 4.4	0134 4.5	0127 6.0	0119 6.4	**2 M**
0707 5.3	0817 5.3	0842 4.7	0917 2.0	0647 0.7	0658 0.7	0700 0.9	0747 1.0	0850 1.2	
1335 1.1	1430 1.3	1432 1.0	1418 0.3	1242 2.0	1332 4.3	1357 4.5	1342 6.1	1336 6.5	
1925 5.1	2030 5.2	2053 4.6	2124 1.8	1907 0.7	1912 0.9	1919 1.1	2004 1.0	2109 1.2	
0152 1.3	0245 1.5	0247 1.2	0230 0.4	0116 1.9	0152 4.2	0215 4.3	0159 5.8	0154 6.2	**3 TU**
0744 5.0	0845 5.1	0907 4.5	0939 1.8	0725 0.8	0728 1.1	0736 1.2	0821 1.3	0917 1.5	
1412 1.5	1457 1.7	1459 1.4	1446 0.5	1357 1.9	1411 4.1	1436 4.3	1414 5.7	1412 6.2	
2003 4.7	2058 4.9	2116 4.3	2145 1.6	1946 0.9	1943 1.2	1956 1.3	2039 1.3	2139 1.6	
0228 1.7	0310 1.9	0311 1.6	0250 0.5	0245 1.8	0237 3.9	0300 4.1	0234 5.4	0233 5.9	**4 W**
0825 4.7	0915 4.9	0932 4.2	0959 1.6	0806 1.0	0802 1.5	0815 1.5	0900 1.7	0947 1.8	
1452 1.8	1527 2.1	1528 1.8	1509 0.6	1521 1.8	1456 3.9	1518 4.1	1452 5.3	1454 5.8	
2048 4.4	2133 4.6	2142 4.0	2209 1.4	2028 1.1	2020 1.6	2036 1.7	2121 1.7	2212 2.0	
0312 2.1	0342 2.3	0341 2.0	0304 0.7	0444 1.6	0330 3.7	0401 3.9	0319 5.0	0321 5.6	**5 TH**
0916 4.3	0956 4.6	1005 4.0	1024 1.5	0852 1.2	0848 1.9	0900 1.9	0949 2.1	1027 2.2	
1546 2.1	1609 2.4	1606 2.1	1539 0.8	1710 1.6	1550 3.7	1615 3.8	1546 4.8	1551 5.3	
2149 4.0	2225 4.4	2230 3.7	2243 1.3	2123 1.3	2114 2.0	2129 2.0	2218 2.1	2257 2.4	
0415 2.3	0430 2.6	0425 2.3	0324 0.8	0657 1.5	0438 3.5	0523 3.7	0424 4.6	0427 5.2	**6 F**
1033 4.1	1100 4.4	1110 3.8	1106 1.4	1016 1.4	0956 2.2	1021 2.3	1059 2.4	1123 2.5	
1708 2.3	1717 2.7	1708 2.4	1646 0.9	1917 1.5	1659 3.5	1739 3.6	1702 4.5	1717 5.0	
2328 3.9	2351 4.2	2356 3.5	2348 1.2	2337 1.4	2235 2.2	2342 2.2	2336 2.4		
0551 2.4	0554 2.8	0543 2.5	0423 0.9	0809 1.5	0610 3.5	0634 3.6	0555 4.5	0000 2.6	**7 SA**
1211 4.1	1229 4.4	1237 3.7	1229 1.4	1230 1.4	1128 2.3	1237 2.3	1227 2.6	0601 5.0	
1841 2.3	1902 2.7	1855 2.4	1945 0.9	2021 1.5	1827 3.5	1854 3.6	1836 4.4	1242 2.6	
								1857 5.0	
0100 4.0	0127 4.3	0132 3.6	0148 1.2	0052 1.3	0012 2.1	0100 2.1	0104 2.4	0126 2.6	**8 SU**
0715 2.3	0744 2.6	0738 2.4	0745 0.9	0841 1.6	0734 3.6	0748 3.8	0723 4.7	0728 5.2	
1324 4.3	1355 4.6	1405 3.9	1424 1.4	1324 1.3	1255 2.1	1333 2.1	1345 2.4	1424 2.4	
1948 2.0	2030 2.3	2026 2.1	2046 0.7	2043 1.5	1943 3.6	2006 3.7	1957 4.7	2009 5.3	
0159 4.3	0242 4.6	0259 3.8	0335 1.4	0139 1.2	0128 1.8	0149 1.8	0213 2.1	0256 2.3	**9 M**
0813 1.9	0856 2.3	0851 2.1	0849 0.8	0845 1.7	0833 3.8	0849 4.0	0827 5.0	0828 5.6	
1415 4.6	1500 4.9	1520 4.2	1541 1.6	1404 1.2	1357 1.8	1415 1.8	1443 2.0	1535 2.0	
2037 1.6	2126 1.9	2122 1.7	2124 0.6	2045 1.7	2037 3.8	2100 4.0	2054 5.1	2058 5.7	
0242 4.7	0335 4.9	0357 4.2	0428 1.6	0218 1.0	0221 1.4	0229 1.6	0304 1.7	0354 1.9	**10 TU**
0857 1.6	0946 1.9	0942 1.7	0934 0.6	0845 1.9	0914 4.0	0933 4.3	0915 5.4	0912 6.0	
1455 5.0	1548 5.2	1612 4.5	1636 1.8	1439 1.0	1442 1.4	1451 1.5	1526 1.6	1624 1.5	
2117 1.3	2211 1.5	2206 1.4	2200 0.4	2046 1.8	2118 4.1	2140 4.2	2135 5.5	2134 6.0	
0318 5.0	0417 5.1	0444 4.5	0514 1.8	0251 0.9	0302 1.1	0304 1.3	0344 1.3	0441 1.5	**11 W**
0935 1.3	1030 1.5	1025 1.3	1015 0.5	0849 2.0	0949 4.3	1009 4.5	0953 5.8	0946 6.3	
1530 5.3	1630 5.4	1657 4.9	1724 2.0	1510 0.8	1521 1.0	1523 1.3	1603 1.2	1706 1.2	
2153 1.0	2252 1.2	2249 1.1	2237 0.3	2050 1.9	2153 4.3	2214 4.4	2207 5.8	2203 6.3	
0350 5.3	0454 5.3	0523 4.7	0557 2.0	0324 0.7	0336 0.8	0338 1.0	0419 1.0	0524 1.2	**12 TH**
1011 1.0	1110 1.2	1108 1.0	1054 0.3	0857 2.0	1020 4.4	1040 4.6	1027 6.0	1018 6.5	
1604 5.5	1709 5.6	1737 4.9	1809 2.1	1543 0.7	1557 0.7	1557 1.0	1638 0.9	1748 1.0	
2228 0.8	2331 1.0	2329 0.8	2315 0.2	2100 2.0	2226 4.4	2247 4.6	2238 6.1	2232 6.5	
0422 5.5	0531 5.5	0600 4.9	0639 2.1	0357 0.6	0412 0.6	0412 0.8	0454 0.8	0604 1.1	**13 F**
1046 0.8	1148 1.0	1148 0.8	1133 0.2	0912 2.1	1051 4.6	1112 4.7	1059 6.2	1048 6.7	O
1638 5.7	1745 5.7	1814 5.0	1853 2.2	1615 0.6	1632 0.6	1630 0.8	1713 0.8	1827 0.9	
2303 0.6			2351 0.1	2117 2.1	2300 4.5	2320 4.7	2311 6.2	2303 6.6	
0455 5.7	0009 0.8	0009 0.7	0717 2.2	0433 0.5	0448 0.5	0448 0.7	0531 0.8	0642 1.0	**14 SA**
1122 0.7	0606 5.6	0636 5.0	1210 0.2	0935 2.1	1123 4.7	1144 4.7	1134 6.3	1120 6.8	
1712 5.8	1226 0.8	1227 0.7	1933 2.2	1651 0.5	1710 0.5	1706 0.7	1749 0.7	1904 0.8	
2339 0.6	1822 5.7	1851 5.1		2147 2.1	2333 4.6	2357 4.7	2348 6.3	2337 6.7	
0530 5.8	0045 0.7	0047 0.6	0028 0.1	0509 0.5	0526 0.4	0524 0.6	0608 0.7	0715 0.9	**15 SU**
1159 0.7	0642 5.7	0711 5.0	0752 2.2	1012 2.1	1155 4.7	1220 4.8	1210 6.3	1154 6.9	
1748 5.8	1302 0.8	1305 0.6	1245 0.2	1728 0.5	1748 0.4	1743 0.7	1827 0.7	1937 0.8	
	1900 5.7	1927 5.1	2009 2.2	2232 2.1					

● ● Time: UT. For British Summer Time (shaded) March 26th to October 29th ADD ONE HOUR ● ●

OCTOBER 2000 TIDE TABLES

•• Time: UT. For British Summer Time (shaded) March 26th to October 29TH ADD ONE HOUR ••

Day	ST MARY'S SCILLY Time	m	PLYMOUTH Time	m	DARTMOUTH Time	m	PORTLAND Time	m	POOLE Time	m	SOUTHAMPTON Time	m	PORTSMOUTH Time	m	SHOREHAM Time	m	DOVER Time	m
16 M	0016	0.7	0121	0.8	0124	0.6	0103	0.1	0547	0.5	0008	4.6	0036	4.7	0027	6.3	0013	6.7
	0606	5.7	0718	5.6	0745	5.0	0825	2.1	1104	2.1	0602	0.5	0601	0.7	0644	0.8	0747	1.0
	1237	0.8	1338	0.8	1342	0.7	1320	0.2	1807	0.6	1228	4.7	1259	4.8	1247	6.3	1230	6.8
	1827	5.7	1936	5.6	2005	5.0	2045	2.1	2334	2.1	1824	0.5	1821	0.7	1906	0.7	2008	0.9
17 TU	0054	0.8	0156	0.9	0200	0.8	0137	0.2	0626	0.6	0045	4.5	0118	4.7	0106	6.2	0051	6.6
	0645	5.6	0755	5.5	0822	4.9	0857	2.1	1211	2.1	0638	0.6	0639	0.8	0724	0.9	0821	1.1
	1318	1.0	1414	1.0	1418	0.9	1354	0.3	1849	0.7	1306	4.6	1340	4.7	1326	6.2	1308	6.7
	1909	5.5	2014	5.4	2043	4.8	2118	1.9			1859	0.7	1901	0.9	1946	0.9	2042	1.1
18 W	0136	1.1	0232	1.2	0236	1.1	0212	0.3	0055	2.0	0130	4.4	0204	4.6	0146	6.1	0133	6.5
	0728	5.4	0832	5.3	0859	4.8	0928	1.9	0709	0.7	0716	0.9	0721	1.1	0805	1.1	0859	1.3
	1403	1.2	1451	1.3	1454	1.2	1430	0.4	1335	2.0	1352	4.4	1425	4.6	1408	5.9	1351	6.3
	1955	5.1	2053	5.1	2122	4.5	2155	1.8	1934	0.8	1939	1.0	1945	1.1	2031	1.1	2121	1.4
19 TH	0223	1.4	0311	1.5	0314	1.4	0251	0.5	0237	1.9	0222	4.2	0256	4.4	0231	5.8	0222	6.2
	0818	5.1	0912	5.1	0940	4.5	1004	1.8	0759	0.9	0801	1.2	0809	1.4	0853	1.4	0943	1.5
	1457	1.5	1536	1.7	1538	1.6	1515	0.6	1521	1.9	1447	4.2	1518	4.4	1457	5.6	1445	6.1
	2051	4.8	2141	4.8	2210	4.2	2241	1.6	2031	0.9	2030	1.3	2039	1.4	2124	1.4	2209	1.7
20 F	0321	1.7	0359	1.9	0401	1.8	0341	0.7	0441	1.9	0328	4.0	0359	4.3	0328	5.4	0324	5.9
	0920	4.7	1006	4.8	1032	4.3	1054	1.7	0904	1.1	0903	1.6	0911	1.7	0955	1.7	1039	1.8
	1607	1.8	1634	2.0	1637	1.8	1623	0.7	1724	1.8	1555	4.0	1623	4.1	1603	5.2	1558	5.7
	2206	4.5	2254	4.5	2317	4.0	2349	1.5	2145	1.1	2141	1.6	2151	1.7	2233	1.7	2315	2.0
21 SA	0439	2.0	0506	2.2	0508	2.1	0507	0.9	0705	1.8	0454	3.9	0529	4.1	0446	5.2	0442	5.6
	1044	4.6	1127	4.6	1149	4.1	1208	1.6	1038	1.2	1028	1.8	1043	1.9	1119	1.8	1154	2.0
	1737	1.8	1757	2.1	1757	2.0	1818	0.8	1938	1.7	1724	3.9	1758	4.0	1732	5.0	1732	5.5
	2341	4.4							2324	1.1	2313	1.6	2329	1.8				
22 SU	0612	1.9	0031	4.5	0049	3.9	0131	1.5	0824	1.8	0627	4.0	0659	4.2	0003	1.8	0043	2.2
	1218	4.6	0642	2.2	0638	2.1	0703	0.9	1212	1.2	1202	1.7	1218	1.9	0621	5.2	0617	5.6
	1901	1.9	1302	4.7	1322	4.2	1348	1.6	2036	1.7	1853	3.9	1929	4.1	1251	1.8	1327	1.9
			1935	1.9	1932	1.8	1957	0.7							1904	5.1	1908	5.7
23 M	0105	4.6	0205	4.7	0219	4.2	0312	1.6	0044	1.1	0040	1.5	0051	1.6	0131	1.6	0215	1.9
	0728	1.6	0812	1.9	0806	1.8	0824	0.8	0844	1.9	0743	4.2	0812	4.4	0742	5.5	0739	5.8
	1331	4.9	1430	5.0	1445	4.5	1518	1.8	1321	1.1	1319	1.4	1330	1.6	1406	1.5	1450	1.6
	2006	1.3	2050	1.5	2049	1.4	2100	0.6	2045	1.9	2002	4.1	2034	4.3	2018	5.4	2018	6.0
24 TU	0206	5.0	0318	5.0	0332	4.5	0417	1.8	0144	0.9	0148	1.1	0154	1.4	0237	1.3	0327	1.6
	0828	1.3	0920	1.5	0917	1.4	0921	0.6	0845	2.0	0838	4.4	0906	4.6	0844	5.8	0839	6.2
	1427	5.3	1536	5.3	1552	4.8	1623	1.9	1413	0.9	1418	1.1	1424	1.3	1505	1.1	1555	1.2
	2100	0.9	2151	1.1	2151	1.0	2148	0.4	2045	2.0	2055	4.3	2121	4.5	2112	5.8	2112	6.3
25 W	0254	5.3	0412	5.3	0429	4.8	0509	2.0	0232	0.7	0242	0.8	0244	1.1	0330	1.0	0429	1.3
	0918	0.9	1016	1.1	1015	1.0	1008	0.5	0846	2.1	0922	4.6	0947	4.7	0933	6.2	0927	6.5
	1513	5.6	1628	5.5	1647	5.0	1716	2.1	1456	0.7	1507	0.8	1509	1.0	1555	0.9	1652	0.9
	2145	0.7	2243	0.8	2244	0.7	2231	0.3	2047	2.1	2137	4.5	2200	4.6	2156	6.1	2154	6.5
26 TH	0337	5.6	0457	5.5	0516	5.0	0555	2.1	0315	0.6	0328	0.5	0328	0.8	0416	0.7	0522	1.1
	1002	0.7	1106	0.9	1105	0.7	1050	0.4	0852	2.2	1002	4.7	1024	4.8	1015	6.3	1007	6.7
	1555	5.7	1712	5.6	1731	5.1	1804	2.2	1537	0.6	1549	0.5	1551	0.8	1638	0.7	1742	0.8
	2227	0.6	2329	0.7	2330	0.6	2311	0.2	2057	2.1	2217	4.6	2239	4.7	2234	6.2	2231	6.6
27 F	0416	5.7	0536	5.6	0556	5.0	0637	2.2	0354	0.5	0410	0.4	0409	0.7	0457	0.6	0608	1.0
	1043	0.6	1148	0.7	1149	0.6	1130	0.3	0906	2.2	1039	4.7	1102	4.8	1054	6.4	1045	6.8
	1634	5.8	1751	5.6	1812	5.1	1848	2.2	1615	0.5	1629	0.4	1630	0.7	1718	0.6	1825	0.8
	2305	0.6					2350	0.1	2115	2.1	2255	4.6	2317	4.7	2312	6.3	2307	6.7
28 SA	0454	5.7	0009	0.7	0011	0.5	0715	2.3	0433	0.5	0449	0.4	0448	0.6	0535	0.6	0645	1.0
	1121	0.7	0612	5.6	0633	5.1	1209	0.2	0931	2.1	1115	4.7	1139	4.8	1131	6.4	1123	6.9
	1711	5.6	1227	0.8	1227	0.6	1926	2.2	1652	0.5	1707	0.4	1707	0.7	1754	0.7	1902	0.8
	2341	0.7	1825	5.6	1848	5.1			2145	2.1	2332	4.6	2355	4.7	2348	6.2	2343	6.7
29 SU ●	0529	5.7	0045	0.8	0047	0.6	0027	0.1	0509	0.6	0525	0.5	0524	0.7	0609	0.7	0717	1.0
	1157	0.8	0645	5.6	0706	5.0	0748	2.2	1006	2.1	1150	4.6	1215	4.7	1205	6.3	1159	6.8
	1747	5.6	1300	0.7	1303	0.7	1247	0.2	1728	0.6	1742	0.5	1743	0.8	1827	0.8	1935	0.9
			1858	5.5	1923	5.0	1958	2.1	2228	2.0								
30 M	0015	0.9	0117	0.9	0119	0.8	0101	0.2	0546	0.6	0009	4.5	0033	4.6	0024	6.1	0018	6.6
	0604	5.5	0715	5.5	0739	5.0	0817	2.1	1052	2.1	0558	0.7	0600	0.9	0643	0.9	0747	1.1
	1232	1.0	1332	1.1	1334	0.9	1321	0.3	1804	0.7	1224	4.5	1251	4.6	1238	6.2	1234	6.7
	1822	5.3	1930	5.4	1955	4.8	2025	2.0	2324	2.0	1811	0.7	1818	0.9	1859	0.9	2006	1.1
31 TU	0048	1.1	0146	1.2	0148	1.1	0132	0.3	0621	0.7	0046	4.4	0112	4.5	0057	6.0	0053	6.5
	0639	5.3	0746	5.4	0809	4.8	0841	2.0	1149	2.0	0628	0.9	0634	1.1	0715	1.1	0816	1.2
	1306	1.2	1402	1.3	1402	1.1	1353	0.4	1838	0.8	1259	4.3	1327	4.5	1308	6.0	1309	6.4
	1857	5.1	2001	5.2	2023	4.6	2048	1.8			1839	0.9	1851	1.1	1931	1.1	2034	1.3

SOUTH COAST OF ENGLAND Time Zone UT

St Mary's * Plymouth * Dartmouth * Portland * Poole * Southampton * Portsmouth * Shoreham * Dover

TIDE TABLES NOVEMBER 2000

ST MARY'S, SCILLY		PLYMOUTH		DARTMOUTH		PORTLAND		POOLE		SOUTHAMPTON		PORTSMOUTH		SHOREHAM		DOVER		Day
Time	m	Time	m	Time	m	Time	m	Time	m	Time	m	Time	m	Time	m	Time	m	
0121	1.4	0215	1.5	0213	1.3	0157	0.4	0031	1.9	0122	4.2	0151	4.4	0130	5.8	0127	6.3	1 W
0715	5.1	0815	5.2	0834	4.6	0901	1.9	0657	0.9	0656	1.2	0709	1.3	0748	1.4	0845	1.5	
1341	1.5	1430	1.7	1429	1.4	1419	0.5	1253	1.9	1334	4.1	1403	4.4	1340	5.7	1343	6.1	
1933	4.8	2031	4.9	2049	4.3	2111	1.6	1915	0.9	1908	1.2	1926	1.3	2005	1.4	2103	1.6	
0154	1.7	0241	1.9	0239	1.6	0212	0.6	0151	1.8	0203	4.0	0233	4.2	0204	5.5	0203	6.0	2 TH
0754	4.8	0845	5.0	0900	4.4	0921	1.7	0733	1.0	0728	1.5	0744	1.6	0827	1.7	0918	1.8	
1419	1.8	1500	2.0	1457	1.8	1442	0.6	1405	1.8	1415	3.9	1440	4.1	1419	5.3	1421	5.8	
2014	4.5	2103	4.7	2116	4.0	2137	1.5	1952	1.0	1943	1.5	2002	1.6	2045	1.7	2136	1.9	
0235	2.0	0312	2.2	0309	1.9	0225	0.7	0333	1.7	0251	3.8	0324	4.0	0247	5.1	0245	5.7	3 F
0840	4.5	0921	4.7	0932	4.1	0945	1.6	0815	1.2	0811	1.8	0824	1.9	0913	2.0	0957	2.1	
1507	2.1	1539	2.3	1534	2.1	1507	0.7	1533	1.6	1503	3.7	1524	3.9	1508	4.9	1509	5.4	
2106	4.2	2148	4.4	2159	3.8	2213	1.3	2037	1.2	2032	1.8	2045	1.9	2136	2.0	2219	2.3	
0328	2.3	0354	2.5	0348	2.3	0246	0.8	0553	1.6	0353	3.6	0440	3.8	0345	4.8	0340	5.4	4 SA
0942	4.3	1012	4.5	1023	3.9	1021	1.5	0916	1.4	0911	2.1	0923	2.2	1016	2.3	1047	2.4	
1613	2.3	1636	2.5	1627	2.3	1557	0.8	1741	1.5	1607	3.6	1633	3.6	1614	4.6	1622	5.0	
2224	4.0	2259	4.2	2313	3.6	2313	1.2	2200	1.3	2140	2.0	2206	2.2	2242	2.3	2315	2.5	
0448	2.4	0501	2.7	0451	2.5	0329	0.9	0727	1.6	0512	3.5	0548	3.8	0502	4.7	0457	5.1	5 SU
1108	4.2	1129	4.4	1144	3.8	1127	1.4	1139	1.4	1033	2.2	1144	2.3	1133	2.5	1153	2.5	
1740	2.3	1758	2.6	1744	2.4	1824	0.9	1943	1.5	1726	3.5	1803	3.6	1739	4.5	1757	4.9	
										2310	2.0							
0000	4.0	0030	4.2	0041	3.6	0051	1.2	0000	1.3	0636	3.6	0006	2.1	0004	2.3	0028	2.6	6 M
0618	2.3	0633	2.7	0622	2.5	0632	1.0	0821	1.6	1159	2.1	0654	3.8	0625	4.7	0627	5.2	
1230	4.3	1256	4.5	1309	3.8	1312	1.4	1244	1.3	1848	3.6	1251	2.2	1251	2.3	1316	2.4	
1856	2.1	1930	2.4	1924	2.3	1952	0.8	2031	1.5			1914	3.7	1901	4.7	1917	5.1	
0110	4.3	0148	4.4	0202	3.8	0242	1.4	0055	1.2	0032	1.9	0103	1.9	0118	2.1	0151	2.4	7 TU
0725	2.1	0800	2.4	0753	2.3	0806	0.9	0842	1.7	0742	3.8	0800	4.0	0734	5.0	0737	5.4	
1329	4.6	1407	4.7	1423	4.1	1447	1.6	1326	1.2	1309	1.8	1335	1.9	1353	2.0	1437	2.1	
1952	1.8	2037	2.0	2030	1.9	2040	0.6	2044	1.6	1952	3.8	2016	3.9	2004	5.0	2011	5.5	
0200	4.6	0247	4.7	0307	4.1	0348	1.6	0137	1.1	0134	1.5	0146	1.7	0214	1.8	0301	2.0	8 W
0815	1.7	0900	2.0	0855	1.9	0857	0.7	0845	1.8	0831	4.0	0853	4.2	0826	5.4	0826	5.8	
1415	4.9	1503	5.0	1525	4.4	1551	1.7	1400	1.1	1401	1.4	1410	1.6	1442	1.6	1536	1.7	
2037	1.4	2128	1.7	2122	1.5	2121	0.4	2045	1.8	2040	4.0	2105	4.1	2049	5.4	2051	5.9	
0239	5.0	0335	5.0	0401	4.4	0436	1.8	0213	0.9	0220	1.2	0224	1.4	0300	1.4	0357	1.6	9 TH
0858	1.4	0949	1.6	0945	1.5	0940	0.6	0845	2.0	0910	4.2	0934	4.4	0909	5.7	0905	6.2	
1454	5.2	1551	5.3	1615	4.7	1645	1.9	1433	0.9	1443	1.1	1445	1.3	1524	1.2	1627	1.3	
2117	1.1	2214	1.3	2209	1.2	2200	0.3	2046	1.9	2121	4.2	2143	4.4	2127	5.8	2124	6.2	
0316	5.3	0418	5.3	0447	4.7	0521	2.0	0248	0.8	0301	0.9	0301	1.1	0341	1.1	0446	1.3	10 F
0938	1.1	1035	1.3	1033	1.1	1021	0.4	0849	2.0	0946	4.4	1008	4.6	0947	6.0	0939	6.4	
1532	5.5	1635	5.5	1702	4.9	1734	2.0	1509	0.7	1524	0.8	1522	1.1	1604	0.9	1713	1.1	
2156	0.9	2258	1.0	2255	0.9	2239	0.2	2051	2.0	2157	4.4	2218	4.5	2203	6.0	2157	6.5	
0352	5.6	0500	5.5	0528	4.9	0605	2.1	0325	0.7	0340	0.7	0339	0.9	0421	0.8	0531	1.1	11 SA
1017	0.9	1118	1.0	1118	0.9	1101	0.3	0857	2.1	1019	4.6	1041	4.7	1024	6.2	1013	6.7	O
1609	5.8	1717	5.6	1746	5.0	1821	2.1	1547	0.6	1604	0.6	1601	0.8	1644	0.7	1757	0.9	
2235	0.7	2340	0.8	2340	0.7	2319	0.1	2103	2.1	2233	4.5	2255	4.7	2242	6.2	2233	6.7	
0429	5.8	0540	5.6	0609	5.1	0646	2.2	0404	0.6	0422	0.5	0419	0.7	0501	0.7	0613	1.0	12 SU
1057	0.7	1200	0.8	1202	0.7	1141	0.2	0915	2.2	1054	4.7	1117	4.8	1103	6.3	1050	6.9	
1648	5.9	1759	5.7	1827	5.1	1905	2.2	1627	0.5	1644	0.4	1642	0.7	1725	0.6	1836	0.9	
2315	0.6					2359	0.1	2128	2.1	2311	4.6	2335	4.8	2324	6.3	2312	6.8	
0507	5.9	0021	0.7	0023	0.6	0726	2.3	0445	0.5	0503	0.5	0500	0.7	0541	0.8	0651	1.0	13 M
1138	0.7	0621	5.7	0647	5.2	1220	0.2	0947	2.2	1131	4.7	1157	4.9	1145	6.4	1129	6.9	
1728	5.9	1241	0.7	1244	0.6	1947	2.2	1708	0.5	1727	0.4	1723	0.6	1807	0.7	1913	0.8	
2356	0.7	1841	5.7	1908	5.1			2209	2.2	2350	4.6					2354	6.8	
0548	5.9	0101	0.7	0104	0.6	0039	0.2	0527	0.6	0545	0.5	0018	4.8	0008	6.4	0727	0.9	14 TU
1221	0.7	0701	5.7	0725	5.2	0803	2.2	1036	2.2	1209	4.7	0542	0.7	0624	0.8	1210	6.9	
1811	5.7	1321	0.7	1326	0.7	1300	0.2	1752	0.5	1808	0.4	1239	4.9	1228	6.4	1948	0.9	
		1924	5.5	1949	5.0	2027	2.1	2315	2.1			1806	0.7	1850	0.8			
0039	0.8	0141	0.8	0146	0.8	0118	0.2	0612	0.6	0033	4.6	0106	4.8	0054	6.3	0038	6.7	15 W
0631	5.7	0742	5.6	0807	5.1	0840	2.2	1144	2.1	0627	0.6	0626	0.9	0709	1.0	0806	1.0	
1306	0.9	1403	0.9	1408	0.8	1341	0.3	1837	0.6	1251	4.6	1324	4.8	1313	6.3	1255	6.7	
1857	5.5	2007	5.3	2032	4.9	2107	2.0			1849	0.6	1850	0.9	1936	0.9	2027	1.1	

● ● Time: UT. For British Summer Time (shaded) March 26th to October 29th ADD ONE HOUR ● ●

NOVEMBER 2000 TIDE TABLES

•• Time: UT. For British Summer Time (shaded) March 26th to October 29TH ADD ONE HOUR ••

Date	ST MARY'S, SCILLY Time	m	PLYMOUTH Time	m	DARTMOUTH Time	m	PORTLAND Time	m	POOLE Time	m	SOUTHAMPTON Time	m	PORTSMOUTH Time	m	SHOREHAM Time	m	DOVER Time	m
16 TH	0125	1.1	0222	1.1	0226	1.1	0200	0.4	0038	2.1	0122	4.5	0155	4.7	0140	6.2	0127	6.6
	0718	5.5	0824	5.4	0848	4.9	0918	2.0	0700	0.8	0711	0.8	0712	1.1	0756	1.1	0848	1.1
	1356	1.1	1446	1.2	1450	1.1	1425	0.4	1310	2.1	1340	4.4	1412	4.6	1400	6.0	1345	6.5
	1947	5.2	2054	5.1	2117	4.6	2151	1.8	1927	0.7	1933	0.8	1938	1.1	2024	1.1	2112	1.3
17 F	0216	1.4	0306	1.4	0310	1.4	0245	0.5	0227	2.0	0217	4.3	0251	4.5	0229	6.0	0220	6.3
	0811	5.2	0912	5.2	0934	4.7	0959	1.9	0754	0.9	0759	1.1	0804	1.4	0848	1.3	0937	1.4
	1453	1.4	1535	1.5	1538	1.4	1517	0.5	1457	1.9	1436	4.2	1506	4.4	1454	5.7	1445	6.1
	2045	4.9	2149	4.8	2210	4.3	2242	1.7	2024	0.9	2025	1.1	2033	1.3	2119	1.3	2204	1.6
18 SA	0315	1.6	0357	1.7	0401	1.7	0339	0.7	0446	1.9	0322	4.2	0402	4.4	0328	5.7	0321	6.1
	0913	4.9	1009	4.9	1029	4.5	1051	1.8	0900	1.1	0900	1.4	0907	1.7	0951	1.6	1036	1.6
	1601	1.6	1634	1.8	1635	1.7	1627	0.7	1706	1.8	1544	4.0	1613	4.2	1559	5.4	1557	5.8
	2156	4.6	2259	4.6	2316	4.1	2351	1.6	2136	1.0	2131	1.3	2142	1.5	2225	1.5	2312	1.9
19 SU	0428	1.8	0503	2.0	0502	1.9	0457	0.9	0705	1.9	0441	4.1	0529	4.3	0440	5.5	0431	5.8
	1030	4.8	1121	4.8	1139	4.3	1202	1.7	1022	1.2	1015	1.6	1027	1.8	1107	1.7	1149	1.8
	1721	1.7	1751	1.9	1747	1.8	1759	0.7	1927	1.7	1706	3.9	1748	4.1	1718	5.2	1721	5.6
	2320	4.5							2258	1.1	2251	1.5	2303	1.7	2344	1.6		
20 M	0550	1.8	0021	4.5	0035	4.1	0119	1.5	0815	1.9	0605	4.1	0643	4.3	0601	5.4	0033	2.0
	1154	4.8	0627	2.1	0620	2.0	0632	0.9	1145	1.2	1138	1.6	1150	1.8	1230	1.6	0552	5.7
	1838	1.6	1245	4.8	1301	4.3	1327	1.7	2029	1.8	1830	3.9	1909	4.1	1842	5.1	1312	1.7
			1912	1.8	1906	1.7	1925	0.7									1845	5.7
21 TU	0039	4.6	0143	4.7	0156	4.2	0243	1.6	0015	1.0	0011	1.4	0021	1.6	0104	1.5	0153	1.9
	0703	1.7	0745	1.9	0738	1.8	0754	0.8	0841	1.9	0718	4.2	0750	4.4	0715	5.5	0709	5.9
	1306	4.9	1406	4.9	1419	4.5	1447	1.7	1254	1.1	1251	1.6	1302	1.7	1343	1.5	1427	1.5
	1942	1.4	2023	1.6	2019	1.5	2029	0.6	2044	1.8	1941	4.1	2012	4.2	1952	5.3	1953	5.9
22 W	0141	4.9	0251	4.9	0306	4.4	0347	1.8	0117	1.0	0119	1.2	0126	1.4	0210	1.3	0300	1.6
	0804	1.4	0852	1.6	0848	1.5	0853	0.7	0845	2.0	0815	4.4	0843	4.5	0815	5.7	0810	6.1
	1403	5.1	1511	5.1	1525	4.7	1551	1.8	1348	0.9	1351	1.2	1358	1.4	1442	1.2	1530	1.3
	2035	1.1	2123	1.4	2122	1.2	2118	0.5	2045	1.9	2036	4.2	2100	4.4	2047	5.6	2047	6.1
23 TH	0231	5.2	0346	5.2	0402	4.7	0439	1.9	0207	0.8	0215	1.0	0218	1.2	0304	1.1	0400	1.4
	0855	1.2	0949	1.3	0947	1.2	0941	0.6	0845	2.1	0901	4.5	0925	4.6	0905	5.9	0900	6.3
	1451	5.3	1603	5.3	1619	4.8	1645	1.9	1433	0.8	1441	0.9	1445	1.2	1532	1.0	1626	1.1
	2121	1.0	2215	1.1	2215	1.0	2201	0.4	2046	2.0	2122	4.4	2142	4.5	2132	5.8	2130	6.3
24 F	0315	5.4	0431	5.3	0449	4.8	0524	2.0	0251	0.7	0303	0.8	0304	1.1	0351	0.9	0451	1.3
	0940	1.0	1039	1.1	1038	1.0	1024	0.5	0848	2.1	0941	4.6	1004	4.7	0949	6.1	0942	6.5
	1533	5.5	1647	5.3	1705	4.9	1733	2.0	1515	0.7	1526	0.7	1528	1.0	1615	0.8	1714	1.0
	2203	0.9	2300	1.0	2302	0.9	2242	0.3	2051	2.0	2201	4.4	2221	4.5	2213	5.9	2209	6.4
25 SA	0354	5.5	0511	5.4	0530	4.9	0606	2.1	0332	0.7	0345	0.7	0346	0.9	0433	0.8	0536	1.2
	1021	0.9	1121	1.0	1122	0.9	1105	0.4	0858	2.1	1019	4.6	1042	4.7	1029	6.2	1022	6.6
	1613	5.5	1726	5.4	1746	4.9	1815	2.0	1554	0.7	1606	0.6	1608	0.9	1654	0.8	1756	1.0
	2241	0.9	2340	1.0	2342	0.9	2321	0.3	2105	2.0	2240	4.5	2300	4.5	2251	6.0	2245	6.5
26 SU	0432	5.6	0546	5.4	0606	4.9	0643	2.1	0411	0.7	0423	0.7	0426	0.9	0510	0.8	0612	1.2
	1100	0.9	1159	1.0	1201	0.9	1145	0.4	0916	2.1	1054	4.6	1118	4.7	1105	6.2	1100	6.6
	1650	5.5	1801	5.4	1823	4.8	1854	2.0	1631	0.6	1641	0.6	1646	0.9	1730	0.8	1831	1.0
	2317	1.0					2359	0.3	2131	2.0	2315	4.5	2339	4.5	2328	6.0	2323	6.5
27 M	0509	5.6	0016	1.0	0019	0.9	0717	2.1	0448	0.7	0500	0.7	0503	1.0	0546	0.9	0645	1.1
	1136	1.0	0618	5.5	0640	4.9	1223	0.3	0944	2.1	1127	4.5	1154	4.7	1140	6.1	1139	6.6
	1726	5.4	1234	1.0	1236	0.9	1927	2.0	1708	0.7	1716	0.7	1723	0.9	1803	0.8	1904	1.1
	2351	1.1	1834	5.3	1858	4.8			2209	2.0	2351	4.4					2359	6.5
28 TU ●	0544	5.5	0050	1.1	0050	1.0	0035	0.3	0525	0.7	0532	0.8	0018	4.5	0003	6.0	0718	1.2
	1211	1.1	0650	5.5	0712	4.9	0746	2.1	1024	2.0	1159	4.4	0540	1.1	0618	1.0	1215	6.5
	1801	5.3	1307	1.1	1308	1.0	1300	0.3	1744	0.7	1746	0.7	1230	4.6	1212	6.1	1935	1.2
			1906	5.3	1931	4.7	1956	1.9	2301	2.0			1758	1.0	1835	1.0		
29 W	0025	1.3	0121	1.2	0121	1.1	0107	0.4	0601	0.8	0026	4.3	0057	4.5	0037	5.9	0034	6.4
	0619	5.4	0721	5.4	0743	4.8	0812	2.0	1113	2.0	0603	1.0	0615	1.2	0650	1.2	0749	1.2
	1245	1.3	1339	1.3	1338	1.2	1333	0.4	1819	0.8	1232	4.3	1305	4.5	1244	5.9	1250	6.3
	1836	5.1	1939	5.1	2002	4.6	2022	1.8			1815	0.9	1832	1.1	1907	1.1	2006	1.3
30 TH	0057	1.4	0152	1.5	0149	1.3	0135	0.5	0004	1.9	0101	4.2	0136	4.4	0111	5.8	0109	6.3
	0654	5.2	0751	5.2	0812	4.7	0836	1.9	0636	0.9	0633	1.2	0649	1.4	0726	1.4	0822	1.4
	1319	1.5	1411	1.6	1408	1.4	1403	0.5	1209	1.9	1307	4.2	1339	4.4	1318	5.7	1324	6.1
	1912	4.9	2010	4.9	2032	4.4	2050	1.7	1854	0.9	1844	1.1	1906	1.3	1942	1.3	2037	1.5

SOUTH COAST OF ENGLAND Time Zone UT

St Mary's * Plymouth * Dartmouth * Portland * Poole * Southampton * Portsmouth * Shoreham * Dover

TIDE TABLES DECEMBER 2000

Day	ST MARY'S, SCILLY Time	m	PLYMOUTH Time	m	DARTMOUTH Time	m	PORTLAND Time	m	POOLE Time	m	SOUTHAMPTON Time	m	PORTSMOUTH Time	m	SHOREHAM Time	m	DOVER Time	m
1 F	0132	1.6	0222	1.7	0218	1.6	0157	0.6	0118	1.9	0140	4.0	0216	4.3	0145	5.6	0144	6.1
	0732	5.0	0822	5.1	0842	4.5	0901	1.8	0712	1.0	0706	1.4	0724	1.6	0804	1.6	0857	1.6
	1356	1.7	1443	1.8	1439	1.6	1428	0.6	1316	1.8	1345	4.0	1415	4.2	1356	5.4	1358	5.8
	1950	4.6	2042	4.7	2102	4.1	2120	1.5	1929	1.0	1918	1.3	1940	1.5	2020	1.5	2112	1.8
2 SA	0209	1.9	0254	2.0	0248	1.8	0214	0.6	0239	1.8	0223	3.9	0257	4.1	0224	5.3	0221	5.9
	0813	4.8	0854	4.9	0912	4.3	0927	1.7	0751	1.1	0746	1.6	0801	1.8	0847	1.8	0934	1.8
	1438	1.9	1520	2.0	1514	1.8	1454	0.6	1431	1.7	1429	3.9	1453	4.0	1440	5.1	1439	5.5
	2034	4.4	2119	4.5	2139	3.9	2156	1.4	2010	1.1	2001	1.5	2019	1.7	2105	1.7	2151	2.0
3 SU	0254	2.1	0332	2.2	0327	2.0	0238	0.7	0420	1.7	0315	3.8	0348	4.0	0312	5.1	0306	5.7
	0902	4.6	0935	4.7	0953	4.1	0959	1.6	0839	1.3	0835	1.8	0847	2.0	0937	2.0	1018	2.1
	1530	2.1	1606	2.2	1558	2.1	1533	0.7	1608	1.6	1523	3.7	1542	3.8	1534	4.9	1533	5.3
	2130	4.2	2209	4.4	2230	3.8	2246	1.3	2103	1.2	2056	1.7	2110	1.9	2157	1.9	2239	2.2
4 M	0354	2.2	0423	2.4	0415	2.2	0320	0.8	0620	1.7	0417	3.7	0457	3.9	0410	4.9	0402	5.4
	1004	4.5	1030	4.6	1050	4.0	1048	1.5	0948	1.3	0940	2.0	0954	2.2	1038	2.1	1112	2.2
	1636	2.1	1705	2.3	1655	2.2	1643	0.7	1811	1.5	1628	3.6	1651	3.7	1639	4.7	1643	5.1
	2242	4.1	2319	4.3	2342	3.7	2359	1.3	2225	1.3	2206	1.8	2230	2.0	2301	2.0	2339	2.4
5 TU	0509	2.3	0529	2.5	0521	2.4	0442	0.9	0742	1.7	0529	3.7	0602	3.9	0519	4.9	0512	5.3
	1118	4.4	1145	4.5	1205	3.9	1208	1.4	1122	1.3	1055	2.0	1127	2.2	1147	2.1	1218	2.3
	1751	2.1	1816	2.3	1807	2.2	1827	0.7	1953	1.5	1743	3.6	1814	3.7	1751	4.7	1759	5.1
									2346	1.2	2323	1.8	2351	1.9				
6 W	0000	4.2	0039	4.4	0058	3.8	0130	1.4	0826	1.7	0639	3.7	0703	4.0	0012	2.0	0049	2.3
	0624	2.2	0646	2.4	0638	2.3	0649	0.9	1224	1.3	1207	1.8	1230	2.0	0628	5.0	0624	5.4
	1229	4.5	1303	4.6	1320	4.0	1343	1.5	2033	1.6	1855	3.7	1920	3.8	1253	1.9	1333	2.1
	1857	1.9	1930	2.1	1924	2.0	1939	0.6							1900	4.9	1903	5.4
7 TH	0105	4.5	0148	4.6	0208	4.0	0251	1.5	0041	1.1	0033	1.6	0048	1.8	0117	1.8	0202	2.1
	0726	1.9	0800	2.1	0755	2.0	0803	0.8	0843	1.8	0737	3.9	0801	4.2	0729	5.2	0725	5.7
	1327	4.8	1409	4.8	1429	4.2	1502	1.6	1311	1.1	1310	1.5	1319	1.7	1352	1.6	1442	1.8
	1952	1.6	2036	1.8	2029	1.7	2033	0.5	2044	1.7	1954	3.9	2018	4.0	1956	5.2	1956	5.7
8 F	0156	4.8	0246	4.8	0310	4.3	0351	1.7	0127	1.0	0131	1.4	0136	1.5	0214	1.4	0307	1.8
	0818	1.6	0903	1.8	0858	1.7	0857	0.6	0845	1.9	0826	4.2	0851	4.4	0821	5.5	0815	6.0
	1416	5.1	1506	5.0	1531	4.5	1604	1.8	1354	0.9	1402	1.2	1404	1.4	1444	1.2	1542	1.5
	2040	1.3	2132	1.5	2126	1.4	2120	0.4	2045	1.8	2043	4.1	2107	4.2	2045	5.6	2042	6.0
9 SA	0241	5.2	0339	5.1	0405	4.6	0444	1.9	0212	0.9	0221	1.1	0223	1.3	0303	1.1	0406	1.5
	0905	1.3	0957	1.4	0955	1.3	0945	0.5	0845	2.0	0908	4.4	0933	4.5	0909	5.9	0859	6.3
	1501	5.4	1600	5.2	1626	4.7	1700	1.9	1437	0.8	1450	0.9	1449	1.1	1531	0.9	1636	1.2
	2125	1.0	2224	1.2	2220	1.0	2206	0.3	2046	2.0	2128	4.3	2150	4.4	2131	5.9	2124	6.3
10 SU	0324	5.5	0428	5.3	0457	4.8	0532	2.0	0256	0.7	0310	0.9	0309	1.0	0351	0.9	0458	1.3
	0950	1.0	1048	1.1	1048	1.0	1030	0.4	0849	2.1	0948	4.5	1012	4.7	0954	6.1	0942	6.6
	1545	5.7	1650	5.4	1719	4.9	1752	2.0	1521	0.6	1536	0.7	1535	0.9	1618	0.8	1727	1.0
	2210	0.8	2312	0.9	2312	0.8	2251	0.2	2055	2.1	2210	4.5	2233	4.6	2218	6.1	2208	6.6
11 M ○	0406	5.8	0515	5.5	0544	5.1	0619	2.2	0342	0.6	0356	0.7	0356	0.8	0437	0.8	0546	1.1
	1036	0.8	1137	0.8	1140	0.8	1116	0.3	0903	2.2	1030	4.6	1054	4.8	1039	6.3	1025	6.8
	1629	5.8	1739	5.5	1807	5.0	1842	2.1	1606	0.5	1623	0.5	1621	0.7	1705	0.7	1812	0.9
	2255	0.7					2337	0.2	2116	2.1	2254	4.6	2318	4.6	2307	6.3	2254	6.8
12 TU	0451	5.9	0000	0.7	0002	0.7	0705	2.2	0427	0.6	0445	0.6	0442	0.7	0524	0.8	0630	1.0
	1122	0.7	0602	5.6	0629	5.2	1201	0.2	0930	2.2	1111	4.7	1138	4.9	1127	6.4	1111	6.9
	1715	5.8	1224	0.7	1227	0.6	1930	2.1	1653	0.5	1710	0.4	1708	0.6	1752	0.7	1855	0.9
	2342	0.7	1828	5.5	1854	5.1			2156	2.2	2339	4.6			2356	6.4	2341	6.8
13 W	0536	5.9	0046	0.7	0050	0.6	0022	0.2	0515	0.6	0532	0.5	0006	4.8	0611	0.9	0714	0.9
	1210	0.7	0648	5.7	0714	5.2	0749	2.3	1017	2.2	1154	4.7	0530	0.7	1215	6.4	1159	6.9
	1801	5.8	1311	0.6	1315	0.6	1247	0.2	1741	0.5	1756	0.3	1224	4.9	1840	0.8	1938	0.9
			1917	5.5	1939	5.0	2017	2.1	2258	2.2			1755	0.6				
14 TH	0029	0.8	0131	0.7	0136	0.7	0108	0.2	0604	0.6	0025	4.6	0055	4.8	0046	6.4	0030	6.8
	0622	5.9	0735	5.6	0741	5.1	0833	2.2	1122	2.2	0620	0.6	0618	0.8	0659	1.0	0758	0.9
	1300	0.7	1357	0.7	1401	0.7	1334	0.3	1829	0.5	1241	4.6	1311	4.8	1305	6.4	1250	6.8
	1849	5.6	2006	5.3	2027	4.9	2103	2.0			1843	0.4	1842	0.7	1930	0.9	2022	1.0
15 F	0118	0.9	0217	0.9	0220	0.9	0154	0.3	0024	2.1	0115	4.6	0147	4.8	0137	6.3	0122	6.7
	0712	5.7	0822	5.5	0843	5.1	0916	2.1	0654	0.7	0707	0.7	0706	1.0	0750	1.1	0845	0.9
	1351	0.9	1444	0.9	1448	0.8	1422	0.3	1247	2.1	1330	4.5	1400	4.7	1355	6.2	1343	6.6
	1940	5.4	2056	5.1	2115	4.7	2151	1.9	1921	0.6	1929	0.6	1932	0.9	2019	1.0	2110	1.1

● ● Time: UT. For British Summer Time (shaded) March 26th to October 29th ADD ONE HOUR ● ●

DECEMBER 2000 TIDE TABLES

•• Time: UT. For British Summer Time (shaded) March 26th to October 29TH ADD ONE HOUR ••

	ST MARY'S, SCILLY		PLYMOUTH		DARTMOUTH		PORTLAND		POOLE		SOUTHAMPTON		PORTSMOUTH		SHOREHAM		DOVER	
	Time	m	Time	m	Time	m	Time	m	Time	m	Time	m	Time	m	Time	m	Time	m
16 SA	0209	1.1	0303	1.1	0307	1.1	0241	0.4	0215	2.1	0210	4.5	0245	4.6	0228	6.2	0214	6.5
	0803	5.5	0911	5.3	0930	4.9	1001	2.0	0747	0.8	0756	0.9	0757	1.2	0844	1.2	0936	1.1
	1445	1.1	1533	1.1	1534	1.1	1514	0.4	1431	2.0	1425	4.3	1453	4.5	1449	5.9	1440	6.3
	2035	5.1	2148	4.9	2205	4.5	2241	1.8	2015	0.7	2018	0.8	2024	1.1	2113	1.1	2203	1.4
17 SU	0304	1.4	0354	1.4	0355	1.4	0333	0.6	0450	2.0	0310	4.3	0404	4.5	0321	6.0	0308	6.3
	0900	5.2	1022	4.7	1022	4.7	1051	1.9	1051	1.9	0849	1.1	0941	1.3	0941	1.3	1032	1.3
	1545	1.4	1627	1.4	1625	1.3	1612	0.5	1637	1.9	1528	4.1	1557	4.3	1546	5.6	1542	6.0
	2136	4.8	2246	4.7	2302	4.3	2338	1.6	2114	0.9	2114	1.0	2121	1.3	2210	1.2	2303	1.6
18 M	0406	1.6	0450	1.7	0448	1.6	0432	0.7	0642	1.9	0417	4.2	0512	4.4	0420	5.7	0407	6.1
	1005	5.0	1103	4.9	1119	4.5	1147	1.8	0950	1.0	0950	1.3	0956	1.6	1045	1.4	1135	1.5
	1651	1.5	1728	1.6	1723	1.5	1721	0.6	1854	1.8	1638	4.0	1721	4.1	1652	5.3	1649	5.8
	2245	4.6	2351	4.6					2222	1.0	2219	1.3	2227	1.5	2316	1.4		
19 TU	0516	1.7	0556	1.8	0007	4.2	0043	1.6	0752	1.9	0529	4.1	0613	4.4	0526	5.6	0009	1.8
	1117	4.8	1212	4.8	0549	1.8	0543	0.8	1103	1.1	1059	1.5	1108	1.7	1156	1.5	0514	5.9
	1801	1.6	1836	1.7	1226	4.3	1252	1.7	2008	1.7	1756	3.9	1833	4.1	1803	5.1	1243	1.6
					1828	1.6	1834	0.6	2334	1.0	2331	1.4	2339	1.6			1802	5.6
20 W	0000	4.6	0103	4.6	0116	4.1	0155	1.6	0831	1.9	0642	4.1	0715	4.3	0027	1.4	0117	1.8
	0627	1.7	0706	1.9	0656	1.8	0701	0.8	1216	1.1	1211	1.5	1222	1.7	0636	5.5	0625	5.8
	1230	4.8	1325	4.7	1339	4.3	1402	1.6	2039	1.7	1909	3.9	1939	4.1	1308	1.5	1351	1.6
	1908	1.6	1944	1.7	1938	1.6	1942	0.6							1914	5.1	1912	5.7
21 TH	0108	4.7	0212	4.7	0225	4.2	0303	1.6	0042	1.0	0042	1.4	0049	1.6	0135	1.4	0223	1.8
	0733	1.6	0811	1.7	0806	1.7	0811	0.9	0844	1.9	0745	4.2	0812	4.4	0738	5.5	0731	5.9
	1333	4.9	1434	4.8	1448	4.4	1509	1.6	1317	1.0	1316	1.4	1326	1.6	1411	1.4	1457	1.5
	2006	1.5	2047	1.6	2045	1.5	2040	0.6	2045	1.8	2012	4.0	2036	4.1	2015	5.2	2012	5.8
22 F	0205	4.9	0312	4.9	0327	4.4	0400	1.7	0139	1.0	0144	1.3	0148	1.5	0235	1.3	0325	1.7
	0830	1.5	0915	1.6	0912	1.6	0908	0.7	0845	1.9	0838	4.3	0900	4.4	0835	5.6	0828	6.0
	1427	5.0	1533	4.9	1549	4.4	1608	1.7	1408	0.9	1414	1.2	1419	1.4	1505	1.2	1555	1.4
	2057	1.3	2142	1.5	2142	1.4	2129	0.5	2045	1.8	2104	4.2	2124	4.2	2107	5.4	2103	5.9
23 SA	0253	5.1	0403	5.0	0419	4.5	0450	1.8	0227	0.9	0237	1.2	0239	1.3	0326	1.2	0421	1.5
	0919	1.3	1009	1.5	1008	1.4	0957	0.6	0846	2.0	0921	4.3	0944	4.5	0924	5.7	0918	6.2
	1515	5.1	1622	5.0	1640	4.5	1700	1.7	1453	0.8	1502	1.1	1506	1.2	1553	1.1	1646	1.3
	2142	1.2	2231	1.3	2233	1.2	2213	0.4	2049	1.9	2148	4.3	2207	4.3	2153	5.6	2147	6.1
24 SU ●	0336	5.3	0447	5.2	0505	4.6	0533	1.9	0312	0.8	0323	1.1	0325	1.2	0411	1.1	0508	1.4
	1003	1.2	1055	1.3	1055	1.2	1041	0.5	0852	2.0	1000	4.4	1023	4.5	1007	5.8	1003	6.3
	1557	5.2	1705	5.1	1724	4.6	1745	1.8	1535	0.8	1544	0.9	1549	1.1	1634	1.0	1730	1.3
	2222	1.2	2314	1.2	2316	1.2	2255	0.4	2100	1.9	2226	4.3	2248	4.4	2235	5.8	2227	6.3
25 M	0416	5.4	0524	5.3	0545	4.7	0614	2.0	0354	0.8	0404	1.0	0408	1.2	0451	1.0	0548	1.3
	1042	1.2	1136	1.2	1138	1.2	1123	0.5	0905	2.0	1036	4.4	1100	4.5	1047	5.9	1043	6.4
	1635	5.2	1742	5.1	1803	4.6	1827	1.8	1615	0.7	1621	0.8	1630	1.0	1712	0.9	1808	1.2
	2300	1.2	2353	1.2	2355	1.1	2336	0.4	2121	2.0	2303	4.4	2326	4.4	2314	5.9	2306	6.4
26 TU	0454	5.4	0559	5.3	0620	4.8	0651	2.0	0433	0.8	0441	1.0	0448	1.1	0528	1.1	0624	1.2
	1120	1.2	1214	1.2	1215	1.1	1203	0.4	0929	2.0	1109	4.4	1136	4.5	1122	6.0	1122	6.4
	1712	5.2	1817	5.1	1840	4.6	1904	1.8	1653	0.7	1655	0.8	1708	1.0	1745	0.9	1841	1.2
	2335	1.2							2154	2.0	2338	4.3			2350	5.9	2343	6.4
27 W	0529	5.4	0030	1.2	0029	1.1	0015	0.3	0510	0.8	0513	1.0	0004	4.5	0602	1.1	0657	1.2
	1154	1.2	0631	5.4	0654	4.8	0724	2.0	1003	2.0	1141	4.3	0525	1.2	1156	6.0	1200	6.3
	1746	5.2	1250	1.2	1249	1.1	1242	0.4	1729	0.7	1727	0.8	1212	4.5	1818	1.0	1913	1.2
			1850	5.1	1915	4.6	1938	1.8	2240	2.0			1744	1.0				
28 TH	0009	1.2	0103	1.2	0101	1.2	0051	0.4	0547	0.8	0012	4.3	0042	4.5	0024	5.9	0019	6.4
	0604	5.4	0702	5.3	0725	4.8	0756	2.0	1047	2.0	0544	1.0	0601	1.2	0635	1.2	0730	1.2
	1228	1.2	1324	1.2	1321	1.1	1318	0.4	1804	0.8	1213	4.3	1247	4.5	1229	5.9	1235	6.3
	1820	5.1	1921	5.1	1948	4.5	2009	1.8	2337	1.9	1758	0.8	1818	1.1	1851	1.1	1945	1.3
29 F	0041	1.3	0136	1.3	0132	1.2	0124	0.4	0621	0.9	0046	4.2	0120	4.4	0057	5.8	0054	6.4
	0638	5.3	0733	5.3	0758	4.8	0825	1.9	1139	1.9	0616	1.1	0634	1.3	0708	1.3	0805	1.3
	1302	1.3	1357	1.4	1353	1.2	1351	0.4	1838	0.8	1246	4.2	1321	4.4	1303	5.8	1308	6.1
	1854	5.0	1952	5.0	2019	4.4	2040	1.7			1829	0.9	1851	1.2	1926	1.1	2018	1.4
30 SA	0115	1.4	0207	1.5	0202	1.2	0153	0.4	0042	1.9	0120	4.2	0157	4.4	0130	5.7	0127	6.3
	0712	5.2	0803	5.2	0829	4.7	0854	1.8	0654	0.9	0649	1.2	0706	1.4	0745	1.4	0840	1.4
	1336	1.4	1429	1.5	1425	1.4	1420	0.4	1235	1.9	1322	4.1	1353	4.3	1339	5.6	1340	6.0
	1928	4.9	2024	4.8	2050	4.3	2112	1.6	1910	0.8	1903	1.0	1922	1.3	2002	1.2	2052	1.5
31 SU	0149	1.6	0239	1.6	0234	1.5	0216	0.5	0147	1.9	0157	4.1	0231	4.3	0204	5.6	0200	6.1
	0749	5.0	0836	5.1	0900	4.5	0922	1.7	0728	1.0	0725	1.3	0739	1.5	0823	1.5	0916	1.5
	1413	1.6	1503	1.7	1457	1.5	1445	0.5	1339	1.8	1402	4.0	1427	4.2	1418	5.4	1414	5.8
	2006	4.7	2057	4.7	2123	4.1	2145	1.5	1947	0.9	1938	1.2	1957	1.4	2039	1.3	2128	1.7

EAST COAST OF ENGLAND Time Zone UT

Margate * Sheerness * London Bridge * Walton-on-the-Naze * Harwich * Lowestoft * Immingham * River Tees * River Tyne

TIDE TABLES JANUARY 2000

1 SA

Location	Time	m	Time	m	Time	m	Time	m
MARGATE	0135	1.5	0738	4.1	1423	1.0	2033	4.1
SHEERNESS	0139	1.6	0809	4.9	1433	1.2	2052	4.9
LONDON BRIDGE	0304	1.7	0924	6.0	1554	1.2	2211	6.2
WALTON-ON-THE-NAZE	0054	1.3	0716	3.6	1350	0.9	2005	3.6
HARWICH	0043	1.2	0716	3.4	1336	0.7	2004	3.4
LOWESTOFT	0503	2.3	1144	0.9	1827	2.2		
IMMINGHAM	0124	6.0	0752	2.3	1419	5.9	2012	2.7
RIVER TEES	0544	1.7	1156	4.4	1812	2.2		
RIVER TYNE	0537	1.7	1146	4.2	1805	2.0		

2 SU

Location	Time	m	Time	m	Time	m	Time	m
MARGATE	0248	1.4	0849	4.1	1523	1.0	2133	4.2
SHEERNESS	0251	1.5	0918	4.9	1534	1.1	2154	5.0
LONDON BRIDGE	0419	1.5	1043	6.1	1658	1.0	2319	6.4
WALTON-ON-THE-NAZE	0211	1.2	0827	3.6	1451	0.9	2106	3.7
HARWICH	0159	1.1	0828	3.4	1439	0.7	2107	3.5
LOWESTOFT	0007	1.2	0615	2.3	1242	0.9	1918	2.3
IMMINGHAM	0233	6.1	0855	2.2	1516	6.1	2117	2.5
RIVER TEES	0014	4.5	0642	1.7	1251	4.5	1911	2.0
RIVER TYNE	0009	4.3	0636	1.7	1243	4.3	1903	1.8

3 M

Location	Time	m	Time	m	Time	m	Time	m
MARGATE	0349	1.2	0949	4.2	1612	0.9	2220	4.3
SHEERNESS	0355	1.4	1017	5.1	1626	1.1	2245	5.2
LONDON BRIDGE	0524	1.3	1145	6.3	1754	0.8		
WALTON-ON-THE-NAZE	0312	1.1	0927	3.7	1541	0.8	2157	3.8
HARWICH	0303	1.0	0930	3.5	1531	0.7	2200	3.6
LOWESTOFT	0105	1.2	0715	2.3	1330	0.9	1958	2.3
IMMINGHAM	0332	6.2	0948	2.1	1603	6.4	2209	2.2
RIVER TEES	0111	4.6	0733	1.7	1341	4.7	2000	1.8
RIVER TYNE	0105	4.4	0724	1.6	1332	4.5	1951	1.7

4 TU

Location	Time	m	Time	m	Time	m	Time	m
MARGATE	0436	1.1	1036	4.3	1649	0.9	2257	4.4
SHEERNESS	0448	1.2	1106	5.2	1710	1.0	2329	5.3
LONDON BRIDGE	0012	6.6	0620	1.0	1234	6.5	1842	0.7
WALTON-ON-THE-NAZE	0403	1.0	1016	3.8	1623	0.8	2240	3.9
HARWICH	0354	0.9	1021	3.6	1614	0.7	2243	3.7
LOWESTOFT	0152	1.1	0804	2.3	1408	0.9	2032	2.4
IMMINGHAM	0420	6.4	1033	2.0	1642	6.6	2254	2.0
RIVER TEES	0201	4.7	0816	1.6	1424	4.8	2042	1.6
RIVER TYNE	0153	4.5	0806	1.5	1413	4.6	2032	1.5

5 W

Location	Time	m	Time	m	Time	m	Time	m
MARGATE	0513	1.0	1118	4.4	1722	0.9	2331	4.5
SHEERNESS	0533	1.0	1148	5.3	1748	0.9		
LONDON BRIDGE	0054	6.7	0707	0.8	1315	6.6	1924	0.7
WALTON-ON-THE-NAZE	0445	0.9	1059	3.8	1700	0.8	2318	3.9
HARWICH	0436	0.8	1103	3.7	1651	0.7	2322	3.7
LOWESTOFT	0233	1.0	0846	2.3	1442	0.9	2101	2.5
IMMINGHAM	0502	6.6	1112	1.8	1718	6.8	2333	1.8
RIVER TEES	0245	4.8	0854	1.5	1503	5.0	2121	1.4
RIVER TYNE	0235	4.6	0844	1.4	1450	4.8	2109	1.3

6 TH ●

Location	Time	m	Time	m	Time	m	Time	m
MARGATE	0549	1.0	1155	4.5	1757	0.9		
SHEERNESS	0007	5.5	0612	0.9	1227	5.5	1824	0.9
LONDON BRIDGE	0130	6.8	0750	0.7	1351	6.7	2004	0.6
WALTON-ON-THE-NAZE	0524	0.8	1138	3.9	1734	0.8	2352	4.0
HARWICH	0514	0.7	1142	3.7	1725	0.7	2357	3.8
LOWESTOFT	0311	0.9	0924	2.4	1513	0.9	2129	2.5
IMMINGHAM	0540	6.7	1148	1.7	1751	7.0		
RIVER TEES	0324	4.9	0930	1.4	1537	5.1	2156	1.3
RIVER TYNE	0313	4.7	0920	1.3	1524	4.9	2145	1.2

7 F

Location	Time	m	Time	m	Time	m	Time	m
MARGATE	0006	4.6	0627	0.8	1233	4.5	1833	0.9
SHEERNESS	0042	5.5	0650	0.8	1303	5.5	1858	0.8
LONDON BRIDGE	0204	6.9	0830	0.6	1426	6.8	2045	0.6
WALTON-ON-THE-NAZE	0558	0.7	1213	3.9	1806	0.8		
HARWICH	0548	0.6	1218	3.8	1757	0.7		
LOWESTOFT	0347	0.8	1000	2.4	1542	0.9	2159	2.5
IMMINGHAM	0012	1.6	0616	6.8	1224	1.6	1824	7.0
RIVER TEES	0400	4.9	1005	1.3	1610	5.1	2230	1.2
RIVER TYNE	0348	4.8	0954	1.3	1555	4.9	2218	1.1

8 SA

Location	Time	m	Time	m	Time	m	Time	m
MARGATE	0042	4.7	0706	0.8	1309	4.5	1911	0.9
SHEERNESS	0117	5.6	0726	0.7	1338	5.6	1933	0.8
LONDON BRIDGE	0238	7.0	0910	0.6	1501	6.9	2124	0.6
WALTON-ON-THE-NAZE	0024	4.0	0632	0.7	1247	4.0	1839	0.8
HARWICH	0031	3.8	0621	0.6	1253	3.8	1828	0.7
LOWESTOFT	0423	0.7	1035	2.3	1614	0.8	2232	2.5
IMMINGHAM	0049	1.5	0651	6.8	1258	1.5	1857	7.1
RIVER TEES	0434	5.0	1039	1.3	1642	5.2	2305	1.1
RIVER TYNE	0423	4.8	1027	1.3	1627	4.9	2252	1.1

9 SU

Location	Time	m	Time	m	Time	m	Time	m
MARGATE	0117	4.7	0742	0.8	1344	4.5	1946	0.9
SHEERNESS	0151	5.6	0802	0.7	1413	5.5	2008	0.8
LONDON BRIDGE	0312	7.0	0948	0.6	1538	7.0	2202	0.7
WALTON-ON-THE-NAZE	0057	4.0	0706	0.7	1321	4.0	1912	0.8
HARWICH	0104	3.8	0654	0.5	1327	3.8	1902	0.7
LOWESTOFT	0500	0.7	1110	2.3	1648	0.8	2307	2.5
IMMINGHAM	0125	1.4	0724	6.8	1333	1.5	1930	7.1
RIVER TEES	0509	4.9	1114	1.3	1716	5.2	2341	1.1
RIVER TYNE	0457	4.8	1059	1.3	1700	4.9	2326	1.0

10 M

Location	Time	m	Time	m	Time	m	Time	m
MARGATE	0151	4.7	0818	0.8	1417	4.5	2020	1.0
SHEERNESS	0224	5.5	0839	0.7	1448	5.5	2043	0.8
LONDON BRIDGE	0348	7.0	1025	0.6	1614	6.9	2237	0.8
WALTON-ON-THE-NAZE	0129	4.0	0741	0.6	1355	4.0	1947	0.8
HARWICH	0136	3.8	0730	0.5	1401	3.8	1936	0.7
LOWESTOFT	0536	0.7	1146	2.3	1724	0.9	2343	2.5
IMMINGHAM	0201	1.4	0758	6.7	1406	1.6	2003	7.0
RIVER TEES	0545	4.9	1150	1.3	1751	5.1		
RIVER TYNE	0532	4.7	1133	1.3	1733	4.9		

11 TU

Location	Time	m	Time	m	Time	m	Time	m
MARGATE	0224	4.6	0851	0.9	1451	4.5	2054	1.0
SHEERNESS	0258	5.4	0915	0.7	1525	5.4	2118	0.9
LONDON BRIDGE	0422	6.9	1059	0.7	1650	6.9	2307	1.0
WALTON-ON-THE-NAZE	0203	4.0	0818	0.6	1432	3.9	2024	0.9
HARWICH	0210	3.8	0806	0.5	1437	3.7	2013	0.7
LOWESTOFT	0615	0.7	1224	2.2	1802	0.9		
IMMINGHAM	0236	1.5	0833	6.6	1441	1.7	2039	6.9
RIVER TEES	0018	1.1	0624	4.8	1227	1.4	1830	5.0
RIVER TYNE	0002	1.1	0609	4.6	1208	1.4	1810	4.8

12 W

Location	Time	m	Time	m	Time	m	Time	m
MARGATE	0258	4.6	0924	0.9	1529	4.4	2131	1.1
SHEERNESS	0333	5.4	0951	0.8	1603	5.3	2153	1.0
LONDON BRIDGE	0455	6.7	1127	0.8	1726	6.8	2334	1.1
WALTON-ON-THE-NAZE	0239	3.9	0857	0.7	1512	3.9	2106	0.9
HARWICH	0246	3.7	0843	0.5	1516	3.7	2052	0.8
LOWESTOFT	0021	2.5	0654	0.7	1306	2.2	1842	1.0
IMMINGHAM	0311	1.6	0910	6.4	1516	1.9	2115	6.7
RIVER TEES	0057	1.2	0706	4.7	1308	1.6	1912	4.9
RIVER TYNE	0039	1.1	0648	4.5	1246	1.5	1851	4.7

13 TH

Location	Time	m	Time	m	Time	m	Time	m
MARGATE	0335	4.5	1001	0.9	1613	4.3	2213	1.2
SHEERNESS	0410	5.3	1027	0.9	1647	5.2	2231	1.1
LONDON BRIDGE	0530	6.6	1156	0.9	1806	6.5		
WALTON-ON-THE-NAZE	0320	3.9	0940	0.7	1557	3.8	2151	1.0
HARWICH	0326	3.7	0925	0.6	1600	3.6	2137	0.9
LOWESTOFT	0100	2.4	0737	0.7	1354	2.2	1929	1.1
IMMINGHAM	0348	1.7	0952	6.3	1557	2.1	2158	6.6
RIVER TEES	0140	1.3	0754	4.6	1354	1.7	2000	4.8
RIVER TYNE	0122	1.2	0734	4.4	1331	1.6	1939	4.6

14 F

Location	Time	m	Time	m	Time	m	Time	m
MARGATE	0421	4.4	1047	1.0	1707	4.2	2306	1.3
SHEERNESS	0454	5.2	1108	1.0	1737	5.1	2320	1.2
LONDON BRIDGE	0006	1.2	0609	6.4	1232	0.9	1854	6.3
WALTON-ON-THE-NAZE	0407	3.8	1030	0.7	1650	3.7	2247	1.1
HARWICH	0412	3.6	1013	0.6	1652	3.5	2231	1.0
LOWESTOFT	0145	2.4	0826	0.7	1452	2.1	2025	1.1
IMMINGHAM	0430	1.9	1042	6.1	1645	2.3	2251	6.4
RIVER TEES	0230	1.4	0848	4.5	1447	1.9	2057	4.6
RIVER TYNE	0211	1.4	0827	4.3	1425	1.8	2035	4.5

15 SA

Location	Time	m	Time	m	Time	m	Time	m
MARGATE	0518	4.3	1147	1.0	1812	4.2		
SHEERNESS	0547	5.1	1201	1.0	1839	5.0		
LONDON BRIDGE	0050	1.3	0700	6.2	1322	1.0	1956	6.1
WALTON-ON-THE-NAZE	0503	3.7	1130	0.8	1751	3.7	2353	1.1
HARWICH	0506	3.5	1115	0.7	1754	3.5	2341	1.0
LOWESTOFT	0237	2.4	0924	0.8	1602	2.1	2133	1.2
IMMINGHAM	0523	2.0	1147	6.0	1746	2.5		
RIVER TEES	0327	1.6	0951	4.4	1551	2.0	2203	4.6
RIVER TYNE	0309	1.5	0928	4.2	1531	1.9	2140	4.5

● ● Time: UT. For British Summer Time (shaded) March 26th to October 29th ADD ONE HOUR ● ●

JANUARY 2000 TIDE TABLES

•• Time: UT. For British Summer Time (shaded) March 26th to October 29th ADD ONE HOUR ••

	MARGATE Time	m	SHEERNESS Time	m	LONDON BRIDGE Time	m	WALTON-ON-THE-NAZE Time	m	HARWICH Time	m	LOWESTOFT Time	m	IMMINGHAM Time	m	RIVER TEES Time	m	RIVER TYNE Time	m
16 SU	0015	1.4	0023	1.3	0151	1.5	0609	3.7	0612	3.5	0345	2.3	0000	6.3	0436	1.6	0418	1.5
	0627	4.2	0653	5.0	0809	6.1	1242	0.8	1228	0.7	1033	0.8	0631	2.1	1058	4.4	1037	4.2
	1306	1.0	1311	1.1	1433	1.1	1903	3.7	1903	3.5	1711	2.2	1304	6.0	1708	2.0	1647	1.8
	1924	4.2	1949	5.0	2113	6.2					2248	1.1	1903	2.5	2315	4.6	2252	4.5
17 M	0136	1.3	0139	1.3	0314	1.5	0106	1.1	0057	1.0	0503	2.4	0118	6.3	0552	1.6	0533	1.5
	0740	4.2	0809	5.0	0933	6.2	0722	3.7	0724	3.5	1142	0.7	0751	2.0	1207	4.6	1148	4.4
	1422	0.9	1432	1.0	1600	1.0	1357	0.7	1341	0.6	1812	2.3	1418	6.2	1827	1.8	1804	1.7
	2035	4.3	2102	5.1	2228	6.4	2016	3.8	2016	3.5			2024	2.2				
18 TU	0250	1.1	0300	1.2	0439	1.2	0221	1.0	0208	0.9	0001	1.0	0233	6.5	0027	4.8	0006	4.6
	0849	4.4	0924	5.2	1050	6.4	0837	3.8	0839	3.6	0611	2.4	0906	1.8	0703	1.4	0644	1.3
	1527	0.8	1550	0.9	1721	0.9	1506	0.6	1448	0.6	1246	0.7	1525	6.5	1311	4.9	1252	4.6
	2139	4.4	2210	5.3	2336	6.7	2124	3.9	2127	3.7	1908	2.3	2139	1.9	1936	1.4	1912	1.4
19 W	0354	0.9	0415	1.0	0558	1.0	0330	0.8	0314	0.7	0110	0.9	0342	6.8	0134	5.0	0112	4.8
	0954	4.5	1033	5.4	1200	6.7	0945	4.0	0951	3.8	0715	2.5	1013	1.5	0805	1.2	0745	1.1
	1625	0.7	1657	0.8	1842	0.8	1605	0.6	1550	0.5	1345	0.7	1623	6.9	1409	5.2	1348	4.9
	2239	4.6	2312	5.5			2223	4.0	2230	3.8	1958	2.4	2245	1.4	2036	1.1	2012	1.0
20 TH	0452	0.7	0524	0.7	0037	6.9	0430	0.6	0415	0.5	0215	0.7	0445	7.1	0233	5.3	0212	5.0
	1058	4.6	1135	5.7	0718	0.7	1045	4.2	1054	3.9	0818	2.5	1112	1.2	0859	1.0	0840	1.0
	1719	0.7	1757	0.6	1300	6.9	1657	0.5	1645	0.4	1439	0.6	1715	7.2	1501	5.4	1438	5.1
	2333	4.7			1949	0.7	2316	4.1	2324	3.9	2046	2.5	2343	1.0	2128	0.7	2107	0.7
21 F ○	0548	0.5	0006	5.7	0131	7.0	0523	0.4	0509	0.3	0313	0.5	0542	7.3	0327	5.5	0306	5.2
	1158	4.7	0626	0.5	0819	0.5	1139	4.3	1148	4.1	0916	2.5	1204	1.1	0948	0.8	0930	0.8
	1811	0.6	1230	5.9	1354	7.1	1743	0.5	1733	0.4	1530	0.6	1801	7.4	1549	5.6	1524	5.3
			1848	0.6	2042	0.6					2132	2.6			2217	0.5	2158	0.5
22 SA	0024	4.8	0056	5.8	0220	7.1	0004	4.2	0014	4.0	0405	0.3	0036	0.7	0417	5.6	0356	5.3
	0642	0.4	0721	0.3	0912	0.2	0612	0.3	0600	0.2	1010	2.6	0634	7.4	1034	0.8	1017	0.8
	1253	4.8	1321	6.0	1443	7.4	1229	4.4	1237	4.2	1617	0.6	1252	1.0	1635	5.7	1610	5.4
	1900	0.6	1936	0.5	2130	0.5	1828	0.6	1818	0.4	2218	2.7	1846	7.5	2304	0.3	2247	0.3
23 SU	0112	4.8	0142	5.9	0305	7.3	0050	4.3	0059	4.1	0454	0.2	0125	0.6	0505	5.6	0445	5.3
	0733	0.2	0811	0.2	0958	0.0	0700	0.2	0646	0.1	1102	2.5	0723	7.3	1118	0.8	1101	0.8
	1343	4.9	1409	6.0	1530	7.6	1315	4.4	1323	4.2	1701	0.7	1336	1.0	1719	5.7	1654	5.4
	1947	0.6	2020	0.5	2212	0.5	1911	0.6	1900	0.4	2303	2.7	1930	7.5	2349	0.4	2333	0.3
24 M	0157	4.9	0227	5.9	0349	7.4	0133	4.3	0142	4.1	0539	0.2	0211	0.6	0551	5.5	0531	5.2
	0821	0.2	0857	0.2	1040	-0.0	0745	0.2	0731	0.0	1151	2.5	0809	7.2	1201	1.0	1143	1.0
	1430	4.9	1454	6.0	1615	7.6	1400	4.3	1406	4.1	1742	0.7	1418	1.2	1803	5.6	1739	5.3
	2031	0.7	2100	0.7	2249	0.6	1953	0.7	1943	0.5	2347	2.7	2012	7.4				
25 TU	0239	4.8	0309	5.8	0433	7.3	0215	4.2	0223	4.0	0624	0.3	0253	0.8	0034	0.5	0018	0.5
	0906	0.3	0940	0.3	1118	0.1	0829	0.2	0815	0.1	1240	2.3	0852	6.9	0636	5.3	0618	5.0
	1512	4.7	1538	5.8	1659	7.5	1443	4.2	1449	4.0	1823	0.8	1455	1.4	1243	1.2	1224	1.1
	2112	0.8	2139	0.8	2323	0.8	2033	0.8	2025	0.6			2053	7.2	1847	5.4	1825	5.1
26 W	0319	4.7	0351	5.6	0514	7.1	0257	4.2	0304	4.0	0031	2.6	0333	1.1	0118	0.8	0101	0.7
	0948	0.4	1019	0.5	1151	0.4	0912	0.3	0859	0.2	0707	0.4	0933	6.6	0722	5.1	0704	4.7
	1553	4.5	1621	5.6	1742	7.1	1527	4.0	1532	3.9	1330	2.2	1532	1.7	1325	1.5	1305	1.4
	2150	1.0	2214	1.0	2354	1.0	2115	0.9	2107	0.7	1903	0.9	2134	6.9	1933	5.2	1912	4.9
27 TH	0359	4.6	0433	5.4	0555	6.8	0339	4.0	0345	3.8	0117	2.5	0411	1.5	0203	1.1	0145	1.1
	1030	0.7	1055	0.7	1221	0.7	0956	0.5	0943	0.3	0751	0.5	1015	6.3	0810	4.8	0751	4.4
	1635	4.3	1706	5.3	1825	6.7	1611	3.8	1616	3.6	1421	2.2	1609	2.1	1409	1.8	1348	1.6
	2231	1.2	2249	1.2			2158	1.0	2151	0.9	1945	1.1	2218	6.5	2023	4.9	2003	4.6
28 F	0442	4.3	0518	5.2	0025	1.3	0425	3.9	0429	3.7	0206	2.4	0451	1.9	0251	1.5	0232	1.4
	1116	0.9	1132	0.9	0638	6.5	1042	0.7	1031	0.5	0839	0.7	1103	6.0	0902	4.5	0843	4.2
	1723	4.1	1752	5.0	1254	1.0	1659	3.6	1703	3.4	1518	2.1	1652	2.4	1459	2.0	1439	1.9
	2321	1.4	2332	1.4	1912	6.4	2248	1.1	2240	1.0	2036	1.2	2311	6.1	2118	4.6	2100	4.3
29 SA	0537	4.1	0608	4.9	0102	1.5	0517	3.7	0519	3.5	0303	2.3	0540	2.3	0345	1.8	0327	1.7
	1213	1.1	1219	1.2	0729	6.1	1139	0.9	1126	0.7	0937	0.9	1201	5.7	1000	4.3	0942	4.0
	1824	3.9	1846	4.8	1337	1.2	1756	3.4	1758	3.3	1624	2.1	1750	2.8	1559	2.2	1546	2.1
					2006	6.1			2343	1.1	2144	1.3			2222	4.4	2207	4.1
30 SU	0030	1.5	0030	1.6	0153	1.7	0621	3.5	0621	3.3	0413	2.2	0021	5.8	0445	2.0	0434	1.9
	0647	3.9	0709	4.7	0831	5.9	1251	1.0	1234	0.9	1051	1.0	0646	2.6	1103	4.2	1050	4.0
	1322	1.2	1323	1.4	1443	1.4	1908	3.3	1905	3.1	1734	2.1	1315	5.6	1713	2.3	1709	2.2
	1936	3.8	1951	4.6	2109	5.9					2318	1.3	1909	2.9	2332	4.3	2323	4.0
31 M	0153	1.5	0148	1.6	0316	1.8	0118	1.3	0103	1.2	0536	2.2	0147	5.7	0554	2.1	0548	2.0
	0805	3.9	0824	4.6	0945	5.8	0741	3.4	0739	3.2	1204	1.1	0803	2.7	1209	4.2	1200	4.0
	1430	1.3	1439	1.4	1606	1.4	1408	1.1	1352	0.9	1839	2.2	1429	5.7	1832	2.2	1828	2.1
	2046	3.9	2103	4.6	2223	5.9	2024	3.4	2021	3.2			2033	2.8				

EAST COAST OF ENGLAND Time Zone UT

Margate * Sheerness * London Bridge * Walton-on-the-Naze * Harwich * Lowestoft * Immingham * River Tees * River Tyne

TIDE TABLES FEBRUARY 2000

MARGATE Time	m	SHEERNESS Time	m	LONDON BRIDGE Time	m	WALTON-ON-THE-NAZE Time	m	HARWICH Time	m	LOWESTOFT Time	m	IMMINGHAM Time	m	RIVER TEES Time	m	RIVER TYNE Time	m	Day
0309	1.4	0312	1.5	0440	1.6	0240	1.2	0228	1.1	0038	1.2	0301	5.8	0039	4.3	0034	4.1	**1 TU**
0916	3.9	0939	4.7	1107	5.9	0855	3.4	0857	3.2	0656	2.2	0910	2.5	0659	2.0	0652	1.9	
1530	1.2	1546	1.3	1710	1.2	1510	1.0	1500	0.9	1300	1.1	1529	6.0	1309	4.4	1301	4.2	
2143	4.1	2208	4.8	2334	6.1	2127	3.5	2127	3.3	1928	2.2	2139	2.5	1936	2.0	1927	1.8	
0409	1.2	0418	1.3	0542	1.3	0341	1.1	0331	0.9	0132	1.1	0359	6.1	0139	4.4	0132	4.3	**2 W**
1013	4.1	1039	5.0	1207	6.1	0953	3.6	0956	3.4	0754	2.2	1003	2.3	0752	1.9	0743	1.7	
1619	1.0	1641	1.2	1804	1.0	1600	1.0	1551	0.9	1343	1.0	1617	6.3	1401	4.6	1350	4.4	
2228	4.2	2300	5.1			2215	3.6	2218	3.5	2006	2.2	2231	2.2	2025	1.8	2013	1.6	
0455	1.1	0511	1.1	0024	6.3	0428	0.9	0418	0.8	0215	0.9	0445	6.3	0229	4.6	0218	4.4	**3 TH**
1059	4.2	1127	5.2	0636	1.1	1039	3.7	1043	3.5	0838	2.3	1048	2.0	0836	1.7	0825	1.6	
1700	1.1	1727	1.0	1252	6.4	1640	0.9	1632	0.8	1418	1.0	1656	6.6	1445	4.8	1430	4.6	
2308	4.4	2345	5.3	1854	0.9	2256	3.8	2300	3.6	2038	2.4	2315	1.9	2106	1.5	2053	1.4	
0535	0.9	0556	0.9	0106	6.5	0507	0.8	0457	0.7	0254	0.8	0524	6.5	0311	4.7	0257	4.6	**4 F**
1139	4.3	1208	5.4	0726	0.9	1119	3.8	1124	3.6	0915	2.3	1127	1.8	0915	1.5	0903	1.4	
1739	1.0	1806	0.9	1331	6.6	1715	0.9	1707	0.7	1451	0.9	1732	6.8	1522	5.0	1505	4.8	
2346	4.5			1941	0.8	2332	3.9	2338	3.7	2108	2.5	2355	1.6	2142	1.2	2128	1.2	
0613	0.8	0024	5.5	0143	6.8	0542	0.7	0531	0.6	0331	0.7	0600	6.7	0347	4.9	0332	4.7	**5 SA**
1218	4.4	0635	0.8	0812	0.7	1155	3.9	1200	3.7	0948	2.3	1205	1.6	0951	1.3	0937	1.3	●
1817	0.9	1245	5.5	1408	6.8	1748	0.8	1739	0.7	1523	0.9	1805	7.0	1555	5.1	1537	4.9	
		1842	0.8	2027	0.6					2139	2.5			2218	1.0	2203	1.0	
0024	4.6	0100	5.6	0220	7.0	0006	4.0	0014	3.7	0407	0.6	0033	1.4	0421	5.0	0405	4.8	**6 SU**
0651	0.7	0712	0.7	0857	0.5	0615	0.6	0604	0.4	1019	2.3	0633	6.8	1025	1.2	1010	1.1	
1254	4.5	1321	5.6	1444	7.0	1230	4.0	1236	3.8	1557	0.8	1241	1.4	1627	5.2	1608	5.0	
1854	0.8	1917	0.7	2111	0.6	1821	0.7	1811	0.6	2213	2.5	1839	7.1	2251	0.9	2236	0.9	
0100	4.7	0135	5.6	0257	7.1	0040	4.0	0048	3.8	0443	0.6	0111	1.2	0453	5.0	0438	4.8	**7 M**
0727	0.6	0749	0.6	0939	0.4	0650	0.5	0638	0.4	1051	2.3	0706	6.9	1100	1.1	1042	1.1	
1329	4.6	1356	5.7	1521	7.2	1304	4.1	1311	3.8	1633	0.7	1317	1.3	1658	5.3	1640	5.0	
1929	0.8	1953	0.7	2151	0.6	1855	0.7	1845	0.5	2248	2.5	1912	7.2	2326	0.8	2309	0.8	
0135	4.7	0209	5.6	0332	7.2	0114	4.1	0122	3.9	0520	0.5	0148	1.1	0527	5.0	0511	4.8	**8 TU**
0801	0.6	0827	0.5	1017	0.4	0726	0.4	0713	0.3	1124	2.3	0740	6.9	1133	1.1	1115	1.0	
1401	4.6	1431	5.7	1556	7.2	1339	4.1	1345	3.9	1709	0.7	1353	1.3	1731	5.3	1713	5.1	
2003	0.8	2029	0.7	2228	0.7	1931	0.6	1919	0.5	2324	2.6	1945	7.2			2343	0.8	
0206	4.7	0242	5.6	0405	7.1	0148	4.1	0156	3.9	0557	0.5	0223	1.1	0000	0.8	0546	4.8	**9 W**
0833	0.6	0903	0.5	1051	0.5	0803	0.4	0748	0.3	1200	2.3	0814	6.9	0602	5.0	1149	1.1	
1434	4.6	1507	5.6	1630	7.1	1415	4.1	1421	3.8	1745	0.8	1427	1.3	1209	1.1	1748	5.0	
2036	0.8	2103	0.7	2258	0.9	2008	0.7	1954	0.5			2020	7.2	1806	5.0			
0237	4.7	0315	5.5	0437	7.0	0224	4.1	0230	3.8	0000	2.5	0257	1.2	0037	0.8	0019	0.8	**10 TH**
0906	0.7	0936	0.6	1119	0.7	0840	0.5	0824	0.3	0633	0.5	0849	6.7	0640	4.9	0623	4.7	
1508	4.5	1544	5.5	1706	7.0	1452	4.0	1458	3.8	1237	2.3	1501	1.5	1246	1.2	1225	1.2	
2111	1.0	2135	0.8	2320	1.1	2045	0.7	2032	0.6	1822	0.8	2055	7.1	1846	5.1	1827	4.9	
0310	4.6	0350	5.5	0510	6.8	0301	4.0	0307	3.8	0038	2.5	0330	1.4	0117	1.0	0057	1.0	**11 F**
0939	0.8	1006	0.7	1139	0.8	0918	0.5	0902	0.4	0712	0.6	0927	6.6	0724	4.8	0705	4.6	
1547	4.4	1623	5.4	1743	6.7	1533	3.9	1539	3.7	1320	2.2	1537	1.7	1327	1.4	1305	1.3	
2149	1.1	2208	0.9	2342	1.1	2127	0.8	2112	0.7	1903	0.9	2135	6.9	1931	5.0	1912	4.8	
0350	4.5	0430	5.4	0548	6.7	0344	4.0	0349	3.7	0120	2.5	0406	1.6	0201	1.2	0141	1.1	**12 SA**
1018	0.9	1039	0.8	1205	0.9	1002	0.6	0945	0.5	0755	0.6	1010	6.3	0814	4.6	0753	4.4	
1635	4.3	1709	5.2	1827	6.4	1621	3.8	1626	3.6	1411	2.1	1619	2.0	1415	1.6	1353	1.5	
2235	1.2	2250	1.0			2215	0.9	2200	0.8	1953	1.0	2223	6.6	2026	4.8	2005	4.7	
0443	4.4	0519	5.2	0021	1.2	0436	3.8	0439	3.6	0210	2.4	0453	1.8	0255	1.4	0233	1.4	**13 SU**
1110	1.0	1124	0.9	0633	6.4	1056	0.7	1039	0.6	0849	0.7	1106	6.0	0914	4.4	0851	4.3	
1735	4.2	1805	5.0	1248	1.0	1718	3.7	1723	3.4	1517	2.1	1714	2.2	1516	1.8	1454	1.7	
2338	1.3	2347	1.2	1921	6.2	2317	1.0	2303	0.9	2057	1.0	2327	6.3	2133	4.6	2109	4.5	
0551	4.2	0622	5.0	0114	1.3	0539	3.7	0542	3.5	0319	2.3	0556	2.1	0401	1.6	0342	1.6	**14 M**
1225	1.1	1231	1.1	0738	6.2	1206	0.8	1151	0.7	0958	0.8	1224	5.9	1024	4.4	1002	4.2	
1847	4.1	1915	4.8	1349	1.2	1827	3.5	1832	3.3	1633	2.1	1830	2.4	1633	1.9	1614	1.8	
				2037	6.1					2217	1.0			2251	4.5	2227	4.4	
0103	1.3	0105	1.3	0230	1.4	0033	1.1	0025	0.9	0442	2.3	0052	6.2	0524	1.7	0506	1.6	**15 TU**
0710	4.2	1401	1.2	0904	6.1	0654	3.6	0657	3.4	1117	0.9	0721	2.2	1140	4.4	1121	4.2	
1353	1.1	2033	4.9	1524	1.3	1327	0.9	1314	0.8	1742	2.2	1351	6.0	1804	1.8	1745	1.7	
2005	4.1			2158	6.2	1947	3.5	1948	3.3	2344	1.0	2002	2.3			2353	4.4	

● ● Time: UT. For British Summer Time (shaded) March 26th to October 29th ADD ONE HOUR ● ●

FEBRUARY 2000 TIDE TABLES

•• Time: UT. For British Summer Time (shaded) March 26th to October 29th ADD ONE HOUR ••

	MARGATE Time	m	SHEERNESS Time	m	LONDON BRIDGE Time	m	WALTON-ON-THE-NAZE Time	m	HARWICH Time	m	LOWESTOFT Time	m	IMMINGHAM Time	m	RIVER TEES Time	m	RIVER TYNE Time	m
16 W	0228	1.1	0237	1.2	0412	1.3	0159	1.0	0146	0.9	0600	2.3	0221	6.2	0013	4.6	0630	1.5
	0832	4.2	0906	5.0	1030	6.3	0819	3.7	0821	3.4	1230	0.9	0848	2.1	0648	1.6	1236	4.4
	1508	1.0	1531	1.1	1656	1.1	1448	0.8	1431	0.7	1845	2.3	1508	6.3	1254	4.6	1903	1.4
	2120	4.3	2151	5.1	2316	6.4	2106	3.7	2108	3.4			2127	1.9	1925	1.5		
17 TH	0342	0.9	0405	1.0	0542	1.0	0318	0.8	0302	0.7	0103	0.8	0341	6.5	0127	4.8	0108	4.6
	0951	4.3	1024	5.3	1148	6.6	0936	3.9	0942	3.6	0717	2.3	1001	1.8	0756	1.4	0737	1.3
	1615	0.9	1646	0.9	1824	1.0	1552	0.7	1540	0.6	1335	0.8	1612	6.7	1358	4.9	1337	4.7
	2227	4.4	2259	5.3			2210	3.8	2217	3.6	1942	2.4	2238	1.4	2027	1.0	2006	1.0
18 F	0448	0.7	0520	0.7	0024	6.7	0422	0.6	0409	0.5	0211	0.6	0446	6.9	0229	5.1	0209	4.9
	1100	4.5	1129	5.6	0709	0.6	1037	4.1	1046	3.8	0824	2.4	1101	1.4	0851	1.1	0832	1.1
	1713	0.8	1747	0.7	1252	6.9	1645	0.6	1635	0.5	1430	0.8	1704	7.0	1451	5.3	1428	5.0
	2324	4.6	2356	5.6	1936	0.8	2303	4.0	2312	3.8	2031	2.5	2336	1.0	2119	0.7	2100	0.7
19 SA O	0545	0.5	0621	0.4	0119	6.9	0515	0.4	0503	0.2	0306	0.4	0539	7.1	0321	5.3	0300	5.1
	1157	4.7	1223	5.8	0810	0.3	1130	4.2	1139	4.0	0916	2.5	1153	1.2	0938	0.9	0920	0.9
	1803	0.7	1838	0.6	1345	7.2	1730	0.6	1721	0.4	1519	0.7	1749	7.3	1539	5.5	1514	5.2
					2030	0.6	2351	4.1			2117	2.6			2206	0.4	2148	0.4
20 SU	0013	4.7	0045	5.8	0208	7.1	0601	0.2	0000	3.9	0354	0.2	0027	0.6	0407	5.5	0347	5.2
	0635	0.3	0713	0.2	0901	0.1	1216	4.3	0548	0.1	1003	2.5	0627	7.3	1021	0.8	1003	0.8
	1246	4.8	1310	6.0	1433	7.4	1812	0.6	1225	4.1	1603	0.6	1239	1.0	1621	5.6	1556	5.4
	1848	0.7	1922	0.5	2116	0.5			1803	0.4	2200	2.7	1831	7.5	2249	0.3	2233	0.3
21 M	0057	4.8	0128	5.9	0251	7.3	0033	4.2	0043	4.0	0438	0.2	0112	0.5	0450	5.5	0430	5.2
	0720	0.2	0758	0.1	0945	-0.0	0645	0.1	0631	-0.0	1047	2.5	0709	7.3	1101	0.8	1043	0.8
	1330	4.8	1354	6.0	1515	7.6	1259	4.4	1307	4.1	1643	0.6	1320	1.0	1701	5.7	1637	5.4
	1929	0.6	2003	0.5	2156	0.5	1852	0.5	1842	0.3	2244	2.7	1912	7.5	2330	0.3	2314	0.3
22 TU	0138	4.9	0209	5.9	0332	7.4	0114	4.3	0124	4.1	0520	0.2	0153	0.5	0530	5.5	0510	5.1
	0801	0.2	0839	0.1	1024	-0.0	0726	0.1	0712	-0.1	1130	2.4	0748	7.2	1139	0.9	1121	0.8
	1410	4.8	1434	6.0	1556	7.6	1339	4.3	1348	4.1	1721	0.7	1357	1.0	1740	5.6	1718	5.3
	2007	0.6	2041	0.6	2231	0.5	1931	0.6	1922	0.4	2326	2.7	1950	7.5			2353	0.4
23 W	0216	4.9	0248	5.8	0410	7.4	0152	4.3	0202	4.1	0559	0.3	0230	0.7	0009	0.5	0550	4.9
	0840	0.3	0916	0.2	1057	0.2	0806	0.2	0752	0.0	1211	2.3	0824	7.0	0608	5.3	1157	1.0
	1446	4.7	1513	5.8	1635	7.4	1418	4.2	1425	4.0	1757	0.7	1431	1.2	1215	1.1	1758	5.1
	2042	0.7	2115	0.7	2300	0.7	2009	0.6	2000	0.4			2027	7.3	1818	5.5		
24 TH	0251	4.8	0325	5.7	0448	7.2	0230	4.2	0239	4.0	0007	2.6	0303	1.0	0048	0.7	0029	0.7
	0915	0.5	0948	0.4	1124	0.5	0843	0.3	0831	0.2	0637	0.4	0857	6.7	0647	5.1	0629	4.7
	1520	4.5	1550	5.6	1712	7.1	1455	4.0	1503	3.8	1251	2.2	1503	1.5	1251	1.3	1231	1.2
	2116	0.9	2145	0.9	2325	0.9	2045	0.7	2038	0.6	1831	0.8	2103	7.0	1858	5.2	1839	4.9
25 F	0326	4.6	0401	5.5	0524	6.9	0309	4.1	0315	3.9	0048	2.5	0333	1.4	0125	1.1	0105	1.0
	0949	0.7	1016	0.7	1146	0.8	0920	0.5	0909	0.4	0714	0.6	0930	6.4	0727	4.8	0709	4.5
	1554	4.3	1626	5.3	1748	6.8	1533	3.8	1539	3.6	1330	2.2	1533	1.8	1328	1.6	1307	1.4
	2152	1.0	2212	1.0	2351	1.1	2122	0.9	2115	0.7	1908	0.9	2140	6.6	1942	4.9	1923	4.6
26 SA	0404	4.4	0438	5.3	0601	6.6	0348	3.9	0352	3.7	0132	2.4	0405	1.8	0203	1.5	0142	1.4
	1027	0.9	1042	0.9	1213	0.9	0958	0.7	0948	0.6	0753	0.8	1006	6.1	0810	4.6	0752	4.2
	1633	4.1	1703	5.0	1827	6.4	1613	3.6	1617	3.4	1414	2.1	1607	2.2	1408	1.9	1349	1.7
	2235	1.2	2244	1.2			2203	1.0	2155	0.9	1951	1.0	2222	6.1	2030	4.6	2012	4.3
27 SU	0451	4.1	0520	5.0	0022	1.2	0432	3.7	0433	3.4	0225	2.2	0442	2.3	0247	1.8	0228	1.7
	1114	1.2	1118	1.2	0646	6.2	1044	1.0	1033	0.8	0839	1.0	1051	5.8	0901	4.3	0842	4.0
	1724	3.9	1748	4.8	1249	1.1	1658	3.4	1700	3.2	1506	2.1	1653	2.6	1457	2.1	1445	2.0
	2333	1.4	2330	1.4	1914	6.1	2256	1.2	2248	1.1	2047	1.1	2321	5.7	2130	4.3	2112	4.0
28 M	0554	3.9	0613	4.7	0103	1.4	0527	3.4	0525	3.2	0332	2.1	0536	2.7	0340	2.1	0328	2.0
	1215	1.4	1214	1.4	0742	5.9	1145	1.2	1132	1.0	0942	1.1	1157	5.5	1002	4.1	0945	3.8
	1831	3.8	1845	4.5	1338	1.4	1757	3.2	1757	3.0	1610	2.0	1802	2.9	1603	2.3	1603	2.2
					2012	5.8					2213	1.2			2242	4.1	2229	3.8
29 TU	0051	1.6	0039	1.6	0157	1.7	0011	1.3	0001	1.2	0455	2.1	0051	5.4	0450	2.4	0451	2.2
	0716	3.7	0724	4.4	0851	5.6	0643	3.2	0641	3.0	1117	1.2	0701	3.0	1113	4.1	1104	3.8
	1328	1.5	1336	1.6	1449	1.7	1315	1.3	1252	1.1	1727	2.1	1328	5.5	1733	2.4	1744	2.1
	1948	3.7	2000	4.4	2118	5.6	1924	3.1	1918	2.9			1942	3.0				

EAST COAST OF ENGLAND Time Zone UT

Margate * Sheerness * London Bridge * Walton-on-the-Naze * Harwich * Lowestoft * Immingham * River Tees * River Tyne

TIDE TABLES MARCH 2000

MARGATE		SHEERNESS		LONDON BRIDGE		WALTON -ON THE- NAZE		HARWICH		LOWESTOFT		IMMINGHAM		RIVER TEES		RIVER TYNE			
Time	m	Time	m	Time	m	Time	m	Time	m	Time	m	Time	m	Time	m	Time	m		
0218	1.5	0221	1.7	0330	1.8	0158	1.3	0141	1.2	0005	1.1	0226	5.5	0000	4.1	2356	3.9	1	W
0839	3.7	0853	4.5	1012	5.6	0818	3.2	0818	3.0	0631	2.1	0829	2.9	0615	2.3	0615	2.1		
1441	1.5	1506	1.6	1626	1.6	1435	1.2	1421	1.1	1230	1.2	1448	5.7	1227	4.2	1222	3.9		
2057	3.9	2123	4.5	2238	5.7	2048	3.2	2047	3.0	1841	2.1	2107	2.7	1901	2.2	1858	1.9		
0333	1.4	0345	1.4	0504	1.6	0312	1.1	0300	1.0	0106	1.0	0333	5.8	0110	4.2	0106	4.0	2	TH
0945	3.7	1006	4.7	1135	5.8	0926	3.4	0929	3.2	0736	2.2	0933	2.6	0724	2.1	0717	1.9		
1545	1.4	1612	1.4	1730	1.4	1532	1.1	1523	1.0	1318	1.1	1545	6.1	1328	4.4	1321	4.2		
2153	4.1	2228	4.9	2351	5.9	2145	3.4	2148	3.2	1930	2.2	2206	2.3	1959	1.9	1949	1.6		
0428	1.2	0445	1.1	0606	1.3	0403	0.9	0351	0.8	0152	0.9	0423	6.2	0204	4.5	0155	4.3	3	F
1035	4.1	1100	5.1	1225	6.2	1015	3.6	1019	3.4	0821	2.2	1023	2.2	0813	1.9	0803	1.7		
1634	1.2	1703	1.1	1825	1.1	1615	1.0	1607	0.9	1355	1.1	1629	6.4	1416	4.7	1403	4.4		
2239	4.3	2317	5.2			2228	3.6	2233	3.4	2008	2.3	2252	1.8	2042	1.5	2030	1.3		
0511	1.0	0533	0.9	0039	6.3	0443	0.8	0431	0.6	0231	0.8	0503	6.5	0248	4.7	0234	4.5	4	SA
1117	4.3	1143	5.4	0700	1.0	1055	3.8	1100	3.6	0856	2.3	1104	1.8	0854	1.6	0841	1.4		
1716	1.1	1745	1.0	1306	6.5	1652	0.8	1642	0.7	1428	0.9	1706	6.7	1456	4.9	1439	4.6		
2320	4.4	2359	5.4	1918	0.9	2307	3.8	2314	3.4	2042	2.4	2333	1.5	2119	1.2	2106	1.1		
0550	0.8	0614	0.7	0118	6.7	0518	0.6	0506	0.5	0308	0.6	0539	6.7	0324	4.9	0309	4.7	5	SU
1155	4.5	1222	5.6	0751	0.7	1131	4.0	1138	3.7	0927	2.3	1143	1.5	0930	1.3	0915	1.2		●
1754	0.9	1822	0.8	1344	6.9	1726	0.7	1716	0.6	1502	0.8	1742	7.0	1531	5.1	1512	4.9		
2359	4.6			2006	0.7	2343	4.0	2351	3.7	2115	2.5			2155	0.9	2139	0.8		
0627	0.6	0036	5.6	0157	7.0	0553	0.5	0540	0.3	0344	0.5	0012	1.2	0358	5.1	0341	4.8	6	M
1231	4.6	0652	0.6	0837	0.5	1207	4.1	1214	3.9	0956	2.3	0612	6.9	1006	1.1	0948	1.0		
1830	0.8	1259	5.7	1421	7.2	1800	0.6	1749	0.5	1538	0.7	1221	1.3	1603	5.3	1544	5.0		
		1858	0.7	2052	0.5					2150	2.5	1815	7.2	2230	0.7	2213	0.6		
0036	4.7	0112	5.7	0233	7.2	0019	4.1	0027	3.9	0421	0.4	0051	1.0	0430	5.2	0414	4.9	7	TU
0702	0.5	0730	0.5	0920	0.3	0629	0.4	0615	0.2	1027	2.4	0645	7.0	1039	0.9	1022	0.9		
1306	4.7	1335	5.8	1457	7.4	1242	4.2	1250	3.9	1615	0.6	1259	1.1	1635	5.4	1616	5.1		
1906	0.7	1935	0.6	2134	0.4	1836	0.5	1824	0.4	2225	2.6	1850	7.4	2304	0.6	2247	0.5		
0110	4.8	0147	5.7	0309	7.4	0054	4.2	0103	3.9	0457	0.4	0127	0.8	0503	5.2	0447	5.0	8	W
0736	0.5	0808	0.4	1000	0.3	0706	0.3	0651	0.2	1059	2.4	0718	7.1	1114	0.9	1055	0.8		
1339	4.8	1410	5.8	1533	7.5	1318	4.2	1326	4.0	1651	0.6	1335	1.0	1709	5.5	1650	5.2		
1941	0.7	2012	0.5	2212	0.5	1912	0.5	1859	0.4	2301	2.6	1924	7.4	2339	0.6	2321	0.5		
0143	4.9	0221	5.8	0342	7.4	0130	4.2	0138	4.0	0533	0.4	0203	0.8	0538	5.2	0521	5.0	9	TH
0810	0.5	0845	0.4	1035	0.4	0742	0.3	0726	0.1	1134	2.4	0752	7.1	1149	0.9	1130	0.8		
1412	4.7	1445	5.8	1608	7.4	1354	4.2	1402	3.9	1727	0.6	1410	1.0	1745	5.5	1727	5.2		
2017	0.7	2046	0.6	2244	0.7	1949	0.5	1934	0.4	2339	2.6	2000	7.4			2357	0.6		
0215	4.8	0254	5.7	0416	7.3	0206	4.2	0213	4.0	0609	0.4	0237	0.9	0016	0.6	0558	4.9	10	F
0845	0.6	0917	0.4	1103	0.6	0819	0.3	0801	0.2	1211	2.3	0827	7.0	0616	5.2	1206	0.9		
1447	4.6	1522	5.7	1643	7.1	1432	4.1	1439	3.9	1805	0.7	1445	1.2	1226	0.9	1806	5.1		
2053	0.8	2118	0.6	2306	1.0	2027	0.6	2012	0.4			2036	7.3	1825	5.3				
0249	4.8	0331	5.7	0451	7.1	0243	4.2	0250	3.9	0018	2.5	0311	1.1	0055	0.8	0034	0.8	11	SA
0920	0.7	0946	0.6	1122	0.8	0857	0.5	0839	0.3	0647	0.5	0903	6.8	0658	5.0	0639	4.7		
1525	4.5	1601	5.5	1721	6.8	1512	4.0	1518	3.7	1252	2.2	1521	1.4	1307	1.1	1245	1.1		
2131	1.0	2151	0.7	2327	1.1	2106	0.7	2052	0.5	1845	0.7	2117	7.0	1912	5.1	1852	4.9		
0330	4.6	0412	5.5	0530	6.8	0326	4.1	0331	3.8	0102	2.5	0347	1.4	0139	1.1	0117	1.0	12	SU
0958	0.9	1018	0.7	1145	0.9	0938	0.6	0921	0.4	0730	0.6	0946	6.5	0748	4.8	0727	4.5		
1610	4.3	1645	5.3	1803	6.5	1557	3.8	1603	3.6	1340	2.2	1602	1.7	1355	1.3	1333	1.3		
2216	1.1	2232	0.9			2154	0.8	2139	0.7	1935	0.8	2206	6.6	2008	4.8	1947	4.7		
0424	4.4	0501	5.3	0002	1.1	0416	3.9	0420	3.6	0156	2.4	0431	1.8	0232	1.4	0209	1.3	13	M
1048	1.1	1103	1.0	0618	6.5	1030	0.8	1015	0.6	0822	0.8	1040	6.1	0847	4.5	0824	4.3		
1708	4.2	1739	5.0	1226	1.1	1652	3.6	1657	3.4	1442	2.1	1655	2.1	1455	1.6	1436	1.5		
2317	1.2	2328	1.1	1857	6.1	2254	0.9	2242	0.8	2039	0.9	2312	6.2	2116	4.6	2054	4.4		
0532	4.2	0606	5.0	0053	1.2	0520	3.7	0523	3.5	0311	2.3	0534	2.2	0338	1.7	0319	1.7	14	TU
1201	1.2	1210	1.2	0723	6.2	1140	1.0	1127	0.8	0933	0.9	1157	5.8	0957	4.4	0937	4.1		
1819	4.0	1850	4.8	1324	1.3	1801	3.4	1806	3.2	1558	2.1	1814	2.3	1613	1.8	1600	1.7		
				2010	6.0					2203	0.9			2238	4.4	2219	4.2		
0045	1.2	0049	1.2	0206	1.4	0013	1.0	0005	1.0	0439	2.2	0045	6.0	0504	1.9	0453	1.8	15	W
0654	4.1	0729	4.9	0848	6.1	0639	3.6	0642	3.3	1102	1.0	0704	2.5	1118	4.3	1103	4.1		
1333	1.3	1345	1.4	1457	1.5	1309	1.0	1255	0.9	1714	2.1	1331	5.8	1750	1.7	1739	1.6		
1941	4.0	2014	4.7	2133	6.1	1927	3.4	1926	3.2	2339	0.9	1945	2.2			2351	4.3		

● ● Time: UT. For British Summer Time (shaded) March 26th to October 29th ADD ONE HOUR ● ●

MARCH 2000 TIDE TABLES

•• Time: UT. For British Summer Time (shaded) March 26th to October 29th ADD ONE HOUR ••

	MARGATE		SHEERNESS		LONDON BRIDGE		WALTON-ON-THE-NAZE		HARWICH		LOWESTOFT		IMMINGHAM		RIVER TEES		RIVER TYNE	
	Time	m	Time	m	Time	m	Time	m	Time	m	Time	m	Time	m	Time	m	Time	m
16 TH	0215	1.1	0230	1.2	0353	1.3	0148	0.9	0133	0.8	0610	2.2	0223	6.1	0005	4.5	0623	1.7
	0825	4.2	0859	5.0	1015	6.3	0811	3.6	0814	3.4	1222	1.0	0837	2.3	0636	1.8	1223	4.3
	1454	1.2	1521	1.2	1635	1.3	1436	1.0	1421	0.9	1824	2.2	1455	6.1	1237	4.5	1857	1.2
	2103	4.2	2138	4.9	2257	6.3	2051	3.5	2054	3.3			2122	1.8	1913	1.4		
17 F	0334	0.8	0403	0.9	0530	0.9	0312	0.7	0257	0.6	0100	0.7	0343	6.4	0120	4.7	0106	4.5
	0951	4.3	1018	5.3	1136	6.7	0928	3.8	0935	3.6	0731	2.3	0951	2.0	0745	1.6	0729	1.4
	1606	1.0	1636	1.0	1807	1.1	1541	0.8	1531	0.7	1328	0.9	1600	6.6	1342	4.8	1326	4.6
	2213	4.4	2248	5.3			2156	3.8	2203	3.5	1925	2.3	2230	1.3	2014	1.0	1959	0.9
18 SA	0442	0.6	0515	0.6	0008	6.7	0413	0.5	0401	0.4	0203	0.5	0444	6.8	0219	5.0	0203	4.8
	1056	4.5	1120	5.6	0656	0.5	1027	4.1	1035	3.8	0826	2.4	1049	1.6	0837	1.3	0821	1.2
	1706	0.9	1735	0.8	1240	7.0	1631	0.7	1623	0.6	1421	0.8	1650	7.0	1436	5.1	1416	4.9
	2310	4.5	2342	5.5	1920	0.8	2248	4.0	2257	3.7	2015	2.4	2324	0.9	2103	0.7	2049	0.6
19 SU O	0537	0.4	0611	0.4	0104	6.9	0502	0.3	0451	0.2	0253	0.3	0531	7.0	0307	5.2	0250	4.9
	1148	4.7	1211	5.9	0755	0.1	1116	4.2	1124	4.0	0909	2.4	1137	1.2	0921	1.1	0905	0.9
	1751	0.8	1822	0.7	1332	7.3	1714	0.6	1705	0.5	1504	0.7	1733	7.2	1521	5.4	1459	5.1
	2357	4.6			2012	0.6	2333	4.1	2342	3.9	2059	2.5			2147	0.5	2133	0.4
20 M	0622	0.3	0028	5.7	0151	7.1	0545	0.2	0533	0.1	0337	0.2	0009	0.6	0348	5.4	0330	5.1
	1232	4.7	0657	0.3	0843	-0.0	1159	4.3	1208	4.1	0948	2.4	0611	7.2	1001	0.9	0945	0.8
	1830	0.7	1254	6.0	1417	7.4	1752	0.6	1744	0.4	1544	0.6	1220	1.0	1600	5.5	1539	5.2
			1903	0.6	2057	0.5					2141	2.6	1812	7.4	2227	0.4	2212	0.3
21 TU	0038	4.7	0109	5.8	0233	7.2	0013	4.2	0024	4.0	0417	0.2	0051	0.5	0427	5.4	0409	5.1
	0700	0.3	0736	0.2	0924	0.0	0624	0.2	0611	-0.0	1025	2.4	0647	7.2	1038	0.9	1021	0.7
	1309	4.8	1333	6.0	1457	7.5	1239	4.3	1247	4.1	1621	0.6	1258	0.9	1637	5.6	1616	5.3
	1906	0.6	1941	0.5	2134	0.5	1830	0.5	1821	0.3	2223	2.6	1849	7.5	2303	0.4	2249	0.4
22 W	0114	4.8	0146	5.9	0310	7.3	0051	4.3	0101	4.1	0455	0.2	0128	0.6	0501	5.4	0445	5.0
	0736	0.3	0812	0.2	1000	0.1	0702	0.2	0649	-0.0	1103	2.4	0721	7.2	1112	0.9	1056	0.8
	1343	4.7	1410	5.9	1533	7.5	1315	4.2	1324	4.0	1657	0.6	1333	1.0	1712	5.5	1654	5.2
	1939	0.6	2016	0.5	2206	0.6	1908	0.5	1859	0.3	2303	2.6	1926	7.4	2339	0.6	2323	0.4
23 TH	0148	4.8	0222	5.9	0345	7.3	0127	4.3	0136	4.1	0531	0.3	0202	0.8	0535	5.3	0520	4.9
	0808	0.4	0845	0.3	1028	0.4	0739	0.3	0726	0.1	1139	2.3	0753	7.0	1145	1.0	1129	0.9
	1414	4.7	1445	5.8	1608	7.3	1351	4.2	1358	3.9	1731	0.6	1405	1.1	1748	5.4	1731	5.0
	2012	0.7	2049	0.6	2233	0.7	1944	0.6	1936	0.4	2342	2.5	2001	7.2			2355	0.8
24 F	0221	4.7	0257	5.7	0419	7.2	0203	4.2	0211	4.0	0604	0.5	0231	1.1	0012	0.9	0554	4.7
	0839	0.6	0915	0.5	1051	0.6	0813	0.4	0801	0.2	1212	2.3	0823	6.9	0609	5.1	1201	1.0
	1443	4.5	1517	5.6	1639	7.1	1424	4.1	1430	3.8	1804	0.7	1434	1.4	1218	1.2	1809	4.8
	2045	0.8	2117	0.8	2254	0.9	2018	0.7	2010	0.5			2035	6.9	1825	5.2		
25 SA	0254	4.6	0330	5.6	0452	6.9	0239	4.1	0244	3.8	0022	2.4	0258	1.4	0045	1.2	0027	1.0
	0910	0.8	0939	0.7	1112	0.8	0845	0.6	0834	0.4	0636	0.7	0853	6.6	0645	4.9	0630	4.5
	1513	4.4	1548	5.4	1712	6.8	1457	3.8	1503	3.6	1246	2.2	1502	1.7	1251	1.4	1234	1.3
	2118	1.0	2141	0.9	2318	0.9	2051	0.8	2043	0.5	1838	0.8	2109	6.5	1906	4.9	1849	4.5
26 SU	0330	4.4	0403	5.3	0527	6.7	0315	3.9	0318	3.7	0104	2.3	0325	1.8	0120	1.5	0100	1.4
	0944	1.0	1003	0.9	1138	0.9	0918	0.8	0908	0.7	0709	0.8	0924	6.3	0724	4.7	0709	4.3
	1548	4.2	1621	5.1	1745	6.5	1531	3.7	1535	3.5	1323	2.2	1533	2.0	1329	1.7	1312	1.5
	2157	1.1	2207	1.1	2349	0.9	2126	0.9	2118	0.8	1917	0.9	2146	6.1	1952	4.6	1935	4.2
27 M	0413	4.2	0441	5.0	0609	6.3	0354	3.6	0355	3.4	0155	2.2	0357	2.3	0200	1.9	0140	1.7
	1027	1.2	1034	1.2	1214	1.0	0956	1.0	0946	0.9	0747	1.0	1003	6.0	0812	4.4	0754	4.1
	1633	4.1	1700	4.9	1826	6.2	1610	3.5	1612	3.3	1409	2.1	1612	2.4	1414	1.9	1400	1.8
	2249	1.3	2246	1.3			2211	1.1	2201	1.0	2007	1.0	2236	5.7	2048	4.3	2030	4.0
28 TU	0509	3.9	0529	4.7	0028	1.1	0442	3.4	0439	3.2	0300	2.1	0442	2.7	0248	2.2	0234	2.0
	1124	1.5	1121	1.5	0700	6.0	1050	1.3	1039	1.1	0838	1.2	1057	5.6	0909	4.2	0851	3.9
	1732	3.8	1750	4.6	1258	1.3	1700	3.2	1657	3.1	1507	2.0	1708	2.8	1512	2.2	1509	2.0
	2359	1.5	2345	1.5	1917	5.9	2315	1.2	2307	1.1	2117	1.1	2357	5.3	2156	4.1	2139	3.8
29 W	0623	3.7	0633	4.4	0116	1.4	0547	3.1	0541	3.0	0421	2.0	0553	3.1	0354	2.4	0351	2.1
	1233	1.6	1233	1.7	0804	5.6	1209	1.4	1155	1.3	1002	1.3	1220	5.4	1018	4.1	1003	3.7
	1848	3.7	1859	4.4	1354	1.6	1810	3.1	1803	2.9	1617	2.0	1843	2.9	1631	2.3	1645	2.1
					2022	5.6					2315	1.1			2313	4.1	2307	3.7
30 TH	0120	1.6	0117	1.7	0216	1.7	0050	1.3	0040	1.1	0553	2.0	0139	5.3	0519	2.5	0527	2.2
	0749	3.7	0759	4.4	0921	5.5	0724	3.0	0721	2.9	1150	1.3	0739	3.1	1133	4.2	1127	3.8
	1348	1.7	1414	1.8	1518	1.9	1345	1.4	1327	1.2	1733	2.0	1354	5.5	1804	2.2	1815	1.9
	2006	3.8	2027	4.4	2140	5.5	1951	3.1	1944	2.9			2024	2.7				
31 F	0242	1.4	0300	1.5	0403	1.7	0227	1.1	0211	1.0	0028	0.9	0255	5.6	0027	4.2	0027	3.9
	0902	3.8	0923	4.6	1045	5.6	0847	3.3	0850	3.1	0704	2.1	0855	2.8	0641	2.3	0641	2.0
	1500	1.5	1533	1.5	1651	1.6	1453	1.1	1440	1.1	1244	1.2	1503	5.9	1240	4.3	1237	4.0
	2109	3.9	2145	4.7	2303	5.7	2103	3.3	2105	3.1	1841	2.1	2130	2.3	1914	1.9	1912	1.6

EAST COAST OF ENGLAND Time Zone UT

Margate * Sheerness * London Bridge * Walton-on-the-Naze * Harwich * Lowestoft * Immingham * River Tees * River Tyne

TIDE TABLES APRIL 2000

MARGATE		SHEERNESS		LONDON BRIDGE		WALTON-ON-THE-NAZE		HARWICH		LOWESTOFT		IMMINGHAM		RIVER TEES		RIVER TYNE			
Time	m	Time	m	Time	m	Time	m	Time	m	Time	m	Time	m	Time	m	Time	m		
0346	1.2	0408	1.2	0526	1.4	0325	0.9	0310	0.8	0117	0.8	0349	6.0	0125	4.4	0121	4.1	1	SA
0958	4.1	1024	5.0	1148	6.0	0940	3.6	0945	3.4	0751	2.2	0950	2.3	0738	2.0	0730	1.7		
1558	1.3	1629	1.2	1751	1.3	1542	1.0	1530	0.9	1323	1.1	1553	6.3	1334	4.6	1326	4.3		
2200	4.2	2241	5.1			2153	3.6	2158	3.3	1929	2.2	2220	1.8	2003	1.6	1956	1.3		
0435	1.0	0500	0.9	0002	6.1	0409	0.7	0354	0.6	0158	0.7	0432	6.4	0212	4.7	0202	4.4	2	SU
1043	4.3	1111	5.4	0627	1.1	1023	3.8	1029	3.6	0827	2.2	1035	1.9	0823	1.7	0810	1.4		
1644	1.1	1714	1.0	1233	6.5	1621	0.8	1610	0.7	1359	0.9	1634	6.7	1418	4.9	1405	4.5		
2245	4.4	2326	5.4	1847	1.0	2235	3.8	2242	3.6	2009	2.3	2303	1.4	2045	1.2	2033	1.0		
0516	0.8	0544	0.7	0046	6.5	0448	0.5	0433	0.4	0236	0.6	0509	6.7	0251	5.0	0238	4.7	3	M
1123	4.5	1152	5.6	0721	0.8	1102	4.0	1109	3.8	0857	2.3	1116	1.5	0902	1.4	0847	1.1		
1724	0.9	1754	0.8	1313	6.9	1659	0.7	1646	0.6	1436	0.8	1712	7.0	1456	5.1	1440	4.8		
2326	4.6			1939	0.8	2315	4.0	2322	3.8	2045	2.4	2345	1.1	2124	0.9	2109	0.7		
0554	0.6	0006	5.6	0127	6.9	0526	0.4	0510	0.3	0315	0.4	0545	6.9	0327	5.0	0312	4.9	4	TU
1200	4.7	0625	0.5	0810	0.5	1140	4.2	1148	3.9	0927	2.4	1157	1.2	0939	1.1	0922	0.9		●
1801	0.7	1231	5.8	1352	7.2	1735	0.5	1723	0.4	1515	0.7	1748	7.2	1532	5.4	1515	5.0		
		1834	0.7	2027	0.6	2353	4.2			2122	2.5			2201	0.7	2145	0.5		
0003	4.8	0045	5.7	0204	7.2	0603	0.3	0001	3.9	0353	0.3	0024	0.8	0401	5.3	0346	5.0	5	W
0630	0.5	0706	0.4	0855	0.3	1218	4.3	0548	0.2	0959	2.4	0619	7.1	1015	0.9	0957	0.7		
1236	4.8	1309	5.9	1430	7.5	1812	0.4	1226	4.0	1554	0.6	1236	0.9	1608	5.6	1550	5.2		
1838	0.6	1913	0.6	2110	0.4			1800	0.3	2200	2.6	1824	7.4	2239	0.5	2221	0.4		
0039	4.9	0121	5.8	0241	7.4	0031	4.3	0039	4.0	0431	0.3	0103	0.6	0436	5.4	0421	5.1	6	TH
0706	0.4	0745	0.3	0936	0.2	0642	0.2	0625	0.1	1033	2.4	0654	7.2	1052	0.8	1033	0.6		
1312	4.9	1346	5.9	1507	7.6	1256	4.3	1304	4.1	1633	0.5	1315	0.8	1645	5.6	1627	5.3		
1917	0.6	1952	0.6	2150	0.4	1851	0.4	1836	0.3	2239	2.6	1901	7.5	2316	0.5	2258	0.4		
0115	5.0	0157	5.8	0318	7.5	0109	4.3	0117	4.1	0509	0.3	0140	0.6	0513	5.4	0457	5.1	7	F
0744	0.4	0822	0.3	1014	0.3	0719	0.2	0702	0.1	1109	2.4	0730	7.2	1130	0.7	1111	0.6		
1350	4.8	1424	5.9	1544	7.5	1333	4.3	1342	4.0	1712	0.5	1352	0.8	1725	5.6	1706	5.2		
1957	0.6	2029	0.5	2225	0.6	1930	0.4	1915	0.3	2318	2.6	1940	7.5	2355	0.6	2336	0.5		
0154	4.9	0235	5.9	0355	7.5	0147	4.3	0155	4.0	0546	0.4	0217	0.8	0554	5.3	0536	5.0	8	SA
0823	0.5	0857	0.4	1045	0.5	0757	0.3	0740	0.2	1148	2.4	0806	7.1	1209	0.8	1150	0.7		
1428	4.7	1502	5.8	1622	7.2	1412	4.2	1420	3.9	1752	0.5	1430	1.0	1810	5.4	1751	5.1		
2037	0.7	2105	0.5	2254	0.7	2009	0.5	1954	0.3			2021	7.3						
0236	4.8	0315	5.8	0436	7.3	0227	4.2	0234	4.0	0002	2.5	0253	1.0	0037	0.9	0015	0.7	9	SU
0903	0.7	0930	0.6	1110	0.8	0836	0.5	0820	0.3	0626	0.5	0845	6.9	0639	5.2	0619	4.8		
1509	4.5	1542	5.6	1703	6.9	1453	4.0	1500	3.8	1230	2.3	1509	1.2	1254	1.0	1233	0.8		
2120	0.9	2142	0.6	2322	0.9	2052	0.6	2038	0.4	1837	0.6	2106	7.0	1901	5.2	1841	4.9		
0323	4.7	0400	5.6	0521	6.9	0312	4.1	0318	3.9	0051	2.4	0331	1.4	0124	1.2	0100	1.0	10	M
0946	1.0	1006	0.8	1138	1.0	0920	0.7	0905	0.5	0710	0.7	0930	6.6	0730	4.9	0709	4.6		
1556	4.4	1628	5.3	1749	6.5	1539	3.8	1545	3.6	1318	2.2	1553	1.5	1345	1.2	1325	1.1		
2209	1.0	2227	0.8	2359	1.0	2142	0.7	2128	0.6	1930	0.6	2202	6.5	2001	4.9	1939	4.6		
0418	4.4	0454	5.4	0613	6.6	0406	3.9	0409	3.7	0154	2.3	0418	1.9	0218	1.6	0156	1.4	11	TU
1039	1.2	1054	1.0	1219	1.2	1014	0.9	1000	0.8	0805	0.9	1027	6.2	0830	4.6	0808	4.3		
1651	4.2	1724	5.0	1845	6.1	1635	3.6	1639	3.4	1418	2.1	1650	1.9	1447	1.5	1432	1.3		
2314	1.1	2327	1.0			2245	0.8	2233	0.7	2036	0.7	2315	6.1	2112	4.6	2051	4.3		
0526	4.2	0601	5.1	0048	1.2	0512	3.7	0514	3.5	0317	2.2	0523	2.4	0326	1.9	0310	1.7	12	W
1151	1.4	1203	1.3	0720	6.3	1124	1.1	1113	1.0	0918	1.0	1142	5.9	0939	4.5	0922	4.1		
1800	4.1	1836	4.8	1316	1.5	1745	3.4	1747	3.2	1532	2.1	1812	2.1	1605	1.6	1558	1.4		
				1954	6.0			2355	0.7	2200	0.7			2232	4.5	2218	4.1		
0039	1.1	0050	1.1	0201	1.3	0006	0.9	0635	3.4	0448	2.2	0050	5.9	0451	2.0	0445	1.8	13	TH
0648	4.1	0724	5.0	0838	6.2	0633	3.6	1239	1.0	1049	1.1	0653	2.6	1058	4.4	1048	4.1		
1319	1.4	1336	1.4	1443	1.6	1253	1.1	1909	3.2	1648	2.1	1315	5.9	1736	1.6	1731	1.3		
1921	4.0	1959	4.8	2112	6.0	1911	3.4			2332	0.6	1948	2.0	2354	4.5	2345	4.2		
0206	1.0	0228	1.0	0339	1.1	0140	0.8	0124	0.6	0620	2.2	0221	6.1	0618	2.0	0609	1.7	14	F
0820	4.2	0851	5.1	1000	6.4	0801	3.7	0804	3.5	1210	1.1	0823	2.4	1214	4.6	1207	4.3		
1440	1.3	1506	1.3	1614	1.4	1418	1.1	1405	1.0	1803	2.2	1438	6.2	1853	1.3	1845	1.1		
2042	4.2	2121	5.0	2235	6.3	2033	3.5	2035	3.3			2110	1.7						
0323	0.7	0354	0.8	0512	0.8	0258	0.6	0245	0.5	0048	0.5	0335	6.6	0103	4.7	0054	4.4	15	SA
0939	4.4	1005	5.4	1118	6.7	0913	3.9	0920	3.7	0727	2.3	0934	2.0	0724	1.7	0713	1.5		
1552	1.1	1619	1.1	1742	1.1	1523	0.9	1513	0.8	1313	1.0	1542	6.5	1318	4.8	1309	4.5		
2153	4.4	2229	5.3	2348	6.6	2136	3.8	2142	3.5	1907	2.3	2213	1.3	1951	1.1	1942	0.8		

● ● Time: UT. For British Summer Time (shaded) March 26th to October 29th ADD ONE HOUR ● ●

APRIL 2000 TIDE TABLES

•• Time: UT. For British Summer Time (shaded) March 26th to October 29th ADD ONE HOUR ••

	MARGATE		SHEERNESS		LONDON BRIDGE		WALTON-ON-THE-NAZE		HARWICH		LOWESTOFT		IMMINGHAM		RIVER TEES		RIVER TYNE	
	Time	m	Time	m	Time	m	Time	m	Time	m	Time	m	Time	m	Time	m	Time	m
16 SU	0428	0.5	0500	0.5	0636	0.4	0357	0.4	0345	0.3	0146	0.4	0430	6.7	0157	4.9	0148	4.6
	1040	4.6	1103	5.7	1221	7.1	1010	4.0	1017	3.9	0815	2.3	1030	1.7	0815	1.5	0803	1.2
	1649	0.9	1715	0.9	1856	0.8	1612	0.8	1603	0.7	1403	0.9	1630	6.8	1410	5.0	1358	4.8
	2250	4.5	2323	5.5			2227	3.9	2236	3.7	1956	2.4	2303	1.0	2039	0.8	2030	0.6
17 M	0520	0.4	0551	0.4	0044	6.9	0443	0.3	0432	0.2	0233	0.3	0512	6.9	0243	5.1	0231	4.8
	1129	4.7	1151	5.8	0733	0.1	1057	4.1	1104	4.0	0853	2.4	1115	1.4	0857	1.3	0845	1.0
	1733	0.8	1800	0.7	1312	7.3	1653	0.7	1645	0.5	1445	0.8	1712	7.1	1454	5.2	1439	4.9
	2335	4.6			1948	0.6	2311	4.1	2320	3.8	2039	2.5	2346	0.8	2120	0.7	2110	0.5
18 TU O	0600	0.4	0007	5.7	0130	7.1	0523	0.3	0511	0.1	0314	0.3	0548	7.0	0322	5.2	0309	4.9
	1209	4.7	0633	0.4	0818	0.1	1138	4.2	1145	4.0	0927	2.4	1156	1.2	0935	1.1	0922	0.9
	1808	0.7	1232	5.9	1356	7.4	1731	0.6	1722	0.4	1522	0.7	1748	7.2	1533	5.3	1518	5.0
			1838	0.6	2031	0.5	2350	4.2			2121	2.5			2157	0.7	2146	0.5
19 W	0013	4.7	0045	5.7	0211	7.2	0600	0.3	0000	3.9	0352	0.3	0024	0.8	0357	5.3	0344	5.0
	0634	0.4	0708	0.4	0857	0.2	1215	4.2	0548	0.1	1000	2.4	0620	7.1	1010	1.0	0957	0.8
	1242	4.7	1309	5.9	1434	7.4	1808	0.5	1223	4.0	1559	0.6	1233	1.1	1609	5.4	1554	5.1
	1840	0.7	1914	0.6	2107	0.5			1759	0.4	2201	2.5	1825	7.3	2232	0.8	2220	0.5
20 TH	0048	4.7	0121	5.8	0247	7.2	0027	4.2	0036	4.0	0427	0.4	0100	0.8	0429	5.3	0418	4.9
	0705	0.5	0741	0.4	0930	0.4	0636	0.3	0623	0.1	1035	2.4	0651	7.1	1043	1.0	1031	0.8
	1312	4.7	1343	5.8	1508	7.3	1250	4.2	1257	4.0	1634	0.6	1308	1.1	1644	5.3	1630	5.0
	1912	0.7	1949	0.5	2138	0.6	1845	0.5	1836	0.3	2242	2.5	1902	7.2	2305	0.9	2252	0.7
21 F	0121	4.7	0156	5.8	0321	7.2	0103	4.2	0111	4.0	0501	0.5	0131	1.0	0500	5.2	0451	4.9
	0735	0.6	0812	0.5	0956	0.6	0710	0.4	0657	0.2	1108	2.4	0722	7.1	1115	1.1	1103	0.9
	1340	4.6	1415	5.8	1539	7.2	1323	4.1	1330	3.9	1708	0.6	1339	1.2	1719	5.2	1706	4.9
	1945	0.7	2023	0.6	2203	0.7	1921	0.6	1911	0.4	2321	2.4	1937	7.1	2336	1.1	2323	0.9
22 SA	0154	4.7	0230	5.7	0352	7.1	0138	4.1	0144	3.9	0532	0.6	0200	1.2	0533	5.1	0524	4.7
	0805	0.7	0841	0.6	1018	0.7	0743	0.6	0731	0.4	1139	2.3	0753	6.9	1148	1.2	1136	1.0
	1408	4.6	1446	5.6	1608	7.0	1354	4.0	1400	3.8	1741	0.7	1409	1.3	1756	5.1	1744	4.9
	2018	0.8	2051	0.8	2226	0.8	1955	0.7	1945	0.5			2011	6.8			2354	1.1
23 SU	0227	4.6	0302	5.5	0424	6.9	0212	4.0	0216	3.8	0000	2.3	0227	1.5	0009	1.3	0557	4.6
	0836	0.9	0906	0.8	1041	0.8	0814	0.8	0803	0.6	0600	0.7	0822	6.7	0609	5.0	1209	1.2
	1437	4.5	1516	5.4	1638	6.8	1425	3.9	1430	3.7	1209	2.3	1437	1.6	1223	1.4	1823	4.5
	2051	0.9	2117	0.9	2251	0.8	2027	0.8	2016	0.6	1815	0.7	2045	6.5	1837	4.9		
24 M	0302	4.4	0336	5.3	0459	6.7	0247	3.8	0249	3.6	0041	2.2	0254	1.8	0045	1.6	0027	1.3
	0909	1.1	0932	1.0	1109	0.9	0844	0.9	0834	0.8	0629	0.9	0854	6.4	0651	4.8	0634	4.4
	1511	4.4	1548	5.2	1711	6.6	1456	3.7	1500	3.5	1243	2.2	1507	1.9	1302	1.6	1246	1.4
	2128	1.1	2143	1.0	2323	0.9	2059	0.9	2048	0.8	1853	0.8	2121	6.1	1924	4.6	1907	4.2
25 TU	0342	4.2	0412	5.1	0539	6.4	0324	3.6	0325	3.5	0130	2.1	0325	2.2	0126	1.9	0105	1.6
	0950	1.3	1003	1.2	1145	1.0	0919	1.1	0909	0.9	0704	1.0	0930	6.1	0737	4.6	0717	4.2
	1554	4.2	1624	5.0	1748	6.3	1532	3.5	1535	3.4	1325	2.2	1544	2.2	1348	1.8	1331	1.6
	2215	1.2	2219	1.2			2139	1.0	2128	0.9	1939	0.9	2207	5.7	2018	4.4	1958	4.0
26 W	0433	4.0	0456	4.8	0000	0.9	0408	3.4	0406	3.3	0233	2.0	0405	2.6	0215	2.2	0154	1.9
	1042	1.5	1046	1.4	0624	6.1	1009	1.3	0957	1.1	0751	1.2	1017	5.8	0833	4.4	0809	4.0
	1648	4.0	1709	4.7	1227	1.2	1618	3.4	1617	3.2	1418	2.1	1633	2.5	1442	2.0	1430	1.8
	2315	1.4	2311	1.4	1832	6.0	2237	1.1	2226	1.0	2039	0.9	2315	5.4	2121	4.2	2100	3.8
27 TH	0535	3.8	0553	4.6	0045	1.1	0505	3.3	0459	3.1	0346	2.0	0502	2.9	0316	2.4	0300	2.1
	1145	1.6	1146	1.7	0718	5.8	1117	1.4	1106	1.3	0854	1.3	1126	5.5	0936	4.3	0912	3.8
	1754	3.8	1811	4.5	1316	1.5	1719	3.2	1712	3.0	1523	2.0	1748	2.7	1550	2.1	1548	1.9
					1926	5.7	2353	1.2	2348	1.0	2203	0.9			2230	4.2	2215	3.7
28 F	0028	1.5	0026	1.5	0138	1.4	0621	3.2	0614	3.0	0504	2.0	0044	5.4	0430	2.4	0427	2.1
	0651	3.8	0707	4.5	0828	5.6	1240	1.4	1231	1.3	1031	1.3	0630	3.1	1043	4.3	1028	3.8
	1257	1.7	1310	1.8	1420	1.8	1841	3.1	1831	2.9	1634	2.0	1253	5.5	1708	2.1	1716	1.8
	1912	3.8	1930	4.4	2040	5.5					2332	0.9	1926	2.6	2338	4.3	2333	3.8
29 SA	0145	1.4	0200	1.4	0250	1.6	0124	1.1	0112	0.9	0615	2.1	0203	5.6	0548	2.3	0549	2.0
	0807	3.9	0828	4.6	0946	5.7	0749	3.3	0747	3.1	1148	1.2	0800	2.8	1148	4.4	1141	3.9
	1409	1.6	1437	1.6	1548	1.8	1400	1.2	1345	1.1	1744	2.1	1409	5.8	1820	1.9	1823	1.5
	2020	3.9	2050	4.6	2205	5.6	2006	3.3	2000	3.1			2040	2.2				
30 SU	0254	1.2	0317	1.2	0424	1.4	0236	0.9	0217	0.7	0029	0.8	0303	6.0	0037	4.5	0034	4.1
	0909	4.1	0936	5.0	1056	6.0	0854	3.6	0856	3.4	0708	2.2	0904	2.4	0652	2.1	0646	1.7
	1512	1.4	1542	1.5	1703	1.5	1457	1.0	1442	0.9	1238	1.1	1506	6.2	1244	4.6	1238	4.2
	2117	4.1	2154	5.0	2314	5.9	2108	3.6	2108	3.3	1842	2.2	2137	1.8	1917	1.6	1912	1.2

EAST COAST OF ENGLAND Time Zone UT

Margate * Sheerness * London Bridge * Walton-on-the-Naze * Harwich * Lowestoft * Immingham * River Tees * River Tyne

TIDE TABLES MAY 2000

	MARGATE Time m	SHEERNESS Time m	LONDON BRIDGE Time m	WALTON-ON-THE-NAZE Time m	HARWICH Time m	LOWESTOFT Time m	IMMINGHAM Time m	RIVER TEES Time m	RIVER TYNE Time m
1 M	0350 1.0	0415 0.9	0536 1.1	0329 0.7	0309 0.5	0115 0.6	0351 6.4	0127 4.8	0121 4.3
	1000 4.3	1030 5.3	1151 6.4	0945 3.9	0948 3.6	0748 2.2	0956 2.0	0743 1.8	0732 1.4
	1605 1.2	1633 1.1	1805 1.2	1545 0.8	1530 0.7	1321 1.0	1554 6.6	1333 4.9	1324 4.5
	2205 4.4	2246 5.3		2157 3.8	2201 3.6	1929 2.3	2227 1.4	2006 1.2	1955 0.9
2 TU	0436 0.8	0506 0.7	0006 6.4	0414 0.5	0356 0.4	0159 0.5	0434 6.7	0211 5.0	0201 4.6
	1045 4.6	1118 5.6	0640 0.8	1029 4.1	1035 3.8	0822 2.3	1043 1.5	0827 1.4	0812 1.1
	1648 0.9	1721 0.8	1238 6.9	1627 0.7	1613 0.6	1404 0.9	1636 6.9	1418 5.2	1404 4.8
	2248 4.6	2332 5.6	1903 0.9	2242 4.0	2248 3.8	2012 2.4	2312 1.0	2049 0.9	2036 0.6
3 W	0518 0.6	0552 0.5	0051 6.8	0456 0.4	0439 0.2	0242 0.4	0514 7.0	0251 5.3	0239 4.9
	1126 4.7	1201 5.8	0737 0.6	1112 4.3	1118 4.0	0856 2.4	1127 1.2	0909 1.1	0852 0.8
	1730 0.7	1805 0.7	1321 7.2	1709 0.5	1654 0.4	1448 0.7	1718 7.2	1459 5.4	1444 5.0
	2327 4.8		1957 0.7	2324 4.2	2332 3.9	2053 2.5	2355 0.8	2131 0.7	2115 0.4
4 TH ●	0557 0.5	0014 5.8	0133 7.1	0536 0.3	0520 0.2	0323 0.3	0552 7.2	0330 5.4	0317 5.0
	1206 4.9	0637 0.4	0827 0.4	1152 4.3	1200 4.1	0931 2.4	1211 0.9	0950 0.9	0932 0.6
	1811 0.6	1242 5.9	1402 7.4	1749 0.4	1736 0.3	1531 0.5	1759 7.4	1541 5.6	1524 5.2
		1849 0.6	2045 0.5			2135 2.6		2212 0.6	2155 0.3
5 F	0008 4.9	0055 5.9	0214 7.4	0006 4.3	0015 4.1	0404 0.3	0037 0.6	0410 5.5	0355 5.1
	0638 0.4	0719 0.4	0911 0.3	0617 0.3	0600 0.1	1008 2.5	0630 7.3	1031 0.8	1012 0.5
	1246 4.9	1323 6.0	1442 7.5	1233 4.4	1242 4.1	1615 0.5	1254 0.8	1624 5.6	1606 5.3
	1854 0.5	1932 0.5	2128 0.4	1831 0.4	1816 0.3	2218 2.6	1841 7.5	2254 0.6	2236 0.4
6 SA	0051 5.0	0136 6.0	0255 7.5	0048 4.4	0057 4.1	0445 0.3	0118 0.6	0451 5.5	0435 5.1
	0720 0.4	0800 0.4	0951 0.4	0657 0.3	0641 0.2	1048 2.5	0709 7.3	1113 0.7	1054 0.5
	1329 4.9	1403 5.9	1523 7.4	1314 4.3	1323 4.1	1659 0.4	1336 0.7	1711 5.6	1651 5.2
	1939 0.5	2015 0.4	2208 0.4	1913 0.4	1858 0.3	2303 2.6	1925 7.5	2337 0.8	2318 0.5
7 SU	0139 5.0	0219 6.0	0338 7.6	0131 4.4	0139 4.1	0527 0.4	0157 0.8	0536 5.5	0518 5.0
	0805 0.6	0839 0.4	1028 0.5	0738 0.4	0722 0.3	1129 2.4	0750 7.2	1158 0.8	1139 0.5
	1414 4.8	1445 5.8	1606 7.3	1355 4.2	1403 4.0	1745 0.4	1418 0.8	1800 5.5	1741 5.1
	2026 0.6	2057 0.4	2246 0.4	1957 0.4	1942 0.3	2352 2.5	2012 7.2		
8 M	0230 4.9	0304 5.9	0424 7.4	0215 4.3	0222 4.0	0609 0.6	0238 1.1	0023 1.0	0003 0.8
	0851 0.8	0918 0.6	1103 0.7	0821 0.6	0806 0.4	1213 2.4	0833 7.0	0624 5.3	0604 4.9
	1500 4.6	1529 5.6	1651 7.0	1439 4.1	1446 3.8	1834 0.4	1502 1.0	1247 0.9	1229 0.6
	2115 0.7	2141 0.5	2324 0.6	2045 0.5	2030 0.3		2105 6.9	1856 5.2	1836 4.8
9 TU	0324 4.7	0354 5.7	0515 7.1	0305 4.2	0309 3.9	0049 2.4	0321 1.5	0113 1.3	0052 1.1
	0940 1.0	1000 0.8	1138 1.0	0907 0.8	0854 0.6	0657 0.7	0921 6.7	0718 5.1	0656 4.7
	1548 4.5	1618 5.4	1741 6.6	1527 3.9	1533 3.7	1303 2.3	1551 1.3	1342 1.1	1324 0.8
	2211 0.9	2230 0.6		2138 0.5	2124 0.4	1930 0.5	2206 6.5	1958 5.0	1937 4.6
10 W	0419 4.5	0451 5.5	0004 0.8	0400 4.0	0403 3.8	0159 2.3	0411 1.9	0209 1.6	0150 1.4
	1036 1.2	1052 1.1	0612 6.8	1003 0.9	0951 0.8	0752 0.9	1019 6.4	0818 4.8	0757 4.4
	1642 4.3	1715 5.1	1221 1.3	1624 3.7	1627 3.5	1401 2.2	1652 1.6	1445 1.3	1431 1.1
	2316 1.0	2333 0.8	1837 6.3	2242 0.6	2228 0.5	2036 0.5	2320 6.2	2106 4.7	2048 4.3
11 TH	0522 4.3	0557 5.2	0054 1.0	0506 3.8	0506 3.6	0320 2.2	0515 2.3	0315 1.9	0301 1.7
	1142 1.4	1157 1.3	0715 6.5	1109 1.1	1058 1.0	0903 1.1	1130 6.1	0925 4.7	0909 4.3
	1745 4.2	1824 5.0	1315 1.5	1731 3.6	1731 3.4	1509 2.2	1809 1.8	1557 1.4	1550 1.2
			1940 6.1	2357 0.7	2344 0.5	2152 0.5		2220 4.6	2207 4.2
12 F	0032 0.9	0051 0.9	0200 1.0	0621 3.7	0622 3.5	0445 2.2	0043 6.0	0432 2.0	0426 1.8
	0639 4.2	0712 5.2	0823 6.4	1229 1.2	1217 1.1	1026 1.1	0634 2.5	1036 4.6	1028 4.2
	1300 1.4	1319 1.4	1427 1.6	1848 3.5	1847 3.3	1623 2.2	1252 6.1	1715 1.4	1712 1.1
	1858 4.1	1939 4.9	2050 6.1			2312 0.5	1930 1.8	2331 4.6	2325 4.2
13 SA	0149 0.8	0215 0.8	0323 1.0	0121 0.6	0106 0.5	0604 2.2	0203 6.1	0549 2.0	0544 1.7
	0802 4.2	0830 5.2	0937 6.5	0739 3.7	0742 3.6	1144 1.1	0755 2.4	1145 4.6	1142 4.3
	1417 1.3	1440 1.3	1548 1.4	1351 1.1	1337 1.0	1738 2.2	1411 6.2	1824 1.3	1821 1.0
	2015 4.2	2057 5.1	2208 6.3	2005 3.6	2005 3.4		2045 1.6		
14 SU	0301 0.7	0330 0.7	0443 0.7	0235 0.5	0221 0.4	0023 0.5	0310 6.3	0034 4.7	0030 4.4
	0915 4.4	0940 5.4	1054 6.7	0849 3.9	0854 3.7	0706 2.3	0906 2.1	0653 1.8	0647 1.5
	1527 1.2	1550 1.1	1706 1.2	1456 1.0	1445 0.9	1248 1.0	1515 6.4	1247 4.8	1244 4.5
	2124 4.4	2203 5.3	2321 6.5	2109 3.8	2114 3.5	1844 2.2	2146 1.4	1920 1.2	1918 0.9
15 M	0405 0.5	0433 0.6	0603 0.5	0332 0.5	0321 0.3	0121 0.5	0403 6.5	0127 4.9	0123 4.5
	1015 4.5	1038 5.6	1157 7.0	0945 4.0	0951 3.8	0754 2.3	1002 1.8	0744 1.6	0737 1.3
	1624 1.0	1646 1.0	1822 0.9	1547 0.9	1538 0.7	1339 0.9	1605 6.7	1339 4.9	1334 4.6
	2222 4.4	2257 5.4		2201 3.9	2209 3.7	1936 2.3	2236 1.2	2007 1.1	2004 0.8

● ● Time: UT. For British Summer Time (shaded) March 26th to October 29th ADD ONE HOUR ● ●

MAY 2000 TIDE TABLES

• • Time: UT. For British Summer Time (shaded) March 26th to October 29th ADD ONE HOUR • •

	MARGATE		SHEERNESS		LONDON BRIDGE		WALTON-ON THE-NAZE		HARWICH		LOWESTOFT		IMMINGHAM		RIVER TEES		RIVER TYNE	
	Time	m	Time	m	Time	m	Time	m	Time	m	Time	m	Time	m	Time	m	Time	m
16 TU O	0455	0.5	0522	0.6	0019	6.8	0419	0.4	0407	0.3	0208	0.5	0445	6.7	0212	5.0	0206	4.6
	1103	4.6	1126	5.7	0701	0.3	1033	4.1	1039	3.9	0830	2.3	1048	1.6	0827	1.5	0820	1.1
	1709	0.9	1731	0.8	1248	7.2	1630	0.8	1621	0.6	1421	0.8	1647	6.8	1424	5.1	1418	4.7
	2309	4.5	2342	5.5	1917	0.7	2247	4.0	2254	3.8	2019	2.4	2318	1.2	2048	1.0	2043	0.8
17 W	0534	0.5	0601	0.6	0106	6.9	0458	0.4	0447	0.3	0248	0.5	0520	6.8	0251	5.1	0244	4.8
	1141	4.6	1207	5.7	0746	0.3	1114	4.1	1120	3.9	0904	2.3	1130	1.4	0906	1.3	0858	1.0
	1744	0.8	1810	0.7	1332	7.2	1709	0.7	1700	0.5	1500	0.7	1725	6.9	1505	5.1	1456	4.8
	2347	4.6			2000	0.6	2327	4.1	2335	3.8	2101	2.4	2354	1.1	2126	1.0	2118	0.8
18 TH	0605	0.6	0021	5.6	0147	7.0	0535	0.5	0523	0.3	0324	0.5	0552	6.9	0327	5.1	0318	4.8
	1213	4.6	0636	0.6	0824	0.4	1151	4.1	1157	3.9	0936	2.4	1207	1.3	0942	1.2	0934	0.9
	1815	0.7	1243	5.7	1409	7.2	1748	0.6	1738	0.4	1537	0.6	1803	7.0	1542	5.2	1533	4.8
			1847	0.7	2037	0.6					2142	2.4			2200	1.1	2151	0.8
19 F	0021	4.6	0057	5.7	0223	7.0	0005	4.1	0012	3.9	0359	0.5	0029	1.1	0359	5.1	0352	4.8
	0634	0.7	0708	0.6	0855	0.6	0609	0.5	0557	0.4	1009	2.4	0624	7.0	1017	1.2	1009	0.9
	1242	4.6	1317	5.7	1442	7.1	1226	4.1	1231	3.9	1614	0.6	1242	1.2	1618	5.1	1610	4.8
	1848	0.7	1924	0.6	2109	0.6	1825	0.6	1815	0.4	2223	2.4	1840	7.0	2233	1.1	2224	0.9
20 SA	0057	4.6	0132	5.7	0256	7.0	0042	4.1	0047	3.9	0431	0.6	0101	1.2	0432	5.1	0425	4.8
	0705	0.7	0740	0.6	0923	0.7	0643	0.6	0631	0.4	1039	2.4	0656	7.0	1051	1.2	1042	0.9
	1311	4.6	1348	5.7	1512	7.0	1258	4.1	1303	3.9	1649	0.6	1316	1.3	1655	5.1	1646	4.7
	1923	0.7	1958	0.6	2137	0.7	1901	0.6	1850	0.5	2302	2.3	1917	6.8	2306	1.3	2256	1.0
21 SU	0132	4.6	0206	5.6	0328	6.9	0116	4.0	0121	3.8	0500	0.7	0132	1.4	0506	5.1	0457	4.7
	0737	0.8	0811	0.7	0949	0.7	0716	0.7	0704	0.6	1109	2.4	0727	6.9	1125	1.2	1116	1.0
	1341	4.6	1420	5.6	1540	6.9	1329	4.0	1333	3.8	1723	0.7	1348	1.4	1733	5.0	1724	4.6
	1959	0.8	2030	0.7	2203	0.7	1936	0.7	1923	0.5	2341	2.3	1952	6.7	2341	1.4	2328	1.2
22 M	0207	4.5	0240	5.5	0401	6.8	0151	3.9	0154	3.7	0527	0.8	0201	1.6	0544	5.0	0531	4.6
	0811	1.0	0839	0.8	1017	0.8	0747	0.9	0736	0.7	1140	2.3	0759	6.8	1203	1.3	1150	1.1
	1412	4.5	1451	5.4	1611	6.8	1359	3.9	1403	3.7	1757	0.7	1419	1.6	1815	4.8	1803	4.4
	2034	0.9	2059	0.8	2232	0.8	2008	0.8	1955	0.6			2027	6.4				
23 TU	0242	4.4	0314	5.3	0437	6.7	0224	3.8	0227	3.6	0022	2.2	0230	1.8	0019	1.6	0001	1.3
	0845	1.1	0909	1.0	1048	0.9	0818	1.0	0807	0.8	0556	0.9	0832	6.6	0626	4.9	0608	4.5
	1447	4.4	1523	5.3	1645	6.6	1430	3.8	1434	3.6	1214	2.3	1451	1.8	1243	1.5	1227	1.2
	2110	1.0	2129	0.9	2304	0.8	2041	0.8	2029	0.7	1835	0.7	2104	6.1	1902	4.6	1845	4.3
24 W	0320	4.3	0351	5.2	0515	6.5	0300	3.7	0302	3.5	0108	2.1	0303	2.1	0101	1.8	0039	1.5
	0923	1.2	0942	1.1	1123	1.0	0854	1.1	0843	0.9	0632	1.0	0908	6.3	0712	4.7	0648	4.3
	1527	4.3	1559	5.1	1721	6.4	1505	3.7	1509	3.5	1254	2.3	1527	2.0	1328	1.6	1309	1.4
	2151	1.1	2205	1.1	2340	0.8	2121	0.9	2109	0.8	1918	0.8	2147	5.9	1953	4.5	1931	4.1
25 TH	0404	4.2	0433	5.0	0557	6.3	0342	3.6	0342	3.4	0203	2.1	0341	2.4	0149	2.0	0124	1.8
	1008	1.4	1022	1.3	1202	1.1	0939	1.2	0927	1.1	0716	1.1	0951	6.1	0803	4.5	0736	4.2
	1615	4.2	1641	4.9	1801	6.2	1548	3.5	1551	3.4	1340	2.2	1612	2.2	1420	1.8	1400	1.5
	2240	1.2	2251	1.2			2211	0.9	2159	0.8	2010	0.8	2242	5.6	2049	4.4	2025	3.9
26 F	0457	4.0	0523	4.8	0021	0.9	0433	3.5	0430	3.3	0306	2.0	0430	2.6	0245	2.2	0220	1.9
	1103	1.5	1113	1.5	0643	6.1	1037	1.3	1024	1.2	0812	1.2	1046	5.8	0900	4.4	0831	4.0
	1712	4.0	1734	4.7	1246	1.3	1643	3.4	1642	3.2	1435	2.1	1710	2.3	1518	1.9	1503	1.6
	2341	1.3	2351	1.3	1847	6.0	2315	1.0	2306	0.8	2112	0.8	2351	5.5	2150	4.3	2127	3.8
27 SA	0600	4.0	0624	4.7	0109	1.1	0536	3.4	0530	3.2	0412	2.0	0534	2.8	0348	2.3	0330	2.0
	1206	1.6	1218	1.6	0739	5.9	1146	1.3	1138	1.2	0922	1.3	1157	5.8	1000	4.4	0936	4.0
	1820	4.0	1840	4.6	1339	1.6	1751	3.4	1745	3.2	1539	2.1	1824	2.3	1624	1.9	1614	1.6
					1945	5.7					2224	0.8			2251	4.4	2235	3.9
28 SU	0051	1.3	0106	1.3	0209	1.3	0027	0.9	0021	0.8	0517	2.1	0105	5.6	0457	2.2	0446	1.9
	0711	4.0	0735	4.7	0850	5.8	0648	3.5	0644	3.3	1040	1.2	0654	2.7	1100	4.5	1043	4.0
	1316	1.5	1335	1.6	1449	1.7	1300	1.2	1251	1.1	1648	2.1	1310	5.9	1730	1.7	1724	1.4
	1929	4.0	1954	4.7	2103	5.7	1906	3.4	1900	3.2	2331	0.7	1939	2.1	2350	4.6	2339	4.1
29 M	0202	1.2	0220	1.1	0325	1.3	0141	0.8	0127	0.7	0614	2.1	0209	5.9	0603	2.1	0552	1.7
	0818	4.1	0845	5.0	1003	6.0	0801	3.6	0757	3.4	1145	1.1	0808	2.5	1157	4.7	1146	4.2
	1425	1.4	1445	1.4	1607	1.5	1407	1.1	1354	0.9	1752	2.2	1415	6.2	1831	1.5	1824	1.2
	2030	4.2	2103	5.0	2220	5.9	2017	3.6	2012	3.4			2045	1.8				
30 TU	0304	1.0	0325	0.9	0442	1.1	0244	0.6	0226	0.5	0028	0.6	0306	6.3	0044	4.8	0035	4.3
	0916	4.3	0947	5.3	1106	6.4	0902	3.9	0901	3.6	0703	2.2	0910	2.1	0700	1.8	0648	1.5
	1524	1.2	1548	1.1	1715	1.2	1504	0.9	1448	0.8	1241	1.0	1511	6.5	1251	4.9	1240	4.5
	2124	4.4	2203	5.3	2323	6.3	2117	3.8	2116	3.6	1848	2.3	2143	1.5	1926	1.0	1915	1.0
31 W	0357	0.8	0424	0.7	0551	0.8	0337	0.5	0318	0.4	0119	0.5	0356	6.6	0133	5.0	0123	4.6
	1007	4.5	1041	5.6	1202	6.8	0954	4.1	0957	3.8	0745	2.3	1006	1.7	0752	1.5	0736	1.2
	1615	1.0	1643	0.9	1821	1.0	1555	0.7	1539	0.6	1332	0.9	1601	6.9	1342	5.1	1329	4.7
	2212	4.6	2257	5.5			2209	4.0	2213	3.8	1938	2.4	2236	1.1	2016	1.0	2002	0.7

EAST COAST OF ENGLAND Time Zone UT

Margate * Sheerness * London Bridge * Walton-on-the-Naze * Harwich * Lowestoft * Immingham * River Tees * River Tyne

TIDE TABLES JUNE 2000

MARGATE		SHEERNESS		LONDON BRIDGE		WALTON-ON-THE-NAZE		HARWICH		LOWESTOFT		IMMINGHAM		RIVER TEES		RIVER TYNE		
Time	m	Time	m	Time	m	Time	m	Time	m	Time	m	Time	m	Time	m	Time	m	
0443	0.6	0518	0.6	0016	6.7	0425	0.4	0408	0.3	0208	0.4	0442	6.9	0219	5.2	0207	4.8	**1 TH**
1054	4.7	1131	5.8	0659	0.7	1042	4.2	1048	4.0	0826	2.4	1058	1.3	0841	1.2	0822	0.9	
1701	0.8	1736	0.7	1251	7.0	1642	0.6	1627	0.5	1422	0.7	1649	7.2	1431	5.4	1415	5.0	
2257	4.7	2345	5.7	1924	0.8	2257	4.2	2305	3.9	2025	2.5	2326	0.9	2103	0.9	2048	0.5	
0528	0.5	0609	0.5	0105	7.0	0510	0.3	0454	0.2	0254	0.4	0527	7.1	0304	5.4	0250	5.0	**2 F**
1139	4.8	1218	5.9	0757	0.5	1128	4.3	1136	4.1	0906	2.4	1148	1.0	0927	1.0	0909	0.7	●
1747	0.6	1827	0.6	1337	7.2	1728	0.5	1715	0.4	1512	0.6	1737	7.3	1520	5.5	1503	5.2	
2344	4.9			2020	0.6	2344	4.3	2354	4.1	2113	2.5			2150	0.8	2133	0.5	
0614	0.5	0033	5.9	0151	7.2	0554	0.4	0539	0.2	0340	0.3	0013	0.8	0349	5.6	0333	5.1	**3 SA**
1224	4.9	0657	0.4	0848	0.5	1212	4.3	1222	4.1	0946	2.5	0609	7.3	1014	0.8	0955	0.5	
1835	0.5	1303	5.9	1422	7.3	1814	0.4	1800	0.3	1601	0.4	1236	0.8	1609	5.6	1551	5.2	
		1916	0.4	2109	0.5					2202	2.6	1827	7.4	2236	0.8	2219	0.5	
0036	5.0	0120	6.0	0238	7.4	0031	4.4	0040	4.1	0425	0.4	0058	0.7	0435	5.6	0416	5.2	**4 SU**
0701	0.5	0742	0.4	0933	0.4	0638	0.4	0624	0.3	1029	2.5	0653	7.3	1102	0.7	1043	0.4	
1313	4.9	1348	5.9	1507	7.3	1257	4.3	1306	4.1	1651	0.3	1324	0.7	1700	5.6	1642	5.2	
1926	0.5	2005	0.3	2155	0.3	1901	0.3	1847	0.2	2254	2.5	1917	7.4	2323	0.9	2306	0.6	
0133	5.0	0207	6.0	0327	7.5	0118	4.4	0127	4.2	0510	0.5	0143	0.9	0523	5.5	0503	5.1	**5 M**
0751	0.6	0826	0.5	1015	0.5	0722	0.5	0709	0.4	1112	2.5	0738	7.2	1151	0.7	1133	0.4	
1403	4.8	1433	5.8	1554	7.2	1342	4.2	1350	4.0	1740	0.3	1411	0.7	1754	5.5	1735	5.1	
2018	0.5	2054	0.3	2239	0.3	1949	0.3	1934	0.2	2348	2.5	2009	7.2			2354	0.8	
0228	4.9	0257	5.9	0417	7.5	0207	4.4	0213	4.1	0556	0.6	0227	1.1	0012	1.1	0551	5.0	**6 TU**
0842	0.8	0910	0.6	1056	0.6	0808	0.6	0755	0.5	1159	2.5	0824	7.1	0613	5.4	1225	0.5	
1452	4.7	1520	5.7	1642	7.1	1428	4.1	1435	3.9	1832	0.3	1500	0.8	1242	0.8	1830	4.9	
2113	0.5	2143	0.4	2323	0.3	2039	0.3	2024	0.2			2105	6.9	1851	5.3			
0321	4.8	0349	5.8	0509	7.3	0258	4.2	0302	4.0	0049	2.4	0313	1.5	0103	1.3	0044	1.1	**7 W**
0933	1.0	0956	0.8	1136	0.9	0856	0.8	0844	0.6	0644	0.8	0914	6.9	0707	5.2	0645	4.8	
1540	4.6	1609	5.5	1733	6.8	1517	4.0	1521	3.8	1249	2.4	1551	1.0	1337	0.9	1321	0.6	
2209	0.6	2235	0.5			2133	0.4	2118	0.3	1926	0.3	2205	6.6	1950	5.1	1930	4.6	
0415	4.6	0445	5.6	0006	0.5	0352	4.1	0354	3.9	0156	2.3	0402	1.8	0157	1.6	0139	1.4	**8 TH**
1026	1.1	1045	1.0	0603	7.1	0948	0.9	0937	0.8	0737	0.9	1008	6.6	0804	5.0	0743	4.6	
1630	4.4	1704	5.3	1218	1.1	1611	3.9	1613	3.7	1344	2.4	1647	1.3	1436	1.1	1421	0.8	
2308	0.7	2332	0.6	1824	6.6	2232	0.5	2216	0.3	2024	0.3	2310	6.3	2052	4.9	2034	4.4	
0512	4.4	0545	5.4	0054	0.7	0451	3.9	0453	3.7	0307	2.2	0458	2.1	0257	1.8	0242	1.6	**9 F**
1122	1.3	1142	1.2	0700	6.8	1048	1.1	1036	1.0	0838	1.1	1109	6.4	0906	4.9	0848	4.5	
1724	4.3	1805	5.2	1305	1.3	1710	3.8	1712	3.6	1445	2.3	1750	1.5	1540	1.2	1528	1.0	
				1920	6.4	2337	0.5	2323	0.4	2130	0.4			2157	4.7	2142	4.2	
0012	0.7	0036	0.7	0148	0.8	0556	3.8	0558	3.6	0421	2.2	0019	6.2	0403	2.0	0352	1.7	**10 SA**
0617	4.2	0650	5.3	0800	6.6	1155	1.2	1144	1.0	0948	1.1	0603	2.3	1010	4.8	0959	4.4	
1228	1.4	1249	1.3	1403	1.5	1817	3.7	1817	3.5	1553	2.2	1221	6.2	1645	1.3	1639	1.1	
1829	4.2	1911	5.1	2021	6.3					2240	0.5	1858	1.7	2300	4.7	2251	4.2	
0122	0.8	0145	0.7	0255	0.9	0051	0.6	0036	0.4	0533	2.2	0128	6.1	0511	2.0	0506	1.7	**11 SU**
0730	4.2	0759	5.2	0906	6.5	0706	3.7	0707	3.6	1104	1.2	0715	2.4	1114	4.7	1109	4.3	
1342	1.4	1401	1.3	1515	1.5	1311	1.2	1258	1.0	1707	2.2	1334	6.2	1749	1.4	1748	1.2	
1940	4.2	2021	5.1	2132	6.2	1928	3.7	1927	3.5	2350	0.6	2006	1.7			2356	4.2	
0230	0.7	0253	0.8	0405	0.8	0202	0.6	0147	0.4	0635	2.2	0233	6.2	0000	4.7	0612	1.6	**12 M**
0840	4.2	0906	5.3	1020	6.5	0816	3.8	0817	3.6	1214	1.1	0826	2.3	0615	1.9	1213	4.4	
1452	1.2	1510	1.2	1627	1.3	1421	1.1	1409	1.0	1817	2.2	1440	6.3	1214	4.8	1845	1.2	
2051	4.2	2129	5.2	2248	6.3	2036	3.7	2038	3.5			2109	1.7	1846	1.3			
0333	0.7	0354	0.8	0515	0.7	0302	0.6	0249	0.4	0051	0.6	0327	6.3	0054	4.7	0051	4.3	**13 TU**
0942	4.3	1006	5.4	1127	6.7	0915	3.8	0918	3.7	0726	2.2	0927	2.1	0711	1.8	0708	1.5	
1554	1.1	1610	1.1	1737	1.1	1520	1.0	1509	0.8	1312	1.0	1536	6.4	1309	4.8	1308	4.5	
2152	4.3	2227	5.3	2350	6.5	2133	3.8	2138	3.6	1915	2.3	2201	1.6	1936	1.3	1933	1.1	
0424	0.7	0445	0.8	0618	0.6	0351	0.6	0340	0.5	0140	0.6	0413	6.4	0142	4.8	0138	4.5	**14 W**
1031	4.4	1057	5.5	1221	6.8	1006	3.9	1010	3.7	0806	2.3	1018	1.9	0759	1.6	0754	1.3	
1643	1.0	1700	1.0	1839	0.9	1609	0.9	1558	0.7	1359	0.9	1623	6.5	1358	4.9	1354	4.5	
2242	4.4	2315	5.4			2223	3.9	2228	3.7	2003	2.3	2246	1.6	2019	1.3	2015	1.1	
0505	0.7	0527	0.8	0041	6.7	0433	0.6	0423	0.5	0221	0.7	0451	6.6	0224	4.9	0218	4.6	**15 TH**
1111	4.5	1140	5.5	0706	0.6	1051	4.0	1054	3.8	0842	2.3	1103	1.7	0842	1.5	0836	1.2	
1721	0.9	1743	0.9	1305	6.9	1651	0.8	1642	0.6	1441	0.8	1705	6.6	1442	4.9	1436	4.6	
2324	4.4	2357	5.4	1926	0.8	2306	3.9	2312	3.7	2047	2.3	2325	1.5	2058	1.3	2052	1.1	

● ● Time: UT. For British Summer Time (shaded) March 26th to October 29th ADD ONE HOUR ● ●

JUNE 2000 TIDE TABLES

•• Time: UT. For British Summer Time (shaded) March 26th to October 29th ADD ONE HOUR ••

	MARGATE		SHEERNESS		LONDON BRIDGE		WALTON-ON-THE-NAZE		HARWICH		LOWESTOFT		IMMINGHAM		RIVER TEES		RIVER TYNE	
	Time	m	Time	m	Time	m	Time	m	Time	m	Time	m	Time	m	Time	m	Time	m
16 F O	0537	0.8	0603	0.8	0124	6.7	0511	0.7	0500	0.5	0258	0.7	0527	6.8	0303	5.0	0255	4.7
	1144	4.5	1218	5.6	0746	0.7	1129	4.0	1133	3.8	0914	2.4	1143	1.6	0921	1.4	0914	1.1
	1755	0.8	1824	0.8	1344	6.9	1731	0.7	1721	0.6	1520	0.7	1745	6.7	1522	5.0	1516	4.7
					2006	0.8	2346	4.0	2351	3.8	2129	2.3			2134	1.3	2127	1.1
17 SA	0001	4.5	0036	5.5	0201	6.8	0546	0.7	0536	0.6	0332	0.7	0001	1.5	0338	5.0	0330	4.8
	0607	0.8	0638	0.8	0821	0.7	1204	4.0	1209	3.8	0945	2.4	0601	6.9	0957	1.3	0951	1.0
	1215	4.6	1254	5.6	1418	6.9	1809	0.7	1758	0.5	1557	0.7	1221	1.5	1600	5.0	1554	4.7
	1830	0.8	1902	0.7	2042	0.7					2209	2.3	1824	6.7	2209	1.3	2201	1.1
18 SU	0038	4.5	0112	5.5	0236	6.8	0024	4.0	0027	3.8	0403	0.8	0036	1.5	0412	5.1	0403	4.8
	0641	0.8	0712	0.7	0854	0.7	0620	0.8	0609	0.6	1015	2.5	0635	6.9	1033	1.2	1025	1.0
	1248	4.6	1327	5.6	1448	6.9	1237	4.0	1242	3.8	1634	0.7	1257	1.4	1638	4.9	1630	4.6
	1908	0.8	1938	0.7	2116	0.7	1845	0.7	1833	0.5	2248	2.3	1900	6.7	2244	1.3	2235	1.1
19 M	0115	4.5	0148	5.5	0309	6.8	0059	3.9	0103	3.8	0431	0.8	0109	1.5	0448	5.1	0436	4.8
	0717	0.9	0745	0.8	0927	0.7	0653	0.8	0642	0.7	1045	2.4	0708	6.9	1110	1.2	1100	1.0
	1322	4.6	1400	5.5	1520	6.9	1309	4.0	1314	3.8	1709	0.6	1333	1.4	1717	4.9	1706	4.6
	1946	0.8	2012	0.7	2148	0.7	1919	0.7	1907	0.5	2326	2.2	1936	6.6	2321	1.4	2308	1.2
20 TU	0151	4.5	0222	5.5	0344	6.8	0133	3.9	0136	3.7	0500	0.8	0141	1.6	0526	5.0	0510	4.7
	0753	1.0	0818	0.8	1000	0.8	0725	0.9	0714	0.7	1117	2.4	0741	6.8	1148	1.3	1133	1.0
	1357	4.5	1433	5.4	1553	6.8	1339	3.9	1345	3.7	1744	0.6	1406	1.5	1757	4.8	1743	4.5
	2023	0.9	2045	0.8	2221	0.8	1953	0.7	1940	0.6			2012	6.5	2359	1.5	2342	1.3
21 W	0226	4.4	0257	5.4	0421	6.7	0206	3.8	0209	3.7	0004	2.2	0214	1.7	0606	5.0	0545	4.7
	0828	1.1	0851	0.9	1034	0.9	0759	1.0	0748	0.8	0532	0.9	0815	6.7	1227	1.3	1210	1.1
	1431	4.5	1506	5.3	1627	6.7	1411	3.8	1416	3.7	1152	2.4	1441	1.6	1839	4.7	1822	4.4
	2057	0.9	2120	0.8	2254	0.8	2027	0.7	2015	0.6	1821	0.7	2048	6.3				
22 TH	0301	4.4	0333	5.3	0457	6.6	0242	3.8	0244	3.6	0044	2.1	0247	1.8	0040	1.6	0018	1.4
	0903	1.2	0926	1.0	1108	1.0	0835	1.0	0824	0.9	0608	0.9	0850	6.5	0648	4.8	0624	4.5
	1508	4.4	1541	5.2	1702	6.6	1446	3.8	1451	3.6	1230	2.4	1517	1.7	1310	1.4	1249	1.2
	2132	1.0	2156	0.9	2328	0.8	2106	0.7	2054	0.6	1901	0.7	2127	6.1	1926	4.6	1905	4.3
23 F	0339	4.3	0412	5.1	0535	6.5	0321	3.7	0322	3.6	0129	2.1	0324	2.1	0124	1.8	0058	1.6
	0941	1.2	1003	1.2	1142	1.1	0916	1.1	0903	0.9	0650	1.0	0929	6.4	0734	4.7	0706	4.4
	1548	4.4	1619	5.1	1738	6.4	1527	3.7	1530	3.5	1312	2.3	1556	1.9	1356	1.5	1333	1.3
	2211	1.0	2236	1.0			2150	0.8	2137	0.7	1945	0.7	2211	6.0	2016	4.5	1951	4.1
24 SA	0424	4.2	0457	5.0	0003	0.9	0406	3.7	0406	3.5	0220	2.1	0405	2.3	0212	1.9	0145	1.7
	1025	1.3	1046	1.3	0615	6.3	1005	1.1	0951	1.0	0739	1.1	1014	6.2	0824	4.6	0754	4.3
	1636	4.3	1704	5.0	1219	1.2	1614	3.7	1617	3.5	1358	2.3	1641	2.0	1447	1.6	1424	1.4
	2258	1.1	2324	1.0	1818	6.2	2242	0.8	2229	0.7	2036	0.7	2304	5.8	2110	4.4	2044	4.0
25 SU	0518	4.1	0548	4.9	0043	0.9	0459	3.6	0458	3.4	0318	2.1	0456	2.5	0307	2.0	0242	1.8
	1118	1.4	1138	1.4	0701	6.2	1102	1.2	1049	1.1	0836	1.2	1109	6.1	0918	4.6	0850	4.2
	1733	4.2	1758	4.9	1303	1.3	1711	3.6	1711	3.4	1451	2.2	1736	2.1	1543	1.7	1524	1.4
	2357	1.1			1906	6.1	2342	0.8	2333	0.7	2134	0.7			2208	4.4	2144	4.0
26 M	0620	4.1	0020	1.1	0133	1.0	0600	3.6	0600	3.4	0422	2.1	0009	5.8	0408	2.1	0348	1.8
	1224	1.4	0648	4.9	0800	6.0	1207	1.2	1159	1.1	0945	1.2	0559	2.5	1017	4.6	0952	4.2
	1837	4.1	1241	1.4	1400	1.5	1816	3.6	1816	3.4	1557	2.2	1215	6.1	1646	1.6	1628	1.4
			1903	4.9	2010	5.9					2240	0.7	1842	2.0	2307	4.5	2248	4.1
27 TU	0109	1.1	0127	1.0	0237	1.1	0051	0.7	0041	0.6	0524	2.1	0118	5.9	0514	2.0	0457	1.8
	0728	4.1	0757	5.0	0913	6.1	0710	3.7	0709	3.5	1057	1.1	0712	2.5	1117	4.7	1057	4.3
	1337	1.4	1352	1.4	1514	1.5	1316	1.1	1308	1.0	1706	2.2	1326	6.2	1751	1.5	1735	1.3
	1944	4.2	2014	5.0	2130	6.0	1927	3.7	1927	3.4	2345	0.7	1954	1.9			2350	4.3
28 W	0220	1.0	0238	0.9	0355	1.0	0200	0.7	0145	0.6	0620	2.2	0222	6.2	0006	4.7	0603	1.6
	0833	4.3	0904	5.2	1024	6.3	0818	3.8	0818	3.6	1203	1.0	0825	2.2	0621	1.8	1200	4.5
	1445	1.2	1503	1.2	1632	1.3	1424	1.0	1411	0.9	1810	2.3	1430	6.5	1218	4.8	1837	1.1
	2045	4.3	2122	5.2	2242	6.3	2036	3.8	2036	3.6			2102	1.6	1853	1.4		
29 TH	0321	0.8	0346	0.8	0509	0.9	0303	0.6	0245	0.5	0043	0.6	0321	6.5	0102	4.9	0048	4.5
	0933	4.5	1007	5.4	1127	6.6	0920	4.0	0923	3.8	0711	2.3	0931	1.8	0722	1.6	0703	1.3
	1544	1.0	1609	1.0	1742	1.1	1524	0.8	1510	0.7	1303	0.9	1531	6.8	1316	5.1	1300	4.7
	2142	4.5	2225	5.4	2345	6.6	2138	4.0	2142	3.7	1908	2.4	2204	1.4	1951	1.2	1933	0.9
30 F	0415	0.7	0449	0.8	0622	0.7	0357	0.5	0342	0.4	0138	0.5	0415	6.8	0155	5.1	0139	4.8
	1027	4.6	1104	5.6	1225	6.8	1015	4.1	1022	3.9	0758	2.4	1032	1.5	0818	1.3	0759	1.0
	1637	0.8	1712	0.8	1856	0.9	1619	0.7	1606	0.5	1401	0.8	1629	7.0	1413	5.3	1356	4.9
	2236	4.6	2323	5.7			2234	4.1	2242	3.9	2003	2.5	2301	1.1	2044	1.0	2027	0.8

EAST COAST OF ENGLAND Time Zone UT

Margate * Sheerness * London Bridge * Walton-on-the-Naze * Harwich * Lowestoft * Immingham * River Tees * River Tyne

TIDE TABLES JULY 2000

MARGATE	SHEERNESS	LONDON BRIDGE	WALTON-ON-THE-NAZE	HARWICH	LOWESTOFT	IMMINGHAM	RIVER TEES	RIVER TYNE		
Time m	Time m	Time m	Time m	Time m	Time m	Time m	Time m	Time m		
0506 0.6	0546 0.6	0043 6.8	0448 0.5	0435 0.4	0230 0.5	0506 7.1	0246 5.4	0228 5.0	**1**	**SA**
1118 4.7	1157 5.8	0733 0.7	1107 4.2	1116 4.0	0843 2.5	1129 1.1	0912 1.0	0852 0.7		
1730 0.7	1810 0.6	1318 7.0	1711 0.5	1658 0.4	1457 0.6	1724 7.2	1507 5.5	1449 5.1		
2332 4.8		2001 0.7	2327 4.3	2336 4.1	2059 2.5	2354 1.0	2134 0.9	2117 0.7		
0557 0.6	0017 5.8	0137 7.1	0536 0.5	0524 0.3	0320 0.5	0554 7.2	0335 5.5	0315 5.1	**2**	**SU**
1209 4.7	0639 0.5	0830 0.6	1156 4.3	1206 4.0	0927 2.5	1224 0.8	1003 0.7	0944 0.5		
1823 0.5	1247 5.8	1407 7.1	1801 0.4	1749 0.3	1551 0.4	1819 7.3	1600 5.6	1542 5.2		●
	1906 0.4	2057 0.5			2154 2.5		2224 0.8	2206 0.6		
0030 4.9	0109 6.0	0228 7.3	0018 4.4	0027 4.2	0409 0.5	0044 0.9	0424 5.6	0401 5.2	**3**	**M**
0648 0.6	0728 0.5	0919 0.5	0622 0.5	0611 0.4	1012 2.6	0640 7.3	1053 0.5	1035 0.3		
1301 4.8	1335 5.9	1455 7.2	1243 4.3	1253 4.1	1643 0.3	1315 0.6	1653 5.6	1633 5.2		
1918 0.4	2000 0.3	2147 0.2	1851 0.3	1838 0.2	2248 2.5	1913 7.3	2312 0.9	2254 0.7		
0128 4.9	0159 6.0	0318 7.5	0108 4.4	0115 4.2	0456 0.6	0132 1.0	0512 5.7	0448 5.3	**4**	**TU**
0739 0.6	0815 0.5	1006 0.5	0709 0.6	0657 0.4	1058 2.6	0727 7.3	1142 0.5	1125 0.2		
1352 4.8	1422 5.9	1542 7.3	1330 4.3	1338 4.1	1733 0.2	1405 0.6	1745 5.5	1726 5.2		
2012 0.3	2051 0.2	2234 0.1	1941 0.2	1926 0.1	2344 2.5	2006 7.2	2359 1.0	2342 0.8		
0222 4.9	0249 6.0	0408 7.6	0157 4.4	0203 4.2	0542 0.7	0218 1.1	0600 5.6	0537 5.2	**5**	**W**
0830 0.7	0901 0.6	1048 0.5	0754 0.7	0742 0.5	1145 2.6	0813 7.3	1233 0.5	1216 0.3		
1440 4.8	1509 5.8	1630 7.3	1415 4.2	1423 4.0	1822 0.1	1453 0.6	1837 5.4	1818 5.0		
2105 0.3	2140 0.2	2318 0.1	2030 0.2	2014 0.1		2058 7.0				
0312 4.8	0339 5.9	0457 7.5	0245 4.3	0250 4.1	0039 2.4	0302 1.4	0048 1.2	0030 1.0	**6**	**TH**
0918 0.8	0946 0.8	1128 0.7	0840 0.8	0828 0.6	0627 0.8	0900 7.1	0651 5.4	0628 5.1		
1525 4.7	1556 5.7	1717 7.1	1502 4.1	1507 4.0	1232 2.6	1541 0.8	1324 0.7	1306 0.5		
2156 0.4	2228 0.3		2120 0.3	2103 0.1	1912 0.2	2150 6.8	1931 5.2	1912 4.8		
0400 4.7	0429 5.7	0000 0.2	0335 4.2	0339 4.0	0138 2.3	0346 1.4	0137 1.4	0118 1.2	**7**	**F**
1004 1.0	1030 0.9	0547 7.3	0927 0.9	0916 0.7	0715 0.9	0948 6.9	0744 5.2	0721 4.9		
1610 4.6	1645 5.5	1206 0.9	1550 4.1	1554 3.9	1322 2.5	1628 1.1	1416 0.9	1359 0.7		
2247 0.5	2315 0.5	1804 6.9	2211 0.4	2155 0.2	2003 0.3	2243 6.5	2027 4.9	2008 4.5		
0449 4.4	0521 5.5	0039 0.5	0426 4.0	0430 3.8	0239 2.2	0432 1.9	0230 1.7	0210 1.5	**8**	**SA**
1051 1.2	1117 1.1	0636 6.9	1018 1.0	1007 0.9	0805 1.0	1041 6.6	0839 5.0	0819 4.6		
1657 4.4	1736 5.3	1244 1.2	1642 3.9	1645 3.7	1417 2.4	1718 1.4	1512 1.2	1454 1.0		
2340 0.7		1853 6.6	2306 0.5	2251 0.4	2057 0.5	2340 6.2	2124 4.7	2106 4.3		
0543 4.2	0006 0.6	0121 0.7	0521 3.8	0524 3.7	0345 2.2	0524 2.2	0327 1.9	0309 1.7	**9**	**SU**
1146 1.3	0617 5.3	0729 6.6	1115 1.1	1105 1.0	0903 1.1	1141 6.3	0939 4.8	0921 4.4		
1754 4.3	1209 1.3	1329 1.4	1739 3.8	1741 3.6	1518 2.3	1815 1.8	1610 1.4	1556 1.3		
	1834 5.1	1947 6.3		2355 0.5	2200 0.6		2223 4.6	2209 4.1		
0042 0.8	0101 0.8	0213 0.9	0009 0.7	0626 3.5	0451 2.1	0042 6.0	0429 2.0	0417 1.8	**10**	**M**
0646 4.1	0717 5.1	0827 6.3	0624 3.7	1212 1.1	1013 1.2	0626 2.4	1040 4.7	1029 4.3		
1254 1.4	1312 1.4	1428 1.5	1223 1.2	1845 3.5	1630 2.3	1251 6.1	1711 1.5	1703 1.4		
1901 4.1	1939 5.0	2050 6.1	1845 3.7		2309 0.7	1918 2.0	2323 4.5	2313 4.1		
0148 0.9	0203 1.0	0319 1.0	0120 0.8	0105 0.6	0556 2.2	0145 5.9	0535 2.0	0530 1.8	**11**	**TU**
0756 4.1	0822 5.0	0935 6.2	0734 3.6	0733 3.4	1134 1.2	0737 2.5	1142 4.6	1137 4.2		
1411 1.4	1421 1.4	1542 1.5	1342 1.2	1328 1.1	1746 2.2	1403 6.0	1811 1.6	1806 1.5		
2014 4.1	2048 5.0	2204 6.1	1958 3.6	1957 3.4		2024 2.1				
0253 1.0	0307 1.1	0426 1.0	0227 0.8	0212 0.7	0016 0.8	0247 6.0	0021 4.5	0015 4.2	**12**	**W**
0902 4.1	0927 5.1	1048 6.3	0842 3.6	0841 3.5	0653 2.2	0849 2.4	0639 2.0	0636 1.7		
1521 1.2	1530 1.3	1653 1.4	1451 1.1	1439 1.0	1245 1.1	1508 6.1	1242 4.6	1239 4.3		
2122 4.1	2154 5.0	2318 6.2	2104 3.7	2106 3.5	1855 2.2	2124 2.1	1906 1.6	1902 1.5		
0351 1.0	0405 1.1	0528 0.9	0322 0.8	0312 0.7	0111 0.9	0341 6.2	0115 4.6	0109 4.3	**13**	**TH**
0958 4.2	1025 5.2	1149 6.4	0939 3.7	0940 3.6	0740 2.3	0950 2.2	0735 1.8	0731 1.6		
1618 1.1	1630 1.2	1757 1.1	1548 1.0	1538 0.9	1339 1.0	1603 6.3	1337 4.7	1334 4.4		
2219 4.2	2250 5.1		2200 3.7	2204 3.5	1951 2.2	2215 2.0	1955 1.6	1949 1.5		
0436 1.0	0454 1.0	0015 6.4	0410 0.8	0400 0.7	0155 0.9	0426 6.4	0203 4.7	0155 4.5	**14**	**F**
1042 4.3	1114 5.3	0623 0.9	1027 3.8	1029 3.6	0819 2.4	1040 2.0	0824 1.6	0817 1.4		
1703 1.0	1721 1.0	1238 6.5	1636 0.9	1626 0.7	1425 0.9	1650 6.4	1426 4.8	1420 4.5		
2305 4.3	2337 5.3	1852 1.0	2248 3.8	2251 3.6	2039 2.3	2259 1.9	2038 1.5	2030 1.4		
0512 1.0	0536 1.0	0101 6.5	0451 0.9	0442 0.7	0233 0.9	0505 6.6	0245 4.9	0235 4.6	**15**	**SA**
1118 4.4	1156 5.4	0709 0.8	1108 3.9	1111 3.7	0852 2.4	1124 1.8	0906 1.4	0857 1.3		
1740 0.9	1805 0.9	1319 6.6	1717 0.8	1707 0.6	1505 0.8	1732 6.5	1509 4.8	1501 4.6		
2345 4.4		1939 0.9	2330 3.9	2333 3.7	2121 2.3	2338 1.7	2116 1.4	2107 1.3		

● ● Time: UT. For British Summer Time (shaded) March 26th to October 29th ADD ONE HOUR ● ●

JULY 2000 TIDE TABLES

•• Time: UT. For British Summer Time (shaded) March 26th to October 29th ADD ONE HOUR ••

Day	MARGATE Time	m	SHEERNESS Time	m	LONDON BRIDGE Time	m	WALTON-ON-THE-NAZE Time	m	HARWICH Time	m	LOWESTOFT Time	m	IMMINGHAM Time	m	RIVER TEES Time	m	RIVER TYNE Time	m
16 SU ○	0546	1.0	0018	5.4	0142	6.6	0527	0.9	0518	0.7	0307	0.9	0541	6.8	0324	5.0	0311	4.7
	1153	4.5	0615	0.9	0751	0.8	1145	4.0	1149	3.8	0922	2.5	1204	1.6	0945	1.3	0935	1.1
	1817	0.8	1234	5.5	1355	6.7	1754	0.7	1744	0.6	1543	0.7	1809	6.6	1548	4.9	1539	4.6
			1845	0.8	2021	0.8					2159	2.3			2153	1.4	2142	1.2
17 M	0023	4.4	0056	5.5	0218	6.7	0007	3.9	0011	3.7	0338	0.9	0015	1.6	0400	5.1	0345	4.8
	0622	0.9	0651	0.9	0832	0.7	0600	0.9	0551	0.7	0952	2.5	0615	6.9	1021	1.2	1009	1.0
	1229	4.6	1309	5.5	1429	6.8	1218	4.0	1224	3.8	1619	0.7	1242	1.4	1625	4.9	1614	4.7
	1854	0.8	1922	0.7	2100	0.7	1828	0.7	1818	0.5	2234	2.3	1845	6.7	2228	1.3	2216	1.2
18 TU	0100	4.5	0131	5.5	0253	6.8	0042	3.9	0046	3.8	0407	0.9	0050	1.6	0434	5.1	0417	4.8
	0700	0.9	0725	0.8	0912	0.7	0633	0.9	0623	0.7	1024	2.5	0649	7.0	1057	1.1	1043	0.9
	1306	4.6	1343	5.6	1503	6.9	1250	4.0	1257	3.8	1654	0.6	1318	1.4	1701	4.9	1648	4.7
	1933	0.8	1957	0.7	2139	0.6	1902	0.6	1851	0.5	2308	2.3	1920	6.7	2304	1.3	2250	1.2
19 W	0136	4.5	0206	5.5	0328	6.9	0115	4.0	0120	3.8	0439	0.8	0124	1.5	0509	5.1	0450	4.8
	0736	0.9	0800	0.8	0950	0.7	0706	0.8	0656	0.7	1057	2.5	0723	7.0	1133	1.1	1117	0.9
	1341	4.6	1417	5.5	1538	6.9	1322	4.0	1329	3.8	1729	0.6	1354	1.3	1737	4.8	1723	4.6
	2009	0.8	2033	0.7	2215	0.7	1936	0.6	1924	0.5	2342	2.3	1954	6.6	2340	1.3	2323	1.2
20 TH	0209	4.5	0240	5.5	0403	6.9	0148	4.0	0153	3.8	0512	0.8	0159	1.6	0544	5.1	0524	4.8
	0810	1.0	0835	0.8	1025	0.8	0740	0.8	0730	0.7	1132	2.5	0757	6.9	1209	1.1	1151	0.9
	1415	4.6	1450	5.5	1612	6.8	1354	4.0	1401	3.8	1803	0.6	1429	1.4	1815	4.8	1759	4.6
	2041	0.8	2109	0.7	2248	0.7	2011	0.6	1959	0.5			2028	6.6			2357	1.3
21 F	0242	4.5	0315	5.5	0438	6.8	0222	4.0	0227	3.8	0017	2.2	0233	1.6	0018	1.4	0559	4.8
	0843	1.0	0910	0.9	1057	0.9	0815	0.9	0804	0.7	0548	0.9	0831	6.8	0621	5.0	1227	1.0
	1448	4.5	1523	5.4	1645	6.7	1428	4.0	1435	3.8	1208	2.5	1503	1.5	1248	1.2	1836	4.5
	2112	0.9	2144	0.7	2318	0.8	2048	0.6	2035	0.5	1840	0.6	2103	6.4	1855	4.7		
22 SA	0315	4.4	0351	5.4	0512	6.7	0259	3.9	0303	3.7	0054	2.2	0306	1.8	0057	1.5	0033	1.4
	0917	1.1	0945	1.0	1126	1.1	0854	0.9	0841	0.8	0627	0.9	0906	6.7	0701	4.9	0637	4.7
	1521	4.5	1557	5.3	1717	6.6	1506	3.9	1511	3.7	1246	2.4	1537	1.6	1328	1.3	1306	1.1
	2145	0.9	2218	0.8	2346	0.8	2127	0.6	2112	0.5	1919	0.6	2141	6.3	1939	4.6	1918	4.4
23 SU	0354	4.4	0430	5.2	0548	6.5	0339	3.9	0342	3.7	0137	2.2	0343	2.0	0139	1.7	0114	1.5
	0954	1.2	1020	1.1	1154	1.1	0935	1.0	0921	0.9	0709	1.0	0944	6.6	0745	4.8	0721	4.6
	1600	4.4	1636	5.2	1751	6.5	1548	3.9	1552	3.7	1327	2.4	1614	1.7	1413	1.4	1350	1.2
	2223	1.0	2254	0.9			2210	0.7	2155	0.6	2002	0.7	2224	6.1	2028	4.5	2004	4.3
24 M	0440	4.3	0515	5.1	0016	0.9	0426	3.8	0429	3.6	0227	2.1	0424	2.2	0227	1.8	0202	1.6
	1039	1.3	1101	1.2	0630	6.4	1024	1.0	1008	1.0	0800	1.1	1030	6.4	0836	4.7	0810	4.5
	1649	4.3	1722	5.1	1229	1.2	1637	3.8	1640	3.6	1413	2.4	1658	1.9	1505	1.5	1441	1.3
	2312	1.0	2338	1.0	1833	6.3	2303	0.8	2247	0.7	2054	0.7	2318	6.0	2124	4.4	2059	4.2
25 TU	0536	4.2	0609	5.0	0056	0.9	0521	3.7	0524	3.5	0330	2.1	0518	2.2	0323	1.9	0300	1.7
	1136	1.4	1154	1.3	0720	6.2	1123	1.1	1109	1.0	0900	1.1	1129	6.3	0936	4.6	0909	4.4
	1751	4.2	1820	5.0	1317	1.3	1736	3.7	1739	3.5	1513	2.3	1757	2.0	1606	1.6	1542	1.4
					1928	6.1			2355	0.7	2156	0.8			2227	4.4	2202	4.2
26 W	0018	1.1	0037	1.1	0151	1.0	0006	0.8	0629	3.5	0439	2.2	0028	5.9	0430	2.0	0410	1.8
	0643	4.1	0714	5.0	0827	6.0	0626	3.7	1224	1.0	1013	1.1	0627	2.4	1043	4.6	1017	4.4
	1251	1.4	1304	1.4	1423	1.4	1232	1.1	1850	3.5	1629	2.3	1243	6.2	1715	1.6	1653	1.4
	1901	4.2	1932	5.0	2046	6.0	1846	3.7			2307	0.8	1912	2.1	2333	4.5	2312	4.2
27 TH	0139	1.1	0154	1.1	0308	1.1	0120	0.8	0109	0.7	0543	2.2	0143	6.1	0547	1.9	0527	1.7
	0755	4.2	0827	5.0	0945	6.1	0739	3.7	0741	3.5	1130	1.1	0748	2.3	1153	4.7	1130	4.4
	1411	1.3	1426	1.3	1551	1.4	1347	1.0	1339	0.9	1741	2.3	1400	6.3	1828	1.5	1807	1.4
	2014	4.3	2050	5.1	2208	6.2	2002	3.8	2004	3.5			2030	1.9				
28 F	0251	1.0	0315	1.0	0436	1.0	0233	0.7	0218	0.6	0015	0.7	0253	6.3	0039	4.7	0019	4.4
	0903	4.3	0938	5.2	1058	6.4	0851	3.8	0853	3.6	0641	2.3	0905	2.0	0701	1.6	0640	1.4
	1520	1.1	1545	1.1	1714	1.1	1500	0.9	1446	0.8	1242	0.9	1513	6.6	1301	4.9	1242	4.6
	2122	4.4	2203	5.3	2322	6.5	2115	3.9	2119	3.7	1848	2.4	2141	1.7	1934	1.3	1915	1.2
29 SA	0353	0.9	0427	0.8	0554	0.9	0336	0.7	0323	0.6	0115	0.7	0356	6.7	0139	5.0	0119	4.7
	1006	4.5	1043	5.5	1206	6.6	0954	4.0	1000	3.8	0734	2.4	1015	1.6	0806	1.3	0745	1.1
	1621	0.9	1656	0.8	1836	0.9	1603	0.7	1550	0.6	1348	0.8	1620	6.9	1404	5.2	1345	4.8
	2227	4.6	2309	5.6			2219	4.1	2227	3.9	1953	2.4	2245	1.4	2032	1.1	2012	1.0
30 SU	0451	0.8	0530	0.7	0030	6.7	0432	0.6	0421	0.5	0212	0.7	0451	7.0	0233	5.3	0212	4.9
	1104	4.6	1142	5.7	0714	0.8	1051	4.1	1100	3.9	0823	2.5	1118	1.1	0902	0.9	0842	0.7
	1720	0.7	1801	0.6	1304	6.8	1700	0.5	1648	0.6	1448	0.6	1720	7.1	1500	5.4	1442	5.1
	2330	4.7			1950	0.6	2316	4.3	2325	4.0	2054	2.5	2341	1.2	2124	0.9	2106	0.8
31 M	0545	0.7	0007	5.8	0128	7.0	0521	0.6	0512	0.5	0305	0.6	0540	7.3	0324	5.5	0301	5.2
	1157	4.7	0626	0.6	0816	0.7	1142	4.2	1151	4.0	0909	2.6	1215	0.8	0953	0.6	0934	0.4
	1816	0.5	1234	5.8	1356	7.0	1751	0.3	1739	0.2	1543	0.3	1815	7.3	1553	5.6	1533	5.2
			1900	0.4	2048	0.3					2149	2.5			2212	0.8	2154	0.7

EAST COAST OF ENGLAND Time Zone UT

Margate * Sheerness * London Bridge * Walton-on-the-Naze * Harwich * Lowestoft * Immingham * River Tees * River Tyne

TIDE TABLES AUGUST 2000

MARGATE		SHEERNESS		LONDON BRIDGE		WALTON-ON-THE-NAZE		HARWICH		LOWESTOFT		IMMINGHAM		RIVER TEES		RIVER TYNE			
Time	m	Time	m	Time	m	Time	m	Time	m	Time	m	Time	m	Time	m	Time	m		
0027	4.8	0100	6.0	0220	7.2	0007	4.4	0017	4.2	0354	0.6	0032	1.0	0412	5.7	0347	5.3	1	TU
0637	0.7	0717	0.6	0908	0.6	0608	0.6	0558	0.4	0955	2.7	0627	7.4	1042	0.4	1024	0.2		●
1248	4.8	1323	5.9	1443	7.1	1229	4.3	1239	4.1	1633	0.2	1306	0.5	1642	5.6	1623	5.3		
1909	0.3	1953	0.2	2139	0.1	1840	0.2	1827	0.1	2241	2.5	1906	7.4	2257	0.8	2241	0.7		
0121	4.9	0149	6.1	0308	7.5	0056	4.5	0104	4.3	0441	0.6	0119	1.0	0457	5.8	0433	5.4	2	W
0726	0.7	0803	0.5	0954	0.5	0653	0.6	0642	0.4	1041	2.7	0712	7.5	1128	0.3	1112	0.1		
1336	4.9	1409	5.9	1529	7.3	1314	4.3	1324	4.1	1720	0.1	1354	0.4	1730	5.6	1711	5.2		
2000	0.2	2042	0.1	2224	-0.1	1927	0.1	1912	-0.0	2330	2.5	1954	7.3	2341	0.9	2324	0.8		
0209	4.9	0236	6.1	0354	7.6	0142	4.4	0149	4.3	0524	0.7	0203	1.0	0542	5.7	0518	5.4	3	TH
0812	0.7	0848	0.6	1036	0.5	0736	0.7	0725	0.5	1126	2.7	0756	7.5	1214	0.4	1158	0.2		
1421	4.9	1453	5.9	1612	7.4	1357	4.3	1406	4.2	1805	0.1	1438	0.5	1816	5.4	1758	5.1		
2047	0.2	2127	0.1	2305	-0.1	2013	0.2	1957	-0.0			2039	7.1						
0254	4.8	0321	6.0	0439	7.5	0227	4.4	0233	4.2	0019	2.4	0243	1.2	0025	1.0	0007	0.9	4	F
0855	0.8	0928	0.7	1112	0.6	0819	0.7	0808	0.5	0606	0.8	0839	7.3	0627	5.6	0605	5.2		
1503	4.8	1536	5.8	1655	7.3	1440	4.3	1448	4.1	1211	2.7	1519	0.7	1300	0.6	1242	0.4		
2132	0.4	2208	0.3	2342	0.2	2057	0.3	2042	0.1	1848	0.2	2122	6.9	1903	5.2	1845	4.8		
0336	4.7	0406	5.8	0524	7.3	0310	4.2	0315	4.0	0108	2.3	0321	1.5	0109	1.3	0049	1.1	5	SA
0935	0.9	1006	0.9	1145	0.8	0901	0.8	0851	0.7	0646	0.9	0921	7.1	0715	5.4	0653	5.0		
1543	4.7	1618	5.6	1738	7.0	1524	4.2	1529	4.0	1257	2.6	1559	1.1	1346	0.9	1327	0.7		
2214	0.6	2246	0.5			2142	0.4	2127	0.2	1932	0.4	2204	6.5	1951	4.9	1932	4.6		
0418	4.5	0450	5.5	0013	0.5	0354	4.0	0400	3.8	0159	2.2	0400	1.8	0154	1.6	0133	1.4	6	SU
1015	1.1	1043	1.1	0607	6.9	0945	1.0	0935	0.8	0729	1.0	1006	6.7	0804	5.1	0743	4.7		
1625	4.5	1702	5.4	1215	1.1	1609	4.0	1612	3.9	1345	2.5	1639	1.5	1434	1.2	1413	1.1		
2257	0.8	2324	0.8	1820	6.7	2228	0.6	2214	0.4	2018	0.6	2250	6.2	2042	4.7	2022	4.3		
0502	4.2	0536	5.2	0044	0.8	0442	3.8	0445	3.6	0254	2.2	0441	2.1	0243	1.8	0222	1.6	7	M
1101	1.3	1124	1.3	0651	6.5	1033	1.1	1023	1.0	0818	1.1	1057	6.3	0900	4.8	0839	4.5		
1715	4.3	1751	5.1	1248	1.3	1659	3.8	1701	3.6	1442	2.4	1724	2.0	1527	1.6	1505	1.5		
2349	1.0			1907	6.4	2321	0.8	2306	0.7	2112	0.8	2343	5.9	2139	4.5	2118	4.1		
0557	4.0	0006	1.0	0121	1.0	0536	3.6	0538	3.4	0357	2.1	0533	2.5	0340	2.1	0323	1.9	8	TU
1201	1.4	0627	5.0	0742	6.2	1133	1.2	1122	1.1	0919	1.2	1202	6.0	1002	4.5	0944	4.2		
1819	4.1	1215	1.5	1331	1.5	1759	3.6	1759	3.4	1551	2.3	1821	2.4	1626	1.8	1607	1.8		
		1849	4.9	2005	6.1					2218	1.0			2240	4.3	2223	4.0		
0054	1.2	0103	1.3	0214	1.3	0029	1.0	0012	0.9	0504	2.1	0050	5.8	0449	2.2	0442	2.0	9	W
0704	3.9	0728	4.8	0841	6.0	0642	3.4	0641	3.3	1046	1.2	0644	2.7	1109	4.4	1057	4.1		
1321	1.5	1326	1.6	1437	1.7	1255	1.3	1240	1.2	1713	2.2	1323	5.8	1732	2.0	1721	1.9		
1936	4.0	2000	4.7	2113	5.9	1915	3.5	1912	3.3	2336	1.1	1936	2.6	2345	4.3	2333	4.0		
0206	1.3	0215	1.4	0334	1.4	0147	1.1	0130	1.0	0612	2.2	0203	5.8	0608	2.2	0604	1.9	10	TH
0817	3.9	0839	4.7	0952	5.9	0801	3.4	0756	3.2	1219	1.1	0810	2.7	1218	4.4	1212	4.1		
1445	1.4	1450	1.5	1609	1.6	1422	1.2	1409	1.1	1837	2.2	1442	5.8	1839	2.0	1830	1.9		
2054	4.0	2118	4.8	2239	5.9	2036	3.5	2036	3.3			2048	2.6						
0313	1.3	0326	1.4	0445	1.3	0253	1.1	0242	1.0	0042	1.1	0309	6.0	0048	4.4	0038	4.2	11	F
0922	4.1	0949	4.9	1112	6.0	0909	3.5	0909	3.3	0708	2.3	0924	2.5	0717	2.0	0709	1.8		
1554	1.2	1603	1.3	1721	1.4	1528	1.1	1518	1.0	1321	1.0	1545	6.0	1321	4.5	1315	4.2		
2158	4.1	2224	5.0	2350	6.1	2139	3.6	2142	3.4	1941	2.2	2148	2.4	1936	1.9	1925	1.8		
0409	1.2	0426	1.3	0545	1.1	0347	1.0	0338	0.9	0131	1.1	0401	6.3	0142	4.6	0131	4.4	12	SA
1013	4.2	1047	5.1	1211	6.2	1003	3.7	1004	3.5	0751	2.3	1021	2.2	0809	1.7	0759	1.6		
1644	1.1	1700	1.1	1822	1.1	1619	0.9	1609	0.8	1407	1.0	1636	6.3	1412	4.6	1404	4.4		
2248	4.2	2316	5.2			2230	3.7	2232	3.6	2029	2.3	2236	2.1	2022	1.7	2010	1.6		
0451	1.2	0514	1.1	0040	6.3	0430	0.9	0422	0.9	0210	1.1	0444	6.6	0229	4.8	0215	4.6	13	SU
1054	4.3	1133	5.3	0638	0.9	1045	3.8	1049	3.6	0827	2.4	1106	1.8	0852	1.5	0840	1.3		
1724	1.0	1748	0.9	1255	6.4	1700	0.8	1650	0.7	1447	1.0	1718	6.5	1457	4.8	1445	4.5		
2329	4.3	2359	5.4	1915	0.9	2311	3.9	2314	3.7	2109	2.3	2317	1.9	2101	1.5	2048	1.4		
0527	1.1	0555	1.0	0121	6.5	0506	0.9	0459	0.8	0244	1.0	0521	6.8	0308	5.0	0251	4.7	14	M
1131	4.5	1213	5.5	0727	0.8	1123	3.9	1128	3.7	0857	2.5	1146	1.6	0930	1.3	0916	1.1		
1800	0.9	1827	0.8	1333	6.6	1735	0.7	1725	0.6	1524	0.7	1754	6.7	1535	4.9	1521	4.7		
				2000	0.8	2347	4.0	2351	3.8	2142	2.4	2354	1.7	2137	1.4	2124	1.3		
0006	4.4	0036	5.5	0157	6.7	0539	0.9	0531	0.8	0315	0.9	0555	7.0	0343	5.1	0324	4.9	15	TU
0603	1.0	0632	0.9	0812	0.7	1157	4.0	1204	3.8	0927	2.5	1224	1.4	1005	1.1	0950	1.0		O
1208	4.6	1249	5.6	1409	6.8	1807	0.6	1757	0.5	1558	0.6	1827	6.8	1609	5.0	1554	4.8		
1836	0.8	1904	0.7	2043	0.6					2214	2.3			2212	1.2	2157	1.2		

● ● Time: UT. For British Summer Time (shaded) March 26th to October 29th ADD ONE HOUR ● ●

AUGUST 2000 TIDE TABLES

•• Time: UT. For British Summer Time (shaded) March 26th to October 29th ADD ONE HOUR ••

	MARGATE		SHEERNESS		LONDON BRIDGE		WALTON-ON-THE-NAZE		HARWICH		LOWESTOFT		IMMINGHAM		RIVER TEES		RIVER TYNE	
	Time	m	Time	m	Time	m	Time	m	Time	m	Time	m	Time	m	Time	m	Time	m
16 W	0042	4.5	0111	5.6	0232	6.9	0021	4.0	0027	3.8	0345	0.9	0030	1.5	0415	5.2	0355	5.0
	0639	0.9	0706	0.6	0854	0.6	0611	0.8	0602	0.7	1000	2.6	0628	7.1	1039	0.9	1023	0.8
	1245	4.7	1324	5.6	1443	7.0	1230	4.1	1238	3.9	1633	0.6	1300	1.2	1641	5.0	1627	4.8
	1912	0.7	1939	0.6	2124	0.5	1840	0.6	1829	0.4	2244	2.4	1859	6.8	2245	1.1	2230	1.1
17 TH	0115	4.6	0145	5.7	0307	7.0	0054	4.1	0100	3.9	0418	0.8	0106	1.4	0446	5.3	0427	5.0
	0714	0.9	0741	0.6	0935	0.6	0644	0.8	0634	0.6	1034	2.6	0701	7.2	1112	0.9	1055	0.7
	1320	4.7	1357	5.7	1518	7.1	1303	4.1	1310	3.9	1706	0.5	1336	1.1	1712	5.0	1659	4.8
	1945	0.7	2015	0.6	2201	0.5	1915	0.5	1902	0.4	2315	2.3	1931	6.9	2318	1.1	2302	1.1
18 F	0147	4.6	0219	5.7	0342	7.1	0127	4.2	0133	3.9	0453	0.8	0141	1.4	0518	5.3	0459	5.0
	0748	0.9	0817	0.8	1012	0.7	0718	0.7	0708	0.6	1109	2.6	0734	7.2	1145	0.9	1128	0.7
	1352	4.7	1430	5.6	1551	7.1	1336	4.2	1343	3.9	1741	0.5	1410	1.1	1746	5.0	1732	4.8
	2018	0.7	2051	0.6	2236	0.6	1950	0.5	1936	0.3	2347	2.3	2003	6.8	2352	1.2	2334	1.1
19 SA	0218	4.6	0254	5.7	0415	7.0	0200	4.2	0206	3.9	0528	0.8	0215	1.4	0551	5.2	0532	5.0
	0820	0.9	0851	0.8	1043	0.8	0754	0.7	0742	0.6	1144	2.6	0807	7.1	1221	0.9	1202	0.8
	1422	4.7	1501	5.6	1622	7.0	1409	4.1	1415	3.9	1815	0.5	1443	1.2	1822	4.9	1807	4.7
	2048	0.8	2124	0.6	2305	0.7	2025	0.5	2010	0.4			2036	6.7				
20 SU	0249	4.6	0328	5.6	0448	6.9	0236	4.2	0242	3.9	0021	2.3	0248	1.5	0028	1.3	0009	1.2
	0853	1.0	0924	0.9	1108	1.0	0830	0.8	0816	0.7	0604	0.9	0841	7.0	0627	5.1	0609	4.9
	1452	4.7	1534	5.5	1653	6.9	1444	4.1	1450	3.9	1221	2.5	1515	1.4	1257	1.1	1238	0.9
	2119	0.9	2155	0.8	2327	0.8	2100	0.6	2045	0.5	1851	0.6	2110	6.6	1902	4.8	1845	4.6
21 M	0324	4.5	0404	5.4	0522	6.7	0313	4.0	0319	3.8	0100	2.3	0321	1.7	0106	1.4	0045	1.3
	0927	1.1	0954	1.0	1128	1.1	0907	0.9	0854	0.8	0643	0.9	0917	6.8	0709	5.0	0650	4.8
	1527	4.6	1610	5.4	1727	6.7	1522	4.0	1528	3.8	1300	2.5	1548	1.6	1339	1.2	1317	1.1
	2154	1.0	2224	0.9	2348	0.9	2139	0.7	2123	0.6	1930	0.7	2149	6.4	1948	4.6	1929	4.5
22 TU	0406	4.4	0445	5.3	0600	6.4	0356	3.9	0401	3.7	0146	2.2	0358	2.0	0151	1.6	0130	1.5
	1008	1.2	1030	1.1	1158	1.1	0951	1.0	0936	0.9	0729	1.0	0959	6.6	0800	4.8	0739	4.6
	1613	4.5	1654	5.3	1806	6.5	1608	3.9	1613	3.7	1345	2.4	1627	1.8	1428	1.5	1404	1.3
	2237	1.1	2300	1.0			2227	0.8	2209	0.7	2018	0.8	2238	6.1	2045	4.4	2021	4.3
23 W	0500	4.2	0535	5.1	0023	0.9	0447	3.6	0451	3.5	0244	2.2	0446	2.2	0246	1.8	0225	1.6
	1101	1.3	1118	1.3	0646	6.2	1046	1.1	1031	1.0	0826	1.0	1055	6.3	0903	4.6	0838	4.5
	1715	4.3	1749	5.1	1242	1.2	1705	3.8	1709	3.6	1445	2.4	1721	2.1	1530	1.7	1505	1.5
	2340	1.2	2357	1.2	1859	6.2	2329	0.9	2313	0.8	2120	0.9	2345	5.9	2151	4.3	2126	4.2
24 TH	0606	4.1	0638	4.9	0112	1.1	0550	3.6	0555	3.4	0357	2.2	0554	2.4	0357	1.9	0338	1.8
	1218	1.4	1229	1.4	0750	5.9	1157	1.1	1148	1.1	0940	1.1	1214	6.1	1018	4.5	0951	4.3
	1830	4.2	1903	5.0	1343	1.4	1816	3.7	1820	3.5	1606	2.3	1839	2.3	1646	1.8	1623	1.7
					2015	6.0					2237	0.9			2306	4.4	2242	4.2
25 F	0108	1.3	0121	1.3	0227	1.3	0047	1.0	0037	0.9	0509	2.2	0112	5.9	0524	1.9	0506	1.7
	0724	4.1	0755	4.9	0913	5.9	0706	3.6	0710	3.4	1108	1.0	0723	2.4	1139	4.5	1115	4.3
	1348	1.3	1401	1.4	1518	1.4	1320	1.1	1312	1.0	1727	2.3	1345	6.1	1812	1.8	1751	1.6
	1954	4.2	2029	5.0	2145	6.1	1939	3.7	1942	3.5	2354	2.3	2009	2.3				
26 SA	0230	1.2	0255	1.2	0412	1.2	0211	1.0	0157	0.9	0613	2.3	0234	6.2	0021	4.6	0000	4.4
	0842	4.2	0915	5.1	1035	6.2	0827	3.7	0830	3.5	1230	0.9	0851	2.1	0650	1.6	0630	1.5
	1505	1.1	1531	1.1	1654	1.1	1445	0.9	1430	0.8	1844	2.4	1509	6.4	1255	4.8	1236	4.5
	2115	4.4	2151	5.3	2309	6.4	2102	3.8	2106	3.6			2127	2.0	1925	1.5	1904	1.4
27 SU	0340	1.0	0414	1.0	0535	1.0	0322	0.9	0309	0.8	0100	0.9	0342	6.6	0127	4.9	0106	4.6
	0951	4.4	1029	5.3	1150	6.5	0939	3.8	0945	3.6	0712	2.4	1007	1.6	0757	1.2	0741	1.4
	1614	0.8	1650	0.8	1826	0.9	1554	0.7	1541	0.6	1341	0.7	1619	6.8	1400	5.1	1341	4.8
	2227	4.6	2301	5.6			2210	4.1	2218	3.9	1956	2.4	2233	1.6	2023	1.3	2003	1.2
28 M	0442	0.9	0520	0.9	0021	6.8	0420	0.8	0410	0.7	0200	0.9	0438	7.0	0222	5.2	0200	5.0
	1051	4.6	1130	5.6	0700	0.8	1037	4.0	1045	3.8	0804	2.5	1110	1.1	0852	0.8	0833	0.7
	1715	0.6	1756	0.5	1251	6.8	1651	0.5	1639	0.4	1440	0.5	1717	7.1	1454	5.4	1435	5.1
	2327	4.7	2359	5.9	1941	0.4	2306	4.3	2315	4.1	2052	2.5	2329	1.3	2112	1.0	2054	1.0
29 TU	0536	0.8	0615	0.7	0119	7.1	0508	0.7	0459	0.6	0252	0.8	0526	7.3	0311	5.5	0247	5.2
	1144	4.7	1221	5.8	0803	0.6	1127	4.2	1137	4.0	0851	2.6	1203	0.7	0940	0.4	0923	0.4
	1808	0.4	1851	0.3	1342	7.1	1739	0.3	1727	0.2	1531	0.3	1806	7.3	1542	5.6	1523	5.2
					2037	0.1	2354	4.4			2140	2.5			2156	0.8	2139	0.8
30 W	0019	4.9	0049	6.0	0209	7.4	0551	0.7	0003	4.2	0339	0.7	0017	1.1	0355	5.7	0330	5.4
	0624	0.7	0703	0.6	0854	0.5	1212	4.3	0542	0.5	0936	2.7	0610	7.6	1024	0.2	1009	0.2
	1232	4.8	1307	5.9	1428	7.2	1824	0.2	1223	4.1	1617	0.2	1251	0.4	1625	5.7	1606	5.3
	1856	0.3	1939	0.2	2125	-0.1			1811	0.0	2225	2.5	1851	7.4	2238	0.7	2221	0.7
31 TH ●	0106	4.9	0134	6.1	0254	7.5	0039	4.5	0048	4.3	0421	0.7	0101	1.0	0437	5.8	0413	5.5
	0707	0.7	0746	0.6	0938	0.4	0633	0.6	0623	0.4	1020	2.8	0652	7.7	1107	0.2	1052	0.1
	1316	4.9	1350	6.0	1511	7.4	1254	4.4	1304	4.4	1700	0.1	1335	0.2	1707	5.6	1649	5.3
	1940	0.3	2023	0.1	2207	-0.1	1908	0.2	1853	-0.0	2308	2.5	1932	7.4	2318	0.8	2301	0.8

EAST COAST OF ENGLAND Time Zone UT

Margate * Sheerness * London Bridge * Walton-on-the-Naze * Harwich * Lowestoft * Immingham * River Tees * River Tyne

TIDE TABLES SEPTEMBER 2000

MARGATE Time m	SHEERNESS Time m	LONDON BRIDGE Time m	WALTON-ON-THE-NAZE Time m	HARWICH Time m	LOWESTOFT Time m	IMMINGHAM Time m	RIVER TEES Time m	RIVER TYNE Time m	
0149 4.9	0216 6.1	0336 7.6	0121 4.4	0130 4.3	0502 0.7	0142 1.0	0518 5.8	0455 5.5	**1 F**
0748 0.7	0826 0.6	1016 0.4	0714 0.7	0703 0.5	1103 2.8	0733 7.6	1148 0.3	1133 0.3	
1357 4.9	1430 6.0	1551 7.4	1335 4.4	1344 4.2	1740 0.2	1415 0.5	1747 5.5	1730 5.1	
2021 0.3	2102 0.2	2244 0.0	1949 0.2	1934 0.0	2351 2.4	2010 7.2	2357 1.0	2339 0.9	
0229 4.8	0257 6.0	0416 7.5	0202 4.3	0209 4.2	0540 0.7	0219 1.1	0557 5.6	0537 5.3	**2 SA**
0826 0.8	0903 0.7	1049 0.6	0754 0.7	0743 0.5	1147 2.7	0812 7.5	1229 0.6	1212 0.5	
1435 4.9	1509 5.9	1630 7.3	1415 4.4	1422 4.2	1820 0.3	1451 0.8	1827 5.3	1812 4.9	
2100 0.5	2138 0.4	2314 0.3	2029 0.4	2014 0.2		2046 7.0			
0305 4.7	0336 5.8	0455 7.2	0241 4.2	0248 4.0	0032 2.3	0253 1.4	0035 1.2	0017 1.1	**3 SU**
0902 0.9	0937 0.9	1116 0.8	0833 0.8	0823 0.6	0617 0.8	0851 7.2	0639 5.4	0621 5.1	
1511 4.8	1547 5.7	1708 7.1	1454 4.3	1500 4.1	1230 2.6	1524 1.2	1309 1.0	1249 0.9	
2135 0.7	2209 0.7	2339 0.7	2108 0.6	2054 0.4	1858 0.5	2121 6.7	1909 5.0	1853 4.7	
0339 4.5	0413 5.5	0533 6.8	0320 4.0	0325 3.8	0114 2.3	0325 1.7	0114 1.5	0055 1.3	**4 M**
0938 1.0	1007 1.1	1141 1.0	0911 0.9	0902 0.8	0655 0.9	0930 6.8	0724 5.1	0706 4.8	
1549 4.6	1625 5.4	1745 6.7	1534 4.1	1539 3.9	1315 2.5	1556 1.7	1350 1.4	1328 1.3	
2212 1.0	2237 0.9		2147 0.8	2133 0.6	1937 0.7	2158 6.3	1954 4.7	1936 4.4	
0417 4.3	0451 5.2	0003 0.9	0400 3.8	0404 3.6	0158 2.2	0400 2.1	0157 1.8	0138 1.6	**5 TU**
1018 1.2	1038 1.3	0611 6.5	0953 1.1	0942 1.0	0739 1.0	1014 6.3	0816 4.7	0757 4.4	
1635 4.3	1707 5.1	1209 1.2	1619 3.8	1621 3.6	1409 2.4	1632 2.2	1435 1.8	1412 1.6	
2256 1.2	2309 1.2	1828 6.4	2231 1.0	2217 0.9	2021 1.0	2242 6.0	2046 4.4	2027 4.2	
0504 4.1	0534 4.9	0035 1.1	0445 3.6	0447 3.4	0250 2.2	0444 2.5	0248 2.1	0233 1.9	**6 W**
1113 1.4	1119 1.5	0654 6.1	1044 1.3	1033 1.1	0833 1.1	1112 5.8	0918 4.4	0857 4.1	
1736 4.1	1759 4.8	1246 1.3	1713 3.5	1711 3.4	1516 2.2	1722 2.7	1530 2.1	1509 2.0	
2355 1.4	2358 1.5	1921 6.0	2330 1.3	2313 1.1	2119 1.1	2344 5.7	2148 4.2	2128 4.0	
0609 3.9	0628 4.7	0119 1.3	0542 3.3	0540 3.2	0353 2.2	0549 2.9	0356 2.3	0349 2.1	**7 TH**
1229 1.6	1224 1.7	0749 5.8	1158 1.4	1144 1.3	0954 1.2	1241 5.5	1031 4.2	1013 3.9	
1856 3.9	1908 4.6	1336 1.6	1827 3.3	1822 3.1	1640 2.2	1841 3.0	1641 2.3	1628 2.2	
		2028 5.7			2248 1.3		2300 4.2	2244 3.9	
0110 1.6	0114 1.7	0223 1.6	0056 1.4	0032 1.3	0505 2.2	0111 5.6	0528 2.3	0527 2.1	**8 F**
0727 3.8	0740 4.5	0856 5.6	0706 3.2	0657 3.1	1148 1.2	0731 3.0	1151 4.2	1139 3.9	
1402 1.6	1403 1.7	1457 1.8	1346 1.4	1330 1.2	1814 2.2	1414 5.6	1806 2.3	1756 2.2	
2023 3.9	2036 4.6	2150 5.6	2002 3.3	2000 3.1		2013 3.0			
0230 1.6	0246 1.7	0404 1.6	0219 1.4	0206 1.2	0012 1.3	0233 5.8	0014 4.3	0002 4.0	**9 SA**
0842 3.9	0906 4.6	1020 5.6	0833 3.3	0829 3.1	0620 2.2	0859 2.7	0654 2.1	0644 1.9	
1521 1.4	1533 1.5	1648 1.6	1500 1.2	1450 1.1	1254 1.0	1524 5.9	1300 4.3	1251 4.1	
2133 4.0	2153 4.8	2320 5.9	2113 3.5	2115 3.3	1922 2.2	2121 2.7	1914 2.2	1900 2.0	
0336 1.5	0357 1.5	0514 1.3	0318 1.2	0310 1.1	0105 1.2	0333 6.2	0115 4.5	0103 4.3	**10 SU**
0940 4.1	1014 4.9	1139 5.9	0932 3.6	0934 3.3	0714 2.3	0957 2.3	0749 1.8	0736 1.6	
1617 1.2	1635 1.2	1754 1.2	1554 1.0	1542 0.9	1341 0.9	1615 6.2	1354 4.6	1342 4.3	
2225 4.2	2248 5.2		2204 3.7	2207 3.5	2009 2.3	2212 2.3	2002 1.9	1947 1.8	
0424 1.3	0449 1.3	0014 6.2	0404 1.1	0356 1.0	0145 1.2	0418 6.5	0203 4.8	0148 4.5	**11 M**
1025 4.3	1104 5.2	0610 1.1	1017 3.8	1021 3.5	0753 2.4	1042 1.9	0830 1.5	0816 1.3	
1659 1.0	1723 1.0	1228 6.3	1634 0.8	1623 0.7	1421 0.8	1656 6.5	1436 4.8	1422 4.5	
2306 4.4	2332 5.4	1848 1.0	2245 3.9	2249 3.7	2046 2.3	2253 2.0	2040 1.7	2026 1.5	
0503 1.2	0531 1.1	0055 6.5	0440 1.0	0433 0.9	0218 1.1	0455 6.8	0242 5.0	0225 4.7	**12 TU**
1104 4.5	1146 5.5	0701 0.9	1055 3.9	1101 3.7	0827 2.5	1122 1.6	0906 1.2	0851 1.1	
1735 0.9	1803 0.8	1307 6.6	1709 0.7	1657 0.6	1457 0.7	1730 6.7	1512 4.9	1457 4.7	
2341 4.5		1936 0.7	2320 4.1	2327 3.8	2118 2.4	2331 1.7	2115 1.4	2100 1.3	
0538 1.0	0010 5.6	0131 6.8	0513 0.8	0505 0.8	0248 1.0	0530 7.0	0316 5.2	0257 4.9	**13 W**
1141 4.6	0608 1.0	0748 0.7	1130 4.1	1138 3.8	0859 2.6	1200 1.3	0939 1.0	0924 0.9	
1809 0.8	1223 5.6	1343 6.9	1741 0.6	1729 0.5	1531 0.6	1802 6.9	1544 5.1	1528 4.9	**O**
	1839 0.7	2019 0.6	2354 4.2		2145 2.4		2149 1.2	2133 1.1	
0015 4.6	0045 5.7	0206 7.0	0546 0.8	0001 3.9	0321 0.9	0007 1.5	0347 5.3	0328 5.1	**14 TH**
0612 0.9	0643 0.9	0832 0.6	1204 4.2	0536 0.7	0933 2.6	0603 7.2	1012 0.8	0957 0.7	
1216 4.8	1258 5.7	1418 7.1	1814 0.5	1212 4.0	1605 0.5	1236 1.1	1614 5.2	1559 5.0	
1843 0.7	1915 0.6	2100 0.4		1801 0.4	2214 2.4	1833 7.0	2221 1.1	2205 1.0	
0047 4.7	0120 5.8	0240 7.2	0028 4.3	0036 4.0	0356 0.8	0043 1.3	0417 5.4	0400 5.2	**15 F**
0646 0.8	0718 0.8	0913 0.5	0620 0.7	0609 0.6	1008 2.7	0635 7.3	1045 0.7	1029 0.6	
1250 4.8	1332 5.8	1451 7.2	1239 4.3	1246 4.0	1639 0.5	1312 1.0	1645 5.2	1631 5.0	
1915 0.7	1951 0.5	2139 0.4	1849 0.4	1835 0.3	2244 2.4	1904 7.1	2254 1.0	2237 0.9	

● ● Time: UT. For British Summer Time (shaded) March 26th to October 29th ADD ONE HOUR ● ●

SEPTEMBER 2000 TIDE TABLES

•• Time: UT. For British Summer Time (shaded) March 26th to October 29th ADD ONE HOUR ••

	MARGATE		SHEERNESS		LONDON BRIDGE		WALTON -ON THE- NAZE		HARWICH		LOWESTOFT		IMMINGHAM		RIVER TEES		RIVER TYNE	
	Time	m	Time	m	Time	m	Time	m	Time	m	Time	m	Time	m	Time	m	Time	m
16 SA	0118	4.8	0154	5.9	0315	7.3	0102	4.3	0109	4.1	0432	0.7	0118	1.2	0448	5.5	0432	5.2
	0720	0.8	0754	0.7	0951	0.6	0655	0.6	0642	0.5	1043	2.7	0708	7.4	1118	0.7	1102	0.6
	1322	4.9	1404	5.8	1524	7.3	1312	4.3	1321	4.1	1714	0.5	1346	1.0	1716	5.2	1703	5.0
	1948	0.7	2027	0.5	2215	0.4	1924	0.4	1909	0.3	2316	2.4	1936	7.1	2327	1.0	2310	0.9
17 SU	0150	4.8	0228	5.8	0348	7.2	0136	4.3	0144	4.0	0508	0.7	0153	1.2	0521	5.4	0506	5.2
	0754	0.9	0830	0.8	1024	0.7	0730	0.7	0717	0.6	1119	2.6	0742	7.4	1152	0.8	1136	0.7
	1353	4.9	1437	5.8	1557	7.2	1346	4.3	1354	4.0	1748	0.5	1418	1.1	1751	5.1	1737	4.9
	2021	0.7	2100	0.5	2245	0.6	1959	0.5	1942	0.4	2351	2.4	2009	7.0			2345	1.0
18 M	0222	4.7	0303	5.7	0422	7.1	0211	4.2	0219	4.0	0544	0.8	0227	1.4	0002	1.1	0543	5.1
	0830	1.0	0901	0.8	1048	0.9	0806	0.7	0752	0.6	1157	2.6	0816	7.2	0558	5.3	1210	0.9
	1425	4.8	1511	5.7	1630	7.1	1421	4.2	1429	4.0	1823	0.6	1451	1.3	1228	1.0	1815	4.8
	2055	0.9	2129	0.8	2305	0.8	2033	0.6	2018	0.5			2042	6.8	1830	5.0		
19 TU	0257	4.6	0339	5.6	0457	6.8	0248	4.1	0255	3.9	0030	2.4	0300	1.6	0040	1.3	0022	1.2
	0906	1.1	0932	1.0	1107	1.0	0843	0.8	0830	0.7	0623	0.8	0854	7.0	0641	5.1	0626	4.9
	1503	4.7	1549	5.6	1706	6.8	1500	4.1	1506	3.9	1238	2.5	1524	1.5	1309	1.2	1249	1.1
	2131	1.0	2157	0.9	2324	0.9	2111	0.8	2056	0.6	1902	0.7	2121	6.6	1916	4.8	1859	4.6
20 W	0339	4.4	0420	5.3	0536	6.5	0329	3.9	0336	3.7	0115	2.3	0338	1.8	0126	1.5	0106	1.4
	0948	1.2	1008	1.1	1137	1.1	0926	0.9	0912	0.8	0709	0.9	0938	6.7	0734	4.8	0717	4.7
	1551	4.5	1634	5.4	1749	6.5	1547	4.0	1551	3.8	1327	2.5	1603	1.9	1359	1.5	1336	1.4
	2215	1.2	2235	1.1	2359	1.1	2157	0.9	2142	0.8	1950	0.8	2209	6.3	2013	4.5	1953	4.4
21 TH	0433	4.2	0509	5.1	0622	6.1	0419	3.8	0425	3.5	0209	2.2	0426	2.2	0223	1.7	0204	1.6
	1041	1.4	1058	1.2	1221	1.2	1021	1.1	1007	1.0	0807	1.0	1037	6.3	0842	4.6	0820	4.4
	1655	4.3	1732	5.1	1844	6.2	1645	3.8	1648	3.6	1433	2.4	1658	2.3	1502	1.8	1440	1.7
	2320	1.4	2334	1.3			2300	1.1	2245	1.0	2053	1.0	2317	6.0	2123	4.4	2100	4.2
22 F	0541	4.1	0613	4.9	0049	1.3	0522	3.6	0527	3.4	0321	2.2	0536	2.4	0337	1.9	0322	1.7
	1202	1.4	1213	1.4	0726	5.8	1135	1.1	1124	1.0	0924	1.0	1205	6.0	1003	4.4	0940	4.3
	1815	4.2	1849	4.9	1323	1.4	1759	3.7	1802	3.4	1600	2.3	1820	2.6	1625	2.0	1607	1.9
					2003	6.0					2217	1.1			2243	4.4	2223	4.2
23 SA	0051	1.5	0103	1.5	0204	1.5	0024	1.2	0013	1.1	0436	2.2	0050	5.9	0512	1.8	0458	1.7
	0702	4.1	0734	4.8	0851	5.8	0642	3.5	0645	3.3	1058	0.9	0714	2.4	1133	4.5	1112	4.3
	1337	1.3	1352	1.4	1502	1.4	1306	1.1	1256	1.0	1728	2.3	1345	6.1	1800	2.0	1743	1.8
	1946	4.2	2019	5.0	2133	6.1	1929	3.7	1930	3.5	2341	1.1	1957	2.5			2346	4.3
24 SU	0217	1.4	0243	1.4	0354	1.4	0156	1.2	0141	1.1	0547	2.3	0219	6.2	0003	4.5	0624	1.4
	0826	4.2	0900	5.0	1017	6.1	0812	3.6	0811	3.4	1223	0.8	0846	2.0	0642	1.5	1233	4.5
	1457	1.0	1527	1.1	1643	1.0	1437	0.9	1421	0.8	1854	2.4	1511	6.4	1251	4.7	1856	1.6
	2112	4.4	2144	5.2	2258	6.5	2054	3.9	2059	3.6			2117	2.2	1915	1.7		
25 M	0330	1.2	0403	1.2	0519	1.0	0309	1.0	0257	0.9	0050	1.1	0329	6.6	0112	4.9	0053	4.7
	0937	4.5	1015	5.3	1134	6.5	0924	3.8	0930	3.6	0651	2.4	1000	1.5	0745	1.1	0727	1.0
	1607	0.7	1645	0.8	1818	0.6	1545	0.6	1532	0.5	1331	0.6	1615	6.8	1351	5.1	1334	4.8
	2221	4.7	2251	5.7			2159	4.1	2207	3.9	1957	2.4	2221	1.8	2009	1.4	1951	1.3
26 TU	0432	1.0	0507	1.0	0009	7.0	0405	0.9	0356	0.8	0148	1.0	0423	7.1	0206	5.2	0146	5.0
	1036	4.6	1115	5.6	0645	0.8	1021	4.0	1029	3.8	0744	2.5	1057	1.0	0836	0.7	0821	0.6
	1706	0.5	1745	0.5	1236	6.9	1637	0.4	1626	0.3	1426	0.4	1707	7.2	1440	5.3	1424	5.1
	2317	4.8	2346	5.9	1927	0.2	2251	4.3	2300	4.1	2044	2.5	2312	1.4	2055	1.1	2038	1.1
27 W	0522	0.8	0558	0.8	0105	7.3	0451	0.8	0442	0.7	0236	0.9	0508	7.4	0252	5.5	0231	5.2
	1127	4.8	1204	5.8	0745	0.5	1108	4.2	1118	4.0	0830	2.7	1146	0.7	0921	0.4	0906	0.4
	1754	0.4	1835	0.3	1326	7.2	1722	0.3	1710	0.2	1513	0.3	1750	7.5	1524	5.5	1506	5.2
					2019	-0.1	2337	4.4	2346	4.2	2124	2.5	2357	1.1	2136	0.9	2120	0.9
28 TH	0004	4.9	0032	6.1	0153	7.5	0531	0.7	0522	0.6	0319	0.8	0549	7.6	0333	5.7	0312	5.4
	0605	0.8	0642	0.7	0834	0.4	1151	4.3	1202	4.1	0915	2.8	1230	0.5	1002	0.3	0948	0.3
	1211	4.9	1247	5.9	1409	7.3	1803	0.3	1751	0.1	1555	0.2	1828	7.4	1603	5.6	1545	5.3
	1836	0.3	1918	0.3	2104	-0.1					2203	2.5			2215	0.8	2158	0.8
29 F	0046	4.9	0113	6.1	0235	7.5	0018	4.4	0027	4.2	0359	0.7	0039	1.0	0412	5.8	0351	5.5
	0643	0.7	0722	0.6	0915	0.4	0611	0.7	0600	0.5	0958	2.8	0628	7.7	1041	0.3	1027	0.3
	1251	4.9	1326	6.0	1449	7.4	1231	4.4	1242	4.2	1635	0.3	1309	0.5	1639	5.6	1623	5.4
	1915	0.4	1955	0.3	2143	0.0	1843	0.3	1829	0.1	2241	2.5	1903	7.4	2251	0.9	2236	0.9
30 SA ●	0123	4.9	0151	6.0	0314	7.5	0057	4.4	0106	4.2	0437	0.7	0117	1.0	0449	5.7	0430	5.4
	0720	0.7	0800	0.6	0951	0.5	0649	0.7	0639	0.5	1041	2.8	0707	7.6	1118	0.5	1103	0.5
	1328	5.0	1403	6.0	1527	7.4	1309	4.4	1318	4.2	1712	0.4	1345	0.7	1715	5.5	1700	5.1
	1950	0.5	2030	0.4	2215	0.3	1921	0.4	1907	0.2	2318	2.5	1937	7.3	2327	1.0	2311	0.9

EAST COAST OF ENGLAND Time Zone UT

Margate * Sheerness * London Bridge * Walton-on-the-Naze * Harwich * Lowestoft * Immingham * River Tees * River Tyne

TIDE TABLES OCTOBER 2000

MARGATE Time m	SHEERNESS Time m	LONDON BRIDGE Time m	WALTON-ON THE-NAZE Time m	HARWICH Time m	LOWESTOFT Time m	IMMINGHAM Time m	RIVER TEES Time m	RIVER TYNE Time m	Day
0157 4.8	0228 5.9	0351 7.3	0134 4.3	0142 4.1	0514 0.7	0151 1.1	0526 5.6	0510 5.2	**1 SU**
0755 0.8	0835 0.7	1021 0.6	0728 0.7	0718 0.5	1123 2.7	0745 7.5	1153 0.8	1138 0.7	
1403 4.9	1440 5.9	1603 7.3	1347 4.4	1354 4.2	1748 0.5	1418 1.0	1750 5.3	1736 5.0	
2024 0.7	2102 0.6	2241 0.5	1957 0.5	1944 0.3	2356 2.4	2010 7.1		2346 1.1	
0228 4.7	0303 5.7	0424 7.1	0210 4.2	0217 4.0	0550 0.8	0224 1.4	0001 1.2	0551 5.0	**2 M**
0829 0.9	0906 0.9	1045 0.8	0805 0.8	0755 0.6	1204 2.6	0822 7.1	0604 5.3	1212 1.0	
1439 4.8	1515 5.7	1637 7.0	1424 4.2	1430 4.0	1822 0.7	1448 1.4	1227 1.2	1814 4.7	
2056 0.9	2129 0.8	2302 0.8	2032 0.7	2020 0.6		2042 6.8	1827 5.1		
0258 4.5	0336 5.5	0457 6.8	0245 4.0	0250 3.8	0031 2.3	0254 1.7	0036 1.5	0021 1.3	**3 TU**
0903 1.0	0933 1.1	1107 1.0	0840 0.9	0830 0.8	0627 0.9	0858 6.7	0646 5.0	0633 4.7	
1515 4.6	1551 5.4	1713 6.7	1502 4.0	1506 3.8	1248 2.4	1515 1.9	1303 1.6	1246 1.4	
2130 1.1	2153 1.1	2326 0.9	2106 1.0	2054 0.8	1856 0.9	2115 6.5	1907 4.8	1854 4.5	
0332 4.3	0409 5.2	0531 6.5	0319 3.8	0324 3.6	0109 2.3	0324 2.1	0115 1.8	0101 1.6	**4 W**
0942 1.2	0958 1.3	1135 1.0	0916 1.1	0906 1.0	0707 1.0	0938 6.2	0735 4.7	0721 4.4	
1558 4.3	1629 5.2	1753 6.4	1543 3.8	1543 3.6	1341 2.3	1548 2.3	1344 2.0	1326 1.8	
2210 1.4	2221 1.3	2358 1.1	2143 1.2	2132 1.0	1934 1.1	2152 6.1	1956 4.5	1939 4.3	
0415 4.1	0446 5.0	0609 6.1	0358 3.6	0400 3.4	0154 2.2	0403 2.5	0203 2.1	0150 1.9	**5 TH**
1032 1.4	1033 1.4	1211 1.2	1000 1.2	0947 1.1	0757 1.1	1030 5.8	0835 4.3	0817 4.1	
1654 4.1	1715 4.8	1842 6.0	1631 3.5	1627 3.3	1448 2.2	1630 2.8	1434 2.3	1418 2.1	
2306 1.6	2304 1.6		2234 1.4	2221 1.3	2023 1.3	2245 5.8	2056 4.3	2036 4.0	
0514 3.9	0534 4.7	0040 1.3	0447 3.4	0443 3.2	0251 2.2	0500 2.9	0306 2.3	0259 2.1	**6 F**
1142 1.6	1128 1.7	0659 5.8	1104 1.4	1051 1.3	0906 1.2	1154 5.4	0948 4.1	0928 3.9	
1808 3.8	1818 4.5	1257 1.4	1735 3.3	1727 3.1	1609 2.1	1738 3.2	1543 2.6	1533 2.3	
		1945 5.7	2350 1.6	2333 1.4	2139 1.4		2209 4.2	2148 3.9	
0017 1.8	0011 1.9	0134 1.6	0555 3.2	0545 3.0	0358 2.2	0008 5.5	0434 2.4	0436 2.1	**7 SA**
0632 3.8	0641 4.4	0804 5.5	1244 1.4	1227 1.3	1103 1.1	0639 3.1	1112 4.1	1056 3.8	
1309 1.6	1300 1.8	1357 1.7	1911 3.2	1906 3.0	1737 2.2	1334 5.4	1715 2.6	1711 2.3	
1938 3.8	1942 4.4	2103 5.5			2333 1.4	1927 3.3	2327 4.2	2313 4.0	
0137 1.8	0152 2.0	0255 1.9	0130 1.5	0109 1.4	0511 2.2	0142 5.6	0611 2.2	0605 2.0	**8 SU**
0752 3.9	0809 4.5	0925 5.4	0736 3.2	0726 3.0	1215 1.0	0820 2.8	1226 4.3	1216 4.0	
1435 1.5	1449 1.6	1558 1.8	1417 1.2	1403 1.1	1849 2.2	1450 5.7	1837 2.4	1826 2.1	
2054 4.0	2109 4.7	2232 5.7	2035 3.4	2036 3.2		2045 3.0			
0251 1.6	0317 1.7	0437 1.6	0239 1.4	0227 1.3	0030 1.3	0252 6.0	0033 4.5	0024 4.2	**9 M**
0857 4.0	0929 4.7	1054 5.7	0849 3.4	0850 3.2	0620 2.3	0922 2.4	0712 1.9	0701 1.7	
1536 1.3	1557 1.3	1718 1.4	1514 1.0	1501 0.9	1305 0.9	1543 6.1	1321 4.5	1310 4.3	
2148 4.2	2210 5.1	2336 6.1	2128 3.7	2132 3.5	1939 2.3	2139 2.5	1929 2.1	1916 1.9	
0346 1.4	0413 1.4	0537 1.3	0328 1.2	0318 1.1	0110 1.2	0342 6.4	0124 4.7	0113 4.4	**10 TU**
0947 4.3	1026 5.1	1151 6.1	0939 3.7	0943 3.5	0710 2.3	1009 1.9	0755 1.6	0743 1.4	
1622 1.1	1647 1.0	1813 1.0	1557 0.8	1544 0.7	1345 0.8	1624 6.5	1403 4.8	1351 4.5	
2230 4.4	2257 5.4		2210 3.9	2216 3.7	2015 2.3	2221 2.1	2010 1.8	1956 1.6	
0429 1.2	0458 1.2	0021 6.4	0407 1.0	0357 0.9	0144 1.1	0421 6.7	0206 5.0	0151 4.7	**11 W**
1030 4.5	1111 5.4	0629 1.0	1020 3.9	1027 3.7	0750 2.4	1051 1.6	0832 1.3	0819 1.1	
1700 0.9	1729 0.8	1233 6.5	1635 0.7	1621 0.6	1422 0.7	1659 6.8	1439 5.0	1424 4.7	
2307 4.6	2337 5.7	1903 0.8	2248 4.1	2254 3.8	2045 2.4	2300 1.8	2046 1.5	2030 1.3	
0506 1.0	0537 1.0	0059 6.8	0443 0.8	0431 0.8	0217 1.0	0457 7.0	0241 5.2	0225 4.9	**12 TH**
1107 4.7	1150 5.6	0718 0.8	1058 4.1	1105 3.9	0826 2.5	1129 1.3	0907 1.0	0853 0.9	
1735 0.8	1808 0.7	1311 6.9	1710 0.5	1655 0.4	1457 0.6	1731 7.0	1512 5.2	1457 4.9	
2341 4.7		1949 0.6	2324 4.3	2331 4.0	2112 2.4	2339 1.5	2121 1.3	2104 1.1	
0541 0.9	0015 5.8	0135 7.1	0518 0.7	0506 0.6	0253 0.9	0532 7.3	0314 5.4	0258 5.1	**13 F** O
1142 4.8	0615 0.9	0803 0.6	1135 4.3	1142 4.0	0903 2.6	1206 1.1	0942 0.8	0927 0.7	
1809 0.7	1227 5.8	1346 7.1	1745 0.5	1730 0.3	1533 0.5	1803 7.1	1543 5.3	1529 5.1	
	1845 0.6	2032 0.4			2142 2.5		2155 1.1	2138 0.9	
0014 4.8	0051 5.9	0211 7.3	0000 4.4	0008 4.1	0331 0.8	0016 1.3	0346 5.5	0330 5.2	**14 SA**
0616 0.8	0652 0.8	0846 0.5	0554 0.6	0541 0.5	0939 2.7	0606 7.4	1016 0.7	1000 0.6	
1216 5.0	1303 5.9	1421 7.3	1212 4.4	1219 4.1	1609 0.5	1242 0.9	1615 5.4	1601 5.1	
1843 0.6	1923 0.6	2112 0.3	1821 0.4	1806 0.3	2213 2.5	1836 7.2	2229 1.0	2212 0.8	
0047 4.9	0127 5.9	0246 7.4	0036 4.4	0044 4.2	0409 0.7	0054 1.1	0419 5.6	0405 5.3	**15 SU**
0653 0.7	0730 0.7	0926 0.5	0630 0.6	0617 0.5	1017 2.7	0641 7.5	1051 0.7	1035 0.6	
1251 5.0	1338 5.9	1457 7.5	1248 4.4	1256 4.1	1645 0.5	1318 0.9	1648 5.4	1635 5.1	
1919 0.6	2000 0.6	2150 0.4	1857 0.4	1841 0.3	2248 2.5	1909 7.3	2303 0.9	2248 0.8	

• • Time: UT. For British Summer Time (shaded) March 26th to October 29th ADD ONE HOUR • •

OCTOBER 2000 TIDE TABLES

•• Time: UT. For British Summer Time (shaded) March 26th to October 29th ADD ONE HOUR ••

	MARGATE Time	m	SHEERNESS Time	m	LONDON BRIDGE Time	m	WALTON-ON-THE-NAZE Time	m	HARWICH Time	m	LOWESTOFT Time	m	IMMINGHAM Time	m	RIVER TEES Time	m	RIVER TYNE Time	m
16 M	0121	4.9	0203	5.9	0322	7.4	0112	4.4	0121	4.1	0448	0.7	0130	1.1	0456	5.6	0442	5.3
	0731	0.8	0807	0.7	1002	0.6	0707	0.6	0654	0.5	1056	2.7	0717	7.5	1126	0.8	1110	0.7
	1327	5.0	1414	5.9	1532	7.5	1324	4.4	1333	4.1	1721	0.5	1354	1.0	1724	5.4	1711	5.1
	1957	0.7	2034	0.6	2222	0.5	1933	0.5	1917	0.4	2325	2.5	1942	7.2	2341	1.0	2325	0.9
17 TU	0159	4.8	0239	5.8	0358	7.2	0148	4.3	0157	4.0	0528	0.7	0207	1.2	0537	5.4	0524	5.2
	0811	0.9	0842	0.8	1032	0.7	0745	0.7	0731	0.6	1137	2.6	0756	7.4	1205	1.0	1148	0.9
	1406	4.9	1451	5.8	1610	7.3	1403	4.3	1410	4.1	1759	0.6	1428	1.2	1806	5.2	1751	4.9
	2036	0.9	2106	0.8	2248	0.8	2009	0.7	1954	0.5			2020	7.0				
18 W	0239	4.7	0318	5.6	0437	6.9	0227	4.1	0235	3.9	0006	2.4	0245	1.4	0023	1.1	0006	1.0
	0852	1.0	0918	0.9	1057	0.9	0825	0.8	0812	0.6	0611	0.7	0839	7.1	0625	5.2	0611	5.0
	1451	4.8	1534	5.7	1653	7.0	1445	4.2	1451	4.0	1223	2.5	1505	1.6	1248	1.3	1230	1.2
	2117	1.1	2140	0.9	2312	1.0	2048	0.8	2036	0.7	1840	0.8	2101	6.7	1854	5.0	1837	4.7
19 TH	0324	4.5	0400	5.4	0519	6.5	0309	4.0	0317	3.7	0050	2.4	0326	1.7	0112	1.4	0055	1.2
	0939	1.2	1000	1.0	1131	1.1	0911	0.9	0858	0.7	0701	0.8	0929	6.7	0722	4.9	0706	4.7
	1545	4.6	1624	5.4	1742	6.6	1534	4.0	1539	3.8	1319	2.4	1548	2.0	1340	1.6	1321	1.5
	2206	1.3	2224	1.2	2350	1.2	2137	1.0	2125	0.9	1930	1.0	2152	6.4	1952	4.7	1933	4.5
20 F	0419	4.3	0452	5.1	0609	6.1	0400	3.8	0406	3.6	0144	2.3	0418	2.0	0212	1.6	0157	1.4
	1039	1.3	1054	1.2	1218	1.2	1009	1.0	0957	0.9	0803	0.8	1036	6.3	0833	4.6	0814	4.4
	1651	4.3	1726	5.2	1842	6.2	1635	3.8	1638	3.6	1435	2.3	1645	2.4	1445	2.0	1429	1.8
	2314	1.5	2326	1.4			2242	1.2	2230	1.1	2036	1.1	2301	6.1	2103	4.5	2043	4.3
21 SA	0526	4.1	0558	4.9	0042	1.5	0505	3.6	0509	3.4	0253	2.2	0533	2.3	0330	1.8	0318	1.6
	1203	1.3	1212	1.3	0715	5.8	1125	1.0	1114	0.9	0921	0.8	1208	6.0	0956	4.4	0937	4.3
	1809	4.2	1844	5.0	1321	1.4	1751	3.7	1752	3.5	1604	2.3	1809	2.7	1610	2.2	1559	2.0
					1959	6.1			2354	1.2	2201	1.2			2224	4.5	2207	4.2
22 SU	0041	1.6	0054	1.6	0159	1.7	0006	1.4	0626	3.3	0408	2.3	0032	1.6	0503	1.7	0451	1.5
	0645	4.1	0719	4.8	0836	5.9	0627	3.5	1243	0.9	1050	0.8	0708	2.2	1123	4.5	1107	4.3
	1330	1.2	1350	1.2	1500	1.3	1257	1.0	1920	3.5	1734	2.3	1343	6.1	1744	2.1	1731	1.9
	1941	4.3	2011	5.1	2121	6.2	1921	3.7			2325	1.2	1942	2.6	2343	4.6	2330	4.4
23 M	0203	1.4	0227	1.5	0337	1.5	0138	1.3	0121	1.2	0521	2.3	0200	6.2	0625	1.4	0611	1.3
	0807	4.3	0844	5.0	0957	6.1	0754	3.6	0751	3.4	1209	0.7	0834	1.9	1236	4.7	1222	4.5
	1448	1.0	1518	1.0	1632	0.9	1424	0.8	1407	0.7	1851	2.4	1501	6.5	1856	1.9	1839	1.7
	2103	4.5	2130	5.4	2242	6.6	2040	3.9	2044	3.7			2100	2.3				
24 TU	0315	1.2	0345	1.3	0459	1.1	0251	1.1	0237	1.0	0033	1.1	0309	6.6	0049	4.9	0036	4.7
	0918	4.5	0957	5.3	1114	6.6	0903	3.8	0908	3.6	0628	2.4	0942	1.4	0725	1.1	0712	1.0
	1555	0.6	1630	0.7	1759	0.4	1528	0.6	1515	0.5	1314	0.5	1601	6.8	1333	5.0	1319	4.8
	2206	4.7	2234	5.7	2351	7.1	2142	4.1	2148	3.9	1945	2.4	2200	1.9	1948	1.6	1933	1.4
25 W	0415	1.0	0446	1.0	0621	0.8	0345	1.0	0335	0.9	0129	1.0	0403	7.0	0143	5.2	0128	4.9
	1017	4.7	1054	5.6	1215	7.0	0959	4.0	1007	3.8	0723	2.5	1037	1.1	0814	0.8	0802	0.7
	1650	0.5	1726	0.5	1905	0.1	1618	0.5	1607	0.3	1406	0.5	1648	7.1	1420	5.3	1405	5.0
	2300	4.8	2326	5.9			2232	4.2	2239	4.1	2027	2.5	2250	1.5	2033	1.3	2018	1.2
26 TH	0503	0.9	0535	0.9	0046	7.4	0430	0.9	0420	0.7	0215	0.9	0447	7.3	0229	5.4	0212	5.2
	1106	4.8	1142	5.8	0721	0.5	1046	4.2	1055	4.0	0809	2.6	1123	0.9	0857	0.6	0845	0.6
	1735	0.4	1811	0.5	1306	7.2	1701	0.4	1649	0.2	1450	0.4	1727	7.2	1500	5.3	1445	5.1
	2343	4.8			1955	-0.0	2316	4.3	2324	4.1	2103	2.5	2333	1.3	2113	1.1	2057	1.0
27 F	0543	0.8	0010	5.9	0133	7.4	0509	0.8	0500	0.6	0257	0.8	0527	7.5	0309	5.6	0252	5.3
	1148	4.9	0616	0.8	0809	0.4	1128	4.3	1138	4.1	0853	2.7	1203	0.8	0936	0.6	0924	0.5
	1812	0.5	1223	5.8	1348	7.3	1739	0.4	1727	0.2	1530	0.4	1800	7.3	1536	5.5	1521	5.2
			1849	0.5	2038	0.1	2356	4.3			2137	2.5			2150	1.0	2135	0.9
28 SA	0021	4.8	0049	5.9	0213	7.4	0548	0.7	0003	4.1	0336	0.7	0013	1.1	0347	5.6	0330	5.3
	0618	0.7	0654	0.7	0848	0.5	1207	4.3	0538	0.5	0936	2.7	0605	7.5	1012	0.6	1000	0.6
	1224	4.9	1301	5.9	1427	7.3	1816	0.4	1216	4.1	1607	0.4	1241	0.8	1610	5.5	1557	5.2
	1845	0.6	1923	0.5	2113	0.3			1803	0.3	2213	2.5	1833	7.3	2225	1.0	2211	0.9
29 SU ●	0053	4.8	0124	5.9	0250	7.3	0033	4.3	0039	4.1	0415	0.7	0051	1.1	0423	5.6	0409	5.3
	0653	0.7	0730	0.7	0923	0.6	0627	0.7	0616	0.5	1019	2.7	0643	7.5	1046	0.8	1033	0.7
	1300	4.9	1337	5.9	1503	7.3	1245	4.3	1253	4.1	1642	0.5	1315	1.0	1642	5.4	1631	5.2
	1918	0.6	1955	0.6	2142	0.5	1852	0.5	1839	0.3	2248	2.5	1906	7.3	2258	1.1	2246	1.0
30 M	0123	4.8	0159	5.8	0324	7.2	0107	4.2	0114	4.0	0451	0.7	0125	1.2	0459	5.4	0447	5.1
	0727	0.8	0806	0.7	0951	0.6	0704	0.7	0654	0.5	1101	2.6	0721	7.3	1118	1.0	1106	0.9
	1336	4.8	1412	5.8	1537	7.2	1322	4.3	1328	4.1	1716	0.7	1346	1.2	1716	5.3	1706	5.0
	1950	0.8	2026	0.7	2206	0.6	1927	0.7	1915	0.5	2322	2.5	1939	7.1	2332	1.2	2321	1.1
31 TU	0153	4.7	0232	5.7	0355	7.0	0141	4.1	0147	3.9	0527	0.8	0157	1.4	0536	5.2	0526	4.9
	0803	0.9	0838	0.9	1015	0.8	0741	0.8	0730	0.6	1142	2.5	0757	7.0	1151	1.3	1139	1.2
	1412	4.7	1448	5.7	1611	7.0	1358	4.1	1403	3.9	1747	0.8	1415	1.6	1751	5.1	1741	4.8
	2022	1.0	2053	0.9	2230	0.8	1959	0.9	1948	0.7	2354	2.4	2010	6.9			2356	1.3

EAST COAST OF ENGLAND Time Zone UT

Margate * Sheerness * London Bridge * Walton-on-the-Naze * Harwich * Lowestoft * Immingham * River Tees * River Tyne

TIDE TABLES NOVEMBER 2000

MARGATE		SHEERNESS		LONDON BRIDGE		WALTON-ON-THE-NAZE		HARWICH		LOWESTOFT		IMMINGHAM		RIVER TEES		RIVER TYNE			
Time	m	Time	m	Time	m	Time	m	Time	m	Time	m	Time	m	Time	m	Time	m		
0223	4.6	0303	5.5	0425	6.8	0212	4.0	0218	3.8	0603	0.9	0227	1.7	0007	1.4	0607	4.6	1	W
0837	1.0	0904	1.0	1039	0.9	0815	0.9	0803	0.8	1226	2.4	0833	6.6	0617	4.9	1212	1.5		
1448	4.5	1522	5.4	1645	6.7	1434	3.9	1437	3.8	1816	1.0	1442	1.9	1226	1.7	1818	4.6		
2055	1.2	2117	1.1	2256	0.9	2030	1.1	2020	0.9			2042	6.6	1831	4.9				
0256	4.4	0334	5.3	0457	6.5	0244	3.8	0249	3.6	0028	2.4	0257	2.0	0045	1.7	0033	1.5	2	TH
0914	1.2	0929	1.2	1109	0.9	0848	1.0	0836	0.9	0642	0.9	0911	6.2	0703	4.6	0652	4.4		
1528	4.3	1559	5.2	1724	6.4	1512	3.7	1513	3.6	1316	2.3	1512	2.3	1305	2.0	1249	1.8		
2133	1.4	2145	1.3	2329	1.1	2103	1.3	2054	1.1	1849	1.1	2117	6.3	1918	4.7	1900	4.4		
0336	4.2	0409	5.0	0533	6.2	0319	3.7	0322	3.5	0108	2.3	0333	2.4	0132	2.0	0118	1.7	3	F
0959	1.4	1001	1.3	1144	1.0	0927	1.2	0915	1.0	0729	1.0	0957	5.8	0800	4.4	0744	4.1		
1617	4.1	1642	4.9	1809	6.1	1556	3.5	1554	3.4	1419	2.2	1551	2.8	1354	2.3	1336	2.1		
2224	1.6	2225	1.6			2149	1.4	2137	1.3	1933	1.3	2203	5.9	2014	4.4	1952	4.2		
0430	4.1	0452	4.8	0009	1.3	0403	3.5	0401	3.3	0200	2.3	0421	2.7	0229	2.2	0217	1.9	4	SA
1100	1.5	1051	1.5	0616	5.9	1022	1.3	1009	1.1	0827	1.0	1104	5.5	0906	4.2	0846	3.9		
1719	3.9	1736	4.6	1227	1.2	1651	3.4	1643	3.2	1532	2.1	1645	3.2	1456	2.6	1442	2.3		
2327	1.8	2322	1.8	1904	5.8	2254	1.6	2241	1.4	2032	1.4	2308	5.7	2121	4.3	2057	4.0		
0537	3.9	0551	4.6	0058	1.6	0501	3.5	0453	3.2	0302	2.2	0536	2.9	0342	2.3	0336	2.0	5	SU
1215	1.6	1203	1.7	0712	5.6	1136	1.3	1128	1.2	0951	1.1	1234	5.4	1021	4.1	1001	3.8		
1837	3.8	1848	4.5	1320	1.5	1803	3.3	1754	3.1	1648	2.1	1810	3.4	1617	2.7	1609	2.4		
				2014	5.6					2203	1.5			2233	4.3	2212	4.0		
0040	1.8	0042	2.0	0159	1.8	0016	1.6	0005	1.5	0411	2.2	0036	5.6	0506	2.2	0504	2.0	6	M
0655	3.9	0707	4.5	0828	5.4	0619	3.2	0606	3.1	1120	1.0	0719	2.8	1134	4.2	1121	3.9		
1334	1.5	1342	1.6	1430	1.7	1309	1.2	1254	1.1	1759	2.2	1354	5.6	1740	2.5	1734	2.3		
1954	3.9	2008	4.6	2131	5.6	1933	3.4	1928	3.2	2332	1.4	1948	3.2	2339	4.4	2327	4.1		
0154	1.7	0214	1.9	0328	1.8	0139	1.4	0124	1.4	0519	2.2	0154	5.8	0617	2.0	0611	1.7	7	TU
0805	4.0	0828	4.6	0951	5.5	0746	3.4	0738	3.1	1216	0.9	0830	2.5	1233	4.4	1222	4.2		
1442	1.3	1501	1.4	1615	1.5	1421	1.0	1402	0.9	1854	2.3	1453	5.9	1843	2.3	1833	2.0		
2056	4.1	2118	4.9	2241	5.9	2039	3.4	2039	3.4			2051	2.8						
0257	1.5	0321	1.6	0448	1.5	0240	1.2	0224	1.2	0020	1.3	0252	6.2	0036	4.6	0025	4.3	8	W
0901	4.2	0935	5.0	1059	5.9	0850	3.6	0848	3.4	0618	2.3	0924	2.1	0709	1.7	0700	1.5		
1536	1.1	1559	1.1	1722	1.2	1513	0.8	1454	0.7	1300	0.8	1539	6.3	1320	4.7	1309	4.4		
2145	4.4	2212	5.3	2336	6.3	2128	3.9	2131	3.6	1933	2.3	2140	2.3	1930	2.0	1917	1.7		
0348	1.3	0414	1.3	0545	1.2	0327	1.0	0311	1.0	0101	1.2	0339	6.6	0122	4.9	0110	4.6	9	TH
0949	4.4	1027	5.3	1150	6.3	0939	3.9	0941	3.6	0707	2.4	1009	1.7	0753	1.4	0740	1.2		
1620	0.9	1647	0.9	1818	0.8	1557	0.6	1539	0.6	1340	0.7	1620	6.7	1400	5.0	1347	4.7		
2228	4.6	2258	5.6			2211	4.1	2216	3.9	2006	2.4	2224	1.9	2012	1.6	1956	1.4		
0430	1.1	0459	1.1	0020	6.7	0409	0.9	0353	0.8	0142	1.0	0420	6.9	0203	5.2	0148	4.8	10	F
1031	4.6	1112	5.6	0639	0.9	1022	4.1	1027	3.8	0750	2.5	1052	1.4	0833	1.1	0818	0.9		
1659	0.7	1731	0.7	1233	6.7	1637	0.5	1619	0.4	1420	0.6	1657	6.9	1437	5.2	1423	4.9		
2307	4.8	2341	5.8	1911	0.6	2252	4.2	2257	4.0	2037	2.5	2306	1.6	2051	1.4	2033	1.2		
0509	0.9	0542	0.9	0101	7.0	0448	0.7	0433	0.6	0224	0.9	0458	7.2	0241	5.4	0226	5.1	11	SA
1109	4.8	1154	5.8	0730	0.7	1104	4.3	1110	4.0	0830	2.6	1133	1.1	0911	0.9	0855	0.8		O
1736	0.6	1813	0.6	1313	7.1	1715	0.5	1659	0.4	1500	0.5	1732	7.2	1512	5.4	1457	5.1		
2344	4.9			2000	0.4	2332	4.4	2339	4.1	2111	2.5	2348	1.3	2128	1.1	2110	1.0		
0548	0.8	0021	5.9	0141	7.3	0527	0.7	0513	0.5	0306	0.8	0537	7.4	0319	5.6	0303	5.2	12	SU
1146	5.0	0624	0.8	0818	0.6	1145	4.4	1152	4.1	0912	2.6	1213	1.0	0949	0.8	0933	0.7		
1814	0.5	1234	5.9	1353	7.3	1754	0.5	1738	0.3	1539	0.5	1808	7.3	1548	5.5	1533	5.2		
		1854	0.6	2045	0.4					2146	2.6			2206	1.0	2149	0.8		
0021	4.9	0101	5.9	0221	7.4	0011	4.4	0019	4.2	0350	0.7	0030	1.1	0358	5.7	0342	5.3	13	M
0629	0.7	0706	0.7	0902	0.5	0607	0.6	0554	0.5	0953	2.7	0617	7.5	1027	0.7	1011	0.6		
1225	5.1	1314	6.0	1433	7.5	1224	4.4	1233	4.2	1619	0.5	1253	0.9	1626	5.6	1610	5.2		
1854	0.5	1934	0.6	2126	0.4	1832	0.5	1817	0.4	2224	2.6	1845	7.4	2246	0.9	2229	0.8		
0100	4.9	0141	5.9	0300	7.4	0050	4.4	0100	4.1	0433	0.6	0111	1.0	0440	5.6	0425	5.3	14	TU
0712	0.7	0748	0.7	0943	0.5	0648	0.6	0634	0.5	1036	2.7	0659	7.5	1107	0.8	1051	0.7		
1309	5.1	1355	6.0	1514	7.6	1306	4.4	1315	4.2	1659	0.6	1332	1.0	1706	5.5	1650	5.2		
1937	0.6	2012	0.6	2203	0.6	1910	0.6	1857	0.4	2303	2.5	1923	7.4	2328	0.9	2312	0.9		
0144	4.9	0221	5.8	0340	7.3	0129	4.3	0139	4.0	0519	0.6	0152	1.1	0527	5.5	0512	5.2	15	W
0758	0.7	0830	0.7	1021	0.5	0730	0.6	0716	0.5	1124	2.6	0743	7.4	1150	1.0	1133	0.9		
1358	5.0	1439	5.9	1558	7.4	1348	4.3	1357	4.1	1741	0.7	1412	1.2	1751	5.4	1734	5.1		
2022	0.8	2051	0.8	2238	0.7	1951	0.7	1938	0.6	2346	2.5	2004	7.2			2359	0.9		

● ● Time: UT. For British Summer Time (shaded) March 26th to October 29th ADD ONE HOUR ● ●

NOVEMBER 2000 TIDE TABLES

•• Time: UT. For British Summer Time (shaded) March 26th to October 29th ADD ONE HOUR ••

	MARGATE Time	m	SHEERNESS Time	m	LONDON BRIDGE Time	m	WALTON-ON-THE-NAZE Time	m	HARWICH Time	m	LOWESTOFT Time	m	IMMINGHAM Time	m	RIVER TEES Time	m	RIVER TYNE Time	m
16 TH	0230	4.7	0303	5.6	0424	7.0	0210	4.1	0220	3.9	0607	0.6	0236	1.2	0015	1.0	0604	5.0
	0847	0.8	0914	0.7	1059	0.7	0815	0.6	0801	0.5	1216	2.5	0833	7.1	0619	5.3	1219	1.2
	1451	4.8	1526	5.7	1647	7.2	1435	4.2	1442	4.0	1826	0.8	1453	1.6	1237	1.3	1824	4.9
	2110	1.1	2131	0.9	2313	1.0	2034	0.9	2023	0.7			2050	6.9	1842	5.2		
17 F	0319	4.5	0349	5.4	0512	6.6	0256	4.0	0304	3.8	0033	2.4	0323	1.5	0108	1.2	0052	1.0
	0941	1.0	1002	0.8	1139	0.9	0906	0.7	0852	0.6	0701	0.6	0930	6.7	0719	5.0	0703	4.8
	1548	4.6	1620	5.5	1741	6.8	1528	4.1	1533	3.9	1320	2.4	1540	2.0	1331	1.7	1314	1.6
	2204	1.3	2219	1.2	2354	1.3	2125	1.1	2115	0.9	1918	1.0	2143	6.6	1940	4.9	1921	4.6
18 SA	0412	4.4	0443	5.2	0605	6.3	0349	3.8	0354	3.6	0127	2.4	0419	1.7	0209	1.4	0155	1.2
	1045	1.1	1100	1.0	1227	1.1	1006	0.8	0952	0.7	0803	0.6	1038	6.4	0828	4.7	0810	4.5
	1650	4.4	1722	5.3	1842	6.5	1630	3.9	1631	3.7	1437	2.3	1638	2.4	1435	2.0	1421	1.8
	2308	1.5	2321	1.4			2228	1.2	2218	1.1	2021	1.2	2248	6.3	2048	4.7	2029	4.5
19 SU	0513	4.2	0548	5.0	0045	1.5	0453	3.7	0454	3.5	0230	2.3	0530	1.9	0322	1.5	0310	1.3
	1159	1.1	1214	1.1	0707	6.1	1117	0.8	1103	0.7	0914	0.7	1201	6.2	0944	4.6	0927	4.3
	1803	4.3	1835	5.1	1330	1.2	1741	3.8	1742	3.6	1601	2.3	1751	2.6	1552	2.1	1542	2.0
					1949	6.3	2343	1.3	2332	1.2	2138	1.3			2202	4.6	2148	4.4
20 M	0023	1.5	0037	1.5	0153	1.6	0606	3.6	0606	3.4	0341	2.3	0009	6.2	0442	1.5	0433	1.4
	0624	4.2	0701	4.9	0817	6.1	1240	0.8	1224	0.7	1031	0.6	0651	1.9	1101	4.6	1048	4.3
	1316	1.0	1337	1.0	1450	1.1	1900	3.8	1900	3.6	1722	2.3	1324	6.2	1715	2.1	1705	1.9
	1925	4.3	1952	5.2	2103	6.4					2257	1.3	1914	2.6	2316	4.7	2306	4.5
21 TU	0140	1.4	0200	1.5	0315	1.5	0107	1.3	0052	1.2	0454	2.3	0132	6.3	0557	1.4	0548	1.2
	0741	4.3	0818	5.0	0932	6.2	0725	3.6	0723	3.5	1145	0.6	0808	1.8	1209	4.7	1158	4.5
	1429	0.8	1455	0.9	1609	0.8	1400	0.7	1343	0.6	1831	2.3	1436	6.4	1826	1.9	1813	1.8
	2040	4.4	2106	5.4	2218	6.6	2015	3.9	2016	3.7			2029	2.4				
22 W	0251	1.3	0314	1.3	0430	1.2	0222	1.2	0206	1.1	0006	1.2	0242	6.6	0021	4.9	0012	4.6
	0851	4.4	0929	5.3	1048	6.5	0836	3.8	0837	3.6	0603	2.4	0915	1.5	0658	1.2	0648	1.1
	1533	0.6	1602	0.7	1727	0.5	1504	0.6	1450	0.5	1249	0.6	1535	6.6	1306	4.9	1255	4.6
	2144	4.6	2209	5.5	2327	6.9	2117	4.0	2121	3.8	1924	2.4	2132	2.1	1922	1.7	1909	1.5
23 TH	0353	1.1	0415	1.1	0547	1.0	0320	1.1	0307	0.9	0104	1.1	0337	6.8	0117	5.0	0106	4.8
	0951	4.6	1028	5.5	1151	6.8	0933	3.9	0939	3.7	0701	2.5	1009	1.4	0748	1.0	0739	1.0
	1628	0.5	1657	0.7	1834	0.3	1555	0.5	1542	0.4	1342	0.6	1621	6.8	1354	5.1	1342	4.8
	2236	4.7	2301	5.7			2209	4.1	2214	3.9	2005	2.4	2224	1.8	2009	1.5	1955	1.3
24 F	0442	0.9	0506	1.0	0023	7.2	0407	0.9	0356	0.8	0153	1.0	0424	7.0	0205	5.2	0153	5.0
	1042	4.7	1117	5.6	0651	0.7	1022	4.1	1030	3.9	0750	2.5	1055	1.2	0831	0.9	0821	0.9
	1712	0.5	1741	0.7	1242	7.0	1638	0.5	1625	0.4	1425	0.6	1700	7.0	1436	5.2	1422	4.9
	2319	4.7	2345	5.7	1925	0.2	2254	4.2	2259	4.0	2040	2.4	2308	1.5	2050	1.3	2036	1.2
25 SA	0522	0.8	0548	0.9	0110	7.2	0449	0.8	0438	0.7	0236	0.9	0505	7.2	0248	5.3	0234	5.0
	1125	4.7	1200	5.7	0740	0.6	1106	4.1	1114	3.9	0835	2.6	1136	1.2	0910	0.9	0859	0.9
	1747	0.6	1817	0.7	1327	7.1	1716	0.6	1703	0.4	1504	0.6	1734	7.1	1512	5.3	1459	5.0
	2354	4.7			2006	0.3	2333	4.2	2339	4.0	2114	2.5	2349	1.4	2127	1.2	2115	1.1
26 SU	0557	0.8	0024	5.7	0151	7.2	0529	0.8	0518	0.6	0316	0.8	0545	7.2	0327	5.4	0313	5.1
	1203	4.8	0627	0.8	0820	0.6	1146	4.2	1154	4.0	0919	2.6	1212	1.2	0945	1.0	0934	0.9
	1818	0.7	1238	5.7	1406	7.1	1751	0.6	1739	0.5	1540	0.6	1807	7.2	1546	5.3	1533	5.1
			1850	0.7	2040	0.5					2148	2.5			2203	1.1	2152	1.0
27 M	0025	4.7	0100	5.7	0226	7.2	0009	4.2	0015	4.0	0356	0.7	0027	1.3	0403	5.3	0351	5.0
	0632	0.7	0705	0.8	0854	0.6	0608	0.7	0557	0.5	1002	2.5	0624	7.2	1018	1.1	1008	1.0
	1239	4.8	1315	5.7	1441	7.1	1224	4.2	1231	4.0	1615	0.7	1246	1.3	1618	5.3	1608	5.0
	1849	0.7	1922	0.7	2110	0.6	1826	0.7	1815	0.5	2221	2.5	1841	7.2	2237	1.2	2227	1.1
28 TU ●	0055	4.7	0133	5.7	0259	7.1	0044	4.1	0049	3.9	0434	0.7	0103	1.4	0439	5.2	0430	4.9
	0708	0.7	0742	0.8	0925	0.6	0645	0.7	0634	0.6	1045	2.5	0702	7.1	1051	1.2	1041	1.1
	1316	4.7	1351	5.7	1515	7.1	1302	4.1	1306	3.9	1645	0.8	1318	1.5	1651	5.2	1642	5.0
	1923	0.8	1954	0.8	2137	0.7	1900	0.8	1849	0.6	2254	2.5	1913	7.1	2312	1.2	2303	1.1
29 W	0127	4.7	0206	5.6	0329	7.0	0116	4.1	0121	3.9	0511	0.8	0136	1.5	0516	5.1	0508	4.8
	0745	0.8	0815	0.8	0953	0.7	0721	0.8	0710	0.6	1126	2.4	0739	6.9	1124	1.4	1113	1.3
	1353	4.6	1426	5.6	1549	6.9	1337	4.0	1341	3.8	1714	0.9	1348	1.7	1727	5.1	1715	4.8
	1957	1.0	2023	0.9	2204	0.8	1932	0.9	1921	0.8	2325	2.5	1945	7.0	2347	1.4	2337	1.2
30 TH	0159	4.6	0237	5.5	0400	6.8	0147	4.0	0152	3.8	0547	0.8	0208	1.7	0557	4.9	0547	4.6
	0821	0.9	0845	1.0	1020	0.8	0755	0.9	0743	0.7	1208	2.3	0815	6.6	1200	1.6	1146	1.5
	1429	4.5	1500	5.4	1625	6.7	1412	3.9	1415	3.7	1742	1.0	1417	1.9	1806	5.0	1751	4.7
	2031	1.2	2051	1.1	2234	0.9	2003	1.1	1953	0.9	2357	2.4	2018	6.7				

EAST COAST OF ENGLAND Time Zone UT

Margate * Sheerness * London Bridge * Walton-on-the-Naze * Harwich * Lowestoft * Immingham * River Tees * River Tyne

TIDE TABLES DECEMBER 2000

Day	MARGATE Time	m	SHEERNESS Time	m	LONDON BRIDGE Time	m	WALTON-ON THE-NAZE Time	m	HARWICH Time	m	LOWESTOFT Time	m	IMMINGHAM Time	m	RIVER TEES Time	m	RIVER TYNE Time	m
1 F	0233	4.5	0309	5.3	0432	6.6	0218	3.9	0222	3.7	0624	0.8	0239	1.9	0026	1.6	0013	1.4
	0857	1.1	0912	1.1	1051	0.9	0828	0.9	0816	0.8	1254	2.2	0851	6.3	0640	4.7	0629	4.4
	1506	4.3	1537	5.2	1703	6.5	1448	3.8	1449	3.6	1814	1.1	1448	2.2	1239	1.9	1222	1.7
	2107	1.3	2122	1.2	2308	1.1	2036	1.2	2026	1.0			2052	6.5	1850	4.8	1830	4.5
2 SA	0310	4.4	0343	5.1	0506	6.4	0251	3.7	0254	3.5	0035	2.4	0314	2.1	0109	1.7	0054	1.5
	0936	1.2	0945	1.2	1125	1.0	0906	1.0	0853	0.9	0706	0.9	0931	6.0	0730	4.4	0715	4.2
	1548	4.2	1617	5.0	1743	6.3	1528	3.6	1527	3.5	1346	2.2	1524	2.5	1324	2.1	1304	1.9
	2149	1.5	2200	1.4	2345	1.2	2118	1.3	2106	1.2	1855	1.2	2132	6.2	1939	4.6	1916	4.3
3 SU	0357	4.2	0423	4.9	0546	6.1	0332	3.6	0333	3.4	0120	2.3	0355	2.4	0159	1.9	0143	1.7
	1023	1.3	1028	1.3	1205	1.1	0952	1.0	0939	0.9	0755	0.9	1021	5.7	0827	4.3	0806	4.1
	1639	4.1	1703	4.8	1829	6.0	1615	3.5	1612	3.4	1446	2.1	1607	2.8	1418	2.3	1357	2.1
	2242	1.6	2247	1.6			2212	1.4	2158	1.3	1946	1.3	2222	5.9	2036	4.4	2010	4.2
4 M	0452	4.1	0511	4.8	0029	1.4	0422	3.5	0420	3.3	0213	2.3	0448	2.6	0257	2.1	0242	1.8
	1122	1.4	1125	1.4	0630	5.9	1051	1.1	1040	1.0	0853	1.0	1126	5.5	0930	4.2	0907	3.9
	1739	4.0	1800	4.7	1251	1.2	1712	3.4	1706	3.3	1551	2.1	1705	3.1	1521	2.5	1503	2.3
	2343	1.7	2347	1.7	1922	5.8	2317	1.4	2306	1.3	2049	1.4	2327	5.8	2139	4.3	2113	4.1
5 TU	0557	4.0	0612	4.6	0119	1.6	0524	3.4	0518	3.2	0315	2.2	0558	2.7	0405	2.1	0352	1.9
	1230	1.4	1235	1.4	0725	5.7	1201	1.1	1153	1.0	1001	1.0	1241	5.6	1035	4.2	1015	3.9
	1848	3.9	1906	4.6	1347	1.4	1821	3.4	1814	3.2	1655	2.1	1821	3.1	1634	2.5	1621	2.3
					2030	5.7					2205	1.4			2242	4.4	2221	4.1
6 W	0053	1.7	0100	1.8	0221	1.8	0029	1.4	0021	1.3	0421	2.2	0043	5.8	0515	2.0	0504	1.8
	0706	4.0	0724	4.7	0841	5.6	0636	3.4	0629	3.2	1109	0.9	0717	2.5	1136	4.4	1121	4.1
	1342	1.3	1351	1.3	1457	1.4	1316	1.0	1303	0.9	1753	2.2	1348	5.8	1745	2.3	1732	2.1
	1957	4.1	2017	4.8	2140	5.6	1934	3.6	1929	3.3	2317	1.3	1942	2.9	2342	4.5	2326	4.2
7 TH	0203	1.6	0215	1.6	0339	1.7	0140	1.3	0127	1.2	0526	2.3	0151	6.1	0617	1.8	0606	1.6
	0810	4.1	0834	4.8	0957	5.8	0749	3.6	0743	3.4	1206	0.8	0824	2.3	1232	4.6	1218	4.3
	1445	1.1	1501	1.2	1617	1.2	1421	0.8	1403	0.7	1842	2.3	1446	6.1	1845	2.1	1829	1.9
	2056	4.3	2121	5.1	2243	6.2	2038	3.8	2036	3.5			2046	2.5				
8 F	0303	1.3	0321	1.4	0451	1.4	0240	1.1	0224	1.0	0015	1.2	0249	6.4	0037	4.8	0021	4.5
	0906	4.3	0937	5.1	1100	6.1	0852	3.8	0849	3.5	0623	2.4	0921	1.9	0711	1.5	0657	1.3
	1537	0.9	1600	1.0	1725	0.9	1516	0.7	1456	0.6	1257	0.7	1536	6.5	1320	4.8	1306	4.6
	2148	4.5	2217	5.4	2339	6.6	2132	4.0	2133	3.8	1925	2.3	2142	2.1	1936	1.8	1917	1.6
9 SA	0354	1.1	0418	1.2	0554	1.1	0332	0.9	0315	0.8	0106	1.1	0339	6.8	0127	5.0	0110	4.7
	0954	4.5	1032	5.4	1154	6.6	0945	4.0	0947	3.8	0714	2.4	1012	1.6	0759	1.3	0742	1.1
	1624	0.8	1654	0.8	1828	0.7	1603	0.6	1545	0.5	1343	0.6	1621	6.8	1404	5.1	1348	4.8
	2236	4.7	2308	5.6			2220	4.2	2224	3.9	2005	2.4	2233	1.7	2022	1.5	2002	1.3
10 SU	0441	0.9	0510	1.0	0029	6.9	0419	0.8	0403	0.7	0156	0.9	0427	7.1	0213	5.3	0156	5.0
	1039	4.7	1122	5.7	0654	0.8	1034	4.2	1039	3.9	0801	2.5	1100	1.3	0844	1.0	0826	0.9
	1707	0.6	1743	0.7	1243	6.9	1647	0.5	1631	0.4	1428	0.6	1704	7.1	1446	5.3	1430	5.0
	2319	4.8	2354	5.8	1927	0.4	2305	4.3	2312	4.0	2044	2.5	2321	1.4	2106	1.2	2046	1.0
11 M O	0525	0.8	0600	0.8	0115	7.1	0504	0.7	0450	0.7	0245	0.8	0513	7.3	0259	5.5	0241	5.2
	1124	4.9	1209	5.8	0751	0.6	1120	4.3	1128	4.1	0848	2.6	1146	1.1	0927	0.9	0909	0.8
	1751	0.6	1830	0.6	1330	7.2	1729	0.5	1715	0.4	1513	0.5	1745	7.3	1528	5.5	1510	5.2
					2020	0.5	2348	4.3	2357	4.1	2123	2.6			2151	0.8	2131	0.8
12 TU	0002	4.9	0039	5.9	0200	7.2	0548	0.6	0536	0.4	0335	0.7	0009	1.1	0345	5.6	0327	5.3
	0612	0.6	0648	0.7	0843	0.5	1206	4.4	1215	4.1	0936	2.6	0600	7.4	1012	0.8	0954	0.8
	1211	5.0	1256	5.9	1415	7.4	1811	0.5	1759	0.4	1557	0.5	1231	1.0	1611	5.6	1551	5.3
	1836	0.6	1914	0.6	2107	0.4					2204	2.6	1827	7.4	2236	0.8	2218	0.7
13 W	0047	4.9	0124	5.9	0244	7.3	0032	4.3	0042	4.1	0424	0.6	0057	1.0	0433	5.6	0415	5.3
	0700	0.6	0737	0.5	0930	0.4	0633	0.5	0621	0.4	1025	2.6	0648	7.5	1056	0.9	1038	0.8
	1303	5.0	1342	6.0	1503	7.5	1252	4.4	1301	4.2	1642	0.6	1316	1.0	1655	5.6	1636	5.3
	1924	0.6	1957	0.6	2151	0.5	1854	0.5	1842	0.5	2247	2.6	1910	7.4	2323	0.7	2306	0.6
14 TH	0135	4.9	0208	5.8	0329	7.3	0115	4.2	0126	4.0	0515	0.5	0144	0.9	0524	5.6	0506	5.3
	0751	0.5	0826	0.5	1017	0.3	0721	0.5	0707	0.3	1118	2.6	0739	7.3	1142	1.0	1124	1.0
	1358	5.0	1430	5.9	1551	7.5	1339	4.4	1348	4.2	1727	0.7	1400	1.2	1742	5.5	1722	5.2
	2013	0.8	2042	0.7	2233	0.6	1937	0.7	1927	0.5	2331	2.6	1954	7.3			2356	0.6
15 F	0224	4.8	0253	5.8	0415	7.1	0200	4.2	0209	3.9	0606	0.4	0232	1.0	0012	0.8	0559	5.1
	0845	0.6	0915	0.5	1101	0.4	0809	0.4	0756	0.3	1215	2.5	0832	7.1	0617	5.4	1213	1.2
	1453	4.9	1521	5.8	1642	7.4	1429	4.3	1435	4.1	1815	0.9	1445	1.5	1230	1.2	1812	5.1
	2104	0.9	2126	0.8	2315	0.8	2024	0.8	2014	0.7			2042	7.1	1833	5.4		

● ● Time: UT. For British Summer Time (shaded) March 26th to October 29th ADD ONE HOUR ● ●

DECEMBER 2000 TIDE TABLES

•• Time: UT. For British Summer Time (shaded) March 26th to October 29th ADD ONE HOUR ••

Date	MARGATE		SHEERNESS		LONDON BRIDGE		WALTON-ON-THE-NAZE		HARWICH		LOWESTOFT		IMMINGHAM		RIVER TEES		RIVER TYNE	
	Time	m	Time	m	Time	m	Time	m	Time	m	Time	m	Time	m	Time	m	Time	m
16 SA	0312	4.7	0342	5.6	0505	6.9	0248	4.1	0255	3.8	0019	2.5	0322	1.1	0105	0.9	0049	0.7
	0941	0.6	1006	0.6	1146	0.5	0902	0.5	0847	0.3	0658	0.4	0927	6.8	0714	5.1	0656	4.9
	1546	4.7	1614	5.7	1735	7.1	1521	4.2	1525	4.0	1318	2.4	1533	1.8	1322	1.5	1306	1.4
	2156	1.1	2214	1.0	2356	1.1	2114	1.0	2104	0.8	1905	1.0	2133	6.9	1928	5.2	1908	4.9
17 SU	0402	4.5	0433	5.4	0556	6.7	0339	3.9	0344	3.7	0110	2.5	0415	1.3	0202	1.1	0147	0.9
	1039	0.7	1101	0.7	1232	0.7	0957	0.5	0942	0.4	0754	0.5	1030	6.5	0815	4.9	0757	4.6
	1642	4.5	1712	5.5	1830	6.8	1618	4.0	1621	3.8	1426	2.3	1624	2.1	1420	1.8	1403	1.7
	2251	1.3	2307	1.2			2209	1.1	2200	1.0	2000	1.1	2230	6.6	2029	4.9	2009	4.7
18 M	0455	4.4	0530	5.2	0041	1.3	0436	3.8	0439	3.6	0208	2.4	0514	1.6	0305	1.2	0251	1.1
	1141	0.8	1201	0.8	0651	6.4	1100	0.6	1044	0.5	0855	0.5	1138	6.3	0921	4.7	0904	4.4
	1744	4.3	1814	5.3	1324	0.8	1719	3.8	1721	3.7	1540	2.2	1724	2.4	1525	2.0	1510	1.9
	2352	1.4			1930	6.6	2312	1.2	2302	1.1	2104	1.2	2338	6.4	2135	4.8	2119	4.6
19 TU	0556	4.3	0009	1.4	0135	1.5	0539	3.7	0540	3.6	0312	2.4	0619	1.8	0413	1.4	0401	1.3
	1249	0.8	0634	5.1	0751	6.3	1211	0.7	1154	0.5	1002	0.6	1250	6.2	1015	4.3	1015	4.3
	1854	4.2	1308	0.9	1425	0.9	1828	3.7	1829	3.6	1653	2.2	1833	2.5	1637	2.1	1624	1.9
			1921	5.2	2035	6.5					2215	1.3			2244	4.7	2232	4.5
20 W	0104	1.4	0118	1.4	0242	1.5	0025	1.3	0013	1.1	0424	2.4	0054	6.3	0522	1.4	0513	1.3
	0705	4.3	0743	5.1	0858	6.3	0648	3.7	0648	3.5	1112	0.7	0730	1.9	1135	4.6	1123	4.3
	1358	0.8	1417	0.9	1534	0.9	1327	0.7	1309	0.6	1800	2.2	1358	6.2	1749	2.0	1737	1.9
	2006	4.2	2030	5.2	2145	6.5	1940	3.7	1939	3.6	2329	1.2	1947	2.5	2351	4.7	2341	4.5
21 TH	0218	1.3	0230	1.4	0354	1.4	0144	1.2	0129	1.1	0538	2.4	0206	6.4	0625	1.4	0618	1.4
	0816	4.3	0854	5.1	1013	6.3	0800	3.7	0800	3.5	1219	0.7	0838	1.9	1235	4.7	1224	4.4
	1503	0.7	1523	0.9	1643	0.8	1433	0.7	1418	0.6	1856	2.3	1500	6.3	1852	1.9	1840	1.7
	2112	4.3	2136	5.3	2256	6.6	2047	3.8	2047	3.6			2057	2.3				
22 F O	0324	1.2	0338	1.3	0506	1.2	0251	1.1	0237	1.0	0036	1.1	0309	6.5	0051	4.8	0042	4.6
	0924	4.3	0957	5.2	1122	6.5	0905	3.8	0908	3.6	0642	2.4	0937	1.8	0720	1.3	0712	1.3
	1601	0.7	1621	0.9	1752	0.7	1529	0.7	1515	0.6	1315	0.7	1551	6.5	1327	4.8	1316	4.6
	2209	4.4	2232	5.4	2356	6.8	2143	3.9	2145	3.7	1942	2.3	2155	2.1	1945	1.7	1933	1.6
23 SA	0421	1.0	0436	1.2	0615	1.0	0346	1.0	0333	0.9	0133	1.0	0402	6.6	0145	4.9	0134	4.7
	1021	4.4	1051	5.3	1218	6.7	1000	3.9	1005	3.7	0737	2.4	1026	1.7	0807	1.3	0758	1.3
	1648	0.7	1708	0.9	1848	0.6	1615	0.7	1603	0.6	1401	0.8	1634	6.7	1413	4.9	1400	4.7
	2254	4.5	2320	5.4			2231	4.0	2234	3.8	2020	2.4	2245	1.9	2031	1.5	2020	1.4
24 SU ●	0506	0.9	0524	1.0	0045	6.9	0433	0.9	0421	0.7	0220	0.9	0448	6.7	0231	5.0	0220	4.8
	1108	4.5	1139	5.4	0709	0.8	1048	4.0	1053	3.8	0825	2.4	1109	1.6	0848	1.3	0838	1.3
	1724	0.8	1747	0.9	1306	6.8	1655	0.7	1644	0.6	1440	0.8	1712	6.9	1454	5.0	1440	4.8
	2330	4.5			1931	0.6	2313	4.0	2316	3.8	2054	2.4	2328	1.7	2112	1.4	2100	1.3
25 M	0544	0.8	0002	5.5	0128	6.9	0515	0.8	0504	0.6	0303	0.8	0530	6.8	0313	5.0	0302	4.8
	1148	4.5	0606	0.9	0753	0.7	1130	4.0	1136	3.8	0910	2.4	1147	1.6	0925	1.3	0914	1.2
	1756	0.8	1220	5.5	1347	6.8	1731	0.8	1721	0.6	1516	0.8	1746	7.0	1530	5.1	1516	4.9
			1822	0.9	2009	0.7	2351	4.0	2354	3.8	2128	2.5			2150	1.2	2139	1.2
26 TU	0003	4.6	0039	5.5	0205	6.9	0554	0.7	0543	0.6	0343	0.8	0009	1.6	0352	5.1	0340	4.8
	0619	0.7	0646	0.8	0831	0.7	1209	4.0	1214	3.8	0954	2.4	0609	6.9	1000	1.3	0949	1.2
	1225	4.6	1258	5.5	1424	6.9	1806	0.8	1756	0.7	1550	0.8	1222	1.6	1603	5.2	1551	4.9
	1828	0.8	1857	0.8	2042	0.7					2200	2.5	1821	7.1	2225	1.2	2215	1.1
27 W	0035	4.7	0114	5.6	0238	7.0	0024	4.0	0030	3.8	0422	0.7	0045	1.5	0428	5.0	0418	4.8
	0656	0.7	0724	0.8	0906	0.6	0631	0.7	0621	0.6	1035	2.4	0648	6.8	1033	1.3	1022	1.3
	1303	4.6	1335	5.6	1459	6.9	1245	4.0	1251	3.8	1620	0.9	1256	1.6	1636	5.2	1624	4.9
	1903	0.9	1930	0.8	2115	0.7	1838	0.8	1830	0.7	2231	2.5	1854	7.1	2300	1.2	2248	1.1
28 TH	0109	4.7	0148	5.5	0309	7.0	0057	4.0	0103	3.8	0458	0.7	0121	1.5	0504	5.0	0454	4.8
	0733	0.7	0759	0.8	0939	0.7	0706	0.7	0655	0.6	1113	2.3	0724	6.8	1106	1.4	1055	1.3
	1340	4.5	1409	5.5	1533	6.9	1320	4.0	1324	3.8	1648	0.9	1327	1.7	1711	5.1	1657	4.9
	1939	0.9	2001	0.9	2148	0.8	1910	0.9	1901	0.8	2303	2.5	1927	7.0	2334	1.2	2322	1.1
29 F	0144	4.6	0220	5.5	0342	6.9	0127	4.0	0133	3.7	0533	0.7	0154	1.6	0541	4.9	0530	4.7
	0811	0.8	0831	0.8	1010	0.7	0739	0.7	0728	0.6	1151	2.3	0757	6.6	1142	1.5	1127	1.4
	1415	4.5	1444	5.4	1609	6.8	1354	3.9	1357	3.7	1716	1.0	1359	1.8	1747	5.1	1730	4.8
	2014	1.1	2033	0.9	2221	0.9	1942	0.9	1933	0.8	2336	2.5	1959	6.9			2356	1.2
30 SA	0218	4.5	0251	5.4	0415	6.7	0158	3.9	0204	3.7	0609	0.7	0227	1.7	0011	1.3	0606	4.5
	0845	0.9	0903	0.9	1042	0.8	0812	0.7	0801	0.6	1229	2.2	0832	6.4	0620	4.7	1201	1.6
	1448	4.4	1518	5.3	1645	6.7	1427	3.8	1430	3.6	1749	1.0	1430	1.9	1218	1.6	1806	4.7
	2048	1.2	2106	1.0	2254	1.0	2017	1.0	2006	0.9			2033	6.7	1826	4.9		
31 SU	0251	4.5	0324	5.3	0449	6.6	0231	3.9	0236	3.6	0012	2.4	0300	1.8	0049	1.4	0033	1.3
	0918	1.0	0936	0.9	1115	0.9	0848	0.8	0836	0.7	0645	0.8	0907	6.3	0702	4.6	0646	4.4
	1524	4.3	1555	5.2	1721	6.5	1503	3.8	1506	3.6	1309	2.2	1503	2.1	1259	1.8	1237	1.7
	2122	1.2	2140	1.2	2328	1.1	2054	1.1	2043	0.9	1827	1.1	2108	6.5	1908	4.8	1845	4.6

SCOTLAND & NORTH WEST ENGLAND Time Zone UT

Leith * Rosyth * Aberdeen * Wick * Lerwick * Ullapool * Oban * Greenock * Liverpool

TIDE TABLES JANUARY 2000

Date	LEITH		ROSYTH		ABERDEEN		WICK		LERWICK		ULLAPOOL		OBAN		GREENOCK		LIVERPOOL	
	Time	m	Time	m	Time	m	Time	m	Time	m	Time	m	Time	m	Time	m	Time	m
1 SA	0424	1.9	0457	1.7	0316	1.6	0112	1.3	0054	0.9	0323	4.2	0201	3.0	0146	0.9	0124	2.5
	1044	4.7	1059	4.8	0943	3.6	0726	2.9	0700	1.8	0919	2.3	0736	1.6	0840	3.1	0708	7.6
	1645	2.2	1650	2.1	1543	1.8	1337	1.6	1327	1.0	1546	4.3	1438	3.1	1418	1.0	1348	2.9
	2315	4.7	2329	4.9	2202	3.7	1944	3.0	1924	1.8	2200	2.0	2047	1.7	2039	3.1	1935	7.7
2 SU	0520	1.8	0554	1.7	0415	1.3	0208	1.3	0150	0.9	0415	4.4	0300	3.1	0250	0.9	0226	2.5
	1145	4.8	1155	4.9	1039	3.7	0824	3.0	0800	1.8	1023	2.2	0839	1.6	0944	3.1	0810	7.8
	1744	2.0	1728	2.0	1642	1.7	1434	1.5	1423	1.0	1637	4.4	1520	3.2	1518	0.9	1448	2.7
					2258	3.7	2043	3.1	2024	1.9	2253	1.9	2137	1.6	2146	3.1	2034	7.9
3 M	0015	4.8	0025	5.0	0503	1.5	0253	1.3	0237	0.9	0459	4.6	0345	3.3	0342	0.8	0319	2.3
	0606	1.7	0633	1.7	1125	3.8	0912	3.2	0849	1.9	1114	2.0	0932	1.5	1035	3.2	0902	8.1
	1238	4.9	1245	5.0	1728	1.6	1519	1.4	1509	1.0	1720	4.5	1556	3.3	1608	0.8	1540	2.5
	1832	1.8	1800	1.8	2345	3.8	2133	3.2	2115	1.9	2336	1.8	2219	1.4	2238	3.1	2124	8.2
4 TU	0106	4.9	0115	5.1	0543	1.4	0331	1.2	0317	0.9	0537	4.7	0424	3.5	0425	0.8	0404	2.1
	0646	1.6	0622	1.6	1205	4.0	0954	3.3	0932	2.0	1156	1.8	1018	1.4	1118	3.3	0945	8.5
	1323	5.0	1327	5.2	1809	1.4	1557	1.3	1548	0.8	1757	4.6	1632	3.4	1650	0.7	1624	2.2
	1913	1.6	1836	1.6			2216	3.2	2157	2.0			2257	1.3	2321	3.1	2206	8.4
5 W	0149	5.0	0158	5.2	0027	3.9	0406	1.2	0354	0.8	0015	1.6	0459	3.6	0503	0.7	0443	1.9
	0723	1.5	0654	1.5	0621	1.3	1031	3.4	1009	2.1	0612	4.9	1059	1.4	1154	3.3	1024	8.7
	1402	5.2	1405	5.3	1241	4.1	1633	1.2	1623	0.8	1234	1.6	1708	3.6	1727	0.6	1703	2.0
	1950	1.4	1918	1.4	1845	1.3	2255	3.3	2236	2.0	1831	4.7	2333	1.2	2359	3.1	2245	8.6
6 TH ●	0227	5.1	0236	5.3	0105	4.0	0440	1.2	0427	0.8	0050	1.5	0533	3.8	0536	0.7	0519	1.8
	0757	1.4	0733	1.3	0656	1.3	1106	3.5	1044	2.1	0644	5.0	1138	1.3	1229	3.4	1100	8.9
	1437	5.3	1441	5.4	1315	4.1	1708	1.1	1655	0.7	1309	1.5	1744	3.7	1801	0.5	1739	1.8
	2024	1.3	2000	1.2	1921	1.1	2331	3.3	2312	2.0	1904	4.8					2320	8.7
7 F	0300	5.2	0312	5.4	0141	4.0	0513	1.1	0459	0.8	0124	1.4	0006	1.1	0034	3.1	0553	1.7
	0833	1.3	0815	1.3	0730	1.2	1139	3.5	1116	2.2	0715	5.1	0607	3.9	0607	0.7	1135	9.1
	1512	5.3	1516	5.5	1347	4.2	1742	1.0	1727	0.7	1343	1.4	1215	1.2	1300	3.4	1814	1.6
	2058	1.2	2043	1.2	1954	1.1			2347	2.0	1936	4.8	1818	3.7	1831	0.5	2354	8.8
8 SA	0334	5.2	0345	5.4	0215	4.1	0006	3.3	0531	0.8	0157	1.4	0039	1.1	0107	3.1	0626	1.6
	0908	1.2	0855	1.2	0803	1.2	0546	1.1	1148	2.2	0746	5.1	0639	3.9	0637	0.7	1209	9.1
	1546	5.3	1551	5.6	1419	4.2	1212	3.5	1800	0.6	1416	1.3	1251	1.2	1332	3.5	1849	1.5
	2133	1.1	2124	1.1	2027	1.0	1815	0.9			2007	4.8	1851	3.7	1902	0.5		
9 SU	0409	5.2	0420	5.4	0250	4.0	0042	3.3	0021	2.0	0229	1.4	0110	1.1	0142	3.1	0027	8.8
	0942	1.2	0934	1.3	0836	1.2	0619	1.1	0605	0.8	0818	5.1	0712	3.9	0710	0.7	0700	1.6
	1620	5.3	1627	5.5	1451	4.2	1247	3.5	1219	2.2	1450	1.3	1326	1.2	1403	3.5	1243	9.1
	2207	1.1	2200	1.1	2101	1.0	1849	0.9	1834	0.6	2040	4.8	1922	3.7	1936	0.4	1925	1.5
10 M	0444	5.2	0456	5.4	0325	4.0	0117	3.3	0055	2.0	0302	1.4	0142	1.1	0218	3.2	0100	8.7
	1017	1.3	1006	1.4	0909	1.2	0653	1.1	0640	0.8	0853	5.0	0745	3.8	0747	0.7	0736	1.7
	1654	5.2	1703	5.5	1526	4.2	1321	3.5	1254	2.1	1525	1.3	1402	1.3	1437	3.5	1318	9.0
	2242	1.1	2225	1.2	2137	1.0	1924	1.0	1912	0.6	2116	4.7	1954	3.6	2014	0.4	2002	1.6
11 TU	0521	5.1	0533	5.3	0403	3.9	0154	3.2	0133	1.9	0337	1.5	0215	1.2	0257	3.2	0136	8.6
	1051	1.4	1029	1.5	0945	1.3	0729	1.2	0718	0.8	0931	4.9	0819	3.7	0827	0.7	0812	1.8
	1730	5.2	1741	5.4	1603	4.1	1358	3.4	1330	2.1	1603	1.4	1441	1.4	1512	3.5	1354	8.9
	2318	1.2	2250	1.2	2215	1.1	2003	1.0	1951	0.7	2157	4.6	2027	3.5	2056	0.5	2039	1.7
12 W	0601	5.0	0615	5.3	0443	3.8	0233	3.1	0212	1.9	0415	1.7	0251	1.3	0339	3.2	0213	8.5
	1125	1.6	1056	1.6	1024	1.4	0808	1.3	0757	0.9	1015	4.8	0857	3.6	0910	0.7	0850	2.1
	1810	5.1	1820	5.3	1645	4.0	1439	3.4	1410	2.0	1644	1.5	1524	1.4	1548	3.4	1433	8.7
	2355	1.4	2324	1.3	2258	1.2	2045	1.1	2034	0.7	2244	4.4	2105	3.3	2142	0.5	2119	1.9
13 TH	0646	4.9	0659	5.1	0529	3.7	0318	3.0	0259	1.8	0458	1.8	0333	1.4	0423	3.2	0254	8.3
	1205	1.7	1134	1.7	1110	1.5	0853	1.4	0844	0.9	1106	4.7	0943	3.4	0957	0.8	0932	2.3
	1856	5.0	1903	5.2	1733	3.9	1524	3.3	1457	2.0	1731	1.7	1613	1.5	1628	3.3	1518	8.5
					2348	1.3	2134	1.1	2124	0.7	2342	4.3	2150	3.2	2235	0.6	2203	2.1
14 F	0041	1.5	0009	1.4	0622	3.7	0409	3.0	0353	1.8	0551	2.0	0424	1.5	0511	3.1	0344	8.0
	0737	4.8	0748	5.0	1206	1.6	0948	1.5	0939	1.0	1208	4.5	1041	3.3	1051	0.9	1021	2.6
	1259	1.9	1225	1.9	1828	3.8	1618	3.2	1555	1.9	1828	1.8	1709	1.6	1715	3.2	1611	8.3
	1948	4.9	1951	5.1			2237	1.2	2224	0.8			2248	3.1	2336	0.6	2257	2.3
15 SA	0139	1.6	0109	1.5	0048	1.3	0510	2.9	0457	1.8	0054	4.2	0526	1.6	0607	3.1	0444	7.9
	0836	4.7	0845	4.9	0725	3.6	1058	1.5	1049	1.0	0656	2.2	1154	3.2	1153	0.9	1124	2.7
	1411	2.0	1341	2.0	1313	1.7	1722	3.2	1706	1.9	1319	4.5	1813	1.6	1819	3.1	1715	8.1
	2050	4.8	2051	5.0	1934	3.8	2351	1.2	2338	0.8	1936	1.9						

● ● Time: UT. For British Summer Time (shaded) March 26th to October 29th ADD ONE HOUR ● ●

JANUARY 2000 TIDE TABLES

•• Time: UT. For British Summer Time (shaded) March 26th to October 29th ADD ONE HOUR ••

Day	LEITH Time	m	ROSYTH Time	m	ABERDEEN Time	m	WICK Time	m	LERWICK Time	m	ULLAPOOL Time	m	OBAN Time	m	GREENOCK Time	m	LIVERPOOL Time	m
16 SU	0252	1.7	0228	1.7	0158	1.4	0619	3.0	0604	1.8	0209	4.2	0004	3.0	0043	0.6	0004	2.4
	0942	4.7	0950	4.9	0835	3.6	1218	1.5	1214	1.0	0815	2.2	0639	1.6	0712	3.0	0557	7.8
	1533	2.0	1517	2.0	1429	1.7	1833	3.2	1820	1.9	1431	4.5	1318	3.3	1303	1.0	1240	2.7
	2200	4.8	2203	5.0	2048	3.8					2050	1.9	1924	1.5	1942	3.0	1829	8.1
17 M	0415	1.7	0412	1.7	0312	1.3	0106	1.2	0054	0.8	0319	4.4	0138	3.1	0154	0.6	0121	2.3
	1053	4.9	1057	5.0	0945	3.8	0730	3.1	0711	1.9	0933	2.0	0757	1.5	0825	3.0	0712	8.0
	1654	1.8	1657	1.8	1544	1.5	1335	1.4	1327	0.9	1541	4.6	1436	3.4	1417	0.9	1400	2.4
	2314	5.0	2318	5.1	2201	3.9	1946	3.2	1931	1.9	2201	1.7	2037	1.3	2104	3.0	1942	8.4
18 TU	0535	1.5	0549	1.5	0421	1.2	0213	1.1	0157	0.7	0421	4.6	0259	3.3	0300	0.5	0236	2.0
	1158	5.1	1159	5.2	1048	4.0	0835	3.2	0812	2.0	1040	1.7	0911	1.3	0936	3.1	0821	8.4
	1804	1.5	1806	1.5	1650	1.3	1442	1.2	1427	0.7	1643	4.8	1541	3.6	1523	0.7	1511	1.9
					2308	4.1	2054	3.4	2037	2.0	2304	1.4	2142	1.1	2215	3.1	2049	8.8
19 W	0022	5.2	0022	5.4	0521	1.1	0311	1.0	0253	0.7	0515	5.0	0400	3.5	0357	0.4	0341	1.6
	0639	1.3	0650	1.3	1142	4.2	0932	3.4	0909	2.1	1139	1.4	1015	1.1	1040	3.2	0922	8.9
	1257	5.3	1255	5.5	1748	1.0	1539	1.0	1521	0.6	1739	5.1	1638	3.8	1620	0.5	1615	1.4
	1905	1.1	1915	1.2			2157	3.5	2139	2.1	2358	1.2	2237	0.8	2318	3.2	2149	9.2
20 TH O	0120	5.5	0120	5.6	0006	4.3	0403	0.9	0344	0.6	0603	5.3	0451	3.8	0448	0.3	0439	1.2
	0735	1.1	0745	1.1	0614	1.0	1024	3.6	1001	2.2	1231	1.0	1111	0.8	1135	3.4	1017	9.3
	1348	5.6	1348	5.7	1232	4.4	1632	0.7	1612	0.4	1830	5.3	1730	3.9	1710	0.3	1712	0.9
	2001	0.8	2021	0.8	1841	0.7	2252	3.6	2236	2.2			2327	0.6			2243	9.5
21 F	0212	5.7	0215	5.8	0100	4.4	0450	0.8	0433	0.6	0048	0.9	0538	4.1	0018	3.3	0531	0.8
	0825	0.9	0838	0.9	0703	0.9	1113	3.8	1051	2.3	0648	5.5	1203	0.7	0536	0.3	1108	9.7
	1436	5.8	1442	5.9	1318	4.5	1721	0.5	1701	0.3	1321	0.7	1817	4.0	1225	3.5	1805	0.5
	2054	0.5	2114	0.5	1931	0.5	2344	3.7	2327	2.2	1917	5.4			1757	0.1	2334	9.7
22 SA	0302	5.9	0308	6.0	0150	4.5	0535	0.8	0519	0.6	0134	0.8	0013	0.4	0112	3.4	0620	0.6
	0912	0.8	0926	0.8	0750	0.8	1200	3.8	1139	2.4	0733	5.6	0622	4.2	0621	0.3	1157	9.9
	1524	5.9	1534	6.0	1403	4.6	1809	0.4	1748	0.2	1406	0.6	1251	0.6	1312	3.7	1854	0.3
	2143	0.3	2203	0.3	2020	0.4					2003	5.4	1900	4.1	1842	0.1		
23 SU	0350	5.9	0400	6.1	0238	4.5	0033	3.7	0016	2.2	0218	0.8	0057	0.4	0201	3.4	0022	9.8
	0957	0.8	1011	0.8	0834	0.8	0618	0.8	0604	0.6	0815	5.6	0703	4.2	0705	0.3	0706	0.6
	1611	5.9	1626	6.0	1448	4.6	1245	3.9	1225	2.4	1451	0.6	1338	0.6	1356	3.8	1242	9.9
	2229	0.3	2248	0.3	2106	0.4	1854	0.5	1835	0.2	2047	5.3	1939	4.0	1927	0.1	1940	0.3
24 M	0438	5.7	0451	6.0	0326	4.4	0119	3.6	0103	2.2	0300	0.9	0139	0.4	0247	3.4	0107	9.6
	1037	0.9	1053	1.0	0917	0.9	0700	0.9	0648	0.6	0859	5.5	0743	4.1	0750	0.3	0748	0.8
	1700	5.8	1717	5.9	1533	4.5	1330	3.8	1311	2.3	1535	0.7	1422	0.8	1439	3.9	1327	9.8
	2312	0.5	2332	0.5	2151	0.5	1939	0.6	1921	0.3	2132	5.1	2016	3.8	2012	0.1	2024	0.5
25 TU	0527	5.5	0541	5.8	0412	4.2	0204	3.5	0147	2.1	0342	1.1	0221	0.6	0329	3.4	0151	9.3
	1112	1.2	1127	1.2	0959	1.1	0740	1.1	0732	0.7	0942	5.3	0821	3.9	0836	0.4	0830	1.1
	1748	5.6	1808	5.7	1619	4.4	1415	3.7	1355	2.2	1618	1.0	1506	1.0	1521	3.9	1409	9.4
	2349	0.8			2236	0.7	2024	0.7	2008	0.4	2218	4.8	2051	3.6	2059	0.3	2106	0.9
26 W	0615	5.3	0012	0.8	0459	4.0	0248	3.3	0230	1.9	0425	1.4	0304	0.8	0410	3.4	0233	8.9
	1141	1.4	0631	5.5	1041	1.3	0821	1.2	0815	0.8	1029	4.9	0900	3.6	0923	0.5	0910	1.5
	1837	5.3	1103	1.4	1707	4.2	1500	3.5	1441	2.1	1701	1.4	1549	1.3	1603	3.8	1451	9.0
			1859	5.5	2321	1.0	2108	1.0	2054	0.6	2309	4.5	2129	3.4	2148	0.4	2147	1.5
27 TH	0021	1.2	0044	1.2	0548	3.8	0333	3.1	0314	1.8	0509	1.7	0348	1.1	0452	3.3	0316	8.4
	0703	5.0	0721	5.2	1127	1.5	0903	1.4	0901	0.9	1121	4.6	0940	3.4	1015	0.7	0952	2.1
	1213	1.7	1145	1.7	1759	3.9	1548	3.3	1527	2.0	1748	1.7	1635	1.6	1645	3.6	1535	8.5
	1927	5.0	1951	5.2			2157	1.2	2145	0.7			2211	3.1	2243	0.7	2230	2.1
28 F	0057	1.5	0030	1.5	0010	1.3	0423	3.0	0401	1.7	0009	4.3	0437	1.4	0536	3.2	0403	8.0
	0754	4.7	0813	4.9	0640	3.6	0954	1.6	0954	1.0	0558	2.1	1027	3.1	1113	0.9	1038	2.6
	1259	2.0	1241	2.0	1221	1.7	1642	3.1	1620	1.8	1227	4.3	1727	1.8	1728	3.4	1624	8.0
	2021	4.8	2045	5.0	1857	3.7	2257	1.4	2242	0.9	1842	2.1	2307	2.9	2348	0.9	2321	2.6
29 SA	0148	1.9	0132	1.9	0107	1.6	0521	2.9	0455	1.7	0120	4.1	0533	1.6	0625	3.0	0457	7.5
	0848	4.5	0908	4.7	0740	3.5	1106	1.7	1105	1.1	0657	2.4	1131	2.9	1222	1.0	1135	7.5
	1407	2.3	1356	2.3	1329	1.9	1747	3.0	1722	1.7	1347	4.1	1831	1.9	1815	3.1	1725	7.5
	2119	4.6	2142	4.8	2005	3.5			2354	1.0	1949	2.3						
30 SU	0303	2.1	0348	2.1	0217	1.8	0009	1.5	0601	1.7	0233	4.1	0040	2.9	0100	1.0	0023	3.0
	0947	4.4	1003	4.6	0847	3.4	0627	2.8	1240	1.1	0817	2.5	0642	1.8	0732	2.8	0606	7.2
	1546	2.4	1540	2.4	1452	2.0	1242	1.7	1839	1.7	1505	4.0	1321	2.9	1337	1.0	1248	3.0
	2225	4.4	2241	4.7	2118	3.5	1900	2.9			2111	2.4	1951	1.9	1917	2.9	1841	7.2
31 M	0429	2.2	0449	2.2	0331	1.8	0124	1.6	0108	1.0	0338	4.1	0221	2.9	0213	1.0	0135	3.1
	1054	4.4	1100	4.6	0954	3.5	0738	2.9	0716	1.7	0945	2.5	0759	1.8	0857	2.8	0722	7.3
	1712	2.2	1651	2.3	1609	1.9	1405	1.6	1355	1.0	1610	4.1	1451	3.0	1448	1.0	1403	3.2
	2338	4.5	2343	4.7	2227	3.5	2011	2.9	1956	1.7	2222	2.2	2106	1.8	2059	2.7	1957	7.3

SCOTLAND & NORTH WEST ENGLAND Time Zone UT
Leith * Rosyth * Aberdeen * Wick * Lerwick * Ullapool * Oban * Greenock * Liverpool
TIDE TABLES FEBRUARY 2000

	LEITH		ROSYTH		ABERDEEN		WICK		LERWICK		ULLAPOOL		OBAN		GREENOCK		LIVERPOOL		
	Time	m	Time	m	Time	m	Time	m	Time	m	Time	m	Time	m	Time	m	Time	m	
	0533	2.1	0527	2.1	0433	1.7	0224	1.5	0208	1.0	0433	4.3	0321	3.1	0317	1.0	0241	2.9	**1 TU**
	1202	4.6	1200	4.8	1054	3.6	0839	3.0	0820	1.8	1051	2.3	0908	1.8	1001	2.9	0829	7.6	
	1810	2.0	1738	2.0	1706	1.7	1500	1.5	1450	0.9	1702	4.3	1542	3.1	1545	0.8	1508	2.9	
					2324	3.6	2109	3.0	2054	1.8	2315	2.0	2159	1.6	2208	2.7	2059	7.7	
	0041	4.6	0043	4.9	0521	1.6	0310	1.4	0256	0.9	0516	4.5	0406	3.3	0406	0.9	0335	2.6	**2 W**
	0623	1.9	0601	1.9	1141	3.8	0927	3.2	0908	1.9	1139	2.0	1002	1.6	1050	3.0	0921	8.0	
	1258	4.8	1254	5.0	1751	1.5	1542	1.3	1532	0.8	1743	4.4	1624	3.3	1631	0.7	1600	2.5	
	1856	1.7	1821	1.8			2157	3.1	2139	1.9	2357	1.8	2242	1.4	2257	2.8	2147	8.0	
	0128	4.8	0133	5.1	0010	3.8	0349	1.3	0336	0.9	0554	4.7	0445	3.5	0447	0.8	0420	2.2	**3 TH**
	0703	1.7	0639	1.7	0602	1.5	1008	3.3	0948	2.0	1218	1.8	1046	1.5	1130	3.2	1004	8.4	
	1342	5.0	1342	5.2	1221	3.9	1619	1.2	1607	0.7	1818	4.6	1703	3.5	1710	0.6	1644	2.1	
	1934	1.5	1904	1.5	1828	1.3	2237	3.2	2218	1.9			2318	1.3	2339	2.9	2227	8.4	
	0207	5.0	0215	5.3	0049	3.9	0424	1.2	0410	0.8	0033	1.6	0520	3.7	0521	0.7	0500	1.9	**4 F**
	0741	1.5	0721	1.5	0639	1.3	1045	3.4	1025	2.1	0627	4.9	1125	1.3	1207	3.3	1042	8.8	
	1419	5.1	1424	5.4	1257	4.1	1653	1.0	1639	0.7	1254	1.5	1738	3.6	1743	0.5	1723	1.7	
	2009	1.3	1950	1.3	1903	1.1	2314	3.3	2254	2.0	1849	4.8	2351	1.1			2303	8.7	
	0242	5.2	0251	5.4	0125	4.0	0457	1.1	0442	0.7	0107	1.4	0554	3.9	0018	3.0	0536	1.6	**5 SA**
	0817	1.3	0804	1.3	0712	1.2	1120	3.5	1058	2.1	0658	5.1	1201	1.2	0551	0.7	1118	9.0	
	1454	5.3	1501	5.6	1330	4.2	1726	0.9	1709	0.6	1327	1.3	1810	3.7	1242	3.4	1800	1.5	●
	2045	1.0	2036	1.1	1936	1.0	2349	3.3	2329	2.0	1919	4.9			1813	0.4	2336	8.9	
	0315	5.3	0326	5.5	0158	4.1	0530	1.1	0515	0.7	0140	1.3	0022	1.0	0054	3.0	0611	1.4	**6 SU**
	0854	1.1	0847	1.2	0745	1.1	1154	3.6	1130	2.2	0728	5.2	0626	4.0	0621	0.6	1152	9.2	
	1529	5.4	1537	5.7	1401	4.2	1758	0.8	1742	0.5	1400	1.1	1235	1.1	1315	3.4	1836	1.2	
	2121	0.9	2117	1.0	2010	0.8					1949	5.0	1840	3.8	1844	0.3			
	0348	5.3	0400	5.6	0231	4.1	0024	3.4	0003	2.0	0212	1.2	0052	0.9	0130	3.1	0010	9.0	**7 M**
	0930	1.0	0926	1.1	0818	1.0	0602	1.0	0548	0.6	0800	5.3	0657	4.0	0654	0.5	0646	1.3	
	1602	5.4	1611	5.7	1433	4.3	1228	3.6	1203	2.2	1432	1.0	1309	1.0	1349	3.5	1227	9.3	
	2156	0.8	2149	0.9	2043	0.8	1830	0.8	1815	0.5	2020	5.0	1909	3.8	1918	0.2	1911	1.1	
	0422	5.3	0434	5.6	0305	4.1	0058	3.4	0036	2.0	0244	1.1	0123	0.9	0207	3.2	0044	9.0	**8 TU**
	1006	1.0	0954	1.1	0851	1.0	0636	1.0	0622	0.6	0833	5.3	0728	4.0	0730	0.4	0721	1.2	
	1635	5.4	1645	5.7	1507	4.3	1303	3.6	1236	2.2	1505	1.0	1343	1.0	1423	3.5	1301	9.3	
	2231	0.8	2207	0.9	2118	0.8	1904	0.7	1850	0.4	2053	4.9	1938	3.8	1954	0.2	1947	1.1	
	0458	5.3	0511	5.6	0339	4.1	0133	3.3	0111	2.0	0318	1.2	0155	0.9	0244	3.2	0118	9.0	**9 W**
	1039	1.1	1012	1.2	0925	1.0	0710	1.0	0658	0.6	0908	5.2	0800	3.9	0807	0.4	0757	1.3	
	1709	5.4	1721	5.7	1542	4.3	1339	3.6	1311	2.1	1540	1.0	1421	1.1	1456	3.5	1336	9.3	
	2303	0.9	2230	0.9	2153	0.8	1939	0.8	1927	0.5	2130	4.8	2009	3.7	2033	0.2	2022	1.2	
	0536	5.2	0549	5.6	0417	4.0	0210	3.3	0148	1.9	0354	1.3	0231	1.0	0321	3.2	0154	8.9	**10 TH**
	1109	1.2	1037	1.3	1002	1.1	0747	1.0	0736	0.7	0948	5.1	0836	3.8	0847	0.4	0833	1.5	
	1747	5.3	1759	5.6	1621	4.2	1417	3.5	1348	2.1	1618	1.2	1501	1.1	1530	3.4	1412	9.1	
	2333	1.0	2301	1.0	2232	0.9	2018	0.9	2008	0.5	2212	4.7	2043	3.6	2116	0.3	2057	1.4	
	0619	5.1	0631	5.4	0459	3.9	0251	3.2	0228	1.9	0433	1.5	0312	1.1	0400	3.2	0232	8.7	**11 F**
	1139	1.4	1112	1.4	1042	1.2	0827	1.1	0818	0.7	1035	4.9	0916	3.6	0930	0.5	0909	1.8	
	1830	5.2	1840	5.5	1706	4.1	1500	3.4	1432	2.0	1701	1.4	1546	1.3	1606	3.3	1454	8.9	
			2340	1.2	2316	1.1	2102	1.0	2054	0.6	2302	4.5	2123	3.4	2204	0.4	2136	1.7	
	0006	1.3	0718	5.2	0547	3.8	0337	3.1	0317	1.8	0520	1.7	0359	1.3	0442	3.2	0316	8.4	**12 SA**
	0706	4.9	1156	1.6	1132	1.4	0915	1.3	0909	0.8	1132	4.6	1005	3.4	1018	0.6	0953	2.1	
	1221	1.6	1927	5.3	1759	4.0	1551	3.3	1525	1.9	1752	1.6	1637	1.4	1648	3.2	1542	8.6	
	1919	5.0					2157	1.2	2148	0.7			2211	3.2	2301	0.5	2223	2.1	
	0054	1.5	0032	1.5	0011	1.3	0433	3.0	0418	1.7	0009	4.3	0456	1.5	0530	3.0	0410	8.1	**13 SU**
	0802	4.8	0810	5.0	0645	3.6	1019	1.4	1013	0.9	0618	2.0	1109	3.2	1118	0.8	1048	2.4	
	1323	1.9	1257	1.8	1235	1.5	1653	3.2	1635	1.8	1245	4.4	1737	1.5	1743	3.0	1642	8.2	
	2020	4.8	2024	5.1	1903	3.8	2312	1.3	2259	0.8	1855	1.9	2319	3.0			2325	2.4	
	0203	1.8	0148	1.8	0121	1.4	0542	2.9	0528	1.7	0132	4.2	0607	1.6	0009	0.6	0520	7.8	**14 M**
	0907	4.6	0915	4.9	0758	3.6	1146	1.5	1140	0.9	0737	2.2	1249	3.1	0630	2.9	1204	2.6	
	1454	2.0	1433	2.0	1357	1.6	1809	3.1	1756	1.8	1407	4.3	1851	1.6	1230	0.9	1800	7.9	
	2134	4.7	2137	4.9	2024	3.7					2015	2.0			1903	2.9			
	0346	1.9	0340	1.9	0245	1.5	0039	1.3	0029	0.8	0255	4.2	0108	3.0	0127	0.7	0048	2.5	**15 TU**
	1023	4.7	1028	4.9	0918	3.6	0700	3.0	0642	1.8	0910	2.1	0738	1.6	0744	2.9	0645	7.8	
	1638	1.9	1637	1.9	1524	1.5	1318	1.4	1309	0.8	1529	4.4	1434	3.2	1354	0.8	1336	2.5	
	2258	4.8	2257	5.0	2148	3.8	1932	3.1	1917	1.8	2143	1.9	2015	1.5	2035	2.3	1924	8.0	

● ● Time: UT. For British Summer Time (shaded) March 26th to October 29th ADD ONE HOUR ● ●

FEBRUARY 2000 TIDE TABLES

•• Time: UT. For British Summer Time (shaded) March 26th to October 29th ADD ONE HOUR ••

	LEITH		ROSYTH		ABERDEEN		WICK		LERWICK		ULLAPOOL		OBAN		GREENOCK		LIVERPOOL	
	Time	m	Time	m	Time	m	Time	m	Time	m	Time	m	Time	m	Time	m	Time	m
16 W	0527	1.8	0538	1.8	0407	1.4	0201	1.3	0144	0.8	0409	4.5	0259	3.2	0242	0.6	0215	2.3
	1139	4.8	1138	5.0	1030	3.8	0815	3.1	0755	1.8	1031	1.8	0909	1.4	0906	2.9	0804	8.1
	1758	1.5	1809	1.6	1640	1.3	1436	1.2	1417	0.7	1639	4.6	1545	3.4	1510	0.7	1457	2.1
							2302	3.9	2048	3.2	2034	1.9	2255	1.7	2130	1.2	2201	2.9	2039	8.4
17 TH	0013	5.0	0006	5.2	0512	1.3	0305	1.2	0245	0.7	0507	4.8	0402	3.5	0345	0.5	0327	1.9
	0633	1.5	0644	1.5	1130	4.0	0918	3.3	0859	2.0	1133	1.4	1018	1.1	1021	3.1	0912	8.6
	1245	5.1	1241	5.3	1742	1.0	1536	0.9	1514	0.5	1736	4.9	1640	3.6	1610	0.5	1606	1.5
	1901	1.1	1921	1.2			2152	3.4	2138	2.0	2351	1.3	2227	0.9	2312	3.0	2142	8.9
18 F	0113	5.3	0108	5.5	0002	4.1	0355	1.0	0337	0.7	0555	5.1	0451	3.8	0437	0.4	0429	1.4
	0727	1.2	0739	1.2	0606	1.1	1012	3.5	0954	2.1	1225	1.0	1111	0.9	1121	3.3	1009	9.2
	1338	5.4	1337	5.6	1221	4.2	1626	0.7	1604	0.4	1823	5.2	1727	3.8	1700	0.3	1705	0.9
	1955	0.7	2016	0.8	1834	0.7	2245	3.5	2230	2.1			2316	0.6			2236	9.3
19 SA **O**	0204	5.6	0203	5.7	0053	4.3	0439	0.9	0423	0.6	0039	1.0	0534	4.0	0011	3.2	0521	0.9
	0814	0.9	0825	1.0	0654	0.9	1101	3.7	1042	2.2	0638	5.4	1158	0.7	0523	0.3	1058	9.6
	1425	5.7	1430	5.9	1306	4.4	1711	0.5	1650	0.2	1311	0.7	1809	4.0	1213	3.5	1755	0.4
	2044	0.4	2103	0.5	1922	0.4	2333	3.6	2317	2.2	1905	5.3	2359	0.4	1744	0.1	2324	9.6
20 SU	0250	5.7	0253	5.9	0139	4.4	0521	0.8	0506	0.5	0122	0.8	0613	4.2	0102	3.3	0608	0.6
	0857	0.8	0906	0.8	0736	0.8	1146	3.8	1127	2.3	0718	5.6	1241	0.6	0606	0.3	1144	9.8
	1510	5.8	1519	6.1	1349	4.6	1754	0.4	1733	0.2	1353	0.5	1845	4.1	1259	3.6	1841	0.2
	2128	0.2	2146	0.3	2006	0.3					1945	5.4			1825	0.0		
21 M	0333	5.8	0341	6.0	0222	4.4	0018	3.6	0000	2.2	0203	0.7	0040	0.3	0148	3.3	0007	9.7
	0938	0.7	0945	0.8	0817	0.8	0600	0.8	0546	0.5	0757	5.6	0649	4.2	0647	0.2	0651	0.5
	1554	5.8	1608	6.1	1430	4.6	1229	3.8	1209	2.3	1433	0.5	1321	0.6	1341	3.7	1226	9.9
	2209	0.2	2227	0.3	2047	0.3	1834	0.4	1815	0.2	2023	5.3	1919	4.0	1906	0.0	1922	0.2
22 TU	0417	5.7	0427	6.0	0303	4.3	0058	3.6	0039	2.1	0241	0.7	0119	0.3	0228	3.4	0048	9.6
	1015	0.7	1018	0.8	0855	0.8	0638	0.8	0626	0.5	0834	5.5	0722	4.1	0727	0.2	0729	0.6
	1639	5.8	1654	6.1	1512	4.5	1310	3.8	1249	2.3	1511	0.6	1359	0.7	1420	3.8	1306	9.8
	2245	0.4	2303	0.5	2126	0.5	1912	0.5	1855	0.3	2101	5.2	1950	3.9	1948	0.1	2000	0.4
23 W	0500	5.5	0512	5.8	0343	4.2	0137	3.4	0118	2.0	0318	0.9	0158	0.5	0305	3.4	0126	9.4
	1045	0.9	1005	1.0	0931	0.9	0714	0.9	0705	0.5	0912	5.3	0754	3.9	0809	0.2	0806	0.9
	1721	5.6	1740	5.9	1552	4.4	1349	3.6	1328	2.2	1548	0.9	1436	0.9	1458	3.8	1343	9.5
	2315	0.7	2330	0.9	2203	0.7	1948	0.7	1936	0.4	2139	4.9	2020	3.7	2030	0.2	2036	0.9
24 TH	0541	5.3	0555	5.5	0423	4.0	0214	3.3	0154	1.9	0356	1.1	0236	0.7	0340	3.3	0202	9.1
	1109	1.2	1031	1.2	1008	1.1	0748	1.0	0742	0.6	0949	4.9	0827	3.7	0852	0.3	0840	1.1
	1804	5.3	1824	5.6	1633	4.2	1429	3.5	1407	2.1	1625	1.2	1512	1.2	1535	3.7	1419	9.1
	2337	1.1	2300	1.2	2240	1.0	2024	0.9	2015	0.6	2218	4.6	2051	3.5	2113	0.4	2109	1.4
25 F	0623	5.0	0637	5.2	0503	3.8	0251	3.1	0231	1.8	0434	1.5	0316	1.0	0415	3.3	0238	8.6
	1133	1.5	1106	1.5	1045	1.3	0824	1.2	0821	0.7	1029	4.6	0900	3.4	0936	0.5	0913	1.8
	1848	5.0	1907	5.3	1718	3.9	1510	3.2	1448	1.9	1704	1.6	1549	1.5	1612	3.5	1456	8.6
			2338	1.5	2320	1.3	2103	1.2	2056	0.7	2305	4.3	2126	3.3	2159	0.6	2142	2.0
26 SA	0005	1.5	0720	4.9	0546	3.6	0333	3.0	0311	1.7	0515	1.9	0359	1.4	0449	3.1	0317	8.1
	0707	4.7	1150	1.8	1130	1.6	0906	1.4	0906	0.9	1118	4.2	0936	3.2	1027	0.7	0948	2.4
	1208	1.8	1954	5.0	1809	3.7	1557	3.0	1533	1.8	1748	2.0	1633	1.7	1647	3.3	1537	8.0
	1935	4.7					2149	1.4	2144	0.9			2210	3.1	2251	0.8	2220	2.6
27 SU	0047	1.8	0032	1.9	0007	1.6	0421	2.8	0357	1.7	0009	4.0	0448	1.6	0525	2.9	0403	7.6
	0755	4.5	0809	4.7	0639	3.4	1004	1.6	1008	1.0	0603	2.2	1023	2.9	1128	0.9	1033	2.9
	1301	2.1	1256	2.2	1227	1.8	1655	2.8	1629	1.6	1237	3.9	1727	1.9	1725	3.0	1629	7.4
	2028	4.4	2048	4.7	1912	3.4	2257	1.6	2249	1.0	1842	2.3	2321	2.9	2357	1.0	2312	3.2
28 M	0151	2.2	0148	2.3	0111	1.8	0522	2.7	0457	1.6	0132	3.9	0551	1.9	0608	2.7	0503	7.1
	0850	4.3	0903	4.5	0743	3.3	1138	1.7	1142	1.0	0709	2.5	1144	2.8	1245	1.0	1138	3.4
	1433	2.4	1426	2.4	1351	1.9	1811	2.7	1746	1.5	1416	3.8	1849	2.0	1809	2.7	1742	6.9
	2131	4.3	2145	4.5	2028	3.3					2006	2.5						
29 TU	0329	2.4	0340	2.4	0236	2.0	0029	1.7	0014	1.0	0252	3.9	0138	2.9	0120	1.2	0031	3.5
	0954	4.2	1002	4.5	0859	3.3	0639	2.7	0618	1.6	0854	2.6	0717	2.0	0721	2.6	0625	7.0
	1636	2.3	1612	2.4	1529	1.9	1327	1.6	1316	1.0	1539	3.9	1420	2.8	1408	1.0	1309	3.5
	2248	4.2	2247	4.5	2150	3.3	1936	2.7	1925	1.6	2147	2.4	2030	1.9	1911	2.5	1915	6.9

SCOTLAND & NORTH WEST ENGLAND Time Zone UT
Leith * Rosyth * Aberdeen * Wick * Lerwick * Ullapool * Oban * Greenock * Liverpool
TIDE TABLES MARCH 2000

	LEITH	ROSYTH	ABERDEEN	WICK	LERWICK	ULLAPOOL	OBAN	GREENOCK	LIVERPOOL	
	Time m	Time m	Time m	Time m	Time m	Time m	Time m	Time m	Time m	
	0503 2.3	0452 2.3	0400 1.9	0152 1.6	0133 1.0	0359 4.1	0256 3.0	0241 1.1	0157 3.3	1 W
	1111 4.3	1103 4.6	1013 3.4	0756 2.8	0743 1.7	1024 2.4	0845 1.9	0918 2.6	0750 7.2	
	1748 2.1	1715 2.2	1639 1.7	1434 1.5	1421 0.9	1639 4.0	1526 3.0	1515 0.9	1430 3.1	
		2357 4.7	2258 3.5	2044 2.8	2031 1.6	2251 2.2	2138 1.7	2128 2.5	2031 7.3	
	0008 4.4	0539 2.1	0458 1.7	0248 1.5	0230 1.0	0450 4.3	0345 3.3	0338 1.0	0304 2.9	2 TH
	0601 2.1	1211 4.8	1111 3.6	0855 3.0	0840 1.8	1116 2.1	0946 1.7	1015 2.8	0852 7.7	
	1224 4.5	1803 1.9	1727 1.5	1520 1.3	1506 0.8	1723 4.3	1612 3.2	1603 0.7	1532 2.6	
	1836 1.8		2348 3.6	2134 3.0	2117 1.7	2335 1.9	2222 1.5	2227 2.6	2124 7.8	
	0102 4.7	0100 4.9	0541 1.5	0329 1.4	0313 0.9	0530 4.5	0425 3.5	0420 0.9	0354 2.4	3 F
	0645 1.8	0624 1.8	1155 3.8	0940 3.1	0923 1.9	1156 1.7	1031 1.5	1100 3.0	0939 8.2	
	1315 4.8	1312 5.1	1806 1.2	1557 1.1	1542 0.7	1757 4.5	1649 3.4	1642 0.5	1620 2.1	
	1915 1.5	1850 1.6		2215 3.1	2156 1.8		2258 1.3	2313 2.8	2204 8.3	
	0142 4.9	0147 5.2	0027 3.8	0404 1.2	0348 0.8	0012 1.6	0500 3.7	0454 0.7	0437 2.0	4 SA
	0722 1.5	0708 1.5	0617 1.3	1019 3.3	1000 2.0	0603 4.8	1108 1.3	1141 3.2	1018 8.7	
	1354 5.0	1400 5.4	1232 3.9	1630 0.9	1613 0.6	1231 1.4	1722 3.6	1716 0.4	1701 1.6	
	1950 1.2	1939 1.3	1839 1.0	2251 3.2	2231 1.9	1827 4.7	2330 1.1	2354 2.9	2240 8.6	
	0217 5.1	0226 5.4	0102 4.0	0436 1.1	0421 0.7	0046 1.3	0533 3.9	0526 0.5	0515 1.6	5 SU
	0758 1.2	0752 1.3	0651 1.1	1056 3.4	1034 2.0	0634 5.0	1142 1.1	1219 3.3	1054 9.1	●
	1430 5.3	1440 5.6	1305 4.1	1702 0.8	1645 0.5	1304 1.1	1752 3.7	1748 0.2	1739 1.3	
	2025 0.9	2025 1.1	1912 0.8	2327 3.3	2305 2.0	1856 4.9			2314 9.0	
	0250 5.3	0302 5.6	0134 4.1	0508 0.9	0453 0.6	0118 1.1	0000 0.9	0034 3.0	0552 1.2	6 M
	0835 0.9	0835 1.1	0724 1.0	1131 3.5	1108 2.1	0704 5.2	0605 4.0	0557 0.4	1130 9.4	
	1505 5.4	1516 5.7	1338 4.2	1734 0.6	1717 0.4	1336 0.9	1214 0.9	1256 3.4	1816 1.0	
	2101 0.7	2103 0.9	1946 0.6		2339 2.0	1924 5.0	1821 3.9	1820 0.1	2348 9.2	
	0324 5.4	0336 5.6	0207 4.2	0001 3.4	0527 0.5	0151 0.9	0029 0.8	0112 3.1	0628 0.9	7 TU
	0912 0.8	0910 0.9	0757 0.8	0541 0.8	1142 2.2	0736 5.3	0636 4.1	0631 0.3	1204 9.6	
	1538 5.5	1550 5.8	1410 4.3	1206 3.6	1751 0.3	1409 0.7	1247 0.8	1331 3.4	1852 0.8	
	2137 0.5	2124 0.7	2020 0.5	1806 0.5		1955 5.1	1848 4.0	1854 0.0		
	0358 5.5	0409 5.8	0240 4.2	0036 3.4	0012 2.0	0223 0.8	0100 0.7	0149 3.2	0022 9.3	8 W
	0948 0.7	0929 0.9	0830 0.8	0615 0.7	0601 0.4	0809 5.4	0707 4.1	0706 0.2	0704 0.8	
	1612 5.6	1624 5.9	1445 4.4	1242 3.6	1215 2.2	1442 0.6	1321 0.8	1405 3.4	1239 9.6	
	2212 0.5	2139 0.7	2054 0.5	1841 0.5	1826 0.3	2028 5.1	1917 4.0	1930 0.0	1927 0.7	
	0434 5.4	0446 5.8	0315 4.2	0111 3.4	0047 2.0	0257 0.8	0135 0.7	0224 3.2	0057 9.4	9 TH
	1022 0.7	0948 0.9	0904 0.8	0651 0.7	0638 0.4	0845 5.3	0739 4.1	0743 0.1	0740 0.9	
	1647 5.6	1700 5.9	1521 4.4	1318 3.6	1251 2.2	1517 0.7	1359 0.8	1439 3.4	1315 9.6	
	2245 0.6	2206 0.8	2129 0.6	1916 0.6	1903 0.3	2104 5.0	1948 3.9	2008 0.0	2002 0.8	
	0513 5.4	0525 5.8	0352 4.1	0147 3.3	0122 2.0	0333 0.9	0212 0.8	0300 3.3	0133 9.3	10 F
	1053 0.9	1016 1.0	0940 0.8	0727 0.8	0716 0.5	0925 5.1	0815 3.9	0821 0.2	0815 1.0	
	1726 5.5	1740 5.8	1601 4.3	1358 3.5	1329 2.1	1554 0.8	1439 0.9	1512 3.4	1353 9.4	
	2312 0.9	2237 0.9	2207 0.7	1954 0.7	1944 0.4	2145 4.8	2021 3.8	2050 0.1	2036 1.1	
	0554 5.2	0607 5.6	0433 4.0	0227 3.2	0201 1.9	0412 1.1	0254 0.9	0336 3.2	0211 9.0	11 SA
	1121 1.1	1051 1.1	1021 1.0	0808 0.9	0759 0.6	1012 4.9	0854 3.7	0903 0.2	0851 1.4	
	1810 5.3	1823 5.6	1647 4.1	1442 3.4	1413 2.0	1636 1.1	1523 1.1	1548 3.3	1433 9.1	
	2342 1.2	2315 1.2	2251 1.0	2037 0.9	2029 0.6	2233 4.5	2100 3.6	2137 0.3	2114 1.5	
	0641 5.0	0652 5.3	0520 3.8	0312 3.1	0247 1.8	0458 1.4	0341 1.2	0415 3.2	0254 8.7	12 SU
	1200 1.4	1133 1.4	1109 1.2	0855 1.0	0849 0.7	1111 4.6	0940 3.4	0951 0.4	0933 1.8	
	1901 5.0	1911 5.3	1740 3.9	1533 3.2	1507 1.9	1724 1.5	1612 1.3	1632 3.1	1521 8.7	
			2345 1.2	2130 1.1	2123 0.7	2339 4.3	2145 3.3	2233 0.5	2159 2.0	
	0025 1.5	0004 1.5	0618 3.6	0406 2.9	0346 1.7	0556 1.8	0437 1.4	0502 3.1	0347 8.2	13 M
	0736 4.8	0744 5.0	1214 1.4	1000 1.2	0954 0.8	1229 4.3	1044 3.1	1051 0.6	1028 2.2	
	1302 1.7	1233 1.7	1848 3.7	1637 3.0	1620 1.7	1827 1.9	1711 1.5	1728 2.9	1622 8.1	
	2003 4.8	2009 5.0		2248 1.3	2235 0.8		2251 3.0	2343 0.7	2300 2.5	
	0137 1.9	0123 2.0	0058 1.5	0515 2.8	0500 1.7	0109 4.1	0552 1.6	0558 2.9	0457 7.7	14 TU
	0842 4.6	0850 4.8	0732 3.5	1135 1.3	1126 0.8	0717 2.0	1252 2.9	1208 0.7	1145 2.6	
	1442 1.9	1423 2.0	1342 1.5	1759 2.9	1744 1.7	1359 4.1	1827 1.6	1844 2.8	1744 7.7	
	2123 4.6	2127 4.8	2016 3.6			1954 2.1				
	0343 2.1	0358 2.1	0232 1.6	0027 1.4	0015 0.9	0240 4.1	0118 2.9	0106 0.8	0027 2.8	15 W
	1003 4.5	1012 4.7	0858 3.5	0639 2.8	0621 1.7	0902 2.0	0739 1.6	0710 2.8	0627 7.6	
	1636 1.8	1650 1.9	1517 1.4	1316 1.2	1300 0.9	1525 4.2	1439 3.0	1339 0.7	1324 2.5	
	2251 4.7	2248 4.9	2145 3.6	1929 2.9	1915 1.7	2136 2.0	2000 1.5	2018 2.7	1915 7.8	

● ● Time: UT. For British Summer Time (shaded) March 26th to October 29th ADD ONE HOUR ● ●

MARCH 2000 TIDE TABLES

•• Time: UT. For British Summer Time (shaded) March 26th to October 29th ADD ONE HOUR ••

Day	LEITH Time	m	ROSYTH Time	m	ABERDEEN Time	m	WICK Time	m	LERWICK Time	m	ULLAPOOL Time	m	OBAN Time	m	GREENOCK Time	m	LIVERPOOL Time	m
16TH	0522	1.9	0531	1.9	0400	1.5	0156	1.3	0137	0.9	0358	4.3	0306	3.2	0227	0.8	0202	2.6
	1126	4.7	1127	4.9	1015	3.7	0800	3.0	0742	1.8	1027	1.7	0918	1.4	0839	2.9	0753	7.9
	1754	1.4	1811	1.5	1634	1.2	1433	1.0	1409	0.6	1635	4.4	1543	3.3	1459	0.6	1449	2.0
					2258	3.8	2047	3.1	2034	1.8	2248	1.7	2120	1.3	2157	2.8	2032	8.2
17F	0007	5.0	0000	5.1	0505	1.3	0258	1.2	0238	0.8	0457	4.7	0401	3.5	0332	0.6	0318	2.0
	0624	1.6	0633	1.6	1117	3.9	0906	3.2	0848	1.9	1125	1.3	1018	1.1	1006	3.0	0902	8.5
	1233	5.0	1233	5.2	1733	0.9	1528	0.8	1505	0.4	1727	4.7	1633	3.5	1558	0.4	1557	1.4
	1853	1.0	1914	1.1	2355	4.0	2145	3.2	2130	1.9	2341	1.3	2215	0.9	2305	3.0	2134	8.8
18SA	0105	5.3	0100	5.4	0556	1.1	0345	1.0	0327	0.6	0542	5.0	0445	3.8	0424	0.5	0418	1.5
	0713	1.3	0725	1.3	1207	4.1	0959	3.4	0942	2.0	1212	0.9	1104	0.9	1109	3.2	0957	9.0
	1327	5.3	1328	5.5	1823	0.6	1614	0.6	1551	0.3	1809	5.0	1715	3.7	1645	0.2	1653	0.8
	1943	0.7	2004	0.8			2234	3.4	2218	2.0			2300	0.7	2359	3.1	2224	9.2
19SU O	0152	5.5	0151	5.6	0042	4.2	0425	0.9	0409	0.5	0025	1.0	0522	4.0	0507	0.4	0508	1.0
	0757	1.0	0806	1.0	0639	0.9	1045	3.6	1027	2.1	0622	5.2	1145	0.7	1158	3.4	1044	9.5
	1412	5.5	1416	5.8	1251	4.3	1654	0.4	1633	0.2	1254	0.6	1751	3.9	1727	0.1	1740	0.5
	2027	0.4	2046	0.5	1906	0.4	2317	3.5	2259	2.1	1848	5.2	2340	0.5			2307	9.5
20M	0233	5.6	0236	5.8	0123	4.3	0503	0.7	0448	0.4	0105	0.8	0555	4.1	0045	3.2	0551	0.7
	0836	0.7	0837	0.8	0718	0.8	1129	3.7	1109	2.2	0659	5.4	1221	0.6	0547	0.2	1126	9.7
	1454	5.7	1502	6.0	1330	4.4	1732	0.4	1712	0.2	1333	0.5	1823	4.0	1242	3.5	1821	0.3
	2106	0.3	2124	0.4	1945	0.3	2357	3.5	2336	2.1	1923	5.3			1806	0.0	2347	9.6
21TU	0313	5.6	0319	5.9	0200	4.3	0538	0.7	0524	0.4	0142	0.6	0018	0.4	0126	3.3	0630	0.6
	0915	0.6	0843	0.7	0755	0.7	1209	3.7	1148	2.2	0733	5.4	0626	4.1	0626	0.1	1205	9.8
	1535	5.7	1546	6.1	1409	4.5	1807	0.4	1750	0.2	1409	0.5	1257	0.6	1321	3.6	1858	0.3
	2143	0.3	2159	0.5	2022	0.4					1957	5.2	1852	4.0	1843	0.0		
22W	0352	5.6	0401	5.9	0237	4.2	0033	3.5	0012	2.0	0218	0.6	0055	0.4	0202	3.3	0024	9.5
	0949	0.6	0910	0.8	0830	0.7	0613	0.7	0601	0.4	0807	5.3	0655	4.0	0704	0.1	0705	0.6
	1615	5.6	1630	6.0	1447	4.4	1247	3.6	1224	2.2	1443	0.6	1330	0.7	1357	3.6	1241	9.6
	2215	0.5	2227	0.7	2056	0.5	1842	0.5	1827	0.3	2030	5.1	1921	4.0	1921	0.1	1932	0.6
23TH	0431	5.4	0442	5.7	0312	4.1	0107	3.4	0045	2.0	0253	0.8	0131	0.6	0235	3.3	0058	9.4
	1018	0.8	0935	0.9	0904	0.8	0647	0.7	0637	0.4	0841	5.1	0724	3.9	0742	0.1	0738	0.9
	1654	5.5	1711	5.8	1524	4.2	1323	3.5	1300	2.1	1517	0.8	1403	0.9	1432	3.6	1315	9.4
	2239	0.8	2156	0.9	2129	0.7	1914	0.7	1902	0.4	2103	4.9	1949	3.8	1959	0.2	2003	1.0
24F	0509	5.2	0520	5.5	0347	4.0	0140	3.3	0118	1.9	0327	1.0	0208	0.8	0306	3.3	0130	9.1
	1039	1.0	1002	1.1	0937	1.0	0720	0.8	0712	0.5	0915	4.8	0754	3.7	0821	0.2	0809	1.2
	1733	5.2	1749	5.5	1603	4.0	1358	3.3	1335	2.0	1551	1.1	1436	1.1	1506	3.5	1348	9.0
	2259	1.1	2224	1.2	2202	1.0	1946	0.9	1936	0.6	2138	4.6	2019	3.7	2037	0.4	2032	1.5
25SA	0546	5.0	0556	5.2	0422	3.8	0213	3.1	0150	1.8	0403	1.3	0245	1.1	0336	3.2	0203	8.7
	1059	1.3	1033	1.4	1012	1.1	0754	1.0	0747	0.6	0950	4.4	0825	3.5	0900	0.4	0839	1.7
	1812	5.0	1828	5.2	1643	3.8	1436	3.1	1412	1.8	1626	1.5	1511	1.4	1539	3.3	1421	8.5
	2324	1.4	2258	1.5	2237	1.2	2019	1.1	2012	0.7	2216	4.3	2052	3.4	2115	0.6	2100	2.0
26SU	0627	4.8	0634	4.9	0500	3.6	0249	3.0	0225	1.8	0440	1.6	0325	1.4	0408	3.1	0238	8.3
	1128	1.6	1109	1.7	1051	1.4	0831	1.2	0827	0.8	1033	4.1	0859	3.3	0942	0.5	0910	2.2
	1856	4.7	1911	4.9	1730	3.6	1519	2.9	1454	1.7	1704	1.8	1550	1.6	1612	3.1	1458	8.0
					2342	1.5	2058	1.3	2053	0.9	2306	4.1	2132	3.2	2154	0.8	2130	2.6
27M	0000	1.8	0721	4.7	0546	3.5	0332	2.8	0307	1.7	0522	2.0	0412	1.7	0440	2.9	0318	7.8
	0711	4.5	1200	2.0	1141	1.6	0921	1.4	0923	0.9	1136	3.8	0939	3.0	1030	0.8	0948	2.7
	1210	1.9	2001	4.6	1827	3.4	1612	2.7	1546	1.6	1751	2.2	1639	1.8	1648	2.9	1543	7.4
	1945	4.4					2155	1.5	2152	1.0			2231	3.0	2242	1.0	2213	3.1
28TU	0054	2.2	0058	2.3	0014	1.8	0426	2.7	0400	1.6	0024	3.8	0511	1.9	0518	2.7	0412	7.3
	0802	4.3	0816	4.5	0645	3.3	1044	1.5	1051	0.9	0618	2.3	1045	2.8	1139	1.0	1042	3.2
	1326	2.3	1340	2.3	1252	1.8	1722	2.6	1654	1.5	1323	3.6	1750	2.0	1730	2.6	1648	6.9
	2044	4.2	2057	4.5	1941	3.2	2326	1.7	2321	1.1	1900	2.5			2354	1.2	2321	3.6
29W	0226	2.5	0236	2.5	0135	2.0	0537	2.6	0509	1.5	0157	3.8	0044	2.9	0606	2.6	0527	6.9
	0901	4.1	0915	4.4	0800	3.2	1233	1.5	1224	0.9	0751	2.4	0634	2.0	1306	1.0	1208	3.5
	1541	2.3	1516	2.4	1433	1.8	1851	2.5	1838	1.5	1457	3.6	1331	2.7	1826	2.4	1821	6.7
	2154	4.1	2158	4.4	2105	3.2					2056	2.5	1940	2.0				
30TH	0421	2.4	0412	2.4	0314	2.0	0106	1.6	0047	1.0	0314	3.8	0221	3.0	0133	1.2	0103	3.6
	1012	4.1	1016	4.5	0921	3.2	0700	2.6	0644	1.5	0942	2.3	0812	2.0	0803	2.5	0700	7.0
	1712	2.1	1642	2.2	1600	1.7	1354	1.4	1335	0.8	1605	3.8	1455	2.9	1426	0.9	1342	3.2
	2317	4.2	2303	4.5	2220	3.3	2008	2.7	2000	1.5	2217	2.3	2103	1.8	2030	2.4	1951	7.0
31F	0530	2.2	0512	2.2	0424	1.8	0213	1.5	0152	0.9	0412	4.1	0314	3.2	0248	1.1	0223	3.2
	1133	4.3	1122	4.6	1028	3.4	0810	2.8	0800	1.6	1042	2.0	0920	1.8	0932	2.7	0812	7.5
	1803	1.7	1739	1.9	1652	1.4	1445	1.2	1426	0.7	1652	4.1	1544	3.1	1521	0.7	1452	2.7
					2314	3.5	2103	2.8	2047	1.7	2305	1.9	2151	1.6	2148	2.6	2049	7.6

SCOTLAND & NORTH WEST ENGLAND Time Zone UT
Leith * Rosyth * Aberdeen * Wick * Lerwick * Ullapool * Oban * Greenock * Liverpool

TIDE TABLES APRIL 2000

LEITH Time	m	ROSYTH Time	m	ABERDEEN Time	m	WICK Time	m	LERWICK Time	m	ULLAPOOL Time	m	OBAN Time	m	GREENOCK Time	m	LIVERPOOL Time	m	Date
0022	4.5	0013	4.8	0509	1.5	0259	1.3	0239	0.8	0456	4.3	0355	3.4	0338	0.9	0320	2.6	**1 SA**
0616	1.8	0602	1.9	1118	3.6	0903	2.9	0847	1.7	1124	1.6	1004	1.5	1024	2.9	0904	8.0	
1235	4.6	1232	4.9	1733	1.2	1525	1.0	1505	0.6	1727	4.3	1621	3.3	1605	0.5	1545	2.1	
1844	1.4	1829	1.6	2355	3.7	2145	3.0	2125	1.8	2343	1.6	2227	1.3	2239	2.8	2132	8.2	
0106	4.8	0109	5.1	0547	1.3	0336	1.1	0318	0.7	0532	4.6	0431	3.6	0418	0.7	0406	2.0	**2 SU**
0655	1.5	0649	1.6	1158	3.8	0945	3.1	0926	1.8	1200	1.3	1040	1.3	1109	3.1	0946	8.6	
1320	4.9	1326	5.2	1808	0.9	1600	0.8	1539	0.5	1758	4.6	1654	3.5	1642	0.3	1630	1.6	
1921	1.1	1918	1.2			2222	3.1	2200	1.9			2259	1.1	2324	2.9	2209	8.7	
0145	5.1	0153	5.4	0031	3.9	0409	0.9	0352	0.6	0018	1.2	0504	3.9	0454	0.5	0448	1.5	**3 M**
0733	1.1	0734	1.3	0621	1.0	1024	3.3	1003	2.0	0604	4.9	1113	1.0	1151	3.2	1024	9.0	
1359	5.2	1409	5.5	1233	4.0	1633	0.6	1613	0.4	1233	0.9	1724	3.7	1716	0.1	1711	1.1	
1957	0.8	2004	1.0	1842	0.7	2258	3.3	2235	2.0	1827	4.9	2330	0.9			2245	9.1	
0221	5.3	0230	5.6	0105	4.1	0442	0.8	0427	0.5	0051	0.9	0536	4.1	0006	3.0	0527	1.1	**4 TU**
0811	0.8	0815	1.0	0656	0.8	1103	3.4	1039	2.1	0636	5.1	1146	0.8	0529	0.3	1100	9.4	
1435	5.4	1447	5.7	1309	4.2	1706	0.4	1648	0.3	1307	0.6	1752	3.9	1230	3.3	1751	0.8	●
2035	0.5	2039	0.7	1917	0.5	2334	3.4	2310	2.0	1857	5.1			1751	0.0	2321	9.4	
0257	5.5	0306	5.8	0139	4.2	0517	0.6	0502	0.4	0125	0.7	0001	0.7	0047	3.1	0606	0.8	**5 W**
0848	0.6	0845	0.8	0731	0.7	1141	3.5	1116	2.1	0709	5.3	0609	4.2	0604	0.1	1138	9.7	
1510	5.6	1523	5.9	1344	4.3	1740	0.3	1724	0.2	1342	0.4	1221	0.7	1309	3.3	1829	0.6	
2112	0.4	2045	0.6	1953	0.4			2345	2.1	1930	5.2	1822	4.1	1827	-0.1	2357	9.6	
0333	5.6	0342	5.9	0214	4.3	0010	3.4	0539	0.3	0200	0.5	0036	0.6	0125	3.2	0644	0.6	**6 TH**
0927	0.5	0858	0.7	0806	0.5	0553	0.5	1154	2.2	0745	5.4	0643	4.2	0640	0.0	1215	9.8	
1547	5.7	1600	6.0	1421	4.4	1220	3.6	1802	0.2	1417	0.3	1258	0.6	1345	3.3	1906	0.5	
2150	0.4	2110	0.6	2029	0.4	1816	0.3			2004	5.2	1854	4.1	1904	-0.1			
0411	5.6	0421	5.9	0250	4.3	0048	3.4	0021	2.1	0236	0.5	0113	0.6	0202	3.2	0034	9.6	**7 F**
1003	0.5	0924	0.7	0843	0.5	0631	0.5	0618	0.3	0824	5.3	0719	4.2	0718	-0.0	0721	0.6	
1626	5.7	1641	6.0	1502	4.4	1300	3.6	1232	2.1	1454	0.4	1338	0.6	1421	3.3	1254	9.8	
2225	0.5	2142	0.7	2106	0.5	1854	0.4	1841	0.3	2042	5.1	1927	4.1	1945	-0.1	1942	0.6	
0451	5.5	0503	5.8	0329	4.2	0126	3.4	0058	2.0	0315	0.6	0154	0.7	0238	3.3	0113	9.5	**8 SA**
1039	0.7	0957	0.8	0923	0.6	0711	0.5	0659	0.3	0908	5.1	0757	4.0	0759	-0.0	0800	0.8	
1709	5.5	1724	5.8	1545	4.3	1342	3.5	1315	2.1	1533	0.6	1420	0.8	1457	3.3	1335	9.6	
2257	0.5	2217	0.9	2148	0.7	1935	0.6	1923	0.4	2125	4.8	2003	3.9	2028	0.1	2018	1.0	
0534	5.3	0546	5.6	0412	4.0	0207	3.2	0139	2.0	0357	0.9	0239	0.9	0315	3.3	0154	9.2	**9 SU**
1115	0.9	1034	0.9	1007	0.8	0755	0.7	0745	0.4	1000	4.8	0839	3.7	0843	0.1	0839	1.1	
1757	5.3	1809	5.6	1634	4.1	1430	3.3	1403	2.0	1616	1.0	1505	1.0	1539	3.2	1419	9.2	
2330	1.2	2256	1.2	2233	0.9	2020	0.6	2010	0.6	2217	4.5	2043	3.7	2117	0.3	2058	1.4	
0622	5.0	0633	5.3	0500	3.8	0253	3.1	0227	1.8	0445	1.2	0330	1.1	0357	3.2	0239	8.8	**10 M**
1200	1.2	1120	1.2	1100	1.0	0848	0.8	0839	0.5	1106	4.4	0927	3.4	0934	0.3	0924	1.6	
1851	5.0	1901	5.3	1733	3.8	1524	3.1	1504	1.8	1706	1.4	1554	1.2	1627	3.1	1510	8.7	
		2346	1.7	2332	1.3	2116	1.1	2107	0.7	2327	4.2	2132	3.4	2215	0.5	2145	2.0	
0018	1.6	0728	4.9	0600	3.6	0348	2.9	0327	1.7	0547	1.6	0430	1.4	0443	3.2	0335	8.3	**11 TU**
0718	4.8	1227	1.6	1209	1.2	1000	1.0	0948	0.6	1228	4.1	1039	3.0	1037	0.4	1022	2.1	
1309	1.5	2006	4.9	1846	3.6	1633	2.9	1618	1.7	1811	1.9	1654	1.5	1726	2.9	1615	8.1	
1957	4.8					2238	1.3	2223	0.9			2245	3.1	2326	0.7	2248	2.5	
0141	2.0	0146	2.1	0049	1.5	0459	2.8	0442	1.7	0058	4.0	0551	1.6	0539	3.0	0447	7.8	**12 W**
0828	4.6	0842	4.7	0717	3.5	1136	1.0	1121	0.7	0713	1.8	1300	2.9	1157	0.6	1142	2.4	
1450	1.7	1504	1.7	1338	1.3	1757	2.8	1739	1.6	1355	4.0	1809	1.6	1839	2.7	1737	7.7	
2118	4.6	2127	4.8	2015	3.5					1944	2.1							
0341	2.1	0400	2.1	0222	1.7	0018	1.4	0005	0.9	0227	4.1	0138	3.0	0048	0.8	0017	2.8	**13 TH**
0949	4.5	1005	4.7	0842	3.5	0622	2.8	0602	1.6	0855	1.8	0746	1.6	0647	2.9	0615	7.7	
1630	1.5	1648	1.5	1509	1.2	1310	1.0	1248	0.6	1517	4.1	1427	3.0	1324	0.6	1315	2.3	
2242	4.7	2244	4.8	2139	3.6	1925	2.8	1911	1.6	2124	2.0	1943	1.5	2016	2.7	1904	7.8	
0506	1.9	0515	1.9	0346	1.5	0144	1.3	0124	0.8	0342	4.2	0256	3.3	0208	0.8	0149	2.6	**14 F**
1110	4.7	1118	4.9	0958	3.6	0742	2.9	0724	1.7	1012	1.5	0912	1.4	0818	2.9	0737	8.0	
1740	1.2	1757	1.2	1622	1.0	1420	0.8	1354	0.5	1622	4.3	1527	3.2	1441	0.6	1436	1.9	
2354	4.9	2352	5.1	2248	3.7	2036	2.9	2021	1.7	2233	1.6	2100	1.3	2148	2.9	2018	8.2	
0605	1.6	0614	1.6	0449	1.3	0243	1.2	0223	0.7	0440	4.5	0347	3.5	0314	0.7	0302	2.1	**15 SA**
1217	5.0	1221	5.1	1100	3.8	0847	3.1	0830	1.8	1108	1.2	1004	1.2	0949	3.1	0845	8.5	
1836	0.9	1857	1.0	1718	0.8	1512	0.6	1448	0.4	1711	4.6	1613	3.4	1540	0.4	1540	1.3	
				2341	3.9	2130	3.1	2112	1.8	2323	1.3	2154	1.0	2248	3.0	2117	8.7	

● ● Time: UT. For British Summer Time (shaded) March 26th to October 29th ADD ONE HOUR ● ●

APRIL 2000 TIDE TABLES

•• Time: UT. For British Summer Time (shaded) March 26th to October 29th ADD ONE HOUR ••

	LEITH Time	m	ROSYTH Time	m	ABERDEEN Time	m	WICK Time	m	LERWICK Time	m	ULLAPOOL Time	m	OBAN Time	m	GREENOCK Time	m	LIVERPOOL Time	m
16 SU	0049	5.2	0049	5.3	0538	1.1	0327	1.0	0309	0.6	0524	4.8	0427	3.7	0405	0.6	0400	1.6
	0652	1.3	0703	1.4	1149	4.0	0940	3.2	0921	1.9	1153	0.9	1045	1.0	1049	3.2	0938	8.9
	1310	5.2	1314	5.4	1804	0.6	1554	0.5	1532	0.3	1751	4.8	1652	3.6	1627	0.3	1633	0.9
	1922	0.7	1946	0.8			2215	3.2	2156	1.9			2237	0.8	2338	3.1	2204	9.0
17 M	0134	5.4	0136	5.5	0024	4.0	0406	0.8	0350	0.5	0006	1.0	0500	3.8	0448	0.4	0448	1.2
	0733	1.0	0740	1.1	0619	0.9	1026	3.4	1006	2.0	0603	5.0	1121	0.8	1137	3.4	1023	9.3
	1354	5.4	1400	5.6	1231	4.2	1631	0.4	1611	0.3	1233	0.7	1726	3.8	1706	0.2	1717	0.7
	2003	0.6	2026	0.7	1844	0.5	2255	3.3	2234	2.0	1826	5.0	2316	0.6			2245	9.3
18 TU O	0213	5.4	0217	5.6	0101	4.1	0440	0.7	0427	0.4	0044	0.8	0530	3.9	0021	3.2	0528	1.0
	0812	0.8	0733	0.9	0657	0.8	1107	3.4	1047	2.1	0637	5.1	1155	0.8	0527	0.2	1103	9.4
	1435	5.5	1443	5.8	1309	4.2	1706	0.4	1648	0.2	1309	0.6	1755	3.9	1218	3.4	1755	0.6
	2039	0.5	2058	0.6	1920	0.5	2331	3.3	2309	2.0	1859	5.1	2353	0.6	1743	0.1	2322	9.4
19 W	0251	5.5	0257	5.7	0136	4.2	0515	0.6	0503	0.4	0121	0.7	0557	3.9	0059	3.2	0604	0.9
	0849	0.7	0806	0.8	0732	0.7	1146	3.4	1124	2.1	0710	5.1	1227	0.8	0604	0.1	1139	9.4
	1513	5.5	1524	5.8	1347	4.3	1739	0.4	1723	0.3	1343	0.6	1824	4.0	1256	3.4	1829	0.7
	2113	0.5	2057	0.7	1954	0.5			2342	2.0	1930	5.1			1819	0.1	2357	9.4
20 TH	0327	5.4	0335	5.7	0209	4.1	0006	3.3	0537	0.4	0155	0.7	0029	0.6	0133	3.3	0638	0.9
	0924	0.7	0839	0.8	0806	0.7	0549	0.6	1200	2.0	0742	5.0	0626	3.9	0641	0.1	1214	9.3
	1551	5.5	1605	5.8	1424	4.2	1222	3.4	1757	0.4	1415	0.6	1300	0.8	1330	3.4	1900	0.9
	2142	0.7	2058	0.8	2026	0.6	1811	0.5			2003	5.0	1852	4.0	1855	0.2		
21 F	0403	5.3	0412	5.5	0242	4.1	0038	3.3	0014	2.0	0228	0.8	0104	0.8	0203	3.3	0030	9.3
	0953	0.8	0910	0.9	0839	0.8	0623	0.6	0612	0.4	0815	4.8	0656	3.8	0717	0.1	0709	1.1
	1628	5.3	1643	5.6	1500	4.1	1257	3.3	1233	2.0	1448	0.8	1332	1.0	1404	3.4	1247	9.1
	2206	0.9	2126	1.0	2058	0.8	1842	0.7	1830	0.5	2034	4.8	1921	3.9	1930	0.3	1930	1.2
22 SA	0439	5.2	0448	5.4	0315	4.0	0109	3.2	0044	1.9	0302	1.0	0140	1.0	0233	3.3	0101	9.1
	1015	1.0	0938	1.1	0912	0.9	0657	0.7	0645	0.5	0848	4.6	0726	3.7	0753	0.2	0740	1.3
	1705	5.1	1719	5.4	1537	3.9	1332	3.1	1308	1.9	1521	1.1	1405	1.1	1436	3.3	1319	8.8
	2228	1.1	2155	1.3	2130	1.0	1914	0.8	1901	0.6	2107	4.6	1952	3.7	2003	0.4	1957	1.6
23 SU	0515	5.0	0522	5.2	0348	3.8	0141	3.1	0115	1.9	0336	1.2	0218	1.2	0303	3.2	0133	8.8
	1035	1.2	1008	1.3	0945	1.0	0730	0.9	0721	0.6	0924	4.3	0757	3.5	0828	0.3	0810	1.7
	1743	4.9	1756	5.1	1616	3.7	1409	3.0	1344	1.8	1555	1.4	1439	1.4	1509	3.1	1351	8.5
	2253	1.4	2227	1.5	2203	1.2	1946	1.0	1935	0.7	2143	4.3	2026	3.6	2037	0.6	2026	2.0
24 M	0553	4.8	0600	5.0	0425	3.7	0216	3.0	0148	1.8	0413	1.5	0257	1.5	0333	3.1	0207	8.4
	1101	1.5	1042	1.6	1024	1.2	0808	1.0	0800	0.7	1007	4.0	0832	3.3	0905	0.5	0842	2.1
	1824	4.7	1837	4.9	1700	3.5	1449	2.8	1425	1.7	1632	1.7	1518	1.6	1542	3.0	1427	8.0
	2326	1.6	2304	1.9	2243	1.5	2023	1.2	2014	0.8	2229	4.1	2106	3.3	2112	0.8	2057	2.5
25 TU	0635	4.6	0645	4.8	0508	3.5	0257	2.8	0229	1.7	0454	1.7	0342	1.7	0405	3.0	0245	8.0
	1140	1.7	1124	1.9	1109	1.4	0854	1.1	0851	0.8	1106	3.8	0912	3.1	0948	0.6	0920	2.5
	1911	4.4	1925	4.6	1754	3.3	1539	2.6	1515	1.6	1715	2.0	1602	1.8	1618	2.8	1509	7.5
			2354	2.2	2333	1.7	2112	1.4	2106	1.0	2333	3.9	2200	3.1	2156	0.9	2138	2.5
26 W	0013	2.1	0736	4.6	0600	3.3	0345	2.7	0318	1.6	0545	2.0	0438	1.9	0442	2.9	0333	7.5
	0723	4.4	1257	2.1	1210	1.6	1003	1.3	1005	0.8	1230	3.6	1009	2.9	1044	0.8	1009	2.9
	1244	2.0	2018	4.5	1859	3.2	1640	2.5	1615	1.5	1814	2.3	1700	1.9	1702	2.7	1606	7.1
	2004	4.2					2229	1.6	2228	1.0			2341	3.0	2255	1.1	2236	3.4
27 TH	0133	2.4	0151	2.4	0041	1.9	0447	2.6	0419	1.5	0057	3.7	0550	2.0	0527	2.7	0438	7.2
	0818	4.2	0833	4.5	0707	3.2	1133	1.3	1130	0.8	0659	2.2	1205	2.7	1200	0.9	1119	3.2
	1428	2.1	1422	2.2	1332	1.6	1757	2.5	1732	1.4	1401	3.6	1828	2.0	1800	2.5	1725	6.8
	2106	4.2	2117	4.4	2015	3.1			2356	1.0	1947	2.4						
28 F	0316	2.4	0316	2.4	0210	1.9	0002	1.6	0534	1.5	0218	3.8	0128	3.0	0015	1.2	0001	3.6
	0923	4.2	0933	4.4	0824	3.2	0600	2.6	1241	0.8	0838	2.1	0719	2.0	0639	2.6	0601	7.1
	1612	2.0	1545	2.1	1500	1.6	1257	1.2	1906	1.5	1515	3.7	1400	2.8	1320	0.9	1246	3.1
	2218	4.2	2218	4.5	2130	3.2	1916	2.5			2124	2.2	2005	1.9	1933	2.5	1853	7.0
29 SA	0440	2.2	0433	2.3	0331	1.8	0121	1.5	0105	0.9	0322	3.9	0229	3.2	0140	1.1	0130	3.3
	1035	4.3	1036	4.6	0935	3.3	0713	2.6	0656	1.6	0951	1.9	0832	1.8	0836	2.7	0718	7.4
	1715	1.7	1659	1.8	1603	1.4	1357	1.1	1336	0.7	1609	3.9	1457	3.0	1427	0.7	1401	2.7
	2328	4.5	2324	4.7	2229	3.4	2017	2.7	2003	1.6	2221	1.9	2103	1.7	2100	2.7	2000	7.5
30 SU	0534	1.8	0530	1.9	0426	1.6	0215	1.3	0157	0.8	0412	4.2	0313	3.4	0245	0.9	0234	2.7
	1143	4.5	1143	4.8	1032	3.5	0814	2.8	0757	1.7	1040	1.5	0921	1.6	0942	2.8	0817	7.9
	1800	1.4	1755	1.5	1650	1.1	1443	0.9	1421	0.6	1648	4.0	1539	3.2	1519	0.5	1500	2.1
					2315	3.7	2105	2.9	2045	1.7	2305	1.6	2144	1.4	2159	2.8	2049	8.1

SCOTLAND & NORTH WEST ENGLAND Time Zone UT
Leith * Rosyth * Aberdeen * Wick * Lerwick * Ullapool * Oban * Greenock * Liverpool

TIDE TABLES MAY 2000

LEITH		ROSYTH		ABERDEEN		WICK		LERWICK		ULLAPOOL		OBAN		GREENOCK		LIVERPOOL			
Time	m	Time	m	Time	m	Time	m	Time	m	Time	m	Time	m	Time	m	Time	m		
0022	4.8	0024	5.0	0509	1.3	0258	1.1	0240	0.7	0453	4.4	0351	3.6	0336	0.7	0327	2.1	1	M
0618	1.5	0620	1.6	1118	3.7	0904	3.0	0845	1.8	1121	1.2	1000	1.3	1033	3.0	0905	8.5		
1236	4.9	1243	5.1	1730	0.8	1522	0.7	1501	0.4	1723	4.5	1614	3.4	1603	0.2	1551	1.6		
1843	1.0	1845	1.2	2355	3.9	2147	3.0	2123	1.8	2343	1.2	2219	1.2	2248	3.0	2132	8.6		
0108	5.1	0114	5.4	0548	1.0	0336	0.9	0320	0.6	0530	4.7	0428	3.8	0418	0.4	0414	1.6	2	TU
0700	1.1	0706	1.3	1158	4.0	0949	3.2	0927	1.9	1159	0.8	1037	1.0	1119	3.1	0948	9.0		
1321	5.2	1331	5.4	1809	0.6	1559	0.5	1539	0.3	1757	4.8	1647	3.1	1643	0.0	1638	1.1		
1924	0.7	1930	0.9			2227	3.2	2201	2.0			2254	0.9	2335	3.1	2212	9.1		
0148	5.3	0157	5.6	0033	4.1	0414	0.7	0358	0.4	0021	0.9	0504	4.0	0458	0.2	0458	1.1	3	W
0742	0.8	0745	1.0	0626	0.8	1032	3.3	1009	2.0	0606	5.0	1115	0.8	1202	3.2	1029	9.4		
1402	5.4	1414	5.7	1238	4.2	1636	0.4	1618	0.2	1236	0.5	1721	3.9	1722	-0.1	1721	0.8		
2005	0.5	1952	0.7	1847	0.4	2306	3.3	2239	2.0	1830	5.0	2332	0.7			2251	9.5		
0228	5.5	0236	5.8	0110	4.2	0452	0.5	0437	0.3	0058	0.6	0542	4.2	0018	3.1	0541	0.8	4	TH
0823	0.6	0808	0.8	0705	0.6	1115	3.5	1051	2.1	0644	5.2	1154	0.6	0537	0.1	1110	9.7	●	
1442	5.6	1455	5.9	1318	4.3	1715	0.3	1658	0.2	1315	0.3	1755	4.1	1244	3.2	1803	0.5		
2047	0.4	2012	0.6	1927	0.3	2345	3.4	2318	2.1	1906	5.2			1802	-0.1	2332	9.7		
0308	5.6	0317	5.9	0148	4.3	0533	0.4	0518	0.3	0137	0.4	0012	0.6	0100	3.2	0623	0.6	5	F
0905	0.4	0831	0.6	0745	0.5	1159	3.5	1133	2.2	0724	5.3	0621	4.2	0617	-0.1	1153	9.9		
1524	5.7	1538	6.0	1401	4.4	1754	0.3	1739	0.2	1354	0.3	1236	0.5	1325	3.3	1844	0.5		
2128	0.4	2045	0.6	2006	0.3			2357	2.1	1945	5.2	1831	4.2	1842	-0.1				
0348	5.6	0359	5.9	0228	4.3	0026	3.4	0600	0.2	0218	0.4	0054	0.6	0139	3.3	0013	9.7	6	SA
0948	0.4	0906	0.6	0827	0.4	0615	0.3	1218	2.1	0809	5.2	0702	4.2	0658	-0.1	0705	0.5		
1608	5.7	1622	6.0	1446	4.4	1244	3.5	1822	0.3	1434	0.4	1318	0.5	1406	3.3	1236	9.8		
2210	0.6	2123	0.7	2049	0.5	1836	0.4			2027	5.1	1909	4.1	1925	-0.0	1924	0.6		
0432	5.5	0444	5.8	0310	4.2	0107	3.4	0039	2.1	0300	0.5	0140	0.7	0218	3.4	0056	9.6	7	SU
1032	0.5	0945	0.7	0912	0.5	0700	0.4	0646	0.3	0859	4.9	0745	4.0	0742	-0.1	0748	0.6		
1656	5.6	1709	5.8	1535	4.2	1331	3.4	1306	2.0	1517	0.6	1403	0.7	1449	3.2	1321	9.6		
2252	0.9	2202	1.0	2134	0.7	1921	0.6	1908	0.4	2115	4.8	1949	4.0	2012	0.1	2004	0.9		
0518	5.3	0530	5.6	0356	4.1	0151	3.3	0124	2.0	0347	0.7	0230	0.9	0259	3.4	0142	9.4	8	M
1119	0.7	1027	0.9	1001	0.6	0750	0.5	0736	0.3	0957	4.6	0831	3.7	0830	0.0	0832	1.0		
1747	5.4	1800	5.6	1629	4.0	1422	3.2	1402	1.9	1603	1.0	1450	0.9	1536	3.2	1409	9.2		
2336	1.2	2245	1.4	2225	1.0	2010	0.8	1959	0.6	2212	4.6	2034	3.7	2104	0.3	2048	1.4		
0609	5.1	0622	5.3	0448	3.9	0241	3.1	0216	1.9	0441	1.0	0324	1.1	0342	3.4	0231	8.9	9	TU
1212	1.0	1202	1.1	1100	0.8	0849	0.6	0835	0.4	1106	4.3	0926	3.3	0925	0.2	0922	1.4		
1845	5.1	1857	5.3	1731	3.8	1521	3.0	1505	1.8	1657	1.4	1541	1.1	1627	3.1	1504	8.7		
		2342	1.7	2326	1.3	2110	1.1	2058	0.8	2324	4.3	2128	3.4	2203	0.6	2139	2.0		
0030	1.6	0723	5.0	0549	3.7	0337	3.0	0318	1.8	0545	1.4	0429	1.4	0430	3.3	0329	8.5	10	W
0709	4.9	1337	1.3	1209	0.9	1003	0.8	0945	0.5	1224	4.1	1043	3.1	1030	0.3	1023	1.8		
1318	1.3	2006	5.0	1845	3.6	1630	2.8	1612	1.7	1803	1.8	1639	1.3	1727	2.9	1609	8.2		
1952	4.8					2227	1.3	2212	0.9			2251	3.2	2312	0.7	2243	2.4		
0142	1.9	0209	2.0	0039	1.5	0446	2.8	0427	1.7	0046	4.1	0550	1.6	0525	3.2	0438	8.1	11	TH
0818	4.7	0839	4.8	0703	3.6	1128	0.8	1107	0.5	0706	1.6	1236	2.9	1144	0.5	1137	2.0		
1444	1.4	1510	1.4	1329	1.1	1748	2.7	1726	1.6	1342	4.0	1751	1.5	1836	2.9	1724	7.9		
2106	4.7	2120	4.9	2004	3.5	2356	1.3	2340	0.9	1928	1.9								
0316	2.0	0339	2.0	0202	1.6	0603	2.8	0540	1.7	0206	4.1	0118	3.2	0026	0.9	0003	2.7	12	F
0933	4.7	0954	4.8	0821	3.5	1251	0.8	1226	0.5	0833	1.6	0728	1.6	0631	3.1	0555	7.9		
1608	1.3	1629	1.3	1450	1.0	1906	2.7	1846	1.6	1457	4.0	1357	3.0	1301	0.5	1257	2.0		
2221	4.7	2230	4.9	2121	3.6					2057	1.9	1914	1.5	2004	2.9	1843	7.9		
0435	1.9	0448	1.8	0320	1.5	0117	1.3	0057	0.8	0318	4.2	0231	3.3	0142	0.9	0125	2.5	13	SA
1047	4.8	1100	4.9	0934	3.6	0717	2.9	0655	1.7	0946	1.4	0843	1.5	0757	3.0	0712	8.1		
1715	1.2	1734	1.1	1559	0.9	1357	0.7	1330	0.5	1600	4.2	1456	3.2	1415	0.5	1410	1.8		
2329	4.9	2333	5.1	2226	3.7	2012	2.8	1954	1.7	2205	1.7	2027	1.3	2123	3.0	1954	8.1		
0535	1.6	0545	1.7	0423	1.4	0218	1.2	0158	0.8	0416	4.4	0321	3.4	0248	0.8	0235	2.2	14	SU
1152	4.9	1200	5.1	1036	3.8	0821	3.0	0802	1.8	1042	1.2	0936	1.3	0922	3.1	0818	8.4		
1809	1.0	1833	1.0	1654	0.8	1448	0.7	1424	0.4	1648	4.4	1543	3.3	1516	0.4	1512	1.5		
				2318	3.8	2105	3.0	2045	1.8	2257	1.4	2123	1.1	2221	3.1	2051	8.5		
0024	5.1	0030	5.2	0513	1.2	0304	1.0	0247	0.7	0502	4.5	0400	3.5	0342	0.6	0333	1.8	15	M
0623	1.4	0635	1.5	1127	3.9	0915	3.1	0856	1.9	1127	1.0	1017	1.2	1023	3.2	0912	8.7		
1247	5.1	1254	5.3	1739	0.8	1530	0.6	1508	0.4	1727	4.6	1622	3.5	1604	0.4	1605	1.3		
1854	0.9	1923	1.0			2150	3.1	2128	1.8	2342	1.2	2208	1.0	2311	3.1	2139	8.8		

● ● Time: UT. For British Summer Time (shaded) March 26th to October 29th ADD ONE HOUR ● ●

MAY 2000 TIDE TABLES

•• Time: UT. For British Summer Time (shaded) March 26th to October 29th ADD ONE HOUR ••

	LEITH Time m	ROSYTH Time m	ABERDEEN Time m	WICK Time m	LERWICK Time m	ULLAPOOL Time m	OBAN Time m	GREENOCK Time m	LIVERPOOL Time m
16TU	0111 5.2	0117 5.3	0000 3.9	0343 0.9	0328 0.6	0541 4.6	0432 3.6	0427 0.4	0421 1.5
	0706 1.1	0647 1.3	0556 1.0	1003 3.2	0942 1.9	1207 0.9	1052 1.0	1112 3.3	0957 8.9
	1333 5.2	1341 5.5	1209 4.0	1605 0.6	1547 0.4	1803 4.8	1656 3.7	1645 0.3	1648 1.2
	1933 0.8	2002 1.0	1818 0.7	2229 3.1	2206 1.9		2248 0.9	2353 3.2	2219 0.8
17W	0151 5.3	0157 5.4	0037 4.0	0418 0.8	0406 0.5	0021 1.0	0500 3.7	0507 0.3	0501 1.4
	0746 1.0	0701 1.2	0634 0.9	1044 3.2	1024 1.9	0616 4.7	1126 1.0	1153 3.3	1037 9.0
	1414 5.3	1423 5.5	1249 4.0	1639 0.6	1622 0.4	1244 0.8	1727 3.8	1722 0.3	1725 1.1
	2008 0.8	2009 1.0	1853 0.7	2305 3.2	2242 1.9	1836 4.8	2326 0.9		2257 9.1
18TH O	0228 5.3	0235 5.5	0111 4.0	0454 0.7	0442 0.5	0059 0.9	0529 3.7	0030 3.2	0538 1.3
	0824 0.9	0737 1.0	0710 0.8	1123 3.2	1102 2.0	0650 4.7	1159 1.0	0545 0.2	1115 9.0
	1453 5.3	1503 5.6	1327 4.0	1711 0.6	1657 0.4	1318 0.8	1757 3.9	1230 3.2	1759 1.2
	2042 0.8	1956 1.0	1927 0.7	2339 3.2	2315 2.0	1908 4.9		1757 0.3	2330 9.1
19F	0304 5.3	0311 5.5	0144 4.0	0529 0.6	0517 0.4	0133 0.9	0003 0.9	0103 3.2	0612 1.3
	0859 0.8	0815 1.0	0745 0.8	1200 3.2	1138 1.9	0723 4.7	0600 3.8	0621 0.2	1149 9.0
	1530 5.3	1542 5.5	1403 4.0	1744 0.7	1730 0.5	1351 0.9	1233 1.0	1305 3.2	1830 1.3
	2112 0.9	2030 1.0	2000 0.8		2346 2.0	1940 4.8	1827 3.9	1831 0.4	
20SA	0339 5.2	0345 5.4	0217 4.0	0012 3.2	0551 0.5	0207 0.9	0039 1.0	0134 3.2	0003 9.1
	0930 0.9	0851 1.1	0819 0.8	0603 0.7	1212 1.9	0757 4.6	0632 3.7	0655 0.2	0644 1.3
	1606 5.2	1618 5.4	1439 3.9	1235 3.1	1802 0.6	1424 1.0	1306 1.1	1338 3.1	1222 8.9
	2139 1.0	2103 1.2	2032 0.9	1816 0.7		2012 4.7	1859 3.9	1904 0.5	1900 1.4
21SU	0414 5.1	0420 5.3	0249 4.0	0043 3.2	0017 2.0	0241 1.0	0117 1.1	0204 3.2	0036 9.0
	0956 1.0	0924 1.2	0852 0.9	0639 0.7	0624 0.5	0831 4.4	0705 3.7	0729 0.3	0715 1.5
	1641 5.1	1654 5.2	1516 3.8	1310 3.0	1246 1.8	1457 1.1	1339 1.2	1410 3.0	1255 8.7
	2205 1.2	2136 1.3	2105 1.1	1848 0.9	1834 0.6	2045 4.6	1932 3.8	1936 0.5	1930 1.7
22M	0450 5.0	0455 5.2	0322 3.9	0116 3.1	0048 1.9	0315 1.2	0154 1.3	0234 3.2	0109 8.8
	1020 1.2	0956 1.3	0927 1.0	0713 0.8	0700 0.6	0909 4.2	0739 3.5	0802 0.3	0748 1.7
	1718 4.9	1730 5.1	1555 3.7	1347 2.9	1322 1.8	1531 1.4	1415 1.3	1443 3.0	1328 8.4
	2233 1.4	2209 1.6	2139 1.2	1921 1.0	1909 0.7	2121 4.4	2007 3.6	2010 0.6	2000 2.0
23TU	0527 4.9	0533 5.1	0358 3.7	0151 3.0	0122 1.9	0352 1.4	0234 1.5	0305 3.2	0144 8.6
	1049 1.3	1030 1.5	1004 1.1	0751 0.9	0740 0.6	0951 4.0	0815 3.4	0839 0.4	0821 2.0
	1757 4.7	1809 4.9	1637 3.5	1427 2.8	1403 1.7	1608 1.6	1451 1.5	1518 2.9	1404 8.1
	2306 1.7	2243 1.8	2218 1.4	1959 1.2	1947 0.8	2205 4.2	2046 3.5	2048 0.7	2034 2.4
24W	0606 4.7	0615 5.0	0439 3.6	0230 2.9	0201 1.8	0433 1.6	0318 1.7	0338 3.1	0221 8.2
	1127 1.5	1110 1.7	1047 1.2	0835 1.0	0827 0.7	1042 3.9	0855 3.2	0921 0.5	0900 2.3
	1841 4.6	1854 4.8	1725 3.4	1512 2.6	1449 1.6	1649 1.8	1532 1.7	1557 2.8	1445 7.8
	2351 1.9	2323 2.0	2303 1.6	2043 1.3	2033 0.9	2259 4.0	2135 3.3	2133 0.9	2115 2.7
25TH	0651 4.5	0702 4.8	0527 3.5	0315 2.8	0247 1.7	0520 1.8	0408 1.8	0415 3.0	0306 7.9
	1222 1.7	1213 1.9	1139 1.4	0930 1.1	0924 0.7	1145 3.7	0944 3.0	1013 0.6	0947 2.6
	1930 4.4	1944 4.6	1821 3.3	1604 2.5	1542 1.5	1740 2.1	1620 1.8	1643 2.8	1533 7.4
				2143 1.4	2135 1.0		2245 3.1	2228 1.0	2206 3.1
26F	0054 2.1	0104 2.3	0000 1.7	0408 2.7	0342 1.6	0006 3.9	0507 1.9	0500 2.9	0400 7.6
	0743 4.4	0753 4.4	0624 3.4	1039 1.1	1034 0.8	0619 1.9	1053 2.9	1116 0.7	1044 2.8
	1338 1.8	1335 1.9	1243 1.4	1708 2.5	1644 1.5	1300 3.6	1724 1.9	1742 2.7	1636 7.2
	2026 4.3	2039 4.6	1926 3.2	2300 1.5	2254 1.0	1849 2.2		2333 1.0	2312 3.3
27SA	0215 2.2	0220 2.3	0111 1.8	0511 2.6	0446 1.6	0119 3.8	0015 3.1	0600 2.8	0507 7.4
	0841 4.3	0848 4.6	0730 3.3	1154 1.1	1145 0.7	0733 1.9	0616 1.9	1225 0.7	1154 2.8
	1500 1.8	1440 1.9	1357 1.4	1817 2.5	1754 1.5	1413 3.7	1227 2.8	1854 2.7	1751 7.2
	2129 4.3	2138 4.6	2034 3.3			2014 2.2	1842 1.9		
28SU	0336 2.1	0335 2.3	0227 1.7	0016 1.4	0011 0.9	0226 3.9	0128 3.2	0044 1.0	0030 3.2
	0945 4.4	0949 4.6	0839 3.4	0618 2.7	0557 1.6	0847 1.8	0726 1.8	0727 2.8	0619 7.6
	1613 1.6	1554 1.8	1505 1.3	1300 1.0	1246 0.7	1514 3.9	1346 2.9	1333 0.6	1307 2.6
	2235 4.5	2240 4.8	2137 3.4	1922 2.6	1903 1.6	2125 2.0	1954 1.7	2009 2.8	1901 7.5
29M	0442 1.9	0445 2.0	0332 1.6	0121 1.3	0111 0.8	0323 4.1	0221 3.3	0153 0.9	0142 2.8
	1050 4.6	1054 4.8	0941 3.5	0722 2.8	0704 1.6	0948 1.5	0849 1.6	0849 2.8	0724 8.0
	1711 1.4	1709 1.5	1602 1.1	1355 0.9	1337 0.6	1604 4.1	1441 3.1	1434 0.4	1412 2.2
	2336 4.8	2340 5.0	2231 3.6	2019 2.8	1957 1.7	2220 1.7	2049 1.5	2115 2.9	2000 8.0
30TU	0536 1.6	0542 1.7	0425 1.3	0215 1.1	0201 0.7	0412 4.4	0306 3.5	0254 0.7	0243 2.3
	1151 4.8	1157 5.1	1035 3.7	0820 2.9	0801 1.8	1038 1.2	0914 1.3	0951 3.0	0821 8.4
	1801 1.1	1806 1.2	1651 0.9	1442 0.7	1424 0.5	1647 4.4	1527 3.4	1527 0.2	1511 1.7
			2318 3.8	2109 3.0	2043 1.8	2306 1.3	2136 1.2	2212 3.0	2052 8.6
31W	0030 5.0	0034 5.3	0512 1.1	0302 0.9	0247 0.6	0457 4.6	0351 3.8	0345 0.5	0337 1.7
	0624 1.2	0629 1.4	1124 3.9	0913 3.1	0852 1.9	1124 0.9	1000 1.1	1044 3.1	0911 8.9
	1244 5.1	1251 5.4	1736 0.7	1527 0.5	1508 0.4	1727 4.7	1609 3.6	1613 0.1	1603 1.3
	1849 0.8	1848 1.0		2154 3.2	2127 2.0	2351 1.0	2220 1.0	2303 3.1	2139 9.0

SCOTLAND & NORTH WEST ENGLAND Time Zone UT
Leith * Rosyth * Aberdeen * Wick * Lerwick * Ullapool * Oban * Greenock * Liverpool

TIDE TABLES JUNE 2000

LEITH	ROSYTH	ABERDEEN	WICK	LERWICK	ULLAPOOL	OBAN	GREENOCK	LIVERPOOL	
Time m	Time m	Time m	Time m	Time m	Time m	Time m	Time m	Time m	
0118 5.3	0122 5.6	0002 4.0	0346 0.7	0330 0.5	0540 4.9	0435 4.0	0431 0.3	0428 1.3	**1 TH**
0712 0.9	0707 1.1	0557 0.8	1003 3.3	0941 2.0	1208 0.6	1046 0.8	1133 3.1	0959 9.3	
1332 5.4	1340 5.6	1211 4.1	1609 0.4	1552 0.3	1806 5.0	1651 3.9	1657 -0.0	1652 0.9	
1937 0.6	1914 0.8	1820 0.5	2239 3.3	2211 2.1		2306 0.8	2351 3.2	2225 9.4	
0202 5.5	0207 5.8	0044 4.2	0431 0.5	0415 0.3	0034 0.7	0520 4.1	0515 0.1	0517 0.9	**2 F**
0759 0.7	0736 0.8	0642 0.6	1053 3.4	1029 2.1	0624 5.1	1131 0.6	1221 3.2	1046 9.6	●
1418 5.6	1428 5.8	1258 4.3	1653 0.4	1636 0.3	1251 0.4	1733 4.0	1741 -0.1	1739 0.7	
2025 0.5	1948 0.7	1905 0.4	2322 3.4	2254 2.1	1847 5.1	2352 0.6		2310 9.6	
0245 5.6	0252 5.9	0127 4.3	0517 0.4	0500 0.3	0118 0.5	0606 4.2	0036 3.3	0604 0.6	**3 SA**
0848 0.5	0813 0.6	0727 0.4	1142 3.5	1118 2.1	0711 5.2	1217 0.5	0558 -0.0	1133 9.8	
1505 5.8	1517 6.0	1345 4.4	1738 0.4	1721 0.3	1336 0.4	1815 4.2	1309 3.2	1824 0.6	
2113 0.5	2030 0.7	1950 0.5		2339 2.1	1930 5.2		1825 -0.0	2357 9.7	
0330 5.7	0339 5.9	0210 4.3	0006 3.5	0547 0.2	0204 0.4	0041 0.6	0120 3.4	0651 0.5	**4 SU**
0937 0.4	0918 0.6	0815 0.4	0604 0.3	1209 2.1	0800 5.1	0651 4.1	0643 -0.1	1221 9.8	
1554 5.8	1606 6.0	1436 4.4	1232 3.5	1808 0.4	1420 0.5	1303 0.5	1357 3.3	1909 0.7	
2200 0.6	2152 0.9	2037 0.6	1824 0.5		2017 5.1	1857 4.2	1912 0.1		
0416 5.6	0428 5.8	0255 4.3	0052 3.4	0024 2.1	0251 0.4	0131 0.7	0203 3.5	0044 9.7	**5 M**
1027 0.4	1047 0.6	0906 0.4	0654 0.3	0636 0.2	0854 4.9	0739 3.9	0730 -0.1	0739 0.5	
1645 5.7	1658 5.9	1528 4.3	1323 3.4	1303 2.1	1506 0.7	1349 0.6	1445 3.3	1311 9.6	
2248 0.9	2221 1.1	2126 0.8	1912 0.6	1857 0.5	2108 5.0	1942 4.0	2000 0.2	1954 0.9	
0506 5.5	0520 5.7	0344 4.2	0139 3.4	0115 2.1	0342 0.6	0224 0.8	0246 3.5	0133 9.5	**6 TU**
1118 0.5	1139 0.7	0959 0.4	0748 0.4	0730 0.2	0952 4.7	0828 3.7	0821 0.0	0828 0.7	
1738 5.5	1752 5.7	1624 4.1	1416 3.2	1400 1.9	1555 1.0	1436 0.8	1534 3.2	1402 9.2	
2335 1.2	2354 1.4	2218 1.0	2002 0.8	1949 0.6	2206 4.8	2030 3.8	2053 0.4	2041 1.3	
0600 5.3	0616 5.4	0437 4.0	0230 3.3	0209 2.0	0436 0.9	0321 1.1	0331 3.5	0224 9.2	**7 W**
1212 0.7	1233 0.9	1057 0.6	0847 0.5	0827 0.3	1057 4.4	0923 3.4	0917 0.1	0920 1.0	
1836 5.2	1851 5.4	1725 3.9	1514 3.0	1457 1.8	1648 1.3	1527 1.0	1626 3.2	1457 8.8	
		2315 1.2	2058 1.1	2046 0.7	2312 4.5	2127 3.6	2149 0.6	2133 1.7	
0024 1.5	0048 1.6	0536 3.9	0325 3.1	0307 1.9	0536 1.1	0422 1.3	0420 3.5	0319 8.8	**8 TH**
0659 5.1	0719 5.2	1159 0.8	0953 0.6	0930 0.4	1206 4.2	1027 3.2	1017 0.3	1017 1.4	
1311 1.0	1334 1.1	1831 3.7	1616 2.9	1556 1.7	1749 1.6	1623 1.2	1721 3.1	1556 8.4	
1938 5.0	1956 5.2		2203 1.2	2149 0.8		2241 3.3	2251 0.7	2231 2.1	
0122 1.8	0151 1.8	0019 1.4	0427 3.0	0408 1.8	0024 4.3	0531 1.5	0513 3.4	0420 8.4	**9 F**
0803 4.9	0827 5.1	0643 3.7	1105 0.7	1040 0.5	0644 1.4	1148 3.0	1123 0.4	1120 1.7	
1419 1.2	1448 1.2	1307 0.9	1723 2.8	1659 1.6	1316 4.1	1726 1.3	1822 3.0	1700 8.0	
2044 4.8	2101 5.0	1939 3.6	2318 1.3	2301 0.9	1859 1.8		2358 0.8	2339 2.4	
0233 1.9	0305 1.9	0129 1.5	0535 2.9	0512 1.8	0137 4.2	0031 3.2	0614 3.3	0527 8.2	**10 SA**
0909 4.8	0932 5.0	0753 3.7	1217 0.8	1154 0.5	0757 1.5	0647 1.6	1234 0.5	1227 1.9	
1532 1.3	1600 1.2	1418 1.0	1832 2.7	1806 1.6	1425 4.0	1309 3.0	1933 3.0	1810 7.9	
2151 4.8	2205 5.0	2048 3.5			2016 1.9	1836 1.4			
0350 1.9	0412 1.9	0242 1.6	0035 1.3	0019 0.9	0247 4.2	0153 3.2	0110 0.8	0050 2.5	**11 SU**
1016 4.8	1034 5.0	0903 3.7	0645 2.9	0621 1.7	0907 1.5	0758 1.6	0727 3.2	0636 8.1	
1638 1.3	1703 1.3	1526 1.1	1324 0.8	1259 0.6	1528 4.1	1415 3.1	1345 0.6	1334 1.9	
2254 4.8	2306 5.0	2153 3.6	1936 2.8	1912 1.6	2128 1.8	1947 1.4	2045 3.0	1918 8.0	
0456 1.8	0509 1.8	0349 1.5	0143 1.2	0127 0.8	0348 4.2	0248 3.3	0218 0.8	0157 2.4	**12 M**
1121 4.9	1133 5.1	1006 3.7	0750 2.9	0728 1.7	1008 1.5	0856 1.5	0847 3.1	0743 8.1	
1734 1.3	1803 1.3	1624 1.1	1418 0.8	1354 0.6	1620 4.3	1507 3.2	1449 0.6	1436 1.9	
2353 4.9		2248 3.7	2033 2.9	2010 1.7	2227 1.7	2047 1.3	2148 3.1	2018 8.2	
0551 1.6	0002 5.1	0445 1.4	0237 1.1	0221 0.7	0439 4.3	0330 3.3	0318 0.6	0258 2.2	**13 TU**
1219 4.9	0556 1.8	1101 3.7	0848 3.0	0828 1.8	1058 1.4	0942 1.4	0952 3.1	0841 8.3	
1821 1.3	1230 5.2	1711 1.0	1501 0.8	1442 0.6	1703 4.4	1551 3.3	1542 0.5	1530 1.8	
	1856 1.3	2333 3.8	2121 3.0	2057 1.8	2317 1.5	2137 1.3	2241 3.1	2109 8.4	
0044 5.0	0053 5.1	0532 1.2	0321 1.0	0307 0.7	0521 4.4	0403 3.4	0407 0.5	0350 2.0	**14 W**
0639 1.4	0608 1.6	1148 3.8	0938 3.0	0918 1.8	1142 1.3	1022 1.3	1045 3.1	0930 8.5	
1309 5.0	1319 5.3	1751 1.0	1539 0.8	1522 0.6	1741 4.6	1627 3.5	1626 0.5	1616 1.7	
1900 1.2	1930 1.4		2203 3.1	2139 1.9		2221 1.2	2325 3.2	2153 8.6	
0128 5.1	0136 5.2	0012 3.9	0400 0.9	0348 0.6	0000 1.4	0434 3.5	0450 0.4	0434 1.8	**15 TH**
0721 1.2	0636 1.4	0613 1.1	1022 3.1	1003 1.9	0600 4.4	1100 1.2	1129 3.1	1013 8.6	
1354 5.1	1403 5.3	1230 3.9	1614 0.8	1600 0.6	1221 1.2	1702 3.6	1705 0.5	1656 1.6	
1931 1.1	1854 1.8	1829 1.0	2240 3.2	2217 1.9	1816 4.7	2302 1.2		2232 8.8	

● ● Time: UT. For British Summer Time (shaded) March 26th to October 29th ADD ONE HOUR ● ●

JUNE 2000 TIDE TABLES

•• Time: UT. For British Summer Time (shaded) March 26th to October 29th ADD ONE HOUR ••

	LEITH		ROSYTH		ABERDEEN		WICK		LERWICK		ULLAPOOL		OBAN		GREENOCK		LIVERPOOL	
	Time	m	Time	m	Time	m	Time	m	Time	m	Time	m	Time	m	Time	m	Time	m
16 F O	0208	5.1	0213	5.3	0048	3.9	0437	0.8	0426	0.6	0039	1.2	0508	3.6	0004	3.2	0513	1.7
	0800	1.1	0715	1.3	0651	1.0	1103	3.1	1042	1.9	0635	4.5	1136	1.1	0529	0.4	1051	8.7
	1433	5.1	1444	5.4	1309	3.9	1648	0.8	1635	0.6	1257	1.1	1735	3.8	1207	3.0	1731	1.6
	2012	1.1	1931	1.3	1904	1.0	2315	3.2	2252	2.0	1849	4.8	2342	1.2	1741	0.5	2308	8.9
17 SA	0245	5.2	0248	5.4	0123	4.0	0513	0.8	0501	0.5	0115	1.2	0542	3.6	0039	3.2	0549	1.6
	0836	1.0	0756	1.2	0727	0.9	1140	3.1	1120	1.9	0709	4.5	1211	1.1	0606	0.3	1128	8.7
	1510	5.1	1521	5.4	1348	3.9	1722	0.8	1708	0.6	1331	1.1	1809	3.8	1243	3.0	1804	1.6
	2045	1.1	2010	1.2	1939	1.0	2349	3.2	2325	2.0	1922	4.8			1815	0.6	2343	9.0
18 SU	0320	5.2	0323	5.4	0156	4.0	0548	0.7	0535	0.5	0151	1.1	0020	1.2	0110	3.2	0623	1.6
	0909	1.0	0836	1.2	0803	0.9	1216	3.1	1155	1.9	0744	4.5	0618	3.7	0639	0.3	1203	8.7
	1545	5.1	1556	5.3	1424	3.9	1756	0.9	1741	0.7	1405	1.2	1245	1.1	1317	3.0	1836	1.6
	2116	1.1	2048	1.3	2012	1.0			2357	2.0	1954	4.7	1842	3.9	1846	0.6		
19 M	0354	5.1	0358	5.4	0229	4.0	0022	3.2	0609	0.5	0224	1.1	0057	1.2	0142	3.3	0017	9.0
	0939	1.0	0916	1.2	0836	0.9	0624	0.7	1230	1.8	0818	4.4	0653	3.6	0711	0.4	0657	1.6
	1619	5.1	1630	5.2	1500	3.8	1252	3.0	1814	0.7	1438	1.2	1320	1.2	1350	3.0	1236	8.6
	2148	1.2	2126	1.4	2045	1.1	1829	0.9			2027	4.7	1916	3.8	1918	0.6	1908	1.7
20 TU	0429	5.1	0434	5.4	0302	3.9	0056	3.2	0028	2.0	0259	1.2	0136	1.3	0212	3.3	0051	8.9
	1010	1.1	0954	1.3	0910	0.9	0659	0.8	0644	0.5	0854	4.3	0728	3.6	0744	0.4	0730	1.6
	1655	5.0	1706	5.2	1537	3.8	1328	3.0	1305	1.8	1512	1.4	1354	1.3	1424	3.0	1310	8.5
	2221	1.3	2202	1.5	2120	1.2	1903	1.0	1848	0.7	2103	4.6	1951	3.7	1953	0.7	1941	1.9
21 W	0505	5.0	0511	5.3	0337	3.9	0130	3.1	0102	1.9	0335	1.3	0214	1.4	0245	3.3	0126	8.7
	1043	1.2	1028	1.4	0947	1.0	0735	0.8	0721	0.6	0931	4.2	0803	3.5	0820	0.4	0806	1.8
	1733	4.9	1745	5.1	1615	3.7	1406	2.9	1342	1.7	1548	1.5	1428	1.4	1502	3.0	1345	8.3
	2256	1.5	2235	1.7	2157	1.3	1939	1.1	1926	0.8	2142	4.4	2029	3.6	2032	0.7	2017	2.1
22 TH	0543	4.9	0551	5.2	0415	3.8	0208	3.1	0139	1.9	0412	1.4	0254	1.5	0319	3.3	0203	8.5
	1120	1.3	1103	1.5	1027	1.1	0815	0.9	0803	0.6	1014	4.1	0839	3.3	0902	0.5	0845	1.9
	1813	4.7	1826	5.0	1658	3.6	1446	2.8	1424	1.7	1627	1.7	1505	1.5	1542	3.0	1423	8.1
	2334	1.8	2307	1.8	2237	1.4	2019	1.2	2007	0.8	2228	4.3	2110	3.4	2116	0.8	2057	2.4
23 F	0624	4.8	0631	5.1	0458	3.7	0248	3.0	0221	1.8	0455	1.5	0339	1.6	0357	3.2	0242	8.3
	1204	1.4	1140	1.6	1111	1.2	0859	1.0	0848	0.6	1104	4.0	0919	3.2	0949	0.5	0927	2.2
	1858	4.6	1911	4.9	1745	3.5	1531	2.7	1511	1.6	1711	1.8	1547	1.6	1628	3.0	1506	7.8
			2347	2.0	2325	1.5	2106	1.3	2055	0.9	2323	4.2	2200	3.3	2205	0.8	2141	2.6
24 SA	0022	1.8	0715	4.9	0547	3.6	0335	2.9	0309	1.7	0544	1.7	0427	1.7	0438	3.1	0329	8.1
	0710	4.7	1231	1.7	1203	1.2	0952	1.0	0941	0.7	1205	3.9	1007	3.0	1043	0.6	1014	2.3
	1259	1.6	2000	4.8	1840	3.4	1624	2.7	1604	1.6	1805	2.0	1637	1.7	1718	2.9	1557	7.6
	1948	4.5					2206	1.4	2153	0.9			2303	3.2	2300	0.9	2233	2.8
25 SU	0123	2.0	0057	2.2	0022	1.6	0429	2.8	0406	1.7	0026	4.1	0524	1.7	0527	3.0	0423	7.9
	0802	4.6	0804	4.8	0643	3.5	1055	1.1	1042	0.7	0642	1.7	1109	3.0	1144	0.6	1109	2.5
	1403	1.6	1339	1.7	1303	1.3	1724	2.6	1705	1.6	1313	3.8	1739	1.7	1816	2.9	1658	7.6
	2046	4.5	2056	4.8	1941	3.4	2315	1.4	2304	0.9	1912	2.1					2337	2.9
26 M	0233	2.0	0225	2.2	0129	1.7	0530	2.8	0511	1.7	0132	4.1	0016	3.2	0002	0.9	0527	7.9
	0900	4.6	0900	4.8	0746	3.5	1203	1.0	1151	0.7	0748	1.7	0624	1.7	0632	2.9	1215	2.4
	1511	1.6	1447	1.7	1409	1.3	1829	2.7	1809	1.6	1420	3.9	1223	3.0	1249	0.6	1806	7.7
	2148	4.6	2157	4.9	2045	3.5					2025	2.0	1848	1.7	1920	2.9		
27 TU	0345	1.9	0339	2.1	0238	1.6	0027	1.3	0021	0.9	0235	4.2	0124	3.3	0108	0.8	0049	2.7
	1003	4.7	1005	4.9	0852	3.6	0635	2.9	0619	1.7	0855	1.6	0729	1.6	0750	2.9	0634	8.0
	1619	1.5	1603	1.6	1515	1.2	1307	0.9	1254	0.6	1520	4.1	1339	3.1	1354	0.5	1325	2.2
	2254	4.7	2259	5.0	2148	3.6	1933	2.8	1912	1.7	2133	1.8	1956	1.5	2028	2.9	1915	8.0
28 W	0452	1.7	0453	1.9	0343	1.4	0133	1.2	0124	0.8	0334	4.3	0224	3.4	0215	0.7	0200	2.4
	1109	4.8	1113	5.1	0957	3.7	0740	3.0	0724	1.8	0957	1.4	0831	1.4	0906	2.9	0739	8.3
	1723	1.3	1721	1.4	1615	1.0	1406	0.8	1350	0.6	1613	4.4	1444	3.3	1455	0.3	1432	1.9
	2354	5.0	2357	5.3	2244	3.8	2032	3.0	2008	1.8	2233	1.5	2057	1.3	2134	3.0	2016	8.4
29 TH	0552	1.4	0551	1.6	0442	1.2	0231	1.0	0218	0.7	0430	4.6	0321	3.6	0315	0.6	0303	2.0
	1212	5.1	1215	5.3	1056	3.9	0842	3.1	0824	1.9	1053	1.1	0929	1.2	1010	3.0	0839	8.7
	1821	1.1	1816	1.2	1709	0.9	1500	0.7	1442	0.5	1702	4.6	1539	3.5	1549	0.2	1532	1.5
					2335	4.0	2125	3.2	2059	1.9	2326	1.2	2154	1.1	2234	3.1	2112	8.9
30 F	0049	5.2	0050	5.5	0535	0.9	0325	0.8	0308	0.5	0521	4.9	0415	3.8	0409	0.4	0402	1.5
	0648	1.1	0636	1.2	1151	4.1	0941	3.3	0920	2.0	1145	0.9	1023	0.9	1108	3.1	0936	9.1
	1309	5.4	1312	5.6	1800	0.7	1549	0.6	1531	0.5	1748	4.9	1630	3.8	1639	0.1	1627	1.1
	1918	0.9	1855	1.1			2215	3.3	2148	2.1			2248	0.9	2327	3.2	2204	9.3

SCOTLAND & NORTH WEST ENGLAND Time Zone UT
Leith * Rosyth * Aberdeen * Wick * Lerwick * Ullapool * Oban * Greenock * Liverpool

TIDE TABLES JULY 2000

Day	LEITH	ROSYTH	ABERDEEN	WICK	LERWICK	ULLAPOOL	OBAN	GREENOCK	LIVERPOOL
	Time m	Time m	Time m	Time m	Time m	Time m	Time m	Time m	Time m
1 SA	0139 5.4 0742 0.8 1400 5.6 2011 0.7	0140 5.7 0720 0.9 1405 5.8 1938 0.9	0023 4.2 0626 0.7 1244 4.3 1850 0.6	0416 0.6 1036 3.4 1638 0.6 2303 3.5	0357 0.4 1015 2.1 1620 0.4 2236 2.1	0017 0.9 0612 5.0 1234 0.7 1834 5.1	0507 3.9 1113 0.7 1718 4.0 2341 0.7	0458 0.2 1203 3.2 1726 0.1	0457 1.1 1029 9.5 1719 0.9 2254 9.6
2 SU ●	0227 5.6 0836 0.5 1451 5.8 2102 0.6	0231 5.8 0854 0.7 1458 6.0 2115 0.9	0109 4.3 0717 0.5 1336 4.4 1939 0.6	0506 0.4 1130 3.5 1725 0.6 2351 3.6	0447 0.3 1109 2.1 1708 0.4 2325 2.2	0106 0.6 0703 5.1 1322 0.6 1920 5.3	0558 4.0 1202 0.5 1805 4.1	0017 3.3 0545 0.1 1257 3.2 1812 0.1	0551 0.7 1120 9.7 1809 0.7 2344 9.7
3 M	0314 5.7 0930 0.3 1541 5.8 2151 0.6	0322 5.9 0950 0.5 1551 6.1 2206 0.9	0155 4.4 0807 0.3 1428 4.4 2027 0.7	0557 0.3 1222 3.5 1813 0.6	0536 0.2 1203 2.1 1757 0.5	0154 0.4 0754 5.2 1409 0.6 2008 5.3	0033 0.6 0647 4.0 1249 0.5 1851 4.2	0104 3.4 0633 -0.0 1350 3.3 1900 0.2	0642 0.4 1211 9.7 1857 0.7
4 TU	0403 5.7 1021 0.2 1632 5.8 2237 0.8	0415 5.9 1041 0.4 1645 6.0 2255 1.0	0242 4.4 0859 0.3 1520 4.3 2115 0.8	0039 3.6 0648 0.2 1314 3.4 1900 0.7	0015 2.2 0627 0.2 1256 2.1 1845 0.5	0243 0.4 0845 5.1 1456 0.7 2057 5.2	0126 0.6 0734 4.0 1335 0.5 1937 4.1	0150 3.6 0720 -0.0 1440 3.3 1948 0.3	0033 9.8 0732 0.4 1301 9.6 1945 0.8
5 W	0454 5.7 1110 0.3 1724 5.6 2321 1.0	0509 5.8 1130 0.5 1739 5.9 2341 1.2	0331 4.4 0950 0.3 1613 4.2 2204 0.9	0127 3.6 0739 0.3 1405 3.3 1947 0.8	0105 2.2 0718 0.2 1348 2.0 1934 0.6	0333 0.5 0938 4.9 1543 0.9 2149 5.0	0218 0.8 0820 3.8 1422 0.6 2024 4.0	0235 3.7 0809 0.0 1528 3.3 2036 0.4	0122 9.7 0821 0.4 1351 9.4 2031 1.0
6 TH	0546 5.5 1158 0.5 1818 5.4	0605 5.7 1218 0.7 1835 5.6	0422 4.3 1042 0.5 1708 4.0 2254 1.1	0215 3.5 0832 0.4 1457 3.1 2036 1.0	0156 2.1 0811 0.3 1439 1.9 2024 0.7	0422 0.7 1033 4.6 1632 1.1 2247 4.8	0309 0.9 0906 3.6 1509 0.8 2113 3.7	0321 3.7 0900 0.1 1615 3.3 2128 0.5	0211 9.5 0909 0.7 1440 9.0 2118 1.4
7 F	0004 1.3 0642 5.3 1247 0.8 1915 5.1	0026 1.5 0703 5.5 1309 0.9 1932 5.4	0516 4.1 1136 0.7 1804 3.8 2348 1.3	0306 3.3 0927 0.6 1550 3.0 2128 1.2	0248 2.0 0905 0.4 1530 1.8 2117 0.8	0514 1.0 1133 4.4 1724 1.4 2351 4.5	0403 1.2 0954 3.3 1600 1.0 2207 3.4	0407 3.7 0955 0.3 1703 3.3 2224 0.6	0300 9.1 0959 1.1 1531 8.6 2209 1.8
8 SA	0048 1.6 0739 5.1 1339 1.2 2012 4.9	0110 1.7 0802 5.3 1408 1.2 2030 5.2	0615 3.9 1233 0.9 1903 3.6	0401 3.2 1027 0.8 1647 2.8 2229 1.3	0342 1.9 1003 0.5 1623 1.7 2216 0.8	0609 1.3 1239 4.2 1821 1.7	0457 1.4 1048 3.1 1654 1.2 2313 3.2	0456 3.6 1056 0.5 1754 3.2 2327 0.7	0352 8.7 1051 1.6 1626 8.2 2303 2.3
9 SU	0141 1.8 0839 4.9 1439 1.5 2112 4.7	0206 2.0 0902 5.1 1518 1.5 2130 5.0	0048 1.5 0718 3.8 1336 1.2 2006 3.5	0501 3.0 1131 1.0 1748 2.8 2342 1.4	0439 1.8 1109 0.6 1721 1.6 2330 0.9	0059 4.3 0710 1.6 1345 4.1 1927 2.0	0557 1.6 1157 3.0 1754 1.4	0548 3.5 1202 0.6 1851 3.1	0449 8.2 1148 2.0 1727 7.8
10 M	0251 2.0 0940 4.8 1548 1.6 2212 4.6	0321 2.1 1001 5.0 1624 1.7 2229 4.9	0157 1.6 0824 3.6 1442 1.3 2111 3.5	0606 2.9 1239 1.1 1852 2.8	0542 1.7 1219 0.7 1824 1.6	0209 4.1 0818 1.8 1451 4.1 2042 2.1	0043 3.1 0701 1.7 1320 3.0 1901 1.5	0035 0.8 0648 3.2 1312 0.7 1959 3.0	0006 2.6 0553 7.9 1251 2.3 1833 7.7
11 TU	0412 2.0 1045 4.7 1652 1.5 2315 4.7	0426 2.1 1101 5.0 1724 1.8 2327 4.9	0309 1.6 0933 3.6 1547 1.4 2212 3.5	0102 1.4 0714 2.9 1342 1.1 1954 2.8	0051 0.9 0651 1.7 1322 0.8 1929 1.7	0317 4.1 0927 1.8 1549 4.1 2155 2.0	0206 3.0 0809 1.7 1430 3.0 2009 1.6	0146 0.8 0801 3.1 1421 0.8 2110 3.0	0114 2.7 0702 7.8 1355 2.4 1940 7.8
12 W	0520 1.9 1149 4.7 1746 1.7	0514 2.0 1200 5.0 1814 1.8	0416 1.6 1035 3.6 1642 1.4 2304 3.7	0211 1.3 0819 2.9 1433 1.1 2050 2.9	0156 0.8 0800 1.7 1415 0.8 2026 1.8	0415 4.1 1028 1.8 1639 4.3 2254 1.9	0300 3.1 0908 1.6 1524 3.2 2109 1.6	0252 0.8 0918 3.0 1521 0.8 2211 3.0	0221 2.7 0808 7.8 1455 2.3 2039 8.0
13 TH	0014 4.8 0615 1.7 1247 4.8 1831 1.6	0022 5.0 0544 1.9 1256 5.1 1806 1.8	0510 1.4 1129 3.7 1727 1.3 2349 3.8	0303 1.2 0915 2.9 1516 1.1 2136 3.0	0249 0.8 0857 1.7 1501 0.8 2114 1.8	0505 4.2 1118 1.7 1721 4.4 2342 1.7	0342 3.2 0957 1.5 1606 3.3 2200 1.5	0348 0.7 1019 2.9 1611 0.7 2300 3.1	0319 2.5 0904 8.0 1546 2.2 2128 8.3
14 F	0105 4.9 0701 1.5 1335 4.9 1911 1.5	0110 5.1 0618 1.7 1344 5.2 1835 1.7	0555 1.3 1215 3.7 1808 1.3	0346 1.1 1003 3.0 1554 1.1 2218 3.2	0333 0.7 0944 1.8 1541 0.8 2155 1.9	0546 4.3 1201 1.5 1758 4.6	0419 3.3 1039 1.4 1645 3.5 2245 1.4	0436 0.6 1109 2.9 1654 0.7 2342 3.1	0409 2.2 0952 8.2 1630 2.0 2211 8.6
15 SA	0148 5.0 0742 1.3 1415 5.0 1948 1.4	0151 5.3 0657 1.5 1424 5.3 1913 1.5	0028 3.9 0635 1.1 1256 3.8 1845 1.2	0424 1.0 1045 3.1 1630 1.0 2254 3.2	0412 0.7 1025 1.9 1618 0.7 2233 2.0	0023 1.5 0623 4.4 1239 1.4 1833 4.7	0457 3.4 1118 1.3 1720 3.7 2326 1.3	0517 0.5 1151 2.9 1730 0.7	0453 2.0 1033 8.4 1709 1.9 2250 8.8

● ● Time: UT. For British Summer Time (shaded) March 26th to October 29th ADD ONE HOUR ● ●

	LEITH Time	m	ROSYTH Time	m	ABERDEEN Time	m	WICK Time	m	LERWICK Time	m	ULLAPOOL Time	m	OBAN Time	m	GREENOCK Time	m	LIVERPOOL Time	m
16 SU O	0227	5.1	0229	5.4	0104	4.0	0500	0.9	0448	0.6	0100	1.4	0534	3.5	0018	3.2	0531	1.8
	0818	1.2	0739	1.3	0712	1.0	1124	3.1	1103	1.9	0657	4.5	1154	1.2	0554	0.4	1111	8.6
	1451	5.1	1501	5.4	1333	3.9	1704	1.0	1651	0.7	1315	1.3	1754	3.8	1228	2.9	1743	1.7
	2022	1.3	1954	1.4	1921	1.1	2330	3.3	2307	2.0	1905	4.8			1803	0.7	2326	8.9
17 M	0302	5.2	0305	5.5	0138	4.0	0534	0.8	0520	0.6	0135	1.2	0005	1.3	0052	3.3	0607	1.6
	0851	1.1	0823	1.2	0746	0.9	1200	3.1	1139	1.9	0729	4.6	0609	3.6	0626	0.4	1146	8.7
	1525	5.1	1536	5.4	1409	3.9	1737	1.0	1724	0.7	1348	1.3	1228	1.1	1303	2.9	1817	1.6
	2057	1.2	2036	1.4	1954	1.1			2339	2.0	1936	4.9	1828	3.9	1833	0.7		
18 TU	0336	5.2	0340	5.5	0210	4.1	0003	3.3	0552	0.5	0209	1.2	0042	1.2	0124	3.3	0000	9.0
	0924	1.0	0904	1.2	0820	0.9	0608	0.8	1212	1.9	0800	4.6	0644	3.7	0656	0.4	0642	1.5
	1558	5.1	1609	5.4	1442	3.9	1234	3.1	1756	0.7	1421	1.3	1301	1.1	1338	3.0	1219	8.7
	2133	1.1	2116	1.4	2027	1.1	1810	1.0			2009	4.9	1902	3.9	1904	0.7	1851	1.6
19 W	0410	5.2	0415	5.5	0242	4.1	0037	3.3	0011	2.0	0242	1.1	0118	1.2	0157	3.4	0034	9.0
	0958	0.9	0942	1.2	0853	0.8	0641	0.7	0624	0.5	0833	4.6	0716	3.6	0727	0.4	0716	1.5
	1633	5.1	1644	5.4	1517	3.9	1309	3.1	1246	1.9	1454	1.3	1333	1.1	1413	3.1	1253	8.7
	2208	1.2	2153	1.4	2100	1.1	1844	1.0	1830	0.7	2042	4.8	1935	3.8	1938	0.6	1924	1.6
20 TH	0445	5.2	0451	5.5	0316	4.0	0111	3.3	0043	2.0	0315	1.1	0153	1.3	0229	3.4	0109	9.0
	1033	1.0	1014	1.2	0927	0.9	0715	0.7	0700	0.5	0906	4.5	0747	3.6	0802	0.4	0751	1.5
	1709	5.1	1720	5.4	1552	3.8	1344	3.0	1321	1.8	1527	1.3	1405	1.2	1449	3.1	1327	8.6
	2242	1.2	2222	1.5	2135	1.2	1918	1.0	1905	0.7	2117	4.7	2009	3.7	2015	0.6	2000	1.7
21 F	0520	5.1	0526	5.4	0352	4.0	0146	3.3	0118	2.0	0350	1.2	0230	1.3	0303	3.4	0143	8.8
	1107	1.0	1040	1.3	1003	0.9	0750	0.8	0736	0.5	0943	4.4	0818	3.5	0840	0.4	0827	1.6
	1747	5.0	1758	5.3	1630	3.8	1420	3.0	1357	1.8	1603	1.5	1439	1.3	1527	3.1	1401	8.4
	2316	1.4	2246	1.6	2212	1.3	1954	1.1	1942	0.7	2157	4.6	2044	3.6	2055	0.6	2037	1.9
22 SA	0557	5.0	0603	5.3	0430	3.9	0223	3.2	0156	1.9	0428	1.3	0309	1.4	0339	3.4	0219	8.7
	1142	1.2	1109	1.3	1042	1.0	0827	0.9	0816	0.6	1025	4.3	0852	3.4	0923	0.4	0905	1.8
	1828	4.9	1839	5.3	1712	3.7	1500	2.9	1439	1.7	1642	1.6	1518	1.4	1608	3.1	1439	8.3
	2352	1.5	2317	1.8	2253	1.4	2035	1.2	2024	0.8	2243	4.5	2124	3.5	2138	0.7	2116	2.2
23 SU	0638	4.9	0644	5.2	0514	3.8	0305	3.1	0239	1.9	0510	1.4	0353	1.5	0416	3.3	0259	8.5
	1221	1.3	1145	1.4	1126	1.1	0911	0.9	0900	0.6	1115	4.2	0931	3.2	1011	0.5	0945	2.0
	1915	4.8	1925	5.1	1759	3.6	1545	2.8	1526	1.7	1727	1.8	1602	1.5	1651	3.1	1522	8.1
			2358	1.9	2341	1.5	2123	1.3	2112	0.8	2339	4.3	2213	3.3	2227	0.7	2200	2.4
24 M	0036	1.7	0729	5.1	0604	3.8	0353	3.0	0329	1.8	0600	1.6	0442	1.5	0457	3.2	0345	8.3
	0725	4.8	1235	1.6	1218	1.2	1004	1.0	0953	0.7	1219	4.0	1020	3.1	1106	0.6	1031	2.2
	1310	1.5	2016	5.0	1854	3.5	1639	2.8	1622	1.7	1824	1.9	1656	1.6	1739	3.0	1615	7.9
	2007	4.7					2224	1.4	2213	0.9			2315	3.2	2322	0.8	2254	2.7
25 TU	0137	1.9	0059	2.1	0041	1.6	0450	3.0	0430	1.8	0045	4.2	0539	1.6	0548	3.1	0442	8.1
	0820	4.8	0821	5.0	0703	3.7	1111	1.1	1057	0.7	0659	1.7	1123	3.0	1209	0.6	1129	2.4
	1413	1.6	1347	1.8	1321	1.3	1742	2.8	1727	1.7	1332	4.0	1800	1.6	1836	3.0	1719	7.8
	2108	4.7	2115	5.0	1959	3.5	2340	1.4	2330	0.9	1935	2.0						
26 W	0253	1.9	0234	2.1	0152	1.6	0557	3.0	0542	1.7	0157	4.2	0032	3.2	0028	0.9	0002	2.7
	0925	4.7	0926	5.0	0812	3.7	1226	1.1	1214	0.8	0809	1.8	0645	1.6	0659	2.9	0551	8.0
	1531	1.7	1512	1.8	1433	1.3	1852	2.9	1834	1.7	1442	4.1	1246	3.0	1319	0.6	1242	2.4
	2215	4.7	2220	5.0	2109	3.6					2054	2.0	1915	1.6	1943	2.9	1835	7.8
27 TH	0417	1.8	0403	2.0	0309	1.5	0059	1.3	0051	0.8	0307	4.3	0154	3.3	0141	0.8	0122	2.6
	1038	4.8	1039	5.1	0927	3.7	0710	3.0	0656	1.8	0923	1.7	0757	1.5	0823	2.9	0707	8.1
	1656	1.6	1651	1.8	1546	1.3	1338	1.1	1324	0.7	1548	4.3	1416	3.2	1429	0.5	1359	2.2
	2324	4.9	2324	5.2	2216	3.8	2000	3.0	1939	1.8	2207	1.7	2033	1.5	2059	2.9	1948	8.2
28 F	0532	1.6	0527	1.7	0420	1.3	0212	1.1	0157	0.7	0413	4.5	0307	3.4	0252	0.7	0237	2.2
	1151	5.0	1148	5.3	1038	3.9	0822	3.1	0805	1.9	1032	1.5	0906	1.3	0942	3.0	0818	8.5
	1808	1.4	1809	1.5	1651	1.1	1442	1.0	1424	0.7	1646	4.6	1526	3.4	1530	0.5	1508	1.8
					2315	4.0	2102	3.2	2038	1.9	2311	1.4	2142	1.2	2209	3.1	2052	8.6
29 SA	0027	5.1	0023	5.4	0521	1.0	0314	0.9	0254	0.6	0513	4.7	0409	3.6	0354	0.5	0344	1.7
	0636	1.2	0634	1.4	1141	4.1	0928	3.3	0909	2.0	1131	1.2	1007	1.0	1050	3.1	0921	8.9
	1254	5.3	1248	5.5	1748	1.0	1537	0.9	1518	0.6	1737	4.9	1622	3.7	1625	0.4	1609	1.4
	1908	1.1	1909	1.3			2157	3.4	2133	2.1			2243	1.0	2309	3.2	2150	9.1
30 SU	0123	5.4	0119	5.6	0007	4.2	0409	0.6	0347	0.4	0006	1.0	0504	3.8	0446	0.3	0445	1.1
	0734	0.8	0748	1.0	0617	0.7	1027	3.4	1009	2.1	0606	5.0	1100	0.7	1152	3.2	1018	9.3
	1348	5.6	1348	5.8	1236	4.3	1627	0.8	1609	0.5	1224	0.9	1712	4.0	1714	0.3	1706	1.0
	2000	0.9	2009	1.1	1840	0.8	2248	3.5	2224	2.2	1824	5.2	2337	0.7			2243	9.5
31 M	0212	5.6	0213	5.8	0055	4.4	0459	0.4	0437	0.3	0057	0.7	0554	4.0	0002	3.4	0541	0.7
	0829	0.4	0848	0.6	0709	0.4	1121	3.5	1103	2.2	0655	5.2	1149	0.5	0534	0.2	1110	9.6
	1439	5.8	1442	6.0	1328	4.4	1714	0.7	1657	0.5	1312	0.7	1759	4.2	1249	3.3	1757	0.8
	2050	0.7	2101	0.9	1928	0.7	2337	3.7	2314	2.3	1909	5.4			1800	0.3	2333	9.8

SCOTLAND & NORTH WEST ENGLAND Time Zone UT
Leith * Rosyth * Aberdeen * Wick * Lerwick * Ullapool * Oban * Greenock * Liverpool

TIDE TABLES AUGUST 2000

	LEITH		ROSYTH		ABERDEEN		WICK		LERWICK		ULLAPOOL		OBAN		GREENOCK		LIVERPOOL		
	Time	m	Time	m	Time	m	Time	m	Time	m	Time	m	Time	m	Time	m	Time	m		
	0300	5.8	0307	6.0	0142	4.5	0548	0.3	0525	0.2	0145	0.4	0028	0.6	0051	3.5	0632	0.3	**1**	**TU**
	0920	0.2	0939	0.4	0758	0.3	1212	3.6	1154	2.2	0742	5.3	0640	4.0	0620	0.1	1200	9.7		●
	1527	5.9	1535	6.2	1418	4.5	1759	0.7	1742	0.5	1357	0.6	1235	0.4	1342	3.4	1845	0.6		
	2136	0.6	2149	0.9	2015	0.7					1954	5.5	1843	4.3	1845	0.3				
	0348	5.9	0400	6.1	0227	4.6	0024	3.8	0003	2.3	0231	0.3	0117	0.5	0139	3.7	0021	9.9	**2**	**W**
	1008	0.1	1025	0.3	0846	0.2	0634	0.2	0612	0.1	0827	5.2	0722	4.0	0706	0.0	0720	0.2		
	1615	5.8	1627	6.2	1506	4.4	1300	3.5	1241	2.1	1442	0.6	1319	0.3	1430	3.4	1247	9.7		
	2220	0.7	2233	0.9	2059	0.8	1842	0.7	1827	0.5	2038	5.4	1925	4.2	1930	0.3	1930	0.6		
	0436	5.8	0452	6.1	0313	4.6	0110	3.7	0049	2.3	0315	0.4	0203	0.6	0223	3.8	0106	9.9	**3**	**TH**
	1053	0.2	1109	0.4	0933	0.3	0721	0.3	0659	0.2	0912	5.1	0801	3.9	0751	0.1	0806	0.2		
	1704	5.7	1718	6.0	1553	4.3	1345	3.4	1327	2.1	1524	0.8	1403	0.4	1514	3.5	1332	9.5		
	2300	0.8	2314	1.1	2142	0.9	1924	0.8	1912	0.5	2123	5.2	2006	4.1	2015	0.4	2013	0.8		
	0526	5.7	0544	5.9	0400	4.4	0155	3.6	0136	2.2	0359	0.6	0248	0.8	0306	3.9	0151	9.7	**4**	**F**
	1135	0.4	1151	0.6	1018	0.4	0806	0.4	0745	0.3	1000	4.8	0838	3.7	0838	0.2	0848	0.6		
	1754	5.4	1807	5.8	1640	4.1	1430	3.3	1411	2.0	1608	1.0	1446	0.6	1555	3.4	1416	9.2		
	2336	1.1	2300	1.4	2225	1.1	2006	1.0	1956	0.6	2212	5.0	2046	3.8	2102	0.4	2055	1.2		
	0616	5.5	0635	5.7	0448	4.3	0241	3.5	0222	2.1	0443	1.0	0332	1.1	0348	3.8	0234	9.3	**5**	**SA**
	1212	0.8	1229	1.0	1103	0.7	0851	0.7	0833	0.4	1051	4.5	0915	3.5	0927	0.4	0930	1.1		
	1843	5.2	1857	5.5	1728	3.9	1515	3.1	1455	1.8	1652	1.3	1531	0.9	1636	3.4	1459	8.7		
			2330	1.6	2311	1.3	2048	1.1	2042	0.7	2306	4.6	2127	3.5	2153	0.6	2137	1.7		
	0009	1.4	0728	5.4	0539	4.0	0329	3.3	0309	2.0	0529	1.4	0417	1.4	0430	3.7	0318	8.8	**6**	**SU**
	0707	5.2	1208	1.4	1151	1.0	0938	0.9	0922	0.6	1150	4.3	0955	3.2	1021	0.6	1014	1.7		
	1248	1.2	1950	5.2	1820	3.7	1603	2.9	1542	1.7	1741	1.7	1619	1.2	1718	3.3	1545	8.2		
	1933	4.9					2138	1.3	2133	0.8			2211	3.2	2250	0.7	2222	2.2		
	0048	1.8	0018	1.9	0003	1.5	0422	3.1	0401	1.8	0011	4.3	0505	1.6	0515	3.5	0406	8.2	**7**	**M**
	0801	4.9	0823	5.1	0637	3.8	1034	1.2	1018	0.8	0620	1.7	1045	3.0	1124	0.8	1101	2.3		
	1333	1.6	1300	1.8	1245	1.4	1657	2.8	1633	1.7	1257	4.1	1712	1.5	1803	3.1	1636	7.8		
	2027	4.7	2045	4.9	1917	3.5	2245	1.5	2239	0.9	1837	2.1	2307	3.0	2357	0.9	2315	2.7		
	0148	2.1	0128	2.2	0106	1.7	0524	2.9	0500	1.7	0127	4.0	0603	1.8	0601	3.2	0503	7.7	**8**	**TU**
	0859	4.7	0921	4.9	0742	3.6	1142	1.3	1126	0.9	0721	2.1	1205	2.9	1234	0.9	1159	2.7		
	1439	2.0	1525	2.1	1350	1.6	1800	2.8	1733	1.6	1409	4.0	1816	1.7	1900	2.9	1741	7.4		
	2125	4.5	2142	4.7	2021	3.4					1951	2.3								
	0321	2.2	0332	2.3	0225	1.8	0015	1.5	0011	1.0	0244	3.9	0045	2.8	0111	0.9	0024	3.1	**9**	**W**
	1003	4.5	1021	4.8	0855	3.5	0636	2.8	0612	1.6	0840	2.2	0716	1.9	0657	3.0	0615	7.3		
	1604	2.1	1634	2.2	1505	1.7	1259	1.4	1243	1.0	1515	4.0	1358	2.9	1350	1.0	1309	3.0		
	2229	4.5	2240	4.7	2130	3.5	1911	2.8	1845	1.7	2120	2.1	1932	1.8	2022	2.8	1857	7.4		
	0453	2.1	0442	2.3	0348	1.8	0146	1.5	0132	0.9	0353	3.9	0236	2.9	0226	0.9	0141	3.1	**10**	**TH**
	1115	4.5	1125	4.8	1008	3.5	0751	2.8	0733	1.6	0959	2.2	0837	1.8	0832	2.8	0735	7.3		
	1715	2.1	1718	2.2	1613	1.7	1406	1.4	1348	1.0	1613	4.2	1505	3.1	1501	1.0	1419	2.9		
	2339	4.5	2341	4.8	2233	3.6	2017	2.9	1956	1.7	2233	2.2	2048	1.8	2139	2.9	2009	7.6		
	0557	1.9	0528	2.1	0451	1.6	0247	1.4	0232	0.9	0448	4.1	0330	3.0	0330	0.8	0251	2.9	**11**	**F**
	1223	4.6	1229	4.9	1109	3.6	0854	2.9	0838	1.7	1057	2.0	0938	1.6	0954	2.7	0842	7.6		
	1809	1.9	1746	2.1	1706	1.6	1456	1.4	1441	0.9	1700	4.4	1551	3.3	1556	1.0	1519	2.6		
					2324	3.7	2110	3.0	2050	1.8	2325	1.9	2146	1.7	2235	3.0	2106	8.0		
	0040	4.7	0039	5.0	0539	1.4	0331	1.2	0318	0.8	0532	4.2	0412	3.2	0419	0.7	0348	2.5	**12**	**SA**
	0645	1.7	0606	1.8	1159	3.7	0945	3.0	0926	1.8	1142	1.8	1024	1.5	1051	2.8	0934	8.0		
	1315	4.8	1321	5.1	1749	1.5	1536	1.3	1524	0.9	1739	4.6	1630	3.5	1639	0.9	1607	2.3		
	1851	1.7	1821	1.9			2154	3.2	2133	1.9			2233	1.5	2318	3.1	2151	8.4		
	0127	4.9	0127	5.2	0007	3.9	0409	1.1	0356	0.7	0006	1.7	0449	3.4	0500	0.6	0434	2.1	**13**	**SU**
	0725	1.4	0645	1.6	0618	1.2	1027	3.1	1006	1.9	0608	4.4	1103	1.3	1134	2.9	1016	8.3		
	1356	5.0	1403	5.3	1239	3.8	1612	1.2	1600	0.8	1221	1.6	1706	3.7	1715	0.6	1648	2.0		
	1927	1.5	1900	1.7	1827	1.3	2232	3.3	2212	2.0	1813	4.7	2313	1.4	2357	3.2	2231	8.8		
	0206	5.1	0209	5.4	0043	4.0	0442	0.9	0429	0.6	0042	1.4	0525	3.5	0535	0.5	0514	1.8	**14**	**M**
	0800	1.2	0725	1.4	0653	1.0	1104	3.2	1044	1.9	0639	4.6	1137	1.1	1212	3.0	1053	8.6		
	1430	5.1	1440	5.4	1315	3.9	1645	1.1	1633	0.6	1256	1.4	1739	3.8	1746	0.6	1724	1.8		
	2003	1.3	1940	1.5	1901	1.2	2308	3.4	2247	2.1	1845	4.9	2349	1.2			2307	9.0		
	0242	5.2	0247	5.6	0117	4.1	0515	0.8	0500	0.6	0116	1.2	0558	3.6	0032	3.3	0549	1.6	**15**	**TU**
	0832	1.0	0806	1.2	0727	0.9	1139	3.2	1118	2.0	0709	4.7	1209	1.0	0606	0.5	1127	8.8		O
	1503	5.2	1516	5.5	1348	4.0	1718	1.0	1703	0.7	1329	1.3	1812	3.9	1249	3.0	1759	1.6		
	2039	1.1	2021	1.3	1934	1.1	2342	3.4	2319	2.1	1915	5.0			1815	0.9	2341	9.2		

● ● Time: UT. For British Summer Time (shaded) March 26th to October 29th ADD ONE HOUR ● ●

AUGUST 2000 TIDE TABLES

•• Time: UT. For British Summer Time (shaded) March 26th to October 29th ADD ONE HOUR ••

	LEITH Time m	ROSYTH Time m	ABERDEEN Time m	WICK Time m	LERWICK Time m	ULLAPOOL Time m	OBAN Time m	GREENOCK Time m	LIVERPOOL Time m
16W	0315 5.3 / 0906 0.8 / 1535 5.3 / 2115 1.0	0322 5.6 / 0845 1.1 / 1546 5.6 / 2100 1.3	0148 4.2 / 0758 0.8 / 1421 4.1 / 2006 1.0	0546 0.7 / 1212 3.3 / 1749 0.9	0530 0.5 / 1151 2.0 / 1735 0.7 / 2350 2.1	0148 1.1 / 0737 4.8 / 1400 1.2 / 1945 5.1	0024 1.1 / 0629 3.7 / 1239 1.0 / 1843 4.0	0106 3.4 / 0635 0.4 / 1324 3.1 / 1845 0.6	0624 1.4 / 1200 8.9 / 1833 1.4
17TH	0348 5.4 / 0940 0.7 / 1609 5.4 / 2150 1.0	0356 5.7 / 0919 1.0 / 1619 5.7 / 2133 1.3	0221 4.2 / 0830 0.7 / 1453 4.1 / 2039 1.0	0015 3.5 / 0618 0.7 / 1245 3.3 / 1821 0.9	0601 0.5 / 1223 2.0 / 1807 0.6	0219 1.0 / 0806 4.8 / 1431 1.1 / 2015 5.1	0057 1.1 / 0657 3.8 / 1309 0.9 / 1914 4.0	0140 3.4 / 0706 0.4 / 1358 3.2 / 1917 0.5	0014 9.3 / 0657 1.2 / 1231 9.0 / 1907 1.4
18F	0421 5.4 / 1015 0.7 / 1643 5.3 / 2224 1.0	0428 5.7 / 0945 1.0 / 1653 5.7 / 2157 1.3	0253 4.2 / 0903 0.7 / 1526 4.0 / 2111 1.0	0048 3.5 / 0649 0.7 / 1319 3.2 / 1854 0.9	0022 2.1 / 0634 0.5 / 1255 2.0 / 1842 0.6	0251 0.9 / 0837 4.8 / 1503 1.1 / 2049 5.0	0130 1.1 / 0725 3.8 / 1340 1.0 / 1945 3.9	0212 3.5 / 0739 0.3 / 1433 3.3 / 1951 0.5	0047 9.3 / 0732 1.2 / 1304 8.9 / 1942 1.4
19SA	0454 5.3 / 1047 0.8 / 1720 5.2 / 2254 1.1	0501 5.6 / 1010 1.0 / 1730 5.6 / 2220 1.4	0327 4.2 / 0936 0.8 / 1601 4.0 / 2145 1.1	0122 3.4 / 0722 0.7 / 1353 3.2 / 1929 1.0	0055 2.1 / 0709 0.5 / 1329 1.9 / 1918 0.7	0324 1.0 / 0911 4.7 / 1537 1.2 / 2126 4.9	0204 1.1 / 0754 3.7 / 1413 1.0 / 2018 3.8	0245 3.5 / 0815 0.3 / 1507 3.3 / 2029 0.5	0120 9.2 / 0806 1.3 / 1337 8.8 / 2016 1.6
20SU	0530 5.3 / 1116 1.0 / 1759 5.1 / 2323 1.3	0538 5.6 / 1039 1.1 / 1809 5.5 / 2249 1.5	0403 4.1 / 1012 0.9 / 1639 3.9 / 2223 1.2	0158 3.4 / 0757 0.8 / 1430 3.1 / 2007 1.1	0130 2.1 / 0746 0.5 / 1406 1.9 / 1957 0.7	0359 1.1 / 0948 4.6 / 1614 1.4 / 2209 4.7	0242 1.1 / 0836 3.6 / 1451 1.2 / 2054 3.6	0318 3.4 / 0854 0.4 / 1543 3.3 / 2109 0.5	0154 9.0 / 0840 1.5 / 1412 8.7 / 2052 1.9
21M	0609 5.2 / 1145 1.2 / 1843 5.0 / 2357 1.5	0618 5.4 / 1112 1.3 / 1854 5.3 / 2327 1.7	0445 4.1 / 1052 1.0 / 1724 3.8 / 2307 1.3	0238 3.3 / 0837 0.9 / 1512 3.0 / 2051 1.2	0210 2.0 / 0828 0.6 / 1450 1.8 / 2043 0.8	0439 1.3 / 1034 4.4 / 1657 1.6 / 2301 4.5	0323 1.3 / 0900 3.4 / 1533 1.3 / 2136 3.4	0351 3.4 / 0938 0.5 / 1621 3.2 / 2153 0.6	0231 8.8 / 0916 1.8 / 1451 8.4 / 2131 2.2
22TU	0655 5.0 / 1224 1.4 / 1934 4.8	0703 5.3 / 1155 1.5 / 1942 5.2	0533 3.9 / 1141 1.2 / 1816 3.7	0324 3.2 / 0924 1.0 / 1603 2.9 / 2147 1.3	0257 1.9 / 0917 0.7 / 1543 1.8 / 2141 0.9	0524 1.5 / 1133 4.2 / 1749 1.9	0410 1.4 / 0944 3.3 / 1624 1.5 / 2231 3.2	0430 3.3 / 1029 0.6 / 1704 3.2 / 2245 0.8	0315 8.5 / 0957 2.1 / 1539 8.1 / 2221 2.5
23W	0051 1.8 / 0751 4.8 / 1324 1.7 / 2034 4.7	0018 1.9 / 0756 5.1 / 1256 1.9 / 2040 5.0	0004 1.5 / 0633 3.8 / 1243 1.4 / 1921 3.6	0421 3.1 / 1030 1.2 / 1706 2.9 / 2308 1.4	0400 1.8 / 1020 0.8 / 1650 1.7 / 2259 0.9	0010 4.3 / 0620 1.8 / 1253 4.1 / 1859 2.1	0505 1.5 / 1041 3.1 / 1729 1.6 / 2354 3.1	0516 3.1 / 1132 0.7 / 1757 3.0 / 2352 0.9	0409 8.2 / 1051 2.5 / 1642 7.8 / 2327 2.8
24TH	0215 2.0 / 0859 4.7 / 1456 1.9 / 2145 4.7	0148 2.1 / 0902 4.9 / 1443 2.1 / 2149 4.9	0119 1.6 / 0747 3.7 / 1404 1.5 / 2039 3.6	0531 3.0 / 1156 1.3 / 1821 2.9	0518 1.8 / 1144 0.9 / 1804 1.7	0132 4.2 / 0733 1.9 / 1418 4.1 / 2029 2.1	0612 1.6 / 1212 3.0 / 1853 1.7	0624 2.9 / 1249 0.8 / 1904 3.0	0520 7.9 / 1206 2.7 / 1804 7.7
25F	0400 1.9 / 1020 4.7 / 1648 1.9 / 2302 4.8	0345 2.1 / 1020 4.9 / 1654 2.0 / 2300 5.0	0248 1.6 / 0913 3.7 / 1530 1.5 / 2156 3.7	0042 1.3 / 0654 3.0 / 1324 1.3 / 1938 3.0	0033 0.9 / 0639 1.8 / 1309 0.9 / 1918 1.8	0254 4.2 / 0901 1.9 / 1534 4.3 / 2157 1.8	0150 3.1 / 0733 1.5 / 1416 3.1 / 2030 1.6	0115 0.9 / 0753 2.9 / 1409 0.8 / 2025 3.0	0055 2.8 / 0646 7.8 / 1335 2.6 / 1929 7.9
26SA	0527 1.6 / 1140 5.0 / 1803 1.6	0535 1.8 / 1133 5.1 / 1810 1.7	0409 1.3 / 1031 3.9 / 1642 1.4 / 2300 3.9	0206 1.1 / 0815 3.1 / 1435 1.2 / 2046 3.2	0145 0.8 / 0759 1.9 / 1415 0.8 / 2024 2.0	0409 4.4 / 1022 1.7 / 1637 4.6 / 2304 1.4	0311 3.2 / 0854 1.3 / 1530 3.4 / 2146 1.3	0237 0.8 / 0926 2.9 / 1517 0.7 / 2147 3.1	0221 2.4 / 0806 8.2 / 1453 2.2 / 2040 8.5
27SU	0012 5.1 / 0632 1.2 / 1245 5.3 / 1900 1.3	0006 5.3 / 0647 1.3 / 1238 5.4 / 1907 1.4	0514 1.0 / 1134 4.1 / 1740 1.1 / 2354 4.2	0309 0.9 / 0924 3.3 / 1530 1.0 / 2144 3.4	0245 0.6 / 0907 2.0 / 1510 0.7 / 2123 2.1	0509 4.7 / 1123 1.4 / 1728 5.0 / 2358 1.0	0410 3.5 / 0957 1.0 / 1622 3.7 / 2244 1.0	0342 0.6 / 1042 3.1 / 1612 0.6 / 2254 3.3	0334 1.7 / 0913 8.7 / 1558 1.6 / 2140 9.1
28M	0109 5.4 / 0727 0.7 / 1339 5.6 / 1948 1.0	0105 5.6 / 0746 0.9 / 1335 5.8 / 1956 1.2	0609 0.7 / 1229 4.3 / 1829 1.0	0401 0.6 / 1020 3.4 / 1616 0.9 / 2234 3.6	0338 0.4 / 1003 2.1 / 1558 0.6 / 2214 2.2	0559 5.0 / 1214 1.1 / 1812 5.3	0500 3.7 / 1048 0.7 / 1708 4.0 / 2333 0.7	0435 0.4 / 1145 3.2 / 1701 0.5 / 2349 3.5	0436 1.1 / 1009 9.2 / 1654 1.2 / 2233 9.6
29TU	0158 5.7 / 0818 0.4 / 1425 5.8 / 2033 0.7	0200 5.8 / 0836 0.5 / 1427 6.0 / 2040 0.9	0041 4.4 / 0657 0.4 / 1317 4.4 / 1914 0.8	0448 0.4 / 1110 3.6 / 1659 0.8 / 2321 3.8	0425 0.3 / 1052 2.2 / 1642 0.5 / 2300 2.3	0046 0.6 / 0642 5.3 / 1259 0.8 / 1854 5.5	0545 3.9 / 1134 0.4 / 1749 4.2	0521 0.2 / 1239 3.4 / 1745 0.4	0530 0.6 / 1100 9.8 / 1744 0.8 / 2320 9.9
30W	0244 5.9 / 0904 0.1 / 1510 5.9 / 2116 0.6	0251 6.1 / 0921 0.3 / 1515 6.2 / 2121 0.8	0125 4.6 / 0743 0.4 / 1401 4.5 / 1956 0.7	0531 0.3 / 1156 3.6 / 1739 0.7	0509 0.2 / 1137 2.2 / 1724 0.5 / 2345 2.4	0130 0.4 / 0723 5.4 / 1341 0.6 / 1933 5.6	0018 0.5 / 0624 4.0 / 1217 0.3 / 1828 4.3	0038 3.6 / 0604 0.1 / 1328 3.5 / 1826 0.4	0618 0.2 / 1145 9.8 / 1829 0.6
31TH ●	0329 6.0 / 0948 0.0 / 1554 5.9 / 2157 0.6	0340 6.2 / 1002 0.2 / 1603 6.2 / 2159 0.8	0208 4.7 / 0826 0.2 / 1443 4.4 / 2036 0.7	0006 3.8 / 0613 0.2 / 1239 3.6 / 1818 0.7	0552 0.2 / 1218 2.2 / 1805 0.5	0212 0.3 / 0803 5.4 / 1421 0.6 / 2012 5.5	0100 0.5 / 0700 4.1 / 1257 0.2 / 1905 4.3	0123 3.8 / 0645 0.1 / 1411 3.5 / 1908 0.3	0003 10.0 / 0702 0.1 / 1227 9.8 / 1910 0.6

SCOTLAND & NORTH WEST ENGLAND Time Zone UT
Leith * Rosyth * Aberdeen * Wick * Lerwick * Ullapool * Oban * Greenock * Liverpool
TIDE TABLES SEPTEMBER 2000

	LEITH		ROSYTH		ABERDEEN		WICK		LERWICK		ULLAPOOL		OBAN		GREENOCK		LIVERPOOL	
	Time	m	Time	m	Time	m	Time	m	Time	m	Time	m	Time	m	Time	m	Time	m
1 F	0414	5.9	0429	6.2	0250	4.6	0049	3.8	0027	2.4	0251	0.4	0140	0.6	0205	3.9	0045	10.0
	1028	0.2	1041	0.4	0907	0.3	0654	0.3	0634	0.2	0842	5.2	0733	4.0	0727	0.2	0742	0.3
	1639	5.7	1649	6.0	1525	4.3	1319	3.5	1259	2.1	1500	0.7	1338	0.4	1450	3.5	1307	9.6
	2233	0.8	2155	1.0	2115	0.8	1857	0.8	1845	0.5	2052	5.3	1939	4.1	1950	0.3	1949	0.8
2 SA	0500	5.8	0516	6.0	0333	4.5	0130	3.7	0109	2.3	0330	0.6	0218	0.8	0244	3.9	0125	9.7
	1103	0.5	1113	0.7	0946	0.5	0732	0.5	0715	0.3	0921	5.0	0805	3.8	0810	0.3	0820	0.7
	1723	5.5	1735	5.8	1606	4.1	1358	3.3	1337	2.0	1539	1.0	1418	0.6	1526	3.5	1346	9.3
	2304	1.0	2218	1.2	2153	1.0	1934	0.9	1925	0.6	2133	5.0	2012	3.8	2033	0.4	2026	1.2
3 SU	0545	5.5	0603	5.7	0416	4.3	0212	3.5	0151	2.2	0408	1.0	0257	1.0	0322	3.8	0203	9.3
	1132	0.9	1041	1.1	1025	0.8	0809	0.8	0757	0.5	1003	4.7	0837	3.6	0854	0.5	0856	1.2
	1807	5.2	1818	5.4	1647	3.9	1436	3.2	1416	1.9	1619	1.3	1459	0.9	1601	3.4	1423	8.8
	2329	1.4	2249	1.5	2233	1.2	2012	1.1	2007	0.7	2216	4.6	2045	3.5	2119	0.5	2103	1.7
4 M	0632	5.2	0649	5.4	0502	4.0	0254	3.3	0234	2.0	0448	1.4	0335	1.3	0400	3.7	0241	8.8
	1157	1.3	1115	1.4	1105	1.2	0848	1.0	0839	0.7	1052	4.3	0912	3.4	0942	0.7	0932	1.9
	1852	4.9	1903	5.1	1732	3.7	1518	3.0	1457	1.8	1701	1.7	1542	1.3	1636	3.3	1503	8.3
			2330	1.8	2318	1.5	2054	1.3	2053	0.9	2310	4.2	2121	3.2	2210	0.7	2140	2.3
5 TU	0000	1.7	0739	5.0	0554	3.7	0342	3.0	0321	1.9	0532	1.8	0418	1.6	0437	3.4	0323	8.2
	0721	4.9	1202	1.9	1151	1.5	0933	1.3	0927	0.9	1159	4.1	0954	3.1	1036	0.9	1010	2.5
	1233	1.8	1952	4.8	1824	3.5	1605	2.9	1542	1.8	1750	2.1	1632	1.6	1713	3.2	1548	7.8
	1941	4.6					2151	1.5	2154	1.0			2204	3.0	2312	0.9	2225	2.9
6 W	0050	2.1	0027	2.2	0015	1.7	0439	2.8	0416	1.7	0036	3.9	0509	1.8	0516	3.2	0414	7.5
	0815	4.6	0834	4.8	0657	3.5	1036	1.5	1030	1.0	0625	2.2	1100	2.9	1142	1.2	1100	3.1
	1330	2.2	1314	2.3	1252	1.8	1704	2.8	1639	1.7	1320	3.9	1733	1.9	1755	2.9	1646	7.3
	2035	4.4	2048	4.6	1927	3.4	2325	1.6	2325	1.1	1856	2.4	2315	2.8			2329	3.3
7 TH	0221	2.4	0212	2.4	0136	1.9	0554	2.7	0529	1.6	0208	3.8	0624	1.9	0028	1.1	0524	7.0
	0918	4.3	0934	4.6	0814	3.3	1206	1.7	1154	1.1	0744	2.5	1327	2.9	0600	2.9	1215	3.5
	1506	2.4	1539	2.6	1414	2.0	1819	2.7	1753	1.7	1437	3.9	1857	2.0	1305	1.3	1807	7.1
	2138	4.3	2148	4.6	2040	3.4					2039	2.5			1858	2.8		
8 F	0427	2.3	0416	2.4	0315	1.9	0115	1.6	0102	1.0	0327	3.8	0210	2.8	0153	1.1	0057	3.5
	1033	4.3	1040	4.6	0936	3.4	0720	2.7	0707	1.6	0927	2.4	0805	1.9	0705	2.6	0700	6.9
	1647	2.4	1642	2.5	1542	2.0	1335	1.6	1316	1.1	1543	4.1	1446	3.0	1432	1.3	1342	3.4
	2251	4.4	2251	4.6	2154	3.5	1937	2.8	1921	1.7	2211	2.3	2030	1.9	2056	2.9	1935	7.3
9 SA	0539	2.1	0512	2.2	0428	1.7	0224	1.4	0207	0.9	0428	4.0	0313	2.9	0303	1.0	0221	3.2
	1154	4.4	1152	4.7	1045	3.5	0831	2.8	0818	1.7	1035	2.2	0918	1.7	0923	2.6	0819	7.3
	1747	2.2	1727	2.3	1643	1.8	1433	1.5	1416	1.0	1635	4.3	1533	3.3	1531	1.2	1451	3.1
					2254	3.6	2039	3.0	2023	1.8	2304	2.0	2134	1.8	2201	2.9	2040	7.8
10 SU	0006	4.6	0000	4.9	0516	1.5	0309	1.2	0254	0.8	0512	4.2	0357	3.1	0354	0.9	0322	2.7
	0627	1.8	0556	1.9	1136	3.7	0923	3.0	0904	1.8	1121	2.0	1005	1.5	1024	2.8	0913	7.8
	1250	4.7	1252	5.0	1727	1.6	1515	1.4	1500	1.0	1715	4.5	1612	3.5	1614	1.1	1542	2.6
	1830	1.9	1806	2.0	2339	3.8	2126	3.1	2108	1.9	2344	1.7	2219	1.6	2248	3.1	2127	8.3
11 M	0059	4.8	0058	5.1	0554	1.3	0345	1.1	0330	0.7	0545	4.4	0433	3.3	0433	0.7	0409	2.2
	0704	1.5	0635	1.6	1215	3.8	1004	3.1	0943	1.9	1158	1.7	1042	1.3	1107	2.9	0954	8.3
	1330	5.0	1336	5.2	1804	1.4	1550	1.2	1536	0.9	1748	4.7	1645	3.7	1648	1.0	1624	2.1
	1906	1.6	1846	1.7			2205	3.3	2146	2.0			2256	1.4	2328	3.3	2206	8.8
12 TU	0139	5.1	0143	5.4	0017	4.0	0418	0.9	0402	0.6	0018	1.4	0506	3.5	0507	0.6	0449	1.8
	0736	1.2	0713	1.3	0628	1.0	1040	3.2	1018	2.0	0615	4.6	1114	1.1	1147	3.1	1030	8.7
	1403	5.2	1413	5.5	1250	4.0	1622	1.1	1608	0.8	1232	1.4	1718	3.9	1718	0.8	1701	1.8
	1941	1.3	1927	1.4	1837	1.2	2241	3.4	2221	2.1	1819	5.0	2329	1.2			2242	9.1
13 W	0214	5.3	0223	5.6	0050	4.1	0449	0.8	0431	0.6	0050	1.2	0536	3.7	0006	3.4	0525	1.4
O	0809	1.0	0751	1.1	0700	0.8	1114	3.3	1051	2.0	0642	4.8	1144	1.0	0537	0.5	1102	8.9
	1436	5.3	1447	5.6	1321	4.1	1653	1.0	1639	0.7	1303	1.2	1749	4.0	1224	3.2	1736	1.5
	2016	1.1	2006	1.2	1909	1.1	2315	3.5	2253	2.2	1848	5.1			1748	0.7	2315	9.4
14 TH	0248	5.4	0259	5.7	0122	4.3	0519	0.7	0501	0.5	0121	0.9	0000	1.0	0043	3.5	0600	1.2
	0842	0.7	0823	0.9	0731	0.7	1146	3.4	1123	2.1	0709	5.0	0605	3.8	0607	0.4	1133	9.1
	1508	5.3	1519	5.7	1353	4.2	1724	0.9	1710	0.6	1335	1.0	1212	0.9	1301	3.3	1811	1.3
	2052	0.9	2040	1.1	1941	0.9	2349	3.6	2324	2.2	1918	5.3	1818	4.1	1818	0.6	2348	9.5
15 F	0321	5.5	0331	5.8	0154	4.3	0549	0.6	0533	0.4	0151	0.8	0031	0.9	0118	3.5	0634	1.0
	0917	0.6	0850	0.8	0803	0.6	1219	3.4	1154	2.1	0738	5.1	0631	3.9	0638	0.3	1206	9.2
	1542	5.5	1551	5.8	1424	4.2	1757	0.8	1743	0.6	1406	0.9	1242	0.8	1336	3.3	1845	1.1
	2128	0.8	2106	1.0	2013	0.9			2357	2.2	1948	5.3	1848	4.1	1851	0.5		

● ● Time: UT. For British Summer Time (shaded) March 26th to October 29th ADD ONE HOUR ● ●

SEPTEMBER 2000 TIDE TABLES

·· Time: UT. For British Summer Time (shaded) March 26th to October 29th ADD ONE HOUR ··

	LEITH Time	m	ROSYTH Time	m	ABERDEEN Time	m	WICK Time	m	LERWICK Time	m	ULLAPOOL Time	m	OBAN Time	m	GREENOCK Time	m	LIVERPOOL Time	m
16 SA	0354	5.6	0403	5.8	0227	4.4	0023	3.6	0606	0.4	0224	0.7	0103	0.9	0151	3.5	0021	9.6
	0951	0.6	0915	0.8	0836	0.6	0621	0.6	1227	2.1	0808	5.1	0659	3.9	0712	0.3	0709	1.0
	1617	5.5	1625	5.8	1457	4.2	1252	3.4	1818	0.6	1438	0.9	1313	0.8	1409	3.4	1238	9.3
	2202	0.8	2128	1.1	2045	0.9	1830	0.8			2021	5.2	1919	4.1	1925	0.4	1921	1.2
17 SU	0427	5.5	0437	5.8	0301	4.4	0058	3.6	0031	2.2	0257	0.7	0138	0.9	0224	3.5	0054	9.5
	1021	0.7	0942	0.7	0909	0.7	0654	0.6	0642	0.5	0841	5.0	0727	3.9	0748	0.3	0742	1.1
	1653	5.4	1703	5.8	1532	4.2	1327	3.3	1300	2.1	1512	1.0	1348	0.9	1443	3.4	1312	9.2
	2233	1.0	2154	1.1	2120	0.9	1906	0.8	1854	0.6	2059	5.1	1952	3.9	2001	0.4	1955	1.4
18 M	0504	5.5	0516	5.7	0339	4.3	0135	3.5	0107	2.2	0332	0.9	0216	0.9	0256	3.4	0130	9.3
	1048	0.9	1011	1.0	0944	0.8	0730	0.7	0719	0.5	0918	4.8	0759	3.8	0826	0.4	0815	1.3
	1733	5.3	1743	5.6	1610	4.1	1404	3.3	1336	2.0	1550	1.2	1427	1.0	1517	3.4	1347	9.0
	2259	1.2	2224	1.2	2157	1.1	1944	0.9	1935	0.7	2142	4.9	2027	3.7	2041	0.5	2030	1.7
19 TU	0546	5.3	0558	5.5	0422	4.2	0216	3.4	0148	2.1	0411	1.1	0257	1.1	0330	3.4	0207	9.1
	1113	1.2	1045	1.2	1024	1.0	0809	0.9	0801	0.7	1003	4.6	0835	3.6	0909	0.5	0850	1.7
	1817	5.1	1827	5.4	1654	3.9	1446	3.1	1418	2.0	1633	1.5	1511	1.2	1554	3.4	1427	8.7
	2333	1.4	2303	1.4	2243	1.2	2028	1.1	2022	0.8	2236	4.6	2109	3.5	2124	0.6	2109	2.0
20 W	0635	5.1	0645	5.3	0512	4.0	0304	3.2	0237	2.0	0456	1.5	0344	1.3	0409	3.3	0251	8.7
	1151	1.5	1127	1.5	1112	1.3	0857	1.1	0851	0.8	1102	4.3	0959	0.7	0959	0.7	0931	2.2
	1907	4.9	1915	5.1	1747	3.7	1536	3.0	1512	1.9	1725	1.8	1604	1.5	1636	3.3	1515	8.3
			2352	1.7	2342	1.4	2127	1.2	2121	0.9	2352	4.3	2203	3.2	2218	0.7	2159	2.5
21 TH	0028	1.7	0739	5.0	0615	3.8	0404	3.0	0343	1.9	0552	1.8	0439	1.5	0500	3.1	0347	8.2
	0733	4.9	1223	2.0	1218	1.5	1003	1.3	0955	1.0	1229	4.1	1015	3.1	1103	0.9	1026	2.6
	1254	1.9	2015	4.9	1855	3.6	1640	2.9	1622	1.8	1839	2.1	1712	1.7	1728	3.2	1619	7.8
	2009	4.7					2256	1.3	2245	0.9			2339	2.9	2329	0.9	2309	2.8
22 F	0205	2.0	0130	2.0	0104	1.6	0520	2.9	0506	1.8	0124	4.1	0548	1.6	0610	2.9	0503	7.7
	0846	4.7	0850	4.8	0737	3.6	1142	1.5	1130	1.0	0711	2.1	1204	2.9	1224	1.0	1145	3.0
	1450	2.2	1446	2.3	1349	1.7	1759	2.9	1742	1.8	1404	4.1	1851	1.8	1833	3.1	1746	7.6
	2124	4.6	2131	4.8	2020	3.6					2021	2.1						
23 SA	0401	1.9	0411	2.0	0240	1.5	0039	1.3	0025	0.9	0251	4.2	0200	3.0	0058	1.0	0044	2.8
	1012	4.7	1012	4.8	0909	3.7	0651	2.9	0635	1.8	0854	2.1	0718	1.6	0740	2.9	0636	7.7
	1646	2.1	1657	2.1	1522	1.7	1318	1.4	1303	1.0	1524	4.3	1432	3.1	1351	1.1	1321	2.9
	2247	4.8	2250	4.9	2141	3.7	1922	3.0	1903	1.9	2154	1.8	2042	1.6	1957	3.0	1916	7.9
24 SU	0523	1.5	0540	1.6	0403	1.3	0202	1.1	0138	0.7	0405	4.4	0310	3.2	0224	0.8	0213	2.3
	1133	5.0	1127	5.0	1027	3.9	0814	3.1	0800	1.9	1016	1.8	0843	1.4	0924	3.0	0759	8.1
	1754	1.7	1803	1.8	1634	1.5	1427	1.3	1408	0.9	1627	4.6	1531	3.4	1501	1.0	1442	2.4
			2358	5.2	2246	4.0	2033	3.2	2014	2.0	2257	1.4	2150	1.2	2130	3.2	2030	8.5
25 M	0000	5.1	0642	1.1	0506	0.9	0301	0.8	0236	0.6	0501	4.7	0403	3.4	0329	0.7	0325	1.6
	0624	1.1	1230	5.4	1128	4.1	0917	3.3	0901	2.0	1113	1.5	0944	1.0	1037	3.2	0905	8.7
	1236	5.3	1854	1.4	1728	1.2	1518	1.1	1500	0.8	1715	5.0	1616	3.8	1557	0.8	1547	1.8
	1845	1.4			2339	4.2	2129	3.4	2110	2.1	2346	1.0	2238	0.7	2239	3.4	2128	9.1
26 TU	0056	5.4	0057	5.5	0557	0.6	0349	0.6	0325	0.4	0545	5.0	0448	3.7	0420	0.5	0424	1.0
	0715	0.7	0735	0.7	1218	4.3	1009	3.4	0951	2.1	1200	1.1	1032	0.7	1133	3.3	0957	9.2
	1326	5.6	1324	5.7	1814	1.0	1600	0.9	1544	0.7	1757	5.3	1656	4.0	1644	0.7	1640	1.2
	1930	1.1	1937	1.1			2218	3.6	2159	2.3			2320	0.7	2333	3.6	2217	9.6
27 W	0142	5.7	0146	5.8	0024	4.4	0431	0.4	0408	0.3	0030	0.6	0527	3.9	0504	0.3	0514	0.6
	0800	0.4	0820	0.5	0642	0.4	1054	3.5	1034	2.2	0624	5.3	1115	0.4	1223	3.5	1043	9.6
	1409	5.8	1409	5.9	1300	4.4	1639	0.8	1624	0.6	1241	0.8	1732	4.2	1726	0.5	1727	0.7
	2012	0.8	2009	0.9	1855	0.9	2303	3.8	2242	2.3	1835	5.5	2359	0.6			2301	9.9
28 TH	0225	5.9	0233	6.1	0106	4.6	0510	0.3	0448	0.3	0109	0.5	0601	4.0	0020	3.7	0558	0.3
	0843	0.2	0859	0.3	0723	0.3	1134	3.6	1114	2.2	0701	5.4	1154	0.3	0544	0.2	1124	9.8
	1450	5.8	1454	6.1	1339	4.5	1717	0.7	1703	0.5	1321	0.7	1806	4.2	1307	3.5	1808	0.7
	2053	0.8	2020	0.7	1934	0.8	2345	3.8	2324	2.4	1911	5.6			1805	0.4	2342	10.0
29 F	0308	5.9	0318	6.2	0145	4.6	0547	0.3	0527	0.3	0148	0.4	0036	0.5	0102	3.8	0637	0.3
	0922	0.2	0934	0.3	0801	0.3	1213	3.6	1151	2.2	0736	5.4	0633	4.1	0623	0.2	1203	9.7
	1530	5.8	1537	6.1	1417	4.4	1754	0.7	1740	0.5	1358	0.6	1233	0.3	1345	3.6	1845	0.7
	2131	0.6	2051	0.7	2011	0.8					1946	5.5	1838	4.2	1845	0.4		
30 SA ●	0350	5.9	0403	6.1	0225	4.6	0025	3.8	0003	2.3	0224	0.5	0111	0.6	0140	3.8	0020	9.9
	0958	0.4	1002	0.5	0838	0.5	0623	0.5	0606	0.3	0811	5.2	0703	4.0	0702	0.3	0714	0.5
	1611	5.7	1620	5.9	1454	4.3	1249	3.5	1227	2.2	1434	0.7	1311	0.5	1421	3.6	1239	9.7
	2206	0.8	2119	0.9	2047	0.8	1830	0.7	1818	0.5	2022	5.2	1908	4.0	1924	0.4	1921	0.9

SCOTLAND & NORTH WEST ENGLAND Time Zone UT
Leith * Rosyth * Aberdeen * Wick * Lerwick * Ullapool * Oban * Greenock * Liverpool

TIDE TABLES OCTOBER 2000

Day	LEITH Time	m	ROSYTH Time	m	ABERDEEN Time	m	WICK Time	m	LERWICK Time	m	ULLAPOOL Time	m	OBAN Time	m	GREENOCK Time	m	LIVERPOOL Time	m
1 SU	0433	5.7	0448	5.9	0305	4.4	0104	3.6	0042	2.3	0259	0.7	0146	0.8	0217	3.8	0057	9.6
	1028	0.7	0939	0.8	0912	0.7	0657	0.6	0644	0.5	0846	5.0	0733	3.9	0742	0.4	0748	0.9
	1651	5.4	1701	5.7	1530	4.2	1324	3.4	1301	2.1	1511	1.0	1348	0.7	1453	3.6	1315	9.3
	2233	1.1	2146	1.1	2122	1.0	1905	0.9	1856	0.6	2057	1.0	1939	3.8	2005	0.4	1955	1.3
2 M	0515	5.4	0530	5.6	0345	4.2	0142	3.4	0120	2.2	0334	1.1	0221	1.0	0252	3.7	0131	9.2
	1050	1.1	1006	1.1	0947	1.0	0730	0.9	0721	0.7	0921	4.7	0803	3.7	0821	0.6	0819	1.5
	1731	5.2	1741	5.3	1607	4.0	1359	3.2	1336	2.0	1548	1.3	1427	1.0	1524	3.5	1348	8.9
	2251	1.4	2216	1.3	2159	1.2	1940	1.0	1935	0.7	2135	4.5	2009	3.6	2046	0.6	2029	1.8
3 TU	0557	5.1	0612	5.3	0428	4.0	0221	3.2	0200	2.0	0410	1.5	0256	1.3	0327	3.5	0206	8.7
	1110	1.5	1037	1.5	1022	1.3	0804	1.1	0757	0.8	1001	4.4	0836	3.5	0901	0.8	0850	2.1
	1812	4.9	1821	5.0	1647	3.8	1436	3.1	1412	1.9	1627	1.7	1509	1.4	1557	3.4	1424	8.5
	2318	1.7	2251	1.7	2239	1.4	2019	1.2	2018	0.9	2220	4.2	2042	3.3	2131	0.8	2102	2.3
4 W	0642	4.8	0657	4.9	0516	3.7	0305	3.0	0243	1.9	0450	1.9	0336	1.6	0403	3.3	0244	8.1
	1142	1.9	1116	1.9	1103	1.6	0842	1.4	0839	1.0	1054	4.2	0915	3.2	0943	1.1	0922	2.7
	1857	4.7	1906	4.8	1733	3.6	1518	2.9	1454	1.8	1711	2.0	1556	1.7	1630	3.2	1505	8.0
	2359	2.0	2337	2.0	2330	1.7	2110	1.4	2115	1.0	2332	3.9	2120	3.0	2223	1.0	2142	2.9
5 TH	0733	4.5	0748	4.6	0615	3.5	0359	2.8	0336	1.7	0537	2.3	0424	1.8	0439	3.1	0330	7.5
	1233	2.3	1212	2.4	1157	1.9	0936	1.6	0937	1.1	1218	3.9	1014	3.0	1033	1.3	1003	3.3
	1949	4.5	2000	4.6	1831	3.4	1612	2.8	1547	1.8	1809	2.4	1656	2.0	1707	3.1	1558	7.4
							2235	1.6	2239	1.1			2218	2.8	2333	1.2	2236	3.4
6 F	0115	2.3	0117	2.4	0042	1.9	0511	2.6	0443	1.6	0122	3.7	0533	2.0	0521	2.8	0435	6.9
	0833	4.3	0847	4.4	0730	3.3	1106	1.8	1103	1.2	0646	2.6	1236	2.9	1146	1.5	1112	3.8
	1401	2.6	1417	2.7	1316	2.1	1723	2.7	1655	1.7	1348	3.9	1820	2.1	1754	2.9	1714	7.0
	2048	4.3	2101	4.4	1945	3.4					1943	2.5						
7 SA	0342	2.4	0336	2.4	0224	1.9	0026	1.6	0015	1.1	0250	3.7	0115	2.7	0100	1.3	0005	3.6
	0943	4.2	0950	4.4	0854	3.3	0640	2.6	0625	1.6	0841	2.6	0718	2.0	0620	2.6	0612	6.7
	1604	2.6	1603	2.6	1457	2.1	1250	1.8	1231	1.2	1503	4.0	1414	3.0	1326	1.6	1254	3.8
	2157	4.3	2205	4.5	2106	3.4	1845	2.8	1827	1.7	2004	2.0	1939	2.0	1939	2.8	1848	7.1
8 SU	0506	2.1	0446	2.2	0351	1.7	0145	1.4	0126	1.0	0356	3.9	0242	2.9	0218	1.2	0137	3.4
	1105	4.3	1100	4.5	1009	3.4	0758	2.7	0748	1.7	1003	2.4	0845	1.8	0834	2.6	0744	7.1
	1715	2.3	1659	2.3	1610	1.9	1400	1.6	1339	1.1	1600	4.2	1504	3.3	1443	1.5	1413	3.4
	2315	4.7	2312	4.7	2213	3.5	1956	2.9	1945	1.8	2231	2.1	2112	1.8	2115	2.9	2002	7.6
9 M	0554	1.8	0536	1.9	0442	1.5	0235	1.2	0216	0.9	0442	4.2	0329	3.1	0314	1.0	0244	2.8
	1210	4.6	1207	4.8	1103	3.6	0851	2.9	0834	1.8	1051	2.1	0935	1.6	0943	2.8	0841	7.7
	1801	2.0	1745	2.0	1657	1.7	1445	1.5	1427	1.0	1643	4.4	1542	3.5	1532	1.3	1508	2.8
					2303	3.7	2048	3.0	2033	1.9	2312	1.7	2154	1.6	2209	3.1	2053	8.2
10 TU	0018	4.8	0018	5.0	0521	1.3	0313	1.1	0254	0.8	0516	4.4	0406	3.3	0355	0.8	0333	2.3
	0632	1.5	0619	1.6	1143	3.8	0933	3.1	0912	1.9	1128	1.8	1012	1.4	1031	3.0	0922	8.2
	1254	4.9	1257	5.1	1733	1.5	1521	1.3	1504	0.9	1718	4.7	1617	3.7	1609	1.1	1552	2.3
	1838	1.7	1828	1.7	2342	3.9	2130	3.2	2112	2.0	2345	1.4	2228	1.4	2254	3.3	2133	8.7
11 W	0102	5.1	0109	5.3	0555	1.0	0346	0.9	0326	0.7	0545	4.7	0438	3.5	0431	0.6	0415	1.8
	0705	1.2	0659	1.3	1218	4.0	1009	3.2	0946	2.0	1202	1.4	1043	1.2	1114	3.2	0957	8.7
	1330	5.2	1339	5.4	1807	1.3	1554	1.1	1537	0.8	1748	4.9	1648	3.9	1643	0.9	1631	1.8
	1914	1.4	1909	1.4			2208	3.4	2148	2.1			2300	1.1	2336	3.4	2209	9.1
12 TH	0140	5.3	0151	5.5	0018	4.1	0418	0.7	0357	0.6	0018	1.1	0506	3.7	0503	0.4	0454	1.4
	0739	0.9	0734	1.0	0627	0.8	1042	3.3	1018	2.1	0612	4.9	1112	1.0	1154	3.3	1030	9.0
	1404	5.4	1415	5.6	1250	4.2	1625	0.8	1609	0.7	1234	1.2	1719	4.0	1716	0.7	1708	1.5
	1950	1.0	1947	1.2	1839	1.1	2244	3.5	2221	2.2	1818	5.2	2330	0.9			2244	9.4
13 F	0216	5.5	0228	5.7	0051	4.3	0448	0.6	0430	0.5	0050	0.8	0534	3.8	0015	3.5	0530	1.1
	0813	0.7	0759	0.8	0700	0.7	1116	3.4	1051	2.2	0640	5.1	1142	0.8	0536	0.3	1103	9.3
	1439	5.6	1448	5.8	1322	4.3	1658	0.8	1643	0.6	1306	0.9	1751	4.2	1233	3.4	1745	1.2
	2027	0.8	2015	1.0	1912	0.9	2321	3.6	2257	2.3	1850	5.3			1748	0.5	2318	9.6
14 SA	0251	5.6	0303	5.8	0125	4.4	0520	0.5	0504	0.4	0122	0.7	0003	0.8	0052	3.5	0607	0.9
	0849	0.6	0820	0.7	0733	0.6	1151	3.5	1125	2.2	0709	5.2	0603	4.0	0609	0.2	1137	9.5
	1515	5.6	1522	5.9	1355	4.4	1732	0.7	1718	0.5	1340	0.7	1214	0.7	1309	3.5	1822	1.0
	2103	0.7	2036	0.9	1947	0.8	2357	3.6	2332	2.3	1922	5.4	1822	4.2	1823	0.4	2354	9.7
15 SU	0326	5.7	0337	5.9	0200	4.5	0554	0.5	0540	0.4	0156	0.8	0037	0.7	0127	3.5	0643	0.9
	0924	0.5	0846	0.6	0807	0.6	1226	3.5	1159	2.2	0742	5.2	0632	4.0	0645	0.2	1212	9.5
	1551	5.6	1559	5.9	1430	4.4	1808	0.7	1756	0.5	1414	0.8	1248	0.7	1344	3.5	1859	1.0
	2139	0.7	2102	0.8	2021	0.8					1958	5.3	1855	4.2	1859	0.3		

13 F — ○

● ● Time: UT. For British Summer Time (shaded) March 26th to October 29th ADD ONE HOUR ● ●

OCTOBER 2000 TIDE TABLES

•• Time: UT. For British Summer Time (shaded) March 26th to October 29th ADD ONE HOUR ••

	LEITH		ROSYTH		ABERDEEN		WICK		LERWICK		ULLAPOOL		OBAN		GREENOCK		LIVERPOOL	
	Time	m	Time	m	Time	m	Time	m	Time	m	Time	m	Time	m	Time	m	Time	m
16 M	0403	5.7	0415	5.9	0239	4.5	0036	3.6	0009	2.3	0231	0.6	0114	0.7	0201	3.5	0030	9.7
	0957	0.7	0917	0.7	0843	0.6	0630	0.6	0617	0.5	0816	5.2	0703	4.0	0722	0.3	0718	1.0
	1629	5.6	1638	5.8	1506	4.3	1303	3.5	1234	2.2	1451	0.9	1326	0.8	1418	3.5	1248	9.5
	2214	0.9	2132	0.9	2059	0.8	1847	0.7	1836	0.6	2039	5.2	1930	4.0	1937	0.3	1936	1.2
17 TU	0444	5.6	0457	5.8	0320	4.4	0117	3.5	0049	2.2	0309	0.8	0154	0.8	0236	3.4	0109	9.5
	1027	0.9	0949	0.9	0921	0.8	0708	0.7	0657	0.6	0856	5.0	0738	3.9	0803	0.4	0754	1.3
	1710	5.4	1721	5.6	1546	4.2	1342	3.4	1312	2.1	1531	1.1	1409	1.0	1454	3.5	1327	9.2
	2248	1.1	2207	1.0	2141	0.9	1929	0.8	1919	0.6	2127	4.9	2009	3.8	2018	0.4	2014	1.5
18 W	0530	5.4	0542	5.6	0406	4.2	0202	3.4	0134	2.1	0349	1.1	0237	1.0	0315	3.3	0150	9.2
	1057	1.3	1026	1.2	1004	1.1	0750	0.9	0742	0.7	0943	4.7	0816	3.7	0848	0.5	0831	1.7
	1756	5.2	1806	5.4	1632	4.0	1426	3.2	1356	2.1	1618	1.4	1457	1.2	1533	3.5	1409	8.9
	2330	1.4	2248	1.3	2230	1.1	2018	1.0	2009	0.7	2227	4.5	2053	3.5	2106	0.5	2057	1.9
19 TH	0622	5.2	0632	5.3	0501	4.0	0254	3.2	0230	2.0	0436	1.5	0325	1.2	0400	3.2	0238	8.7
	1139	1.7	1109	1.6	1057	1.4	0840	1.2	0834	0.9	1047	4.4	0901	3.4	0940	0.8	0915	2.2
	1848	5.0	1857	5.1	1727	3.8	1518	3.1	1451	2.0	1714	1.7	1554	1.5	1617	3.5	1501	8.4
			2342	1.6	2335	1.3	2123	1.1	2114	0.8	2349	4.2	2152	3.1	2203	0.7	2151	2.3
20 F	0036	1.6	0730	5.0	0609	3.8	0357	3.0	0342	1.9	0536	1.9	0421	1.4	0457	3.1	0337	8.1
	0724	4.9	1210	2.0	1208	1.7	0952	1.4	0943	1.0	1218	4.2	1005	3.2	1046	1.0	1012	2.7
	1255	2.1	2001	4.8	1839	3.6	1623	3.0	1605	1.9	1833	2.0	1709	1.7	1709	3.3	1608	8.0
	1954	4.7					2257	1.2	2240	0.9			2351	2.9	2318	0.9	2304	2.6
21 SA	0212	1.8	0209	1.8	0100	1.4	0518	2.9	0503	1.8	0120	4.1	0531	1.6	0608	3.0	0457	7.7
	0840	4.7	0847	4.7	0736	3.6	1133	1.6	1121	1.1	0700	2.2	1239	3.0	1206	1.2	1134	3.0
	1451	2.3	1509	2.2	1339	1.8	1744	2.9	1726	1.8	1351	4.2	1900	1.7	1812	3.2	1734	7.8
	2112	4.7	2126	4.7	2004	3.6					2016	2.0						
22 SU	0354	1.7	0415	1.7	0232	1.4	0033	1.1	0014	0.8	0244	4.2	0150	3.0	0044	0.9	0037	2.6
	1004	4.8	1008	4.8	0903	3.7	0648	2.9	0630	1.8	0844	2.2	0700	1.5	0739	3.0	0627	7.7
	1630	2.1	1643	2.0	1509	1.8	1306	1.5	1249	1.1	1509	4.4	1424	3.2	1328	1.2	1309	2.9
	2233	4.8	2243	4.9	2124	3.8	1906	3.0	1846	1.9	2141	1.7	2039	1.5	1936	3.2	1900	8.0
23 M	0509	1.4	0528	1.3	0351	1.2	0150	1.0	0124	0.7	0353	4.4	0255	3.1	0205	0.8	0200	2.1
	1120	5.0	1120	5.0	1017	3.9	0804	3.1	0749	1.9	1000	1.9	0824	1.3	0917	3.1	0745	8.1
	1734	1.8	1745	1.7	1618	1.6	1412	1.3	1352	1.0	1611	4.7	1518	3.5	1440	1.1	1427	2.4
	2342	5.1	2348	5.2	2228	4.0	2014	3.2	1956	2.0	2239	1.3	2138	1.2	2111	3.3	2012	8.5
24 TU	0606	1.1	0627	0.9	0450	0.9	0245	0.8	0220	0.6	0445	4.7	0345	3.4	0310	0.7	0308	1.6
	1220	5.3	1220	5.3	1114	4.1	0902	3.2	0845	2.0	1054	1.5	0924	1.0	1021	3.3	0848	8.7
	1824	1.5	1835	1.4	1710	1.3	1501	1.2	1442	1.0	1658	4.9	1600	3.7	1538	1.0	1529	1.9
					2321	4.2	2110	3.4	2051	2.1	2327	1.0	2221	1.0	2219	3.5	2109	9.1
25 W	0038	5.4	0044	5.5	0539	0.7	0330	0.6	0306	0.5	0527	5.0	0427	3.6	0401	0.5	0404	1.1
	0655	0.8	0718	0.7	1200	4.2	0950	3.4	0930	2.1	1139	1.2	1010	0.8	1114	3.4	0939	9.1
	1308	5.5	1309	5.6	1754	1.1	1541	1.0	1525	0.7	1739	5.2	1637	3.9	1624	0.8	1620	1.4
	1907	1.2	1915	1.2			2158	3.6	2139	2.2			2259	0.8	2312	3.6	2157	9.4
26 TH	0124	5.6	0132	5.7	0006	4.4	0409	0.5	0348	0.4	0009	0.8	0503	3.8	0444	0.4	0451	0.8
	0738	0.6	0801	0.6	0621	0.6	1031	3.5	1011	2.2	0604	5.2	1051	0.6	1200	3.5	1021	9.4
	1349	5.7	1352	5.7	1239	4.3	1618	0.9	1603	0.6	1221	1.0	1709	4.0	1706	0.6	1703	1.1
	1948	0.9	1923	1.0	1834	1.0	2242	3.7	2222	2.3	1815	5.3	2334	0.7	2357	3.7	2239	9.7
27 F	0206	5.7	0215	5.9	0045	4.5	0445	0.5	0426	0.4	0047	0.7	0535	3.9	0523	0.4	0533	0.7
	0817	0.5	0836	0.5	0659	0.6	1109	3.5	1048	2.2	0639	5.3	1130	0.5	1240	3.6	1101	9.6
	1427	5.7	1433	5.8	1315	4.4	1654	0.8	1641	0.6	1259	0.8	1739	4.1	1745	0.5	1743	1.1
	2028	0.8	1947	0.8	1911	0.9	2323	3.7	2302	2.3	1850	5.3					2318	9.7
28 SA	0248	5.8	0258	6.0	0124	4.5	0519	0.5	0503	0.4	0123	0.6	0009	0.7	0036	3.7	0609	0.7
	0854	0.5	0847	0.6	0734	0.6	1145	3.5	1123	2.2	0712	5.3	0606	4.0	0600	0.4	1138	9.6
	1506	5.7	1512	5.8	1350	4.4	1730	0.7	1718	0.6	1335	0.8	1208	0.6	1316	3.6	1819	1.0
	2106	0.8	2021	0.8	1947	0.8			2340	2.3	1924	5.2	1809	4.0	1823	0.4	2354	9.6
29 SU ●	0328	5.7	0340	5.9	0203	4.4	0002	3.6	0539	0.5	0157	0.7	0042	0.8	0113	3.7	0643	0.9
	0927	0.7	0841	0.7	0809	0.7	0553	0.6	1156	2.2	0745	5.2	0635	4.0	0637	0.4	1212	9.5
	1545	5.6	1553	5.7	1424	4.3	1220	3.5	1755	0.6	1411	0.9	1245	0.7	1348	3.6	1854	1.2
	2139	0.9	2053	0.9	2023	0.9	1806	0.8			1957	5.1	1839	3.9	1901	0.4		
30 M	0408	5.5	0422	5.7	0241	4.3	0039	3.5	0017	2.2	0230	0.9	0115	0.9	0148	3.6	0030	9.4
	0954	0.9	0909	0.9	0842	0.9	0626	0.8	0613	0.6	0818	5.0	0705	3.9	0715	0.5	0715	1.2
	1622	5.4	1631	5.5	1459	4.2	1253	3.4	1228	2.2	1445	1.1	1321	0.9	1420	3.6	1245	9.3
	2206	1.1	2123	1.1	2057	1.0	1842	0.9	1832	0.7	2032	4.8	1909	3.8	1939	0.5	1927	1.5
31 TU	0447	5.3	0502	5.5	0320	4.1	0116	3.3	0054	2.1	0305	1.2	0149	1.1	0223	3.5	0103	9.0
	1013	1.2	0939	1.2	0914	1.1	0658	1.0	0648	0.8	0851	4.8	0736	3.8	0751	0.7	0745	1.7
	1659	5.2	1708	5.3	1533	4.1	1327	3.3	1301	2.1	1521	1.3	1400	1.2	1451	3.6	1318	9.0
	2224	1.4	2153	1.3	2133	1.2	1917	1.0	1909	0.8	2109	4.5	1941	3.6	2018	0.6	2000	1.9

SCOTLAND & NORTH WEST ENGLAND Time Zone UT

Leith * Rosyth * Aberdeen * Wick * Lerwick * Ullapool * Oban * Greenock * Liverpool

TIDE TABLES NOVEMBER 2000

LEITH Time m	ROSYTH Time m	ABERDEEN Time m	WICK Time m	LERWICK Time m	ULLAPOOL Time m	OBAN Time m	GREENOCK Time m	LIVERPOOL Time m	
0527 5.1	0542 5.2	0401 3.9	0154 3.2	0132 2.0	0339 1.5	0224 1.3	0257 3.3	0137 8.6	**1 W**
1036 1.5	1009 1.5	0948 1.4	0730 1.2	0721 0.9	0927 4.6	0810 3.6	0826 0.9	0814 2.2	
1737 5.0	1745 5.0	1609 3.9	1402 3.2	1336 2.0	1559 1.6	1439 1.5	1522 3.5	1353 8.6	
2248 1.6	2227 1.6	2211 1.4	1955 1.2	1950 0.9	2151 4.2	2014 3.4	2057 0.8	2032 2.3	
0609 4.8	0623 4.9	0445 3.7	0236 3.0	0213 1.9	0417 1.9	0302 1.5	0332 3.2	0213 8.1	**2 TH**
1107 1.9	1045 1.8	1027 1.6	0806 1.4	0759 1.1	1012 4.3	0849 3.4	0902 1.1	0845 2.7	
1820 4.8	1827 4.8	1651 3.7	1442 3.0	1415 1.9	1641 1.9	1525 1.7	1554 3.4	1432 8.1	
2327 1.9	2308 1.9	2257 1.6	2042 1.3	2042 1.0	2249 3.9	2052 3.1	2142 1.0	2109 2.8	
0657 4.6	0710 4.6	0539 3.5	0325 2.8	0303 1.8	0500 2.2	0346 1.7	0409 3.0	0255 7.6	**3 F**
1151 2.2	1129 2.2	1115 1.9	0850 1.2	0850 1.2	1115 4.1	0942 3.1	0944 1.3	0924 3.2	
1908 4.5	1919 4.6	1743 3.5	1530 2.9	1504 1.9	1733 2.2	1621 2.0	1631 3.2	1519 7.7	
		2357 1.7	2149 1.5	2154 1.0		2145 2.9	2238 1.1	2158 3.2	
0027 2.1	0018 2.2	0645 3.3	0427 2.7	0402 1.7	0018 3.8	0444 1.9	0453 2.8	0351 7.1	**4 SA**
0751 4.4	0804 4.4	1221 2.1	1005 1.8	1009 1.2	0558 2.5	1121 3.0	1040 1.5	1019 3.7	
1305 2.5	1320 2.5	1851 3.4	1605 1.8	1605 1.8	1244 3.9	1736 2.1	1715 3.0	1624 7.3	
2005 4.4	2018 4.5		2321 1.5	2316 1.0	1846 2.4	2330 2.7	2351 1.2	2309 3.5	
0212 2.3	0210 2.3	0119 1.8	0546 2.6	0519 1.6	0152 3.7	0609 2.0	0553 2.7	0511 6.8	**5 SU**
0854 4.3	0904 4.3	0802 3.3	1142 1.8	1136 1.2	0730 2.6	1318 3.0	1158 1.6	1145 3.9	
1449 2.6	1459 2.6	1351 2.2	1745 2.8	1720 1.7	1406 4.0	1910 2.1	1823 2.9	1746 7.1	
2109 4.3	2120 4.4	2008 3.4			2026 2.4				
0405 2.2	0348 2.2	0249 1.8	0047 1.4	0029 1.0	0306 3.9	0142 2.8	0110 1.2	0037 3.4	**6 M**
1003 4.3	1007 4.4	0915 3.4	0705 2.7	0654 1.7	0909 2.5	0748 1.9	0728 2.7	0642 6.9	
1621 2.4	1617 2.4	1515 2.0	1305 1.7	1248 1.2	1511 4.1	1419 3.2	1325 1.6	1316 3.6	
2218 4.4	2224 4.6	2118 3.5	1859 2.8	1844 1.8	2139 2.1	2026 1.9	2015 2.9	1905 7.4	
0505 1.9	0454 1.9	0353 1.6	0147 1.3	0125 0.9	0359 4.1	0244 3.0	0217 1.0	0150 3.0	**7 TU**
1112 4.5	1112 4.6	1015 3.6	0806 2.9	0751 1.8	1007 2.2	0849 1.7	0853 2.9	0750 7.4	
1717 2.1	1712 2.1	1612 1.8	1401 1.6	1343 1.1	1600 4.3	1503 3.4	1433 1.4	1419 3.1	
2324 4.7	2330 4.8	2216 3.7	1958 3.0	1945 1.9	2227 1.8	2113 1.7	2124 3.1	2004 7.9	
0548 1.6	0545 1.6	0438 1.3	0231 1.1	0209 0.8	0438 4.3	0325 3.2	0308 0.8	0246 2.4	**8 W**
1206 4.8	1210 5.0	1102 3.8	0852 3.0	0832 1.9	1050 1.9	0930 1.5	0949 3.1	0838 8.0	
1800 1.8	1800 1.8	1654 1.6	1444 1.4	1426 1.0	1640 4.6	1539 3.6	1523 1.1	1510 2.5	
		2302 3.9	2047 3.2	2030 2.0	2306 1.5	2150 1.4	2216 3.3	2050 8.5	
0017 5.0	0027 5.1	0516 1.1	0309 0.9	0247 0.7	0511 4.6	0400 3.4	0351 0.6	0334 1.9	**9 TH**
0627 1.3	0630 1.3	1140 4.0	0931 3.2	0908 2.0	1127 1.6	1004 1.3	1037 3.3	0918 8.5	
1251 5.1	1257 5.3	1732 1.3	1521 1.2	1503 0.8	1715 4.9	1613 3.8	1605 0.9	1554 2.0	
1841 1.4	1843 1.5	2342 4.1	2130 3.3	2110 2.1	2342 1.2	2224 1.2	2302 3.4	2131 8.9	
0102 5.3	0113 5.4	0552 0.9	0342 0.8	0323 0.6	0541 4.9	0431 3.6	0429 0.4	0418 1.5	**10 F**
0704 1.0	0709 1.0	1216 4.2	1009 3.4	0943 2.1	1203 1.3	1037 1.1	1121 3.4	0955 9.0	
1331 5.4	1339 5.6	1808 1.1	1556 1.0	1540 0.7	1749 5.1	1647 4.0	1643 0.7	1636 1.6	
1920 1.1	1922 1.2		2212 3.5	2149 2.2		2258 0.9	2344 3.4	2210 9.3	
0142 5.5	0154 5.6	0020 4.3	0417 0.7	0359 0.5	0018 0.9	0502 3.8	0506 0.3	0459 1.1	**11 SA**
0742 0.8	0736 0.8	0628 0.7	1045 3.5	1019 2.2	0612 5.1	1111 0.9	1202 3.4	1032 9.3	**O**
1409 5.6	1417 5.7	1251 4.3	1632 0.6	1618 0.6	1238 1.0	1722 4.2	1721 0.5	1718 1.2	
2000 0.8	1949 0.9	1845 0.9	2253 3.6	2230 2.3	1824 5.3	2335 0.7		2248 9.6	
0222 5.7	0233 5.8	0058 4.4	0452 0.6	0437 0.5	0054 0.7	0535 4.0	0024 3.4	0539 0.9	**12 SU**
0821 0.7	0754 0.7	0705 0.6	1124 3.6	1057 2.3	0645 5.3	1148 0.7	0542 0.2	1110 9.6	
1448 5.7	1455 5.9	1328 4.4	1710 0.7	1657 0.5	1316 0.8	1758 4.2	1241 3.5	1759 1.0	
2039 0.8	2012 0.8	1923 0.8	2334 3.7	2310 2.3	1902 5.4		1758 0.4	2329 9.8	
0302 5.8	0314 5.9	0139 4.5	0530 0.6	0516 0.5	0131 0.6	0013 0.6	0103 3.4	0619 0.8	**13 M**
0900 0.7	0824 0.7	0743 0.6	1202 3.6	1134 2.3	0721 5.3	0609 4.1	0621 0.2	1149 9.7	
1527 5.7	1536 5.9	1406 4.4	1751 0.6	1737 0.5	1354 0.7	1227 0.7	1319 3.6	1840 0.9	
2121 0.7	2043 0.7	2003 0.7		2353 2.3	1942 5.4	1836 4.2	1837 0.3		
0344 5.8	0357 5.9	0221 4.5	0018 3.7	0557 0.6	0210 0.6	0054 0.6	0143 3.4	0010 9.8	**14 TU**
0939 0.8	0859 0.7	0823 0.7	0610 0.6	1213 2.3	0800 5.3	0645 4.1	0702 0.3	0658 0.9	
1608 5.6	1618 5.6	1445 4.4	1242 3.6	1821 0.5	1436 0.8	1311 0.7	1357 3.6	1230 9.6	
2204 0.8	2120 0.7	2045 0.7	1834 0.6		2029 5.2	1917 4.1	1919 0.3	1922 1.0	
0429 5.7	0442 5.8	0308 4.4	0103 3.6	0039 2.3	0251 0.8	0136 0.7	0224 3.4	0053 9.6	**15 W**
1020 1.0	0936 1.0	0906 0.9	0653 0.8	0641 0.7	0844 5.1	0724 4.0	0746 0.4	0738 1.2	
1652 5.5	1703 5.6	1528 4.3	1325 3.5	1255 2.2	1521 1.0	1358 0.9	1435 3.7	1313 9.4	
2250 0.9	2200 0.9	2133 0.8	1921 0.6	1909 0.6	2122 4.9	2000 3.8	2005 0.3	2005 1.3	

● ● Time: UT. For British Summer Time (shaded) March 26th to October 29th ADD ONE HOUR ● ●

NOVEMBER 2000 TIDE TABLES

•• Time: UT. For British Summer Time (shaded) March 26th to October 29th ADD ONE HOUR ••

	LEITH Time	m	ROSYTH Time	m	ABERDEEN Time	m	WICK Time	m	LERWICK Time	m	ULLAPOOL Time	m	OBAN Time	m	GREENOCK Time	m	LIVERPOOL Time	m
16TH	0518	5.5	0531	5.6	0359	4.2	0153	3.4	0131	2.2	0336	1.1	0221	0.8	0309	3.3	0139	9.3
	1103	1.3	1017	1.3	0954	1.1	0739	1.0	0729	0.8	0936	4.9	0807	3.8	0835	0.6	0819	1.6
	1741	5.3	1752	5.4	1617	4.1	1412	3.4	1344	2.1	1611	1.2	1451	1.2	1517	3.7	1400	9.1
	2342	1.2	2247	1.1	2228	1.0	2016	0.8	2003	0.6	2226	4.6	2050	3.5	2057	0.5	2054	1.6
17F	0614	5.3	0624	5.3	0457	4.0	0248	3.2	0232	2.0	0426	1.5	0310	1.1	0400	3.3	0232	8.8
	1154	1.7	1104	1.6	1050	1.4	0833	1.3	0824	0.9	1042	4.6	0857	3.6	0930	0.8	0907	2.1
	1836	5.1	1848	5.1	1714	3.9	1506	3.2	1443	2.0	1711	1.5	1552	1.4	1603	3.6	1455	8.7
					2333	1.1	2125	1.0	2109	0.7	2342	4.3	2153	3.2	2157	0.6	2151	2.0
18SA	0045	1.4	0054	1.4	0607	3.8	0354	3.0	0339	1.9	0527	1.9	0406	1.3	0459	3.2	0333	8.3
	0717	5.0	0727	5.0	1200	1.7	0942	1.5	0932	1.1	1204	4.4	1006	3.3	1033	1.0	1006	2.5
	1302	2.0	1314	2.0	1824	3.8	1610	3.1	1553	2.0	1827	1.8	1708	1.6	1655	3.5	1600	8.3
	1942	4.9	1959	4.9			2249	1.1	2227	0.7			2336	3.0	2307	0.7	2301	2.2
19SU	0205	1.6	0224	1.5	0051	1.2	0510	2.9	0451	1.8	0104	4.2	0513	1.4	0606	3.1	0446	7.9
	0830	4.8	0842	4.9	0726	3.7	1110	1.6	1057	1.1	0645	2.1	1221	3.2	1145	1.2	1122	2.8
	1430	2.2	1456	2.1	1321	1.8	1724	3.1	1706	1.9	1328	4.4	1845	1.6	1757	3.4	1717	8.1
	2057	4.8	2118	4.8	1943	3.7			2351	0.7	1954	1.8						
20M	0331	1.5	0357	1.4	0212	1.2	0013	1.0	0608	1.8	0222	4.2	0118	3.0	0024	0.8	0021	2.2
	0945	4.9	0956	4.9	0845	3.7	0630	2.9	1221	1.1	0816	2.2	0633	1.5	0728	3.1	0606	7.9
	1557	2.1	1617	1.9	1442	1.8	1237	1.6	1820	1.9	1445	4.5	1359	3.3	1301	1.2	1246	2.8
	2211	4.9	2228	4.9	2058	3.8	1841	3.1			2113	1.7	2012	1.5	1915	3.4	1835	8.2
21TU	0443	1.4	0505	1.1	0327	1.2	0126	1.0	0100	0.7	0330	4.4	0226	3.1	0139	0.8	0136	2.0
	1056	5.0	1102	5.0	0954	3.8	0740	3.0	0721	1.9	0932	2.0	0752	1.3	0851	3.2	0720	8.1
	1703	1.9	1718	1.7	1551	1.6	1345	1.4	1327	1.0	1548	4.6	1455	3.5	1413	1.2	1400	2.4
	2318	5.1	2330	5.2	2204	4.0	1948	3.2	1929	2.0	2213	1.5	2110	1.3	2044	3.4	1945	8.5
22W	0541	1.2	0605	1.0	0427	1.0	0222	0.9	0157	0.6	0424	4.6	0318	3.3	0246	0.7	0242	1.7
	1156	5.2	1200	5.2	1051	4.0	0838	3.2	0818	2.0	1030	1.7	0854	1.2	0954	3.3	0822	8.5
	1757	1.6	1810	1.5	1646	1.4	1438	1.3	1420	0.9	1638	4.8	1539	3.6	1515	1.0	1502	2.1
					2259	4.1	2047	3.3	2028	2.1	2303	1.3	2155	1.2	2153	3.5	2043	8.8
23TH	0016	5.3	0027	5.4	0515	0.9	0307	0.8	0245	0.6	0506	4.8	0401	3.5	0339	0.6	0337	1.4
	0630	1.1	0658	0.9	1137	4.1	0925	3.3	0905	2.0	1118	1.5	0944	1.0	1047	3.4	0914	8.8
	1245	5.3	1251	5.4	1733	1.3	1520	1.1	1505	0.8	1720	4.9	1615	3.7	1604	0.8	1554	1.7
	1842	1.4	1852	1.4	2346	4.2	2136	3.4	2118	2.1	2345	1.1	2233	1.0	2247	3.6	2133	9.1
24F	0106	5.4	0115	5.5	0557	0.9	0345	0.8	0326	0.6	0544	5.0	0438	3.6	0424	0.5	0424	1.2
	0712	1.0	0742	0.9	1217	4.2	1007	3.4	0945	2.1	1200	1.3	1027	0.9	1133	3.5	0958	9.1
	1328	5.5	1335	5.5	1813	1.1	1558	1.0	1545	0.7	1757	5.0	1645	3.8	1648	0.6	1639	1.5
	1924	1.2	1852	1.2			2221	3.5	2203	2.2			2309	1.0	2332	3.6	2216	9.2
25SA	0149	5.5	0200	5.6	0027	4.3	0421	0.8	0403	0.6	0024	1.0	0511	3.8	0504	0.5	0506	1.2
	0749	0.9	0812	0.9	0635	0.9	1045	3.5	1023	2.2	0619	5.1	1106	0.9	1213	3.5	1037	9.3
	1407	5.5	1414	5.5	1252	4.3	1636	0.9	1624	0.7	1239	1.2	1715	3.8	1727	0.5	1719	1.4
	2005	1.1	1921	1.0	1851	1.0	2303	3.5	2243	2.2	1833	5.1	2343	0.9			2255	9.3
26SU	0230	5.5	0241	5.7	0107	4.3	0454	0.8	0439	0.6	0100	1.0	0542	3.9	0012	3.5	0542	1.2
	0824	0.9	0742	0.9	0709	0.9	1121	3.5	1058	2.2	0652	5.2	1145	0.9	0541	0.5	1114	9.3
	1445	5.5	1451	5.6	1327	4.3	1712	0.9	1700	0.6	1316	1.1	1745	3.8	1248	3.6	1756	1.4
	2043	1.0	1957	1.0	1928	1.0	2342	3.5	2321	2.2	1908	5.0			1806	0.5	2332	9.2
27M	0309	5.5	0321	5.6	0145	4.3	0527	0.9	0515	0.7	0135	1.1	0017	0.9	0048	3.5	0615	1.3
	0857	1.0	0815	0.9	0744	0.9	1155	3.5	1131	2.2	0725	5.2	0612	3.9	0618	0.6	1148	9.3
	1522	5.5	1529	5.5	1400	4.3	1748	0.9	1737	0.7	1351	1.2	1222	1.0	1321	3.6	1830	1.4
	2118	1.1	2035	1.0	2004	1.0			2358	2.1	1942	4.9	1818	3.8	1843	0.5		
28TU ●	0347	5.4	0400	5.5	0224	4.2	0018	3.4	0548	0.8	0209	1.2	0051	1.0	0124	3.4	0007	9.1
	0924	1.2	0849	1.1	0817	1.1	0601	1.0	1203	2.2	0757	5.1	0645	3.9	0653	0.7	0647	1.5
	1558	5.4	1606	5.4	1433	4.2	1228	3.5	1813	0.7	1427	1.3	1300	1.1	1351	3.6	1222	9.2
	2145	1.2	2109	1.1	2039	1.1	1824	0.9			2017	4.7	1850	3.7	1919	0.6	1904	1.6
29W	0424	5.2	0438	5.3	0301	4.0	0055	3.3	0035	2.1	0242	1.3	0124	1.1	0158	3.3	0041	8.8
	0949	1.4	0921	1.3	0850	1.2	0633	1.1	0621	0.9	0831	4.9	0718	3.8	0727	0.8	0717	1.8
	1633	5.2	1641	5.3	1507	4.1	1301	3.4	1236	2.2	1502	1.4	1338	1.3	1423	3.6	1256	9.0
	2207	1.3	2142	1.3	2114	1.2	1900	1.0	1850	0.8	2054	4.5	1924	3.6	1955	0.6	1936	1.9
30TH	0502	5.1	0515	5.1	0340	3.9	0133	3.2	0111	2.0	0317	1.6	0200	1.2	0232	3.2	0115	8.8
	1016	1.6	0954	1.5	0924	1.4	0707	1.2	0655	0.9	0906	4.7	0752	3.7	0800	0.9	0747	2.1
	1710	5.1	1718	5.2	1542	4.0	1336	3.3	1309	2.1	1539	1.6	1418	1.5	1454	3.5	1330	8.7
	2235	1.5	2215	1.5	2151	1.3	1938	1.1	1929	0.8	2133	4.3	1959	3.4	2031	0.7	2010	2.2

SCOTLAND & NORTH WEST ENGLAND Time Zone UT
Leith * Rosyth * Aberdeen * Wick * Lerwick * Ullapool * Oban * Greenock * Liverpool
TIDE TABLES DECEMBER 2000

	LEITH		ROSYTH		ABERDEEN		WICK		LERWICK		ULLAPOOL		OBAN		GREENOCK		LIVERPOOL	
	Time	*m*	*Time*	*m*	*Time*	*m*	*Time*	*m*	*Time*	*m*	*Time*	*m*	*Time*	*m*	*Time*	*m*	*Time*	*m*
1 F	0541	4.9	0554	4.9	0421	3.8	0212	3.0	0151	1.9	0354	1.8	0236	1.4	0307	3.1	0150	8.2
	1048	1.8	1028	1.7	1000	1.6	0742	1.4	0732	1.0	0946	4.5	0830	3.5	0836	1.0	0819	2.5
	1749	4.9	1757	5.0	1621	3.9	1414	3.2	2014	0.9	1618	1.8	1501	1.7	1527	3.4	1407	8.4
	2311	1.7	2255	1.6	2232	1.4	2020	1.2			2220	4.1	2037	3.2	2112	1.0	2047	2.5
2 SA	0624	4.7	0637	4.7	0509	3.6	0256	2.9	0235	1.8	0433	2.1	0315	1.6	0346	3.0	0229	7.8
	1128	2.0	1107	2.0	1044	1.8	0823	1.5	0815	1.1	1036	4.3	0917	3.3	0918	1.2	0857	2.9
	1834	4.7	1843	4.8	1706	3.7	1457	3.1	1431	1.9	1704	2.0	1550	1.8	1603	3.3	1450	8.0
			2348	1.8	2321	1.6	2112	1.3	2109	0.9	2319	4.0	2122	3.0	2200	0.9	2130	2.8
3 SU	0001	1.9	0726	4.6	0603	3.5	0348	2.8	0326	1.7	0521	2.3	0401	1.8	0431	3.0	0315	7.5
	0713	4.5	1204	2.3	1136	1.9	0917	1.7	0913	1.2	1139	4.2	1021	3.1	1009	1.3	0944	3.2
	1224	2.3	1934	4.6	1802	3.6	1548	3.0	1524	1.8	1800	2.2	1648	2.0	1645	3.2	1541	7.7
	1925	4.6					2218	1.4	2215	1.0			2223	2.9	2259	1.0	2224	3.0
4 M	0111	2.0	0109	2.0	0022	1.7	0449	2.7	0425	1.7	0036	3.9	0501	1.9	0527	2.9	0415	7.2
	0808	4.4	0820	4.5	0706	3.4	1030	1.8	1029	1.2	0624	2.5	1151	3.1	1109	1.4	1045	3.5
	1341	2.4	1351	2.4	1243	2.1	1649	2.9	1625	1.8	1256	4.1	1758	2.0	1739	3.1	1645	7.4
	2022	4.5	2031	4.6	1907	3.5	2333	1.4	2327	1.0	1911	2.3	2352	2.8			2332	3.1
5 TU	0234	2.1	0219	2.0	0133	1.7	0558	2.7	0534	1.7	0154	3.9	0620	1.9	0006	1.1	0527	7.1
	0909	4.4	0919	4.5	0813	3.4	1150	1.8	1148	1.2	0747	2.5	1312	3.1	0635	2.9	1203	3.5
	1505	2.4	1506	2.4	1400	2.0	1756	2.9	1735	1.8	1407	4.1	1912	1.9	1218	1.4	1756	7.5
	2124	4.5	2133	4.6	2016	3.5					2027	2.2			1857	3.0		
6 W	0352	1.9	0332	1.9	0245	1.6	0042	1.3	0030	0.9	0300	4.0	0126	2.9	0115	1.0	0045	2.9
	1012	4.6	1021	4.6	0918	3.5	0704	2.8	0645	1.7	0904	2.4	0737	1.8	0749	3.0	0640	7.3
	1618	2.2	1620	2.2	1511	1.9	1300	1.6	1253	1.1	1507	4.3	1409	3.3	1330	1.3	1319	3.2
	2227	4.6	2236	4.7	2120	3.6	1900	3.0	1844	1.8	2130	2.0	2012	1.7	2023	3.0	1903	7.8
7 TH	0453	1.7	0448	1.7	0344	1.4	0139	1.2	0122	0.9	0351	4.2	0228	3.0	0217	0.8	0151	2.6
	1115	4.7	1121	4.9	1013	3.7	0801	3.0	0741	1.8	1001	2.1	0834	1.7	0857	3.1	0742	7.7
	1715	1.9	1719	1.9	1606	1.7	1357	1.5	1345	1.0	1557	4.5	1454	3.5	1434	1.1	1421	2.7
	2328	4.9	2337	5.0	2215	3.8	1959	3.1	1942	1.9	2221	1.7	2102	1.5	2130	3.1	2000	8.2
8 F	0543	1.5	0548	1.5	0433	1.2	0225	1.1	0207	0.8	0433	4.5	0314	3.2	0309	0.6	0249	2.1
	1209	5.0	1215	5.2	1100	3.9	0850	3.2	0826	2.0	1048	1.8	0920	1.4	0955	3.2	0833	8.3
	1804	1.6	1809	1.6	1654	1.6	1444	1.3	1429	0.9	1640	4.8	1536	3.7	1527	0.9	1515	2.2
					2305	4.0	2051	3.3	2033	2.0	2306	1.4	2145	1.3	2224	3.2	2051	8.7
9 SA	0023	5.1	0031	5.2	0517	1.0	0308	0.9	0249	0.7	0511	4.8	0354	3.5	0356	0.4	0341	1.7
	0630	1.2	0637	1.2	1143	4.1	0934	3.3	0909	2.1	1132	1.5	1002	1.2	1046	3.3	0919	8.8
	1258	5.3	1303	5.4	1738	1.2	1527	1.1	1512	0.8	1722	5.0	1618	3.9	1613	0.7	1605	1.8
	1850	1.3	1853	1.3	2351	4.2	2141	3.4	2120	2.1	2348	1.1	2228	1.0	2313	3.3	2138	9.1
10 SU	0112	5.4	0120	5.5	0600	0.9	0348	0.8	0331	0.6	0548	5.1	0433	3.7	0439	0.3	0428	1.3
	0714	1.0	0715	1.0	1224	4.3	1017	3.5	0951	2.2	1214	1.2	1045	1.0	1133	3.4	1003	9.2
	1342	5.5	1347	5.7	1821	1.0	1610	0.9	1554	0.6	1804	5.2	1700	4.0	1656	0.5	1653	1.3
	1935	1.1	1927	1.0			2229	3.6	2207	2.2			2311	0.8	2359	3.3	2223	9.5
11 M	0157	5.6	0206	5.8	0036	4.4	0430	0.7	0414	0.6	0030	0.9	0512	4.0	0521	0.2	0515	1.0
	0758	0.9	0739	0.8	0642	0.8	1100	3.6	1033	2.3	0627	5.3	1129	0.8	1215	3.5	1048	9.5
	1425	5.6	1430	5.8	1305	4.4	1654	0.7	1639	0.5	1257	0.9	1743	4.1	1739	0.3	1739	1.0
	2021	0.8	1959	0.8	1905	0.8	2317	3.7	2254	2.3	1848	5.3	2354	0.6			2309	9.7
12 TU	0242	5.8	0253	5.9	0123	4.5	0512	0.7	0458	0.6	0112	0.8	0553	4.1	0044	3.4	0559	0.9
	0845	0.8	0813	0.8	0726	0.7	1142	3.7	1115	2.3	0707	5.4	1215	0.7	0604	0.2	1132	9.7
	1507	5.7	1515	5.9	1346	4.5	1739	0.6	1724	0.5	1341	0.8	1827	4.1	1257	3.6	1826	0.8
	2110	0.7	2040	0.8	1951	0.6			2344	2.3	1935	5.4			1822	0.2	2356	9.8
13 W	0329	5.8	0341	6.0	0210	4.5	0006	3.7	0543	0.6	0156	0.8	0038	0.6	0131	3.4	0643	0.9
	0931	0.8	0854	0.8	0811	0.8	0557	0.8	1159	2.3	0751	5.4	0635	4.2	0648	0.3	1218	9.8
	1551	5.7	1603	5.9	1430	4.5	1227	3.7	1812	0.4	1427	0.7	1303	0.7	1339	3.7	1913	0.8
	2200	0.6	2216	0.6	2039	0.6	1828	0.6			2024	5.3	1912	4.0	1907	0.2		
14 TH	0418	5.8	0430	5.9	0300	4.5	0055	3.6	0036	2.3	0240	0.9	0123	0.6	0219	3.4	0043	9.7
	1018	1.0	0932	1.0	0857	0.9	0643	0.9	0630	0.7	0839	5.3	0718	4.1	0735	0.4	0727	1.0
	1639	5.6	1652	5.7	1515	4.4	1312	3.7	1246	2.3	1515	0.8	1354	0.8	1421	3.8	1305	9.6
	2251	0.7	2309	0.6	2130	0.6	1919	0.6	1902	0.4	2118	5.1	1959	3.8	1956	0.2	2001	0.9
15 F	0509	5.6	0522	5.8	0354	4.3	0147	3.5	0130	2.2	0327	1.1	0209	0.7	0309	3.4	0133	9.4
	1106	1.2	1050	1.3	0948	1.1	0732	1.0	0720	0.8	0931	5.2	0804	4.0	0824	0.6	0813	1.3
	1729	5.5	1745	5.5	1606	4.3	1401	3.6	1338	2.2	1606	1.0	1448	1.0	1505	3.8	1354	9.4
	2342	0.8			2224	0.7	2014	0.7	1957	0.5	2218	4.8	2049	3.6	2048	0.3	2051	1.1

• • Time: UT. For British Summer Time (shaded) March 26th to October 29th ADD ONE HOUR • •

DECEMBER 2000 TIDE TABLES

• • Time: UT. For British Summer Time (shaded) March 26th to October 29th ADD ONE HOUR • •

	LEITH Time	m	ROSYTH Time	m	ABERDEEN Time	m	WICK Time	m	LERWICK Time	m	ULLAPOOL Time	m	OBAN Time	m	GREENOCK Time	m	LIVERPOOL Time	m
16SA	0603	5.4	0001	0.8	0451	4.1	0242	3.3	0227	2.1	0418	1.4	0258	0.8	0400	3.3	0226	9.0
	1154	1.5	0618	5.5	1041	1.3	0824	1.2	0814	0.9	1031	4.9	0856	3.7	0918	0.7	0902	1.7
	1825	5.3	1209	1.5	1701	4.2	1454	3.5	1435	2.2	1703	1.3	1547	1.2	1552	3.8	1448	9.1
			1844	5.3	2324	0.9	2116	0.8	2057	0.6	2324	4.6	2145	3.3	2145	0.4	2146	1.4
17SU	0038	1.1	0057	1.0	0554	3.9	0342	3.2	0326	1.9	0514	1.7	0351	1.0	0454	3.3	0322	8.6
	0703	5.2	0719	5.3	1141	1.6	0922	1.4	0912	1.0	1140	4.7	0958	3.5	1015	0.9	0957	2.1
	1246	1.8	1306	1.7	1804	4.0	1553	3.3	1536	2.1	1806	1.6	1652	1.4	1644	3.7	1546	8.7
	1927	5.1	1950	5.1			2225	0.9	2202	0.6			2254	3.1	2248	0.6	2246	1.7
18M	0141	1.3	0205	1.2	0030	1.1	0447	3.0	0427	1.9	0035	4.4	0450	1.2	0552	3.2	0424	8.2
	0809	5.0	0825	5.1	0702	3.8	1032	1.5	1019	1.0	0619	2.0	1125	3.3	1120	1.0	1100	2.4
	1349	2.0	1418	1.9	1248	1.7	1659	3.2	1639	2.0	1255	4.6	1806	1.6	1741	3.6	1650	8.4
	2033	5.0	2058	5.0	1914	3.9	2339	1.0	2316	0.7	1917	1.7			2357	0.7	2351	2.0
19TU	0252	1.5	0324	1.3	0140	1.2	0556	3.0	0531	1.8	0148	4.3	0022	3.0	0658	3.2	0533	8.0
	0916	4.9	0931	5.0	0812	3.7	1151	1.6	1139	1.1	0733	2.1	0558	1.4	1230	1.1	1211	2.6
	1506	2.1	1538	1.9	1401	1.8	1808	3.2	1746	1.9	1409	4.5	1314	3.2	1848	3.4	1759	8.2
	2142	5.0	2203	5.0	2026	3.9					2031	1.8	1924	1.6				
20W	0404	1.5	0433	1.3	0251	1.3	0051	1.1	0028	0.7	0257	4.3	0143	3.0	0109	0.8	0100	2.1
	1022	4.9	1034	5.0	0921	3.7	0703	3.0	0639	1.8	0851	2.1	0712	1.4	0811	3.2	0643	7.9
	1621	2.0	1643	1.9	1514	1.7	1307	1.5	1254	1.0	1518	4.5	1425	3.3	1343	1.1	1323	2.6
	2248	5.0	2305	5.1	2134	3.9	1917	3.2	1856	1.9	2139	1.8	2031	1.5	2007	3.4	1909	8.2
21TH	0507	1.5	0536	1.3	0356	1.3	0152	1.1	0129	0.8	0356	4.5	0246	3.1	0218	0.8	0206	2.0
	1124	5.0	1134	5.0	1021	3.8	0805	3.1	0743	1.9	0959	2.0	0820	1.4	0919	3.2	0749	8.1
	1725	1.9	1739	1.8	1618	1.6	1411	1.4	1356	0.9	1615	4.6	1516	3.3	1450	0.9	1429	2.4
	2351	5.1			2236	3.9	2020	3.2	2002	2.0	2235	1.7	2124	1.4	2121	3.3	2013	8.2
22F	0600	1.5	0003	5.2	0449	1.3	0242	1.1	0221	0.8	0445	4.6	0336	3.3	0318	0.7	0306	1.9
	1220	5.1	0633	1.3	1112	3.9	0857	3.2	0836	1.9	1054	1.8	0917	1.3	1018	3.3	0845	8.4
	1818	1.7	1229	5.1	1711	1.5	1502	1.3	1448	0.9	1704	4.7	1556	3.4	1545	0.8	1527	2.2
			1823	1.7	2327	4.0	2115	3.3	2058	2.0	2323	1.6	2209	1.3	2221	3.3	2108	8.5
23SA	0046	5.1	0057	5.3	0534	1.2	0323	1.1	0306	0.8	0526	4.8	0418	3.4	0407	0.7	0357	1.8
	0644	1.4	0719	1.3	1155	4.0	0943	3.3	0922	2.0	1142	1.7	1006	1.2	1107	3.4	0934	8.6
	1308	5.2	1317	5.2	1756	1.3	1545	1.2	1532	0.8	1745	4.7	1629	3.5	1633	0.7	1616	1.9
	1905	1.5	1828	1.5			2203	3.3	2146	2.0			2248	1.2	2311	3.3	2155	8.7
24SU ●	0134	5.2	0145	5.4	0013	4.0	0400	1.1	0345	0.8	0005	1.4	0453	3.6	0450	0.7	0440	1.7
	0723	1.4	0649	1.3	0614	1.2	1024	3.4	1002	2.1	0603	5.0	1048	1.2	1149	3.4	1017	8.9
	1351	5.3	1357	5.4	1233	4.1	1623	1.0	1612	0.7	1224	1.5	1700	3.5	1715	0.6	1659	1.8
	1948	1.3	1901	1.3	1837	1.2	2247	3.4	2229	2.1	1823	4.8	2324	1.1	2353	3.2	2237	8.8
25M	0216	5.3	0227	5.4	0055	4.1	0434	1.1	0422	0.8	0043	1.4	0525	3.7	0529	0.7	0518	1.6
	0759	1.3	0718	1.3	0650	1.2	1100	3.5	1039	2.2	0638	5.1	1129	1.2	1226	3.5	1055	9.0
	1430	5.3	1435	5.4	1309	4.2	1700	1.0	1650	0.7	1303	1.4	1733	3.6	1754	0.5	1738	1.7
	2026	1.2	1941	1.1	1915	1.1	2326	3.4	2308	2.1	1858	4.8	2359	1.1			2315	8.8
26TU	0255	5.3	0305	5.4	0133	4.1	0509	1.1	0457	0.8	0118	1.3	0558	3.8	0031	3.2	0553	1.6
	0832	1.3	0756	1.2	0725	1.2	1136	3.5	1114	2.2	0711	5.1	1207	1.2	0605	0.7	1131	9.1
	1506	5.3	1511	5.5	1342	4.2	1736	1.0	1726	0.7	1339	1.4	1807	3.7	1259	3.5	1813	1.6
	2100	1.2	2021	1.1	1951	1.1			2345	2.1	1932	4.8			1831	0.5	2351	8.8
27W	0330	5.3	0342	5.4	0211	4.1	0003	3.3	0531	0.8	0152	1.4	0033	1.0	0106	3.2	0625	1.7
	0903	1.3	0834	1.2	0759	1.2	0542	1.1	1147	2.2	0743	5.1	0630	3.9	0639	0.8	1206	9.1
	1540	5.3	1546	5.5	1415	4.2	1209	3.5	1800	0.7	1413	1.4	1245	1.2	1330	3.5	1848	1.7
	2130	1.2	2100	1.1	2025	1.1	1812	1.0			2006	4.8	1841	3.7	1905	0.5		
28TH	0405	5.2	0417	5.3	0247	4.0	0039	3.3	0020	2.0	0226	1.4	0106	1.1	0141	3.1	0025	8.7
	0933	1.3	0911	1.3	0832	1.3	0616	1.2	0603	0.8	0815	5.0	0704	3.9	0711	0.8	0656	1.7
	1614	5.2	1621	5.4	1448	4.2	1242	3.5	1218	2.2	1447	1.4	1322	1.3	1402	3.5	1239	9.0
	2157	1.2	2137	1.2	2059	1.1	1847	1.0	1834	0.7	2039	4.7	1915	3.6	1938	0.6	1920	1.7
29F	0440	5.1	0452	5.2	0323	3.9	0115	3.2	0054	2.0	0300	1.5	0140	1.2	0215	3.1	0058	8.6
	1004	1.4	0946	1.4	0905	1.4	0648	1.2	0636	0.9	0849	4.9	0739	3.8	0744	0.8	0727	1.9
	1649	5.2	1656	5.4	1521	4.1	1316	3.4	1250	2.1	1521	1.5	1400	1.4	1433	3.5	1313	8.9
	2227	1.3	2212	1.3	2133	1.1	1921	1.0	1909	0.7	2114	4.6	1949	3.5	2012	0.6	1953	1.9
30SA	0516	5.0	0528	5.1	0400	3.9	0151	3.1	0130	1.9	0333	1.7	0214	1.3	0251	3.1	0132	8.4
	1037	1.6	1020	1.6	0939	1.4	0722	1.3	0711	0.9	0924	4.8	0814	3.7	0820	0.9	0800	2.1
	1726	5.0	1733	5.2	1557	4.0	1351	3.3	1324	2.1	1558	1.6	1438	1.5	1506	3.5	1348	8.7
	2302	1.4	2247	1.4	2209	1.2	1958	1.1	1948	0.8	2152	4.4	2023	3.4	2049	0.6	2028	2.0
31SU	0556	4.9	0608	5.0	0439	3.7	0229	3.0	0208	1.9	0409	1.8	0248	1.4	0330	3.1	0207	8.2
	1112	1.6	1053	1.7	1017	1.6	0759	1.4	0748	1.0	1005	4.7	0853	3.5	0859	0.9	0836	2.4
	1805	4.9	1812	5.1	1636	3.9	1430	3.3	1403	2.0	1637	1.7	1519	1.6	1542	3.4	1425	8.4
	2341	1.5	2324	1.5	2251	1.3	2038	1.2	2030	0.8	2235	4.3	2059	3.2	2131	0.7	2106	2.2

WEST COAST ENGLAND, WALES & IRELAND Time Zone UT
Holyhead * Milford Haven * Swansea * Avonmouth * Dublin * Belfast * Londonderry * Galway * Cobh

TIDE TABLES JANUARY 2000

HOLYHEAD		MILFORD HAVEN		SWANSEA		AVONMOUTH		DUBLIN		BELFAST		LONDON-DERRY		GALWAY		COBH		Day
Time	m	Time	m	Time	m	Time	m	Time	m	Time	m	Time	m	Time	m	Time	m	
0012	1.8	0152	5.4	0200	7.4	0236	10.3	0106	1.3	0054	0.8	0426	2.3	0103	4.2	0057	3.3	**1 SA**
0635	4.6	0815	2.3	0809	3.0	0854	3.6	0754	3.5	0718	2.9	1007	1.2	0707	2.0	0735	1.2	
1236	2.1	1421	5.5	1428	7.6	1506	10.5	1331	1.5	1324	1.0	1645	2.5	1330	4.1	1336	3.3	
1855	4.7	2054	2.1	2047	2.9	2132	3.4	2013	3.7	1923	3.1	2327	1.1	1939	1.8	2009	1.2	
0112	1.8	0258	5.5	0306	7.7	0345	10.6	0204	1.3	0149	0.8	0518	2.4	0202	4.3	0203	3.4	**2 SU**
0733	4.7	0919	2.1	0911	2.8	1007	3.3	0847	3.6	0809	3.0	1109	1.1	0806	1.9	0839	1.1	
1336	2.0	1524	5.7	1530	7.9	1612	10.9	1430	1.4	1418	0.9	1736	2.5	1427	4.2	1438	3.4	
1952	4.8	2150	1.9	2144	2.7	2239	3.0	2107	3.7	2018	3.2			2029	1.7	2105	1.1	
0203	1.7	0354	5.8	0401	8.1	0445	11.1	0253	1.2	0239	0.8	0009	1.0	0250	4.4	0301	3.5	**3 M**
0820	4.9	1012	1.9	1003	2.6	1108	2.8	0933	3.7	0856	3.1	0603	2.5	0854	1.7	0932	1.1	
1426	1.8	1616	5.9	1622	8.2	1709	11.3	1520	1.3	1507	0.8	1202	1.1	1514	4.3	1529	3.5	
2039	4.9	2237	1.7	2231	2.4	2335	2.5	2154	3.7	2106	3.2	1820	2.5	2114	1.6	2153	1.0	
0247	1.5	0441	6.1	0447	8.5	0534	11.7	0336	1.1	0322	0.8	0047	0.9	0333	4.6	0349	3.6	**4 TU**
0900	5.1	1057	1.6	1048	2.3	1159	2.3	1012	3.8	0937	3.2	0645	2.6	0938	1.5	1017	1.0	
1508	1.6	1701	6.1	1706	8.5	1756	11.7	1603	1.2	1551	0.7	1247	1.0	1557	4.4	1612	3.6	
2119	5.0	2318	1.5	2313	2.2			2234	3.7	2151	3.2	1859	2.5	2154	1.5	2234	0.9	
0324	1.4	0522	6.3	0528	8.7	0023	2.1	0415	1.1	0401	0.7	0122	0.9	0412	4.7	0431	3.7	**5 W**
0936	5.3	1137	1.4	1129	2.1	0617	12.1	1048	3.9	1016	3.3	0724	2.7	1018	1.3	1056	0.9	
1545	1.4	1747	6.3	1747	8.7	1245	1.9	1642	1.1	1631	0.7	1327	0.9	1636	4.5	1651	3.7	
2156	5.1	2356	1.4	2351	2.0	1837	12.1	2311	3.8	2231	3.2	1934	2.5	2233	1.4	2312	0.8	
0359	1.3	0600	6.4	0606	8.9	0106	1.8	0451	1.0	0436	0.7	0156	0.9	0449	4.8	0510	3.8	**6 TH**
1009	5.4	1215	1.3	1208	1.9	0656	12.4	1122	4.0	1052	3.4	0759	2.8	1055	1.2	1133	0.8	**●**
1619	1.3	1818	6.4	1824	8.8	1327	1.7	1718	1.0	1708	0.6	1404	0.9	1714	4.6	1727	3.7	
2229	5.2					1914	12.3	2345	3.8	2309	3.2	2006	2.6	2308	1.3	2348	0.7	
0431	1.3	0030	1.3	0027	1.9	0147	1.7	0526	0.9	0509	0.7	0227	0.8	0525	4.9	0546	3.9	**7 F**
1042	5.5	0635	6.6	0642	9.0	0731	12.6	1155	4.0	1125	3.4	0833	2.8	1131	1.1	1209	0.8	
1652	1.2	1250	1.2	1245	1.8	1406	1.6	1752	0.9	1742	0.6	1439	0.9	1750	4.7	1801	3.7	
2302	5.2	1851	6.4	1859	8.9	1948	12.4			2343	3.2	2037	2.6	2342	1.2			
0503	1.2	0104	1.2	0100	1.8	0224	1.6	0020	3.8	0541	0.7	0257	0.8	0600	4.9	0024	0.7	**8 SA**
1115	5.5	0708	6.6	0717	9.1	0805	12.7	0600	0.9	1157	3.5	0904	2.8	1206	1.0	0622	3.9	
1726	1.2	1324	1.1	1319	1.7	1444	1.6	1230	4.0	1814	0.6	1514	0.9	1824	4.7	1244	0.7	
2336	5.2	1924	6.4	1933	8.9	2021	12.5	1826	0.9			2109	2.6			1836	3.8	
0537	1.2	0137	1.2	0132	1.7	0300	1.6	0055	3.7	0018	3.2	0328	0.8	0017	1.2	0100	0.7	**9 SU**
1149	5.5	0741	6.6	0750	9.0	0838	12.7	0635	0.9	0614	0.7	0936	2.8	0635	4.9	0657	3.9	
1800	1.1	1358	1.2	1351	1.7	1519	1.6	1305	4.0	1230	3.5	1551	0.9	1239	1.0	1319	0.7	
		1957	6.4	2004	8.8	2055	12.5	1900	0.9	1848	0.6	2143	2.6	1900	4.6	1910	3.7	
0010	5.2	0211	1.3	0202	1.7	0332	1.7	0132	3.7	0052	3.2	0401	0.8	0051	1.3	0135	0.7	**10 M**
0612	1.3	0815	6.5	0822	8.9	0912	12.6	0710	1.0	0650	0.7	1011	2.8	0711	4.8	0732	3.9	
1225	5.5	1433	1.2	1422	1.6	1552	1.7	1342	3.9	1303	3.5	1630	0.9	1315	1.1	1354	0.7	
1836	1.2	2031	6.3	2036	8.7	2130	12.4	1936	0.9	1924	0.6	2222	2.5	1936	4.6	1945	3.7	
0047	5.1	0245	1.4	0231	1.7	0403	1.9	0212	3.6	0130	3.2	0439	0.9	0128	1.4	0210	0.8	**11 TU**
0648	1.4	0850	6.4	0854	8.8	0948	12.4	0748	1.0	0728	0.7	1048	2.8	0748	4.8	0808	3.8	
1303	5.4	1509	1.4	1454	1.7	1624	1.9	1423	3.8	1341	3.5	1712	1.0	1353	1.2	1431	0.7	
1915	1.2	2107	6.2	2109	8.5	2205	12.1	2015	0.9	2004	0.6	2305	2.5	2015	4.5	2023	3.7	
0127	5.0	0321	1.5	0304	1.9	0433	2.1	0256	3.5	0211	3.2	0520	0.9	0208	1.5	0247	0.8	**12 W**
0729	1.5	0928	6.3	0930	8.6	1024	12.0	0829	1.1	0811	0.7	1131	2.8	0829	4.6	0846	3.7	
1344	5.3	1548	1.5	1530	1.8	1655	2.2	1506	3.7	1421	3.5	1759	1.0	1435	1.3	1511	0.8	
1958	1.3	2147	6.0	2147	8.3	2242	11.7	2100	1.0	2048	0.6	2354	2.4	2057	4.4	2105	3.6	
0211	4.9	0401	1.7	0343	2.1	0505	2.4	0345	3.5	0256	3.2	0608	1.0	0253	1.6	0329	0.9	**13 TH**
0815	1.6	1012	6.1	1012	8.3	1104	11.5	0917	1.2	0858	0.8	1221	2.7	0914	4.5	0930	3.6	
1430	5.1	1631	1.7	1615	2.1	1730	2.5	1556	3.7	1508	3.4	1852	1.1	1522	1.4	1557	0.9	
2048	1.4	2233	5.8	2233	8.0	2324	11.2	2153	1.0	2139	0.7			2145	4.2	2153	3.5	
0303	4.7	0449	1.9	0433	2.3	0543	2.7	0440	3.4	0347	3.1	0051	2.3	0345	1.8	0420	1.0	**14 F**
0909	1.8	1103	5.9	1105	8.1	1150	11.1	1014	1.3	0951	0.9	0703	1.0	1006	4.4	1022	3.5	
1525	5.0	1724	1.8	1710	2.4	1813	2.8	1652	3.6	1601	3.4	1320	2.6	1617	1.5	1652	1.0	
2146	1.5	2330	5.6	2331	7.8			2254	1.1	2236	0.7	1953	1.1	2243	4.1	2249	3.4	
0406	4.6	0550	2.1	0539	2.6	0013	10.8	0543	3.4	0445	3.1	0201	2.2	0450	1.9	0521	1.0	**15 SA**
1015	1.9	1206	5.8	1210	7.9	0631	3.0	1121	1.4	1053	0.9	0807	1.1	1109	4.2	1123	3.4	
1631	4.9	1830	2.0	1822	2.6	1249	10.8	1757	3.6	1703	3.3	1431	2.6	1724	1.6	1757	1.0	
2254	1.6					1909	3.0			2339	0.8	2105	1.1	2353	4.1	2355	3.4	

● ● Time: UT. For British Summer Time (shaded) March 26th to October 29th ADD ONE HOUR ● ●

JANEUARY 2000 TIDE TABLES

•• Time: UT. For British Summer Time (shaded) March 26th to October 29TH ADD ONE HOUR ••

	HOLYHEAD Time	m	MILFORD HAVEN Time	m	SWANSEA Time	m	AVONMOUTH Time	m	DUBLIN Time	m	BELFAST Time	m	LONDONDERRY Time	m	GALWAY Time	m	COBH Time	m
16 SU	0519	4.7	0041	5.6	0045	7.6	0121	10.6	0000	1.1	0551	3.1	0324	2.2	0605	1.8	0633	1.0
	1128	1.8	0704	2.2	0700	2.7	0737	3.3	0651	3.5	1203	1.1	0925	1.1	1223	1.6	1232	3.4
	1745	4.9	1318	5.8	1326	7.9	1407	10.8	1229	1.3	1812	3.3	1551	2.6	1836	1.6	1909	1.0
			1946	2.0	1942	2.5	2028	3.1	1907	3.7			2221	1.0				
17 M	0005	1.5	0158	5.7	0205	7.8	0243	10.8	0106	1.0	0049	0.8	0442	2.3	0106	4.3	0107	3.4
	0633	4.8	0826	2.0	0821	2.5	0907	3.2	0756	3.6	0701	3.1	1048	1.0	0719	1.6	0751	0.9
	1239	1.6	1434	5.9	1443	8.1	1525	11.3	1334	1.2	1316	1.0	1703	2.7	1335	4.3	1346	3.4
	1856	5.1	2103	1.8	2058	2.2	2157	2.7	2015	3.9	1925	3.3	2328	0.9	1945	1.4	2023	0.8
18 TU	0112	1.3	0311	6.0	0319	8.3	0359	11.5	0206	0.9	0157	0.8	0545	2.5	0211	4.5	0221	3.6
	0737	5.1	0940	1.6	0931	2.0	1036	2.6	0856	3.8	0809	3.3	1200	0.9	0823	1.3	0903	0.7
	1345	1.4	1544	6.2	1553	8.6	1636	12.0	1434	1.0	1424	0.9	1804	2.8	1439	4.6	1456	3.6
	2000	5.3	2210	1.4	2203	1.8	2317	2.1	2116	4.0	2035	3.4			2044	1.2	2129	0.7
19 W	0212	1.1	0416	6.4	0423	8.9	0506	12.3	0303	0.8	0259	0.7	0024	0.8	0307	4.8	0327	3.8
	0833	5.3	1044	1.2	1033	1.6	1155	2.0	0951	4.1	0909	3.4	0639	2.7	0919	1.0	1004	0.5
	1442	1.0	1646	6.6	1654	9.1	1742	12.7	1530	0.7	1524	0.7	1300	0.7	1535	4.9	1557	3.8
	2057	5.5	2309	1.0	2302	1.3			2212	4.2	2138	3.4	1858	2.8	2137	0.9	2227	0.5
20 TH O	0306	0.9	0513	6.8	0519	9.4	0030	1.5	0354	0.7	0355	0.6	0114	0.7	0358	5.1	0424	4.0
	0924	5.6	1140	1.0	1130	1.1	0609	13.0	1041	4.3	1005	3.6	0727	2.8	1010	0.6	1059	0.3
	1536	0.7	1742	6.9	1750	9.5	1304	1.3	1623	0.6	1620	0.5	1355	0.6	1627	5.2	1650	4.0
	2149	5.7			2354	0.9	1841	13.2	2306	4.3	2236	3.5	1948	2.9	2226	0.7	2320	0.3
21 F	0355	0.7	0002	0.7	0612	9.8	0133	1.0	0443	0.6	0447	0.5	0159	0.6	0447	5.4	0516	4.1
	1012	5.8	0605	7.1	1223	0.8	0704	13.6	1130	4.4	1056	3.7	0812	3.0	1058	0.4	1150	0.2
	1625	0.7	1233	0.5	1841	9.7	1403	0.9	1713	0.4	1711	0.4	1445	0.6	1716	5.3	1739	4.1
	2239	5.8	1832	7.1			1934	13.6	2356	4.3	2329	3.5	2035	2.9	2312	0.6		
22 SA	0442	0.6	0051	0.5	0043	0.7	0227	0.7	0530	0.6	0536	0.5	0242	0.5	0535	5.5	0009	0.2
	1058	6.0	0654	7.3	0700	9.9	0754	13.9	1216	4.5	1145	3.8	0854	3.0	1145	0.3	0605	4.2
	1713	0.3	1321	0.3	1311	0.7	1454	0.6	1801	0.3	1800	0.3	1533	0.6	1803	5.3	1238	0.2
	2327	5.8	1920	7.2	1928	9.8	2022	13.8					2121	2.8	2357	0.5	1826	4.1
23 SU	0527	0.6	0137	0.4	0127	0.7	0313	0.6	0044	4.3	0019	3.5	0324	0.5	0621	5.5	0057	0.2
	1144	6.0	0739	7.4	0746	9.9	0839	14.0	0615	0.6	0624	0.5	0936	3.0	1230	0.3	0651	4.3
	1800	0.3	1407	0.3	1355	0.7	1537	0.6	1301	4.5	1231	3.8	1619	0.7	1850	5.3	1324	0.2
			2004	7.1	2011	9.4	2106	13.8	1848	0.4	1847	0.2	2205	2.7			1911	4.1
24 M	0013	5.7	0221	0.5	0207	0.8	0353	0.7	0131	4.2	0107	3.4	0406	0.6	0042	0.6	0142	0.3
	0612	0.7	0823	7.2	0829	9.7	0922	13.9	0700	0.7	0709	0.6	1016	3.0	0707	5.4	0736	4.2
	1230	5.9	1450	0.5	1434	0.9	1615	0.9	1347	4.4	1318	3.8	1704	0.7	1315	0.5	1409	0.3
	1846	0.5	2047	6.9	2051	9.4	2148	13.4	1936	0.5	1933	0.3	2249	2.6	1936	5.1	1955	4.0
25 TU	0059	5.5	0303	0.7	0245	1.1	0427	1.0	0218	4.0	0154	3.3	0447	0.7	0126	0.8	0226	0.3
	0657	0.9	0906	7.0	0909	9.4	1003	13.4	0745	0.9	0755	0.6	1057	2.9	0753	5.2	0820	4.1
	1315	5.7	1531	0.8	1512	1.2	1646	1.3	1434	4.3	1404	3.7	1750	0.9	1400	0.7	1451	0.4
	1933	0.8	2129	6.6	2130	9.0	2227	12.8	2024	0.7	2020	0.3	2334	2.5	2021	4.8	2039	3.9
26 W	0145	5.2	0343	1.1	0323	1.4	0458	1.5	0306	3.8	0242	3.1	0530	0.8	0211	1.1	0309	0.5
	0742	1.2	0947	6.6	0948	9.0	1044	12.7	0833	1.1	0842	0.7	1139	2.7	0839	4.9	0903	3.9
	1401	5.4	1611	1.2	1549	1.7	1715	1.9	1524	4.1	1452	3.5	1837	1.0	1446	1.1	1534	0.6
	2021	1.1	2210	6.2	2209	8.5	2306	12.0	2115	0.9	2108	0.5			2108	4.5	2123	3.7
27 TH	0231	4.9	0423	1.5	0403	1.9	0527	2.1	0357	3.6	0331	3.0	0022	2.3	0259	1.4	0351	0.7
	0830	1.5	1029	6.2	1030	8.5	1122	11.8	0924	1.3	0932	0.9	0615	0.9	0927	4.5	0948	3.7
	1448	5.1	1652	1.7	1631	2.2	1745	2.5	1620	3.8	1544	3.4	1227	2.6	1536	1.4	1618	0.8
	2112	1.5	2254	5.8	2253	8.0	2345	11.2	2210	1.2	2200	0.7	1930	1.1	2158	4.2	2209	3.5
28 F	0322	4.7	0506	1.9	0451	2.5	0557	2.8	0454	3.4	0425	2.9	0118	2.2	0351	1.7	0438	0.9
	0924	1.8	1115	5.8	1116	8.0	1203	11.0	1024	1.4	1027	1.0	0706	1.1	1020	4.2	1036	3.4
	1542	4.8	1739	2.1	1722	2.7	1816	3.1	1721	3.7	1639	3.2	1324	2.4	1632	1.7	1708	1.0
	2209	1.8	2345	5.4	2346	7.5			2310	1.3	2257	0.8	2030	1.2	2256	4.0	2300	3.3
29 SA	0421	4.4	0600	2.3	0551	3.0	0027	10.4	0556	3.3	0524	2.8	0225	2.1	0454	2.0	0530	1.1
	1028	2.1	1211	5.4	1214	7.5	0633	3.4	1130	1.6	1131	1.0	0806	1.2	1124	3.9	1130	3.2
	1648	4.5	1839	2.4	1829	3.2	1251	10.3	1827	3.5	1740	3.1	1444	2.2	1741	2.0	1805	1.2
	2315	1.8					1858	3.7					2140	1.2				
30 SU	0534	4.4	0049	5.2	0054	7.2	0124	9.8	0015	1.5	0001	0.9	0339	2.2	0006	3.9	0000	3.2
	1143	2.3	0710	2.5	0705	3.3	0727	3.9	0700	3.3	0625	2.8	0918	1.2	0613	2.1	0634	1.3
	1806	4.4	1321	5.2	1325	7.2	1357	9.8	1244	1.6	1239	1.1	1614	2.2	1243	3.8	1236	3.1
			1956	2.5	1948	3.4	2011	4.1	1933	3.5	1842	3.0	2246	1.2	1857	2.0	1912	1.2
31 M	0027	2.1	0206	5.1	0212	7.2	0242	9.7	0121	1.5	0106	1.0	0446	2.2	0120	3.9	0111	3.1
	0648	4.4	0831	2.5	0821	3.5	0906	4.1	0801	3.4	0724	2.9	1036	1.2	0732	2.0	0746	1.3
	1259	2.2	1440	5.2	1442	7.3	1518	9.9	1356	1.5	1343	1.2	1721	2.2	1357	3.8	1349	3.1
	1921	4.5	2111	2.3	2101	3.2	2149	3.8	2035	3.5	1943	3.0	2342	1.1	2004	1.9	2020	1.2

WEST COAST ENGLAND, WALES & IRELAND Time Zone UT
Holyhead * Milford Haven * Swansea * Avonmouth * Dublin * Belfast * Londonderry * Galway * Cobh

TIDE TABLES FEBRUARY 2000

HOLYHEAD Time	m	MILFORD HAVEN Time	m	SWANSEA Time	m	AVONMOUTH Time	m	DUBLIN Time	m	BELFAST Time	m	LONDONDERRY Time	m	GALWAY Time	m	COBH Time	m	Day
0132	2.0	0320	5.4	0322	7.5	0400	10.2	0221	1.4	0204	1.0	0542	2.4	0222	4.0	0222	3.2	**1 TU**
0751	4.6	0940	2.2	0927	3.1	1026	3.5	0857	3.6	0819	3.0	1142	1.1	0834	1.8	0852	1.2	
1401	2.0	1548	5.4	1548	7.6	1630	10.4	1456	1.4	1440	0.9	1812	2.3	1457	4.0	1454	3.1	
2019	4.6	2210	2.1	2201	2.9	2256	3.1	2129	3.6	2039	3.0			2057	1.8	2117	1.1	
0224	1.8	0417	5.7	0418	7.9	0502	11.0	0312	1.3	0255	0.9	0028	1.0	0313	4.2	0321	3.3	**2 W**
0839	4.9	1035	1.9	1021	2.7	1124	2.7	0946	3.7	0909	3.1	0629	2.5	0924	1.6	0945	1.0	
1449	1.7	1640	5.7	1642	7.9	1727	11.1	1543	1.2	1529	0.8	1236	1.0	1544	4.1	1544	3.3	
2104	4.8	2257	1.8	2250	2.5	2351	2.4	2215	3.6	2128	3.0	1854	2.4	2142	1.6	2205	0.9	
0306	1.6	0503	6.0	0505	8.3	0551	11.7	0354	1.1	0339	0.8	0109	0.9	0356	4.4	0407	3.5	**3 TH**
0918	5.1	1119	1.6	1108	2.4	1216	2.1	1028	3.8	0953	3.2	0710	2.6	1006	1.3	1030	0.9	
1528	1.5	1723	6.0	1726	8.3	1814	11.7	1624	1.1	1612	0.7	1320	0.9	1624	4.3	1627	3.4	
2142	5.0	2338	1.5	2332	2.2			2255	3.7	2212	3.1	1930	2.4	2221	1.4	2248	0.8	
0342	1.4	0542	6.3	0545	8.7	0040	1.9	0433	1.0	0418	0.8	0145	0.8	0435	4.6	0448	3.6	**4 F**
0951	5.3	1158	1.3	1150	2.0	0634	12.2	1105	3.9	1032	3.3	0748	2.7	1042	1.1	1110	0.7	
1603	1.3	1800	6.2	1806	8.6	1304	1.7	1700	0.9	1650	0.6	1359	0.9	1701	4.5	1706	3.6	
2215	5.1					1854	12.2	2330	3.7	2251	3.1	2003	2.5	2256	1.2	2328	0.6	
0414	1.2	0014	1.3	0009	1.8	0126	1.6	0508	0.9	0452	0.7	0219	0.7	0510	4.7	0527	3.8	**5 SA**
1024	5.4	0617	6.5	0624	8.9	0712	12.6	1139	3.9	1107	3.4	0823	2.8	1116	0.9	1149	0.6	●
1635	1.1	1233	1.1	1227	1.7	1349	1.5	1733	0.9	1724	0.5	1435	0.8	1735	4.6	1742	3.7	
2246	5.2	1834	6.4	1842	8.9	1931	12.5			2326	3.2	2033	2.6	2328	1.0			
0446	1.1	0048	1.1	0044	1.6	0209	1.5	0002	3.7	0524	0.6	0251	0.7	0544	4.9	0006	0.5	**6 SU**
1057	5.6	0651	6.7	0659	9.1	0748	12.8	0541	0.8	1139	3.4	0854	2.9	1148	0.8	0603	3.9	
1708	0.9	1308	1.0	1302	1.4	1431	1.3	1210	4.0	1756	0.5	1510	0.8	1807	4.7	1226	0.5	
2318	5.3	1907	6.6	1915	9.0	2006	12.7	1803	0.8	2359	3.2	2104	2.6			1818	3.7	
0518	1.0	0121	1.0	0115	1.4	0248	1.4	0033	3.8	0557	0.5	0321	0.7	0000	0.9	0043	0.5	**7 M**
1130	5.6	0724	6.8	0733	9.2	0822	13.0	0612	0.8	1209	3.5	0926	2.9	0617	4.9	0639	3.9	
1741	0.9	1342	0.9	1334	1.2	1509	1.2	1242	4.0	1828	0.4	1545	0.7	1220	0.7	1303	0.5	
2351	5.3	1940	6.6	1947	9.1	2039	12.9	1834	0.7			2136	2.6	1840	4.8	1853	3.8	
0552	0.9	0154	0.9	0145	1.2	0324	1.3	0106	3.8	0032	3.2	0353	0.7	0033	0.8	0119	0.5	**8 TU**
1205	5.6	0757	6.8	0805	9.3	0857	13.2	0644	0.8	0631	0.5	0958	2.9	0651	5.0	0713	3.9	
1815	0.8	1415	0.9	1405	1.1	1545	1.2	1316	4.0	1242	3.5	1621	0.7	1254	0.7	1338	0.5	
		2014	6.6	2018	9.1	2115	13.0	1906	0.7	1903	0.4	2211	2.6	1914	4.7	1927	3.8	
0026	5.3	0229	0.9	0215	1.2	0357	1.3	0142	3.7	0106	3.3	0427	0.7	0107	0.9	0154	0.5	**9 W**
0627	1.0	0833	6.8	0837	9.2	0933	13.1	0718	0.8	0708	0.5	1033	2.9	0727	4.9	0748	3.9	
1242	5.6	1451	0.9	1436	1.1	1617	1.3	1354	4.0	1318	3.5	1659	0.8	1329	0.7	1413	0.5	
1851	0.9	2049	6.6	2050	9.0	2149	12.8	1943	0.7	1940	0.4	2249	2.5	1950	4.7	2003	3.8	
0103	5.2	0303	1.1	0245	1.3	0427	1.5	0221	3.7	0145	3.3	0506	0.7	0145	1.0	0230	0.6	**10 TH**
0705	1.1	0909	6.7	0911	9.1	1008	12.7	0757	0.8	0748	0.5	1112	2.8	0806	4.8	0825	3.8	
1320	5.5	1527	1.1	1509	1.3	1645	1.6	1436	3.9	1357	3.5	1741	0.8	1407	0.9	1450	0.6	
1931	1.0	2127	6.4	2125	8.8	2224	12.4	2025	0.7	2022	0.4	2331	2.4	2030	4.6	2042	3.7	
0142	5.1	0341	1.3	0321	1.5	0454	1.8	0307	3.6	0227	3.2	0551	0.8	0225	1.1	0308	0.7	**11 F**
0748	1.2	0949	6.5	0949	8.8	1045	12.2	0842	0.9	0833	0.6	1157	2.7	0849	4.7	0906	3.7	
1403	5.3	1606	1.3	1548	1.6	1714	2.0	1524	3.8	1443	3.5	1828	0.9	1450	1.1	1531	0.7	
2017	1.1	2209	6.1	2206	8.5	2301	11.8	2115	0.9	2109	0.5			2114	4.4	2127	3.6	
0229	4.9	0424	1.6	0405	1.9	0525	2.2	0400	3.5	0316	3.2	0020	2.3	0312	1.3	0353	0.8	**12 SA**
0837	1.4	1035	6.2	1036	8.4	1125	11.6	0936	1.1	0924	0.8	0642	0.9	0937	4.4	0953	3.6	
1453	5.1	1652	1.7	1636	2.0	1749	2.4	1621	3.7	1536	3.4	1252	2.5	1541	1.3	1621	0.8	
2110	1.4	2259	5.8	2258	8.0	2344	11.2	2215	1.0	2203	0.7	1922	1.0	2206	4.2	2218	3.5	
0325	4.7	0516	1.9	0502	2.4	0605	2.6	0503	3.5	0413	3.1	0121	2.1	0411	1.6	0450	0.9	**13 SU**
0939	1.6	1133	5.8	1136	8.0	1215	11.0	1043	1.2	1023	0.9	0743	1.0	1037	4.2	1050	3.4	
1556	4.9	1752	2.0	1742	2.5	1835	2.8	1728	3.7	1637	3.2	1402	2.4	1644	1.6	1722	0.9	
2218	1.6							2327	1.1	2309	0.8	2029	1.1	2312	4.0	2321	3.3	
0439	4.6	0005	5.6	0008	7.7	0042	10.7	0616	3.5	0521	3.0	0248	2.1	0527	1.7	0601	1.0	**14 M**
1056	1.8	0628	2.1	0622	2.8	0700	3.1	1200	1.3	1136	1.0	0905	1.1	1152	4.1	1159	3.2	
1715	4.8	1246	5.6	1253	7.7	1330	10.6	1846	3.7	1752	3.1	1536	2.3	1804	1.7	1838	1.0	
2336	1.7	1912	2.1	1909	2.8	1945	3.3					2154	1.1					
0605	4.6	0127	5.5	0135	7.6	0207	10.5	0042	1.2	0026	0.9	0436	2.1	0034	4.0	0037	3.3	**15 TU**
1218	1.7	0800	2.1	0756	2.8	0830	3.4	0732	3.6	0638	3.1	1050	1.1	0656	1.6	0726	1.0	
1839	4.8	1411	5.6	1421	7.7	1457	10.7	1315	1.2	1258	1.0	1704	2.4	1316	4.1	1321	3.2	
				2042	2.0	2127	3.2	2001	3.8	1914	3.1	2318	1.0	1927	1.6	2001	0.9	

● ● Time: UT. For British Summer Time (shaded) March 26th to October 29th ADD ONE HOUR ● ●

FEBRUARY 2000 TIDE TABLES

•• Time: UT. For British Summer Time (shaded) March 26th to October 29TH ADD ONE HOUR ••

	HOLYHEAD Time m	MILFORD HAVEN Time m	SWANSEA Time m	AVONMOUTH Time m	DUBLIN Time m	BELFAST Time m	LONDONDERRY Time m	GALWAY Time m	COBH Time m
16 W	0055 1.6	0253 5.7	0301 7.9	0334 10.9	0151 1.1	0143 0.9	0547 2.3	0153 4.2	0202 3.4
	0721 4.9	0927 1.8	0918 2.4	1014 3.0	0839 3.8	0752 3.2	1210 0.9	0812 1.4	0847 0.8
	1333 1.4	1532 5.9	1541 8.1	1618 11.3	1424 1.0	1413 0.9	1808 2.5	1428 4.4	1440 3.4
	1953 5.0	2158 1.6	2154 2.2	2257 2.5	2108 3.9	2030 3.2		2035 1.3	2115 0.7
17 TH	0202 1.3	0406 6.1	0412 8.5	0451 11.8	0254 1.0	0250 0.8	0019 0.8	0257 4.6	0315 3.6
	0823 5.2	1036 1.3	1027 1.8	1139 2.2	0939 4.0	0857 3.3	0639 2.6	0912 1.0	0952 0.5
	1436 1.0	1638 6.3	1647 8.7	1731 12.2	1524 0.8	1516 0.7	1309 0.7	1528 4.7	1545 3.6
	2052 5.3	2300 1.2	2254 1.6		2207 4.1	2135 3.3	1900 2.6	2130 1.0	2215 0.5
18 F	0257 1.0	0504 6.6	0512 9.1	0015 1.7	0347 0.8	0347 0.7	0109 0.7	0350 4.9	0414 3.8
	0915 5.5	1133 0.8	1125 1.3	0558 12.7	1033 4.2	0954 3.5	0724 2.8	1003 0.6	1048 0.3
	1528 0.7	1733 6.7	1742 9.2	1252 1.4	1617 0.5	1611 0.5	1359 0.6	1619 5.0	1639 3.8
	2143 5.5	2352 0.7	2347 1.1	1833 13.0	2300 4.2	2231 3.4	1946 2.7	2218 0.7	2309 0.3
19 SA O	0345 0.8	0554 7.0	0603 9.6	0121 1.0	0435 0.7	0437 0.6	0153 0.6	0438 5.2	0506 4.0
	1001 5.8	1222 0.5	1216 0.9	0654 13.4	1121 4.4	1044 3.7	0805 2.9	1048 0.3	1138 0.2
	1615 0.4	1820 7.0	1831 9.6	1351 0.8	1704 0.4	1700 0.3	1444 0.5	1705 5.2	1727 4.0
	2228 5.7			1923 13.5	2347 4.2	2321 3.5	2029 2.8	2301 0.5	2357 0.1
20 SU	0429 0.6	0039 0.4	0033 0.8	0213 0.5	0518 0.6	0523 0.5	0234 0.5	0522 5.4	0552 4.2
	1045 5.9	0640 7.3	0650 9.8	0742 13.8	1204 4.5	1130 3.8	0844 3.0	1130 0.1	1224 0.1
	1658 0.3	1307 0.3	1300 0.5	1440 0.5	1748 0.3	1744 0.2	1526 0.5	1748 5.2	1812 4.1
	2310 5.7	1903 7.2	1915 9.8	2007 13.8			2109 2.8	2342 0.4	
21 M	0510 0.5	0121 0.3	0113 0.6	0258 0.4	0029 4.2	0005 3.5	0313 0.5	0606 5.4	0042 0.1
	1127 6.0	0722 7.3	0732 9.9	0824 14.0	0600 0.6	0606 0.5	0921 3.0	1211 0.1	0636 4.2
	1740 0.3	1348 0.2	1339 0.6	1521 0.4	1245 4.4	1213 3.8	1605 0.5	1830 5.2	1307 0.1
	2351 5.7	1945 7.1	1953 9.7	2047 13.9	1830 0.4	1827 0.2	2148 2.7		1854 4.1
22 TU	0551 0.5	0200 0.3	0149 0.7	0336 0.4	0109 4.1	0046 3.4	0351 0.5	0022 0.4	0124 0.1
	1208 5.9	0802 7.3	0809 9.8	0903 14.0	0639 0.6	0647 0.5	0957 2.9	0647 5.3	0717 4.2
	1821 0.5	1427 0.4	1413 0.8	1555 0.6	1325 4.4	1255 3.8	1642 0.6	1251 0.3	1348 0.2
		2023 7.0	2028 9.6	2124 13.7	1912 0.5	1907 0.3	2226 2.6	1912 5.1	1933 4.0
23 W	0032 5.5	0238 0.5	0222 0.9	0407 0.7	0146 3.9	0125 3.3	0427 0.6	0103 0.6	0203 0.3
	0630 0.7	0839 7.0	0845 9.6	0939 13.6	0718 0.7	0727 0.6	1033 2.8	0729 5.1	0756 4.1
	1248 5.7	1502 0.7	1445 1.1	1623 1.1	1405 4.2	1336 3.7	1718 0.8	1331 0.5	1425 0.4
	1901 0.7	2059 6.7	2102 9.3	2200 13.1	1952 0.7	1948 0.4	2303 2.5	1953 4.8	2012 3.9
24 TH	0110 5.3	0312 0.9	0255 1.2	0433 1.2	0224 3.8	0204 3.2	0505 0.7	0142 0.8	0240 0.4
	0710 1.0	0915 6.7	0918 9.2	1014 12.9	0759 0.9	0807 0.6	1109 2.6	0810 4.8	0833 3.9
	1327 5.4	1535 1.1	1516 1.5	1646 1.6	1447 4.0	1419 3.6	1756 0.9	1412 0.9	1501 0.5
	1942 1.1	2135 6.3	2135 8.8	2232 12.3	2036 0.9	2028 0.6	2342 2.3	2034 4.5	2051 3.8
25 F	0149 5.0	0346 1.3	0330 1.6	0455 1.8	0305 3.6	0245 3.1	0544 0.8	0224 1.1	0316 0.6
	0751 1.3	0951 6.3	0953 8.7	1045 12.0	0843 1.1	0849 0.8	1147 2.4	0852 4.5	0911 3.7
	1407 5.1	1607 1.5	1551 2.0	1707 2.2	1535 3.8	1505 3.4	1836 1.0	1454 1.3	1538 0.8
	2024 1.4	2211 5.9	2211 8.4	2302 11.4	2123 1.2	2112 0.7		2117 4.2	2130 3.6
26 SA	0230 4.8	0421 1.7	0408 2.2	0518 2.4	0352 3.5	0330 3.0	0026 2.2	0309 1.5	0354 0.9
	0836 1.7	1029 5.8	1031 8.2	1116 11.1	0936 1.3	0937 0.9	0627 0.9	0938 4.1	0951 3.4
	1451 4.7	1643 2.0	1631 2.6	1730 2.8	1631 3.6	1555 3.2	1231 2.2	1542 1.7	1618 1.0
	2112 1.8	2253 5.5	2254 7.8	2333 10.6	2219 1.4	2201 0.9	1927 1.1	2205 3.9	2214 3.3
27 SU	0319 4.5	0503 2.1	0457 2.8	0544 3.0	0451 3.4	0423 2.9	0122 2.1	0403 1.8	0437 1.1
	0930 2.0	1115 5.4	1118 7.6	1151 10.2	1041 1.5	1034 1.0	0719 1.1	1032 3.8	1036 3.2
	1547 4.4	1730 2.4	1724 3.2	1800 3.4	1740 3.4	1654 3.0	1335 2.0	1642 2.0	1706 1.2
	2212 2.2	2347 5.1	2351 7.3		2325 1.6	2300 1.1	2033 1.2	2306 3.7	2306 3.1
28 M	0424 4.3	0602 2.5	0602 3.3	0015 9.8	0602 3.3	0525 2.8	0244 2.0	0515 2.1	0532 1.3
	1043 2.3	1218 5.0	1221 7.1	0621 3.7	1158 1.6	1145 1.1	0827 1.2	1147 3.5	1133 3.0
	1707 4.2	1843 2.7	1842 3.6	1245 9.5	1853 3.3	1759 2.9	1549 1.9	1807 2.2	1809 1.3
	2331 2.3			1846 4.1			2200 1.2		
29 TU	0551 4.2	0105 4.9	0109 7.0	0130 9.2	0038 1.6	0012 1.2	0415 2.1	0027 3.6	0014 3.0
	1212 2.3	0735 2.7	0726 3.6	0726 4.4	0715 3.3	0633 2.8	1006 1.2	0651 2.1	0645 1.4
	1843 4.2	1348 4.8	1344 6.9	1414 9.2	1319 1.5	1302 1.1	1715 2.0	1323 3.5	1250 2.9
		2024 2.7	2012 3.7	2034 4.5	2003 3.3	1906 2.9	2315 1.1	1936 2.1	1925 1.3

WEST COAST ENGLAND, WALES & IRELAND Time Zone UT
Holyhead * Milford Haven * Swansea * Avonmouth * Dublin * Belfast * Londonderry * Galway * Cobh

TIDE TABLES MARCH 2000

HOLYHEAD		MILFORD HAVEN		SWANSEA		AVONMOUTH		DUBLIN		BELFAST		LONDON-DERRY		GALWAY		COBH		
Time	m	Time	m	Time	m	Time	m	Time	m	Time	m	Time	m	Time	m	Time	m	
0054	2.3	0240	5.0	0234	7.1	0310	9.4	0149	1.5	0122	1.1	0520	2.2	0150	3.7	0136	3.0	1 W
0712	4.4	0905	2.5	0846	3.4	0944	4.1	0822	3.4	0737	2.9	1133	1.1	0811	1.9	0806	1.3	
1330	2.1	1518	5.1	1508	7.1	1550	9.7	1429	1.4	1407	1.0	1804	2.1	1437	3.7	1412	2.9	
1956	4.4	2139	2.4	2127	3.3	2221	3.7	2103	3.4	2007	2.9			2040	1.9	2037	1.2	
0157	2.0	0350	5.4	0344	7.5	0427	10.3	0248	1.4	0222	1.1	0009	1.0	0251	3.9	0247	3.2	2 TH
0809	4.7	1008	2.1	0950	3.0	1052	3.0	0918	3.6	0834	3.0	0610	2.4	0906	1.6	0910	1.1	
1424	1.8	1616	5.4	1612	7.6	1657	10.6	1520	1.2	1501	0.9	1228	1.0	1527	3.9	1512	3.1	
2044	4.7	2233	2.0	2221	2.8	2320	2.7	2154	3.5	2100	2.9	1844	2.2	2127	1.6	2133	1.0	
0242	1.7	0438	5.8	0436	8.0	0522	11.3	0333	1.2	0311	0.9	0051	0.9	0336	4.2	0339	3.4	3 F
0852	5.0	1055	1.7	1041	2.5	1147	2.2	1005	3.7	0924	3.1	0652	2.5	0948	1.3	1000	0.9	
1504	1.5	1659	5.8	1700	8.1	1747	11.5	1600	1.0	1546	0.7	1311	0.9	1607	4.2	1600	3.3	
2121	4.9	2314	1.6	2306	2.3			2235	3.6	2147	3.0	1918	2.4	2203	1.3	2220	0.8	
0318	1.4	0517	6.2	0519	8.5	0013	2.0	0411	1.0	0352	0.8	0129	0.7	0415	4.4	0423	3.6	4 SA
0927	5.2	1134	1.3	1124	2.0	0607	12.1	1042	3.8	1006	3.2	0730	2.7	1022	1.0	1044	0.7	
1539	1.2	1736	6.2	1740	8.6	1239	1.6	1634	0.9	1624	0.6	1348	0.7	1641	4.4	1640	3.5	
2153	5.1	2351	1.2	2344	1.8	1830	12.2	2309	3.7	2227	3.1	1951	2.5	2236	1.0	2303	0.6	
0351	1.2	0553	6.5	0558	8.9	0103	1.5	0445	0.9	0429	0.7	0203	0.6	0448	4.6	0502	3.8	5 SU
1000	5.4	1210	1.0	1203	1.5	0648	12.7	1115	3.9	1042	3.3	0804	2.8	1054	0.8	1124	0.5	
1611	0.9	1810	6.5	1816	9.0	1327	1.3	1705	0.8	1659	0.4	1424	0.6	1712	4.6	1718	3.7	●
2224	5.3					1907	12.7	2339	3.8	2303	3.2	2021	2.6	2306	0.8	2343	0.4	
0423	0.9	0025	0.9	0019	1.3	0149	1.2	0515	0.8	0503	0.6	0236	0.5	0521	4.9	0539	3.9	6 M
1033	5.6	0627	6.8	0634	9.3	0725	13.1	1145	3.9	1114	3.3	0836	2.9	1124	0.5	1203	0.4	
1643	0.7	1245	0.8	1238	1.1	1412	1.0	1733	0.6	1731	0.3	1458	0.6	1743	4.7	1755	3.8	
2254	5.4	1844	6.7	1851	9.3	1944	13.0			2335	3.2	2052	2.6	2337	0.6			
0455	0.7	0100	0.7	0052	1.0	0232	1.0	0008	3.8	0536	0.5	0309	0.5	0554	5.0	0021	0.4	7 TU
1106	5.7	0701	7.0	0709	9.5	0801	13.4	0544	0.7	1145	3.4	0909	2.9	1155	0.4	0615	4.0	
1716	0.6	1320	0.6	1311	0.8	1454	0.8	1215	4.0	1804	0.3	1533	0.5	1815	4.9	1241	0.3	
2327	5.5	1918	6.9	1924	9.5	2019	13.4	1803	0.5			2124	2.6			1831	3.9	
0529	0.6	0134	0.6	0124	0.8	0310	0.9	0039	3.9	0008	3.3	0342	0.5	0009	0.5	0059	0.3	8 W
1142	5.7	0736	7.1	0743	9.7	0837	13.6	0615	0.6	0610	0.4	0942	2.9	0628	5.1	0651	4.0	
1751	0.6	1354	0.5	1343	0.7	1531	0.8	1248	4.1	1218	3.5	1607	0.5	1228	0.3	1318	0.3	
		1953	7.0	1957	9.6	2054	13.5	1836	0.5	1839	0.2	2157	2.6	1848	4.9	1906	3.9	
0001	5.5	0209	0.6	0154	0.8	0345	0.9	0112	3.9	0042	3.3	0418	0.5	0044	0.5	0135	0.4	9 TH
0605	0.6	0812	7.1	0817	9.7	0913	13.5	0651	0.5	0647	0.4	1017	2.8	0705	5.1	0727	4.0	
1218	5.7	1430	0.6	1415	0.7	1603	0.9	1327	4.1	1255	3.5	1644	0.6	1303	0.4	1354	0.4	
1827	0.6	2029	6.9	2030	9.5	2129	13.3	1914	0.5	1916	0.2	2234	2.5	1925	4.9	1943	3.9	
0038	5.4	0245	0.7	0227	0.9	0414	1.1	0152	3.9	0120	3.3	0457	0.5	0121	0.6	0212	0.4	10 F
0643	0.7	0849	6.9	0851	9.5	0949	13.2	0730	0.6	0727	0.4	1056	2.7	0744	5.0	0803	4.0	
1257	5.6	1506	0.8	1448	1.0	1630	1.2	1411	4.1	1336	3.5	1724	0.6	1341	0.6	1430	0.5	
1906	0.7	2106	6.7	2106	9.2	2204	12.9	1957	0.6	1958	0.3	2314	2.4	2004	4.7	2022	3.8	
0118	5.3	0322	1.0	0303	1.2	0439	1.4	0238	3.8	0203	3.3	0541	0.7	0201	0.8	0250	0.5	11 SA
0725	0.9	0929	6.7	0930	9.1	1026	12.6	0816	0.7	0812	0.5	1142	2.6	0827	4.8	0844	3.8	
1341	5.4	1545	1.1	1526	1.4	1657	1.6	1501	4.0	1423	3.4	1808	0.8	1424	0.9	1510	0.6	
1951	1.0	2148	6.4	2146	8.8	2240	12.2	2046	0.8	2045	0.5			2048	4.5	2106	3.7	
0203	5.1	0404	1.3	0345	1.7	0508	1.9	0332	3.7	0252	3.2	0000	2.2	0248	1.1	0335	0.7	12 SU
0815	1.2	1015	6.3	1015	8.6	1105	11.8	0911	0.9	0902	0.6	0631	0.8	0915	4.5	0930	3.6	
1431	5.1	1629	1.5	1612	2.0	1728	2.2	1601	3.8	1518	3.3	1236	2.4	1513	1.3	1558	0.8	
2045	1.3	2236	6.0	2236	8.2	2322	11.4	2148	1.0	2139	0.7	1859	0.9	2139	4.2	2156	3.5	
0259	4.8	0456	1.7	0439	2.3	0545	2.4	0436	3.6	0350	3.1	0057	2.1	0346	1.4	0430	0.9	13 M
0918	1.5	1111	5.8	1113	8.0	1154	11.0	1021	1.1	1003	0.8	0735	1.0	1015	4.2	1026	3.4	
1536	4.8	1727	2.0	1714	2.6	1811	2.7	1712	3.7	1624	3.1	1351	2.2	1617	1.6	1659	0.9	
2153	1.7	2342	5.6	2344	7.7					2303	1.2	2248	0.9	2003	1.0	2245	4.0	2259	3.3	
0413	4.6	0609	2.1	0559	2.9	0018	10.7	0553	3.5	0500	3.0	0231	2.0	0505	1.7	0542	1.0	14 TU
1039	1.7	1227	5.4	1232	7.5	0637	3.0	1144	1.2	1121	0.9	0917	1.1	1134	4.0	1136	3.2	
1703	4.6	1851	2.2	1848	3.1	1308	10.3	1836	3.6	1745	3.0	1552	2.1	1744	1.8	1817	1.0	
2319	1.8					1918	3.4					2133	1.1					
0546	4.6	0108	5.4	0115	7.4	0145	10.3	0025	1.3	0015	1.0	0447	2.1	0012	3.9	0018	3.2	15 W
1208	1.6	0748	2.2	0742	3.0	0808	3.5	0715	3.6	0621	3.0	1118	1.0	0644	1.6	0710	1.0	
1835	4.7	1359	5.4	1408	7.4	1439	10.3	1305	1.2	1250	0.9	1713	2.2	1306	4.0	1303	3.1	
		2030	2.1	2028	2.9	2106	3.4	1914	3.7	1914	3.0	2312	1.0	1918	1.7	1945	1.0	

● ● Time: UT. For British Summer Time (shaded) March 26th to October 29th ADD ONE HOUR ● ●

MARCH 2000 TIDE TABLES

•• Time: UT. For British Summer Time (shaded) March 26th to October 29TH ADD ONE HOUR ••

	HOLYHEAD		MILFORD HAVEN		SWANSEA		AVONMOUTH		DUBLIN		BELFAST		LONDON-DERRY		GALWAY		COBH	
	Time	m	Time	m	Time	m	Time	m	Time	m	Time	m	Time	m	Time	m	Time	m
16TH	0045	1.7	0242	5.6	0248	7.7	0318	10.6	0141	1.2	0136	1.0	0548	2.3	0142	4.1	0149	3.3
	0709	4.8	0919	1.8	0911	2.6	0958	3.0	0827	3.8	0739	3.1	1224	0.8	0806	1.3	0833	0.9
	1326	1.4	1524	5.7	1533	7.9	1607	11.0	1418	1.0	1406	0.8	1809	2.4	1424	4.2	1427	3.3
	1950	4.9	2148	1.7	2145	2.4	2241	2.6	2103	3.8	2029	3.1			2029	1.4	2102	0.7
17F	0154	1.5	0355	6.0	0403	8.3	0441	11.6	0245	1.1	0242	0.9	0012	0.8	0248	4.4	0303	3.6
	0813	5.1	1027	1.3	1020	2.0	1127	2.1	0930	4.0	0843	3.3	0633	2.5	0904	1.0	0939	0.6
	1427	1.0	1628	6.2	1639	8.5	1721	12.0	1518	0.7	1506	0.6	1314	0.6	1521	4.6	1531	3.6
	2047	5.2	2248	1.2	2245	1.7			2203	4.0	2130	3.2	1856	2.5	2121	1.0	2203	0.5
18SA	0248	1.1	0451	6.5	0500	8.9	0001	1.7	0339	0.9	0336	0.7	0100	0.7	0339	4.7	0401	3.8
	0903	5.4	1121	0.9	1115	1.4	0547	12.5	1023	4.2	0939	3.5	0713	2.7	0951	0.6	1034	0.4
	1517	0.7	1718	6.6	1730	9.1	1238	1.3	1608	0.6	1557	0.4	1357	0.5	1607	4.8	1624	3.8
	2132	5.4	2337	0.8	2334	1.2	1819	12.9	2252	4.1	2221	3.3	1938	2.6	2204	0.7	2254	0.3
19SU O	0332	0.8	0539	6.9	0549	9.4	0103	0.9	0424	0.8	0423	0.6	0142	0.5	0424	5.0	0451	4.0
	0946	5.7	1206	0.5	1202	1.0	0639	13.3	1109	4.3	1027	3.6	0751	2.8	1031	0.3	1122	0.2
	1600	0.5	1803	6.9	1815	9.5	1333	0.7	1651	0.5	1642	0.3	1435	0.4	1649	5.0	1709	4.0
	2212	5.6					1906	13.4	2333	4.1	2306	3.4	2017	2.7	2244	0.5	2341	0.2
20M	0412	0.6	0021	0.5	0016	0.9	0154	0.5	0503	0.7	0505	0.5	0221	0.5	0505	5.2	0535	4.1
	1026	5.8	0621	7.2	0633	9.7	0724	13.6	1148	4.4	1110	3.7	0827	2.9	1110	0.2	1206	0.2
	1639	0.4	1246	0.3	1242	0.8	1419	0.5	1731	0.4	1724	0.3	1510	0.4	1729	5.1	1752	4.1
	2249	5.6	1842	7.1	1854	9.7	1947	13.7			2345	3.4	2054	2.7	2322	0.3		
21TU	0450	0.5	0059	0.4	0053	0.7	0236	0.4	0009	4.1	0544	0.5	0257	0.4	0545	5.2	0023	0.2
	1105	5.9	0700	7.2	0711	9.8	0802	13.8	0541	0.6	1151	3.7	0900	2.9	1148	0.2	0615	4.2
	1717	0.4	1324	0.3	1316	0.8	1457	0.5	1225	4.3	1802	0.3	1544	0.4	1807	5.1	1245	0.2
	2326	5.6	1920	7.1	1930	9.7	2023	13.8	1809	0.5			2128	2.6			1831	4.1
22W	0527	0.5	0136	0.4	0126	0.8	0311	0.5	0042	4.0	0020	3.4	0333	0.4	0000	0.3	0102	0.2
	1142	5.8	0736	7.2	0745	9.8	0837	13.8	0616	0.6	0621	0.5	0933	2.8	0624	5.2	0653	4.1
	1754	0.5	1357	0.4	1347	0.9	1528	0.7	1300	4.2	1230	3.7	1615	0.5	1224	0.3	1322	0.3
			1954	7.0	2002	9.6	2057	13.6	1844	0.6	1838	0.4	2200	2.6	1845	5.0	1908	4.0
23TH	0003	5.5	0209	0.5	0157	0.9	0339	0.7	0113	3.9	0053	3.5	0406	0.5	0037	0.5	0137	0.4
	0603	0.7	0811	7.0	0818	9.6	0911	13.5	0651	0.7	0657	0.5	1006	2.7	0703	5.0	0728	4.0
	1220	5.6	1430	0.7	1415	1.1	1553	1.0	1335	4.1	1307	3.6	1645	0.6	1301	0.6	1356	0.4
	1829	0.8	2028	6.7	2033	9.4	2129	13.2	1920	0.8	1914	0.5	2233	2.5	1924	4.8	1944	4.0
24F	0038	5.3	0241	0.8	0227	1.2	0403	1.1	0145	3.8	0127	3.3	0439	0.6	0115	0.7	0209	0.5
	0640	0.9	0844	6.7	0848	9.2	0942	12.9	0729	0.8	0733	0.6	1038	2.5	0742	4.7	0802	3.9
	1256	5.3	1500	1.0	1445	1.5	1614	1.5	1413	4.0	1346	3.5	1715	0.7	1339	0.9	1428	0.6
	1905	1.1	2100	6.4	2103	9.0	2157	12.5	1958	1.0	1950	0.6	2306	2.4	2001	4.6	2018	3.8
25SA	0112	5.1	0312	1.2	0259	1.6	0423	1.5	0223	3.7	0203	3.2	0515	0.7	0154	1.0	0241	0.7
	0717	1.2	0916	6.3	0920	8.8	1011	12.1	0810	1.0	0812	0.7	1112	2.3	0821	4.4	0835	3.7
	1331	5.0	1529	1.4	1516	1.9	1633	2.0	1457	3.8	1428	3.3	1750	0.9	1417	1.3	1500	0.8
	1942	1.4	2133	6.1	2136	8.6	2224	11.6	2041	1.2	2029	0.8	2345	2.2	2041	4.3	2054	3.6
26SU	0149	4.9	0344	1.6	0334	2.1	0444	2.1	0308	3.6	0244	3.1	0555	0.9	0235	1.4	0314	0.9
	0757	1.5	0950	5.9	0954	8.3	1037	11.2	0858	1.2	0855	0.8	1151	2.1	0902	4.1	0910	3.5
	1410	4.7	1600	1.9	1551	2.5	1654	2.5	1550	3.5	1515	3.2	1832	1.0	1459	1.7	1535	1.0
	2024	1.8	2209	5.6	2214	8.0	2251	10.7	2133	1.4	2112	1.0			2123	4.0	2134	3.4
27M	0232	4.6	0421	2.0	0415	2.7	0509	2.7	0401	3.4	0333	3.0	0033	2.1	0322	1.7	0354	1.1
	0845	1.9	1029	5.4	1035	7.7	1106	10.3	1000	1.4	0947	1.0	0642	1.0	0949	3.8	0951	3.3
	1500	4.4	1640	2.3	1635	3.1	1721	3.1	1656	3.5	1610	3.0	1242	1.9	1551	2.0	1618	1.2
	2117	2.2	2255	5.2	2303	7.5	2324	9.9	2241	1.6	2205	1.1	1926	1.1	2215	3.7	2222	3.2
28TU	0327	4.4	0512	2.4	0512	3.3	0542	3.4	0509	3.3	0430	2.9	0141	2.0	0425	2.0	0444	1.3
	0950	2.2	1122	5.0	1129	7.2	1148	9.5	1118	1.5	1053	1.1	0743	1.1	1053	3.5	1042	3.0
	1612	4.1	1740	2.7	1742	3.6	1800	3.8	1814	3.2	1715	2.8	1453	1.7	1711	2.2	1715	1.3
	2231	2.4							2358	1.7	2312	1.2	2047	1.2	2327	3.5	2324	3.0
29W	0447	4.2	0005	4.9	0012	7.0	0021	9.2	0630	3.2	0539	2.8	0326	2.0	0559	2.1	0551	1.4
	1117	2.3	0635	2.7	0632	3.6	0631	4.1	1239	1.5	1212	1.1	0920	1.2	1233	3.4	1154	2.9
	1754	4.1	1247	4.7	1246	6.8	1306	8.9	1928	3.2	1824	2.8	1653	1.8	1856	2.2	1831	1.3
			1922	2.8	1918	3.8	1900	4.5					2228	1.2				
30TH	0003	2.4	0145	4.9	0139	6.9	0212	9.0	0114	1.6	0030	1.3	0445	2.1	0102	3.5	0045	3.0
	0619	4.3	0819	2.6	0759	3.6	0832	4.4	0743	3.3	0648	2.8	1111	1.1	0733	2.0	0715	1.4
	1244	2.1	1432	4.8	1417	6.9	1500	9.2	1353	1.4	1324	1.0	1740	2.0	1404	3.6	1321	2.9
	1918	4.3	2057	2.6	2042	3.6	2135	4.2	2033	3.3	1929	2.8	2333	1.0	2009	2.0	1951	1.2
31F	0117	2.2	0309	5.2	0259	7.2	0344	9.9	0218	1.5	0139	1.2	0537	2.3	0215	3.7	0204	3.1
	0728	4.5	0930	2.2	0909	3.1	1015	3.4	0844	3.4	0751	2.9	1206	0.9	0833	1.7	0829	1.2
	1345	1.8	1539	5.2	1531	7.3	1617	10.2	1446	1.2	1421	0.9	1818	2.1	1459	3.9	1432	3.1
	2012	4.6	2156	2.1	2143	3.0	2244	3.1	2125	3.5	2026	2.9			2057	1.7	2055	1.0

WEST COAST ENGLAND, WALES & IRELAND Time Zone UT
Holyhead * Milford Haven * Swansea * Avonmouth * Dublin * Belfast * Londonderry * Galway * Cobh

TIDE TABLES APRIL 2000

HOLYHEAD		MILFORD HAVEN		SWANSEA		AVONMOUTH		DUBLIN		BELFAST		LONDON-DERRY		GALWAY		COBH		
Time	m	Time	m	Time	m	Time	m	Time	m	Time	m	Time	m	Time	m	Time	m	
0207	1.8	0401	5.6	0357	7.8	0445	11.0	0304	1.3	0233	1.0	0020	0.9	0304	4.0	0303	3.4	**1 SA**
0816	4.8	1020	1.8	1004	2.5	1112	2.3	0932	3.5	0844	3.0	0620	2.5	0915	1.4	0925	0.9	
1430	1.4	1625	5.7	1624	7.9	1711	11.3	1527	1.0	1509	0.7	1248	0.8	1538	4.1	1524	3.4	
2050	4.8	2241	1.7	2230	2.3	2340	2.2	2207	3.3	2115	3.0	1851	2.3	2134	1.3	2147	0.8	
0246	1.5	0443	6.1	0444	8.4	0533	12.0	0341	1.1	0318	0.8	0100	0.7	0342	4.3	0350	3.6	**2 SU**
0855	5.1	1101	1.3	1049	1.9	1207	1.6	1011	3.7	0929	3.1	0658	2.6	0950	1.0	1012	0.7	
1506	1.1	1703	6.2	1706	8.5	1757	12.2	1600	0.8	1549	0.6	1325	0.6	1611	4.4	1609	3.6	
2123	5.1	2319	1.2	2310	1.7			2241	3.7	2156	3.1	1925	2.4	2206	1.0	2233	0.6	
0321	1.1	0520	6.5	0524	8.9	0033	1.6	0413	0.9	0357	0.7	0136	0.6	0417	4.6	0431	3.9	**3 M**
0930	5.4	1139	0.9	1130	1.4	0616	12.7	1044	3.8	1007	3.2	0734	2.8	1021	0.7	1055	0.5	
1540	0.8	1739	6.6	1745	9.1	1300	1.2	1630	0.7	1626	0.4	1401	0.5	1642	4.7	1649	3.8	
2154	5.3	2357	0.9	2348	1.2	1837	12.8	2310	3.8	2233	3.2	1958	2.5	2238	0.7	2315	0.5	
0354	0.8	0557	6.9	0603	9.4	0123	1.1	0443	0.7	0434	0.5	0212	0.5	0451	4.9	0510	4.0	**4 TU**
1004	5.6	1216	0.6	1207	0.9	0657	13.2	1115	3.9	1043	3.3	0809	2.9	1053	0.4	1136	0.4	●
1614	0.6	1815	6.9	1821	9.5	1348	0.9	1700	0.5	1701	0.3	1436	0.4	1713	4.9	1727	4.0	
2227	5.5					1917	13.3	2339	3.9	2307	3.3	2032	2.6	2309	0.4	2356	0.4	
0429	0.6	0033	0.6	0024	0.8	0209	0.8	0515	0.6	0511	0.4	0249	0.4	0526	5.1	0548	4.1	**5 W**
1039	5.7	0634	7.1	0641	9.8	0736	13.6	1148	4.1	1118	3.4	0845	2.9	1126	0.3	1216	0.3	
1648	0.4	1254	0.4	1244	0.6	1432	0.6	1733	0.4	1737	0.2	1512	0.4	1747	5.1	1806	4.1	
2300	5.6	1853	7.1	1858	9.8	1954	13.6			2342	3.3	2106	2.6	2344	0.3			
0504	0.5	0111	0.4	0059	0.6	0250	0.6	0012	4.0	0548	0.3	0327	0.3	0603	5.2	0036	0.3	**6 TH**
1117	5.8	0712	7.3	0719	9.9	0815	13.8	0549	0.4	1154	3.5	0921	2.9	1201	0.2	0627	4.2	
1724	0.4	1331	0.3	1319	0.5	1511	0.5	1224	4.2	1814	0.2	1548	0.4	1822	5.1	1254	0.3	
2337	5.6	1930	7.2	1934	9.9	2032	13.8	1809	0.3			2142	2.6			1844	4.1	
0542	0.4	0149	0.4	0134	0.6	0327	0.6	0048	4.0	0019	3.4	0406	0.4	0020	0.3	0115	0.3	**7 F**
1157	5.8	0751	7.2	0757	9.9	0853	13.8	0627	0.4	0627	0.3	1000	2.8	0642	5.2	0705	4.2	
1803	0.4	1409	0.4	1354	0.6	1545	0.6	1306	4.2	1235	3.5	1625	0.4	1238	0.3	1333	0.4	
		2009	7.1	2011	9.8	2109	13.6	1850	0.4	1854	0.2	2219	2.5	1900	5.1	1923	4.1	
0016	5.6	0227	0.5	0210	0.8	0358	0.8	0130	4.0	0100	3.4	0448	0.4	0059	0.4	0154	0.4	**8 SA**
0624	0.5	0831	7.0	0835	9.7	0931	13.4	0711	0.4	0709	0.3	1042	2.6	0723	5.1	0744	4.1	
1239	5.7	1448	0.7	1430	0.9	1614	1.0	1353	4.1	1320	3.4	1705	0.5	1318	0.6	1413	0.5	
1846	0.6	2048	6.8	2049	9.4	2146	13.1	1935	0.5	1938	0.4	2300	2.4	1942	4.9	2004	4.0	
0059	5.4	0308	0.8	0248	1.1	0425	1.2	0218	3.9	0145	3.3	0535	0.6	0142	0.6	0236	0.5	**9 SU**
0710	0.7	0913	6.7	0916	9.2	1010	12.7	0800	0.6	0756	0.4	1131	2.4	0809	4.8	0827	3.9	
1326	5.4	1529	1.1	1510	1.4	1641	1.5	1447	4.0	1410	3.3	1749	0.6	1403	0.9	1455	0.6	
1933	1.0	2133	6.5	2133	8.9	2225	12.4	2027	0.8	2027	0.5	2346	2.3	2028	4.7	2050	3.8	
0147	5.2	0353	1.2	0333	1.7	0455	1.7	0313	3.8	0236	3.2	0629	0.8	0232	1.0	0323	0.7	**10 M**
0803	1.0	1001	6.2	1003	8.6	1054	11.8	0858	0.8	0849	0.6	1230	2.2	0900	4.5	0915	3.7	
1421	5.1	1615	1.5	1557	2.1	1714	2.0	1550	3.8	1509	3.1	1840	0.8	1455	1.4	1545	0.8	
2030	1.4	2224	6.0	2224	8.3	2311	11.5	2130	1.1	2125	0.8			2121	4.3	2142	3.6	
0245	4.9	0448	1.7	0430	2.3	0533	2.3	0419	3.7	0337	3.1	0045	2.1	0333	1.4	0419	0.9	**11 TU**
0909	1.4	1100	5.7	1103	7.9	1147	10.9	1012	1.0	0954	0.7	0741	0.9	1003	4.2	1012	3.4	
1530	4.7	1716	2.0	1702	2.7	1758	2.7	1706	3.6	1621	3.0	1358	2.0	1601	1.7	1646	1.0	
2140	1.9	2330	5.6	2333	7.7			2248	1.3	2240	1.0	1942	0.9	2229	4.1	2246	3.4	
0401	4.7	0603	2.0	0552	2.9	0011	10.7	0538	3.6	0449	3.0	0231	2.1	0455	1.6	0531	1.1	**12 W**
1031	1.5	1217	5.4	1222	7.4	0629	2.9	1133	1.1	1117	0.8	0948	1.0	1124	4.0	1123	3.2	
1658	4.6	1841	2.2	1838	3.2	1300	10.3	1828	3.6	1748	2.9	1553	2.0	1733	1.9	1804	1.1	
2308	1.9					1906	3.3					2109	1.0	2357	3.9			
0532	4.6	0056	5.4	0103	7.4	0133	10.4	0009	1.4	0009	1.0	0432	2.2	0635	1.6	0007	3.3	**13 TH**
1158	1.5	0740	2.1	0733	3.0	0759	3.3	0659	3.7	0609	3.0	1117	0.8	1257	4.0	0657	1.1	
1828	4.6	1348	5.3	1356	7.4	1427	10.3	1255	1.1	1243	0.8	1702	2.2	1909	1.8	1249	3.2	
		2015	2.1	2015	3.0	2050	3.3	1946	3.6	1912	2.9	2248	1.0			1930	1.0	
0031	1.8	0226	5.6	0233	7.6	0303	10.7	0127	1.3	0125	1.0	0528	2.4	0127	4.1	0135	3.4	**14 F**
0654	4.8	0905	1.8	0859	2.6	0941	2.8	0811	3.8	0721	3.1	1215	0.6	0751	1.3	0817	0.9	
1313	1.3	1509	5.7	1518	7.8	1552	11.0	1407	0.9	1353	0.6	1754	2.3	1412	4.3	1409	3.4	
1939	4.9	2131	1.7	2130	2.4	2221	2.5	2054	3.8	2021	3.0	2351	0.8	2015	1.5	2044	0.8	
0139	1.5	0337	6.0	0345	8.2	0424	11.6	0232	1.2	0227	0.8	0612	2.5	0232	4.4	0247	3.6	**15 SA**
0756	5.1	1009	1.3	1004	2.0	1105	2.0	0914	4.0	0824	3.3	1300	0.5	0845	1.0	0921	0.7	
1412	1.0	1609	6.1	1621	8.4	1703	12.0	1505	0.7	1450	0.5	1839	2.5	1504	4.5	1512	3.6	
2033	5.1	2229	1.3	2227	1.9	2338	1.7	2151	3.9	2118	3.1			2103	1.2	2144	0.6	

● ● Time: UT. For British Summer Time (shaded) March 26th to October 29th ADD ONE HOUR ● ●

APRIL 2000 TIDE TABLES

•• Time: UT. For British Summer Time (shaded) March 26th to October 29TH ADD ONE HOUR ••

	HOLYHEAD	MILFORD HAVEN	SWANSEA	AVONMOUTH	DUBLIN	BELFAST	LONDONDERRY	GALWAY	COBH
	Time m	Time m	Time m	Time m	Time m	Time m	Time m	Time m	Time m
16 SU	0230 1.2	0431 6.4	0442 8.8	0527 12.4	0324 1.0	0318 0.7	0039 0.7	0321 4.6	0343 3.9
	0845 5.3	1100 1.0	1056 1.5	1213 1.3	1007 4.1	0918 3.4	0651 2.6	0929 0.7	1015 0.5
	1459 0.8	1657 6.5	1710 9.0	1758 12.7	1552 0.6	1538 0.4	1339 0.4	1548 4.8	1603 3.8
	2115 5.3	2316 0.9	2312 1.4		2238 3.9	2205 3.2	1919 2.5	2144 0.9	2235 0.4
17 M	0313 1.0	0517 6.8	0528 9.2	0039 1.0	0407 0.9	0403 0.6	0122 0.6	0403 4.8	0430 4.0
	0926 5.5	1142 0.7	1139 1.2	0618 13.0	1051 4.2	1006 3.5	0728 2.7	1008 0.5	1101 0.4
	1539 0.6	1739 6.8	1751 9.4	1307 0.9	1633 0.6	1621 0.3	1414 0.4	1627 4.9	1648 4.0
	2151 5.4	2357 0.7	2352 1.1	1843 13.1	2315 4.0	2245 3.3	1957 2.6	2222 0.6	2319 0.4
18 TU O	0351 0.8	0557 6.9	0609 9.5	0127 0.8	0445 0.8	0443 0.5	0200 0.5	0442 5.0	0513 4.1
	1004 5.6	1220 0.6	1216 1.1	0700 13.2	1129 4.2	1048 3.6	0803 2.7	1045 0.4	1142 0.4
	1616 0.6	1817 6.9	1829 9.6	1351 0.9	1710 0.6	1659 0.3	1446 0.4	1705 5.0	1729 4.0
	2226 5.5			1921 13.3	2347 3.9	2319 3.3	2031 2.6	2259 0.5	
19 W	0427 0.7	0033 0.6	0027 1.0	0208 0.7	0520 0.7	0521 0.5	0236 0.5	0521 5.0	0000 0.4
	1041 5.6	0634 7.0	0645 9.6	0736 13.3	1202 4.1	1127 3.6	0836 2.7	1121 0.4	0551 4.1
	1651 0.6	1254 0.5	1249 1.1	1427 0.9	1744 0.6	1735 0.4	1515 0.4	1742 5.1	1221 0.4
	2300 5.5	1853 6.9	1903 9.6	1956 13.4		2351 3.4	2103 2.6	2336 0.5	1806 4.1
20 TH	0503 0.7	0108 0.6	0100 1.1	0241 0.8	0015 3.9	0556 0.5	0310 0.5	0559 5.0	0036 0.5
	1118 5.6	0709 6.9	0719 9.5	0810 13.3	0554 0.7	1203 3.5	0907 2.6	1157 0.5	0627 4.1
	1725 0.7	1327 0.6	1319 1.2	1457 1.0	1234 4.1	1809 0.5	1542 0.5	1818 5.0	1254 0.5
	2335 5.5	1926 6.9	1935 9.5	2028 13.3	1817 0.7		2133 2.5		1842 4.0
21 F	0539 0.8	0141 0.7	0131 1.2	0309 0.9	0043 3.9	0023 3.4	0342 0.5	0012 0.6	0109 0.6
	1153 5.4	0742 6.8	0751 9.3	0842 13.2	0628 0.7	0630 0.5	0938 2.5	0637 4.8	0700 4.0
	1759 0.9	1358 0.8	1348 1.4	1522 1.2	1308 4.0	1239 3.5	1609 0.6	1233 0.8	1327 0.6
		1959 6.7	2006 9.3	2059 13.1	1851 0.8	1842 0.6	2203 2.5	1855 4.9	1915 4.0
22 SA	0009 5.3	0212 0.9	0202 1.4	0333 1.1	0115 3.9	0055 3.4	0414 0.6	0049 0.8	0139 0.7
	0614 1.0	0814 6.5	0821 9.1	0912 12.7	0705 0.8	0705 0.6	1009 2.3	0715 4.6	0731 3.9
	1227 5.2	1428 1.1	1418 1.7	1543 1.4	1345 3.9	1317 3.4	1639 0.7	1309 1.0	1357 0.8
	1833 1.1	2030 6.4	2036 9.0	2127 12.5	1927 1.0	1915 0.7	2236 2.4	1932 4.7	1949 3.8
23 SU	0042 5.2	0244 1.2	0233 1.8	0355 1.4	0154 3.8	0130 3.3	0448 0.7	0127 1.1	0209 0.9
	0650 1.2	0846 6.2	0853 8.7	0941 12.0	0746 0.9	0742 0.7	1042 2.2	0753 4.4	0803 3.7
	1303 5.0	1458 1.4	1448 2.0	1604 1.8	1429 3.7	1357 3.3	1712 0.8	1345 1.4	1427 0.9
	1909 1.4	2102 6.1	2109 8.6	2154 11.7	2009 1.2	1953 0.8	2313 2.3	2009 4.4	2024 3.7
24 M	0118 5.0	0316 1.5	0308 2.2	0418 1.9	0239 3.7	0209 3.3	0527 0.8	0207 1.4	0242 1.0
	0729 1.6	0918 5.9	0926 8.3	1008 11.2	0833 1.1	0823 0.8	1121 2.0	0832 4.1	0837 3.6
	1340 4.7	1530 1.8	1521 2.5	1627 2.3	1520 3.5	1442 3.1	1751 0.9	1425 1.7	1502 1.0
	1948 1.7	2137 5.8	2145 8.2	2221 10.9	2100 1.4	2034 1.0	2357 2.2	2049 4.1	2103 3.5
25 TU	0158 4.8	0353 1.9	0347 2.6	0443 2.4	0330 3.5	0254 3.2	0612 0.9	0251 1.7	0321 1.2
	0814 1.7	0956 5.5	1004 7.8	1037 10.5	0931 1.3	0912 0.9	1209 1.9	0917 3.8	0917 3.4
	1427 4.4	1606 2.2	1602 3.0	1654 2.8	1621 3.3	1533 3.0	1838 1.0	1513 2.0	1543 1.2
	2036 2.1	2219 5.4	2230 7.6	2253 10.2	2204 1.5	2123 1.1		2136 3.9	2148 3.4
26 W	0248 4.5	0440 2.3	0437 3.1	0516 3.0	0431 3.4	0347 3.0	0053 2.1	0348 1.9	0409 1.3
	0910 2.0	1042 5.1	1053 7.3	1115 9.7	1042 1.4	1010 1.0	0707 1.1	1012 3.6	1006 3.2
	1529 4.2	1658 2.6	1658 3.4	1730 3.4	1734 3.2	1632 2.9	1324 1.7	1621 2.2	1637 1.3
	2139 2.3	2317 5.1	2329 7.2	2341 9.5	2318 1.6	2222 1.2	1938 1.1	2236 3.7	2245 3.2
27 TH	0354 4.3	0548 2.6	0546 3.4	0600 3.6	0543 3.2	0447 2.9	0211 2.1	0505 2.0	0512 1.4
	1024 2.1	1152 4.8	1200 6.9	1216 9.2	1156 1.4	1120 1.1	0821 1.1	1132 3.5	1109 3.1
	1656 4.1	1818 2.8	1822 3.8	1822 4.0	1847 3.2	1738 2.8	1541 1.8	1756 2.3	1745 1.3
	2303 2.4					2333 1.3	2100 1.2	2357 3.6	2357 3.1
28 F	0518 4.3	0041 4.9	0046 7.0	0106 9.2	0030 1.6	0552 2.9	0340 2.1	0633 2.0	0627 1.4
	1145 2.0	0718 2.6	0707 3.4	0711 4.0	0657 3.2	1230 1.0	1006 1.1	1307 3.6	1228 3.0
	1824 4.2	1325 4.8	1321 6.9	1354 9.2	1304 1.3	1842 2.8	1647 1.9	1918 2.1	1902 1.3
		1956 2.6	1948 3.5	1955 4.2	1951 3.3		2227 1.1		
29 SA	0021 2.2	0207 5.1	0204 7.2	0248 9.7	0133 1.5	0045 1.2	0444 2.2	0118 3.7	0114 3.2
	0633 4.5	0836 2.3	0820 3.1	0916 3.6	0758 3.3	0656 2.9	1118 0.9	0741 1.7	0742 1.3
	1253 1.8	1445 5.1	1439 7.2	1523 10.0	1359 1.2	1331 0.9	1732 2.1	1412 3.8	1342 3.2
	1924 4.5	2105 2.3	2054 3.1	2151 3.4	2045 3.4	1942 2.9	2327 1.0	2012 1.8	2010 1.1
30 SU	0120 2.2	0310 5.6	0309 7.7	0357 10.7	0222 1.3	0145 1.1	0533 2.4	0216 4.0	0218 3.4
	0729 4.8	0933 1.9	0918 2.5	1027 2.6	0848 3.4	0753 3.0	1207 0.8	0829 1.4	0843 1.0
	1344 1.4	1539 5.6	1538 7.9	1624 11.0	1442 1.0	1422 0.7	1812 2.2	1455 4.1	1442 3.2
	2009 4.8	2157 1.8	2146 2.3	2255 2.5	2128 3.5	2033 3.0		2054 1.4	2107 0.9

WEST COAST ENGLAND, WALES & IRELAND Time Zone UT
Holyhead * Milford Haven * Swansea * Avonmouth * Dublin * Belfast * Londonderry * Galway * Cobh

TIDE TABLES MAY 2000

HOLYHEAD Time m	MILFORD HAVEN Time m	SWANSEA Time m	AVONMOUTH Time m	DUBLIN Time m	BELFAST Time m	LONDON-DERRY Time m	GALWAY Time m	COBH Time m	
0205 1.5	0359 6.0	0400 8.3	0451 11.8	0301 1.1	0236 0.9	0016 0.8	0300 4.3	0310 3.7	**1 M**
0814 5.0	1020 1.4	1008 1.9	1127 1.8	0930 3.6	0842 3.1	0617 2.6	0909 1.1	0935 0.8	
1426 1.1	1623 6.1	1626 8.5	1716 12.0	1518 0.8	1508 0.6	1249 0.6	1532 4.4	1531 3.7	
2046 5.1	2242 1.3	2231 1.7	2354 1.8	2205 3.6	2118 3.1	1850 2.4	2130 1.1	2157 0.7	
0245 1.2	0442 6.5	0447 8.9	0540 12.6	0336 0.9	0321 0.7	0100 0.6	0339 4.6	0356 3.9	**2 TU**
0854 5.3	1103 1.0	1052 1.3	1224 1.3	1007 3.7	0927 3.2	0658 2.7	0945 0.7	1022 0.6	
1505 0.8	1705 6.6	1709 9.1	1803 12.8	1553 0.6	1549 0.4	1329 0.5	1606 4.7	1615 3.9	
2121 5.3	2324 0.9	2313 1.2		2238 3.8	2159 3.2	1928 2.5	2205 0.7	2244 0.5	
0323 0.8	0524 6.9	0530 9.4	0051 1.2	0410 0.7	0403 0.6	0142 0.4	0418 4.9	0439 4.1	**3 W**
0933 5.6	1145 0.6	1135 0.9	0625 13.2	1044 3.9	1009 3.3	0738 2.8	1021 0.5	1106 0.4	
1542 0.5	1745 7.0	1751 9.6	1318 0.9	1628 0.5	1630 0.3	1407 0.4	1642 5.0	1658 4.1	
2157 5.5		2354 0.8	1847 13.3	2312 3.9	2238 3.3	2006 2.6	2241 0.5	2328 0.4	
0401 0.6	0006 0.6	0613 9.8	0141 0.8	0447 0.5	0445 0.4	0224 0.3	0457 5.1	0521 4.2	**4 TH**
1012 5.7	0606 7.2	1216 0.6	0709 13.6	1123 4.1	1051 3.4	0818 2.9	1057 0.3	1150 0.4	**●**
1621 0.4	1227 0.4	1832 9.9	1406 0.6	1706 0.3	1711 0.2	1445 0.3	1718 5.2	1741 4.2	
2235 5.7	1827 7.2		1930 13.7	2348 4.1	2318 3.4	2044 2.7	2319 0.3		
0442 0.4	0048 0.4	0035 0.6	0227 0.6	0527 0.4	0527 0.3	0308 0.3	0538 5.3	0012 0.4	**5 F**
1054 5.8	0648 7.3	0656 10.0	0752 13.8	1205 4.2	1134 3.5	0900 2.8	1136 0.3	0603 4.3	
1702 0.3	1309 0.3	1257 0.5	1449 0.5	1747 0.3	1753 0.2	1524 0.3	1757 5.3	1233 0.4	
2315 5.7	1909 7.3	1913 10.0	2011 13.8			2124 2.7	2359 0.2	1823 4.2	
0524 0.4	0130 0.4	0116 0.6	0307 0.5	0029 4.1	0000 3.5	0352 0.3	0621 5.3	0055 0.4	**6 SA**
1138 5.8	0732 7.2	0739 9.9	0834 13.8	0609 0.3	0611 0.3	0944 2.7	1216 0.4	0645 4.2	
1745 0.4	1351 0.4	1337 0.7	1527 0.6	1251 4.2	1221 3.4	1604 0.3	1839 5.2	1315 0.4	
2359 5.7	1951 7.2	1955 9.8	2051 13.7	1831 0.4	1836 0.3	2204 2.6		1906 4.2	
0610 0.5	0214 0.5	0157 0.8	0343 0.7	0114 4.2	0044 3.5	0439 0.4	0042 0.4	0139 0.4	**7 SU**
1225 5.6	0816 7.0	0822 9.6	0917 13.4	0657 0.3	0657 0.3	1030 2.6	0706 5.1	0728 4.1	
1831 0.7	1433 0.7	1418 1.0	1600 0.9	1342 4.2	1310 3.4	1646 0.4	1300 0.7	1358 0.5	
	2036 6.9	2039 9.5	2133 13.2	1919 0.6	1924 0.4	2248 2.5	1924 5.1	1951 4.1	
0045 5.5	0259 0.8	0242 1.2	0415 1.1	0205 4.1	0133 3.4	0530 0.5	0130 0.6	0224 0.6	**8 M**
0701 0.6	0903 6.7	0908 9.2	1000 12.8	0751 0.5	0748 0.4	1123 2.4	0756 4.9	0813 4.0	
1317 5.4	1518 1.0	1502 1.5	1632 1.4	1439 4.0	1406 3.2	1731 0.6	1348 1.0	1445 0.6	
1922 1.0	2124 6.6	2126 9.0	2218 12.5	2013 0.8	2018 0.6	2336 2.4	2014 4.8	2039 4.0	
0138 5.3	0348 1.1	0330 1.7	0450 1.6	0302 4.0	0227 3.3	0628 0.7	0223 0.9	0315 0.7	**9 TU**
0758 0.9	0954 6.2	0958 8.6	1048 11.9	0852 0.7	0845 0.5	1226 2.2	0851 4.6	0903 3.8	
1416 5.1	1609 1.5	1552 2.1	1708 2.0	1544 3.8	1509 3.1	1822 0.7	1444 1.4	1536 0.8	
2021 1.4	2218 6.2	2221 8.4	2308 11.7	2117 1.1	2120 0.8		2110 4.5	2134 3.8	
0239 5.1	0446 1.5	0430 2.2	0532 2.2	0408 3.8	0330 3.2	0036 2.3	0327 1.3	0412 0.9	**10 W**
0905 1.2	1054 5.8	1058 8.0	1145 11.2	1003 0.9	0953 0.6	0745 0.8	0954 4.3	1001 3.6	
1527 4.8	1710 1.9	1658 2.6	1755 2.5	1658 3.6	1624 2.9	1350 2.1	1551 1.7	1638 0.9	
2130 1.7	2323 5.8	2327 7.9		2231 1.3	2236 0.9	1921 0.9	2218 4.2	2238 3.6	
0351 4.9	0558 1.9	0548 2.7	0009 11.1	0522 3.8	0439 3.1	0204 2.2	0445 1.5	0521 1.0	**11 TH**
1021 1.3	1206 5.5	1212 7.5	0628 2.7	1120 1.0	1111 0.6	0930 0.9	1111 4.1	1110 3.4	
1648 4.6	1827 2.1	1825 3.0	1251 10.6	1815 3.6	1745 2.9	1522 2.1	1715 1.9	1750 1.0	
2250 1.8			1900 3.0	2348 1.4	2355 1.0	2036 1.0	2339 4.1	2354 3.5	
0512 4.8	0039 5.6	0047 7.6	0121 10.8	0638 3.7	0551 3.1	0346 2.3	0612 1.5	0638 1.1	**12 F**
1140 1.4	0721 1.9	0715 2.8	0748 2.9	1236 1.0	1227 0.6	1048 0.8	1236 4.1	1228 3.3	
1809 4.6	1326 5.4	1335 7.4	1407 10.6	1929 3.6	1900 3.0	1630 2.1	1843 1.8	1908 1.0	
	1951 2.0	1951 2.9	2027 3.0			2202 1.0			
0008 1.8	0159 5.3	0209 7.7	0240 10.9	0103 1.4	0104 0.9	0450 2.4	0102 4.1	0112 3.5	**13 SA**
0628 4.9	0839 1.7	0833 2.5	0912 2.6	0748 3.8	0700 3.2	1146 0.7	0724 1.4	0752 1.0	
1250 1.2	1441 5.7	1452 7.8	1525 11.0	1346 0.9	1331 0.5	1724 2.3	1346 4.3	1342 3.4	
1916 4.8	2103 1.8	2102 2.5	2149 2.5	2035 3.7	2002 3.2	2312 0.9	1948 1.6	2018 0.9	
0113 1.6	0308 6.0	0318 8.1	0356 11.5	0209 1.3	0203 0.8	0539 2.5	0206 4.3	0221 3.7	**14 SU**
0730 5.0	0941 1.5	0936 2.1	1029 2.1	0850 3.9	0800 3.2	1232 0.6	0818 1.2	0855 0.8	
1348 1.1	1541 6.0	1553 8.3	1634 11.7	1443 0.8	1426 0.4	1811 2.4	1439 4.5	1445 3.6	
2009 5.0	2200 1.5	2157 2.0	2303 1.9	2130 3.7	2055 3.1		2037 1.3	2118 0.7	
0206 1.4	0403 6.3	0413 8.6	0459 12.1	0301 1.1	0254 0.7	0006 0.8	0256 4.5	0318 3.8	**15 M**
0821 5.2	1031 1.2	1027 1.8	1137 1.6	0943 4.0	0853 3.3	0621 2.5	0902 1.0	0949 0.7	
1435 1.0	1630 6.3	1642 8.7	1729 12.3	1530 0.8	1514 0.4	1310 0.5	1522 4.6	1537 3.8	
2051 5.1	2248 1.2	2243 1.7		2215 3.8	2139 3.2	1852 2.5	2119 1.1	2209 0.6	

● ● Time: UT. For British Summer Time (shaded) March 26th to October 29th ADD ONE HOUR ● ●

MAY 2000 TIDE TABLES

•• Time: UT. For British Summer Time (shaded) March 26th to October 29TH ADD ONE HOUR ••

Date	HOLYHEAD Time	m	MILFORD HAVEN Time	m	SWANSEA Time	m	AVONMOUTH Time	m	DUBLIN Time	m	BELFAST Time	m	LONDONDERRY Time	m	GALWAY Time	m	COBH Time	m
16TU	0251	1.2	0449	6.5	0500	8.9	0005	1.5	0345	1.0	0339	0.6	0053	0.7	0339	4.6	0406	4.0
	0903	5.3	1113	1.0	1109	1.5	0550	12.5	1028	4.0	0941	3.4	0659	2.5	0942	0.9	1035	0.6
	1515	0.9	1712	6.5	1724	9.1	1233	1.4	1610	0.7	1556	0.4	1344	0.5	1601	4.8	1623	3.9
	2127	5.3	2329	1.0	2324	1.5	1815	12.6	2252	3.8	2218	3.2	1930	2.5	2158	0.9	2254	0.6
17W	0330	1.0	0530	6.6	0541	9.1	0054	1.3	0424	0.9	0420	0.5	0133	0.6	0419	4.7	0448	4.0
	0942	5.3	1151	0.9	1147	1.5	0632	12.6	1106	4.0	1024	3.4	0736	2.5	1019	0.8	1116	0.6
	1552	0.8	1751	6.6	1801	9.3	1317	1.4	1646	0.8	1634	0.4	1415	0.5	1639	4.9	1703	4.0
	2202	5.3					1853	12.7	2322	3.9	2252	3.3	2004	2.5	2236	0.8	2333	0.6
18TH O	0406	0.9	0006	0.9	0000	1.4	0135	1.3	0501	0.9	0457	0.5	0211	0.6	0457	4.8	0525	4.0
	1018	5.4	0608	6.6	0618	9.2	0709	12.7	1139	3.9	1103	3.4	0809	2.5	1055	0.8	1153	0.7
	1627	0.9	1226	0.9	1221	1.5	1354	1.4	1720	0.8	1709	0.5	1444	0.5	1716	4.9	1741	4.0
	2236	5.4	1827	6.7	1836	9.3	1928	12.7	2351	3.9	2324	3.3	2037	2.5	2314	0.7		
19F	0442	0.9	0041	0.9	0034	1.5	0209	1.3	0536	1.0	0533	0.5	0245	0.6	0536	4.7	0009	0.7
	1054	5.3	0643	6.6	0654	9.1	0744	12.7	1212	3.9	1139	3.4	0842	2.4	1131	0.9	0600	4.0
	1700	0.9	1259	0.9	1253	1.6	1425	1.4	1753	0.8	1742	0.6	1511	0.6	1753	4.9	1227	0.7
	2310	5.4	1900	6.7	1910	9.3	2001	12.9			2357	3.4	2108	2.5	2351	0.8	1816	4.0
20SA	0517	1.0	0115	0.9	0108	1.6	0239	1.3	0021	3.9	0607	0.6	0317	0.6	0614	4.7	0042	0.8
	1130	5.2	0717	6.5	0727	9.0	0816	12.7	0612	0.8	1215	3.3	0912	2.3	1207	1.0	0632	3.9
	1733	1.1	1331	1.0	1324	1.7	1454	1.4	1246	3.8	1814	0.7	1538	0.6	1829	4.8	1259	0.8
	2344	5.3	1933	6.6	1942	9.1	2033	12.8	1828	0.9			2139	2.5			1851	3.9
21SU	0552	1.1	0148	1.0	0141	1.7	0307	1.3	0054	3.9	0029	3.4	0349	0.7	0028	0.9	0112	0.9
	1204	5.1	0750	6.4	0759	8.8	0848	12.4	0649	0.8	0642	0.6	0944	2.3	0652	4.5	0704	3.8
	1807	1.2	1403	1.2	1356	1.9	1518	1.5	1324	3.8	1252	3.3	1607	0.7	1243	1.2	1330	0.9
			2006	6.4	2015	8.9	2103	12.4	1906	1.0	1848	0.7	2211	2.5	1906	4.7	1925	3.8
22M	0018	5.2	0221	1.2	0215	1.9	0333	1.5	0133	3.9	0104	3.4	0424	0.7	0106	1.1	0144	1.0
	0628	1.2	0822	6.2	0832	8.6	0917	12.0	0730	0.9	0718	0.7	1018	2.2	0730	4.4	0736	3.7
	1239	4.9	1434	1.5	1427	2.1	1542	1.8	1407	3.6	1331	3.2	1641	0.7	1320	1.4	1402	0.9
	1842	1.4	2039	6.2	2048	8.6	2132	11.9	1948	1.1	1924	0.8	2248	2.4	1943	4.5	2000	3.9
23TU	0054	5.1	0255	1.5	0249	2.2	0358	1.8	0217	3.8	0142	3.4	0503	0.8	0145	1.3	0218	1.1
	0706	1.4	0856	5.9	0905	8.2	0947	11.4	0815	1.0	0759	0.7	1057	2.1	0809	4.2	0812	3.6
	1318	4.7	1507	1.7	1500	2.4	1608	2.2	1455	3.5	1413	3.1	1718	0.8	1400	1.7	1437	1.0
	1921	1.7	2114	5.9	2124	8.2	2203	11.2	2035	1.3	2004	0.9	2329	2.3	2022	4.1	2039	3.6
24W	0133	4.9	0333	1.8	0327	2.5	0427	2.2	0306	3.6	0224	3.3	0546	0.9	0229	1.5	0257	1.2
	0749	1.6	0932	5.6	0942	7.9	1020	10.8	0907	1.2	0844	0.8	1144	2.0	0852	4.0	0851	3.5
	1402	4.5	1544	2.0	1538	2.7	1637	2.6	1549	3.4	1500	3.0	1802	0.9	1445	1.9	1518	1.1
	2006	1.9	2154	5.6	2206	7.8	2237	10.6	2130	1.4	2051	1.0			2106	4.1	2122	3.5
25TH	0219	4.7	0416	2.1	0411	2.8	0500	2.7	0358	3.4	0310	3.2	0017	2.3	0318	1.7	0342	1.3
	0839	1.8	1015	5.3	1026	7.5	1058	10.2	1006	1.3	0935	0.9	0636	1.0	0941	3.8	0937	3.4
	1455	4.4	1630	2.3	1626	3.1	1713	3.0	1651	3.2	1552	2.9	1242	1.9	1542	2.1	1607	1.2
	2100	2.1	2244	5.4	2257	7.5	2321	10.1	2233	1.5	2144	1.1	1852	1.0	2158	3.9	2214	3.4
26F	0315	4.6	0511	2.3	0507	3.0	0542	3.1	0457	3.3	0402	3.1	0115	2.2	0418	1.8	0439	1.3
	0939	1.9	1111	5.1	1121	7.2	1149	9.8	1109	1.3	1033	0.9	0736	1.0	1042	3.7	1034	3.2
	1603	4.2	1731	2.5	1733	3.3	1800	3.4	1757	3.2	1650	2.9	1400	1.8	1654	2.1	1707	1.3
	2208	2.2	2348	5.3	2359	7.3			2338	1.6	2245	1.2	1952	1.1	2300	3.8	2315	3.3
27SA	0423	4.5	0620	2.4	0616	3.1	0024	9.8	0600	3.3	0458	3.0	0225	2.2	0527	1.8	0545	1.3
	1048	1.9	1224	5.0	1230	7.1	0639	3.4	1209	1.3	1136	0.9	0851	1.0	1156	3.7	1141	3.2
	1719	4.3	1848	2.5	1851	3.2	1259	9.7	1900	3.2	1751	2.9	1525	1.9	1811	2.1	1815	1.3
	2321	2.1					1905	3.7			2350	1.2	2106	1.1				
28SU	0534	4.6	0103	5.3	0109	7.4	0145	10.0	0037	1.5	0558	3.0	0337	2.3	0012	3.8	0023	3.4
	1156	1.7	0733	2.2	0727	2.9	0800	3.4	0701	3.3	1236	0.8	1010	1.0	0636	1.7	0654	1.2
	1827	4.5	1340	5.2	1343	7.3	1421	10.1	1303	1.2	1850	2.9	1631	2.0	1308	3.9	1251	3.3
			2004	2.3	2000	2.9	2036	3.5	1955	3.3			2221	1.0	1915	1.9	1923	1.1
29M	0026	1.9	0212	5.6	0216	7.7	0302	10.6	0129	1.4	0054	1.1	0439	2.4	0119	4.0	0129	3.5
	0637	4.8	0839	1.9	0830	2.4	0927	2.8	0757	3.4	0658	3.0	1114	0.8	0735	1.4	0758	1.1
	1254	1.4	1445	5.6	1448	7.8	1533	10.9	1351	1.0	1333	0.7	1724	2.2	1403	4.1	1354	3.5
	1921	4.7	2107	1.9	2100	2.3	2159	2.8	2043	3.4	1945	3.0	2325	0.8	2007	1.5	2025	1.0
30TU	0120	1.6	0311	6.0	0315	8.3	0406	11.5	0215	1.2	0151	1.0	0532	2.5	0214	4.3	0227	3.7
	0731	5.0	0935	1.5	0926	1.9	1038	2.1	0845	3.5	0755	3.1	1206	0.7	0823	1.2	0856	0.9
	1344	1.1	1540	6.1	1545	8.5	1633	11.8	1436	0.8	1425	0.6	1811	2.3	1448	4.4	1451	3.7
	2007	5.0	2201	1.5	2151	1.9	2308	2.0	2126	3.6	2037	3.1			2051	1.2	2121	0.8
31W	0208	1.2	0403	6.4	0409	8.8	0502	12.4	0257	1.0	0245	0.8	0020	0.6	0302	4.6	0320	3.9
	0818	5.3	1026	1.1	1016	1.4	1143	1.5	0932	3.7	0848	3.2	0621	2.7	0907	0.9	0948	0.7
	1430	0.8	1630	6.5	1635	9.1	1728	12.6	1518	0.6	1515	0.5	1252	0.5	1530	4.7	1542	3.9
	2049	5.3	2251	1.1	2240	1.3			2206	3.8	2125	3.3	1856	2.5	2133	0.8	2213	0.6

WEST COAST ENGLAND, WALES & IRELAND Time Zone UT
Holyhead * Milford Haven * Swansea * Avonmouth * Dublin * Belfast * Londonderry * Galway * Cobh

TIDE TABLES JUNE 2000

	HOLYHEAD	MILFORD HAVEN	SWANSEA	AVONMOUTH	DUBLIN	BELFAST	LONDONDERRY	GALWAY	COBH
	Time m	Time m	Time m	Time m	Time m	Time m	Time m	Time m	Time m
1 TH	0253 0.9	0453 6.8	0459 9.3	0013 1.5	0340 0.7	0334 0.6	0111 0.5	0347 4.9	0409 4.1
	0903 5.5	1115 0.8	1105 1.0	0554 13.0	1017 3.9	0939 3.3	0709 2.7	0949 0.6	1038 0.5
	1514 0.6	1718 6.9	1722 9.5	1245 1.1	1601 0.5	1602 0.4	1336 0.4	1611 5.0	1631 4.1
	2131 5.5	2340 0.7	2328 0.9	1818 13.2	2248 4.0	2212 3.4	1939 2.6	2215 0.5	2303 0.5
2 F ●	0337 0.6	0541 7.0	0548 9.7	0112 1.0	0424 0.5	0423 0.5	0200 0.4	0432 5.1	0456 4.2
	0949 5.7	1203 0.5	1152 0.7	0645 13.4	1103 4.1	1030 3.4	0755 2.8	1032 0.5	1126 0.4
	1558 0.4	1804 7.1	1809 9.8	1339 0.8	1645 0.4	1648 0.3	1418 0.3	1654 5.2	1718 4.2
	2214 5.7			1906 13.6	2330 4.1	2258 3.5	2023 2.7	2258 0.3	2351 0.4
3 SA	0423 0.5	0028 0.5	0015 0.7	0204 0.7	0509 0.4	0510 0.4	0249 0.3	0518 5.2	0542 4.3
	1036 5.8	0629 7.2	0637 9.8	0733 13.7	1151 4.2	1120 3.4	0842 2.8	1115 0.4	1212 0.4
	1643 0.4	1250 0.4	1239 0.7	1428 0.6	1730 0.4	1736 0.3	1501 0.3	1737 5.3	1806 4.3
	2259 5.8	1851 7.2	1857 9.9	1953 13.8		2345 3.5	2106 2.7	2343 0.3	
4 SU	0511 0.4	0116 0.4	0103 0.7	0251 0.6	0015 4.2	0559 0.3	0338 0.3	0605 5.2	0039 0.4
	1124 5.8	0718 7.2	0725 9.8	0821 13.6	0557 0.3	1212 3.4	0930 2.7	1200 0.5	0628 4.2
	1730 0.5	1336 0.5	1324 0.8	1512 0.6	1242 4.2	1824 0.4	1543 0.3	1823 5.3	1300 0.4
	2346 5.8	1939 7.2	1944 9.8	2039 13.7	1818 0.5		2150 2.7		1852 4.2
5 M	0600 0.4	0204 0.5	0151 0.8	0333 0.7	0103 4.3	0033 3.6	0428 0.4	0030 0.3	0126 0.4
	1216 5.6	0806 7.0	0814 9.5	0907 13.4	0648 0.3	0649 0.3	1019 2.6	0654 5.1	0715 4.2
	1820 0.7	1424 0.7	1410 1.0	1552 0.9	1335 4.2	1306 3.3	1627 0.4	1247 0.7	1347 0.5
		2027 7.0	2032 9.5	2125 13.4	1908 0.6	1915 0.5	2236 2.7	1912 5.2	1941 4.2
6 TU	0036 5.7	0253 0.7	0239 1.1	0412 1.0	0155 4.2	0124 3.5	0521 0.5	0121 0.5	0215 0.5
	0654 0.5	0855 6.7	0903 9.2	0954 12.9	0744 0.4	0742 0.3	1112 2.4	0745 4.9	0803 4.1
	1311 5.4	1512 1.0	1457 1.4	1630 1.3	1433 4.0	1403 3.2	1713 0.5	1338 1.0	1436 0.6
	1912 0.9	2116 6.8	2121 9.1	2212 12.8	2002 0.8	2011 0.6	2325 2.6	2003 4.9	2030 4.1
7 W	0130 5.5	0344 1.0	0330 1.5	0451 1.4	0251 4.2	0219 3.5	0620 0.7	0215 0.8	0306 0.7
	0751 0.7	0947 6.4	0953 8.7	1044 12.3	0844 0.5	0840 0.3	1212 2.3	0841 4.7	0854 3.9
	1409 5.1	1603 1.3	1548 1.8	1709 1.8	1535 3.8	1507 3.1	1803 0.6	1433 1.3	1527 0.7
	2009 1.3	2209 6.4	2215 8.6	2303 12.2	2102 1.1	2112 0.8		2059 4.7	2124 3.9
8 TH	0228 5.3	0439 1.3	0425 1.9	0533 1.9	0353 4.0	0318 3.4	0020 2.5	0315 1.1	0401 0.8
	0853 1.0	1042 6.0	1048 8.2	1136 11.6	0948 0.7	0943 0.4	0727 0.8	0940 4.4	0949 3.7
	1513 4.9	1659 1.6	1647 2.3	1753 2.2	1642 3.7	1616 3.0	1320 2.2	1535 1.6	1625 0.8
	2112 1.5	2308 6.1	2314 8.2	2358 11.6	2208 1.3	2218 0.9	1857 0.8	2200 4.4	2224 3.7
9 F	0333 5.1	0542 1.6	0530 2.3	0623 2.3	0500 3.9	0422 3.3	0127 2.4	0421 1.3	0503 1.0
	1001 1.2	1144 5.7	1151 7.7	1233 11.1	1057 0.9	1051 0.5	0845 0.9	1047 4.2	1051 3.5
	1623 4.7	1804 1.9	1758 2.6	1848 2.6	1751 3.6	1726 2.9	1434 2.1	1646 1.8	1728 0.9
	2222 1.7				2317 1.4	2328 0.9	2000 0.9	2310 4.2	2330 3.6
10 SA	0443 4.9	0012 5.8	0020 7.8	0059 11.2	0609 3.8	0527 3.2	0245 2.3	0535 1.5	0609 1.0
	1110 1.3	0650 1.8	0643 2.6	0724 2.6	1206 1.0	1159 0.5	1000 0.9	1200 4.1	1158 3.5
	1736 4.6	1252 5.5	1301 7.5	1338 10.8	1859 3.5	1833 2.9	1544 2.1	1804 1.8	1836 1.0
	2334 1.8	1915 2.0	1915 2.7	1954 2.8			2112 0.9		
11 SU	0554 4.9	0121 5.8	0131 7.7	0207 11.0	0027 1.4	0034 0.9	0358 2.3	0026 4.1	0040 3.6
	1217 1.4	0800 1.8	0755 2.6	0833 2.6	0715 3.8	0631 3.2	1102 0.8	0645 1.5	0718 1.1
	1842 4.7	1402 5.6	1413 7.7	1448 10.9	1312 1.0	1301 0.5	1643 2.2	1310 4.2	1307 3.5
		2024 1.9	2024 2.6	2107 2.7	2002 3.5	1931 2.9	2223 0.9	1913 1.7	1945 1.0
12 M	0040 1.7	0230 5.8	0239 7.9	0318 11.2	0134 1.4	0133 0.8	0457 2.3	0133 4.1	0148 3.6
	0659 4.9	0903 1.7	0858 2.4	0944 2.5	0818 3.8	0730 3.2	1151 0.8	0744 1.4	0822 1.0
	1317 1.3	1505 5.8	1517 8.0	1556 11.2	1411 1.0	1357 0.5	1734 2.3	1406 4.3	1412 3.5
	1938 4.8	2125 1.8	2121 2.3	2218 2.5	2058 3.6	2023 3.0	2325 0.9	2008 1.5	2046 0.9
13 TU	0138 1.6	0329 5.9	0339 8.2	0422 11.5	0233 1.3	0226 0.7	0547 2.4	0228 4.2	0247 3.7
	0754 5.0	0957 1.6	0952 2.2	1051 2.3	0914 3.8	0824 3.2	1233 0.7	0832 1.3	0918 0.9
	1408 1.3	1558 6.0	1609 8.4	1654 11.6	1500 1.0	1446 0.5	1819 2.3	1454 4.4	1508 3.7
	2024 4.9	2216 1.6	2210 2.1	2322 2.2	2145 3.7	2108 3.1		2054 1.4	2139 0.9
14 W	0227 1.4	0420 6.1	0428 8.5	0517 11.8	0322 1.2	0314 0.7	0018 0.8	0315 4.3	0337 3.8
	0841 5.0	1042 1.4	1038 2.0	1151 2.1	1002 3.8	0914 3.2	0631 2.4	0915 1.2	1006 0.9
	1451 1.2	1645 6.2		1743 11.9	1543 1.0	1530 0.5	1309 0.7	1535 4.6	1556 3.8
	2104 5.1	2301 1.4	2254 1.9		2225 3.7	2148 3.2	1900 2.4	2137 1.2	2226 0.8
15 TH	0310 1.3	0504 6.2	0512 8.6	0015 2.0	0405 1.1	0357 0.6	0104 0.8	0357 4.4	0421 3.8
	0922 5.1	1123 1.3	1118 1.9	0603 12.0	1043 3.8	0959 3.2	0711 2.4	0955 1.2	1048 0.8
	1530 1.2	1726 6.3	1734 8.9	1239 1.9	1621 0.9	1610 0.6	1343 0.6	1615 4.7	1639 3.8
	2141 5.2	2341 1.3	2334 1.9	1825 12.2	2259 3.8	2226 3.3	1939 2.5	2217 1.0	2306 0.8

● ● Time: UT. For British Summer Time (shaded) March 26th to October 29th ADD ONE HOUR ● ●

JUNE 2000 TIDE TABLES

•• Time: UT. For British Summer Time (shaded) March 26th to October 29TH ADD ONE HOUR ••

	HOLYHEAD	MILFORD HAVEN	SWANSEA	AVONMOUTH	DUBLIN	BELFAST	LONDON-DERRY	GALWAY	COBH
	Time m	Time m	Time m	Time m	Time m	Time m	Time m	Time m	Time m
16 F ○	0348 1.2	0545 6.3	0553 8.7	0100 1.8	0445 1.0	0437 0.6	0145 0.7	0438 4.5	0459 3.8
	1000 5.1	1200 1.2	1156 1.9	0644 12.1	1120 3.8	1040 3.2	0748 2.3	1033 1.1	1126 0.8
	1606 1.1	1803 6.4	1812 9.0	1320 1.8	1658 0.9	1646 0.6	1415 0.6	1653 4.8	1718 3.9
	2216 5.3			1903 12.4	2331 3.9	2300 3.3	2014 2.5	2256 1.0	2342 0.9
17 SA	0425 1.2	0018 1.2	0012 1.8	0139 1.7	0522 0.9	0515 0.6	0221 0.7	0517 4.5	0535 3.8
	1036 5.1	0622 6.4	0630 8.8	0721 12.2	1154 3.7	1118 3.2	0821 2.3	1111 1.1	1201 0.8
	1639 1.1	1236 1.2	1232 1.9	1357 1.7	1734 0.9	1719 0.7	1445 0.6	1730 4.8	1754 3.9
	2250 5.3	1839 6.5	1848 9.0	1939 12.5		2335 3.4	2047 2.5	2334 0.9	
18 SU	0500 1.1	0054 1.1	0049 1.8	0215 1.6	0003 3.9	0550 0.6	0255 0.7	0556 4.5	0017 0.9
	1111 5.1	0657 6.3	0706 8.7	0756 12.2	0600 0.9	1154 3.2	0853 2.3	1148 1.2	0609 3.8
	1712 1.2	1310 1.2	1306 1.9	1430 1.7	1230 3.7	1751 0.7	1514 0.6	1808 4.8	1235 0.8
	2324 5.3	1914 6.5	1924 8.9	2012 12.5	1811 0.9		2118 2.5		1830 3.9
19 M	0534 1.2	0129 1.2	0125 1.9	0248 1.6	0039 3.9	0008 3.4	0328 0.7	0012 1.0	0050 0.9
	1145 5.0	0731 6.3	0741 8.6	0829 12.2	0638 0.9	0624 0.6	0924 2.3	0634 4.5	0642 3.8
	1746 1.3	1343 1.3	1339 2.0	1501 1.7	1307 3.7	1230 3.2	1544 0.7	1224 1.3	1308 0.9
	2358 5.3	1948 6.4	1958 8.8	2044 12.3	1848 1.0	1824 0.7	2151 2.5	1845 4.7	1905 3.8
20 TU	0609 1.2	0203 1.3	0200 1.9	0318 1.6	0117 3.9	0042 3.4	0403 0.7	0049 1.0	0124 1.0
	1221 4.9	0804 6.2	0815 8.5	0900 12.0	0716 0.9	0659 0.6	0958 2.2	0712 4.4	0716 3.7
	1821 1.4	1416 1.4	1411 2.1	1530 1.8	1347 3.6	1307 3.1	1616 0.7	1301 1.4	1342 0.9
		2021 6.3	2032 8.6	2116 12.1	1927 1.0	1900 0.8	2226 2.5	1921 4.6	1941 3.8
21 W	0034 5.2	0238 1.4	0233 2.0	0348 1.8	0157 3.8	0118 3.4	0441 0.8	0127 1.2	0159 1.0
	0647 1.3	0837 6.0	0848 8.3	0933 11.7	0757 1.0	0736 0.6	1036 2.2	0749 4.3	0751 3.7
	1258 4.8	1449 1.6	1443 2.2	1558 2.1	1430 3.5	1346 3.1	1651 0.8	1339 1.5	1418 0.9
	1859 1.5	2056 6.1	2106 8.4	2150 11.7	2009 1.1	1939 0.8	2303 2.5	2000 4.4	2018 3.7
22 TH	0112 5.1	0315 1.6	0309 2.1	0419 2.0	0239 3.7	0156 3.4	0522 0.8	0206 1.3	0236 1.1
	0727 1.4	0912 5.8	0922 8.1	1007 11.4	0839 1.0	0818 0.7	1118 2.1	0829 4.1	0829 3.6
	1339 4.7	1526 1.8	1518 2.4	1629 2.3	1516 3.4	1429 3.1	1732 0.8	1421 1.7	1456 1.0
	1940 1.7	2133 6.0	2144 8.1	2226 11.3	2054 1.2	2022 0.9	2345 2.5	2041 4.3	2058 3.6
23 F	0154 5.0	0354 1.8	0346 2.3	0452 2.3	0325 3.6	0237 3.3	0608 0.9	0250 1.4	0319 1.1
	0811 1.5	0952 5.6	1000 7.8	1045 11.0	0925 1.1	0903 0.7	1206 2.1	0912 4.0	0912 3.5
	1424 4.6	1606 2.0	1557 2.6	1703 2.6	1606 3.3	1515 3.0	1816 0.9	1509 1.8	1540 1.1
	2027 1.8	2217 5.8	2227 7.9	2306 10.9	2143 1.4	2110 0.9		2126 4.1	2144 3.5
24 SA	0242 4.8	0439 2.0	0431 2.5	0530 2.6	0413 3.5	0323 3.2	0033 2.4	0338 1.5	0408 1.2
	0900 1.6	1039 5.5	1047 7.6	1127 10.6	1016 1.1	0952 0.7	0659 0.9	1001 3.9	1001 3.4
	1518 4.5	1655 2.2	1649 2.8	1743 2.9	1700 3.3	1605 3.0	1303 2.0	1603 1.9	1632 1.1
	2122 1.9	2309 5.6	2318 7.7	2354 10.6	2239 1.4	2203 1.0	1908 0.9	2218 4.0	2236 3.5
25 SU	0338 4.7	0533 2.1	0527 2.6	0615 2.9	0505 3.4	0413 3.2	0129 2.4	0433 1.6	0504 1.2
	0959 1.6	1136 5.4	1144 7.5	1220 10.4	1112 1.1	1048 0.8	0758 1.0	1059 3.9	1059 3.4
	1621 4.4	1756 2.3	1754 2.9	1833 3.1	1759 3.2	1700 3.0	1412 2.0	1708 1.9	1731 1.2
	2227 2.0				2337 1.4	2303 1.1	2009 1.0	2318 4.0	2336 3.5
26 M	0441 4.7	0011 5.6	0020 7.6	0055 10.4	0603 3.4	0509 3.2	0236 2.4	0537 1.6	0607 1.2
	1103 1.6	0636 2.1	0633 2.6	0713 3.0	1209 1.1	1147 0.8	0907 1.0	1206 3.9	1202 3.4
	1730 4.5	1245 5.4	1251 7.5	1327 10.4	1859 3.3	1800 3.0	1527 2.0	1818 1.8	1836 1.1
	2334 1.9	1906 2.2	1907 2.7	1939 3.2			2121 0.9		
27 TU	0548 4.8	0119 5.7	0127 7.8	0210 10.7	0036 1.4	0006 1.1	0346 2.4	0027 4.0	0041 3.5
	1207 1.4	0745 2.0	0742 2.4	0830 2.9	0703 3.4	0611 3.1	1020 0.9	0642 1.5	0713 1.1
	1834 4.7	1355 5.6	1402 7.8	1445 10.8	1305 1.0	1248 0.7	1636 2.1	1312 4.1	1309 1.1
		2018 2.0	2015 2.4	2104 3.0	1956 3.4	1901 3.1	2237 0.9	1921 1.6	1944 1.0
28 W	0038 1.6	0227 5.9	0234 8.1	0323 11.3	0131 1.2	0112 1.0	0452 2.5	0132 4.2	0145 3.6
	0651 4.9	0852 1.7	0847 2.1	0951 2.5	0804 3.6	0715 3.2	1124 0.8	0742 1.3	0818 1.0
	1306 1.2	1500 5.9	1507 8.3	1554 11.5	1358 0.9	1348 0.7	1736 2.2	1409 4.3	1413 3.6
	1931 4.9	2124 1.7	2117 2.0	2226 2.4	2049 3.6	2000 3.2	2345 0.7	2017 1.3	2048 0.9
29 TH	0136 1.4	0329 6.2	0336 8.6	0427 12.0	0225 1.0	0213 0.9	0551 2.6	0230 4.5	0248 3.8
	0748 5.2	0954 1.4	0946 1.6	1105 1.9	0902 3.8	0818 3.3	1219 0.6	0835 1.0	0918 0.8
	1400 1.0	1600 6.3	1606 8.8	1657 12.3	1450 0.7	1445 0.6	1829 2.4	1459 4.6	1514 3.8
	2022 5.2	2224 1.3	2214 1.5	2339 1.8	2140 3.8	2057 3.3		2108 1.0	2148 0.7
30 F	0229 1.0	0427 6.6	0435 9.0	0528 12.6	0317 0.8	0310 0.7	0046 0.6	0322 4.7	0344 4.0
	0841 5.4	1051 1.0	1042 1.2	1214 1.4	0957 4.0	0918 3.3	0646 2.7	0925 0.8	1014 0.6
	1451 0.8	1655 6.7	1700 9.3	1754 12.9	1540 0.6	1540 0.5	1309 0.5	1547 4.9	1609 4.0
	2111 5.5	2321 0.9	2309 1.1		2228 4.0	2151 3.4	1918 2.6	2157 0.6	2242 0.5

WEST COAST ENGLAND, WALES & IRELAND Time Zone UT
Holyhead * Milford Haven * Swansea * Avonmouth * Dublin * Belfast * Londonderry * Galway * Cobh

TIDE TABLES JULY 2000

HOLYHEAD Time m	MILFORD HAVEN Time m	SWANSEA Time m	AVONMOUTH Time m	DUBLIN Time m	BELFAST Time m	LONDONDERRY Time m	GALWAY Time m	COBH Time m	
0320 0.7 0933 5.6 1541 0.6 2158 5.7	0523 6.8 1145 0.7 1748 7.0	0530 9.4 1135 1.0 1753 9.6	0046 1.3 0625 13.1 1317 1.0 1849 13.4	0408 0.6 1050 4.1 1629 0.5 2317 4.2	0405 0.5 1015 3.4 1633 0.5 2242 3.6	0142 0.5 0738 2.7 1356 0.4 2006 2.7	0413 5.0 1013 0.6 1634 5.2 2245 0.4	0436 4.1 1106 0.5 1702 4.1 2334 0.4	**1 SA**
0410 0.5 1024 5.7 1630 0.5 2246 5.8	0014 0.6 0615 7.0 1236 0.6 1838 7.2	0002 0.9 0624 9.6 1226 0.8 1845 9.8	0147 1.0 0719 13.4 1413 0.8 1941 13.7	0458 0.4 1142 4.2 1718 0.5	0457 0.4 1111 3.4 1724 0.4 2333 3.6	0235 0.4 0827 2.7 1441 0.4 2051 2.8	0503 5.1 1100 0.5 1722 5.3 2333 0.2	0526 4.2 1157 0.4 1751 4.2	**2 SU** ●
0500 0.3 1115 5.7 1718 0.5 2335 5.9	0106 0.4 0706 7.1 1325 0.5 1927 7.3	0054 0.8 0715 9.7 1315 0.8 1935 9.8	0240 0.7 0810 13.6 1503 0.7 2030 13.8	0005 4.3 0549 0.3 1234 4.2 1806 0.5	0549 0.3 1205 3.4 1814 0.5	0327 0.4 0917 2.7 1525 0.3 2136 2.8	0553 5.2 1148 0.5 1810 5.3	0024 0.4 0615 4.2 1246 0.3 1841 4.3	**3 M**
0551 0.3 1206 5.7 1807 0.6	0156 0.4 0756 7.0 1413 0.6 2016 7.2	0145 0.8 0805 9.5 1402 0.9 2024 9.6	0328 0.7 0859 13.5 1548 0.8 2117 13.6	0054 4.4 0641 0.2 1327 4.2 1856 0.6	0023 3.7 0640 0.2 1300 3.4 1905 0.5	0417 0.4 1006 2.6 1609 0.4 2221 2.8	0021 0.2 0642 5.2 1236 0.6 1900 5.3	0114 0.4 0702 4.2 1335 0.4 1930 4.2	**4 TU**
0025 5.8 0643 0.4 1259 5.5 1857 0.8	0245 0.5 0844 6.9 1501 0.8 2104 7.0	0233 0.9 0852 9.3 1448 1.1 2112 9.3	0412 0.8 0945 13.3 1627 1.0 2203 13.3	0143 4.4 0733 0.3 1420 4.1 1946 0.8	0113 3.7 0731 0.2 1354 3.3 1957 0.6	0508 0.5 1055 2.5 1654 0.5 2307 2.8	0110 0.4 0733 5.0 1324 0.8 1950 5.1	0203 0.4 0750 4.1 1424 0.4 2018 4.1	**5 W**
0116 5.7 0736 0.6 1351 5.2 1949 1.1	0333 0.8 0932 6.6 1548 1.1 2153 6.7	0319 1.2 0939 8.9 1533 1.5 2159 8.9	0450 1.1 1032 12.8 1704 1.4 2250 12.7	0236 4.3 0827 0.4 1515 3.9 2039 1.0	0205 3.6 0824 0.2 1451 3.1 2051 0.7	0600 0.6 1147 2.4 1740 0.6 2355 2.7	0200 0.6 0824 4.8 1415 1.1 2042 4.8	0251 0.5 0839 4.0 1512 0.5 2109 4.0	**6 TH**
0209 5.5 0830 0.8 1447 5.0 2045 1.4	0422 1.1 1021 6.2 1637 1.4 2243 6.3	0406 1.6 1026 8.5 1623 1.9 2248 8.5	0527 1.6 1118 12.1 1742 1.9 2337 12.1	0330 4.2 0924 0.6 1614 3.7 2136 1.2	0259 3.5 0921 0.3 1551 3.0 2149 0.8	0655 0.8 1242 2.2 1830 0.7	0253 0.9 0917 4.5 1509 1.4 2136 4.5	0342 0.7 0929 3.8 1603 0.7 2201 3.8	**7 F**
0305 5.2 0930 1.1 1546 4.7 2145 1.6	0512 1.5 1113 5.9 1730 1.7 2337 6.0	0458 2.0 1118 8.0 1720 2.4 2343 8.0	0606 2.0 1206 11.4 1823 2.4	0430 4.0 1024 0.8 1715 3.5 2238 1.4	0356 3.4 1019 0.4 1651 2.9 2251 0.8	0048 2.5 0755 0.9 1344 2.1 1924 0.8	0349 1.2 1014 4.3 1609 1.6 2236 4.2	0436 0.9 1023 3.7 1658 0.8 2258 3.7	**8 SA**
0406 5.0 1032 1.4 1651 4.6 2252 1.8	0609 1.8 1210 5.6 1830 2.0	0558 2.4 1218 7.7 1826 2.7	0027 11.4 0649 2.5 1258 10.9 1911 2.9	0533 3.8 1125 1.0 1817 3.4 2344 1.5	0456 3.3 1121 0.6 1752 2.9 2355 0.9	0151 2.4 0900 1.0 1451 2.1 2025 0.9	0452 1.4 1117 4.1 1718 1.8 2344 4.0	0533 1.0 1121 3.5 1757 1.0	**9 SU**
0512 4.8 1137 1.6 1759 4.5	0037 5.7 0711 2.0 1315 5.5 1938 2.1	0045 7.7 0705 2.7 1325 7.5 1936 2.8	0124 10.9 0742 3.0 1400 10.5 2014 3.2	0637 3.7 1229 1.2 1918 3.4	0557 3.2 1224 0.6 1851 2.9	0303 2.3 1006 1.0 1557 2.1 2134 1.0	0600 1.6 1227 4.0 1832 1.8	0000 3.5 0636 1.1 1224 3.4 1902 1.1	**10 M**
0002 1.9 0622 4.7 1241 1.7 1903 4.6	0144 5.5 0818 2.1 1423 5.5 2045 2.1	0153 7.6 0813 2.8 1433 7.6 2040 2.8	0229 10.6 0851 3.2 1509 10.5 2129 3.2	0052 1.5 0741 3.6 1330 1.2 2017 3.5	0057 0.9 0657 3.1 1322 0.7 1944 2.9	0417 2.2 1104 0.9 1657 2.1 2245 1.0	0056 3.9 0707 1.7 1331 4.1 1938 1.7	0106 3.4 0741 1.2 1331 3.4 2008 1.1	**11 TU**
0108 1.9 0727 4.7 1339 1.6 1957 4.8	0251 5.6 0920 2.0 1526 5.6 2145 2.0	0259 7.7 0915 2.7 1533 7.9 2137 2.6	0339 10.6 1003 3.1 1615 10.8 2239 2.9	0200 1.4 0841 3.6 1427 1.2 2110 3.6	0155 0.8 0754 3.1 1416 0.7 2033 3.0	0519 2.2 1154 0.9 1748 2.2 2348 1.0	0200 4.0 0804 1.6 1425 4.2 2033 1.6	0212 3.5 0842 1.1 1435 3.5 2107 1.1	**12 W**
0206 1.7 0821 4.7 1428 1.6 2043 4.9	0351 5.7 1014 1.8 1619 5.9 2236 1.7	0357 8.0 1007 2.5 1624 8.2 2227 2.4	0442 11.0 1109 2.7 1712 11.3 2337 2.5	0258 1.3 0935 3.6 1515 1.2 2157 3.7	0248 0.8 0847 3.1 1504 0.7 2118 3.1	0610 2.2 1238 0.8 1835 2.3	0254 4.0 0853 1.5 1512 4.3 2120 1.4	0308 3.5 0935 1.0 1529 3.6 2157 1.0	**13 TH**
0253 1.6 0906 4.8 1510 1.5 2123 5.1	0442 5.9 1100 1.6 1705 6.1 2321 1.5	0446 8.2 1053 2.3 1709 8.5 2312 2.2	0536 11.4 1203 2.3 1800 11.8	0347 1.2 1022 3.6 1559 1.1 2238 3.8	0335 0.7 0935 3.1 1547 0.7 2200 3.2	0040 0.9 0655 2.2 1317 0.7 1917 2.4	0340 4.2 0937 1.4 1554 4.5 2203 1.2	0354 3.6 1020 1.0 1615 3.7 2239 1.0	**14 F**
0334 1.4 0945 4.9 1548 1.4 2158 5.2	0525 6.1 1140 1.5 1745 6.3	0530 8.4 1135 2.1 1751 8.7 2354 2.1	0027 2.1 0622 11.7 1251 2.0 1842 12.1	0430 1.1 1103 3.6 1639 1.0 2239 3.9	0418 0.6 1018 3.1 1625 0.7 2239 3.3	0124 0.8 0734 2.3 1353 0.7 1955 2.5	0423 4.3 1018 1.3 1634 4.6 2243 1.1	0436 3.7 1100 0.9 1656 3.7 2318 0.9	**15 SA**

● ● Time: UT. For British Summer Time (shaded) March 26th to October 29th ADD ONE HOUR ● ●

JULY 2000 TIDE TABLES

•• Time: UT. For British Summer Time (shaded) March 26th to October 29TH ADD ONE HOUR ••

	HOLYHEAD		MILFORD HAVEN		SWANSEA		AVONMOUTH		DUBLIN		BELFAST		LONDON-DERRY		GALWAY		COBH	
	Time	m	Time	m	Time	m	Time	m	Time	m	Time	m	Time	m	Time	m	Time	m
16 SU O	0410	1.3	0000	1.4	0611	8.5	0112	1.9	0510	1.0	0457	0.6	0204	0.8	0503	4.4	0512	3.7
	1021	5.0	0604	6.2	1213	2.0	0703	11.9	1140	3.7	1058	3.1	0809	2.3	1056	1.2	1138	0.8
	1621	1.3	1217	1.3	1830	8.8	1333	1.8	1717	1.0	1700	0.7	1426	0.7	1712	4.7	1734	3.8
	2232	5.3	1822	6.4			1921	12.3	2349	3.9	2314	3.4	2030	2.6	2321	0.9	2354	0.9
17 M	0444	1.2	0037	1.3	0033	1.9	0154	1.7	0547	0.9	0533	0.6	0239	0.8	0541	4.4	0548	3.8
	1054	5.1	0640	6.3	0648	8.6	0740	12.1	1215	3.7	1135	3.1	0840	2.3	1133	1.1	1214	0.8
	1654	1.2	1252	1.3	1249	1.9	1413	1.7	1754	0.9	1732	0.7	1457	0.7	1749	4.7	1810	3.8
	2305	5.4	1857	6.5	1906	8.9	1956	12.4			2348	3.4	2102	2.6	2357	0.9		
18 TU	0517	1.1	0112	1.2	0109	1.8	0233	1.6	0023	4.0	0606	0.6	0312	0.7	0617	4.5	0030	0.9
	1127	5.1	0714	6.3	0724	8.6	0813	12.2	0622	0.9	1209	3.1	0909	2.3	1208	1.1	0622	3.8
	1727	1.2	1325	1.2	1322	1.8	1449	1.7	1249	3.7	1804	0.7	1526	0.7	1825	4.7	1249	0.8
	2339	5.4	1930	6.5	1941	8.8	2029	12.5	1829	0.9			2133	2.6			1846	3.8
19 W	0551	1.1	0146	1.2	0143	1.7	0309	1.6	0057	3.9	0020	3.4	0346	0.7	0031	0.9	0105	0.9
	1201	5.1	0746	6.3	0757	8.6	0846	12.3	0657	0.8	0639	0.5	0940	2.3	0652	4.4	0657	3.8
	1801	1.2	1358	1.3	1354	1.8	1522	1.7	1324	3.6	1243	3.2	1556	0.7	1242	1.2	1324	0.8
			2003	6.5	2014	8.8	2102	12.5	1904	0.9	1838	0.7	2205	2.6	1901	4.7	1921	3.8
20 TH	0013	5.4	0220	1.2	0215	1.7	0342	1.6	0133	3.9	0053	3.4	0421	0.7	0106	0.9	0140	0.9
	0625	1.1	0818	6.2	0828	8.5	0919	12.2	0730	0.8	0712	0.5	1014	2.3	0727	4.4	0731	3.8
	1236	5.0	1431	1.3	1424	1.8	1554	1.8	1401	3.6	1318	3.2	1629	0.7	1318	1.2	1359	0.8
	1836	1.3	2037	6.4	2046	8.7	2136	12.3	1939	1.0	1915	0.7	2239	2.6	1937	4.6	1956	3.8
21 F	0050	5.3	0254	1.3	0246	1.7	0414	1.7	0210	3.8	0127	3.4	0500	0.8	0141	1.0	0216	0.9
	0702	1.2	0852	6.2	0900	8.4	0953	12.1	0805	0.8	0750	0.5	1051	2.3	0803	4.3	0807	3.7
	1313	4.9	1506	1.5	1454	1.9	1623	1.9	1441	3.5	1357	3.2	1706	0.7	1355	1.3	1435	0.9
	1914	1.4	2112	6.3	2119	8.5	2211	12.0	2015	1.0	1955	0.7	2316	2.6	2015	4.5	2033	3.8
22 SA	0128	5.2	0330	1.5	0319	1.8	0444	2.0	0250	3.7	0206	3.4	0541	0.8	0219	1.1	0254	0.9
	0741	1.2	0929	6.0	0933	8.3	1027	11.7	0842	0.9	0830	0.5	1133	2.2	0842	4.2	0846	3.7
	1353	4.8	1542	1.6	1529	2.0	1653	2.2	1524	3.5	1439	3.1	1747	0.8	1436	1.5	1513	0.9
	1955	1.5	2151	6.2	2157	8.3	2247	11.6	2057	1.1	2039	0.8	2358	2.6	2056	4.3	2114	3.7
23 SU	0210	5.1	0409	1.7	0357	2.0	0515	2.3	0333	3.6	0248	3.4	0627	0.9	0301	1.2	0337	1.0
	0824	1.3	1009	5.9	1014	8.1	1105	11.3	0927	0.9	0915	0.6	1221	2.1	0925	4.1	0930	3.6
	1439	4.7	1624	1.8	1612	2.3	1726	2.5	1612	3.4	1525	3.1	1834	0.8	1522	1.6	1558	1.0
	2043	1.7	2236	6.0	2242	8.1	2327	11.2	2145	1.2	2127	0.9			2142	4.2	2200	3.6
24 M	0258	5.0	0455	1.8	0445	2.2	0551	2.6	0422	3.6	0336	3.3	0048	2.5	0350	1.3	0427	1.1
	0916	1.4	1058	5.7	1104	7.8	1147	10.9	1019	1.0	1007	0.7	0719	0.9	1015	4.0	1015	3.5
	1533	4.6	1715	2.0	1707	2.5	1806	2.8	1706	3.4	1618	3.1	1318	2.1	1619	1.7	1652	1.1
	2141	1.8	2330	5.8	2337	7.9			2243	1.3	2223	1.0	1930	0.9	2237	4.1	2255	3.5
25 TU	0356	4.8	0551	2.0	0545	2.5	0015	10.8	0518	3.5	0432	3.3	0149	2.4	0448	1.5	0525	1.1
	1017	1.5	1200	5.6	1207	7.7	0636	2.9	1121	1.1	1105	0.8	0821	1.0	1116	4.0	1120	3.4
	1639	4.6	1820	2.2	1819	2.7	1242	10.6	1807	3.4	1717	3.1	1430	2.0	1727	1.7	1756	1.1
	2250	1.8					1858	3.1	2350	1.3	2327	1.0	2038	0.9	2345	4.0	2358	3.5
26 W	0506	4.8	0036	5.7	0045	7.8	0123	10.6	0624	3.5	0536	3.2	0305	2.3	0557	1.5	0633	1.1
	1127	1.5	0700	2.1	0700	2.5	0740	3.1	1226	1.1	1210	0.8	0933	1.0	1227	4.0	1228	3.4
	1754	4.7	1313	5.5	1322	7.7	1359	10.6	1915	3.5	1824	3.1	1557	2.0	1843	1.6	1909	1.1
			1938	2.1	1938	2.6	2015	3.3					2202	0.9				
27 TH	0003	1.7	0151	5.7	0200	7.9	0245	10.8	0057	1.3	0038	1.0	0426	2.4	0059	4.1	0109	3.5
	0619	4.8	0818	2.0	0816	2.4	0911	3.0	0735	3.6	0646	3.2	1050	0.9	0709	1.4	0746	1.1
	1236	1.4	1430	5.7	1438	8.0	1521	11.0	1330	1.0	1319	0.8	1713	2.2	1336	4.2	1342	3.5
	1903	4.8	2058	1.9	2052	2.3	2153	2.9	2021	3.6	1931	3.2	2326	0.8	1952	1.4	2023	0.9
28 F	0112	1.5	0305	6.0	0313	8.3	0400	11.4	0202	1.1	0149	0.9	0536	2.5	0207	4.3	0221	3.6
	0728	5.0	0931	1.7	0926	2.0	1036	2.4	0843	3.8	0758	3.2	1155	0.8	0813	1.2	0856	0.9
	1340	1.2	1539	6.1	1546	8.6	1632	11.8	1430	0.9	1425	0.8	1814	2.4	1437	4.5	1453	3.7
	2003	5.1	2208	1.5	2158	1.8	2315	2.2	2120	3.8	2036	3.3			2052	1.0	2130	0.7
29 SA	0214	1.2	0412	6.3	0419	8.7	0509	12.2	0303	0.8	0254	0.8	0035	0.7	0307	4.6	0326	3.8
	0829	5.3	1035	1.3	1027	1.5	1151	1.8	0945	3.9	0906	3.3	0635	2.6	0909	1.0	0957	0.7
	1437	1.0	1641	6.5	1646	9.1	1738	12.6	1527	0.8	1525	0.7	1250	0.6	1530	4.8	1554	3.9
	2057	5.4	2309	1.0	2258	1.3			2215	4.1	2134	3.5	1906	2.6	2145	0.7	2227	0.5
30 SU	0309	0.8	0512	6.7	0518	9.2	0030	1.6	0358	0.6	0352	0.6	0134	0.6	0401	4.9	0421	4.0
	0924	5.5	1132	0.9	1124	1.1	0613	12.8	1042	4.1	1006	3.4	0728	2.7	1001	0.7	1052	0.5
	1529	0.8	1736	6.9	1742	9.5	1302	1.3	1618	0.7	1620	0.6	1339	0.5	1621	5.1	1649	4.1
	2146	5.7			2354	1.0	1837	13.2	2306	4.3	2228	3.6	1953	2.8	2235	0.5	2321	0.4
31 M	0400	0.5	0004	0.7	0613	9.5	0136	1.1	0451	0.4	0445	0.4	0227	0.5	0452	5.1	0512	4.1
	1015	5.7	0605	7.0	1215	0.8	0710	13.3	1135	4.2	1103	3.4	0817	2.7	1049	0.5	1144	0.3
	1618	0.6	1224	0.6	1834	9.8	1402	0.8	1707	0.6	1712	0.5	1424	0.4	1709	5.3	1739	4.2
	2233	5.9	1827	7.2			1930	13.7	2354	4.4	2318	3.7	2037	2.9	2322	0.1		

WEST COAST ENGLAND, WALES & IRELAND Time Zone UT
Holyhead * Milford Haven * Swansea * Avonmouth * Dublin * Belfast * Londonderry * Galway * Cobh

TIDE TABLES AUGUST 2000

HOLYHEAD		MILFORD HAVEN		SWANSEA		AVONMOUTH		DUBLIN		BELFAST		LONDONDERRY		GALWAY		COBH		
Time	m	Time	m	Time	m	Time	m	Time	m	Time	m	Time	m	Time	m	Time	m	
0449	0.3	0055	0.4	0046	0.7	0232	0.7	0540	0.3	0536	0.3	0315	0.4	0541	5.2	0011	0.3	1 TU
1103	5.7	0655	7.1	0704	9.7	0800	13.6	1225	4.2	1155	3.4	0903	2.7	1136	0.4	0601	4.2	●
1704	0.5	1313	0.4	1304	0.7	1454	0.6	1754	0.6	1800	0.5	1508	0.4	1757	5.4	1233	0.3	
2321	6.0	1915	7.4	1924	9.9	2019	13.9					2119	2.9			1828	4.3	
0537	0.2	0144	0.3	0134	0.6	0321	0.5	0041	4.5	0007	3.8	0403	0.4	0008	0.1	0100	0.3	2 W
1151	5.7	0742	7.2	0751	9.7	0847	13.8	0628	0.2	0624	0.2	0948	2.7	0628	5.2	0648	4.3	
1750	0.6	1359	0.4	1348	0.7	1539	0.5	1312	4.2	1245	3.4	1551	0.4	1220	0.4	1321	0.2	
		2001	7.3	2009	9.8	2104	14.0	1839	0.6	1848	0.5	2200	2.9	1844	5.4	1915	4.3	
0007	6.0	0230	0.4	0218	0.7	0402	0.5	0127	4.5	0055	3.8	0448	0.5	0053	0.2	0146	0.3	3 TH
0624	0.3	0827	7.0	0834	9.5	0930	13.6	0716	0.3	0712	0.2	1032	2.6	0715	5.1	0733	4.2	
1238	5.6	1443	0.6	1430	0.9	1617	0.7	1400	4.1	1334	3.3	1633	0.4	1305	0.6	1406	0.3	
1836	0.7	2045	7.2	2053	9.6	2147	13.7	1925	0.7	1934	0.6	2242	2.9	1930	5.2	2000	4.2	
0054	5.8	0312	0.6	0257	1.0	0437	0.9	0213	4.4	0142	3.7	0533	0.6	0138	0.4	0231	0.5	4 F
0712	0.5	0909	6.8	0915	9.2	1011	13.2	0803	0.4	0759	0.3	1116	2.4	0800	4.9	0818	4.1	
1325	5.3	1525	0.9	1509	1.2	1649	1.1	1446	3.9	1422	3.2	1715	0.5	1351	0.8	1451	0.4	
1922	0.9	2128	6.8	2133	9.2	2227	13.1	2011	0.9	2021	0.6	2324	2.7	2018	4.9	2045	4.1	
0141	5.6	0354	1.0	0336	1.4	0508	1.4	0301	4.2	0231	3.6	0618	0.8	0224	0.7	0316	0.6	5 SA
0800	0.8	0952	6.4	0956	8.8	1051	12.5	0852	0.7	0847	0.4	1202	2.3	0848	4.6	0903	4.0	
1412	5.1	1606	1.3	1550	1.7	1719	1.7	1535	3.7	1512	3.1	1759	0.7	1438	1.2	1536	0.6	
2010	1.3	2212	6.4	2215	8.7	2308	12.3	2100	1.1	2112	0.7			2106	4.6	2131	3.9	
0230	5.3	0436	1.4	0418	1.9	0536	2.0	0353	4.0	0323	3.4	0009	2.5	0312	1.1	0402	0.8	6 SU
0850	1.2	1036	6.0	1039	8.3	1130	11.6	0943	0.9	0939	0.5	0706	0.9	0937	4.3	0949	3.8	
1503	4.8	1650	1.7	1636	2.2	1748	2.4	1627	3.6	1604	3.0	1253	2.2	1530	1.5	1621	0.8	
2103	1.6	2257	6.0	2301	8.2	2348	11.4	2155	1.3	2206	0.9	1847	0.8	2158	4.2	2219	3.7	
0322	4.9	0520	1.9	0506	2.4	0606	2.7	0451	3.8	0418	3.3	0100	2.3	0407	1.5	0451	1.1	7 M
0945	1.6	1124	5.6	1129	7.8	1212	10.8	1039	1.2	1034	0.7	0801	1.0	1033	4.1	1039	3.5	
1559	4.6	1739	2.1	1732	2.7	1822	3.0	1724	3.4	1700	2.9	1354	2.1	1631	1.8	1712	1.1	
2205	1.9	2348	5.6	2354	7.7			2258	1.5	2308	0.9	1942	1.0	2300	3.9	2313	3.4	
0425	4.6	0614	2.2	0606	2.9	0032	10.6	0554	3.6	0518	3.1	0209	2.1	0513	1.8	0546	1.3	8 TU
1049	1.9	1223	5.3	1231	7.5	0643	3.3	1141	1.4	1136	0.9	0906	1.1	1139	3.9	1137	3.4	
1707	4.4	1843	2.4	1841	3.1	1302	10.1	1827	3.4	1800	2.9	1508	2.0	1748	1.9	1812	1.2	
2318	2.1					1906	3.7					2049	1.1					
0540	4.4	0053	5.3	0100	7.4	0130	10.0	0009	1.6	0015	1.0	0345	2.0	0016	3.7	0016	3.3	9 W
1200	2.0	0725	2.5	0721	3.2	0739	3.9	0703	3.4	0620	3.0	1018	1.1	0630	1.9	0652	1.4	
1822	4.5	1336	5.2	1344	7.3	1412	9.8	1247	1.5	1241	0.9	1622	2.1	1253	3.9	1245	3.3	
		2003	2.5	1956	3.2	2027	4.0	1932	3.4	1900	2.9	2211	1.1	1910	1.9	1922	1.3	
0036	2.1	0211	5.2	0215	7.3	0248	9.8	0126	1.5	0121	1.0	0504	2.0	0134	3.7	0129	3.2	10 TH
0700	4.4	0844	2.4	0836	3.2	0915	3.9	0809	3.4	0721	3.0	1120	1.0	0740	1.9	0802	1.3	
1309	2.0	1454	5.3	1457	7.5	1534	10.0	1353	1.5	1342	1.0	1724	2.2	1359	4.0	1359	3.3	
1930	4.6	2118	2.3	2104	3.1	2201	3.7	2034	3.5	1956	3.0	2327	1.1	2016	1.7	2031	1.3	
0144	2.0	0326	5.4	0325	7.5	0409	10.2	0236	1.4	0221	0.9	0600	2.1	0238	3.8	0236	3.3	11 F
0804	4.5	0948	2.2	0939	3.0	1034	3.3	0911	3.5	0819	3.0	1212	0.9	0837	1.8	0903	1.2	
1406	1.9	1557	5.6	1557	7.9	1643	10.8	1451	1.4	1436	0.9	1814	2.3	1453	4.1	1502	3.4	
2022	4.8	2216	2.0	2202	2.8	2306	2.9	2130	3.6	2047	3.1			2108	1.5	2127	1.2	
0236	1.7	0423	5.6	0422	7.8	0512	10.9	0330	1.3	0312	0.8	0025	1.0	0327	4.0	0329	3.4	12 SA
0853	4.7	1039	1.9	1030	2.6	1133	2.6	1004	3.5	0910	3.0	0644	2.2	0924	1.6	0952	1.1	
1452	1.7	1646	6.0	1647	8.2	1737	11.5	1539	1.2	1523	0.9	1255	0.8	1538	4.3	1552	3.5	
2103	5.1	2303	1.7	2251	2.5			2216	3.8	2133	3.2	1857	2.5	2151	1.3	2213	1.1	
0318	1.5	0508	5.9	0509	8.2	0000	2.2	0415	1.1	0357	0.7	0111	0.9	0410	4.2	0412	3.6	13 SU
0931	4.9	1121	1.6	1114	2.3	0602	11.5	1048	3.6	0956	3.1	0721	2.3	1005	1.4	1035	0.9	
1529	1.5	1727	6.3	1730	8.6	1224	2.1	1621	1.1	1603	0.8	1333	0.7	1618	4.5	1634	3.7	
2139	5.2	2343	1.5	2333	2.1	1822	12.1	2256	3.9	2215	3.3	1936	2.6	2229	1.1	2254	0.9	
0352	1.3	0546	6.2	0551	8.5	0049	1.8	0453	1.0	0436	0.6	0149	0.8	0448	4.3	0451	3.7	14 M
1004	5.0	1159	1.4	1153	2.0	0645	12.0	1125	3.6	1036	3.1	0754	2.4	1041	1.2	1115	0.8	
1602	1.3	1803	6.6	1809	8.8	1312	1.8	1659	1.0	1639	0.8	1407	0.7	1654	4.6	1712	3.8	
2211	5.4					1901	12.5	2330	3.9	2251	3.3	2010	2.7	2303	0.9	2331	0.8	
0424	1.1	0019	1.2	0012	1.8	0135	1.6	0527	0.9	0511	0.6	0224	0.7	0523	4.5	0527	3.8	15 TU
1035	5.1	0621	6.4	0627	8.7	0721	12.2	1157	3.7	1112	3.1	0824	2.4	1115	1.0	1152	0.7	O
1633	1.2	1228	1.3	1228	1.8	1355	1.6	1733	0.9	1711	0.7	1439	0.6	1730	4.7	1749	3.9	
2243	5.5	1837	6.6	1845	9.0	1937	12.7			2324	3.4	2042	2.7	2336	0.7			

● ● Time: UT. For British Summer Time (shaded) March 26th to October 29th ADD ONE HOUR ● ●

AUGUST 2000 TIDE TABLES

•• Time: UT. For British Summer Time (shaded) March 26th to October 29TH ADD ONE HOUR ••

	HOLYHEAD		MILFORD HAVEN		SWANSEA		AVONMOUTH		DUBLIN		BELFAST		LONDON-DERRY		GALWAY		COBH	
	Time	m	Time	m	Time	m	Time	m	Time	m	Time	m	Time	m	Time	m	Time	m
16 W	0455	1.0	0053	1.1	0048	1.6	0218	1.5	0002	4.0	0542	0.5	0257	0.7	0556	0.9	0008	0.8
	1106	5.2	0653	6.5	0701	8.8	0755	12.5	0559	0.8	1145	3.2	0853	2.5	1147	0.9	0602	3.9
	1705	1.1	1305	1.1	1301	1.6	1435	1.6	1227	3.7	1742	0.6	1508	0.6	1803	4.8	1228	0.7
	2315	5.5	1909	6.7	1918	9.1	2010	12.8	1804	0.9	2354	3.4	2112	2.8			1824	4.0
17 TH	0527	0.9	0125	1.0	0121	1.4	0256	1.4	0033	4.0	0613	0.5	0329	0.7	0007	0.7	0044	0.7
	1137	5.2	0724	6.6	0733	8.9	0827	12.7	0627	0.7	1216	3.2	0921	2.5	0628	4.6	0636	3.9
	1737	1.0	1338	1.1	1331	1.5	1511	1.5	1257	3.7	1814	0.6	1536	0.6	1218	0.9	1303	0.7
	2349	5.5	1942	6.8	1950	9.1	2043	12.9	1835	0.8			2141	2.8	1836	4.8	1858	4.0
18 F	0600	0.9	0158	1.0	0151	1.3	0331	1.3	0104	4.0	0025	3.4	0401	0.7	0039	0.6	0119	0.7
	1210	5.2	0757	6.6	0803	9.0	0900	12.8	0657	0.7	0645	0.4	0952	2.5	0700	4.6	0709	3.9
	1810	1.1	1410	1.1	1400	1.4	1544	1.5	1330	3.7	1249	3.2	1609	0.6	1251	0.9	1338	0.7
			2015	6.8	2021	9.1	2117	12.9	1906	0.8	1849	0.6	2213	2.8	1911	4.8	1932	4.0
19 SA	0024	5.5	0232	1.1	0221	1.3	0403	1.4	0138	3.9	0058	3.5	0436	0.7	0112	0.7	0154	0.8
	0633	0.9	0830	6.5	0834	8.9	0933	12.7	0728	0.7	0720	0.4	1027	2.4	0734	4.6	0744	3.9
	1245	5.2	1444	1.2	1429	1.5	1613	1.7	1406	3.7	1325	3.3	1644	0.6	1327	1.0	1412	0.7
	1846	1.1	2048	6.7	2053	9.0	2151	12.6	1940	0.8	1927	0.6	2248	2.7	1947	4.7	2007	3.9
20 SU	0100	5.4	0304	1.2	0251	1.4	0431	1.7	0216	3.9	0136	3.5	0515	0.7	0148	0.8	0229	0.8
	0710	1.0	0904	6.4	0906	8.8	1006	12.3	0804	0.7	0759	0.4	1105	2.4	0811	4.5	0820	3.9
	1322	5.1	1518	1.4	1502	1.6	1639	2.0	1446	3.7	1405	3.3	1724	0.7	1405	1.2	1448	0.8
	1925	1.3	2125	6.5	2128	8.8	2225	12.1	2020	0.9	2009	0.7	2330	2.6	2027	4.5	2045	3.8
21 M	0139	5.3	0342	1.4	0326	1.7	0457	2.0	0259	3.8	0218	3.4	0558	0.8	0227	1.0	0307	0.9
	0751	1.2	0942	6.2	0944	8.5	1040	11.8	0847	0.8	0842	0.5	1148	2.2	0852	4.3	0901	3.8
	1404	4.9	1557	1.6	1540	1.9	1706	2.3	1533	3.6	1450	3.2	1811	0.8	1448	1.4	1529	0.9
	2011	1.5	2206	6.2	2210	8.5	2300	11.5	2106	1.0	2056	0.8			2112	4.4	2129	3.7
22 TU	0225	5.1	0423	1.7	0409	2.0	0527	2.4	0350	3.7	0306	3.4	0018	2.5	0313	1.3	0353	1.0
	0840	1.4	1027	5.9	1030	8.2	1118	11.2	0939	1.0	0932	0.7	0648	0.9	0939	4.2	0948	3.6
	1454	4.8	1644	1.9	1630	2.3	1740	2.7	1627	3.5	1542	3.2	1240	2.1	1542	1.6	1620	1.0
	2106	1.7	2257	5.9	2303	8.1	2343	10.9	2205	1.2	2151	0.9	1906	0.9	2206	4.1	2221	3.6
23 W	0322	4.9	0515	2.0	0505	2.5	0606	2.8	0449	3.6	0403	3.3	0119	2.3	0410	1.5	0449	1.2
	0941	1.6	1125	5.6	1131	7.8	1206	10.7	1043	1.1	1030	0.8	0746	1.0	1039	4.0	1046	3.5
	1600	4.6	1746	2.2	1740	2.8	1826	3.1	1731	3.5	1643	3.1	1349	2.0	1651	1.7	1724	1.1
	2218	1.8							2318	1.3	2256	1.0	2015	1.0	2315	4.0	2325	3.4
24 TH	0436	4.7	0003	5.6	0012	7.7	0045	10.4	0600	3.6	0511	3.2	0242	2.2	0524	1.7	0600	1.2
	1056	1.7	0627	2.2	0624	2.8	0701	3.3	1158	1.2	1142	1.0	0858	1.0	1155	4.0	1157	3.4
	1724	4.6	1242	5.5	1252	7.6	1321	10.3	1847	3.5	1755	3.1	1533	2.0	1818	1.7	1843	1.2
	2342	1.8	1913	2.3	1912	2.9	1938	3.6					2153	1.0				
25 F	0602	4.7	0127	5.5	0137	7.6	0215	10.4	0037	1.3	0015	1.1	0424	2.2	0038	4.0	0042	3.4
	1217	1.7	0757	2.2	0757	2.8	0837	3.5	0721	3.6	0630	3.2	1027	1.0	0648	1.7	0723	1.2
	1845	4.8	1410	5.6	1419	7.8	1454	10.6	1312	1.2	1300	1.0	1708	2.2	1316	4.1	1321	3.4
			2046	2.1	2039	2.6	2131	3.3	2001	3.7	1910	3.2	2333	0.9	1940	1.5	2007	1.0
26 SA	0100	1.6	0253	5.7	0301	8.0	0342	10.9	0150	1.1	0135	1.0	0536	2.4	0156	4.2	0205	3.5
	0720	4.9	0921	1.9	0915	2.4	1016	2.8	0835	3.8	0750	3.2	1142	0.8	0803	1.4	0841	1.0
	1329	1.5	1530	6.0	1535	8.3	1616	11.4	1419	1.1	1413	0.9	1807	2.4	1424	4.4	1440	3.6
	1951	5.1	2201	1.6	2151	2.1	2300	2.5	2107	3.9	2019	3.3			2045	1.1	2118	0.8
27 SU	0206	1.2	0405	5.9	0412	8.5	0458	11.8	0255	0.9	0242	0.8	0039	0.7	0259	4.5	0313	3.7
	0824	5.2	1027	1.4	1020	1.8	1138	2.0	0939	3.9	0900	3.3	0632	2.5	0901	1.1	0945	0.7
	1428	1.2	1633	6.5	1638	9.0	1727	12.4	1518	0.9	1515	0.8	1237	0.7	1521	4.8	1543	3.9
	2046	5.4	2302	1.1	2252	1.5			2204	4.1	2119	3.5	1855	2.7	2137	0.7	2216	0.6
28 M	0301	0.8	0503	6.6	0511	9.1	0019	1.7	0351	0.6	0340	0.6	0132	0.6	0352	4.8	0409	4.0
	0916	5.5	1122	1.0	1115	1.2	0604	12.7	1036	4.1	1000	3.4	0720	2.7	0951	0.8	1041	0.5
	1518	0.9	1727	7.0	1733	9.5	1251	1.3	1609	0.8	1608	0.7	1324	0.5	1610	5.1	1637	4.1
	2134	5.7	2354	0.6	2345	1.0	1828	13.3	2255	4.3	2213	3.6	1938	2.9	2224	0.3	2308	0.4
29 TU	0349	0.5	0554	7.0	0603	9.6	0125	0.9	0442	0.4	0431	0.4	0218	0.5	0440	5.1	0459	4.2
	1003	5.7	1212	0.6	1204	0.8	0700	13.4	1126	4.2	1052	3.4	0804	2.8	1036	0.5	1131	0.3
	1603	0.7	1814	7.3	1822	9.9	1350	0.7	1656	0.7	1656	0.6	1408	0.4	1656	5.4	1726	4.3
	2218	6.0					1919	13.8	2341	4.5	2301	3.7	2018	3.0	2306	0.1	2357	0.3
30 W	0434	0.3	0042	0.4	0033	0.7	0219	0.5	0527	0.4	0518	0.3	0301	0.4	0524	5.2	0545	4.3
	1047	5.7	0639	7.2	0649	9.8	0747	13.8	1211	4.2	1139	3.5	0846	2.8	1118	0.3	1218	0.2
	1646	0.5	1257	0.4	1248	0.6	1439	0.4	1739	0.6	1741	0.5	1449	0.4	1740	5.5	1812	4.4
	2302	6.1	1859	7.5	1907	10.0	2003	14.1			2347	3.8	2057	3.0	2348	0.0		
31 TH ●	0518	0.2	0126	0.3	0116	0.6	0305	0.3	0024	4.5	0603	0.2	0341	0.4	0608	5.3	0042	0.3
	1130	5.7	0722	7.3	0731	9.9	0829	13.9	0610	0.2	1223	3.4	0926	2.7	1200	0.3	0629	4.4
	1728	0.5	1339	0.4	1328	0.6	1521	0.3	1252	4.2	1824	0.5	1529	0.4	1823	5.4	1303	0.2
	2345	6.0	1940	7.4	1948	10.0	2045	14.1	1819	0.6			2134	3.0			1855	4.4

WEST COAST ENGLAND, WALES & IRELAND Time Zone UT
Holyhead * Milford Haven * Swansea * Avonmouth * Dublin * Belfast * Londonderry * Galway * Cobh

TIDE TABLES SEPTEMBER 2000

Day	HOLYHEAD Time m	MILFORD HAVEN Time m	SWANSEA Time m	AVONMOUTH Time m	DUBLIN Time m	BELFAST Time m	LONDONDERRY Time m	GALWAY Time m	COBH Time m
1 F	0600 0.3	0206 0.4	0154 0.7	0343 0.4	0105 4.5	0031 3.8	0420 0.5	0029 0.1	0124 0.3
	1212 5.6	0803 7.2	0810 9.7	0907 13.8	0652 0.3	0645 0.2	1004 2.6	0651 5.2	0711 4.3
	1810 0.7	1418 0.5	1404 0.8	1556 0.6	1332 4.1	1304 3.4	1607 0.5	1241 0.5	1344 0.3
		2020 7.2	2027 9.8	2123 13.9	1900 0.7	1906 0.6	2211 2.9	1906 5.2	1936 4.3
2 SA	0027 5.9	0244 0.6	0228 0.9	0414 0.8	0146 4.4	0115 3.7	0457 0.7	0109 0.4	0206 0.5
	0642 0.6	0841 6.9	0846 9.4	0944 13.4	0733 0.5	0727 0.3	1042 2.5	0733 5.0	0751 4.2
	1253 5.4	1456 0.8	1439 1.1	1624 1.0	1410 3.9	1345 3.3	1645 0.6	1322 0.7	1424 0.5
	1851 0.9	2058 6.9	2103 9.4	2200 13.3	1941 0.8	1948 0.6	2248 2.7	1949 4.9	2017 4.1
3 SU	0109 5.6	0320 1.0	0301 1.4	0439 1.4	0228 4.2	0158 3.6	0534 0.8	0151 0.8	0245 0.7
	0724 0.9	0918 6.5	0921 9.0	1019 12.6	0815 0.8	0809 0.5	1120 2.4	0815 4.7	0832 4.1
	1334 5.2	1532 1.2	1515 1.6	1648 1.7	1451 3.8	1426 3.2	1725 0.7	1406 1.1	1503 0.7
	1935 1.2	2136 6.5	2139 8.9	2234 12.4	2024 1.0	2031 0.7	2326 2.5	2033 4.6	2057 3.9
4 M	0152 5.2	0354 1.5	0336 1.9	0502 2.1	0314 4.0	0245 3.4	0614 1.0	0235 1.2	0324 0.9
	0807 1.3	0957 6.1	0958 8.5	1051 11.7	0900 1.0	0853 0.7	1202 2.2	0900 4.4	0912 3.9
	1417 4.9	1608 1.7	1554 2.1	1712 2.4	1535 3.6	1512 3.1	1809 0.9	1452 1.5	1542 0.9
	2021 1.6	2215 6.0	2218 8.4	2306 11.3	2115 1.2	2119 0.9		2121 4.2	2138 3.7
5 TU	0238 4.8	0430 2.0	0416 2.5	0524 2.8	0407 3.7	0336 3.3	0009 2.2	0324 1.6	0406 1.1
	0856 1.8	1038 5.7	1041 8.0	1124 10.7	0953 1.3	0942 0.9	0700 1.1	0951 4.1	0957 3.6
	1506 4.6	1649 2.2	1641 2.8	1736 3.1	1628 3.5	1604 3.0	1254 2.1	1548 1.8	1626 1.2
	2117 2.0	2259 5.5	2304 7.8	2341 10.4	2216 1.4	2216 1.0	1859 1.0	2218 3.8	2224 3.4
6 W	0334 4.5	0515 2.4	0508 3.1	0551 3.4	0512 3.5	0435 3.1	0108 2.0	0424 2.0	0454 1.4
	0956 2.1	1130 5.3	1118 7.5	1203 9.9	1055 1.5	1040 1.1	0801 1.2	1051 3.8	1048 3.4
	1610 4.4	1747 2.6	1745 3.3	1810 3.8	1734 3.4	1705 2.9	1411 2.0	1703 2.1	1719 1.4
	2230 2.3	2359 5.1			2330 1.6	2327 1.1	2005 1.2	2333 3.6	2321 3.2
7 TH	0453 4.2	0624 2.7	0005 7.3	0029 9.6	0627 3.3	0540 2.9	0321 1.9	0549 2.2	0556 1.5
	1112 2.3	1245 5.0	0623 3.6	0630 4.1	1206 1.7	1151 1.2	0926 1.2	1211 3.7	1154 3.2
	1733 4.3	1917 2.8	1251 7.2	1310 9.3	1848 3.4	1811 2.9	1548 2.1	1841 2.1	1830 1.5
	2358 2.3		1909 3.6	1906 4.5			2143 1.2		
8 F	0629 4.2	0127 4.9	0126 7.0	0153 9.1	0054 1.6	0042 1.1	0457 2.0	0109 3.6	0038 3.1
	1235 2.3	0805 2.8	0754 3.7	0754 4.7	0740 3.3	0647 2.9	1047 1.2	0718 2.1	0713 1.5
	1854 4.5	1421 5.1	1416 7.2	1453 9.4	1321 1.6	1303 1.2	1658 2.2	1331 3.8	1318 3.2
		2050 2.6	2030 3.5	2126 4.4	1958 3.5	1915 3.0	2316 1.2	1957 1.7	1949 1.5
9 SA	0117 2.1	0301 5.1	0251 7.2	0336 9.5	0212 1.5	0149 1.0	0548 2.1	0221 3.8	0200 3.2
	0743 4.4	0923 2.5	0909 3.4	1005 4.0	0848 3.4	0748 2.9	1145 1.0	0821 1.9	0826 1.4
	1341 2.1	1534 5.5	1527 7.6	1615 10.2	1427 1.5	1403 1.1	1749 2.4	1432 4.0	1431 3.3
	1954 4.7	2154 2.2	2135 3.1	2239 3.3	2100 3.6	2012 3.0		2051 1.6	2054 1.3
10 SU	0212 1.9	0402 5.5	0357 7.6	0446 10.5	0308 1.3	0244 0.9	0012 1.0	0312 4.0	0300 3.3
	0833 4.7	1017 2.1	1005 2.9	1106 3.0	0943 3.5	0843 3.0	0627 2.2	0907 1.7	0921 1.2
	1428 1.9	1624 5.9	1621 8.1	1712 11.3	1518 1.3	1453 1.0	1229 0.9	1518 4.3	1524 3.5
	2038 5.0	2241 1.8	2226 2.6	2333 2.4	2151 3.7	2103 3.1	1831 2.6	2132 1.4	2144 1.1
11 M	0253 1.5	0445 5.9	0445 8.1	0537 11.4	0351 1.1	0329 0.7	0053 0.9	0351 4.2	0345 3.6
	0909 4.9	1059 1.7	1049 2.4	1159 2.2	1027 3.6	0930 3.0	0700 2.4	0945 1.4	1007 1.0
	1505 1.6	1703 6.3	1703 8.5	1757 12.1	1559 1.2	1535 0.9	1307 0.8	1557 4.5	1608 3.7
	2113 5.2	2320 1.5	2308 2.1		2231 3.8	2145 3.2	1908 2.7	2206 1.1	2226 0.9
12 TU	0327 1.3	0522 6.2	0524 8.5	0024 1.8	0427 0.9	0408 0.6	0128 0.8	0426 4.4	0425 3.8
	0941 5.1	1135 1.4	1127 1.9	0619 12.1	1103 3.7	1010 3.1	0732 2.5	1019 1.2	1048 0.8
	1537 1.3	1738 6.6	1742 8.9	1248 1.7	1635 1.0	1611 0.8	1342 0.7	1631 4.7	1647 3.9
	2145 5.4	2354 1.2	2345 1.7	1836 12.6	2305 3.9	2223 3.3	1942 2.8	2238 0.8	2305 0.8
13 W O	0357 1.0	0555 6.5	0600 8.9	0112 1.4	0459 0.8	0442 0.5	0202 0.7	0457 4.6	0502 3.9
	1009 5.3	1208 1.1	1202 1.6	0656 12.5	1133 3.7	1045 3.2	0801 2.6	1051 0.9	1127 0.7
	1608 1.1	1811 6.8	1817 9.2	1333 1.5	1706 0.9	1644 0.7	1414 0.6	1703 4.8	1723 4.0
	2216 5.6			1912 12.9	2334 3.9	2255 3.3	2014 2.9	2308 0.6	2342 0.7
14 TH	0428 0.9	0027 1.0	0020 1.3	0156 1.3	0526 0.7	0513 0.5	0234 0.6	0528 4.8	0537 4.0
	1039 5.4	0627 6.7	0633 9.2	0730 12.8	1200 3.8	1117 3.2	0830 2.6	1121 0.8	1203 0.6
	1639 1.0	1241 1.0	1234 1.3	1414 1.3	1734 0.8	1716 0.6	1445 0.6	1736 5.0	1758 4.1
	2248 5.7	1843 7.0	1851 9.4	1946 13.2		2325 3.4	2044 2.9	2338 0.5	
15 F	0459 0.8	0100 0.8	0053 1.1	0236 1.1	0002 4.0	0544 0.4	0306 0.6	0559 4.8	0019 0.6
	1109 5.4	0700 6.8	0706 9.4	0803 13.1	0553 0.6	1148 3.3	0859 2.6	1151 0.7	0611 4.1
	1710 0.9	1314 0.9	1304 1.1	1452 1.2	1227 3.8	1748 0.5	1515 0.5	1808 5.0	1239 0.6
	2322 5.7	1916 7.1	1923 9.6	2020 13.3	1803 0.7	2356 3.5	2115 2.9		1832 4.2

• • Time: UT. For British Summer Time (shaded) March 26th to October 29th ADD ONE HOUR • •

SEPTEMBER 2000 TIDE TABLES

•• Time: UT. For British Summer Time (shaded) March 26th to October 29TH ADD ONE HOUR ••

	HOLYHEAD		MILFORD HAVEN		SWANSEA		AVONMOUTH		DUBLIN		BELFAST		LONDON-DERRY		GALWAY		COBH	
	Time	m	Time	m	Time	m	Time	m	Time	m	Time	m	Time	m	Time	m	Time	m
16 SA	0531	0.7	0133	0.8	0124	1.0	0313	1.1	0033	4.0	0616	0.4	0338	0.6	0009	0.5	0055	0.6
	1142	5.4	0732	6.9	0736	9.4	0836	13.2	0621	0.6	1220	3.3	0929	2.6	0630	4.9	0645	4.1
	1744	0.9	1348	0.8	1334	1.1	1527	1.2	1257	3.9	1824	0.5	1549	0.6	1224	0.7	1315	0.6
	2357	5.7	1950	7.0	1955	9.6	2054	13.3	1834	0.7			2148	2.9	1843	5.0	1906	4.1
17 SU	0605	0.8	0207	0.8	0154	1.0	0346	1.1	0107	4.1	0030	3.5	0412	0.6	0042	0.6	0130	0.7
	1216	5.4	0806	6.9	0808	9.4	0910	13.1	0654	0.6	0651	0.4	1003	2.6	0704	4.9	0720	4.1
	1820	0.9	1421	1.0	1405	1.2	1557	1.4	1333	3.9	1255	3.4	1626	0.6	1259	0.8	1350	0.7
			2025	6.9	2028	9.4	2129	13.0	1910	0.7	1902	0.5	2224	2.8	1920	4.9	1942	4.1
18 M	0033	5.6	0242	1.0	0225	1.2	0414	1.5	0147	4.0	0109	3.5	0450	0.7	0117	0.7	0205	0.8
	0642	0.9	0842	6.7	0842	9.2	0943	12.7	0733	0.6	0730	0.4	1040	2.5	0742	4.8	0757	4.1
	1254	5.3	1457	1.2	1438	1.4	1622	1.8	1415	3.9	1336	3.4	1708	0.7	1337	1.0	1426	0.8
	1900	1.1	2103	6.7	2104	9.1	2203	12.5	1952	0.8	1944	0.6	2307	2.6	2001	4.7	2020	4.0
19 TU	0114	5.4	0318	1.3	0300	1.5	0439	1.9	0233	4.0	0153	3.4	0533	0.8	0157	1.0	0242	0.9
	0724	1.1	0920	6.4	0919	8.9	1018	12.1	0817	0.8	0814	0.6	1123	2.3	0823	4.6	0836	3.9
	1336	5.1	1536	1.5	1516	1.8	1648	2.2	1503	3.8	1422	3.3	1756	0.9	1421	1.2	1507	0.9
	1947	1.3	2144	6.3	2145	8.7	2239	11.7	2042	0.9	2031	0.7	2357	2.4	2048	4.5	2103	3.8
20 W	0201	5.2	0359	1.7	0342	2.0	0506	2.4	0327	3.8	0244	3.3	0622	0.9	0243	1.3	0327	1.0
	0813	1.4	1004	6.0	1005	8.4	1055	11.4	0910	1.0	0904	0.7	1215	2.2	0912	4.3	0924	3.8
	1427	4.9	1623	1.9	1605	2.4	1720	2.7	1600	3.7	1515	3.2	1854	1.0	1516	1.5	1557	1.1
	2045	1.6	2236	5.9	2239	8.1	2323	11.0	2143	1.1	2127	0.9			2145	4.2	2155	3.6
21 TH	0301	4.9	0452	2.1	0437	2.6	0542	2.9	0432	3.7	0344	3.2	0103	2.2	0342	1.7	0424	1.2
	0916	1.7	1103	5.5	1107	7.8	1144	10.7	1018	1.2	1006	1.0	0720	1.0	1013	4.1	1022	3.6
	1536	4.7	1729	2.3	1716	2.9	1805	3.2	1709	3.6	1619	3.1	1325	2.1	1630	1.8	1703	1.2
	2200	1.8	2345	5.5	2351	7.6			2303	1.3	2236	1.0	2012	1.1	2257	4.0	2301	3.4
22 F	0422	4.7	0609	2.4	0602	3.1	0026	10.3	0551	3.6	0459	3.0	0248	2.1	0503	1.9	0538	1.3
	1038	1.9	1226	5.4	1234	7.5	0638	3.5	1141	1.4	1124	1.1	0833	1.1	1134	4.0	1136	3.4
	1706	4.6	1906	2.4	1900	3.1	1302	10.2	1830	3.6	1736	3.1	1539	2.1	1808	1.8	1827	1.3
	2331	1.8					1919	3.7					2227	1.1				
23 SA	0557	4.7	0118	5.3	0125	7.4	0159	10.1	0027	1.2	0004	1.0	0435	2.2	0029	4.0	0024	3.3
	1206	1.9	0749	2.4	0747	3.1	0818	3.7	0716	3.6	0627	3.0	1012	1.1	0640	1.9	0708	1.3
	1833	4.8	1402	5.5	1409	7.7	1439	10.4	1300	1.4	1252	1.1	1707	2.3	1304	4.2	1307	3.4
			2044	2.1	2034	2.8	2118	3.4	1948	3.7	1856	3.2	2347	0.9	1935	1.5	1955	1.1
24 SU	0053	1.5	0249	5.6	0255	7.8	0331	10.7	0144	1.1	0127	0.9	0536	2.4	0151	4.3	0152	3.5
	0717	4.9	0914	2.0	0910	2.6	1003	3.0	0830	3.8	0748	3.1	1129	0.9	0757	1.6	0829	1.1
	1320	1.6	1523	6.0	1527	8.3	1606	11.3	1411	1.3	1404	1.0	1757	2.6	1415	4.5	1429	3.6
	1941	5.2	2156	1.6	2146	2.2	2250	2.5	2055	4.0	2005	3.3			2036	1.1	2106	0.9
25 M	0157	1.1	0358	6.1	0405	8.5	0450	11.8	0248	0.8	0232	0.7	0039	0.7	0251	4.6	0301	3.7
	0818	5.2	1018	1.5	1012	1.9	1126	2.0	0934	3.9	0855	3.2	0624	2.6	0852	1.2	0933	0.8
	1418	1.3	1623	6.5	1629	9.0	1718	12.5	1509	1.1	1503	0.9	1222	0.8	1509	4.9	1531	3.9
	2033	5.5	2252	1.1	2244	1.5			2152	4.2	2103	3.5	1839	2.8	2124	0.7	2203	0.6
26 TU	0249	0.8	0451	6.6	0500	9.1	0007	1.5	0342	0.6	0326	0.5	0123	0.6	0340	4.9	0355	4.0
	0906	5.5	1109	1.0	1103	1.3	0553	12.8	1027	4.1	0950	3.3	0707	2.7	0937	0.9	1027	0.5
	1505	1.0	1712	7.0	1720	9.5	1236	1.1	1558	0.9	1552	0.7	1307	0.6	1554	5.2	1623	4.2
	2118	5.8	2340	0.7	2333	1.0	1815	13.3	2241	4.3	2155	3.7	1918	3.0	2206	0.4	2253	0.4
27 W	0334	0.5	0538	7.0	0547	9.6	0109	0.8	0428	0.4	0413	0.4	0203	0.5	0423	5.2	0443	4.2
	0947	5.6	1155	0.6	1148	0.9	0644	13.5	1113	4.2	1036	3.4	0747	2.8	1018	0.6	1115	0.4
	1546	0.7	1757	7.3	1805	9.9	1331	0.6	1641	0.8	1637	0.6	1348	0.6	1637	5.4	1709	4.4
	2200	6.0					1902	13.8	2324	4.4	2241	3.8	1954	3.0	2245	0.2	2339	0.3
28 TH	0415	0.4	0023	0.4	0015	0.7	0159	0.5	0510	0.4	0457	0.3	0239	0.5	0504	5.3	0527	4.4
	1026	5.7	0619	7.2	0629	9.9	0727	13.8	1152	4.2	1118	3.5	0824	2.8	1057	0.4	1200	0.3
	1625	0.6	1236	0.5	1227	0.7	1418	0.4	1720	0.7	1718	0.6	1427	0.5	1718	5.5	1752	4.4
	2240	6.0	1837	7.4	1846	10.1	1943	14.0			2324	3.8	2030	3.0	2324	0.2		
29 F	0454	0.4	0102	0.4	0053	0.7	0242	0.5	0003	4.4	0537	0.3	0313	0.5	0544	5.3	0021	0.4
	1104	5.7	0659	7.3	0707	10.0	0805	13.9	0548	0.4	1156	3.5	0900	2.8	1136	0.4	0608	4.4
	1704	0.6	1315	0.4	1303	0.7	1457	0.5	1227	4.1	1758	0.5	1503	0.5	1759	5.4	1241	0.3
	2320	6.0	1916	7.4	1924	10.0	2020	14.0	1757	0.7			2104	3.0			1832	4.4
30 SA ●	0533	0.5	0139	0.6	0127	0.8	0316	0.7	0040	4.4	0005	3.8	0345	0.6	0002	0.3	0100	0.5
	1142	5.6	0736	7.2	0742	9.8	0840	13.8	0625	0.5	0615	0.4	0933	2.7	0624	5.2	0647	4.4
	1743	0.7	1351	0.6	1337	0.9	1528	0.7	1300	4.1	1231	3.4	1539	0.6	1215	0.6	1319	0.3
			1952	7.2	1958	9.8	2055	13.8	1834	0.7	1836	0.6	2137	2.8	1839	5.2	1910	4.3

WEST COAST ENGLAND, WALES & IRELAND Time Zone UT
Holyhead * Milford Haven * Swansea * Avonmouth * Dublin * Belfast * Londonderry * Galway * Cobh

TIDE TABLES OCTOBER 2000

	HOLYHEAD		MILFORD HAVEN		SWANSEA		AVONMOUTH		DUBLIN		BELFAST		LONDONDERRY		GALWAY		COBH	
	Time	m	Time	m	Time	m	Time	m	Time	m	Time	m	Time	m	Time	m	Time	m
1 SU	0000	5.8	0212	0.7	0157	1.1	0344	1.0	0117	4.3	0045	3.7	0416	0.7	0039	0.6	0137	0.6
	0610	0.8	0811	6.9	0815	9.6	0915	13.4	0702	0.7	0653	0.5	1006	2.6	0703	5.1	0724	4.3
	1220	5.5	1425	0.9	1409	1.2	1554	1.2	1333	4.0	1307	3.4	1614	0.7	1254	0.8	1354	0.6
	1822	1.0	2027	6.8	2031	9.4	2129	13.2	1912	0.8	1914	0.6	2211	2.6	1921	4.9	1946	4.1
2 M	0039	5.5	0245	1.1	0228	1.5	0407	1.5	0156	4.1	0125	3.6	0447	0.8	0118	1.0	0212	0.8
	0648	1.1	0845	6.6	0848	9.2	0946	12.7	0739	0.9	0731	0.7	1039	2.5	0743	4.8	0800	4.1
	1257	5.3	1458	1.3	1442	1.7	1616	1.7	1410	3.9	1344	3.3	1651	0.8	1335	1.1	1428	0.8
	1902	1.3	2101	6.4	2104	9.0	2200	12.3	1954	1.0	1954	0.8	2245	2.4	2003	4.6	2021	3.9
3 TU	0117	5.2	0316	1.5	0300	2.0	0427	2.1	0239	3.9	0209	3.4	0521	1.0	0158	1.4	0245	1.0
	0727	1.5	0919	6.2	0921	8.7	1015	11.8	0821	1.1	0810	0.8	1117	2.4	0825	4.5	0838	3.9
	1336	5.0	1531	1.7	1518	2.2	1637	2.4	1452	3.8	1426	3.2	1731	1.0	1419	1.5	1503	1.0
	1945	1.6	2136	6.0	2139	8.4	2229	11.3	2042	1.2	2038	0.9	2324	2.2	2047	4.2	2058	3.7
4 W	0158	4.8	0348	2.0	0335	2.6	0447	2.8	0330	3.6	0257	3.2	0603	1.1	0242	1.8	0321	1.2
	0810	1.9	0957	5.8	1000	8.2	1043	10.8	0911	1.4	0854	1.0	1203	2.3	0911	4.2	0918	3.7
	1420	4.7	1609	2.2	1600	2.8	1700	3.0	1543	3.6	1514	3.1	1820	1.1	1511	1.9	1542	1.3
	2035	2.0	2215	5.5	2221	7.9	2257	10.3	2142	1.4	2130	1.0			2139	3.9	2139	3.5
5 TH	0248	4.5	0427	2.4	0419	3.2	0511	3.4	0435	3.4	0352	3.0	0014	2.0	0339	2.2	0405	1.4
	0903	2.3	1043	5.3	1050	7.6	1114	9.9	1015	1.6	0945	1.2	0656	1.2	1006	3.9	1005	3.4
	1517	4.5	1700	2.6	1657	3.7	1730	3.7	1648	3.5	1612	3.0	1309	2.1	1621	2.2	1630	1.5
	2141	2.3	2309	5.0	2315	7.3	2336	9.4	2257	1.5	2236	1.2	1922	1.3	2248	3.6	2231	3.2
6 F	0402	4.2	0526	2.8	0526	3.7	0545	4.1	0553	3.3	0457	2.9	0213	1.8	0502	2.4	0502	1.6
	1018	2.5	1152	5.0	1159	7.1	1209	9.1	1130	1.8	1052	1.3	0812	1.3	1121	3.8	1106	3.2
	1636	4.4	1824	2.9	1818	3.8	1816	4.4	1806	3.4	1718	3.0	1454	2.1	1759	2.2	1736	1.6
	2309	2.4									2355	1.2	2100	1.3			2342	3.1
7 SA	0545	4.1	0034	4.7	0033	6.9	0052	8.8	0021	1.6	0606	2.8	0433	1.9	0030	3.6	0618	1.6
	1149	2.6	0712	3.0	0704	4.0	0642	4.8	0709	3.3	1210	1.4	0954	1.3	0644	2.4	1227	3.2
	1806	4.4	1333	5.0	1327	7.0	1401	8.9	1249	1.7	1828	3.0	1620	2.3	1251	3.8	1900	1.6
			2011	2.8	1948	3.7	2012	4.8	1921	3.4			2251	1.2	1924	2.1		
8 SU	0035	2.2	0223	4.9	0206	6.9	0252	9.0	0139	1.4	0108	1.1	0519	2.1	0154	3.8	0111	3.1
	0709	4.4	0846	2.7	0830	3.7	0926	4.7	0818	3.3	0712	2.8	1104	1.2	0753	2.2	0740	1.5
	1303	2.3	1458	5.3	1448	7.3	1537	9.7	1338	1.6	1320	1.3	1712	2.5	1400	4.0	1349	3.3
	1914	4.7	2120	2.4	2059	3.3	2206	3.8	2025	3.5	1930	3.0	2343	1.1	2019	1.8	2013	1.4
9 M	0135	1.9	0330	5.3	0321	7.4	0410	10.0	0236	1.3	0205	1.0	0555	2.3	0245	4.0	0221	3.3
	0800	4.6	0944	2.3	0931	3.1	1034	3.5	0915	3.5	0809	2.9	1151	1.0	0840	1.9	0844	1.3
	1354	2.0	1550	5.8	1545	7.9	1636	10.9	1450	1.4	1414	1.1	1754	2.6	1447	4.2	1448	3.5
	2002	5.0	2209	1.9	2152	2.7	2301	2.7	2117	3.6	2024	3.1			2100	1.5	2108	1.2
10 TU	0218	1.6	0414	5.8	0411	8.0	0502	11.1	0318	1.1	0251	0.8	0021	0.9	0323	4.3	0312	3.6
	0838	4.9	1027	1.9	1016	2.5	1127	2.5	0958	3.6	0857	3.0	0628	2.4	0918	1.5	0933	1.1
	1433	1.7	1630	6.2	1630	8.4	1723	11.9	1530	1.2	1459	1.0	1231	0.9	1525	4.5	1535	3.8
	2039	5.2	2248	1.5	2235	2.1	2352	1.9	2157	3.7	2109	3.2	1832	2.8	2134	1.2	2154	1.0
11 W	0253	1.3	0450	6.2	0451	8.5	0545	12.0	0352	0.9	0331	0.7	0057	0.8	0356	4.6	0354	3.8
	0909	5.1	1104	1.5	1054	1.9	1216	1.8	1032	3.7	0937	3.1	0700	2.6	0950	1.3	1017	0.9
	1506	1.4	1706	6.6	1708	9.0	1803	12.6	1603	1.1	1538	0.8	1308	0.7	1600	4.7	1615	4.0
	2113	5.5	2324	1.2	2312	1.6			2231	3.8	2147	3.3	1907	2.9	2205	0.9	2235	0.8
12 TH	0325	1.0	0524	6.6	0527	9.1	0041	1.4	0421	0.8	0407	0.5	0131	0.6	0426	4.8	0432	4.0
	0939	5.3	1139	1.1	1130	1.5	0624	12.6	1101	3.8	1013	3.2	0730	2.7	1021	1.0	1057	0.7
	1538	1.1	1740	6.9	1745	9.4	1303	1.4	1633	0.9	1613	0.7	1342	0.6	1632	5.0	1653	4.1
	2146	5.6	2358	0.9	2348	1.2	1841	13.1	2300	3.9	2221	3.3	1940	3.0	2235	0.7	2314	0.6
13 F **O**	0357	0.9	0557	6.9	0602	9.5	0127	1.2	0448	0.7	0440	0.4	0204	0.6	0456	5.0	0509	4.2
	1009	5.5	1214	0.9	1203	1.2	0700	13.0	1128	3.9	1046	3.3	0802	2.8	1051	0.8	1136	0.6
	1609	0.9	1815	7.1	1820	9.7	1348	1.2	1701	0.8	1648	0.6	1418	0.6	1705	5.1	1730	4.3
	2219	5.8					1918	13.4	2330	4.0	2254	3.4	2013	3.0	2306	0.5	2353	0.6
14 SA	0429	0.7	0033	0.7	0023	0.9	0211	1.0	0518	0.6	0514	0.4	0237	0.5	0527	5.1	0545	4.3
	1040	5.6	0632	7.1	0636	9.7	0736	13.4	1157	4.0	1118	3.4	0833	2.8	1124	0.6	1215	0.6
	1643	1.0	1249	0.7	1236	1.0	1428	1.1	1732	0.7	1724	0.6	1453	0.5	1739	5.2	1806	4.3
	2254	5.8	1850	7.2	1855	9.9	1954	13.6			2328	3.5	2048	3.0	2339	0.5		
15 SU	0503	0.6	0109	0.6	0057	0.8	0250	0.9	0003	4.1	0548	0.3	0312	0.5	0600	5.2	0030	0.6
	1115	5.6	0708	7.1	0711	9.8	0812	13.5	0550	0.5	1153	3.4	0906	2.8	1157	0.6	0621	4.3
	1719	0.7	1325	0.7	1310	0.9	1506	1.0	1229	4.0	1800	0.5	1530	0.5	1817	5.2	1252	0.6
	2332	5.8	1927	7.2	1931	9.9	2031	13.6	1807	0.6			2124	2.9			1842	4.3

• • Time: UT. For British Summer Time (shaded) March 26th to October 29th ADD ONE HOUR • •

OCTOBER 2000 TIDE TABLES

•• Time: UT. For British Summer Time (shaded) March 26th to October 29TH ADD ONE HOUR ••

	HOLYHEAD Time m	MILFORD HAVEN Time m	SWANSEA Time m	AVONMOUTH Time m	DUBLIN Time m	BELFAST Time m	LONDONDERRY Time m	GALWAY Time m	COBH Time m
16 M	0539 0.7 1151 5.6 1758 0.8	0145 0.7 0745 7.1 1402 0.8 2005 7.1	0130 0.9 0745 9.8 1345 1.0 2008 9.7	0325 1.0 0848 13.4 1538 1.2 2109 13.3	0042 4.1 0627 0.5 1307 4.1 1848 0.6	0006 3.5 0626 0.4 1231 3.5 1841 0.5	0347 0.6 0942 2.7 1611 0.6 2205 2.8	0013 0.6 0636 5.2 1235 0.7 1857 5.1	0107 0.6 0658 4.3 1330 0.6 1920 4.2
17 TU	0012 5.7 0619 0.9 1232 5.5 1842 1.0	0222 0.9 0823 6.9 1441 1.1 2045 6.8	0205 1.1 0822 9.5 1421 1.3 2047 9.3	0355 1.3 0924 13.0 1606 1.6 2146 12.7	0126 4.1 0708 0.6 1351 4.0 1933 0.7	0048 3.5 0707 0.5 1314 3.4 1925 0.5	0426 0.7 1020 2.6 1656 0.7 2251 2.6	0051 0.8 0716 5.0 1316 0.9 1941 4.9	0145 0.7 0737 4.2 1409 0.8 2000 4.1
18 W	0057 5.5 0704 1.1 1318 5.3 1933 1.2	0301 1.2 0904 6.6 1524 1.4 2131 6.3	0242 1.5 0903 9.1 1503 1.8 2132 8.8	0421 1.8 1001 12.4 1634 2.0 2227 11.9	0216 4.0 0755 0.8 1442 3.9 2027 0.8	0136 3.4 0753 0.6 1403 3.4 2015 0.7	0510 0.8 1104 2.5 1748 0.9 2346 2.4	0133 1.1 0800 4.8 1403 1.2 2031 4.6	0225 0.9 0820 4.1 1453 0.9 2045 3.9
19 TH	0148 5.2 0757 1.5 1412 5.0 2035 1.5	0345 1.7 0952 6.2 1615 1.9 2226 5.9	0325 2.1 0951 8.5 1554 2.4 2227 8.1	0451 2.3 1043 11.6 1709 2.6 2315 11.0	0315 3.8 0852 1.1 1543 3.8 2135 1.0	0230 3.2 0846 0.8 1459 3.3 2115 0.8	0600 0.9 1157 2.4 1851 1.1	0223 1.5 0851 4.6 1502 1.6 2131 4.3	0312 1.0 0909 3.9 1546 1.1 2139 3.7
20 F	0254 4.9 0903 1.8 1524 4.8 2154 1.7	0442 2.1 1055 5.7 1727 2.2 2339 5.5	0422 2.7 1056 7.9 1709 3.0 2342 7.5	0531 2.9 1138 10.8 1758 3.2	0426 3.7 1004 1.4 1656 3.7 2257 1.2	0336 3.1 0953 1.1 1606 3.2 2230 0.9	0100 2.2 0659 1.1 1312 2.3 2035 1.2	0326 1.9 0956 4.3 1619 1.8 2248 4.1	0410 1.2 1009 3.6 1653 1.2 2247 3.4
21 SA	0419 4.7 1027 2.0 1654 4.8 2322 1.7	0603 2.4 1218 5.5 1903 2.3	0552 3.2 1224 7.5 1854 3.2	0023 10.3 0630 3.5 1257 10.3 1918 3.6	0549 3.6 1127 1.5 1818 3.7	0459 2.9 1118 1.2 1724 3.1 2358 0.9	0259 2.2 0812 1.2 1533 2.3 2236 1.1	0451 2.1 1119 4.2 1759 1.8	0525 1.3 1124 3.5 1816 1.3
22 SU	0551 4.7 1154 2.0 1818 4.9	0111 5.4 0741 2.4 1351 5.6 2034 2.0	0116 7.4 0737 3.2 1357 7.7 2025 2.8	0149 10.2 0808 3.6 1427 10.6 2105 3.2	0018 1.1 0710 3.6 1248 1.5 1933 3.8	0629 3.0 1243 1.2 1841 3.2	0425 2.3 0948 1.2 1647 2.5 2338 0.9	0021 4.2 0631 2.0 1250 4.3 1921 1.5	0010 3.4 0653 1.3 1254 3.5 1939 1.2
23 M	0040 1.4 0707 4.9 1306 1.7 1924 5.2	0238 5.7 0901 2.0 1507 6.1 2142 1.6	0244 7.8 0857 2.6 1513 8.2 2134 2.2	0318 10.8 0945 2.9 1551 11.5 2230 2.3	0134 1.0 0822 3.8 1358 1.3 2039 4.0	0115 0.8 0744 3.1 1351 1.0 1948 3.3	0520 2.5 1105 1.0 1734 2.7	0141 4.4 0744 1.7 1400 4.6 2018 1.2	0135 3.5 0812 1.1 1413 3.7 2048 0.9
24 TU	0142 1.1 0803 4.9 1401 1.4 2016 5.5	0342 6.1 1002 1.5 1605 6.5 2235 1.1	0351 8.4 0957 2.0 1612 8.9 2228 1.6	0433 11.8 1105 2.0 1700 12.5 2344 1.5	0236 0.6 0924 3.9 1455 1.2 2136 4.2	0216 0.6 0845 3.2 1445 0.9 2045 3.5	0024 0.7 0606 2.7 1158 0.9 1815 2.9	0236 4.7 0835 1.4 1451 4.9 2103 0.9	0242 3.8 0916 0.8 1514 4.0 2145 0.7
25 W	0232 0.9 0848 5.4 1447 1.1 2100 5.7	0433 6.6 1051 1.1 1652 6.8 2320 0.8	0442 9.1 1045 1.4 1701 9.4 2313 1.2	0533 12.7 1212 1.2 1754 13.2	0327 0.6 1013 4.0 1542 1.0 2224 4.3	0308 0.5 0934 3.3 1533 0.7 2135 3.6	0103 0.6 0646 2.8 1243 0.7 1851 3.0	0321 5.0 0918 1.1 1535 5.1 2143 0.6	0336 4.0 1009 0.5 1605 4.2 2233 0.5
26 TH	0315 0.7 0927 5.6 1527 0.9 2139 5.8	0517 6.9 1134 0.8 1735 7.1	0527 9.5 1127 1.1 1744 9.8 2353 0.9	0043 1.0 0621 13.3 1306 0.8 1839 13.5	0410 0.6 1054 4.1 1623 0.9 2305 4.3	0353 0.4 1017 3.4 1616 0.6 2220 3.7	0139 0.6 0724 2.8 1324 0.6 1927 3.0	0402 5.2 0957 0.8 1616 5.3 2221 0.5	0424 4.2 1056 0.5 1649 4.3 2318 0.5
27 F	0353 0.6 1003 5.7 1605 0.8 2218 5.8	0000 0.6 0557 7.1 1213 0.7 1814 7.2	0606 9.8 1205 1.0 1823 9.9	0132 0.8 0703 13.5 1350 0.8 1918 13.6	0449 0.6 1130 4.1 1700 0.8 2342 4.3	0433 0.4 1054 3.5 1656 0.6 2301 3.7	0211 0.6 0759 2.9 1401 0.6 2001 3.0	0441 5.3 1036 0.7 1656 5.3 2258 0.5	0506 4.4 1139 0.4 1730 4.4 2357 0.5
28 SA	0430 0.6 1039 5.7 1642 0.8 2257 5.8	0036 0.6 0634 7.1 1249 0.6 1851 7.1	0028 1.0 0642 9.9 1239 1.0 1858 9.8	0212 0.9 0739 13.6 1427 0.9 1954 13.6	0524 0.6 1200 4.1 1736 0.8	0512 0.4 1129 3.5 1733 0.6 2340 3.7	0240 0.6 0831 2.8 1436 0.6 2033 2.9	0519 5.4 1114 0.7 1736 5.3 2335 0.7	0545 4.4 1218 0.5 1808 4.3
29 SU ●	0506 0.8 1116 5.6 1720 0.9 2334 5.6	0110 0.7 0709 7.0 1324 0.8 1926 7.0	0100 1.1 0715 9.8 1312 1.2 1932 9.6	0245 1.1 0813 13.5 1458 1.1 2028 13.4	0016 4.2 0559 0.7 1230 4.1 1812 0.8	0548 0.5 1202 3.5 1810 0.6	0308 0.7 0902 2.8 1510 0.7 2105 2.7	0557 5.3 1152 0.8 1815 5.1	0035 0.6 0623 4.3 1253 0.6 1843 4.2
30 M	0542 1.0 1151 5.5 1757 1.1	0143 0.9 0743 6.9 1357 1.0 2000 6.7	0130 1.4 0748 9.5 1344 1.5 2004 9.3	0312 1.3 0846 13.3 1524 1.3 2101 13.0	0051 4.1 0633 0.8 1303 4.1 1849 0.9	0018 3.6 0623 0.6 1236 3.5 1846 0.7	0335 0.8 0933 2.7 1543 0.8 2137 2.6	0012 0.9 0635 5.1 1230 1.0 1854 4.9	0109 0.8 0658 4.3 1326 0.8 1917 4.1
31 TU	0011 5.4 0617 1.3 1227 5.3 1835 1.3	0215 1.2 0816 6.6 1430 1.3 2033 6.4	0200 1.7 0820 9.2 1417 1.8 2036 8.9	0336 1.7 0917 12.7 1547 1.8 2132 12.2	0128 4.0 0710 1.0 1339 4.0 1930 1.0	0057 3.5 0657 0.8 1312 3.5 1924 0.8	0404 0.9 1005 2.7 1618 0.9 2211 2.4	0049 1.2 0713 4.9 1310 1.3 1936 4.6	0141 0.9 0733 4.1 1357 1.0 1950 3.9

WEST COAST ENGLAND, WALES & IRELAND Time Zone UT
Holyhead * Milford Haven * Swansea * Avonmouth * Dublin * Belfast * Londonderry * Galway * Cobh

TIDE TABLES NOVEMBER 2000

HOLYHEAD		MILFORD HAVEN		SWANSEA		AVONMOUTH		DUBLIN		BELFAST		LONDONDERRY		GALWAY		COBH		
Time	m	Time	m	Time	m	Time	m	Time	m	Time	m	Time	m	Time	m	Time	m	
0048	5.1	0245	1.5	0232	2.1	0357	2.1	0212	3.8	0137	3.4	0437	1.0	0127	1.6	0212	1.1	1 W
0654	1.6	0849	6.3	0853	8.8	0946	11.9	0751	1.2	0734	0.9	1042	2.6	0753	4.7	0809	3.9	
1303	5.1	1503	1.7	1451	2.3	1609	2.3	1421	3.9	1351	3.4	1658	1.0	1352	1.6	1430	1.1	
1915	1.6	2106	6.0	2110	8.5	2200	11.3	2018	1.2	2006	0.9	2248	2.2	2018	4.3	2024	3.7	
0127	4.8	0316	2.0	0306	2.5	0418	2.7	0301	3.6	0222	3.2	0517	1.1	0209	1.9	0245	1.2	2 TH
0733	1.9	0925	5.9	0930	8.3	1013	11.0	0839	1.4	0815	1.1	1125	2.4	0836	4.4	0846	3.7	
1344	4.9	1539	2.1	1531	2.7	1633	2.9	1512	3.7	1436	3.3	1745	1.2	1440	1.9	1506	1.3	
2001	1.9	2143	5.5	2148	7.9	2227	10.5	2116	1.3	2054	1.0	2336	2.1	2106	4.0	2103	3.5	
0212	4.5	0353	2.4	0345	3.1	0443	3.2	0402	3.4	0314	3.0	0606	1.3	0300	2.2	0326	1.4	3 F
0821	2.2	1007	5.5	1015	7.8	1048	10.1	0941	1.6	0903	1.2	1222	2.3	0925	4.1	0930	3.5	
1434	4.7	1627	2.5	1620	3.2	1703	3.5	1612	3.5	1527	3.2	1842	1.3	1541	2.1	1552	1.5	
2058	2.2	2230	5.1	2237	7.4	2303	9.7	2226	1.5	2152	1.1			2206	3.8	2151	3.3	
0315	4.3	0444	2.7	0440	3.6	0516	3.8	0516	3.3	0413	2.9	0051	1.9	0410	2.5	0418	1.5	4 SA
0924	2.5	1105	5.2	1115	7.3	1127	9.4	1054	1.7	1000	1.3	0709	1.4	1028	3.9	1025	3.4	
1540	4.5	1735	2.8	1729	3.6	1745	4.1	1723	3.4	1627	3.1	1341	2.3	1701	2.2	1651	1.6	
2212	2.3	2339	4.8	2343	7.0			2341	1.5	2301	1.2	1959	1.4	2330	3.7	2253	3.2	
0444	4.2	0604	3.0	0605	3.9	0000	9.0	0631	3.2	0518	2.8	0314	1.9	0545	2.5	0527	1.6	5 SU
1048	2.6	1229	5.0	1232	7.0	0604	4.5	1209	1.8	1111	1.4	0830	1.4	1148	3.9	1135	3.2	
1703	4.5	1909	2.8	1854	3.7	1253	9.0	1837	3.4	1733	3.0	1513	2.4	1827	2.2	1806	1.6	
2334	2.2					1851	4.6					2140	1.3					
0612	4.3	0115	4.8	0107	6.8	0140	8.9	0052	1.4	0013	1.1	0424	2.1	0102	3.8	0012	3.2	6 M
1207	2.5	0745	2.8	0735	3.7	0727	4.4	0738	3.3	0624	2.8	0956	1.3	0705	2.3	0645	1.6	
1818	4.6	1357	5.2	1351	7.2	1437	9.4	1317	1.7	1223	1.4	1618	2.5	1306	4.0	1254	3.3	
		2027	2.5	2009	3.4	2106	4.2	1942	3.4	1836	3.0	2251	1.2	1930	1.9	1921	1.5	
0041	2.0	0236	5.1	0227	7.2	0312	9.6	0150	1.3	0114	1.0	0507	2.3	0202	4.1	0127	3.3	7 TU
0712	4.6	0854	2.5	0843	3.3	0940	4.1	0833	3.4	0724	2.9	1057	1.2	0759	2.1	0755	1.4	
1306	2.2	1500	5.3	1457	7.7	1545	10.4	1410	1.5	1324	1.2	1707	2.7	1402	4.2	1400	3.5	
1915	4.9	2123	2.1	2107	2.8	2215	3.2	2033	3.5	1933	3.1	2337	1.0	2015	1.6	2024	1.3	
0131	1.7	0328	5.6	0326	7.8	0412	10.6	0233	1.1	0205	0.9	0545	2.5	0244	4.3	0227	3.5	8 W
0756	4.8	0945	2.0	0933	2.7	1041	3.0	0918	3.5	0814	3.0	1145	1.0	0839	1.8	0853	1.2	
1351	1.8	1547	6.0	1547	8.3	1638	11.4	1451	1.3	1415	1.1	1749	2.8	1445	4.5	1454	3.7	
1959	5.1	2207	1.7	2154	2.2	2310	2.3	2116	3.6	2022	3.1			2054	1.3	2115	1.0	
0212	1.4	0410	6.1	0412	8.4	0501	11.7	0309	1.0	0249	0.7	0018	0.8	0318	4.6	0315	3.8	9 TH
0832	5.1	1027	1.6	1016	2.0	1135	2.2	0954	3.7	0858	3.1	0621	2.6	0915	1.4	0942	0.9	
1429	1.5	1627	6.5	1630	8.9	1724	12.3	1524	1.2	1500	0.9	1228	0.8	1522	4.7	1539	3.9	
2038	5.4	2248	1.3	2236	1.6			2152	3.7	2106	3.2	1829	2.9	2127	1.1	2201	0.8	
0248	1.1	0448	6.5	0452	9.0	0003	1.7	0340	0.8	0330	0.6	0055	0.7	0350	4.9	0359	4.0	10 F
0906	5.4	1106	1.2	1055	1.5	0545	12.5	1025	3.8	0939	3.2	0657	2.8	0948	1.1	1027	0.8	
1506	1.2	1706	6.8	1711	9.4	1227	1.6	1557	1.0	1542	0.8	1309	0.7	1558	5.0	1621	4.1	
2115	5.6	2327	0.9	2316	1.2	1806	13.0	2227	3.9	2146	3.3	1907	3.0	2201	0.8	2245	0.7	
0324	0.8	0527	6.9	0530	9.5	0054	1.3	0412	0.7	0408	0.5	0132	0.6	0423	5.1	0439	4.2	11 SA
0939	5.6	1146	0.9	1133	1.1	0627	13.1	1056	3.9	1016	3.4	0733	2.9	1022	0.9	1109	0.6	O
1542	0.9	1746	7.1	1751	9.8	1307	1.1	1630	0.8	1621	0.6	1350	0.6	1636	5.2	1702	4.3	
2151	5.8			2354	0.9	1849	13.4	2303	4.0	2226	3.4	1945	3.1	2236	0.7	2327	0.6	
0400	0.7	0006	0.7	0609	9.9	0142	1.0	0447	0.5	0447	0.4	0209	0.5	0457	5.3	0520	4.3	12 SU
1014	5.7	0606	7.1	1212	0.9	0709	13.5	1129	4.1	1054	3.5	0809	2.9	1058	0.7	1151	0.6	
1620	0.7	1226	0.7	1831	10.0	1402	1.0	1707	0.6	1702	0.5	1431	0.5	1714	5.3	1742	4.3	
2230	5.9	1827	7.3			1930	13.7	2341	4.2	2307	3.5	2024	3.1	2312	0.6			
0439	0.6	0046	0.6	0033	0.8	0225	0.8	0524	0.5	0526	0.4	0246	0.5	0534	5.4	0008	0.6	13 M
1052	5.8	0646	7.2	0649	10.0	0749	13.7	1206	4.2	1133	3.5	0846	2.9	1136	0.6	0600	4.4	
1700	0.7	1306	0.6	1251	0.9	1444	0.9	1748	0.5	1744	0.4	1514	0.6	1755	5.3	1233	0.5	
2312	5.8	1908	7.3	1912	10.0	2012	13.7			2350	3.5	2106	3.0	2351	0.7	1822	4.3	
0519	0.7	0127	0.6	0112	0.8	0305	0.9	0024	4.2	0608	0.4	0324	0.6	0614	5.4	0048	0.6	14 TU
1133	5.6	0727	7.2	0729	9.9	0829	13.6	0606	0.5	1215	3.6	0924	2.9	1217	0.7	0641	4.3	
1744	0.7	1348	0.7	1331	1.0	1522	1.1	1248	4.2	1828	0.4	1559	0.7	1839	5.3	1315	0.6	
2357	5.7	1951	7.1	1954	9.8	2053	13.4	1833	0.5			2151	2.8			1903	4.2	
0603	0.8	0208	0.8	0151	1.1	0340	1.2	0113	4.2	0037	3.5	0406	0.6	0033	0.9	0130	0.7	15 W
1218	5.7	0810	7.0	0811	9.7	0909	13.3	0651	0.6	0653	0.5	1006	2.8	0657	5.3	0724	4.3	
1833	0.9	1433	0.9	1413	1.3	1556	1.4	1336	4.2	1304	3.5	1648	0.8	1358	0.7	1358	0.7	
		2036	6.8	2038	9.4	2136	12.9	1923	0.6	1916	0.5	2241	2.7	1927	5.1	1947	4.1	

• • Time: UT. For British Summer Time (shaded) March 26th to October 29th ADD ONE HOUR • •

NOVEMBER 2000 TIDE TABLES

•• Time: UT. For British Summer Time (shaded) March 26th to October 29TH ADD ONE HOUR ••

	HOLYHEAD	MILFORD HAVEN	SWANSEA	AVONMOUTH	DUBLIN	BELFAST	LONDON-DERRY	GALWAY	COBH
	Time m	Time m	Time m	Time m	Time m	Time m	Time m	Time m	Time m
16TH	0047 5.5	0252 1.2	0233 1.5	0412 1.6	0207 4.0	0129 3.3	0451 0.8	0119 1.2	0215 0.8
	0652 1.1	0856 6.7	0856 9.2	0953 12.7	0742 0.8	0742 0.7	1052 2.7	0745 5.1	0809 4.1
	1308 5.5	1521 1.3	1459 1.7	1630 1.9	1430 4.1	1353 3.5	1744 1.0	1354 1.1	1445 0.8
	1927 1.1	2126 6.4	2126 8.8	2222 12.2	2021 0.7	2009 0.6	2339 2.5	2021 4.8	2035 3.9
17F	0144 5.2	0341 1.5	0319 2.0	0447 2.1	0309 3.9	0227 3.2	0542 0.9	0212 1.6	0304 0.9
	0748 1.5	0948 6.3	0948 8.7	1041 12.0	0840 1.1	0839 0.9	1148 2.6	0839 4.8	0900 3.9
	1406 5.2	1616 1.7	1553 2.0	1709 2.4	1531 4.0	1451 3.4	1853 1.1	1454 1.4	1539 1.0
	2030 1.3	2223 6.0	2222 8.2	2315 11.4	2129 0.9	2112 0.7		2122 4.5	2130 3.7
18SA	0251 4.9	0439 1.9	0418 2.6	0530 2.7	0421 3.7	0337 3.0	0054 2.3	0315 1.9	0402 1.1
	0853 1.8	1051 6.0	1051 8.1	1138 11.3	0951 1.4	0948 1.0	0639 1.1	0943 4.5	1000 3.7
	1515 5.0	1724 2.0	1706 2.7	1802 2.9	1643 3.9	1557 3.3	1300 2.5	1608 1.7	1643 1.1
	2145 1.5	2332 5.6	2333 7.7		2245 1.0	2226 0.7	2034 1.2	2235 4.3	2234 3.5
19SU	0409 4.8	0554 2.2	0540 3.0	0018 10.8	0539 3.6	0458 2.9	0233 2.3	0434 2.1	0512 1.2
	1011 2.0	1205 5.8	1209 7.7	0630 3.1	1109 1.5	1109 1.1	0749 1.2	1100 4.4	1112 3.6
	1635 4.9	1848 2.1	1836 2.9	1248 10.9	1800 3.8	1710 3.2	1446 2.5	1734 1.7	1758 1.2
	2304 1.5			1914 3.2		2345 0.7	2210 1.1	2359 4.3	2351 3.5
20M	0532 4.8	0051 5.5	0056 7.5	0133 10.6	0001 1.0	0620 2.9	0354 2.4	0604 2.1	0631 1.2
	1131 2.0	0718 2.2	0714 3.0	0751 3.2	0654 3.6	1225 1.1	0912 1.2	1224 4.4	1231 3.6
	1753 5.0	1326 5.8	1333 7.7	1406 11.0	1226 1.5	1821 3.3	1609 2.6	1852 1.6	1915 1.1
		2009 1.9	2001 2.7	2039 2.9	1912 3.9		2311 1.0		
21TU	0017 1.4	0211 5.7	0218 7.7	0251 10.9	0114 1.0	0056 0.7	0451 2.5	0115 4.5	0108 3.5
	0644 4.9	0835 2.0	0832 2.7	0915 2.8	0803 3.7	0728 3.0	1029 1.1	0718 1.9	0746 1.1
	1241 1.8	1439 6.0	1448 8.1	1524 11.5	1336 1.4	1329 1.0	1702 2.7	1334 4.5	1347 3.7
	1900 5.2	2115 1.6	2109 2.3	2157 2.4	2017 4.0	1926 3.3	2357 0.8	1951 1.4	2023 1.0
22W	0118 1.2	0315 6.0	0326 8.2	0404 11.6	0215 0.9	0155 0.6	0539 2.6	0212 4.7	0216 3.7
	0741 5.1	0936 1.6	0933 2.2	1031 2.2	0903 3.8	0825 3.1	1127 1.0	0812 1.6	0851 0.9
	1338 1.6	1539 6.3	1548 8.6	1632 12.2	1434 1.3	1424 0.8	1745 2.8	1428 4.7	1450 3.9
	1954 5.4	2209 1.3	2204 1.9	2309 1.9	2114 4.1	2023 3.4		2037 1.2	2121 0.8
23TH	0209 1.1	0408 6.4	0418 8.8	0504 12.3	0306 0.8	0246 0.5	0036 0.8	0258 4.9	0312 3.9
	0827 5.3	1027 1.3	1021 1.8	1139 1.7	0951 3.9	0913 3.3	0620 2.7	0856 1.3	0947 0.7
	1426 1.3	1628 6.6	1638 9.1	1727 12.6	1522 1.1	1512 0.7	1215 0.9	1514 4.9	1542 4.0
	2040 5.5	2254 1.1	2249 1.6		2202 4.1	2113 3.5	1825 2.9	2118 1.0	2211 0.7
24F	0253 1.0	0453 6.6	0503 9.2	0010 1.5	0348 0.7	0331 0.5	0110 0.7	0339 5.1	0401 4.1
	0906 5.4	1111 1.1	1103 1.5	0554 12.7	1032 4.0	0954 3.4	0658 2.8	0937 1.1	1034 0.6
	1508 1.2	1712 6.8	1721 9.4	1233 1.4	1604 1.0	1556 0.7	1258 0.8	1556 5.0	1627 4.1
	2121 5.6	2334 1.0	2329 1.4	1813 12.9	2244 4.1	2159 3.6	1902 2.9	2157 1.0	2254 0.6
25SA	0332 0.9	0533 6.8	0542 9.5	0059 1.4	0426 0.8	0412 0.5	0141 0.7	0418 5.2	0445 4.2
	0943 5.5	1150 1.0	1142 1.4	0636 12.9	1106 4.0	1031 3.4	0733 2.8	1016 1.0	1117 0.6
	1547 1.1	1751 6.8	1800 9.5	1318 1.4	1642 0.9	1636 0.6	1336 0.8	1636 5.0	1708 4.1
	2200 5.6			1854 13.0	2321 4.1	2241 3.6	1936 2.8	2235 0.9	2335 0.7
26SU	0409 1.0	0011 0.9	0005 1.4	0140 1.5	0501 0.8	0450 0.6	0209 0.7	0456 5.2	0524 4.2
	1018 5.6	0611 6.8	0619 9.6	0713 13.0	1136 4.1	1106 3.5	0806 2.8	1054 0.9	1155 0.7
	1624 1.0	1227 1.0	1218 1.4	1357 1.4	1719 0.9	1714 0.6	1412 0.8	1715 5.0	1745 4.1
	2237 5.5	1829 6.8	1836 9.4	1930 13.0	2355 4.1	2320 3.5	2009 2.7	2312 1.0	
27M	0444 1.0	0045 1.0	0038 1.5	0215 1.5	0536 0.9	0524 0.6	0237 0.8	0533 5.2	0011 0.7
	1054 5.6	0647 6.8	0654 9.5	0748 13.1	1207 4.1	1139 3.5	0837 2.8	1133 1.0	0601 4.2
	1701 1.1	1302 1.0	1252 1.5	1429 1.5	1756 0.9	1751 0.6	1445 0.8	1755 4.9	1230 0.8
	2314 5.4	1904 6.7	1911 9.3	2005 12.9		2357 3.5	2041 2.7	2349 1.2	1820 4.0
28TU ●	0518 1.2	0118 1.1	0109 1.7	0245 1.6	0030 4.0	0558 0.7	0304 0.8	0611 5.1	0044 0.8
	1129 5.5	0721 6.7	0727 9.4	0822 13.0	0611 0.9	1212 3.6	0908 2.8	1212 1.1	0636 4.1
	1738 1.2	1336 1.1	1325 1.7	1458 1.6	1239 4.1	1826 0.7	1518 0.9	1834 4.8	1302 0.9
	2350 5.2	1938 6.5	1944 9.1	2039 12.6	1834 0.9		2112 2.6		1852 3.9
29W	0553 1.3	0151 1.3	0141 1.9	0311 1.8	0107 3.9	0034 3.4	0333 0.9	0027 1.4	0115 0.9
	1204 5.4	0754 6.6	0800 9.1	0854 12.6	0648 1.0	0632 0.8	0941 2.8	0649 5.0	0711 4.0
	1815 1.4	1409 1.3	1359 1.9	1525 1.8	1317 4.0	1248 3.5	1553 1.0	1251 1.3	1333 1.0
		2011 6.3	2016 8.8	2109 12.2	1915 1.0	1903 0.7	2147 2.5	1915 4.6	1925 3.8
30TH	0025 5.1	0223 1.5	0212 2.1	0336 2.1	0148 3.7	0113 3.3	0406 1.0	0104 1.5	0147 1.0
	0628 1.5	0828 6.3	0834 8.8	0924 12.0	0729 1.2	0707 0.9	1017 2.7	0728 4.8	0745 3.9
	1239 5.3	1444 1.6	1434 2.2	1551 2.2	1359 3.9	1325 3.5	1632 1.1	1333 1.5	1405 1.1
	1853 1.5	2045 6.0	2050 8.4	2139 11.5	2000 1.1	1942 0.8	2225 2.3	1956 4.4	1959 3.7

WEST COAST ENGLAND, WALES & IRELAND Time Zone UT
Holyhead * Milford Haven * Swansea * Avonmouth * Dublin * Belfast * Londonderry * Galway * Cobh

TIDE TABLES DECEMBER 2000

	HOLYHEAD	MILFORD HAVEN	SWANSEA	AVONMOUTH	DUBLIN	BELFAST	LONDON-DERRY	GALWAY	COBH
	Time m	Time m	Time m	Time m	Time m	Time m	Time m	Time m	Time m
1 F	0103 4.9 0706 1.8 1318 5.1 1935 1.7	0255 1.8 0903 6.0 1520 1.9 2121 5.7	0245 2.4 0909 8.4 1511 2.5 2126 8.0	0359 2.5 0954 11.3 1617 2.6 2209 10.9	0236 3.6 0815 1.3 1446 3.8 2051 1.2	0154 3.2 0745 1.0 1406 3.4 2026 0.9	0445 1.1 1058 2.6 1717 1.2 2310 2.2	0145 1.9 0809 4.6 1416 1.7 2039 4.2	0220 1.1 0822 3.8 1441 1.2 2036 3.6
2 SA	0145 4.7 0749 2.0 1402 4.9 2023 1.9	0330 2.1 0942 5.8 1602 2.2 2201 5.4	0322 2.7 0949 8.0 1553 2.8 2207 7.6	0426 2.9 1026 10.7 1648 3.1 2244 10.3	0330 3.4 0909 1.5 1539 3.6 2150 1.3	0239 3.1 0830 1.1 1451 3.3 2115 1.0	0530 1.2 1147 2.5 1809 1.2	0230 2.1 0853 4.3 1506 1.9 2129 4.0	0258 1.2 0903 3.6 1523 1.3 2120 3.4
3 SU	0237 4.5 0840 2.1 1455 4.7 2121 2.1	0414 2.4 1029 5.5 1654 2.4 2254 5.1	0406 3.1 1037 7.6 1645 3.2 2259 7.2	0459 3.4 1106 10.1 1727 3.5 2330 9.8	0431 3.3 1012 1.6 1638 3.5 2252 1.4	0330 3.0 0920 1.2 1541 3.2 2211 1.0	0008 2.1 0622 1.3 1246 2.5 1910 1.3	0325 2.3 0944 4.2 1605 2.0 2228 3.9	0344 1.3 0951 3.5 1615 1.4 2213 3.3
4 M	0342 4.3 0945 2.4 1600 4.6 2228 2.1	0512 2.6 1130 5.3 1800 2.6	0506 3.4 1137 7.3 1752 3.3	0541 3.8 1201 9.7 1817 3.9	0539 3.2 1118 1.7 1742 3.4 2354 1.4	0427 2.9 1018 1.3 1636 3.1 2312 1.0	0127 2.1 0725 1.3 1357 2.5 2024 1.3	0434 2.4 1044 4.0 1712 2.1 2342 3.9	0442 1.4 1048 3.4 1717 1.4 2317 3.2
5 TU	0457 4.3 1058 2.4 1712 4.6 2336 2.0	0003 5.0 0627 2.7 1243 5.3 1915 2.5	0005 7.0 0624 3.5 1247 7.3 1905 3.2	0032 9.5 0637 4.2 1318 9.6 1929 4.1	0644 3.3 1220 1.7 1845 3.4	0527 2.9 1123 1.3 1736 3.1	0255 2.1 0839 1.3 1511 2.5 2142 1.2	0552 2.4 1154 4.0 1821 2.0	0549 1.4 1154 3.3 1826 1.4
6 W	0609 4.5 1206 2.2 1818 4.8	0121 5.1 0746 2.6 1354 5.5 2023 2.2	0120 7.1 0740 3.3 1356 7.5 2012 2.9	0154 9.6 0800 4.2 1439 10.1 2103 3.6	0051 1.3 0741 3.3 1315 1.6 1942 3.4	0015 1.0 0628 2.9 1227 1.2 1836 3.1	0403 2.2 0952 1.2 1612 2.6 2245 1.1	0054 4.0 0700 2.2 1301 4.1 1918 1.8	0027 3.3 0700 1.4 1303 3.4 1933 1.2
7 TH	0036 1.7 0705 4.7 1302 1.9 1913 5.0	0228 5.4 0851 2.2 1454 5.8 2119 1.9	0229 7.6 0842 2.8 1457 8.0 2109 2.4	0310 10.3 0935 3.6 1544 11.0 2216 2.9	0139 1.2 0829 3.5 1401 1.4 2030 3.5	0112 0.9 0724 3.0 1327 1.1 1933 3.1	0456 2.4 1054 1.1 1705 2.8 2335 0.9	0150 4.2 0751 1.9 1357 4.3 2006 1.5	0133 3.4 0805 1.2 1405 3.6 2033 1.0
8 F	0127 1.5 0751 5.0 1351 1.6 2001 5.2	0324 5.9 0945 1.8 1546 6.2 2209 1.5	0327 8.2 0934 2.3 1551 8.6 2159 1.9	0412 11.2 1045 2.7 1640 11.9 2318 2.1	0221 1.0 0912 3.6 1443 1.2 2115 3.7	0204 0.8 0816 3.1 1421 1.0 2026 3.2	0542 2.6 1148 0.9 1753 2.9	0234 4.5 0835 1.6 1443 4.6 2049 1.3	0232 3.6 0903 1.0 1500 3.8 2127 0.9
9 SA	0212 1.2 0833 5.3 1435 1.3 2045 5.5	0412 6.3 1034 1.4 1634 6.6 2257 1.1	0416 8.8 1021 1.7 1639 9.1 2246 1.4	0506 12.2 1146 2.0 1733 12.7	0302 0.9 0950 3.8 1523 1.0 2157 3.9	0253 0.7 0904 3.3 1512 0.8 2116 3.3	0021 0.8 0626 2.7 1239 0.8 1839 3.0	0313 4.8 0916 1.3 1527 4.9 2130 1.0	0324 3.9 0955 0.8 1550 4.0 2216 0.7
10 SU	0255 0.9 0913 5.5 1518 1.0 2129 5.7	0458 6.7 1121 1.0 1721 6.9 2342 0.8	0503 9.4 1107 1.3 1727 9.6 2332 1.0	0018 1.5 0556 12.9 1244 1.5 1822 13.2	0342 0.7 1028 4.0 1604 0.8 2241 4.1	0339 0.6 0950 3.4 1559 0.7 2205 3.4	0103 0.5 0708 2.8 1327 0.6 1923 3.0	0352 5.0 0957 1.0 1610 5.1 2211 0.8	0412 4.1 1044 0.6 1636 4.1 2303 0.6
11 M O	0337 0.7 0954 5.7 1602 0.8 2213 5.8	0544 7.0 1207 0.8 1808 7.1	0548 9.7 1153 1.0 1813 9.8	0112 1.1 0644 13.4 1337 1.1 1910 13.6	0423 0.6 1108 4.1 1648 0.6 2326 4.2	0425 0.5 1034 3.5 1646 0.6 2254 3.5	0144 0.6 0750 2.9 1414 0.6 2009 3.0	0432 5.3 1038 0.7 1654 5.3 2252 0.7	0458 4.2 1131 0.5 1721 4.2 2348 0.5
12 TU	0421 0.6 1036 5.8 1647 0.6 2300 5.8	0028 0.6 0629 7.2 1254 0.6 1854 7.2	0016 0.8 0633 9.9 1239 0.9 1900 9.9	0203 0.9 0730 13.7 1426 0.9 1957 13.7	0506 0.5 1150 4.3 1733 0.4	0511 0.4 1119 3.6 1733 0.4 2342 3.5	0225 0.5 0831 3.0 1502 0.6 2054 3.0	0514 5.4 1121 0.6 1740 5.4 2336 0.8	0543 4.3 1217 0.4 1806 4.2
13 W	0506 0.7 1121 5.9 1735 0.6 2349 5.8	0114 0.6 0715 7.3 1340 0.6 1942 7.1	0101 0.8 0718 9.9 1325 0.9 1947 9.8	0249 0.8 0816 13.8 1512 1.0 2044 13.6	0014 4.3 0551 0.5 1236 4.3 1822 0.4	0557 0.5 1206 3.7 1821 0.4	0307 0.6 0914 3.0 1551 0.7 2142 2.9	0558 5.5 1206 0.6 1828 5.3	0034 0.5 0629 4.3 1303 0.4 1851 4.2
14 TH	0553 0.8 1209 5.8 1826 0.6	0200 0.7 0802 7.2 1428 0.7 2030 6.9	0145 0.9 0805 9.8 1412 1.0 2034 9.5	0332 1.0 0902 13.6 1554 1.2 2130 13.2	0105 4.2 0639 0.6 1325 4.3 1915 0.4	0033 3.4 0645 0.5 1254 3.8 1912 0.4	0351 0.6 0958 3.0 1643 0.8 2234 2.7	0021 0.9 0645 5.4 1254 0.7 1918 5.2	0120 0.5 0715 4.3 1349 0.5 1937 4.1
15 F	0041 5.6 0643 1.0 1300 5.7 1921 0.8	0247 0.9 0851 6.9 1518 1.0 2121 6.6	0230 1.2 0853 9.4 1459 1.3 2122 9.0	0411 1.3 0948 13.2 1633 1.5 2218 12.7	0200 4.1 0731 0.7 1418 4.3 2012 0.5	0127 3.3 0737 0.6 1346 3.6 2006 0.4	0437 0.7 1045 2.9 1739 0.9 2330 2.6	0110 1.1 0735 5.3 1347 0.9 2011 5.0	0206 0.6 0802 4.2 1437 0.6 2026 4.0

● ● Time: UT. For British Summer Time (shaded) March 26th to October 29th ADD ONE HOUR ● ●

DECEMBER 2000 TIDE TABLES

•• Time: UT. For British Summer Time (shaded) March 26th to October 29TH ADD ONE HOUR ••

	HOLYHEAD		MILFORD HAVEN		SWANSEA		AVONMOUTH		DUBLIN		BELFAST		LONDON-DERRY		GALWAY		COBH	
	Time	m	Time	m	Time	m	Time	m	Time	m	Time	m	Time	m	Time	m	Time	m
16SA	0137	5.3	0336	1.2	0316	1.6	0450	1.7	0300	3.9	0226	3.2	0527	0.8	0203	1.4	0257	0.7
	0737	1.3	0942	6.7	0943	9.0	1037	12.7	0827	1.0	0833	0.8	1138	2.8	0829	5.0	0853	4.0
	1356	5.5	1612	1.3	1551	1.8	1715	1.9	1518	4.2	1442	3.5	1844	1.1	1443	1.2	1530	0.7
	2020	1.0	2215	6.2	2214	8.5	2309	12.1	2115	0.7	2106	0.5			2108	4.7	2118	3.8
17SU	0238	5.1	0430	1.6	0410	2.1	0533	2.1	0406	3.8	0331	3.0	0036	2.4	0300	1.6	0351	0.8
	0836	1.5	1039	6.3	1039	8.5	1130	12.0	0930	1.3	0936	0.9	0621	1.0	0927	4.8	0948	3.8
	1457	5.3	1711	1.6	1651	2.2	1801	2.3	1624	4.0	1544	3.4	1240	2.7	1545	1.4	1627	0.9
	2125	1.2	2314	5.9	2313	8.0			2222	0.9	2211	0.5	2000	1.1	2211	4.5	2217	3.6
18M	0345	4.9	0532	1.9	0516	2.5	0003	11.5	0516	3.6	0443	2.9	0151	2.3	0406	1.9	0452	0.9
	0944	1.8	1141	6.0	1143	8.0	0622	2.5	1040	1.4	1046	1.0	0723	1.1	1033	4.5	1051	3.7
	1606	5.1	1818	1.8	1803	2.6	1229	11.5	1734	3.9	1649	3.3	1357	2.6	1656	1.6	1731	1.0
	2234	1.4					1856	2.6	2332	1.0	2320	0.6	2123	1.1	2321	4.4	2322	3.5
19TU	0457	4.7	0020	5.7	0022	7.6	0105	11.0	0626	3.6	0555	2.9	0308	2.3	0522	2.0	0600	1.0
	1056	1.9	0642	2.0	0634	2.8	0722	2.8	1152	1.5	1156	1.0	0833	1.2	1147	4.4	1200	3.5
	1718	5.0	1249	5.9	1255	7.8	1334	11.2	1843	3.9	1756	3.3	1519	2.6	1811	1.6	1840	1.0
	2344	1.5	1929	1.9	1920	2.7	2000	2.8					2230	1.1				
20W	0609	4.8	0130	5.6	0139	7.6	0214	10.9	0042	1.0	0027	0.6	0413	2.4	0036	4.4	0032	3.5
	1207	1.9	0755	2.0	0751	2.8	0833	2.9	0732	3.6	0700	3.0	0947	1.1	0639	1.9	0712	1.0
	1827	5.0	1400	5.8	1409	7.9	1445	11.2	1303	1.5	1301	0.9	1626	2.6	1301	4.4	1311	3.5
			2038	1.9	2033	2.6	2112	2.8	1948	3.9	1900	3.3	2322	1.0	1916	1.6	1949	1.0
21TH	0048	1.5	0239	5.8	0250	7.9	0325	11.1	0145	1.0	0129	0.6	0507	2.5	0140	4.5	0142	3.5
	0712	4.9	0902	1.9	0858	2.5	0947	2.8	0832	3.7	0757	3.0	1054	1.1	0742	1.8	0821	1.0
	1311	1.8	1506	6.0	1515	8.1	1554	11.4	1406	1.4	1359	0.9	1719	2.6	1403	4.4	1419	3.6
	1929	5.1	2137	1.7	2133	2.4	2224	2.6	2048	3.9	1959	3.3			2010	1.5	2051	0.9
22F	0145	1.4	0338	6.0	0348	8.3	0429	11.5	0239	1.0	0223	0.6	0005	0.9	0232	4.6	0245	3.7
	0803	5.0	0959	1.7	0953	2.3	1057	2.5	0924	3.8	0847	3.1	0554	2.6	0834	1.6	0921	0.9
	1406	1.6	1602	6.1	1611	8.5	1655	11.8	1500	1.3	1451	0.8	1149	1.0	1454	4.5	1517	3.7
	2021	5.1	2228	1.5	2224	2.1	2330	2.3	2139	3.9	2052	3.3	1804	2.6	2056	1.4	2145	0.8
23SA	0233	1.3	0428	6.2	0438	8.7	0524	11.9	0324	1.0	0310	0.6	0042	0.9	0317	4.8	0338	3.8
	0848	5.2	1048	1.5	1040	2.0	1157	2.2	1007	3.9	0930	3.3	0636	2.7	0919	1.4	1011	0.8
	1453	1.4	1650	6.3	1658	8.7	1746	12.0	1546	1.2	1538	0.7	1236	1.0	1539	4.6	1605	3.8
	2106	5.2	2312	1.4	2306	1.9			2224	3.9	2140	3.4	1845	2.6	2138	1.3	2232	0.8
24SU ●	0314	1.3	0512	6.4	0521	9.0	0024	2.1	0404	1.0	0354	0.7	0117	0.9	0357	4.9	0424	3.9
	0927	5.3	1130	1.3	1122	1.9	0610	12.3	1044	4.0	1009	3.4	0714	2.7	1001	1.3	1055	0.8
	1535	1.3	1733	6.4	1740	8.9	1245	1.9	1627	1.1	1621	0.7	1318	0.9	1621	4.7	1647	3.9
	2147	5.2	2351	1.3	2345	1.8	1831	12.3	2303	3.9	2224	3.4	1923	2.6	2218	1.3	2312	0.8
25M	0352	1.2	0553	6.5	0600	9.1	0108	1.9	0442	1.0	0432	0.7	0148	0.8	0437	5.0	0506	3.9
	1003	5.4	1209	1.2	1201	1.8	0651	12.5	1118	4.0	1046	3.4	0749	2.8	1042	1.1	1134	0.8
	1612	1.2	1812	6.5	1819	9.0	1327	1.8	1706	1.0	1700	0.6	1356	0.9	1702	4.7	1725	3.8
	2224	5.2					1911	12.4	2339	3.9	2303	3.4	1957	2.6	2257	1.3	2350	0.8
26TU	0427	1.2	0027	1.2	0021	1.8	0147	1.8	0518	1.0	0507	0.7	0218	0.8	0516	5.0	0543	3.9
	1038	5.5	0630	6.6	0637	9.2	0729	12.7	1150	4.1	1121	3.5	0822	2.8	1121	1.1	1209	0.8
	1648	1.2	1245	1.2	1238	1.8	1405	1.7	1745	0.9	1736	0.6	1430	0.9	1741	4.7	1800	3.8
	2300	5.2	1848	6.5	1855	8.9	1948	12.5			2341	3.3	2030	2.6	2334	1.3		
27W	0501	1.2	0101	1.2	0055	1.8	0222	1.8	0014	3.9	0540	0.7	0248	0.8	0554	5.0	0024	0.8
	1112	5.5	0705	6.6	0712	9.1	0804	12.7	0554	1.0	1155	3.5	0854	2.8	1159	1.1	0618	3.9
	1724	1.2	1321	1.2	1313	1.8	1439	1.7	1224	4.1	1812	0.7	1503	0.9	1820	4.7	1242	0.8
	2333	5.2	1923	6.4	1930	8.9	2022	12.4	1822	0.9			2101	2.5			1833	3.8
28TH	0534	1.3	0134	1.3	0127	1.9	0254	1.8	0050	3.8	0016	3.3	0317	0.9	0012	1.3	0056	0.8
	1145	5.5	0739	6.5	0746	9.0	0837	12.5	0632	1.0	0612	0.8	0927	2.8	0632	5.0	0653	3.9
	1758	1.3	1354	1.3	1347	1.9	1511	1.8	1300	4.1	1229	3.6	1538	1.0	1237	1.2	1315	0.9
			1955	6.3	2002	8.7	2054	12.2	1901	1.0	1846	0.7	2133	2.5	1858	4.6	1906	3.7
29F	0008	5.1	0206	1.4	0159	1.9	0323	2.0	0128	3.7	0052	3.2	0349	0.9	0048	1.4	0128	0.8
	0608	1.4	0812	6.4	0820	8.8	0909	12.3	0711	1.0	0646	0.8	1001	2.8	0709	4.8	0727	3.8
	1220	5.4	1428	1.4	1421	1.9	1540	2.0	1339	4.0	1303	3.5	1615	1.0	1315	1.3	1347	0.9
	1833	1.3	2028	6.1	2034	8.5	2124	11.9	1941	1.0	1921	0.7	2209	2.4	1936	4.5	1939	3.7
30SA	0043	5.0	0239	1.5	0230	2.1	0350	2.2	0209	3.6	0129	3.2	0424	1.0	0126	1.6	0201	0.8
	0644	1.5	0845	6.3	0853	8.6	0939	11.9	0751	1.2	0722	0.9	1038	2.8	0747	4.7	0802	3.8
	1257	5.3	1502	1.6	1454	2.1	1609	2.2	1421	3.8	1339	3.5	1655	1.1	1354	1.4	1421	0.9
	1911	1.5	2101	6.0	2106	8.3	2155	11.6	2022	1.1	2000	0.7	2249	2.4	2015	4.4	2015	3.7
31SU	0121	4.8	0312	1.7	0303	2.2	0417	2.5	0254	3.5	0209	3.1	0503	1.0	0206	1.7	0236	1.0
	0722	1.7	0921	6.1	0927	8.3	1012	11.5	0834	1.3	0802	0.9	1119	2.7	0820	4.5	0839	3.7
	1336	5.1	1539	1.8	1528	2.3	1639	2.5	1505	3.7	1418	3.4	1741	1.1	1433	1.5	1459	1.0
	1951	1.6	2137	5.8	2141	8.0	2229	11.1	2106	1.2	2042	0.8	2335	2.3	2055	4.2	2054	3.5

DENMARK, GERMANY, HOLLAND & BELGIUM Time Zone -0100
Esbjerg * Helgoland * Cuxhaven * Hoek van Holland * Rotterdam * Vlissingen * Antwerpen * Dunkerque * Calais

TIDE TABLES JANUARY 2000

	esbjerg	HELGOLAND	CUXHAVEN	HOEK VAN HOLLAND	ROTTERDAM	VLISSINGEN	ANTWERPEN	DUNKERQUE	CALAIS
	Time m	Time m	Time m	Time m	Time m	Time m	Time m	Time m	Time m
1 SA	0357 0.3	0655 2.5	0206 0.7	0421 0.4	0555 0.5	0356 1.0	0503 1.1	0309 1.6	0300 2.3
	1031 1.7	1354 0.6	0801 3.0	1058 1.7	1202 1.7	1011 3.9	1120 4.8	0902 5.0	0827 5.9
	1646 0.2	1941 2.3	1509 0.6	1642 0.2	1814 0.2	1634 0.7	1746 0.6	1543 1.5	1534 2.1
	2318 1.5		2045 2.7	2333 1.8		2247 4.0	2358 5.0	2133 5.0	2103 5.9
2 SU	0508 0.3	0217 0.7	0333 0.7	0518 0.4	0040 1.8	0507 1.0	0615 1.0	0416 1.5	0404 2.2
	1138 1.7	0809 2.5	0912 2.9	1159 1.7	0725 0.5	1112 4.0	1227 4.9	1001 5.1	0929 6.0
	1749 0.3	1505 0.6	1622 0.6	1736 0.3	1305 1.7	1735 0.7	1851 0.5	1644 1.3	1632 1.9
		2055 2.3	2157 2.8		1936 0.3	2342 4.1		2227 5.2	2202 6.1
3 M	0018 1.6	0333 0.7	0450 0.7	0027 1.9	0138 1.8	0602 0.9	0100 5.2	0512 1.3	0456 2.0
	0612 0.3	0922 2.4	1024 2.9	0611 0.4	0835 0.4	1205 4.1	0721 0.8	1051 5.3	1025 6.2
	1238 1.7	1606 0.6	1724 0.5	1250 1.8	1401 1.7	1823 0.7	1324 5.2	1734 1.2	1720 1.8
	1843 0.2	2200 2.4	2305 2.9	1826 0.3	2044 0.4		1949 0.4	2312 5.4	2253 6.3
4 TU	0111 1.7	0435 0.6	0551 0.5	0114 1.9	0230 1.8	0030 4.2	0151 5.4	0600 1.1	0540 1.8
	0707 0.3	1024 2.5	1129 2.9	0657 0.3	0939 0.4	0648 0.7	0815 0.5	1134 5.4	1112 6.4
	1330 1.7	1658 0.6	1816 0.4	1335 1.9	1451 1.7	1250 4.2	1413 5.4	1818 1.1	1801 1.6
	1930 0.2	2253 2.5		1912 0.3	2145 0.5	1904 0.6	2037 0.3	2354 5.5	2335 6.4
5 W	0154 1.7	0527 0.5	0001 3.0	0156 1.9	0314 1.8	0112 4.3	0236 5.5	0642 1.0	0620 1.6
	0754 0.2	1115 2.5	0643 0.4	0739 0.3	1126 0.5	0728 0.6	0902 0.4	1214 5.5	1152 6.6
	1415 1.7	1743 0.5	1224 3.0	1415 2.0	1533 1.7	1330 4.4	1456 5.6	1858 1.0	1839 1.5
	2010 0.2	2338 2.6	1902 0.4	1955 0.3		1942 0.6	2121 0.3		
6 TH ●	0233 1.8	0612 0.4	0048 3.1	0235 2.0	0000 0.5	0149 4.4	0315 5.6	0033 5.6	0012 6.6
	0835 0.2	1200 2.5	0730 0.4	0816 0.3	0352 1.7	0806 0.5	0943 0.3	0721 0.9	0658 1.5
	1454 1.7	1824 0.5	1310 3.0	1451 2.0	1114 0.5	1406 4.5	1534 5.7	1253 5.6	1228 6.7
	2047 0.2		1944 0.4	2038 0.4	1612 1.7	2017 0.6	2159 0.4	1935 1.0	1918 1.4
7 F	0308 1.8	0017 2.7	0130 3.1	0312 2.0	0047 0.6	0224 4.5	0351 5.6	0109 5.6	0046 6.7
	0913 0.1	0654 0.4	0812 0.3	0847 0.2	0427 1.7	0843 0.4	1021 0.4	0758 0.9	0736 1.4
	1530 1.7	1239 2.5	1353 2.9	1525 2.1	1200 0.5	1441 4.5	1609 5.6	1330 5.6	1302 6.8
	2122 0.1	1903 0.5	2024 0.4	2127 0.4	1647 1.7	2051 0.5	2233 0.5	2010 1.0	1955 1.4
8 SA	0341 1.8	0054 2.7	0210 3.2	0347 2.0	0126 0.6	0258 4.5	0425 5.5	0145 5.7	0118 6.8
	0949 0.1	0733 0.4	0851 0.3	0914 0.2	0502 1.7	0918 0.4	1055 0.5	0832 0.8	0813 1.4
	1603 1.7	1317 2.5	1434 3.0	1559 2.1	1305 0.5	1514 4.6	1642 5.6	1404 5.6	1335 6.8
	2155 0.1	1940 0.5	2101 0.4	2345 0.3	1723 1.8	2124 0.5	2304 0.5	2042 1.0	2031 1.4
9 SU	0414 1.8	0127 2.7	0248 3.2	0419 2.0	0201 0.6	0331 4.5	0458 5.5	0217 5.7	0149 6.8
	1024 0.1	0809 0.4	0930 0.3	0942 0.2	0537 1.7	0952 0.4	1128 0.5	0905 0.9	0848 1.4
	1636 1.6	1352 2.5	1513 2.9	1632 2.1	1344 0.4	1547 4.6	1715 5.6	1436 5.6	1406 6.8
	2229 0.1	2015 0.5	2137 0.4		1800 1.8	2200 0.5	2336 0.7	2115 1.0	2105 1.5
10 M	0448 1.8	0200 2.7	0324 3.2	0024 0.3	0054 0.7	0404 4.5	0531 5.5	0247 5.7	0219 6.8
	1057 0.1	0845 0.4	1006 0.4	0450 1.9	0613 1.8	1028 0.3	1202 0.5	0936 0.9	0921 1.5
	1709 1.6	1425 2.5	1550 2.9	1012 0.1	1421 0.4	1621 4.6	1749 5.6	1507 5.6	1436 6.8
	2303 0.0	2050 0.5	2212 0.4	1706 2.1	1838 1.9	2236 0.6		2147 1.0	2136 1.5
11 TU	0522 1.7	0233 2.7	0359 3.2	0105 0.3	0000 0.7	0438 4.4	0011 0.7	0320 5.7	0251 6.8
	1132 0.0	0920 0.4	1041 0.3	0521 1.9	0651 1.8	1105 0.3	0605 5.5	1010 0.9	0953 1.5
	1743 1.5	1459 2.5	1626 2.9	1045 0.1	1312 0.4	1656 4.5	1238 0.4	1542 5.7	1508 6.7
	2338 0.0	2124 0.4	2248 0.4	1742 2.1	1918 1.9	2315 0.6	1824 5.7	2221 1.1	2210 1.6
12 W	0557 1.7	0306 2.8	0433 3.2	0144 0.3	0139 0.6	0514 4.3	0046 0.6	0357 5.7	0325 6.8
	1208 0.0	0956 0.4	1117 0.3	0557 1.9	0732 1.8	1143 0.4	0640 5.6	1047 0.9	1029 1.6
	1818 1.5	1534 2.5	1701 2.9	1121 0.1	1448 0.3	1735 4.4	1314 0.3	1621 5.7	1546 6.7
		2201 0.4	2324 0.4	1821 2.0	2001 2.0	2354 0.6	1902 5.7	2300 1.1	2249 1.7
13 TH	0015 0.0	0345 2.8	0507 3.2	0223 0.3	0242 0.5	0554 4.3	0124 0.6	0439 5.7	0406 6.7
	0633 1.7	1035 0.4	1155 0.3	0636 1.8	0817 1.9	1224 0.4	0719 5.6	1128 1.0	1112 1.7
	1247 0.0	1616 2.5	1740 2.9	1207 0.0	1359 0.2	1821 4.3	1353 0.3	1707 5.6	1630 6.6
	1857 1.4	2243 0.5		1908 2.0	2051 2.0		1945 5.6	2345 1.3	2336 1.9
14 F	0058 0.0	0432 2.8	0004 0.4	0200 0.4	0344 0.5	0039 0.7	0206 0.6	0530 5.5	0454 6.5
	0715 1.6	1121 0.4	0551 3.3	0724 1.8	0909 1.9	0642 4.1	0805 5.5	1218 1.2	1204 1.8
	1332 0.0	1707 2.5	1239 0.3	1312 0.0	1511 0.2	1311 0.4	1438 0.3	1803 5.4	1725 6.4
	1943 1.4	2333 0.5	1827 3.0	2006 1.9	2152 2.0	1918 4.2	2038 5.5		
15 SA	0148 0.0	0528 2.8	0051 0.4	0223 0.3	0545 0.4	0132 0.8	0257 0.7	0042 1.4	0033 2.0
	0806 1.6	1216 0.3	0645 3.3	0827 1.8	1017 1.8	0744 4.0	0903 5.3	0629 5.3	0554 6.3
	1426 0.0	1808 2.5	1329 0.3	1422 0.0	1637 0.2	1408 0.5	1533 0.4	1306 1.3	1306 1.9
	2044 1.4		1924 3.0	2123 1.9	2308 2.0	2031 4.1	2149 5.3	1909 5.2	1833 6.2

● ● Time Zone -0100. For UT subtract 1 hour. For European summer time (shaded) 26/3-29/10 add 1 hour ● ●

JANUARY 2000 TIDE TABLES

• • Time Zone -0100. For UT subtract 1 hour. For European summer time (shaded) 26/3-29/10 add 1 hour • •

Day	ESBJERG Time	m	HELGOLAND Time	m	CUXHAVEN Time	m	HOEK VAN HOLLAND Time	m	ROTTERDAM Time	m	VLISSINGEN Time	m	ANTWERPEN Time	m	DUNKERQUE Time	m	CALAIS Time	m
16 SU	0246	0.1	0035	0.5	0147	0.4	0311	0.3	0644	0.4	0236	0.8	0359	0.8	0154	1.5	0138	2.1
	0912	1.6	0633	2.8	0748	3.3	0951	1.7	1136	1.8	0900	4.0	1022	5.2	0741	5.2	0708	6.2
	1530	0.1	1320	0.3	1430	0.2	1524	0.0	1833	0.2	1518	0.6	1641	0.5	1436	1.4	1413	1.9
	2157	1.4	1915	2.6	2027	3.1	2237	1.9			2145	4.1	2309	5.3	2024	5.2	1951	6.2
17 M	0356	0.1	0145	0.4	0255	0.3	0409	0.3	0020	2.0	0351	0.8	0513	0.8	0310	1.4	0248	2.1
	1026	1.6	0743	2.8	0855	3.3	1106	1.7	0745	0.3	1014	4.1	1140	5.2	0857	5.2	0825	6.3
	1644	0.1	1428	0.2	1541	0.0	1628	0.1	1245	1.9	1642	0.5	1802	0.6	1549	1.3	1527	1.8
	2312	1.5	2021	2.7	2132	3.2	2343	1.9	1954	0.1	2254	4.2			2137	5.3	2104	6.4
18 TU	0513	0.1	0258	0.3	0412	0.2	0510	0.3	0121	2.0	0516	0.7	0018	5.5	0422	1.2	0403	1.9
	1142	1.6	0851	2.8	1002	3.4	1210	1.9	0842	0.3	1121	4.2	0641	0.8	1005	5.4	0934	6.5
	1756	0.0	1535	0.1	1652	0.0	1730	0.1	1343	2.0	1756	0.4	1246	5.5	1657	1.1	1640	1.6
			2124	2.8	2236	3.3			2100	0.3	2356	4.4	1924	0.5	2239	5.5	2208	6.6
19 W	0024	1.6	0406	0.1	0524	0.0	0042	2.0	0215	2.1	0625	0.5	0119	5.7	0527	1.0	0514	1.6
	0626	0.0	0954	2.9	1106	3.5	0603	0.3	0937	0.3	1220	4.5	0759	0.6	1103	5.7	1035	6.8
	1257	1.7	1636	0.0	1756	-0.1	1306	2.0	1435	2.1	1854	0.3	1344	5.7	1757	0.9	1749	1.4
	1900	0.0	2222	2.9	2336	3.5	1824	0.2	2112	0.3			2030	0.4	2333	5.8	2306	6.9
20 TH O	0130	1.7	0507	0.0	0627	-0.2	0135	2.0	0302	2.1	0050	4.5	0213	5.8	0623	0.7	0620	1.3
	0730	-0.1	1053	2.9	1207	3.5	0645	0.3	0831	0.3	0721	0.3	0900	0.4	1154	5.9	1133	7.1
	1408	1.7	1732	0.0	1854	-0.2	1357	2.1	1523	2.2	1312	4.7	1436	5.9	1851	0.7	1852	1.1
	1957	0.0	2315	3.0			1909	0.2	2230	0.4	1946	0.3	2125	0.4				
21 F	0230	1.7	0604	-0.1	0032	3.5	0225	2.0	0346	2.1	0140	4.7	0304	5.8	0021	5.9	0002	7.1
	0827	-0.1	1147	2.9	0725	-0.3	0726	0.2	0903	0.2	0813	0.2	0953	0.3	0715	0.5	0719	1.0
	1510	1.7	1824	-0.1	1305	3.4	1446	2.2	1608	2.2	1401	4.8	1526	6.0	1243	6.0	1229	7.3
	2048	0.0			1947	-0.2	1951	0.3	2122	0.3	2034	0.2	2215	0.4	1939	0.6	1948	0.9
22 SA	0324	1.8	0005	3.0	0125	3.5	0314	2.0	0430	2.1	0228	4.7	0351	5.8	0109	6.0	0057	7.3
	0920	-0.2	0656	-0.2	0818	-0.3	0807	0.1	0944	0.2	0903	0.0	1042	0.2	0803	0.4	0812	0.8
	1604	1.7	1237	2.8	1358	3.4	1533	2.2	1221	0.4	1449	4.9	1613	6.0	1331	6.1	1323	7.4
	2136	0.0	1912	-0.1	2036	-0.2	2033	0.3	1653	2.2	2120	0.3	2300	0.5	2026	0.6	2038	0.8
23 SU	0412	1.8	0051	3.0	0215	3.5	0403	2.0	0016	0.5	0314	4.7	0438	5.8	0154	6.0	0148	7.3
	1009	-0.2	0745	-0.2	0907	-0.3	0850	0.0	0512	2.1	0950	0.0	1127	0.1	0850	0.3	0859	0.8
	1652	1.6	1323	2.8	1447	3.3	1621	2.2	1030	0.1	1536	4.9	1700	6.1	1418	6.1	1414	7.4
	2221	-0.1	1957	0.0	2122	-0.2	2117	0.4	1738	2.2	2203	0.4	2343	0.5	2110	0.7	2121	0.8
24 M	0456	1.8	0134	3.0	0259	3.5	0451	2.0	0107	0.5	0400	4.7	0524	5.8	0239	6.0	0235	7.3
	1054	-0.2	0829	-0.2	0952	-0.3	0935	0.0	0555	2.1	1036	0.0	1210	0.1	0936	0.3	0940	0.8
	1736	1.6	1405	2.7	1529	3.2	1709	2.2	1122	0.1	1623	4.8	1747	6.0	1505	6.0	1500	7.3
	2305	-0.1	2037	0.0	2203	-0.1	2205	0.4	1824	2.2	2245	0.5			2153	0.8	2200	0.9
25 TU	0537	1.8	0215	3.0	0339	3.5	1023	0.0	0203	0.5	0446	4.6	0023	0.5	0325	6.0	0318	7.2
	1139	-0.1	0910	-0.1	1034	-0.2	1757	2.1	0639	2.1	1119	0.0	0610	5.8	1021	0.4	1018	0.9
	1814	1.5	1443	2.6	1607	3.1	2259	0.5	1218	0.0	1711	4.7	1251	0.0	1551	5.9	1542	7.1
	2348	-0.1	2115	0.1	2242	0.0			1909	2.2	2327	0.6	1833	5.9	2236	0.9	2238	1.2
26 W	0617	1.8	0254	3.0	0415	3.5	0625	1.9	0043	0.4	0533	4.5	0102	0.5	0411	5.9	0400	7.0
	1223	-0.1	0948	0.0	1112	-0.1	1117	0.0	0722	2.0	1202	0.1	0656	5.7	1106	0.6	1057	1.2
	1850	1.5	1521	2.6	1642	3.1	1846	2.0	1319	0.0	1800	4.5	1331	0.0	1638	5.7	1624	6.8
			2151	0.1	2316	0.1			1954	2.1			1920	5.7	2321	1.1	2317	1.5
27 TH	0030	-0.1	0334	2.9	0450	3.4	0130	0.4	0146	0.4	0009	0.7	0142	0.6	0458	5.7	0443	6.7
	0657	1.7	1026	0.2	1148	0.1	0713	1.9	0807	2.0	0621	4.3	0742	5.5	1154	0.9	1139	1.5
	1306	0.0	1601	2.5	1718	3.0	1224	0.0	1422	0.1	1245	0.1	1412	0.1	1727	5.4	1710	6.5
	1927	1.4	2227	0.3	2348	0.2	1937	1.9	2042	2.0	1851	4.3	2008	5.4				
28 F	0115	0.0	0418	2.8	0530	3.3	0153	0.4	0252	0.4	0056	0.8	0224	0.7	0009	1.3	0000	1.8
	0741	1.7	1105	0.3	1223	0.3	0803	1.8	0857	1.9	0712	4.1	0830	5.2	0550	5.4	0531	6.4
	1353	0.0	1646	2.4	1800	2.9	1357	0.0	1526	0.1	1334	0.4	1457	0.3	1245	1.2	1226	1.9
	2009	1.4	2309	0.4			2032	1.8	2139	1.8	1945	4.0	2058	5.1	1821	5.1	1802	6.1
29 SA	0203	0.1	0508	2.6	0021	0.4	0245	0.3	0402	0.4	0152	0.9	0312	0.9	0105	1.6	0051	2.2
	0830	1.6	1151	0.5	0618	3.1	0900	1.7	0958	1.7	0810	3.9	0923	4.9	0650	5.1	0628	6.0
	1445	0.1	1740	2.3	1300	0.5	1506	0.1	1634	0.2	1431	0.6	1552	0.5	1343	1.5	1322	2.2
	2104	1.4			1851	2.7	2135	1.7	2250	1.7	2048	3.8	2155	4.8	1927	4.8	1903	5.8
30 SU	0301	0.2	0001	0.6	0106	0.4	0345	0.3	0518	0.4	0259	1.0	0416	1.1	0209	1.7	0151	2.4
	0933	1.5	0608	2.4	0717	2.9	1009	1.6	1118	1.6	0921	3.7	1027	4.6	0804	4.8	0733	5.8
	1547	0.2	1251	0.7	1353	0.7	1612	0.1	1749	0.3	1536	0.8	1657	0.7	1447	1.6	1426	2.4
	2213	1.4	1847	2.2	1955	2.6	2250	1.6			2202	3.7	2310	4.6	2043	4.7	2012	5.6
31 M	0412	0.2	0116	0.8	0214	0.8	0445	0.3	0003	1.6	0410	1.0	0527	1.1	0319	1.8	0257	2.5
	1046	1.5	0722	2.3	0827	2.7	1122	1.6	0636	0.4	1034	3.7	1151	4.5	0920	4.8	0843	5.7
	1657	0.2	1411	0.8	1523	0.8	1712	0.2	1230	1.5	1645	0.8	1804	0.8	1553	1.6	1533	2.4
	2324	1.4	2007	2.2	2110	2.6	2356	1.6	1906	0.4	2309	3.7			2151	4.8	2120	5.7

DENMARK, GERMANY, HOLLAND & BELGIUM Time Zone -0100
Esbjerg * Helgoland * Cuxhaven * Hoek van Holland * Rotterdam * Vlissingen * Antwerpen * Dunkerque * Calais

TIDE TABLES FEBRUARY 2000

ESBJERG Time m	HELGOLAND Time m	CUXHAVEN Time m	HOEK VAN HOLLAND Time m	ROTTERDAM Time m	VLISSINGEN Time m	ANTWERPEN Time m	DUNKERQUE Time m	CALAIS Time m	
0530 0.2	0251 0.8	0407 0.8	0542 0.3	0108 1.6	0522 0.9	0029 4.6	0427 1.6	0404 2.4	**1 TU**
1157 1.5	0847 2.2	0945 2.6	1222 1.7	0746 0.4	1136 3.8	0639 1.0	1021 5.0	0949 5.8	
1803 0.2	1530 0.7	1649 0.7	1810 0.2	1335 1.6	1748 0.8	1259 4.8	1656 1.5	1636 2.2	
	2127 2.3	2227 0.6		2015 0.4		1909 0.7	2246 5.0	2221 5.9	
0028 1.5	0409 0.7	0524 0.7	0051 1.7	0207 1.6	0005 3.9	0127 4.9	0526 1.4	0502 2.1	**2 W**
0636 0.2	1003 2.3	1103 2.7	0634 0.2	0848 0.4	0621 0.8	0744 0.8	1112 5.2	1046 6.1	
1300 1.5	1633 0.6	1751 0.6	1312 1.8	1431 1.6	1228 4.0	1351 5.1	1748 1.3	1729 1.9	
1859 0.2	2232 2.4	2335 2.8	1902 0.3	2124 0.5	1838 0.7	2007 0.6	2333 5.2	2312 6.2	
0123 1.6	0507 0.5	0622 0.5	0137 1.8	0258 1.6	0051 4.1	0213 5.1	0615 1.1	0552 1.8	**3 TH**
0730 0.1	1101 2.3	1206 2.8	0717 0.2	0946 0.4	0709 0.6	0837 0.6	1157 5.4	1133 6.4	
1353 1.5	1724 0.5	1841 0.4	1354 1.8	1519 1.6	1311 4.2	1435 5.3	1834 1.2	1816 1.7	
1945 0.1	2321 2.5		1945 0.3	2336 0.5	1921 0.6	2054 0.6		2354 6.5	
0209 1.6	0555 0.4	0029 3.0	0218 1.8	0340 1.7	0130 4.2	0254 5.3	0015 5.4	0638 1.6	**4 F**
0814 0.0	1148 2.4	0711 0.3	0750 0.2	1103 0.4	0749 0.5	0921 0.5	0658 0.9	1212 6.6	
1437 1.5	1808 0.4	1257 2.9	1430 1.9	1558 1.7	1348 4.4	1512 5.5	1238 5.5	1900 1.5	
2025 0.0		1926 0.3	2021 0.3		1957 0.6	2134 0.6	1914 1.0		
0247 1.7	0003 2.6	0115 3.1	0255 1.9	0025 0.5	0206 4.4	0330 5.4	0052 5.5	0030 6.7	**5 SA**
0853 0.0	0638 0.3	0754 0.2	0817 0.1	0415 1.7	0824 0.4	1000 0.4	0737 0.8	0721 1.4	
1514 1.5	1229 2.5	1342 3.0	1505 2.0	1218 0.4	1422 4.5	1548 5.6	1315 5.6	1248 6.8	●
2102 0.0	1848 0.3	2007 0.2	2054 0.3	1633 1.8	2031 0.5	2210 0.5	1951 1.0	1942 1.3	
0321 1.7	0041 2.7	0157 3.2	0329 1.9	0105 0.5	0239 4.5	0405 5.6	0127 5.6	0104 6.8	**6 SU**
0930 -0.1	0718 0.2	0836 0.1	0842 0.1	0449 1.7	0858 0.3	1036 0.4	0812 0.7	0803 1.3	
1547 1.5	1306 2.5	1423 3.0	1539 2.0	1259 0.4	1454 4.6	1622 5.7	1348 5.7	1320 6.9	
2136 -0.1	1927 0.2	2047 0.1	2133 0.3	1709 1.8	2106 0.4	2246 0.5	2024 0.9	2022 1.3	
0356 1.7	0116 2.7	0236 3.2	0401 1.9	0142 0.4	0312 4.5	0439 5.7	0157 5.7	0134 6.9	**7 M**
1004 -0.1	0754 0.2	0915 0.1	0909 0.0	0524 1.8	0934 0.2	1113 0.3	0846 0.6	0840 1.2	
1620 1.5	1341 2.5	1502 3.0	1613 2.1	1339 0.3	1527 4.6	1656 5.8	1418 5.7	1349 7.0	
2211 -0.1	2003 0.1	2125 0.1	2353 0.3	1745 1.9	2142 0.4	2324 0.5	2056 0.9	2057 1.3	
0431 1.7	0149 2.7	0314 3.2	0432 1.9	0220 0.4	0345 4.6	0513 5.7	0226 5.8	0203 7.0	**8 TU**
1039 -0.2	0830 0.1	0951 0.0	0939 0.0	0600 1.8	1012 0.1	1151 0.2	0918 0.6	0913 1.2	
1654 1.5	1414 2.5	1539 3.0	1647 2.1	1418 0.2	1601 4.6	1730 5.8	1447 5.8	1418 7.0	
2245 -0.2	2038 0.2	2201 0.1	2200 0.3	1824 2.0	2221 0.4		2129 0.8	2128 1.3	
0507 1.6	0221 2.8	0350 3.3	0503 1.9	0257 0.4	0418 4.6	0001 0.4	0257 6.0	0230 7.1	**9 W**
1113 -0.2	0905 0.1	1027 0.0	1011 0.0	0638 1.9	1050 0.1	0547 5.8	0952 0.6	0943 1.2	
1727 1.4	1445 2.5	1613 3.0	1723 2.1	1455 0.2	1636 4.6	1229 0.2	1520 5.9	1448 7.0	
2321 -0.2	2112 0.2	2237 0.1	2228 0.3	1903 2.0	2300 0.4	1805 5.9	2203 0.8	2157 1.4	
0541 1.6	0254 2.8	0424 3.3	0538 1.9	0053 0.5	0453 4.5	0038 0.5	0333 6.0	0303 7.1	**10 TH**
1148 -0.2	0939 0.1	1103 0.0	1048 0.0	0717 1.9	1128 0.2	0621 5.8	1027 0.6	1015 1.3	
1757 1.4	1518 2.6	1648 3.0	1801 2.0	1329 0.2	1714 4.5	1305 0.2	1558 5.9	1523 7.0	
2357 -0.2	2148 0.2	2312 0.0	2306 0.3	1944 2.1	2337 0.5	1842 5.8	2239 0.9	2231 1.5	
0613 1.6	0330 2.9	0458 3.3	0616 1.9	0151 0.5	0531 4.4	0112 0.5	0414 6.0	0341 7.0	**11 F**
1225 -0.2	1016 0.1	1139 0.0	1130 -0.1	0759 2.0	1206 0.2	0657 5.8	1106 0.7	1052 1.4	
1829 1.4	1554 2.6	1722 3.0	1843 2.0	1443 0.2	1756 4.4	1340 0.3	1641 5.8	1604 6.8	
	2226 0.2	2349 0.1	2354 0.3	2030 2.1		1921 5.7	2320 1.0	2312 1.6	
0037 -0.2	0412 2.9	0536 3.3	0700 1.9	0246 0.4	0018 0.5	0148 0.6	0500 5.8	0426 6.8	**12 SA**
0648 1.6	1057 0.2	1217 0.0	1224 -0.1	0846 2.0	0615 4.3	0739 5.6	1152 0.9	1138 1.6	
1306 -0.2	1639 2.6	1803 3.1	1934 1.9	1500 0.3	1247 0.3	1418 0.3	1731 5.6	1654 6.6	
1908 1.4	2311 0.2			2122 2.0	1847 4.3	2009 5.5			
0123 -0.2	0503 2.8	0030 0.1	0104 0.3	0512 0.4	0104 0.6	0231 0.7	0010 1.2	0003 1.9	**13 SU**
0734 1.5	1145 0.2	0624 3.3	0754 1.8	0943 1.9	0710 4.2	0831 5.4	0554 5.5	0521 6.5	
1355 -0.1	1734 2.6	1301 0.1	1348 -0.1	1624 0.1	1339 0.4	1507 0.5	1251 1.2	1234 1.8	
2001 1.4		1853 3.1	2044 1.8	2228 1.9	1954 4.1	2113 5.2	1833 5.2	1758 6.2	
0218 -0.1	0005 0.3	0120 0.1	0240 0.2	0555 0.3	0205 0.7	0329 0.8	0118 1.4	0105 2.1	**14 M**
0837 1.5	0604 2.7	0721 3.3	0913 1.7	1057 1.9	0824 4.0	0945 5.1	0704 5.2	0635 6.2	
1457 0.0	1245 0.3	1355 0.2	1503 0.0	1755 0.1	1448 0.5	1612 0.7	1406 1.4	1343 2.0	
2115 1.4	1839 2.5	1953 3.0	2206 1.7	2345 1.8	2113 3.9	2238 5.0	1953 5.0	1922 6.0	
0327 -0.1	0112 0.3	0221 0.2	0345 0.2	0652 0.3	0321 0.8	0444 0.9	0239 1.5	0219 2.2	**15 TU**
1000 1.5	0714 2.7	0826 3.2	1039 1.7	1214 1.9	0947 4.0	1112 5.1	0831 5.1	0803 6.1	
1612 0.0	1354 0.3	1504 0.2	1618 0.1	1923 0.2	1619 0.6	1736 0.8	1526 1.4	1502 2.1	
2239 1.4	1948 2.6	2059 3.1	2321 1.7		2232 3.9	2355 5.1	2118 5.0	2047 6.1	

• • Time Zone -0100. For UT subtract 1 hour. For European summer time (shaded) 26/3-29/10 add 1 hour • •

FEBRUARY 2000 TIDE TABLES

• • Time Zone -0100. For UT subtract 1 hour. For European summer time (shaded) 26/3-29/10 add 1 hour • •

	ESBJERG		HELGOLAND		CUXHAVEN		HOEK VAN HOLLAND		ROTTERDAM		VLISSINGEN		ANTWERPEN		DUNKERQUE		CALAIS	
	Time	m	Time	m	Time	m	Time	m	Time	m	Time	m	Time	m	Time	m	Time	m
16 W	0450	-0.1	0229	0.2	0341	0.2	0457	0.2	0054	1.8	0458	0.7	0622	0.9	0400	1.4	0343	2.1
	1125	1.5	0826	2.7	0935	3.2	1151	1.8	0746	0.3	1104	4.1	1226	5.2	0951	5.2	0921	6.3
	1733	0.0	1507	0.2	1622	0.1	1744	0.2	1320	1.9	1742	0.5	1907	0.7	1641	1.3	1628	1.9
			2057	2.7	2206	3.2			2037	0.2	2342	4.1			2228	5.2	2157	6.4
17 TH	0000	1.5	0345	0.1	0501	0.0	0027	1.7	0153	1.9	0614	0.5	0103	5.3	0511	1.1	0507	1.8
	0612	-0.1	0936	2.7	1043	3.2	0557	0.2	0738	0.3	1209	4.3	0746	0.6	1054	5.5	1027	6.6
	1250	1.5	1615	0.1	1733	0.0	1253	1.9	1416	2.0	1843	0.4	1330	5.5	1746	1.0	1746	1.5
	1845	0.0	2200	2.8	2310	3.3	2004	0.2	2051	0.3			2017	0.6	2324	5.5	2300	6.7
18 F	0114	1.5	0451	0.0	0610	-0.1	0124	1.8	0244	1.9	0041	4.3	0201	5.5	0612	0.7	0618	1.4
	0720	-0.2	1038	2.7	1149	3.2	0639	0.2	0805	0.2	0712	0.3	0849	0.4	1148	5.8	1127	6.9
	1405	1.5	1715	0.0	1836	-0.1	1346	2.0	1506	2.1	1303	4.5	1427	5.7	1841	0.8	1850	1.2
	1944	-0.1	2257	2.8			2202	0.2	2203	0.3	1935	0.3	2113	0.5			2356	7.0
19 SA O	0218	1.6	0550	-0.2	0011	3.3	0216	1.8	0329	2.0	0131	4.5	0254	5.6	0014	5.7	0715	1.0
	0818	-0.3	1133	2.7	0710	-0.3	0715	0.1	1111	0.3	0803	0.0	0942	0.2	0704	0.5	1222	7.2
	1504	1.5	1808	-0.1	1249	3.2	1435	2.1	1552	2.1	1352	4.7	1516	5.8	1236	6.0	1942	0.9
	2036	-0.1	2348	2.9	1931	-0.2	1942	0.3	2059	0.3	2021	0.2	2203	0.5	1930	0.7		
20 SU	0312	1.7	0642	-0.2	0108	3.4	0304	1.9	0412	2.0	0216	4.6	0340	5.7	0057	5.9	0046	7.2
	0908	-0.3	1222	2.7	0803	-0.3	0752	0.0	0920	0.1	0850	-0.1	1030	0.2	0751	0.3	0804	0.8
	1554	1.5	1856	-0.1	1343	3.2	1521	2.1	1636	2.2	1437	4.8	1602	5.9	1321	6.1	1311	7.3
	2122	-0.2			2020	-0.2	2018	0.3	2139	0.3	2105	0.3	2246	0.5	2013	0.6	2027	0.8
21 M	0359	1.7	0034	2.9	0158	3.4	0832	0.0	0453	2.0	0259	4.7	0424	5.7	0139	6.0	0131	7.3
	0954	-0.3	0727	-0.2	0851	-0.3	1605	2.1	1251	0.3	0934	-0.1	1112	0.1	0836	0.2	0845	0.7
	1636	1.5	1305	2.6	1430	3.1	2059	0.3	1718	2.2	1520	4.8	1645	6.0	1403	6.1	1354	7.4
	2205	-0.2	1939	-0.1	2105	-0.2			2224	0.3	2145	0.3	2325	0.4	2054	0.6	2104	0.8
22 TU	0441	1.7	0115	2.9	0241	3.4	0915	-0.1	0535	2.1	0341	4.7	0506	5.8	0219	6.1	0212	7.3
	1036	-0.3	0809	-0.2	0933	-0.3	1648	2.1	1054	0.0	1016	-0.1	1151	0.0	0918	0.2	0921	0.7
	1713	1.5	1342	2.6	1509	3.1	2142	0.4	1802	2.2	1602	4.8	1727	6.0	1445	6.1	1433	7.3
	2245	-0.2	2018	0.0	2145	-0.2			2314	0.3	2224	0.4			2133	0.7	2137	0.9
23 W	0519	1.7	0153	2.9	0318	3.4	1000	0.0	0145	0.5	0421	4.7	0002	0.4	0300	6.0	0248	7.3
	1116	-0.2	0847	-0.1	1012	-0.2	1729	2.0	0616	2.1	1054	0.0	0547	5.8	0959	0.3	0952	0.9
	1745	1.4	1417	2.6	1542	3.0	2231	0.4	1149	0.0	1643	4.7	1228	-0.1	1526	5.9	1509	7.2
	2324	-0.2	2052	0.0	2220	-0.1			1844	2.1	2300	0.4	1809	6.0	2211	0.8	2207	1.1
24 TH	0554	1.7	0229	2.9	0349	3.3	0553	1.9	0009	0.4	0502	4.6	0038	0.4	0341	6.0	0324	7.2
	1154	-0.2	0921	0.0	1046	0.0	1049	0.0	0657	2.0	1131	0.1	0627	5.8	1039	0.5	1024	1.1
	1815	1.4	1451	2.6	1612	3.0	1810	2.0	1252	0.1	1724	4.5	1303	-0.1	1606	5.8	1546	7.0
			2124	0.1	2251	0.0	2333	0.3	1925	2.0	2336	0.5	1849	5.8	2249	1.0	2239	1.4
25 F	0003	-0.2	0305	2.8	0420	3.3	0633	1.9	0112	0.4	0542	4.4	0113	0.4	0423	5.8	0403	6.9
	0628	1.6	0951	0.2	1115	0.1	1147	0.0	0738	2.0	1206	0.2	0708	5.6	1118	0.8	1058	1.4
	1231	-0.1	1525	2.5	1642	3.0	1854	1.9	1400	0.1	1806	4.3	1339	0.0	1649	5.5	1625	6.7
	1842	1.4	2155	0.2	2318	0.1			2006	1.9			1930	5.5	2329	1.2	2314	1.7
26 SA	0041	-0.2	0343	2.7	0454	3.2	0133	0.2	0224	0.4	0015	0.6	0148	0.5	0507	5.5	0444	6.6
	0701	1.5	1022	0.3	1140	0.3	0715	1.8	0819	1.9	0624	4.2	0749	5.3	1200	1.1	1136	1.8
	1309	-0.1	1604	2.4	1718	2.9	1302	0.0	1505	0.2	1245	0.4	1415	0.2	1734	5.2	1709	6.3
	1912	1.4	2230	0.4	2345	0.3	1941	1.8	2048	1.7	1850	4.0	2013	5.2			2356	2.1
27 SU	0122	-0.1	0427	2.5	0538	3.0	0207	0.2	0333	0.4	0058	0.7	0227	0.7	0014	1.5	0533	6.2
	0739	1.5	1057	0.5	1207	0.5	0806	1.7	0905	1.7	0712	4.0	0835	5.0	0557	5.1	1224	2.2
	1350	0.0	1651	2.3	1804	2.7	1416	0.1	1609	0.3	1334	0.6	1459	0.5	1250	1.4	1804	5.8
	1954	1.3	2312	0.6			2036	1.6	2141	1.6	1942	3.7	2101	4.8	1828	4.8		
28 M	0209	0.0	0521	2.3	0021	0.5	0307	0.2	0440	0.4	0202	0.9	0318	1.0	0111	1.7	0048	2.4
	0829	1.4	1144	0.7	0633	2.7	0908	1.6	1009	1.5	0814	3.7	0929	4.6	0701	4.8	0635	5.7
	1441	0.1	1753	2.2	1246	0.7	1542	0.1	1717	0.4	1446	0.8	1602	0.9	1350	1.7	1322	2.5
	2053	1.3			1905	2.5	2145	1.5	2310	1.4	2053	3.5	2200	4.4	1940	4.5	1915	5.5
29 TU	0312	0.1	0013	0.8	0112	0.7	0414	0.2	0551	0.4	0324	1.0	0436	1.2	0219	1.9	0152	2.6
	0946	1.3	0633	2.1	0741	2.5	1031	1.5	1149	1.4	0943	3.5	1041	4.3	0827	4.6	0752	5.5
	1552	0.2	1256	0.9	1345	0.9	1649	0.2	1830	0.4	1600	0.9	1718	1.0	1457	1.8	1430	2.6
	2223	1.3	1913	2.1	2019	2.4	2315	1.4	0034	1.4	2227	3.4	2339	4.2	2107	4.4	2033	5.4

DENMARK, GERMANY, HOLLAND & BELGIUM Time Zone -0100

Esbjerg * Helgoland * Cuxhaven * Hoek van Holland * Rotterdam * Vlissingen * Antwerpen * Dunkerque * Calais

TIDE TABLES MARCH 2000

esbjerg		HELGOLAND		CUXHAVEN		HOEK VAN HOLLAND		ROTTERDAM		VLISSINGEN		ANTWERPEN		DUNKERQUE		CALAIS		Day
Time	m	Time	m	Time	m	Time	m	Time	m	Time	m	Time	m	Time	m	Time	m	
0439	0.1	0155	0.9	0239	0.9	0513	0.2	0702	0.4	0439	1.0	0554	1.1	0332	1.8	0305	2.6	**1 W**
1116	1.3	0805	2.0	0903	2.4	1149	1.5	1305	1.4	1104	3.6	1228	4.4	0945	4.7	0909	5.6	
1716	0.2	1444	0.9	1600	1.0	1749	0.2	1943	0.4	1710	0.9	1827	1.1	1609	1.8	1544	2.5	
2344	1.4	2045	2.1	2142	2.5					2334	3.6			2215	4.6	2145	5.6	
0601	0.1	0339	0.8	0455	0.8	0022	1.5	0142	1.4	0548	0.8	0057	4.5	0443	1.6	0418	2.4	**2 TH**
1228	1.3	0937	2.1	1030	2.5	0606	0.2	0809	0.4	1201	3.8	0704	1.0	1045	5.0	1015	5.8	
1824	0.1	1605	0.7	1723	0.7	1245	1.7	1408	1.5	1810	0.8	1325	4.8	1714	1.5	1652	2.2	
		2202	2.3	2301	2.7	1845	0.2	2057	0.4			1931	0.9	2306	4.9	2242	6.0	
0047	1.4	0444	0.5	0558	0.5	0112	1.6	0238	1.5	0024	3.8	0145	4.8	0542	1.3	0521	2.0	**3 F**
0700	-0.1	1041	2.2	1142	2.6	0649	0.1	0912	0.4	0643	0.6	0806	0.8	1133	5.2	1106	6.2	
1327	1.4	1700	0.5	1817	0.5	1328	1.8	1458	1.6	1246	4.1	1408	5.1	1806	1.3	1749	1.8	
1916	0.0	2256	2.4			2128	0.2	2252	0.4	1857	0.6	2023	0.8	2350	5.2	2328	6.4	
0138	1.5	0532	0.3	0003	2.9	0154	1.7	0321	1.6	0105	4.1	0225	5.1	0630	1.0	0614	1.6	**4 SA**
0747	-0.1	1128	2.4	0647	0.3	0720	0.1	1019	0.3	0725	0.4	0852	0.6	1215	5.5	1148	6.6	
1414	1.4	1745	0.3	1236	2.8	1405	1.9	1538	1.7	1324	4.3	1445	5.4	1849	1.1	1838	1.5	
1959	-0.1	2339	2.6	1903	0.2	2003	0.2	2352	0.4	1934	0.5	2105	0.7					
0221	1.5	0614	0.2	0051	3.0	0230	1.8	0357	1.7	0141	4.3	0302	5.4	0028	5.5	0006	6.7	**5 SU**
0827	-0.2	1208	2.5	0730	0.1	0744	0.1	1137	0.3	0800	0.3	0933	0.5	0711	0.7	0700	1.3	
1452	1.4	1826	0.2	1321	3.0	1440	2.0	1614	1.8	1357	4.5	1521	5.7	1251	5.7	1224	6.8	●
2036	-0.2			1945	0.1	2024	0.3			2009	0.4	2145	0.5	1927	0.9	1922	1.2	
0258	1.5	0018	2.7	0135	3.2	0303	1.8	0035	0.3	0215	4.5	0338	5.7	0101	5.7	0040	7.0	**6 M**
0903	-0.3	0653	0.0	0812	-0.1	0808	0.0	0430	1.8	0835	0.2	1012	0.3	0748	0.6	0743	1.1	
1526	1.4	1245	2.6	1402	3.1	1514	2.0	1231	0.2	1430	4.6	1556	5.9	1323	5.8	1256	7.0	
2113	-0.2	1905	0.1	2026	0.0	2039	0.3	1649	1.9	2044	0.3	2224	0.4	2001	0.6	2003	1.1	
0334	1.5	0054	2.8	0215	3.3	0335	1.9	0115	0.3	0248	4.6	0414	5.9	0130	5.8	0110	7.1	**7 TU**
0939	-0.3	0730	0.0	0851	-0.2	0835	0.0	0505	1.9	0912	0.1	1052	0.1	0822	0.4	0822	1.0	
1600	1.4	1320	2.6	1441	3.2	1548	2.1	1317	0.2	1503	4.7	1632	6.0	1351	5.9	1325	7.2	
2148	-0.3	1942	0.0	2105	-0.2	2056	0.3	1726	2.0	2122	0.2	2305	0.3	2035	0.7	2039	1.0	
0412	1.5	0128	2.8	0254	3.4	0407	1.9	0156	0.2	0321	4.7	0449	6.0	0200	6.0	0138	7.2	**8 W**
1015	-0.3	0807	-0.1	0929	-0.2	0906	-0.1	0542	1.9	0951	0.0	1133	0.0	0857	0.4	0857	1.0	
1635	1.4	1353	2.6	1518	3.2	1624	2.1	1400	0.1	1538	4.7	1707	6.1	1422	6.0	1354	7.2	
2225	-0.3	2018	0.0	2142	-0.2	2123	0.3	1804	2.1	2202	0.2	2345	0.2	2109	0.6	2112	1.1	
0448	1.5	0202	2.9	0331	3.4	0441	1.9	0236	0.2	0355	4.7	0523	6.1	0233	6.1	0207	7.3	**9 TH**
1051	-0.3	0843	-0.1	1006	-0.2	0940	-0.1	0619	2.0	1030	0.0	1213	0.0	0932	0.4	0927	1.0	
1708	1.4	1424	2.6	1554	3.2	1700	2.1	1442	0.1	1614	4.7	1742	6.1	1457	6.1	1425	7.2	
2301	-0.4	2054	0.0	2219	-0.2	2157	0.2	1843	2.1	2242	0.3			2144	0.6	2142	1.1	
0523	1.5	0236	2.9	0407	3.4	0516	2.0	0313	0.2	0430	4.7	0024	0.3	0309	6.2	0241	7.3	**10 F**
1126	-0.3	0918	-0.1	1042	-0.2	1019	-0.1	0658	2.0	1109	0.1	0558	6.0	1009	0.4	0959	1.1	
1736	1.4	1457	2.7	1628	3.2	1739	2.0	1520	0.1	1652	4.6	1251	0.1	1535	6.1	1500	7.1	
2339	-0.4	2130	0.0	2255	-0.2	2237	0.2	1923	2.1	2321	0.3	1819	5.9	2221	0.7	2215	1.3	
0554	1.5	0312	2.9	0443	3.4	0555	2.0	0348	0.3	0509	4.6	0100	0.5	0350	6.1	0319	7.1	**11 SA**
1203	-0.3	0954	0.0	1118	-0.2	1103	-0.1	0739	2.1	1148	0.1	0636	5.9	1048	0.6	1036	1.2	
1806	1.4	1533	2.7	1703	3.2	1821	1.9	1554	0.1	1733	4.5	1326	0.1	1618	5.9	1542	6.9	
		2208	0.0	2332	-0.2	2325	0.2	2006	2.0			1900	5.7	2302	1.0	2255	1.5	
0018	-0.4	0354	2.9	0521	3.4	0639	1.9	0418	0.3	0000	0.4	0134	0.6	0436	5.9	0404	6.9	**12 SU**
0628	1.4	1033	0.1	1154	-0.1	1157	-0.1	0824	2.0	0553	4.5	0718	5.7	1133	0.8	1120	1.5	
1243	-0.2	1615	2.7	1740	3.2	1909	1.8	1621	0.1	1228	0.2	1402	0.5	1707	5.6	1632	6.6	
1843	1.3	2251	0.0					2054	1.9	1823	4.3	1945	5.4	2350	1.1	2344	1.8	
0104	-0.4	0443	2.8	0011	-0.1	0025	0.2	0411	0.3	0045	0.5	0215	0.7	0529	5.6	0500	6.5	**13 M**
0715	1.4	1118	0.2	0605	3.3	0732	1.8	0916	2.0	0647	4.3	0808	5.4	1230	1.1	1215	1.8	
1332	-0.2	1706	2.6	1236	0.0	1354	0.0	1621	0.1	1319	0.4	1447	0.7	1808	5.1	1739	6.1	
1936	1.3	2342	0.1	1827	3.1	2017	1.7	2153	1.8	1928	4.0	2046	5.0					
0200	-0.3	0542	2.7	0057	0.0	0222	0.1	0426	0.3	0145	0.6	0309	0.9	0055	1.4	0045	2.1	**14 TU**
0822	1.3	1214	0.3	0659	3.2	0854	1.7	1024	1.9	0803	4.0	0919	5.1	0640	5.2	0619	6.1	
1432	-0.1	1809	2.6	1326	0.2	1501	0.0	1717	0.2	1430	0.6	1549	0.9	1345	1.4	1324	2.1	
2049	1.3			1923	3.1	2146	1.5	2312	1.7	2053	3.8	2212	4.8	1933	4.8	1910	5.9	
0310	-0.2	0048	0.2	0157	0.1	0329	0.2	0524	0.2	0309	0.7	0423	1.0	0218	1.6	0201	2.3	**15 W**
0950	1.3	0651	2.5	0802	3.1	1023	1.7	1148	1.8	0931	3.9	1049	5.0	0816	5.0	0754	6.0	
1551	0.0	1324	0.3	1432	0.3	1630	0.1	1848	0.2	1609	0.7	1715	1.0	1509	1.5	1450	2.2	
2218	1.3	1918	2.5	2028	3.0	2306	1.5			2218	3.7	2334	4.9	2108	4.8	2039	5.9	

• • Time Zone -0100. For UT subtract 1 hour. For European summer time (shaded) 26/3-29/10 add 1 hour • •

MARCH 2000 TIDE TABLES

• • Time Zone -0100. For UT subtract 1 hour. For European summer time (shaded) 26/3-29/10 add 1 hour • •

Day	ESBJERG Time	m	HELGOLAND Time	m	CUXHAVEN Time	m	HOEK VAN HOLLAND Time	m	ROTTERDAM Time	m	VLISSINGEN Time	m	ANTWERPEN Time	m	DUNKERQUE Time	m	CALAIS Time	m
16TH	0440	-0.2	0207	0.2	0318	0.1	0448	0.2	0030	1.7	0449	0.6	0608	0.9	0342	1.4	0336	2.2
	1122	1.3	0805	2.5	0911	3.0	1139	1.8	0618	0.2	1054	4.0	1209	5.1	0942	5.2	0914	6.2
	1719	0.0	1442	0.3	1557	0.2	1851	0.1	1300	1.9	1732	0.6	1851	0.9	1631	1.4	1627	2.0
	2344	1.4	2031	2.6	2137	3.1			2024	0.3	2333	3.9			2220	5.0	2150	6.2
17F	0603	-0.3	0327	0.1	0443	0.0	0016	1.5	0133	1.7	0604	0.4	0045	5.1	0459	1.1	0506	1.8
	1251	1.4	0918	2.5	1022	3.0	0709	0.1	0704	0.2	1201	4.3	0733	0.6	1047	5.5	1021	6.5
	1833	-0.1	1556	0.2	1714	0.1	1242	1.9	1359	2.0	1833	0.4	1316	5.4	1739	1.1	1743	1.5
			2139	2.7	2245	3.1	2110	0.1	2015	0.3			2002	0.6	2316	5.4	2251	6.6
18SA	0103	1.5	0436	0.0	0553	-0.1	0115	1.6	0226	1.8	0032	4.1	0147	5.4	0601	0.7	0611	1.3
	0710	-0.3	1023	2.5	1131	3.0	0631	0.1	0742	0.2	0702	0.2	0835	0.3	1139	5.8	1119	6.8
	1400	1.4	1657	0.1	1817	0.0	1335	2.0	1450	2.1	1254	4.5	1413	5.7	1833	0.8	1839	1.1
	1931	-0.2	2239	2.7	2351	3.2	2208	0.1	2130	0.4	1923	0.3	2058	0.5			2344	6.9
19SU O	0207	1.5	0533	-0.1	0652	-0.2	0204	1.7	0312	1.9	0119	4.3	0239	5.6	0002	5.6	0703	1.0
	0805	-0.4	1117	2.6	1233	3.0	0700	0.1	0819	0.1	0750	0.0	0927	0.1	0653	0.4	1209	7.1
	1453	1.4	1750	0.0	1912	-0.2	1421	2.0	1535	2.1	1339	4.6	1502	5.9	1225	6.0	1927	0.9
	2021	-0.2	2330	2.8			1933	0.3	2039	0.4	2006	0.3	2145	0.4	1918	0.7		
20M	0259	1.6	0622	-0.2	0049	3.3	0248	1.8	0353	2.0	0200	4.5	0324	5.7	0042	5.8	0030	7.1
	0852	-0.4	1203	2.6	0743	-0.3	0736	0.0	0859	0.1	0833	-0.1	1012	0.1	0738	0.2	0746	0.8
	1536	1.4	1836	-0.1	1324	3.1	1503	2.1	1617	2.1	1420	4.7	1545	5.9	1305	6.1	1252	7.2
	2106	-0.3			2000	-0.2	2003	0.3	2117	0.3	2045	0.3	2227	0.4	1957	0.6	2006	0.8
21TU	0342	1.6	0015	2.8	0138	3.3	0814	0.0	0433	2.0	0239	4.6	0404	5.7	0118	6.0	0109	7.3
	0935	-0.4	0706	-0.1	0829	-0.2	1544	2.1	0942	0.1	0912	-0.1	1051	0.0	0818	0.2	0824	0.7
	1613	1.4	1243	2.5	1408	3.0	2040	0.3	1657	2.1	1459	4.8	1624	6.0	1342	6.1	1330	7.3
	2145	-0.3	1918	0.0	2044	-0.2			2200	0.3	2123	0.3	2303	0.3	2035	0.6	2039	0.9
22W	0419	1.6	0054	2.8	0219	3.2	0854	0.0	0513	2.0	0317	4.7	0443	5.8	0155	6.0	0144	7.3
	1013	-0.3	0745	-0.1	0910	-0.1	1623	2.0	1029	0.1	0951	-0.1	1127	0.0	0857	0.2	0854	0.8
	1645	1.4	1318	2.5	1444	3.0	2121	0.3	1737	2.1	1537	4.7	1703	6.0	1420	6.0	1403	7.3
	2224	-0.3	1955	0.0	2122	-0.1			2247	0.3	2159	0.3	2339	0.3	2112	0.6	2107	1.0
23TH	0454	1.6	0129	2.7	0253	3.2	0445	2.0	0553	2.0	0354	4.7	0521	5.9	0233	6.0	0217	7.3
	1049	-0.3	0820	0.0	0946	0.0	0938	0.0	1121	0.1	1026	0.0	1202	0.0	0934	0.4	0922	0.8
	1713	1.4	1349	2.5	1514	3.0	1700	2.0	1816	2.0	1614	4.6	1742	6.0	1457	5.9	1436	7.2
	2300	-0.3	2028	0.1	2156	0.0	2206	0.3	2339	0.3	2234	0.3			2146	0.7	2133	1.1
24F	0527	1.6	0202	2.7	0321	3.2	0519	2.0	0632	2.0	0431	4.6	0012	0.3	0312	6.0	0250	7.2
	1124	-0.2	0849	0.2	1016	0.1	1024	0.0	1224	0.2	1058	0.1	0559	5.8	1009	0.6	0950	1.1
	1739	1.4	1419	2.6	1539	3.0	1736	1.9	1854	1.9	1650	4.5	1234	0.0	1536	5.8	1509	7.0
	2336	-0.3	2058	0.1	2224	0.1	2258	0.3			2307	0.4	1818	5.8	2220	0.9	2201	1.3
25SA	0557	1.5	0235	2.7	0348	3.1	0554	1.9	0039	0.3	0507	4.5	0044	0.3	0351	5.8	0325	7.0
	1156	-0.2	0916	0.3	1041	0.3	1118	0.1	0709	1.9	1128	0.3	0635	5.6	1043	0.8	1019	1.4
	1804	1.4	1451	2.5	1603	3.0	1812	1.8	1341	0.2	1725	4.3	1305	0.1	1615	5.5	1545	6.7
			2126	0.2	2248	0.2			1930	1.8	2339	0.5	1854	5.5	2254	1.1	2232	1.6
26SU	0010	-0.3	0310	2.6	0421	3.0	0130	0.2	0158	0.3	0544	4.3	0115	0.4	0431	5.6	0403	6.7
	0627	1.4	0942	0.4	1100	0.4	0629	1.9	0746	1.8	1200	0.4	0712	5.4	1119	1.1	1052	1.7
	1228	-0.1	1526	2.5	1636	2.9	1223	0.1	1444	0.3	1802	4.1	1336	0.3	1655	5.2	1624	6.4
	1832	1.4	2157	0.2	2314	0.3	1851	1.7	2006	1.7			1932	5.2	2331	1.3	2307	1.9
27M	0046	-0.2	0350	2.4	0502	2.8	0058	0.1	0301	0.3	0014	0.6	0148	0.6	0515	5.2	0445	6.3
	0658	1.3	1012	0.5	1127	0.5	0711	1.8	0824	1.7	0624	4.1	0754	5.1	1202	1.4	1133	2.1
	1304	-0.1	1609	2.4	1720	2.8	1321	0.1	1539	0.4	1236	0.6	1412	0.6	1741	4.9	1711	5.9
	1908	1.4	2235	0.5	2348	0.5	1939	1.6	2043	1.5	1846	3.8	2015	4.8			2355	2.3
28TU	0128	-0.1	0439	2.2	0553	2.6	0144	0.1	0400	0.4	0057	0.8	0228	0.8	0019	1.6	0539	5.8
	0742	1.3	1052	0.7	1203	0.7	0812	1.6	0907	1.5	0718	3.7	0843	4.8	0609	4.8	1228	2.5
	1347	0.0	1703	2.2	1816	2.6	1513	0.2	1641	0.4	1332	0.9	1459	0.9	1258	1.7	1815	5.5
	1959	1.3	2327	0.7			2050	1.4	2130	1.3	1949	3.5	2109	4.5	1842	4.5		
29W	0221	0.0	0546	2.0	0033	0.7	0337	0.2	0505	0.4	0230	1.0	0323	1.1	0124	1.8	0059	2.6
	0847	1.2	1151	0.9	0658	2.4	0932	1.5	1027	1.3	0837	3.5	0945	4.4	0727	4.5	0656	5.5
	1447	0.1	1819	2.1	1254	0.9	1625	0.2	1752	0.5	1521	1.0	1615	1.2	1406	1.9	1337	2.7
	2113	1.3			1929	2.4	2214	1.3	2348	1.2	2120	3.3	2218	4.2	2010	4.3	1941	5.3
30TH	0342	0.0	0051	0.9	0137	0.9	0442	0.2	0615	0.4	0357	1.0	0459	1.2	0237	1.9	0212	2.7
	1027	1.1	0716	1.9	0818	2.3	1103	1.5	1228	1.4	1018	3.5	1121	4.3	0859	4.5	0822	5.4
	1617	0.1	1335	1.0	1412	1.0	1726	0.2	1910	0.5	1633	1.0	1739	1.3	1518	1.9	1453	2.6
	2250	1.3	1951	2.1	2051	2.4	2342	1.4			2253	3.4			2132	4.4	2101	5.5
31F	0515	0.0	0253	0.8	0406	0.9	0536	0.1	0106	1.3	0506	0.8	0007	4.2	0351	1.7	0330	2.5
	1149	1.2	0854	2.0	0945	2.4	1209	1.6	0727	0.4	1126	3.7	0615	1.1	1006	4.8	0934	5.7
	1740	0.1	1523	0.8	1641	0.9	1827	0.2	1334	1.5	1736	0.8	1245	4.6	1629	1.7	1609	2.3
			2115	2.2	2213	2.6			2028	0.4	2350	3.7	1844	1.2	2230	4.8	2204	5.9

DENMARK, GERMANY, HOLLAND & BELGIUM Time Zone -0100
Esbjerg * Helgoland * Cuxhaven * Hoek van Holland * Rotterdam * Vlissingen * Antwerpen * Dunkerque * Calais

TIDE TABLES APRIL 2000

esbjerg	HELGOLAND	CUXHAVEN	HOEK VAN HOLLAND	ROTTERDAM	VLISSINGEN	ANTWERPEN	DUNKERQUE	CALAIS	
Time m	Time m	Time m	Time m	Time m	Time m	Time m	Time m	Time m	
0003 1.3 0622 -0.2 1251 1.3 1839 -0.1	0406 0.6 1005 2.2 1625 0.6 2215 2.4	0522 0.6 1103 2.6 1742 0.6 2321 2.8	0039 1.5 0619 0.1 1256 1.8 2052 0.1	0204 1.4 0836 0.3 1426 1.7 2150 0.3	0607 0.6 1214 4.0 1827 0.6	0106 4.6 0720 0.9 1332 5.0 1942 1.0	0458 1.4 1058 5.1 1729 1.4 2316 5.1	0442 2.1 1030 6.1 1713 1.9 2252 6.3	**1 SA**
0100 1.4 0712 -0.3 1342 1.3 1925 -0.2	0457 0.3 1054 2.4 1712 0.3 2302 2.6	0613 0.3 1200 2.9 1831 0.3	0122 1.6 0648 0.1 1335 1.9 2145 0.1	0250 1.6 0944 0.2 1509 1.8 2305 0.3	0033 4.0 0654 0.4 1253 4.3 1906 0.5	0151 5.0 0815 0.7 1412 5.4 2030 0.7	0552 1.1 1141 5.5 1816 1.1 2354 5.4	0540 1.6 1113 6.6 1806 1.5 2332 6.7	**2 SU**
0147 1.4 0754 -0.3 1424 1.3 2006 -0.2	0540 0.1 1135 2.5 1755 0.1 2344 2.7	0014 3.1 0658 0.0 1248 3.1 1915 0.0	0158 1.7 0709 0.1 1411 2.0 1948 0.2	0329 1.7 1054 0.2 1547 2.0 2358 0.2	0110 4.3 0731 0.3 1327 4.5 1942 0.4	0230 5.4 0900 0.5 1449 5.8 2115 0.5	0637 0.7 1218 5.7 1857 0.8	0629 1.3 1151 6.9 1852 1.2	**3 M**
0229 1.4 0833 -0.4 1500 1.4 2045 -0.3	0621 -0.1 1213 2.6 1836 0.0	0101 3.3 0741 -0.2 1330 3.2 1957 0.0	0232 1.8 0733 0.0 1446 2.1 1957 0.2	0405 1.8 1157 0.1 1624 2.1	0145 4.5 0807 0.1 1402 4.7 2020 0.3	0307 5.8 0943 0.2 1527 6.1 2159 0.3	0027 5.7 0717 0.5 1250 5.9 1934 0.6	0006 7.0 0713 1.0 1224 7.2 1934 1.0	**4 TU** ●
0309 1.5 0911 -0.4 1537 1.4 2124 -0.4	0023 2.8 0700 -0.1 1250 2.7 1916 -0.1	0145 3.4 0822 -0.3 1412 3.3 2039 -0.3	0306 1.9 0802 0.0 1522 2.1 2021 0.2	0044 0.2 0441 1.9 1250 0.1 1702 2.1	0219 4.6 0846 0.0 1437 4.8 2100 0.2	0345 6.1 1027 0.0 1604 6.3 2242 0.1	0059 5.9 0755 0.3 1321 6.1 2011 0.5	0039 7.2 0754 0.9 1255 7.3 2013 0.9	**5 W**
0349 1.5 0948 -0.4 1614 1.4 2203 -0.4	0101 2.9 0739 -0.2 1325 2.7 1955 -0.1	0227 3.5 0902 -0.3 1451 3.3 2119 -0.3	0341 2.0 0836 -0.1 1600 2.1 2054 0.2	0128 0.1 0518 2.0 1338 0.0 1741 2.1	0254 4.8 0927 0.0 1514 4.9 2142 0.1	0421 6.2 1109 -0.1 1641 6.3 2325 0.1	0132 6.1 0833 0.3 1356 6.2 2048 0.5	0110 7.4 0832 0.9 1328 7.3 2049 1.0	**6 TH**
0430 1.5 1027 -0.4 1649 1.4 2242 -0.4	0139 2.9 0818 -0.2 1400 2.8 2033 -0.2	0308 3.5 0941 -0.3 1530 3.3 2157 -0.4	0417 2.0 0913 -0.1 1639 2.1 2132 0.2	0210 0.1 0557 2.1 1423 0.0 1821 2.1	0331 4.8 1009 0.0 1551 4.8 2224 0.2	0458 6.3 1152 0.0 1719 6.3	0208 6.2 0911 0.3 1433 6.2 2126 0.5	0144 7.4 0907 0.9 1403 7.3 2124 1.0	**7 F**
0508 1.5 1104 -0.4 1719 1.4 2322 -0.5	0216 2.9 0855 -0.1 1435 2.8 2112 -0.2	0347 3.5 1018 -0.3 1606 3.3 2236 -0.3	0455 2.0 0955 0.0 1718 2.0 2215 0.1	0249 0.1 0637 2.1 1504 0.0 1900 2.1	0409 4.8 1050 0.0 1632 4.7 2306 0.2	0007 0.2 0536 6.2 1232 0.1 1758 6.0	0247 6.2 0950 0.3 1515 6.1 2206 0.6	0221 7.3 0943 1.0 1442 7.1 2201 1.2	**8 SA**
0542 1.4 1143 -0.3 1750 1.4	0255 2.9 0933 0.0 1512 2.8 2151 -0.1	0425 3.5 1055 -0.2 1642 3.3 2314 -0.3	0536 2.0 1042 0.0 1801 1.9 2305 0.1	0324 0.2 0718 2.1 1542 0.1 1942 2.0	0450 4.7 1131 0.2 1715 4.5 2348 0.3	0046 0.4 0616 6.0 1310 0.4 1841 5.7	0330 6.1 1032 0.5 1559 5.9 2249 0.8	0303 7.1 1024 1.2 1527 6.9 2243 1.4	**9 SU**
0005 -0.4 0621 1.4 1226 -0.3 1830 1.4	0338 2.8 1012 0.0 1554 2.8 2235 -0.1	0505 3.4 1133 -0.1 1719 3.3 2354 -0.2	0622 2.0 1142 0.1 1852 1.7	0350 0.2 0803 2.1 1613 0.2 2028 1.9	0536 4.6 1214 0.3 1806 4.2	0124 0.6 0701 5.7 1348 0.6 1930 5.3	0418 5.9 1118 0.8 1650 5.5 2339 1.1	0352 6.8 1110 1.4 1622 6.5 2333 1.7	**10 M**
0052 -0.4 0713 1.3 1315 -0.2 1925 1.4	0427 2.7 1056 0.2 1645 2.7 2326 0.0	0548 3.3 1213 0.0 1803 3.2	0008 0.1 0719 1.9 1412 0.1 2009 1.6	0301 0.2 0854 2.0 1600 0.2 2124 1.7	0036 0.4 0634 4.3 1307 0.5 1917 3.9	0206 0.7 0754 5.4 1434 0.8 2033 5.0	0513 5.5 1215 1.1 1754 5.1	0455 6.4 1206 1.8 1737 6.1	**11 TU**
0150 -0.4 0824 1.2 1417 -0.1 2039 1.3	0524 2.6 1149 0.3 1744 2.6	0040 -0.1 0639 3.1 1301 0.2 1858 3.2	0210 0.1 0849 1.8 1506 0.1 2134 1.5	0347 0.2 0959 1.9 1640 0.2 2242 1.6	0139 0.5 0757 4.1 1424 0.7 2041 3.7	0259 0.9 0907 5.1 1533 1.0 2154 4.8	0043 1.3 0629 5.2 1330 1.5 1925 4.7	0035 2.0 0622 6.1 1315 2.1 1909 5.9	**12 W**
0305 -0.3 0951 1.2 1538 0.0 2206 1.4	0030 0.1 0630 2.4 1257 0.4 1852 2.6	0139 0.1 0739 3.0 1406 0.3 2001 3.1	0315 0.1 1011 1.8 1731 0.2 2251 1.4	0444 0.1 1125 1.8 1743 0.3	0306 0.6 0921 4.0 1600 0.7 2203 3.7	0412 0.9 1030 5.0 1655 1.1 2312 4.8	0203 1.5 0807 5.0 1456 1.6 2057 4.8	0154 2.2 0749 6.0 1445 2.2 2028 5.9	**13 TH**
0433 -0.3 1122 1.2 1705 0.0 2332 1.4	0148 0.2 0743 2.4 1418 0.4 2006 2.6	0259 0.1 0847 2.9 1531 0.3 2110 3.1	0442 0.1 1127 1.8 1951 0.1	0004 1.6 0543 0.1 1239 1.9 2010 0.3	0438 0.5 1042 4.1 1719 0.6 2318 3.9	0551 0.8 1148 5.2 1828 0.9	0329 1.4 0930 5.2 1620 1.4 2206 5.0	0332 2.1 0903 6.2 1619 1.9 2136 6.2	**14 F**
0551 -0.3 1242 1.3 1816 -0.1	0308 0.1 0857 2.4 1533 0.3 2116 2.6	0422 0.1 0958 2.9 1650 0.2 2220 3.1	0001 1.5 0709 0.1 1228 1.9 2101 0.1	0109 1.7 0639 0.1 1339 2.0 2149 0.3	0550 0.3 1148 4.3 1818 0.5	0024 5.1 0712 0.5 1257 5.5 1939 0.7	0446 1.1 1033 5.5 1727 1.1 2300 5.3	0454 1.7 1008 6.4 1727 1.5 2235 6.5	**15 SA**

• • Time Zone -0100. For UT subtract 1 hour. For European summer time (shaded) 26/3-29/10 add 1 hour • •

APRIL 2000 TIDE TABLES

• • Time Zone -0100. For UT subtract 1 hour. For European summer time (shaded) 26/3-29/10 add 1 hour • •

Day	ESBJERG Time m	HELGOLAND Time m	CUXHAVEN Time m	HOEK VAN HOLLAND Time m	ROTTERDAM Time m	VLISSINGEN Time m	ANTWERPEN Time m	DUNKERQUE Time m	CALAIS Time m
16 SU	0049 1.5 / 0655 -0.4 / 1345 1.4 / 1914 -0.2	0415 0.0 / 1002 2.4 / 1635 0.1 / 2217 2.7	0531 0.0 / 1108 2.9 / 1754 0.1 / 2327 3.1	0057 1.6 / 0905 0.0 / 1318 2.0 / 2122 0.1	0204 1.8 / 0725 0.1 / 1431 2.0 / 2044 0.4	0015 4.1 / 0645 0.1 / 1239 4.5 / 1905 0.4	0125 5.4 / 0812 0.2 / 1353 5.7 / 2035 0.4	0548 0.7 / 1124 5.7 / 1818 0.8 / 2343 5.6	0553 1.3 / 1103 6.7 / 1819 1.2 / 2325 6.8
17 M	0151 1.5 / 0747 -0.4 / 1433 1.4 / 2003 -0.2	0510 -0.1 / 1055 2.5 / 1727 0.1 / 2309 2.7	0628 -0.1 / 1209 3.0 / 1848 -0.1	0145 1.7 / 0647 0.1 / 1402 2.0 / 2130 0.1	0251 1.9 / 1013 0.2 / 1515 2.1 / 2157 0.4	0100 4.3 / 0730 0.0 / 1321 4.6 / 1945 0.3	0216 5.6 / 0903 0.1 / 1441 5.9 / 2121 0.3	0636 0.4 / 1206 5.9 / 1900 0.7	0641 1.0 / 1151 6.9 / 1903 1.0
18 TU O	0239 1.5 / 0831 -0.3 / 1512 1.4 / 2045 -0.3	0558 -0.1 / 1140 2.5 / 1813 0.0 / 2352 2.7	0025 3.2 / 0718 -0.2 / 1300 3.0 / 1936 -0.1	0235 2.0 / 0821 0.1 / 1441 2.0 / 2146 0.1	0333 1.9 / 0842 0.1 / 1556 2.1 / 2101 0.3	0139 4.5 / 0809 0.0 / 1359 4.6 / 2022 0.3	0301 5.7 / 0947 0.0 / 1523 6.0 / 2202 0.3	0021 5.8 / 0718 0.3 / 1243 6.0 / 1938 0.6	0007 7.0 / 0721 0.9 / 1230 7.1 / 1939 1.0
19 W	0318 1.5 / 0911 -0.3 / 1545 1.4 / 2124 -0.3	0640 0.0 / 1218 2.5 / 1854 0.0	0113 3.2 / 0803 -0.1 / 1341 3.0 / 2019 0.0	0306 1.9 / 0757 0.1 / 1521 2.0 / 2024 0.3	0412 2.0 / 0923 0.1 / 1634 2.0 / 2140 0.3	0216 4.6 / 0847 0.0 / 1436 4.7 / 2058 0.3	0342 5.8 / 1025 0.0 / 1603 6.1 / 2239 0.2	0056 5.9 / 0757 0.3 / 1318 6.0 / 2014 0.6	0043 7.1 / 0756 0.9 / 1303 7.1 / 2009 1.0
20 TH	0353 1.5 / 0947 -0.3 / 1612 1.5 / 2200 -0.3	0030 2.6 / 0718 0.1 / 1251 2.5 / 1932 0.1	0153 3.1 / 0842 0.0 / 1415 3.0 / 2057 0.0	0342 2.0 / 0836 0.1 / 1557 2.0 / 2104 0.3	0451 2.0 / 1006 0.2 / 1712 2.0 / 2224 0.3	0253 4.7 / 0921 0.1 / 1512 4.7 / 2134 0.3	0420 5.9 / 1101 0.0 / 1639 6.0 / 2314 0.2	0131 5.9 / 0833 0.4 / 1354 5.9 / 2048 0.7	0115 7.2 / 0824 0.9 / 1333 7.1 / 2036 1.1
21 F	0427 1.5 / 1021 -0.2 / 1640 1.5 / 2236 -0.3	0104 2.6 / 0751 0.2 / 1321 2.5 / 2004 0.2	0226 3.0 / 0917 0.2 / 1444 3.0 / 2131 0.1	0417 2.0 / 0919 0.1 / 1632 2.0 / 2148 0.2	0528 1.9 / 1054 0.2 / 1748 1.9 / 2314 0.3	0329 4.7 / 0955 0.2 / 1547 4.6 / 2209 0.3	0457 5.9 / 1135 0.1 / 1715 5.9 / 2348 0.2	0208 5.9 / 0908 0.5 / 1430 5.9 / 2122 0.8	0147 7.2 / 0851 1.1 / 1405 7.0 / 2102 1.2
22 SA	0500 1.5 / 1053 -0.2 / 1708 1.5 / 2310 -0.3	0136 2.6 / 0819 0.3 / 1351 2.5 / 2034 0.3	0255 3.0 / 0946 0.3 / 1509 3.0 / 2200 0.2	0450 2.0 / 1005 0.2 / 1705 1.9 / 2236 0.2	0606 1.9 / 1151 0.3 / 1824 1.8	0403 4.6 / 1027 0.3 / 1621 4.5 / 2242 0.4	0533 5.8 / 1206 0.2 / 1750 5.7	0245 5.8 / 0941 0.7 / 1507 5.7 / 2154 0.9	0220 7.1 / 0918 1.2 / 1437 6.9 / 2129 1.4
23 SU	0530 1.4 / 1124 -0.2 / 1735 1.5 / 2344 -0.2	0209 2.5 / 0844 0.4 / 1422 2.5 / 2103 0.3	0324 2.9 / 1009 0.4 / 1534 3.0 / 2224 0.3	0522 2.0 / 1058 0.2 / 1738 1.8 / 2329 0.2	0012 0.3 / 0642 1.8 / 1321 0.4 / 1858 1.7	0438 4.5 / 1056 0.4 / 1654 4.3 / 2312 0.4	0018 0.3 / 0606 5.6 / 1233 0.3 / 1824 5.5	0323 5.7 / 1012 0.9 / 1545 5.5 / 2226 1.1	0254 6.9 / 0945 1.4 / 1512 6.7 / 2157 1.6
24 M	0559 1.4 / 1155 -0.1 / 1803 1.4	0243 2.4 / 0909 0.5 / 1457 2.5 / 2133 0.4	0357 2.9 / 1030 0.5 / 1606 2.9 / 2251 0.4	0555 1.9 / 1213 0.2 / 1812 1.8	0134 0.3 / 0717 1.7 / 1421 0.4 / 1931 1.6	0512 4.3 / 1126 0.5 / 1728 4.1 / 2344 0.5	0046 0.4 / 0642 5.4 / 1303 0.5 / 1858 5.2	0401 5.5 / 1045 1.1 / 1623 5.3 / 2300 1.3	0330 6.7 / 1015 1.7 / 1548 6.5 / 2230 1.8
25 TU	0018 -0.2 / 0630 1.3 / 1230 -0.1 / 1839 1.4	0321 2.3 / 0940 0.6 / 1536 2.4 / 2209 0.5	0436 2.7 / 1057 0.5 / 1645 2.8 / 2324 0.5	0017 0.1 / 0632 1.9 / 1259 0.2 / 1851 1.6	0228 0.3 / 0753 1.7 / 1507 0.5 / 2007 1.5	0549 4.1 / 1201 0.7 / 1808 3.9	0118 0.5 / 0720 5.2 / 1337 0.7 / 1938 5.0	0442 5.2 / 1123 1.3 / 1705 5.0 / 2342 1.5	0409 6.4 / 1053 2.0 / 1630 6.1 / 2314 2.2
26 W	0057 -0.2 / 0711 1.2 / 1310 0.0 / 1926 1.4	0407 2.2 / 1019 0.7 / 1626 2.3 / 2257 0.7	0524 2.6 / 1134 0.7 / 1738 2.7	0104 0.1 / 0720 1.7 / 1352 0.2 / 1951 1.5	0316 0.3 / 0833 1.6 / 1559 0.5 / 2048 1.4	0023 0.7 / 0637 3.9 / 1248 0.9 / 1903 3.6	0156 0.6 / 0805 5.0 / 1420 0.9 / 2026 4.7	0531 4.9 / 1213 1.6 / 1758 4.7	0456 6.0 / 1145 2.3 / 1725 5.7
27 TH	0145 -0.2 / 0809 1.1 / 1401 0.0 / 2030 1.3	0508 2.0 / 1113 0.8 / 1733 2.2	0007 0.7 / 0623 2.4 / 1222 0.8 / 1845 2.5	0157 0.1 / 0847 1.6 / 1602 0.2 / 2125 1.3	0413 0.4 / 0927 1.4 / 1709 0.5 / 2154 1.2	0117 0.8 / 0751 3.6 / 1404 1.1 / 2025 3.4	0242 0.8 / 0901 4.7 / 1513 1.1 / 2129 4.4	0039 1.7 / 0636 4.7 / 1318 1.8 / 1911 4.4	0015 2.4 / 0602 5.6 / 1253 2.5 / 1843 5.5
28 F	0251 -0.1 / 0931 1.1 / 1514 0.1 / 2151 1.3	0008 0.8 / 0628 1.9 / 1234 0.8 / 1856 2.1	0104 0.8 / 0736 2.3 / 1328 1.0 / 2003 2.5	0314 0.1 / 1006 1.6 / 1700 0.2 / 2246 1.3	0521 0.4 / 1137 1.4 / 1838 0.5	0312 0.9 / 0916 3.6 / 1552 1.0 / 2154 3.4	0345 1.0 / 1015 4.5 / 1629 1.3 / 2254 4.2	0149 1.8 / 0758 4.6 / 1430 1.8 / 2034 4.5	0129 2.6 / 0727 5.5 / 1407 2.5 / 2007 5.5
29 SA	0419 -0.1 / 1059 1.1 / 1642 0.1 / 2310 1.3	0150 0.8 / 0756 2.0 / 1422 0.8 / 2018 2.2	0237 0.8 / 0855 2.4 / 1522 0.9 / 2121 2.6	0502 0.1 / 1122 1.7 / 1804 0.2 / 2354 1.5	0019 1.3 / 0643 0.3 / 1253 1.5 / 1958 0.4	0421 0.8 / 1037 3.7 / 1654 0.9 / 2304 3.6	0511 1.0 / 1143 4.7 / 1746 1.2	0300 1.7 / 0915 4.8 / 1539 1.7 / 2142 4.7	0243 2.4 / 0844 5.7 / 1521 2.3 / 2114 5.9
30 SU	0533 -0.2 / 1205 1.2 / 1751 0.0	0314 0.6 / 0911 2.2 / 1536 0.6 / 2124 2.4	0427 0.6 / 1010 2.6 / 1653 0.6 / 2230 2.9	0544 0.1 / 1217 1.8 / 2010 0.1	0122 1.4 / 0801 0.2 / 1348 1.7 / 2110 0.3	0522 0.6 / 1133 4.0 / 1748 0.7 / 2354 4.0	0015 4.6 / 0623 0.9 / 1246 5.1 / 1849 1.0	0407 1.5 / 1012 5.1 / 1642 1.4 / 2233 5.1	0354 2.1 / 0942 6.1 / 1627 1.9 / 2206 6.3

DENMARK, GERMANY, HOLLAND & BELGIUM Time Zone -0100

Esbjerg * Helgoland * Cuxhaven * Hoek van Holland * Rotterdam * Vlissingen * Antwerpen * Dunkerque * Calais

TIDE TABLES MAY 2000

Day	esbjerg Time	m	HELGOLAND Time	m	CUXHAVEN Time	m	HOEK VAN HOLLAND Time	m	ROTTERDAM Time	m	VLISSINGEN Time	m	ANTWERPEN Time	m	DUNKERQUE Time	m	CALAIS Time	m
1 M	0013	1.4	0412	0.3	0528	0.3	0043	1.6	0212	1.6	0614	0.4	0109	5.1	0507	1.1	0456	1.7
	0628	-0.3	1007	2.4	1112	2.9	0606	0.1	0910	0.2	1216	4.3	0727	0.7	1059	5.4	1030	6.5
	1300	1.3	1631	0.3	1750	0.3	1300	1.9	1435	1.9	1832	0.5	1333	5.5	1736	1.1	1724	1.5
	1845	-0.2	2218	2.6	2330	3.1	2112	0.1	2218	0.2			1949	0.7	2315	5.4	2249	6.7
2 TU	0106	1.4	0500	0.1	0619	0.0	0122	1.7	0256	1.8	0035	4.2	0153	5.5	0558	0.8	0549	1.3
	0715	-0.3	1053	2.6	1205	3.1	0630	0.1	1015	0.1	0657	0.3	0823	0.4	1138	5.8	1110	6.9
	1348	1.4	1719	0.1	1839	0.0	1339	2.0	1517	2.0	1255	4.6	1415	5.9	1822	0.8	1814	1.2
	1931	-0.2	2305	2.8			1903	0.3	2318	0.1	1912	0.4	2042	0.5	2351	5.7	2327	7.1
3 W	0155	1.5	0545	-0.1	0021	3.4	0200	1.9	0336	1.9	0112	4.5	0234	5.9	0643	0.5	0637	1.1
	0759	-0.4	1135	2.7	0706	-0.2	0659	0.0	1120	0.1	0738	0.2	0912	0.2	1215	6.0	1148	7.2
	1430	1.4	1804	0.0	1253	3.3	1418	2.1	1557	2.1	1333	4.8	1456	6.2	1905	0.6	1900	1.1
	2015	-0.3	2348	2.9	1926	-0.2	1923	0.2			1954	0.3	2131	0.2				
4 TH ●	0242	1.5	0628	-0.2	0111	3.5	0236	2.0	0010	0.1	0151	4.7	0314	6.2	0028	5.9	0005	7.3
	0841	-0.4	1215	2.8	0751	-0.3	0733	0.0	0414	2.0	0820	0.1	0959	0.0	0726	0.4	0722	0.9
	1512	1.4	1848	-0.2	1338	3.4	1457	2.2	1220	0.1	1411	4.9	1536	6.4	1252	6.1	1225	7.3
	2059	-0.4			2011	-0.3	1954	0.2	1636	2.2	2037	0.2	2218	0.1	1947	0.5	1944	1.0
5 F	0327	1.5	0032	2.9	0157	3.6	0315	2.1	0058	0.1	0229	4.8	0354	6.4	0106	6.0	0043	7.4
	0923	-0.4	0711	-0.2	0834	-0.4	0810	0.0	0454	2.1	0903	0.0	1045	-0.1	0809	0.3	0806	0.9
	1554	1.4	1255	2.8	1421	3.4	1536	2.1	1314	0.0	1451	4.9	1616	6.4	1331	6.2	1304	7.3
	2142	-0.4	1930	-0.2	2054	-0.4	2030	0.2	1716	2.1	2122	0.1	2304	0.1	2028	0.5	2026	1.0
6 SA	0414	1.5	0114	2.9	0242	3.5	0355	2.1	0143	0.1	0309	4.9	0434	6.4	0145	6.1	0124	7.4
	1004	-0.4	0752	-0.2	0915	-0.4	0851	0.0	0534	2.1	0947	0.0	1129	0.0	0851	0.3	0848	0.9
	1633	1.5	1334	2.8	1503	3.4	1618	2.1	1403	0.1	1532	4.9	1657	6.3	1413	6.1	1346	7.3
	2225	-0.4	2012	-0.2	2136	-0.4	2112	0.1	1757	2.1	2207	0.1	2348	0.1	2110	0.5	2108	1.0
7 SU	0459	1.5	0157	2.9	0325	3.5	0437	2.1	0224	0.1	0351	4.9	0516	6.3	0228	6.1	0207	7.3
	1045	-0.3	0833	-0.1	0956	-0.3	0936	0.1	0616	2.1	1031	0.1	1212	0.2	0933	0.4	0930	0.9
	1708	1.5	1413	2.9	1542	3.4	1700	2.0	1448	0.1	1615	4.7	1741	6.0	1457	6.0	1432	7.1
	2309	-0.4	2054	-0.2	2217	-0.4	2158	0.1	1838	2.0	2253	0.1			2153	0.6	2150	1.1
8 M	0542	1.4	0239	2.9	0407	3.4	0521	2.1	0300	0.2	0436	4.8	0031	0.3	0315	6.0	0256	7.1
	1127	-0.3	0912	-0.1	1036	-0.2	1028	0.2	0659	2.1	1115	0.2	0601	6.1	1018	0.6	1015	1.1
	1744	1.5	1454	2.9	1621	3.4	1747	1.8	1529	0.1	1703	4.5	1254	0.4	1545	5.8	1524	6.8
	2355	-0.4	2136	-0.2	2258	-0.4	2251	0.1	1921	1.9	2339	0.2	1827	5.7	2239	0.7	2236	1.3
9 TU	0627	1.4	0324	2.8	0449	3.3	0611	2.1	0308	0.2	0527	4.6	0114	0.4	0406	5.8	0354	6.8
	1213	-0.2	0954	0.0	1115	-0.1	1137	0.2	0744	2.1	1203	0.4	0651	5.8	1106	0.8	1103	1.4
	1828	1.5	1537	2.8	1700	3.4	1844	1.7	1603	0.2	1759	4.2	1336	0.6	1640	5.4	1628	6.5
			2222	-0.1	2341	-0.3	2357	0.1	2006	1.8			1921	5.3	2331	1.0	2327	1.5
10 W	0046	-0.4	0412	2.7	0533	3.2	0718	2.0	0224	0.1	0032	0.3	0200	0.6	0506	5.5	0505	6.5
	0722	1.3	1038	0.1	1156	0.0	1457	0.2	0835	2.0	0633	4.4	0750	5.5	1204	1.1	1200	1.7
	1304	-0.1	1626	2.8	1745	3.3	2009	1.6	1518	0.3	1259	0.6	1424	0.8	1748	5.1	1742	6.2
	1924	1.5	2313	0.0					2059	1.7	1913	4.0	2027	5.1				
11 TH	0146	-0.3	0506	2.5	0028	-0.1	0154	0.0	0315	0.1	0138	0.4	0254	0.7	0034	1.2	0029	1.8
	0829	1.2	1129	0.3	0621	3.1	0841	1.9	0939	1.9	0751	4.2	0859	5.3	0624	5.2	0621	6.2
	1406	-0.1	1723	2.7	1242	0.1	1614	0.2	1604	0.3	1415	0.7	1521	1.0	1316	1.4	1309	2.0
	2034	1.4			1836	3.2	2118	1.5	2212	1.6	2026	3.8	2137	4.9	1914	4.9	1857	6.0
12 F	0259	-0.3	0014	0.1	0125	0.0	0301	0.0	0412	0.0	0257	0.4	0403	0.7	0150	1.3	0145	2.0
	0946	1.2	0607	2.4	0717	2.9	0954	1.9	1102	1.9	0906	4.1	1011	5.2	0752	5.1	0735	6.1
	1523	0.0	1232	0.3	1343	0.3	1758	0.2	1706	0.3	1541	0.8	1633	1.0	1438	1.5	1433	2.1
	2153	1.5	1827	2.6	1936	3.1	2229	1.5	2334	1.6	2141	3.8	2248	5.0	2036	4.9	2008	6.0
13 SA	0418	-0.3	0126	0.2	0238	0.1	0536	0.0	0515	0.1	0417	0.4	0524	0.6	0311	1.3	0313	2.0
	1106	1.3	0715	2.3	0820	2.8	1106	1.9	1214	1.9	1021	4.2	1124	5.2	0909	5.2	0843	6.2
	1642	-0.1	1348	0.4	1501	0.3	1932	0.2	1939	0.3	1657	0.7	1754	0.9	1558	1.4	1556	1.9
	2312	1.5	1937	2.6	2042	3.1	2336	1.6			2252	3.9	2357	5.1	2142	5.1	2112	6.2
14 SU	0530	-0.3	0240	0.2	0354	0.1	0708	0.0	0042	1.6	0527	0.3	0640	0.4	0426	1.1	0428	1.7
	1219	1.3	0826	2.3	0927	2.8	1207	1.9	0618	0.1	1124	4.3	1230	5.4	1010	5.4	0945	6.4
	1751	-0.1	1502	0.3	1619	0.3	2037	0.1	1315	1.9	1755	0.6	1908	0.7	1703	1.1	1700	1.6
			2048	2.6	2151	3.1			2109	0.3	2349	4.1			2236	5.3	2210	6.4
15 M	0026	1.5	0346	0.1	0502	0.1	0032	1.7	0138	1.7	0621	0.2	0058	5.4	0525	0.8	0525	1.4
	0631	-0.3	0932	2.3	1036	2.8	0839	0.0	0718	0.1	1215	4.4	0742	0.2	1100	5.6	1040	6.6
	1318	1.4	1606	0.2	1724	0.1	1256	2.0	1408	2.0	1841	0.5	1327	5.7	1754	0.9	1751	1.3
	1850	-0.2	2151	2.6	2257	3.1	2131	0.2	2227	0.3			2006	0.5	2320	5.5	2300	6.7

● ● Time Zone -0100. For UT subtract 1 hour. For European summer time (shaded) 26/3-29/10 add 1 hour ● ●

MAY 2000 TIDE TABLES

• • Time Zone -0100. For UT subtract 1 hour. For European summer time (shaded) 26/3-29/10 add 1 hour • •

	ESBJERG		HELGOLAND		CUXHAVEN		HOEK VAN HOLLAND		ROTTERDAM		VLISSINGEN		ANTWERPEN		DUNKERQUE		CALAIS	
	Time	m	Time	m	Time	m	Time	m	Time	m	Time	m	Time	m	Time	m	Time	m
16 TU	0125	1.5	0442	0.1	0600	0.0	0120	1.8	0227	1.8	0035	4.3	0151	5.6	0613	0.6	0612	1.1
	0722	-0.3	1027	2.4	1137	2.9	0633	0.1	0951	0.2	0705	0.2	0834	0.1	1142	5.8	1126	6.7
	1405	1.4	1700	0.1	1821	0.1	1339	2.0	1454	2.0	1258	4.5	1417	5.9	1836	0.7	1833	1.2
	1939	-0.2	2244	2.6	2357	3.1	2213	0.2	2325	0.3	1921	0.4	2054	0.3	2357	5.7	2342	6.8
17 W	0212	1.5	0530	0.1	0650	0.0	0202	1.8	0312	1.9	0115	4.4	0237	5.7	0654	0.5	0651	1.1
	0806	-0.2	1113	2.5	1228	2.9	0706	0.2	1029	0.3	0743	0.2	0918	0.0	1219	5.8	1204	6.8
	1442	1.5	1748	0.1	1910	0.0	1419	2.0	1534	1.9	1336	4.6	1500	6.0	1915	0.7	1908	1.2
	2022	-0.2	2329	2.6					1938	0.3	2231	0.4	1957	0.4	2136	0.2		
18 TH O	0251	1.5	0613	0.1	0046	3.0	0242	1.9	0351	1.9	0153	4.5	0319	5.8	0033	5.7	0018	6.9
	0845	-0.2	1152	2.5	0735	0.1	0744	0.2	1122	0.3	0818	0.2	0957	0.0	0733	0.6	0725	1.1
	1512	1.5	1831	0.1	1311	3.0	1457	2.0	1612	1.9	1413	4.6	1540	6.0	1254	5.8	1237	6.9
	2101	-0.2			1954	0.1	2015	0.2	2340	0.4	2034	0.3	2215	0.1	1951	0.7	1939	1.2
19 F	0325	1.5	0009	2.5	0127	3.0	0318	2.0	0429	1.8	0230	4.6	0358	5.9	0109	5.7	0051	7.0
	0920	-0.1	0651	0.2	0815	0.2	0824	0.2	1216	0.4	0853	0.3	1035	0.1	0808	0.7	0754	1.2
	1542	1.5	1227	2.5	1347	2.9	1534	2.0	1648	1.8	1449	4.6	1618	6.0	1330	5.8	1308	6.9
	2139	-0.2	1909	0.2	2033	0.2	2056	0.2	2210	0.3	2111	0.3	2251	0.2	2027	0.8	2006	1.3
20 SA	0400	1.5	0044	2.4	0203	2.9	0353	2.0	0506	1.8	0306	4.6	0436	5.8	0146	5.7	0123	7.0
	0954	-0.1	0724	0.3	0850	0.3	0909	0.3	1317	0.5	0927	0.3	1109	0.2	0842	0.8	0822	1.3
	1612	1.6	1259	2.5	1419	2.9	1609	2.0	1724	1.7	1524	4.6	1654	5.8	1407	5.7	1339	6.9
	2215	-0.2	1945	0.3	2109	0.2	2140	0.2	2256	0.3	2148	0.3	2326	0.2	2100	0.8	2035	1.4
21 SU	0436	1.5	0118	2.4	0238	2.8	0426	2.0	0543	1.8	0342	4.6	0510	5.7	0224	5.6	0156	6.9
	1027	-0.1	0754	0.4	0920	0.4	0958	0.3	1117	0.5	1000	0.4	1140	0.4	0915	0.9	0851	1.4
	1643	1.6	1331	2.5	1449	2.9	1642	1.9	1758	1.7	1557	4.5	1727	5.6	1444	5.6	1412	6.8
	2250	-0.2	2017	0.3	2140	0.3	2358	0.1	2352	0.4	2221	0.4	2357	0.4	2133	0.9	2103	1.5
22 M	0508	1.4	0152	2.4	0312	2.8	0458	2.0	0618	1.7	0415	4.5	0544	5.5	0301	5.5	0230	6.8
	1058	-0.1	0823	0.4	0946	0.5	1257	0.2	1232	0.5	1030	0.5	1208	0.5	0946	1.0	0920	1.6
	1714	1.5	1403	2.5	1519	2.9	1714	1.8	1832	1.6	1630	4.3	1759	5.4	1521	5.5	1446	6.7
	2324	-0.2	2048	0.4	2209	0.4	2305	0.1			2253	0.4			2205	1.1	2133	1.6
23 TU	0539	1.4	0227	2.3	0346	2.7	0531	2.0	0116	0.4	0449	4.4	0024	0.5	0339	5.4	0304	6.6
	1130	-0.1	0851	0.5	1012	0.5	1333	0.2	0654	1.7	1101	0.6	0618	5.4	1018	1.1	0951	1.7
	1745	1.5	1438	2.5	1551	2.9	1746	1.8	1312	0.5	1705	4.2	1236	0.7	1557	5.3	1522	6.5
	2358	-0.2	2119	0.4	2237	0.4	2348	0.1	1906	1.6	2324	0.5	1833	5.2	2238	1.2	2206	1.8
24 W	0611	1.3	0305	2.3	0424	2.7	0607	1.9	0058	0.3	0525	4.2	0054	0.5	0418	5.3	0342	6.4
	1204	0.0	0924	0.5	1042	0.5	1409	0.3	0730	1.7	1137	0.7	0654	5.3	1055	1.3	1027	1.9
	1821	1.5	1516	2.4	1627	2.8	1823	1.7	1258	0.5	1743	4.0	1310	0.9	1637	5.1	1601	6.3
			2156	0.5	2311	0.5			1943	1.5			1910	5.1	2316	1.3	2248	2.0
25 TH	0036	-0.1	0348	2.2	0506	2.6	0035	0.0	0132	0.3	0003	0.5	0132	0.5	0502	5.1	0425	6.2
	0651	1.2	1003	0.6	1119	0.6	0651	1.8	0812	1.6	0609	4.0	0736	5.2	1139	1.4	1115	2.1
	1244	0.0	1602	2.4	1713	2.7	1336	0.3	1346	0.5	1221	0.8	1351	0.8	1724	4.9	1649	6.0
	1905	1.4	2242	0.6	2353	0.6	1908	1.6	2026	1.5	1831	3.8	1954	5.0			2343	2.2
26 F	0120	-0.1	0440	2.1	0557	2.5	0126	0.0	0237	0.3	0050	0.6	0216	0.5	0005	1.5	0520	5.9
	0743	1.2	1052	0.7	1205	0.7	0757	1.7	0903	1.6	0709	3.9	0824	5.0	0555	4.9	1217	2.3
	1331	0.0	1700	2.3	1812	2.7	1539	0.3	1615	0.5	1315	0.9	1439	0.9	1234	1.6	1751	5.8
	2000	1.4	2341	0.6			2038	1.5	2123	1.4	1940	3.6	2048	4.8	1823	4.8		
27 SA	0214	-0.1	0546	2.0	0045	0.6	0221	0.1	0414	0.3	0153	0.7	0309	0.5	0106	1.6	0050	2.3
	0848	1.2	1159	0.7	0659	2.5	0919	1.7	1030	1.5	0824	3.9	0927	4.9	0701	4.8	0629	5.8
	1430	0.0	1810	2.3	1303	0.7	1634	0.3	1809	0.5	1435	1.0	1537	1.0	1341	1.7	1325	2.4
	2106	1.4			1921	2.7	2151	1.4	2315	1.3	2055	3.6	2200	4.7	1933	4.7	1904	5.8
28 SU	0322	-0.1	0057	0.6	0154	0.6	0321	0.1	0545	0.3	0321	0.7	0412	0.7	0214	1.6	0159	2.3
	1001	1.2	0700	2.1	0809	2.5	1029	1.7	1206	1.6	0938	3.8	1044	5.0	0813	4.9	0743	5.8
	1542	0.0	1322	0.7	1421	0.7	1736	0.2	1927	0.4	1558	0.9	1645	1.0	1449	1.6	1433	2.2
	2217	1.4	1924	2.3	2033	2.8	2300	1.5			2207	3.7	2318	4.9	2044	4.8	2015	5.9
29 M	0436	-0.1	0216	0.5	0321	0.5	0425	0.1	0036	1.5	0430	0.6	0524	0.6	0320	1.4	0306	2.0
	1111	1.3	0813	2.2	0918	2.7	1132	1.9	0724	0.2	1043	4.1	1156	5.2	0919	5.1	0848	6.1
	1656	0.0	1442	0.5	1552	0.5	1918	0.2	1309	1.8	1659	0.7	1755	0.9	1554	1.4	1538	2.0
	2324	1.4	2033	2.5	2142	2.9	2358	1.6	2033	0.3	2308	4.0			2144	5.1	2115	6.3
30 TU	0539	-0.2	0322	0.3	0436	0.3	0512	0.1	0133	1.6	0529	0.4	0023	5.2	0422	1.2	0409	1.7
	1212	1.3	0915	2.4	1022	2.9	1223	2.0	0836	0.1	1136	4.3	0635	0.5	1013	5.4	0943	6.5
	1759	-0.1	1545	0.3	1703	0.3	2036	0.2	1400	2.0	1752	0.6	1253	5.6	1654	1.1	1639	1.7
			2133	2.6	2245	3.2			2136	0.2	2357	4.3	1903	0.7	2234	5.4	2205	6.7
31 W	0024	1.5	0418	0.0	0536	0.0	0045	1.8	0221	1.8	0621	0.3	0115	5.6	0519	0.9	0506	1.4
	0635	-0.3	1008	2.6	1120	3.1	0552	0.1	0940	0.1	1222	4.6	0742	0.4	1100	5.7	1030	6.8
	1307	1.4	1641	0.1	1800	0.0	1308	2.1	1447	2.1	1842	0.4	1342	6.0	1748	0.9	1734	1.4
	1855	-0.2	2227	2.8	2342	3.4	1825	0.3	2237	0.1			2009	0.4	2318	5.7	2251	7.0

DENMARK, GERMANY, HOLLAND & BELGIUM Time Zone -0100
Esbjerg * Helgoland * Cuxhaven * Hoek van Holland * Rotterdam * Vlissingen * Antwerpen * Dunkerque * Calais

TIDE TABLES JUNE 2000

esbjerg		HELGOLAND		CUXHAVEN		HOEK VAN HOLLAND		ROTTERDAM		VLISSINGEN		ANTWERPEN		DUNKERQUE		CALAIS			
Time	m	Time	m	Time	m	Time	m	Time	m	Time	m	Time	m	Time	m	Time	m		
0120	1.5	0509	-0.1	0629	-0.2	0128	1.9	0306	1.9	0042	4.5	0203	5.9	0611	0.6	0600	1.2	1	TH
0725	-0.3	1057	2.7	1213	3.3	0631	0.1	1045	0.1	0709	0.2	0841	0.2	1145	5.9	1115	7.1		
1358	1.5	1731	-0.1	1853	-0.2	1351	2.1	1530	2.1	1306	4.8	1428	6.2	1837	0.7	1827	1.2		
1946	-0.2	2316	2.9			1857	2.1	2334	0.1	1930	0.3	2105	0.3			2336	7.2		
0215	1.5	0557	-0.2	0036	3.5	0210	2.0	0348	2.0	0124	4.7	0248	6.2	0001	5.9	0652	1.0	2	F
0813	-0.3	1142	2.8	0719	-0.3	0710	0.1	1151	0.1	0755	0.1	0933	0.1	0700	0.5	1200	7.2		
1448	1.5	1820	-0.2	1303	3.4	1433	2.2	1611	2.1	1348	4.9	1512	6.4	1227	6.1	1917	1.1		●
2036	-0.3			1942	-0.4	1933	0.2	2357	0.1	2017	0.2	2156	0.1	1924	0.5				
0309	1.5	0004	2.9	0128	3.5	0254	2.1	0430	2.1	0207	4.9	0331	6.3	0044	6.0	0021	7.3	3	SA
0900	-0.3	0643	-0.2	0806	-0.4	0751	0.1	1034	0.2	0842	0.1	1021	0.1	0746	0.4	0743	0.9		
1534	1.5	1227	2.8	1351	3.4	1517	2.1	1652	2.1	1432	4.9	1556	6.3	1311	6.1	1247	7.3		
2124	-0.3	1907	-0.3	2030	-0.5	2013	0.2	2257	0.3	2105	0.1	2244	0.1	2009	0.5	2007	1.0		
0402	1.5	0052	2.9	0218	3.5	0337	2.2	0512	2.1	0251	4.9	0415	6.4	0128	6.0	0110	7.3	4	SU
0945	-0.3	0729	-0.2	0852	-0.4	0836	0.1	1054	0.3	0928	0.1	1108	0.1	0832	0.4	0833	0.9		
1618	1.5	1310	2.8	1436	3.4	1601	2.0	1346	0.1	1517	4.8	1641	6.2	1357	6.0	1336	7.2		
2211	-0.4	1954	-0.3	2116	-0.5	2057	0.1	1734	2.0	2153	0.1	2331	0.1	2055	0.5	2055	1.0		
0453	1.5	0139	2.8	0305	3.4	0422	2.2	0003	0.2	0337	4.9	0502	6.3	0215	6.0	0202	7.2	5	M
1030	-0.2	0812	-0.2	0936	-0.3	0923	0.2	0556	2.1	1015	0.2	1154	0.3	0918	0.5	0921	0.9		
1700	1.6	1353	2.9	1520	3.4	1648	1.9	1434	0.2	1603	4.7	1728	6.0	1444	5.9	1430	7.1		
2259	-0.4	2039	-0.3	2201	-0.5	2145	0.1	1817	2.0	2242	0.1			2142	0.5	2143	1.0		
0542	1.5	0224	2.8	0350	3.3	0510	2.2	0121	0.2	0426	4.8	0018	0.2	0305	6.0	0300	7.1	6	TU
1115	-0.2	0855	-0.1	1018	-0.3	1016	0.3	0641	2.1	1101	0.3	0551	6.1	1005	0.7	1009	1.0		
1742	1.6	1436	2.9	1601	3.4	1739	1.8	1517	0.2	1655	4.5	1238	0.4	1536	5.8	1530	6.9		
2348	-0.4	2124	-0.3	2245	-0.4	2237	0.1	1900	1.9	2332	0.1	1819	5.7	2230	0.6	2231	1.1		
0632	1.4	0309	2.7	0433	3.2	0604	2.1	0100	0.1	0521	4.7	0104	0.2	0400	5.8	0401	6.9	7	W
1202	-0.2	0938	0.0	1100	-0.2	1412	0.2	0727	2.1	1151	0.5	0644	5.9	1054	0.9	1059	1.2		
1829	1.6	1521	2.8	1643	3.4	1845	1.7	1430	0.3	1754	4.3	1323	0.6	1633	5.5	1630	6.7		
		2210	-0.2	2330	-0.4	2339	0.0	1946	1.8			1915	5.5	2322	0.8	2322	1.3		
0039	-0.3	0355	2.6	0516	3.1	0714	2.0	0152	0.0	0026	0.1	0153	0.3	0501	5.6	0503	6.7	8	TH
0724	1.3	1021	0.0	1142	-0.1	1513	0.3	0818	2.0	0627	4.5	0742	5.7	1150	1.1	1152	1.5		
1253	-0.1	1608	2.8	1727	3.4	1953	1.7	1436	0.3	1246	0.6	1411	0.7	1736	5.3	1731	6.5		
1922	1.6	2258	-0.1					2037	1.8	1900	4.2	2014	5.3						
0137	-0.3	0445	2.5	0016	-0.2	0133	0.0	0247	0.0	0127	0.2	0245	0.4	0022	1.0	0019	1.6	9	F
0821	1.3	1109	0.1	0602	3.0	0821	2.0	0919	2.0	0734	4.4	0843	5.5	0610	5.3	0605	6.4		
1351	-0.1	1700	2.7	1227	0.0	1643	0.3	1530	0.3	1352	0.7	1504	0.9	1255	1.3	1253	1.8		
2024	1.6	2353	0.0	1815	3.3	2052	1.6	2141	1.7	2003	4.0	2115	5.2	1848	5.1	1833	6.3		
0242	-0.2	0539	2.3	0108	-0.1	0243	0.0	0345	0.0	0233	0.3	0345	0.4	0131	1.1	0125	1.8	10	SA
0926	1.3	1204	0.2	0652	2.9	0927	1.9	1033	1.9	0841	4.3	0947	5.3	0724	5.2	0709	6.2		
1457	0.0	1800	2.6	1319	0.1	1750	0.3	1633	0.4	1504	0.8	1606	0.9	1408	1.5	1404	2.0		
2132	1.6			1910	3.2	2157	1.6	2259	1.6	2110	4.0	2218	5.1	2002	5.1	1936	6.2		
0351	-0.2	0055	0.1	0209	0.1	0354	0.0	0450	0.0	0342	0.3	0452	0.4	0243	1.2	0239	1.9	11	SU
1033	1.3	0640	2.2	0748	2.8	1036	1.9	1143	1.9	0949	4.2	1054	5.2	0837	5.2	0812	6.2		
1609	0.0	1311	0.3	1424	0.2	1853	0.2	1805	0.4	1619	0.8	1715	0.9	1522	1.4	1518	2.0		
2242	1.6	1905	2.5	2012	3.0	2304	1.6			2218	4.0	2326	5.1	2109	5.1	2039	6.2		
0458	-0.2	0204	0.2	0318	0.2	0455	0.1	0008	1.6	0453	0.3	0600	0.4	0354	1.1	0351	1.8	12	M
1139	1.4	0748	2.2	0851	2.7	1138	1.9	0601	0.1	1053	4.2	1201	5.3	0939	5.3	0913	6.2		
1718	0.0	1424	0.3	1540	0.3	1958	0.2	1245	1.9	1723	0.7	1827	0.8	1628	1.3	1623	1.8		
2350	1.6	2015	2.5	2118	2.9			2006	0.3	2318	4.1			2206	5.3	2137	6.3		
0559	-0.2	0311	0.2	0427	0.2	0003	1.7	0109	1.7	0550	0.3	0029	5.2	0454	1.0	0450	1.6	13	TU
1238	1.4	0854	2.2	0957	2.7	0542	0.1	0724	0.1	1147	4.3	0706	0.3	1032	5.4	1009	6.3		
1819	-0.1	1533	0.3	1651	0.2	1230	1.9	1341	1.9	1813	0.6	1300	5.5	1722	1.1	1715	1.6		
		2121	2.4	2225	2.9	2054	0.2	2132	0.3			1931	0.6	2254	5.4	2230	6.4		
0051	1.6	0410	0.2	0527	0.2	0053	1.8	0203	1.7	0008	4.2	0124	5.4	0545	0.9	0539	1.4	14	W
0652	-0.1	0955	2.3	1101	2.8	0620	0.2	0844	0.2	0636	0.4	0801	0.2	1116	5.5	1058	6.5		
1327	1.5	1633	0.2	1751	0.2	1316	1.9	1431	1.9	1233	4.4	1352	5.7	1809	0.9	1759	1.5		
1912	-0.1	2219	2.4	2327	2.9	1858	0.3	2250	0.3	1856	0.5	2024	0.4	2336	5.5	2316	6.6		
0141	1.5	0501	0.2	0620	0.2	0139	1.9	0251	1.8	0053	4.3	0214	5.6	0627	0.8	0619	1.4	15	TH
0738	-0.1	1046	2.4	1157	2.8	0658	0.2	0951	0.3	0715	0.4	0848	0.2	1156	5.6	1139	6.6		
1407	1.5	1724	0.2	1844	0.1	1358	1.9	1515	1.8	1315	4.4	1439	5.8	1850	0.8	1836	1.5		
1959	-0.1	2309	2.4			1930	0.2	2345	0.3	1935	0.5	2110	0.2			2356	6.7		

● ● Time Zone -0100. For UT subtract 1 hour. For European summer time (shaded) 26/3-29/10 add 1 hour ● ●

JUNE 2000 TIDE TABLES

• • Time Zone -0100. For UT subtract 1 hour. For European summer time (shaded) 26/3-29/10 add 1 hour • •

	ESBJERG		HELGOLAND		CUXHAVEN		HOEK VAN HOLLAND		ROTTERDAM		VLISSINGEN		ANTWERPEN		DUNKERQUE		CALAIS	
	Time	m	Time	m	Time	m	Time	m	Time	m	Time	m	Time	m	Time	m	Time	m
16 F	0223	1.5	0547	0.2	0021	2.8	0220	1.9	0333	1.7	0133	4.4	0259	5.7	0014	5.6	0655	1.4
O	0818	0.0	1130	2.4	0707	0.2	0739	0.2	1048	0.4	0752	0.4	0931	0.1	0707	0.9	1215	6.6
	1442	1.6	1811	0.2	1244	2.9	1438	1.9	1553	1.7	1354	4.5	1521	5.8	1233	5.6	1910	1.5
	2041	-0.1	2352	2.3	1931	0.1	2009	0.2	2316	0.4	2013	0.4	2152	0.2	1928	0.8		
17 SA	0301	1.5	0627	0.3	0107	2.8	0258	2.0	0412	1.7	0212	4.5	0339	5.8	0051	5.6	0030	6.7
	0856	0.0	1209	2.4	0750	0.2	0822	0.3	1139	0.5	0827	0.4	1010	0.2	0744	0.9	0727	1.4
	1516	1.6	1852	0.2	1324	2.9	1516	2.0	1629	1.7	1431	4.5	1559	5.8	1311	5.6	1248	6.7
	2120	-0.1			2014	0.2	2049	0.2	2351	0.5	2051	0.3	2232	0.2	2006	0.8	1942	1.5
18 SU	0339	1.5	0032	2.3	0148	2.7	0334	2.0	0448	1.7	0249	4.5	0418	5.7	0130	5.5	0105	6.7
	0931	0.0	0705	0.3	0828	0.3	0911	0.3	1226	0.6	0903	0.5	1047	0.3	0819	1.0	0800	1.5
	1550	1.6	1245	2.4	1402	2.8	1553	1.9	1703	1.6	1506	4.5	1635	5.6	1348	5.6	1321	6.7
	2157	-0.1	1931	0.3	2053	0.2	2128	0.2	2248	0.4	2129	0.3	2309	0.3	2041	0.9	2015	1.5
19 M	0415	1.5	0109	2.3	0227	2.7	0409	2.0	0524	1.7	0324	4.5	0453	5.6	0207	5.5	0138	6.7
	1006	0.0	0739	0.4	0903	0.4	1148	0.3	1306	0.6	0936	0.5	1119	0.5	0853	1.0	0832	1.6
	1624	1.6	1320	2.4	1438	2.8	1627	1.9	1738	1.6	1541	4.5	1709	5.5	1425	5.5	1354	6.7
	2233	-0.1	2006	0.3	2128	0.3	2201	0.1	2355	0.4	2205	0.4	2340	0.5	2115	1.0	2047	1.6
20 TU	0450	1.5	0145	2.2	0305	2.7	0442	2.0	0600	1.7	0358	4.5	0526	5.5	0245	5.5	0212	6.7
	1039	-0.1	0812	0.4	0935	0.4	1231	0.3	1220	0.6	1009	0.6	1148	0.7	0925	1.1	0903	1.6
	1657	1.6	1354	2.4	1513	2.8	1700	1.8	1813	1.6	1615	4.4	1742	5.3	1500	5.5	1428	6.7
	2308	-0.1	2041	0.3	2202	0.3	2236	0.1			2237	0.4			2147	1.0	2119	1.6
21 W	0523	1.4	0220	2.2	0342	2.6	0515	2.0	0118	0.4	0432	4.4	0009	0.5	0321	5.4	0246	6.6
	1111	-0.1	0845	0.4	1006	0.4	1313	0.3	0636	1.7	1042	0.6	0600	5.4	0957	1.1	0936	1.7
	1730	1.6	1428	2.4	1548	2.8	1730	1.8	1300	0.6	1648	4.3	1217	0.8	1536	5.5	1502	6.6
	2342	-0.1	2114	0.3	2234	0.3	2315	0.1	1848	1.6	2310	0.4	1815	5.3	2219	1.1	2153	1.7
22 TH	0557	1.4	0256	2.2	0419	2.6	0549	2.0	0130	0.3	0506	4.3	0040	0.5	0357	5.4	0321	6.5
	1145	-0.1	0918	0.4	1039	0.4	1354	0.3	0715	1.7	1118	0.6	0634	5.4	1031	1.2	1012	1.8
	1807	1.5	1504	2.4	1622	2.8	1803	1.7	1357	0.6	1724	4.2	1251	0.7	1612	5.4	1538	6.5
			2150	0.4	2308	0.4			1927	1.6	2346	0.4	1850	5.3	2255	1.1	2231	1.8
23 F	0018	-0.1	0334	2.2	0457	2.6	0002	0.1	0105	0.3	0546	4.2	0115	0.4	0436	5.3	0359	6.4
	0634	1.3	0956	0.4	1115	0.4	0629	1.9	0757	1.7	1200	0.7	0712	5.4	1110	1.3	1053	1.9
	1223	-0.1	1545	2.4	1700	2.8	1435	0.3	1516	0.6	1806	4.0	1329	0.7	1653	5.3	1619	6.4
	1847	1.5	2230	0.4	2347	0.4	1843	1.7	2010	1.6			1928	5.3	2337	1.2	2318	1.9
24 SA	0057	-0.1	0418	2.1	0539	2.6	0053	0.0	0152	0.2	0028	0.5	0156	0.4	0521	5.2	0444	6.3
	0718	1.3	1039	0.5	1157	0.4	0716	1.9	0845	1.8	0633	4.1	0755	5.3	1156	1.4	1145	2.0
	1306	-0.1	1633	2.4	1748	2.8	1518	0.3	1420	0.5	1246	0.8	1412	0.7	1742	5.2	1708	6.2
	1933	1.5	2319	0.4			1933	1.6	2102	1.6	1856	3.9	2014	5.2				
25 SU	0142	-0.1	0512	2.1	0032	0.4	0145	0.0	0303	0.2	0118	0.5	0242	0.3	0028	1.3	0014	2.0
	0810	1.2	1133	0.5	0630	2.6	0823	1.8	0949	1.7	0735	4.0	0848	5.3	0615	5.1	0539	6.1
	1356	-0.1	1733	2.4	1246	0.4	1445	0.3	1743	0.5	1342	0.8	1503	0.7	1254	1.5	1244	2.1
	2027	1.5			1847	2.8	2048	1.6	2215	1.5	2002	3.8	2113	5.1	1842	5.1	1808	6.1
26 M	0237	-0.1	0018	0.4	0126	0.3	0237	0.0	0439	0.2	0218	0.5	0336	0.4	0130	1.4	0115	2.0
	0910	1.3	0615	2.2	0729	2.6	0937	1.8	1115	1.7	0845	4.0	0956	5.2	0718	5.1	0644	6.1
	1455	0.0	1238	0.5	1346	0.4	1533	0.3	1853	0.4	1448	0.8	1602	0.7	1401	1.5	1347	2.1
	2130	1.5	1840	2.4	1952	2.9	2205	1.6	2345	1.6	2112	3.9	2228	5.1	1949	5.0	1916	6.1
27 TU	0342	-0.1	0125	0.3	0231	0.3	0332	0.0	0648	0.2	0327	0.5	0439	0.4	0236	1.4	0219	2.0
	1017	1.3	0722	2.2	0833	2.7	1044	1.9	1227	1.8	0953	4.1	1110	5.3	0827	5.1	0754	6.1
	1604	0.0	1351	0.4	1458	0.3	1627	0.3	1957	0.3	1600	0.8	1710	0.7	1509	1.4	1451	2.0
	2236	1.5	1948	2.5	2100	3.0	2312	1.7			2220	4.0	2339	5.3	2057	5.1	2025	6.3
28 W	0451	-0.1	0234	0.2	0345	0.1	0429	0.1	0052	1.7	0441	0.5	0551	0.4	0342	1.2	0323	1.8
	1124	1.4	0827	2.4	0937	2.9	1145	2.0	0803	0.1	1057	4.3	1215	5.6	0932	5.3	0900	6.4
	1715	0.0	1501	0.2	1615	0.1	1715	0.3	1327	1.9	1711	0.6	1824	0.7	1615	1.2	1555	1.8
	2343	1.5	2054	2.6	2205	3.1			2057	0.2	2321	4.2			2158	5.3	2127	6.5
29 TH	0555	-0.2	0337	0.0	0454	-0.1	0009	1.8	0148	1.8	0547	0.4	0041	5.5	0445	1.0	0427	1.6
	1227	1.4	0927	2.5	1038	3.1	0522	0.1	0907	0.1	1152	4.5	0706	0.4	1030	5.6	0957	6.7
	1821	-0.1	1604	0.0	1723	-0.1	1238	2.0	1418	2.0	1813	0.5	1312	5.9	1716	1.0	1658	1.6
			2154	2.7	2307	3.3	1758	0.3	2156	0.2			1939	0.3	2251	5.6	2222	6.8
30 F	0048	1.6	0435	-0.1	0554	-0.2	0101	1.9	0238	1.9	0014	4.5	0136	5.8	0544	0.8	0529	1.4
	0654	-0.2	1021	2.7	1136	3.2	0611	0.1	1013	0.1	0644	0.2	0814	0.3	1121	5.8	1051	6.9
	1327	1.5	1702	-0.2	1823	-0.3	1327	2.1	1504	2.0	1242	4.7	1404	6.1	1812	0.8	1758	1.4
	1921	-0.2	2249	2.8			1838	0.3	2257	0.2	1909	0.3	2042	0.3	2341	5.8	2315	7.1

DENMARK, GERMANY, HOLLAND & BELGIUM Time Zone -0100
Esbjerg * Helgoland * Cuxhaven * Hoek van Holland * Rotterdam * Vlissingen * Antwerpen * Dunkerque * Calais

TIDE TABLES JULY 2000

esbjerg	HELGOLAND	CUXHAVEN	HOEK VAN HOLLAND	ROTTERDAM	VLISSINGEN	ANTWERPEN	DUNKERQUE	CALAIS	Day
Time m	Time m	Time m	Time m	Time m	Time m	Time m	Time m	Time m	
0152 1.6	0529 -0.2	0006 3.4	0149 2.0	0324 2.0	0103 4.7	0227 6.0	0638 0.7	0629 1.2	**1 SA**
0749 -0.2	1112 2.7	0650 -0.4	0656 0.1	0936 0.2	0736 0.2	0911 0.2	1209 5.9	1143 7.1	
1424 1.6	1756 -0.3	1230 3.3	1415 2.1	1548 2.0	1331 4.8	1454 6.1	1904 0.6	1857 1.2	
2017 -0.2	2342 2.8	1918 -0.4	1918 0.2	2216 0.3	2000 0.2	2138 0.2			
0255 1.6	0620 -0.2	0102 3.4	0236 2.1	0408 2.1	0151 4.8	0315 6.2	0028 5.9	0008 7.2	**2 SU**
0840 -0.2	1201 2.8	0742 -0.4	0739 0.2	1050 0.3	0824 0.2	1003 0.2	0728 0.6	0727 1.0	
1516 1.6	1848 -0.4	1322 3.3	1502 2.0	1630 2.0	1418 4.8	1541 6.1	1256 6.0	1236 7.2	●
2109 -0.3		2011 -0.5	2000 0.1	2337 0.3	2051 0.1	2229 0.2	1953 0.5	1954 1.0	
0353 1.6	0033 2.7	0156 3.3	0323 2.2	0452 2.1	0239 4.9	0403 6.2	0116 6.0	0103 7.3	**3 M**
0929 -0.2	0709 -0.2	0833 -0.4	0824 0.3	1146 0.4	0912 0.2	1051 0.3	0817 0.6	0824 0.9	
1606 1.6	1248 2.8	1412 3.3	1549 2.0	1714 2.0	1505 4.8	1629 6.0	1344 6.0	1331 7.2	
2200 -0.3	1938 -0.4	2100 -0.6	2043 0.1		2141 0.0	2318 0.1	2042 0.4	2048 0.9	
0447 1.5	0122 2.7	0246 3.3	0410 2.2	0041 0.2	0327 4.9	0451 6.2	0206 6.0	0200 7.3	**4 TU**
1016 -0.2	0755 -0.2	0919 -0.4	0910 0.3	0538 2.2	1000 0.3	1139 0.4	0904 0.6	0915 0.9	
1653 1.7	1334 2.8	1500 3.3	1639 1.9	1237 0.4	1554 4.7	1718 5.9	1433 5.9	1428 7.2	
2249 -0.3	2025 -0.4	2148 -0.6	2129 0.0	1757 2.0	2231 0.0		2130 0.4	2136 0.9	
0538 1.5	0208 2.6	0333 3.2	0500 2.2	0152 0.2	0417 4.9	0006 0.1	0257 6.0	0257 7.2	**5 W**
1103 -0.1	0839 -0.2	1003 -0.4	1000 0.4	0624 2.2	1047 0.4	0540 6.2	0951 0.7	1002 0.9	
1738 1.7	1418 2.8	1544 3.3	1732 1.8	1330 0.4	1644 4.6	1224 0.4	1524 5.9	1522 7.1	
2338 -0.3	2110 -0.4	2233 -0.6	2218 0.0	1841 2.0	2321 0.0	1807 5.8	2218 0.5	2223 0.9	
0626 1.4	0252 2.6	0416 3.1	0554 2.1	0024 0.0	0511 4.7	0053 0.1	0351 5.9	0350 7.1	**6 TH**
1148 -0.1	0921 -0.2	1046 -0.3	1057 0.5	0711 2.1	1135 0.5	0632 6.0	1039 0.9	1047 1.1	
1824 1.7	1502 2.8	1625 3.3	1830 1.8	1434 0.4	1738 4.5	1308 0.5	1617 5.8	1613 6.9	
	2154 -0.3	2316 -0.5	2314 0.0	1927 1.9		1859 5.7	2309 0.6	2309 1.1	
0027 -0.3	0335 2.5	0457 3.0	0653 2.1	0121 0.0	0012 0.0	0139 0.1	0445 5.7	0442 6.9	**7 F**
0712 1.4	1003 -0.1	1126 -0.3	1548 0.3	0800 2.1	0609 4.6	0725 5.8	1130 1.0	1134 1.3	
1236 -0.1	1547 2.8	1706 3.3	1926 1.8	1355 0.4	1224 0.6	1352 0.6	1712 5.6	1704 6.7	
1911 1.7	2238 -0.2	2359 -0.3		2014 1.9	1834 4.3	1952 5.5		2357 1.3	
0118 -0.2	0418 2.4	0539 2.9	0030 0.0	0221 0.0	0103 0.1	0227 0.1	0003 0.8	0534 6.6	**8 SA**
0758 1.3	1045 0.0	1206 -0.2	0752 2.0	0853 2.0	0708 4.4	0819 5.6	0543 5.5	1224 1.6	
1327 -0.1	1635 2.7	1751 3.2	1632 0.3	1456 0.4	1318 0.7	1440 0.7	1226 1.2	1757 6.5	
2003 1.6	2324 -0.1		2021 1.8	2109 1.8	1932 4.2	2046 5.3	1810 5.4		
0213 -0.2	0506 2.3	0042 -0.2	0215 0.0	0321 0.0	0158 0.2	0318 0.2	0103 1.0	0052 1.6	**9 SU**
0850 1.3	1133 0.1	0623 2.8	0851 1.9	0956 1.9	0807 4.3	0916 5.4	0645 5.2	0630 6.3	
1424 0.0	1727 2.6	1250 0.0	1502 0.4	1602 0.4	1418 0.8	1534 0.8	1328 1.4	1322 1.9	
2100 1.6		1840 3.1	2119 1.7	2216 1.7	2033 4.1	2145 5.1	1917 5.2	1856 6.2	
0312 -0.1	0017 0.1	0131 0.0	0316 0.0	0427 0.1	0257 0.4	0415 0.4	0206 1.2	0154 1.9	**10 M**
0947 1.3	0601 2.2	0713 2.7	0956 1.9	1106 1.8	0911 4.1	1019 5.2	0754 5.1	0731 6.1	
1527 0.0	1230 0.2	1342 0.2	1555 0.3	1718 0.4	1524 0.9	1636 0.9	1436 1.5	1427 2.1	
2203 1.6	1828 2.4	1936 2.9	2226 1.7	2330 1.7	2139 4.0	2250 5.0	2028 5.1	1958 6.1	
0415 0.0	0118 0.3	0230 0.2	0415 0.1	0542 0.1	0403 0.5	0516 0.5	0312 1.3	0302 2.0	**11 TU**
1048 1.4	0704 2.1	0812 2.6	1103 1.8	1212 1.7	1016 4.0	1128 5.1	0903 5.0	0834 6.0	
1636 0.1	1339 0.3	1452 0.3	1651 0.3	1852 0.4	1637 0.8	1742 0.9	1543 1.5	1534 2.1	
2308 1.5	1937 2.3	2041 2.7	2330 1.7		2244 4.0	2359 5.0	2133 5.1	2100 6.0	
0519 0.0	0228 0.3	0343 0.3	0512 0.2	0036 1.6	0510 0.6	0621 0.5	0415 1.3	0406 2.0	**12 W**
1149 1.5	0814 2.1	0918 2.6	1202 1.8	0706 0.2	1117 4.1	1233 5.1	1002 5.1	0934 6.0	
1745 0.1	1456 0.3	1613 0.3	1744 0.3	1312 1.7	1740 0.8	1853 0.8	1645 1.3	1633 2.0	
	2049 2.2	2151 2.6		2006 0.4	2342 4.1		2227 5.2	2159 6.1	
0012 1.5	0336 0.4	0453 0.3	0027 1.8	0136 1.6	0604 0.6	0100 5.2	0512 1.3	0500 1.8	**13 TH**
0618 0.0	0923 2.1	1026 2.6	0603 0.2	0821 0.3	1210 4.2	0725 0.5	1051 5.3	1030 6.1	
1245 1.5	1606 0.3	1723 0.3	1253 1.8	1409 1.7	1830 0.6	1330 5.3	1738 1.2	1724 1.9	
1845 0.1	2157 2.2	2300 2.6	1832 0.2	2115 0.4		1955 0.6	2314 5.3	2251 6.3	
0109 1.5	0434 0.3	0552 0.3	0117 1.8	0231 1.7	0033 4.2	0154 5.4	0600 1.2	0547 1.7	**14 F**
0710 0.0	1023 2.2	1128 2.7	0650 0.3	1037 0.4	0649 0.6	0820 0.4	1136 5.4	1117 6.3	
1335 1.6	1704 0.2	1821 0.2	1340 1.9	1457 1.7	1257 4.3	1418 5.5	1824 1.0	1806 1.7	
1937 0.0	2254 2.2		1913 0.2	2316 0.4	1915 0.5	2047 0.4	2357 5.4	2336 6.4	
0200 1.5	0524 0.3	0001 2.6	0201 1.9	0318 1.7	0117 4.3	0241 5.6	0642 1.1	0627 1.6	**15 SA**
0755 0.0	1114 2.3	0643 0.2	0733 0.3	1153 0.4	0729 0.6	0907 0.4	1216 5.5	1157 6.4	
1418 1.6	1754 0.2	1222 2.7	1422 1.9	1539 1.6	1337 4.4	1502 5.6	1906 1.0	1845 1.6	
2023 0.0	2343 2.2	1912 0.1	1951 0.2	2250 0.4	1955 0.4	2132 0.3			

● ● Time Zone -0100. For UT subtract 1 hour. For European summer time (shaded) 26/3-29/10 add 1 hour ● ●

JULY 2000 TIDE TABLES

• • Time Zone -0100. For UT subtract 1 hour. For European summer time (shaded) 26/3-29/10 add 1 hour • •

	ESBJERG		HELGOLAND		CUXHAVEN		HOEK VAN HOLLAND		ROTTERDAM		VLISSINGEN		ANTWERPEN		DUNKERQUE		CALAIS	
	Time	m	Time	m	Time	m	Time	m	Time	m	Time	m	Time	m	Time	m	Time	m
16SU O	0243	1.5	0609	0.3	0053	2.6	0240	2.0	0359	1.6	0157	4.4	0322	5.7	0037	5.5	0015	6.6
	0835	0.0	1157	2.3	0729	0.2	0815	0.3	1039	0.6	0806	0.5	0948	0.4	0721	1.1	0706	1.6
	1456	1.7	1839	0.2	1309	2.8	1502	1.9	1615	1.6	1415	4.4	1541	5.6	1254	5.5	1233	6.6
	2103	0.0			1957	0.1	2027	0.1	2345	0.5	2034	0.4	2213	0.3	1945	0.9	1924	1.6
17M	0322	1.5	0026	2.2	0139	2.6	0316	2.0	0435	1.6	0233	4.5	0400	5.7	0116	5.5	0050	6.6
	0912	0.0	0651	0.3	0811	0.2	0858	0.3	1118	0.6	0842	0.5	1026	0.5	0759	1.1	0743	1.5
	1531	1.7	1237	2.3	1351	2.8	1539	1.9	1649	1.6	1450	4.5	1617	5.6	1332	5.5	1306	6.7
	2142	-0.1	1920	0.2	2039	0.1	2058	0.1			2111	0.3	2251	0.4	2022	0.9	2001	1.5
18TU	0358	1.5	0105	2.2	0221	2.6	0351	2.0	0034	0.5	0307	4.5	0434	5.7	0154	5.5	0124	6.7
	0947	0.0	0728	0.2	0850	0.2	1120	0.3	0511	1.7	0916	0.5	1100	0.6	0833	1.1	0820	1.5
	1606	1.7	1313	2.4	1431	2.8	1613	1.9	1119	0.6	1524	4.5	1651	5.5	1407	5.6	1339	6.7
	2217	-0.1	1957	0.2	2118	0.1	2129	0.1	1724	1.6	2146	0.3	2324	0.4	2056	0.9	2038	1.5
19W	0432	1.5	0141	2.2	0300	2.6	0424	2.0	0112	0.4	0340	4.5	0507	5.6	0229	5.5	0157	6.7
	1021	0.0	0804	0.2	0927	0.2	1206	0.3	0546	1.7	0950	0.5	1130	0.7	0906	1.1	0854	1.5
	1640	1.6	1347	2.4	1509	2.8	1645	1.9	1148	0.7	1557	4.5	1724	5.5	1440	5.6	1411	6.8
	2251	-0.1	2032	0.2	2154	0.1	2200	0.1	1759	1.6	2220	0.3	2356	0.5	2128	0.9	2112	1.5
20TH	0506	1.4	0214	2.2	0337	2.6	0457	2.0	0157	0.4	0412	4.5	0541	5.6	0301	5.6	0227	6.7
	1054	-0.1	0839	0.2	1001	0.2	1251	0.3	0623	1.8	1024	0.5	1203	0.7	0937	1.1	0927	1.6
	1715	1.6	1420	2.4	1544	2.8	1713	1.8	1228	0.6	1629	4.4	1757	5.5	1512	5.7	1442	6.8
	2324	-0.1	2106	0.2	2228	0.1	2233	0.1	1835	1.7	2254	0.3			2200	0.9	2143	1.5
21F	0540	1.4	0246	2.2	0413	2.6	0530	2.0	0048	0.4	0446	4.5	0029	0.4	0333	5.6	0258	6.7
	1127	-0.1	0912	0.2	1036	0.2	1333	0.3	0700	1.8	1101	0.6	0614	5.6	1009	1.1	0959	1.6
	1751	1.6	1453	2.4	1618	2.8	1743	1.8	1319	0.6	1703	4.3	1236	0.7	1545	5.7	1513	6.8
	2357	-0.1	2139	0.2	2302	0.1	2309	0.1	1913	1.7	2329	0.3	1830	5.5	2234	0.9	2216	1.6
22SA	0615	1.4	0319	2.2	0448	2.6	0606	2.0	0158	0.3	0521	4.4	0103	0.4	0408	5.6	0332	6.7
	1203	-0.1	0947	0.2	1110	0.2	1415	0.3	0741	1.9	1139	0.6	0649	5.6	1044	1.1	1033	1.7
	1827	1.6	1529	2.4	1652	2.9	1819	1.8	1416	0.6	1739	4.3	1312	0.6	1623	5.7	1549	6.7
			2215	0.2	2336	0.1	2350	0.1	1954	1.8			1904	5.5	2312	1.0	2254	1.7
23SU	0033	-0.1	0357	2.2	0524	2.7	0646	2.0	0127	0.2	0007	0.3	0139	0.3	0448	5.6	0411	6.6
	0651	1.3	1025	0.2	1147	0.2	1454	0.3	0826	1.9	0602	4.3	0727	5.6	1124	1.2	1115	1.7
	1242	-0.1	1610	2.5	1731	2.9	1900	1.8	1515	0.5	1220	0.6	1349	0.6	1706	5.6	1631	6.6
	1905	1.5	2257	0.2					2042	1.8	1821	4.2	1944	5.5	2356	1.1	2340	1.8
24M	0113	-0.1	0441	2.2	0015	0.1	0044	0.0	0225	0.2	0049	0.4	0218	0.3	0536	5.4	0458	6.5
	0731	1.3	1109	0.2	0605	2.7	0736	1.9	0918	1.9	0651	4.2	0813	5.5	1213	1.3	1206	1.9
	1326	-0.1	1702	2.4	1229	0.2	1408	0.3	1552	0.5	1307	0.7	1433	0.6	1759	5.4	1723	6.4
	1948	1.5	2345	0.2	1820	2.9	1953	1.7	2139	1.7	1913	4.1	2033	5.4				
25TU	0200	-0.1	0536	2.2	0100	0.1	0154	0.0	0355	0.2	0139	0.4	0305	0.3	0051	1.3	0036	1.9
	0822	1.3	1204	0.2	0655	2.7	0842	1.9	1027	1.8	0755	4.1	0912	5.4	0634	5.3	0556	6.3
	1418	-0.1	1803	2.4	1318	0.1	1446	0.3	1815	0.4	1404	0.7	1527	0.7	1316	1.5	1305	2.1
	2045	1.5			1919	2.9	2106	1.7	2254	1.7	2022	4.0	2141	5.2	1903	5.2	1827	6.2
26W	0258	-0.1	0045	0.2	0154	0.1	0254	0.0	0606	0.2	0242	0.5	0403	0.5	0157	1.4	0138	2.0
	0927	1.3	0640	2.3	0754	2.8	0959	1.9	1145	1.8	0909	4.1	1029	5.3	0743	5.1	0709	6.1
	1523	0.0	1310	0.2	1419	0.1	1540	0.3	1916	0.3	1514	0.8	1632	0.8	1429	1.5	1410	2.1
	2154	1.5	1912	2.4	2024	2.9	2229	1.7			2138	4.0	2300	5.2	2017	5.2	1945	6.2
27TH	0407	0.0	0151	0.2	0300	0.0	0357	0.0	0012	1.7	0400	0.2	0516	0.6	0309	1.4	0245	1.9
	1041	1.4	0747	2.3	0859	2.9	1110	1.9	0728	0.2	1021	4.1	1142	5.4	0859	5.2	0827	6.2
	1638	0.0	1422	0.1	1533	0.0	1642	0.3	1254	1.9	1635	0.7	1753	0.8	1542	1.4	1520	2.0
	2310	1.5	2021	2.5	2132	3.0	2339	1.8	2015	0.3	2251	4.1			2130	5.3	2059	6.4
28F	0521	0.0	0300	0.0	0414	-0.1	0504	0.1	0117	1.8	0521	0.5	0012	5.4	0419	1.2	0357	1.8
	1154	1.5	0852	2.5	1003	3.0	1213	1.9	0836	0.2	1128	4.3	0639	0.6	1006	5.4	0935	6.4
	1754	-0.1	1533	-0.1	1650	-0.1	1740	0.3	1351	1.9	1752	0.6	1248	5.6	1651	1.2	1632	1.8
			2127	2.6	2238	3.1			2112	0.3	2354	4.4	1918	0.6	2233	5.5	2204	6.7
29SA	0026	1.5	0406	-0.1	0524	-0.2	0039	1.9	0213	2.0	0626	0.4	0115	5.7	0524	1.0	0509	1.6
	0630	-0.1	0953	2.6	1103	3.1	0603	0.2	0947	0.2	1226	4.4	0754	0.5	1104	5.6	1036	6.7
	1302	1.5	1639	-0.2	1757	-0.3	1309	1.9	1442	2.0	1854	0.4	1347	5.8	1753	0.9	1742	1.5
	1903	-0.1	2227	2.6	2341	3.2	1826	0.2	2105	0.3			2027	0.4	2328	5.8	2303	7.0
30SU	0139	1.6	0506	-0.2	0626	-0.3	0133	2.0	0303	2.0	0049	4.6	0212	5.9	0621	0.9	0617	1.3
	0730	-0.1	1048	2.7	1202	3.2	0651	0.2	0941	0.3	0721	0.3	0855	0.3	1156	5.8	1132	7.0
	1406	1.6	1738	-0.4	1858	-0.5	1401	1.9	1528	2.0	1318	4.6	1440	5.9	1848	0.6	1848	1.2
	2003	-0.2	2324	2.6			1906	0.2	2254	0.3	1949	0.2	2126	0.3			2359	7.2
31M	0247	1.6	0600	-0.3	0041	3.2	0223	2.1	0349	2.1	0139	4.8	0303	6.1	0018	6.0	0720	1.1
	0825	-0.1	1140	2.7	0723	-0.4	0731	0.3	1048	0.4	0811	0.2	0949	0.2	0714	0.7	1227	7.2
	1503	1.7	1832	-0.5	1258	3.3	1451	1.9	1611	2.0	1406	4.7	1530	5.9	1244	5.9	1947	1.0
	2058	-0.2			1954	-0.6	1945	0.1	2348	0.3	2039	0.0	2218	0.2	1939	0.4		

DENMARK, GERMANY, HOLLAND & BELGIUM Time Zone -0100
Esbjerg * Helgoland * Cuxhaven * Hoek van Holland * Rotterdam * Vlissingen * Antwerpen * Dunkerque * Calais

TIDE TABLES AUGUST 2000

esbjerg	HELGOLAND	CUXHAVEN	HOEK VAN HOLLAND	ROTTERDAM	VLISSINGEN	ANTWERPEN	DUNKERQUE	CALAIS	Day
Time m	Time m	Time m	Time m	Time m	Time m	Time m	Time m	Time m	
0345 1.6	0017 2.6	0137 3.2	0311 2.2	0434 2.2	0227 4.9	0352 6.1	0107 6.1	0054 7.3	1 TU ●
0915 -0.1	0651 -0.3	0815 -0.4	0811 0.3	0945 0.3	0859 0.2	1039 0.4	0803 0.7	0815 0.9	
1554 1.7	1230 2.8	1351 3.3	1539 1.9	1654 2.0	1454 4.7	1617 5.9	1331 6.0	1321 7.3	
2148 -0.3	1923 -0.5	2045 -0.6	2027 0.0	2209 0.1	2129 -0.1	2306 0.2	2028 0.3	2039 0.8	
0438 1.5	0105 2.6	0229 3.1	0358 2.2	0519 2.2	0315 4.9	0439 6.2	0156 6.1	0148 7.4	2 W
1002 -0.1	0738 -0.3	0903 -0.5	0853 0.4	1233 0.5	0945 0.3	1124 0.5	0849 0.7	0903 0.8	
1642 1.7	1315 2.8	1440 3.3	2110 0.0	1737 2.0	1539 4.7	1703 5.9	1418 6.0	1412 7.3	
2236 -0.3	2009 -0.5	2133 -0.6		2258 0.1	2216 -0.1	2352 0.1	2115 0.3	2124 0.7	
0526 1.5	0149 2.5	0315 3.0	0445 2.2	0605 2.2	0402 4.9	0526 6.2	0245 6.1	0239 7.3	3 TH
1046 -0.1	0821 -0.3	0947 -0.4	0938 0.5	1325 0.5	1030 0.4	1207 0.5	0934 0.7	0946 0.8	
1727 1.7	1359 2.8	1524 3.3	2156 0.0	1821 2.1	1625 4.7	1749 5.9	1504 6.0	1459 7.3	
2322 -0.2	2052 -0.4	2216 -0.6		2352 0.0	2303 -0.1		2201 0.3	2205 0.8	
0609 1.5	0230 2.5	0357 3.0	0533 2.1	0650 2.2	0450 4.8	0036 0.0	0332 6.0	0325 7.2	4 F
1130 -0.1	0902 -0.3	1028 -0.4	1027 0.5	1425 0.5	1112 0.5	0612 6.1	1018 0.8	1025 1.0	
1809 1.7	1440 2.8	1604 3.3	1801 1.9	1904 2.1	1712 4.6	1248 0.5	1551 6.0	1543 7.1	
	2133 -0.3	2257 -0.5	2246 0.0		2346 0.0	1836 5.8	2248 0.5	2245 0.9	
0006 -0.2	0308 2.4	0433 2.9	0623 2.1	0052 0.0	0539 4.6	0117 0.0	0419 5.8	0409 7.0	5 SA
0646 1.4	0939 -0.2	1106 -0.3	1130 0.5	0735 2.1	1154 0.6	0700 5.9	1103 1.0	1104 1.2	
1213 -0.1	1521 2.7	1642 3.2	1850 1.9	1317 0.4	1800 4.5	1328 0.6	1638 5.8	1627 6.9	
1850 1.7	2211 -0.2	2334 -0.3	2345 0.0	1948 2.0		1922 5.6	2336 0.6	2326 1.2	
0050 -0.1	0347 2.4	0509 2.9	0715 2.0	0155 0.0	0030 0.2	0158 0.1	0508 5.6	0454 6.7	6 SU
0723 1.4	1017 -0.1	1141 -0.2	1351 0.4	0821 2.0	0631 4.4	0748 5.7	1151 1.2	1146 1.6	
1258 -0.1	1603 2.6	1720 3.1	1941 1.9	1423 0.4	1239 0.7	1410 0.7	1728 5.6	1715 6.6	
1931 1.7	2250 0.0			2035 1.9	1852 4.3	2011 5.4			
0136 0.0	0430 2.3	0009 -0.1	0134 0.1	0259 0.1	0115 0.3	0242 0.2	0027 1.0	0011 1.6	7 M
0802 1.4	1057 0.0	0548 2.8	0809 1.9	0912 1.9	0725 4.2	0838 5.4	0600 5.3	0545 6.3	
1345 0.0	1651 2.5	1216 0.0	1423 0.3	1530 0.4	1330 0.8	1457 0.8	1244 1.4	1234 1.9	
2018 1.6	2332 0.2	1804 3.0	2036 1.8	2130 1.8	1948 4.1	2103 5.1	1826 5.3	1809 6.2	
0225 0.1	0518 2.2	0046 0.1	0237 0.1	0405 0.2	0209 0.5	0332 0.4	0122 1.3	0103 2.0	8 TU
0851 1.4	1145 0.2	0633 2.7	0909 1.8	1016 1.7	0824 4.0	0933 5.0	0702 5.0	0643 6.0	
1441 0.1	1747 2.3	1256 0.2	1516 0.3	1641 0.4	1433 0.9	1553 0.9	1345 1.6	1330 2.3	
2115 1.5		1857 2.7	2141 1.7	2242 1.6	2054 3.9	2203 4.8	1936 5.0	1912 5.9	
0323 0.1	0024 0.4	0129 0.3	0342 0.1	0516 0.3	0311 0.7	0431 0.7	0223 1.5	0203 2.2	9 W
0952 1.4	0618 2.1	0728 2.5	1019 1.7	1131 1.6	0933 3.8	1042 4.8	0816 4.8	0748 5.7	
1548 0.2	1249 0.4	1351 0.4	1616 0.3	1757 0.4	1544 1.0	1700 1.0	1452 1.7	1433 2.4	
2223 1.5	1855 2.1	2000 2.5	2256 1.7		2208 3.8	2323 4.7	2054 4.9	2019 5.8	
0431 0.2	0134 0.5	0236 0.5	0445 0.2	0000 1.6	0421 0.8	0536 0.8	0328 1.6	0311 2.3	10 TH
1101 1.4	0730 2.0	0836 2.4	1130 1.7	0633 0.3	1045 3.8	1204 4.7	0928 4.8	0856 5.7	
1706 0.3	1415 0.5	1527 0.5	1715 0.3	1242 1.5	1700 0.9	1812 1.0	1601 1.7	1542 2.4	
2334 1.5	2015 2.0	2115 2.4		1911 0.4	2315 3.9		2159 5.0	2126 5.8	
0541 0.2	0257 0.6	0414 0.6	0001 1.7	0109 1.5	0529 0.8	0038 4.9	0433 1.6	0418 2.3	11 F
1207 1.5	0849 2.0	0950 2.4	0544 0.3	0747 0.4	1146 3.9	0647 0.8	1026 5.0	0959 5.8	
1818 0.3	1542 0.4	1658 0.4	1230 1.7	1345 1.5	1804 0.8	1307 4.9	1704 1.5	1645 2.2	
	2137 2.0	2234 2.4	1807 0.2	2016 0.4		1927 0.8	2253 5.2	2226 6.0	
0042 1.5	0409 0.5	0527 0.5	0056 1.8	0212 1.6	0012 4.1	0135 5.2	0530 1.4	0515 2.0	12 SA
0642 0.1	1001 2.1	1102 2.5	0636 0.3	0901 0.5	0624 0.7	0752 0.7	1115 5.1	1054 6.1	
1306 1.6	1648 0.3	1803 0.3	1321 1.8	1442 1.6	1236 4.1	1357 5.2	1757 1.3	1738 2.0	
1916 0.1	2242 2.1	2345 2.5	1851 0.2	2115 0.4	1855 0.6	2025 0.6	2339 5.4	2315 6.3	
0139 1.5	0506 0.4	0622 0.3	0141 1.9	0305 1.6	0059 4.3	0221 5.4	0618 1.3	0602 1.8	13 SU
0731 0.1	1058 2.2	1203 2.7	0721 0.3	1134 0.5	0708 0.7	0844 0.6	1157 5.3	1138 6.3	
1354 1.6	1739 0.2	1854 0.1	1405 1.8	1528 1.6	1318 4.3	1440 5.4	1842 1.1	1824 1.7	
2003 0.0	2333 2.2		1928 0.2	2236 0.4	1937 0.5	2111 0.4		2357 6.5	
0227 1.5	0552 0.2	0042 2.6	0219 2.0	0348 1.7	0138 4.4	0301 5.6	0021 5.5	0645 1.6	14 M
0814 0.1	1144 2.3	0710 0.2	0758 0.3	1221 0.5	0745 0.6	0925 0.6	0700 1.2	1215 6.6	
1436 1.7	1823 0.1	1254 2.8	1442 1.9	1604 1.6	1355 4.4	1518 5.5	1236 5.5	1906 1.5	
2044 0.0		1940 0.0	2000 0.1		2015 0.4	2151 0.4	1923 0.9		
0306 1.5	0016 2.2	0128 2.7	0254 2.0	0020 0.4	0212 4.5	0337 5.7	0100 5.6	0033 6.7	15 TU O
0851 0.0	0634 0.2	0754 0.1	0833 0.4	0423 1.7	0820 0.6	1002 0.6	0738 1.1	0727 1.5	
1512 1.7	1224 2.4	1339 2.9	1518 1.9	1428 0.6	1428 4.5	1553 5.6	1312 5.6	1249 6.8	
2121 -0.1	1903 0.0	2021 -0.1	2027 0.1	1637 1.7	2048 0.3	2227 0.4	2000 0.8	1947 1.4	

• • Time Zone -0100. For UT subtract 1 hour. For European summer time (shaded) 26/3-29/10 add 1 hour • •

AUGUST 2000 TIDE TABLES

• • Time Zone -0100. For UT subtract 1 hour. For European summer time (shaded) 26/3-29/10 add 1 hour • •

	ESBJERG Time	m	HELGOLAND Time	m	CUXHAVEN Time	m	HOEK VAN HOLLAND Time	m	ROTTERDAM Time	m	VLISSINGEN Time	m	ANTWERPEN Time	m	DUNKERQUE Time	m	CALAIS Time	m
16W	0339	1.5	0054	2.2	0209	2.7	0327	2.1	0051	0.4	0245	4.6	0411	5.8	0136	5.7	0106	6.8
	0926	0.0	0712	0.1	0833	0.0	0905	0.4	0456	1.8	0854	0.5	1036	0.6	0812	1.0	0806	1.4
	1545	1.7	1300	2.4	1419	2.9	1550	1.9	1333	0.5	1501	4.6	1627	5.7	1345	5.7	1321	6.9
	2155	-0.1	1939	0.0	2100	-0.1	2055	0.1	1709	1.7	2122	0.2	2302	0.4	2034	0.7	2024	1.3
17TH	0412	1.5	0128	2.3	0248	2.8	0400	2.1	0123	0.4	0316	4.6	0444	5.8	0207	5.7	0136	6.9
	0959	-0.1	0749	0.1	0911	0.0	0933	0.4	0530	1.9	0928	0.5	1110	0.6	0844	1.0	0842	1.3
	1620	1.7	1333	2.4	1457	2.9	1620	1.9	1103	0.6	1533	4.6	1700	5.7	1415	5.8	1350	7.0
	2229	-0.1	2015	0.0	2136	-0.1	2124	0.1	1744	1.8	2157	0.3	2337	0.3	2106	0.7	2059	1.3
18F	0445	1.5	0200	2.3	0324	2.8	0433	2.1	0200	0.3	0348	4.6	0518	5.9	0236	5.8	0205	6.9
	1033	-0.1	0824	0.1	0947	0.0	0949	0.4	0606	1.9	1004	0.5	1146	0.6	0915	1.0	0914	1.3
	1656	1.7	1406	2.5	1533	2.9	1649	1.9	1127	0.6	1604	4.6	1733	5.8	1444	5.9	1417	7.0
	2301	-0.1	2048	0.0	2211	-0.1	2154	0.1	1820	1.8	2233	0.2			2138	0.7	2129	1.3
19SA	0518	1.4	0230	2.3	0359	2.8	0506	2.1	0236	0.3	0421	4.6	0012	0.3	0306	5.8	0233	7.0
	1106	-0.1	0857	0.1	1021	0.0	1012	0.4	0644	2.0	1041	0.5	0551	5.8	0947	1.0	0942	1.4
	1731	1.6	1437	2.5	1606	3.0	1720	1.9	1203	0.6	1637	4.5	1221	0.6	1516	6.0	1446	7.0
	2333	-0.1	2121	0.0	2245	-0.1	2228	0.1	1857	1.9	2309	0.2	1805	5.8	2211	0.7	2158	1.4
20SU	0550	1.4	0300	2.3	0432	2.8	0541	2.1	0107	0.3	0455	4.6	0048	0.3	0339	5.9	0303	6.9
	1140	-0.1	0931	0.1	1056	0.0	1045	0.4	0722	2.0	1118	0.5	0624	5.8	1021	1.0	1012	1.5
	1803	1.6	1510	2.5	1640	3.0	1754	1.9	1242	0.5	1712	4.5	1255	0.6	1553	6.0	1520	7.0
			2155	0.0	2318	-0.1	2306	0.0	1936	2.0	2345	0.3	1839	5.7	2247	0.8	2231	1.5
21M	0007	-0.1	0334	2.3	0505	2.8	0619	2.0	0212	0.3	0533	4.5	0121	0.4	0418	5.8	0340	6.8
	0619	1.4	1007	0.1	1131	0.0	1127	0.4	0804	2.0	1155	0.6	0700	5.7	1058	1.1	1049	1.6
	1218	-0.1	1548	2.5	1715	3.0	1834	1.9	1432	0.5	1751	4.4	1328	0.7	1635	5.9	1600	6.8
	1833	1.6	2233	0.0	2354	-0.1	2353	0.0	2020	2.0			1916	5.7	2328	1.0	2312	1.6
22TU	0045	-0.1	0414	2.4	0541	2.8	0703	2.0	0331	0.2	0022	0.4	0155	0.4	0504	5.6	0424	6.6
	0652	1.4	1048	0.1	1209	0.0	1219	0.3	0851	2.0	0618	4.4	0742	5.6	1142	1.2	1134	1.8
	1259	-0.1	1636	2.5	1758	3.0	1921	1.9	1530	0.5	1238	0.6	1406	0.7	1724	5.7	1648	6.6
	1911	1.5	2317	0.1					2109	1.9	1838	4.3	2001	5.5				
23W	0129	0.0	0504	2.4	0035	0.0	0054	0.1	0333	0.2	0109	0.5	0236	0.5	0019	1.2	0003	1.8
	0737	1.4	1137	0.1	0626	2.8	0759	1.9	0948	1.9	0715	4.2	0835	5.3	0558	5.4	0520	6.3
	1349	-0.1	1734	2.5	1254	0.0	1403	0.3	1721	0.4	1332	0.7	1455	0.8	1241	1.4	1231	2.0
	2006	1.5			1852	2.9	2024	1.8	2213	1.9	1942	4.1	2101	5.2	1825	5.4	1752	6.2
24TH	0223	0.0	0010	0.2	0123	0.0	0224	0.1	0510	0.2	0210	0.6	0331	0.7	0126	1.4	0106	2.0
	0842	1.4	0605	2.3	0722	2.8	0920	1.8	1103	1.8	0832	4.0	0950	5.1	0709	5.1	0636	6.0
	1451	0.0	1239	0.1	1350	0.0	1509	0.3	1814	0.4	1443	0.8	1600	0.9	1357	1.6	1339	2.2
	2122	1.5	1842	2.4	1956	2.9	2157	1.7	2336	1.8	2106	4.0	2226	5.1	1946	5.1	1918	6.0
25F	0333	0.1	0116	0.2	0224	0.1	0339	0.2	0651	0.2	0334	0.7	0447	0.9	0245	1.5	0219	2.1
	1006	1.4	0713	2.4	0826	2.9	1043	1.7	1222	1.8	0954	3.9	1115	5.1	0836	5.0	0806	6.0
	1611	0.0	1353	0.1	1501	0.0	1621	0.3	1912	0.3	1615	0.8	1728	1.0	1518	1.5	1456	2.2
	2250	1.5	1955	2.4	2104	2.9	2318	1.8			2230	4.0	2348	5.2	2113	5.2	2045	6.2
26SA	0455	0.1	0230	0.1	0341	0.1	0504	0.2	0050	1.9	0506	0.7	0618	0.9	0401	1.4	0340	2.0
	1129	1.5	0823	2.4	0932	3.0	1156	1.7	0807	0.3	1112	4.0	1229	5.3	0954	5.1	0924	6.2
	1738	0.0	1511	0.0	1624	-0.1	1730	0.3	1327	1.8	1741	0.6	1904	0.8	1633	1.3	1620	2.0
			2106	2.5	2213	3.0			1922	0.3	2342	4.3			2223	5.5	2154	6.5
27SU	0016	1.5	0342	0.0	0458	-0.1	0025	1.9	0151	2.0	0615	0.5	0100	5.5	0511	1.2	0503	1.7
	0612	0.1	0929	2.6	1036	3.1	0730	0.3	0932	0.3	1215	4.3	0739	0.7	1055	5.4	1027	6.6
	1245	1.6	1621	-0.2	1739	-0.3	1257	1.8	1422	1.9	1845	0.4	1333	5.6	1739	1.0	1738	1.6
	1852	-0.1	2211	2.5	2319	3.0	1815	0.2	1947	0.3			2016	0.5	2320	5.8	2255	6.9
28M	0136	1.5	0446	-0.1	0606	-0.2	0121	2.0	0245	2.1	0039	4.6	0200	5.8	0611	1.0	0614	1.3
	0717	0.0	1028	2.7	1138	3.2	0945	0.3	0925	0.4	0711	0.4	0843	0.5	1147	5.7	1124	7.0
	1353	1.7	1721	-0.4	1842	-0.5	1350	1.8	1509	2.0	1308	4.5	1428	5.7	1835	0.6	1843	1.2
	1953	-0.2	2309	2.6			1852	0.2	2021	0.2	1939	0.1	2115	0.3			2350	7.2
29TU	0242	1.6	0542	-0.2	0022	3.1	0211	2.2	0332	2.2	0130	4.8	0252	6.0	0010	6.0	0712	1.0
	0812	0.0	1121	2.7	0704	-0.3	0721	0.4	1029	0.5	0759	0.3	0937	0.5	0703	0.8	1215	7.2
	1451	1.7	1816	-0.4	1237	3.3	1439	1.9	1552	2.0	1354	4.5	1517	5.8	1233	5.9	1937	0.8
	2046	-0.2			1937	-0.6	1929	0.1	2100	0.1	2027	0.0	2206	0.2	1926	0.4		
30W	0336	1.6	0000	2.6	0119	3.1	0257	2.2	0416	2.2	0215	4.9	0339	6.1	0057	6.2	0041	7.4
	0900	-0.1	0633	-0.3	0757	-0.4	0755	0.4	1125	0.5	0844	0.3	1024	0.5	0749	0.7	0802	0.8
	1542	1.8	1210	2.8	1331	3.3	2008	0.0	1634	2.1	1437	4.7	1601	5.9	1315	6.1	1303	7.4
	2134	-0.2	1904	-0.5	2027	-0.6			2142	0.1	2112	-0.1	2251	0.1	2012	0.2	2023	0.7
31TH ●	0423	1.6	0045	2.5	0209	3.0	0342	2.2	0459	2.3	0258	4.9	0423	6.2	0140	6.2	0129	7.4
	0945	-0.1	0718	-0.3	0844	-0.4	0833	0.5	1003	0.4	0926	0.4	1106	0.5	0833	0.7	0845	0.7
	1627	1.8	1254	2.8	1419	3.3	2049	0.0	1715	2.1	1518	4.8	1644	5.9	1357	6.2	1348	7.4
	2218	-0.2	1948	-0.4	2113	-0.6			2230	0.1	2156	-0.1	2333	0.1	2057	0.2	2103	0.6

DENMARK, GERMANY, HOLLAND & BELGIUM Time Zone -0100
Esbjerg * Helgoland * Cuxhaven * Hoek van Holland * Rotterdam * Vlissingen * Antwerpen * Dunkerque * Calais

TIDE TABLES SEPTEMBER 2000

	esbjerg		HELGOLAND		CUXHAVEN		HOEK VAN HOLLAND		ROTTERDAM		VLISSINGEN		ANTWERPEN		DUNKERQUE		CALAIS		
	Time	m	Time	m	Time	m	Time	m	Time	m	Time	m	Time	m	Time	m	Time	m	
	0504	1.5	0126	2.5	0253	3.0	0424	2.2	0542	2.3	0340	4.9	0506	6.2	0223	6.2	0212	7.4	**1 F**
	1027	-0.1	0800	-0.3	0927	-0.4	0915	0.5	1051	0.4	1006	0.4	1146	0.5	0914	0.7	0921	0.8	
	1708	1.8	1335	2.8	1501	3.2	2133	0.0	1757	2.2	1600	4.8	1726	5.9	1439	6.2	1429	7.4	
	2300	-0.1	2029	-0.3	2154	-0.5			2323	0.1	2236	0.0			2140	0.3	2139	0.7	
	0541	1.5	0203	2.5	0330	3.0	0507	2.1	0624	2.2	0423	4.8	0012	0.1	0306	6.1	0251	7.3	**2 SA**
	1107	-0.1	0838	-0.2	1006	-0.3	1000	0.5	1421	0.5	1045	0.5	0548	6.1	0954	0.8	0955	0.9	
	1745	1.8	1413	2.7	1537	3.2	1729	2.0	1839	2.2	1642	4.7	1223	0.5	1521	6.1	1508	7.3	
	2339	-0.1	2105	-0.2	2230	-0.3	2220	0.1			2315	0.1	1807	5.9	2221	0.5	2212	0.9	
	0611	1.5	0236	2.5	0403	2.9	0549	2.1	0022	0.1	0505	4.6	0049	0.1	0348	5.9	0330	7.1	**3 SU**
	1146	-0.1	0913	-0.1	1040	-0.2	1051	0.5	0706	2.1	1122	0.6	0630	6.0	1033	1.0	1027	1.2	
	1820	1.7	1450	2.7	1609	3.1	1809	2.0	1241	0.4	1723	4.6	1300	0.5	1603	6.0	1547	7.0	
			2138	-0.1	2303	-0.1	2312	0.1	1921	2.1	2351	0.3	1849	5.7	2303	0.7	2247	1.2	
	0017	0.0	0312	2.4	0433	2.9	0632	2.0	0130	0.1	0548	4.4	0125	0.2	0430	5.7	0411	6.7	**4 M**
	0639	1.5	0946	0.0	1111	-0.1	1325	0.4	0747	2.0	1200	0.7	0712	5.7	1115	1.2	1103	1.5	
	1226	0.0	1529	2.6	1643	3.0	1854	1.9	1349	0.4	1807	4.4	1336	0.6	1648	5.7	1630	6.7	
	1854	1.6	2209	0.1	2331	0.1			2002	2.0			1931	5.5	2346	1.1	2326	1.6	
	0054	0.1	0349	2.4	0506	2.8	0020	0.2	0236	0.2	0028	0.5	0202	0.3	0517	5.3	0456	6.4	**5 TU**
	0708	1.5	1021	0.1	1139	0.1	0720	1.9	0829	1.9	0633	4.2	0755	5.4	1200	1.4	1144	1.9	
	1307	0.0	1612	2.4	1724	2.9	1342	0.3	1457	0.4	1242	0.8	1415	0.8	1739	5.3	1719	6.3	
	1930	1.6	2242	0.3	2357	0.3	1945	1.8	2045	1.9	1856	4.1	2016	5.2					
	0136	0.2	0433	2.3	0548	2.7	0143	0.2	0339	0.3	0114	0.7	0244	0.6	0036	1.4	0011	2.0	**6 W**
	0745	1.5	1101	0.3	1212	0.3	0815	1.8	0915	1.7	0726	3.9	0842	5.0	0610	5.0	0550	5.9	
	1354	0.1	1703	2.2	1814	2.6	1435	0.3	1603	0.4	1340	0.9	1503	1.0	1255	1.7	1233	2.3	
	2017	1.5	2324	0.5			2048	1.7	2139	1.7	1957	3.8	2109	4.8	1842	5.0	1819	5.8	
	0224	0.3	0529	2.1	0029	0.5	0304	0.3	0443	0.4	0221	0.9	0339	0.9	0133	1.7	0106	2.4	**7 TH**
	0842	1.4	1156	0.5	0642	2.5	0922	1.6	1027	1.5	0835	3.6	0938	4.6	0721	4.6	0657	5.6	
	1456	0.3	1809	2.0	1256	0.5	1544	0.3	1711	0.5	1500	1.1	1611	1.1	1400	1.9	1334	2.6	
	2129	1.4			1917	2.4	2209	1.6	2313	1.5	2122	3.6	2219	4.5	2006	4.7	1933	5.6	
	0332	0.3	0024	0.7	0117	0.7	0420	0.3	0554	0.5	0338	1.1	0452	1.1	0239	1.9	0212	2.6	**8 F**
	1006	1.5	0642	2.0	0749	2.4	1051	1.5	1204	1.4	1004	3.5	1115	4.4	0848	4.5	0814	5.4	
	1621	0.3	1324	0.7	1409	0.7	1647	0.3	1821	0.5	1618	1.0	1730	1.2	1512	1.9	1446	2.7	
	2257	1.4	1937	1.9	2034	2.2	2332	1.6			2245	3.7			2126	4.8	2049	5.6	
	0456	0.3	0208	0.8	0253	0.9	0523	0.4	0039	1.5	0451	1.0	0010	4.6	0349	1.8	0327	2.6	**9 SA**
	1127	1.5	0810	2.0	0909	2.4	1203	1.6	0709	0.6	1117	3.7	0606	1.2	0957	4.7	0925	5.6	
	1747	0.3	1515	0.6	1633	0.7	1742	0.3	1318	1.4	1731	0.9	1239	4.6	1624	1.7	1603	2.5	
			2114	1.9	2203	2.2			1931	0.5	2347	3.9	1850	1.0	2227	5.0	2156	5.8	
	0012	1.4	0342	0.7	0500	0.7	0031	1.8	0148	1.5	0555	0.9	0110	4.9	0456	1.7	0438	2.3	**10 SU**
	0609	0.3	0934	2.1	1030	2.5	0618	0.4	0827	0.6	1211	3.9	0719	1.0	1050	5.0	1025	5.9	
	1233	1.6	1626	0.4	1741	0.4	1257	1.7	1420	1.5	1829	0.7	1331	4.9	1725	1.5	1706	2.1	
	1849	0.1	2224	2.1	2324	2.4	1827	0.2	2036	0.5			1957	0.8	2315	5.3	2250	6.1	
	0114	1.5	0442	0.5	0559	0.5	0116	1.9	0243	1.6	0035	4.2	0156	5.3	0551	1.4	0534	1.9	**11 M**
	0703	0.2	1035	2.3	1139	2.7	0705	0.4	1059	0.5	0644	0.8	0815	0.9	1133	5.3	1112	6.3	
	1326	1.7	1716	0.2	1831	0.2	1340	1.8	1507	1.6	1253	4.2	1412	5.2	1815	1.1	1757	1.7	
	1937	0.0	2314	2.2			1903	0.2	2142	0.4	1913	0.5	2044	0.6	2357	5.6	2333	6.5	
	0203	1.5	0529	0.3	0021	2.6	0153	2.0	0325	1.8	0112	4.4	0234	5.6	0635	1.2	0621	1.6	**12 TU**
	0747	0.1	1121	2.4	0646	0.2	0741	0.4	1146	0.5	0722	0.6	0857	0.8	1212	5.5	1151	6.6	
	1409	1.7	1758	0.1	1230	2.9	1416	1.9	1544	1.7	1329	4.4	1450	5.5	1856	0.9	1842	1.4	
	2017	0.0	2354	2.3	1915	0.0	1931	0.2	2316	0.3	1949	0.4	2123	0.5					
	0243	1.5	0610	0.2	0106	2.8	0227	2.1	0400	1.9	0146	4.5	0309	5.8	0036	5.8	0009	6.8	**13 W**
	0824	0.1	1200	2.5	0729	0.1	0808	0.4	1224	0.4	0756	0.6	0933	0.6	0713	1.0	0703	1.3	**O**
	1447	1.7	1836	0.0	1315	3.0	1449	1.9	1617	1.8	1401	4.5	1524	5.7	1246	5.7	1224	6.9	
	2053	0.0			1956	-0.1	1955	0.1			2021	0.3	2159	0.4	1933	0.7	1924	1.2	
	0315	1.5	0030	2.4	0146	2.9	0300	2.1	0012	0.4	0218	4.7	0342	5.9	0109	5.9	0041	7.0	**14 TH**
	0900	0.0	0648	0.1	0809	-0.1	0827	0.4	0434	2.0	0829	0.5	1009	0.5	0747	0.9	0742	1.1	
	1521	1.7	1236	2.6	1356	3.1	1520	2.0	1300	0.4	1433	4.6	1558	5.9	1316	5.8	1254	7.1	
	2127	-0.1	1913	-0.1	2034	-0.2	2021	0.1	1650	1.9	2055	0.2	2235	0.3	2007	0.6	2002	1.1	
	0347	1.5	0104	2.5	0224	3.0	0333	2.2	0057	0.3	0249	4.8	0416	6.1	0138	5.9	0110	7.1	**15 F**
	0933	0.0	0726	0.0	0848	-0.1	0844	0.4	0509	2.0	0904	0.5	1046	0.5	0819	0.9	0819	1.1	
	1556	1.7	1310	2.6	1434	3.2	1551	2.0	1337	0.4	1505	4.7	1632	6.0	1345	6.0	1322	7.2	
	2201	-0.1	1949	-0.1	2111	-0.2	2049	0.1	1724	1.9	2130	0.2	2313	0.2	2040	0.6	2037	1.1	

• • Time Zone -0100. For UT subtract 1 hour. For European summer time (shaded) 26/3-29/10 add 1 hour • •

SEPTEMBER 2000 TIDE TABLES

• • Time Zone -0100. For UT subtract 1 hour. For European summer time (shaded) 26/3-29/10 add 1 hour • •

Date	ESBJERG Time	m	HELGOLAND Time	m	CUXHAVEN Time	m	HOEK VAN HOLLAND Time	m	ROTTERDAM Time	m	VLISSINGEN Time	m	ANTWERPEN Time	m	DUNKERQUE Time	m	CALAIS Time	m
16 SA	0420	1.5	0136	2.5	0301	3.0	0406	2.2	0139	0.3	0321	4.8	0450	6.1	0206	6.0	0136	7.1
	1008	-0.1	0801	0.0	0925	-0.1	0906	0.4	0545	2.1	0942	0.4	1125	0.4	0851	0.8	0852	1.2
	1633	1.7	1343	2.6	1512	3.2	1622	2.0	1415	0.3	1537	4.7	1705	6.1	1415	6.1	1349	7.2
	2234	-0.1	2024	-0.1	2147	-0.2	2121	0.1	1800	2.0	2208	0.2	2351	0.2	2113	0.6	2108	1.1
17 SU	0453	1.5	0207	2.5	0336	3.0	0441	2.2	0221	0.2	0355	4.8	0524	6.1	0237	6.1	0205	7.1
	1042	-0.1	0836	0.0	1001	-0.1	0936	0.4	0623	2.1	1020	0.5	1203	0.5	0925	0.8	0921	1.3
	1707	1.7	1416	2.7	1548	3.2	1655	2.0	1453	0.3	1611	4.7	1738	6.0	1448	6.2	1419	7.2
	2308	-0.1	2057	0.0	2222	-0.2	2157	0.1	1837	2.0	2246	0.3			2148	0.6	2138	1.2
18 M	0523	1.5	0238	2.5	0410	3.0	0517	2.1	0301	0.2	0430	4.7	0028	0.3	0313	6.1	0237	7.1
	1118	-0.1	0912	0.0	1036	-0.1	1013	0.4	0701	2.1	1058	0.5	0558	6.0	1000	0.9	0952	1.4
	1736	1.6	1451	2.7	1623	3.2	1731	2.0	1528	0.4	1646	4.7	1238	0.6	1527	6.2	1454	7.1
	2342	0.0	2132	0.0	2257	-0.1	2236	0.1	1916	2.1	2322	0.3	1813	6.0	2225	0.7	2211	1.4
19 TU	0548	1.5	0311	2.5	0443	3.0	0555	2.1	0337	0.2	0509	4.6	0102	0.5	0353	6.0	0315	6.9
	1156	-0.1	0948	0.0	1112	-0.1	1057	0.3	0741	2.1	1135	0.6	0635	5.9	1038	1.0	1029	1.5
	1806	1.6	1529	2.7	1659	3.1	1812	2.0	1347	0.5	1727	4.6	1311	0.8	1609	6.0	1535	6.9
			2209	0.1	2332	-0.1	2324	0.1	1958	2.1			1851	5.8	2306	0.9	2252	1.5
20 W	0019	0.0	0349	2.6	0518	3.0	0638	2.0	0408	0.3	0000	0.5	0134	0.6	0438	5.7	0400	6.6
	0621	1.5	1028	0.0	1150	-0.1	1148	0.3	0825	2.0	0552	4.4	0717	5.6	1122	1.2	1114	1.8
	1238	-0.1	1615	2.6	1740	3.1	1858	2.0	1509	0.4	1217	0.6	1345	0.9	1658	5.8	1625	6.6
	1845	1.6	2251	0.2					2045	2.1	1813	4.4	1936	5.6	2357	1.2	2344	1.8
21 TH	0103	0.1	0437	2.5	0010	0.0	0024	0.2	0354	0.3	0045	0.6	0213	0.8	0533	5.3	0457	6.2
	0706	1.5	1116	0.1	0600	3.0	0731	1.9	0916	1.9	0647	4.2	0808	5.3	1219	1.5	1211	2.0
	1328	0.0	1712	2.5	1233	0.0	1259	0.3	1542	0.4	1311	0.8	1433	1.0	1800	5.4	1733	6.1
	1942	1.5	2342	0.2	1831	3.0	2000	1.9	2144	2.0	1916	4.1	2035	5.2			
22 F	0157	0.1	0536	2.5	0056	0.1	0218	0.2	0433	0.3	0148	0.8	0307	1.0	0105	1.5	0048	2.1
	0812	1.5	1216	0.1	0654	3.0	0854	1.7	1026	1.7	0807	3.9	0921	5.0	0647	4.9	0621	5.9
	1433	0.1	1819	2.4	1327	0.1	1449	0.3	1644	0.3	1426	0.9	1538	1.1	1336	1.6	1321	2.2
	2109	1.4			1933	2.9	2139	1.8	2305	1.9	2048	3.9	2200	5.0	1928	5.1	1909	5.9
23 SA	0309	0.2	0047	0.3	0154	0.2	0339	0.3	0539	0.3	0323	0.9	0424	1.2	0228	1.6	0206	2.2
	0943	1.5	0645	2.5	0757	3.0	1027	1.6	1153	1.7	0938	3.8	1051	4.9	0826	4.8	0800	5.8
	1558	0.1	1331	0.1	1439	0.1	1609	0.3	1743	0.3	1609	0.9	1713	1.1	1501	1.6	1446	2.2
	2245	1.4	1933	2.4	2041	2.9	2306	1.8			2218	4.0	2329	5.1	2104	5.2	2039	6.1
24 SU	0438	0.2	0205	0.3	0313	0.2	0616	0.3	0027	1.9	0458	0.8	0603	1.1	0351	1.6	0337	2.1
	1112	1.6	0757	2.5	0905	3.1	1144	1.6	0743	0.4	1100	3.9	1210	5.1	0946	5.0	0916	6.1
	1730	0.0	1453	0.0	1606	0.0	1831	0.3	1303	1.9	1733	0.6	1853	0.8	1621	1.3	1619	2.0
			2048	2.4	2151	2.9			1836	0.3	2333	4.3			2215	5.5	2148	6.4
25 M	0018	1.5	0321	0.2	0437	0.1	0015	2.0	0132	2.0	0606	0.6	0044	5.5	0503	1.3	0503	1.7
	0600	0.2	0906	2.6	1012	3.2	0839	0.3	0921	0.4	1205	4.2	0726	0.9	1046	5.4	1018	6.5
	1233	1.7	1604	-0.1	1721	-0.2	1246	1.7	1400	1.9	1836	0.3	1317	5.5	1728	0.9	1734	1.5
	1842	-0.1	2154	2.5	2300	3.0	1807	0.3	1919	0.2			2003	0.5	2311	5.9	2246	6.8
26 TU	0133	1.6	0427	0.0	0545	-0.1	0109	2.1	0227	2.2	0030	4.6	0145	5.8	0603	1.0	0606	1.2
	0703	0.1	1008	2.7	1116	3.3	0939	0.3	0855	0.5	0659	0.5	0828	0.6	1135	5.7	1112	6.9
	1342	1.8	1703	-0.3	1822	-0.3	1336	1.8	1449	2.0	1254	4.4	1412	5.7	1824	0.6	1831	1.0
	1941	-0.1	2251	2.6			1838	0.2	1958	0.2	1926	0.1	2100	0.2	2358	6.1	2338	7.1
27 W	0232	1.6	0523	-0.1	0003	3.1	0157	2.2	0313	2.2	0116	4.8	0237	6.1	0651	0.8	0657	0.9
	0757	0.0	1102	2.8	0644	-0.2	0711	0.5	1002	0.5	0744	0.4	0920	0.5	1217	6.0	1159	7.2
	1439	1.8	1756	-0.3	1216	3.3	1421	1.9	1532	2.1	1336	4.6	1459	5.9	1911	0.3	1919	0.8
	2030	-0.1	2339	2.6	1917	-0.4	1912	0.1	2038	0.1	2010	0.0	2148	0.1			
28 TH	0320	1.6	0612	-0.1	0058	3.1	0240	2.2	0356	2.3	0157	4.9	0321	6.2	0040	6.3	0024	7.3
	0842	0.0	1149	2.8	0735	-0.3	0738	0.5	0858	0.4	0824	0.4	1005	0.5	0733	0.7	0742	0.8
	1525	1.8	1842	-0.3	1309	3.3	1949	0.1	1613	2.1	1416	4.7	1541	5.9	1255	6.1	1242	7.4
	2115	-0.1			2005	-0.4			2120	0.1	2051	0.0	2230	0.1	1955	0.2	2000	0.6
29 F	0400	1.6	0021	2.6	0145	3.1	0321	2.2	0437	2.3	0237	4.9	0403	6.2	0120	6.3	0105	7.4
	0924	0.0	0656	-0.1	0821	-0.3	0814	0.5	0939	0.4	0903	0.4	1045	0.5	0813	0.6	0819	0.8
	1606	1.8	1231	2.8	1355	3.3	2029	0.1	1653	2.2	1454	4.8	1621	6.0	1333	6.2	1321	7.4
	2155	0.0	1924	-0.3	2048	-0.3			2206	0.1	2130	0.0	2309	0.1	2036	0.3	2036	0.7
30 SA ●	0435	1.6	0058	2.6	0225	3.1	0401	2.2	0518	2.2	0316	4.9	0442	6.2	0158	6.2	0142	7.3
	1004	0.0	0736	-0.1	0903	-0.2	0854	0.5	1024	0.4	0941	0.5	1122	0.5	0851	0.7	0851	0.9
	1642	1.8	1309	2.8	1433	3.2	1621	2.1	1733	2.2	1533	4.8	1700	6.0	1412	6.2	1357	7.4
	2233	0.0	2000	-0.1	2127	-0.2	2111	0.1	2255	0.2	2207	0.1	2345	0.1	2115	0.4	2107	0.8

DENMARK, GERMANY, HOLLAND & BELGIUM Time Zone -0100
Esbjerg * Helgoland * Cuxhaven * Hoek van Holland * Rotterdam * Vlissingen * Antwerpen * Dunkerque * Calais

TIDE TABLES OCTOBER 2000

Day	esbjerg Time	m	HELGOLAND Time	m	CUXHAVEN Time	m	HOEK VAN HOLLAND Time	m	ROTTERDAM Time	m	VLISSINGEN Time	m	ANTWERPEN Time	m	DUNKERQUE Time	m	CALAIS Time	m
1 SU	0505	1.6	0132	2.6	0259	3.0	0439	2.1	0557	2.2	0354	4.8	0521	6.2	237	6.1	0218	7.2
	1042	0.0	0812	0.0	0940	-0.1	0937	0.5	1114	0.4	1017	0.5	1157	0.5	0928	0.8	0921	1.0
	1716	1.8	1344	2.7	1505	3.2	1658	2.1	1813	2.2	1612	4.8	1739	5.9	1451	6.1	1433	7.3
	2308	0.1	2033	0.1	2201	0.0	2157	0.2	2351	0.2	2241	0.3			2152	0.6	2137	1.0
2 M	0530	1.6	0203	2.6	0326	3.0	0517	2.1	0636	2.1	0433	4.6	0019	0.2	0316	5.9	0253	7.0
	1119	0.0	0845	0.1	1012	0.0	1024	0.4	1209	0.4	1051	0.6	0600	6.0	1005	1.0	0949	1.2
	1747	1.7	1418	2.6	1533	3.1	1734	2.1	1852	2.1	1649	4.6	1230	0.5	1532	6.0	1510	7.0
	2342	0.1	2102	0.2	2229	0.2	2245	0.2			2312	0.5	1817	5.8	2229	0.9	2208	1.3
3 TU	0555	1.6	0235	2.6	0351	3.0	0554	2.0	0100	0.3	0509	4.5	0051	0.3	0357	5.7	0330	6.8
	1156	0.1	0915	0.2	1100	0.2	1118	0.4	0713	2.0	1124	0.7	0637	5.7	1042	1.2	1021	1.5
	1816	1.7	1454	2.5	1604	3.0	1812	2.0	1315	0.4	1727	4.4	1303	0.6	1614	5.7	1549	6.7
			2128	0.3	2250	0.3	2344	0.3	1930	2.0	2344	0.6	1855	5.5	2306	1.2	2241	1.7
4 W	0015	0.2	0309	2.5	0420	3.0	0633	1.9	0209	0.4	0548	4.2	0122	0.5	0439	5.4	0411	6.4
	0621	1.6	0946	0.3	1105	0.3	1224	0.3	0750	1.8	1200	0.8	0715	5.4	1121	1.4	1056	1.9
	1233	0.1	1534	2.4	1644	2.8	1854	1.9	1423	0.4	1809	4.2	1337	0.7	1700	5.4	1633	6.3
	1846	1.6	2156	0.5	2312	0.5			2009	1.9			1936	5.2	2350	1.5	2321	2.1
5 TH	0051	0.3	0351	2.4	0501	2.8	0051	0.3	0306	0.5	0021	0.8	0158	0.8	0527	5.0	0459	6.0
	0654	1.6	1022	0.5	1135	0.5	0719	1.8	0826	1.7	0631	3.9	0757	5.0	1209	1.7	1141	2.3
	1315	0.2	1621	2.2	1733	2.6	1322	0.3	1524	0.4	1245	0.9	1416	0.9	1754	5.0	1727	5.9
	1925	1.5	2232	0.7	2343	0.6	1952	1.8	2050	1.7	1903	3.9	2023	4.9				
6 F	0133	0.3	0442	2.3	0554	2.7	0159	0.4	0405	0.6	0112	1.1	0243	1.1	0044	1.8	0013	2.5
	0742	1.6	1110	0.7	1215	0.7	0827	1.6	0908	1.5	0731	3.6	0848	4.6	0628	4.6	0602	5.6
	1408	0.3	1724	2.0	1835	2.4	1443	0.3	1625	0.5	1411	1.1	1510	1.1	1311	1.9	1242	2.6
	2027	1.4	2324	0.9			2112	1.7	2148	1.5	2021	3.6	2124	4.6	1911	4.7	1842	5.5
7 SA	0230	0.4	0551	2.1	0029	0.9	0354	0.4	0510	0.6	0258	1.3	0353	1.4	0151	2.0	0119	2.7
	0854	1.5	1227	0.8	0702	2.5	0949	1.5	1100	1.3	0900	3.4	0957	4.3	0754	4.4	0724	5.3
	1527	0.4	1851	1.9	1315	0.9	1617	0.3	1732	0.5	1539	1.1	1640	1.3	1422	2.0	1354	2.7
	2210	1.4			1951	2.2	2245	1.6			2201	3.5	2305	4.4	2042	4.7	2005	5.4
8 SU	0357	0.5	0056	1.0	0135	1.0	0500	0.4	0000	1.5	0414	1.2	0520	1.5	0302	2.0	0236	2.7
	1036	1.5	0721	2.1	0822	2.4	1122	1.5	0629	0.6	1036	3.5	1151	4.3	0916	4.5	0843	5.5
	1703	0.3	1432	0.8	1546	0.9	1714	0.3	1241	1.3	1650	1.0	1803	1.2	1535	1.9	1514	2.6
	2335	1.4	2034	1.9	2121	2.3	2356	1.7	1845	0.5	2312	3.8			2151	4.9	2118	5.7
9 M	0524	0.4	0300	0.9	0418	1.0	0558	0.4	0112	1.6	0520	1.1	0033	4.7	0413	1.8	0354	2.4
	1151	1.6	0851	2.2	0946	2.5	1222	1.6	0753	0.6	1136	3.8	0633	1.3	1015	4.8	0948	5.8
	1812	0.2	1550	0.6	1706	0.6	1801	0.3	1343	1.5	1752	0.8	1253	4.7	1642	1.6	1627	2.2
			2151	2.1	2245	2.5			2000	0.5			1913	1.0	2243	5.2	2215	6.1
10 TU	0039	1.5	0408	0.7	0524	0.7	0043	1.9	0208	1.7	0002	4.1	0121	5.1	0514	1.5	0457	2.0
	0625	0.3	0957	2.3	1059	2.8	0828	0.4	0918	0.5	0613	0.9	0735	1.1	1102	5.2	1038	6.3
	1248	1.7	1641	0.4	1757	0.3	1307	1.9	1433	1.6	1220	4.1	1337	5.1	1737	1.2	1722	1.7
	1902	0.1	2240	2.3	2345	2.8	1836	0.2	2109	0.4	1840	0.6	2006	0.7	2326	5.6	2300	6.5
11 W	0130	1.6	0456	0.4	0613	0.4	0122	2.0	0252	1.9	0041	4.4	0200	5.5	0602	1.2	0546	1.5
	0712	0.2	1045	2.5	1154	3.0	0924	0.3	1045	0.4	0654	0.7	0821	0.9	1140	5.5	1118	6.7
	1335	1.7	1724	0.2	1841	0.1	1343	1.9	1513	1.8	1257	4.3	1415	5.5	1821	0.9	1809	1.3
	1942	0.0	2321	2.5			1900	0.2	2218	0.4	1918	0.5	2048	0.5			2336	6.8
12 TH	0211	1.6	0539	0.2	0031	3.0	0157	2.1	0331	2.0	0115	4.6	0236	5.8	0003	5.8	0630	1.2
	0751	0.1	1126	2.7	0657	0.2	0746	0.4	1137	0.4	0727	0.6	0900	0.7	0642	1.0	1152	7.0
	1415	1.7	1803	0.0	1241	3.2	1416	1.9	1548	1.9	1330	4.5	1451	5.8	1214	5.7	1851	1.1
	2019	0.0	2357	2.6	1922	-0.1	1921	0.2	2326	0.3	1951	0.4	2127	0.4	1900	0.7		
13 F O	0246	1.6	0618	0.1	0112	3.2	0230	2.2	0407	2.1	0147	4.7	0311	6.1	0036	6.0	0009	7.1
	0829	0.1	1204	2.8	0739	0.0	0748	0.5	1222	0.3	0802	0.5	0939	0.5	0718	0.8	0712	1.1
	1453	1.8	1841	0.0	1324	3.3	1448	2.0	1624	2.0	1403	4.7	1527	6.0	1244	5.9	1223	7.2
	2055	0.0			2003	-0.2	1948	0.2			2026	0.3	2206	0.2	1936	0.6	1932	1.0
14 SA	0320	1.6	0032	2.7	0153	3.3	0305	2.2	0024	0.3	0220	4.9	0346	6.3	0106	6.1	0039	7.2
	0906	0.0	0657	0.0	0819	-0.1	0807	0.4	0444	2.2	0839	0.5	1020	0.4	0753	0.8	0751	1.0
	1530	1.8	1242	2.8	1406	3.4	1521	2.1	1306	0.3	1436	4.8	1602	6.2	1314	6.1	1252	7.3
	2130	0.0	1919	-0.1	2042	-0.2	2018	0.1	1700	2.1	2104	0.2	2246	0.1	2012	0.5	2009	1.0
15 SU	0354	1.6	0106	2.7	0231	3.3	0340	2.3	0114	0.2	0254	4.9	0421	6.4	0137	6.2	0109	7.3
	0942	0.0	0736	0.0	0859	-0.2	0836	0.4	0521	2.2	0918	0.4	1101	0.3	0828	0.7	0826	1.1
	1609	1.8	1318	2.8	1446	3.4	1557	2.1	1348	0.3	1511	4.9	1637	6.3	1347	6.2	1323	7.3
	2206	0.0	1956	0.0	2120	-0.2	2052	0.1	1737	2.1	2144	0.2	2327	0.1	2049	0.5	2044	1.0

• • Time Zone -0100. For UT subtract 1 hour. For European summer time (shaded) 26/3-29/10 add 1 hour • •

OCTOBER 2000 TIDE TABLES

• • Time Zone -0100. For UT subtract 1 hour. For European summer time (shaded) 26/3-29/10 add 1 hour • •

Day	ESBJERG Time	m	HELGOLAND Time	m	CUXHAVEN Time	m	HOEK VAN HOLLAND Time	m	ROTTERDAM Time	m	VLISSINGEN Time	m	ANTWERPEN Time	m	DUNKERQUE Time	m	CALAIS Time	m
16 M	0428	1.6	0140	2.8	0309	3.3	0417	2.2	0201	0.2	0330	4.9	0457	6.3	0212	6.2	0140	7.2
	1021	0.0	0814	0.0	0938	-0.2	0910	0.4	0600	2.2	1000	0.4	1142	0.4	0905	0.7	0900	1.2
	1645	1.7	1355	2.8	1525	3.4	1633	2.2	1428	0.3	1547	4.9	1713	6.3	1424	6.2	1357	7.3
	2243	0.0	2033	0.0	2157	-0.1	2131	0.2	1816	2.1	2224	0.3			2127	0.6	2118	1.1
17 TU	0459	1.6	0214	2.8	0345	3.3	0455	2.2	0245	0.2	0409	4.8	0006	0.3	0250	6.1	0216	7.1
	0851	0.0	0851	0.0	1015	-0.2	0950	0.3	0639	2.1	1040	0.5	0535	6.2	0942	0.8	0935	1.3
	1718	1.7	1433	2.8	1603	3.4	1712	2.2	1505	0.3	1626	4.8	1220	0.5	1504	6.2	1435	7.1
	2320	0.1	2109	0.1	2234	-0.1	2215	0.2	1856	2.2	2303	0.4	1751	6.2	2206	0.7	2157	1.3
18 W	0527	1.6	0249	2.8	0421	3.3	0535	2.1	0324	0.3	0449	4.7	0042	0.5	0332	6.0	0257	6.9
	1139	0.0	0930	0.0	1054	-0.1	1036	0.3	0718	2.1	1121	0.5	0615	5.9	1024	1.0	1015	1.5
	1751	1.6	1514	2.8	1642	3.3	1754	2.1	1535	0.4	1708	4.7	1257	0.7	1549	6.0	1520	6.8
			2148	0.2	2311	0.0	2305	0.3	1939	2.2	2344	0.4	1833	5.9	2250	0.9	2240	1.5
19 TH	0000	0.1	0329	2.8	0457	3.3	0620	2.0	0359	0.3	0535	4.4	0119	0.8	0419	5.7	0346	6.5
	0603	1.6	1012	0.1	1133	-0.1	1130	0.3	0802	2.0	1206	0.6	0659	5.6	1110	1.2	1103	1.7
	1224	0.0	1600	2.7	1725	3.2	1843	2.1	1420	0.4	1758	4.4	1336	0.9	1641	5.7	1615	6.5
	1836	1.6	2230	0.3	2350	0.1			2025	2.1			1921	5.6	2342	1.3	2333	1.8
20 F	0045	0.2	0416	2.8	0539	3.3	0012	0.3	0414	0.4	0032	0.7	0200	1.0	0517	5.3	0450	6.1
	0651	1.6	1100	0.1	1217	0.0	0715	1.8	0851	1.9	0632	4.1	0753	5.2	1208	1.4	1201	2.0
	1318	0.1	1655	2.6	1814	3.1	1242	0.3	1509	0.3	1303	0.7	1424	1.0	1747	5.4	1733	6.1
	1942	1.5	2320	0.4			1952	1.9	2122	2.0	1907	4.2	2024	5.3				
21 SA	0141	0.3	0513	2.7	0035	0.3	0229	0.4	0401	0.4	0138	0.9	0254	1.2	0051	1.6	0039	2.1
	0801	1.6	1200	0.2	0630	3.2	0851	1.6	0956	1.7	0757	3.8	0909	4.9	0637	4.9	0622	5.8
	1425	0.1	1800	2.5	1311	0.1	1435	0.3	1607	0.3	1424	0.8	1530	1.1	1324	1.6	1313	2.2
	2111	1.5			1912	3.0	2131	1.9	2242	2.0	2041	4.0	2146	5.1	1921	5.1	1909	5.9
22 SU	0254	0.3	0024	0.4	0132	0.4	0454	0.4	0500	0.4	0318	1.0	0409	1.3	0215	1.7	0200	2.2
	0930	1.6	0620	2.7	0732	3.2	1013	1.6	1124	1.7	0924	3.7	1032	4.9	0817	4.8	0752	5.9
	1553	0.1	1314	0.2	1423	0.2	1558	0.3	1708	0.2	1600	0.8	1705	1.1	1449	1.6	1443	2.2
	2246	1.5	1912	2.4	2018	3.0	2252	1.9			2206	4.1	2309	5.1	2053	5.2	2030	6.1
23 M	0424	0.3	0140	0.5	0240	0.5	0705	0.4	0005	2.0	0446	0.9	0543	1.2	0340	1.6	0334	2.0
	1059	1.7	0732	2.7	0839	3.2	1128	1.6	0642	0.4	1045	3.9	1149	5.1	0933	5.1	0903	6.2
	1718	0.1	1433	0.1	1545	0.1	1833	0.3	1237	1.8	1719	0.6	1835	0.8	1609	1.3	1613	1.8
			2025	2.5	2127	3.0			1806	0.2	2319	4.3			2202	5.5	2136	6.4
24 TU	0012	1.6	0257	0.4	0412	0.3	0000	2.0	0110	2.1	0551	0.7	0024	5.4	0453	1.3	0451	1.6
	0543	0.3	0842	2.7	0947	3.3	0829	0.3	0857	0.4	1148	4.2	0704	0.9	1031	5.4	1003	6.5
	1221	1.8	1542	0.1	1657	0.0	1228	1.7	1336	1.9	1819	0.3	1255	5.4	1715	0.9	1719	1.4
	1827	0.0	2131	2.5	2236	3.1	2027	0.2	1859	0.2			1942	0.4	2257	5.9	2233	6.8
25 W	0120	1.6	0403	0.2	0521	0.1	0053	2.1	0205	2.2	0014	4.6	0125	5.8	0549	1.0	0548	1.2
	0645	0.2	0946	2.8	1053	3.3	0928	0.3	0812	0.5	0641	0.6	0806	0.7	1118	5.7	1055	6.8
	1327	1.8	1640	-0.1	1758	-0.1	1317	1.8	1426	2.0	1235	4.4	1350	5.7	1809	0.6	1812	1.0
	1923	0.0	2227	2.6	2338	3.1	1824	0.3	1942	0.2	1907	0.2	2037	0.2	2342	6.1	2321	7.0
26 TH	0213	1.7	0500	0.1	0619	0.0	0138	2.2	0252	2.2	0057	4.7	0216	6.0	0634	0.7	0636	1.0
	0737	0.1	1040	2.9	1152	3.4	1021	0.4	0928	0.5	0724	0.5	0857	0.5	1158	6.0	1140	7.1
	1420	1.9	1731	-0.1	1851	-0.2	1400	2.0	1510	2.1	1315	4.6	1436	5.9	1854	0.4	1856	0.8
	2009	0.0	2315	2.7			1857	0.2	2245	0.3	1948	0.1	2124	0.1				
27 F	0256	1.7	0548	0.0	0031	3.2	0219	2.2	0334	2.2	0136	4.8	0300	6.2	0021	6.2	0004	7.2
	0822	0.1	1127	2.8	0711	0.0	0724	0.5	1036	0.5	0803	0.5	0941	0.4	0715	0.6	0716	0.9
	1503	1.9	1816	0.0	1244	3.4	1441	2.0	1551	2.1	1354	4.7	1518	6.0	1234	6.1	1220	7.2
	2051	0.1	2355	2.7	1939	-0.1	1933	0.2	2102	0.2	2027	0.2	2206	0.1	1934	0.4	1934	0.8
28 SA	0331	1.7	0633	0.1	0117	3.2	0259	2.2	0414	2.2	0215	4.8	0341	6.2	0057	6.2	0041	7.2
	0903	0.1	1208	2.8	0757	0.0	0758	0.5	0921	0.4	0839	0.5	1021	0.4	0752	0.6	0751	0.9
	1539	1.9	1856	0.1	1328	3.3	1519	2.1	1630	2.1	1431	4.8	1558	6.0	1310	6.1	1256	7.3
	2129	0.1			2021	0.0	2012	0.2	2144	0.3	2103	0.2	2243	0.2	2012	0.5	2007	0.8
29 SU	0400	1.7	0031	2.7	0154	3.2	0337	2.2	0452	2.2	0251	4.8	0419	6.2	0133	6.1	0115	7.2
●	0942	0.1	0712	0.1	0838	0.1	0837	0.4	1003	0.4	0915	0.5	1057	0.4	0829	0.7	0821	1.0
	1612	1.9	1245	2.7	1405	3.2	1556	2.1	1709	2.1	1509	4.8	1636	6.0	1348	6.1	1330	7.3
	2204	0.2	1932	0.2	2058	0.0	2054	0.3	2230	0.3	2136	0.3	2318	0.2	2049	0.6	2036	1.0
30 M	0427	1.7	0103	2.7	0225	3.1	0414	2.1	0530	2.1	0329	4.8	0457	6.1	0211	6.0	0148	7.1
	1018	0.1	0748	0.2	0915	0.2	0920	0.4	1050	0.4	0951	0.5	1132	0.4	0905	0.8	0848	1.2
	1646	1.8	1318	2.7	1436	3.1	1631	2.1	1748	2.1	1545	4.8	1714	5.9	1426	6.0	1404	7.1
	2238	0.2	2003	0.3	2130	0.3	2139	0.3	2321	0.4	2209	0.5	2351	0.3	2124	0.8	2104	1.2
31 TU	0454	1.8	0133	2.7	0250	3.1	0449	2.1	0607	2.0	0405	4.6	0533	5.9	0249	5.9	0222	6.9
	1055	0.1	0821	0.3	0947	0.3	1005	0.4	1142	0.4	1025	0.6	1205	0.5	0939	1.0	0915	1.4
	1717	1.8	1352	2.6	1504	3.0	1706	2.1	1826	2.0	1622	4.6	1751	5.8	1506	5.8	1439	7.0
	2310	0.3	2029	0.5	2156	0.5	2227	0.4			2239	0.6			2158	1.0	2133	1.4

DENMARK, GERMANY, HOLLAND & BELGIUM Time Zone -0100
Esbjerg * Helgoland * Cuxhaven * Hoek van Holland * Rotterdam * Vlissingen * Antwerpen * Dunkerque * Calais

TIDE TABLES NOVEMBER 2000

esbjerg		HELGOLAND		CUXHAVEN		HOEK VAN HOLLAND		ROTTERDAM		VLISSINGEN		ANTWERPEN		DUNKERQUE		CALAIS		
Time	m	Time	m	Time	m	Time	m	Time	m	Time	m	Time	m	Time	m	Time	m	
0522	1.8	0205	2.7	0313	3.1	0524	2.0	0019	0.5	0440	4.5	0021	0.5	0328	5.7	0257	6.7	**1 W**
1130	0.2	0851	0.4	1014	0.4	1054	0.3	0642	1.9	1057	0.7	0609	5.6	1014	1.2	0945	1.6	
1745	1.7	1427	2.5	1536	3.0	1741	2.1	1240	0.4	1658	4.5	1235	0.6	1545	5.6	1516	6.7	
2342	0.3	2054	0.5	2215	0.6	2323	0.4	1903	1.9	2309	0.7	1827	5.5	2232	1.2	2203	1.7	
0549	1.7	0239	2.6	0344	3.1	0559	1.9	0130	0.6	0515	4.3	0049	0.7	0408	5.4	0336	6.5	**2 TH**
1206	0.2	0921	0.5	1038	0.5	1145	0.3	0717	1.8	1130	0.8	0644	5.3	1049	1.4	1017	1.8	
1813	1.6	1505	2.4	1615	2.8	1819	2.0	1344	0.4	1736	4.3	1306	0.7	1629	5.4	1557	6.4	
		2122	0.6	2238	0.6			1939	1.8	2344	0.9	1904	5.3	2309	1.5	2239	2.0	
0016	0.3	0318	2.6	0424	3.0	0025	0.4	0226	0.6	0554	4.0	0122	0.9	0452	5.1	0418	6.1	**3 F**
0621	1.7	0955	0.6	1108	0.6	0638	1.8	0751	1.7	1208	0.9	0722	5.1	1130	1.6	1057	2.2	
1245	0.3	1550	2.3	1702	2.7	1238	0.3	1439	0.4	1822	4.0	1342	0.8	1718	5.1	1645	6.0	
1850	1.5	2157	0.8	2312	0.8	1906	1.9	2018	1.7			1948	5.0	2358	1.7	2327	2.4	
0054	0.4	0404	2.4	0515	2.9	0122	0.4	0319	0.6	0027	1.1	0202	1.1	0545	4.8	0512	5.7	**4 SA**
0705	1.7	1040	0.7	1148	0.8	0733	1.7	0830	1.6	0645	3.7	0807	4.8	1225	1.8	1155	2.5	
1330	0.3	1647	2.1	1800	2.5	1332	0.3	1536	0.5	1259	1.0	1426	1.0	1821	4.8	1748	5.6	
1943	1.4	2246	0.9	2357	0.9	2024	1.8	2106	1.6	1930	3.7	2042	4.8					
0142	0.4	0506	2.3	0618	2.7	0329	0.5	0424	0.7	0131	1.3	0254	1.3	0101	1.9	0033	2.6	**5 SU**
0806	1.6	1145	0.9	1242	0.9	0900	1.5	0920	1.4	0802	3.5	0908	4.5	0656	4.6	0626	5.5	
1433	0.4	1803	2.0	1910	2.4	1438	0.3	1642	0.5	1454	1.1	1527	1.1	1333	2.0	1309	2.6	
2103	1.4					2142	1.7	2257	1.5	2053	3.6	2154	4.6	1941	4.7	1909	5.5	
0249	0.5	0000	1.1	0057	1.1	0434	0.5	0548	0.7	0331	1.3	0406	1.5	0212	2.0	0148	2.7	**6 M**
0927	1.6	0627	2.2	0734	2.6	1018	1.5	1148	1.4	0929	3.4	1032	4.4	0818	4.5	0748	5.5	
1600	0.4	1324	0.9	1407	1.0	1642	0.3	1757	0.5	1604	1.0	1657	1.2	1444	1.9	1425	2.5	
2239	1.4	1933	2.0	2031	2.4	2302	1.8			2219	3.7	2326	4.6	2059	4.8	2027	5.6	
0419	0.5	0153	1.0	0238	1.1	0535	0.4	0028	1.6	0436	1.2	0531	1.4	0322	1.9	0303	2.4	**7 TU**
1053	1.6	0753	2.3	0855	2.7	1133	1.6	0721	0.6	1046	3.6	1157	4.6	0927	4.8	0859	5.7	
1717	0.3	1454	0.7	1609	0.8	1732	0.3	1258	1.5	1706	0.9	1813	1.0	1551	1.7	1537	2.2	
2349	1.5	2055	2.2	2151	2.6			1921	0.4	2318	4.0			2159	5.1	2129	6.0	
0532	0.4	0317	0.8	0432	0.9	0001	1.9	0127	1.8	0532	1.0	0031	5.0	0426	1.6	0409	2.0	**8 W**
1158	1.7	0905	2.4	1008	2.9	0736	0.4	0836	0.5	1138	4.0	0638	1.2	1020	5.1	0953	6.2	
1814	0.2	1554	0.5	1710	0.5	1225	1.7	1352	1.7	1758	0.7	1252	5.0	1651	1.3	1638	1.8	
		2153	2.4	2255	2.9	1805	0.3	2036	0.3			1915	0.8	2245	5.5	2218	6.4	
0044	1.6	0413	0.6	0530	0.6	0045	2.0	0216	2.0	0002	4.3	0118	5.4	0520	1.3	0504	1.6	**9 TH**
0627	0.3	1000	2.6	1109	3.2	0845	0.4	0945	0.4	0617	0.8	0734	1.0	1102	5.4	1037	6.6	
1251	1.7	1642	0.3	1759	0.2	1306	1.8	1437	1.8	1219	4.3	1336	5.4	1741	1.0	1729	1.4	
1900	0.1	2238	2.6	2348	3.2	1823	0.3	2142	0.3	1841	0.5	2006	0.6	2325	5.8	2257	6.8	
0130	1.6	0500	0.4	0619	0.3	0124	2.1	0259	2.1	0040	4.6	0159	5.8	0605	1.0	0552	1.3	**10 F**
0712	0.2	1047	2.8	1201	3.4	0940	0.4	1047	0.3	0655	0.7	0823	0.7	1138	5.7	1114	6.9	
1338	1.8	1725	0.1	1845	0.0	1342	2.0	1518	2.0	1256	4.5	1416	5.8	1824	0.8	1815	1.1	
1942	0.1	2318	2.8			1847	0.2	2246	0.3	1919	0.4	2051	0.4			2333	7.0	
0212	1.7	0545	0.2	0033	3.4	0200	2.2	0339	2.2	0116	4.8	0238	6.1	0000	6.0	0637	1.1	**11 SA**
0755	0.1	1130	2.9	0705	0.1	0712	0.5	1142	0.3	0733	0.6	0908	0.5	0646	0.8	1149	7.2	
1421	1.8	1807	0.0	1248	3.5	1418	2.1	1556	2.1	1332	4.7	1454	6.1	1212	5.9	1859	1.0	O
2021	0.1	2357	2.9	1929	-0.1	1918	0.2	2349	0.2	1957	0.3	2135	0.2	1906	0.6			
0251	1.7	0628	0.1	0118	3.5	0238	2.3	0417	2.2	0153	4.9	0316	6.3	0035	6.1	0008	7.2	**12 SU**
0837	0.1	1212	3.0	0750	-0.1	0739	0.4	1232	0.3	0814	0.5	0953	0.3	0726	0.7	0720	1.1	
1504	1.8	1848	0.0	1335	3.6	1455	2.2	1634	2.1	1409	4.9	1533	6.3	1247	6.1	1224	7.3	
2101	0.1			2012	-0.2	1952	0.2			2039	0.3	2218	0.1	1946	0.6	1941	1.0	
0330	1.7	0036	2.9	0200	3.6	0316	2.3	0048	0.2	0230	5.0	0355	6.4	0111	6.2	0044	7.3	**13 M**
0919	0.1	0710	0.0	0833	-0.1	0812	0.4	0457	2.2	0857	0.4	1038	0.3	0806	0.6	0801	1.1	
1548	1.8	1254	3.0	1419	3.6	1534	2.2	1319	0.3	1448	5.0	1612	6.4	1324	6.1	1301	7.3	
2142	0.1	1930	0.0	2053	-0.1	2030	0.2	1714	2.2	2121	0.3	2302	0.2	2027	0.5	2022	1.0	
0407	1.7	0114	3.0	0241	3.6	0356	2.3	0140	0.2	0310	4.9	0435	6.4	0150	6.2	0122	7.2	**14 TU**
1002	0.1	0752	0.0	0915	-0.2	0836	0.4	0536	2.2	0942	0.4	1121	0.3	0847	0.7	0842	1.1	
1630	1.8	1335	3.0	1503	3.6	1614	2.3	1403	0.3	1528	5.0	1653	6.4	1405	6.2	1342	7.2	
2222	0.1	2010	0.1	2134	-0.1	2112	0.3	1755	2.2	2204	0.3	2345	0.3	2109	0.6	2103	1.1	
0442	1.7	0151	3.0	0321	3.5	0437	2.2	0227	0.3	0351	4.8	0516	6.2	0232	6.1	0204	7.1	**15 W**
1045	0.1	0833	0.0	0957	-0.2	0934	0.4	0617	2.1	1027	0.4	1204	0.4	0929	0.7	0923	1.2	
1712	1.7	1418	2.9	1545	3.5	1657	2.3	1441	0.4	1610	4.9	1736	6.3	1449	6.1	1426	7.1	
2303	0.1	2050	0.1	2214	0.0	2200	0.3	1837	2.2	2248	0.5			2151	0.7	2147	1.2	

• • Time Zone -0100. For UT subtract 1 hour. For European summer time (shaded) 26/3-29/10 add 1 hour • •

NOVEMBER 2000 TIDE TABLES

• • Time Zone -0100. For UT subtract 1 hour. For European summer time (shaded) 26/3-29/10 add 1 hour • •

	ESBJERG		HELGOLAND		CUXHAVEN		HOEK VAN HOLLAND		ROTTERDAM		VLISSINGEN		ANTWERPEN		DUNKERQUE		CALAIS	
	Time	m	Time	m	Time	m	Time	m	Time	m	Time	m	Time	m	Time	m	Time	m
16TH	0517	1.7	0230	3.0	0359	3.5	0521	2.0	0311	0.3	0436	4.6	0026	0.5	0317	5.9	0251	6.8
	1130	0.0	0916	0.0	1038	-0.1	1023	0.3	0658	2.0	1112	0.4	0600	5.9	1013	0.9	1008	1.3
	1755	1.7	1501	2.9	1627	3.4	1742	2.2	1508	0.3	1657	4.7	1247	0.6	1537	6.0	1517	6.8
	2346	0.2	2130	0.2	2253	0.1	2254	0.4	1921	2.2	2333	0.6	1822	6.0	2238	0.9	2235	1.4
17F	0557	1.7	0312	3.0	0438	3.5	0609	1.9	0349	0.4	0525	4.4	0107	0.7	0408	5.7	0347	6.5
	1218	0.0	1000	0.0	1121	-0.1	1118	0.2	0742	2.0	1202	0.5	0650	5.6	1102	1.0	1057	1.5
	1846	1.6	1548	2.8	1711	3.3	1837	2.1	1354	0.3	1753	4.5	1331	0.7	1633	5.7	1621	6.5
			2214	0.3	2334	0.2			2009	2.2			1915	5.7	2331	1.2	2329	1.6
18SA	0034	0.2	0400	3.0	0521	3.5	0218	0.4	0326	0.4	0024	0.8	0152	0.9	0509	5.3	0457	6.2
	0650	1.7	1049	0.1	1206	0.0	0717	1.7	0831	1.9	0629	4.1	0748	5.3	1200	1.3	1156	1.8
	1313	0.1	1640	2.7	1758	3.2	1232	0.2	1442	0.2	1302	0.6	1423	0.8	1742	5.4	1739	6.2
	1951	1.5	2303	0.4			1958	2.0	2106	2.1	1909	4.3	2020	5.4				
19SU	0131	0.3	0454	2.9	0019	0.3	0333	0.5	0330	0.4	0130	1.0	0246	1.1	0037	1.5	0033	1.9
	0757	1.7	1146	0.2	0611	3.5	0842	1.7	0933	1.8	0748	3.9	0859	5.0	0628	5.0	0618	6.1
	1421	0.1	1739	2.6	1300	0.1	1421	0.2	1539	0.2	1418	0.7	1528	0.9	1312	1.4	1306	2.0
	2109	1.5			1852	3.1	2116	2.0	2221	2.0	2028	4.2	2133	5.2	1909	5.2	1858	6.1
20M	0241	0.3	0001	0.5	0114	0.4	0507	0.5	0428	0.4	0258	1.0	0355	1.2	0157	1.6	0151	2.1
	0917	1.7	0556	2.8	0709	3.4	0951	1.6	1054	1.7	0903	3.9	1011	5.0	0756	5.0	0733	6.0
	1540	0.1	1253	0.2	1405	0.2	1546	0.2	1640	0.1	1539	0.6	1648	0.8	1433	1.4	1430	2.0
	2232	1.5	1845	2.5	1953	3.0	2231	2.0	2339	2.0	2145	4.2	2247	5.2	2033	5.3	2010	6.2
21TU	0402	0.3	0112	0.5	0224	0.4	0658	0.4	0537	0.5	0421	1.0	0515	1.2	0320	1.6	0315	2.0
	1039	1.8	0704	2.8	0812	3.3	1102	1.7	1207	1.8	1018	4.0	1123	5.1	0910	5.1	0840	6.2
	1657	0.1	1405	0.2	1518	0.2	1829	0.2	1744	0.1	1655	0.5	1806	0.7	1551	1.2	1551	1.8
	2348	1.6	1954	2.5	2058	3.0	2338	2.0			2254	4.3	2359	5.4	2141	5.5	2115	6.3
22W	0517	0.3	0227	0.5	0342	0.4	0806	0.3	0044	2.1	0527	0.8	0633	1.0	0431	1.3	0427	1.7
	1156	1.8	0814	2.8	0919	3.3	1203	1.8	0817	0.4	1120	4.1	1229	5.3	1009	5.4	0941	6.4
	1803	0.1	1513	0.2	1628	0.1	1958	0.2	1308	1.9	1755	0.4	1914	0.4	1656	0.9	1654	1.4
			2101	2.5	2205	3.1			1845	0.2	2349	4.5			2236	5.7	2212	6.6
23TH	0052	1.7	0334	0.4	0451	0.3	0030	2.1	0140	2.1	0618	0.7	0100	5.6	0527	1.0	0523	1.4
	0620	0.2	0920	2.8	1025	3.3	0903	0.4	0939	0.4	1209	4.3	0738	0.8	1057	5.7	1034	6.7
	1301	1.9	1612	0.2	1730	0.1	1253	1.9	1401	2.0	1843	0.3	1324	5.6	1748	0.7	1746	1.1
	1857	0.1	2200	2.6	2308	3.1	1816	0.3	1939	0.2			2010	0.3	2321	5.9	2302	6.8
24F	0144	1.7	0433	0.3	0551	0.2	0116	2.1	0229	2.2	0035	4.6	0152	5.8	0613	0.8	0609	1.2
	0713	0.2	1016	2.8	1126	3.3	0948	0.4	1049	0.4	0700	0.6	0831	0.5	1138	5.8	1120	6.9
	1354	1.9	1704	0.2	1823	0.1	1337	2.0	1448	2.0	1252	4.5	1413	5.7	1833	0.6	1830	1.0
	1945	0.2	2249	2.7			1846	0.3	2225	0.3	1924	0.3	2057	0.2			2345	6.9
25SA	0225	1.7	0524	0.2	0002	3.2	0158	2.1	0312	2.1	0115	4.6	0238	6.0	0000	6.0	0649	1.1
	0800	0.2	1105	2.8	0645	0.2	0715	0.5	1009	0.5	0739	0.6	0916	0.4	0654	0.7	1200	7.0
	1436	1.9	1749	0.2	1219	3.3	1419	2.0	1530	2.0	1333	4.6	1457	5.9	1215	5.9	1908	1.0
	2026	0.2	2331	2.7	1911	0.1	1922	0.3	2306	0.4	2001	0.4	2139	0.2	1912	0.6		
26SU	0259	1.8	0610	0.3	0048	3.2	0239	2.1	0352	2.1	0154	4.7	0320	6.0	0036	6.0	0021	7.0
	0842	0.2	1148	2.7	0732	0.2	0750	0.4	1122	0.6	0817	0.5	0957	0.3	0732	0.7	0724	1.2
	1512	1.8	1830	0.3	1304	3.2	1459	2.1	1609	2.0	1411	4.7	1538	5.9	1251	5.9	1235	7.0
	2103	0.2			1954	0.3	2002	0.3	2357	0.5	2036	0.4	2218	0.2	1950	0.7	1940	1.1
27M	0328	1.8	0008	2.7	0127	3.2	0318	2.1	0430	2.0	0232	4.7	0400	6.0	0112	6.0	0054	6.9
	0921	0.2	0652	0.3	0815	0.3	0829	0.4	0948	0.4	0854	0.5	1036	0.3	0809	0.8	0753	1.2
	1546	1.8	1225	2.6	1342	3.1	1536	2.1	1231	0.6	1449	4.7	1618	5.9	1328	5.9	1309	7.0
	2139	0.3	1906	0.4	2032	0.4	2045	0.4	1648	2.0	2109	0.5	2254	0.3	2025	0.8	2009	1.2
28TU ●	0357	1.8	0042	2.7	0200	3.2	0354	2.1	0053	0.6	0309	4.7	0437	5.9	0149	5.9	0126	6.9
	1000	0.2	0730	0.4	0854	0.4	0911	0.3	0506	1.9	0930	0.5	1112	0.3	0845	0.9	0821	1.4
	1621	1.8	1300	2.6	1417	3.0	1612	2.1	1031	0.4	1526	4.7	1655	5.9	1406	5.9	1342	7.0
	2212	0.3	1938	0.5	2105	0.5	2130	0.4	1727	1.9	2142	0.6	2327	0.4	2100	1.0	2037	1.4
29W	0428	1.9	0113	2.7	0229	3.2	0430	2.1	0011	0.6	0345	4.6	0513	5.7	0227	5.8	0200	6.8
	1036	0.2	0804	0.5	0928	0.5	0954	0.3	0542	1.8	1006	0.5	1145	0.5	0919	1.0	0850	1.5
	1653	1.8	1335	2.6	1450	3.0	1646	2.1	1119	0.4	1602	4.6	1730	5.7	1445	5.7	1411	6.8
	2245	0.3	2007	0.6	2132	0.6	2221	0.5	1804	1.9	2215	0.7	2357	0.4	2132	1.1	2106	1.5
30TH	0459	1.8	0146	2.7	0257	3.1	0504	2.0	0017	0.6	0419	4.4	0547	5.5	0306	5.6	0234	6.7
	1112	0.2	0836	0.5	0957	0.6	1036	0.3	0618	1.8	1039	0.6	1215	0.6	0952	1.1	0919	1.6
	1723	1.7	1410	2.5	1524	2.9	1721	2.1	1212	0.4	1637	4.5	1806	5.5	1525	5.6	1453	6.7
	2318	0.3	2034	0.6	2155	0.7	2319	0.5	1841	1.8	2245	0.8			2205	1.2	2136	1.7

DENMARK, GERMANY, HOLLAND & BELGIUM Time Zone -0100
Esbjerg * Helgoland * Cuxhaven * Hoek van Holland * Rotterdam * Vlissingen * Antwerpen * Dunkerque * Calais

TIDE TABLES DECEMBER 2000

	esbjerg	m	HELGOLAND	m	CUXHAVEN	m	HOEK VAN HOLLAND	m	ROTTERDAM	m	VLISSINGEN	m	ANTWERPEN	m	DUNKERQUE	m	CALAIS	m
1 F	0529	1.8	0220	2.7	0329	3.1	0538	1.9	0018	0.7	0454	4.3	0024	0.8	0345	5.5	0310	6.5
	1146	0.3	0907	0.6	1025	0.6	1119	0.2	0652	1.7	1111	0.7	0621	5.3	1026	1.3	0951	1.8
	1751	1.6	1448	2.4	1601	2.8	1757	2.0	1259	0.4	1713	4.3	1244	0.7	1606	5.4	1530	6.5
	2351	0.3	2105	0.7	2221	0.7			1917	1.8	2318	0.9	1841	5.3	2239	1.4	2210	1.9
2 SA	0601	1.8	0257	2.7	0406	3.1	0012	0.5	0052	0.7	0530	4.1	0055	0.9	0424	5.3	0349	6.3
	1222	0.3	0942	0.6	1056	0.7	0613	1.8	0727	1.7	1145	0.7	0657	5.1	1103	1.4	1029	2.0
	1827	1.5	1529	2.3	1643	2.7	1207	0.2	1332	0.4	1754	4.1	1317	0.7	1649	5.2	1612	6.2
			2141	0.8	2256	0.8	1839	2.0	1957	1.8	2359	1.0	1921	5.2	2321	1.6	2253	2.2
3 SU	0027	0.3	0340	2.6	0449	3.0	0100	0.5	0133	0.7	0614	3.9	0133	1.0	0509	5.1	0435	6.1
	0642	1.7	1024	0.7	1134	0.8	0655	1.7	0808	1.6	1228	0.8	0737	5.0	1148	1.6	1120	2.2
	1303	0.3	1618	2.2	1733	2.7	1258	0.2	1423	0.4	1847	3.9	1357	0.7	1739	5.0	1703	5.9
	1912	1.5	2227	0.9	2339	0.9	1936	1.9	2043	1.7			2006	5.0			2352	2.4
4 M	0110	0.3	0433	2.5	0544	2.9	0154	0.5	0300	0.7	0048	1.1	0217	1.1	0012	1.8	0530	5.8
	0733	1.7	1117	0.8	1224	0.8	0807	1.6	0857	1.6	0713	3.7	0826	4.8	0604	4.9	1226	2.4
	1352	0.3	1720	2.2	1833	2.6	1352	0.2	1542	0.4	1324	0.9	1446	0.8	1245	1.7	1806	5.7
	2012	1.4	2327	1.0			2051	1.8	2151	1.7	1956	3.8	2104	4.8	1840	4.8		
5 TU	0203	0.4	0539	2.4	0034	1.0	0406	0.5	0509	0.6	0154	1.2	0310	1.2	0118	1.9	0102	2.5
	0835	1.6	1228	0.8	0651	2.8	0921	1.6	1021	1.5	0824	3.6	0933	4.7	0710	4.7	0639	5.7
	1454	0.3	1834	2.2	1327	0.9	1451	0.2	1705	0.4	1454	1.0	1545	0.8	1352	1.8	1336	2.4
	2125	1.4			1943	2.6	2200	1.8	2335	1.7	2108	3.8	2218	4.8	1950	4.8	1920	5.7
6 W	0308	0.4	0048	1.0	0146	1.0	0506	0.5	0648	0.6	0333	1.2	0414	1.2	0227	1.8	0211	2.4
	0946	1.6	0655	2.4	0805	2.9	1030	1.6	1206	1.5	0937	3.6	1051	4.7	0821	4.8	0753	5.8
	1607	0.3	1349	0.8	1452	0.8	1558	0.3	1844	0.3	1607	0.9	1657	0.8	1459	1.6	1444	2.2
	2241	1.5	1951	2.3	2055	2.7	2307	1.9			2218	3.9	2330	5.0	2059	5.0	2030	5.9
7 TH	0424	0.4	0214	0.9	0319	0.9	0630	0.4	0043	1.8	0436	1.1	0527	1.1	0333	1.7	0317	2.1
	1057	1.7	0809	2.5	0917	3.0	1133	1.7	0800	0.4	1044	3.9	1158	5.0	0926	5.0	0857	6.0
	1715	0.3	1459	0.6	1612	0.6	1657	0.3	1309	1.7	1706	0.7	1810	0.7	1601	1.4	1547	1.9
	2347	1.5	2057	2.5	2203	2.9			2003	0.3	2315	4.2			2157	5.3	2127	6.2
8 F	0532	0.3	0323	0.7	0438	0.7	0003	2.0	0139	2.0	0530	0.9	0030	5.3	0433	1.4	0417	1.8
	1200	1.7	0912	2.7	1022	3.2	0806	0.4	0903	0.3	1136	4.1	0637	0.9	1018	5.3	0950	6.4
	1812	0.2	1556	0.4	1713	0.3	1224	1.8	1400	1.8	1759	0.6	1253	5.3	1659	1.1	1645	1.6
			2151	2.7	2301	3.2	1739	0.3	2109	0.2			1917	0.6	2245	5.6	2215	6.6
9 SA	0043	1.6	0420	0.4	0538	0.4	0048	2.1	0227	2.1	0003	4.5	0121	5.7	0527	1.1	0512	1.5
	0630	0.2	1007	2.9	1121	3.4	0628	0.5	1003	0.3	0619	0.7	0742	0.7	1103	5.6	1036	6.7
	1257	1.8	1647	0.2	1806	0.1	1309	1.9	1446	2.0	1221	4.4	1341	5.7	1751	0.9	1737	1.3
	1902	0.1	2239	2.8	2354	3.4	1816	0.2	2211	0.2	1846	0.5	2014	0.4	2327	5.8	2300	6.9
10 SU	0134	1.7	0511	0.2	0631	0.1	0132	2.2	0310	2.2	0046	4.7	0206	6.0	0616	0.9	0603	1.3
	0722	0.2	1057	3.0	1214	3.6	0645	0.4	1101	0.3	0706	0.6	0838	0.5	1144	5.8	1119	7.0
	1350	1.8	1735	0.1	1856	-0.1	1351	2.1	1528	2.1	1304	4.6	1426	6.0	1838	0.7	1828	1.2
	1950	0.1	2324	3.0			1855	0.2	2317	0.2	1931	0.4	2106	0.3			2342	7.1
11 M O	0222	1.7	0600	0.1	0042	3.6	0214	2.2	0352	2.2	0129	4.8	0251	6.2	0009	6.0	0652	1.2
	0812	0.1	1145	3.0	0721	-0.1	0718	0.4	1158	0.3	0752	0.5	0929	0.3	0703	0.7	1203	7.2
	1442	1.8	1821	0.0	1306	3.7	1433	2.2	1610	2.1	1347	4.8	1510	6.2	1225	6.0	1918	1.0
	2036	0.1			1943	-0.1	1935	0.2			2016	0.3	2154	0.2	1924	0.6		
12 TU	0307	1.8	0008	3.0	0130	3.6	0257	2.2	0024	0.3	0211	4.9	0335	6.3	0051	6.1	0027	7.2
	0900	0.0	0647	0.0	0809	-0.2	0756	0.3	0433	2.2	0839	0.3	1018	0.2	0748	0.6	0741	1.1
	1533	1.8	1232	3.0	1355	3.6	1515	2.3	1250	0.3	1430	4.9	1554	6.3	1308	6.1	1248	7.3
	2121	0.1	1906	0.0	2030	-0.2	2016	0.3	1653	2.2	2102	0.3	2242	0.2	2009	0.6	2006	1.0
13 W	0351	1.8	0051	3.1	0215	3.7	0340	2.2	0122	0.3	0254	4.9	0418	6.2	0134	6.1	0112	7.2
	0947	0.0	0733	-0.1	0856	-0.2	0837	0.3	0515	2.1	0927	0.3	1106	0.2	0832	0.6	0830	1.1
	1623	1.8	1318	3.0	1442	3.6	1600	2.3	1121	0.4	1514	5.0	1639	6.4	1352	6.1	1336	7.2
	2206	0.1	1951	0.1	2114	-0.1	2101	0.3	1736	2.2	2148	0.3	2327	0.3	2054	0.6	2055	1.0
14 TH	0433	1.8	0133	3.1	0259	3.7	0425	2.1	0213	0.3	0339	4.8	0504	6.1	0219	6.0	0201	7.1
	1034	0.0	0819	-0.1	0941	-0.1	0922	0.2	0557	2.1	1015	0.2	1152	0.3	0917	0.6	0917	1.0
	1712	1.7	1403	2.9	1529	3.5	1646	2.3	1233	0.3	1600	4.9	1725	6.3	1439	6.1	1427	7.1
	2250	0.1	2034	0.1	2157	-0.1	2150	0.4	1821	2.2	2235	0.4			2139	0.7	2142	1.0
15 F	0514	1.8	0215	3.1	0342	3.7	0512	2.0	0258	0.3	0427	4.6	0012	0.5	0308	5.9	0255	7.0
	1122	0.0	0904	-0.1	1026	-0.2	1011	0.2	0640	2.0	1105	0.2	0552	5.9	1003	0.6	1004	1.1
	1800	1.7	1448	2.9	1613	3.4	1736	2.2	1233	0.4	1651	4.8	1239	0.3	1531	6.0	1524	7.0
	2336	0.1	2116	0.1	2239	0.0	2245	0.5	1906	2.2	2322	0.6	1815	6.1	2226	0.9	2231	1.2

• • Time Zone -0100. For UT subtract 1 hour. For European summer time (shaded) 26/3-29/10 add 1 hour • •

DECEMBER 2000 TIDE TABLES

• • Time Zone -0100. For UT subtract 1 hour. For European summer time (shaded) 26/3-29/10 add 1 hour • •

	ESBJERG		HELGOLAND		CUXHAVEN		HOEK VAN HOLLAND		ROTTERDAM		VLISSINGEN		ANTWERPEN		DUNKERQUE		CALAIS	
	Time	m	Time	m	Time	m	Time	m	Time	m	Time	m	Time	m	Time	m	Time	m
16SA	0559	1.8	0259	3.1	0423	3.7	0607	1.9	0339	0.4	0520	4.4	0057	0.6	0400	5.8	0353	6.8
	1212	0.0	0949	-0.1	1110	-0.2	1104	0.1	0725	2.0	1157	0.3	0644	5.7	1054	0.8	1054	1.2
	1851	1.6	1533	2.8	1656	3.4	1835	2.2	1326	0.2	1749	4.6	1327	0.4	1627	5.8	1625	6.8
			2200	0.2	2321	0.0			1956	2.2			1909	5.8	2318	1.1	2322	1.4
17SU	0024	0.2	0345	3.1	0506	3.7	0227	0.4	0316	0.5	0014	0.7	0143	0.8	0459	5.5	0453	6.6
	0650	1.8	1036	0.0	1156	-0.1	0718	1.8	0813	1.9	0622	4.2	0741	5.4	1149	1.0	1148	1.4
	1306	0.0	1621	2.7	1741	3.3	1211	0.1	1418	0.1	1254	0.3	1418	0.5	1732	5.5	1727	6.5
	1946	1.5	2245	0.3			1946	2.1	2051	2.2	1858	4.4	2009	5.6				
18M	0118	0.2	0434	3.0	0005	0.1	0334	0.5	0300	0.4	0113	0.9	0235	0.9	0018	1.3	0020	1.7
	0748	1.8	1127	0.1	0552	3.6	0820	1.8	0909	1.9	0727	4.1	0842	5.3	0606	5.3	0556	6.4
	1406	0.1	1713	2.6	1245	0.0	1406	0.1	1516	0.1	1357	0.4	1516	0.5	1254	1.1	1250	1.7
	2048	1.5	2336	0.3	1829	3.2	2052	2.0	2157	2.1	2005	4.3	2112	5.3	1844	5.3	1833	6.3
19TU	0219	0.2	0530	2.9	0054	0.2	0522	0.4	0400	0.4	0223	1.0	0334	1.1	0130	1.5	0126	1.9
	0855	1.8	1225	0.2	0645	3.5	0921	1.7	1020	1.8	0833	4.0	0945	5.1	0721	5.2	0702	6.2
	1514	0.1	1812	2.5	1340	0.1	1516	0.1	1618	0.1	1505	0.5	1621	0.6	1408	1.2	1400	1.8
	2156	1.5			1923	3.0	2200	2.0	2309	2.0	2112	4.2	2220	5.2	2000	5.2	1939	6.2
20W	0329	0.3	0037	0.4	0151	0.4	0623	0.4	0511	0.4	0338	1.0	0442	1.1	0245	1.5	0240	2.0
	1006	1.8	0633	2.8	0743	3.4	1028	1.7	1133	1.8	0941	4.0	1052	5.1	0836	5.2	0807	6.2
	1623	0.2	1330	0.3	1444	0.3	1624	0.2	1726	0.1	1618	0.5	1728	0.6	1521	1.2	1515	1.8
	2304	1.5	1916	2.5	2024	3.0	2306	2.0			2220	4.2	2330	5.2	2110	5.3	2044	6.2
21TH	0442	0.3	0148	0.5	0303	0.4	0726	0.4	0014	2.0	0451	0.9	0553	1.0	0357	1.4	0351	1.9
	1118	1.8	0741	2.7	0847	3.3	1131	1.8	0717	0.4	1046	4.1	1200	5.1	0940	5.3	0910	6.2
	1728	0.2	1438	0.4	1553	0.3	1912	0.2	1237	1.8	1724	0.5	1836	0.5	1627	1.1	1622	1.6
			2024	2.5	2129	3.0			1841	0.2	2320	4.3			2209	5.4	2145	6.3
22F	0009	1.6	0300	0.5	0417	0.4	0003	2.0	0112	2.0	0549	0.8	0033	5.3	0458	1.2	0451	1.7
	0548	0.2	0849	2.7	0954	3.2	0827	0.4	0833	0.4	1142	4.2	0704	0.9	1033	5.5	1008	6.4
	1224	1.8	1541	0.4	1657	0.3	1227	1.8	1334	1.9	1815	0.5	1259	5.3	1723	1.0	1718	1.5
	1827	0.2	2129	2.5	2234	3.0	1809	0.3	1958	0.2			1939	0.4	2259	5.5	2239	6.4
23SA	0105	1.7	0406	0.4	0523	0.4	0054	2.0	0206	2.0	0011	4.3	0129	5.5	0548	1.0	0542	1.5
	0647	0.2	0952	2.6	1058	3.1	0915	0.4	0958	0.4	0637	0.7	0803	0.6	1119	5.6	1100	6.6
	1322	1.8	1636	0.4	1754	0.3	1316	1.9	1426	1.9	1231	4.3	1352	5.5	1809	0.9	1804	1.4
	1917	0.2	2224	2.6	2333	3.1	1842	0.3	2042	0.3	1859	0.5	2030	0.4	2341	5.6	2326	6.6
24SU ●	0151	1.7	0502	0.4	0621	0.3	0140	2.0	0253	1.9	0057	4.4	0218	5.6	0632	0.9	0624	1.4
	0739	0.2	1047	2.6	1156	3.1	0715	0.4	0944	0.5	0719	0.6	0854	0.5	1200	5.7	1143	6.7
	1409	1.8	1725	0.4	1845	0.3	1401	2.0	1512	1.9	1315	4.4	1439	5.6	1851	0.9	1844	1.3
	2001	0.2	2312	2.6			1921	0.4	2233	0.5	1937	0.5	2115	0.3				
25M	0229	1.8	0552	0.4	0024	3.1	0223	2.0	0334	1.9	0138	4.5	0303	5.7	0019	5.7	0005	6.6
	0824	0.2	1133	2.6	0712	0.3	0748	0.3	1103	0.5	0759	0.5	0938	0.3	0712	0.8	0700	1.4
	1450	1.8	1809	0.4	1246	3.0	1443	2.0	1553	1.9	1357	4.5	1522	5.7	1237	5.7	1221	6.8
	2042	0.2	2354	2.7	1930	0.4	2003	0.4	2323	0.6	2013	0.6	2157	0.3	1929	0.9	1918	1.4
26TU	0303	1.8	0637	0.4	0108	3.1	0304	2.0	0412	1.8	0217	4.5	0343	5.8	0057	5.7	0039	6.7
	0906	0.2	1215	2.5	0757	0.4	0826	0.3	1205	0.6	0837	0.5	1018	0.3	0751	0.8	0733	1.5
	1527	1.7	1848	0.5	1329	3.0	1521	2.1	1632	1.8	1435	4.6	1603	5.8	1315	5.7	1254	6.8
	2118	0.2			2012	0.4	2047	0.4			2048	0.6	2234	0.4	2005	1.0	1950	1.5
27W	0336	1.8	0030	2.7	0146	3.1	0344	2.0	0013	0.7	0254	4.5	0421	5.7	0133	5.7	0111	6.7
	0945	0.2	0718	0.4	0839	0.4	0904	0.2	0448	1.8	0915	0.4	1057	0.3	0827	0.9	0803	1.5
	1602	1.7	1254	2.5	1409	2.9	1558	2.1	1018	0.4	1512	4.6	1640	5.7	1354	5.6	1328	6.8
	2153	0.2	1924	0.5	2048	0.5	2135	0.4	1709	1.8	2122	0.6	2309	0.5	2039	1.1	2020	1.5
28TH	0409	1.8	0105	2.7	0221	3.1	0421	2.0	0103	0.7	0330	4.5	0457	5.6	0211	5.7	0144	6.7
	1021	0.2	0755	0.5	0917	0.5	0941	0.2	0524	1.7	0952	0.4	1132	0.4	0902	0.9	0834	1.5
	1635	1.7	1329	2.4	1445	2.9	1633	2.1	1101	0.4	1548	4.6	1715	5.6	1432	5.6	1401	6.8
	2227	0.2	1957	0.6	2121	0.6			1747	1.8	2155	0.6	2339	0.7	2112	1.1	2051	1.6
29F	0442	1.8	0139	2.7	0254	3.1	0000	0.4	0203	0.7	0404	4.4	0530	5.4	0248	5.6	0217	6.7
	1057	0.2	0830	0.5	0951	0.5	0454	1.9	0600	1.7	1026	0.5	1202	0.5	0935	1.0	0905	1.6
	1706	1.6	1404	2.4	1521	2.8	1016	0.2	1149	0.4	1621	4.5	1748	5.5	1509	5.6	1436	6.7
	2259	0.2	2029	0.6	2151	0.6	1706	2.1	1824	1.8	2227	0.7			2144	1.2	2121	1.7
30SA	0513	1.8	0212	2.7	0328	3.1	0044	0.4	0015	0.7	0437	4.3	0006	0.8	0324	5.6	0251	6.7
	1130	0.2	0902	0.5	1023	0.6	0525	1.9	0635	1.7	1057	0.5	0603	5.3	1006	1.1	0937	1.6
	1735	1.6	1439	2.4	1557	2.8	1054	0.1	1228	0.4	1654	4.4	1230	0.5	1545	5.5	1509	6.6
	2331	0.2	2100	0.6	2221	0.6	1739	2.0	1901	1.8	2300	0.7	1822	5.4	2215	1.2	2154	1.7
31SU	0547	1.8	0247	2.6	0402	3.1	0127	0.4	0022	0.7	0511	4.2	0036	0.8	0359	5.5	0326	6.6
	1203	0.1	0935	0.6	1054	0.6	0555	1.8	0712	1.7	1128	0.5	0637	5.2	1040	1.1	1012	1.7
	1808	1.5	1515	2.4	1634	2.8	1136	0.1	1257	0.4	1730	4.3	1301	0.5	1622	5.4	1545	6.5
			2135	0.6	2254	0.6	1816	2.0	1940	1.8	2337	0.8	1858	5.3	2251	1.3	2231	1.9

FRANCE, SPAIN, PORTUGAL & GIBRALTAR Time Zone -0100
Dieppe * Le Havre * Cherbourg * St Helier * St Malo * Brest * Pointe de Grave * Lisboa * Gibraltar

TIDE TABLES JANUARY 2000

DIEPPE		LE HAVRE		CHERBOURG		ST HELIER JERSEY		ST MALO		BREST		POINTE DE GRAVE		LISBOA		GIBRALTAR		
Time	m	Time	m	Time	m	Time	m	Time	m	Time	m	Time	m	Time	m	Time	m	
0136	2.3	0653	6.6	0442	4.9	0254	8.3	0247	9.2	0706	2.7	0112	4.3	0558	1.5	0506	0.4	**1 SA**
0737	7.3	1325	2.7	1132	2.5	0930	3.8	0924	4.2	1317	5.6	0653	2.0	1230	3.1	1130	0.8	
1416	2.4	1915	6.4	1706	4.9	1521	9.3	1512	9.3	1945	2.6	1340	4.4	1828	1.3	1742	0.3	
2009	7.2					2207	3.6	2201	4.0			1931	1.9					
0251	2.3	0154	2.6	0003	2.3	0403	8.5	0351	9.5	0152	5.6	0207	4.4	0103	3.2	0002	0.8	**2 SU**
0839	7.5	0803	6.7	0551	5.1	1038	3.6	1027	4.0	0809	2.6	0753	1.9	0652	1.4	0551	0.3	
1527	2.4	1425	2.5	1236	2.3	1627	8.6	1614	9.6	1417	5.7	1433	4.4	1327	3.2	1216	0.8	
2108	7.5	2033	6.5	1813	5.0	2309	3.3	2257	3.7	2039	2.4	2024	1.8	1912	1.2	1821	0.3	
0353	2.1	0248	2.4	0100	2.2	0500	8.9	0446	9.9	0243	5.4	0254	4.6	0152	3.3	0046	0.8	**3 M**
0931	7.8	0902	6.9	0644	5.3	1135	3.2	1121	3.6	0900	2.3	0845	1.8	0736	1.2	0631	0.3	
1621	1.9	1516	2.2	1327	2.1	1722	8.9	1706	9.9	1506	5.9	1517	4.6	1415	3.3	1257	0.9	
2155	7.8	2130	6.8	1905	5.2			2344	3.4	2124	2.2	2110	1.7	1951	1.1	1857	0.3	
0441	1.9	0336	2.2	0145	2.0	0000	3.0	0533	10.3	0327	6.1	0333	4.7	0236	3.4	0126	0.8	**4 TU**
1015	8.1	0945	7.1	0727	5.6	0548	9.3	1206	3.2	0944	2.1	0929	1.6	0815	1.1	0709	0.3	
1704	1.7	1600	2.0	1410	1.9	1224	2.8	1751	10.2	1547	6.1	1554	4.7	1458	3.3	1335	0.9	
2236	8.1	2209	7.0	1948	5.4	1809	9.3			2205	2.0	2151	1.6	2027	1.0	1933	0.2	
0522	1.7	0418	2.1	0226	1.8	0045	2.7	0027	3.1	0406	6.3	0409	4.9	0316	3.5	0203	0.9	**5 W**
1054	8.4	1015	7.3	0806	5.8	0630	9.7	0614	10.6	1024	1.9	1009	1.5	0851	1.0	0745	0.3	
1743	1.5	1642	1.8	1448	1.7	1306	2.4	1248	2.9	1624	6.3	1629	4.8	1538	3.4	1412	0.9	
2315	8.3	2239	7.2	2027	5.6	1850	9.6	1833	10.5	2242	1.9	2227	1.5	2103	0.9	2009	0.2	
0600	1.6	0459	1.9	0303	1.7	0124	2.4	0107	2.9	0442	6.5	0443	5.0	0354	3.6	0240	0.9	**6 TH**
1130	8.6	1035	7.4	0843	5.9	0709	9.9	0652	10.9	1100	1.8	1046	1.4	0927	0.9	0821	0.2	●
1820	1.3	1722	1.7	1525	1.5	1344	2.2	1330	2.6	1659	6.4	1702	4.9	1615	3.4	1449	0.9	
2351	8.5	2305	7.3	2104	5.7	1927	9.8	1910	10.8	2316	1.8	2303	1.4	2137	0.9	2046	0.2	
0636	1.5	0540	1.8	0340	1.6	0201	2.2	0148	2.7	0515	6.6	0517	5.1	0430	3.6	0316	0.9	**7 F**
1206	8.7	1059	7.5	0918	6.0	0744	10.1	0728	11.1	1136	1.7	1121	1.4	1002	0.8	0857	0.2	
1856	1.2	1802	1.6	1600	1.4	1421	2.1	1410	2.4	1732	6.5	1735	4.9	1651	3.4	1526	0.9	
		2332	7.4	2139	5.8	2003	9.9	1945	11.0	2351	1.7	2337	1.4	2212	0.8	2122	0.2	
0027	8.6	0620	1.8	0415	1.6	0236	2.1	0227	2.6	0549	6.7	0551	5.1	0505	3.7	0353	0.9	**8 SA**
0712	1.4	1128	7.6	0952	6.0	0818	10.2	0802	11.3	1210	1.6	1157	1.3	1036	0.8	0933	0.2	
1241	8.7	1841	1.6	1636	1.3	1455	1.9	1449	2.3	1805	6.5	1809	4.9	1726	3.4	1603	0.9	
1931	1.2			2212	5.8	2036	10.0	2020	11.1					2246	0.8	2158	0.2	
0101	8.6	0002	7.5	0451	1.6	0309	2.1	0305	2.5	0024	1.7	0011	1.4	0539	3.6	0430	0.9	**9 SU**
0746	1.4	0700	1.8	1024	6.0	0850	10.2	0834	11.4	0623	6.7	0625	5.1	1112	0.8	1008	0.2	
1315	8.7	1158	7.6	1712	1.3	1529	1.9	1527	2.2	1245	1.6	1232	1.3	1759	3.4	1641	0.9	
2006	1.1	1918	1.5	2245	5.8	2109	9.9	2052	11.2	1838	6.4	1842	4.9	2321	0.8	2233	0.2	
0135	8.5	0030	7.5	0527	1.6	0342	2.0	0340	2.5	0100	1.8	0046	1.4	0611	3.6	0508	0.9	**10 M**
0821	1.4	0737	1.8	1055	5.9	0922	10.1	0906	11.4	0657	6.6	0700	5.1	1148	0.8	1044	0.2	
1349	8.6	1226	7.6	1748	1.4	1603	2.0	1602	2.3	1321	1.7	1308	1.3	1831	3.3	1720	0.9	
2040	1.2	1954	1.6	2317	5.7	2142	9.8	2124	11.1	1912	6.3	1918	4.8	2358	0.9	2309	0.2	
0209	8.5	0054	7.4	0603	1.7	0415	2.3	0414	2.7	0136	1.9	0123	1.5	0644	3.5	0547	0.9	**11 TU**
0855	1.5	0813	1.9	1128	5.9	0956	10.0	0938	11.3	0733	6.5	0737	5.0	1227	0.9	1122	0.2	
1423	8.4	1254	7.5	1826	1.5	1637	2.3	1636	2.5	1400	1.8	1345	1.4	1906	3.3	1802	0.8	
2115	1.3	2029	1.7	2352	5.6	2217	9.6	2158	10.9	1949	6.2	1955	4.7			2349	0.2	
0245	8.3	0121	7.3	0641	1.9	0449	2.6	0446	2.9	0216	2.0	0203	1.5	0039	1.0	0630	0.9	**12 W**
0931	1.6	0848	2.0	1205	5.7	1032	9.7	1013	11.1	0812	6.3	0818	4.8	0719	3.5	1206	0.3	
1500	8.2	1330	7.4	1906	1.6	1714	2.5	1710	2.8	1442	2.0	1427	1.5	1310	1.0	1849	0.8	
2153	1.5	2105	1.8			2255	9.3	2236	10.6	2030	6.0	2038	4.5	1945	3.2			
0324	8.1	0200	7.1	0032	5.4	0528	2.9	0520	3.3	0300	2.2	0247	1.6	0125	1.1	0035	0.3	**13 TH**
1011	1.8	0927	2.1	0723	2.0	1112	9.3	1054	10.6	0856	6.1	0906	4.7	0801	3.3	0718	0.8	
1543	8.0	1416	7.2	1248	5.5	1756	2.9	1748	3.2	1529	2.2	1515	1.6	1400	1.1	1258	0.3	
2236	1.8	2147	2.0	1951	1.8	2339	9.0	2321	10.2	2118	5.8	2132	4.4	2033	3.1	1945	0.8	
0412	7.9	0252	6.9	0121	5.3	0614	3.3	0603	3.7	0351	2.4	0339	1.7	0221	1.2	0130	0.3	**14 F**
1059	2.1	1014	2.3	0812	2.2	1202	9.0	1145	10.1	0948	5.9	1005	4.5	0854	3.2	0814	0.8	
1636	7.6	1516	6.9	1343	5.3	1846	3.3	1839	3.6	1624	2.3	1611	1.7	1502	1.2	1402	0.3	
2329	2.0	2238	2.2	2044	2.0					2218	5.6	2242	4.3	2134	3.1	2051	0.8	
0511	7.6	0402	6.8	0221	5.1	0034	8.7	0021	9.8	0451	2.5	0442	1.8	0331	1.3	0240	0.3	**15 SA**
1158	2.3	1110	2.5	0914	2.3	0712	3.5	0703	4.0	1054	5.8	1118	4.5	1001	3.2	0918	0.8	
1744	7.4	1633	6.7	1449	5.2	1306	8.7	1253	9.7	1726	2.4	1715	1.8	1614	1.2	1521	0.3	
		2339	2.3	2148	2.1	1950	3.4	1949	3.9	2330	5.6			2248	3.1	2204	0.8	

• • Time Zone -0100. For UT subtract 1 hour. For European summer time (shaded) 26/3-29/10 add 1 hour • •

JANUARY 2000 TIDE TABLES

• • Time Zone -0100. For UT subtract 1 hour. For European summer time (shaded) 26/3-29/10 add 1 hour • •

	DIEPPE		LE HAVRE		CHERBOURG		ST HELIER JERSEY		ST MALO		BREST		POINTE DE GRAVE		LISBOA		GIBRALTAR	
	Time	m	Time	m	Time	m	Time	m	Time	m	Time	m	Time	m	Time	m	Time	m
16 SU	0033	2.2	0524	6.7	0330	5.1	0145	8.6	0137	9.6	0600	2.5	0000	4.3	0449	1.3	0359	0.3
	0623	7.5	1217	2.5	1026	2.3	0827	3.6	0821	4.1	1209	5.8	0551	1.8	1120	3.2	1027	0.8
	1315	2.3	1757	6.7	1602	5.1	1424	8.7	1416	9.6	1837	2.4	1235	4.5	1727	1.1	1642	0.2
	1903	7.4			2300	2.1	2109	3.4	2109	3.8			1826	1.7			2318	0.8
17 M	0155	2.2	0050	2.3	0442	5.2	0305	8.8	0258	9.8	0048	5.8	0115	4.5	0006	3.2	0511	0.2
	0739	7.7	0639	6.9	1142	2.1	0951	3.3	0945	3.7	0714	2.3	0703	1.7	0603	1.2	1135	0.9
	1440	2.1	1333	2.3	1718	5.3	1545	9.0	1536	10.0	1326	6.0	1345	4.7	1238	3.3	1748	0.2
	2018	7.7	1909	7.0			2229	3.0	2227	3.3	1948	2.1	1935	1.6	1833	1.0		
18 TU	0313	1.9	0208	2.2	0012	1.9	0421	9.3	0411	10.4	0200	6.1	0219	4.8	0116	3.4	0023	0.8
	0849	8.1	0738	7.2	0554	5.5	1108	2.7	1101	3.1	0824	2.0	0810	1.5	0708	0.9	0611	0.2
	1551	1.6	1452	2.0	1253	1.7	1657	9.5	1646	10.7	1434	6.3	1448	4.9	1346	3.5	1238	0.9
	2126	8.2	2012	7.2	1832	5.5	2339	2.4	2335	2.7	2054	1.8	2038	1.4	1932	0.8	1845	0.1
19 W	0418	1.5	0324	1.8	0120	1.6	0527	9.9	0514	11.2	0303	6.5	0316	5.0	0216	3.6	0120	0.8
	0952	8.6	0830	7.5	0700	5.8	1215	2.0	1208	2.3	0927	1.6	0911	1.2	0805	0.7	0705	0.1
	1653	1.2	1604	1.5	1356	1.3	1802	10.1	1748	11.4	1533	6.7	1545	5.1	1445	3.6	1335	0.9
	2225	8.7	2128	7.5	1936	5.8					2151	1.4	2134	1.2	2024	0.7	1936	0.0
20 TH	0518	1.1	0433	1.5	0220	1.3	0042	1.8	0037	2.0	0358	6.9	0409	5.3	0310	3.9	0213	0.9
O	1048	9.0	0917	7.8	0758	6.1	0627	10.6	0611	11.9	1023	1.2	1006	1.0	0857	0.5	0755	0.1
	1751	0.8	1707	1.1	1452	0.9	1315	1.4	1309	1.7	1627	7.0	1636	5.3	1539	3.8	1428	1.0
	2318	9.0	2251	7.7	2031	6.1	1859	10.7	1842	12.0	2244	1.1	2226	1.0	2114	0.6	2025	0.0
21 F	0615	0.8	0532	1.2	0314	1.0	0139	1.3	0135	1.5	0449	7.2	0458	5.5	0400	4.0	0303	1.0
	1139	9.3	1105	7.9	0850	6.4	0719	11.1	0703	12.4	1115	0.9	1057	0.9	0945	0.4	0843	0.0
	1845	0.4	1802	0.7	1543	0.7	1409	0.9	1405	1.1	1716	7.2	1725	5.4	1628	3.9	1520	1.0
			2351	7.9	2121	6.3	1951	11.1	1933	12.3	2334	0.9	2315	0.9	2200	0.5	2112	-0.0
22 SA	0008	9.3	0624	0.9	0403	0.8	0230	1.0	0228	1.1	0537	7.4	0546	5.6	0448	4.1	0352	1.0
	0709	0.5	1205	8.1	0938	6.5	0808	11.4	0752	12.7	1204	0.7	1146	0.8	1033	0.4	0930	0.0
	1228	9.5	1851	0.5	1631	0.5	1500	0.7	1456	0.8	1803	7.3	1811	5.4	1715	3.9	1609	1.0
	1936	0.2			2208	6.4	2037	11.2	2021	12.5					2245	0.5	2157	0.0
23 SU	0054	9.4	0042	8.0	0451	0.8	0317	0.9	0316	0.9	0021	0.9	0002	0.9	0533	4.1	0439	1.0
	0757	0.4	0712	0.8	1023	6.6	0853	11.5	0837	12.8	0624	7.4	0631	5.5	1118	0.4	1017	1.0
	1314	9.5	1255	8.1	1717	0.5	1545	0.7	1542	0.8	1251	0.8	1233	0.8	1759	3.8	1657	1.0
	2021	0.1	1936	0.5	2251	6.3	2121	11.2	2104	12.4	1848	7.2	1856	5.3	2328	0.6	2243	0.0
24 M	0139	9.4	0130	8.0	0534	0.9	0400	1.0	0400	1.1	0107	1.0	0047	0.9	0616	4.1	0527	1.0
	0840	0.4	0754	0.9	1106	6.5	0935	11.3	0919	12.6	0707	7.3	0715	5.4	1202	0.6	1103	0.1
	1357	9.3	1339	8.0	1800	0.7	1627	0.9	1624	1.0	1336	1.0	1318	0.9	1842	3.7	1745	0.9
	2103	0.2	2017	0.6	2333	6.1	2201	10.8	2145	12.0	1930	6.9	1939	5.1			2327	0.1
25 TU	0222	9.2	0212	7.9	0616	1.1	0440	1.3	0439	1.5	0151	1.2	0132	1.0	0011	0.7	0614	0.9
	0920	0.6	0834	1.1	1146	6.2	1013	10.9	0959	12.1	0749	7.0	0759	5.2	0659	3.9	1151	0.1
	1439	9.0	1416	7.8	1842	1.0	1706	1.4	1701	1.5	1419	1.3	1403	1.0	1245	0.8	1833	0.9
	2141	0.5	2054	1.0			2239	10.3	2224	11.5	2012	6.6	2022	4.9	1925	3.5		
26 W	0303	8.8	0249	7.7	0013	5.9	0518	1.8	0515	2.0	0234	1.6	0218	1.2	0055	0.9	0013	0.2
	0957	0.9	0911	1.5	0657	1.5	1051	10.3	1038	11.5	0830	6.6	0843	4.9	0742	3.7	0702	0.9
	1520	8.6	1443	7.5	1226	5.9	1742	2.0	1736	2.2	1503	1.7	1448	1.3	1331	1.0	1240	0.2
	2217	0.9	2130	1.6	1922	1.4	2315	9.7	2303	10.8	2054	6.2	2108	4.6	2009	3.3	1923	0.8
27 TH	0344	8.4	0321	7.3	0054	5.6	0553	2.5	0548	2.7	0318	2.0	0305	1.5	0142	1.2	0103	0.3
	1033	1.4	0946	1.9	0737	1.8	1127	9.6	1118	10.7	0912	6.2	0930	4.6	0830	3.4	0752	0.8
	1602	8.1	1502	7.1	1307	5.5	1818	2.7	1809	3.0	1548	2.2	1537	1.6	1421	1.2	1337	0.3
	2254	1.5	2205	2.0	2003	1.8	2354	9.0	2345	10.1	2139	5.8	2159	4.3	2059	3.1	2017	0.7
28 F	0428	7.8	0349	7.0	0138	5.2	0631	3.1	0625	3.4	0405	2.4	0356	1.7	0236	1.4	0202	0.3
	1113	1.9	1025	2.4	0821	2.2	1209	8.9	1203	9.9	0959	5.7	1025	4.3	0923	3.2	0848	0.8
	1648	7.4	1544	6.7	1354	5.2	1857	3.3	1849	3.7	1638	2.6	1631	1.8	1519	1.4	1451	0.3
	2336	2.1	2247	2.5	2049	2.2					2233	5.4	2302	4.1	2158	3.0	2120	0.7
29 SA	0520	7.2	0431	6.6	0230	5.0	0041	8.4	0037	9.4	0500	2.8	0454	2.0	0345	1.6	0324	0.3
	1200	2.4	1115	2.8	0914	2.5	0718	3.7	0712	4.1	1058	5.4	1133	4.1	1028	3.0	0951	0.8
	1751	6.9	1643	6.4	1451	4.8	1303	8.2	1300	9.2	1741	2.9	1734	2.0	1629	1.5	1624	0.3
					2342	2.9	1949	3.9	1942	4.3	2343	5.2			2309	2.9	2231	0.7
30 SU	0027	2.6	0533	6.4	0333	4.8	0145	8.0	0144	8.9	0609	2.9	0014	4.0	0503	1.6	0449	0.4
	0635	6.9	1221	3.0	1022	2.7	0821	4.1	0814	4.5	1218	5.2	0601	2.1	1144	2.9	1100	0.7
	1300	2.8	1800	6.1	1601	4.6	1418	7.8	1415	8.7	1857	2.9	1250	4.0	1739	1.5	1732	0.3
	1919	6.7			2257	2.7	2101	4.1	2052	4.6			1844	2.1			2341	0.7
31 M	0139	2.8	0053	3.0	0453	4.8	0309	7.8	0303	8.8	0106	5.3	0124	4.1	0022	3.0	0550	0.3
O	0757	6.8	0646	6.3	1142	2.7	0942	4.1	0930	4.6	0727	2.9	0727	2.1	0615	1.5	1203	0.8
	1430	2.8	1333	3.0	1730	4.7	1543	7.8	1534	8.7	1342	5.3	1357	4.1	1255	2.9	1822	0.3
	2033	6.8	1924	6.2			2222	4.0	2209	4.5	2006	2.8	1949	2.0	1839	1.5		

FRANCE, SPAIN, PORTUGAL & GIBRALTAR Time Zone -0100
Dieppe * Le Havre * Cherbourg * St Helier * St Malo * Brest * Pointe de Grave * Lisboa * Gibraltar
TIDE TABLES FEBRUARY 2000

DIEPPE		LE HAVRE		CHERBOURG		ST HELIER JERSEY		ST MALO		BREST		POINTE DE GRAVE		LISBOA		GIBRALTAR		Day
Time	m	Time	m	Time	m	Time	m	Time	m	Time	m	Time	m	Time	m	Time	m	
0308	2.8	0201	2.9	0015	2.6	0425	8.1	0414	9.1	0214	5.5	0221	4.3	0124	3.1	0038	0.7	1 TU
0859	7.1	0759	6.5	0610	4.9	1059	3.8	1042	4.2	0831	2.7	0814	2.0	0710	1.4	0637	0.3	
1544	2.5	1436	2.7	1253	2.4	1654	8.2	1642	9.1	1442	5.5	1451	4.3	1352	3.1	1254	0.8	
2128	7.2	2042	6.4	1842	4.9	2330	3.6	2312	4.1	2100	2.6	2043	1.9	1927	1.3	1903	0.2	
0408	2.4	0259	2.7	0117	2.3	0524	8.6	0511	9.6	0305	5.8	0308	4.5	0214	3.3	0124	0.8	2 W
0948	7.5	0857	6.8	0706	5.2	1158	3.2	1141	3.8	0921	2.4	0906	1.8	0755	1.2	0716	0.3	
1635	2.1	1530	2.4	1345	2.1	1748	8.7	1734	9.6	1528	5.8	1534	4.5	1439	3.2	1337	0.8	
2214	7.6	2134	6.8	1932	5.1					2143	2.3	2128	1.7	2008	1.2	1941	0.2	
0454	2.1	0349	2.3	0204	2.1	0022	3.0	0004	3.6	0346	6.1	0348	4.7	0257	3.4	0204	0.8	3 TH
1031	7.9	0938	7.1	0749	5.5	0610	9.1	0557	10.1	1003	2.1	0948	1.6	0834	1.0	0752	0.2	
1718	1.7	1618	2.0	1427	1.8	1245	2.7	1230	3.2	1606	6.1	1612	4.7	1520	3.3	1415	0.9	
2254	8.0	2212	7.1	2013	5.4	1833	9.1	1817	10.2	2221	2.0	2207	1.5	2045	1.0	2016	0.1	
0536	1.7	0437	2.1	0245	1.8	0106	2.6	0050	3.1	0424	6.4	0425	4.9	0336	3.5	0241	0.9	4 F
1110	8.3	1010	7.4	0827	5.7	0651	9.6	0636	10.6	1041	1.8	1027	1.4	0911	0.9	0827	0.2	
1758	1.4	1704	1.5	1506	1.5	1327	2.2	1314	2.7	1642	6.3	1647	4.8	1558	3.4	1451	0.9	
2331	8.4	2245	7.3	2050	5.6	1911	9.6	1855	10.7	2257	1.8	2244	1.4	2121	0.9	2050	0.1	
0616	1.5	0524	1.8	0322	1.6	0146	2.2	0133	2.6	0458	6.6	0500	5.1	0412	3.6	0315	0.9	5 SA
1147	8.6	1040	7.6	0903	5.9	0727	9.9	0712	11.1	1117	1.6	1103	1.3	0945	0.8	0900	0.1	
1838	1.1	1748	1.5	1542	1.2	1406	1.9	1357	2.2	1721	6.5	1721	4.9	1633	3.5	1527	0.9	●
		2317	7.5	2124	5.8	1947	9.9	1932	11.1	2332	1.6	2318	1.3	2155	0.7	2122	0.1	
0008	8.6	0607	1.4	0358	1.4	0223	1.9	0215	2.2	0532	6.8	0535	5.2	0446	3.7	0350	0.9	6 SU
0655	1.2	1109	7.7	0936	6.0	0802	10.2	0748	11.5	1151	1.4	1137	1.2	1019	0.7	0932	0.1	
1224	8.8	1830	1.3	1618	1.1	1443	1.6	1438	1.8	1748	6.6	1754	5.0	1706	3.5	1602	0.9	
1916	0.9	2348	7.6	2156	5.9	2021	10.1	2006	11.4			2352	1.2	2230	0.7	2154	0.1	
0044	8.8	0648	1.5	0434	1.3	0258	1.7	0255	2.0	0007	1.5	0609	5.2	0518	3.8	0424	0.9	7 M
0733	1.1	1131	7.8	1007	6.1	0836	10.5	0821	11.8	0606	6.9	1211	1.1	1054	0.6	1004	0.1	
1259	8.9	1908	1.2	1654	1.0	1518	1.5	1517	1.6	1227	1.3	1827	5.0	1738	3.5	1637	0.9	
1954	0.8			2227	6.0	2054	10.3	2039	11.6	1821	6.7			2304	0.6	2226	0.1	
0119	8.8	0000	7.6	0509	1.2	0331	1.6	0333	1.8	0042	1.4	0026	1.1	0551	3.8	0459	0.9	8 TU
0809	1.0	0726	1.4	1038	6.2	0909	10.6	0854	11.9	0640	6.9	0643	5.2	1128	0.6	1036	0.1	
1334	8.8	1152	7.8	1730	1.0	1551	1.5	1554	1.5	1303	1.3	1246	1.1	1809	3.5	1714	0.9	
2029	0.8	1944	1.2	2257	6.0	2129	10.4	2112	11.7	1855	6.7	1859	4.9	2340	0.7	2258	0.1	
0153	8.8	0012	7.6	0545	1.3	0404	1.7	0408	1.9	0119	1.5	0101	1.2	0623	3.7	0535	0.9	9 W
0844	1.0	0800	1.5	1109	6.2	0944	10.6	0926	11.9	0715	6.9	0718	5.1	1205	0.6	1112	0.1	
1409	8.8	1220	7.8	1806	1.1	1625	1.6	1629	1.7	1341	1.4	1322	1.1	1842	3.5	1752	0.9	
2103	0.9	2018	1.3	2330	5.9	2203	10.3	2145	11.6	1930	6.6	1933	4.8			2333	0.1	
0227	8.7	0041	7.6	0621	1.4	0438	1.8	0441	2.2	0157	1.6	0139	1.2	0018	0.6	0614	0.9	10 TH
0918	1.2	0833	1.6	1144	6.0	1019	10.3	1000	11.6	0752	6.7	0754	5.0	0657	3.6	1149	0.1	
1444	8.6	1255	7.7	1843	1.3	1700	1.8	1702	2.1	1421	1.6	1402	1.2	1245	0.8	1834	0.8	
2138	1.1	2049	1.4			2239	10.0	2220	11.2	2009	6.4	2012	4.7	1919	3.4			
0304	8.5	0119	7.4	0006	5.8	0514	2.2	0513	2.6	0239	1.8	0222	1.3	0101	0.9	0012	0.2	11 F
0954	1.4	0906	1.7	0700	1.6	1057	9.9	1036	11.2	0833	6.4	0837	4.8	0736	3.5	0657	0.8	
1522	8.3	1339	7.5	1224	5.8	1736	2.3	1737	2.7	1504	1.9	1447	1.4	1331	0.9	1233	0.2	
2215	1.5	2124	1.7	1924	1.5	2318	9.6	2300	10.8	2051	6.1	2058	4.5	2003	3.3	1923	0.8	
0345	8.2	0208	7.2	0049	5.6	0554	2.7	0549	3.1	0326	2.1	0312	1.5	0152	1.1	0100	0.2	12 SA
1035	1.7	0945	2.0	0745	1.9	1140	9.4	1120	10.6	0920	6.1	0931	4.6	0825	3.3	0748	0.8	
1608	7.9	1436	7.2	1312	5.6	1819	2.8	1818	3.3	1554	2.1	1540	1.6	1427	1.1	1327	0.2	
2300	1.8	2208	2.0	2011	1.8			2349	10.1	2144	5.8	2200	4.3	2059	3.2	2022	0.7	
0436	7.8	0314	6.9	0143	5.3	0005	9.1	0636	3.7	0421	2.3	0411	1.7	0257	1.2	0203	0.3	13 SU
1127	2.1	1036	2.3	0840	2.1	0643	3.2	1218	9.9	1020	5.8	1043	4.4	0930	3.2	0849	0.8	
1709	7.5	1554	6.8	1415	5.2	1235	8.9	1916	3.8	1654	2.4	1644	1.8	1537	1.2	1445	0.3	
		2304	2.3	2112	2.1	1915	3.3			2253	5.6	2325	4.2	2213	3.1	2136	0.7	
0000	2.2	0445	6.7	0251	5.1	0108	8.6	0057	9.6	0530	2.5	0522	1.8	0418	1.3	0336	0.3	14 M
0545	7.4	1141	2.5	0952	2.2	0752	3.5	0746	4.1	1138	5.6	1211	4.3	1054	3.1	1004	0.7	
1239	2.4	1733	6.7	1532	5.0	1350	8.5	1340	9.4	1807	2.6	1759	1.8	1659	1.3	1630	0.2	
1832	7.2			2228	2.2	2034	3.6	2036	4.1					2342	3.1	2300	0.7	
0125	2.4	0017	2.5	0412	5.1	0231	8.4	0227	9.4	0020	5.6	0054	4.3	0545	1.2	0508	0.2	15 TU
0711	7.3	0615	6.7	1117	2.2	0923	3.5	0918	4.0	0650	2.5	0642	1.8	1224	3.1	1125	0.8	
1418	2.1	1304	2.5	1700	5.0	1521	8.5	1518	9.5	1307	5.7	1333	4.5	1816	1.2	1749	0.2	
1957	7.3	1900	6.8	2354	2.1	2206	3.4	2206	3.8	1928	2.4	1917	1.8					

• • Time Zone -0100. For UT subtract 1 hour. For European summer time (shaded) 26/3-29/10 add 1 hour • •

FEBRUARY 2000 TIDE TABLES

• • Time Zone -0100. For UT subtract 1 hour. For European summer time (shaded) 26/3-29/10 add 1 hour • •

	DIEPPE		LE HAVRE		CHERBOURG		ST HELIER JERSEY		ST MALO		BREST		POINTE DE GRAVE		LISBOA		GIBRALTAR	
	Time	m	Time	m	Time	m	Time	m	Time	m	Time	m	Time	m	Time	m	Time	m
16 W	0256	2.2	0145	2.5	0538	5.2	0401	8.7	0355	9.9	0145	5.8	0207	4.6	0102	3.3	0016	0.8
	0831	7.6	0727	7.0	1240	1.9	1051	3.0	1050	3.5	0810	2.2	0758	1.6	0657	1.0	0614	0.2
	1537	1.9	1436	2.2	1827	5.3	1646	9.0	1639	10.1	1424	6.0	1442	4.7	1338	3.3	1236	0.8
	2112	7.8	2014	7.1			2326	2.8	2326	3.1	2041	2.0	2026	1.5	1921	1.0	1848	0.1
17 TH	0406	1.7	0312	2.1	0111	1.8	0516	9.4	0506	10.7	0253	6.3	0309	4.9	0206	3.6	0117	0.8
	0939	8.2	0828	7.3	0653	5.6	1204	2.3	1203	2.6	0917	1.7	0903	1.3	0757	0.8	0707	0.1
	1642	1.3	1554	1.7	1348	1.4	1754	9.7	1742	11.0	1525	6.4	1539	5.0	1437	3.5	1335	0.9
	2213	8.4	2133	7.4	1931	5.6					2141	1.6	2124	1.3	2015	0.8	1936	0.1
18 F	0509	1.2	0423	1.6	0212	1.4	0031	2.0	0030	2.3	0349	6.7	0402	5.2	0300	3.8	0209	0.9
	1037	8.7	0938	7.6	0751	5.9	0617	10.2	0604	11.6	1013	1.3	0958	1.0	0848	0.6	0754	0.1
	1741	0.7	1657	1.1	1443	1.0	1305	1.5	1303	1.5	1617	6.8	1629	5.2	1528	3.7	1427	1.0
	2306	8.9	2242	7.7	2024	6.0	1850	10.4	1836	11.7	2233	1.2	2215	1.0	2103	0.6	2021	0.0
19 SA O	0606	0.7	0521	1.1	0305	1.0	0127	1.4	0127	1.5	0439	7.1	0449	5.4	0348	4.0	0257	1.0
	1127	9.1	1058	7.9	0841	6.2	0708	10.9	0655	12.3	1103	0.9	1047	0.8	0935	0.4	0839	-0.0
	1834	0.3	1749	0.7	1532	0.6	1358	0.9	1356	1.0	1704	7.1	1714	5.3	1614	3.8	1514	1.0
	2354	9.3	2339	8.0	2109	6.2	1938	10.9	1924	12.3	2321	0.9	2302	0.9	2147	0.5	2103	-0.0
20 SU	0656	0.4	0611	0.8	0351	0.8	0217	0.9	0216	1.1	0524	7.4	0533	5.5	0432	4.1	0341	1.0
	1213	9.4	1154	8.1	0925	6.5	0754	11.3	0741	12.7	1149	0.7	1131	0.7	1017	0.4	0921	-0.0
	1921	0.1	1836	0.4	1617	0.4	1446	0.6	1443	0.6	1747	7.3	1755	5.3	1657	3.9	1558	1.0
					2151	6.3	2021	11.2	2008	12.5			2345	0.8	2228	0.5	2144	-0.0
21 M	0038	9.4	0027	8.1	0435	0.7	0301	0.7	0301	0.8	0006	0.8	0614	5.5	0514	4.1	0424	1.0
	0741	0.2	0655	0.7	1006	6.5	0836	11.5	0823	12.8	0606	7.4	1214	0.7	1057	0.4	1002	-0.0
	1256	9.5	1241	8.1	1659	0.5	1528	0.5	1525	0.6	1232	0.7	1834	5.3	1737	3.9	1641	1.0
	2003	0.0	1917	0.4	2230	6.3	2101	11.3	2048	12.5	1827	7.2			2307	0.5	2222	0.0
22 TU	0119	9.5	0111	8.1	0515	0.7	0341	0.7	0341	0.8	0047	0.8	0027	0.8	0554	4.1	0504	1.0
	0821	0.2	0735	0.8	1044	6.5	0915	11.4	0901	12.7	0645	7.3	0652	5.4	1135	0.5	1041	0.0
	1336	9.4	1321	8.1	1737	0.6	1606	0.7	1603	0.8	1312	0.9	1254	0.8	1815	3.8	1722	1.0
	2040	0.1	1954	0.6	2307	6.2	2137	11.0	2124	12.2	1905	7.0	1911	5.1	2345	0.6	2300	0.0
23 W	0157	9.3	0148	7.9	0552	1.0	0417	1.0	0416	1.1	0127	1.1	0108	0.9	0633	3.9	0544	1.0
	0856	0.4	0809	1.0	1119	6.3	0950	11.1	0936	12.3	0722	7.1	0729	5.2	1212	0.7	1120	0.1
	1414	9.2	1352	7.8	1813	1.0	1639	1.1	1636	1.3	1351	1.2	1334	0.9	1853	3.6	1802	0.9
	2113	0.5	2027	1.0	2342	6.0	2211	10.6	2157	11.8	1941	6.7	1946	4.9			2336	0.1
24 TH	0234	9.0	0217	7.7	0627	1.3	0449	1.4	0447	1.7	0205	1.4	0148	1.0	0023	0.8	0624	0.9
	0927	0.8	0840	1.4	1154	6.0	1022	10.5	1010	11.7	0757	6.7	0803	4.9	0710	3.7	1158	0.1
	1449	8.8	1348	7.6	1846	1.4	1709	1.7	1704	2.0	1427	1.6	1413	1.2	1249	0.9	1842	0.8
	2144	0.9	2054	1.5			2242	10.0	2230	11.1	2015	6.3	2021	4.6	1931	3.4		
25 F	0309	8.5	0226	7.4	0016	5.7	0519	2.1	0515	2.4	0242	1.8	0229	1.3	0102	1.0	0014	0.2
	0957	1.2	0906	1.8	0700	1.7	1054	9.8	1043	10.9	0832	6.2	0839	4.6	0750	3.4	0705	0.8
	1524	8.2	1409	7.3	1229	5.6	1736	2.4	1731	2.8	1505	2.1	1455	1.5	1328	1.2	1239	0.2
	2214	1.4	2119	2.0	1918	1.8	2314	9.3	2304	10.4	2051	5.9	2100	4.4	2012	3.2	1924	0.8
26 SA	0344	8.0	0240	7.1	0053	5.4	0548	2.8	0544	3.2	0321	2.3	0313	1.6	0145	1.3	0057	0.3
	1030	1.8	0934	2.3	0733	2.1	1127	9.0	1118	10.1	0909	5.8	0920	4.2	0833	3.1	0750	0.8
	1601	7.6	1452	6.9	1308	5.2	1805	3.2	1801	3.6	1545	2.6	1541	1.8	1415	1.4	1328	0.3
	2248	2.0	2151	2.5	1953	2.2	2350	8.6	2343	9.5	2135	5.5	2149	4.1	2100	3.0	2015	0.7
27 SU	0423	7.3	0324	6.7	0136	5.1	0624	3.5	0620	3.9	0406	2.7	0403	1.9	0240	1.5	0155	0.3
	1108	2.3	1013	2.7	0815	2.5	1209	8.2	1203	9.2	0956	5.3	1015	4.0	0930	2.9	0846	0.7
	1646	6.9	1546	6.4	1357	4.8	1843	3.9	1842	4.3	1637	3.0	1637	2.1	1516	1.6	1452	0.4
	2331	2.6	2236	3.0	2038	2.6					2234	5.2	2300	3.9	2206	2.8	2124	0.6
28 M	0517	6.7	0421	6.4	0234	4.8	0039	7.9	0038	8.7	0506	3.0	0506	2.1	0357	1.7	0356	0.4
	1158	2.8	1109	3.2	0912	2.7	0715	4.1	0712	4.6	1107	5.0	1142	3.8	1049	2.7	1005	0.6
	1803	6.4	1657	6.1	1506	4.5	1312	7.5	1311	8.4	1751	3.2	1748	2.3	1639	1.7	1652	0.4
			2343	3.3	2145	2.8	1947	4.4	1944	4.9					2331	2.8	2256	0.6
29 TU	0029	3.1	0539	6.1	0351	4.6	0206	7.4	0205	8.3	0005	5.0	0028	3.9	0528	1.6	0528	0.4
	0656	6.4	1228	3.3	1034	2.8	0838	4.4	0827	5.0	0632	3.1	0623	2.2	1218	2.8	1133	0.7
	1312	3.1	1828	6.0	1639	4.4	1454	7.3	1451	8.2	1255	5.0	1316	3.8	1800	1.6	1759	0.3
	1948	6.3			2318	2.9	2125	4.5	2112	5.1	1924	3.1	1908	2.2				

FRANCE, SPAIN, PORTUGAL & GIBRALTAR Time Zone -0100
Dieppe * Le Havre * Cherbourg * St Helier * St Malo * Brest * Pointe de Grave * Lisboa * Gibraltar

TIDE TABLES MARCH 2000

	DIEPPE		LE HAVRE		CHERBOURG		ST HELIER JERSEY		ST MALO		BREST		POINTE DE GRAVE		LISBOA		GIBRALTAR	
	Time	m	Time	m	Time	m	Time	m	Time	m	Time	m	Time	m	Time	m	Time	m
1 W	0202	3.2	0109	3.3	0528	4.6	0349	7.5	0339	8.4	0139	5.2	0143	4.0	0049	2.9	0015	0.7
	0819	6.6	0703	6.2	1207	2.7	1017	4.2	1000	4.8	0757	3.0	0739	2.1	0641	1.5	0621	0.3
	1456	3.0	1353	3.1	1815	4.6	1626	7.6	1616	8.5	1416	5.2	1422	4.0	1326	2.9	1238	0.7
	2055	6.7	1954	6.2			2258	4.1	2242	4.7	2032	2.8	2013	2.0	1900	1.4	1845	0.3
2 TH	0330	2.9	0224	3.0	0044	2.6	0458	8.1	0447	9.0	0239	5.5	0239	4.3	0146	3.1	0108	0.7
	0918	7.0	0812	6.5	0639	4.9	1130	3.6	1118	4.2	0856	2.6	0838	1.9	0732	1.3	0702	0.3
	1601	2.4	1459	2.7	1315	2.3	1726	8.2	1713	9.2	1506	5.6	1509	4.3	1415	3.1	1323	0.8
	2146	7.3	2057	6.7	1910	5.0	2358	3.4	2345	4.0	2119	2.5	2103	1.8	1945	1.2	1923	0.2
3 F	0424	2.3	0324	2.6	0139	2.2	0547	8.7	0534	9.8	0323	5.9	0323	4.6	0231	3.3	0147	0.8
	1005	7.6	0903	6.9	0726	5.2	1221	2.9	1211	3.4	0939	2.2	0924	1.6	0812	1.1	0736	0.2
	1649	1.9	1553	2.2	1401	1.9	1810	8.9	1757	10.0	1545	5.9	1549	4.6	1457	3.2	1400	0.8
	2228	7.8	2143	7.1	1951	5.3					2158	2.1	2144	1.5	2024	1.0	1957	0.1
4 SA ●	0509	1.8	0415	2.1	0221	1.8	0044	2.7	0032	3.3	0400	6.3	0402	4.8	0311	3.5	0221	0.8
	1045	8.1	0942	7.3	0804	5.6	0628	9.4	0615	10.5	1017	1.8	1003	1.4	0848	0.9	0809	0.1
	1733	1.4	1642	1.8	1441	1.5	1306	2.3	1256	2.7	1619	6.3	1625	4.8	1533	3.4	1435	0.9
	2307	8.3	2221	7.4	2027	5.6	1849	9.5	1835	10.7	2234	1.7	2221	1.3	2100	0.8	2028	0.1
5 SU	0552	1.4	0503	1.8	0259	1.5	0125	2.2	0115	2.5	0435	6.6	0439	5.1	0347	3.7	0254	0.9
	1124	8.6	1014	7.6	0839	5.9	0705	9.9	0651	11.2	1053	1.5	1039	1.2	0923	0.7	0839	0.1
	1815	1.0	1727	1.4	1518	1.1	1346	1.7	1339	2.0	1653	6.6	1700	5.0	1608	3.5	1508	0.9
	2345	8.7	2256	7.6	2100	5.8	1925	10.0	1911	11.3	2309	1.4	2255	1.1	2134	0.7	2059	0.1
6 M	0634	1.0	0548	1.4	0336	1.2	0204	1.7	0158	1.9	0509	6.9	0513	5.2	0421	3.8	0327	0.9
	1202	8.9	1035	7.8	0911	6.1	0740	10.4	0727	11.8	1129	1.2	1113	1.0	0957	0.5	0910	0.1
	1855	0.7	1809	1.1	1554	0.9	1424	1.4	1421	1.4	1726	6.8	1733	5.1	1641	3.6	1542	0.9
			2317	7.7	2131	6.0	2000	10.4	1946	11.8	2345	1.2	2329	1.0	2209	0.5	2129	0.1
7 TU	0022	9.0	0629	1.2	0412	1.0	0241	1.4	0239	1.5	0544	7.1	0548	5.3	0454	3.9	0400	1.0
	0714	0.9	1051	7.9	0943	6.3	0816	10.8	0803	12.2	1205	1.0	1147	0.9	1031	0.5	0942	0.0
	1239	9.1	1849	1.0	1630	0.8	1501	1.1	1500	1.1	1800	7.0	1805	5.1	1713	3.7	1617	1.0
	1934	0.5	2306	7.8	2202	6.2	2035	10.8	2021	12.1					2244	0.5	2200	0.0
8 W	0058	9.1	0706	1.1	0448	1.0	0316	1.2	0318	1.2	0022	1.1	0003	0.9	0527	3.9	0434	1.0
	0752	0.7	1115	8.0	1015	6.4	0851	11.0	0836	12.4	0619	7.2	0621	5.3	1106	0.4	1014	0.0
	1315	9.1	1925	1.0	1707	0.7	1536	1.0	1539	1.0	1242	1.0	1222	0.9	1746	3.7	1653	0.9
	2012	0.5	2332	7.8	2233	6.3	2111	10.9	2054	12.2	1835	7.0	1838	5.1	2321	0.5	2232	0.0
9 TH	0133	9.1	0742	1.1	0524	1.0	0350	1.1	0354	1.3	0100	1.1	0039	0.9	0602	3.8	0510	0.9
	0828	0.7	1147	8.0	1048	6.4	0927	11.1	0909	12.3	0655	7.1	0657	5.2	1142	0.5	1048	0.0
	1351	9.1	1959	1.1	1744	0.9	1609	1.0	1615	1.2	1320	1.1	1259	0.9	1821	3.7	1730	0.9
	2047	0.7			2306	6.2	2146	10.8	2127	12.1	1911	6.9	1912	5.0			2306	0.1
10 F	0208	9.0	0006	7.8	0601	1.1	0424	1.3	0429	1.6	0139	1.2	0118	1.0	0000	0.6	0548	0.9
	0903	0.9	0814	1.3	1124	6.3	1004	10.8	0943	12.1	0733	6.9	0734	5.1	0638	3.7	1124	0.1
	1426	8.9	1224	6.3	1821	1.1	1644	1.4	1650	1.7	1400	1.3	1339	1.0	1222	0.6	1811	0.9
	2121	0.9	2030	1.3	2343	6.1	2222	10.5	2202	11.7	1949	6.7	1950	4.8	1858	3.6	2342	0.1
11 SA	0244	8.8	0046	7.6	0640	1.4	0500	1.7	0502	2.1	0221	1.5	0202	1.1	0042	0.8	0629	0.9
	0938	1.2	0845	1.5	1203	6.0	1042	10.3	1019	11.5	0813	6.6	0817	4.8	0719	3.6	1203	0.1
	1504	8.5	1309	7.6	1902	1.4	1720	1.9	1724	2.4	1443	1.7	1424	1.2	1307	0.8	1855	0.8
	2158	1.3	2103	1.6			2300	9.9	2239	11.1	2031	6.3	2036	4.6	1942	3.4		
12 SU	0324	8.4	0135	7.4	0026	5.8	0538	2.3	0536	2.8	0307	1.8	0251	1.3	0132	1.0	0025	0.2
	1018	1.6	0921	1.8	0724	1.6	1124	9.6	1100	10.8	0900	6.2	0911	4.6	0809	3.4	0716	0.8
	1548	8.1	1406	7.2	1252	5.6	1800	2.6	1803	3.2	1533	2.1	1517	1.5	1400	1.1	1251	0.2
	2242	1.8	2144	2.0	1948	1.8	2344	9.3	2324	10.4	2122	5.9	2137	4.4	2038	3.2	1948	0.7
13 M	0412	7.9	0241	7.0	0118	5.5	0625	2.9	0620	3.5	0403	2.2	0351	1.6	0236	1.2	0122	0.2
	1108	2.1	1009	2.2	0819	2.0	1216	8.9	1154	9.9	1000	5.8	1026	4.3	0915	3.1	0814	0.7
	1648	7.5	1537	6.8	1354	5.2	1854	3.3	1855	3.9	1633	2.4	1621	1.8	1512	1.3	1400	0.2
	2340	2.3	2239	2.4	2049	2.2					2232	5.6	2307	4.2	2153	3.1	2059	0.7
14 TU	0522	7.3	0426	6.6	0227	5.1	0043	8.6	0029	9.5	0512	2.5	0505	1.8	0401	1.3	0257	0.3
	1223	2.4	1115	2.6	0932	2.2	0732	3.5	0726	4.1	1123	5.5	1201	4.2	1044	3.0	0931	0.7
	1814	7.1	1729	6.6	1517	4.9	1331	8.3	1318	9.1	1749	2.5	1741	1.9	1641	1.4	1557	0.3
			2355	2.8	2210	2.4	2012	3.8	2015	4.4					2327	3.1	2230	0.7
15 W	0110	2.6	0600	6.6	0354	5.0	0210	8.2	0207	9.1	0004	5.5	0043	4.3	0536	1.3	0451	0.3
	0654	7.1	1247	2.7	1103	2.2	0906	3.6	0905	4.3	0637	2.5	0630	1.8	1217	3.1	1104	0.7
	1404	2.4	1854	6.7	1655	4.9	1512	8.2	1512	9.1	1259	5.5	1328	4.3	1806	1.3	1730	0.2
	1944	7.2			2344	2.3	2151	3.6	2157	4.2	1916	2.5	1905	1.9			2357	0.7

• • Time Zone -0100. For UT subtract 1 hour. For European summer time (shaded) 26/3-29/10 add 1 hour • •

MARCH 2000 TIDE TABLES

• • Time Zone -0100. For UT subtract 1 hour. For European summer time (shaded) 26/3-29/10 add 1 hour • •

Day	DIEPPE Time	m	LE HAVRE Time	m	CHERBOURG Time	m	ST HELIER JERSEY Time	m	ST MALO Time	m	BREST Time	m	POINTE DE GRAVE Time	m	LISBOA Time	m	GIBRALTAR Time	m
16TH	0242	2.3	0134	2.7	0530	5.1	0350	8.5	0347	9.6	0135	5.7	0200	4.5	0050	3.3	0600	0.2
	0818	7.4	0716	6.8	1231	1.9	1041	3.1	1047	3.7	0802	2.2	0750	1.6	0651	1.1	1224	0.8
	1524	1.9	1427	2.3	1821	5.2	1639	8.8	1636	9.9	1417	5.9	1436	4.6	1330	3.3	1830	0.2
	2100	7.7	2012	7.0			2315	3.0	2320	3.4	2031	2.2	2017	1.6	1913	1.1		
17F	0355	1.8	0303	2.2	0103	1.9	0506	9.2	0458	10.5	0243	6.2	0300	4.8	0153	3.5	0102	0.8
	0928	8.0	0827	7.2	0645	5.4	1154	2.3	1157	2.7	0907	1.8	0854	1.3	0749	0.8	0653	0.1
	1630	1.3	1542	1.7	1337	1.4	1744	9.6	1735	10.8	1515	6.3	1530	4.9	1425	3.5	1323	0.8
	2201	8.3	2130	7.3	1921	5.6					2129	1.7	2114	1.3	2005	0.9	1917	0.1
18SA	0457	1.2	0409	1.6	0202	1.4	0019	2.1	0021	2.4	0336	6.6	0351	5.1	0245	3.8	0153	0.9
	1024	8.6	0948	7.5	0739	5.8	0604	10.0	0554	11.4	1000	1.3	0946	1.0	0836	0.6	0737	0.1
	1727	0.7	1639	1.1	1430	1.0	1251	1.6	1251	1.7	1603	6.7	1616	5.1	1512	3.7	1412	0.9
	2251	8.8	2233	7.7	2009	5.9	1835	10.3	1824	11.7	2218	1.2	2202	1.0	2050	0.7	1958	0.1
19SU O	0551	0.7	0503	1.1	0250	1.0	0112	1.4	0112	1.6	0423	7.0	0436	5.3	0330	3.9	0236	0.9
	1112	9.0	1051	7.8	0824	6.1	0652	10.7	0641	12.1	1046	1.0	1031	0.8	0918	0.5	0818	0.0
	1816	0.3	1730	0.7	1515	0.7	1342	1.0	1339	1.1	1646	7.0	1657	5.2	1555	3.8	1455	1.0
	2336	9.2	2324	7.9	2051	6.2	1920	10.9	1907	12.2	2303	0.9	2245	0.8	2130	0.6	2036	0.0
20M	0638	0.4	0550	0.8	0333	0.8	0159	1.0	0157	1.0	0505	7.2	0515	5.4	0412	4.0	0317	1.0
	1154	9.3	1140	8.0	0906	6.4	0735	11.1	0723	12.5	1129	0.8	1112	0.7	0956	0.4	0855	-0.0
	1900	0.1	1813	0.5	1557	0.5	1425	0.7	1422	0.7	1726	7.2	1734	5.2	1635	3.9	1535	1.0
					2129	6.3	2000	11.2	1947	12.5	2345	0.8	2325	0.7	2207	0.5	2112	0.0
21TU	0016	9.4	0008	8.0	0414	0.7	0240	0.7	0239	0.8	0544	7.3	0552	5.4	0452	4.0	0354	1.0
	0719	0.3	0632	0.7	0943	6.4	0814	11.3	0802	12.7	1209	0.8	1151	0.7	1031	0.5	0931	-0.0
	1234	9.4	1222	8.0	1635	0.6	1504	0.6	1501	0.7	1803	7.2	1809	5.2	1712	3.9	1612	1.0
	1939	0.1	1852	0.6	2205	6.3	2036	11.2	2024	12.5					2242	0.5	2146	0.0
22W	0054	9.4	0046	8.0	0451	0.8	0317	0.7	0316	0.9	0024	0.9	0004	0.7	0529	4.0	0430	1.0
	0756	0.3	0709	0.8	1018	6.4	0850	11.3	0837	12.5	0620	7.2	0626	5.2	1105	0.6	1006	0.0
	1312	9.3	1258	7.9	1710	0.8	1538	0.8	1536	1.0	1245	1.0	1227	0.8	1748	3.8	1648	1.0
	2014	0.3	1927	0.6	2238	6.3	2110	11.1	2057	12.2	1837	7.0	1840	5.1	2317	0.6	2219	0.1
23TH	0130	9.3	0118	7.8	0524	1.0	0349	0.9	0348	1.3	0100	1.1	0042	0.7	0605	3.8	0503	0.9
	0828	0.6	0739	1.1	1051	6.3	0923	11.0	0910	12.1	0654	7.0	0657	5.1	1138	0.7	1039	0.1
	1346	9.1	1233	7.7	1742	1.1	1608	1.1	1606	1.5	1321	1.3	1303	1.0	1821	3.7	1721	0.9
	2044	0.7	1954	1.3	2309	6.1	2141	10.7	2128	11.8	1909	6.8	1910	4.9	2351	0.8	2251	0.1
24F	0203	9.0	0133	7.6	0556	1.3	0419	1.4	0417	1.8	0134	1.4	0118	1.0	0639	3.6	0536	0.9
	0856	0.9	0804	1.4	1122	6.0	0954	10.5	0941	11.6	0725	6.6	0727	4.8	1211	0.9	1112	0.1
	1419	8.7	1247	7.5	1811	1.5	1634	1.7	1631	2.1	1354	1.7	1339	1.2	1856	3.5	1754	0.8
	2110	1.1	2016	1.7	2341	5.9	2210	10.2	2157	11.2	1941	6.4	1941	4.7			2324	0.2
25SA	0235	8.5	0112	7.4	0625	1.7	0446	1.9	0442	2.4	0208	1.8	0155	1.3	0027	1.0	0609	0.8
	0922	1.3	0825	1.8	1154	5.7	1023	9.9	1010	10.9	0756	6.2	0757	4.5	0715	3.4	1145	0.2
	1451	8.3	1330	7.3	1839	1.9	1659	2.3	1655	2.8	1426	2.1	1415	1.5	1245	1.1	1827	0.8
	2137	1.5	2037	2.1			2238	9.5	2227	10.5	2013	6.0	2014	4.4	1932	3.3	2357	0.2
26SU	0306	8.0	0151	7.2	0013	5.6	0512	2.6	0508	3.1	0242	2.2	0234	1.6	0106	1.2	0643	0.7
	0951	1.7	0851	2.2	0655	2.0	1052	9.1	1040	10.1	0830	5.8	0830	4.2	0753	3.1	1221	0.2
	1522	7.7	1415	7.0	1230	5.3	1724	3.1	1721	3.6	1501	2.5	1456	1.8	1325	1.3	1905	0.7
	2208	2.1	2106	2.5	1909	2.2	2308	8.8	2257	9.7	2051	5.6	2054	4.2	2014	3.1		
27M	0339	7.4	0237	6.8	0051	5.2	0543	3.3	0539	3.8	0324	2.6	0320	1.9	0153	1.4	0035	0.3
	1026	2.2	0926	2.6	0732	2.3	1126	8.3	1113	9.3	0911	5.4	0916	4.0	0842	2.9	0724	0.7
	1600	7.1	1506	6.6	1314	4.9	1756	3.8	1754	4.3	1546	2.9	1545	2.1	1417	1.6	1307	0.3
	2246	2.6	2148	3.0	1950	2.6	2345	8.0	2336	8.9	2142	5.3	2154	3.9	2110	2.9	1953	0.6
28TU	0421	6.8	0331	6.4	0143	4.8	0627	4.0	0620	4.6	0417	3.0	0417	2.1	0300	1.6	0130	0.4
	1111	2.7	1015	3.1	0823	2.6	1215	7.5	1203	8.4	1012	5.0	1032	3.7	0954	2.7	0823	0.6
	1654	6.4	1611	6.2	1420	4.5	1847	4.4	1844	5.0	1651	3.2	1653	2.3	1534	1.9	1437	0.4
	2338	3.1	2248	3.4	2051	2.9					2300	5.0	2326	3.8	2233	2.8	2108	0.6
29W	0534	6.3	0443	6.1	0300	4.5	0053	7.3	0048	8.2	0530	3.2	0531	2.2	0434	1.7	0356	0.4
	1214	3.1	1126	3.4	0937	2.8	0739	4.5	0726	5.1	1151	4.8	1224	3.7	1130	2.7	0959	0.6
	1844	6.1	1739	6.0	1551	4.4	1351	7.0	1351	7.9	1823	3.3	1817	2.3	1709	1.7	1645	0.4
					2221	3.0	2018	4.8	2006	5.4							2257	0.6
30TH	0055	3.4	0012	3.5	0435	4.5	0300	7.2	0248	8.1	0045	5.0	0056	3.9	0001	2.8	0526	0.4
	0724	6.3	0612	6.0	1112	2.7	0920	4.5	0905	5.2	0706	3.1	0654	2.2	0600	1.5	1139	0.6
	1352	3.1	1258	3.3	1733	4.5	1547	7.3	1535	8.2	1334	5.0	1343	3.9	1248	2.8	1749	0.3
	2007	6.4	1911	6.2	2357	2.7	2209	4.5	2155	5.2	1951	3.0	1933	2.1	1822	1.6		
31F O	0238	3.1	0144	3.3	0558	4.8	0421	7.7	0406	8.7	0200	5.3	0200	4.2	0107	3.0	0014	0.7
	0834	6.7	0730	6.1	1231	2.4	1048	3.9	1041	4.6	0818	2.7	0800	1.9	0657	1.3	0615	0.7
	1516	2.6	1419	2.8	1836	4.9	1651	8.0	1638	9.0	1432	5.4	1436	4.4	1342	3.0	1237	0.7
	2106	7.0	2021	6.6			2321	3.7	2312	4.4	2045	2.6	2028	1.8	1913	1.3	1833	0.3

FRANCE, SPAIN, PORTUGAL & GIBRALTAR Time Zone -0100
Dieppe * Le Havre * Cherbourg * St Helier * St Malo * Brest * Pointe de Grave * Lisboa * Gibraltar

TIDE TABLES APRIL 2000

	DIEPPE Time	m	LE HAVRE Time	m	CHERBOURG Time	m	ST HELIER JERSEY Time	m	ST MALO Time	m	BREST Time	m	POINTE DE GRAVE Time	m	LISBOA Time	m	GIBRALTAR Time	m	Day
	0345	2.5	0251	2.7	0102	2.3	0512	8.5	0459	9.5	0249	5.7	0250	4.5	0156	3.2	0100	0.7	**1 SA**
	0928	7.4	0827	6.8	0650	5.1	1145	3.1	1141	3.7	0905	2.3	0851	1.6	0740	1.1	0653	0.2	
	1612	2.0	1519	2.3	1325	1.9	1736	8.7	1724	9.9	1512	5.8	1519	4.5	1424	3.2	1320	0.8	
	2154	7.7	2111	7.1	1918	5.2					2126	2.2	2112	1.6	1954	1.0	1909	0.2	
	0436	1.9	0346	2.2	0148	1.9	0011	2.9	0004	3.4	0328	6.2	0332	4.8	0237	3.4	0139	0.8	**2 SU**
	1014	8.0	0909	7.2	0730	5.5	0554	9.2	0542	10.4	0945	1.8	0931	1.3	0818	0.8	0727	0.2	
	1700	1.4	1611	1.8	1407	1.5	1232	2.4	1228	2.7	1548	6.3	1557	4.8	1502	3.4	1357	0.8	
	2236	8.3	2151	7.4	1953	5.6	1817	9.5	1803	10.8	2204	1.7	2150	1.3	2032	0.8	1943	0.1	
	0522	1.3	0435	1.7	0228	1.5	0054	2.2	0049	2.6	0405	6.6	0410	5.0	0315	3.6	0214	0.9	**3 M**
	1056	8.6	0936	7.6	0806	5.8	0633	10.0	0621	11.2	1023	1.4	1009	1.1	0854	0.6	0800	0.1	
	1745	0.9	1658	1.4	1447	1.1	1316	1.7	1312	1.9	1624	6.6	1632	5.0	1537	3.6	1434	0.9	
	2316	8.8	2220	7.6	2027	5.9	1855	10.2	1842	11.5	2242	1.3	2227	1.1	2109	0.6	2017	0.1	
	0606	0.9	0521	1.4	0306	1.2	0136	1.6	0133	1.8	0442	6.9	0446	5.2	0351	3.8	0249	0.9	**4 TU**
	1136	9.0	0951	7.8	0839	6.2	0712	10.6	0700	11.9	1101	1.1	1045	0.9	0930	0.5	0834	0.1	●
	1828	0.6	1742	1.1	1525	0.9	1357	1.2	1355	1.3	1700	6.9	1706	5.1	1612	3.7	1511	0.9	
	2356	9.1	2207	7.8	2100	6.2	1933	10.8	1920	12.1	2320	1.0	2303	0.9	2145	0.5	2050	0.1	
	0649	0.7	0603	1.1	0345	0.9	0217	1.2	0215	1.3	0519	7.2	0523	5.3	0428	3.9	0325	1.0	**5 W**
	1215	9.2	1013	8.0	0914	6.4	0751	11.1	0738	12.4	1139	0.9	1121	0.8	1006	0.4	0908	0.0	
	1910	0.5	1824	0.9	1604	0.7	1437	0.9	1438	0.9	1736	7.1	1741	5.2	1648	3.8	1548	1.0	
			2229	7.9	2133	6.4	2012	11.2	1957	12.5	2359	0.9	2339	0.8	2223	0.4	2124	0.0	
	0034	9.3	0643	1.0	0424	0.8	0255	0.9	0257	1.0	0557	7.3	0600	5.3	0505	3.9	0402	1.0	**6 TH**
	0730	0.5	1043	8.1	0950	6.5	0830	11.4	0815	12.6	1219	0.8	1158	0.8	1043	0.4	0943	-0.0	
	1254	9.3	1903	0.9	1642	0.7	1515	0.7	1518	0.8	1814	7.2	1816	5.2	1724	3.9	1626	1.0	
	1950	0.5	2301	8.0	2209	6.5	2050	11.3	2033	12.6					2301	0.4	2158	0.0	
	0112	9.3	0721	1.0	0503	0.8	0333	0.8	0336	1.0	0039	0.8	0018	0.8	0542	3.9	0439	1.0	**7 F**
	0809	0.6	1119	8.0	1027	6.5	0909	11.4	0851	12.6	0636	7.3	0637	5.3	1121	0.5	1018	-0.0	
	1332	9.2	1939	1.0	1722	0.8	1551	0.8	1557	1.0	1300	1.0	1238	0.8	1802	3.8	1705	0.9	
	2028	0.6	2339	7.9	2245	6.4	2128	11.2	2108	12.4	1852	7.1	1854	5.1	2342	0.5	2235	0.0	
	0149	9.2	0756	1.1	0543	0.9	0409	1.0	0413	1.3	0121	1.0	0100	0.8	0624	3.8	0518	0.9	**8 SA**
	0847	0.7	1200	7.9	1107	6.3	0949	11.1	0927	12.2	0716	7.0	0718	5.1	1203	0.6	1056	0.0	
	1410	9.0	2012	1.3	1803	1.1	1628	1.2	1634	1.6	1342	1.2	1320	1.0	1843	3.7	1745	0.9	
	2106	0.9			2325	6.2	2206	10.8	2145	12.0	1933	6.8	1935	4.9			2313	0.1	
	0227	8.9	0022	7.7	0626	1.2	0448	1.4	0449	1.9	0206	1.3	0147	1.0	0027	0.7	0600	0.9	**9 SU**
	0925	1.0	0830	1.4	1151	6.0	1030	10.5	1004	11.6	0800	6.7	0806	4.8	0709	3.6	1136	0.1	
	1451	8.6	1249	7.5	1846	1.4	1706	1.8	1711	2.3	1427	1.6	1408	1.2	1249	0.9	1829	0.8	
	2146	1.3	2048	1.6			2246	10.2	2223	11.4	2018	6.4	2024	4.7	1930	3.5	2356	0.1	
	0309	8.4	0115	7.3	0011	5.9	0528	2.1	0527	2.6	0255	1.7	0239	1.3	0120	0.8	0646	0.8	**10 M**
	1008	1.4	0907	1.7	0712	1.5	1114	9.7	1046	10.8	0850	6.2	0903	4.5	0803	3.3	1222	0.1	
	1538	8.1	1356	7.1	1243	5.6	1748	2.6	1751	3.2	1519	2.0	1503	1.5	1344	1.1	1920	0.7	
	2233	1.8	2129	2.1	1936	1.8	2331	9.4	2309	10.5	2112	6.0	2131	4.4	2029	3.3			
	0401	7.9	0232	6.9	0106	5.5	0617	2.8	0612	3.4	0353	2.1	0341	1.5	0227	1.2	0050	0.2	**11 TU**
	1102	1.9	0955	2.2	0809	1.9	1208	8.9	1142	9.8	0954	5.7	1022	4.3	0911	3.1	0742	0.7	
	1641	7.5	1608	6.8	1349	5.2	1842	3.3	1844	4.0	1621	2.4	1609	1.8	1457	1.4	1324	0.2	
	2335	2.2	2224	2.5	2039	2.2					2224	5.6	2301	4.3	2144	3.2	2024	0.7	
	0512	7.3	0425	6.7	0218	5.1	0031	8.7	0014	9.6	0503	2.4	0455	1.7	0355	1.3	0214	0.3	**12 W**
	1218	2.3	1103	2.6	0923	2.1	0724	3.4	0718	4.1	1116	5.4	1156	4.2	1038	3.0	0854	0.7	
	1804	7.1	1728	6.6	1513	4.8	1325	8.3	1312	9.0	1737	2.6	1729	1.9	1630	1.5	1505	0.3	
			2346	2.9	2201	2.4	2001	4.5	2003	4.5	2354	5.5			2312	3.2	2151	0.7	
	0100	2.5	0548	6.6	0345	5.0	0159	8.3	0155	9.1	0627	2.5	0032	4.3	0529	1.2	0411	0.3	**13 TH**
	0640	7.1	1240	2.7	1052	2.1	0857	3.6	0857	4.3	1248	5.5	0620	1.7	1205	3.1	1030	0.7	
	1347	2.3	1848	6.7	1648	4.9	1502	8.2	1503	9.1	1903	2.5	1318	4.3	1756	1.3	1646	0.3	
	1930	7.2			2333	2.3	2136	3.7	2144	4.3			1852	1.9			2323	0.7	
	0225	2.2	0126	2.7	0517	5.1	0335	8.5	0332	9.6	0121	5.7	0146	4.5	0033	3.3	0529	0.3	**14 F**
	0803	7.3	0706	6.8	1216	1.8	1025	3.1	1033	3.7	0748	2.2	0738	1.6	0641	1.1	1155	0.7	
	1505	1.8	1412	2.3	1806	5.2	1624	8.8	1620	9.9	1402	5.8	1422	4.6	1313	3.3	1751	0.2	
	2044	7.7	2007	7.0			2256	3.0	2303	3.5	2015	2.2	2002	1.6	1900	1.1			
	0338	1.7	0245	2.2	0047	1.9	0447	9.2	0440	10.4	0226	6.1	0245	4.8	0134	3.5	0032	0.8	**15 SA**
	0912	7.9	0824	7.1	0627	5.4	1133	2.4	1139	2.7	0850	1.8	0839	1.3	0734	0.9	0623	0.2	
	1610	1.2	1520	1.7	1319	1.4	1724	9.5	1715	10.7	1457	6.2	1513	4.8	1406	3.5	1257	0.8	
	2142	8.3	2119	7.3	1902	5.5	2357	2.3			2111	1.7	2057	1.3	1949	0.9	1840	0.2	

• • Time Zone -0100. For UT subtract 1 hour. For European summer time (shaded) 26/3-29/10 add 1 hour • •

APRIL 2000 TIDE TABLES

• • Time Zone -0100. For UT subtract 1 hour. For European summer time (shaded) 26/3-29/10 add 1 hour • •

	DIEPPE		LE HAVRE		CHERBOURG		ST HELIER JERSEY		ST MALO		BREST		POINTE DE GRAVE		LISBOA		GIBRALTAR	
	Time	m	Time	m	Time	m	Time	m	Time	m	Time	m	Time	m	Time	m	Time	m
16 SU	0438	1.1	0347	1.7	0143	1.5	0542	9.9	0000	2.5	0317	6.5	0333	5.0	0225	3.7	0123	0.9
	1005	8.4	0939	7.4	0718	5.7	1228	1.7	0532	11.2	0940	1.4	0927	1.1	0818	0.7	0706	0.2
	1705	0.7	1615	1.2	1409	1.1	1812	10.2	1229	1.9	1542	6.6	1557	5.0	1451	3.7	1345	0.9
	2230	8.8	2215	7.7	1947	5.8			1801	11.5	2158	1.4	2143	1.1	2031	0.8	1921	0.2
17 M	0529	0.7	0438	1.2	0230	1.2	0048	1.7	0048	1.8	0401	6.8	0416	5.1	0309	3.8	0205	0.9
	1051	8.9	1034	7.7	0802	6.0	0629	10.5	0617	11.8	1024	1.1	1010	0.9	0855	0.6	0745	0.1
	1752	0.5	1703	0.9	1452	0.9	1316	1.3	1312	1.4	1623	6.9	1635	5.1	1532	3.8	1425	0.9
	2312	9.1	2303	7.9	2027	6.1	1855	10.7	1842	11.9	2240	1.1	2224	0.9	2108	0.7	1957	0.1
18 TU O	0613	0.5	0524	1.0	0311	1.0	0133	1.3	0130	1.4	0442	7.0	0454	5.2	0350	3.9	0242	0.9
	1131	9.1	1119	7.8	0841	6.2	0710	10.8	0657	12.1	1104	1.0	1048	0.8	0930	0.6	0819	0.1
	1834	0.4	1745	0.9	1532	0.8	1358	1.1	1353	1.3	1700	7.0	1709	5.1	1609	3.8	1503	0.9
	2351	9.2	2343	7.9	2103	6.2	1933	10.9	1920	12.1	2320	1.0	2303	0.8	2143	0.6	2031	0.1
19 W	0653	0.5	0603	1.0	0349	0.9	0213	1.1	0209	1.3	0519	7.0	0527	5.2	0427	3.9	0316	0.9
	1209	9.2	1158	7.8	0917	6.3	0748	11.0	0735	12.2	1142	1.0	1125	0.8	1003	0.6	0853	0.1
	1912	0.5	1823	1.0	1608	0.9	1435	1.0	1430	1.3	1736	7.0	1741	5.1	1645	3.8	1536	0.9
			0058	7.8	2136	6.3	2009	11.0	1955	12.1	2357	1.1	2339	0.9	2217	0.6	2104	0.1
20 TH	0028	9.2	0638	1.1	0424	1.0	0248	1.1	0245	1.4	0554	6.9	0558	5.1	0503	3.8	0348	0.9
	0728	0.6	1124	7.6	0950	6.2	0823	10.9	0809	12.0	1218	1.2	1200	0.9	1034	0.7	0926	0.1
	1245	9.1	1854	1.2	1641	1.1	1506	1.2	1504	1.6	1809	6.9	1810	5.0	1720	3.8	1609	0.9
	1945	0.7	2345	7.6	2208	6.2	2042	10.9	2028	11.9					2250	0.7	2137	0.1
21 F	0103	9.1	0706	1.3	0457	1.2	0320	1.2	0318	1.7	0033	1.2	0015	1.0	0539	3.7	0418	0.9
	0759	0.8	1135	7.5	1022	6.1	0856	10.7	0842	11.7	0626	6.7	0627	4.9	1106	0.8	0958	0.1
	1319	8.9	1919	1.6	1712	1.3	1536	1.4	1533	2.0	1251	1.4	1234	1.1	1754	3.7	1639	0.9
	2013	1.0	2356	7.5	2239	6.1	2112	10.6	2058	11.6	1840	6.7	1839	4.9	2323	0.8	2209	0.1
22 SA	0135	8.8	0730	1.6	0527	1.4	0349	1.5	0345	2.1	0106	1.5	0051	1.1	0612	3.5	0448	0.9
	0826	1.1	1218	7.4	1054	5.9	0926	10.3	0912	11.3	0657	6.5	0654	4.7	1138	0.9	1030	0.1
	1351	8.6	1940	1.9	1740	1.6	1602	1.8	1559	2.5	1322	1.8	1308	1.3	1827	3.5	1710	0.8
	2039	1.3			2310	5.9	2141	10.2	2127	11.1	1911	6.4	1908	4.7	2358	1.0	2241	0.2
23 SU	0205	8.5	0036	7.4	0557	1.7	0416	2.0	0412	2.6	0139	1.8	0126	1.5	0647	3.3	0518	0.8
	0851	1.4	0751	1.8	1127	5.7	0955	9.8	0940	10.8	0727	6.2	0724	4.5	1212	1.1	1103	0.1
	1421	8.2	1303	7.2	1809	1.9	1627	2.4	1623	3.0	1354	2.1	1342	1.5	1902	3.3	1741	0.8
	2105	1.7	2004	2.2	2342	5.6	2208	9.6	2154	10.6	1943	6.1	1940	4.5			2314	0.2
24 M	0235	8.1	0119	7.2	0628	1.9	0445	2.5	0438	3.1	0212	2.1	0203	1.5	0036	1.1	0549	0.8
	0920	1.7	0818	2.1	1201	5.3	1024	9.1	1008	10.2	0800	5.8	0757	4.3	0724	3.1	1138	0.2
	1453	7.8	1348	7.0	1841	2.3	1654	3.0	1648	3.6	1427	2.5	1421	1.8	1251	1.3	1815	0.8
	2135	2.1	2035	2.5			2236	8.9	2222	10.0	2021	5.8	2020	4.3	1941	3.1	2349	0.3
25 TU	0306	7.6	0205	6.9	0018	5.3	0515	3.2	0506	3.7	0252	2.5	0246	1.8	0121	1.3	0624	0.7
	0954	2.1	0853	2.5	0705	2.2	1055	8.4	1038	9.5	0840	5.4	0841	4.1	0809	2.9	1217	0.3
	1527	7.3	1438	6.7	1244	5.0	1725	3.7	1718	4.2	1511	2.8	1507	2.0	1338	1.5	1855	0.7
	2212	2.5	2116	2.9	1921	2.6	2309	8.2	2254	9.3	2107	5.4	2114	4.1	2030	3.0		
26 W	0344	7.1	0256	6.6	0106	4.9	0556	3.8	0542	4.3	0341	2.8	0338	2.0	0220	1.5	0031	0.3
	1036	2.5	0939	2.9	0753	2.5	1137	7.7	1118	8.8	0934	5.1	0948	3.8	0910	2.7	0709	0.7
	1615	6.7	1536	6.3	1345	4.7	1810	4.3	1758	4.8	1608	3.1	1607	2.2	1443	1.6	1309	0.3
	2301	2.9	2212	3.3	2018	2.8			2343	8.6	2212	5.1	2233	4.0	2138	2.8	1948	0.7
27 TH	0442	6.6	0359	6.2	0216	4.6	0000	7.6	0636	4.9	0445	3.0	0444	2.1	0340	1.6	0135	0.4
	1133	2.9	1043	3.2	0859	2.6	0655	4.3	1236	8.2	1053	4.9	1127	3.8	1033	2.7	0809	0.6
	1739	6.4	1652	6.1	1507	4.5	1253	7.2	1905	5.3	1722	3.2	1722	2.3	1612	1.7	1436	0.4
			2327	3.4	2137	2.9	1923	4.7			2338	5.0			2301	2.8	2059	0.7
28 F	0008	3.2	0521	6.1	0341	4.6	0143	7.3	0129	8.3	0602	3.0	0001	4.0	0506	1.5	0323	0.4
	0620	6.4	1204	3.2	1021	2.6	0819	4.4	0801	5.1	1227	5.0	0600	2.1	1154	2.8	0939	0.6
	1254	3.0	1825	6.2	1633	4.6	1442	7.3	1430	8.2	1846	3.0	1253	3.9	1732	1.6	1611	0.4
	1908	6.5			2303	2.7	2100	4.6	2047	5.3			1839	2.2			2227	0.7
29 SA	0139	3.0	0053	3.3	0459	4.7	0321	7.6	0306	8.6	0100	5.2	0113	4.2	0014	3.0	0449	0.4
	0739	6.7	0645	6.3	1138	2.4	0947	4.0	0942	4.7	0720	2.7	0709	1.9	0610	1.3	1112	0.7
	1422	2.6	1327	2.8	1743	4.8	1557	7.9	1545	8.9	1339	5.3	1354	4.2	1255	3.0	1715	0.3
	2015	7.0	1939	6.6			2224	4.0	2220	4.1	1954	2.7	1941	1.9	1830	1.3	2341	0.7
30 SU	0257	2.5	0207	2.8	0013	2.4	0422	8.3	0409	9.4	0200	5.6	0208	4.5	0109	3.2	0545	0.2
	0842	7.3	0746	6.7	0559	5.1	1054	3.3	1055	3.8	0818	2.3	0806	1.6	0659	1.1	1217	0.7
	1527	2.1	1434	2.3	1239	2.0	1650	8.7	1638	9.8	1429	5.7	1440	4.5	1342	3.2	1805	0.2
	2110	7.7	2031	7.0	1831	5.2	2324	3.1	2322	3.6	2044	2.2	2030	1.6	1918	1.1		

FRANCE, SPAIN, PORTUGAL & GIBRALTAR Time Zone -0100
Dieppe * Le Havre * Cherbourg * St Helier * St Malo * Brest * Pointe de Grave * Lisboa * Gibraltar

TIDE TABLES   MAY 2000

Day	DIEPPE Time	m	LE HAVRE Time	m	CHERBOURG Time	m	ST HELIER JERSEY Time	m	ST MALO Time	m	BREST Time	m	POINTE DE GRAVE Time	m	LISBOA Time	m	GIBRALTAR Time	m
1 M	0356	1.9	0306	2.2	0106	2.0	0511	9.1	0500	10.3	0248	6.1	0254	4.7	0156	3.4	0036	0.8
	0934	7.9	0829	7.1	0645	5.4	1148	2.5	1149	2.9	0906	1.9	0852	1.4	0742	0.9	0632	0.2
	1621	1.5			1327	1.6	1736	9.5	1724	10.7	1511	6.2	1521	4.8	1424	3.4	1308	0.8
	2159	8.3	2108	7.4	1912	5.6					2128	1.8	2114	1.3	2000	0.8	1848	0.2
2 TU	0447	1.4	0359	1.7	0151	1.6	0015	2.4	0012	2.7	0330	6.5	0336	5.0	0239	3.6	0123	0.9
	1022	8.5	0854	7.5	0726	5.8	0556	9.9	0545	11.2	0948	1.4	0933	1.1	0821	0.7	0714	0.1
	1710	1.0	1622	1.4	1412	1.2	1238	1.8	1237	2.0	1551	6.6	1600	5.0	1503	3.6	1354	0.9
	2244	8.8	2113	7.7	1949	6.0	1820	10.3	1807	11.6	2210	1.3	2154	1.1	2040	0.6	1930	0.1
3 W	0535	0.9	0448	1.4	0235	1.2	0103	1.7	0100	1.9	0411	6.9	0417	5.2	0320	3.8	0206	0.9
	1106	8.9	0915	7.8	0806	6.1	0640	10.6	0627	11.9	1030	1.1	1014	0.9	0900	0.5	0754	0.1
	1757	0.7	1711	1.1	1454	1.0	1325	1.2	1324	1.4	1630	7.0	1638	5.2	1542	3.8	1436	0.9
	2327	9.2	2131	7.9	2027	6.3	1903	10.9	1849	12.2	2253	1.0	2235	0.9	2121	0.5	2010	0.1
4 TH ●	0621	0.7	0536	1.1	0318	1.0	0148	1.1	0146	1.3	0453	7.2	0457	5.3	0401	3.9	0248	1.0
	1150	9.2	0945	8.0	0846	6.4	0724	11.1	0710	12.4	1113	0.8	1054	0.8	0940	0.4	0835	0.0
	1843	0.6	1757	1.0	1536	0.8	1410	0.9	1409	1.0	1712	7.2	1717	5.3	1623	3.9	1519	0.9
			2202	8.0	2106	6.5	1946	11.3	1930	12.6	2336	0.8	2317	0.8	2202	0.4	2050	0.0
5 F	0009	9.4	0620	1.0	0400	0.8	0232	0.8	0231	1.0	0535	7.3	0539	5.4	0444	3.9	0330	1.0
	0706	0.6	1020	8.0	0927	6.5	0809	11.4	0751	12.6	1157	0.8	1136	0.8	1021	0.4	0915	-0.0
	1232	9.3	1840	1.0	1620	0.8	1453	0.7	1454	0.9	1753	7.3	1757	5.3	1705	4.0	1601	0.9
	1928	0.6	2239	8.0	2147	6.6	2029	11.5	2010	12.7					2245	0.4	2130	0.0
6 SA	0051	9.4	0702	1.0	0444	0.8	0315	0.7	0315	1.0	0021	0.8	0000	0.8	0527	3.9	0413	1.0
	0751	0.6	1100	7.9	1011	6.5	0852	11.4	0832	12.6	0618	7.2	0622	5.3	1103	0.5	0955	-0.0
	1314	9.2	1225	7.7	1703	0.9	1534	0.8	1537	1.1	1241	0.9	1219	0.9	1748	3.9	1644	0.9
	2012	0.7	1921	1.1	2229	6.5	2111	11.4	2050	12.6	1836	7.2	1839	5.2	2330	0.5	2212	0.0
7 SU	0132	9.2	0052	7.6	0529	0.9	0356	0.9	0357	1.2	0106	0.9	0047	0.8	0613	3.8	0456	0.9
	0834	0.7	0742	1.1	1057	6.3	0936	11.1	0912	12.2	0703	7.0	0708	5.1	1148	0.7	1037	0.0
	1357	9.0	1147	7.7	1748	1.1	1615	1.2	1618	1.6	1327	1.1	1306	1.0	1833	3.8	1727	0.9
	2054	0.9	2000	1.3	2315	6.3	2153	11.0	2130	12.2	1921	6.9	1927	5.1			2255	0.1
8 M	0215	8.9	0130	7.5	0615	1.1	0439	1.3	0439	1.7	0155	1.2	0136	1.0	0018	0.7	0542	0.9
	0918	0.9	0821	1.3	1147	6.0	1021	10.5	0954	11.6	0751	6.6	0800	4.9	0703	3.6	1121	0.1
	1442	8.7	1321	7.3	1836	1.5	1657	1.8	1700	2.3	1416	1.5	1356	1.3	1236	0.9	1814	0.8
	2140	1.2	2040	1.6			2236	10.3	2212	11.5	2011	6.5	2022	4.8	1924	3.6	2343	0.1
9 TU	0302	8.5	0203	7.3	0004	6.0	0523	1.9	0521	2.4	0247	1.5	0231	1.2	0114	0.9	0630	0.8
	1006	1.2	0903	1.6	0706	1.4	1109	9.8	1041	10.8	0845	6.2	0902	4.6	0800	3.4	1211	0.1
	1534	8.2	1515	7.1	1242	5.6	1742	2.5	1743	3.0	1509	1.9	1452	1.5	1334	1.1	1906	0.8
	2230	1.6	2125	2.1	1930	1.8	2325	9.6	2302	10.7	2108	6.1	2129	4.6	2023	3.5		
10 W	0357	8.0	0318	7.0	0102	5.6	0615	2.6	0609	3.2	0345	1.9	0333	1.5	0222	1.1	0040	0.2
	1101	1.6	0954	2.0	0804	1.7	1205	9.0	1139	9.9	0949	5.8	1017	4.4	0906	3.2	0726	0.7
	1636	7.7	1612	6.9	1348	5.3	1838	3.2	1836	3.8	1611	2.3	1557	1.8	1447	1.4	1312	0.2
	2330	2.0	2223	2.5	2033	2.1					2216	5.8	2250	4.5	2133	3.3	2007	0.7
11 TH	0504	7.5	0421	6.8	0211	5.3	0024	8.9	0006	9.9	0452	2.2	0443	1.6	0348	1.2	0156	0.3
	1207	1.9	1102	2.4	0913	2.0	0720	3.1	0712	3.8	1104	5.5	1140	4.3	1023	3.1	0833	0.7
	1750	7.4	1721	6.7	1503	5.0	1315	8.5	1302	9.3	1722	2.5	1712	1.9	1615	1.4	1433	0.3
			2340	2.7	2148	2.3	1950	3.6	1948	4.3	2335	5.6			2251	3.3	2121	0.7
12 F	0042	2.2	0536	6.7	0328	5.1	0142	8.6	0134	9.4	0608	2.3	0011	4.4	0512	1.2	0330	0.3
	0621	7.3	1225	2.4	1033	2.0	0839	3.3	0836	4.0	1225	5.5	0600	1.7	1142	3.1	0957	0.7
	1321	2.0	1835	6.8	1626	5.0	1438	8.4	1434	9.3	1839	2.4	1255	4.4	1736	1.4	1559	0.3
	1907	7.4			2309	2.2	2112	3.5	2115	4.2			1829	1.8			2242	0.7
13 SA	0157	2.1	0104	2.6	0450	5.1	0306	8.6	0300	9.6	0054	5.7	0121	4.6	0006	3.3	0449	0.3
	0739	7.4	0651	6.8	1149	1.9	0956	3.0	1002	3.7	0723	2.1	0713	1.6	0619	1.1	1118	0.7
	1436	1.8	1344	2.2	1739	5.2	1553	8.8	1547	9.8	1335	5.8	1357	4.5	1247	3.3	1706	0.3
	2018	7.7	1948	7.0			2225	3.1	2230	3.6	1948	2.2	1936	1.6	1838	1.2	2351	0.8
14 SU	0309	1.7	0216	2.2	0021	2.0	0416	9.1	0407	10.2	0159	6.0	0220	4.7	0109	3.5	0546	0.3
	0846	7.8	0806	7.0	0558	5.3	1101	3.0	1106	3.0	0824	1.9	0813	1.4	0710	1.0	1222	0.8
	1542	1.4	1448	1.8	1251	1.6	1653	9.4	1643	10.0	1430	6.1	1448	4.7	1340	3.4	1757	0.3
	2116	8.2	2055	7.3	1835	5.5	2327	2.5	2327	2.9	2045	1.9	2032	1.4	1927	1.1		
15 M	0410	1.3	0315	1.8	0117	1.7	0512	9.6	0500	10.8	0251	6.3	0309	4.9	0200	3.6	0044	0.8
	0939	8.2	0916	7.2	0651	5.6	1157	2.1	1155	2.4	0913	1.6	0902	1.2	0752	0.9	0630	0.2
	1636	1.0	1543	1.5	1342	1.4	1742	9.9	1730	11.0	1515	6.4	1532	4.9	1425	3.6	1312	0.8
	2203	8.6	2151	7.5	1920	5.7					2132	1.6	2118	1.2	2007	0.9	1840	0.2

• • Time Zone -0100. For UT subtract 1 hour. For European summer time (shaded) 26/3-29/10 add 1 hour • •

MAY 2000 TIDE TABLES

• • Time Zone -0100. For UT subtract 1 hour. For European summer time (shaded) 26/3-29/10 add 1 hour • •

	DIEPPE		LE HAVRE		CHERBOURG		ST HELIER JERSEY		ST MALO		BREST		POINTE DE GRAVE		LISBOA		GIBRALTAR	
	Time	m	Time	m	Time	m	Time	m	Time	m	Time	m	Time	m	Time	m	Time	m
16TU	0501	1.0	0407	1.5	0203	1.4	0018	2.1	0014	2.3	0336	6.5	0351	4.9	0245	3.7	0127	0.9
	1025	8.6	1010	7.4	0735	5.8	0600	10.0	0546	11.2	0957	1.5	0945	1.1	0828	0.8	0709	0.2
	1724	0.9	1630	1.3	1425	1.2	1245	1.8	1239	2.1	1556	6.6	1610	5.0	1506	3.7	1353	0.8
	2246	8.8	2236	7.6	1959	5.9	1826	10.3	1811	11.4	2215	1.4	2200	1.1	2044	0.8	1918	0.2
17W	0545	0.9	0452	1.3	0245	1.3	0103	1.8	0056	2.0	0416	6.6	0429	5.0	0325	3.7	0204	0.9
	1106	8.8	1054	7.5	0814	5.9	0642	10.3	0627	11.5	1037	1.4	1023	1.1	0902	0.8	0745	0.2
	1805	0.8	1712	1.3	1504	1.2	1327	1.6	1318	2.0	1634	6.7	1644	5.0	1544	3.7	1430	0.9
	2325	9.0	2314	7.7	2035	6.1	1905	10.5	1849	11.6	2254	1.3	2239	1.1	2118	0.8	1954	0.2
18TH O	0624	0.9	0532	1.3	0323	1.2	0144	1.6	0135	2.0	0453	6.6	0503	4.9	0403	3.7	0239	0.9
	1144	8.9	1130	7.5	0851	6.0	0721	10.4	0705	11.5	1115	1.4	1059	1.1	0934	0.8	0820	0.1
	1842	1.0	1749	1.4	1539	1.3	1403	1.6	1355	2.1	1709	6.7	1715	5.0	1621	3.8	1504	0.9
			2344	7.6	2109	6.2	1941	10.6	1925	11.6	2332	1.3	2315	1.1	2152	0.8	2030	0.2
19F	0001	9.0	0606	1.4	0358	1.3	0219	1.6	0212	2.0	0528	6.6	0533	4.9	0440	3.6	0311	0.9
	0700	1.0	1157	7.4	0925	6.0	0757	10.4	0741	11.4	1150	1.5	1133	1.2	1006	0.8	0855	0.1
	1220	8.8	1821	1.6	1613	1.4	1436	1.7	1430	2.2	1743	6.7	1745	5.0	1656	3.7	1537	0.9
	1915	1.2	2301	7.5	2142	6.1	2015	10.5	2000	11.5			2351	1.2	2226	0.8	2106	0.2
20SA	0036	8.8	0635	1.6	0431	1.4	0251	1.6	0246	2.2	0008	1.4	0601	4.8	0516	3.6	0343	0.9
	0731	1.1	1123	7.4	0959	5.9	0830	10.3	0815	11.2	0601	6.5	1208	1.3	1039	0.9	0930	0.1
	1254	8.6	1847	1.8	1645	1.6	1506	1.8	1501	2.5	1224	1.6	1814	4.9	1730	3.6	1610	0.9
	1945	1.4	2336	7.5	2215	6.1	2046	10.4	2031	11.3	1816	6.6			2300	0.9	2142	0.2
21SU	0109	8.6	0700	1.7	0503	1.5	0322	1.8	0317	2.4	0042	1.6	0027	1.3	0551	3.4	0415	0.8
	0800	1.3	1204	7.3	1033	5.8	0902	10.0	0846	11.0	0633	6.3	0630	4.7	1112	1.0	1006	0.1
	1327	8.4	1913	2.0	1715	1.8	1535	2.1	1530	2.9	1256	1.8	1242	1.4	1805	3.5	1643	0.8
	2012	1.6			2247	5.9	2116	10.0	2101	11.0	1848	6.4	1845	4.8	2336	1.0	2217	0.2
22M	0141	8.4	0017	7.4	0535	1.7	0352	2.1	0346	2.7	0115	1.8	0102	1.4	0627	3.3	0448	0.8
	0827	1.5	0727	1.9	1107	5.6	0933	9.6	0916	10.6	0705	6.1	0701	4.6	1147	1.1	1042	0.1
	1359	8.2	1248	7.2	1748	2.0	1603	2.5	1557	3.1	1328	2.1	1316	1.6	1840	3.4	1717	0.8
	2041	1.8	1942	2.2	2320	5.7	2145	9.6	2130	10.7	1921	6.2	1919	4.7			2253	0.2
23TU	0212	8.1	0059	7.3	0609	1.9	0423	2.5	0415	3.0	0150	2.0	0139	1.5	0014	1.1	0523	0.8
	0857	1.7	0758	2.1	1142	5.4	1003	9.2	0945	10.3	0739	5.8	0737	4.4	0703	3.1	1118	0.2
	1431	7.9	1330	7.1	1823	2.2	1633	2.9	1625	3.5	1403	2.3	1354	1.7	1225	1.2	1753	0.8
	2112	2.0	2016	2.4	2356	5.4	2214	9.1	2158	10.3	1959	5.9	1959	4.5	1917	3.3	2330	0.2
24W	0244	7.8	0142	7.0	0647	2.1	0456	3.0	0445	3.4	0229	2.3	0220	1.7	0057	1.2	0600	0.8
	0931	1.9	0833	2.3	1224	5.1	1036	8.7	1016	9.8	0818	5.6	0821	4.2	0745	3.0	1158	0.2
	1506	7.5	1415	6.8	1903	2.4	1706	3.4	1654	3.9	1445	2.6	1438	1.9	1310	1.4	1833	0.8
	2149	2.3	2057	2.7			2248	8.6	2230	9.8	2042	5.6	2048	4.4	2000	3.1		
25TH	0321	7.4	0227	6.8	0040	5.1	0535	3.4	0518	3.9	0314	2.5	0307	1.8	0149	1.4	0013	0.3
	1012	2.2	0918	2.6	0733	2.3	1115	8.2	1055	9.3	0907	5.3	0918	4.1	0835	2.8	0642	0.7
	1551	7.2	1505	6.6	1317	4.8	1748	3.9	1730	4.3	1536	2.8	1530	2.1	1406	1.5	1245	0.3
	2234	2.5	2148	3.0	1955	2.6	2332	8.1	2314	9.3	2136	5.4	2151	4.2	2054	3.0	1919	0.7
26F	0412	7.0	0321	6.5	0139	4.9	0624	3.8	0603	4.3	0408	2.7	0403	1.9	0254	1.4	0106	0.3
	1104	2.4	1015	2.8	0830	2.4	1211	7.8	1152	8.9	1009	5.1	1034	4.0	0938	2.8	0733	0.7
	1654	6.9	1608	6.3	1424	4.7	1845	4.2	1823	4.7	1636	2.9	1633	2.1	1517	1.6	1345	0.3
	2333	2.8	2252	3.1	2100	2.7					2243	5.3	2306	4.2	2200	3.0	2014	0.7
27SA	0526	6.8	0430	6.3	0248	4.8	0040	7.8	0024	8.9	0511	2.7	0507	2.0	0409	1.4	0215	0.3
	1209	2.6	1122	2.9	0936	2.4	0728	4.0	0709	4.0	1122	5.1	1155	4.0	1050	2.8	0840	0.7
	1811	6.9	1730	6.3	1535	4.7	1330	7.7	1319	8.7	1745	2.9	1742	2.1	1635	1.5	1456	0.3
					2212	2.7	2000	4.3	1944	4.9	2356	5.3			2311	3.0	2120	0.7
28SU	0046	2.8	0003	3.0	0358	4.8	0208	7.9	0156	8.9	0620	2.6	0018	4.3	0517	1.3	0333	0.3
	0643	6.9	0551	6.3	1046	2.3	0844	3.8	0839	4.5	1236	5.3	0614	1.9	1157	3.0	1000	0.7
	1327	2.5	1234	2.7	1641	4.9	1451	8.0	1442	9.0	1854	2.7	1302	4.2	1742	1.4	1607	0.3
	1921	7.2	1848	6.6	2321	2.4	2121	3.9	2116	4.5			1847	1.9			2231	0.8
29M	0206	2.5	0115	2.7	0501	5.1	0322	8.4	0312	9.4	0104	5.6	0121	4.5	0015	3.2	0444	0.3
	0751	7.3	0658	6.7	1149	2.0	0957	3.3	1000	3.9	0725	2.3	0715	1.7	0614	1.1	1119	0.7
	1439	2.1	1343	2.3	1738	5.2	1556	8.7	1548	9.8	1338	5.7	1357	4.5	1253	3.2	1709	0.3
	2023	7.7	1942	6.9			2231	3.3	2230	3.3	1956	2.3	1945	1.7	1837	1.2	2339	0.8
30TU	0312	2.0	0219	2.3	0021	2.1	0422	9.1	0413	10.2	0202	6.0	0214	4.7	0111	3.4	0544	0.2
	0852	7.8	0745	7.0	0557	5.4	1101	2.7	1103	3.1	0821	1.9	0809	1.5	0703	0.9	1224	0.8
	1540	1.6	1445	1.9	1245	1.7	1652	9.5	1642	10.6	1430	6.1	1444	4.7	1342	3.4	1804	0.2
	2119	8.3	2016	7.3	1827	5.6	2332	2.5	2330	2.9	2049	1.8	2036	1.4	1927	0.9		
31W	0409	1.5	0319	1.8	0114	1.7	0517	9.8	0506	11.0	0253	6.4	0303	4.9	0201	3.6	0038	0.9
	0947	8.4	0818	6.3	0647	5.8	1158	2.0	1158	2.3	0912	1.5	0859	1.3	0749	0.7	0636	0.1
	1634	1.2	1544	1.5	1336	1.4	1744	10.2	1731	11.4	1517	6.5	1529	5.0	1430	3.6	1321	0.8
	2210	8.8	2038	7.6	1912	6.0					2139	1.4	2124	1.2	2013	0.7	1855	0.2

FRANCE, SPAIN, PORTUGAL & GIBRALTAR Time Zone -0100
Dieppe * Le Havre * Cherbourg * St Helier * St Malo * Brest * Pointe de Grave * Lisboa * Gibraltar

TIDE TABLES   JUNE 2000

DIEPPE		LE HAVRE		CHERBOURG		ST HELIER JERSEY		ST MALO		BREST		POINTE DE GRAVE		LISBOA		GIBRALTAR		Day
Time	m	Time	m	Time	m	Time	m	Time	m	Time	m	Time	m	Time	m	Time	m	
0503	1.1	0415	1.5	0204	1.4	0027	1.8	0024	2.2	0342	6.7	0349	5.1	0251	3.7	0132	0.9	1 TH
1037	8.8	0850	7.7	0735	6.1	0609	10.5	0556	11.7	1001	1.2	0945	1.1	0833	0.6	0726	0.1	
1726	1.0	1640	1.3	1424	1.2	1252	1.5	1251	1.7	1603	6.9	1612	5.2	1516	3.8	1412	0.9	
2259	9.1	2107	7.8	1958	6.3	1834	10.9	1819	12.1	2227	1.1	2211	1.0	2058	0.5	1943	0.1	
0554	0.8	0509	1.2	0252	1.1	0120	1.3	0115	1.6	0429	7.0	0436	5.3	0339	3.8	0222	0.9	2 F
1126	9.1	0926	7.8	0823	6.3	0700	11.0	0644	12.2	1049	1.0	1030	0.9	0918	0.5	0813	0.0	●
1818	0.6	1733	1.1	1513	1.0	1344	1.1	1342	1.3	1650	7.1	1657	5.4	1603	3.9	1500	0.9	
2346	9.3	2144	8.0	2044	6.5	1923	11.3	1906	12.5	2316	0.8	2258	0.8	2144	0.4	2030	0.1	
0645	0.7	0600	1.0	0341	0.9	0210	1.2	0207	1.2	0517	7.1	0522	5.3	0427	3.9	0312	1.0	3 SA
1212	9.2	1124	7.7	0912	6.4	0750	11.3	0731	12.4	1136	0.9	1117	0.9	1003	0.5	0900	0.0	
1908	0.7	1821	1.1	1601	0.9	1433	0.9	1432	1.2	1736	7.2	1742	5.4	1649	4.0	1548	0.9	
		2226	7.9	2131	6.6	2010	11.5	1951	12.7			2346	0.8	2231	0.4	2118	0.1	
0033	9.4	0648	0.9	0429	0.8	0259	0.8	0257	1.1	0005	0.8	0610	5.3	0516	3.9	0400	0.9	4 SU
0736	0.6	1146	7.7	1001	6.4	0839	11.3	0818	12.4	0605	7.1	1204	0.9	1048	0.5	0947	0.1	
1259	9.2	1909	1.1	1649	0.9	1519	0.9	1520	1.2	1225	0.9	1830	5.4	1736	4.0	1635	0.9	
1958	0.7			2219	6.5	2057	11.4	2036	12.6	1824	7.2			2319	0.5	2206	0.1	
0118	9.3	0015	7.7	0518	0.8	0345	0.9	0345	1.2	0054	0.8	0036	0.8	0606	3.8	0448	0.9	5 M
0824	0.6	0733	1.0	1052	6.3	0927	11.1	0903	12.1	0654	7.0	0700	5.2	1136	0.7	1034	0.1	
1346	9.3	1332	7.7	1739	1.1	1605	1.2	1606	1.5	1315	1.1	1254	1.0	1825	3.9	1723	0.9	
2046	0.8	1954	1.3	2309	6.4	2143	11.1	2121	12.3	1913	7.0	1921	5.3			2255	0.1	
0206	9.0	0039	7.6	0607	0.9	0433	1.2	0430	1.5	0145	1.0	0127	1.0	0011	0.6	0539	0.9	6 TU
0912	0.7	0818	1.1	1144	6.1	1014	10.6	0949	11.7	0744	6.7	0754	5.0	0657	3.7	1123	0.1	
1435	8.8	1421	7.6	1828	1.4	1650	1.6	1651	2.0	1405	1.4	1345	1.2	1227	0.9	1813	0.9	
2134	1.0	2039	1.5			2229	10.6	2206	11.7	2004	6.7	2017	5.1	1916	3.8	2348	0.1	
0254	8.7	0229	7.5	0000	6.1	0520	1.7	0515	2.0	0237	1.3	0221	1.1	0107	0.8	0630	0.8	7 W
1000	0.9	0904	1.4	0659	1.2	1103	10.0	1037	11.0	0837	6.3	0853	4.8	0751	3.5	1215	0.1	
1526	8.5	1510	7.4	1238	5.8	1737	2.2	1736	2.6	1458	1.7	1440	1.4	1323	1.1	1906	0.8	
2223	1.2	2125	1.8	1921	1.7	2317	10.0	2256	11.1	2059	6.4	2118	4.9	2011	3.6			
0347	8.3	0317	7.3	0054	5.8	0610	2.2	0603	2.7	0333	1.7	0319	1.3	0212	1.0	0047	0.2	8 TH
1051	1.1	0954	1.7	0754	1.5	1154	9.4	1132	10.3	0936	6.0	0959	4.6	0850	3.3	0726	0.8	
1622	8.1	1603	7.2	1336	5.5	1830	2.8	1824	3.2	1555	2.0	1540	1.6	1430	1.3	1313	0.2	
2315	1.6	2218	2.2	2018	2.0			2354	10.4	2159	6.0	2226	4.7	2113	3.5	2003	0.8	
0446	7.9	0411	7.0	0154	5.5	0010	9.3	0656	3.3	0433	2.0	0422	1.5	0326	1.2	0154	0.3	9 F
1145	1.5	1051	2.0	0854	1.8	0706	2.7	1238	9.8	1039	5.7	1110	4.4	0957	3.2	0828	0.7	
1724	7.8	1703	7.0	1439	5.2	1252	8.9	1923	3.7	1658	2.3	1646	1.8	1548	1.4	1419	0.3	
		2321	2.4	2123	2.2	1929	3.2			2305	5.8	2338	4.6	2222	3.3	2106	0.8	
0013	1.8	0514	6.8	0259	5.2	0112	8.9	0102	9.8	0539	2.2	0530	1.6	0442	1.2	0309	0.3	10 SA
0553	7.6	1157	2.2	1002	1.9	0809	3.1	0801	3.6	1149	5.6	1220	4.4	1106	3.2	0938	0.7	
1245	1.7	1807	6.9	1548	5.1	1400	8.6	1351	9.5	1806	2.4	1755	1.8	1703	1.4	1529	0.3	
1834	7.6			2233	2.3	2036	3.4	2032	3.9					2333	3.3	2212	0.8	
0118	2.0	0030	2.5	0409	5.1	0224	8.7	0216	9.7	0016	5.7	0046	4.5	0546	1.2	0421	0.3	11 SU
0706	7.5	0621	6.7	1112	2.0	0916	3.1	0914	3.7	0647	2.2	0638	1.6	1212	3.2	1049	0.7	
1354	1.8	1306	2.2	1700	5.0	1509	8.7	1501	9.6	1257	5.7	1323	4.5	1807	1.3	1633	0.3	
1944	7.7	1913	6.9	2344	2.2	2145	3.3	2143	3.8	1914	2.3	1902	1.7			2315	0.8	
0230	1.9	0138	2.3	0520	5.2	0334	8.8	0324	9.8	0124	5.8	0148	4.6	0036	3.4	0520	0.3	12 M
0814	7.6	0732	6.8	1216	1.9	1021	3.0	1020	3.4	0750	2.1	0739	1.6	0639	1.1	1153	0.7	
1504	1.7	1409	2.0	1800	5.1	1613	9.0	1602	10.0	1357	5.8	1417	4.6	1309	3.3	1728	0.3	
2044	7.9	2019	7.0			2248	3.0	2245	3.4	2013	2.1	2000	1.6	1859	1.2			
0336	1.7	0239	2.1	0045	2.0	0436	9.1	0422	10.2	0221	5.9	0240	4.6	0131	3.4	0010	0.8	13 TU
0910	7.9	0843	6.9	0618	5.3	1118	2.7	1114	3.1	0843	2.0	0832	1.5	0722	1.1	0607	0.3	
1603	1.5	1506	1.9	1309	1.8	1707	9.4	1654	10.4	1446	6.0	1503	4.7	1357	3.5	1245	0.8	
2135	8.2	2118	7.2	1850	5.5	2344	2.6	2335	3.0	2104	1.9	2051	1.5	1942	1.1	1815	0.3	
0430	1.5	0332	1.8	0135	1.8	0528	9.4	0512	10.5	0309	6.1	0326	4.7	0218	3.5	0057	0.8	14 W
0958	8.2	0940	7.1	0707	5.5	1209	2.5	1200	2.8	0929	1.8	0917	1.4	0800	1.0	0648	0.2	
1652	1.4	1554	1.7	1355	1.7	1754	9.7	1739	10.7	1530	6.2	1544	4.8	1440	3.6	1330	0.8	
2219	8.5	2204	7.3	1931	5.7					2149	1.8	2136	1.4	2020	1.0	1858	0.3	
0515	1.3	0418	1.7	0218	1.6	0032	2.4	0020	2.7	0351	6.2	0405	4.7	0301	3.5	0139	0.8	15 TH
1041	8.6	1025	7.2	0750	5.6	0614	9.6	0557	10.7	1011	1.8	0957	1.4	0835	1.0	0727	0.2	
1735	1.4	1638	1.7	1436	1.6	1254	2.3	1242	2.7	1609	6.4	1619	4.9	1521	3.6	1411	0.8	
2300	8.6	2240	7.4	2009	5.9	1837	9.9	1821	10.9	2230	1.7	2216	1.4	2056	1.0	1939	0.3	

● ● Time Zone -0100. For UT subtract 1 hour. For European summer time (shaded) 26/3-29/10 add 1 hour ● ●

JUNE 2000 TIDE TABLES

• • Time Zone -0100. For UT subtract 1 hour. For European summer time (shaded) 26/3-29/10 add 1 hour • •

	DIEPPE		LE HAVRE		CHERBOURG		ST HELIER JERSEY		ST MALO		BREST		POINTE DE GRAVE		LISBOA		GIBRALTAR	
	Time	m	Time	m	Time	m	Time	m	Time	m	Time	m	Time	m	Time	m	Time	m
16 F O	0556	1.3	0459	1.6	0258	1.5	0115	2.1	0101	2.6	0430	6.3	0439	4.8	0342	3.5	0217	0.8
	1121	8.5	1100	7.3	0829	5.7	0656	9.8	0639	10.8	1050	1.7	1035	1.4	0909	0.9	0806	0.2
	1814	1.4	1716	1.8	1513	1.6	1333	2.2	1321	2.7	1647	6.5	1652	4.9	1559	3.6	1448	0.8
	2337	8.6	2303	7.4	2046	6.0	1915	10.1	1900	11.0	2309	1.6	2254	1.3	2131	0.9	2018	0.2
17 SA	0633	1.3	0536	1.7	0335	1.5	0153	2.0	0141	2.5	0506	6.3	0512	4.8	0420	3.5	0254	0.8
	1158	8.5	1121	7.3	0906	5.8	0734	9.9	0718	10.8	1126	1.7	1111	1.4	0942	0.9	0845	0.2
	1849	1.5	1751	1.8	1549	1.7	1409	2.1	1359	2.7	1722	6.5	1724	5.0	1636	3.7	1525	0.8
			2256	7.4	2121	6.0	1951	10.1	1936	11.1	2346	1.6	2330	1.3	2206	0.9	2057	0.2
18 SU	0013	8.6	0609	1.7	0409	1.5	0228	1.9	0219	2.5	0541	6.3	0542	4.7	0457	3.4	0330	0.8
	0707	1.4	1125	7.3	0942	5.8	0809	9.9	0754	10.8	1200	1.7	1145	1.4	1017	0.9	0923	0.2
	1233	8.5	1824	1.9	1623	1.7	1442	2.1	1435	2.8	1757	6.5	1755	5.0	1712	3.6	1601	0.8
	1921	1.6	2326	7.5	2156	6.0	2025	10.1	2010	11.0					2242	0.9	2136	0.2
19 M	0048	8.5	0642	1.8	0444	1.5	0301	2.0	0255	2.6	0021	1.6	0006	1.4	0533	3.4	0407	0.8
	0739	1.4	1157	7.3	1018	5.7	0843	9.8	0827	10.8	0614	6.2	0614	4.7	1051	1.0	1000	0.1
	1308	8.4	1857	2.0	1657	1.8	1515	2.2	1509	2.8	1234	1.8	1220	1.5	1747	3.6	1636	0.8
	1952	1.7			2230	5.9	2057	10.0	2042	11.0	1830	6.4	1829	4.9	2318	0.9	2213	0.2
20 TU	0121	8.4	0003	7.4	0518	1.6	0334	2.1	0329	2.6	0055	1.7	0042	1.4	0609	3.3	0443	0.8
	0810	1.4	0715	1.8	1052	5.6	0915	9.6	0859	10.7	0647	6.1	0647	4.7	1127	1.0	1038	0.1
	1342	8.2	1233	7.3	1732	1.9	1546	2.4	1541	2.9	1309	2.0	1255	1.5	1821	3.5	1712	0.8
	2024	1.7	1931	2.1	2303	5.8	2128	9.7	2112	10.9	1904	6.3	1904	4.9	2355	1.0	2251	0.2
21 W	0154	8.2	0040	7.4	0554	1.7	0406	2.3	0401	2.8	0130	1.9	0118	1.5	0644	3.2	0520	0.8
	0842	1.5	0748	1.9	1127	5.5	0948	9.4	0930	10.5	0721	6.0	0723	4.6	1205	1.1	1115	0.2
	1415	8.1	1311	7.2	1808	2.0	1618	2.7	1612	3.1	1344	2.1	1333	1.6	1857	3.4	1748	0.8
	2056	1.8	2007	2.2	2339	5.6	2200	9.4	2142	10.7	1940	6.1	1942	4.8			2328	0.2
22 TH	0227	8.1	0118	7.3	0631	1.8	0441	2.6	0433	3.0	0208	2.0	0157	1.5	0036	1.1	0558	0.8
	0916	1.6	0824	2.1	1204	5.3	1021	9.1	1002	10.3	0759	5.8	0803	4.4	0721	3.1	1153	0.2
	1450	7.9	1348	7.1	1847	2.2	1651	3.0	1642	3.4	1424	2.3	1412	1.7	1246	1.2	1827	0.8
	2132	2.0	2045	2.4			2233	9.1	2215	10.4	2020	5.9	2025	4.6	1934	3.3		
23 F	0304	7.8	0157	7.1	0017	5.4	0517	2.9	0506	3.3	0249	2.2	0239	1.6	0121	1.2	0009	0.2
	0954	1.8	0903	2.2	0713	2.0	1057	8.8	1039	10.0	0841	5.6	0850	4.3	0802	3.0	0639	0.8
	1530	7.7	1430	6.9	1247	5.1	1730	3.3	1716	3.7	1509	2.5	1458	1.8	1334	1.3	1235	0.2
	2213	2.1	2130	2.5	1931	2.4	2313	8.8	2254	10.1	2106	5.7	2115	4.5	2017	3.2	1910	0.8
24 SA	0348	7.6	0242	6.8	0103	5.2	0559	3.2	0545	3.6	0336	2.4	0327	1.7	0213	1.3	0056	0.7
	1039	2.0	0951	2.4	0800	2.1	1142	8.5	1124	9.6	0931	5.4	0947	4.2	0851	3.0	0727	0.8
	1621	7.5	1521	6.7	1339	5.0	1816	3.6	1759	4.0	1600	2.6	1551	1.9	1433	1.4	1324	0.3
	2303	2.3	2221	2.7	2024	2.5			2347	9.7	2159	5.6	2215	4.4	2109	3.1	1958	0.8
25 SU	0445	7.3	0339	6.6	0159	5.1	0004	8.5	0636	3.9	0430	2.4	0421	1.8	0315	1.3	0152	0.3
	1133	2.2	1046	2.5	0856	2.2	0650	3.5	1227	9.3	1031	5.4	1056	4.2	0950	3.0	0825	0.8
	1722	7.3	1627	6.5	1440	4.9	1240	8.3	1900	4.3	1659	2.7	1651	2.0	1542	1.4	1422	0.3
			2321	2.7	2125	2.5	1915	3.8			2302	5.5	2324	4.4	2212	3.1	2055	0.8
26 M	0003	2.5	0451	6.5	0303	5.1	0110	8.4	0058	9.4	0530	2.4	0523	1.8	0424	1.3	0258	0.3
	0553	7.2	1148	2.5	0958	2.2	0752	3.5	0748	4.0	1138	5.4	1208	4.2	1057	3.0	0935	0.7
	1238	2.3	1744	6.6	1545	5.0	1351	8.4	1344	9.3	1803	2.6	1755	1.9	1653	1.4	1529	0.3
	1830	7.4			2232	2.4	2026	3.7	2020	4.3					2321	3.2	2200	0.8
27 TU	0115	2.4	0025	2.6	0409	5.1	0225	8.5	0218	9.5	0010	5.6	0033	4.4	0529	1.2	0410	0.3
	0703	7.3	0606	6.7	1102	2.1	0905	3.3	0906	3.8	0636	2.3	0627	1.7	1204	3.2	1051	0.7
	1351	2.2	1255	2.3	1648	5.2	1504	8.7	1458	9.7	1247	5.6	1312	4.4	1758	1.2	1639	0.3
	1938	7.7	1849	6.9	2338	2.2	2142	3.3	2139	3.8	1909	2.3	1900	1.8			2308	0.8
28 W	0230	2.1	0133	2.3	0513	5.3	0337	9.0	0330	10.0	0118	5.8	0136	4.6	0028	3.3	0518	0.2
	0812	7.7	0708	6.9	1205	1.9	1018	2.9	1019	3.3	0740	2.1	0729	1.6	0627	1.0	1202	0.8
	1501	1.9	1403	2.1	1747	5.5	1612	9.3	1603	10.4	1351	6.0	1410	4.7	1306	3.4	1743	0.2
	2042	8.1	1937	7.2			2254	2.7	2249	3.2	2013	2.0	2001	1.5	1857	1.0		
29 TH	0336	1.7	0241	2.0	0040	1.9	0442	9.6	0433	10.7	0221	6.2	0234	4.8	0130	3.5	0014	0.9
	0915	8.2	0756	7.3	0615	5.6	1124	2.3	1122	2.7	0841	1.7	0827	1.4	0721	0.8	0620	0.1
	1603	1.5	1510	1.6	1304	1.6	1713	10.0	1701	11.1	1448	6.4	1503	5.0	1402	3.6	1305	0.9
	2141	8.6	2016	7.5	1843	5.9	2357	2.1	2352	2.5	2112	1.6	2058	1.3	1950	0.8	1842	0.2
30 F	0436	1.3	0347	1.6	0139	1.5	0544	10.2	0531	11.3	0318	6.5	0328	5.1	0228	3.6	0115	0.9
	1012	8.6	0838	7.5	0712	5.9	1226	1.8	1222	2.1	0936	1.4	0921	1.2	0812	0.7	0716	0.1
	1701	1.2	1615	1.5	1401	1.4	1811	10.6	1756	11.8	1542	6.7	1553	5.2	1455	3.8	1400	0.9
	2236	9.0	2055	7.7	1937	6.2					2207	1.2	2152	1.1	2041	0.6	1936	0.2

FRANCE, SPAIN, PORTUGAL & GIBRALTAR Time Zone -0100
Dieppe * Le Havre * Cherbourg * St Helier * St Malo * Brest * Pointe de Grave * Lisboa * Gibraltar

TIDE TABLES JULY 2000

DIEPPE	LE HAVRE	CHERBOURG	ST HELIER JERSEY	ST MALO	BREST	POINTE DE GRAVE	LISBOA	GIBRALTAR	Day
Time m	Time m	Time m	Time m	Time m	Time m	Time m	Time m	Time m	
0533 1.0	0448 1.3	0233 1.2	0057 1.5	0051 1.9	0411 6.8	0420 5.2	0322 3.7	0212 0.9	1 SA
1106 9.0	0922 7.7	0809 6.1	0642 10.7	0626 11.8	1030 1.1	1012 1.1	0900 0.6	0809 0.0	
1758 1.0	1715 1.3	1455 1.2	1323 1.4	1320 1.7	1633 7.0	1642 5.4	1547 3.9	1453 0.9	
2328 9.2	2137 7.9	2030 6.4	1905 11.0	1848 12.3	2300 0.9	2244 0.9	2130 0.5	2029 0.1	
0630 0.8	0545 1.0	0327 0.9	0154 1.1	0149 1.4	0503 7.0	0511 5.3	0415 3.8	0306 0.9	2 SU
1157 9.2	1042 7.8	0902 6.3	0736 11.0	0718 12.2	1121 1.0	1103 1.0	0948 0.5	0900 0.0	●
1854 0.8	1810 1.1	1548 1.0	1417 1.1	1415 1.4	1724 7.2	1732 5.5	1636 4.0	1544 0.9	
	2327 7.9	2121 6.5	1957 11.3	1939 12.5	2352 0.8	2335 0.8	2220 0.4	2120 0.1	
0018 9.3	0638 0.8	0418 0.7	0247 0.8	0244 1.1	0553 7.1	0601 5.3	0505 3.9	0357 1.0	3 M
0724 0.5	1227 7.9	0954 6.4	0828 11.2	0808 12.3	1212 0.9	1152 0.9	1036 0.5	0949 0.0	
1246 9.3	1900 1.0	1639 1.0	1508 1.0	1507 1.2	1814 7.3	1821 5.5	1725 4.1	1633 1.0	
1948 0.7	2340 7.9	2211 6.6	2045 11.4	2027 12.6			2309 0.4	2210 0.1	
0106 9.3	0726 0.7	0507 0.7	0337 0.7	0335 1.0	0043 0.7	0025 0.8	0554 3.8	0448 0.9	4 TU
0815 0.4	1320 7.9	1044 6.3	0917 11.1	0856 12.2	0643 7.0	0651 5.3	1124 0.6	1038 0.0	
1334 9.2	1947 1.0	1727 1.0	1556 1.1	1556 1.2	1302 1.0	1241 1.0	1813 4.0	1722 1.0	
2036 0.6		2300 6.5	2132 11.3	2113 12.5	1903 7.2	1912 5.4		2301 0.1	
0154 9.2	0133 7.9	0556 0.8	0425 0.9	0421 1.1	0133 0.8	0115 0.9	0000 0.5	0539 0.9	5 W
0902 0.4	0812 0.8	1133 6.2	1003 10.9	0942 11.9	0732 6.8	0742 5.1	0643 3.7	1127 0.1	
1422 9.1	1409 7.8	1816 1.2	1642 1.3	1640 1.5	1351 1.2	1330 1.1	1213 0.8	1812 0.9	
2123 0.7	2032 1.2	2348 6.3	2217 10.9	2158 12.1	1951 6.9	2003 5.3	1901 3.9	2353 0.1	
0241 9.0	0219 7.8	0645 1.0	0511 1.3	0505 1.5	0222 1.1	0205 1.0	0052 0.7	0630 0.9	6 TH
0946 0.5	0855 1.0	1221 5.9	1048 10.4	1027 11.5	0821 6.6	0833 4.9	0732 3.6	1216 0.1	
1509 8.8	1457 7.7	1904 1.5	1727 1.8	1723 2.0	1441 1.5	1421 1.2	1305 0.9	1902 0.9	
2206 0.9	2115 1.5		2301 10.4	2243 11.5	2040 6.6	2055 5.1	1951 3.7		
0329 8.7	0304 7.6	0036 6.0	0556 1.8	0548 2.1	0312 1.4	0257 1.2	0148 0.9	0048 0.2	7 F
1030 0.8	0939 1.3	0733 1.3	1133 9.8	1114 10.8	0911 6.2	0929 4.7	0824 3.4	0724 0.8	
1557 8.5	1543 7.4	1310 5.7	1811 2.3	1805 2.6	1532 1.8	1515 1.4	1402 1.1	1309 0.2	
2251 1.2	2200 1.8	1954 1.8	2346 9.7	2330 10.9	2131 6.2	2153 4.8	2045 3.5	1954 0.9	
0418 8.2	0349 7.3	0126 5.7	0642 2.4	0631 2.7	0404 1.8	0352 1.4	0250 1.1	0148 0.2	8 SA
1115 1.2	1025 1.7	0825 1.7	1219 9.2	1205 10.2	1004 5.9	1030 4.5	0921 3.3	0821 0.8	
1651 8.1	1632 7.1	1403 5.4	1859 2.9	1851 3.2	1626 2.1	1612 1.6	1507 1.3	1406 0.2	
2338 1.6	2249 2.2	2048 2.1			2227 5.9	2255 4.6	2145 3.3	2050 0.9	
0515 7.8	0439 6.9	0221 5.4	0036 9.1	0024 10.2	0501 2.2	0451 1.6	0357 1.3	0256 0.3	9 SU
1204 1.7	1118 2.1	0921 2.0	0731 2.9	0721 3.3	1104 5.6	1135 4.4	1024 3.1	0922 0.8	
1751 7.7	1724 6.9	1502 5.1	1312 8.7	1304 9.7	1726 2.4	1715 1.8	1619 1.4	1512 0.3	
	2347 2.5	2149 2.4	1953 3.3	1944 3.7	2330 5.6		2252 3.2	2149 0.8	
0032 2.0	0537 6.7	0322 5.1	0135 8.7	0127 9.7	0604 2.4	0003 4.4	0503 1.3	0409 0.3	10 M
0623 7.4	1219 2.4	1024 2.2	0827 3.3	0819 3.7	1211 5.5	0556 1.8	1130 3.1	1029 0.7	
1303 2.0	1824 6.7	1609 5.1	1417 8.5	1411 9.4	1832 2.5	1241 4.3	1728 1.4	1622 0.3	
1902 7.5		2258 2.5	2056 3.5	2048 4.0		1821 1.9		2251 0.8	
0139 2.2	0053 2.6	0432 5.0	0245 8.4	0236 9.4	0040 5.5	0109 4.3	0000 3.2	0513 0.3	11 TU
0736 7.3	0644 6.5	1132 2.3	0932 3.5	0925 3.9	0710 2.5	0700 1.8	0602 1.3	1135 0.7	
1416 2.2	1324 2.5	1719 5.1	1527 8.5	1518 9.4	1318 5.5	1342 4.4	1233 3.2	1725 0.3	
2009 7.5	1929 6.7		2204 3.5	2154 3.9	1938 2.5	1926 1.9	1827 1.4	2351 0.8	
0256 2.2	0158 2.5	0006 2.4	0355 8.5	0344 9.5	0148 5.5	0209 4.4	0101 3.2	0606 0.3	12 W
0839 7.5	0759 6.6	0544 5.1	1037 3.4	1029 3.8	0811 2.4	0759 1.8	0651 1.3	1233 0.8	
1527 2.2	1425 2.4	1234 2.3	1632 8.7	1620 9.7	1417 5.7	1434 4.5	1329 3.3	1818 0.3	
2106 7.7	2034 6.8	1819 5.3	2309 3.3	2255 3.6	2036 2.3	2023 1.8	1917 1.3		
0357 2.0	0255 2.3	0106 2.2	0457 8.7	0444 9.7	0244 5.7	0300 4.4	0154 3.2	0043 0.8	13 TH
0933 7.7	0906 6.7	0643 5.2	1136 3.1	1124 3.5	0903 2.2	0850 1.7	0734 1.2	0650 0.3	
1621 2.0	1518 2.3	1327 2.1	1727 9.1	1713 10.0	1506 5.9	1518 4.6	1416 3.4	1322 0.8	
2154 8.0	2126 7.0	1908 5.5		2348 3.3	2126 2.1	2112 1.7	1959 1.2	1903 0.3	
0447 1.8	0345 2.1	0154 2.0	0003 2.9	0535 10.0	0330 5.8	0344 4.5	0241 3.3	0130 0.8	14 F
1018 8.0	0954 6.9	0731 5.4	0550 9.0	1211 3.3	0948 2.1	0934 1.6	0812 1.1	0730 0.2	
1706 1.9	1606 2.1	1412 2.0	1227 2.8	1759 10.4	1549 6.1	1557 4.8	1500 3.5	1406 0.8	
2237 8.2	2202 7.2	1950 5.7	1814 9.4		2209 2.0	2156 1.6	2037 1.1	1945 0.3	
0530 1.7	0430 1.9	0236 1.8	0051 2.6	0035 3.1	0412 6.0	0421 4.6	0323 3.3	0212 0.8	15 SA
1100 8.2	1029 7.1	0812 5.6	0636 9.3	0620 10.3	1028 1.9	1014 1.6	0848 1.0	0809 0.2	
1748 1.8	1648 2.0	1451 1.9	1310 2.5	1255 3.1	1628 6.3	1633 4.9	1539 3.5	1445 0.8	
2316 8.4	2221 7.3	2028 5.9	1855 9.7	1841 10.6	2249 1.8	2235 1.5	2114 1.0	2024 0.2	

• • Time Zone -0100. For UT subtract 1 hour. For European summer time (shaded) 26/3-29/10 add 1 hour • •

JULY 2000 TIDE TABLES

• • Time Zone -0100. For UT subtract 1 hour. For European summer time (shaded) 26/3-29/10 add 1 hour • •

	DIEPPE		LE HAVRE		CHERBOURG		ST HELIER JERSEY		ST MALO		BREST		POINTE DE GRAVE		LISBOA		GIBRALTAR	
	Time	m	Time	m	Time	m	Time	m	Time	m	Time	m	Time	m	Time	m	Time	m
16SU O	0609	1.5	0512	1.8	0313	1.6	0132	2.3	0118	2.8	0448	6.1	0454	4.7	0403	3.4	0251	0.8
	1138	8.3	1051	7.3	0851	5.7	0716	9.6	0700	10.5	1106	1.8	1051	1.5	0924	0.9	0847	0.9
	1825	1.7	1729	2.0	1529	1.8	1349	2.3	1336	2.9	1704	6.4	1706	5.0	1618	3.6	1521	0.9
	2354	8.5	2241	7.5	2105	6.0	1933	9.9	1918	10.9	2326	1.7	2312	1.4	2149	0.9	2101	0.2
17M	0645	1.4	0551	1.7	0350	1.5	0209	2.1	0200	2.6	0523	6.2	0527	4.8	0439	3.4	0329	0.9
	1215	8.4	1112	7.4	0927	5.8	0753	9.7	0737	10.7	1141	1.8	1126	1.4	0959	0.9	0924	0.1
	1901	1.6	1809	1.9	1604	1.7	1425	2.2	1417	2.7	1739	6.5	1740	5.1	1654	3.6	1557	0.9
			2311	7.6	2140	6.0	2008	10.0	1954	11.0			2347	1.3	2224	0.8	2137	0.2
18TU	0029	8.6	0629	1.7	0425	1.4	0245	2.0	0239	2.4	0001	1.6	0559	4.8	0515	3.4	0405	0.9
	0721	1.3	1142	7.5	1001	5.8	0827	9.8	0812	10.8	0557	6.3	1200	1.4	1033	0.9	0959	0.1
	1250	8.5	1847	1.8	1639	1.7	1459	2.2	1454	2.6	1215	1.7	1813	5.1	1728	3.6	1632	0.9
	1936	1.6	2343	7.6	2213	6.0	2040	10.1	2027	11.1	1812	6.5			2300	0.8	2212	0.2
19W	0104	8.6	0706	1.6	0500	1.4	0319	1.9	0316	2.3	0036	1.6	0021	1.3	0549	3.4	0441	0.9
	0755	1.3	1213	7.5	1034	5.8	0900	9.8	0844	10.9	0629	6.3	0632	4.8	1109	0.9	1033	0.1
	1324	8.5	1924	1.8	1715	1.7	1532	2.2	1530	2.6	1249	1.8	1235	1.4	1801	3.6	1706	0.9
	2009	1.5			2245	6.0	2112	10.0	2057	11.2	1845	6.5	1848	5.1	2335	0.8	2246	0.2
20TH	0138	8.5	0015	7.6	0535	1.5	0352	2.0	0351	2.3	0110	1.6	0057	1.3	0621	3.3	0517	0.9
	0828	1.3	0741	1.7	1106	5.7	0931	9.8	0915	10.9	0703	6.2	0706	4.8	1145	0.9	1107	0.2
	1357	8.4	1242	7.4	1750	1.8	1604	2.3	1603	2.6	1324	1.8	1310	1.4	1833	3.5	1742	0.9
	2042	1.5	1959	1.9	2317	5.9	2145	9.9	2128	11.2	1920	6.4	1923	5.0			2321	0.2
21F	0211	8.4	0045	7.5	0611	1.6	0425	2.1	0424	2.4	0146	1.7	0132	1.3	0012	0.9	0554	0.8
	0902	1.3	0815	1.7	1139	5.6	1004	9.6	0947	10.8	0737	6.1	0741	4.7	0654	3.3	1142	0.2
	1432	8.3	1310	7.4	1826	1.9	1637	2.4	1635	2.8	1402	2.0	1347	1.5	1223	1.0	1819	0.9
	2117	1.6	2033	2.0	2350	5.8	2218	9.7	2200	11.0	1957	6.3	2000	4.9	1906	3.4	2359	0.2
22SA	0246	8.3	0117	7.4	0649	1.7	0500	2.4	0457	2.7	0225	1.9	0210	1.4	0051	1.0	0635	0.8
	0937	1.5	0849	1.8	1215	5.5	1039	9.4	1021	10.6	0815	6.0	0820	4.5	0729	3.2	1219	0.2
	1508	8.2	1342	7.2	1905	2.1	1712	2.7	1707	3.1	1442	2.1	1427	1.6	1305	1.1	1900	0.9
	2153	1.8	2109	2.1			2254	9.5	2236	10.7	2036	6.1	2042	4.7	1944	3.3		
23SU	0324	8.1	0156	7.2	0028	5.6	0536	2.7	0532	3.0	0307	2.0	0253	1.5	0137	1.1	0042	0.2
	1016	1.7	0927	2.0	0730	1.9	1118	9.1	1100	10.3	0857	5.8	0905	4.4	0810	3.1	0721	0.8
	1549	8.0	1424	7.0	1257	5.4	1752	3.0	1743	3.4	1528	2.3	1514	1.7	1355	1.2	1303	0.2
	2236	2.0	2151	2.3	1950	2.3	2336	9.1	2319	10.3	2123	5.9	2132	4.6	2030	3.3	1946	0.8
24M	0411	7.8	0246	7.0	0115	5.4	0619	3.0	0614	3.0	0356	2.2	0342	1.6	0231	1.2	0133	0.3
	1102	2.0	1012	2.2	0818	2.1	1204	8.8	1150	9.9	0949	5.6	1003	4.3	0902	3.1	0817	0.8
	1640	7.7	1523	6.8	1351	5.2	1841	3.4	1831	3.8	1621	2.4	1609	1.8	1457	1.3	1359	0.3
	2327	2.2	2241	2.5	2044	2.4					2219	5.7	2236	4.4	2127	3.2	2040	0.8
25TU	0509	7.5	0354	6.7	0215	5.3	0031	8.8	0015	9.8	0451	2.3	0440	1.8	0337	1.2	0238	0.3
	1157	2.2	1107	2.4	0915	2.2	0712	3.3	0711	3.8	1051	5.6	1117	4.3	1008	3.1	0924	0.7
	1744	7.5	1640	6.7	1454	5.2	1306	8.6	1256	9.6	1723	2.5	1714	1.9	1611	1.3	1510	0.3
			2342	2.6	2149	2.4	1945	3.6	1938	4.0	2327	5.6	2351	4.4	2239	3.1	2144	0.8
26W	0031	2.4	0519	6.6	0326	5.2	0141	8.6	0131	9.5	0556	2.4	0547	1.8	0449	1.2	0358	0.3
	0621	7.3	1212	2.5	1021	2.3	0822	3.4	0824	3.9	1205	5.6	1234	4.4	1124	3.1	1039	0.7
	1309	2.3	1803	6.7	1606	5.2	1421	8.6	1415	9.6	1833	2.4	1825	1.8	1726	1.2	1631	0.3
	1858	7.5			2302	2.3	2104	3.5	2058	3.9					2357	3.2	2255	0.8
27TH	0153	2.3	0053	2.5	0441	5.2	0301	8.7	0256	9.7	0044	5.7	0107	4.5	0559	1.1	0517	0.2
	0739	7.5	0642	6.8	1133	2.2	0943	3.2	0943	3.6	0707	2.3	0657	1.7	1238	3.3	1154	0.8
	1430	2.2	1327	2.4	1717	5.4	1540	9.0	1533	10.0	1321	5.8	1345	4.6	1834	1.1	1743	0.2
	2012	7.8	1912	7.0			2226	3.5	2220	3.5	1947	2.2	1936	1.7				
28F	0312	2.0	0210	2.2	0015	2.0	0419	9.1	0412	10.2	0158	6.0	0215	4.7	0111	3.3	0005	0.8
	0852	7.9	0748	7.1	0556	5.5	1100	2.8	1057	3.1	0817	2.0	0804	1.6	0700	0.9	0621	0.2
	1542	1.9	1445	2.1	1243	1.9	1652	9.6	1642	10.7	1428	6.2	1445	4.9	1343	3.5	1257	0.8
	2120	8.3	2006	7.3	1825	5.7	2339	2.4	2333	2.8	2054	1.8	2041	1.4	1934	0.8	1843	0.2
29SA	0418	1.6	0327	1.8	0122	1.7	0530	9.8	0518	10.9	0303	6.3	0315	4.9	0215	3.5	0109	0.9
	0955	8.4	0845	7.4	0703	5.8	1209	2.1	1205	2.5	0919	1.6	0904	1.4	0756	0.8	0716	0.1
	1645	1.5	1558	1.8	1348	1.6	1756	10.2	1742	11.4	1528	6.6	1541	5.2	1441	3.7	1354	0.9
	2220	8.7	2051	7.7	1926	6.1					2154	1.4	2139	1.2	2029	0.6	1936	0.1
30SU	0520	1.1	0436	1.4	0221	1.2	0043	1.7	0039	2.1	0400	6.7	0410	5.2	0311	3.7	0206	0.9
	1051	8.8	0957	7.7	0801	6.1	0631	10.4	0616	11.6	1016	1.3	0959	1.2	0847	0.6	0807	0.0
	1745	1.1	1704	1.4	1445	1.3	1309	1.6	1307	1.8	1622	7.0	1633	5.4	1533	3.9	1446	0.9
	2314	9.1	2136	7.9	2021	6.4	1853	10.8	1838	12.0	2248	1.0	2233	1.0	2119	0.4	2027	0.1
31M	0618	0.7	0536	1.0	0315	0.9	0142	1.1	0139	1.4	0451	7.0	0501	5.3	0403	3.8	0300	1.0
	1143	9.2	1116	7.9	0854	6.3	0726	10.9	0709	12.1	1109	1.0	1050	1.0	0936	0.5	0854	0.0
	1843	0.8	1800	1.1	1537	1.0	1405	1.1	1403	1.3	1712	7.3	1722	5.6	1623	4.1	1535	1.0
			2300	8.0	2112	6.6	1945	11.3	1929	12.6	2339	0.7	2323	0.8	2208	0.3	2115	0.0

FRANCE, SPAIN, PORTUGAL & GIBRALTAR Time Zone -0100
Dieppe * Le Havre * Cherbourg * St Helier * St Malo * Brest * Pointe de Grave * Lisboa * Gibraltar
TIDE TABLES AUGUST 2000

Day	DIEPPE Time	m	LE HAVRE Time	m	CHERBOURG Time	m	ST HELIER JERSEY Time	m	ST MALO Time	m	BREST Time	m	POINTE DE GRAVE Time	m	LISBOA Time	m	GIBRALTAR Time	m
1 TU ●	0004	9.4	0627	0.6	0406	0.7	0236	0.7	0233	0.9	0541	7.1	0549	5.4	0451	3.9	0351	1.0
	0712	0.4	1215	8.1	0942	6.5	0816	11.2	0759	12.4	1158	0.8	1139	0.9	1022	0.5	0942	-0.0
	1232	9.4	1850	0.8	1626	0.9	1456	0.9	1455	1.0	1800	7.4	1809	5.6	1710	4.1	1623	1.0
	1935	0.5			2159	6.7	2033	11.5	2016	12.8					2255	0.3	2203	0.0
2 W	0052	9.5	0028	8.1	0454	0.6	0326	0.6	0323	0.6	0029	0.6	0011	0.7	0537	3.9	0440	1.0
	0801	0.2	0715	0.5	1028	6.5	0902	11.3	0845	12.5	0627	7.2	0635	5.4	1108	0.5	1027	0.0
	1318	9.5	1306	8.1	1712	0.9	1543	0.8	1542	0.9	1246	0.8	1225	0.9	1755	4.1	1710	1.0
	2021	0.4	1934	0.8	2244	6.7	2117	11.5	2100	12.8	1847	7.4	1855	5.6	2341	0.4	2251	0.1
3 TH	0137	9.5	0118	8.1	0539	0.7	0412	0.6	0407	0.7	0115	0.7	0057	0.8	0622	3.8	0528	1.0
	0845	0.2	0757	0.5	1112	6.4	0945	11.1	0927	12.3	0712	7.0	0720	5.3	1153	0.6	1112	0.1
	1403	9.4	1353	8.1	1757	1.0	1626	1.0	1624	1.1	1332	1.0	1312	0.9	1840	4.0	1756	1.0
	2103	0.4	2015	0.9	2327	6.5	2158	11.2	2142	12.5	1930	7.1	1940	5.4			2338	0.1
4 F	0221	9.3	0203	8.0	0622	0.9	0453	1.0	0447	1.1	0200	0.9	0142	0.9	0027	0.6	0616	0.9
	0925	0.5	0836	0.8	1154	6.2	1025	10.7	1007	11.9	0756	6.8	0805	5.1	0706	3.7	1157	0.1
	1445	9.1	1435	7.9	1839	1.3	1706	1.4	1702	1.5	1417	1.3	1357	1.1	1238	0.8	1843	1.0
	2142	0.7	2054	1.2			2237	10.7	2221	11.9	2014	6.8	2025	5.2	1925	3.8		
5 SA	0303	8.9	0242	7.7	0008	6.2	0532	1.5	0524	1.7	0245	1.3	0229	1.1	0113	0.9	0027	0.2
	1003	0.7	0914	1.2	0705	1.3	1103	10.1	1047	11.3	0839	6.4	0851	4.8	0751	3.5	0706	0.9
	1527	8.7	1513	7.6	1236	5.9	1744	2.0	1738	2.2	1502	1.7	1445	1.3	1326	1.0	1244	0.2
	2221	1.1	2131	1.6	1922	1.7	2315	10.0	2302	11.2	2057	6.4	2112	4.8	2012	3.5	1932	0.9
6 SU	0345	8.5	0314	7.4	0051	5.8	0609	2.3	0600	2.5	0330	1.8	0317	1.4	0203	1.1	0122	0.2
	1041	1.2	0950	1.7	0748	1.7	1141	9.5	1128	10.5	0924	6.0	0942	4.5	0840	3.3	0758	0.8
	1611	8.2	1548	7.2	1321	5.5	1822	2.7	1815	2.9	1549	2.1	1536	1.6	1420	1.3	1338	0.2
	2259	1.6	2209	2.1	2007	2.1	2356	9.3	2345	10.4	2143	5.9	2205	4.5	2104	3.3	2024	0.9
7 M	0431	7.9	0345	7.0	0137	5.4	0646	3.0	0638	3.2	0418	2.3	0409	1.7	0300	1.3	0230	0.3
	1121	1.8	1030	2.3	0835	2.2	1224	8.8	1217	9.8	1015	5.6	1040	4.3	0936	3.1	0857	0.8
	1701	7.6	1624	6.9	1411	5.2	1906	3.4	1857	3.6	1642	2.5	1632	1.8	1525	1.4	1451	0.3
	2343	2.1	2255	2.6	2059	2.5					2238	5.5	2309	4.2	2206	3.1	2123	0.8
8 TU	0530	7.3	0434	6.6	0232	5.1	0044	8.5	0039	9.5	0515	2.6	0509	1.9	0407	1.5	0357	0.3
	1209	2.3	1121	2.8	0929	2.5	0733	3.6	0725	3.9	1118	5.4	1150	4.2	1042	3.0	1006	0.7
	1809	7.2	1715	6.5	1512	5.0	1321	8.2	1318	9.2	1745	2.7	1736	2.0	1641	1.5	1621	0.4
			2356	2.9	2203	2.7	2002	3.9	1953	4.2	2350	5.2			2319	2.9	2230	0.8
9 W	0039	2.6	0542	6.3	0341	4.8	0151	8.0	0149	9.0	0625	2.8	0025	4.1	0518	1.5	0510	0.3
	0652	6.9	1229	3.1	1037	2.7	0836	4.0	0828	4.4	1236	5.3	0617	2.1	1155	3.0	1118	0.7
	1313	2.8	1823	6.4	1629	4.9	1439	8.0	1436	8.9	1900	2.8	1301	4.1	1754	1.5	1730	0.4
	1930	7.0			2320	2.8	2117	4.1	2104	4.5			1848	2.1			2336	0.8
10 TH	0203	2.8	0111	3.0	0509	4.8	0316	7.8	0311	8.8	0115	5.2	0138	4.1	0032	2.9	0604	0.3
	0808	6.9	0704	6.2	1155	2.7	0955	4.1	0944	4.5	0739	2.8	0725	2.1	0621	1.5	1222	0.8
	1445	2.8	1343	3.0	1750	5.1	1600	8.1	1553	9.0	1349	5.4	1404	4.3	1300	3.1	1822	0.3
	2036	7.2	1936	6.5			2236	3.8	2221	4.3	2010	2.7	1955	2.0	1854	1.4		
11 F	0324	2.6	0221	2.8	0035	2.6	0433	8.1	0424	9.1	0223	5.4	0237	4.2	0132	3.0	0034	0.8
	0908	7.2	0826	6.4	0624	5.0	1109	3.7	1055	4.2	0839	2.6	0824	2.0	0711	1.3	0648	0.3
	1551	2.6	1446	2.8	1301	2.5	1705	8.6	1655	9.5	1445	5.7	1454	4.5	1354	3.2	1313	0.8
	2130	7.5	2039	6.7	1848	5.3	2341	3.4	2326	3.9	2105	2.4	2051	1.9	1940	1.2	1903	0.3
12 SA	0419	2.3	0318	2.5	0130	2.3	0532	8.6	0521	9.5	0313	5.6	0324	4.4	0221	3.1	0121	0.8
	0957	7.6	0924	6.7	0716	5.3	1206	3.3	1151	3.8	0927	2.3	0912	1.8	0753	1.2	0725	0.2
	1640	2.3	1539	2.5	1351	2.3	1755	9.1	1743	10.0	1530	6.0	1536	4.7	1439	3.4	1354	0.8
	2215	7.9	2122	7.0	1933	5.6					2150	2.1	2136	1.7	2020	1.1	1940	0.3
13 SU	0504	1.9	0407	2.2	0214	2.0	0031	2.8	0017	3.4	0354	5.9	0401	4.6	0304	3.2	0202	0.9
	1039	8.0	1002	7.1	0757	5.5	0619	9.0	0606	10.0	1008	2.1	0954	1.6	0830	1.0	0800	0.2
	1723	2.0	1627	2.2	1431	2.0	1251	2.8	1237	3.3	1609	6.2	1613	4.9	1519	3.5	1431	0.9
	2256	8.2	2152	7.3	2011	5.8	1837	9.5	1824	10.5	2229	1.9	2215	1.5	2056	0.9	2015	0.2
14 M	0545	1.6	0451	1.9	0252	1.7	0113	2.4	0101	2.9	0430	6.1	0436	4.7	0342	3.3	0239	0.9
	1118	8.3	1030	7.3	0833	5.7	0659	9.4	0644	10.5	1045	1.9	1030	1.5	0906	0.9	0834	0.1
	1802	1.7	1711	2.0	1508	1.8	1331	2.4	1320	2.9	1645	6.5	1648	5.0	1556	3.6	1506	0.9
	2333	8.5	2220	7.5	2047	6.0	1915	9.9	1901	10.9	2305	1.7	2251	1.4	2130	0.8	2048	0.2
15 TU O	0623	1.4	0533	1.7	0327	1.5	0152	2.1	0142	2.5	0503	6.3	0509	4.9	0418	3.4	0313	0.9
	1154	8.5	1056	7.5	0908	5.9	0735	9.8	0720	10.9	1119	1.7	1106	1.4	0940	0.8	0907	0.1
	1839	1.5	1752	1.8	1543	1.6	1409	2.1	1400	2.5	1718	6.6	1721	5.2	1631	3.6	1539	0.9
			2248	7.7	2120	6.1	1949	10.1	1936	11.3	2339	1.5	2325	1.2	2204	0.7	2119	0.2

• • Time Zone -0100. For UT subtract 1 hour. For European summer time (shaded) 26/3-29/10 add 1 hour • •

AUGUST 2000 TIDE TABLES

• • Time Zone -0100. For UT subtract 1 hour. For European summer time (shaded) 26/3-29/10 add 1 hour • •

	DIEPPE		LE HAVRE		CHERBOURG		ST HELIER JERSEY		ST MALO		BREST		POINTE DE GRAVE		LISBOA		GIBRALTAR	
	Time	m	Time	m	Time	m	Time	m	Time	m	Time	m	Time	m	Time	m	Time	m
16W	0009	8.7	0613	1.5	0403	1.3	0229	1.8	0222	2.1	0536	6.5	0540	5.0	0452	3.5	0348	0.9
	0700	1.2	1122	7.6	0940	6.0	0808	10.0	0754	11.2	1153	1.6	1139	1.3	1014	0.7	0939	0.1
	1229	8.7	1831	1.6	1618	1.5	1443	1.9	1439	2.2	1751	6.7	1754	5.2	1704	3.7	1611	0.9
	1916	1.3	2315	7.8	2151	6.2	2021	10.3	2008	11.5			2358	1.2	2237	0.7	2151	0.2
17TH	0045	8.8	0651	1.4	0437	1.2	0303	1.7	0301	1.8	0012	1.4	0612	5.0	0524	3.5	0422	0.9
	0736	1.0	1142	7.7	1010	6.1	0840	10.2	0826	11.4	0608	6.5	1212	1.3	1048	0.7	1009	0.1
	1303	8.8	1908	1.5	1652	1.5	1516	1.8	1516	2.0	1227	1.5	1827	5.2	1736	3.7	1645	1.0
	1952	1.2	2339	7.8	2221	6.3	2054	10.5	2039	11.7	1824	6.8			2311	0.6	2224	0.2
18F	0118	8.8	0725	1.3	0512	1.2	0336	1.6	0337	1.7	0047	1.4	0031	1.1	0554	3.5	0457	0.9
	0812	1.0	1158	7.7	1039	6.1	0912	10.3	0857	11.5	0640	6.6	0645	4.9	1123	0.7	1041	0.1
	1337	8.8	1942	1.5	1727	1.5	1548	1.8	1551	2.0	1302	1.5	1245	1.3	1807	3.7	1719	0.9
	2026	1.2			2251	6.2	2127	10.5	2110	11.7	1857	6.7	1900	5.1	2345	0.7	2257	0.2
19SA	0152	8.8	0004	7.8	0546	1.3	0409	1.7	0412	1.8	0122	1.4	0106	1.2	0626	3.4	0535	0.9
	0845	1.1	0758	1.4	1109	6.0	0945	10.2	0928	11.5	0713	6.5	0715	4.9	1159	0.8	1113	0.2
	1410	8.7	1222	7.6	1801	1.7	1621	1.9	1624	2.2	1339	1.6	1321	1.3	1839	3.6	1756	0.9
	2059	1.4	2015	1.6	2322	6.1	2200	10.3	2142	11.6	1932	6.6	1934	5.0			2333	0.2
20SU	0225	8.6	0035	7.8	0622	1.5	0441	1.9	0445	2.2	0200	1.6	0142	1.2	0023	0.8	0615	0.9
	0918	1.3	0829	1.5	1142	5.9	1018	10.0	1000	11.2	0749	6.3	0750	4.7	0659	3.4	1149	0.2
	1444	8.6	1254	7.6	1839	1.8	1654	2.2	1656	2.6	1418	1.8	1400	1.4	1239	0.9	1836	0.9
	2133	1.5	2046	1.8	2358	6.0	2235	10.0	2215	11.2	2009	6.4	2012	4.9	1915	3.4		
21M	0300	8.4	0113	7.6	0700	1.8	0515	2.3	0518	2.7	0240	1.8	0223	1.4	0105	0.9	0014	0.2
	0953	1.6	0902	1.8	1221	5.7	1054	9.7	1036	10.8	0828	6.1	0830	4.6	0738	3.3	0701	0.8
	1521	8.3	1336	7.3	1920	2.1	1731	2.7	1728	3.1	1502	2.1	1445	1.5	1325	1.0	1232	0.3
	2211	1.8	2121	2.0			2314	9.5	2254	10.7	2053	6.1	2058	4.7	1959	3.3	1924	0.9
22TU	0342	8.1	0200	7.3	0042	5.7	0554	2.8	0555	3.2	0327	2.1	0310	1.6	0155	1.1	0104	0.3
	1034	1.9	0941	2.1	0745	2.0	1136	9.2	1119	10.3	0915	5.9	0923	4.4	0827	3.2	0757	0.8
	1606	8.0	1430	7.0	1310	5.5	1815	3.2	1809	3.6	1553	2.3	1539	1.7	1424	1.2	1329	0.3
	2257	2.2	2206	2.3	2011	2.3			2343	10.0	2146	5.8	2200	4.4	2056	3.1	2020	0.8
23W	0434	7.6	0306	6.9	0139	5.4	0002	9.0	0644	3.8	0421	2.3	0408	1.8	0300	1.2	0214	0.3
	1127	2.3	1032	2.4	0840	2.3	0643	3.3	1218	9.7	1016	5.7	1039	4.3	0933	3.1	0905	0.7
	1706	7.6	1548	6.7	1414	5.3	1231	8.7	1908	4.0	1655	2.5	1645	1.9	1539	1.3	1453	0.3
			2304	2.6	2117	2.4	1915	3.6			2256	5.6	2324	4.3	2212	3.0	2128	0.8
24TH	0000	2.5	0445	6.6	0255	5.1	0109	8.5	0055	9.4	0527	2.5	0518	1.9	0418	1.3	0354	0.3
	0548	7.3	1137	2.7	0951	2.5	0752	3.7	0754	4.2	1136	5.6	1210	4.3	1057	3.0	1025	0.7
	1239	2.6	1732	6.6	1534	5.2	1349	8.4	1342	9.3	1809	2.5	1802	1.9	1705	1.3	1632	0.3
	1827	7.3			2237	2.4	2039	3.7	2032	4.2					2342	3.1	2245	0.8
25F	0130	2.6	0020	2.7	0424	5.1	0240	8.3	0235	9.3	0024	5.5	0053	4.4	0539	1.2	0518	0.2
	0718	7.2	0628	6.7	1114	2.4	0923	3.7	0922	4.1	0645	2.5	0636	1.9	1221	3.2	1142	0.8
	1412	2.5	1300	2.7	1700	5.3	1521	8.4	1516	9.6	1303	5.7	1331	4.5	1822	1.1	1742	0.3
	1954	7.5	1855	6.8			2212	3.4	2207	3.8	1932	2.3	1921	1.8			2357	0.9
26SA	0257	2.2	0151	2.5	0001	2.2	0411	8.8	0405	9.8	0148	5.8	0208	4.6	0102	3.2	0616	0.2
	0837	7.7	0744	7.0	0551	5.3	1049	3.1	1048	3.5	0803	2.2	0751	1.7	0648	1.0	1245	0.9
	1530	2.1	1431	2.4	1233	2.1	1643	9.2	1634	10.4	1418	6.1	1437	4.8	1331	3.4	1837	0.2
	2106	8.0	1958	7.2	1819	5.6	2330	2.6	2329	3.0	2044	1.9	2031	1.5	1926	0.8		
27SU	0408	1.7	0318	2.0	0113	1.7	0524	9.5	0513	10.7	0254	6.2	0309	4.9	0206	3.4	0100	0.9
	0943	8.3	0851	7.3	0700	5.7	1159	2.4	1159	2.7	0909	1.8	0854	1.5	0745	0.8	0706	0.1
	1636	1.5	1550	1.9	1340	1.7	1748	10.0	1736	11.3	1518	6.6	1533	5.2	1428	3.7	1339	0.9
	2208	8.6	2049	7.6	1920	6.0					2144	1.4	2130	1.2	2019	0.6	1925	0.1
28M	0510	1.1	0427	1.4	0212	1.2	0035	1.8	0033	2.1	0349	6.7	0402	5.1	0300	3.6	0154	1.0
	1039	0.8	1003	7.7	0754	6.1	0623	10.3	0609	11.6	1004	1.3	0948	1.2	0836	0.6	0751	0.1
	1736	1.0	1653	1.4	1435	1.3	1259	1.7	1258	1.8	1610	7.0	1623	5.4	1519	3.9	1428	1.0
	2301	9.1	2135	7.9	2011	6.4	1842	10.8	1829	12.1	2236	1.0	2221	0.9	2107	0.4	2010	0.1
29TU	0606	0.6	0523	0.8	0303	0.9	0131	1.1	0129	1.3	0439	7.0	0448	5.3	0348	3.8	0243	1.0
	1129	9.3	1107	8.0	0841	6.4	0714	10.9	0659	12.2	1054	1.0	1036	1.0	0922	0.5	0833	0.0
	1830	0.6	1745	1.0	1524	1.0	1352	1.1	1351	1.2	1658	7.4	1709	5.6	1606	4.1	1514	1.1
	2349	9.5	2319	8.1	2057	6.6	1930	11.3	1916	12.7	2324	0.7	2308	0.8	2152	0.3	2054	0.0
30W	0657	0.2	0612	0.5	0351	0.6	0222	0.7	0218	0.7	0524	7.3	0533	5.4	0433	3.9	0330	1.1
	1214	9.6	1201	8.2	0925	6.6	0800	11.3	0744	12.6	1141	0.8	1121	0.8	1005	0.4	0915	0.0
	1918	0.3	1833	0.7	1609	0.8	1440	0.8	1438	0.8	1742	7.5	1751	5.6	1651	4.1	1558	1.1
					2141	6.8	2015	11.6	2000	13.0			2351	0.7	2234	0.3	2136	0.0
31TH ●	0033	9.6	0015	8.2	0434	0.6	0308	0.5	0304	0.5	0009	0.6	0614	5.4	0515	3.9	0415	1.1
	0742	0.1	0655	0.4	1006	6.6	0842	11.5	0826	12.7	0606	7.3	1205	0.8	1047	0.4	0955	0.0
	1257	9.6	1248	8.3	1651	0.8	1523	0.7	1521	0.7	1225	0.7	1833	5.6	1733	4.1	1641	1.1
	2000	0.3	1914	0.7	2221	6.8	2056	11.7	2041	12.9	1824	7.5			2315	0.4	2218	0.1

FRANCE, SPAIN, PORTUGAL & GIBRALTAR Time Zone -0100
Dieppe * Le Havre * Cherbourg * St Helier * St Malo * Brest * Pointe de Grave * Lisboa * Gibraltar

TIDE TABLES SEPTEMBER 2000

Day	DIEPPE Time	m	LE HAVRE Time	m	CHERBOURG Time	m	ST HELIER JERSEY Time	m	ST MALO Time	m	BREST Time	m	POINTE DE GRAVE Time	m	LISBOA Time	m	GIBRALTAR Time	m
1 F	0115	9.6	0101	8.2	0515	0.7	0349	0.6	0345	0.6	0052	0.7	0034	0.7	0556	3.8	0500	1.0
	0822	0.1	0735	0.5	1045	6.5	0921	11.3	0905	12.6	0647	7.2	0653	5.3	1035	0.5	1035	0.1
	1338	9.5	1330	8.2	1732	1.0	1603	0.9	1600	0.9	1308	0.9	1248	0.8	1814	3.9	1724	1.1
	2039	0.4	1952	0.8	2259	6.6	2134	11.4	2119	12.6	1904	7.2	1912	5.4	2354	0.6	2300	0.1
2 SA	0155	9.4	0140	8.1	0554	1.0	0427	0.9	0421	1.0	0133	1.0	0115	0.9	0636	3.7	0543	1.0
	0858	0.4	0811	0.8	1122	6.3	0957	10.9	0941	12.1	0725	6.9	0731	5.1	1207	0.7	1114	0.2
	1416	9.3	1406	7.9	1810	1.3	1639	1.3	1635	1.4	1348	1.2	1330	1.0	1855	3.7	1807	1.0
	2114	0.7	2026	1.2	2336	6.3	2209	10.9	2154	12.0	1942	6.9	1950	5.1			2342	0.2
3 SU	0233	9.1	0210	7.8	0631	1.4	0500	1.5	0454	1.7	0212	1.4	0157	1.1	0033	0.8	0627	0.9
	0932	0.8	0842	1.3	1159	6.0	1030	10.3	1015	11.5	0803	6.5	0810	4.9	0715	3.5	1155	0.2
	1453	8.8	1433	7.6	1847	1.7	1711	2.0	1706	2.1	1429	1.7	1412	1.3	1248	0.9	1851	0.9
	2147	1.1	2055	1.6			2242	10.1	2230	11.3	2019	6.4	2028	4.8	1936	3.5		
4 M	0310	8.5	0206	7.4	0012	5.9	0530	2.3	0524	2.5	0252	1.9	0239	1.4	0114	1.1	0028	0.3
	1004	1.3	0909	1.8	0707	1.9	1103	9.6	1051	10.7	0841	6.1	0851	4.6	0758	3.3	0715	0.8
	1530	8.3	1439	7.3	1236	5.7	1742	2.7	1738	2.9	1510	2.1	1457	1.6	1333	1.2	1242	0.3
	2220	1.7	2124	2.1	1924	2.2	2316	9.3	2306	10.4	2058	5.9	2110	4.4	2022	3.2	1941	0.8
5 TU	0348	7.9	0239	7.0	0053	5.5	0559	3.1	0555	3.4	0334	2.4	0325	1.8	0200	1.3	0127	0.4
	1038	2.0	0938	2.4	0744	2.4	1138	8.8	1130	9.8	0924	5.7	0939	4.3	0847	3.1	0811	0.8
	1610	7.6	1509	6.9	1321	5.3	1817	3.5	1813	3.8	1557	2.6	1548	1.9	1428	1.4	1350	0.4
	2257	2.3	2159	2.7	2006	2.6	2356	8.4	2351	9.4	2145	5.4	2204	4.1	2119	2.9	2041	0.8
6 W	0434	7.2	0330	6.6	0143	5.1	0636	3.9	0634	4.2	0424	2.8	0420	2.1	0301	1.6	0314	0.4
	1119	2.6	1018	3.0	0830	2.8	1224	8.1	1223	9.0	1022	5.3	1046	4.0	0951	2.9	0923	0.7
	1704	6.9	1602	6.5	1418	5.0	1906	4.1	1901	4.5	1656	2.9	1650	2.2	1545	1.6	1600	0.4
	2345	2.8	2250	3.2	2103	2.9					2254	5.1	2327	3.9	2234	2.8	2157	0.7
7 TH	0551	6.6	0438	6.2	0252	4.7	0055	7.7	0057	8.6	0534	3.1	0529	2.3	0424	1.7	0448	0.4
	1214	3.1	1121	3.4	0936	3.0	0734	4.5	0732	4.9	1146	5.1	1213	4.0	1111	2.8	1048	0.7
	1840	6.5	1714	6.2	1536	4.8	1345	7.6	1348	8.4	1817	3.1	1805	2.3	1716	1.6	1715	0.4
					2224	3.0	2024	4.5	2012	5.0							2315	0.8
8 F	0054	3.2	0008	3.4	0430	4.6	0237	7.3	0239	8.3	0037	5.0	0102	3.9	0000	2.8	0543	0.3
	0730	6.5	0607	6.0	1109	3.1	0908	4.7	0856	5.2	0703	3.1	0647	2.3	0546	1.6	1159	0.8
	1348	3.3	1252	3.6	1716	4.8	1533	7.6	1527	8.5	1319	5.2	1330	4.1	1228	2.9	1803	0.4
	2002	6.7	1839	6.2	2358	2.8	2203	4.4	2147	4.9	1942	2.9	1923	2.2	1828	1.4		
9 SA	0242	3.1	0142	3.3	0605	4.8	0413	7.7	0406	8.6	0201	5.2	0210	4.1	0108	2.9	0014	0.8
	0839	6.8	0740	6.2	1234	2.8	1044	4.3	1030	4.8	0815	2.9	0756	2.2	0646	1.4	0624	0.3
	1516	3.0	1415	3.3	1825	5.1	1645	8.2	1635	9.1	1422	5.5	1426	4.3	1327	3.1	1248	0.8
	2103	7.1	1954	6.5			2318	3.8	2307	4.4	2042	2.6	2025	2.0	1918	1.3	1840	0.3
10 SU	0347	2.6	0251	2.8	0104	2.5	0514	8.3	0503	9.2	0253	5.5	0258	4.3	0158	3.0	0057	0.9
	0933	7.3	0852	6.6	0657	5.2	1145	3.6	1133	4.2	0904	2.5	0848	1.9	0731	1.2	0658	0.3
	1610	2.5	1515	2.8	1327	2.4	1735	8.8	1723	9.7	1508	5.9	1510	4.6	1413	3.3	1325	0.9
	2151	7.6	2049	6.9	1911	5.4			2358	3.6	2127	2.3	2112	1.8	1958	1.0	1912	0.3
11 M	0434	2.1	0342	2.4	0148	2.1	0008	3.1	0545	9.9	0332	5.9	0337	4.6	0240	3.2	0133	0.9
	1015	7.8	0936	7.0	0736	5.5	0558	8.9	1218	3.5	0945	2.2	0930	1.7	0809	1.0	0730	0.2
	1654	2.5	1603	2.3	1407	2.0	1229	3.0	1801	10.4	1545	6.2	1548	4.9	1453	3.4	1357	0.9
	2232	8.1	2128	7.3	1948	5.8	1815	9.4			2204	1.9	2151	1.5	2033	0.9	1942	0.2
12 TU	0515	1.6	0427	1.9	0225	1.7	0050	2.5	0039	2.9	0406	6.2	0412	4.8	0317	3.3	0206	0.9
	1053	8.3	1010	7.4	0810	5.8	0636	9.5	0621	10.6	1020	1.9	1006	1.5	0844	0.9	0800	0.2
	1735	1.6	1647	1.9	1442	1.7	1309	2.4	1258	2.9	1620	6.5	1623	5.1	1530	3.6	1429	1.0
	2309	8.6	2158	7.6	2021	6.0	1851	9.9	1836	11.0	2239	1.6	2225	1.3	2106	0.7	2012	0.2
13 W O	0555	1.2	0509	1.6	0300	1.4	0129	2.0	0120	2.3	0439	6.5	0445	5.0	0351	3.5	0239	1.0
	1129	8.7	1039	7.6	0842	6.0	0710	10.0	0655	11.2	1054	1.6	1040	1.3	0918	0.7	0830	0.2
	1814	1.3	1728	1.6	1517	1.5	1346	2.0	1338	2.3	1653	6.8	1657	5.2	1604	3.7	1500	1.0
	2345	8.9	2221	7.8	2053	6.2	1924	10.4	1911	11.6	2312	1.4	2259	1.2	2139	0.6	2042	0.2
14 TH	0634	1.0	0549	1.3	0335	1.2	0206	1.7	0200	1.8	0510	6.7	0516	5.1	0424	3.5	0312	1.0
	1204	9.0	1057	7.8	0912	6.2	0743	10.4	0729	11.6	1128	1.4	1113	1.2	0951	0.6	0859	0.1
	1853	1.1	1808	1.4	1551	1.3	1421	1.9	1418	1.9	1726	7.0	1730	5.3	1637	3.7	1533	1.0
			2239	7.9	2124	6.4	1957	10.7	1944	12.0	2346	1.2	2331	1.1	2212	0.5	2112	0.2
15 F	0021	9.1	0627	1.2	0410	1.1	0242	1.4	0239	1.5	0542	6.8	0548	5.1	0455	3.6	0347	1.0
	0712	0.9	1057	7.8	0941	6.3	0816	10.7	0802	12.0	1203	1.3	1146	1.1	1025	0.5	0929	0.1
	1239	9.1	1845	1.3	1627	1.3	1456	1.6	1456	1.6	1759	7.0	1803	5.3	1709	3.7	1606	1.0
	1930	1.0	2300	8.0	2153	6.5	2031	10.9	2017	12.2					2245	0.5	2145	0.2

• • Time Zone -0100. For UT subtract 1 hour. For European summer time (shaded) 26/3-29/10 add 1 hour • •

SEPTEMBER 2000 TIDE TABLES

• • Time Zone -0100. For UT subtract 1 hour. For European summer time (shaded) 26/3-29/10 add 1 hour • •

	DIEPPE	LE HAVRE	CHERBOURG	ST HELIER JERSEY	ST MALO	BREST	POINTE DE GRAVE	LISBOA	GIBRALTAR
	Time m	Time m	Time m	Time m	Time m	Time m	Time m	Time m	Time m
16 SA	0057 9.1	0703 1.1	0445 1.1	0315 1.3	0318 1.4	0021 1.1	0004 1.0	0527 3.6	0423 1.0
	0749 0.9	1115 7.9	1011 6.4	0850 10.8	0834 12.1	0615 6.9	0618 5.1	1100 0.5	1000 0.2
	1314 9.1	1921 1.3	1701 1.3	1530 1.5	1533 1.6	1239 1.3	1220 1.1	1742 3.7	1642 1.0
	2006 1.0	2327 8.1	2224 6.5	2106 11.0	2049 12.2	1833 7.0	1835 5.3	2320 0.5	2218 0.2
17 SU	0130 9.1	0737 1.2	0520 1.2	0348 1.4	0354 1.5	0058 1.2	0039 1.1	0559 3.6	0500 0.9
	0824 1.0	1145 7.9	1041 6.4	0924 10.8	0906 12.0	0649 6.8	0650 5.0	1136 0.6	1033 0.2
	1347 9.0	1953 1.4	1737 1.4	1603 1.6	1608 1.8	1316 1.4	1256 1.2	1816 3.6	1719 1.0
	2039 1.2		2257 6.4	2141 10.8	2121 12.0	1909 6.9	1910 5.1	2357 0.6	2253 0.2
18 M	0204 8.9	0001 8.0	0557 1.4	0421 1.6	0428 1.9	0136 1.4	0116 1.2	0634 3.5	0542 0.9
	0858 1.2	0808 1.4	1115 6.2	0958 10.5	0939 11.7	0725 6.7	0724 4.9	1217 0.7	1109 0.2
	1421 8.8	1220 7.8	1815 1.6	1636 1.9	1641 2.3	1356 1.6	1336 1.3	1854 3.5	1801 0.9
	2114 1.4	2023 1.6	2334 6.2	2217 10.4	2155 11.6	1947 6.6	1948 4.9		2333 0.2
19 TU	0239 8.6	0040 7.8	0635 1.7	0456 2.1	0502 2.5	0217 1.7	0157 1.3	0039 0.8	0628 0.8
	0933 1.5	0839 1.7	1154 6.0	1034 10.0	1014 11.2	0805 6.4	0806 4.7	0715 3.4	1151 0.3
	1457 8.5	1303 7.5	1857 1.9	1713 2.5	1714 2.9	1441 1.9	1423 1.5	1303 0.9	1850 0.9
	2151 1.7	2055 1.9		2256 9.7	2233 10.9	2030 6.2	2036 4.7	1940 3.3	
20 W	0320 8.2	0128 7.4	0018 5.8	0534 2.8	0538 3.3	0303 2.1	0246 1.6	0128 1.0	0022 0.3
	1014 2.0	0915 2.0	0720 2.1	1115 9.4	1055 10.6	0851 6.0	0859 4.5	0805 3.2	0724 0.8
	1541 8.0	1357 7.2	1242 5.7	1757 3.1	1753 3.6	1533 2.2	1518 1.7	1401 1.1	1247 0.3
	2237 2.2	2138 2.3	1948 2.2	2343 9.0	2320 10.1	2125 5.8	2142 4.4	2040 3.1	1950 0.8
21 TH	0412 7.7	0234 6.9	0117 5.4	0623 3.4	0624 4.0	0400 2.4	0345 1.9	0233 1.3	0134 0.3
	1107 2.4	1004 2.5	0817 2.4	1208 8.7	1150 9.8	0954 5.7	1020 4.3	0914 3.1	0834 0.7
	1641 7.5	1518 6.7	1348 5.3	1858 3.7	1851 4.2	1638 2.5	1627 1.9	1521 1.3	1422 0.4
	2343 2.5	2236 2.7	2057 2.4			2241 5.5	2315 4.2	2203 3.0	2105 0.8
22 F	0530 7.2	0439 6.5	0239 5.1	0053 8.3	0032 9.2	0510 2.7	0500 2.0	0358 1.4	0336 0.3
	1226 2.7	1112 2.9	0934 2.6	0736 4.0	0736 4.5	1121 5.5	1200 4.3	1042 3.0	1000 0.8
	1809 7.2	1716 6.6	1517 5.1	1330 8.2	1319 9.2	1757 2.6	1750 2.0	1655 1.3	1619 0.3
		2359 2.9	2224 2.4	2028 3.9	2020 4.5			2336 3.0	2229 0.8
23 SA	0119 2.7	0621 6.6	0419 5.0	0234 8.1	0229 9.0	0017 5.4	0049 4.3	0528 1.3	0500 0.2
	0705 7.1	1245 3.0	1105 2.5	0914 4.0	0913 4.5	0634 2.7	0624 2.0	1210 3.2	1121 0.8
	1402 2.6	1843 6.7	1654 5.2	1515 8.4	1509 9.4	1255 5.7	1324 4.5	1816 1.1	1727 0.3
	1941 7.3		2353 2.2	2206 3.5	2206 4.1	1924 2.4	1913 1.8		2342 0.9
24 SU	0247 2.2	0143 2.6	0550 5.3	0409 8.6	0403 9.7	0142 5.7	0203 4.6	0054 3.2	0555 0.2
	0827 7.6	0739 6.9	1227 2.2	1042 3.3	1045 3.8	0754 2.3	0741 1.8	0640 1.1	1223 0.9
	1520 2.1	1424 2.6	1812 5.6	1637 9.1	1627 10.3	1409 6.1	1428 4.9	1318 3.4	1816 0.2
	2056 7.9	1951 7.1		2322 2.7	2324 3.1	2035 1.9	2023 1.5	1918 0.8	
25 M	0357 1.6	0308 2.0	0104 1.7	0517 9.5	0506 10.7	0245 6.2	0300 4.9	0154 3.4	0041 1.0
	0931 8.3	0851 7.3	0651 5.7	1148 2.5	1150 2.7	0857 1.8	0842 1.5	0736 0.9	0640 0.2
	1625 1.5	1537 1.9	1330 1.7	1737 10.0	1724 11.3	1506 6.6	1521 5.2	1414 3.7	1314 1.0
	2155 8.6	2055 7.5	1909 6.0			2131 1.4	2118 1.2	2008 0.6	1900 0.2
26 TU	0456 0.9	0411 1.3	0200 1.2	0022 1.8	0021 2.0	0336 6.7	0348 5.1	0244 3.6	0131 1.0
	1024 8.9	0959 7.7	0740 6.1	0610 10.3	0556 11.7	0950 1.4	0934 1.2	0823 0.6	0721 0.1
	1721 0.9	1636 1.3	1421 1.2	1244 1.7	1243 1.8	1555 7.1	1609 5.4	1502 3.9	1359 1.0
	2245 9.1	2212 7.9	1957 6.4	1827 10.8	1813 12.2	2220 1.0	2206 0.9	2051 0.4	1940 0.1
27 W	0548 0.5	0503 0.8	0247 0.9	0115 1.2	0111 1.2	0421 7.1	0432 5.3	0329 3.8	0215 1.1
	1110 9.4	1055 8.0	0824 6.4	0656 11.0	0641 12.3	1036 1.0	1019 1.0	0906 0.5	0759 0.1
	1811 0.5	1725 0.9	1506 0.9	1333 1.1	1330 1.2	1639 7.3	1651 5.5	1547 4.0	1440 1.1
	2330 9.5	2310 8.1	2039 6.6	1912 11.3	1857 12.7	2304 0.8	2248 0.8	2132 0.3	2019 0.1
28 TH	0635 0.2	0549 0.5	0330 0.7	0201 0.8	0156 0.8	0503 7.3	0512 5.4	0410 3.9	0258 1.1
	1153 9.6	1143 8.2	0903 6.6	0738 11.4	0722 12.7	1121 0.8	1102 0.8	0945 0.4	0836 0.1
	1855 0.3	1809 0.7	1548 0.8	1418 0.9	1414 0.8	1721 7.5	1730 5.6	1628 4.0	1521 1.1
		2358 8.2	2118 6.7	1953 11.6	1938 12.9	2345 0.7	2329 0.7	2209 0.4	2057 0.1
29 F	0012 9.7	0631 0.5	0411 0.7	0243 0.7	0238 0.7	0542 7.3	0549 5.4	0450 3.9	0339 1.1
	0717 0.2	1225 8.2	0941 6.7	0817 11.5	0801 12.8	1202 0.8	1142 0.8	1023 0.4	0912 0.1
	1233 9.7	1849 0.7	1628 0.9	1457 0.9	1454 0.8	1800 7.4	1807 5.5	1709 4.0	1559 1.1
	1936 0.3	2321 8.0	2155 6.7	2031 11.6	2016 12.8			2245 0.5	2133 0.1
30 SA ●	0051 9.6	0709 0.7	0449 0.9	0321 0.8	0317 0.9	0025 0.8	0008 0.8	0528 3.8	0417 1.0
	0755 0.3	1303 8.1	1016 6.6	0853 11.3	0837 12.6	0619 7.2	0624 5.3	1100 0.5	0946 0.2
	1311 9.5	1924 1.0	1705 1.1	1534 1.0	1531 1.1	1241 1.0	1222 0.9	1747 3.8	1636 1.0
	2011 0.5		2230 6.5	2106 11.3	2051 12.5	1836 7.1	1842 5.3	2321 0.6	2209 0.2

FRANCE, SPAIN, PORTUGAL & GIBRALTAR Time Zone -0100
Dieppe * Le Havre * Cherbourg * St Helier * St Malo * Brest * Pointe de Grave * Lisboa * Gibraltar
TIDE TABLES OCTOBER 2000

DIEPPE		LE HAVRE		CHERBOURG		ST HELIER JERSEY		ST MALO		BREST		POINTE DE GRAVE		LISBOA		GIBRALTAR		Day
Time	m	Time	m	Time	m	Time	m	Time	m	Time	m	Time	m	Time	m	Time	m	
0128	9.4	0008	7.9	0524	1.2	0354	1.2	0351	1.4	0103	1.1	0046	1.0	0605	3.7	0455	1.0	**1 SU**
0828	0.7	0740	1.1	1050	6.4	0926	11.0	0911	12.1	0654	7.0	0657	5.1	1136	0.7	1021	0.2	
1346	9.3	1330	7.8	1739	1.4	1606	1.4	1604	1.7	1318	1.3	1301	1.1	1824	3.6	1714	1.0	
2043	0.9	1953	1.3	2304	6.3	2139	10.8	2124	11.9	1910	6.8	1914	5.0	2355	0.8	2245	0.2	
0203	9.0	0112	7.7	0557	1.6	0424	1.7	0421	2.1	0139	1.6	0124	1.2	0642	3.5	0533	0.9	**2 M**
0859	1.1	0806	1.6	1123	6.2	0957	10.4	0942	11.5	0728	6.6	0730	4.9	1213	0.9	1055	0.3	
1420	8.8	1252	7.6	1812	1.8	1636	2.0	1633	2.3	1355	1.7	1341	1.3	1903	3.4	1753	0.9	
2112	1.3	2016	1.7	2338	5.9	2210	10.1	2157	11.2	1943	6.4	1946	4.7			2322	0.3	
0236	8.5	0109	7.4	0627	2.0	0450	2.5	0447	2.9	0214	2.0	0202	1.5	0030	1.1	0613	0.8	**3 TU**
0927	1.6	0827	2.0	1157	5.8	1026	9.7	1014	10.8	0802	6.2	0804	4.6	0720	3.3	1133	0.4	
1453	8.3	1333	7.3	1845	2.2	1703	2.8	1700	3.1	1433	2.2	1421	1.6	1253	1.1	1836	0.8	
2141	1.8	2039	2.2			2240	9.3	2229	10.3	2018	5.9	2021	4.4	1945	3.1			
0311	7.9	0157	7.1	0015	5.5	0515	3.2	0513	3.7	0251	2.5	0244	1.9	0111	1.3	0005	0.4	**4 W**
0957	2.1	0852	2.5	0658	2.5	1056	8.9	1047	9.9	0841	5.8	0845	4.3	0804	3.1	0700	0.8	
1527	7.6	1418	7.0	1236	5.4	1734	3.5	1730	3.9	1515	2.6	1508	2.0	1342	1.4	1218	0.4	
2215	2.3	2110	2.7	1921	2.5	2314	8.4	2304	9.4	2059	5.4	2105	4.1	2036	2.8	1931	0.7	
0348	7.2	0248	6.7	0100	5.1	0546	4.0	0546	4.5	0336	2.9	0333	2.2	0203	1.5	0111	0.5	**5 TH**
1035	2.7	0930	3.0	0739	2.9	1133	8.1	1127	9.1	0932	5.4	0943	4.1	0900	2.9	0806	0.7	
1609	7.0	1511	6.6	1328	5.0	1818	4.2	1812	4.7	1609	3.0	1604	2.2	1449	1.6	1351	0.5	
2259	2.8	2155	3.1	2012	2.9			2357	8.5	2200	5.0	2218	3.8	2147	2.7	2051	0.7	
0445	6.6	0348	6.2	0207	4.7	0003	7.6	0634	5.2	0439	3.2	0438	2.4	0320	1.7	0341	0.5	**6 F**
1124	3.2	1024	3.5	0841	3.1	0636	4.7	1241	8.3	1050	5.1	1112	4.0	1019	2.8	0938	0.7	
1724	6.4	1617	6.2	1446	4.7	1241	7.4	1915	5.3	1724	3.2	1718	2.4	1626	1.6	1627	0.5	
2359	3.3	2303	3.5	2129	3.0	1930	4.7			2341	4.8			2318	2.6	2224	0.7	
0633	6.3	0511	6.0	0344	4.5	0146	7.1	0146	8.0	0611	3.3	0011	3.8	0459	1.7	0455	0.4	**7 SA**
1240	3.5	1150	3.8	1015	3.2	0809	5.0	0755	5.6	1232	5.1	0600	2.4	1145	2.8	1105	0.7	
1911	6.3	1744	6.0	1627	4.7	1454	7.3	1439	8.2	1900	3.1	1242	4.0	1751	1.5	1719	0.4	
				2305	2.9	2115	4.7	2054	5.4			1839	2.3			2330	0.8	
0139	3.3	0043	3.5	0530	4.7	0342	7.4	0328	8.3	0125	5.0	0131	4.0	0033	2.8	0538	0.4	**8 SU**
0755	6.5	0651	6.1	1151	3.0	1002	4.7	0945	5.4	0738	3.1	0716	2.3	0612	1.5	1157	0.8	
1425	3.3	1332	3.5	1750	4.9	1615	7.9	1557	8.7	1348	5.4	1347	4.3	1250	3.0	1755	0.4	
2022	6.7	1911	6.3			2241	4.1	2230	4.8	2009	2.8	1948	2.1	1846	1.3			
0301	2.8	0210	3.1	0023	2.6	0444	8.1	0428	9.0	0222	5.4	0224	4.3	0127	3.0	0014	0.9	**9 M**
0854	7.1	0812	6.5	0627	5.1	1111	4.0	1100	4.6	0833	2.7	0813	2.0	0701	1.3	0612	0.3	
1530	2.7	1439	3.0	1252	2.5	1704	8.6	1648	9.5	1436	5.8	1435	4.6	1339	3.2	1234	0.9	
2116	7.3	2015	6.7	1839	5.3	2333	3.4	2326	3.9	2054	2.4	2037	1.8	1927	1.1	1827	0.3	
0355	2.2	0306	2.5	0112	2.1	0527	8.8	0511	9.8	0301	5.8	0305	4.6	0208	3.2	0049	0.9	**10 TU**
0941	7.7	0905	7.0	0706	5.4	1156	3.2	1147	3.7	0912	2.3	0857	1.7	0740	1.1	0642	0.3	
1618	2.1	1530	2.4	1334	2.1	1742	9.3	1727	10.3	1514	6.2	1515	4.9	1420	3.4	1307	0.9	
2200	8.0	2101	7.2	1916	5.7					2132	2.0	2118	1.5	2003	0.8	1856	0.3	
0440	1.6	0352	2.0	0151	1.7	0016	2.6	0008	3.0	0335	6.2	0341	4.8	0245	3.3	0122	1.0	**11 W**
1021	8.3	0943	7.4	0739	5.8	0603	9.5	0548	10.7	0948	1.9	0935	1.5	0816	0.8	0712	0.2	
1702	1.6	1615	1.9	1411	1.7	1236	2.5	1227	2.9	1549	6.5	1553	5.1	1457	3.5	1339	1.0	
2239	8.5	2133	7.5	1950	6.0	1818	10.0	1803	11.1	2207	1.6	2154	1.3	2036	0.7	1926	0.2	
0522	1.2	0436	1.6	0227	1.4	0057	2.0	0049	2.3	0408	6.6	0415	5.0	0319	3.5	0156	1.0	**12 TH**
1059	8.8	1015	7.7	0810	6.1	0638	10.1	0623	11.4	1024	1.6	1010	1.3	0851	0.7	0742	0.2	
1743	1.2	1658	1.6	1447	1.5	1316	2.0	1308	2.2	1623	6.9	1628	5.3	1533	3.7	1412	1.0	
2318	9.0	2149	7.8	2021	6.3	1854	10.5	1839	11.8	2242	1.3	2227	1.1	2110	0.5	1957	0.2	
0604	0.9	0519	1.3	0304	1.2	0136	1.6	0130	1.7	0441	6.9	0448	5.2	0353	3.6	0231	1.0	**13 F** O
1136	9.1	1008	7.8	0840	6.3	0714	10.7	0659	12.0	1100	1.3	1044	1.1	0926	0.5	0813	0.2	
1824	0.9	1740	1.3	1523	1.2	1354	1.6	1349	1.7	1658	7.1	1703	5.4	1607	3.8	1446	1.1	
2355	9.2	2203	8.0	2054	6.5	1930	11.0	1915	12.2	2318	1.1	2302	1.0	2145	0.4	2030	0.1	
0645	0.8	0600	1.1	0341	1.0	0215	1.3	0212	1.3	0515	7.1	0521	5.2	0427	3.7	0307	1.0	**14 SA**
1213	9.3	1017	7.9	0911	6.5	0750	11.0	0734	12.4	1136	1.1	1119	1.0	1001	0.5	0845	0.1	
1905	0.8	1820	1.2	1600	1.1	1432	1.3	1430	1.4	1734	7.2	1737	5.4	1642	3.8	1522	1.0	
		2227	8.1	2126	6.6	2007	11.2	1951	12.5	2356	1.0	2337	1.0	2220	0.4	2103	0.1	
0033	9.3	0639	1.1	0418	1.0	0251	1.2	0252	1.2	0551	7.1	0554	5.3	0501	3.8	0345	1.0	**15 SU**
0724	0.8	1043	8.0	0943	6.6	0826	11.2	0809	12.5	1215	1.1	1156	1.0	1039	0.5	0918	0.2	
1250	9.3	1857	1.2	1638	1.1	1509	1.2	1510	1.4	1811	7.2	1813	5.3	1719	3.8	1600	1.0	
1944	0.9	2259	8.1	2200	6.6	2045	11.3	2027	12.5					2257	0.5	2138	0.1	

• • Time Zone -0100. For UT subtract 1 hour. For European summer time (shaded) 26/3-29/10 add 1 hour • •

OCTOBER 2000 TIDE TABLES

• • Time Zone -0100. For UT subtract 1 hour. For European summer time (shaded) 26/3-29/10 add 1 hour • •

	DIEPPE		LE HAVRE		CHERBOURG		ST HELIER JERSEY		ST MALO		BREST		POINTE DE GRAVE		LISBOA		GIBRALTAR	
	Time	m	Time	m	Time	m	Time	m	Time	m	Time	m	Time	m	Time	m	Time	m
16 M	0109	9.2	0715	1.2	0456	1.1	0327	1.2	0332	1.4	0034	1.1	0015	1.0	0538	3.7	0424	1.0
	0803	0.9	1117	8.0	1018	6.6	0903	11.2	0844	12.4	0627	7.1	0629	5.2	1118	0.5	0954	0.2
	1326	9.2	1933	1.3	1717	1.2	1545	1.4	1548	1.6	1256	1.2	1236	1.1	1758	3.7	1640	1.0
	2021	1.0	2336	8.0	2238	6.5	2124	11.0	2102	12.2	1850	7.0	1851	5.2	2336	0.6	2215	0.2
17 TU	0146	9.0	0749	1.4	0535	1.4	0403	1.5	0409	1.8	0115	1.3	0054	1.2	0617	3.6	0506	0.9
	0840	1.2	1156	7.8	1054	6.4	0940	10.8	0919	12.1	0706	6.9	0708	5.1	1200	0.7	1033	0.2
	1402	9.0	2006	1.5	1757	1.4	1621	1.8	1625	2.1	1339	1.5	1320	1.2	1841	3.5	1724	0.9
	2059	1.3			2319	6.2	2203	10.5	2139	11.7	1931	6.7	1935	5.0			2257	0.2
18 W	0224	8.7	0020	7.7	0617	1.7	0440	2.1	0446	2.5	0159	1.6	0139	1.4	0020	0.8	0554	0.9
	0919	1.5	0823	1.6	1137	6.1	1018	10.3	0956	11.5	0749	6.6	0753	4.9	0701	3.5	1116	0.3
	1442	8.6	1242	7.6	1843	1.7	1701	2.4	1702	2.8	1427	1.8	1409	1.4	1249	0.9	1815	0.9
	2140	1.6	2040	1.8			2245	9.8	2218	11.0	2018	6.3	2027	4.7	1932	3.3	2345	0.3
19 TH	0308	8.2	0112	7.3	0008	5.8	0521	2.8	0524	3.3	0248	2.1	0230	1.6	0111	1.0	0651	0.8
	1004	1.9	0900	2.1	0706	2.1	1101	9.5	1039	10.8	0840	6.2	0852	4.6	0755	3.3	1213	0.3
	1528	8.1	1340	7.1	1228	5.7	1748	3.1	1744	3.5	1522	2.2	1507	1.7	1351	1.1	1919	0.8
	2231	2.0	2124	2.2	1938	2.0	2336	9.0	2307	10.1	2117	5.8	2139	4.4	2036	3.1		
20 F	0404	7.7	0238	6.8	0112	5.4	0613	3.5	0613	4.1	0348	2.5	0333	1.9	0217	1.3	0056	0.4
	1103	2.4	0951	2.5	0806	2.4	1157	8.8	1135	9.9	0946	5.8	1017	4.4	0905	3.1	0803	0.8
	1632	7.5	1518	6.7	1338	5.3	1852	3.7	1843	4.2	1629	2.5	1618	1.9	1513	1.2	1348	0.4
	2341	2.4	2224	2.6	2048	2.3					2236	5.5	2312	4.3	2158	3.0	2039	0.8
21 SA	0522	7.2	0445	6.6	0236	5.1	0049	8.3	0024	9.2	0500	2.7	0448	2.1	0345	1.4	0257	0.4
	1221	2.6	1101	2.9	0925	2.6	0727	4.0	0725	4.6	1112	5.6	1151	4.4	1030	3.1	0930	0.8
	1759	7.2	1706	6.6	1507	5.1	1321	8.3	1307	9.2	1748	2.6	1740	1.9	1648	1.2	1552	0.4
			2351	2.8	2214	2.3	2023	3.9	2014	4.5					2327	3.0	2207	0.8
22 SU	0107	2.5	0612	6.6	0412	5.1	0229	8.2	0221	9.1	0009	5.5	0040	4.4	0518	1.3	0430	0.3
	0652	7.2	1238	2.9	1054	2.5	0903	4.0	0903	4.6	0622	2.7	0612	2.0	1154	3.2	1051	0.9
	1347	2.5	1832	6.7	1641	5.2	1503	8.5	1454	9.5	1242	5.8	1310	4.6	1806	1.0	1700	0.3
	1927	7.3			2339	2.1	2154	3.5	2155	4.0	1912	2.3	1901	1.8			2321	0.9
23 M	0229	2.1	0130	2.5	0536	5.3	0357	8.7	0348	9.7	0129	5.8	0148	4.6	0040	3.2	0524	0.3
	0811	7.7	0731	6.9	1213	2.1	1026	3.4	1029	3.8	0739	2.3	0727	1.8	0628	1.1	1153	0.9
	1503	2.0	1408	2.5	1757	5.5	1621	9.2	1609	10.3	1354	6.2	1412	4.9	1301	3.4	1749	0.3
	2039	7.9	1946	7.1			2305	2.7	2306	3.1	2019	1.9	2007	1.5	1904	0.8		
24 TU	0338	1.5	0246	2.0	0047	1.7	0459	9.5	0446	10.7	0228	6.2	0244	4.9	0136	3.4	0017	1.0
	0913	8.3	0843	7.3	0635	5.7	1130	2.6	1130	2.8	0840	1.9	0826	1.5	0721	0.9	0607	0.2
	1607	1.4	1515	1.9	1313	1.7	1718	10.0	1703	11.2	1448	6.6	1504	5.1	1355	3.7	1242	1.0
	2137	8.5	2100	7.4	1851	5.9			2359	2.2	2112	1.5	2100	1.2	1951	0.6	1830	0.2
25 W	0435	0.9	0346	1.4	0140	1.3	0001	2.0	0533	11.5	0316	6.6	0330	5.1	0224	3.6	0103	1.0
	1003	8.9	0945	7.7	0721	6.0	0548	10.3	1219	2.0	0930	1.5	0915	1.2	0806	0.7	0645	0.2
	1700	0.8	1610	1.4	1402	1.3	1222	1.9	1750	12.0	1535	6.9	1550	5.3	1442	3.8	1324	1.0
	2225	9.0	2203	7.8	1936	6.2	1806	10.6			2158	1.2	2145	1.0	2031	0.5	1906	0.2
26 TH	0525	0.5	0437	1.0	0226	1.0	0051	1.5	0045	1.5	0359	7.0	0411	5.3	0307	3.8	0144	1.1
	1048	9.3	1036	7.9	0802	6.3	0632	10.8	0616	12.2	1015	1.2	1000	1.0	0846	0.6	0721	0.2
	1748	0.5	1659	1.0	1445	1.1	1309	1.4	1303	1.5	1618	7.2	1630	5.4	1525	3.9	1401	1.1
	2308	9.3	2254	7.9	2017	6.4	1848	11.1	1832	12.4	2241	1.0	2226	1.0	2109	0.5	1942	0.1
27 F	0609	0.4	0522	0.8	0307	0.9	0135	1.2	0127	1.2	0439	7.2	0448	5.3	0347	3.8	0222	1.1
	1129	9.5	1121	8.0	0839	6.5	0712	11.1	0655	12.5	1057	1.2	1040	0.9	0923	0.5	0755	0.2
	1830	0.5	1742	0.9	1526	1.0	1351	1.2	1345	1.3	1657	7.2	1707	5.4	1606	3.9	1437	1.1
	2348	9.5	2338	8.0	2054	6.5	1928	11.4	1912	12.5	2321	1.0	2305	1.0	2143	0.5	2016	0.1
28 SA	0650	0.5	0603	0.9	0346	0.9	0214	1.1	0207	1.3	0516	7.2	0524	5.3	0425	3.9	0258	1.0
	1207	9.5	1200	8.0	0915	6.6	0749	11.2	0733	12.5	1137	1.1	1120	0.9	0959	0.5	0829	0.2
	1909	0.6	1821	1.0	1604	1.0	1430	1.2	1424	1.3	1734	7.1	1742	5.3	1645	3.8	1511	1.0
					2130	6.5	2005	11.2	1948	12.4	2358	1.1	2342	1.0	2216	0.6	2050	0.2
29 SU ●	0026	9.4	0015	7.9	0422	1.1	0249	1.3	0244	1.6	0552	7.1	0556	5.2	0502	3.8	0332	1.0
	0727	0.7	0639	1.1	0948	6.5	0824	11.1	0808	12.3	1215	1.2	1157	1.0	1034	0.6	0902	0.2
	1244	9.4	1231	7.8	1639	1.2	1503	1.4	1500	1.6	1809	6.9	1813	5.1	1721	3.7	1544	1.0
	1942	0.8	1854	1.2	2204	6.4	2039	11.0	2024	12.0					2249	0.7	2123	0.2
30 M	0102	9.2	0008	7.7	0455	1.4	0321	1.6	0317	2.0	0034	1.4	0018	1.2	0537	3.7	0406	1.0
	0759	1.0	0709	1.5	1021	6.4	0857	10.9	0842	11.9	0626	6.9	0627	5.1	1109	0.7	0935	0.2
	1318	9.1	1227	7.6	1712	1.5	1535	1.7	1531	2.1	1251	1.5	1235	1.2	1758	3.5	1616	0.9
	2013	1.1	1921	1.5	2238	6.0	2112	10.6	2056	11.6	1842	6.6	1843	4.9	2322	0.9	2157	0.2
31 TU	0136	8.8	0002	7.5	0526	1.8	0348	2.0	0345	2.5	0108	1.7	0054	1.4	0613	3.5	0439	0.9
	0827	1.4	0732	1.8	1053	6.2	0927	10.4	0912	11.4	0658	6.6	0657	4.9	1145	0.9	1009	0.2
	1351	8.7	1220	7.5	1743	1.8	1603	2.1	1600	2.6	1326	1.8	1312	1.4	1835	3.3	1650	0.9
	2040	1.4	1942	1.8	2311	5.8	2142	10.0	2127	11.0	1913	6.3	1912	4.7	2357	1.1	2232	0.3

FRANCE, SPAIN, PORTUGAL & GIBRALTAR Time Zone -0100
Dieppe * Le Havre * Cherbourg * St Helier * St Malo * Brest * Pointe de Grave * Lisboa * Gibraltar

TIDE TABLES NOVEMBER 2000

DIEPPE Time m	LE HAVRE Time m	CHERBOURG Time m	ST HELIER JERSEY Time m	ST MALO Time m	BREST Time m	POINTE DE GRAVE Time m	LISBOA Time m	GIBRALTAR Time m	Day
0209 8.4	0047 7.4	0555 2.1	0415 2.6	0412 3.1	0141 2.1	0130 1.6	0650 3.4	0515 0.8	1 W
0854 1.8	0754 2.2	1126 5.8	0955 9.8	0942 10.8	0731 6.3	0730 4.7	1223 1.1	1044 0.3	
1422 8.2	1303 7.3	1815 2.1	1632 2.7	1627 3.2	1401 2.2	1351 1.7	1914 3.1	1727 0.8	
2108 1.8	2006 2.2	2347 5.5	2212 9.3	2157 10.3	1946 5.9	1945 4.4		2310 0.4	
0241 7.9	0133 7.1	0627 2.4	0442 3.2	0436 3.8	0215 2.5	0209 1.9	0035 1.3	0556 0.8	2 TH
0923 2.2	0821 2.5	1203 5.5	1024 9.1	1012 10.1	0808 5.9	0808 4.5	0730 3.2	1124 0.4	
1454 7.7	1348 7.1	1851 2.4	1703 3.4	1655 3.9	1441 2.6	1434 1.9	1307 1.3	1814 0.8	
2141 2.2	2037 2.5		2243 8.5	2229 9.6	2025 5.5	2027 4.2	2000 2.9	2358 0.4	
0316 7.4	0220 6.8	0030 5.1	0512 3.9	0506 4.4	0257 2.9	0254 2.1	0121 1.5	0650 0.7	3 F
0958 2.6	0858 2.9	0706 2.8	1057 8.4	1045 9.4	0854 5.5	0900 4.3	0819 3.0	1219 0.5	
1531 7.2	1437 6.7	1250 5.1	1743 4.0	1730 4.5	1530 2.9	1525 2.1	1405 1.5	1921 0.7	
2221 2.6	2119 2.9	1937 2.7	2324 7.8	2309 8.8	2118 5.2	2128 4.0	2102 2.7		
0403 6.8	0313 6.4	0130 4.8	0557 4.5	0545 5.0	0352 3.2	0351 2.3	0224 1.6	0123 0.5	4 SA
1045 3.0	0949 3.3	0802 3.0	1145 7.7	1132 8.7	0958 5.2	1015 4.1	0925 2.8	0804 0.7	
1626 6.6	1534 6.3	1359 4.8	1842 4.5	1822 5.0	1633 3.1	1629 2.3	1526 1.6	1411 0.5	
2315 3.0	2218 3.3	2044 2.8			2236 4.9	2305 3.9	2221 2.6	2051 0.7	
0522 6.4	0421 6.2	0252 4.6	0039 7.3	0024 8.2	0506 3.3	0505 2.4	0354 1.7	0323 0.5	5 SU
1148 3.3	1102 3.6	0922 3.1	0709 4.9	0649 5.5	1124 5.1	1142 4.1	1045 2.8	0930 0.7	
1800 6.4	1649 6.1	1525 4.7	1333 7.3	1313 8.3	1752 3.1	1744 2.3	1654 1.5	1600 0.5	
	2340 3.4	2206 2.8	2009 4.7	1944 5.3			2341 2.7	2216 0.8	
0033 3.2	0554 6.1	0424 4.6	0236 7.3	0217 8.2	0015 5.0	0035 4.0	0518 1.6	0429 0.4	6 M
0650 6.5	1231 3.5	1050 3.0	0851 4.9	0827 5.5	0633 3.2	0621 2.3	1157 2.9	1040 0.8	
1318 3.3	1819 6.2	1648 4.8	1517 7.6	1451 8.5	1248 5.3	1255 4.3	1758 1.3	1653 0.4	
1921 6.6		2324 2.6	2138 4.3	2124 5.0	1912 2.9	1854 2.1		2314 0.8	
0202 2.9	0108 3.1	0536 4.9	0351 7.8	0331 8.8	0130 5.3	0137 4.2	0041 2.9	0513 0.4	7 TU
0758 6.9	0721 6.4	1200 2.6	1014 4.3	1001 4.9	0742 2.9	0724 2.1	0618 1.4	1130 0.9	
1438 2.8	1348 3.0	1749 5.1	1615 8.3	1554 9.2	1348 5.6	1351 4.5	1254 3.1	1733 0.4	
2025 7.1	1933 6.5		2242 3.7	2236 4.2	2008 2.5	1951 1.9	1845 1.1	2358 0.9	
0307 2.3	0215 2.6	0024 2.2	0440 8.6	0423 9.6	0218 5.7	0224 4.5	0127 3.1	0551 0.3	8 W
0854 7.5	0822 6.9	0622 5.3	1110 3.5	1101 4.0	0830 2.5	0815 1.8	0703 1.2	1211 0.9	
1536 2.2	1446 2.5	1251 2.2	1659 9.0	1642 10.1	1433 6.0	1437 4.8	1339 3.3	1809 0.3	
2118 7.8	2026 7.0	1833 5.5	2333 2.9	2327 3.3	2051 2.1	2037 1.6	1926 0.9		
0400 1.8	0309 2.1	0110 1.8	0521 9.4	0506 10.5	0257 6.1	0305 4.8	0207 3.3	0038 1.0	9 TH
0942 8.2	0906 7.3	0700 5.7	1157 2.8	1148 3.1	0911 2.1	0857 1.6	0743 0.9	0626 0.3	
1624 1.6	1536 2.0	1334 1.8	1739 9.8	1724 11.0	1513 6.4	1518 5.0	1421 3.5	1250 1.0	
2205 8.4	2102 7.4	1912 5.8			2131 1.7	2117 1.4	2003 0.7	1844 0.2	
0446 1.3	0358 1.7	0151 1.5	0018 2.2	0012 2.4	0334 6.5	0342 5.0	0245 3.5	0117 1.0	10 F
1025 8.8	0939 7.6	0734 6.0	0602 10.1	0546 11.4	0951 1.7	0936 1.3	0822 0.7	0700 0.2	
1711 1.2	1624 1.6	1415 1.5	1241 2.1	1233 2.3	1551 6.8	1557 5.2	1500 3.6	1328 1.0	
2248 8.9	2115 7.7	1948 6.2	1821 10.5	1806 11.7	2210 1.4	2155 1.2	2041 0.6	1920 0.2	
0532 1.0	0446 1.3	0232 1.2	0103 1.7	0057 1.8	0411 6.9	0418 5.2	0322 3.7	0157 1.0	11 SA
1107 9.1	0927 7.8	0808 6.3	0642 10.7	0627 12.0	1031 1.3	1015 1.2	0900 0.6	0736 0.2	O
1755 0.9	1710 1.3	1455 1.2	1324 1.6	1318 1.8	1630 7.1	1636 5.4	1540 3.7	1407 1.1	
2329 9.2	2134 7.9	2025 6.4	1902 11.0	1846 12.2	2251 1.1	2233 1.1	2118 0.5	1957 0.1	
0616 0.8	0532 1.2	0312 1.1	0145 1.3	0142 1.4	0449 7.1	0455 5.3	0401 3.8	0237 1.0	12 SU
1148 9.4	0948 7.9	0844 6.5	0723 11.2	0706 12.5	1112 1.1	1055 1.0	0940 0.5	0813 0.1	
1840 0.8	1755 1.1	1536 1.1	1407 1.3	1403 1.4	1711 7.2	1715 5.4	1621 3.8	1448 1.1	
	2204 8.0	2103 6.5	1945 11.3	1927 12.5	2332 1.0	2313 1.0	2157 0.4	2034 0.1	
0010 9.3	0615 1.1	0354 1.1	0227 1.2	0226 1.3	0530 7.3	0533 5.4	0441 3.9	0318 1.0	13 M
0700 0.8	1021 8.0	0921 6.6	0804 11.4	0745 12.7	1155 1.0	1136 1.0	1021 0.4	0851 0.1	
1228 9.4	1837 1.1	1618 1.0	1448 1.2	1447 1.3	1752 7.3	1757 5.4	1703 3.8	1530 1.0	
1924 0.8	2241 8.0	2145 6.5	2027 11.3	2007 12.5		2355 1.0	2238 0.5	2113 0.1	
0051 9.3	0657 1.2	0436 1.1	0308 1.2	0310 1.4	0015 1.0	0615 5.3	0522 3.9	0402 1.0	14 TU
0744 0.9	1100 7.9	1001 6.6	0843 11.4	0825 12.6	0611 7.2	1221 1.0	1104 0.5	0931 0.2	
1309 9.3	1918 1.1	1702 1.1	1530 1.3	1530 1.5	1239 1.1	1840 5.3	1747 3.7	1615 1.0	
2007 0.9	2324 7.8	2228 6.4	2110 11.1	2047 12.3	1836 7.1		2321 0.6	2154 0.1	
0133 9.1	0054 7.6	0521 1.3	0348 1.5	0352 1.8	0059 1.2	0039 1.2	0606 3.8	0448 0.9	15 W
0827 1.1	0737 1.4	1044 6.5	0927 11.0	0905 12.3	0654 7.0	0659 5.2	1151 0.6	1014 0.2	
1350 9.1	1144 7.8	1747 1.2	1612 1.5	1612 1.9	1327 1.3	1309 1.2	1835 3.6	1704 0.9	
2051 1.1	1957 1.4	2315 6.2	2154 10.6	2128 11.8	1921 6.8	1929 5.0		2240 0.2	

• • Time Zone -0100. For UT subtract 1 hour. For European summer time (shaded) 26/3-29/10 add 1 hour • •

NOVEMBER 2000 TIDE TABLES

• •Time Zone -0100. For UT subtract 1 hour. For European summer time (shaded) 26/3-29/10 add 1 hour • •

	DIEPPE		LE HAVRE		CHERBOURG		ST HELIER JERSEY		ST MALO		BREST		POINTE DE GRAVE		LISBOA		GIBRALTAR	
	Time	m	Time	m	Time	m	Time	m	Time	m	Time	m	Time	m	Time	m	Time	m
16TH	0216	8.8	0123	7.5	0607	1.6	0430	2.0	0434	2.4	0146	1.5	0127	1.4	0007	0.8	0539	0.9
	0913	1.4	0817	1.7	1132	6.2	1009	10.5	0946	11.8	0742	6.7	0750	5.0	0655	3.6	1103	0.3
	1434	8.7	1236	7.5	1836	1.5	1656	2.1	1655	2.5	1400	1.3	1400	1.3	1242	0.8	1800	0.9
	2139	1.4	2038	1.6			2241	9.9	2212	11.1	2012	6.4	2026	4.8	1929	3.4	2333	0.3
17F	0304	8.4	0239	7.2	0009	5.8	0515	2.7	0517	3.1	0239	1.9	0221	1.6	0100	1.0	0639	0.9
	1003	1.7	0859	2.0	0659	1.9	1056	9.8	1032	11.0	0836	6.4	0852	4.8	0750	3.5	1206	0.3
	1524	8.2	1351	7.2	1227	5.8	1746	2.8	1742	3.2	1514	2.0	1500	1.6	1345	1.0	1906	0.8
	2232	1.7	2124	2.0	1933	1.7	2334	9.2	2305	10.3	2113	6.0	2136	4.5	2031	3.2		
18SA	0401	7.9	0336	7.0	0112	5.5	0609	3.3	0607	3.8	0337	2.3	0322	1.8	0206	1.2	0045	0.3
	1100	2.0	0951	2.4	0759	2.2	1152	9.1	1130	10.2	0940	6.0	1009	4.6	0855	3.3	0749	0.8
	1626	7.7	1537	6.9	1333	5.5	1849	3.3	1839	3.8	1618	2.3	1606	1.7	1504	1.1	1336	0.4
	2334	2.0	2224	2.3	2039	2.0					2225	5.7	2258	4.4	2145	3.1	2024	0.8
19SU	0510	7.5	0444	6.8	0226	5.2	0042	8.6	0018	9.5	0445	2.5	0433	2.0	0330	1.4	0227	0.4
	1206	2.3	1059	2.7	0911	2.4	0718	3.7	0713	4.3	1056	5.8	1131	4.6	1011	3.2	0909	0.8
	1742	7.4	1656	6.8	1450	5.2	1306	8.7	1250	9.6	1731	2.4	1722	1.8	1632	1.2	1524	0.4
			2341	2.5	2155	2.1	2007	3.5	1957	4.1	2346	5.6			2303	3.1	2147	0.8
20M	0045	2.1	0558	6.8	0348	5.1	0204	8.5	0152	9.3	0600	2.6	0017	4.4	0457	1.4	0356	0.4
	0629	7.5	1221	2.7	1031	2.4	0840	3.8	0836	4.3	1217	5.9	0549	1.9	1129	3.3	1024	0.9
	1321	2.2	1815	6.8	1612	5.2	1433	8.6	1421	9.6	1848	2.3	1245	4.7	1745	1.1	1636	0.3
	1902	7.4			2313	2.0	2127	3.3	2124	3.9			1837	1.7			2258	0.9
21TU	0200	1.9	0103	2.3	0507	5.3	0324	8.6	0313	9.7	0102	5.8	0124	4.6	0015	3.2	0454	0.3
	0745	7.7	0710	7.0	1146	2.1	0956	3.4	0956	3.8	0714	2.4	0701	1.8	0607	1.2	1124	0.9
	1436	1.9	1339	2.4	1727	5.4	1548	9.1	1535	10.1	1327	6.1	1348	4.8	1236	3.4	1725	0.3
	2015	7.8	1929	7.0			2234	2.9	2233	3.2	1954	2.0	1942	1.5	1843	0.9	2354	0.9
22W	0309	1.5	0215	2.0	0021	1.7	0427	9.3	0414	10.4	0203	6.1	0220	4.8	0112	3.4	0539	0.3
	0847	8.2	0820	7.2	0609	5.5	1100	2.8	1057	3.1	0815	2.0	0802	1.6	0701	1.0	1212	1.0
	1541	1.4	1445	2.1	1248	1.8	1648	9.6	1633	10.8	1424	6.4	1442	5.0	1333	3.6	1805	0.3
	2113	8.3	2042	7.2	1826	5.7	2331	2.4	2327	2.6	2048	1.7	2036	1.4	1929	0.8		
23TH	0409	1.1	0314	1.6	0115	1.5	0519	9.9	0503	11.1	0252	6.4	0307	5.0	0201	3.6	0039	1.0
	0939	8.6	0921	7.5	0657	5.8	1154	2.3	1148	2.4	0906	1.7	0853	1.4	0746	0.9	0617	0.3
	1635	1.0	1540	1.5	1339	1.5	1738	10.1	1721	11.4	1512	6.6	1528	5.1	1421	3.7	1254	1.0
	2202	8.7	2144	7.5	1914	5.9					2134	1.4	2122	1.2	2009	0.7	1841	0.2
24F	0458	0.9	0406	1.3	0202	1.3	0021	2.0	0013	2.1	0336	6.7	0348	5.1	0245	3.7	0118	1.0
	1024	9.0	1012	7.7	0739	6.1	0605	10.4	0547	11.6	0952	1.5	0938	1.2	0826	0.8	0653	0.2
	1722	0.8	1630	1.3	1424	1.3	1242	1.9	1232	2.0	1555	6.8	1609	5.2	1504	3.7	1330	1.0
	2245	9.0	2233	7.6	1955	6.1	1822	10.4	1805	11.7	2217	1.4	2203	1.2	2045	0.7	1915	0.2
25SA	0543	0.8	0452	1.2	0243	1.2	0106	1.8	0055	1.9	0415	6.9	0426	5.2	0324	3.8	0155	1.0
	1105	9.2	1055	7.8	0817	6.2	0645	10.7	0627	11.9	1035	1.4	1019	1.2	0903	0.7	0727	0.2
	1804	0.8	1714	1.2	1504	1.2	1324	1.7	1313	1.9	1635	6.8	1646	5.1	1545	3.7	1404	1.0
	2325	9.1	2315	7.7	2033	6.2	1903	10.6	1845	11.8	2257	1.4	2242	1.2	2118	0.7	1948	0.2
26SU	0623	0.9	0533	1.3	0322	1.3	0145	1.7	0134	2.0	0453	6.9	0500	5.2	0403	3.8	0230	1.0
	1144	9.2	1131	7.7	0852	6.3	0724	10.8	0706	11.9	1115	1.4	1058	1.2	0938	0.7	0801	0.2
	1842	0.9	1753	1.3	1542	1.3	1402	1.7	1352	2.0	1712	6.8	1719	5.1	1624	3.6	1437	1.0
			2350	7.7	2110	6.2	1941	10.6	1924	11.7	2334	1.5	2318	1.2	2151	0.8	2023	0.2
27M	0003	9.0	0610	1.5	0358	1.4	0220	1.8	0212	2.2	0529	6.9	0533	5.1	0440	3.8	0303	1.0
	0700	1.1	1157	7.6	0927	6.3	0759	10.8	0742	11.8	1152	1.5	1136	1.2	1012	0.7	0836	0.2
	1221	9.1	1826	1.5	1618	1.3	1436	1.7	1429	2.2	1746	6.7	1750	5.0	1701	3.6	1510	0.9
	1917	1.1			2145	6.1	2016	10.5	2000	11.5			2354	1.3	2224	0.8	2058	0.2
28TU ●	0040	8.9	0013	7.5	0431	1.6	0251	1.9	0245	2.5	0009	1.6	0603	5.1	0516	3.7	0338	0.9
	0732	1.3	0640	1.7	1000	6.2	0832	10.6	0817	11.5	0603	6.8	1212	1.3	1047	0.8	0912	0.2
	1255	8.9	1127	7.5	1651	1.5	1508	1.9	1503	2.4	1228	1.6	1819	4.8	1738	3.4	1544	0.9
	1948	1.3	1854	1.7	2220	5.9	2049	10.2	2033	11.2	1819	6.5			2258	0.9	2134	0.2
29W	0115	8.6	0002	7.4	0503	1.8	0321	2.2	0316	2.8	0042	1.8	0029	1.5	0551	3.6	0413	0.9
	0801	1.6	0706	2.0	1033	6.1	0903	10.3	0849	11.2	0636	6.6	0634	5.0	1123	0.9	0948	0.3
	1328	8.6	1204	7.5	1723	1.7	1539	2.2	1533	2.8	1303	1.9	1249	1.6	1814	3.3	1620	0.8
	2015	1.5	1919	1.9	2254	5.7	2121	9.9	2106	10.8	1851	6.3	1850	4.7	2333	1.0	2212	0.3
30TH	0148	8.3	0036	7.3	0535	2.0	0350	2.6	0345	3.2	0115	2.1	0104	1.6	0627	3.4	0451	0.8
	0828	1.8	0733	2.2	1107	5.8	0933	9.9	0920	10.8	0709	6.4	0707	4.8	1201	1.0	1026	0.3
	1400	8.3	1245	7.4	1755	1.9	1610	2.6	1603	3.1	1337	2.1	1327	1.6	1851	3.1	1659	0.8
	2044	1.7	1946	2.1	2330	5.5	2152	9.4	2136	10.4	1924	6.0	1924	4.5			2253	0.3

FRANCE, SPAIN, PORTUGAL & GIBRALTAR Time Zone -0100
Dieppe * Le Havre * Cherbourg * St Helier * St Malo * Brest * Pointe de Grave * Lisboa * Gibraltar

TIDE TABLES DECEMBER 2000

	DIEPPE		LE HAVRE		CHERBOURG		ST HELIER JERSEY		ST MALO		BREST		POINTE DE GRAVE		LISBOA		GIBRALTAR		Day
	Time	m	Time	m	Time	m	Time	m	Time	m	Time	m	Time	m	Time	m	Time	m	
	0220	8.0	0116	7.2	0608	2.3	0420	3.0	0412	3.6	0149	2.3	0142	1.8	0010	1.2	0533	0.8	**1 F**
	0857	2.0	0803	2.4	1143	5.6	1003	9.3	0948	10.4	0745	6.1	0745	4.7	0705	3.3	1108	0.4	
	1432	7.9	1327	7.2	1831	2.1	1642	3.1	1632	3.5	1415	2.4	1406	1.8	1242	1.2	1743	0.8	
	2116	1.9	2018	2.3			2224	8.8	2206	9.9	2002	5.7	2003	4.4	1933	3.0	2339	0.4	
	0254	7.6	0158	7.0	0009	5.2	0451	3.5	0440	4.0	0227	2.6	0224	2.0	0052	1.3	0621	0.8	**2 SA**
	0932	2.3	0841	2.7	0646	2.5	1036	8.8	1020	9.9	0827	5.8	0831	4.5	0746	3.1	1158	0.4	
	1507	7.5	1410	6.9	1224	5.3	1720	3.6	1704	4.0	1457	2.6	1452	1.9	1331	1.3	1839	0.8	
	2154	2.1	2058	2.6	1914	2.3	2300	8.3	2242	9.4	2046	5.4	2054	4.2	2020	2.8			
	0335	7.3	0244	6.7	0058	5.0	0531	4.0	0514	4.4	0315	2.9	0312	2.1	0144	1.5	0039	0.4	**3 SU**
	1014	2.6	0928	3.0	0733	2.7	1115	8.2	1059	9.4	0917	5.5	0929	4.3	0836	3.0	0719	0.8	
	1553	7.1	1459	6.6	1318	5.0	1806	4.0	1745	4.4	1549	2.9	1545	2.1	1431	1.4	1306	0.4	
	2242	2.5	2150	2.8	2008	2.5	2351	7.8	2332	8.9	2144	5.2	2204	4.0	2119	2.7	1948	0.7	
	0431	6.9	0339	6.5	0200	4.7	0624	4.4	0602	4.8	0413	3.1	0412	2.2	0251	1.6	0157	0.4	**4 M**
	1108	2.9	1027	3.2	0835	2.8	1215	7.8	1157	8.9	1020	5.3	1040	4.3	0939	2.9	0825	0.8	
	1658	6.8	1558	6.3	1424	4.8	1908	4.3	1845	4.7	1651	3.0	1646	2.1	1544	1.5	1430	0.4	
	2342	2.7	2254	3.0	2113	2.6					2257	5.1	2326	4.0	2230	2.8	2104	0.8	
	0543	6.8	0451	6.3	0312	4.7	0104	7.6	0050	8.6	0521	3.1	0518	2.2	0409	1.6	0315	0.4	**5 TU**
	1218	3.0	1136	3.2	0948	2.8	0736	4.6	0715	5.1	1133	5.3	1154	4.3	1048	2.9	0933	0.8	
	1815	6.7	1715	6.2	1535	4.8	1343	7.7	1326	8.8	1800	2.9	1752	2.1	1656	1.4	1547	0.4	
					2223	2.5	2024	4.3	2009	4.7					2338	2.9	2215	0.8	
	0058	2.7	0006	2.9	0421	4.8	0230	7.8	0217	8.8	0014	5.2	0039	4.2	0521	1.5	0416	0.4	**6 W**
	0654	6.9	0617	6.4	1058	2.7	0900	4.4	0847	4.9	0633	3.0	0624	2.1	1155	3.1	1034	0.9	
	1338	2.8	1248	2.9	1642	5.0	1503	8.1	1447	9.1	1243	5.5	1259	4.4	1754	1.2	1645	0.4	
	1927	7.0	1836	6.4	2327	2.3	2138	3.9	2133	4.3	1906	2.6	1855	1.9			2315	0.8	
	0213	2.4	0116	2.6	0522	5.1	0338	8.4	0324	9.4	0120	5.5	0136	4.4	0036	3.0	0506	0.3	**7 TH**
	0800	7.4	0727	6.7	1200	2.4	1012	3.8	1004	4.2	0736	2.6	0724	1.9	0618	1.3	1127	0.9	
	1448	2.3	1354	2.5	1739	5.3	1604	8.7	1551	9.8	1343	5.9	1354	4.7	1252	3.2	1733	0.3	
	2030	7.5	1939	6.8			2242	3.2	2238	3.5	2003	2.3	1950	1.7	1845	1.0			
	0316	2.0	0220	2.2	0024	2.0	0433	9.1	0420	10.2	0212	5.9	0225	4.7	0125	3.3	0006	0.9	**8 F**
	0858	8.0	0817	7.1	0612	5.5	1112	3.1	1104	3.4	0829	2.2	0815	1.7	0708	1.0	0551	0.3	
	1546	1.6	1454	2.1	1254	2.0	1657	9.4	1644	10.6	1434	6.2	1443	4.9	1342	3.4	1215	1.0	
	2127	8.1	2023	7.1	1830	5.6	2337	2.6	2333	2.8	2053	1.9	2039	1.5	1930	0.8	1817	0.2	
	0410	1.5	0318	1.8	0114	1.7	0524	9.9	0509	11.1	0259	6.4	0309	4.9	0211	3.5	0053	0.9	**9 SA**
	0951	8.5	0845	7.4	0656	5.8	1205	2.4	1157	2.6	0918	1.8	0903	1.4	0754	0.8	0635	0.2	
	1639	1.4	1550	1.7	1342	1.6	1748	10.1	1733	11.4	1521	6.6	1529	5.1	1430	3.5	1303	1.0	
	2218	8.6	2049	7.4	1917	5.9					2140	1.5	2124	1.3	2013	0.7	1900	0.1	
	0501	1.2	0413	1.5	0202	1.4	0029	2.0	0023	2.1	0343	6.8	0352	5.2	0256	3.7	0139	1.0	**10 SU**
	1039	9.0	0900	7.6	0739	6.1	0612	10.5	0557	11.8	1005	1.4	0949	1.2	0839	0.6	0717	0.2	
	1729	1.0	1643	1.4	1430	1.3	1256	1.8	1248	2.0	1606	6.9	1614	5.3	1517	3.7	1348	1.0	
	2306	9.0	2118	7.7	2003	6.2	1836	10.7	1821	11.9	2226	1.2	2209	1.1	2057	0.5	1942	0.1	
	0551	1.0	0506	1.3	0249	1.2	0119	1.5	0114	1.7	0428	7.1	0436	5.3	0341	3.8	0225	1.0	**11 M** O
	1125	9.2	0931	7.8	0822	6.4	0659	11.0	0642	12.3	1051	1.2	1036	1.1	0923	0.5	0800	0.1	
	1819	1.0	1735	1.2	1517	1.0	1345	1.4	1339	1.5	1653	7.1	1659	5.4	1604	3.8	1436	1.0	
	2351	9.2	2154	7.8	2049	6.3	1926	11.1	1907	12.3	2312	1.1	2254	1.1	2140	0.5	2026	0.1	
	0641	0.9	0557	1.2	0336	1.1	0207	1.3	0204	1.5	0513	7.3	0519	5.4	0426	3.9	0312	1.0	**12 TU**
	1210	9.4	1009	7.9	0907	6.5	0746	11.3	0727	12.6	1139	1.0	1122	1.0	1009	0.4	0845	0.1	
	1909	0.7	1824	1.0	1558	1.0	1433	1.1	1430	1.3	1739	7.2	1745	5.4	1651	3.8	1524	1.0	
			2328	7.7	2137	6.4	2014	11.2	1954	12.4	2359	1.0	2340	1.0	2224	0.5	2111	0.1	
	0036	9.3	0645	1.2	0424	1.1	0254	1.2	0253	1.4	0600	7.3	0606	5.5	0512	4.0	0400	1.0	**13 W**
	0731	0.9	1054	7.9	0954	6.6	0832	11.4	0812	12.7	1228	1.0	1210	1.0	1055	0.4	0930	0.1	
	1255	9.3	1910	1.0	1652	0.8	1520	1.1	1518	1.3	1827	7.1	1833	5.3	1739	3.8	1614	1.0	
	1959	0.7	2351	7.7	2226	6.4	2101	11.1	2039	12.3					2310	0.6	2158	0.1	
	0122	9.2	0731	1.3	0512	1.1	0339	1.4	0340	1.6	0047	1.1	0027	1.1	0559	3.9	0450	0.9	**14 TH**
	0821	0.9	1239	7.7	1042	6.6	0918	11.2	0857	12.5	0647	7.2	0654	5.4	1144	0.5	1020	0.2	
	1341	9.2	1956	1.1	1740	0.9	1606	1.3	1605	1.5	1318	1.1	1300	1.0	1829	3.7	1706	0.9	
	2047	0.7			2315	6.2	2148	10.8	2124	11.9	1915	6.9	1924	5.2	2358	0.7	2249	0.2	
	0209	9.0	0153	7.7	0600	1.3	0424	1.7	0426	1.9	0136	1.3	0117	1.2	0648	3.8	0543	0.9	**15 F**
	0909	1.0	0816	1.4	1131	6.3	1003	10.8	0941	12.1	0736	7.0	0746	5.3	1236	0.7	1115	0.2	
	1428	8.9	1357	7.6	1830	1.1	1654	1.7	1651	1.9	1409	1.3	1352	1.2	1921	3.5	1803	0.9	
	2135	0.9	2040	1.2			2236	10.3	2210	11.4	2006	6.6	2019	5.0			2345	0.2	

• • Time Zone -0100. For UT subtract 1 hour. For European summer time (shaded) 26/3-29/10 add 1 hour • •

DECEMBER 2000 TIDE TABLES

• • Time Zone -0100. For UT subtract 1 hour. For European summer time (shaded) 26/3-29/10 add 1 hour • •

Day	DIEPPE Time	m	LE HAVRE Time	m	CHERBOURG Time	m	ST HELIER JERSEY Time	m	ST MALO Time	m	BREST Time	m	POINTE DE GRAVE Time	m	LISBOA Time	m	GIBRALTAR Time	m
16 SA	0257	8.7	0242	7.5	0007	5.9	0511	2.2	0511	2.4	0228	1.6	0209	1.4	0051	0.9	0642	0.9
	0957	1.2	0901	1.7	0651	1.5	1050	10.3	1028	11.5	0828	6.7	0844	5.1	0739	3.7	1218	0.3
	1518	8.6	1445	7.5	1223	6.0	1743	2.2	1737	2.4	1502	1.6	1447	1.3	1335	0.9	1906	0.8
	2224	1.1	2127	1.5	1923	1.3	2326	9.7	2300	10.7	2101	6.2	2121	4.7	2016	3.4		
17 SU	0350	8.3	0333	7.3	0102	5.6	0601	2.7	0558	3.0	0323	2.0	0306	1.6	0151	1.1	0051	0.3
	1047	1.5	0950	2.0	0746	1.8	1141	9.7	1121	10.8	0925	6.3	0948	4.9	0837	3.5	0745	0.3
	1612	8.1	1537	7.2	1320	5.7	1837	2.7	1827	3.0	1600	2.0	1548	1.5	1443	1.0	1333	0.3
	2315	1.4	2218	1.8	2021	1.6					2202	5.9	2230	4.6	2119	3.2	2015	0.8
18 M	0448	8.0	0430	7.1	0202	5.4	0020	9.1	0000	10.1	0423	2.3	0409	1.7	0303	1.3	0209	0.3
	1142	1.7	1045	2.2	0847	2.1	0658	3.2	0652	3.6	1028	6.0	1100	4.7	0943	3.4	0852	0.9
	1715	7.7	1638	7.0	1421	5.4	1239	9.1	1224	10.2	1703	2.0	1654	1.7	1600	1.2	1502	0.3
			2318	2.1	2125	1.9	1939	3.1	1927	3.5	2310	5.7	2342	4.5	2229	3.1	2127	0.8
19 TU	0012	1.7	0532	7.0	0309	5.2	0124	8.7	0111	9.7	0529	2.4	0518	1.8	0422	1.4	0329	0.3
	0555	7.7	1151	2.4	0956	2.2	0804	3.5	0757	3.9	1139	5.9	1211	4.6	1055	3.3	1000	0.9
	1243	2.0	1745	6.8	1530	5.2	1347	8.8	1336	9.8	1812	2.3	1803	1.7	1712	1.2	1618	0.3
	1827	7.5			2235	2.0	2045	3.3	2038	3.7					2339	3.2	2236	0.8
20 W	0118	1.8	0026	2.2	0422	5.1	0235	8.7	0225	9.6	0023	5.7	0050	4.5	0536	1.3	0434	0.3
	0708	7.7	0636	6.9	1109	2.2	0914	3.5	0909	3.9	0639	2.5	0627	1.8	1206	3.3	1101	0.9
	1355	2.0	1301	2.4	1645	5.2	1501	8.8	1450	9.8	1251	5.9	1318	4.7	1813	1.2	1713	0.3
	1941	7.6	1854	6.8	2345	2.0	2153	3.2	2148	3.5	1921	2.3	1909	1.7			2336	0.8
21 TH	0232	1.8	0135	2.1	0533	5.3	0345	8.9	0333	9.9	0130	5.8	0150	4.6	0042	3.3	0524	0.3
	0815	7.9	0743	7.0	1217	2.1	1021	3.2	1015	3.5	0745	2.3	0732	1.7	0636	1.2	1153	0.9
	1508	1.8	1408	2.2	1754	5.3	1609	9.0	1555	10.1	1355	6.0	1416	4.7	1307	3.4	1757	0.3
	2044	7.8	2009	6.9			2255	2.9	2248	3.2	2020	2.1	2008	1.6	1903	1.1		
22 F	0338	1.6	0238	2.0	0045	1.8	0445	9.2	0430	10.3	0225	6.1	0242	4.7	0136	3.4	0025	0.9
	0911	8.2	0849	7.2	0630	5.5	1121	2.9	1112	3.1	0841	2.1	0828	1.6	0725	1.1	0607	0.3
	1607	1.5	1507	1.9	1314	1.9	1707	9.3	1651	10.5	1449	6.2	1507	4.8	1400	3.4	1238	0.9
	2137	8.1	2118	7.0	1851	5.4	2350	2.6	2339	2.9	2110	2.0	2058	1.5	1945	1.0	1835	0.2
23 SA	0431	1.4	0333	1.8	0137	1.7	0536	9.6	0520	10.8	0313	6.3	0327	4.9	0223	3.5	0108	0.9
	1000	8.4	0944	7.3	0717	5.7	1214	2.5	1201	2.8	0930	1.9	0917	1.5	0807	1.0	0645	0.3
	1657	1.3	1600	1.7	1403	1.7	1757	9.6	1740	10.8	1535	6.3	1551	4.9	1445	3.5	1318	0.9
	2224	8.4	2210	7.2	1937	5.6					2155	1.8	2142	1.4	2023	1.0	1910	0.2
24 SU ●	0518	1.3	0422	1.7	0221	1.6	0038	2.4	0024	2.7	0356	6.5	0406	5.0	0306	3.6	0148	0.9
	1043	8.6	1027	7.4	0757	5.9	0621	10.0	0605	11.1	1015	1.8	1000	1.4	0845	0.9	0723	0.2
	1741	1.2	1647	1.6	1445	1.5	1300	2.2	1245	2.6	1617	6.4	1629	4.9	1528	3.5	1357	0.9
	2306	8.6	2252	7.3	2018	5.7	1842	9.9	1824	10.9	2236	1.7	2221	1.4	2057	0.9	1947	0.2
25 M	0600	1.3	0506	1.7	0302	1.6	0120	2.2	0106	2.6	0435	6.6	0442	5.0	0345	3.7	0225	0.9
	1124	8.7	1101	7.5	0836	6.0	0702	10.2	0646	11.2	1056	1.7	1040	1.4	0921	0.9	0800	0.2
	1821	1.2	1728	1.6	1524	1.4	1340	2.1	1328	2.5	1654	6.5	1703	4.9	1607	3.5	1433	0.9
	2345	8.6	2325	7.3	2057	5.8	1922	10.0	1906	11.0	2314	1.7	2258	1.4	2132	0.9	2024	0.2
26 TU	0637	1.4	0545	1.8	0339	1.6	0157	2.1	0146	2.7	0512	6.7	0515	5.0	0424	3.7	0302	0.9
	1201	8.7	1117	7.5	0912	6.1	0739	10.3	0724	11.3	1134	1.7	1118	1.4	0957	0.8	0837	0.2
	1857	1.3	1805	1.6	1600	1.4	1416	2.0	1407	2.5	1730	6.5	1733	4.8	1645	3.5	1510	0.9
			2345	7.3	2133	5.8	1959	10.1	1943	11.0	2350	1.7	2334	1.4	2206	0.9	2102	0.2
27 W	0022	8.6	0620	1.9	0414	1.6	0231	2.1	0224	2.7	0546	6.6	0546	5.1	0500	3.7	0339	0.9
	0711	1.5	1118	7.5	0946	6.1	0815	10.3	0800	11.2	1209	1.7	1154	1.4	1031	0.8	0915	0.2
	1237	8.7	1837	1.7	1634	1.4	1450	2.0	1444	2.5	1803	6.4	1803	4.8	1721	3.4	1548	0.9
	1929	1.3	2354	7.4	2208	5.8	2033	10.0	2018	10.9					2240	0.9	2140	0.2
28 TH	0057	8.5	0651	2.0	0448	1.7	0303	2.2	0257	2.8	0024	1.8	0009	1.5	0535	3.6	0416	0.9
	0742	1.6	1151	7.5	1021	6.0	0847	10.2	0833	11.1	0620	6.6	0618	5.0	1106	0.9	0952	0.2
	1311	8.5	1908	1.8	1707	1.5	1523	2.1	1518	2.6	1244	1.8	1230	1.4	1757	3.3	1625	0.9
	1959	1.4			2242	5.7	2106	9.8	2051	10.8	1835	6.3	1834	4.8	2315	0.9	2219	0.3
29 F	0130	8.4	0023	7.4	0520	1.8	0334	2.3	0329	2.9	0056	1.9	0044	1.5	0609	3.5	0454	0.9
	0811	1.7	0723	2.1	1054	5.9	0918	10.0	0904	11.0	0653	6.5	0651	5.0	1142	0.9	1030	0.3
	1343	8.4	1227	7.5	1741	1.6	1555	2.3	1548	2.7	1317	1.9	1305	1.5	1834	3.2	1703	0.8
	2028	1.4	1938	1.8	2316	5.6	2137	9.6	2121	10.6	1907	6.2	1908	4.7	2351	1.0	2257	0.3
30 SA	0203	8.2	0058	7.4	0554	1.9	0405	2.6	0358	3.1	0129	2.1	0119	1.6	0642	3.4	0533	0.8
	0840	1.7	0755	2.2	1127	5.7	0948	9.7	0933	10.8	0726	6.3	0727	4.9	1220	1.0	1110	0.3
	1415	8.2	1304	7.4	1815	1.7	1627	2.6	1619	2.9	1352	2.1	1342	1.5	1906	3.1	1744	0.8
	2059	1.5	2010	2.0	2351	5.4	2208	9.3	2151	10.4	1941	6.0	1944	4.6			2338	0.3
31 SU	0236	8.0	0134	7.3	0629	2.1	0436	2.9	0427	3.3	0205	2.3	0157	1.7	0029	1.1	0614	0.8
	0912	1.9	0830	2.3	1202	5.5	1020	9.3	1003	10.6	0803	6.1	0806	4.7	0717	3.3	1152	0.3
	1449	8.0	1342	7.2	1853	1.9	1701	2.9	1650	3.2	1430	2.3	1421	1.6	1300	1.1	1829	0.8
	2133	1.7	2045	2.1			2241	8.9	2224	10.1	2019	5.8	2025	4.4	1942	3.0		

USE OF TIDE TABLES AND CURVES

Calculation of times and heights of tides is by no means precise and there are differences to be found in tables published by different authorities. In addition, a wind from a steady direction or unusually high or low barometric pressures can cause quite large variations in times and heights. It therefore makes very little sense to calculate too scrupulously and very often the old twelfths rule ($\frac{1}{12}$ in the first hour, $\frac{2}{12}$ in the second hour, $\frac{3}{12}$ in the third hour, $\frac{3}{12}$ in the fourth hour, $\frac{2}{12}$ in the fifth hour and $\frac{1}{12}$ in the sixth hour) will be perfectly adequate.

However, it may be felt that the best use possible should be made of the published data so that any uncertainties are reduced to natural or unavoidable causes. Hence these notes. Heights calculated by whatever method must be added to the charted depth.

Standard Ports

Say one needs the height of tide at 1650UT at Shoreham on Wednesday 16th February 2000. The tables give LW at 1423 of 1.3m and HW at 2039 of 5.5m. Go to the tidal curve for Shoreham and mark the LW height of 1.3m on the bottom line and the HW height of 5.5 on the top line of the graticule to the left of the curve. Draw a diagonal line between these two points. Mark the HW time on the bottom line under the curve and work backwards to 1650 and erect a perpendicular from this time to the curve (mid neap/spring lines). Draw a horizontal away to the diagonal and from thence another perpendicular to the top line of the graticule. This shows that the height of tide at 1230 is 2.5m. Incidentally, the twelfths rule would have given $4\frac{1}{2}$ twelfths for the $2\frac{1}{2}$ hours after LW, ie $\frac{9}{24}$ of (5·5-1·3)m range or 1·6m above 1·3m LW giving a height of 2.9m.

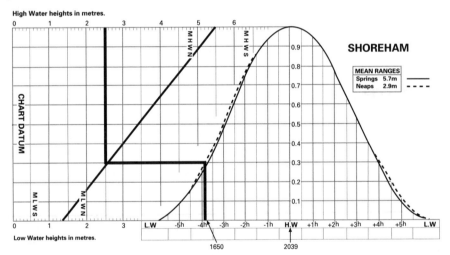

Secondary Ports

The procedure is the same after the times and heights of HW and LW for the secondary port are calculated using the difference tables. Thus: find the times and heights of daytime HW and LW at Orford Haven Bar, on the East coast of England, on Tuesday 20th June 2000.

Note that the secondary port tables have two columns for HW differences and two for LW differences. Note, especially, that the times in bold opposite the standard port are discrete, ie having found Orford Haven Bar and looked above to the bold times, the HW difference when HW Walton-on-the Naze is either 0100 or 1300 is -0026 or when HW Walton-on-the-Naze is either 0700 or 1900 the difference is -0030. At any time between 0700 and 1300, for example, the difference is found by interpolation between -0026 and -0030. This can be done by eye, by calculation or by drawing a straight line graph.

Similarly when LW Walton-on-the-Naze is either 0100 or 1300, the correction is -0036 and when LW Walton-on-the-Naze is either 0700 or 1900, the correction is -0038. HW heights at Walton-on-the-Naze of 4.2m and 3.4m give differences at Orford Haven Bar of -1.0m and -0.8m and LW heights of 1.1m and 0.4m give differences of -0.1m and 0.0m

On 20th June 2000, HW Walton-on-the-Naze is at 1339 (3.9m) and LW is at 0725 (0.9m). Hence, by interpolation, the HW correction for Orford Haven Bar is -0027 (-0.9m) making HW Orford Haven Bar 1339 -0027 = 1312 (3.0m) and LW correction Orford Haven Bar is -0038 (-0.1m) making LW Orford Haven Bar 0725 -0038 = 0647 (0.8m).

ST MARY'S, SCILLY ISLES

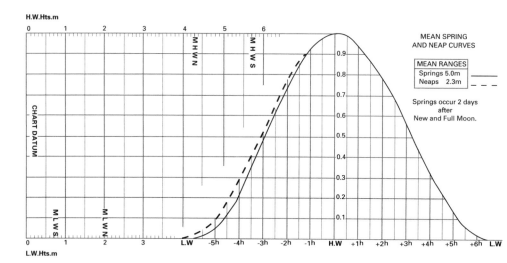

H.W.Hts.m

MEAN SPRING
AND NEAP CURVES

MEAN RANGES
Springs 5.0m
Neaps 2.3m

Springs occur 2 days
after
New and Full Moon.

L.W.Hts.m

PLYMOUTH

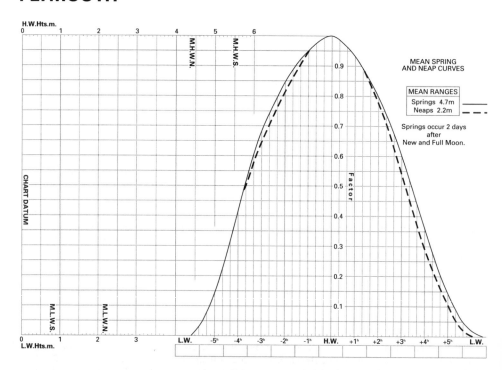

H.W.Hts.m.

MEAN SPRING
AND NEAP CURVES

MEAN RANGES
Springs 4.7m
Neaps 2.2m

Springs occur 2 days
after
New and Full Moon.

L.W.Hts.m.

DARTMOUTH

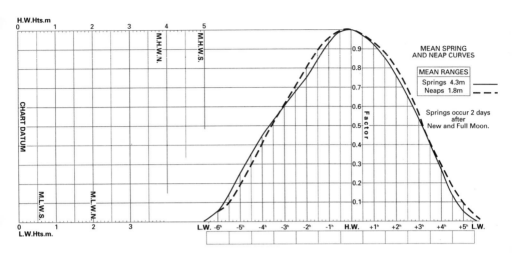

MEAN SPRING
AND NEAP CURVES

MEAN RANGES
Springs 4.3m
Neaps 1.8m

Springs occur 2 days
after
New and Full Moon.

PORTLAND

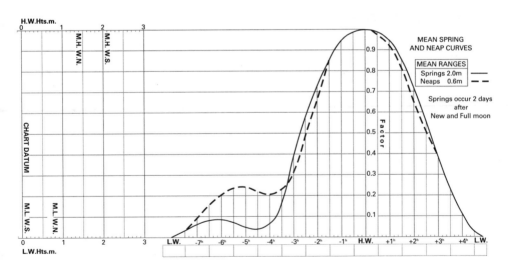

MEAN SPRING
AND NEAP CURVES

MEAN RANGES
Springs 2.0m
Neaps 0.6m

Springs occur 2 days
after
New and Full moon

POOLE

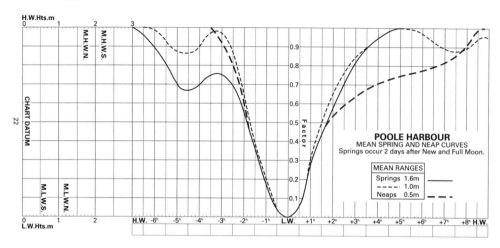

POOLE HARBOUR
MEAN SPRING AND NEAP CURVES
Springs occur 2 days after New and Full Moon.

MEAN RANGES	
Springs	1.6m
	1.0m
Neaps	0.5m

SOUTHAMPTON

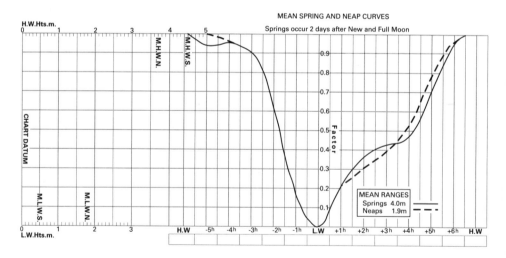

MEAN SPRING AND NEAP CURVES
Springs occur 2 days after New and Full Moon

MEAN RANGES	
Springs	4.0m
Neaps	1.9m

PORTSMOUTH

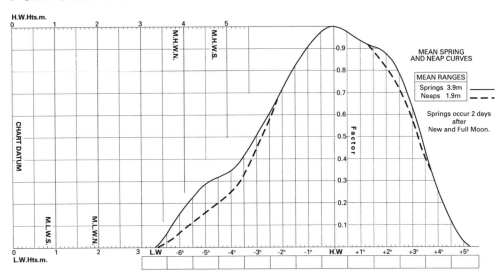

H.W.Hts.m.

MEAN SPRING
AND NEAP CURVES

MEAN RANGES
Springs 3.9m
Neaps 1.9m

Springs occur 2 days
after
New and Full Moon.

CHART DATUM

M.H.W.N. M.H.W.S.

M.L.W.S. M.L.W.N.

Factor

L.W -6ʰ -5ʰ -4ʰ -3ʰ -2ʰ -1ʰ H.W +1ʰ +2ʰ +3ʰ +4ʰ +5ʰ

L.W.Hts.m.

SHOREHAM

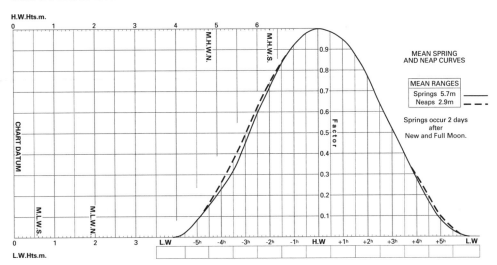

H.W.Hts.m.

MEAN SPRING
AND NEAP CURVES

MEAN RANGES
Springs 5.7m
Neaps 2.9m

Springs occur 2 days
after
New and Full Moon.

CHART DATUM

M.H.W.N. M.H.W.S.

M.L.W.S. M.L.W.N.

Factor

L.W -5ʰ -4ʰ -3ʰ -2ʰ -1ʰ H.W +1ʰ +2ʰ +3ʰ +4ʰ +5ʰ L.W

L.W.Hts.m.

DOVER

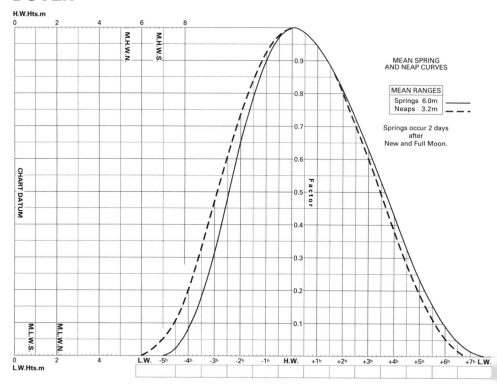

MEAN SPRING
AND NEAP CURVES

MEAN RANGES
Springs 6.0m
Neaps 3.2m

Springs occur 2 days
after
New and Full Moon.

MARGATE

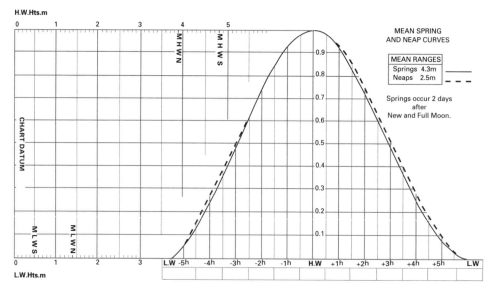

MEAN SPRING
AND NEAP CURVES

MEAN RANGES
Springs 4.3m
Neaps 2.5m

Springs occur 2 days
after
New and Full Moon.

SHEERNESS

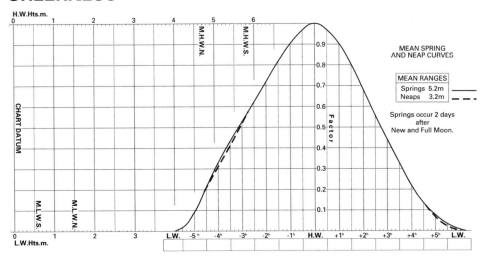

MEAN SPRING
AND NEAP CURVES

MEAN RANGES
Springs 5.2m
Neaps 3.2m

Springs occur 2 days
after
New and Full Moon.

LONDON BRIDGE

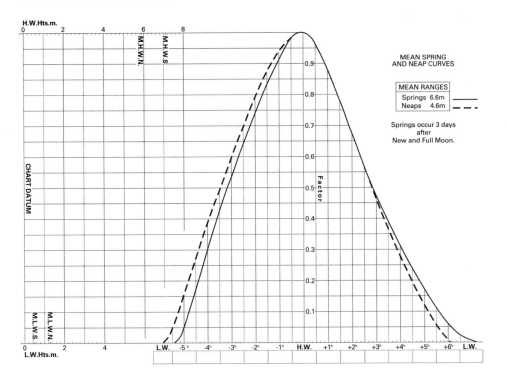

MEAN SPRING
AND NEAP CURVES

MEAN RANGES
Springs 6.6m
Neaps 4.6m

Springs occur 3 days
after
New and Full Moon.

WALTON-ON-THE-NAZE

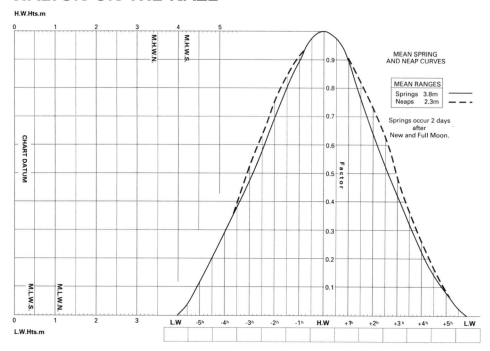

MEAN SPRING
AND NEAP CURVES

MEAN RANGES
Springs 3.8m
Neaps 2.3m

Springs occur 2 days
after
New and Full Moon.

HARWICH

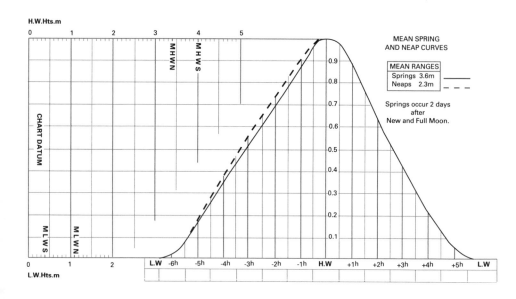

MEAN SPRING
AND NEAP CURVES

MEAN RANGES
Springs 3.6m
Neaps 2.3m

Springs occur 2 days
after
New and Full Moon.

LOWESTOFT

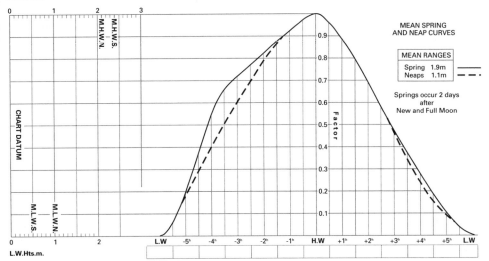

IMMINGHAM

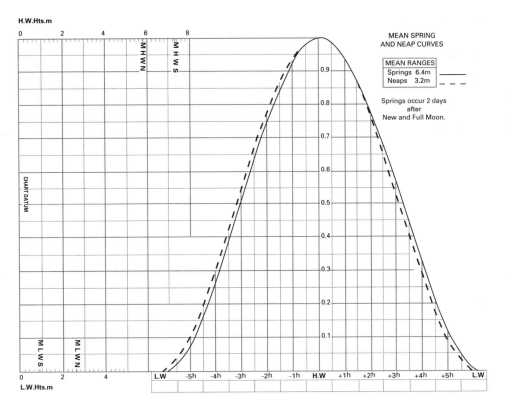

RIVER TEES

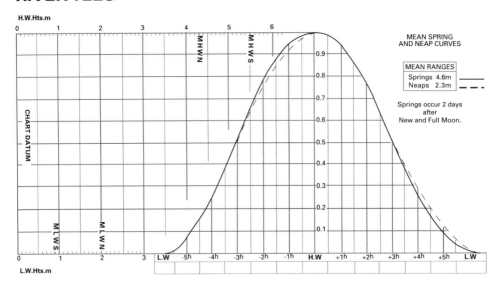

MEAN SPRING
AND NEAP CURVES

MEAN RANGES
Springs 4.6m
Neaps 2.3m

Springs occur 2 days
after
New and Full Moon.

RIVER TYNE

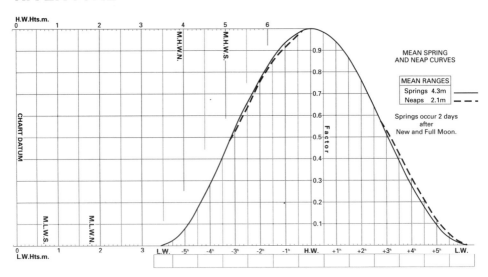

MEAN SPRING
AND NEAP CURVES

MEAN RANGES
Springs 4.3m
Neaps 2.1m

Springs occur 2 days
after
New and Full Moon.

LEITH

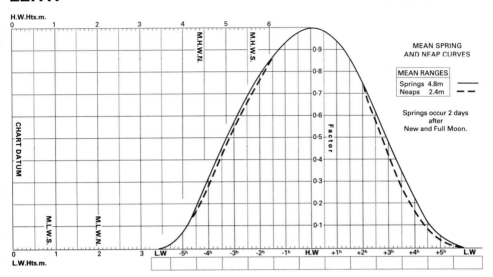

ROSYTH

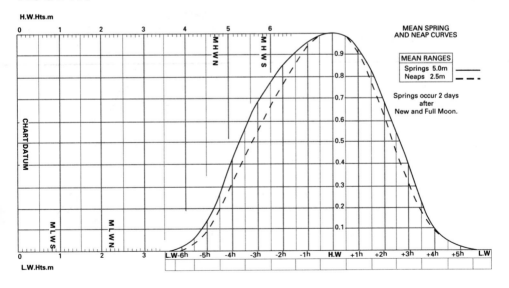

ABERDEEN

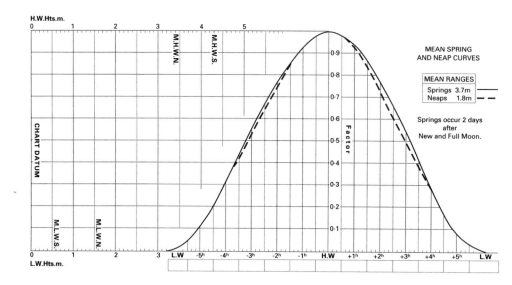

MEAN SPRING
AND NEAP CURVES

MEAN RANGES
Springs 3.7m
Neaps 1.8m

Springs occur 2 days
after
New and Full Moon.

WICK

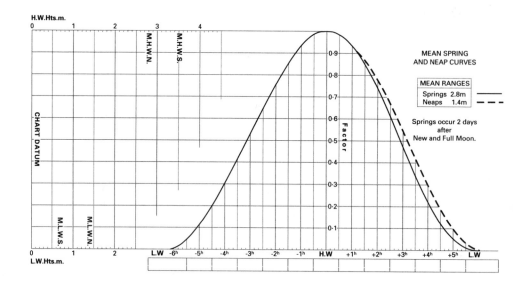

MEAN SPRING
AND NEAP CURVES

MEAN RANGES
Springs 2.8m
Neaps 1.4m

Springs occur 2 days
after
New and Full Moon.

LERWICK

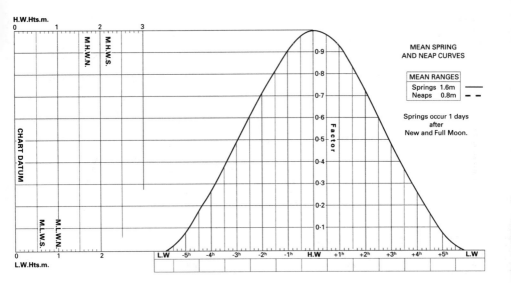

H.W.Hts.m.

CHART DATUM

M.H.W.N. M.H.W.S.

M.L.W.N. M.L.W.S.

Factor

L.W -5ʰ -4ʰ -3ʰ -2ʰ -1ʰ H.W +1ʰ +2ʰ +3ʰ +4ʰ +5ʰ L.W

L.W.Hts.m.

MEAN SPRING
AND NEAP CURVES

MEAN RANGES
Springs 1.6m
Neaps   0.8m

Springs occur 1 days
after
New and Full Moon.

ULLAPOOL

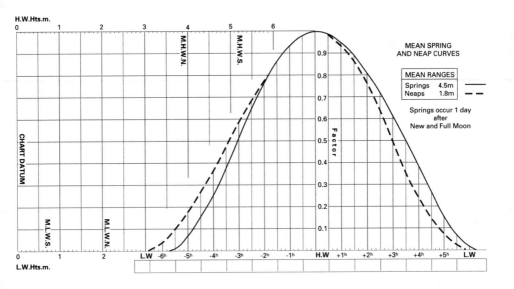

H.W.Hts.m.

CHART DATUM

M.H.W.N. M.H.W.S.

M.L.W.S. M.L.W.N.

Factor

L.W -6ʰ -5ʰ -4ʰ -3ʰ -2ʰ -1ʰ H.W +1ʰ +2ʰ +3ʰ +4ʰ +5ʰ L.W

L.W.Hts.m.

MEAN SPRING
AND NEAP CURVES

MEAN RANGES
Springs 4.5m
Neaps   1.8m

Springs occur 1 day
after
New and Full Moon

OBAN

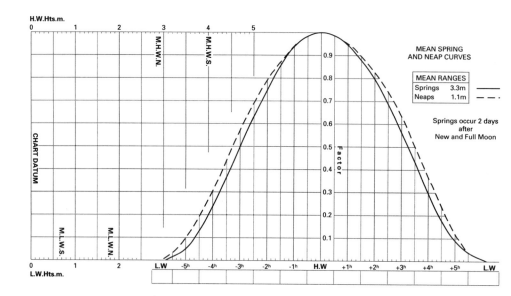

GREENOCK

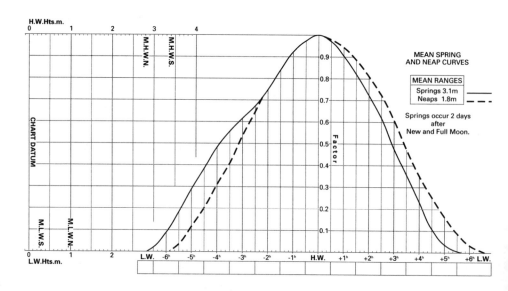

LIVERPOOL

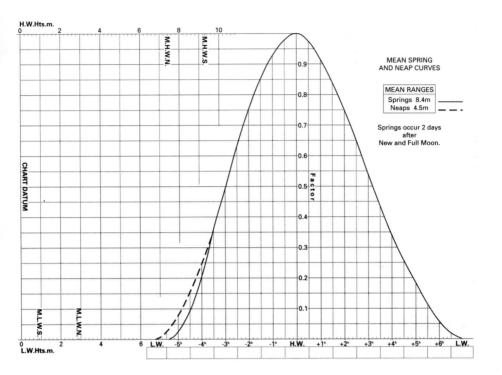

MEAN SPRING
AND NEAP CURVES

MEAN RANGES

| Springs | 8.4m | ——— |
| Neaps | 4.5m | – – – |

Springs occur 2 days
after
New and Full Moon.

HOLYHEAD

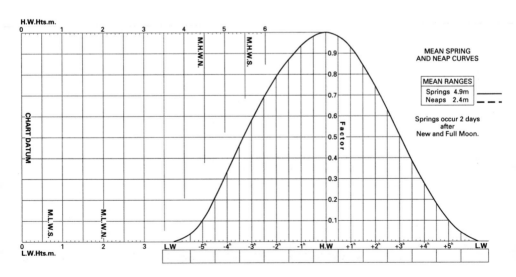

MEAN SPRING
AND NEAP CURVES

MEAN RANGES

| Springs | 4.9m | ——— |
| Neaps | 2.4m | – – – |

Springs occur 2 days
after
New and Full Moon.

MILFORD HAVEN

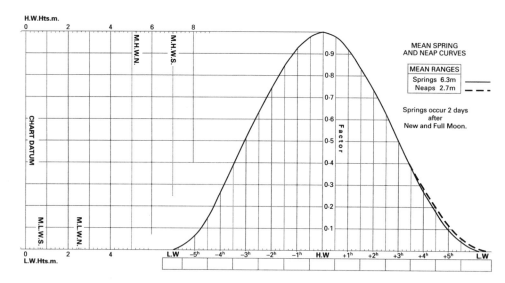

H.W.Hts.m.

MEAN SPRING
AND NEAP CURVES

MEAN RANGES
Springs 6.3m
Neaps 2.7m

Springs occur 2 days
after
New and Full Moon.

SWANSEA

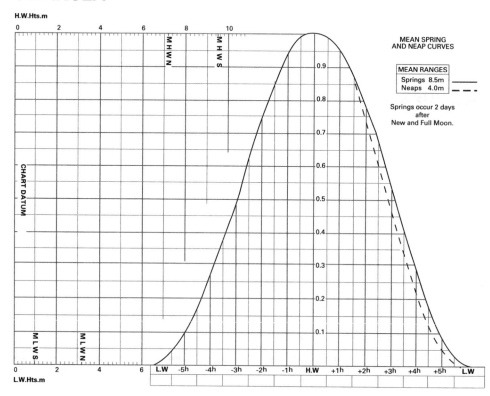

H.W.Hts.m

MEAN SPRING
AND NEAP CURVES

MEAN RANGES
Springs 8.5m
Neaps 4.0m

Springs occur 2 days
after
New and Full Moon.

AVONMOUTH

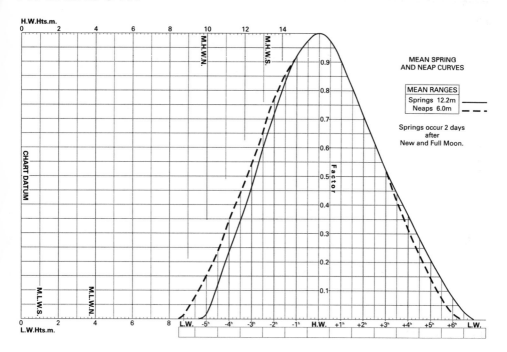

MEAN SPRING
AND NEAP CURVES

MEAN RANGES
Springs 12.2m
Neaps 6.0m

Springs occur 2 days
after
New and Full Moon.

DUBLIN

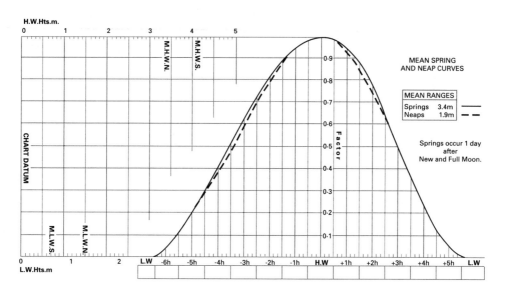

MEAN SPRING
AND NEAP CURVES

MEAN RANGES
Springs 3.4m
Neaps 1.9m

Springs occur 1 day
after
New and Full Moon.

BELFAST

H. W. Hts.m.

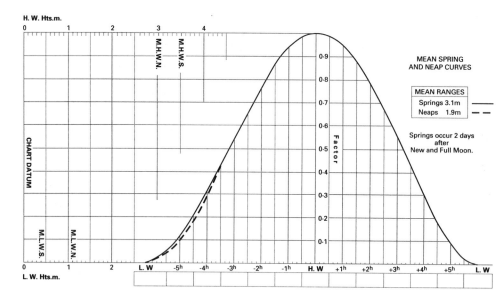

MEAN SPRING
AND NEAP CURVES

MEAN RANGES
Springs 3.1m
Neaps   1.9m

Springs occur 2 days
after
New and Full Moon.

L. W. Hts.m.

LONDONDERRY

H.W.Hts.m

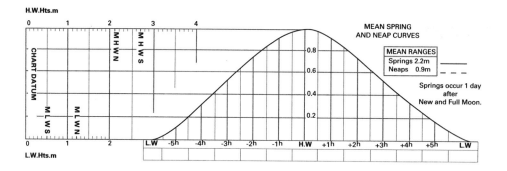

MEAN SPRING
AND NEAP CURVES

MEAN RANGES
Springs 2.2m
Neaps   0.9m

Springs occur 1 day
after
New and Full Moon.

L.W.Hts.m

GALWAY

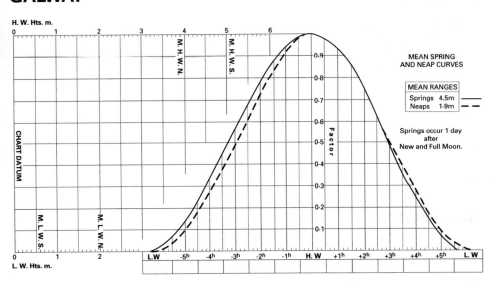

H. W. Hts. m.

MEAN SPRING
AND NEAP CURVES

MEAN RANGES
Springs 4.5m
Neaps 1.9m

Springs occur 1 day
after
New and Full Moon.

CHART DATUM

L. W. Hts. m.

COBH

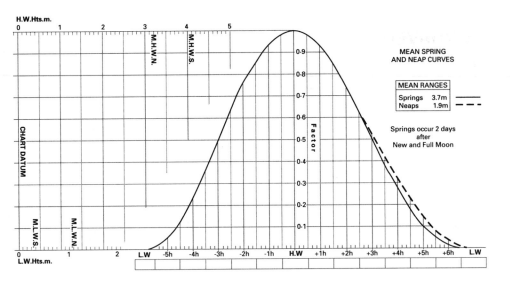

H.W.Hts.m.

MEAN SPRING
AND NEAP CURVES

MEAN RANGES
Springs 3.7m
Neaps 1.9m

Springs occur 2 days
after
New and Full Moon

CHART DATUM

L.W.Hts.m.

ESBJERG

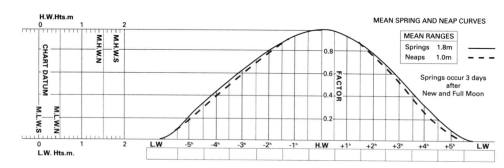

HELGOLAND

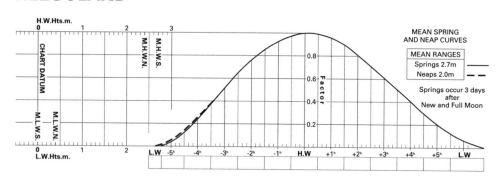

CUXHAVEN

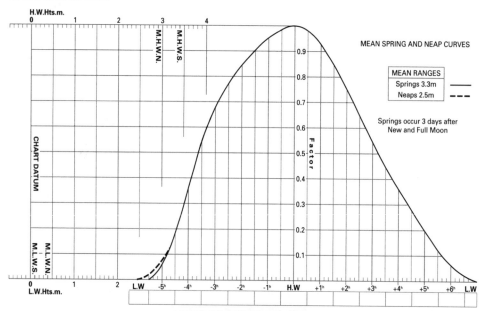

HOEK VAN HOLLAND

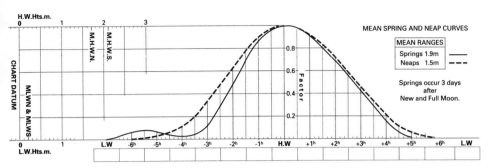

MEAN SPRING AND NEAP CURVES

MEAN RANGES
Springs 1.9m ——
Neaps 1.5m - - -

Springs occur 3 days
after
New and Full Moon.

ROTTERDAM

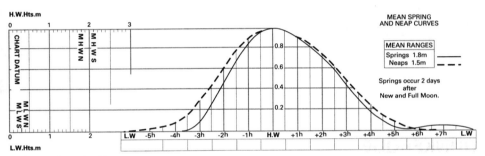

MEAN SPRING
AND NEAP CURVES

MEAN RANGES
Springs 1.8m ——
Neaps 1.5m - - -

Springs occur 2 days
after
New and Full Moon.

NB - There are often two Low Waters.
When this occurs the times shown in the Tide Tables are midway between the two.

VLISSINGEN

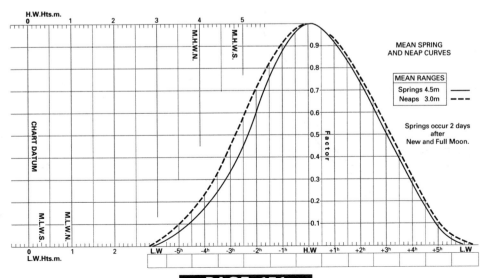

MEAN SPRING
AND NEAP CURVES

MEAN RANGES
Springs 4.5m ——
Neaps 3.0m - - -

Springs occur 2 days
after
New and Full Moon.

ANTWERPEN

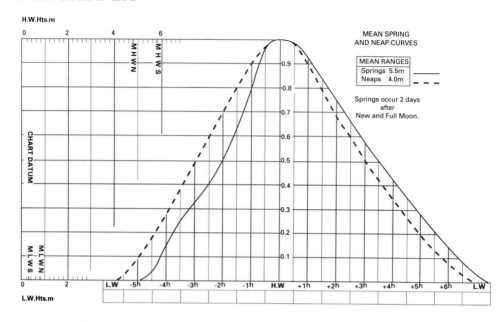

DUNKERQUE

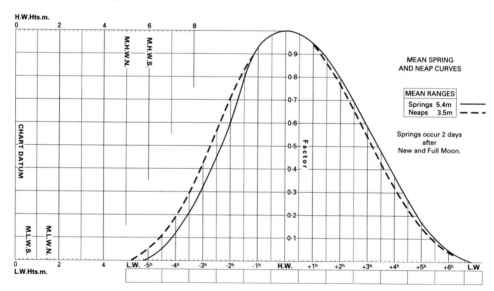

CALAIS

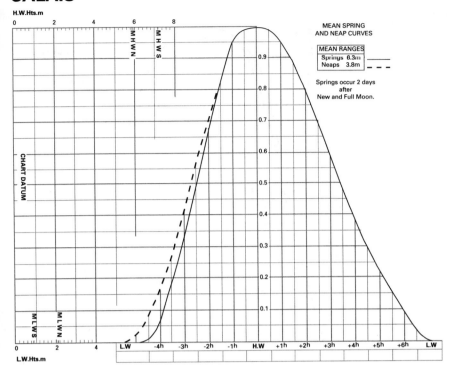

MEAN SPRING
AND NEAP CURVES

MEAN RANGES
Springs 6.3m
Neaps 3.8m

Springs occur 2 days
after
New and Full Moon.

DIEPPE

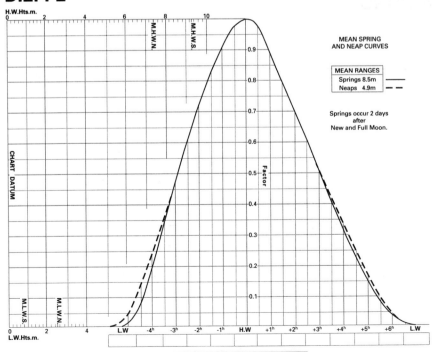

MEAN SPRING
AND NEAP CURVES

MEAN RANGES
Springs 8.5m
Neaps 4.9m

Springs occur 2 days
after
New and Full Moon.

LE HAVRE

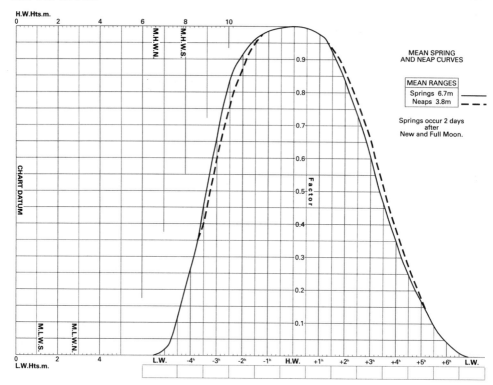

CHERBOURG

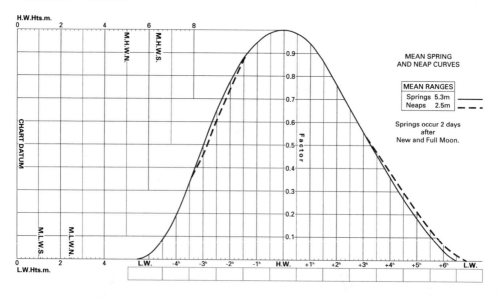

ST HELIER

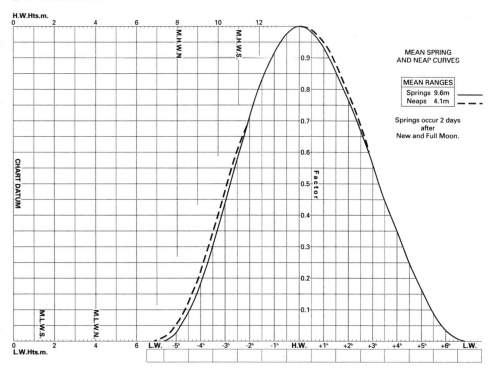

MEAN SPRING
AND NEAP CURVES

MEAN RANGES	
Springs 9.6m	
Neaps 4.1m	

Springs occur 2 days
after
New and Full Moon.

ST MALO

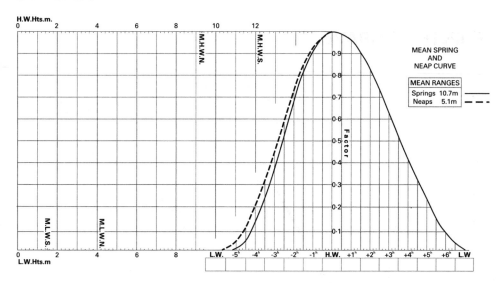

MEAN SPRING
AND
NEAP CURVE

MEAN RANGES	
Springs 10.7m	
Neaps 5.1m	

BREST

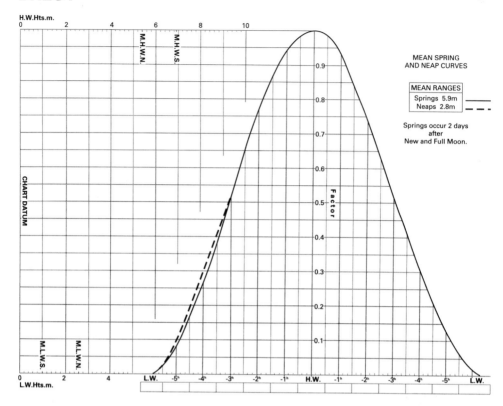

MEAN SPRING
AND NEAP CURVES

MEAN RANGES	
Springs 5.9m	————
Neaps 2.8m	– – –

Springs occur 2 days
after
New and Full Moon.

POINTE DE GRAVE

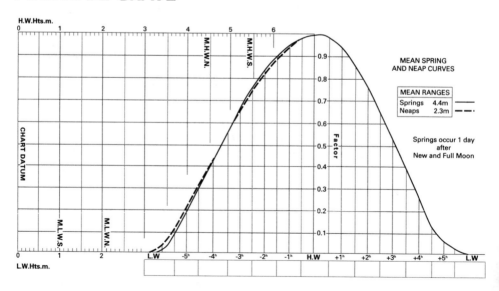

MEAN SPRING
AND NEAP CURVES

MEAN RANGES	
Springs 4.4m	————
Neaps 2.3m	– – –

Springs occur 1 day
after
New and Full Moon

LISBOA

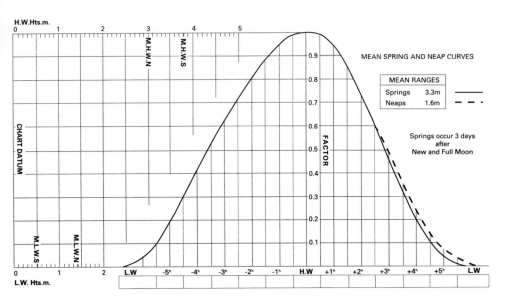

MEAN SPRING AND NEAP CURVES

MEAN RANGES	
Springs	3.3m
Neaps	1.6m

Springs occur 3 days
after
New and Full Moon

GIBRALTAR

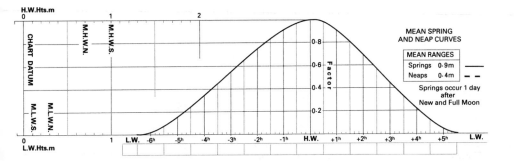

MEAN SPRING
AND NEAP CURVES

MEAN RANGES	
Springs	0·9m
Neaps	0·4m

Springs occur 1 day
after
New and Full Moon

SECONDARY PORTS & TIDAL DIFFERENCES
South Coast UK

Location	Lat	Long	High Water 0000 / 1200	High Water 0600 / 1800	Low Water 0000 / 1200	Low Water 0600 / 1800	MHWS	MHWN	MLWN	MLWS
PLYMOUTH, DEVONPORT	50 22N	4 11W	and	and	and	and	5.5	4.4	2.2	0.8
standard port			1200	1800	1200	1800				
ISLES OF SCILLY, ST. MARY'S	49 55N	6 19W	*standard port*				5.7	4.3	2.0	0.7
Penzance Newlyn	50 06N	5 33W	-0055	-0115	-0035	-0035	+0.1	0.0	-0.2	0.0
Porthleven	50 05N	5 19W	-0050	-0105	-0030	-0025	0.0	-0.1	-0.2	0.0
Lizard Point	49 57N	5 12W	-0045	-0100	-0030	-0030	-0.2	-0.2	-0.3	-0.2
Coverack	50 01N	5 05W	-0030	-0050	-0020	-0015	-0.2	-0.2	-0.3	-0.2
Helford River (Entrance)	50 05N	5 05W	-0030	-0035	-0015	-0010	-0.2	-0.2	-0.3	-0.2
Falmouth	50 09N	5 03W	-0025	-0045	-0010	-0010	-0.2	-0.2	-0.3	-0.2
Truro	50 16N	5 03W	-0020	-0025	*dries*	*dries*	-2.0	-2.0	*dries*	
Mevagissey	50 16N	4 47W	-0015	-0020	-0010	-0005	-0.1	-0.1	-0.2	-0.1
Par	50 21N	4 42W	-0010	-0015	-0010	-0005	-0.4	-0.4	-0.4	-0.2
Fowey	50 20N	4 38W	-0010	-0015	-0010	-0005	-0.1	-0.1	-0.2	-0.2
Lostwithiel	50 24N	4 40W	+0005	-0010	*dries*	*dries*	-4.1	-4.1	*dries*	
Looe	50 21N	4 27W	-0010	-0010	-0005	-0005	-0.1	-0.2	-0.2	-0.2
Whitsand Bay	50 20N	4 15W	0000	0000	0000	0000	0.0	+0.1	-0.1	+0.2
Saltash	50 24N	4 12W	0000	+0010	0000	-0005	+0.1	+0.1	+0.1	+0.1
Cargreen	50 26N	4 12W	0000	+0010	+0020	+0020	0.0	0.0	-0.1	0.0
Cotehele Quay	50 29N	4 13W	0000	+0020	+0045	+0045	-0.9	-0.9	-0.8	-0.4
Lopwell	50 28N	4 09W	*no data*	*no data*	*dries*	*dries*	-2.6	-2.7	*dries*	
Jupiter Point	50 23N	4 14W	+0010	+0005	0000	-0005	0.0	0.0	+0.1	0.0
St. Germans	50 23N	4 18W	0000	0000	+0020	+0020	-0.3	-0.1	0.0	+0.2
Turnchapel	50 22N	4 07W	0000	0000	+0010	-0015	0.0	+0.1	+0.2	+0.1
Bovisand Pier .	50 20N	4 08W	0000	-0020	0000	-0010	-0.2	-0.1	0.0	+0.1
River Yealm Entrance	50 18N	4 04W	+0006	+0006	+0002	+0002	-0.1	-0.1	-0.1	-0.1
			0100 / 1300	0600 / 1800	0100 / 1300	0600 / 1800				
PLYMOUTH, DEVONPORT	50 22N	4 11W	and	and	and	and	5.5	4.4	2.2	0.8
standard port			1300	1800	1300	1800				
Salcombe	50 13N	3 47W	0000	+0010	+0005	-0005	-0.2	-0.3	-0.1	-0.1
Start Point	50 13N	3 39W	+0015	+0015	+0005	+0010	-0.1	-0.2	+0.1	+0.2
River Dart										
Dartmouth	50 21N	3 34W	+0015	+0025	0000	-0005	-0.6	-0.6	-0.2	-0.2
Greenway Quay	50 23N	3 35W	+0030	+0045	+0025	+0005	-0.6	-0.6	-0.2	-0.2
Totnes	50 26N	3 41W	+0030	+0040	+0115	+0030	-2.0	-2.1	*dries*	
Torquay	50 28N	3 31W	+0025	+0045	+0010	0000	-0.6	-0.7	-0.2	-0.1
Teignmouth *Approaches*	50 33N	3 30W	+0025	+0040	0000	0000	-0.7	-0.8	-0.3	-0.2
Teignmouth *Shaldon Bridge*	50 33N	3 31W	+0035	+0050	+0020	+0020	-0.9	-0.9	-0.2	0.0
Exmouth *Approaches*	50 36N	3 23W	+0030	+0050	+0015	+0005	-0.9	-1.0	-0.5	-0.3
River Exe										
Exmouth Dock	50 37N	3 25W	+0035	+0055	+0050	+0020	-1.5	-1.6	-0.9	-0.6
Starcross	50 38N	3 27W	+0040	+0110	+0055	+0025	-1.4	-1.5	-0.8	-0.1
Topsham	50 41N	3 28W	+0045	+0105	*no data*	*no data*	- 1.5	-1.6	*no data*	
Lyme Regis	50 43N	2 56W	+0040	+0100	+0005	-0005	-1.2	-1.3	-0.5	-0.2
Bridport *West Bay*	50 42N	2 45W	+0025	+0040	0000	0000	-1.4	-1.4	-0.6	-0.2
Chesil Beach	50 37N	2 33W	+0040	+0055	-0005	+0010	-1.6	-1.5	-0.5	0.0
Chesil Cove	50 34N	2 28W	+0035	+0050	-0010	+0005	-1.5	-1.6	-0.5	-0.2
			0100 / 1300	0700 / 1900	0100 / 1300	0700 / 1900				
PORTLAND	50 34N	2 26W	and	and	and	and	2.1	1.4	0.8	0.1
standard port			1300	1900	1300	1900				
Lulworth Cove	50 37N	2 15W	+0005	+0015	-0005	0000	+0.1	+0.1	+0.2	+0.1
Mupe Bay	50 37N	2 13W	+0005	+0015	-0005	0000	+0.1	+0.1	+0.2	+0.1
			0000 / 1200	0600 / 1800	0500 / 1700	1100 / 2300				
PORTSMOUTH	50 48N	1 07W	and	and	and	and	4.7	3.8	1.9	0.8
standard port			1200	1800	1700	2300				
Swanage	50 37N	1 57W	-0250	+0105	-0105	-0105	-2.7	-2.2	-0.7	-0.3
Poole Harbour Entrance	50 40N	1 56W	-0230	+0115	-0045	-0020	-2.5	-2.1	-0.6	-0.2
POOLE, TOWN QUAY	50 43N	1 59W	*standard port*				2.2	1.7	1.2	0.6
Pottery Pier	50 42N	1 59W	-0150	+0200	-0010	0000	-2.7	-2.1	-0.6	0.0
Wareham *River Frome*	50 41N	2 06W	-0140	+0205	+0110	+0035	-2.5	-2.1	-0.7	+0.1
Cleavel Point	50 40N	2 00W	-0220	+0130	-0025	-0015	-2.6	-2.3	-0.7	-0.3
Bournemouth	50 43N	1 52W	-0240	+0055	-0050	-0030	-2.7	-2.2	-0.8	-0.3
Christchurch *Entrance*	50 43N	1 45W	-0230	+0030	-0035	-0035	-2.9	-2.4	-1.2	-0.2
Christchurch *Quay*	50 44N	1 46W	-0210	+0100	+0105	+0055	-2.9	-2.4	-1.0	0.0
Christchurch *Tuckton*	50 44N	1 47W	-0205	+0110	+0110	+0105	-3.0	-2.5	-1.0	+0.1
Hurst Point	50 42N	1 33W	-0115	-0005	-0030	-0025	-2.0	-1.5	-0.5	-0.1

Location	Lat	Long	High Water		Low Water		MHW...			
Lymington	50 46N	1 32W	-0110	+0005	-0020	-0020	-1.7			
Bucklers Hard	50 48N	1 25W	-0040	-0010	+0010	-0010	-1.0	-0.8		
Stansore Point	50 47N	1 21W	-0050	-0010	-0005	-0010	-0.8	-0.5		
Isle of Wight										
Yarmouth	50 42N	1 30W	-0105	+0005	-0025	-0030	-1.7	-1.4	-0.3	
Totland Bay	50 41N	1 33W	-0130	-0045	-0040	-0040	-2.1	-1.6	-0.4	0.0
Freshwater	50 40N	1 31W	-0210	+0025	-0040	-0020	-2.1	-1.5	-0.4	0.0
Ventnor	50 36N	1 12W	-0025	-0030	-0025	-0030	-0.8	-0.6	-0.2	+0.2
Sandown	50 39N	1 09W	0000	+0005	+0010	+0025	-0.6	-0.5	-0.2	0.0
Foreland *Lifeboat Slip*	50 41N	1 04W	-0005	0000	+0005	+0010	-0.1	-0.1	0.0	+0.1
Bembridge Harbour	50 42N	1 06W	-0010	+0005	+0020	0000	-1.6	-1.5	-1.4	-0.6
Ryde	50 44N	1 07W	-0010	+0010	-0005	-0010	-0.2	-0.1	0.0	+0.1
Medina River										
Cowes	50 46N	1 18W	-0015	+0015	0000	-0020	-0.5	-0.3	-0.1	0.0
Folly Inn	50 44N	1 17W	-0015	+0015	0000	-0020	-0.6	-0.4	-0.1	+0.2
Newport	50 42N	1 17W	*no data*	*no data*	*no data*	*no data*	-0.6	-0.4	+0.1	+0.8
SOUTHAMPTON *standard port*	50 54N	1 24W	0400 and 1600	1100 and 2300	0000 and 1200	0600 and 1800	4.5	3.7	1.8	0.5
Calshot Castle	50 49N	1 18W	0000	+0025	0000	0000	0.0	0.0	+0.2	+0.3
Redbridge	50 55N	1 28W	-0020	+0005	0000	-0005	-0.1	-0.1	-0.1	-0.1
River Hamble										
Warsash	50 51N	1 18W	+0020	+0010	+0010	0000	0.0	+0.1	+0.1	+0.3
Bursledon	50 53N	1 18W	+0020	+0020	+0010	+0010	+0.1	+0.1	+0.2	+0.2
PORTSMOUTH *standard port*	50 48N	1 07W	0500 and 1700	1000 and 2200	0000 and 1200	0600 and 1800	4.7	3.8	1.9	0.8
Lee-on-the-Solent	50 48N	1 12W	-0005	+0005	-0015	-0010	-0.2	-0.1	+0.1	+0.2
Chichester Harbour										
Entrance	50 47N	0 56W	-0010	+0005	+0015	+0020	+0.2	+0.2	0.0	+0.1
Northney	50 50N	0 58W	+0020	+0010	0000	+0005	0.0	-0.2	-0.2	-0.4
Bosham	50 50N	0 52W	+0010	+0005	*no data*	*no data*	0.0	-0.1	*no data*	
Itchenor	50 48N	0 52W	+0005	0000	-0010	+0005	-0.1	-0.2	-0.2	-0.3
Dell Quay	50 49N	0 49W	+0015	+0010	*no data*	*no data*	0.0	-0.1	*no data*	
Selsey Bill	50 43N	0 47W	-0005	-0005	+0035	+0035	+0.6	+0.6	0.0	0.0
Nab Tower	50 40N	0 57W	+0015	0000	+0015	+0015	-0.2	0.0	+0.2	0.0
SHOREHAM *standard port*	50 50N	0 15W	0500 and 1700	1000 and 2200	0000 and 1200	0600 and 1800	6.3	4.8	1.9	0.6
Pagham	50 46N	0 43W	+0015	0000	-0015	-0025	-0.7	-0.5	-0.1	-0.1
Bognor Regis	50 47N	0 40W	+0010	-0005	-0005	-0020	-0.6	-0.5	-0.2	-0.1
River Arun										
Littlehampton *Entrance*	50 48N	0 32W	+0010	0000	-0005	-0010	-0.4	-0.4	-0.2	-0.2
Littlehampton *Norfolk Wharf*	50 48N	0 33W	+0015	+0005	0000	+0045	-0.7	-0.7	-0.3	+0.2
Arundel	50 51N	0 33W	*no data*	+0120	*no data*	*no data*	-3.1	-2.8	*no data*	
Worthing	50 48N	0 22W	+0010	0000	-0005	-0010	-0.1	-0.2	0.0	0.0
Brighton	50 49N	0 08W	-0010	-0005	-0005	-0005	+0.3	+0.1	0.0	-0.1
Newhaven	50 47N	0 04E	-0015	-0010	0000	0000	+0.4	+0.2	0.0	-0.2
Eastbourne	50 46N	0 17E	-0010	-0005	+0015	+0020	+1.1	+0.6	+0.2	+0.1
DOVER *standard port*	51 07N	1 19E	0000 and 1200	0600 and 1800	0100 and 1300	0700 and 1900	6.8	5.3	2.1	0.8
Hastings	50 51N	0 35E	0000	-0010	-0030	-0030	+0.8	+0.5	+0.1	-0.1
Rye *Approaches*	50 55N	0 47E	+0005	-0010	*no data*	*no data*	+1.0	+0.7	*no data*	
Rye *Harbour*	50 56N	0 46E	+0005	-0010	*dries*	*dries*	-1.4	-1.7	*dries*	
Dungeness	50 54N	0 58E	-0010	-0015	-0020	-0010	+1.0	+0.6	+0.4	+0.1
Folkestone	51 05N	1 12E	-0020	-0005	-0010	-0010	+0.4	+0.4	0.0	-0.1
Deal	51 13N	1 25E	+0010	+0020	+0010	+0005	-0.6	-0.3	0.0	0.0
Richborough	51 18N	1 21E	+0015	+0015	+0030	+0030	-3.4	-2.6	-1.7	-0.7
Ramsgate	51 20N	1 25E	+0030	+0030	+0017	+0007	-1.6	-1.3	-0.7	-0.2

EAST COAST ENGLAND

Location	Lat	Long	High Water		Low Water		MHW...			
MARGATE *standard port*	51 23N	1 23E	0100 and 1300	0700 and 1900	0100 and 1300	0700 and 1900	4.8	3.9	1.4	0.5
Broadstairs	51 21N	1 27E	-0020	-0008	+0007	+0010	-0.2	-0.2	-0.1	-0.1
Herne Bay	51 23N	1 07E	+0034	+0022	+0015	+0032	+0.4	+0.4	0.0	0.0
Whitstable *Approaches*	51 22N	1 02E	+0042	+0029	+0025	+0050	+0.6	+0.6	+0.1	0.0

	Lat	Long	High Water		Low Water		MHWS	MHWN	MLWN	MLWS
	27N	0 45E	0200 and 1400	0800 and 2000	0200 and 1400	0700 and 1900	5.8	4.7	1.5	0.6
	51 22N	0 46E	-0007	0000	0000	+0016	0.0	0.0	0.0	-0.1
	51 19N	0 54E	no data	no data	no data	no data	-0.2	-0.2	no data	
	51 25N	0 39E	+0002	+0002	0000	+0005	+0.2	+0.1	0.0	0.0
	51 23N	0 38E	+0016	+0008	no data	no data	+0.1	0.0	no data	
	51 24N	0 36E	+0004	+0004	0000	+0010	+0.2	+0.1	0.0	-0.1
Chau. aches	51 24N	0 33E	+0010	+0012	+0012	+0018	+0.3	+0.1	-0.1	-0.2
Upnor	51 25N	0 32E	+0015	+0015	+0015	+0025	+0.2	+0.2	-0.1	-0.1
Rochester Stroo. Pier	51 24N	0 30E	+0018	+0018	+0018	+0028	+0.2	+0.2	-0.2	-0.3
Wouldham	51 21N	0 27E	+0030	+0025	+0035	+0120	-0.2	-0.3	-1.0	-0.3
New Hythe	51 19N	0 28E	+0035	+0035	+0220	+0240	-1.6	-1.7	-1.2	-0.3
Allington Lock	51 17N	0 30E	+0050	+0035	no data	no data	-2.1	-2.2	-1.3	-0.4
River Thames										
Southend-on-Sea	51 31N	0 43E	-0005	0000	0000	+0005	0.0	0.0	-0.1	-0.1
Coryton	51 30N	0 31E	+0005	+0010	+0010	+0015	+0.4	+0.3	+0.1	-0.1
LONDON BRIDGE	51 30N	0 05W	0300 and 1500	0900 and 2100	0400 and 1600	1100 and 2300	7.1	5.9	1.3	0.5
standard port										
Albert Bridge	51 29N	0 10W	+0025	+0020	+0105	+0110	-0.9	-0.8	-0.7	-0.4
Hammersmith Bridge	51 29N	0 14W	+0040	+0035	+0205	+0155	-1.4	-1.3	-1.0	-0.5
Kew Bridge	51 29N	0 17W	+0055	+0050	+0255	+0235	-1.8	-1.8	-1.2	-0.5
Richmond Lock	51 28N	0 19W	+0105	+0055	+0325	+0305	-2.2	-2.2	-1.3	-0.5
SHEERNESS	51 27N	0 45E	0200 and 1400	0700 and 1900	0100 and 1300	0700 and 1900	5.8	4.7	1.5	0.6
standard port										
Thames Estuary Shivering Sand	51 30N	1 05E	-0025	-0019	-0008	-0026	-0.6	-0.6	-0.1	-0.1
MARGATE	51 23N	1 23E	0100 and 1300	0700 and 1900	0100 and 1300	0700 and 1900	4.8	3.9	1.4	0.5
standard port										
SE Long Sand	51 32N	1 21E	-0006	-0003	-0004	-0004	0.0	+0.1	0.0	-0.1
WALTON-ON-THE-NAZE	51 51N	1 16E	0000 and 1200	0600 and 1800	0500 and 1700	1100 and 2300	4.2	3.4	1.1	0.4
standard port										
Whitaker Beacon	51 40N	1 06E	+0022	+0024	+0033	+0027	+0.6	+0.5	+0.2	+0.1
Holliwell Point	51 38N	0 56E	+0034	+0037	+0100	+0037	+1.1	+0.9	+0.3	+0.1
River Roach Rochford	51 35N	0 43E	+0050	+0040	dries	dries	-0.8	-1.1	dries	
River Crouch										
Burnham-on-Crouch	51 37N	0 48E	+0050	+0035	+0115	+0050	+1.0	+0.8	-0.1	-0.2
North Fambridge	51 38N	0 41E	+0115	+0050	+0130	+0100	+1.1	+0.8	0.0	-0.1
Hullbridge	51 38N	0 38E	+0115	+0050	+0135	+0105	+1.1	+0.8	0.0	-0.1
Battlesbridge	51 37N	0 34E	+0120	+0110	dries	dries	-1.8	-2.0	dries	
River Blackwater										
Bradwell Waterside	51 45N	0 53E	+0035	+0023	+0047	+0004	+1.0	+0.8	+0.2	0.0
Osea Island	51 43N	0 46E	+0057	+0045	+0050	+0007	+1.1	+0.9	+0.1	0.0
Maldon	51 44N	0 42E	+0107	+0055	no data	no data	-1.3	-1.1	no data	
West Mersea	51 47N	0 54E	+0035	+0015	+0055	+0010	+0.9	+0.4	+0.1	+0.1
River Colne										
Brightlingsea	51 48N	1 00E	+0025	+0021	+0046	+0004	+0.8	+0.4	+0.1	0.0
Colchester	51 53N	0 56E	+0035	+0025	dries	dries	0.0	-0.3	dries	
Clacton-on-Sea	51 47N	1 09E	+0012	+0010	+0025	+0008	+0.3	+0.1	+0.1	+0.1
Bramble Creek	51 53N	1 14E	+0010	-0007	-0005	+0010	+0.3	+0.3	+0.3	+0.3
Sunk Head	51 46N	1 30E	0000	+0002	-0002	+0002	-0.3	-0.3	-0.1	-0.1
HARWICH	51 57N	1 17E	0000 and 1200	0600 and 1800	0000 and 1200	0600 and 1800	4.0	3.4	1.1	0.4
standard port										
River Stour Mistley	51 57N	1 05E ·	+0025	+0025	0000	+0020	+0.2	0.0	-0.1	-0.1
River Orwell Ipswich	52 03N	1 10E	+0015	+0025	0000	+0010	+0.2	0.0	-0.1	-0.1
WALTON-ON-THE-NAZE	51 51N	1 16E	0100 and 1300	0700 and 1900	0100 and 1300	0700 and 1900	4.2	3.4	1.1	0.4
standard port										
Felixstowe Pier	51 57N	1 21E	-0008	-0010	-0020	-0020	-0.4	-0.3	-0.1	0.0
River Deben										
Woodbridge Haven	51 59N	1 24E	0000	-0005	-0020	-0025	-0.5	-0.5	-0.1	+0.1
Woodbridge	52 05N	1 19E	+0045	+0025	+0025	-0020	-0.2	-0.3	-0.2	0.0

Location	Lat	Long	High Water		Low Water					
Bawdsey	52 00N	1 26E	-0016	-0020	-0030	-0032	-0.			
Orford Haven										
Bar	52 02N	1 28E	-0026	-0030	-0036	-0038	-1.0	-0.8		
Orford Quay	52 05N	1 32E	+0040	+0040	+0055	+0055	-1.4	-1.1		
Slaughden Quay	52 08N	1 36E	+0105	+0105	+0125	+0125	-1.3	-0.8	-0.1	
Iken Cliffs	52 09N	1 31E	+0130	+0130	+0155	+0155	-1.3	-1.0	0.0	+0.
			0300	0900	0200	0800				
LOWESTOFT	52 28N	1 45E	and	and	and	and	2.4	2.1	1.0	0.5
standard port			1500	2100	1400	2000				
Orford Ness	52 05N	1 35E	+0135	+0135	+0135	+0125	+0.4	+0.6	-0.1	0.0
Aldeburgh	52 09N	1 36E	+0130	+0130	+0115	+0120	+0.3	+0.2	-0.1	-0.2
Minsmere Sluice	52 14N	1 38E	+0110	+0110	+0110	+0110	0.0	-0.1	-0.2	-0.2
Southwold	52 19N	1 40E	+0105	+0105	+0055	+0055	0.0	0.0	-0.1	0.0
Great Yarmouth										
Gorleston-on-Sea	52 34N	1 44E	-0035	-0035	-0030	-0030	0.0	0.0	0.0	0.0
Britannia Pier	52 36N	1 45E	-0100	-0100	-0040	-0040	0.0	0.0	0.0	0.0
Caister-on-Sea	52 39N	1 44E	-0120	-0120	-0100	-0100	0.0	-0.1	0.0	0.0
Winterton-on-Sea	52 43N	1 42E	-0225	-0215	-0135	-0135	+0.8	+0.5	+0.2	+0.1
			0100	0700	0100	0700				
IMMINGHAM	53 38N	0 11E	and	and	and	and	7.3	5.8	2.6	0.9
standard port			1300	1900	1300	1900				
Cromer	52 56N	1 18E	+0050	+0030	+0050	+0130	-2.1	-1.7	-0.5	-0.1
Blakeney Bar	52 59N	0 59E	+0035	+0025	+0030	+0040	-1.6	-1.3	no data	
Blakeney	52 57N	1 01E	+0115	+0055	no data	no data	-3.9	-3.8	no data	
Wells Bar	52 59N	0 49E	+0020	+0020	+0020	+0020	-1.3	-1.0	no data	
Wells	52 57N	0 51E	+0035	+0045	+0340	+0310	-3.8	-3.8	no data	
Burnham Overy Staithe	52 58N	0 48E	+0045	+0055	no data	no data	-5.0	-4.9	no data	
The Wash										
Hunstanton	52 56N	0 29E	+0010	+0020	+0105	+0025	+0.1	-0.2	-0.1	0.0
West Stones	52 50N	0 21E	+0025	+0025	+0115	+0040	-0.3	-0.4	-0.3	+0.2
King's Lynn	52 45N	0 24E	+0030	+0030	+0305	+0140	-0.5	-0.8	-0.8	+0.1
Wisbech Cut	52 48N	0 13E	+0020	+0025	+0200	+0030	-0.3	-0.7	-0.4 no data	
Lawyer's Creek	52 53N	0 05E	+0010	+0020	no data	no data	-0.3	-0.6	no data	
Tabs Head	52 56N	0 05E	0000	+0005	+0125	+0020	+0.2	-0.2	-0.2	-0.2
Boston	52 58N	0 01W	0000	+0010	+0140	+0050	-0.5	-1.0	-0.9	-0.5
Skegness	53 09N	0 21E	+0010	+0015	+0030	+0020	-0.4	-0.5	-0.1	0.0
Inner Dowsing Light Tower	53 20N	0 34E	0000	0000	+0010	+0010	-0.9	-0.7	-0.1	+0.3
River Humber										
Bull Sand Fort	53 34N	0 04E	-0020	-0030	-0035	-0015	-0.4	-0.3	+0.1	+0.2
Grimsby	53 35N	0 04W	-0003	-0011	-0015	-0002	-0.3	-0.2	0.0	+0.1
Hull King George Dock	53 44N	0 16W	+0010	+0010	+0021	+0017	+0.3	+0.2	-0.1	-0.2
Hull Albert Dock	53 44N	0 21W	+0019	+0019	+0033	+0027	+0.3	+0.1	-0.1	-0.2
Humber Bridge	53 43N	0 27W	+0027	+0022	+0049	+0039	-0.1	-0.4	-0.7	-0.6
River Trent										
Burton Stather	53 39N	0 42W	+0105	+0045	+0335	+0305	-2.1	-2.3	-2.3	dries
Flixborough Wharf	53 37N	0 42W	+0120	+0100	+0400	+0340	-2.3	-2.6	dries	
Keadby	53 36N	0 44W	+0135	+0120	+0425	+0410	-2.5	-2.8	dries	
Owston Ferry	53 29N	0 46W	+0155	+0145	dries	dries	-3.5	-3.9	dries	
River Ouse										
Blacktoft	53 42N	0 43W	+0100	+0055	+0325	+0255	-1.6	-1.8	-2.2	-1.1
Goole	53 42N	0 52W	+0130	+0115	+0355	+0350	-1.6	-2.1	-1.9	-0.6
			0000	0600	0000	0600				
RIVER TEES ENTRANCE	54 38N	1 09W	and	and	and	and	5.5	4.3	2.0	0.9
standard port			1200	1800	1200	1800				
Bridlington	54 05N	0 11W	+0100	+0050	+0055	+0050	+0.6	+0.4	+0.3	+0.2
Filey Bay	54 13N	0 16W	+0042	+0042	+0047	+0034	+0.3	+0.6	+0.4	+0.1
Scarborough	54 17N	0 23W	+0040	+0040	+0030	+0030	+0.2	+0.3	+0.3	0.0
Whitby	54 29N	0 37W	+0015	+0030	+0020	+0005	+0.1	0.0	-0.1	-0.1
River Tees										
Middlesborough Dock Entrance	54 35N	1 13W	0000	+0002	0000	-0003	+0.1	+0.2	+0.1	-0.1
Tees Bridge Newport	54 34N	1 16W	-0002	+0004	+0005	-0003	+0.1	+0.2	0.0	-0.1
Hartlepool	54 41N	1 11W	-0004	-0004	-0006	-0006	-0.1	-0.1	-0.2	-0.1
Seaham	54 50N	1 19W	-0015	-0015	-0015	-0015	-0.3	-0.2	0.0	-0.2
Sunderland	54 55N	1 21W	-0017	-0017	-0016	-0016	-0.3	-0.1	0.0	-0.1
			0200	0800	0100	0800				
R. TYNE, N. SHIELDS	55 01N	1 26W	and	and	and	and	5. 0	3.9	1.8	0.7
standard port			1400	2000	1300	2000				
River Tyne Newcastle-upon-Tyne	54 58N	1 36W	+0003	+0003	+0008	+0008	+0.3	+0.2	+0.1	+0.1
Blyth	55 07N	1 29W	+0005	-0007	-0001	+0009	0.0	0.0	-0.1	+0.1

	Long	High Water		Low Water		MHWS	MHWN	MLWN	MLWS
	1 32W	-0010	-0010	-0020	-0020	+0.1	+0.1	0.0	+0.1
...N	1 34W	-0023	-0015	-0023	-0014	0.0	+0.2	+0.2	+0.1
...34N	1 38W	-0048	-0044	-0058	-0102	-0.2	-0.2	-0.2	0.0
...40N	1 47W	-0043	-0039	-0105	-0110	-0.2	-0.2	-0.3	-0.1
...5 47N	2 00W	-0053	-0053	-0109	-0109	-0.3	-0.1	-0.5	-0.1
		0000	**0600**	**0200**	**0800**				
	53 24N	3 01W	and	and	and	and	9.3	7.4	2.9	0.9
		1200	**1800**	**1400**	**2000**				
Por...	54 50N	5 07W	+0018	+0026	0000	-0035	-5.5	-4.4	-2.0	-0.6
Wigtown...									
Drummore	54 41N	4 53W	+0030	+0040	+0015	+0020	-3.4	-2.5	-0.9	-0.3
Port William	54 43N	4 40W	+0030	+0030	+0025	0000	-2.9	-2.2	-0.8	no data
Isle of Whithorn	54 42N	4 22W	+0020	+0025	+0025	+0005	-2.4	-2.0	-0.8	-0.2
Garlieston	54 47N	4 21W	+0025	+0035	+0030	+0005	-2.3	-1.7	-0.5	no data
Solway Firth									
Kirkcudbright Bay	54 48N	4 04W	+0015	+0015	+0010	0000	-1.8	-1.5	-0.5	-0.1
Hestan Islet	54 50N	3 48W	+0025	+0025	+0020	+0025	-1.0	-1.1	-0.5	0.0
Southerness Point	54 52N	3 36W	+0030	+0030	+0030	+0010	-0.7	-0.7	no data	
Annan Waterfoot	54 58N	3 16W	+0050	+0105	+0220	+0310	-2.2	-2.6	-2.7	
Torduff Point	54 58N	3 09W	+0105	+0140	+0520	+0410	-4.1	-4.9		
Redkirk	54 59N	3 06W	+0110	+0215	+0715	+0445	-5.5	-6.2		
Silloth	54 52N	3 24W	+0030	+0040	+0045	+0055	-0.1	-0.3	-0.6	-0.1
Maryport	54 43N	3 30W	+0017	+0032	+0020	+0005	-0.7	-0.8	-0.4	0.0
Workington	54 39N	3 34W	+0020	+0020	+0020	+0010	-1.2	-1.1	-0.3	0.0
Whitehaven	54 33N	3 36W	+0005	+0015	+0010	+0005	-1.3	-1.1	-0.5	+0.1
Tarn Point	54 17N	3 25W	+0005	+0005	+0010	0000	-1.0	-1.0	-0.4	0.0
Duddon Bar	54 09N	3 20W	+0003	+0003	+0008	+0002	-0.8	-0.8	-0.3	0.0
Barrow-in-Furness	54 06N	3 12W	+0009	+0015	+0015	+0011	-0.1	-0.1	- 0.1	+0.1
Ulverston	54 11N	3 04W	+0020	+0040	no data	no data	0.0	-0.1	no data	
Arnside	54 12N	2 51W	+0100	+0135	no data	no data	+0.5	+0.2	no data	
Morecambe	54 04N	2 52W	+0005	+0010	+0030	+0015	+0.2	0.0	0.0	+0.2
Heysham	54 02N	2 55W	+0005	+0005	+0015	0000	+0.1	0.0	0.0	+0.2
River Lune Glasson Dock	54 00N	2 51W	+0020	+0030	+0220	+0240	-2.7	-3.0	no data	
Lancaster	54 03N	2 49W	+0110	+0030	dries	dries	-5.0	-4.9	dries	
River Wyre									
Wyre Lighthouse	53 57N	3 02W	-0010	-0010	+0005	0000	-0.1	-0.1	no data	
Fleetwood	53 56N	3 00W	-0008	-0008	-0003	-0003	-0.1	-0.1	+0.1	+0.3
Blackpool	53 49N	3 04W	-0015	-0005	-0005	-0015	-0.4	-0.4	-0.1	+0.1
River Ribble Preston	53 46N	2 45W	+0010	+0010	+0335	+0310	-4.0	-4.1	-2.8	-0.8
Liverpool Bay									
Southport	53 39N	3 01W	-0020	-0010	no data	no data	-0.3	-0.3	no data	
Formby	53 32N	3 07W	-0015	-0010	-0020	-0020	-0.3	-0.1	0.0	+0.1
River Mersey									
Gladstone Dock	53 27N	3 01W	-0003	-0003	-0003	-0003	-0.1	-0.1	0.0	-0.1
Eastham	53 19N	2 57W	+0010	+0010	+0009	+0009	+0.3	+0.1	-0.1	-0.3
Hale Head	53 19N	2 48W	+0030	+0025	no data	no data	-2.4	-2.5	no data	
Widnes	53 21N	2 44W	+0040	+0045	+0400	+0345	-4.2	-4.4	-2.5	-0.3
Fiddler's Ferry	53 22N	2 39W	+0100	+0115	+0540	+0450	-5.9	-6.3	-2.4	-0.4
River Dee									
Hilbre Island	53 23N	3 13W	-0015	-0012	-0010	-0015	-0.3	-0.2	+0.2	+0.4
Mostyn Docks	53 19N	3 16W	-0020	-0015	-0020	-0020	-0.8	-0.7	no data	
Connah's Quay	53 13N	3 03W	0000	+0015	+0355	+0340	-4.6	-4.4	dries	
Chester	53 12N	2 54W	+0105	+0105	+0500	+0500	-5.3	-5.4	dries	
Isle of Man									
Peel	54 14N	4 42W	-0015	+0010	0000	-0010	-4.0	-3.2	-1.4	-0.4
Ramsey	54 19N	4 22W	+0005	+0015	-0005	-0015	-1.9	-1.5	-0.6	0.0
Douglas	54 09N	4 28W	+0005	+0015	-0015	-0025	-2.4	-2.0	-0.5	-0.1
Port St. Mary	54 04N	4 44W	+0005	+0015	-0010	-0030	-3.4	-2.6	-1.3	-0.4
Calf Sound	54 04N	4 48W	+0005	+0005	-0015	-0025	-3.2	-2.6	-0.9	-0.3
Port Erin	54 05N	4 46W	-0005	+0015	-0010	-0050	-4.1	-3.2	-1.3	-0.5

Wales

	Long	High Water		Low Water		MHWS	MHWN	MLWN	MLWS
Colwyn Bay	53 18N	3 43W	-0015	-0020	no data	no data	-1.5	-1.3	no data	
Llandudno	53 20N	3 50W	-0015	-0020	-0030	-0035	-1.7	-1.4	-0.7	-0.3
		0000	**0600**	**0500**	**1100**				
HOLYHEAD	53 19N	4 37W	and	and	and	and	5.6	4.4	2.0	0.7
standard port		**1200**	**1800**	**1700**	**2300**				
Conwy	53 17N	3 50W	+0025	+0035	+0120	+0105	+2.3	+1.8	+0.6	+0.4
Menai Strait									
Beaumaris	53 16N	4 05W	+0025	+0010	+0055	+0035	+2.0	+1.6	+0.5	+0.1
Menai Bridge	53 13N	4 09W	+0030	+0010	+0100	+0035	+1.7	+1.4	+0.3	0.0

Location	Lat	Long	High Water		Low Water		MHWS	MHWN	MLWN	MLWS
Port Dinorwic	53 11N	4 13W	-0015	-0025	+0030	0000	0.0	0.0	0.0	+0.1
Caernarfon	53 09N	4 16W	-0030	-0030	+0015	-0005	-0.4	-0.4	-0.1	-0.1
Fort Belan	53 07N	4 20W	-0040	-0015	-0025	-0005	-1.0	-0.9	-0.2	-0.1
Trwyn Dinmor	53 19N	4 03W	+0025	+0015	+0050	+0035	+1.9	+1.5	+0.5	+0.2
Moelfre	53 20N	4 14W	+0025	+0020	+0050	+0035	+1.9	+1.4	+0.5	+0.2
Amlwch	53 25N	4 20W	+0020	+0010	+0035	+0025	+1.6	+ 1.3	+0.5	+0.2
Cemaes Bay	53 25N	4 27W	+0020	+0025	+0040	+0035	+1.0	+0.7	+0.3	+0.1
Trearddur Bay	53 16N	4 37W	-0045	-0025	-0015	-0015	-0.4	-0.4	0.0	+0.1
Porth Trecastell	53 12N	4 30W	-0045	-0025	-0005	-0015	-0.6	-0.6	0.0	0.0
Llanddwyn Island	53 08N	4 25W	-0115	-0055	-0030	-0020	-0.7	-0.5	-0.1	0.0
Trefor	53 00N	4 25W	-0115	-0100	-0030	-0020	-0.8	-0.9	-0.2	-0.1
Porth Dinllaen	52 57N	4 34W	-0120	-0105	-0035	-0025	-1.0	-1.0	-0.2	-0.2
Porth Ysgaden	52 54N	4 39W	-0125	-0110	-0040	-0035	-1.1	-1.0	-0.1	-0.1
Bardsey Island	52 46N	4 47W	-0220	-0240	-0145	-0140	-1.2	-1.2	-0.5	-0.1
MILFORD HAVEN *standard port*	51 42N	5 03W	0100 and 1300	0800 and 2000	0100 and 1300	0700 and 1900	7.0	5.2	2.5	0.7
Cardigan Bay										
Aberdaron	52 48N	4 43W	+0210	+0200	+0240	+0310	-2.4	-1.9	-0.6	-0.2
St. Tudwal's Roads	52 49N	4 29W	+0155	+0145	+0240	+0310	-2.2	-1.9	-0.7	-0.2
Pwllheli	52 53N	4 24W	+0210	+0150	+0245	+0320	-2.0	- 1.8	-0.6	-0.2
Criccieth	52 55N	4 14W	+0210	+0155	+0255	+0320	-2.0	-1.8	-0.7	-0.3
Porthmadog	52 55N	4 08W	+0235	+0210	*no data*	*no data*	-1.9	-1.8	*no data*	
Barmouth	52 43N	4 03W	+0215	+0205	+0310	+0320	-2.0	-1.7	-0.7	0.0
Aberdovey	52 32N	4 03W	+0215	+0200	+0230	+0305	-2.0	-1.7	-0.5	0.0
Aberystwyth	52 24N	4 05W	+0145	+0130	+0210	+0245	-2.0	-1.7	-0.7	0.0
New Quay	52 13N	4 21W	+0150	+0125	+0155	+0230	-2.1	-1.8	-0.6	-0.1
Aberporth	52 08N	4 33W	+0135	+0120	+0150	+0220	-2.1	-1.8	-0.6	-0.1
Port Cardigan	52 07N	4 42W	+0140	+0120	+0220	+0130	-2.3	-1.8	-0.5	0.0
Cardigan *Town*	52 05N	4 40W	+0220	+0150	*no data*	*no data*	-2.2	-1.6	*no data*	
Fishguard	52 00N	4 58W	+0115	+0100	+0110	+0135	-2.2	-1.8	-0.5	+0.1
Porthgain	51 57N	5 11W	+0055	+0045	+0045	+0100	-2.5	-1.8	-0.6	0.0
Ramsey Sound	51 53N	5 19W	+0030	+0030	+0030	+0030	-1.9	-1.3	-0.3	0.0
Solva	51 52N	5 12W	+0015	+0010	+0035	+0015	-1.5	-1.0	-0.2	0.0
Little Haven	51 46N	5 06W	+0010	+0010	+0025	+0015	-1.1	-0.8	-0.2	0.0
Martin's Haven	51 44N	5 15W	+0010	+0010	+0015	+0015	-0.8	-0.5	+0.1	+0.1
Skomer Island	51 44N	5 17W	-0005	-0005	+0005	+0005	-0.4	-0.1	0.0	0.0
Dale Roads	51 42N	5 09W	-0005	-0005	-0008	-0008	0.0	0.0	0.0	-0.1
Cleddau River										
Neyland	51 42N	4 57W	+0002	+0010	0000	0000	0.0	0.0	0.0	0.0
Black Tar	51 45N	4 54W	+0010	+0020	+0005	0000	+0.1	+0.1	0.0	-0.1
Haverfordwest	51 48N	4 58W	+0010	+0025	*dries*	*dries*	-4.8	-4.9	*dries*	
Stackpole Quay	51 37N	4 54W	-0005	+0025	-0010	-0010	+0.9	+0.7	+0.2	+0.3
Tenby	51 40N	4 42W	-0015	-0010	-0015	-0020	+1.4	+1.1	+0.5	+0.2
Towy River										
Ferryside	51 46N	4 22W	0000	-0010	+0220	0000	-0.3	-0.7	-1.7	-0.6
Carmarthen	51 51N	4 18W	+0010	0000	*dries*	*dries*	-4.4	-4.8	*dries*	
Burry Inlet										
Burry Port	51 41N	4 15W	+0003	+0003	+0007	+0007	+1.6	+1.4	+0.5	+0.4
Llanelli	51 40N	4 10W	-0003	-0003	+0150	+0020	+0.8	+0.6	*no data*	
Mumbles	51 34N	3 58W	+0005	+0010	-0020	-0015	+2.3	+1.7	+0.6	+0.2
River Neath Entrance	51 37N	3 51W	0000	+0013	*dries*	*dries*	+2.7	+2.1	*dries*	
Port Talbot	51 35N	3 49W	+0003	+0005	-0010	-0003	+2.6	+2.2	+1.0	+0.5
Porthcawl	51 28N	3 42W	+0005	+0010	-0010	-0005	+2.9	+2.3	+0.8	+0.3
BRISTOL, AVONMOUTH *standard port*	51 30N	2 44W	0600 and 1800	1100 and 2300	0300 and 1500	0800 and 2000	13.2	9.8	3.8	1.0
Barry	51 23N	3 16W	-0030	-0015	-0125	-0030	-1.8	-1.3	+0.2	0.0
Flat Holm	51 23N	3 07W	-0015	-0015	-0045	-0045	-1.3	-1.1	-0.2	+0.2
Steep Holm	51 20N	3 06W	-0020	-0020	-0050	-0050	-1.6	-1.2	-0.2	-0.2
Cardiff	51 27N	3 09W	-0015	-0015	-0100	-0030	-1.0	-0.6	+0.1	0.0
Newport	51 33N	2 59W	-0020	-0010	0000	-0020	-1.1	-1.0	-0.6	-0.7
River Wye Chepstow	51 39N	2 40W	+0020	+0020	*no data*	*no data*	*no data*		*no data*	
BRISTOL, AVONMOUTH *standard port*	51 30N	2 44W	0000 and 1200	0600 and 1800	0000 and 1200	0700 and 1900	13.2	9.8	3.8	1.0

WEST COAST ENGLAND
River Severn

Location	Lat	Long	High Water		Low Water		MHWS	MHWN	MLWN	MLWS
Sudbrook	51 35N	2 43W	+0010	+0010	+0025	+0015	+0.2	+0.1	-0.1	+0.1
Beachley *Aust*	51 36N	2 38W	+0010	+0015	+0040	+0025	-0.2	-0.2	-0.5	-0.3

Location	Lat	Long	High Water		Low Water		MHWS	MHWN	MLWN	MLWS
Inward Rocks	51 39N	2 37W	+0020	+0020	+0105	+0045	-1.0	-1.1	-1.4	-0.6
Narlwood Rocks	51 39N	2 36W	+0025	+0025	+0120	+0100	-1.9	-2.0	-2.3	-0.8
White House	51 40N	2 33W	+0025	+0025	+0145	+0120	-3.0	-3.1	-3.6	-1.0
Berkeley	51 42N	2 30W	+0030	+0045	+0245	+0220	-3.8	-3.9	-3.4	-0.5
Sharpness Dock	51 43N	2 29W	+0035	+0050	+0305	+0245	-3.9	-4.2	-3.3	-0.4
Wellhouse Rock	51 44N	2 29W	+0040	+0055	+0320	+0305	-4.1	-4.4	-3.1	-0.2
Epney	51 42N	2 24W	+0130	no data	no data	no data	-9.4	no data	no data	
Minsterworth	51 50N	2 23W	+0140	no data	no data	no data	-10.1	no data	no data	
Llanthony	51 51N	2 21W	+0215	no data	no data	no data	-10.7	no data	no data	
			0200	**0800**	**0300**	**0800**				
BRISTOL, AVONMOUTH	51 30N	2 44W	and	and	and	and	**13.2**	**9.8**	**3.8**	**1.0**
standard port			**1400**	**2000**	**1500**	**2000**				
River Avon										
Shirehampton	51 29N	2 41W	0000	0000	+0035	+0010	-0.7	-0.7	-0.8	0.0
Sea Mills	51 29N	2 39W	+0005	+0005	+0105	+0030	-1.4	-1.5	-1.7	-0.1
Cumberland Basin *Entrance*	51 27N	2 37W	+0010	+0010	dries	dries	-2.9	-3.0	dries	
Portishead	51 30N	2 45W	-0002	0000	no data	no data	-0.1	-0.1	no data	
Clevedon	51 27N	2 52W	-0010	-0020	-0025	-0015	-0.4	-0.2	+0.2	0.0
St Thomas Head	51 24N	2 56W	0000	0000	-0030	-0030	-0.4	-0.2	+0.1	+0.1
English & Welsh Grounds	51 28N	2 59W	-0008	-0008	-0030	-0030	-0.5	-0.8	-0.3	0.0
Weston-super-Mare	51 21N	2 59W	-0020	-0030	-0130	-0030	-1.2	-1.0	-0.8	-0.2
River Parrett										
Burnham	51 14N	3 00W	-0020	-0025	-0030	0000	-2.3	-1.9	-1.4	-1.1
Bridgwater	51 08N	3 00W	-0015	-0030	+0305	+0455	-8.6	-8.1	dries	
Hinkley Point	51 13N	3 08W	-0020	-0025	-0100	-0040	-1.7	-1.4	-0.2	-0.2
Watchet	51 11N	3 20W	-0035	-0050	-0145	-0040	-1.9	-1.5	+0.1	+0.1
Minehead	51 13N	3 28W	-0037	-0052	-0155	-0045	-2.6	-1.9	-0.2	0.0
Porlock Bay	51 13N	3 38W	-0045	-0055	-0205	-0050	-3.0	-2.2	-0.1	-0.1
Lynmouth	51 14N	3 49W	-0055	-0115	no data	no data	-3.6	-2.7	no data	
			0100	**0700**	**0100**	**0700**				
MILFORD HAVEN	51 42N	5 03W	and	and	and	and	**7.0**	**5.2**	**2.5**	**0.7**
standard port			**1300**	**1900**	**1300**	**1900**				
Ilfracombe	51 13N	4 07W	-0016	-0016	-0041	-0031	+2.3	+1.8	+0.6	+0.3
Rivers Taw & Torridge										
Appledore	51 03N	4 12W	-0020	-0025	+0015	-0045	+0.5	0.0	-0.9	-0.5
Yelland Marsh	51 04N	4 10W	-0010	-0015	+0100	-0015	+0.1	-0.4	-1.2	-0.6
Fremington	51 05N	4 07W	-0010	-0015	+0030	-0030	-1.1	-1.8	-2.2	-0.5
Barnstaple	51 05N	4 04W	0000	-0015	-0155	-0245	-2.9	-3.8	-2.2	-0.4
Bideford	51 01N	4 12W	-0020	-0025	0000	0000	-1.1	-1.6	-2.5	-0.7
Clovelly	51 00N	4 24W	-0030	-0030	-0020	-0040	+1.3	+1.1	+0.2	+0.2
Lundy	51 10N	4 40W	-0030	-0030	-0020	-0040	+1.0	+0.7	+0.2	+0.1
Bude	50 50N	4 33W	-0040	-0040	-0035	-0045	+0.7	+0.6	no data	
Boscastle	50 41N	4 42W	-0045	-0010	-0110	-0100	+0.3	+0.4	+0.2	+0.2
Port Isaac	50 35N	4 50W	-0100	-0100	-0100	-0100	+0.5	+0.6	0.0	+0.2
			0100	**0700**	**0100**	**0700**				
MILFORD HAVEN	51 42N	5 03W	and	and	and	and	**7.0**	**5.2**	**2.5**	**0.7**
standard port			**1300**	**1900**	**1300**	**1900**				
River Camel										
Padstow	50 33N	4 56W	-0055	-0050	-0040	-0050	+0.3	+0.4	+0.1	+0.1
Wadebridge	50 31N	4 50W	-0052	-0052	+0235	+0245	-3.8	-3.8	-2.5	-0.4
Newquay	50 25N	5 05W	-0100	-0110	-0105	-0050	0.0	+0.1	0.0	-0.1
Perranporth	50 21N	5 09W	-0100	-0110	-0110	-0050	-0.1	0.0	0.0	+0.1
St. Ives	50 13N	5 28W	-0050	-0115	-0105	-0040	-0.4	-0.3	-0.1	-0.1
Cape Cornwall	50 08N	5 42W	-0130	-0145	-0120	-0120	-1.0	-0.9	-0.5	-0.1
Sennen Cove	50 04N	5 42W	-0130	-0145	-0125	-0125	-0.9	-0.4	no data	
IRELAND			**0000**	**0700**	**0000**	**0500**				
DUBLIN, NORTH WALL	53 21N	6 13W	and	and	and	and	**4.1**	**3.4**	**1.5**	**0.7**
standard port			**1200**	**1900**	**1200**	**1700**				
Courtown	52 39N	6 13W	-0328	-0242	-0158	-0138	-2.8	-2.4	-0.5	0.0
Arklow	52 47N	6 08W	-0315	-0201	-0140	-0134	-2.7	-2.2	-0.6	-0.1
Wicklow	52 59N	6 02W	-0019	-0019	-0024	-0026	-1.4	-1.1	-0.4	0.0
Greystones	53 09N	6 04W	-0008	-0008	-0008	-0008	-0.5	-0.4	no data	
Dun Laoghaire	53 18N	6 08W	-0006	-0001	-0002	-0003	0.0	0.0	0.0	+0.1
Dublin Bar	53 21N	6 09W	-0006	-0001	-0002	-0003	0.0	0.0	0.0	+0.1
Howth	53 23N	6 04W	-0007	-0005	+0001	+0005	0.0	-0.1	-0.2	-0.2
Malahide	53 27N	6 09W	+0002	+0003	+0009	+0009	+0.1	-0.2	-0.4	-0.2
Balbriggan	53 37N	6 11W	-0021	-0015	+0010	+0002	+0.3	+0.2	no data	
River Boyne Bar	53 43N	6 14W	-0005	0000	+0020	+0030	+0.9	+0.8	+0.4	+0.3
Dunany Point	53 52N	6 14W	-0028	-0018	-0008	-0006	+0.7	+0.9	no data	
DUNDALK SOLDIERS POINT	54 00N	6 21W	-0010	-0010	0000	+0045	+1.0	+0.8	+0.1	-0.1

NORTHERN IREL...

Location	Lat	Long	High Water		Low Water					
Carlingford Lough										
Cranfield Point	54 0..3W		-0027	-0011	+0005	-0...				
Warrenpoint			-0020	-0010	+0025	+0...				
Newry *Victoria Lock*			-0010	-0010	+0025	dries				

			0...00	0700	0000	06...				
BELFAST	54 36N	5 55W	and	and	and	an...				
standard port			...00	1900	1200	180...				
Kilkeel	54 03N	5 59W	+0...	0700	+0010	+001...			+0.1	
Newcastle	54 12N	5 53W	+0025	1900	+0010	+0040		+1.0	no data	
Killough Harbour	54 15N	5 38W	0000	...030	+0020	no data	+1.7	+1.2	+0.6	+0.3
Ardglass	54 16N	5 36W	+0010	+0...	no data	+0010				
Strangford Lough						...005			+0.1	+0.1
Killard Point	54 19N	5 31W	+0011	+0021	+0...	+0025	+1.0	+0.8	-0.2	0.0
Strangford	54 22N	5 33W	+0147	+0157	+0148	...08	+0.1	+0.1	-0.3	-0.1
Quoile Barrier	54 22N	5 41W	+0150	+0200	+0150		+0.2	+0.2	no data	
Killyleagh	54 24N	5 39W	+0157	+0207	+0211	+0231	0.3	+0.3		
South Rock	54 24N	5 25W	+0023	+0023	+0025	+0025	+1.0	+0.8	+0.1	+0.1
Portavogie	54 28N	5 26W	+0010	+0020	+0010	+0020	+1.2	+0.9	+0.3	+0.2
Donaghadee	54 38N	5 32W	+0020	+0020	+0023	+0023	+0.5	+0.4	0.0	+0.1
Carrickfergus	54 43N	5 48W	+0005	+0005	+0005	+0005	-0.3	-0.3	-0.2	-0.1
Larne	54 51N	5 47W	+0005	0000	+0010	-0005	-0.7	-0.5	-0.3	0.0
Red Bay	55 04N	6 03W	+0022	-0010	+0007	-0017	-1.9	-1.5	-0.8	-0.2
Cushendun	55 08N	6 02W	+0010	-0030	0000	-0025	-1.7	-1.5	-0.6	-0.2

			0200	0900	0300	0700				
LONDONDERRY	55 00N	7 19W	and	and	and	and	2.7	2.1	1.2	0.5
standard port			1400	2100	1500	1900				
Ballycastle Bay	55 12N	6 14W	+0053	-0147	-0125	+0056	-1.5	-1.0	-0.5	-0.2

			0200	0800	0500	1100				
LONDONDERRY	55 00N	7 19W	and	and	and	and	2.7	2.1	1.2	0.5
standard port			1400	2000	1700	2300				
Portrush	55 12N	6 40W	-0105	-0105	-0105	-0105	-0.8	-0.7	-0.4	0.1
Coleraine	55 08N	6 40W	-0030	-0130	-0110	-0020	-0.5	-0.3	-0.3	-0.1
Lough Foyle							-0.4	-0.2	no data	
Warren Point	55 13N	6 57W	-0121	-0139	-0156	-0132	-0.4	-0.2	-0.2	- 0.1
Moville	55 11N	7 03W	-0046	-0058	-0108	-0052	-0.4	-0.3	-0.3	-0.2
Quigley's Point	55 07N	7 11W	-0025	-0040	-0025	-0040	-0.3	-0.3	-0.2	-0.1
Culmore Point	55 03N	7 15W	-0010	-0030	-0020	-0040				

IRELAND

River Foyle							+0.1	+0.2	no data	
Culdaff Bay	55 18N	7 09W	-0136	-0156	-0206	-0146				

			0200	0900	0200	0800				
GALWAY	53 16N	9 03W	and	and	and	and	5.1	3.9	2.0	0.6
standard port			1400	2100	1400	2000				
Inishtrahull	55 26N	7 14W	+0100	+0100	+0115	+0200	-1.8	-1.4	-0.4	-0.2
Portmore	55 22N	7 20W	+0120	+0120	+0135	+0135	-1.3	-1.1	-0.4	-0.1
Trawbreaga Bay	55 19N	7 23W	+0115	+0059	+0109	+0125	-1.1	-0.8	no data	
Lough Swilly							-0.8	-0.7	-0.1	-0.1
Rathmullan	55 05N	7 31W	+0125	+0050	+0126	+0118	-1.1	-0.9	-0.5	-0.1
Fanad Head	55 16N	7 38W	+0115	+0040	+0125	+0120				
Mulroy Bay							-1.2	-1.0	no data	
Bar	55 15N	7 46W	+0108	+0052	+0102	+0118	-2.2	-1.7	no data	
Fanny's Bay	55 12N	7 49W	+0145	+0129	+0151	+0207	-3.1	-2.3	no data	
Seamount Bay	55 11N	7 44W	+0210	+0154	+0226	+0242	-3.7	-2.8	no data	
Cranford Bay	55 09N	7 42W	+0329	+0313	+0351	+0407				
Sheephaven							-1.1	-0.9	no data	
Downies Bay	55 11N	7 50W	+0057	+0043	+0053	+0107	-1.2	-0.9	no data	
Inishbofin Bay	55 10N	8 10W	+0040	+0026	+0032	+0046				

			0600	1100	0000	0700				
GALWAY	53 16N	9 03W	and	and	and	and	5.1	3.9	2.0	0.6
standard port			1800	2300	1200	1900				
Gweedore Harbour	55 04N	8 19W	+0048	+0100	+0055	+0107	-1.3	-1.0	-0.5	-0.1
Burtonport	54 59N	8 26W	+0042	+0055	+0115	+0055	-1.2	-1.0	-0.6	-0.1
Loughros More Bay	54 47N	8 30W	+0042	+0054	+0046	+0058	-1.1	-0.9	no data	

	Lat	Long	High Water		Low		MHWS	MHWN	MLWN	MLWS
					35		-1.0	-0.9	-0.5	0.0
					+0104		-1.2	-0.9	no data	
...Salt Hill Quay	54 38N	8 26W	+0040	+0050	+0059		-1.4	-1.0	-0.4	-0.2
...more	54 38N	8 13W	+0038	+0050 +2	+0054		-1.0	-0.9	-0.5	-0.1
...Harbour Oyster Island	54 28N	8 27W	+0036	+00 +0111	+0123		-1.2	-0.9	no data	
...ysadare Bay Culleenamore	54 18N	8 34W	+0043	+0030	+0050		-1.3	-1.2	-0.7	-0.2
Killala Bay Inishcrone	54 16N	8 36W	+0059	+0040	+0050		-1.4	-1.1	-0.4	-0.1
Broadhaven	54 13N	9 06W	+0035							
Blacksod Bay	54 16N	9 53W	+00							
Blacksod Quay				+0035	+0040	+0040	-1.2	-1.0	-0.6	-0.2
Bull's Mouth	54 06N	10 03W	+01	+0057	+0109	+0105	-1.5	-1.0	-0.6	-0.1
Clare Island	54 02N	9 55W	+0019	+0013	+0029	+0023	-1.0	-0.7	-0.4	-0.1
Westport Bay	53 48N	9 5?								
Inishraher			+0030	+0012	+0058	+0026	-0.6	-0.5	-0.3	-0.1
Killary Harbour	53 48N	9 53W	+0021	+0015	+0035	+0029	-1.0	-0.8	-0.4	-0.1
Inishbofin Bofin Harbour	53 ?N	10 13W	+0013	+0009	+0021	+0017	-1.0	-0.8	-0.4	-0.1
Clifden Bay	53 29N	10 04W	+0005	+0005	+0016	+0016	-0.7	-0.5	no data	
Slyne Head	53 24N	10 14W	+0002	+0002	+0010	+0010	-0.7	-0.5	no data	
Roundstone Bay	53 23N	9 55W	+0003	+0003	+0008	+0008	-0.7	-0.5	-0.3	-0.1
Kilkieran Cove	53 20N	9 44W	+0005	+0005	+0016	+0016	-0.3	-0.2	-0.1	0.0
Aran Islands Killeany Bay	53 07N	9 39W	-0008	-0008	+0003	+0003	-0.4	-0.3	-0.2	-0.1
Liscannor	52 56N	9 23W	-0003	-0007	+0006	+0002	-0.4	-0.3	no data	
Seafield Point	52 48N	9 30W	-0006	-0014	+0004	-0004	-0.5	-0.4	no data	
Kilrush	52 38N	9 30W	+0025	+0016	+0046	+0014	-0.1	-0.2	-0.3	-0.1
Limerick Dock	52 40N	8 38W	+0135	+0141	+0141	+0219	+1.0	+0.7	-0.8	-0.2
COBH *standard port*	51 51N	8 18W	0500 and 1700	1100 and 2300	0500 and 1700	1100 and 2300	4.1	3.2	1.3	0.4
Tralee Bay Fenit Pier	52 16N	9 52W	-0057	-0017	-0029	-0109	+0.5	+0.2	+0.3	+0.1
Smerwick Harbour	52 12N	10 24W	-0107	-0027	-0041	-0121	-0.3	-0.4	no data	
Dingle Harbour	52 07N	10 15W	-0111	-0041	-0049	-0119	-0.1	0.0	+0.3	+0.4
Castlemaine Hbr										
Cromane Point	52 09N	9 54W	-0026	-0006	-0017	-0037	+0.4	+0.2	+0.4	+0.2
Valentia Harbour										
Knights Town	51 56N	10 18W	-0118	-0038	-0056	-0136	-0.6	-0.4	-0.1	0.0
Ballinskelligs Bay										
Castle	51 49N	10 16W	-0119	-0039	-0054	-0134	-0.5	-0.5	-0.1	0.0
Kenmare River										
West Cove	51 46N	10 03W	-0113	-0033	-0049	-0129	-0.6	-0.5	-0.1	0.0
Dunkerron Harbour	51 52N	9 38W	-0117	-0027	-0050	-0140	-0.2	-0.3	+0.1	0.0
Coulagh Bay										
Ballycrovane Hbr	51 43N	9 57W	-0116	-0036	-0053	-0133	-0.6	-0.5	-0.1	0.0
Black Ball Harbour	51 36N	10 02W	-0115	-0035	-0047	-0127	-0.7	-0.6	-0.1	+0.1
Bantry Bay										
Castletown Bearhaven	51 39N	9 54W	-0048	-0012	-0025	-0101	-0.9	-0.6	-0.1	0.0
Bantry	51 41N	9 28W	-0045	-0025	-0040	-0105	-0.9	-0.8	-0.2	0.0
Dunmanus Bay										
Dunbeacon Harbour	51 37N	9 33W	-0057	-0025	-0032	-0104	-0.8	-0.7	-0.3	-0.1
Dunmanus Harbour	51 32N	9 40W	-0107	-0031	-0044	-0120	-0.7	-0.6	-0.2	0.0
Crookhaven	51 28N	9 43W	-0057	-0033	-0048	-0112	-0.8	-0.6	-0.4	-0.1
Schull	51 31N	9 32W	-0040	-0015	-0015	-0110	-0.9	-0.6	-0.2	0.0
Baltimore	51 29N	9 23W	-0025	-0005	-0010	-0050	-0.6	-0.3	+0.1	+0.2
Castletownshend	51 32N	9 10W	-0020	-0030	-0020	-0050	-0.4	-0.2	+0.1	+0.3
Clonakilty Bay	51 35N	8 50W	-0033	-0011	-0019	-0041	-0.3	-0.2	no data	
Courtmacsherry	51 38N	8 42W	-0029	-0007	+0005	-0017	-0.4	-0.3	-0.2	-0.1
Kinsale	51 42N	8 31W	-0019	-0005	-0009	-0023	-0.2	0.0	+0.1	+0.2
Roberts Cove	51 45N	8 19W	-0005	-0005	-0005	-0005	-0.1	0.0	0.0	+0.1
Cork Harbour										
Ringaskiddy	51 50N	8 19W	+0005	+0020	+0007	+0013	+0.1	+0.1	+0.1	+0.1
Marino Point	51 53N	8 20W	0000	+0010	0000	+0010	+0.1	+0.1	0.0	0.0
Cork City	51 54N	8 27W	+0005	+0010	+0020	+0010	+0.4	+0.4	+0.3	+0.2
Ballycotton	51 50N	8 01W	-0011	+0001	+0003	-0009	0.0	0.0	-0.1	0.0
Youghal	51 57N	7 51W	0000	+0010	+0010	0000	-0.2	-0.1	-0.1	-0.1
Dungarvan Harbour	52 05N	7 34W	+0004	+0012	+0007	-0001	0.0	+0.1	-0.2	0.0
Waterford Harbour										
Dunmore East	52 09N	6 59W	+0008	+0003	0000	0000	+0.1	0.0	+0.1	+0.2
Cheekpoint	52 16N	7 00W	+0022	+0020	+0020	+0020	+0.3	+0.2	+0.2	+0.1
Kilmokea Point	52 17N	7 00W	+0026	+0022	+0020	+0020	+0.2	+0.1	+0.1	+0.1
Waterford	52 16N	7 07W	+0057	+0057	+0046	+0046	+0.4	+0.3	-0.1	+0.1

Location	Lat	Long	High Water		Low Water		MHWS	MHWN	MLWN	MLWS
New Ross	52 24N	6 57W	+0100	+0030	+0055	+0130	+0.3	+0.4	+0.3	+0.4
Baginbun Head	52 10N	6 50W	+0003	+0003	-0008	-0008	-0.2	-0.1	+0.2	+0.2
Great Saltee	52 07N	6 38W	+0019	+0009	-0004	+0006	-0.3	-0.4	no data	
Carnsore Point	52 10N	6 22W	+0029	+0019	-0002	+0008	-1.1	-1.0	no data	
Rosslare Harbour	52 15N	6 21W	+0045	+0035	+0015	-0005	-2.2	-1.8	-0.5	-0.1
Wexford Harbour	52 20N	6 27W	+0126	+0126	+0118	+0108	-2.1	-1.7	-0.3	+0.1

SCOTLAND

Location	Lat	Long	High Water		Low Water		MHWS	MHWN	MLWN	MLWS
			0300	0900	0300	0900				
LEITH	55 59N	3 11W	and	and	and	and	5.6	4.4	2.0	0.8
standard port			1500	2100	1500	2100				
Eyemouth	55 52N	2 05W	-0015	-0025	-0014	-0004	-0.9	-0.8	no data	
Dunbar	56 00N	2 31W	-0005	-0010	+0010	+0017	-0.4	-0.3	-0.1	-0.1
Fidra	56 04N	2 47W	-0001	0000	-0002	+0001	-0.2	-0.2	0.0	0.0
Cockenzie	55 58N	2 57W	-0007	-0015	-0013	-0005	-0.2	0.0	no data	
Granton	55 59N	3 13W	0000	0000	0000	0000	0.0	0.0	0.0	0.0
			0300	1000	0300	0900				
ROSYTH	56 01N	3 27W	and	and	and	and	5.8	4.7	2.2	0.8
standard port			1500	2200	1500	2100				
River Forth										
Grangemouth	56 02N	3 41W	+0025	+0010	-0052	-0015	-0.1	-0.2	-0.3	-0.3
Kincardine	56 04N	3 43W	+0015	+0030	-0030	-0030	0.0	-0.2	-0.5	-0.3
Alloa	56 07N	3 48W	+0040	+0040	+0025	+0025	-0.2	-0.5	no data	-0.7
Stirling	56 07N	3 56W	+0100	+0100	no data	no data	-2.9	-3.1	-2.3	-0.7
			0300	0900	0300	0900				
LEITH	55 59N	3 11W	and	and	and	and	5.6	4.4	2.0	0.8
standard port			1500	2100	1500	2100				
Firth of Forth										
Burntisland	56 03N	3 14W	+0013	+0004	-0002	+0007	+0.1	0.0	+0.1	+0.2
Kirkcaldy	56 09N	3 09W	+0005	0000	-0004	-0001	-0.3	-0.3	-0.2	-0.2
Methil	56 11N	3 00W	-0005	-0001	-0001	-0001	-0.1	-0.1	-0.1	-0.1
Anstruther Easter	56 13N	2 42W	-0018	-0012	-0006	-0008	-0.3	-0.2	0.0	0.0
			0000	0600	0100	0700				
ABERDEEN	57 09N	2 05W	and	and	and	and	4.3	3.4	1.6	0.6
standard port			1200	1800	1300	1900				
River Tay										
Bar	56 27N	2 38W	+0100	+0100	+0050	+0110	+0.9	+0.8	+0.3	+0.1
Dundee	56 27N	2 58W	+0140	+0120	+0055	+0145	+1.1	+0.9	+0.3	+0.1
Newburgh	56 21N	3 14W	+0215	+0200	+0250	+0335	-0.2	-0.4	-1.1	-0.5
Perth	56 24N	3 27W	+0220	+0225	+0510	+0530	-0.9	-1.4	-1.2	-0.3
Arbroath	56 33N	2 35W	+0056	+0037	+0034	+0055	+0.7	+0.7	+0.2	+0.1
Montrose	56 42N	2 27W	+0055	+0055	+0030	+0040	+0.5	+0.4	+0.2	0.0
Stonehaven	56 58N	2 12W	+0013	+0008	+0013	+0009	+0.2	+0.2	+0.1	0.0
Peterhead	57 30N	1 46W	-0035	-0045	-0035	-0040	-0.5	-0.3	-0.1	-0.1
Fraserburgh	57 41N	2 00W	-0105	-0115	-0120	-0110	-0.6	-0.5	-0.2	0.0
			0200	0900	0400	0900				
ABERDEEN	57 09N	2 05W	and	and	and	and	4.3	3.4	1.6	0.6
standard port			1400	2100	1600	2100				
Banff	57 40N	2 31W	-0100	-0150	-0150	-0050	-0.4	-0.2	-0.1	+0.2
Whitehills	57 41N	2 35W	-0122	-0137	-0117	-0127	-0.4	-0.3	+0.1	+0.1
Buckie	57 40N	2 58W	-0130	-0145	-0125	-0140	-0.2	-0.2	0.0	+0.1
Lossiemouth	57 43N	3 18W	-0125	-0200	-0130	-0130	-0.2	-0.2	0.0	0.0
Burghead	57 42N	3 29W	-0120	-0150	-0135	-0120	-0.2	-0.2	0.0	0.0
Nairn	57 36N	3 52W	-0120	-0150	-0135	-0130	0.0	-0.1	0.0	+0.1
McDermott Base	57 36N	3 59W	-0110	-0140	-0120	-0115	-0.1	-0.1	+0.1	+0.3
			0300	1000	0000	0700				
ABERDEEN	57 09N	2 05W	and	and	and	and	4.3	3.4	1.6	0.6
standard port			1500	2200	1200	1900				
Inverness Firth										
Fortrose	57 35N	4 08W	-0125	-0125	-0125	-0125	0.0	0.0	no data	
Inverness	57 30N	4 15W	-0115	-0120	-0115	-0105	+0.4	+0.2	+0.1	+0.1
Cromarty Firth										
Cromarty	57 42N	4 03W	-0130	-0135	-0135	-0120	0.0	-0.1	0.0	+0.1
Invergordon	57 41N	4 10W	-0125	-0135	-0135	-0115	0.0	-0.1	-0.1	0.0
Dingwall	57 36N	4 25W	-0105	-0120	no data	no data	0.0	0.0	no data	

SECONDARY PORT TIDAL DATA

Location	Lat	Long	High Water		Low Water		MHWS	MHWN	MLWN	MLWS
			0300	0800	0200	0800				
ABERDEEN	57 09N	2 05W	and	and	and	and	4.3	3.4	1.6	0.6
standard port			1500	2000	1400	2000				
Dornoch Firth										
Portmahomack	57 50N	3 50W	-0120	-0210	-0140	-0110	-0.2	-0.1	+0.1	+0.1
Meikle Ferry	57 51N	4 08W	-0100	-0140	-0120	-0055	+0.1	0.0	-0.1	0.0
Golspie	57 58N	3 59W	-0130	-0215	-0155	-0130	-0.3	-0.3	-0.1	0.0
			0000	0700	0200	0700				
WICK	58 26N	3 05W	and	and	and	and	3.5	2.8	1.4	0.7
standard port			1200	1900	1400	1900				
Helmsdale	58 07N	3 39W	+0025	+0015	+0035	+0030	+0.4	+0.3	+0.1	0.0
Duncansby Head	58 39N	3 02W	-0115	-0115	-0110	-0110	-0.4	-0.4	no data	
Orkney Islands										
Muckle Skerry	58 41N	2 55W	-0025	-0025	-0020	-0020	-0.9	-0.8	-0.4	-0.3
Burray Ness	58 51N	2 52W	+0005	+0005	+0015	+0015	-0.2	-0.3	-0.1	-0.1
Deer Sound	58 58N	2 50W	-0040	-0040	-0035	-0035	-0.3	-0.3	-0.1	-0.1
Kirkwall	58 59N	2 58W	-0042	-0042	-0041	-0041	-0.5	-0.4	-0.1	-0.1
Loth	59 12N	2 42W	-0052	-0052	-0058	-0058	-0.1	0.0	+0.3	+0.4
Kettletoft Pier	59 14N	2 36W	-0025	-0025	-0015	-0015	0.0	0.0	+0.2	+0.2
Rapness	59 15N	2 52W	-0205	-0205	-0205	-0205	+0.1	0.0	+0.2	0.0
Pierowall	59 19N	2 58W	-0150	-0150	-0145	-0145	+0.2	0.0	0.0	-0.1
Tingwall	59 05N	3 02W	-0200	-0125	-0145	-0125	-0.4	-0.4	-0.1	-0.1
Stromness	58 58N	3 18W	-0225	-0135	-0205	-0205	+0.1	-0.1	0.0	0.0
St. Mary's	58 54N	2 55W	-0140	-0140	-0140	-0140	-0.2	-0.2	0.0	-0.1
Widewall Bay	58 49N	3 01W	-0155	-0155	-0150	-0150	+0.1	-0.1	-0.1	-0.3
Bur Wick	58 44N	2 58W	-0100	-0100	-0150	-0150	-0.1	-0.1	+0.2	+0.1
			0000	0600	0100	0800				
LERWICK	60 09N	1 08W	and	and	and	and	2.1	1.7	0.9	0.5
standard port			1200	1800	1300	2000				
Fair Isle	59 32N	1 36W	-0006	-0015	-0031	-0037	+0.1	0.0	+0.1	+0.1
Shetland Islands										
Sumburgh *Grutness Voe*	59 53N	1 17W	+0006	+0008	+0004	-0002	-0.3	-0.3	-0.2	-0.1
Dury Voe	60 21N	1 10W	-0015	-0015	-0010	-0010	0.0	-0.1	0.0	-0.2
Out Skerries	60 25N	0 45W	-0025	-0025	-0010	-0010	+0.1	0.0	0.0	-0.1
Toft Pier	60 28N	1 12W	-0105	-0100	-0125	-0115	+0.2	+0.1	-0.1	-0.1
Burra Voe *Yell Sound*	60 30N	1 03W	-0025	-0025	-0025	-0025	+0.2	+0.1	0.0	-0.1
Mid Yell	60 36N	1 03W	-0030	-0020	-0035	-0025	+0.3	+0.2	+0.2	+0.1
Balta Sound	60 45N	0 50W	-0055	-0055	-0045	-0045	+0.2	+0.1	0.0	-0.1
Burra Firth	60 48N	0 52W	-0110	-0110	-0115	-0115	+0.4	+0.2	0.0	0.0
Bluemull Sound	60 42N	1 00W	-0135	-0135	-0155	-0155	+0.5	+0.2	+0.1	0.0
Sullom Voe	60 27N	1 18W	-0135	-0125	-0135	-0120	0.0	0.0	-0.2	-0.2
Hillswick	60 29N	1 29W	-0220	-0220	-0200	-0200	-0.1	-0.1	-0.1	-0.1
Scalloway	60 08N	1 16W	-0150	-0150	-0150	-0150	-0.5	-0.4	-0.3	0.0
Bay of Quendale	59 54N	1 20W	-0025	-0025	-0030	-0030	-0.4	-0.3	0.0	+0.1
Foula	60 07N	2 03W	-0140	-0130	-0140	-0120	-0.1	-0.1	0.0	0.0
			0200	0700	0100	0700				
WICK	58 26N	3 05W	and	and	and	and	3.5	2.8	1.4	0.7
Standard port			1400	1900	1300	1900				
Stroma	58 40N	3 08W	-0115	-0115	-0110	-0110	-0.4	-0.5	-0.1	-0.2
Gills Bay	58 38N	3 10W	-0150	-0150	-0202	-0202	+0.7	+0.7	+0.6	+0.3
Scrabster	58 37N	3 33W	-0255	-0225	-0240	-0230	+1.5	+1.2	+0.8	+0.3
Sule Skerry	59 05N	4 24W	-0320	-0255	-0315	-0250	+0.4	+0.3	+0.2	+0.1
Loch Eriboll Portnancon	58 30N	4 42W	-0340	-0255	-0315	-0255	+1.6	+1.3	+0.8	+0.4
Kyle of Durness	58 36N	4 47W	-0350	-0350	-0315	-0315	+1.1	+0.7	+0.4	-0.1
Rona	59 08N	5 49W	-0410	-0345	-0330	-0340	-0.1	-0.2	-0.2	-0.1
			0100	0700	0300	0900				
ULLAPOOL	57 54N	5 10W	and	and	and	and	5.2	3.9	2.1	0.7
standard port			1300	1900	1500	2100				
Outer Hebrides										
Stornoway	58 12N	6 23W	-0010	-0010	-0010	-0010	-0.4	-0.2	-0.1	0.0
Loch Shell	58 00N	6 25W	-0023	-0010	-0010	-0027	-0.4	-0.3	-0.2	0.0
E. Loch Tarbert	57 54N	6 48W	-0035	-0020	-0020	-0030	-0.2	-0.2	0.0	+0.1
Loch Maddy	57 36N	7 06W	-0054	-0024	-0026	-0040	-0.4	-0.3	-0.2	0.0
Loch Carnan	57 22N	7 16W	-0100	-0020	-0030	-0050	-0.7	-0.7	-0.2	-0.1
Loch Skiport	57 20N	7 16W	-0110	-0035	-0034	-0034	-0.6	-0.6	-0.4	-0.2
Loch Boisdale	57 09N	7 16W	-0105	-0040	-0030	-0050	-1.1	-0.9	-0.4	-0.2

PAGE 188

Location	Lat	Long	High Water		Low Water		MHWS	MHWN	MLWN	MLWS
Barra *North Bay*	57 00N	7 24W	-0113	-0041	-0044	-0058	-1.0	-0.7	-0.3	-0.1
Castle Bay	56 57N	7 29W	-0125	-0050	-0055	-0110	-0.9	-0.8	-0.4	-0.1
Barra Head	56 47N	7 38W	-0125	-0050	-0055	-0105	-1.2	-0.9	-0.3	+0.1
Shillay	57 31N	7 41W	-0113	-0053	-0057	-0117	-1.0	-0.9	-0.8	-0.3
Balivanich	57 29N	7 23W	-0113	-0027	-0041	-0055	-1.1	-0.8	-0.6	-0.2
Scolpaig	57 39N	7 29W	-0043	-0043	-0050	-0050	-1.4	-1.1	-0.6	0.0
Leverburgh	57 46N	7 01W	-0051	-0030	-0025	-0035	-0.6	-0.4	-0.2	-0.1
W. Loch Tarbert	57 55N	6 55W	-0025	-0025	-0056	-0056	-1.5	-1.1	-0.6	0.0
Little Bernera	58 16N	6 52W	-0031	-0021	-0027	-0037	-0.9	-0.8	-0.5	-0.2
Carloway	58 17N	6 47W	-0050	+0010	-0045	-0025	-1.0	-0.7	-0.5	-0.1
			0000	**0600**	**0300**	**0900**				
ULLAPOOL	57 54N	5 10W	and	and	and	and	**5.2**	**3.9**	**2.1**	**0.7**
standard port			**1200**	**1800**	**1500**	**2100**				
St Kilda *Village Bay*	57 48N	8 34W	-0050	-0050	-0055	-0055	-1.8	-1.4	-0.9	-0.3
Flannan Isles	58 16N	7 36W	-0036	-0026	-0026	-0036	-1.3	-0.9	-0.7	-0.2
Rockall	57 36N	13 41W	-0105	-0105	-0115	-0115	-2.2	-1.7	-1.0	-0.2
Loch Bervie	58 27N	5 03W	+0030	+0010	+0010	+0020	-0.3	-0.3	-0.2	0.0
Loch Laxford	58 24N	5 05W	+0015	+0015	+0005	+0005	-0.3	-0.4	-0.2	0.0
Eddrachillis Bay										
Badcall Bay	58 19N	5 08W	+0005	+0005	+0005	+0005	-0.7	-0.5	-0.5	+0.2
Loch Nedd	58 14N	5 10W	0000	0000	0000	0000	-0.3	-0.2	-0.2	0.0
Loch Inver	58 09N	5 18W	-0005	-0005	-0005	-0005	-0.2	0.0	0.0	+0.1
Summer Isles *Tanera Mor*	58 01N	5 24W	-0005	-0005	-0010	-0010	-0.1	+0.1	0.0	+0.1
Loch Ewe Mellon Charles	57 51N	5 38W	-0010	-0010	-0010	-0010	-0.1	-0.1	-0.1	0.0
Loch Gairloch Gairloch	57 43N	5 41W	-0020	-0020	-0010	-0010	0.0	+0.1	-0.3	-0.1
Loch Torridon Shieldaig	57 31N	5 39W	-0020	-0020	-0015	-0015	+0.4	+0.3	+0.1	0.0
Inner Sound Applecross	57 26N	5 49W	-0010	-0015	-0010	-0010	0.0	0.0	0.0	+0.1
Loch Carron Plockton	57 20N	5 39W	+0005	-0025	-0005	-0010	+0.5	+0.5	+0.5	+0.2
Rona *Loch a' Bhraige*	57 35N	5 58W	-0020	0000	-0010	0000	-0.1	-0.1	-0.1	-0.2
Skye										
Broadford Bay	57 15N	5 54W	-0015	-0015	-0010	-0015	+0.2	+0.1	+0.1	0.0
Portree	57 24N	6 11W	-0025	-0025	-0025	-0025	+0.1	-0.2	-0.2	0.0
Loch Snizort (Uig Bay)	57 35N	6 22W	-0045	-0020	-0005	-0025	+0.1	-0.4	-0.2	0.0
Loch Dunvegan	57 27N	6 38W	-0105	-0030	-0020	-0040	0.0	-0.1	0.0	0.0
Loch Harport	57 20N	6 25W	-0115	-0035	-0020	-0100	-0.1	-0.1	0.0	+0.1
Soay *Camus nan Gall*	57 09N	6 13W	-0055	-0025	-0025	-0045	-0.4	-0.2	*no data*	
Loch Alsh										
Kyle of Lochalsh	57 17N	5 43W	-0040	-0020	-0005	-0025	0.0	-0.1	-0.2	-0.2
Dornie Bridge	57 17N	5 31W	-0040	-0010	-0005	-0020	+0.1	-0.1	0.0	0.0
Kyle Rhea *Glenelg Bay*	57 13N	5 38W	-0105	-0035	-0035	-0055	-0.4	-0.4	-0.9	-0.1
Loch Hourn	57 06N	5 34W	-0125	-0050	-0040	-0110	-0.2	-0.1	-0.1	+0.1
			0000	**0600**	**0100**	**0700**				
OBAN	56 25N	5 29W	and	and	and	and	**4.0**	**2.9**	**1.8**	**0.7**
standard port			**1200**	**1800**	**1300**	**1900**				
Loch Nevis										
Inverie Bay	57 02N	5 41W	+0030	+0020	+0035	+0020	+1.0	+0.9	+0.2	0.0
Mallaig	57 00N	5 50W	+0017	+0017	+0017	+0017	+1.0	+0.7	+0.3	+0.1
Eigg *Bay of Laig*	56 55N	6 10W	+0015	+0030	+0040	+0005	+0.7	+0.6	-0.2	- 0.2
Loch Moidart	56 47N	5 53W	+0015	+0015	+0040	+0020	+0.8	+0.6	- 0.2	-0.2
Coll *Loch Eatharna*	56 37N	6 31W	+0025	+0010	+0015	+0025	+0.4	+0.3	*no data*	
Tiree *Gott Bay*	56 31N	6 48W	0000	+0010	+0005	+0010	0.0	+0.1	0.0	0.0
			0100	**0700**	**0100**	**0800**				
OBAN	56 25N	5 29W	and	and	and	and	**4.0**	**2.9**	**1.8**	**0.7**
standard port			**1300**	**1900**	**1300**	**2000**				
Mull										
Carsaig Bay	56 19N	5 59W	-0015	-0005	-0030	+0020	+0.1	+0.2	0.0	-0.1
Iona	56 19N	6 23W	-0010	-0005	-0020	+0015	0.0	+0.1	-0.3	-0.2
Bunessan	56 19N	6 14W	-0015	-0015	-0010	-0015	+0.3	+0.1	0.0	-0.1
Ulva Sound	56 29N	6 08W	-0010	-0015	0000	-0005	+0.4	+0.3	0.0	-0.1
Loch Sunart Salen	56 42N	5 47W	-0015	+0015	+0010	+0005	+0.6	+0.5	-0.1	-0.1
Sound of Mull										
Tobermory	56 37N	6 04W	+0025	+0010	+0015	+0025	+0.4	+0.4	0.0	0.0
Salen	56 31N	5 57W	+0045	+0015	+0020	+0030	+0.2	+0.2	-0.1	0.0
Loch Aline	56 32N	5 46W	+0012	+0012	*no data*	*no data*	+0.5	+0.3	*no data*	
Craignure	56 28N	5 42W	+0030	+0005	+0010	+0015	0.0	+0.1	-0.1	-0.1
Loch Linnhe										
Corran	56 43N	5 14W	+0007	+0007	+0004	+0004	+0.4	+0.4	-0.1	0.0

SECONDARY PORT TIDAL DATA

Location	Lat	Long	High Water		Low Water		MHWS	MHWN	MLWN	MLWS
Corpach	56 50N	5 07W	0000	+0020	+0040	0000	0.0	0.0	-0.2	-0.2
Loch Eil Head	56 51N	5 20W	+0025	+0045	+0105	+0025	no data		no data	
Loch Leven Head	56 43N	5 00W	+0045	+0045	+0045	+0045	no data		no data	
Loch Linnhe Port Appin	56 33N	5 25W	-0005	-0005	-0030	0000	+0.2	+0.2	+0.1	+0.1
Loch Creran										
Barcaldine Pier	56 32N	5 19W	+0010	+0020	+0040	+0015	+0.1	+0.1	0.0	+0.1
Loch Creran Head	56 33N	5 16W	+0015	+0025	+0120	+0020	-0.3	-0.3	-0.4	-0.3
Loch Etive										
Dunstaffnage Bay	56 27N	5 26W	+0005	0000	0000	+0005	+0.1	+0.1	+0.1	+0.1
Connel	56 27N	5 24W	+0020	+0005	+0010	+0015	-0.3	-0.2	-0.1	+0.1
Bonawe	56 27N	5 13W	+0150	+0205	+0240	+0210	-2.0	-1.7	-1.3	-0.5
Seil Sound	56 18N	5 35W	-0035	-0015	-0040	-0015	-1.3	-0.9	-0.7	-0.3
Colonsay Scalasaig	56 04N	6 10W	-0020	-0005	-0015	+0005	-0.1	-0.2	-0.2	-0.2
Jura Glengarrisdale Bay	56 06N	5 47W	-0020	0000	-0010	0000	-0.4	-0.2	0.0	-0.2
Islay										
Rubha A'Mhail	55 56N	6 07W	-0020	0000	+0005	-0015	-0.3	-0.1	-0.3	-0.1
Ardnave Point	55 52N	6 20W	-0035	+0010	0000	-0025	-0.4	-0.2	-0.3	-0.1
Orsay	55 41N	6 31W	-0110	-0110	-0040	-0040	-1.4	-0.6	-0.5	-0.2
Bruichladdich	55 48N	6 22W	-0100	-0005	-0110	-0040	-1.7	-1.4	-0.4	+0.1
Port Ellen	55 38N	6 11W	-0530	-0050	-0045	-0530	-3.1	-2.1	-1.3	-0.4
Port Askaig	55 51N	6 06W	-0110	-0030	-0020	-0020	-1.9	-1.4	-0.8	-0.3
Sound of Jura										
Craighouse	55 50N	5 57W	-0230	-0250	-0150	-0230	-3.0	-2.4	-1.3	-0.6
Loch Melfort	56 15N	5 29W	-0055	-0025	-0040	-0035	-1.2	-0.8	-0.5	-0.1
Loch Beag	56 09N	5 36W	-0110	-0045	-0035	-0045	-1.6	-1.2	-0.8	-0.4
Carsaig Bay	56 02N	5 38W	-0105	-0040	-0050	-0050	-2.1	-1.6	-1.0	-0.4
Sound of Gigha	55 41N	5 44W	-0450	-0210	-0130	-0410	-2.5	-1.6	-1.0	-0.1
Machrihanish	55 25N	5 45W	-0520	-0350	-0340	-0540	Mean range 0.5 metres			
			0000	**0600**	**0000**	**0600**				
GREENOCK	55 57N	4 46W	and	and	and	and	**3.4**	**2.8**	**1.0**	**0.3**
standard port			**1200**	**1800**	**1200**	**1800**				
Firth of Clyde										
Southend, Kintyre	55 19N	5 38W	-0030	-0010	+0005	+0035	-1.3	-1.2	-0.5	-0.2
Campbeltown	55 25N	5 36W	-0025	-0005	-0015	+0005	-0.5	-0.3	+0.1	+0.2
Carradale	55 36N	5 28W	-0015	-0005	-0005	+0005	-0.3	-0.2	+0.1	+0.1
Loch Ranza	55 43N	5 18W	-0015	-0005	-0010	-0005	-0.4	-0.3	-0.1	0.0
Loch Fyne										
East Loch Tarbert	55 52N	5 24W	-0005	-0005	0000	-0005	+0.2	+0.1	0.0	0.0
Inveraray	56 14N	5 04W	+0011	+0011	+0034	+0034	-0.1	+0.1	-0.5	-0.2
Kyles of Bute										
Rubha Bodach	55 55N	5 09W	-0020	-0010	-0007	-0007	-0.2	-0.1	+0.2	+0.2
Tighnabruich	55 55N	5 13W	+0007	-0010	-0002	-0015	0.0	+0.2	+0.4	+0.5
Firth of Clyde - continued										
Millport	55 45N	4 56W	-0005	-0025	-0025	-0005	0.0	-0.1	0.0	+0.1
Rothesay Bay	55 51N	5 03W	-0020	-0015	-0010	-0002	+0.2	+0.2	+0.2	+0.2
Wemyss Bay	55 53N	4 53W	-0005	-0005	-0005	-0005	0.0	0.0	+0.1	+0.1
Loch Long										
Coulport	56 03N	4 53W	-0011	-0011	-0008	-0008	0.0	0.0	0.0	0.0
Lochgoilhead	56 10N	4 54W	+0015	0000	-0005	-0005	-0.2	-0.3	-0.3	-0.3
Arrochar	56 12N	4 45W	-0005	-0005	-0005	-0005	0.0	0.0	-0.1	-0.1
Gareloch										
Rosneath	56 01N	4 47W	-0005	-0005	-0005	-0005	0.0	-0.1	0.0	0.0
Faslane	56 04N	4 49W	-0010	-0010	-0010	-0010	0.0	0.0	-0.1	-0.2
Garelochhead	56 05N	4 50W	0000	0000	0000	0000	0.0	0.0	0.0	-0.1
River Clyde										
Helensburgh	56 00N	4 44W	0000	0000	0000	0000	0.0	0.0	0.0	0.0
Port Glasgow	55 56N	4 41W	+0010	+0005	+0010	+0020	+0.2	+0.1	0.0	0.0
Bowling	55 56N	4 29W	+0020	+0010	+0030	+0055	+0.6	+0.5	+0.3	+0.1
Renfrew	55 53N	4 23W	+0025	+0015	+0035	+0100	+0.9	+0.8	+0.5	+0.2
Glasgow	55 51N	4 16W	+0025	+0015	+0035	+0105	+1.3	+1.2	+0.6	+0.4
Firth of Clyde - continued										
Brodick Bay	55 35N	5 08W	0000	0000	+0005	+0005	-0.2	-0.2	0.0	0.0
Lamlash	55 32N	5 07W	-0016	-0036	-0024	-0004	-0.2	-0.2	no data	
Ardrossan	55 38N	4 49W	-0020	-0010	-0010	-0010	-0.2	-0.2	+0.1	+0.1
Irvine	55 36N	4 41W	-0020	-0020	-0030	-0010	-0.3	-0.3	-0.1	0.0
Troon	55 33N	4 41W	-0025	-0025	-0020	-0020	-0.2	-0.2	0.0	0.0
Ayr	55 28N	4 39W	-0025	-0025	-0030	-0015	-0.4	-0.3	+0.1	+0.1
Girvan	55 15N	4 52W	-0025	-0040	-0035	-0010	-0.3	-0.3	-0.1	0.0
Loch Ryan Stranraer	54 55N	5 03W	-0020	-0020	-0017	-0017	-0.4	-0.4	-0.4	-0.2

Location	Lat	Long	High Water		Low Water		MHWS	MHWN	MLWN	MLWS

DENMARK

Location	Lat	Long	High Water				Low Water			
ESBJERG	55 28N	8 27E	0300 and 1500	0700 and 1900	0100 and 1300	0800 and 2000	I.8	1.4	0.4	0.0
standard port										
Hirtshals	57 36N	9 58E	+0055	+0320	+0340	+0100	-1.5	-1.1	-0.3	0.0
Hanstholm	57 08N	8 36E	+0100	+0340	+0340	+0130	-1.5	-1.1	-0.3	0.0
Thyborøn	56 42N	8 13E	+0120	+0230	+0410	+0210	-1.4	-1.1	-0.3	0.0
Torsminde	56 22N	8 07E	+0045	+0050	+0040	+0010	-1.2	-0.9	-0.3	0.0
Hvide Sande	56 00N	8 07E	0000	+0010	-0015	-0025	-1.0	-0.7	-0.3	0.0
Blavandshuk	55 33N	8 05E	-0120	-0110	-0050	-0100	0.0	0.0	-0.1	0.0
Gradyb Bar	55 26N	8 15E	-0130	-0115	*no data*	*no data*	-0.3	-0.2	-0.1	0.0
Rømø Havn	55 05N	8 34E	-0040	-0005	0000	-0020	+0.2	+0.2	-0.1	0.0
Hojer	54 58N	8 40E	-0020	+0015	*no data*	*no data*	+0.6	+0.7	0.0	0.0

GERMANY

Location	Lat	Long	High Water				Low Water			
HELGOLAND	54 11N	7 53E	0100 and 1300	0600 and 1800	0100 and 1300	0800 and 2000	2.7	2.4	0.4	0.0
standard port										
Lister Tief List	55 01N	8 27E	+0252	+0240	+0201	+0210	-0.8	-0.6	-0.2	0.0
Hörnum	54 46N	8 18E	+0223	+0218	+0131	+0137	-0.5	-0.4	-0.2	0.0
Amrum-Hafen	54 38N	8 23E	+0138	+0137	+0128	+0134	+0.2	+0.2	0.0	0.0
Dagebüll	54 44N	8 41E	+0226	+0217	+0211	+0225	+0.5	+0.5	-0.1	0.0
Suderoogsand	54 25N	8 30E	+0116	+0102	+0038	+0122	+0.4	+0.3	0.0	-0.1
Hever Husum	54 28N	9 02E	+0205	+0152	+0118	+0200	+1.1	+1.0	0.0	0.0
Suederhoeft	54 16N	8 42E	+0103	+0056	+0051	+0112	+0.7	+0.6	+0.1	0.0
Eidersperrwerk	54 16N	8 51E	+0120	+0115	+0130	+0155	+0.7	+0.6	0.0	0.0
Linnenplate	54 13N	8 40E	+0047	+0046	+0034	+0046	+0.7	+0.6	+0.1	0.0
Büsum	54 07N	8 52E	+0054	+0049	-0001	+0027	+0.9	+0.8	+0.1	0.0
			0200 and 1400	0800 and 2000	0200 and 1400	0900 and 2100				
CUXHAVEN	53 52N	8 43E					3.4	2.9	0.4	0.1
standard port										
River Elbe										
Grober Vogelsand	54 00N	8 29E	-0044	-0046	-0101	-0103	0.0	0.0	+0.1	0.0
Scharhörn	53 58N	8 28E	-0045	-0047	-0101	-0103	0.0	0.0	0.0	-0.1
Brunsbüttel	53 53N	9 08E	+0057	+0105	+0121	+0112	-0.3	-0.2	-0.2	-0.1
Glückstadt	53 47N	9 25E	+0205	+0214	+0220	+0213	-0.3	-0.2	-0.2	0.0
Stadersand	53 38N	9 32E	+0241	+0245	+0300	+0254	-0.1	0.0	-0.3	0.0
Schulau	53 34N	9 42E	+0304	+0315	+0337	+0321	0.0	+0.1	-0.3	-0.2
Seemannshoeft	53 32N	9 53E	+0324	+0332	+0403	+0347	+0.1	+0.2	-0.4	-0.2
Hamburg	53 33N	9 58E	+0338	+0346	+0422	+0406	+0.2	+0.3	-0.4	-0.3
Harburg	53 28N	10 00E	+0344	+0350	+0430	+0416	+0.3	+0.4	-0.4	-0.3
Wangerooge East	53 46N	7 58E	-0108	-0109	-0116	-0023	0.0	0.0	+0.1	0.0
Bremerhaven	53 33N	8 34E	+0019	+0034	-0024	-0012	+0.7	+0.7	0.0	-0.1
Wilhelmshaven	53 31N	8 09E	-0005	-0015	-0055	-0050	+0.9	+0.9	+0.1	-0.1
Hooksiel	53 39N	8 05E	-0033	-0038	-0100	-0101	+0.5	+0.4	+0.1	0.0
			0200 and 1400	0700 and 1900	0200 and 1400	0800 and 2000				
HELGOLAND	54 11N	7 53E					2.7	2.4	0.4	0.0
standard port										
East Frisian islands and coast										
Spiekeroog	53 45N	7 41E	+0003	-0003	-0031	-0012	+0.4	+0.3	0.0	0.0
Neuharlingersiel	53 42N	7 42E	+0014	+0008	-0024	-0013	+0.6	+0.5	+0.1	0.0
Langeoog	53 43N	7 30E	+0003	-0001	-0034	-0018	+0.3	+0.2	0.0	0.0
Norderney *Riffgat*	53 42N	7 10E	-0024	-0030	-0056	-0045	+0.1	0.0	0.0	0.0
Norddeich Hafen	53 37N	7 10E	-0018	-0017	-0029	-0012	+0.2	+0.1	0.0	0.0
River Ems										
Memmert	53 38N	6 53E	-0032	-0038	-0114	-0103	+0.2	+0.1	0.0	0.0
Borkum *Fischerbalje*	53 33N	6 45E	-0048	-0052	-0124	-0105	0.0	0.0	0.0	0.0
Emshorn	53 30N	6 51E	-0037	-0041	-0108	-0047	+0.1	+0.1	0.0	0.0
Knock	53 20N	7 02E	+0018	+0005	-0028	+0004	+0.6	+0.6	0.0	0.0
Emden	53 20N	7 11E	+0041	+0028	-0011	+0022	+0.9	+0.8	0.0	0.0

NETHERLANDS

Location	Lat	Long	High Water				Low Water			
HELGOLAND	54 11N	7 53E	0200 and 1400	0700 and 1900	0200 and 1400	0800 and 2000	2.7	2.4	0.4	0.0
standard port										
Nieuwe Statenzijl	53 14N	7 13E	+0110	+0135	*no data*	*no data*	+1.1	+1.0	*no data*	
Delfzijl	53 20N	6 56E	+0020	-0005	-0040	0000	+0.9	+0.8	+0.3	+0.3
Eemshaven	53 26N	6 52E	-0025	-0045	-0115	-0045	+0.5	+0.4	+0.3	+0.3
Schiermonnikoog	53 28N	6 12E	-0120	-0130	-0240	-0220	+0.2	+0.2	+0.3	+0.3

Location	Lat	Long	High Water		Low Water		MHWS	MHWN	MLWN	MLWS
Waddenzee										
Lauwersoog	53 25N	6 12E	-0130	-0145	-0235	-0220	+0.2	+0.2	+0.3	+0.3
Nes	53 26N	5 47E	-0135	-0150	-0245	-0225	+0.1	+0.1	+0.2	+0.2
Holwerd	53 24N	5 53E	-0120	-0135	-0155	-0135	+0.3	+0.3	+0.4	+0.4
West Terschelling	53 22N	5 13E	-0220	-0250	-0335	-0310	-0.4	-0.3	+0.1	+0.2
Vlieland-haven	53 18N	5 06E	-0250	-0320	-0355	-0330	-0.3	-0.3	+0.1	+0.2
Harlingen	53 10N	5 25E	-0155	-0245	-0210	-0130	-0.4	-0.4	-0.1	+0.2
Kornwerderzand	53 04N	5 20E	-0210	-0315	-0300	-0215	-0.5	-0.5	-0.1	+0.2
Den Oever	52 56N	5 00E	-0245	-0410	-0400	-0305	-0.8	-0.7	0.0	+0.2
Oude Schild	53 02N	4 51E	-0310	-0420	-0445	-0400	-1.0	-0.9	0.0	+0.2
Den Helder	52 58N	4 45E	-0410	-0520	-0520	-0430	-1.0	-0.9	0.0	+0.2
Noordwinning *Platform K13-a*	53 13N	3 13E	-0420	-0430	-0520	-0530	-1.0	-1.1	+0.1	+0.1
			0300	**0900**	**0400**	**1000**				
VLISSINGEN	51 27N	3 36E	and	and	and	and	4.8	3.9	0.9	0.3
standard port			**1500**	**2100**	**1600**	**2200**				
IJmuiden	52 28N	4 35E	+0145	+0140	+0305	+0325	-2.7	-2.2	-0.6	-0.1
Scheveningen	52 06N	4 16E	+0105	+0100	+0220	+0245	-2.6	-2.1	-0.6	-0.1
Europlatform	52 00N	3 17E	+0005	-0005	-0030	-0055	-2.7	-2.2	-0.6	-0.1
Nieuwe Waterweg Maassluis	51 55N	4 15E	+0155	+0115	+0100	+0310	-2.7	-2.1	-0.6	0.0
Nieuwe Maas Vlaardingen	51 54N	4 21E	+0150	+0120	+0130	+0330	-2.7	-2.1	-0.6	-0.1
Lek										
Krimpen Aan de Lek	51 55N	4 38E	+0225	+0200	+0325	+0445	-3.1	-2.5	-0.7	-0.l
Streefkerk	51 55N	4 45E	+0305	+0310	+0400	+0510	-3.3	-2.5	-0.6	0.0
Schoonhoven	51 57N	4 51E	+0415	+0315	+0435	+0545	-3.1	-2.4	-0.5	+0.1
Oude Maas										
Spijkenisse	51 52N	4 20E	+0145	+0120	+0145	+0310	-2.9	-2.3	-0.7	-0.1
Goidschalxoord	51 50N	4 27E	+0200	+0140	+0240	+0410	-3.4	-2.7	-0.7	-0.1
De Kil 's-Gravendeel	51 47N	4 38E	+0400	+0310	+0425	+0525	-4.0	-3.2	-0.6	0.0
Merwede										
Dordrecht	51 49N	4 39E	+0205	+0300	+0405	+0505	-3.8	-3.1	-0.7	0.0
Werkendam	51 49N	4 53E	+0425	+0410	+0550	+0650	-4.1	-3.3	-0.6	0.0
Haringvlietsluizen	51 50N	4 02E	+0015	+0015	+0015	-0020	-1.8	-1.6	-0.5	0.0
Ooster Schelde										
Roompot	51 37N	3 40E	-0015	+0005	+0005	-0020	-1.2	-1.0	-0.3	0.0
Stavenisse	51 36N	4 01E	+0150	+0120	+0055	+0115	-1.3	-0.9	-0.5	0.0
Lodijkse Gat	51 30N	4 12E	+0145	+0125	+0105	+0115	-0.7	-0.4	-0.3	0.0
Zijpe Philipsdam *West*	51 40N	4 11E	+0215	+0125	+0100	+0110	-1.2	-0.8	-0.5	-0.1
Walcheren Westkapelle	51 31N	3 27E	-0025	-0015	-0010	-0025	-0.6	-0.5	-0.1	0.0
Westerschelde										
Terneuzen	51 20N	3 50E	+0020	+0020	+0020	+0030	+0.3	+0.3	0.0	0.0
Hansweert	51 27N	4 00E	+0100	+0050	+0040	+0100	+0.6	+0.6	0.0	0.0
Bath	51 24N	4 13E	+0125	+0115	+0115	+0140	+1.0	+0.9	0.0	0.0

BELGIUM

Location	Lat	Long	High Water		Low Water		MHWS	MHWN	MLWN	MLWS
Zeebrugge	51 21N	3 12E	-0035	-0027	-0015	-0040	0.0	0.0	+0.2	+0.1
Blankenberge	51 19N	3 07E	-0045	-0045	-0018	-0043	+0.1	+0.1	+0.2	+0.1
Oostende	51 14N	2 56E	-0054	-0046	-0023	-0048	+0.2	+0.3	+0.2	+0.1
Nieuwpoort	51 09N	2 43E	-0106	-0058	-0025	-0050	+0.5	+0.4	+0.3	+0.1
			0000	**0500**	**0000**	**0600**				
ANTWERPEN, PROSPERPOLDER			and	and	and	and	5.8	4.8	0.8	0.3
standard port	51 21N	4 14E	**1200**	**1700**	**1200**	**1800**				
Boudewijnsluis	51 17N	4 20E	+0013	+0005	+0025	+0020	0.0	+0.1	0.0	0.0
Royersluis	51 14N	4 24E	+0030	+0015	+0045	+0041	+0.2	+0.3	0.0	0.0
Boom	51 05N	4 22E	+0125	+0110	+0155	+0150	-0.2	0.0	-0.4	-0.2
Gentbrugge	51 03N	3 44E	+0430	+0415	+0630	+0600	-3.9	-3.3	-1.1	-0.4

FRANCE

Location	Lat	Long	High Water		Low Water		MHWS	MHWN	MLWN	MLWS
			0200	**0800**	**0200**	**0900**				
DUNKERQUE	51 03N	2 22E	and	and	and	and	6.0	5.0	l.5	0.6
standard port			**1400**	**2000**	**1400**	**2100**				
Gravelines	51 01N	2 06E	-0005	-0015	-0005	+0005	+0.3	+0.1	-0.1	-0.1
Sandettie Bank	51 09N	1 47E	-0015	-0025	-0020	-0005	+0.1	-0.1	-0.1	-0.1
Wissant	50 53N	1 40E	-0035	-0050	-0030	-0010	+2.0	+1.5	+0.8	+0.4
			0100	**0600**	**0100**	**0700**				
DIEPPE	49 56N	1 05E	and	and	and	and	9.3	7.4	2.5	0.8
standard port			**1300**	**1800**	**1300**	**1900**				
Boulogne	50 44N	1 35E	+0014	+0027	+0035	+0033	-0.4	-0.2	+0.1	+0.3
Le Touquet, Étaples	50 31N	1 35E	+0007	+0017	+0032	+0032	+0.2	+0.3	+0.4	+0.4
Berck	50 24N	1 34E	+0007	+0017	+0028	+0028	+0.5	+0.5	+0.4	+0.4

Location	Lat	Long	High Water		Low Water		MHWS	MHWN	MLWN	MLWS
La Somme										
Le Hourdel	50 13N	1 34E	+0020	+0020	*no data*	*no data*	+0.8	+0.6	*no data*	
St Valéry	50 11N	1 37E	+0035	+0035	*no data*	*no data*	+0.9	+0.7	*no data*	
Cayeux	50 11N	1 29E	0000	+0005	+0015	+0010	+0.5	+0.6	+0.4	+0.4
Le Tréport	50 04N	1 22E	+0005	0000	+0007	+0007	+0.1	+0.1	0.0	+0.1
St. Valéry-en-Caux	49 52N	0 42E	-0005	-0005	-0015	-0020	-0.5	-0.4	-0.1	-0.1
Fécamp	49 46N	0 22E	-0015	-0010	-0030	-0040	-1.0	-0.6	+0.3	+0.4
Etretat	49 42N	0 12E	-0020	-0020	-0045	-0050	-1.2	-0.8	+0.3	+0.4
			0000	0500	0000	0700				
LE HAVRE	49 29N	0 07E	and	and	and	and	7.9	6.6	2.8	1.2
standard port			1200	1700	1200	1900				
Antifer *Le Havre*	49 39N	0 09E	+0025	+0015	+0005	-0007	+0.1	0.0	0.0	0.0
La Seine										
Honfleur	49 25N	0 14E	-0135	-0135	+0015	+0040	+0.1	+0.1	+0.1	+0.3
Tancarville	49 28N	0 28E	-0105	-0100	+0105	+0140	-0.1	-0.1	0.0	+1.0
Quillebeuf	49 28N	0 32E	-0045	-0050	+0120	+0200	0.0	0.0	+0.2	+1.4
Vatteville	49 29N	0 40E	+0005	-0020	+0225	+0250	0.0	-0.1	+0.8	+2.3
Caudebec	49 32N	0 44E	+0020	-0015	+0230	+0300	-0.3	-0.2	+0.9	+2.4
Heurteauville	49 27N	0 49E	+0110	+0025	+0310	+0330	-0.5	-0.2	+1.1	+2.7
Duclair	49 29N	0 53E	+0225	+0150	+0355	+0410	-0.4	-0.3	+1.4	+3.3
Rouen	49 27N	1 06E	+0440	+0415	+0525	+0525	-0.2	-0.1	+1.6	+3.6
Trouville	49 22N	0 05E	-0100	-0010	0000	+0005	+0.4	+0.3	+0.3	+0.1
Dives	49 18N	0 05W	-0100	-0010	0000	0000	+0.3	+0.2	+0.2	+0.1
Ouistreham	49 17N	0 15W	-0045	-0010	-0005	0000	-0.3	-0.3	-0.2	-0.3
Courseulles-sur-Mer	49 20N	0 27W	-0045	-0015	-0020	-0025	-0.5	-0.5	-0.1	-0.1
Arromanches	49 21N	0 37W	-0055	-0025	-0027	-0035	-0.6	-0.6	-0.2	-0.2
Port-en-Bessin	49 21N	0 45W	-0055	-0030	-0030	-0035	-0.7	-0.7	-0.2	-0.1
Alpha-Baie de Seine	49 49N	0 20W	+0030	+0020	-0005	-0020	-1.0	-0.9	-0.4	-0.2
			0300	1000	0400	1000				
CHERBOURG	49 39N	1 38W	and	and	and	and	6.4	5.0	2.5	1.1
standard port			1500	2200	1600	2200				
Rade de la Capelle	49 25N	1 05W	+0115	+0050	+0130	+0117	+0.8	+0.9	+0.1	+0.1
Iles Saint Marcouf	49 30N	1 08W	+0118	+0052	+0125	+0110	+0.6	+0.7	+0.1	+0.1
St. Vaast-la-Hougue	49 34N	1 16W	+0120	+0050	+0120	+0115	+0.3	+0.5	0.0	-0.1
Barfleur	49 40N	1 15W	+0110	+0055	+0052	+0052	+0.1	+0.3	0.0	0.0
Omonville	49 42N	1 50W	-0010	-0010	-0015	-0015	-0.1	-0.1	0.0	0.0
Goury	49 43N	1 57W	-0100	-0040	-0105	-0120	+1.7	+1.6	+1.0	+0.3

CHANNEL ISLANDS

			0300	0900	0200	0900				
ST. HELIER	49 11N	2 07W	and	and	and	and	11.0	8.1	4.0	1.4
standard port			1500	2100	1400	2100				
Alderney Braye	49 43N	2 12W	+0050	+0040	+0025	+0105	-4.8	-3.4	-1.5	-0.5
Sark Maseline Pier	49 26N	2 21W	+0005	+0015	+0005	+0010	-2.1	-1.5	-0.6	-0.3
Guernsey St. Peter Port	49 27N	2 31W	0000	+0012	-0008	+0002	-1.7	-1.1	-0.4	0.0
Jersey										
St. Catherine Bay	49 13N	2 01W	0000	+0010	+0010	+0010	0.0	-0.1	0.0	+0.1
Bouley Bay	49 14N	2 05W	+0002	+0002	+0004	+0004	-0.3	-0.3	-0.1	-0.1
Les Ecrehou	49 17N	1 56W	+0105	+0109	+0111	+0109	-0.2	+0.1	-0.2	0.0
Les Minquiers	48 57N	2 08W	+0046	+0042	+0059	+0052	+0.5	+0.6	+0.1	+0.1

FRANCE

			0100	0800	0300	0800				
ST. MALO	48 38N	2 02W	and	and	and	and	12.2	9.3	4.2	1.5
standard port			1300	2000	1500	2000				
Iles Chausey	48 52N	1 49W	+0005	+0005	+0015	+0015	+0.8	+0.7	+0.6	+0.4
Diélette	49 33N	1 52W	+0045	+0035	+0020	+0035	-2.5	-1.9	-0.7	-0.3
Carteret	49 22N	1 47W	+0030	+0020	+0015	+0030	-1.6	-1.2	-0.5	-0.2
Portbail	49 18N	1 45W	+0030	+0025	+0025	+0030	-0.8	-0.6	-0.2	-0.1
St. Germain sur Ay	49 14N	1 36W	+0025	+0025	+0035	+0035	-0.7	-0.5	0.0	+0.1
Le Sénéquet	49 05N	1 40W	+0015	+0015	+0023	+0023	-0.3	-0.3	+0.1	+0.1
Regnéville sur Mer	49 01N	1 33W	+0010	+0010	+0030	+0020	+0.4	+0.3	+0.2	0.0
Granville	48 50N	1 36W	+0005	+0005	+0020	+0010	+0.7	+0.5	+0.3	+0.1
Cancale	48 40N	1 51W	-0002	-0002	+0010	+0010	+0.8	+0.6	+0.3	+0.1
Ile des Hebihens	48 37N	2 11W	-0002	-0002	-0005	-0005	-0.2	-0.2	-0.1	-0.1
St. Cast	48 38N	2 15W	-0002	-0002	-0005	-0005	-0.2	-0.2	-0.1	-0.1
Erquy	48 38N	2 28W	-0010	-0005	-0023	-0017	-0.6	-0.5	0.0	0.0
Dahouët	48 35N	2 34W	-0010	-0010	-0025	-0020	-0.9	-0.7	-0.2	-0.2
Le Légué *(buoy)*	48 34N	2 41W	-0005	-0005	-0025	-0015	-0.8	-0.5	-0.2	-0.1
Binic	48 36N	2 49W	-0008	-0008	-0030	-0015	-0.8	-0.7	-0.2	-0.2

Location	Lat	Long	High Water		Low Water		MHWS	MHWN	MLWN	MLWS
Portrieux	48 38N	2 49W	-0010	-0005	-0025	-0015	-1.0	-0.7	-0.2	-0.1
Paimpol	48 47N	3 02W	-0005	-0010	-0035	-0025	-1.4	-0.9	-0.4	-0.1
Ile de Bréhat	48 51N	3 00W	-0008	-0013	-0040	-0037	-1.8	-1.3	-0.4	-0.2
Les Héaux de Bréhat	48 55N	3 05W	-0018	-0017	-0050	-0050	-2.4	-1.7	-0.6	-0.2
Lézardrieux	48 47N	3 06W	-0010	-0010	-0047	-0037	-1.7	-1.3	-0.5	-0.2
Port-Béni	48 51N	3 10W	-0017	-0022	-0100	-0045	-2.4	-1.6	-0.5	-0.1
Tréguier	48 47N	3 13W	-0005	-0010	-0055	-0040	-2.3	-1.6	-0.6	-0.2
Perros-Guirec	48 49N	3 28W	-0030	-0040	-0115	-0055	-2.9	-1.9	-0.8	-0.2
Ploumanac'h	48 50N	3 29W	-0023	-0033	-0112	-0053	-2.9	-1.9	-0.6	-0.1

Location	Lat	Long	High Water		Low Water		MHWS	MHWN	MLWN	MLWS
			0000	0600	0000	0600				
BREST	48 23N	4 30W	and	and	and	and	6.9	5.4	2.6	1.0
standard port			1200	1800	1200	1800				
Trébeurden	48 46N	3 35W	+0100	+0110	+0120	+0100	+2.3	+1.9	+0.9	+0.4
Locquirec	48 42N	3 38W	+0058	+0108	+0120	+0100	+2.2	+1.8	+0.8	+0.3
Anse de Primel	48 43N	3 50W	+0100	+0110	+0120	+0100	+2.1	+1.7	+0.8	+0.3
Rade de Morlaix Morlaix	48 41N	3 53W	+0055	+0105	+0115	+0055	+2.0	+1.7	+0.8	+0.3
Roscoff	48 43N	3 58W	+0055	+0105	+0115	+0055	+1.9	+1.6	+0.8	+0.3
Ile de Batz	48 44N	4 00W	+0045	+0100	+0105	+0055	+2.0	+1.6	+0.9	+0.4
Brignogan	48 40N	4 19W	+0040	+0045	+0058	+0038	+1.5	+1.2	+0.6	+0.2
L'Aber Vrac'h Ile Cézon	48 36N	4 34W	+0030	+0030	+0040	+0035	+0.8	+0.7	+0.2	0.0
Aber Benoit	48 35N	4 37W	+0022	+0025	+0035	+0020	+1.0	+0.9	+0.4	+0.2
Portsall	48 34N	4 43W	+0015	+0020	+0025	+0015	+0.6	+0.5	+0.1	0.0
L'Aber Ildut	48 28N	4 45W	+0010	+0010	+0023	+0010	+0.4	+0.3	0.0	0.0
Ouessant Baie de Lampaul	48 27N	5 06W	+0005	+0005	-0005	+0003	0.0	-0.1	-0.1	0.0
Molene	48 24N	4 58W	+0012	+0012	+0017	+0017	+0.4	+0.3	+0.2	+0.1
Le Conquet	48 22N	4 47W	-0005	0000	+0007	+0007	-0.1	-0.1	-0.1	0.0
Le Trez Hir	48 21N	4 42W	-0010	-0005	-0008	-0008	-0.3	-0.3	-0.1	0.0
Camaret	48 16N	4 36W	-0010	-0010	-0013	-0013	-0.3	-0.3	-0.1	0.0
Morgat	48 13N	4 30W	-0008	-0008	-0020	-0010	-0.4	-0.4	-0.2	0.0
Douarnenez	48 06N	4 19W	-0010	-0015	-0018	-0008	-0.5	-0.5	-0.3	-0.1
Ile de Sein	48 02N	4 51W	-0005	-0005	-0010	-0005	-0.7	-0.6	-0.2	-0.1
Audierne	48 01N	4 33W	-0035	-0030	-0035	-0030	-1.7	-1.3	-0.6	-0.2
Le Guilvinec	47 48N	4 17W	-0010	-0025	-0025	-0015	-1.8	-1.4	-0.6	-0.1
Lesconil	47 48N	4 13W	-0008	-0028	-0028	-0018	-1.9	-1.4	-0.6	-0.1
Pont l'Abbe River Loctudy	47 50N	4 10W	-0013	-0033	-0035	-0025	-1.9	-1.5	-0.7	-0.2
Odet River										
Bénodet	47 53N	4 07W	0000	-0020	-0023	-0013	-1.7	-1.3	-0.5	-0.1
Corniguel	47 58N	4 06W	+0015	+0010	-0015	-0010	-2.0	-1.6	-1.0	-0.7
Concarneau	47 52N	3 55W	-0010	-0030	-0030	-0020	-1.9	-1.5	-0.7	-0.2
Iles de Glenan Ile de Penfret	47 44N	3 57W	-0005	-0030	-0028	-0018	-1.9	-1.5	-0.7	-0.2
Port Louis	47 42N	3 21W	+0004	-0021	-0022	-0012	-1.8	-1.4	-0.6	-0.1
Lorient	47 45N	3 21W	+0003	-0022	-0020	-0010	-1.8	-1.4	-0.6	-0.2
Hennebont	47 48N	3 17W	+0015	-0017	+0005	+0003	-1.9	-1.5	-0.8	-0.2
Ile de Groix Port Tudy	47 39N	3 27W	0000	-0025	-0025	-0015	-1.8	-1.4	-0.6	-0.1
Port d'Etel	47 39N	3 12W	+0020	-0010	+0030	+0010	-2.0	-1.3	-0.4	+0.5
Port-Haliguen	47 29N	3 06W	+0015	-0020	-0015	-0010	-1.7	-1.3	-0.6	-0.3
Port Maria	47 29N	3 08W	+0010	-0025	-0025	-0015	-1.6	-1.3	-0.6	-0.1
Belle-Ile Le Palais	47 21N	3 09W	+0007	-0028	-0025	-0020	-1.8	-1.4	-0.7	-0.3
Crac'h River La Trinité	47 35N	3 01W	+0020	-0020	-0015	-0005	-1.5	-1.1	-0.5	-0.2
Morbihan										
Port-Navalo	47 33N	2 55W	+0030	-0005	-0010	-0005	-2.0	-1.5	-0.8	-0.3
Auray	47 40N	2 59W	+0055	0000	+0020	+0005	-2.0	-1.4	-0.8	-0.2
Arradon	47 37N	2 50W	+0155	+0145	+0145	+0130	-3.7	-2.7	-1.6	-0.5
Vannes	47 39N	2 46W	+0220	+0200	+0200	+0125	-3.6	-2.7	-1.6	-0.5
Le Logeo	47 33N	2 51W	+0155	+0140	+0145	+0125	-3.7	-2.7	-1.6	-0.5
Port du Crouesty	47 32N	2 54W	+0013	-0022	-0017	-0012	-1.6	-1.2	-0.6	-0.3
Ile de Houat	47 24N	2 57W	+0010	-0025	-0020	-0015	-1.7	-1.3	-0.6	-0.3
Ile de Hoedic	47 20N	2 52W	+0010	-0035	-0027	-0022	-1.8	-1.4	-0.7	-0.3
Pénerf	47 31N	2 37W	+0020	-0025	-0015	-0015	-1.5	-1.1	-0.6	-0.3
Tréhiguier	47 30N	2 27W	+0035	-0020	-0005	-0010	-1.4	-1.0	-0.5	-0.3
Le Croisic	47 18N	2 31W	+0015	-0040	-0020	-0015	-1.5	-1.1	-0.6	-0.3
Le Pouliguen	47 17N	2 25W	+0020	-0025	-0020	-0025	-1.5	-1.1	-0.6	-0.3
Le Grand-Charpentier	47 13N	2 19W	+0015	-0045	-0025	-0020	-1.5	-1.1	-0.6	-0.3
Pornichet	47 16N	2 21W	+0020	-0045	-0022	-0022	-1.4	-1.0	-0.5	-0.2
La Loire										
St. Nazaire	47 16N	2 12W	+0030	-0040	-0010	-0010	-1.1	-0.8	-0.4	-0.2
Donges	47 18N	2 05W	+0035	-0035	+0005	+0005	-1.0	-0.7	-0.5	-0.4
Cordemais	47 17N	1 54W	+0055	-0005	+0105	+0030	-0.7	-0.5	-0.7	-0.4
Le Pellerin	47 12N	1 46W	+0110	+0010	+0145	+0100	-0.7	-0.5	-0.9	-0.4
Nantes *Chantenay*	47 12N	1 35W	+0135	+0055	+0215	+0125	-0.6	-0.3	-0.8	-0.1

Location	Lat	Long	High Water		Low Water		MHWS	MHWN	MLWN	MLWS
			0500	1100	0500	1100				
BREST	48 23N	4 30W	and	and	and	and	6.9	5.4	2.6	1.0
standard port			1700	2300	1700	2300				
Pointe de Saint-Gildas	47 08N	2 15W	-0045	+0025	-0020	-0020	-1.3	-1.0	-0.5	-0.2
Pornic	47 06N	2 07W	-0050	+0030	-0010	-0010	-1.1	-0.8	-0.4	-0.2
Ile de Noirmoutier L'Herbaudière	47 02N	2 18W	-0047	+0023	-0020	-0020	-1.4	-1.0	-0.5	-0.2
Fromentine	46 54N	2 10W	-0050	+0020	-0020	+0010	-1.6	-1.2	-0.7	-0.0
Ile de Yeu Port Joinville	46 44N	2 21W	-0040	+0015	-0030	-0035	-1.9	-1.4	-0.7	-0.3
St. Gilles-Croix-de-Vie	46 41N	1 56W	-0030	+0015	-0032	-0032	-1.8	-1.3	-0.6	-0.3
Les Sables d'Olonne	46 30N	1 48W	-0030	+0015	-0035	-0035	-1.7	-1.3	-0.6	-0.3
			0000	0600	0500	1200				
POINTE DE GRAVE	45 34N	1 04W	and	and	and	and	5.4	4.4	2.1	1.0
standard port			1200	1800	1700	2400				
Ile de Ré St Martin	46 12N	1 22W	+0015	-0030	-0025	-0020	+0.6	+0.5	+0.3	-0.1
La Pallice	46 10N	1 13W	+0015	-0030	-0025	-0020	+0.6	+0.5	+0.3	-0.1
La Rochelle	46 09N	1 09W	+0015	-0030	-0025	-0020	+0.6	+0.5	+0.3	-0.1
Ile d'Aix	46 01N	1 10W	+0015	-0040	-0030	-0025	+0.7	+0.5	+0.3	-0.1
La Charente Rochefort	45 57N	0 58W	+0035	-0010	+0030	+0125	+1.1	+0.9	+0.1	-0.2
Le Chapus	45 51N	1 11W	+0015	-0040	-0025	-0015	+0.6	+0.6	+0.4	+0.2
La Cayenne	45 47N	1 08W	+0030	-0015	-0010	-0005	+0.2	+0.2	+0.3	0.0
Pointe de Gatseau	45 48N	1 14W	+0005	-0005	-0015	-0025	-0.1	-0.1	+0.2	+0.2
La Gironde										
Royan	45 37N	1 00W	0000	-0005	-0005	-0005	-0.3	-0.2	0.0	0.0
Richard	45 27N	0 56W	+0018	+0018	+0028	+0033	-0.1	-0.1	-0.4	-0.5
Lamena	45 20N	0 48W	+0035	+0045	+0100	+0125	+0.2	+0.1	-0.5	-0.3
Pauillac	45 12N	0 45W	+0100	+0100	+0135	+0205	+0.1	0.0	-1.0	-0.5
La Reuille	45 03N	0 36W	+0135	+0145	+0230	+0305	-0.2	-0.3	-1.3	-0.7
La Garonne										
Le Marquis	45 00N	0 33W	+0145	+0150	+0247	+0322	-0.3	-0.4	- 1.5	-0.9
Bordeaux	44 52N	0 33W	+0200	+0225	+0330	+0405	-0.1	-0.2	-1.7	-1.0
La Dordogne Libourne	44 55N	0 15W	+0250	+0305	+0525	+0540	-0.7	-0.9	-2.0	-0.4
Bassin d' Arcachon										
Cap Ferret	44 37N	1 15W	-0015	+0005	-0005	+0015	-1.4	-1.2	-0.8	-0.5
Arcachon *Eyrac*	44 40N	1 10W	+0010	+0025	0000	+0020	-1.1	-1.0	-0.8	-0.6
L'Adour Boucau	43 31N	1 31W	-0030	-0035	-0025	-0040	-1.2	-1.1	-0.4	-0.3
St Jean de Luz Socoa	43 24N	1 41W	-0040	-0045	-0030	-0045	-1.1	-1.1	-0.6	-0.4

SPAIN

Location	Lat	Long	High Water		Low Water		MHWS	MHWN	MLWN	MLWS
Pasajes	43 20N	1 56W	-0050	-0030	-0015	-0045	-1.2	-1.3	-0.5	-0.5
San Sebastian	43 19N	1 59W	-0110	-0030	-0020	-0040	-1.2	-1.2	-0.5	-0.4
Guetaria	43 18N	2 12W	-0110	-0030	-0020	-0040	-1.0	-1.0	-0.5	-0.4
Lequeitio	43 22N	2 30W	-0115	-0035	-0025	-0045	-1.2	-1.2	-0.5	-0.4
Bermeo	43 25N	2 43W	-0055	-0015	-0005	-0025	-0.8	-0.7	-0.5	-0.4
Abra de Bilbao	43 21N	3 02W	-0125	-0045	-0035	-0055	-1.2	-1.2	-0.5	-0.4
Portugalete *Bilbao*	43 20N	3 02W	-0100	-0020	-0010	-0030	-1.2	-1.2	-0.5	-0.4
Castro Urdiales	43 23N	3 13W	-0040	-0120	-0020	-0110	-1.4	-1.5	-0.6	-0.6
Ria de Santona	43 26N	3 28W	-0005	-0045	+0015	-0035	-1.4	-1.4	-0.6	-0.6
Santander	43 28N	3 47W	-0020	-0100	0000	-0050	-1.3	-1.4	-0.6	-0.6
Ria de Suances	43 27N	4 03W	0000	-0030	+0020	-0020	-1.5	-1.5	-0.6	-0.6
San Vicente de la Barquera	43 23N	4 24W	-0020	-0100	0000	-0050	-1.5	-1.5	-0.6	-0.6
Ria de Tina Mayor	43 24N	4 31W	-0020	-0100	0000	-0050	-1.4	-1.5	-0.6	-0.6
Ribadesella	43 28N	5 04W	+0005	-0020	+0020	-0020	-1.4	-1.3	-0.6	-0.4
Gijon	43 34N	5 42W	-0005	-0030	+0010	-0030	-1.4	-1.3	-0.6	-0.4
Luanco	43 37N	5 47W	-0010	-0035	+0005	-0035	-1.4	-1.3	-0.6	-0.4
Aviles	43 35N	5 56W	-0100	-0040	-0015	-0050	-1.5	-1.4	-0.7	-0.5
San Esteban de Pravia	43 34N	6 05W	-0005	-0030	+0010	-0030	-1.4	-1.3	-0.6	-0.4
Luarca	43 33N	6 32W	+0010	-0015	+0025	-0015	-1.2	-1.1	-0.5	-0.3
Ribadeo	43 33N	7 02W	+0010	-0015	+0025	-0015	-1.4	-1.3	-0.6	-0.4
Ria de Vivero	43 43N	7 36W	+0010	-0015	+0025	-0015	-1.4	-1.4	-0.6	-0.4
Santa Marta de Ortigueira	43 41N	7 51W	-0020	0000	+0020	-0010	-1.3	-1.2	-0.6	-0.4
El Ferrol del Caudillo	43 28N	8 16W	-0045	-0100	-0010	-0105	-1.6	-1.4	-0.7	-0.4
La Coruna	43 22N	8 24W	-0110	-0050	-0030	-0100	-1.6	-1.6	-0.6	-0.5
Ria de Corme	43 16N	8 58W	-0025	-0005	+0015	-0015	-1.7	-1.6	-0.6	-0.5
Ria de Camarinas	43 08N	9 11W	-0120	-0055	-0030	-0100	-1.6	-1.6	-0.6	-0.5
			0500	1000	0300	0800				
LISBOA	38 42N	9 08W	and	and	and	and	3.8	3.0	1.4	0.5
standard port			1700	2200	1500	2000				
Corcubion	42 57N	9 12W	+0055	+0110	+0120	+0135	-0.5	-0.4	-0.2	0.0
Muros	42 46N	9 03W	+0050	+0105	+0115	+0130	-0.3	-0.3	-0.1	0.0

SECONDARY PORT TIDAL DATA

Location	Lat	Long	High Water		Low Water		MHWS	MHWN	MLWN	MLWS
Ria de Arosa Villagarcia	42 37N	8 47W	+0040	+0100	+0110	+0120	-0.3	-0.2	-0.1	0.0
Ria de Pontevedra Marin	42 24N	8 42W	+0050	+0110	+0120	+0130	-0.5	-0.4	-0.2	0.0
Vigo	42 15N	8 43W	+0040	+0100	+0105	+0125	-0.4	-0.3	-0.1	0.0
Bayona	42 07N	8 51W	+0035	+0050	+0100	+0115	-0.3	-0.3	-0.1	0.0
La Guardia	41 54N	8 53W	+0040	+0055	+0105	+0120	-0.5	-0.4	-0.2	-0.1
			0400	**0900**	**0400**	**0900**				
LISBOA	38 42N	9 08W	and	and	and	and	**3.8**	**3.0**	**1.4**	**0.5**
standard port			**1600**	**2100**	**1600**	**2100**				

PORTUGAL Zone UT (GMT)

Location	Lat	Long	High Water		Low Water		MHWS	MHWN	MLWN	MLWS
Viana do Castelo	41 41N	8 50W	-0020	0000	+0010	+0015	-0.3	-0.3	0.0	0.0
Esposende	41 32N	8 47W	-0020	0000	+0010	+0015	-0.6	-0.5	-0.1	0.0
Povoa de Varzim	41 22N	8 46W	-0020	0000	+0010	+0015	-0.3	-0.3	0.0	0.0
Porto de Leixoes	41 11N	8 42W	-0025	-0010	0000	+0010	-0.3	-0.3	-0.1	0.0
Rio Douro										
Entrance	41 09N	8 40W	-0010	+0005	+0015	+0025	-0.6	-0.5	-0.1	0.0
Oporto *Porto*	41 08N	8 37W	+0002	+0002	+0040	+0040	-0.5	-0.4	-0.1	+0.1
Barra de Aveiro	40 39N	8 45W	+0005	+0010	+0010	+0015	-0.6	-0.4	0.0	+0.2
Figueira da Foz	40 09N	8 51W	-0015	0000	+0010	+0020	-0.5	-0.4	-0.1	0.0
Nazare *Pederneira*	39 36N	9 05W	-0030	-0015	-0005	+0005	-0.5	-0.4	-0.1	+0.1
Peniche	39 21N	9 22W	-0035	-0015	-0005	0000	-0.3	-0.3	-0.1	+0.1
Ericeira	38 58N	9 25W	-0040	-0025	-0010	-0010	-0.4	-0.3	-0.1	+0.1
River Tagus (Rio Tejo)										
Cascais	38 42N	9 25W	-0040	-0025	-0015	-0010	-0.3	-0.3	+0.1	+0.2
Paco de Arcos	38 41N	9 18W	-0020	-0030	-0005	-0005	-0.4	-0.4	-0.1	0.0
Alcochete	38 45N	8 58W	+0010	+0010	+0010	+0010	+0.5	+0.4	+0.2	+0.1
Vila Franca de Xira	38 57N	8 59W	+0045	+0040	+0100	+0140	+0.3	+0.2	-0.1	+0.4
Sesimbra	38 26N	9 07W	-0045	-0030	-0020	-0010	-0.4	-0.4	0.0	+0.1
Setubal	38 30N	8 54W	-0020	-0015	-0005	+0005	-0.4	-0.3	-0.1	0.0
Porto de Sines	37 57N	8 53W	-0050	-0030	-0020	-0010	-0.5	-0.4	-0.1	+0.1
Milfontes	37 43N	8 47W	-0040	-0030 *no data*	*no data*	-0.1	-0.1	+0.1	+0.2
Arrifana	37 17N	8 52W	-0030	-0020 *no data*	*no data*	-0.1	0.0	0.0	+0.2
Enseada de Belixe	37 01N	8 58W	-0050	-0030	-0020	-0015	+0.3	+0.2	+0.3	+0.3
Lagos	37 06N	8 40W	-0100	-0040	-0030	-0025	-0.5	-0.4	-0.1	+0.1
Portimao	37 07N	8 32W	-0100	-0040	-0030	-0025	-0.5	-0.4	0.0	+0.2
Ponta do Altar	37 06N	8 31W	-0100	-0040	-0030	-0025	-0.3	-0.3	0.0	+0.1
Enseada de Albufeira	37 05N	8 15W	-0035	+0015	-0005	0000	-0.2	-0.2	+0.1	+0.2
Cabo de Santa Maria	36 58N	7 52W	-0050	-0030	-0015	+0005	-0.5	-0.4	-0.1	+0.1
Rio Guadiana										
Vila Real de Santo António	37 11N	7 25W	-0050	-0015	-0010	0000	-0.5	-0.4	-0.1	+0.1
			0500	**1000**	**0500**	**1100**				
LISBOA	38 42N	9 08W	and	and	and	and	**3.8**	**3.0**	**1.4**	**0.5**
standard port			**1700**	**2200**	**1700**	**2300**				

Spain Zone -0100

Location	Lat	Long	High Water		Low Water		MHWS	MHWN	MLWN	MLWS
Ayamonte	37 13N	7 25W	+0005	+0015	+0025	+0045	-0.7	-0.6	0.0	-0.1
Ria de Huelva										
Bar	37 08N	6 52W	0000	+0015	+0035	+0030	-0.6	-0.5	-0.2	-0.1
Huelva, Muelle de Fabrica	37 15N	6 58W	+0010	+0025	+0045	+0040	-0.3	-0.3	-0.2	0.0
Rio Guadalquivir										
Bar	36 45N	6 26W	-0005	+0005	+0020	+0030	-0.6	-0.5	-0.1	-0.1
Bonanza	36 48N	6 20W	+0025	+0040	+0100	+0120	-0.8	-0.6	-0.3	0.0
Corta de los Jerónimos	37 08N	6 06W	+0210	+0230	+0255	+0345	-1.2	-0.9	-0.4	0.0
Sevilla	37 23N	6 00W	+0400	+0430	+0510	+0545	-1.7	-1.2	-0.5	0.0
Rota	36 37N	6 21W	-0010	+0010	+0025	+0015	-0.7	-0.6	-0.3	-0.1
Puerto de Santa Maria	36 36N	6 13W	+0006	+0006	+0027	+0027	-0.6	-0.4	-0.3	-0.1
Cadiz										
Puerto Cadiz	36 32N	6 17W	0000	+0020	+0040	+0025	-0.5	-0.5	-0.2	0.0
La Carraca	36 30N	6 11W	+0020	+0050	+0100	+0040	-0.5	-0.4	-0.1	0.0
Cabo Trafalgar	36 11N	6 02W	-0003	-0003	+0026	+0026	-1.4	-1.1	0.5	-0.1
Rio Barbate	36 11N	5 55W	+0016	+0016	+0045	+0045	-1.9	-1.5	-0.4	+0.1
Punta Camarinal	36 05N	5 48W	-0007	-0007	+0013	+0013	-1.7	-1.4	-0.6	-0.2

GIBRALTAR

Location	Lat	Long	High Water		Low Water		MHWS	MHWN	MLWN	MLWS
			0000	**0700**	**0100**	**0600**				
GIBRALTAR	36 08N	5 21W	and	and	and	and	**1.0**	**0.7**	**0.3**	**0.1**
standard port			**1200**	**1900**	**1300**	**1800**				
Tarifa	36 00N	5 36W	-0038	-0038	-0042	-0042	+0.4	+0.3	+0.3	+0.2
Punta Carnero	36 04N	5 26W	-0010	-0010	0000	0000	0.0	+0.1	+0.1	+0.1
Algeciras	36 07N	5 27W	-0010	-0010	-0010	-0010	+0.1	+0.2	+0.1	+0.1

ENGLISH CHANNEL AND SOUTH BRITTANY

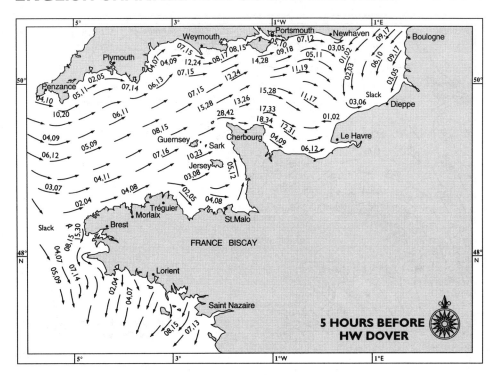

5 HOURS BEFORE
HW DOVER

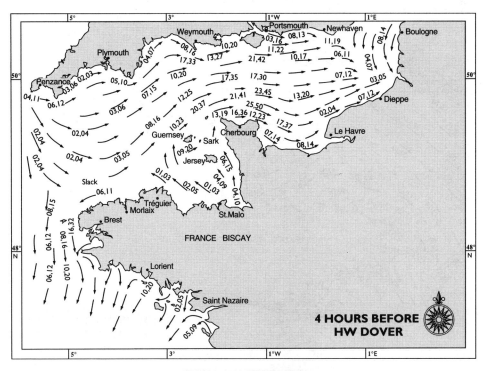

4 HOURS BEFORE
HW DOVER

ENGLISH CHANNEL AND SOUTH BRITTANY

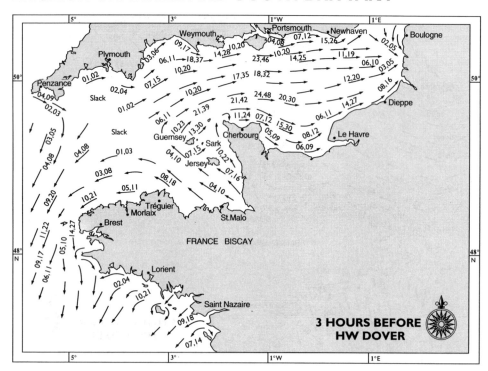

3 HOURS BEFORE
HW DOVER

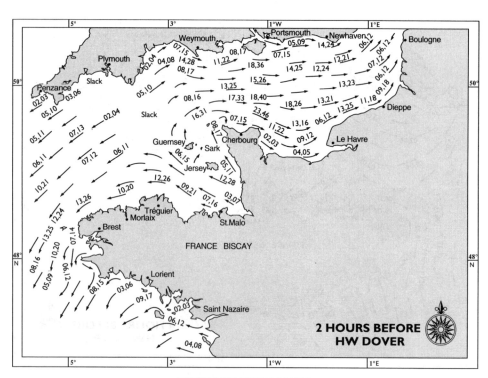

2 HOURS BEFORE
HW DOVER

ENGLISH CHANNEL AND SOUTH BRITTANY

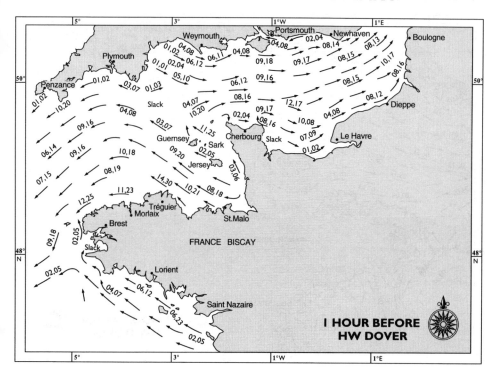

I HOUR BEFORE
HW DOVER

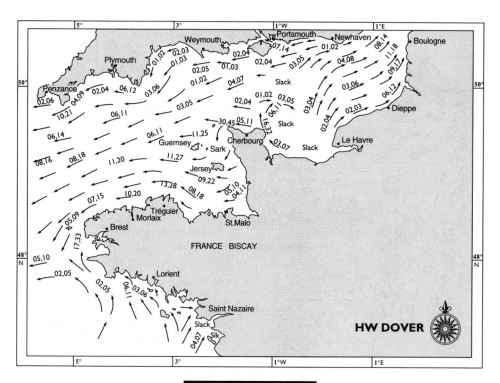

HW DOVER

ENGLISH CHANNEL AND SOUTH BRITTANY

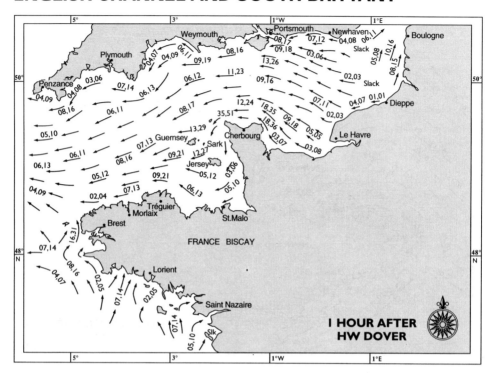

I HOUR AFTER
HW DOVER

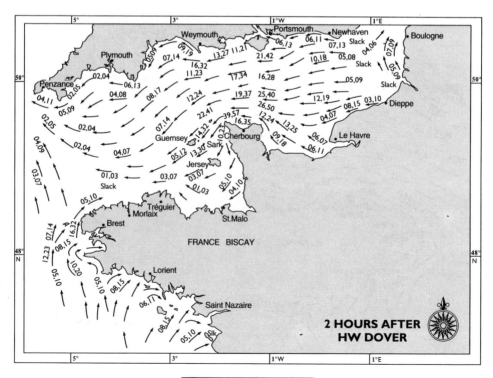

2 HOURS AFTER
HW DOVER

ENGLISH CHANNEL AND SOUTH BRITTANY

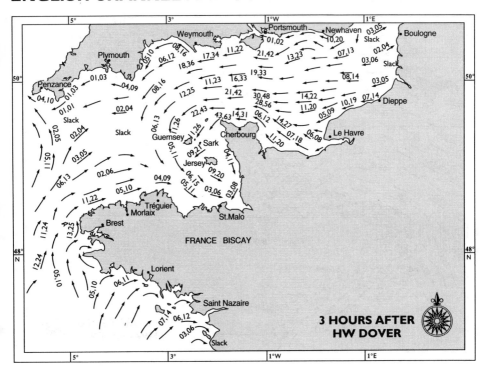

3 HOURS AFTER HW DOVER

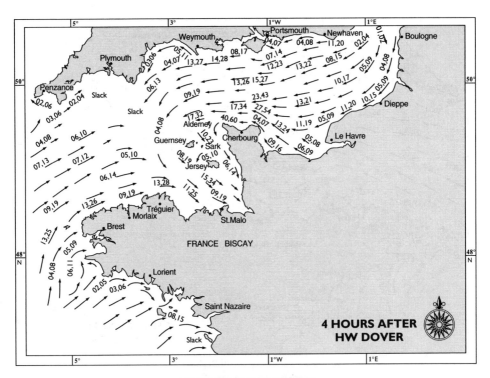

4 HOURS AFTER HW DOVER

ENGLISH CHANNEL AND SOUTH BRITTANY

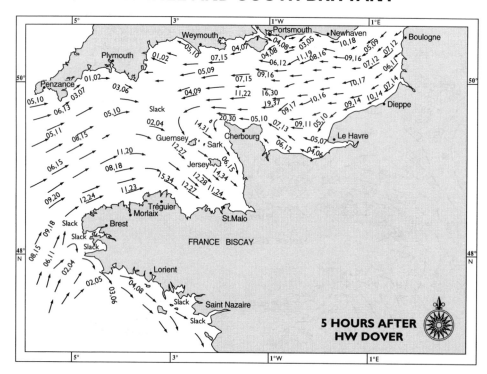

5 HOURS AFTER
HW DOVER

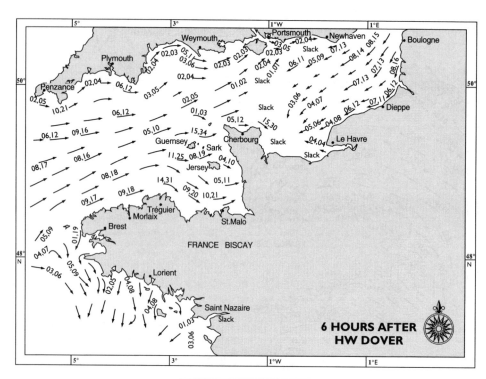

6 HOURS AFTER
HW DOVER

PORTLAND

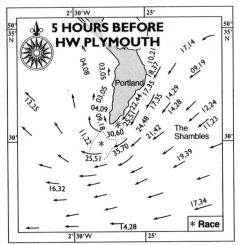

5 HOURS BEFORE HW PLYMOUTH

* Race

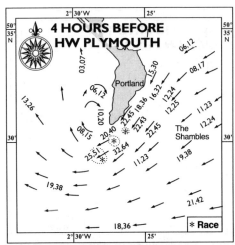

4 HOURS BEFORE HW PLYMOUTH

* Race

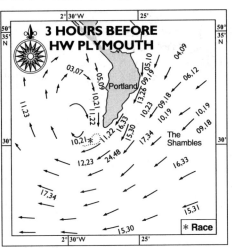

3 HOURS BEFORE HW PLYMOUTH

* Race

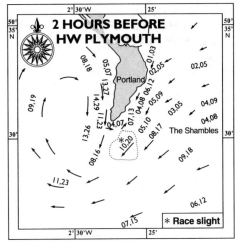

2 HOURS BEFORE HW PLYMOUTH

* Race slight

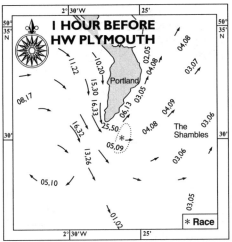

1 HOUR BEFORE HW PLYMOUTH

* Race

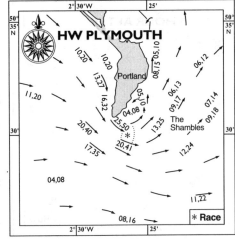

HW PLYMOUTH

* Race

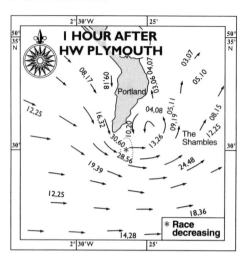

1 HOUR AFTER HW PLYMOUTH

* Race decreasing

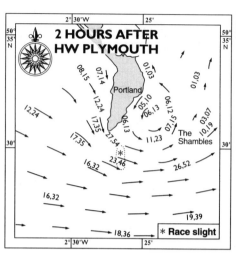

2 HOURS AFTER HW PLYMOUTH

* Race slight

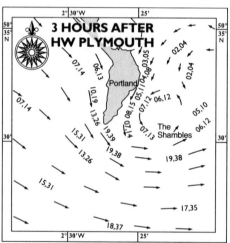

3 HOURS AFTER HW PLYMOUTH

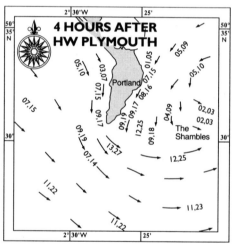

4 HOURS AFTER HW PLYMOUTH

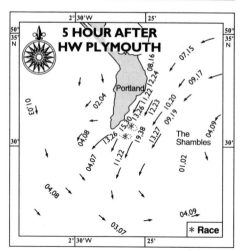

5 HOUR AFTER HW PLYMOUTH

* Race

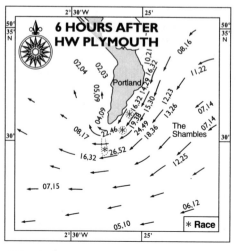

6 HOURS AFTER HW PLYMOUTH

* Race

ISLE OF WIGHT

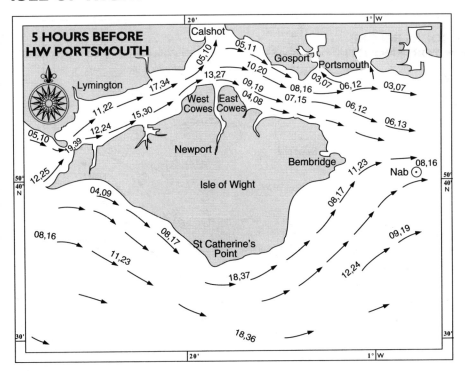

5 HOURS BEFORE HW PORTSMOUTH

Calshot
Lymington
Gosport
Portsmouth
West Cowes East Cowes
Newport
Bembridge
Nab
Isle of Wight
St Catherine's Point

05,10
05,11
10,20
13,27
09,19
04,08
08,16
07,15
03,07
06,12
03,07
06,12
06,13
17,34
11,22
15,30
12,24
05,10
19,39
12,25
04,09
08,16
11,23
08,17
11,23
08,17
09,19
12,24
18,37
18,36

20'   1° W
50° 40' N

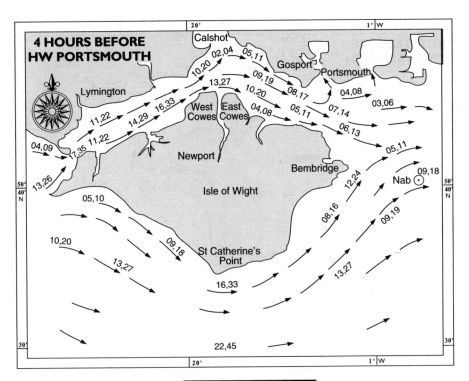

4 HOURS BEFORE HW PORTSMOUTH

Calshot
Lymington
Gosport
Portsmouth
West Cowes East Cowes
Newport
Bembridge
Nab
Isle of Wight
St Catherine's Point

02,04
05,11
10,20
09,19
08,17
04,08
13,27
10,20
05,11
04,08
07,14
03,06
06,13
05,11
09,18
17,35
11,22
11,22
14,29
16,33
04,09
13,26
05,10
10,20
13,27
09,18
16,33
22,45
08,16
12,24
09,19
13,27
09,19

20'   1° W
50° 40' N

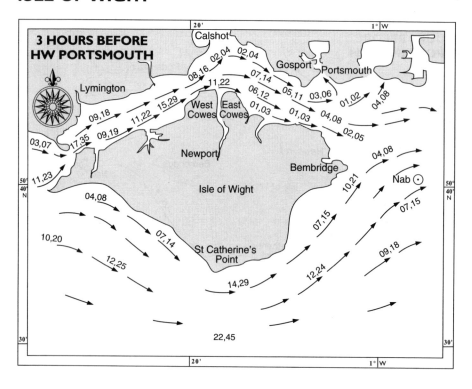

3 HOURS BEFORE HW PORTSMOUTH

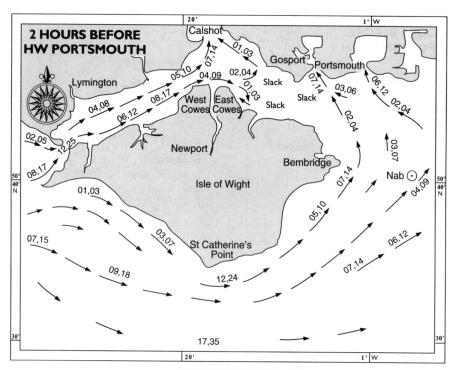

2 HOURS BEFORE HW PORTSMOUTH

ISLE OF WIGHT

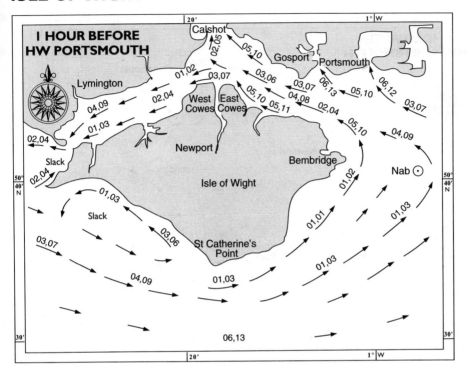

I HOUR BEFORE HW PORTSMOUTH

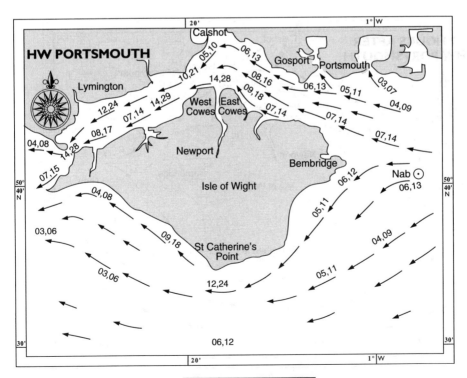

HW PORTSMOUTH

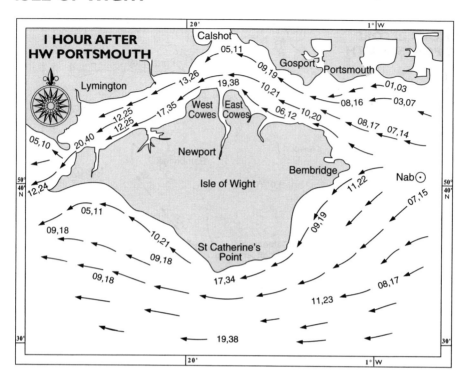

I HOUR AFTER HW PORTSMOUTH

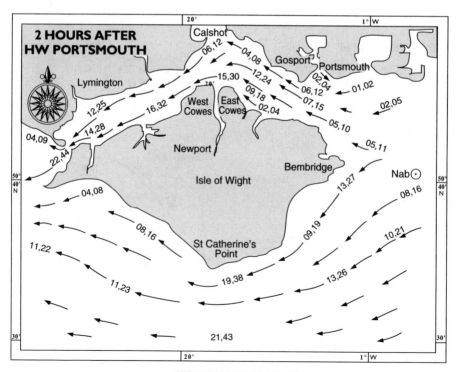

2 HOURS AFTER HW PORTSMOUTH

ISLE OF WIGHT

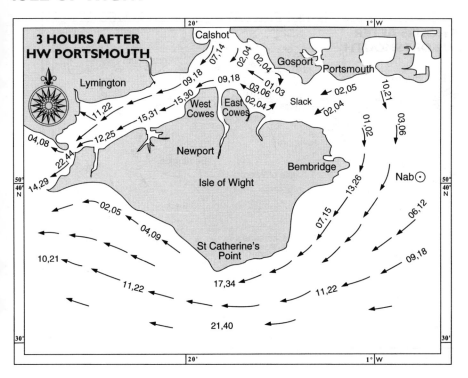

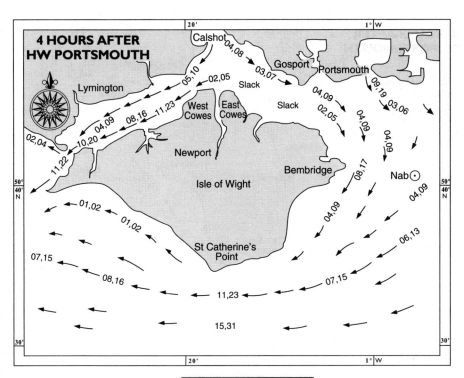

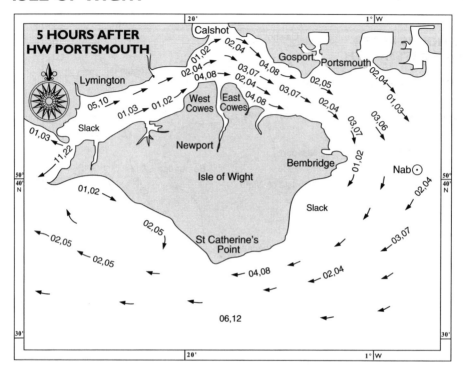

5 HOURS AFTER HW PORTSMOUTH

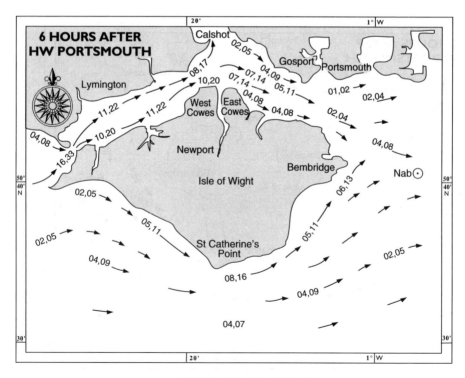

6 HOURS AFTER HW PORTSMOUTH

CHANNEL ISLES

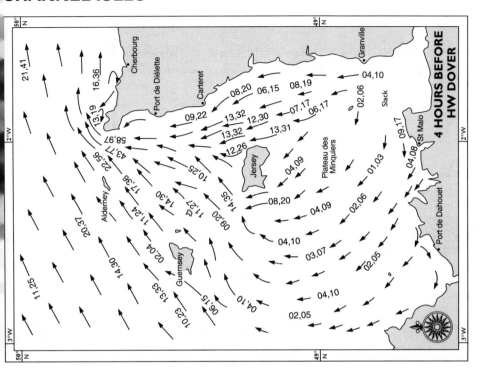

4 HOURS BEFORE HW DOVER

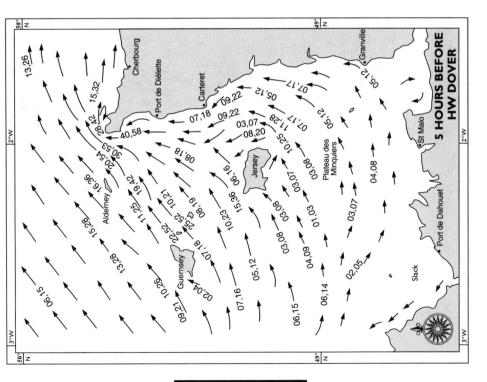

5 HOURS BEFORE HW DOVER

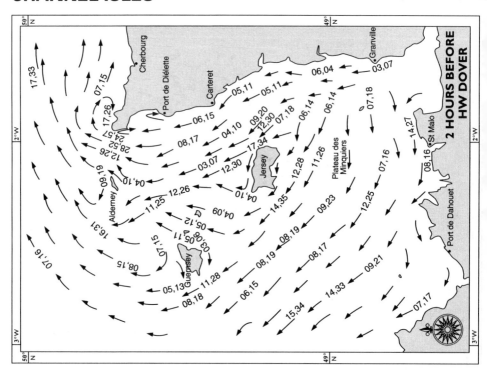

2 HOURS BEFORE HW DOVER

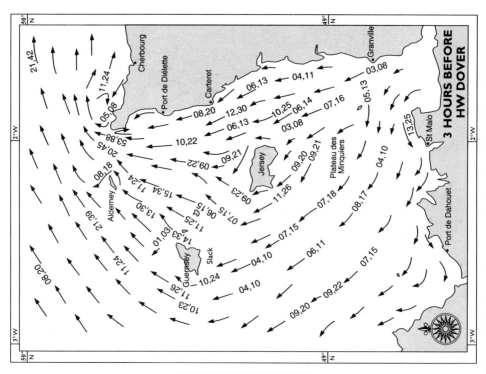

3 HOURS BEFORE HW DOVER

CHANNEL ISLES

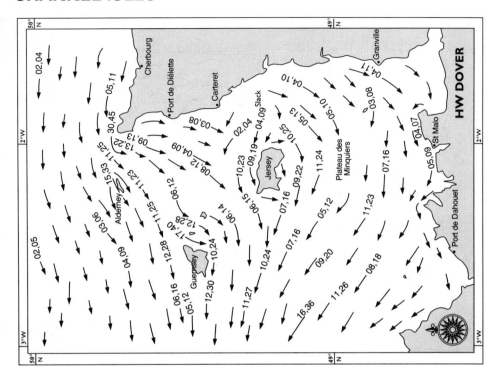

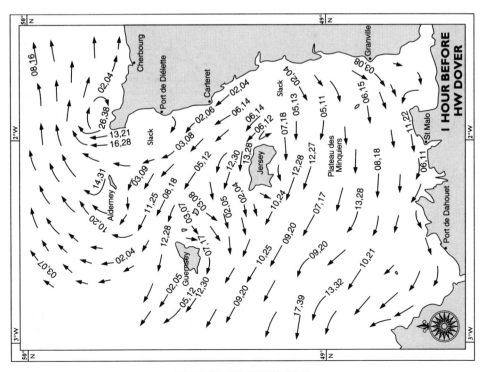

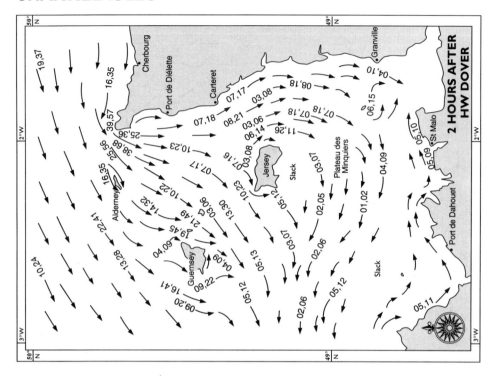

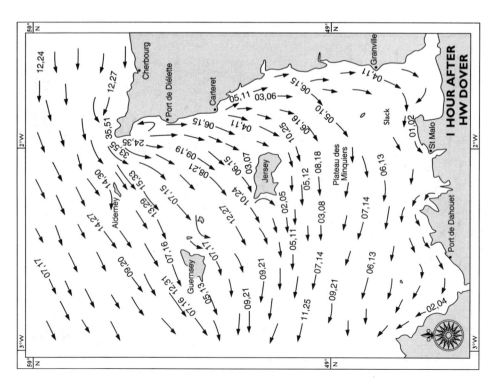

CHANNEL ISLES

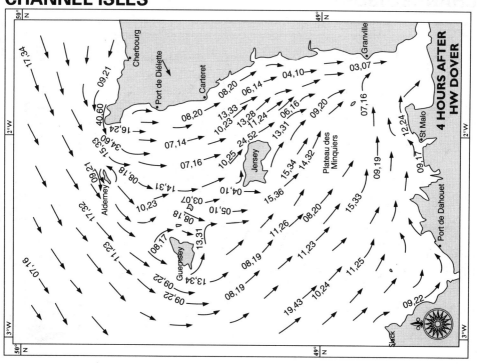

4 HOURS AFTER HW DOVER

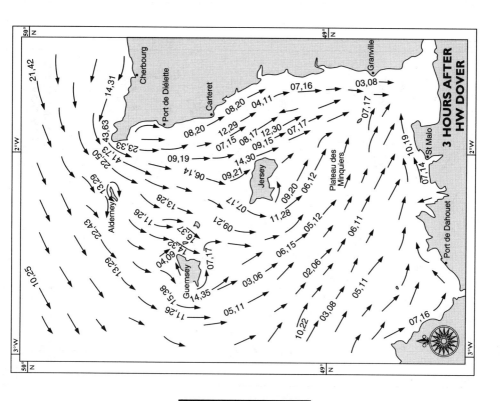

3 HOURS AFTER HW DOVER

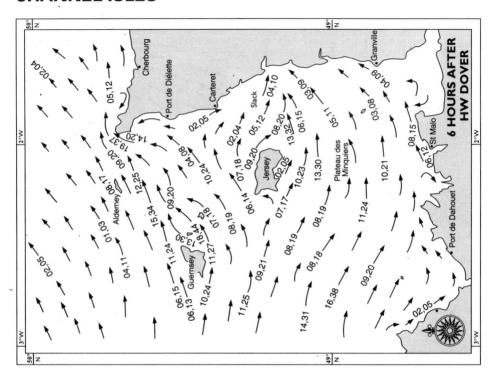

6 HOURS AFTER HW DOVER

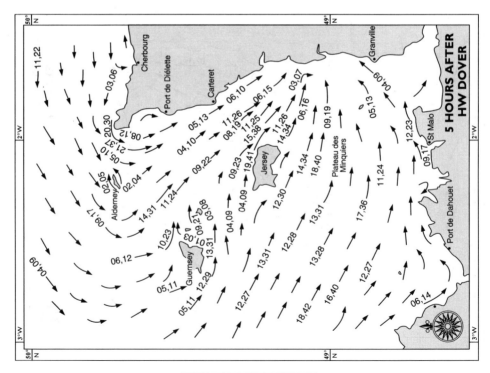

5 HOURS AFTER HW DOVER

NORTH SEA

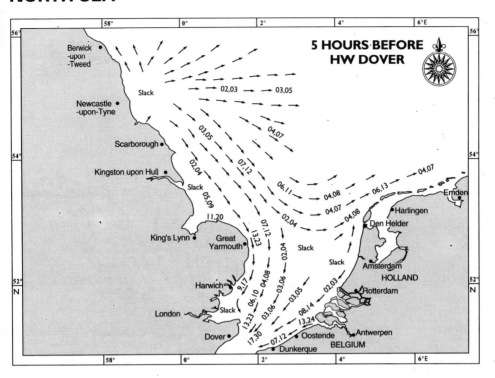

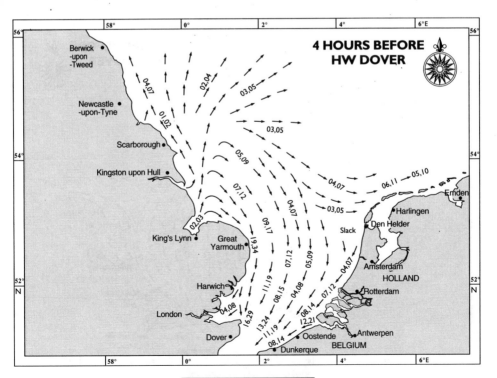

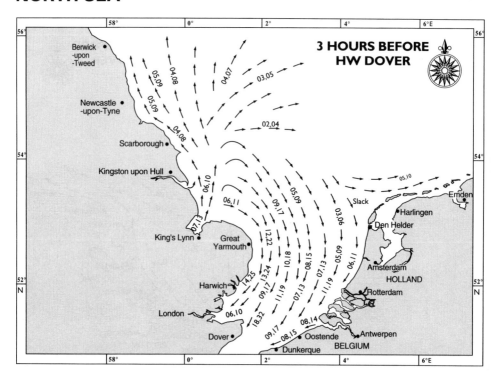

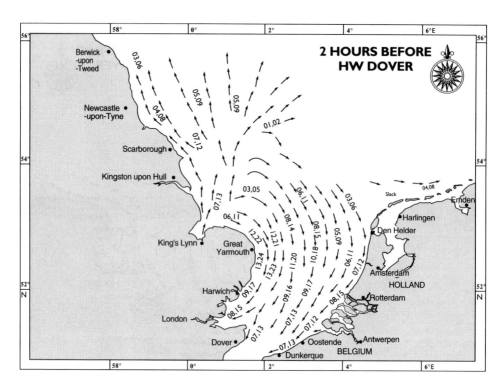

NORTH SEA

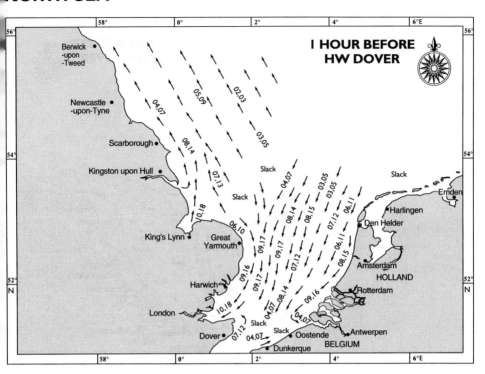

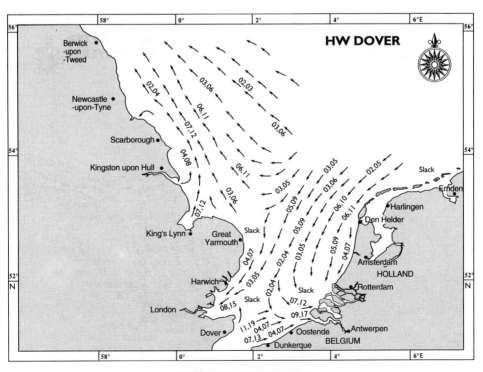

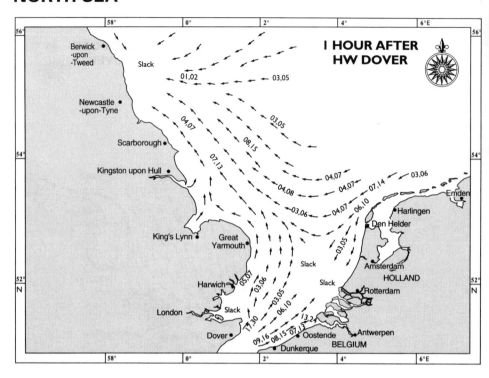

I HOUR AFTER HW DOVER

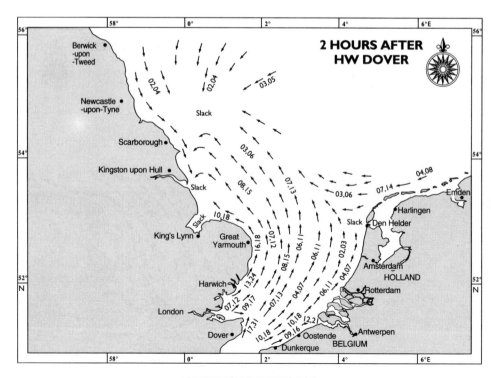

2 HOURS AFTER HW DOVER

NORTH SEA

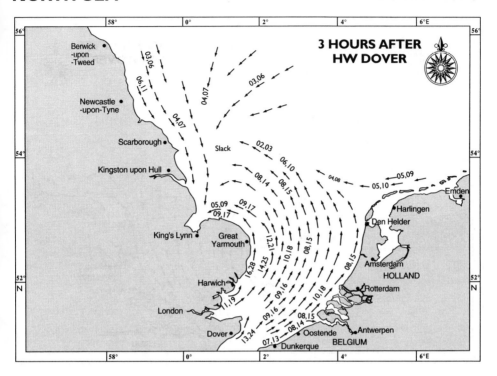

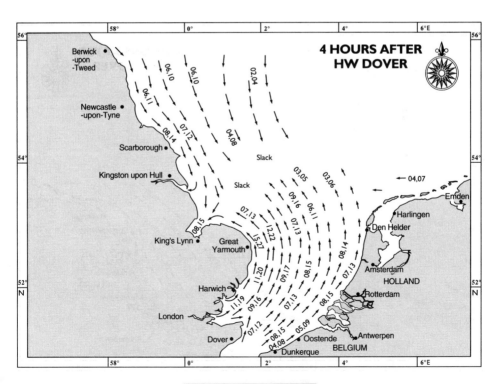

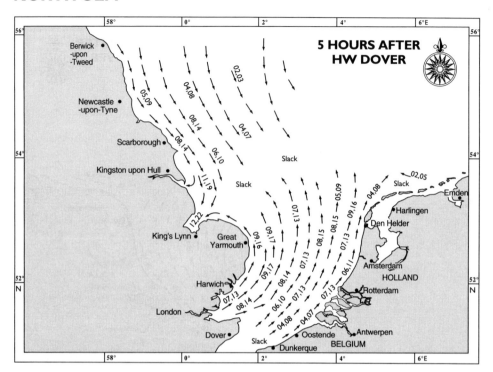

5 HOURS AFTER HW DOVER

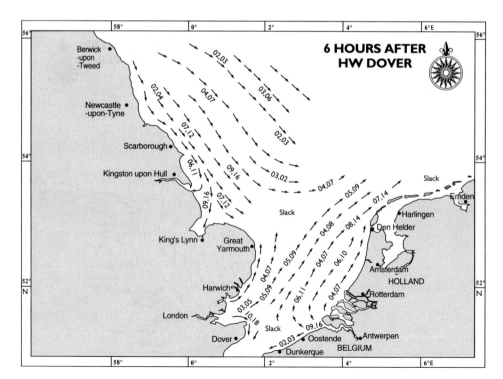

6 HOURS AFTER HW DOVER

SCOTLAND

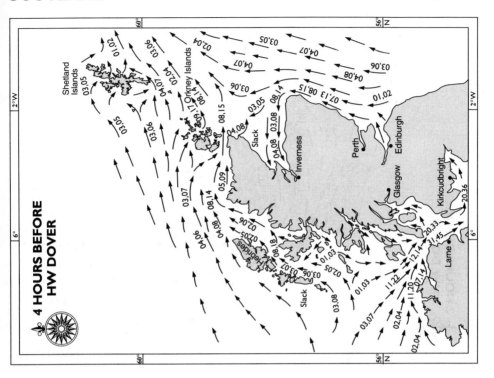

4 HOURS BEFORE HW DOVER

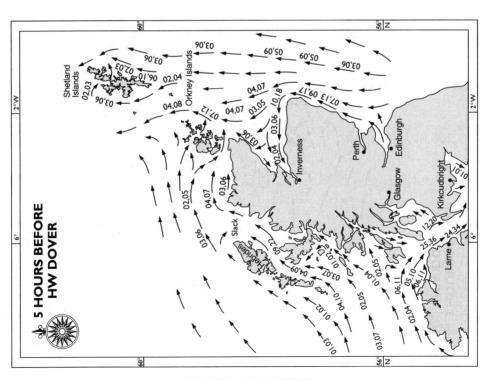

5 HOURS BEFORE HW DOVER

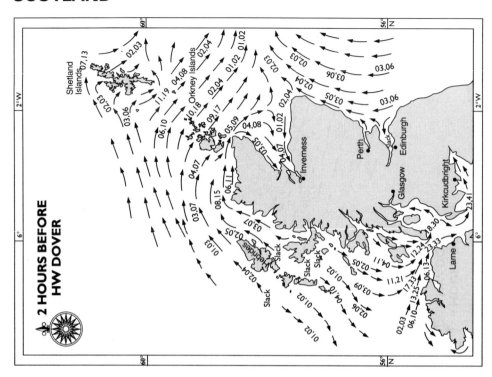

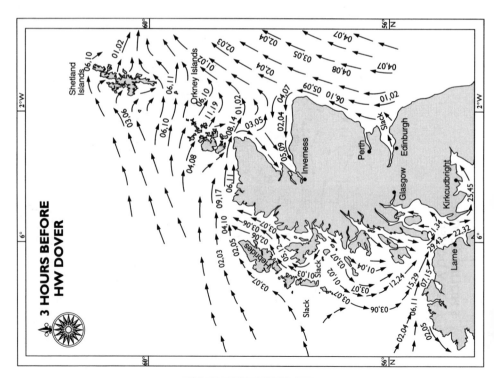

SCOTLAND

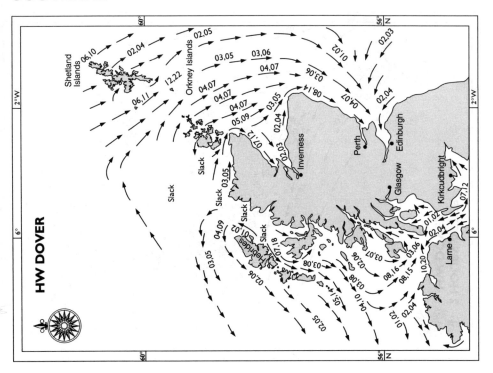

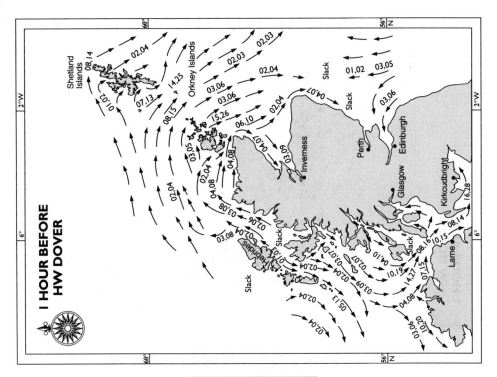

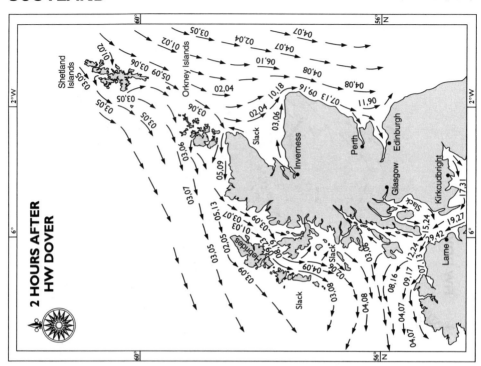

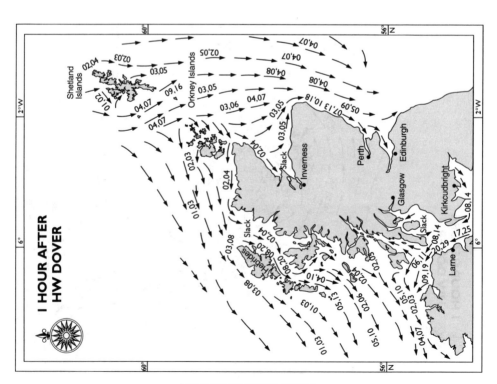

SCOTLAND

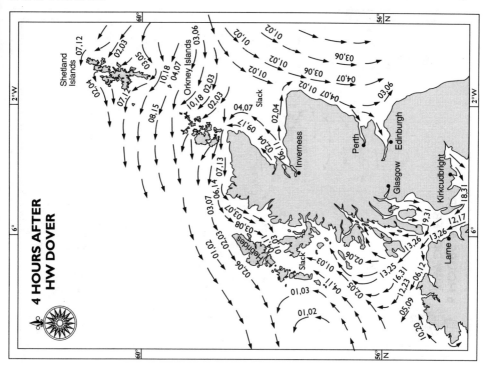

4 HOURS AFTER HW DOVER

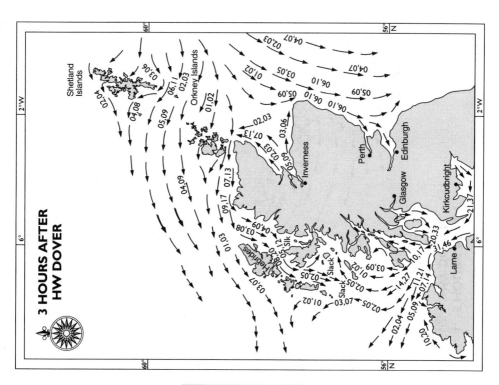

3 HOURS AFTER HW DOVER

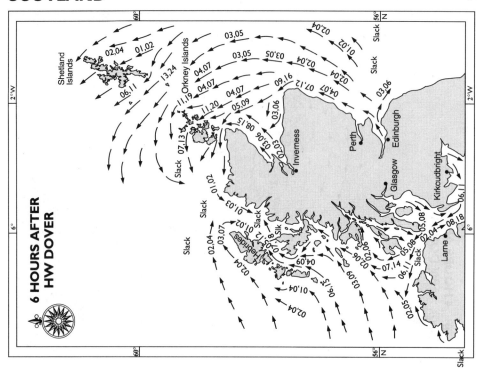

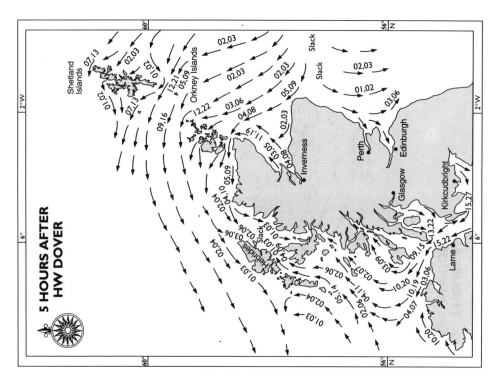

CELTIC SEA, IRISH SEA AND WEST IRELAND

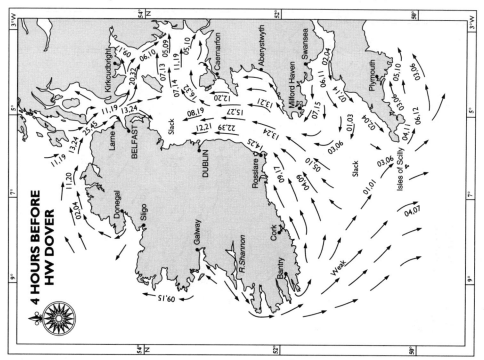

4 HOURS BEFORE HW DOVER

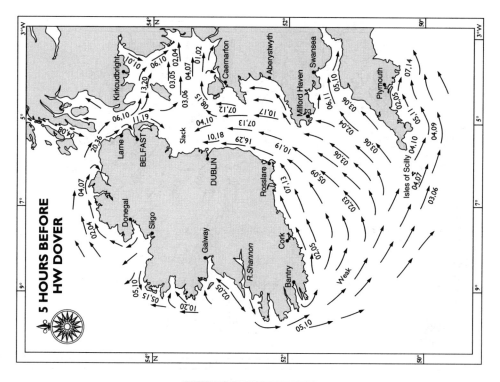

5 HOURS BEFORE HW DOVER

CELTIC SEA, IRISH SEA AND WEST IRELAND

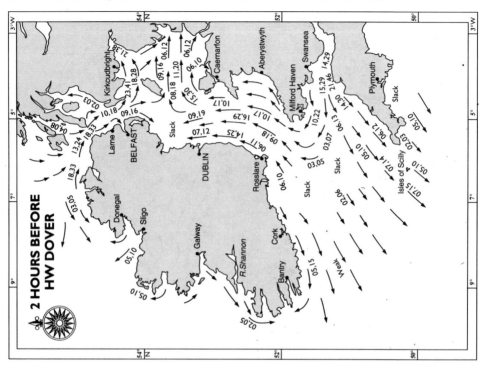

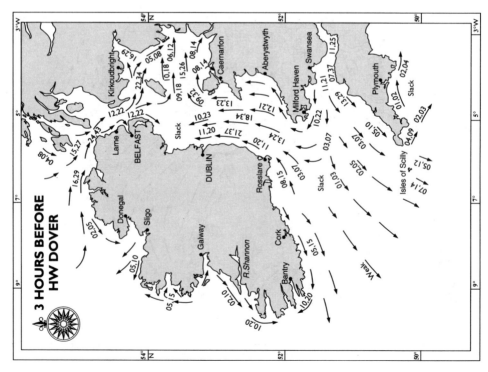

CELTIC SEA, IRISH SEA AND WEST IRELAND

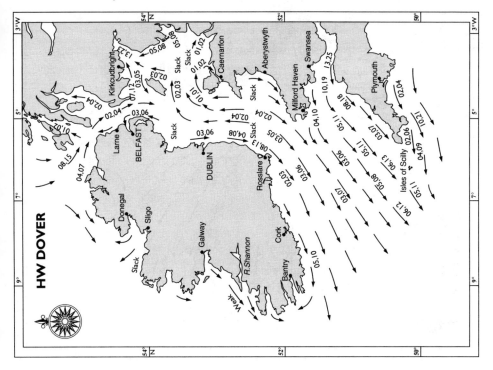

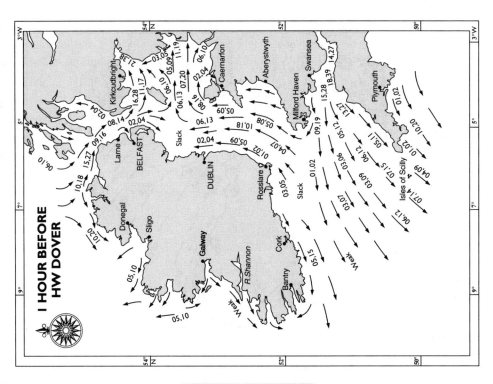

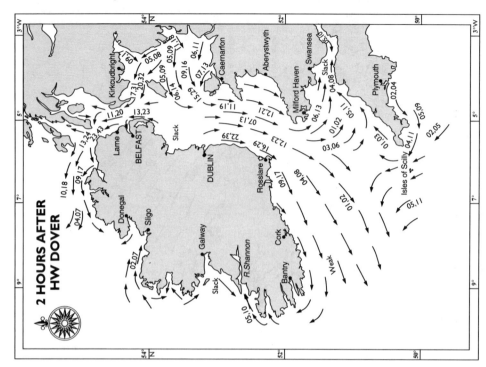

2 HOURS AFTER HW DOVER

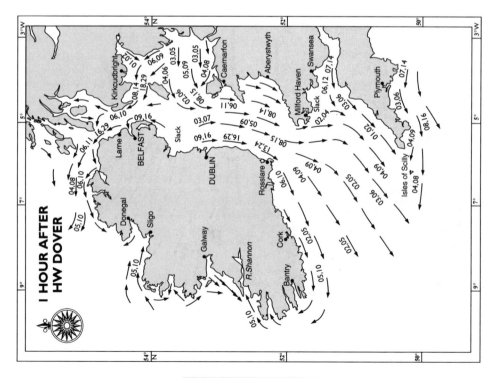

1 HOUR AFTER HW DOVER

CELTIC SEA, IRISH SEA AND WEST IRELAND

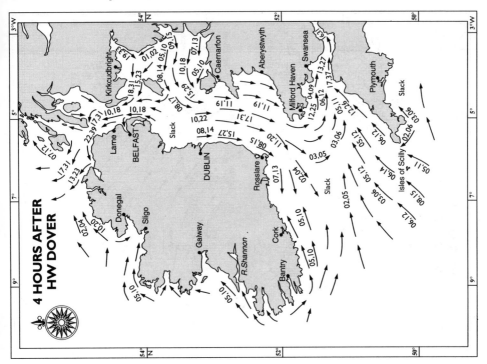

4 HOURS AFTER HW DOVER

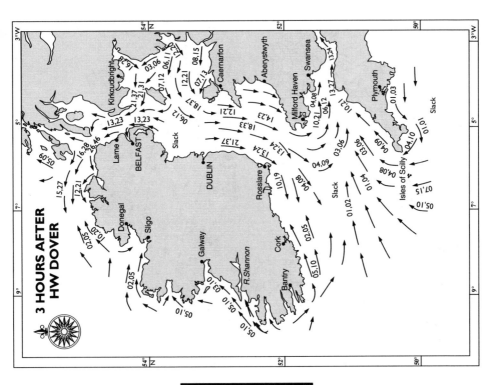

3 HOURS AFTER HW DOVER

CELTIC SEA, IRISH SEA AND WEST IRELAND

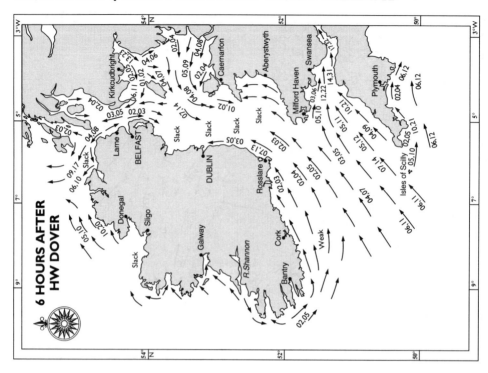

6 HOURS AFTER HW DOVER

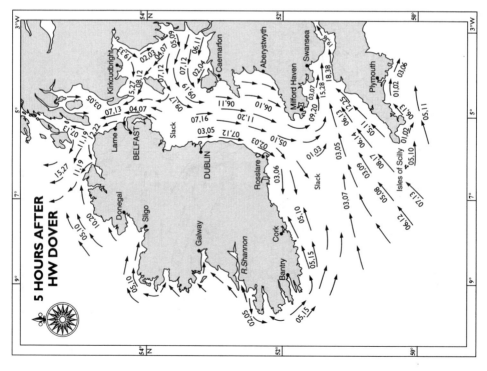

5 HOURS AFTER HW DOVER

AREA PLANNERS

England, Scotland, Ireland, Wales, France, Belgium, Holland
Germany, Denmark, Spain & Portugal

Ports, waypoints, principal lights, DGPS beacons, courses and distances

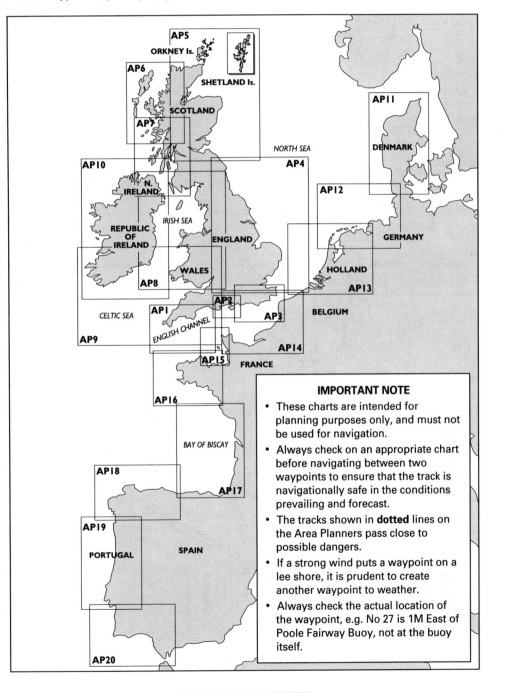

AP5
ORKNEY Is.
AP6
SHETLAND Is.
SCOTLAND
AP7
AP11
NORTH SEA
DENMARK
AP10
AP4
N. IRELAND
AP12
IRISH SEA
REPUBLIC OF IRELAND
ENGLAND
GERMANY
WALES
HOLLAND
AP8
AP13
AP1
CELTIC SEA
AP2
AP3
BELGIUM
AP9
ENGLISH CHANNEL
AP14
AP15
FRANCE
AP16
BAY OF BISCAY
AP18
AP17
AP19
PORTUGAL
SPAIN
AP20

IMPORTANT NOTE

- These charts are intended for planning purposes only, and must not be used for navigation.
- Always check on an appropriate chart before navigating between two waypoints to ensure that the track is navigationally safe in the conditions prevailing and forecast.
- The tracks shown in **dotted** lines on the Area Planners pass close to possible dangers.
- If a strong wind puts a waypoint on a lee shore, it is prudent to create another waypoint to weather.
- Always check the actual location of the waypoint, e.g. No 27 is 1M East of Poole Fairway Buoy, not at the buoy itself.

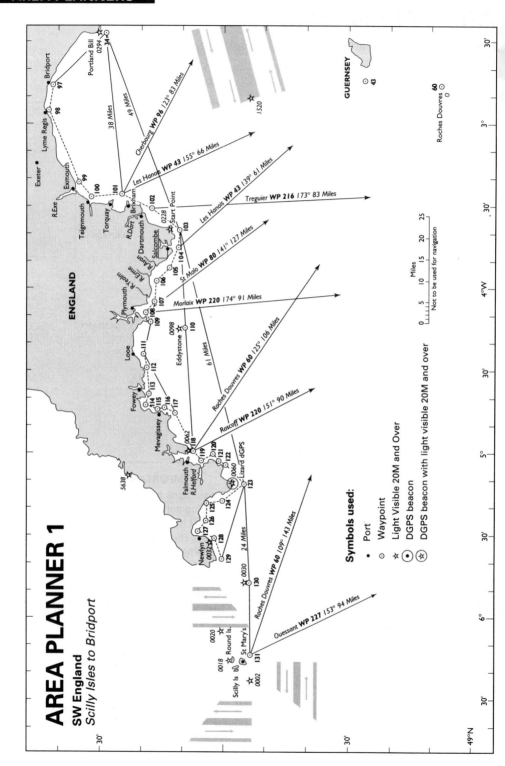

AREA PLANNER 1

SW England
Scilly Isles to Bridport

Symbols used:

- • Port
- ⊙ Waypoint
- ☆ Light Visible 20M and Over
- ⊛ DGPS beacon
- ⊛ DGPS beacon with light visible 20M and over

Cherbourg **WP 96** 123° 83 Miles

Les Hanois **WP 43** 155° 66 Miles

Les Hanois **WP 43** 139° 61 Miles

Treguier **WP 216** 173° 83 Miles

St.Malo **WP 80** 141° 127 Miles

Morlaix **WP 220** 174° 91 Miles

Roches Douvres **WP 60** 125° 106 Miles

Roscoff **WP 220** 151° 90 Miles

Roches Douvres **WP 60** 109° 143 Miles

Ouessant **WP 227** 153° 94 Miles

38 Miles

49 Miles

61 Miles

24 Miles

ENGLAND

GUERNSEY

Roches Douvres 60

Exeter
Lyme Regis
Bridport
Portland Bill
R.Exe
Exmouth
Teignmouth
Torquay
Brixham
R.Dart
Dartmouth
Salcombe
R.Avon
R.Erme
R.Yealm
Plymouth
Eddystone
Looe
Fowey
Mevagissey
Falmouth
R.Helford
Lizard dGPS
Newlyn
Round Is.
St. Mary's
Scilly Is

Start Point

Miles
0 5 10 15 20 25
Not to be used for navigation

AREA PLANNER 1
WAYPOINTS
England South West - *Scilly Isles to Bridport*

34	Portland Bill - *5M S of*	50°25'·82N	02°27'·30W
43	Guernsey SW - *1·8M W Les Hanois*	49°26'·16N	02°45'·00W
60	Roches Douvres Lt - *2·5M NE*	49°08'·24N	02°45'·96W
80	St Malo - *1·3M NW Grande Jardin Lt. Bn*	48°41'·10N	02°06'·40W
96	Cherbourg - *0·5M N of W ent*	49°40'·95N	01°39'·35W
97	Bridport - *1M S of entrance*	50°41'·50N	02°45'·70W
98	Lyme Regis - *1M SSE on ldg Lts*	50°42'·80N	02°54'·80W
99	River Exe - *0·3M S of E Exe Lt By*	50°35'·67N	03°22'·30W
100	Teignmouth - *1M E of Bar*	50°32'·30N	03°27'·80W
101	Torbay - *1·7M NE of Berry Hd*	50°25'·10N	03°27'·00W
102	Dartmouth - *2M 150° from ent*	50°18'·25N	03°31'·60W
103	Start Point - *2M S of*	50°11'·30N	03°38'·47W
104	Salcombe - *1·5M S of bar*	50°11'·62N	03°46'·60W
105	Bolt Tail - *1·3M SW of R Avon*	50°13'·60N	03°53'·60W
106	River Erme - *1·5M SSW of Battisborough 1.*	50°16'·80N	03°58'·50W
107	R Yealm -*1·2M SW of Yealm Hd*	50°17'·30N	04°05'·70W
108	Plymouth - *0·9M S of W end of brkwtr*	50°19'·13N	04°09'·50W
109	Rame Hd - *0·2M S of*	50°18'·15N	04°13'·30W
110	Eddystone - *1M S of*	50°09'·80N	04°15'·85W
111	Looe - *1·5M SE of entrance*	50°19'·80N	04°25'·20W
112	Polperro - *0·7M S of*	50°19'·00N	04°30'·80W
113	Fowey - *1·5M SSW of ent*	50°18'·20N	04°39'·50W
114	Charlestown - *1M SE of*	50°19'·00N	04°44'·10W
115	Mevagissey - *0·8M E of*	50°16'·10N	04°45'·50W
116	Gwineas Lt By - *0·2M E of*	50°14'·40N	04°45'·00W
117	Dodman Pt - *1·3M SSE of*	50°11'·90N	04°47'·00W
118	Falmouth - *0·8M S of St Anthony Hd*	50°07'·64N	05°00'·90W
119	Helford River -*1M E of ent*	50°05'·70N	05°04'·00W
120	Manacles - *0·2M E of*	50°02'·80N	05°01'·50W
121	Coverack - *1M E of*	50°01'·30N	05°04'·30W
122	Black Hd - *0·7M SE of*	49°59'·70N	05°05'·30W
123	Lizard - *2M S of*	49°55'·58N	05°l 2'·07W
124	Porth Mellin - *1·7M W of*	50°00'·80N	05°l 8'·50W
125	Porthleven - *0·4M SW of*	50°04'·50N	05°l 9'·70W
126	Mountamopus By - *0·2M S*	50°04'·40N	05°26'·20W
127	Penzance - *1·5M SE of and for Mousehole*	50°06'·00N	05°30'·00W
128	Tater Du Lt -*1·5M ESE*	50°02'·50N	05°32'·60W
129	Runnel Stone Lt By - *0·3M S*	50°00'·85N	05°40'·30W
130	Wolf Rk - *2M S of*	49°54'·65N	05°48'·50W
131	St Mary's, Scilly - *2M E of St Mary's Sound*	49°54'·00N	06°l 5'·00W
216	Treguier - *4·1M N of Pointe de Chateau*	48°56'·20N	03°14'·30W
220	Roscoff - *6M NNE of ent*	48°49'·10N	03°54'·30W
227	Ushant Creac'h Lt - *3·5M NW*	48°30'·00N	05°11'·30W

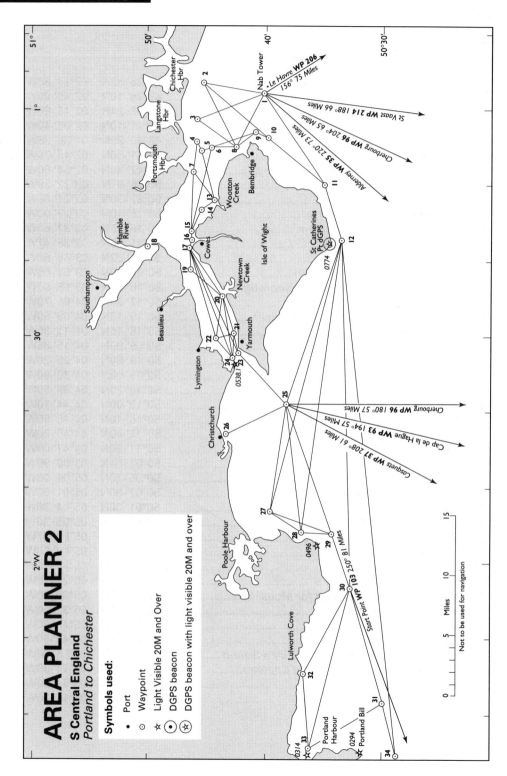

AREA PLANNER 2

2°W

S Central England
Portland to Chichester

Symbols used:

- • Port
- ⊙ Waypoint
- ☆ Light Visible 20M and Over
- ⊙ DGPS beacon
- ⊛ DGPS beacon with light visible 20M and over

Nab Tower

• Le Havre **WP 206** 156° 75 Miles

St Vaast **WP 214** 188° 66 Miles

Cherbourg **WP 96** 204° 65 Miles

Alderney **WP 35** 220° 73 Miles

Chichester Hbr

Langstone Hbr

Portsmouth Hbr

Wootton Creek

Bembridge

Hamble River

Cowes

Isle of Wight

Newtown Creek

St Catherines Pt dGPS
0774

Southampton

Beaulieu

Yarmouth

Lymington
0538.l

Christchurch

Cherbourg **WP 96** 180° 57 Miles

Cap de la Hague **WP 93** 194° 57 Miles

Casquets **WP 37** 208° 61 Miles

Poole Harbour

0496

Start Point **WP 103** 250° 81 Miles

Luworth Cove

Portland Harbour
0294 Portland Bill

0314

| 0 | 5 | 10 | 15 |
| | Miles | | |

Not to be used for navigation

51°

50'

1°

40'

50°30'

30'

AREA PLANNER 2

WAYPOINTS

England South Central - *Portland to Chichester*

1	Nab Tower - *0·5M NW of*	50°40'·38N	00°57'·55W
2	Chichester Bar Bn - *0·5M S of*	50°45'·38N	00°56'·37W
3	Langstone Fairway Buoy - *0·5M S of*	50°45'·78N	01°01'·27W
4	Main Passage - *Dolphin gap off Southsea*	50°45'·98N	01°04'·02W
5	Horse Sand Buoy - *Portsmouth ch*	50°45'·49N	01°05'·18W
6	Forts- *midway between the two*	50°44'·70N	01°05'·00W
7	Gilkicker Point - *0·3M S of*	50°46'·00N	01°08'·40W
8	Bembridge Tide Gauge	50°42'·43N	01°04'·93W
9	Bembridge Ledge Buoy	50°41'·12N	01°02'·72W
10	West Princessa Buoy - *S of Bembridge*	50°40'·12N	01°03'·58W
11	Dunnose Head - *1M off*	50°35'·00N	01°10'·00W
12	St Catherine's Point - *1M S of*	50°33'·52N	01°17'·80W
13	Wootton Beacon	50°44'·51N	01°12'·05W
14	Peel Bank Buoy - *east Solent*	50°45'·58N	01°13'·25W
15	Old Castle Point - *0·3M N of*	50°46'·30N	01°16'·50W
16	Cowes entrance	50°46'·20N	01°17'·85W
17	Egypt Point - *0·4M N of*	50°46'·20N	01°18'·70W
18	Hamble Point Buoy	50°50'·12N	01°18'·58W
19	Beaulieu Spit Beacon - *0·3M off*	50°46'·83N	01°21'·50W
20	Newtown - *0·5M NW of ent*	50°43'·87N	01°25'·20W
21	Yarmouth ent - *0·4M N of*	50°42'·80N	01°30'·00W
22	Lymington, Jack in the basket - *seaward mark*	50°44'·24N	01°30'·48W
23	Hurst Narrows - *midway*	50°42'·20N	01°32'·40W
24	Keyhaven - *0·2M E of entrance*	50°42'·80N	01°32'·80W
25	Fairway Buoy - *Needles channel*	50°38'·20N	01°38'·90W
26	Christchurch - *0·3M E of ent*	50°43'·44N	01°43'·80W
27	Poole Fairway Buoy - *1M E of*	50°38'·97N	01°53'·21W
28	Swanage - *0·7M NE of pier*	50°37'·00N	01°56'·00W
29	Anvil Point - *1·5M SE of*	50°34'·30N	01°56'·00W
30	St Albans Head - *1·5M S of*	50°33'·20N	02°03'·30W
31	East Shambles - *1M SE of*	50°30'·00N	02°18'·90W
32	Lulworth Cove - *0·1M S of ent*	50°36'·87N	02°14'·80W
33	Weymouth - *1M E of ent*	50°36'·60N	02°25'·00W
34	Portland Bill - *5M S of*	50°25'·82N	02°27'·30W
35	Alderney - Bray Harbour - *1M NNE of*	49°45'·00N	02°10'·75W
37	Casquets - *1M W of*	49°43'·38N	02°24'·06W
93	Cap de La Hague - *2M W of*	49°43'·37N	02°00'·00W
96	Cherbourg - *0·5M N of W ent*	49°40'·95N	01°39'·35W
103	Start Point - *2M S of*	50°11'·30N	03°38'·47W
206	Le Havre - *0·5M NE of Le Havre LHA*	49°32'·00N	00°09'·20W
214	St-Vaast-la-Hougue - *3·0 M ENE of entrance*	49°36'·40N	01°11'·00W

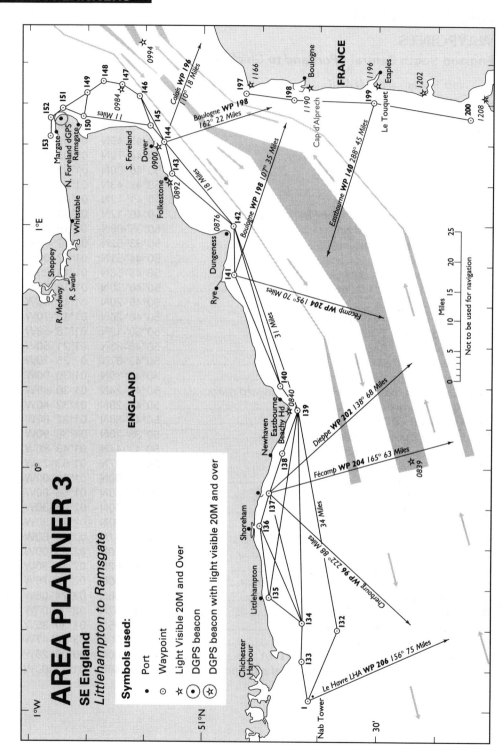

AREA PLANNER 3

SE England
Littlehampton to Ramsgate

Symbols used:

- Port
- Waypoint
- Light Visible 20M and Over
- DGPS beacon
- DGPS beacon with light visible 20M and over

Not to be used for navigation

AREA PLANNER 3
WAYPOINTS
England South East - *Littlehampton to Ramsgate*

1	Nab Tower - *0·5M NW of*	50°40'·38N	00°57'·55W
96	Cherbourg - *0·5M N of W entrance*	49°40'·95N	01°39'·35W
132	Owers - *0·5M S of*	50°36'·80N	00°40'·60W
133	Boulder Lt by - *0·1M N of*	50°41'·60N	00°49'·03W
134	East Borough Hd Lt By - *0·1M N of*	50°41'·60N	00°39'·00W
135	Littlehampton entrance - *1M 165°of on leading Lts*	50°47'·00N	00°32'·00W
136	Shoreham entrance - *1M S of on leading Lts*	50°48'·50N	00°l 4'·65W
137	Brighton entrance - *1M S of*	50°47'·50N	00°06'·30W
138	Newhaven entrance - *1M S of*	50°45'·50N	00°03'·60E
139	Beachy Hd - *1·5M S of*	50°42'·50N	00°14'·60W
140	Eastbourne - *1·2M SE of Langney Pt*	50°46'·25N	00°21'·10E
141	Rye - *0·1M S of Rye Fairway By*	50°53'·90N	00°48'·13E
142	Dungeness - *1M SE of*	50°54'·00N	00°59'·65E
143	Folkestone - *0·5M SE of breakwater*	51°04'·17N	01°l 2'·35E
144	Dover - *1·2M SE of Western entrance*	51°05'·80N	01°21'·10E
145	South Foreland - *2M E of*	51°08·70N	01°26'·25E
146	South Goodwin Lt By - *0·2M SE of*	51°l 0'·43N	01°32'·59E
147	East Goodwin Lt Float - *0·8M W of*	51°l 3'·23N	01°35'·20E
148	East Goodwin Lt By - *0·2M E of*	51°l 6'·00N	01°35'·92E
149	Goodwin Knoll - *1M SE of*	51°l 8'·84N	01°33'·43E
150	Ramsgate - *1M E of; and for Pegwell Bay*	51°l 9'·47N	01°27'·13E
151	North Foreland - *1M E of*	51°22'·50N	01°28'·70E
152	Foreness Pt - *1M NNE of*	51°24'·46N	01°26'·36E
153	Margate - *0·7M N of*	51°24'·10N	01°22'·50E
197	Cap Gris-Nez - *2·0 M NW of headland*	50°53'·30N	01°32'·50E
198	Boulogne - *2·0 M WNW of entrance*	50°45'·30N	01°31'·50E
199	Étaples - *3·0M W of Le Touquet point*	50°32'·20N	01°30'·80E
200	St Valéry-sur-Somme - *5M WNW Le Hourdel Pt*	50°15'·30N	01°27'·10E
202	Dieppe - *1M NW of entrance*	49°57'·00N	01°04'·00E
204	Fécamp - *1M NW of entrance*	49°46'·70N	00°20'·80E
206	Le Havre - *0·5M NE of Le Havre LHA*	49°32'·00N	00°09'·20W

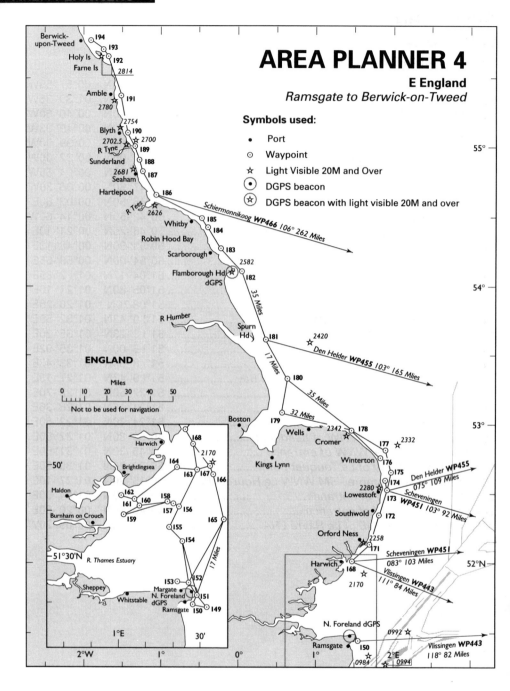

AREA PLANNER 4

E England
Ramsgate to Berwick-on-Tweed

Symbols used:

- • Port
- ⊙ Waypoint
- ☆ Light Visible 20M and Over
- ⊙̇ DGPS beacon
- ☆̇ DGPS beacon with light visible 20M and over

Berwick-upon-Tweed • 194
193
Holy Is ☆ 192
Farne Is 2814
Amble • ☆ 191
2780
2754
Blyth ☆ 190
2702.5 ☆ 2700
R Tyne 189
Sunderland • 188
2681 ☆ 187
Seaham
Hartlepool • 186
R Tees 2626
185
Schiermonnikoog **WP466** 106° 262 Miles
Whitby • 184
Robin Hood Bay •
Scarborough • 183
2582
Flamborough Hd ☆̇ 182
dGPS
35 Miles
R Humber
Spurn Hd 181
2420
☆ Den Helder **WP455** 103° 165 Mlies
17 Miles
ENGLAND
180
35 Miles
Miles
0 10 20 30 40 50
Not to be used for navigation
32 Miles
Boston •
179
Wells • 2342 178
Cromer • 177 2332
176
Winterton 175
Den Helder **WP455**
075° 109 Miles
174
2280 Scheveningen
Lowestoft ☆ 173 **WP451** 103° 92 Miles
Southwold • 172
Orford Ness •
2258
171
Scheveningen **WP451**
Harwich • 168 083° 103 Miles
☆ Vlissingen **WP443**
2170 111° 84 Miles

Kings Lynn •

55°

54°

53°

52°N

Harwich •
168
2170
Brightlingsea •
164
163 167 166
Maldon •
162
161 160 158
157 156
Burnham on Crouch •
159
155
154
165
17 Miles
51°30'N R. Thames Estuary
153 152
Margate •
Sheppey • N. Foreland 151
Whitstable • dGPS
Ramsgate 150 149
1°E
30'
2°W 1° 0°

N. Foreland dGPS
0992 ☆
Ramsgate • 150
0984 2°E
☆ 0994
Vlissingen **WP443**
118° 82 Miles
1°

AREA PLANNER 4
WAYPOINTS
England East - *Ramsgate to Berwick-on-Tweed*

149	Goodwin Knoll - *1M SE of*	51°18'·83N	01°33'·40E
150	Ramsgate -*1M E Pegwell Bay*	51°19'·47N	01°27'·13E
151	North Foreland - *1M E*	51°22'·50N	01°28'·70E
152	Foreness Pt - *1M NNE of*	51°24'·46N	01°26'·36E
153	Margate - *0·7M N of*	51°24'·10N	01°22'·50E
154	Fisherman's Gat - *SE turning waypoint*	51°33'·30N	01°25'·00E
155	Fisherman's Gat - *NW turning waypoint*	51°36'·30N	01°20'·70E
156	Black Deep/Sunk Sand - *turning waypoint*	51°40'·94N	01°25'·00E
157	Barrow No 2 Lt By - *0·3M NE*	51°42'·16N	01°23'·34E
158	Barrow No 3 Lt By - *0·3M N*	51°42'·29N	01°20'·35E
159	Whitaker channel - *for River Crouch (6M)*	51°40'·40N	01°05'·30E
160	Swin Spitway Lt By - *0·1M SSW*	51°41'·83N	01°08'·36E
161	Spitway North - *turning waypt*	51°43'·70N	01°07'·10E
162	Colne,Blackwater - *0·3M W Eagle Lt By*	51°44'·10N	01°03'·43E
163	NE Gunfleet Lt By - *0·5M NW of*	51°50'·25N	01°27'·35E
164	Medusa Lt By - *0·3M SW of*	51°51'·00N	01°20'·00E
165	Kentish Knock Lt By - *0·2M E*	51°38'·50N	01°40'·80E
166	Trinity Lt By - *0·6M N of*	51°49'·65N	01°36'·45E
167	Sunk Lt F - *0·2M SW of*	51°50'·87N	01°34'·80E
168	Cork Lt By - *1M E Harwich Yt ch ent*	51°55'·35N	01°29'·00E
171	Orfordness - *1·5M ESE of*	52°04'·20N	01°37'·00E
172	Southwold - *2M ESE of ent*	52°18'·00N	01°43'·70E
173	Lowestoft - *2·8M E of ent*	52°28'·30N	01°50'·10E
174	Gt Yarmouth - *0·5M WNW of S Corton SCM*	52°32'·07N	01°49'·36E
175	Gt Yarmouth - *4·7M E of ent*	52°34'·33N	01°52'·10E
176	Winterton - *0·5M NE Cockle ECM*	52°44'·40N	01°44'·20E
177	Winterton - *5·2M NE of*	52°46'·90N	01°48'·50E
178	Cromer - *3·0M NNE of Lt*	52°58'·15N	01°21'·20E
179	North Well Lt By - *0·5M NE*	53°03'·35N	00°28'·60E
180	Inner Dowsing Lt By - *0·5M NE of*	53°20'·10N	00°34'·50E
181	Spurn Head - *2·6M E of Spurn Lightship*	53°34'·80N	00°17'·70E
182	Flamborough Head - *2·0 M E*	54°07'·10N	00°01'·10W
183	Scarborough - *1·0M E of ent*	54°16'·87N	00°21'·56W
184	Robin Hood's Bay - *2·6M NE*	54°26'·40N	00°27'·30W
185	Whitby - *1·6M N of ent*	54°31'·10N	00°36'·60W
186	River Tees - *Fairway Buoy*	54°40'·93N	01°06'·38W
187	Seaham - *0·9M E of ent*	54°50'·40N	01°17'·70W
188	Sunderland - *1·7M E of ent*	54°55'·25N	01°18'·10W
189	R Tyne - *1·7 M E by N of ent*	55°01'·15N	01°21'·10W
190	Blyth - *1·5M E of entrance*	55°07'·00N	01°26'·50W
191	Amble - *2·5M NE of ent*	55°21'·85N	01°30'·70W
192	Farne Island - *2·0 M NE of Longstone Lt*	55°40'·00N	01°33'·95W
193	Holy Island - *1·0M NE of Emmanuel Hd*	55°41'·95N	01°45'·50W
194	Berwick-upon-Tweed - *1·5M E of Breakwater*	55°45'·90N	01°56'·30W
443	Breskens/Vlissingen - *1·4M NE Niewe Sluis Lt*	51°25'·50N	03°32'·80E
451	Scheveningen - *0·7M NW harbour ent*	52°07'·00N	04°14'·80E
455	Den Helder - *1·2M S Kijkduin Lt*	52°56'·90N	04°41'·90E
458	Noorderhaaks Is - *3·2M WSW*	52°57'·30N	04°33'·70E
466	Ameland - *2·9M NNW E end*	53°30'·40N	06°00'·00E

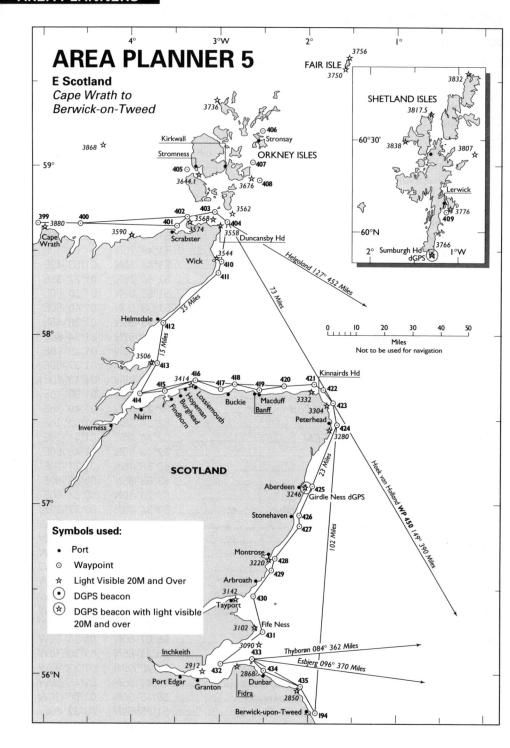

AREA PLANNER 5

E Scotland
Cape Wrath to Berwick-on-Tweed

FAIR ISLE
3756
3750

SHETLAND ISLES
3832
3817.5

60°30'
3838
3807

Kirkwall
Stronsay
406

ORKNEY ISLES
407

Stromness
3868
405
3644.1
3676
408

Lerwick
3776
409

59°

60°N

2° Sumburgh Hd
dGPS
3766
1°W

399   400
3880
Cape
Wrath
3590
402 403
401 3568 3562
3574 404
Scrabster 3558 Duncansby Hd

Helgoland 127° 452 Miles

Wick
3544
410
411

73 Miles

0   10   20   30   40   50
Miles
Not to be used for navigation

Helmsdale
412

25 Miles

15 Miles

58°

3506
413

3414 416
415 418
417 419 420 421
414 Lossiemouth 422
Nairn Hopeman Buckie Macduff 3332
Burghead Banff
Findhorn 3304
Peterhead 423
424
3280

Kinnairds Hd

Inverness

SCOTLAND

Hoek van Holland WP 450 149° 390 Miles

23 Miles

Aberdeen 425
3246 Girdle Ness dGPS

57°

Stonehaven 426
427

102 Miles

Symbols used:

- • Port
- ⊙ Waypoint
- ☆ Light Visible 20M and Over
- ⊙ DGPS beacon
- ⍟ DGPS beacon with light visible 20M and over

Montrose 428
3220 429

Arbroath
3142
430
Tayport

Fife Ness
3102 431

Inchkeith
3090 433

Thyborøn 084° 362 Miles
Esbjerg 096° 370 Miles

2912 432 434
56°N
Port Edgar 2868 435
Granton Dunbar
Fidra
2850

Berwick-upon-Tweed 194

AREA PLANNER 5

WAYPOINTS

Scotland East - *Cape Wrath to Berwick-upon- Tweed*

194	Berwick-upon - Tweed - *1·5M E*	55°45'·90N	01°56'·30W
399	Cape Wrath - *2M NW of*	58°38'·90N	05°02'·80W
400	Whiten Head - *4·4M N of*	58°39'·20N	04°34'·90W
401	Scrabster - *1·4M NE of Holborn Hd*	58°38'·60N	03°30'·70W
402	Dunnet Head Lt -*1·7M NW of*	58°41'·60N	03°24'·30W
403	Pentl'd Firth - *1·5M NE by N Stroma*	58°43'·00N	03°05'·40W
404	Duncansby Head - *2M NE of*	58°39'·80N	02°58'·40W
405	Stromness - *2·8M NW Graemsay Lt.*	58°57'·10N	03°23'·70W
406	Stronsay - *0·8M NW Ness Lt.*	59°10'·00N	02°35'·80W
407	Kirkwall - *1·5M NW of Mull Hd*	58°59'·40N	02°40'·40W
408	Copinsay Lt - *2·5M E of*	58°54'·10N	02°35'·10W
409	Lerwick - *1·1M SW of Bressay Lt*	60°06'·60N	01°08'·60W
410	Wick - *1·6M E of South Hd*	58°25'·80N	03°01'·00W
411	Scarlet Hd - *2M E by S*	58°21'·90N	03°02'·50W
412	Helmsdale - *1·8M SE of ent*	58°05'·50N	03°36'·80W
413	Tarbat Ness Lt - *2M E of*	57°51'·80N	03°42'·70W
414	Inverness - *0·5 NE of Frwy By*	57°40'·30N	03°53'·30W
415	Findhorn - *2·2M NW of bay*	57°41'·45N	03°40'·00W
416	Lossiemouth - *1·7M N*	57°45'·20N	03°16'·70W
417	Buckie - *2·0M WNW*	57°41'·70N	03°00'·90W
418	Scar Nose - *1·6M N*	57°44'·00N	02°50'·90W
419	Banff - *1·3M N of Meavie Pt*	57°41'·60N	02°31'·40W
420	Troup Head - *1·8M N*	57°43'·50N	02°17'·70W
421	Kinnairds Head - *1·6M N*	57°43'·50N	02°00'·20W
422	Cairnbulg Point Lt - *1·9M NE*	57°42'·20N	01°53'·70W
423	Rattray Head Lt - *1·8M ENE*	57°37'·40N	01°45'·90W
424	Peterhead - *2·1M ESE*	57°29'·30N	01°42'·60W
425	Aberdeen - *2M E by N Girdle Ness*	57°08'·80N	01°59'·00W
426	Stonehaven - *2M E*	56°57'·60N	02°08'·20W
427	Todhead Point Lt - *2·5M E*	56°53'·10N	02°08'·30W
428	Montrose - *2·1M E Scurdie Ness Lt*	56°42'·10N	02°22'·40W
429	Red Head - *1·8M E of*	56°37'·40N	02°25'·30W
430	Tayport - *0·5M E Fairway By*	56°29'·25N	02°37'·24W
431	Fife Ness - *2·8M ESE*	56°15'·95N	02°30'·30W
432	Granton - *0·5M N Inchkeith By*	56°04'·00N	03°00'·00W
433	Bass Rock Lt - *1·5M N*	56°06'·10N	02°38'·40W
434	Dunbar - *1·5M NNE*	56°01'·76N	02°30'·20W
435	St Abb's Head Lt - *1·5M NE*	55°56'·10N	02°06'·40W
450	Hoek van Holland - *1·2M WNW*	51°59'·90N	04°01'·00E

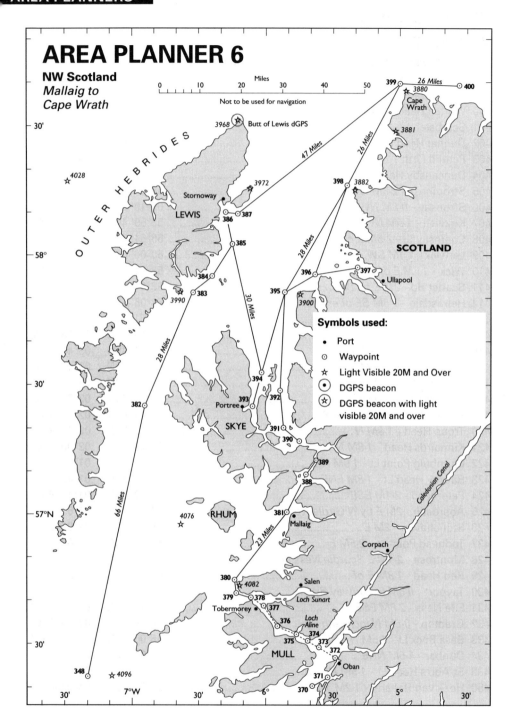

AREA PLANNER 6

NW Scotland
Mallaig to
Cape Wrath

Miles

0   10   20   30   40   50

Not to be used for navigation

399   26 Miles   400
☆ 3880
Cape
Wrath

3968 (★) Butt of Lewis dGPS

☆ 3881

47 Miles

26 Miles

☆ 4028

3972

398   3882 ☆

Stornoway

LEWIS   ⊙387
386

O U T E R   H E B R I D E S

385

28 Miles

SCOTLAND

58°

384   ⊙
383

3990

396   ⊙397
• Ullapool

395
☆
3900

30 Miles

Symbols used:

- Port
⊙ Waypoint
☆ Light Visible 20M and Over
⊙ DGPS beacon
(★) DGPS beacon with light
visible 20M and over

28 Miles

30'

394

393   392
Portree •

SKYE   391

382 ⊙

390

389

388

57°N

66 Miles

4076
☆

RHUM

381 •
Mallaig

Caledonian Canal

23 Miles

Corpach

380 ⊙
☆ 4082   Salen •

379   ⊙378
Tobermorey •   377   Loch Sunart

376   Loch
Aline
374
375   373

30'

MULL   372
• Oban

348 ⊙   ☆ 4096   371 ⊙

370 ⊙

30'   7°W   30'   6°   30'   5°   30'

AREA PLANNER 6
WAYPOINTS
Scotland North West - *Mallaig to Cape Wrath*

348	Skerryvore Lt - *6·8M W by N of*	56°20'·80N	07°18'·80W
370	Sound of Insh - *1M SSW of Insh Island*	56°17'·60N	05°41'·00W
371	Kerrera Sound - *0·7M SSW of Rubha Seanach*	56°21'·70N	05°33'·90W
372	Oban - *0·5M WNW of Maiden Isle*	56°26'·00N	05°30'·30W
373	Between Lady's Rock and Eilean Musdile	56°27'·20N	05°36'·70W
374	Sound of Mull - *1·6M SE of Ardtornish Pt*	56°30'·15N	05°42'·75W
375	Loch Aline - *0·7M S by W of entrance*	56°31'·30N	05°46'·80W
376	Sound of Mull - *1·8M N of Salen*	56°33'·00N	05°56'·30W
377	Tobermory - *0·9M NE of harbour entrance*	56°38'·40N	06°02'·40W
378	Ardmore Point (Mull) - *0·7M N of*	56°40'·00N	06°07'·60W
379	Point of Ardnamurchan - *2·8M S of*	56°40'·90N	06°13'·30W
380	Point of Ardnamurchan - *1·3M W of*	56°43'·60N	06°15'·90W
381	Mallaig - *1·5 miles WNW of harbour entrance*	57°01'·00N	05°52'·10W
382	Neist Point Lt - *4·0M W of*	57°25'·45N	06°54'·50W
383	Sound of Shiant - *2·2M E of Eilean Glas Lt Ho*	57°51'·20N	06°34'·40W
384	Sound of Shiant - *0·3M NW of Shiants Lt By*	57°54'·80N	06°26'·00W
385	Kebock Head - *2·3M E of*	58°02'·40N	06°17'·00W
386	Stornoway - *1·2M SE of harbour entrance*	58°10'·30N	06°20'·60W
387	Chicken Head - *1·2M S of*	58°09'·80N	06°15'·10W
388	Sandaig Islands Lt - *0·6M W by N of*	57°10'·25N	05°43'·20W
389	Kyle Rhea (S appr) - *0·6M W of Glenelg*	57°12'·75N	05°38'·80W
390	Loch Alsh (W appr) - *1·0M NW of entrance*	57°17'·20N	05°46'·10W
391	Crowlin Islands - *1·5 M W of*	57°20'·70N	05°53'·80W
392	Inner Sound - *1·7M E Rubha Ard Ghlaisen*	57°29'·55N	05°55'·50W
393	Portree - *1·8M E of town*	57°25'·00N	06°08'·00W
394	Sd of Raasay - *3·1M SE of Rubha nam Brathairean*	57°33'·30N	06°03'·80W
395	Rubha Reidh - *3·0M W of*	57°51'·60N	05°54'·40W
396	Greenstone Point - *1·6M NW of*	57°56'·60N	05°39'·20W
397	Ullapool - *1·7M NE of Cailleach Head Lt*	57°56'·90N	05°21'·80W
398	Stoerhead Lt - *2M NW of*	58°15'·80N	05°26'·80W
399	Cape Wrath - *2M NW of*	58°38'·90N	05°02'·80W
400	Whiten Head - *4·4M N of*	58°39'·20N	04°34'·90W

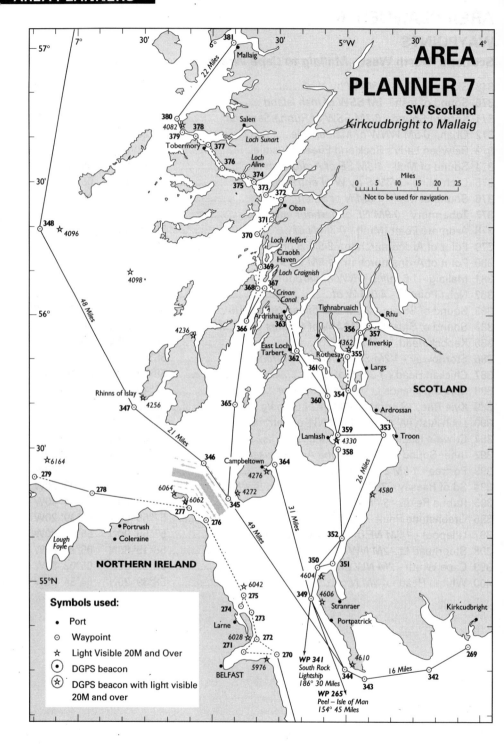

AREA PLANNER 7
SW Scotland
Kirkcudbright to Mallaig

Miles
0   5   10   15   20   25
Not to be used for navigation

SCOTLAND

NORTHERN IRELAND

Symbols used:
- Port
- ⊙ Waypoint
- ☆ Light Visible 20M and Over
- ⊙ DGPS beacon
- ⊛ DGPS beacon with light visible 20M and over

WP 341
South Rock
Lightship
186° 30 Miles

WP 265
Peel – Isle of Man
154° 45 Miles

AREA PLANNER 7

WAYPOINTS

Scotland South West - *Kirkcudbright to Mallaig*

265	Peel - *1·0M NW Hbr ent*	54°14'·50N	04°42'·50W
269	Kirkcudbright - *1·5M S Little Ross Lt*	54°44'·50N	04°05'·00W
270	Mew Island Lt - *1·3M ENE*	54°42'·30N	05°29'·90W
271	Belfast - *0·7M ENE No.1 SHM*	54°42'·00N	05°45'·20W
272	Black Head Lt - *1·3M ENE*	54°46'·50N	05°39'·20W
273	Isle of Muck - *1·1M NE*	54°51'·70N	05°41'·85W
274	Larne Lough - *1M N of Barr's Pt*	54°52'·50N	05°46'·80W
275	East Maiden Lt - *1·7M SW*	54°54'·50N	05°45'·50W
276	Torr Head - *0·6M ENE of*	55°12'·20N	06°02'·80W
277	Fair Head - *0·9M N of*	55°14'·60N	06°09'·00W
278	Lough Foyle - *4·8M NNE Inishowen Hd Lt*	55°17'·90N	06°52'·20W
279	Malin Head - *2·0M NNE*	55°25'·00N	07°21'·20W
341	South Rock Lt V - *1·1M E of*	54°24'·30N	05°20'·00W
342	Burrow Head - *2·0 M S of*	54°38'·70N	04°23'·00W
343	Mull of Galloway Lt - *1·7M S of*	54°36'·40N	04°51'·50W
344	Crammag Head Lt - *1·8M SW of*	54°38'·60N	05°00'·00W
345	Mull of Kintyre Lt - *2·5M SW of*	55°16'·90N	05°51'·30W
346	Mull of Kintyre Lt - *10·3M NW of*	55°25'·50N	06°01'·50W
347	Rhinns of Islay Lt - *2·2M SW of*	55°38'·85N	06°33'·50W
348	Skerryvore Lt - *6·8M W by N of*	56°20'·80N	07°18'·80W
349	Killantringan Lt - *4·2M NW of*	54°54'·20N	05°14'·70W
350	Corsewall Pt Lt - *1·8M WNW of*	55°01'·20N	05°12'·20W
351	Stranraer - *1·0M NNW ent to Loch Ryan*	55°02'·40N	05°05'·10W
352	Bennane Head - *1·5M NW of*	55°09'·25N	05°01'·80W
353	Troon - *2·1M W of harbour ent*	55°33'·10N	04°44'·70W
354	Little Cumbrae Island Lt - *0·8M SW of*	55°42'·75N	04°59'·00W
355	Rothesay - *Ent to Rothesay Sound*	55°50'·90N	04°59'·60W
356	Firth of Clyde, Cloch Point Lt - *1·3M WSW of*	55°55'·95N	04°54'·75W
357	R. Clyde, Kempock Point - *0·9M WNW of*	55°58'·10N	04°50'·50W
358	Lamlash - *1·0M SE of S ent*	55°29'·80N	05°03'·60W
359	Lamlash - *1·0M E of N ent*	55°32'·90N	05°03'·00W
360	Isle of Arran - *2·0M NNE of Sannox Bay*	55°41'·60N	05°08'·00W
361	West Kyle - *1·0M E Lamont Shelf IDM*	55°48'·35N	05°11'·80W
362	East Loch Tarbert - *1·0 E of Loch*	55°52'·20N	05°22'·00W
363	Ardrishaig - *1·3 SSE of hbr ent*	55°59'·50N	05°25'·60W
364	Campbeltown - *1·0 NE of Loch ent*	55°26'·40N	05°31'·00W
365	Gigha Island - *1·5M W of Cath Sgeir WCM*	55°39'·70N	05°50'·00W
366	Sound of Jura - *2·5M NW of Island of Danna*	55°58'·80N	05°45'·50W
367	Loch Crinan - *0·6M NW of Ardnoe Point*	56°06'·00N	05°35'·40W
368	Sound of Jura - *2·0M SSW Reisa an t-Sruith I. Lt*	56°06'·00N	05°39'·90W
369	Sound of Luing - *0·5M WSW of Ardluing SHM By*	56°11'·00N	05°39'·40W
370	Sound of Insh - *1M SSW of Insh Island*	56°17'·60N	05°41'·00W
371	Kerrera Sound - *0·7M SSW of Rubha Seanach*	56°21'·70N	05°33'·90W
372	Oban - *0·5M WNW of Maiden Isle*	56°26'·00N	05°30'·30W
373	Between Lady's Rock and Eilean Musdile	56°27'·20N	05°36'·70W
374	Sound of Mull - *1·6M SE of Ardtornish Point*	56°30'·15N	05°42'·75W
375	Loch Aline - *0·7M S by W of ent*	56°31'·30N	05°46'·80W
376	Sound of Mu - *1·8M N of Salen*	56°33'·00N	05°56'·30W
377	Tobermory - *0·9M NE of hbr ent*	56°38'·40N	06°02'·40W
378	Ardmore Pt (Mull) - *0·7M N of*	56°40'·00N	06°07'·60W
379	Pt of Ardnamurchan - *2·8M S*	56°40'·90N	06°13'·30W
380	Pt of Ardnamurchan - *1·3M W*	56°43'·60N	06°15'·90W
381	Mallaig - *1·5M WNW of hbr ent*	57°01'·00N	05°52'·10W

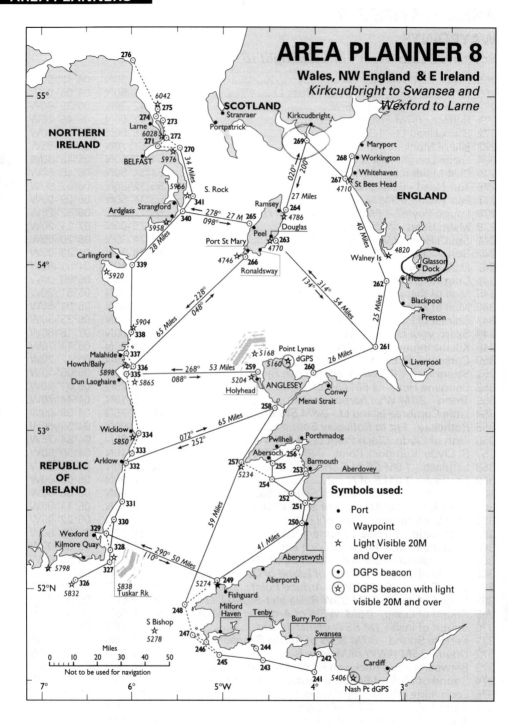

AREA PLANNER 8
Wales, NW England & E Ireland
Kirkcudbright to Swansea and Wexford to Larne

276

6042
☆ 275
274
Larne • 6028 273
271 272
BELFAST 5976
270
34 Miles
5966
341
Strangford
Ardglass 340
5958
278° 27 M
098°
28 Miles
339
Carlingford
☆5920

SCOTLAND
Stranraer
Portpatrick
Kirkcudbright
269
020°
200°
Maryport
268 Workington
Whitehaven
267 St Bees Head
4710

NORTHERN
IRELAND

ENGLAND

S. Rock
Ramsey
264
☆4786
265
Peel
Douglas
Port St Mary
Port St Mary ☆263
4770
4746 ☆266
Ronaldsway

27 Miles

40 Miles

Walney Is
4820
Glasson
Dock
262
Fleetwood
Blackpool
Preston

54 Miles

25 Miles

228°
048°
65 Miles

134°
314°

5904
338
Malahide 337
Howth/Baily 336
5898 335
Dun Laoghaire ☆5865

☆5168
Point Lynas
dGPS
5160 ☆
260
268° 53 Miles 259
088°
5204 ☆
Holyhead
ANGLESEY
258
Menai Strait
Conwy

26 Miles

261
Liverpool

072°
252°
65 Miles

Wicklow
☆334
5850
333
Arklow 332
Pwllheli Porthmadog
Abersoch 256
257 255
5234 253
254
252
251
250

Barmouth
Aberdovey

REPUBLIC
OF
IRELAND

331
330
329
Wexford
Kilmore Quay 328
☆5798
327
326
☆5832 5838
Tuskar Rk

290° 50 Miles
110°
59 Miles
41 Miles

Aberystwyth
5274 ☆ 249
Fishguard
248
S Bishop
☆5278
247
246
245
243
241 5406 ☆
Nash Pt dGPS

Aberporth

Milford
Haven
Tenby
244
Burry Port
Swansea
242
Cardiff

Symbols used:

- • Port
- ⊙ Waypoint
- ☆ Light Visible 20M and Over
- ⦿ DGPS beacon
- ⊛ DGPS beacon with light visible 20M and over

Miles
0 10 20 30 40 50
Not to be used for navigation

55°
54°
53°
52°N
7°   6°   5°W   4°   3°

AREA PLANNER 8

WAYPOINTS

NW England, Wales & E Ireland - *Kirkcudbright to Swansea*

241 Ledge SCM - *2M S*	51°28'·00N	03°58'·60W
242 Swansea - *1M SE Mumbles Hd*	51°33'·40N	03°57'·00W
243 Caldey Island - *7M SE*	51°32'·20N	04°35'·20W
244 Tenby - *1M SE Caldey Is*	51°37'·20N	04°39'·60W
245 Crow Rock - *1·3M S of*	51°35'·40N	05°03'·50W
246 Milford Haven - *1·1M S St Ann's Hd*	51°39'·70N	05°10'·60W
247 Skokholm Is Lt - *1·6M W of*	51°41'·60N	05°19'·70W
248 South Bishop Is Lt - *3·0M NW of*	51°53'·30N	05°27'·80W
249 Fishguard - *1·5M N Strumble Hd*	52°03'·40N	05°04'·20W
250 Aberystwyth - *1·5M W*	52°24'·40N	04°08'·00W
251 Aberdovey - *1·5M W of hbr bar*	52°31'·70N	04°07'·10W
252 Sarn-y-Bwch WCM - *1·1M W*	52°34'·80N	04°15'·10W
253 Barmouth - *1·2M W of hbr bar*	52°42'·60N	04°05'·60W
254 Causeway WCM - *2M SW*	52°39'·90N	04°28'·00W
255 Abersoch - *1·2M SE St Tudwal's Is Lt*	52°47'·20N	04°26'·80W
256 Porthmadog - *1·1M SW Frwy By*	52°52'·70N	04°12'·50W
257 Bardsey Island light - *4M NNW*	52°48'·60N	04°50'·30W
258 Menai Strait - *1·4M SW Llanddwyn Is*	53°07'·30N	04°26'·80W
259 Holyhead - *1M N of W Bkwtr*	53°21'·00N	04°37'·00W
260 Menai Strait - *1·2M N of Puffin Is*	53°20'·50N	04°01'·50W
261 Liverpool - *0·7M S of Bar Lt V*	53°31'·30N	03°20'·90W
262 Fleetwood - *2M SW Lune Dp By*	53°54'·10N	03°13'·00W
263 Douglas - *1·1M W of Douglas Hd*	54°08'·70N	04°26'·00W
264 Ramsey - *1·3M ENE of S bkwtr*	54°19'·90N	04°20'·20W
265 Peel - *1M NW entrance*	54°14'·50N	04°42'·50W
266 Pt St Mary - *1·2M S of Kallow Pt*	54°02'·90N	04°43'·80W
267 St Bees Head Lt - *2M W of*	54°30'·80N	03°41'·50W
268 Workington - *1M WNW of bkwtr*	54°39'·40N	03°36'·30W
269 Kirkcudbright - *1·5M S Little Ross Lt*	54°44'·50N	04°05'·00W
270 Mew Island Lt - *1·3M ENE*	54°42'·30N	05°29'·90W
271 Belfast - *0·7M ENE No.1 SHM*	54°42'·00N	05°45'·20W
272 Black Head Lt - *1·3M ENE*	54°46'·50N	05°39'·20W
273 Isle of Muck - *1·1M NE*	54°51'·70N	05°41'·85W
274 Larne Lough - *1M N of Barr's pt*	54°52'·50N	05°46'·80W
275 East Maiden Lt - *1·7M SW*	54°54'·50N	05°45'·50W
276 Torr Head - *0·6M ENE of*	55°12'·20N	06°02'·80W
326 Coningbeg Lt - *0·4M N of*	52°02'·80N	06°39'·30W
327 Carnsore Point - *3·2M ESE of*	52°09'·40N	06°16'·40W
328 Greenore Point - *1·8M E of*	52°14'·70N	06°15'·90W
329 Wexford - *1·6M E of entrance*	52°20'·50N	06°19.30'W
330 W Blackwater Pt - *0·4M W of*	52°25'·80N	06°14'·00W
331 Cahore Point - *1·7MSE of*	52°32'·50N	06°09'·90W
332 Arklow - *1·2M E by S*	52°47'·40N	06°06'·40W
333 Mizen Head (E coast) - *1M ESE*	52°51'·00N	06°01'·90W
334 Wicklow - *2·6M E of*	52°58'·90N	05°57'·80W
335 Dun Laoghaire - *2·2M NE of*	53°19'·60N	06°04'·60W
336 Ben of Howth - *1·4M E of*	53°22'·40N	06°00'·50W
337 Malahide - *1·5M E of Bar*	53°27'·00N	06°04'·80W
338 Rockabill Lt - *1·2M WSW*	53°35'·30N	06°02'·00W
339 Carlingford Lough	53°58'·40N	06°00'·00W
340 Strangford Lough	54°18'·40N	05°27'·70W
341 South Rock Lt V - *1·1M E of*	54°24'·30N	05°20'·00W

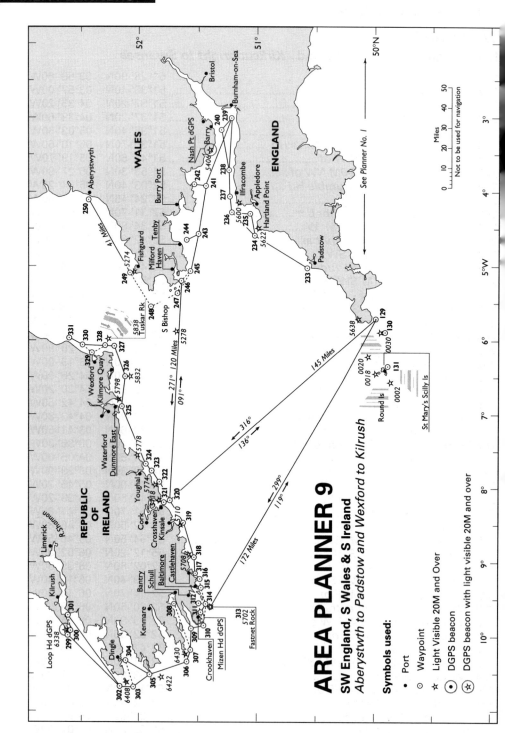

AREA PLANNER 9

SW England, S Wales & S Ireland
Aberystwyth to Padstow and Wexford to Kilrush

Symbols used:

- • Port
- ⊙ Waypoint
- ☆ Light Visible 20M and Over
- ⊙ DGPS beacon
- ⊛ DGPS beacon with light visible 20M and over

AREA planner 9

WAYPOINTS

SW England, S Wales and S Ireland - *Aberystwyth to Padstow*

129	Runnel Stone Lt By - *0·3M S of*	50°00'·85N	05°40'·30W
130	Wolf Rk Lt - *2M S of*	49°54'·65N	05°48'·50W
131	St Mary's, Scilly - *2M E of St Mary's*	49°54'·00N	06°I 5.00'W
233	Padstow - *2M NW of Stepper Point*	50°35'·70N	04°59'·10W
234	Hartland Point - *2·5M NW of*	51°02'·80N	04°34'·40W
235	River Taw - *1·6M NW Bideford By*	51°06'·20N	04°18'·20W
236	Morte Point - *2·5M NNW of*	51°13'·60N	04°15'·80W
237	Ilfracombe - *1·5M N*	51°14'·20N	04°06'·80W
238	Foreland Point - *1·5 miles N*	51°16'·20N	03°47'·20W
239	Burnham on Sea - *2·6M N*	51°15'·30N	03°07'·80W
240	Barry & R. Severn - *2·9M SSW ent*	51°21'·00N	03°17'·30W
241	Ledge SCM By - *2M S of*	51°28'·00N	03°58'·60W
242	Swansea - *1M SE Mumbles Hd*	51°33'·40N	03°57'·00W
243	Caldey Island - *7 miles SE*	51°32'·20N	04°35'·20W
244	Tenby - *1M SE Caldey Island*	51°37'·20N	04°39'·60W
245	Crow Rock - *1·3M S of*	51°35'·40N	05°03'·50W
246	Milford Haven - *1·1M S St Ann's Hd*	51°39'·70N	05°10'·60W
247	Skokholm Island Lt - *1·6M W of*	51°41'·60N	05°19'·70W
248	South Bishop Is Lt - *3·0M NW*	51°53'·30N	05°27'·80W
249	Fishguard - *1·5M N Strumble Hd*	52°03'·40N	05°04'·20W
250	Aberystwyth - *1·6M W of ent*	52°24'·40N	04°08'·00W
299	Loop Head Lt - *1·6M W of*	52°33'·70N	09°58'·60W
300	Loop Head Lt - *1·4 miles S of*	52°32'·30N	09°55'·80W
301	Kilrush - *0·9M S of Kilcredaun Lt*	52°33'·90N	09°42'·50W
302	Tearaght Island Lt - *2·5M NW*	52°06'·20N	10°42'·50W
303	Great Foze Rock - *1·8M SW*	52°00'·00N	10°43'·20W
304	Dingle - *1·2M S of Reenbeg Point*	52°05'·60N	10°15'·80W
305	Bray Head - *1·4M W of*	51°52'·80N	10°28'·00W
306	The Bull Island Lt - *1·7M SW*	51°34'·30N	10°20'·10W
307	Crow Head - *1·9MS of*	51°32'·90N	10°09'·40W
308	Bantry - *0·8M SW Whiddy Island*	51°40'·00N	09°32'·80W
309	Sheep's Head Lt - *1·5M W of*	51°32'·30N	09°53'·40W
310	Mizen Head Lt (SW) - *2M SSW*	51°25'·00N	09°50'·30W
311	Crookhaven - *1M ESE Streek Hd*	51°27'·80N	09°40'·30W
312	Schull - *1M S of Long Island Lt*	51°29'·20N	09°32'·00W
313	The Fastnet Rock Lt	51°23'·33N	09°36'·16W
314	Cape Clear - *1·6M SW of*	51°24'·20N	09°32'·90W
315	Baltimore - *1·5M S harbour ent*	51°26'·90N	09°23'·50W
316	Toe Head - *1·5M S of*	51°27'·40N	09°13'·00W
317	Castle Haven - *1M SE of ent*	51°30.30'N	09°09.80'W
318	Galley Head - *1·4M S of*	51°30'·40N	08°57'·20W
319	Old Hd of Kinsale Lt - *1·5M SSE*	51°34'·90N	08°30'·80W
320	Cork Landfall By - *0·4M E of*	51°43'·00N	08°14'·80W
321	Roche's Point Lt - *1·2M S of*	51°46'·40N	08°15'·40W
322	Ballycotton Island Lt - *1·2M S*	51°48'·40N	07°58'·80W
323	Youghal, S - *IM SE Capel Island*	51°52'·40N	07°50'·00W
324	Youghal, SE - *2M SE Blackball PHB*	51°54'·80N	07°45'·60W
325	Waterford - *1·4M SSE Dunmore E*	52°07'·40N	06°58'·80W
326	Coningbeg Lt V - *2·4M N of*	52°02'·80N	06°39'·30W
327	Carnsore Point - *3·2M ESE of*	52°09'·40N	06°16'·40W
328	Greenore Point - *1·8M E of*	52°14'·70N	06°15'·90W
329	Wexford - *1·6M E of entrance*	52°20'·50N	06°19'·30W
330	W Blackwater Pt Mk - *0·4M W*	52°25'·80N	06°14'·00W
331	Cahore Point - *1·7 miles SE of*	52°32'·50N	06°09'·90W

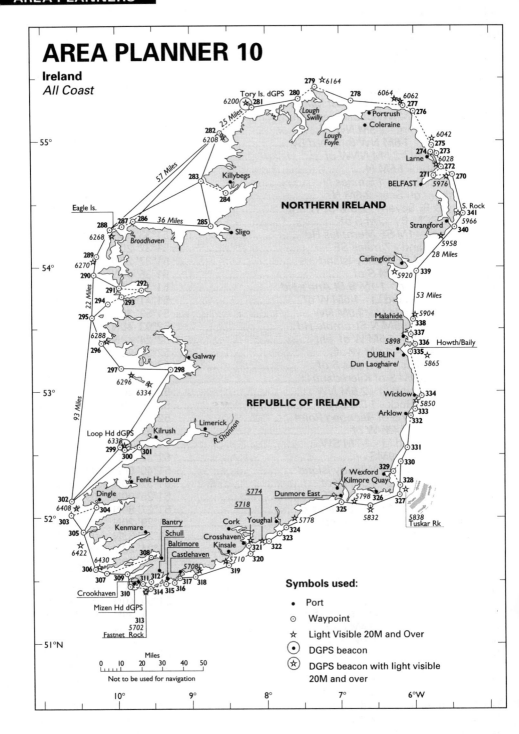

AREA PLANNER 10

Ireland
All Coast

279 ☆6164
Tory Is. dGPS 280   278   6064   6062
6200 ☆281   6028☆277
                                              Ø276
                        Lough   Portrush
                        Swilly   ● Coleraine
282
6208
                        Lough   6042
                        Foyle   Ø275
                                              274Ø273
                                          Larne● 6028
57 Miles   271Ø272
283   Killybegs   BELFAST● 5976 270
284
                    NORTHERN IRELAND   S. Rock
Eagle Is.   ☆341
288 287 286 36 Miles 285   5966
6268 ☆   Broadhaven   ● Sligo   Strangford● 340
289   5958
6270☆   28 Miles
290   Carlingford
      292   ☆5920 Ø339
291
294   53 Miles
      293
295
6288   Malahide ☆5904
296   Ø338
                                                 Ø337
297   298   ● Galway   5898 Ø336 Howth/Baily
6296 ☆   Ø335
     6334   DUBLIN   5865
                            Dun Laoghaire/
REPUBLIC OF IRELAND
                    Limerick   Wicklow● Ø334
Loop Hd dGPS   Kilrush   ☆5850
633B   ● R.Shannon   Arklow● 333
299   Ø332
300   301
                                          Ø331
         ● Fenit Harbour   Ø330
                            Wexford● 329
302   Kilmore Quay● Ø328
6408   ● Dingle   5774 Dunmore East 5798 Ø326
304   5718   325 Ø327
303   Cork Youghal 5832
305   Kenmare Bantry   ☆5778   5838
6422 ☆   Schull   Crosshaven● 324   Tuskar Rk
6430   Baltimore Kinsale 323
306   Castlehaven ●321 322
307 309 311 312   5708 320
   310   314 315 316 317 318 319
Crookhaven   5710
   Mizen Hd dGPS
      313
      5702
   Fastnet Rock

Symbols used:

● Port

⊙ Waypoint

☆ Light Visible 20M and Over

⊙ DGPS beacon

☆ DGPS beacon with light visible 20M and over

Miles
0 10 20 30 40 50
Not to be used for navigation

AREA planner 10
WAYPOINTS
Ireland

270	Mew Is Lt - 1·3M ENE .... 54°42'·30N	05°29'·90W	
271	Belfast -		
	0·7M ENE No.1 By .... 54°42'·00N	05°45'·20W	
272	Black Hd Lt -		
	1·3 miles ENE .... 54°46'·50N	05°39'·20W	
273	Isle of Muck - 1·1M NE ..... 54°51'·70N	05°41'·85W	
274	Larne Lough -		
	1M N of Barr's pt .... 54°52'·50N	05°46'·80W	
275	E Maiden Lt - 1·7M SW .... 54°54'·50N	05°45'·50W	
276	Torr Head - 0·6M ENE of .. 55°12'·20N	06°02'·80W	
277	Fair Head - 0·9M N of .... 55°14'·60N	06°09'·00W	
278	L. Foyle		
	4·8M NNE Inishowen Lt ... 55°17'·90N	06°52'·20W	
279	Malin Head - 2M NNE ...... 55°25'·00N	07°21'·20W	
280	Lough Swilly - 1M N of ent	55°18'·20N	
	07°34'·30W		
281	Tory Island - 1·2M SE of ... 55°14'·00N	08°11'·00W	
282	Rinrawros Pt Lt,		
	Aran - 1·3M NW .... 55°01'·75N	08°35'·40W	
283	Rathlin O'Birne Is Lt -		
	1·9M WSW .... 54°39'·20N	08°52'·90W	
284	Killibegs -		
	2·4M WNW S.John's Pt Lt 54°34'·70N	08°31'·80W	
285	Sligo -		
	2·7M N of Aughris Hd ..... 54°19'·50N	08°45'·30W	
286	The Stags rocks -		
	1·3M N of .... 54°23'·40N	09°47'·40W	
287	Broadhaven -		
	1M N of the bay .... 54°20'·40N	09°56'·00W	
288	Eagle Island - 1·4M NW of 54°17'·80N	10°07'·40W	
289	Black Rock -		
	2·7M NE by N of .... 54°06'·20N	10°16'·60W	
290	Achill Head - 1·4M SW .... 53°57'·30N	10°17'·90W	
291	Clew Bay -		
	1M SW Achillbeg Is Lt .... 53°50'·80N	09°57'·90W	
292	Westport -		
	1·5M WSW Inishgort Lt ...... 53°49'·00N	09°42'·60W	
293	Clew Bay -		
	1·5M NW Roonah Hd .... 53°46'·90N	09°57'·90W	
294	Inishturk Island -		
	1·2M NW .... 53°43'·60N	10°08'·80W	
295	Inishshark Island -		
	1·8M W of .... 53°36'·50N	10°21'·00W	
296	Slyne Head Lt - 1·6M SW . 53°22'·90N	10°16'·00W	
297	Rock Is Lt -		
	5·3M NW by W of .... 53°11'·80N	09°58'·60W	
298	Galway -		
	2·3M N Black Hd Lt .... 53°11'·50N	09°15'·40W	
299	Loop Head Lt - 1·6M W of 52°33'·70N	09°58'·60W	
300	Loop Head Lt - 1·4M S of . 52°32'·30N	09°55'·80W	
301	Kilrush -		
	9M S Kilcredaun Hd Lt .... 52°33'·90N	09°42'·50W	
302	Tearaght Island Lt -		
	2·5M NW .... 52°06'·20N	10°42'·50W	
303	Great Foze Rk - 1·8M SW . 52°00'·00N	10°43'·20W	
304	Dingle -		
	1·2M S of Reenbeg Pt .... 52°05'·60N	10°15'·80W	
305	Bray Head - 1·4M W of ..... 51°52'·80N	10°28'·00W	
306	The Bull Island Lt -		
	1·7M SW .... 51°34'·30N	10°20'·10W	
307	Crow Head - 1·9M S of ..... 51°32'·90N	10°09'·40W	
308	Bantry -		
	0·8M SW Whiddy Is .... 51°40'·00N	09°32'·80W	
309	Sheep's Head Lt -		
	1·5M W of .... 51°32'·30N	09°53'·40W	
310	Mizen Head Lt (SW)-		
	2M SSW .... 51°25'·00N	09°50'·30W	
311	Crookhaven -		
	1M ESE Streek Hd .... 51°27'·80N	09°40'·30W	
312	Schull -		
	M S of Long Is Lt .... 51°29'·20N	09°32'·00W	
313	The Fastnet Rock .... 51°23'·33N	09°36'·16W	
314	Cape Clear - 1·6M SW of .. 51°24'·20N	09°32'·90W	
315	Baltimore - 1·5M S .... 51°26'·90N	09°23'·50W	
316	Toe Head - 1·5M S of .... 51°27'·40N	09°13'·00W	
317	Castle Haven - 1M SE .... 51°30'·30N	09°09'·80W	
318	Galley Head - 1·4M S of ... 51°30'·40N	08°57'·20W	
319	Old Hd of Kinsale Lt -		
	1·5M SSE .... 51°34'·90N	08°30'·80W	
320	Cork Landfall By -		
	0·4M E of .... 51°43'·00N	08°14'·80W	
321	Roche's Point Lt -		
	·2M S of .... 51°46'·40N	08°15'·40W	
322	Ballycotton Island Lt -		
	1·2M S .... 51°48'·40N	07°58'·80W	
323	Youghal,		
	IM SE Capel Island .... 51°52'·40N	07°50'·00W	
324	Youghal, SE -		
	2M SE Blackball PHB .... 51°54'·80N	07°45'·60W	
325	Waterford -		
	1·4M SSE Dunmore E .... 52°07'·40N	06°58'·80W	
326	Coningbeg Lt V -		
	0·4M N .... 52°02'·80N	06°39'·30W	
327	Carnsore Point -		
	3·2M ESE .... 52°09'·40N	06°16'·40W	
328	Greenore Point -		
	1·8M E of .... 52°14'·70N	06°15'·90W	
329	Wexford - 1·6M E .... 52°20'·50N	06°19'·30W	
330	W Blackwater Pt Mk -		
	0·4M W .... 52°25'·80N	06°14'·00W	
331	Cahore Point -		
	1·7 miles SE of .... 52°32'·50N	06°09'·90W	
332	Arklow - 1·2M E by S .... 52°47'·40N	06°06'·40W	
333	Mizen Head (E coast) -		
	1M ESE .... 52°51'·00N	06°01'·90W	
334	Wicklow - 2·6M E .... 52°58'·90N	05°57'·80W	
335	Dun Laoghaire - 2·2M NE . 53°19'·60N	06°04'·60W	
336	Ben of Howth - 1·4M E of . 53°22'·40N	06°00'·50W	
337	Malahide - 1·5M E of Bar .. 53°27'·00N	06°04'·80W	
338	Rockabill - 1·2M WSW ...... 53°35'·30N	06°02'·00W	
339	Carlingford Lough .... 53°58'·40N	06°00'·00W	
340	Strangford Lough .... 54°18'·40N	05°27'·70W	
341	South Rock Lt V - 1·1M E .. 54°24'·30N	05°20'·00W	

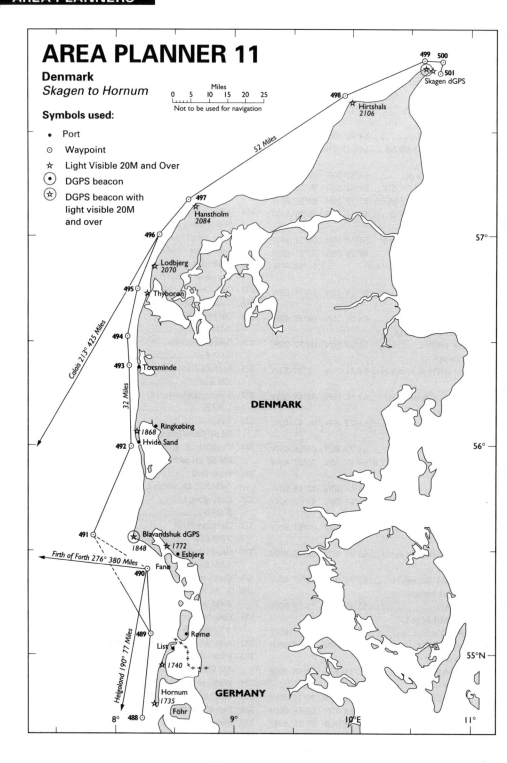

AREA PLANNER 11

Denmark
Skagen to Hornum

Miles
0 5 10 15 20 25

Not to be used for navigation

Symbols used:

- ● Port
- ⊙ Waypoint
- ☆ Light Visible 20M and Over
- ⊙ DGPS beacon
- ✪ DGPS beacon with light visible 20M and over

499 500
✪ ⊙ 501
Skagen dGPS

498 ⊙

☆ Hirtshals
2106

52 Miles

497
☆
Hanstholm
2084

496

☆ Lodbjerg
2070

495 ☆ Thyborøn

494 ⊙

493 ⊙ ● Torsminde

DENMARK

● Ringkøbing
☆ 1868
● Hvide Sand

492 ⊙

Colos 213° 425 Miles

32 Miles

491 ⊙
☆ Blåvandshuk dGPS
1848
☆ 1772
● Esbjerg

Firth of Forth 276° 380 Miles

● Fanø
490 ⊙

489 ⊙ ● Rømø

List
☆ 1740

Helgoland 190° 77 Miles

Hornum
☆ 1735
Föhr

GERMANY

488 ⊙

57°

56°

55°N

8°   9°   10°E   11°

AREA planner 11
WAYPOINTS
Denmark & NW Germany - *Skagen to Hornum*

488 Hornum - *1·2M W of Holtknobsloch landfall buoy* ...... 54°41'·10N   08°08'·40E
489 Rømø - *0·4M W of Lister Tief landfall buoy* .... 55°05'·40N   08°16'·40E
490 Esbjerg - *0·5M SW of Grådyb landfall buoy* .... 55°24'·30N   08°11'·00E
491 Slugen chan N - *9·6M W by N Blavands Huk Lt* .... 55°35'·40N   07°48'·40E
492 Hvide Sande - *2·7M W of harbour entrance* .... 56°00'·00N   08°02'·50E
493 Torsminde - *2·7 M W of harbour entrance* .... 56°22'·50N   08°02'·30E
494 Bovbjerg lt - *2·6M W* .... 56°30'·80N   08°03'·00E
495 Thyborøn - *0·7M W landfall buoy* .... 56°42'·50N   08°07'·40E
496 Nørre Vorupør Lt - *3·2M W* .... 56°57'·20N   08°16'·40E
497 Hanstholm - *1·0M NW landfall buoy* .... 57°08'·80N   08°33'·70E
498 Hirtshals - *2·3M N by W harbour entrance* .... 57°38'·00N   09°56'·50E
499 Skagen W Lt - *2·2M N* .... 57°47'·10N   10°35'·70E
500 Skagen *landfall buoy No.1 - 0·7M S* .... 57°46'·40N   10°46'·00E
501 Skagen - *3·3M E Skagen Lt* .... 57°44'·00N   10°43'·50E

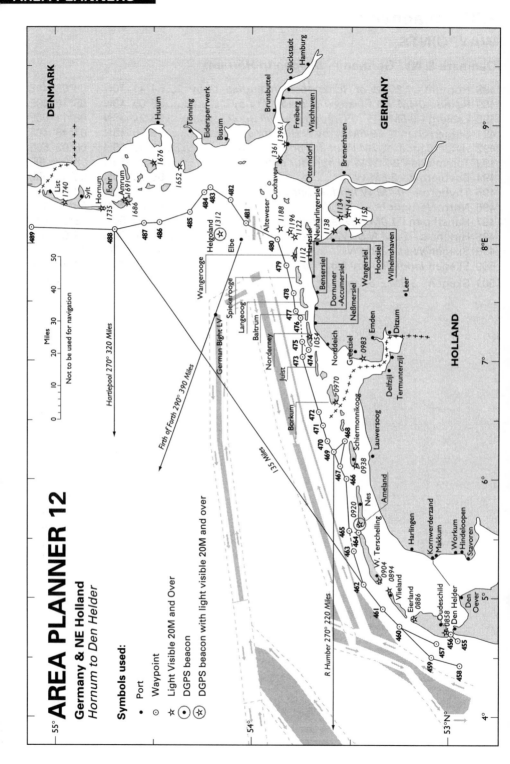

AREA PLANNER 12

Germany & NE Holland
Hornum to Den Helder

Symbols used:

- Port
- ⊙ Waypoint
- ☆ Light Visible 20M and Over
- ⊙ DGPS beacon
- ⊛ DGPS beacon with light visible 20M and over

AREA PLANNER 12
WAYPOINTS
Germany & N Holland - *Hornum to Den Helder*

455	Den Helder - *1·2M SW Kijkduin Lt*	52°56'·90N	04°41'·90E
456	Den Helder - *1·1M N by E Kijkduin Lt*	52°58'·40N	04°44'·10E
457	Molengat Channel - *N ent*	53°03'·00N	04°41'·00E
458	Noorderhaaks I. - *3·2M WSW*	52°57'·30N	04°33'·70E
459	Texel - *0·3M W Molengat NCM*	53°03'·70N	04°39'·00E
460	Vlieland - *2·8M W of SW end of I.*	53°13'·50N	04°46'·60E
461	Vlieland - *W ent to Stortemelk ch*	53°19'·10N	04°55'·20E
462	Terschelling - *0·4M NW Otto ECM*	53°25'·00N	05°06'·10E
463	Terschelling - *W ent to Westgat buoyed ch*	53°27'·80N	05°24'·00E
464	Borndiep Channel - *1·4M WNW Ameland Lt*	53°27'·60N	05°35'·60E
465	Ameland Lt - *2·5M N*	53°29'·50N	05°37'·40E
466	Ameland - *2·9M NNE of E end*	53°30'·40N	06°00'·00E
467	Schiermonnikoog N ent - *Westgat buoyed ch*	53°32'·50N	06°08'·40E
468	Schiermonnikoog E ent - *Lauwers buoyed ch*	53°33'·20N	06°17'·00E
469	Verkenningston Hubertgat SWM - *0·2M S*	53°34'·70N	06°14'·40E
470	Westereems Verkenningston SWM - *0·2M SE*	53°36'·80N	06°19'·80E
471	Riffgat SWM - *0·2M SE*	53°38'·80N	06°27'·40E
472	Osterems SWM - *0·2M S*	53°41'·70N	06°36'·20E
473	Schluchter SWM - *0·2M S*	53°44'·60N	07°04'·20E
474	Norderney - *1·5M N by W of W end of I.*	53°43'·80N	07°07'·00E
475	Norderney - *Dovetief SWM 0·5M S*	53°45'·20N	07°09'·80E
476	Baltrum - *1·7M N by E of Baltrum*	53°45'·00N	07°22'·40E
477	Langeoog - *0·2M N of Accumer Ee SWM*	53°47'·40N	07°27'·40E
478	Spiekeroog - *0·2M N Otzumer Balje SWM*	53°48'·25N	07°37'·40E
479	Wangerooge - *0·2M N of Harle SWM*	53°49'·00N	07°49'·00E
480	Neue Weser Channel - *3·5M W by S Alte Weser Lt*	53°50'·90N	08°01'·90E
481	Elbe Channel - *0·3M W Scharhörnriff N NCM*	53°59'·00N	08°10'·70E
482	Busum S Channel - *0·2M W Süderpiep SWM*	54°06'·00N	08°21'·60E
483	Busum N Channel - *0·2M W of Norderpiep By*	54°11'·50N	08°28'·30E
484	Eidersperrwerk - *0·2M W of Eider SWM*	54°14'·60N	08°27'·20E
485	Husum- *0·2M W Hever SWM*	54°20'·40N	08°18'·60E
486	Amrun - *0·2M W of Rütergat SWM*	54°31'·00N	08°11'·80E
487	Hornum - *0·2M W of Vortrapptief SWM*	54°35'·00N	08°11'·80E
488	Hornum - *2M W Holtknobsloch SWM*	54°40'·86N	08°07'·06E
489	Rømø - *0·4M W Lister Tief SWM*	55°05'·40N	08°16'·10E

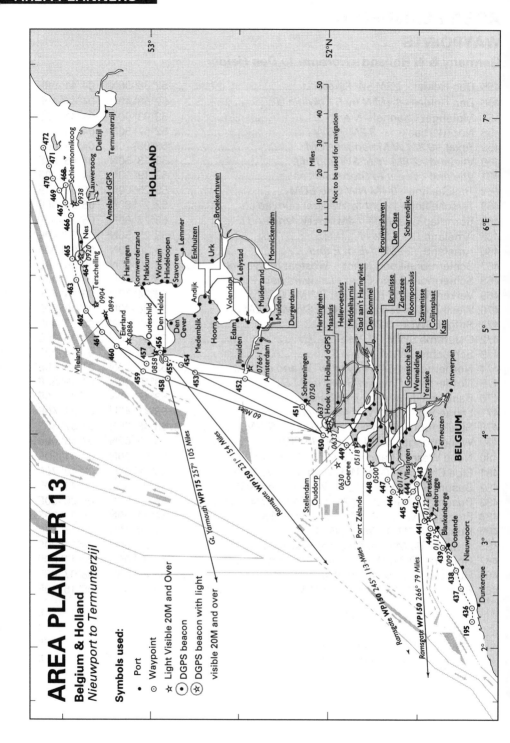

AREA PLANNER 13

Belgium & Holland
Nieuwport to Termunterzijl

Symbols used:

- Port
- ⊙ Waypoint
- ☆ Light Visible 20M and Over
- ⊙ DGPS beacon
- ☆ DGPS beacon with light
  visible 20M and over

AREA planner 13
WAYPOINTS
Belgium & NW Holland - *Nieuwport to Termunterzijl*

150	Ramsgate - *1M E of*	51°l 9'·47N	01°27'·13E
175	Gt Yarmouth - *4·7M E*	52°34'·33N	01°52'·10E
195	Dunkerque - *2M NW of*	51°05'·00N	02°18'·40E
436	Dunkerque - *1·7M NE by E*	51°04'·20N	02°23'·50E
437	Trapegeer SHM - *0·6M N*	051°09'·10N	02°34'·50E
438	Nieuwpoort - *0·9M NW by W*	51°09'·80N	02°41'·80E
439	Oostende - *0·5M NW*	51°14'·70N	02°54'·50E
440	Blankenberge - *0·8M NW*	51°19'·60N	03°05'·60E
441	Zeebrugge - *0·6M NW*	51°22'·30N	03°10'·80E
442	Ft Maisonnueve WCM - *0·3M NE*	51°24'·50N	03°21'·60E
443	Vlissingen - *1·4M NE Niewe Sluis Lt*	51°25'·50N	03°32'·80E
444	Trawl SCM - *0·4M N*	51°26'·70N	03°28'·30E
445	West Kapelle Lt - *4M W by S*	51°31'·30N	03°20'·50E
446	Domburg - *2M NW*	51°35'·60N	03°28'·00E
447	Roompotsluis - *S chnl 5M off*	51°36'·20N	03°33'·20E
448	Geul Van de Banjaard - *N ent*	51°44'·00N	03°33'·00E
449	Haringvlietsluizen - *to S Channel*	51°51'·60N	03°53'·20E
450	Hoek van Holland - *1·2M WNW*	52°00'·10N	04°00'·30E
451	Scheveningen - *0·7M NW*	52°07'·00N	04°14'·80E
452	IJmuiden - *0·7M W by N ent*	52°28'·10N	04°31'·10E
453	Petten WCM - *0·4M W*	52°47'·50N	04°36'·20E
454	Grote Kaap Lt - *0·9M W*	52°52'·90N	04°41'·40E
455	Den Helder - *1·2M SW Kijkduin Lt*	52°56'·90N	04°41'·90E
456	Den Helder - *1·1M N*	52°58'·40N	04°44'·10E
457	Molengat Channel - *N entrance*	53°03'·00N	04°41'·00E
458	Noorderhaaks I. - *3·2M WSW*	52°57'·30N	04°33'·70E
459	Texel - *0·3M W Molengat NCM*	53°03'·70N	04°39'·00E
460	Vlieland - *2·8M W of SW end of I.*	53°13'·50N	04°46'·60E
461	Vlieland - *W ent to Stortemelk chnl*	53°19'·10N	04°55'·20E
462	Terschelling - *0·4M NW Otto ECM*	53°25'·00N	05°06'·10E
463	Terschelling - *W ent*	53°27'·80N	05°24'·00E
464	Borndiep Channel - *1·4M WNW*	53°27'·60N	05°35'·60E
465	Ameland Lt - *2·5M N*	53°29'·50N	05°37'·40E
466	Ameland - *2·9M NNE of E end*	53°30'·40N	06°00'·00E
467	Schiermonnikoog - *N ent*	53°32'·50N	06°08'·40E
468	Schiermonnikoog - *E ent*	53°33'·20N	06°17'·00E
469	Verkenningston Hubertgat By	53°34'·70N	06°14'·40E
470	Westereems Verkenningston By	53°36'·80N	06°19'·80E
471	Riffgat landfall buoy - *0·2M SE*	53°38'·80N	06°27'·40E
472	Osterems landfall By - *0·2M S*	53°41'·70N	06°36'·20E

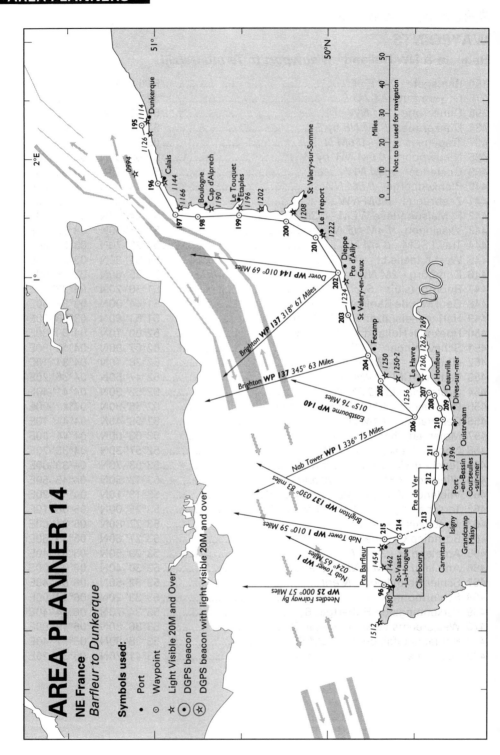

AREA PLANNER 14

NE France
Barfleur to Dunkerque

Symbols used:

- Port
- ☉ Waypoint
- ☆ Light Visible 20M and Over
- ⊙ DGPS beacon
- ⊛ DGPS beacon with light visible 20M and over

Not to be used for navigation

Miles
0   10   20   30   40   50

51°
50°N
2°E
1°

Dunkerque
195 1114
196 1126
Calais 1144
197 1166
Boulogne
198 Cap d'Alprech 1190
199 Le Touquet 1196
Etaples 1202
St Valery-sur-Somme
200 1208
Le Treport
201 1222
Dieppe
202 Pte d'Ailly
Dover WP 144 010° 69 Miles
203 1234
St Valery-en-Caux
Brighton WP 137 318° 67 Miles
204 Fecamp 1250
205 1250-2
Brighton WP 137 345° 63 Miles
Le Havre 1256
206 207 1260, 1262, 1269
Eastbourne WP 140 015° 76 Miles
208 Honfleur
209 Deauville
210 Dives-sur-mer
Nab Tower WP 1 336° 75 Miles
211 Ouistreham
212 Pte de Ver 1396
Brighton WP 137 030° 83 miles
Port-en-Bessin
Courseulles-sur-mer
213
Nab Tower WP 1 010° 59 Miles
214 215
Isigny
Grandcamp
Maisy
Nab Tower WP 1 024° 65 Miles
Pte Barfleur 1454
1462
St-Vaast-La-Hougue
Carentan
Cherbourg
Needles Fairway by WP 25 000° 57 Miles
96 1480
1512

AREA planner 14
WAYPOINTS
France North - *Barfleur to Dunkerque*

1	Nab Tower - *0·5M NW*	50°40'·38N	00°57'·55W
25	Fairway Buoy - *Needles channel*	50°38'·20N	01°38'·90W
96	Cherbourg - *0·5M N of W ent*	49°40'·95N	01°39'·35W
137	Brighton entrance - *1M S of*	50°47'·50N	00°06'·30W
140	Eastbourne - *1·2M SE Langney Pt*	50°46'·25N	00°21'·10E
141	Rye - *0·1M S of Fairway By*	50°53'·90N	00°48'·13E
144	Dover - *1·2M SE of W ent*	51°05'·80N	01°21'·10E
195	Dunkerque - *2M NW of ent*	51°05'·00N	02°18'·40E
196	Calais - *2M NW of ent*	50°59'·20N	01°47'·70E
197	Cap Gris-Nez - *2M NW*	50°53'·30N	01°32'·50E
198	Boulogne - *2M WNW of ent*	50°45'·30N	01°31'·50E
199	Étaples - *3M W of Le Touquet Pt*	50°32'·20N	01°30'·80E
200	St Valéry-sur-Somme - *5M WNW*	50°15'·30N	01°27'·10E
201	Le Trèport - *2M NW of ent*	50°05'·40N	01°20'·40E
202	Dieppe - *1M NW of ent*	49°57'·00N	01°04'·00E
203	St Valéry-en-Caux - *2M N of ent*	49°54'·50N	00°42'·30E
204	Fécamp - *1M NW of ent*	49°46'·70N	00°20'·80E
205	Cap D'Antifer - *1·8M NW*	49°42'·40N	00°07'·80E
206	Le Havre - *0·5M NE of LHA*	49°32'·00N	00°09'·20W
207	Honfleur - *7·5M W of ent*	49°27'·00N	00°02'·50E
208	Deauville - *3M NNW of ent*	49°24'·50N	00°02'·20E
209	Dives-sur-Mer - *3M NNW*	49°20'·70N	00°07'·00W
210	Ouistreham - *3·6M NNE of ent*	49°21'·00N	00°11'·40W
211	Courseulles-sur-Mer - *3M N*	49°23'·40N	00°27'·00W
212	Port-en-Bessin - *3M NNW*	49°24'·00N	00°43'·60W
213	Grandcamp Maisy - *4M NW*	49°26'·70N	01°06'·30W
214	St-Vaast-la-Hougue - *3M ENE*	49°36'·40N	01°11'·00W
215	Barfleur - *2M NE*	49°42'·00N	01°13'·30W

AREA PLANNER 15

N Central France & Channel Isles
Cherbourg to Lézardrieux

Symbols used:

- • Port
- ⊙ Waypoint
- ☆ Light Visible 20M and Over
- ⊙ DGPS beacon
- ⊛ DGPS beacon with light visible 20M and over

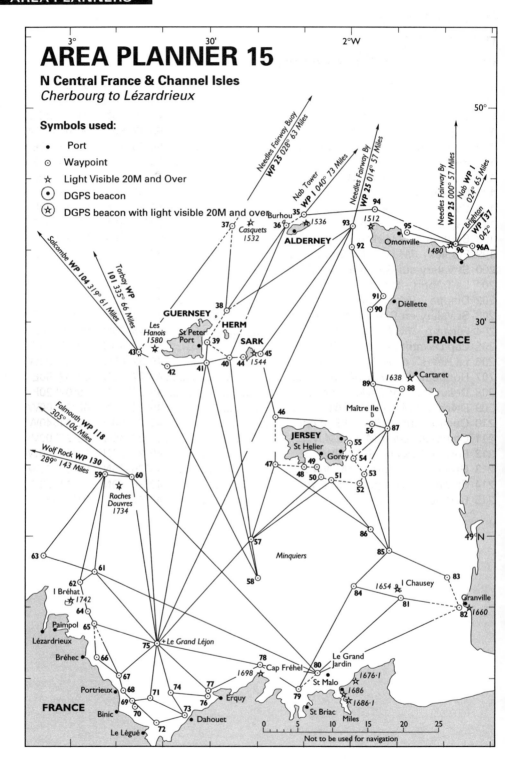

AREA PLANNER 15

WAYPOINTS

France North Central & Channel Islands - *Cherbourg to Lezardrieux*

1   Nab Tower -
    0·5 mile north-west .... 50°40'·38N   00°57'·55W
25 Fairway Buoy -
    Needles channel .... 50°38'·20N   01°38'·90W
35 Alderney - Bray Harbour-
    1M NNE.......................... 49°45'·00N   02°10'·75W
36 The Swinge -
    turning way point .... 49°43'·50N   02°14'·40W
37 Casquets -*1 mile W of* .... 49°43'·38N   02°24'·06W
38 Guernsey NE -
    1·2m E of Beaucette .... 49°30'·13N   02°28'·30W
39 St Peter Port -
    0·5M E of ent .... 49°27'·40N   02°30'·70W
40 Big Russel - *mid way south* 49°25'·30N   02°26'·00W
41 Guernsey -
    1M SE of St Martin's Pt ..... 49°24'·66N   02°30'·53W
42 Guernsey -
    1·5M S of Pleinmont Pt ..... 49°24'·00N   02°40'·00W
43 Guernsey -
    1·8M W of Les Hanois .... 49°26'·16N   02°45'·00W
44 Sark - *0·3M S of Brecou* .... 49°25'·47N   02°23'·30W
45 Sark -
    1M E of Creux Harbour ..... 49°25'·80N   02°19'·00W
46 Jersey -
    1·75M NW of Grosnez Pt... 49°16'·60N   02°16'·75W
47 Jersey -
    1M WSW of La Corbiere ... 49°10'·46N   02°16'·32W
48 Jersey -
    0·15M S of Normant Pt ..... 49°09'·80N   02°10'·00W
49 St Helier -
    0·3M S of Breakwater .... 49°09'·97N   02°07'·33W
50 St Helier -
    0·3M S of Demie de Ras.... 49°08'·77N   02°06'·06W
51 SE Jersey -
    1st turning pt going E .... 49°08'·05N   02°03'·35W
52 SE Jersey -
    2nd turning pt to Gorey .... 49°07'·60N   01°57'·90W
53 SE Jersey -
    3rd turning pt to Gorey ..... 49°08'·70N   01°57'·20W
54 Gorey Entrance -
    298°, 1·6 miles .... 49°11'·10N   01°59'·12W
55 St Catherine, Jersey -
    0·5M SE .... 49°13'·10N   02°00'·00W
56 Les Écrehou -
    1·4M S of Maitre lle Bn ..... 49°15'·70N   01°55'·50W
57 Minquiers NCM -
    0·1M W............................ 48°59'·70N   02°20'·65W
58 SW Minquiers WCM -
    0·1M SW .... 48°54'·34N   02°19'·42W
59 Roches Douvres Lt -
    3M NW of......................... 49°08'·60N   02°52'·10W
60 Roches Douvres Lt -
    2·5M NE .... 49°08'·10N   02°46'·20W
61 Lezardrieux -
    1·5m N La Horaire Bn .... 48°55'·07N   02°55'·15W
62 Lezardrieux Appr -
    1·7M NNE .... 48°53'·60N   02°58'·18W
63 Les Héaux de Brehat -
    3M N of .... 48°57'·60N   03°05'·10W
64 Ile de Brehat -
    2·5M E by S of .... 48°49'·70N   02°56'·00W

65 Paimpol - *1M E of*
    Les Charpentiers Bn .... 48°47'·90N   02°54'·40W
66 Bréhec -
    0·8M E of Le Taureau Mk .. 48°43·60'N   02°54'·00W
67 lle Harbour Light -
    1M NW of......................... 48°40·75'N   02°49'·60W
68 St Quay Portrieux -
    0·2M E of ent..................... 48°38'·90N   02°48'·55W
69 La Roselière WCM -
    0·3M S .... 48°37'·25N   02°46'·40W
70 Binic -
    2M 080° from Breakwater . 48°36'·50N   02°45'·85W
71 Caffa ECM By - *0·3M SE*.... 48°37'·68N   02°42'·68W
72 Le Legué Buoy -
    0·2M NW .... 48°34'·52N   02°41'·28W
73 Dahouet - *1M NW of ent* ... 48°35'·50N   02°35'·20W
74 Rohein WCM Bn -
    0·6M SW .... 48°38'·50N   02°38'·40W
75 Grand Léjon Lt Bn -
    0·7M W............................. 48°44'·90N   02°40'·80W
76 Erquy-*1M W of* .... 48°38'·10N   02°30'·00W
77 Cap d'Erquy -
    1·0M WNW of .... 48°38'·95N   02°30'·00W
78 Cap Frehel Lt - *1·1M N of* .. 48°42'·50N   02°19'·07W
79 St Briac -
    2M off on approach .... 48°38'·40N   02°10'·90W
80 St Malo - *1·3M NW*
    Le Grande Jardin Bn .... 48°41'·10N   02°06'·40W
81 Iles Chausey -
    1M S of entrance .... 48°51'·10N   01°49'·00W
82 Granville -
    0·7M SW of Granville Lt .... 48°49'·62N   01°37'·55W
83 Iles Chausey -
    0·5M E of Anvers ECM ..... 48°54'·00N   01°40'·00W
84 SE Minquiers ECM -
    1M SE .... 48°53'·20N   01°58'·90W
85 Les Ardentes ECM By -
    0·2M E .... 48°57'·90N   01°51'·15W
86 NE Minquiers ECM -
    0·1M NE .... 49°00'·97N   01°55'·11W
87 Les Écrehou SE -
    0·4M SE of
    Écrevière By .... 49°15'·10N   01°51'·65W
88 Cartaret - *1·75M SW* .... 49°20'·90N   01°49'·20W
89 Cartaret - *0·3M SW*
    Trois Grunes WCM By...... 49°21'·65N   01°55'·30W
90 Cap de Flamanville -
    2M W of .... 49°31'·65N   01°56'·30W
91 Diellette -
    1M NW of on transit .... 49°33'·80N   01°53'·00W
92 Cap de La Hague -
    4M SSW of .... 49°40'·54N   02°01'·55W
93 Cap de La Hague -
    2M W of .... 49°43'·37N   02°00'·28W
94 Cap de La Hague -
    1·5M N of
    La Plate Lt .... 49°45'·50N   01°55'·70W
95 Omonville -
    1M E of, in white sec .... 49°42'·55N   01°48'·25W
96 Cherbourg -
    0·5M N of W ent .... 49°40'·95N   01°39'·35W
96a Cherbourg -
    0·5M N of E ent .... 49°40'·87N   01°35'·80W
101 Tor Bay -
    1·7M NE of Berry Hd .... 50°25'·10N   03°27'·00W
104 Salcombe - *1·5M S of bar* . 50°11'·62N   03°46'·60W
118 Falmouth -
    0·8M S of St Anthony Hd.. 50°07'·64N   05°00'·90W
130 Wolf Rk - *2 miles S of* .... 49°54'·65N   05°48'·50W

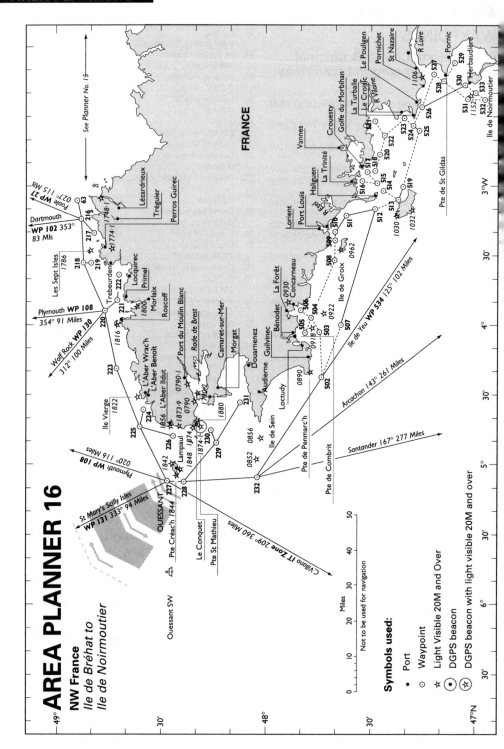

AREA PLANNER 16

NW France
Ile de Bréhat to
Ile de Noirmoutier

FRANCE

Symbols used:
- Port
- Waypoint
- Light Visible 20M and Over
- DGPS beacon
- DGPS beacon with light visible 20M and over

Not to be used for navigation

Miles

See Planner No. 15

AREA PLANNER 16

WAYPOINTS

France North West & Biscay - *Douarnenez to Ile de Noirmoutier*

27	Poole Fairway Buoy - *1M E*	50°39'·00N	01°53'·20W
63	Les Héaux de Brehat - *3M N*	48°57'·60N	03°05'·10W
102	Dartmouth - *2M 150° from ent*	50°18'·25N	03°31'·60W
108	Plymouth - *0·9M S of W brkwtr*	50°19'·13N	04°09'·50W
130	Wolf Rk - *2MS of*	49°54'·65N	05°48'·50W
131	St Mary's, Scilly - *2M E of St Mary's Sound*	49°54'·00N	06°l 5'·00W
216	Treguier - *4·1M N of Pte de Chateau*	48º56'·20N	03º14'·30W
217	Perros Guirec - *2·3M NNW of Port Blanc*	48º52'·30N	03º20'·20W
218	Ile Bono Light - *4M NW*	48º55'·50N	03º33'·90W
219	Ploumanach - *2·7M E of Les Triagoz*	48º52'·30N	03º34'·60W
220	Roscoff - *6M NNE of ent*	48º49'·10N	03º54'·30W
221	Morlaix & Primel - *2·2M NW Pte de Primel*	48º45'·00N	03º51'·20W
222	Trebeurden - *1·5M S of Le Crapaud*	48º45'·20N	03º40'·50W
223	Pte de Beg-Pol Lt - *4M N*	48º44'·70N	04º20'·80W
224	L'Aber Wrach, L'Aber Benoit - *1M W of Libenter WCM*	48º37'·60N	04º39'·90W
225	Gr Basse de Portsall WCM - *1·6M N of*	48º38'·30N	04º45'·90W
226	Chenal du Four - *3·9M W of L'Aber Ildut ent*	48º28'·30N	04º51'·30W
227	Ushant Creach Lt - *3·5M NW*	48º30'·00N	05º11'·30W
228	Ushant - *4·9M WSW Lampaul*	48º25'·30N	05º12'·30W
229	Vandrée WCM - *4·8M W*	48º15'·30N	04º55'·00W
230	Chenal du Four, S Ent - *3·5M WSW ent Rade de Brest*	48º17'·20N	04º48'·20W
231	Douarnenez - *1·5M SW Basse Vieille IDM*	48º07'·30N	04º37'·20W
232	Chaussée de Sein WCM - *1·6M SW*	48º02'·90N	05º09.60'W
502	Guilvinec - *5·5M SW hbr ent*	47°44'·30N	04°23'·50W
503	Concarneau appr - *2·3M SW I. aux Moutons Lt*	47°44'·80N	04°03'·90W
504	Concarneau appr - *2·1M ENE I. aux Moutons*	47°47'·50N	03°58'·80W
505	Benodet - *3·0M S by E river mouth*	47°48'·90N	04°05'·40W
506	Concarneau - *2·0M SSW hbr ent*	47°50'·40N	03°56'·50W
507	I de Glenan - *3M S Jument de Glénan Lt By*	47°38'·50N	04°01'·30W
508	Lorient - *3·0M NW by W Pen Men Lt*	47°40'·50N	03°34'·20W
509	Lorient Passe de L'Ouest - *0·5M SW ent*	47°40'·50N	03°25'·70W
510	Lorient S.Chan - *1·5M S by W ent*	47°40'·40N	03°22'·50W
511	R. Etel - *3M SW river mouth*	47°36'·60N	03°15'·70W
512	Quiberon Peninsula - *3·0M W*	47°28'·90N	03°11'·80W
513	Belle I - Le Palais - *1·3M NE hbr ent*	47°21'·60N	03°07'·50W
514	P. de la Teignouse SW ent - *0·7M SW*	47°25'·20N	03°05'·20W
515	P. de la Teignouse NE ent - *0·7M E*	47°26'·90N	03°00'·50W
516	La Trinite-sur-mer - *1·5M S by E ent*	47°32'·70N	02°59'·80W
517	Golfe du Morbihan - *2·2M S Ent ch*	47°31'·00N	02°55'·20W
518	Chimère SCM - *0·5M SW*	47°28'·60N	02°54'·60W
519	Pointe de Kerdonis Lt - *2M NE*	47°20'·20N	03°01'·50W
520	Pointe de S. Jacques Lt - *1·8M S*	47°27'·40N	02°47'·40W
521	R. Vilaine - *0·7M S Les Mâts SCM*	47°28'·50N	02°34'·80W
522	Ile Dumet Lt - *1·5M W*	47°24'·80N	02°39'·30W
523	La Turballe - *2M N Pte du Croisic*	47°19'·80N	02°32'·90W
524	Plateau du Four - *1·6M ESE Le Four Lt*	47°17'·40N	02°35'·80W
525	Plateau du Four - *0·4M S Goué-Vas*	47°14'·60N	02°38'·10W
526	Le Pouliguen *2M W by S of Pt de Penchâteau*	47°15'·00N	02°27'·90W
527	St. Nazaire - *3·5M Pte Aiguillon Lt*	47°11'·40N	02°17'·60W
528	St. Nazaire - *6·1M Pte Aiguillon Lt*	47°09'·00N	02°19'·30W
529	Pornic - *2·1M WSW Pornic hbr ent*	47°05'·70N	02°10'·00W
530	L'Herbaudière - *1·5M N by E hbr ent*	47°03'·10N	02°17'·50W
531	Ile du Pilier Lt - *1·8M W*	47°02'·60N	02°24'·10W
532	Chaussée des Boeufs - *SW ent.*	46°56'·70N	02°24'·10W
533	Ile Noirmoutier - *SW ent Chenal de la Grise*	47°01'·10N	02°20'·80W

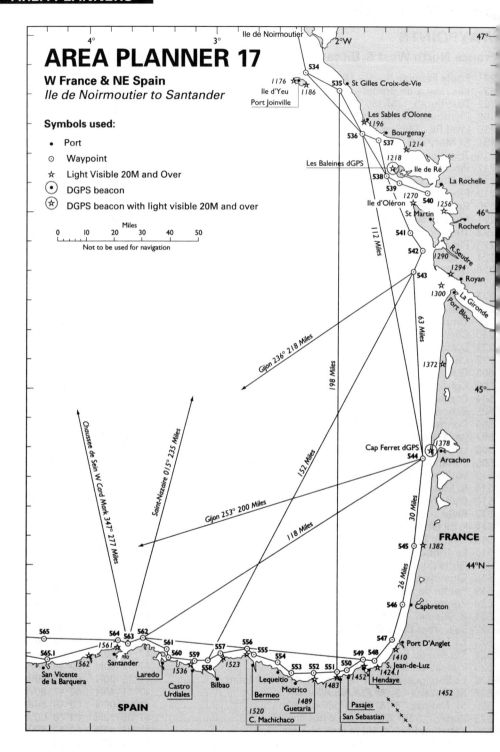

AREA PLANNER 17
W France & NE Spain
Ile de Noirmoutier to Santander

Symbols used:

- • Port
- ⊙ Waypoint
- ☆ Light Visible 20M and Over
- ⦿ DGPS beacon
- ⊛ DGPS beacon with light visible 20M and over

Miles
0   10   20   30   40   50
Not to be used for navigation

AREA PLANNER 17
WAYPOINTS
France-Biscay & NE Spain - *Ile de Nourmontier to Santander*

534	Ile d'Yeu, Port Joinville - *2·4M N by E harbour ent*	46°46'·00N	02°19'·60W
535	St. Gilles-Croix-da-Vie - *3M SW ent*	46°39'·70N	01°59'·60W
536	Les Sables-d'Olonne - *3·7M SW ent*	46°26'·30N	01°49'·60W
537	Bourgenay - *1·4M SW SWM*	46°24'·40N	01°43'·20W
538	Ile de Ré - *3·0M SW Les Baleines Lt*	46°12'·70N	01°37'·10W
539	La Rochelle appr. chan. - *6·5M NW Pte Chassiron*	46°07'·40N	01°31'·60W
540	La Rochelle Ldg Lts - *6M SW by W harbour ent*	46°06'·00N	01°17'·30W
541	Ile d'Oleron - *3·7M SW Pte Chardonnière*	45°54'·60N	01°26'·70W
542	R. Seudre - *3·0M W Pointe de Gatseau*	45°47'·80N	01°18'·80W
543	R. Gironde-ent chan - *7M SW Pte de la Coubre*	45°38'·20N	01°22'·60W
544	Bassin d'Arcachon - *N ent - 5M SW Cap Ferret Lt*	44°35'·00N	01°19'·80W
545	Contis Lt - *3·5M W*	44°05'·70N	01°23'·80W
546	Capbreton - *1·9M W by N harbour ent*	43°39'·80N	01°29'·50W
547	Port d'Anglet - *1·7M WNW hbr brkwtr*	43°32'·80N	01°33'·70W
548	St Jean-de-Luz - *1·5M NNW harbour ent*	43°25'·50N	01°40'·80W
549	Hendaye - *1·8M N Cabo Higuer Lt*	43°25'·40N	01°47'·70W
550	Pasajes - *2·0M N harbour entrance*	43°22'·30N	01°55'·80W
551	San Sebastian - *2·2M N entrance to bay*	43°21'·80N	01°59'·70W
552	Guetaria - *1·8 M N I. de San Antón*	43°20'·50N	02°11'·80W
553	Motrico - *1·8M NE hbr ent*	43°20'·10N	02°21'·00W
554	Lequeitio - *1·8M NNE hbr ent*	43°23'·60N	02°28'·60W
555	Bermeo - *2·2M NNE*	43°27'·40N	02°41'·40W
556	Cabo Machichaco Lt - *1·9M N*	43°29'·20N	02°45'·10W
557	Cabo Villano Lt - *2·3M N*	43°28'·30N	02°56'·60W
558	Abra de Bilbao - *2·0M N of ent*	43°24'·80N	03°04'·80W
559	Castro Urdiales - *1·9M NW of harbour ent*	43°24'·40N	03°11'·00W
560	Laredo - *2M NW Canto de Laredo*	43°26'·80N	03°22'·50W
561	Punta del Pescador - *1·9M NW*	43°29'·10N	03°24'·20W
562	Cabo Ajo Lt - *2·2M N*	43°32'·90N	03°35'·30W
563	Santander - *1·7M N I. de S. Marina*	43°30'·20N	03°43'·70W
564	Cabo Mayor Lt - *1·7M N*	43°31'·10N	03°47'·40W
565	S Vicente de la Barquera Lt - *9·3M N*	43°33'·00N	04°23'·50W

AREA PLANNER 18

NW Spain
Llaneres to Cabo Silleiro

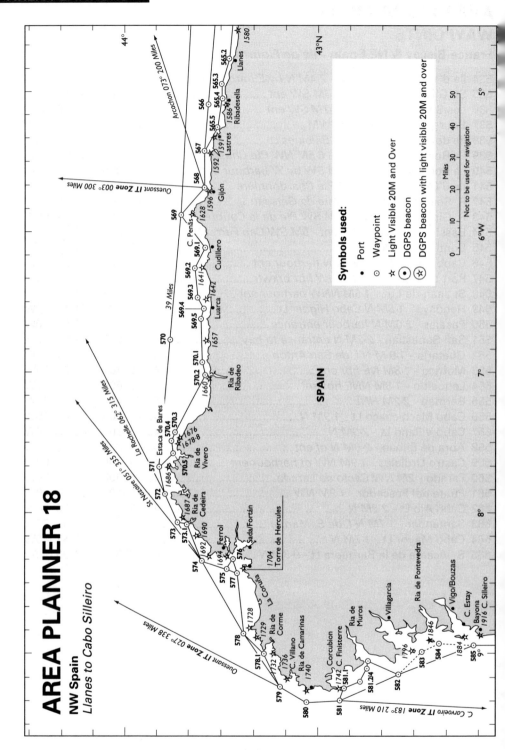

Symbols used:

- • Port
- ⊙ Waypoint
- ☆ Light Visible 20M and Over
- ⊙ DGPS beacon
- ⊛ DGPS beacon with light visible 20M and over

Miles

0 10 20 30 40 50

Not to be used for navigation

SPAIN

Arcachon 073° 200 Miles

Ouessant TT Zone 003° 300 Miles

39 Miles

La Rochelle 062° 315 Miles

St Nazaire 051° 335 Miles

Ouessant TT Zone 027° 338 Miles

C Carvoeiro TT Zone 183° 210 Miles

Llanes 1580
565.2
565.3
566
565.4
565.5
1586 Ribadesella
1591 Lastres
1592
567
568
1596 Gijón
1628
569
C. Peñas
569.1
1641 Cudillero
569.2
569.3
1642
569.4 Luarca
569.5
1657
570.1
570.2 570.1
570.2
1660 Ria de Ribadeo
Estaca de Bares
570.3
570.4
1676
1678·8
570.5
571 Ria de Vivero
1686
572
1687 Ria de Cedeira
573.1
1692 1690 Ferrol
573
1694 Sada/Fortán
574
575 La Coruña
577 576
1704 Torre de Hercules
1728
578 Ria de Corme
1729
578.1
1732 Ria de Camariñas
1736
C. Villano
579 1740
C. Finisterre
1742
581.1 Corcubion
580 581 581.2/4
Ria de Muros
582
Villagarcia
1796 583
584 Ria de Pontevedra
1846
1884 Vigo/Bouzas
585 C. Estay
1916 C. Silleiro Bayona

44°
43°N

5°
6°W
7°
8°
9°

PAGE 270

AREA PLANNER 18
WAYPOINTS
NW Spain - *Llanes to Cabo Silleiro*

565.2	Llanes - *1·5 M N of hbr ent*	43°26'·70N	04°44'·90W
565.3	Cabo de Mar - *1·5 M N of headland*	43°29'·20N	04°55'·70W
566	Punta de Somos Lt - *6·3M N*	43°34'·70N	05°05'·00W
566.1	Ribadesella - *1·5 M N of hbr ent*	43°29'·60N	05°03'·90W
566.2	Lastres - *1·5 M NE of hbr ent*	43°32'·00N	05°14'·33W
567	Tazones Lt - *2·7M N*	43°35'·60N	05°24'·00W
568	Gijon - *1·9M ENE breakwater* Lt	43°35'·00N	05°38'·20W
569	Cabo Peñas Lt - *3·1M N*	43°42'·50N	05°50'·80W
569.1	Cudillero - *1·5 M N of hbr ent*	43°35'·47N	06°08'·86W
569.2	Cabo Vidio - *1·7 M N of light*	43°37'·30N	06°14'·82W
569.3	Cabo Busto - *1·5 M N of light*	43°35'·69N	06°28'·23W
569.4	Luarca - *1·5 M N of hbr ent*	43°34'·54N	06°32'·21W
569.5	Romanellas - *1·5 M N of headland*	43°35'·97N	06°37'·67W
570	Cabo San Augustin Lt - *11·8M N*	43°45'·80N	06°44'·00W
570.1	Cabo S Sebastian - *1·75 M N of light*	43°36'·23N	06°56'·81W
570.2	Ribadeo - *1·75 M N of Ria ent*	43°35'·21N	07°02'·21W
570.3	Los Farallones Is - *1·5 M N of*	43°44'·90N	07°26'·36W
570.4	Pta Roncadoira - *1·8 M N of lt*	43°45'·81N	07°31'·59W
570.5	Vivero - *3·5 M N of Pta de Faro*	43°46'·30N	07°35'·00W
571	Pta de la Estaca de Bares Lt - *2·0M N*	43°49'·30N	07°41'·10W
572	Pta de los Aguillones Lt - 2·5M N	43°48'·80N	07°52'·10W
573	Pta Candelaria Lt - *2·1M NW*	43°44'·30N	08°04'·70W
573.1	Cedeira - *0·5 M W of Pta Lameda*	43°40'·94N	08°05'·16W
574	Cabo Prior Lt - *3·4M NW*	43°36'·70N	08°21'·50W
575	Cabo Prioriño Chico Lt - *4·4M WNW*	43°29'·40N	08°25'·80W
576	El Ferrol appro - *1·4M SW C. Prioriño Chico* Lt	43°26'·70N	08°21'·80W
577	La Coruña - *3·3M NW Torre de Hercules* Lt	43°25'·10N	08°28'·00W
578	Sisargas Is Lt - *2·9M NW*	43°23'·70N	08°53'·50W
578.1	Corme - *1·8 M W of Pta del Roncundo*	43°16'·57N	09°01'·86W
579	Cabo Villano Lt - *3·6M NW*	43°11'·50N	09°16'·60W
579.1	Camariñas - *1·9 M NW of Pta de la Barca*	43°08'·20N	09°14'·95W
580	Cabo Toriñana Lt - *2·7M W*	43°03'·30N	09°21'·50W
581	Cabo Finisterre Lt - *4M W*	42°52'·80N	09°21'·60W
581.1	Corcubion - *1·5 M S of Cabo Finisterre*	42°51'·50N	09°16'·20W
581.2	Bajo de los Meixidos - *1 M W of*	42°45'·60N	09°14'·10W
581.3	Los Bruyos Is - *2 M SW of*	42°42'·80N	09°10'·30W
581.4	Muros - *1·8 M SSW of Pta Queixal*	42°42'·80N	09°05'·70W
582	Cabo Corrubedo Lt - *4·2M WSW*	42°33'·40N	09°10'·60W
583	Villagarcia - *2·5M S Isla Salvora* Lt	42°25'·50N	09°00'·70W
584	Vigo - NW appr - *5·0M W Pta Couso* Lt	42°18'·60N	08°58'·00W
585	Vigo/Bayona - SW appr - *3·8M NW C Silleiro* Lt	42°08'·70N	08°57'·50W

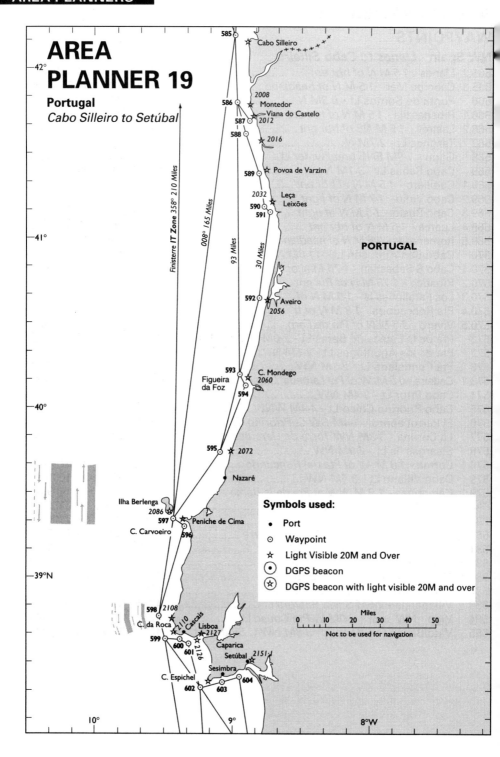

AREA PLANNER 19

42°

Portugal
Cabo Silleiro to Setúbal

585 — Cabo Silleiro
+ + + + + +

2008
586 — Montedor
587 — Viana do Castelo
2012
588 — 2016

589 — Povoa de Varzim

2032 — Leça
590 — Leixões
591

Finisterre IT Zone 358° 210 Miles
008° 165 Miles
93 Miles
30 Miles

41°

PORTUGAL

592 — Aveiro
2056

593 — C. Mondego
Figueira — 2060
da Foz
594

40°

595 — 2072

Nazaré

Ilha Berlenga
2086
597 — Peniche de Cima
C. Carvoeiro — 596

39°N

Symbols used:

- • Port
- ⊙ Waypoint
- ☆ Light Visible 20M and Over
- ⦿ DGPS beacon
- ⊛ DGPS beacon with light visible 20M and over

598 — 2108
C. da Roca — Cascais
2110
599 — Lisboa
600 — 2127
601 — 2126
Caparica
Setúbal — 2151
Sesimbra
C. Espichel
602 — 603 — 604

Miles
0   10   20   30   40   50
Not to be used for navigation

10°   9°   8°W

AREA PLANNER 19
WAYPOINTS
Portugal - *Cabo Silleiro to Setubal*

585	Vigo/Bayona - SW appro - *3·8M NW C Silleiro Lt*	42°08'·70N	08°57'·50W
586	Montedor Lt - *3·8M W*	41°44'·90N	08°57'·50W
587	Viano do Castelo (Ldg Lts) - *1·2M from breakwater*	41°39'·20N	08°51'·00W
588	Viano do Castelo (Ldg Lts) - *5·5M from breakwater*	41°35'·00N	08°52'·00W
589	Póvoa de Varzim - *1·6M WSW harbour entrance*	41°21'·50N	08°48'·10W
590	Porto de Leixões - *2M W breakwater*	41°10'·20N	08°45'·00W
591	Porto - *1·5M W river mouth*	41°08'·50N	08°42'·80W
592	Aveiro - *2·0M W breakwater*	40°38'·60N	08°48'·20W
593	Cabo Mondego Lt - *3·2M W*	40°11'·30N	08°58'·10W
594	Figueira da Foz - *2·1M W breakwater*	40°08'·60N	08°55'·00W
595	Nazaré - *2·8M W of harbour entrance*	39°35'·40N	09°08'·40W
596	Peniche de Cima - *1·5M SW of harbour entrance*	39°20'·00N	09°23'·84W
597	Cabo Carvoeiro Lt - *3·0M W by N*	39°22'·50N	09°28'·30W
598	Cabo da Roca Lt - *3·5M W*	38°47'·00N	09°34'·20W
599	Cabo Raso Lt - *3·3M SW*	38°40'·40N	09°32'·10W
600	Cascais - *1·5M S S· Marta Lt*	38°40'·00N	09°25'·20W
601	Lisboa (Ldg Lts) - *5·0M SW Gibalta Lt*	38°38'·60N	09°20'·50W
602	Cabo Espichel Lt - *3·2M SW*	38°22'·50N	09°15'·40W
603	Sesimbra (Ldg Lts) - *1·5M S harbour entrance*	38°24'·80N	09°06'·10W
604	Sétubal (Ldg Lts) - *3·5M SW Outão Lt*	38°26'·80N	08°58'·60W

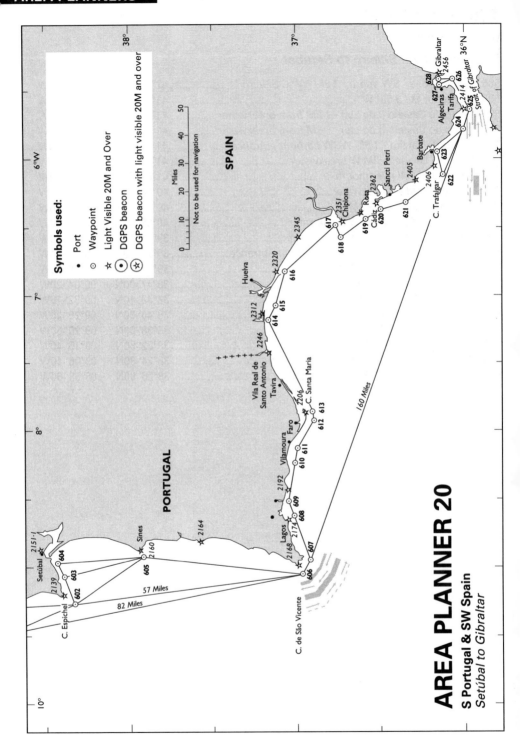

AREA PLANNER 20

S Portugal & SW Spain
Setúbal to Gibraltar

Symbols used:
- • Port
- ⊙ Waypoint
- ☆ Light Visible 20M and Over
- ⊙ DGPS beacon
- ⊛ DGPS beacon with light visible 20M and over

Miles

0 10 20 30 40 50

Not to be used for navigation

PORTUGAL

SPAIN

Setúbal
2151·1
604
603
602
2139
C. Espichel
57 Miles
82 Miles
Sines
2160
605
606
607
2168
Lagos
2174
608
609
2192
610 611
Vilamoura
Faro
612 613
C. Santa Maria
2206
614
2312
615
2320
616
Huelva
2345
617
618
2351
Chipiona
619
Rota
2362
620
Cádiz
621
2405
Sancti Petri
2406
622
C. Trafalgar
623
Barbate
2414
624
625 Strait of Gibraltar 36°N
626
627 Algeciras
Tarifa
628 Gibraltar
2456
160 Miles
Vila Real de Santo António
Tavira
2246
2164
C. de São Vicente

38°
37°
36°N

10°
8°
7°
6°W

AREA PLANNER 20
WAYPOINTS
S Portugal & SW Spain - *Setubal to Gibraltar*

602	Cabo Espichel - *3·2M SW*	38°22'·50N	09°15'·40W
603	Sesimbra (Ldg Lts) - *1·5M S harbour entrance*	38°24'·80N	09°06'·10W
604	Sétubal (Ldg Lts) - *3·5M SW Outão Lt*	38°26'·80N	08°58'·60W
605	Sines - *1M W of breakwater*	37°56'·30N	08°54'·60W
606	Cabo de São Vicente Lt - *3·0M SW*	36°59'·50N	09°02'·50W
607	Pta de Sagres Lt - *2·5M S*	36°57'·20N	08°56'·80W
608	Lagos - *1·4M SE Punta da Piedade Lt*	37°04'·00N	08°38'·80W
609	Portimão - *2·0M S harbour entrance*	37°04'·40N	08°31'·50W
610	Albufeira Lt - *2·6M S*	37°02'·60N	08°14'·80W
611	Vilamoura - *1·6M SSW harbour entrance*	37°02'·60N	08°08'·20W
612	I. da Barreta - *2·0M SW*	36°56'·50N	07°57'·30W
613	Faro/Olhào - *1·0M SSW entrance channel*	36°56'·70N	07°52'·60W
614	Santo António - *2·0M S river mouth*	37°08'·50N	07°23'·60W
615	Fish Haven off Ria Higuerita - *1·2M S*	37°05'·80N	07°20'·00W
616	Huelva - *1M S river mouth*	37°05'·60N	06°49'·60W
617	Chipiona/Sanlúcar (Ldg Lts)- *0·5M WSW By*	36°45'·70N	06°27'·50W
618	Punta del Perro Lt - *3·2M W*	36°44'·80N	06°30'·40W
619	Bahia de Cádiz - *2·2M SSW Punta Candor*	36°36'·10N	06°24'·80W
620	Cadiz - *1·6M W by S Castillo de San Sebastián*	36°31'·40N	06°20'·80W
621	Sancti Petri - *3M SW chan. entrance*	36°21'·00N	06°15'·30W
622	Cabo Trafalgar Lt - *3·6M SW*	36°08'·50N	06°05'·20W
623	Barbate - *1·1M S end of breakwater*	36°09'·70N	05°55'·40W
624	Punta Paloma Lt - *4·7M SSW*	35°59'·50N	05°45'·00W
625	Tarifa - *1·3M S I. de Tarifa Lt*	35°58'·80N	05°36'·40W
626	Punta Carnero Lt - *1·8M SE*	36°03'·40N	05°24'·00W
627	Algeciras - *1·2M SE end of breakwater*	36°08'·20N	05°24'·40W
628	Gibraltar - *0·8M SW E Head pier*	36°08'·60N	05°22'·80W

2.6   SUN AND MOON TABLES – RISING, SETTING AND TWILIGHTS

2.6.1   Rising and Setting Phenomena

The tables of Sunrise, Sunset and Twilights, Moonrise and Moonset and Phases of the Moon (see Table 2(9)) enable the degree of darkness around twilight and throughout the night to be estimated.

2.6.2   Contents of Tables 2(7), 2(8) and 2(9)

Table 2 (7) provides Local Mean Times (LMT) for every third day of the year, of morning Nautical Twilight, Sunrise, Sunset and evening Civil Twilight for latitude 50°N and latitude variations (v). Use the left-hand sign in the tabular entry for v for Sunrise, and the right-hand sign for Sunset. The latitude corrections in Table 2 (8) for Sunrise, Sunset and Twilights, enable the LMT for latitudes in the range 30°N to 60°N to be found.

Table 2 (9) gives times of Moonrise and Moonset for each day for latitude 50°N and latitude variations (v). The latitude correction table enables the LMT for latitudes in the range 30°N to 60°N to be found. The tabular values are for the Greenwich Meridian, and are approximately the LMT of the corresponding phenomena for the other meridians. Expressing the longitude in time, the UT is obtained from:

$$UT = LMT \begin{smallmatrix} + \text{ west} \\ - \text{ east} \end{smallmatrix} \text{ longitude}$$

For Moonrise and Moonset a further small correction of one minute for every seven degrees of longitude is also required, which is added to the LMT if west, subtracted if east.

At Sunrise and Sunset the upper limb of the Sun is on the horizon at sea level. The Sun's zenith distance is 96° for Civil Twilight and 102° for Nautical Twilight. At Civil Twilight the brightest stars are visible and the horizon is clearly defined. At Nautical Twilight the horizon is not visible.

At Moonrise and Moonset the Moon's upper limb is on the horizon at sea level.

2.6.3   Example (a): The Sun – rising, setting and twilights

Find the UT of the beginning of morning Nautical Twilight, Sunrise, Sunset and the end of evening Civil Twilight on 22 January 2000 for latitude 36°07'N, longitude 18°20'E.

From table 2(7), for 22 January, $v = + 30$ for the beginning of Nautical Twilight, $v = + 52$ for Sunrise; $v = - 52$ for Sunset and $v = - 41$ for the end of Civil Twilight. From table 2 (8) the latitude corrections for Nautical Twilight, Sunrise, Sunset and Civil Twilight are $- 22$ mins, $- 40$ mins, $+ 40$ mins and $+ 31$ mins respectively. Note that for Sunset, the sign of the correction has to be reversed because v is minus.

Convert longitude from degrees and minutes of arc to whole minutes of time, by multiplying the degrees of longitude by 4 and adding a further correction of 0 mins, 1 min, 2 mins, 3 mins or 4 mins when the minutes of longitude are in the range 0' to 7', 8' to 22', 23' to 37', 38' to 52' or 53' to 59', respectively. The longitude equivalent in time of 18°20'E is $- (18 \times 4 + 1) = - 73m$.

Remarks	Naut Twilight		Sunrise		Sunset		Civil Twilight	
Tabular value, 22 Jan	06h	31m	07h	47m	16h	36m	17h	13m
Corr'n for latitude		– 22m		– 40m		+ 40m		+ 31m
LMT	06h	09m	07h	07m	17h	16m	17h	44m
Corr'n for longitude	– 1h	13m	– 1h	13m	– 1h	13m	– 1h	13m
UT of phenomenon	04h	56m	05h	54m	16h	03m	16h	31m

2.6.4   Example (b): The Moon – rising and setting

Find the UT of Moonrise and Moonset on 30 January 2000 for latitude 36°07'N, longitude 06°30'W. From Table 2(9) for 30 January, $v = + 41$ for Moonrise and $v = - 44$ for Moonset. The latitude correction for Moonrise and Moonset is $- 31$ mins and $+ 33$ mins, respectively. Note the reversal of the sign of the correction for Moonset, because v is minus.

Using the method in example (a), the longitude equivalent in time of 06°30'W is + 26mins.

Remarks	Moonrise		Moonset	
Tabular value, 30 Jan	02h	34m	12h	12m
Corr'n for latitude		– 31m		+ 33m
LMT	02h	03m	12h	45m
Corr'n for longitude		+ 26m		+ 26m
UT of phenomenon	02h	29m	13h	11m

These times can be increased by +1min to allow for the effect of longitude on the LMT of the phenomenon. See text at end of Table 2 (9) for the instructions.

2000 – SUNRISE, SUNSET and TWILIGHTS

Date	Naut Twi	v	Sun-rise	v	Sun-set	Civil Twi	v	Date	Naut Twi	v	Sun-rise	v	Sun-set	Civil Twi	v
	h m		h m		h m	h m			h m		h m		h m	h m	
Jan 1	06 39	+39	07 59	+63 –	16 08	16 46	– 51	Jul 2	02 08	–115	03 56	– 67 +	20 12	20 56	+84
4	06 39	39	07 58	62	16 11	16 49	50	5	02 11	113	03 58	66	20 11	20 54	82
7	06 39	38	07 58	61	16 15	16 53	49	8	02 15	110	04 01	65	20 09	20 52	81
10	06 38	37	07 56	59	16 19	16 56	48	11	02 20	107	04 03	64	20 07	20 50	79
13	06 37	35	07 55	58	16 23	17 00	46	14	02 25	104	04 07	62	20 04	20 47	77
16	06 35	+34	07 52	+56 –	16 27	17 04	– 45	17	02 30	–101	04 10	– 60 +	20 02	20 43	+75
19	06 33	32	07 50	54	16 32	17 08	43	20	02 36	97	04 14	58	19 58	20 39	72
22	06 31	30	07 47	52	16 36	17 13	41	23	02 42	94	04 17	56	19 55	20 35	70
25	06 28	29	07 44	50	16 41	17 17	39	26	02 48	90	04 21	54	19 51	20 30	67
28	06 25	27	07 40	47	16 46	17 22	37	29	02 54	86	04 25	52	19 47	20 26	64
31	06 22	+25	07 36	+45 –	16 51	17 26	– 34	Aug 1	03 00	– 82	04 30	– 50 +	19 42	20 21	+62
Feb 3	06 18	22	07 32	42	16 56	17 31	32	4	03 06	78	04 34	47	19 37	20 15	59
6	06 14	20	07 27	40	17 02	17 36	30	7	03 12	74	04 38	45	19 32	20 10	56
9	06 10	18	07 22	37	17 07	17 41	27	10	03 18	70	04 43	42	19 27	20 04	53
12	06 05	15	07 17	34	17 12	17 46	25	13	03 24	67	04 47	39	19 22	19 58	50
15	06 01	+13	07 12	+31 –	17 17	17 51	– 22	16	03 30	– 63	04 51	– 37 +	19 16	19 52	+47
18	05 56	10	07 06	29	17 22	17 56	19	19	03 36	59	04 56	34	19 10	19 45	44
21	05 50	7	07 01	26	17 27	18 00	17	22	03 42	55	05 00	31	19 04	19 39	41
24	05 45	5	06 55	23	17 32	18 05	14	25	03 48	52	05 05	28	18 58	19 32	38
27	05 39	+ 2	06 49	20	17 38	18 10	11	28	03 53	48	05 09	26	18 52	19 26	35
Mar 1	05 33	– 1	06 43	+17 –	17 43	18 15	– 8	31	03 59	– 45	05 14	– 23 +	18 46	19 19	+31
4	05 27	4	06 37	14	17 47	18 20	5	Sep 3	04 04	41	05 18	20	18 39	19 13	28
7	05 21	7	06 30	11	17 52	18 25	– 3	6	04 09	38	05 23	17	18 33	19 06	25
10	05 14	10	06 24	8	17 57	18 30	0	9	04 15	34	05 27	14	18 26	18 59	22
13	05 08	13	06 18	6	18 02	18 34	+ 3	12	04 20	31	05 32	11	18 20	18 52	19
16	05 01	–16	06 11	+ 3 –	18 07	18 39	+ 6	15	04 25	– 28	05 36	– 9 +	18 13	18 46	+17
19	04 54	19	06 05	0	18 12	18 44	9	18	04 30	25	05 41	6	18 06	18 39	14
22	04 48	22	05 58	– 3 +	18 16	18 49	12	21	04 35	22	05 45	– 3 +	18 00	18 32	11
25	04 41	25	05 51	6	18 21	18 54	15	24	04 39	18	05 50	0	17 53	18 25	8
28	04 34	28	05 45	9	18 26	18 59	18	27	04 44	15	05 54	+ 3 –	17 47	18 19	5
31	04 27	–32	05 38	–12 +	18 31	19 03	+ 21	30	04 49	– 12	05 59	+ 6 –	17 40	18 12	+ 2
Apr 3	04 19	35	05 32	15	18 35	19 08	24	Oct 3	04 54	9	06 03	9	17 34	18 06	– 1
6	04 12	38	05 26	18	18 40	19 13	27	6	04 58	6	06 08	12	17 27	17 59	4
9	04 05	42	05 19	21	18 45	19 18	30	9	05 03	4	06 13	14	17 21	17 53	7
12	03 58	45	05 13	23	18 50	19 23	33	12	05 08	– 1	06 17	17	17 15	17 47	9
15	03 51	–49	05 07	–26 +	18 54	19 29	+ 37	15	05 12	+ 2	06 22	+ 20 –	17 08	17 41	–12
18	03 43	53	05 01	29	18 59	19 34	40	18	05 17	5	06 27	23	17 02	17 35	15
21	03 36	56	04 55	32	19 04	19 39	43	21	05 21	7	06 32	26	16 56	17 29	18
24	03 29	60	04 49	35	19 08	19 44	46	24	05 26	10	06 37	29	16 51	17 24	20
27	03 22	64	04 43	37	19 13	19 49	49	27	05 30	13	06 42	31	16 45	17 19	23
30	03 15	–68	04 38	–40 +	19 18	19 54	+ 52	30	05 35	+ 15	06 47	+ 34 –	16 40	17 14	–25
May 3	03 08	71	04 33	43	19 22	19 59	55	Nov 2	05 39	18	06 52	37	16 35	17 09	28
6	03 01	75	04 27	45	19 27	20 04	58	5	05 44	20	06 57	40	16 30	17 04	30
9	02 55	79	04 23	48	19 31	20 10	61	8	05 48	22	07 02	42	16 25	17 00	33
12	02 48	83	04 18	50	19 36	20 14	64	11	05 52	24	07 07	45	16 21	16 56	35
15	02 42	–87	04 14	–53 +	19 40	20 19	+ 67	14	05 57	+ 26	07 12	+ 47 –	16 17	16 52	–37
18	02 36	91	04 10	55	19 44	20 24	69	17	06 01	28	07 16	49	16 13	16 49	39
21	02 30	95	04 06	57	19 48	20 29	72	20	06 05	30	07 21	52	16 10	16 46	41
24	02 25	98	04 03	59	19 52	20 33	74	23	06 09	32	07 26	54	16 07	16 43	43
27	02 20	102	04 00	61	19 55	20 37	77	26	06 13	34	07 30	56	16 04	16 41	45
30	02 15	–105	03 57	–63 +	19 59	20 41	+ 79	29	06 16	+ 35	07 34	+ 58 –	16 02	16 39	–46
Jun 2	02 11	108	03 55	64	20 02	20 45	80	Dec 2	06 20	36	07 38	59	16 00	16 38	48
5	02 08	111	03 53	65	20 04	20 48	82	5	06 23	38	07 42	61	15 59	16 37	49
8	02 05	113	03 52	67	20 07	20 51	83	8	06 26	38	07 46	62	15 58	16 36	50
11	02 02	115	03 51	67	20 09	20 53	85	11	06 29	39	07 49	63	15 58	16 36	51
14	02 01	–117	03 50	–68 +	20 11	20 55	+ 85	14	06 31	+ 40	07 51	+ 64 –	15 58	16 37	–52
17	02 00	118	03 50	69	20 12	20 56	86	17	06 34	40	07 54	64	15 59	16 37	52
20	02 00	118	03 50	69	20 13	20 57	86	20	06 35	40	07 56	64	16 00	16 39	52
23	02 01	118	03 51	69	20 13	20 58	86	23	06 37	40	07 57	64	16 04	16 40	52
26	02 02	118	03 52	68	20 13	20 58	85	26	06 38	40	07 58	64	16 04	16 42	52
29	02 05	–116	03 54	–68 +	20 13	20 57	+ 85	29	06 39	+ 40	07 59	+ 63 –	16 06	16 44	–51
Jul 2	02 08	–115	03 56	–67 +	20 12	20 56	+ 84	Jan 1	06 39	+ 39	07 59	+ 63 –	16 09	16 47	–51

2000 – SUNRISE, SUNSET and TWILIGHTS

Corrections to Sunrise and Sunset

N. Lat	30°	35°	40°	45°	50°	52°	54°	56°	58°	60°
v	m	m	m	m	m	m	m	m	m	m
0	0	0	0	0	0	0	0	0	0	0
2	-2	-2	-1	-1	0	0	+1	+1	+2	+2
4	4	3	2	1	0	+1	1	2	3	4
6	6	5	4	2	0	1	2	3	4	6
8	8	6	5	3	0	1	2	4	6	7
10	-10	-8	-6	-3	0	+1	+3	+5	+7	+9
12	12	10	7	4	0	2	4	6	8	11
14	14	11	8	4	0	2	4	7	10	13
16	16	13	9	5	0	2	5	8	11	15
18	18	14	10	6	0	3	6	9	12	16
20	-20	-16	-12	-6	0	+3	+6	+10	+14	+18
22	22	18	13	7	0	3	7	11	15	20
24	24	19	14	8	0	4	7	12	16	22
26	26	21	15	8	0	4	8	13	18	24
28	28	22	16	9	0	4	9	14	19	26
30	-30	-24	-17	-10	0	+4	+9	+15	+21	+28
32	32	26	19	10	0	5	10	16	22	30
34	34	27	20	11	0	5	11	17	24	32
36	36	29	21	11	0	5	11	18	25	34
38	38	31	22	12	0	6	12	19	27	36
40	-40	-32	-23	-13	0	+6	+13	+20	+28	+38
42	42	34	24	13	0	6	13	21	30	40
44	44	35	26	14	0	7	14	22	31	42
46	46	37	27	15	0	7	15	23	33	44
48	48	39	28	15	0	7	15	24	35	47
50	-50	-40	-29	-16	0	+8	+16	+26	+36	+49
52	52	42	30	17	0	8	17	27	38	51
54	54	44	32	17	0	8	17	28	40	54
56	56	45	33	18	0	9	18	29	42	56
58	58	47	34	19	0	9	19	30	43	59
60	-60	-49	-35	-19	0	+9	+20	+32	+45	+62
62	62	50	36	20	0	10	20	33	47	64
64	64	52	38	21	0	10	21	34	49	67
66	66	53	39	22	0	10	22	36	51	70
68	68	55	40	22	0	11	23	37	54	74
70	-70	-57	-41	-23	0	+11	+24	+38	+56	+77

If v is negative reverse the sign of the correction

Corrections to Nautical Twilight

N. Lat	30°	35°	40°	45°	50°	52°	54°	56°	58°	60°
v	m	m	m	m	m	m	m	m	m	m
+40	-40	-31	-22	-12	0	+5	+11	+17	+24	+31
30	30	23	16	9	0	4	8	12	17	22
20	20	15	10	5	0	2	5	7	10	13
+10	-10	-7	-5	-2	0	+1	+2	+3	+3	+4
0	0	+1	+1	+1	0	-1	-1	-2	-3	-4
-10	+10	+9	+7	+4	0	-2	-4	-7	-10	-13
20	20	17	13	7	0	3	7	12	17	23
30	30	25	18	10	0	5	11	17	24	33
40	40	33	24	14	0	7	14	23	33	44
50	50	41	30	17	0	-8	18	29	42	57
-60	+60	+49	+37	+21	0	-10	-22	-36	-52	-73
70	70	58	43	24	0	12	27	44	65	95
80	80	66	49	28	0	15	32	54	83	-136
90	90	75	56	32	0	17	39	67	-116	TAN
100	100	83	63	37	0	20	47	-88	TAN	TAN
-110	+110	+92	+70	+42	0	-24	-59	TAN	TAN	TAN
-120	+120	+101	+78	+47	0	-29	-81	TAN	TAN	TAN

Corrections to Civil Twilight

N. Lat	30°	35°	40°	45°	50°	52°	54°	56°	58°	60°
v	m	m	m	m	m	m	m	m	m	m
-50	+50	+40	+28	+15	0	-7	-15	-24	-33	-44
40	40	32	23	12	0	6	12	18	26	34
30	30	24	17	9	0	4	8	13	19	25
20	20	16	11	6	0	3	5	8	12	15
-10	+10	+8	+5	+3	0	-1	-2	-4	-5	-7
0	0	0	0	0	0	0	+1	+1	+2	+2
+10	-10	-8	-6	-4	0	+2	4	6	8	11
20	20	16	12	7	0	3	7	11	15	20
30	30	24	18	10	0	5	10	16	22	30
40	40	33	24	13	0	6	13	21	30	41
+50	-50	-41	-30	-17	0	+8	+17	+27	+39	+52
60	60	49	36	20	0	10	21	33	48	66
70	70	57	42	24	0	12	25	41	60	84
80	80	66	49	27	0	14	30	49	74	110
83	83	68	50	29	0	14	32	52	80	121
+86	-86	-71	-52	-30	0	+15	+33	+56	+86	+137

The times on the opposite page are the local mean times (LMT) of morning nautical twilight, sunrise, sunset and evening civil twilight for latitude 50°N, together with their variations v. The variations are the differences in minutes of time between the time of the phenomenon for latitudes 50°N and 30°N. The sign on the left-handside of v (between sunrise and sunset) applies to sunrise, and the sign on the right-hand side applies to sunset. The LMT of the phenomenon for latitudes between 30°N and 60°N is found by applying the corrections in the tables above to the tabulated times as follows:

Sunrise and sunset: To determine the LMT of sunrise or sunset, take out the tabulated time and v corresponding to the required date. Using v and latitude as arguments in the table of "Corrections to Sunrise and Sunset", extract the correction. This table is for positive v. If v is minus, reverse the sign of the correction. Apply the correction to the tabulated time.

Nautical twilight: To determine the LMT of morning nautical twilight, follow the same method as for sunrise and sunset, but use the table of "Corrections to Nautical Twilight". This table includes both positive and negative values of v. The entry TAN stands for Twilight All Night, because the Sun does not reach an altitude of –12°.

Civil twilight: To determine the LMT of evening civil twilight follow the same method as for nautical twilight, but use the table of "Corrections to Civil Twilight". This table includes both positive and negative values of v.

Convert LMT to UT by adding the longitude in time if west (+), or subtracting if east (–).

Examples of the use of these tables are given on p. 276.

Table 2 (9)

2000 – MOONRISE and MOONSET

Day	JANUARY Rise	v	Set	v	MARCH Rise	v	Set	v	MAY Rise	v	Set	v	JULY Rise	v	Set	v
	h m		h m		h m		h m		h m		h m		h m		h m	
1	02 38	+25	13 16	−29	04 10	+60	12 49	−59	03 53	+9	15 53	−3	03 34	−61	19 57	+63
2	03 41	35	13 41	39	04 55	57	13 44	56	04 17	−4	17 09	+11	04 36	62	20 57	60
3	04 44	45	14 10	47	05 34	52	14 46	49	04 41	17	18 27	25	05 48	58	21 45	52
4	05 44	52	14 45	54	06 07	43	15 51	40	05 09	30	19 47	38	07 06	48	22 22	40
5	06 41	58	15 25	59	06 36	33	16 59	29	05 41	43	21 06	50	08 25	36	22 53	28
6	07 33	+60	16 12	−60	07 02	+22	18 10	−17	06 21	−53	22 22	+59	09 43	−22	23 19	+15
7	08 19	58	17 05	57	07 26	+10	19 22	−4	07 10	60	23 29	62	10 57	−9	23 42	+2
8	08 59	53	18 05	51	07 50	−2	20 35	+9	08 08	62	24 26	59	12 09	+4	24 03	−10
9	09 33	46	19 08	43	08 14	15	21 49	22	09 16	58	00 26	59	13 19	17	00 03	10
10	10 03	36	20 14	32	08 40	27	23 04	35	10 28	49	01 12	52	14 26	29	00 26	22
11	10 29	+26	21 22	−21	09 11	−39	24 19	+46	11 43	−38	01 48	+42	15 32	+40	00 49	−33
12	10 53	14	22 31	−9	09 47	49	00 19	46	12 56	25	02 18	30	16 36	50	01 15	43
13	11 16	+2	23 42	+4	10 31	57	01 32	55	14 09	−13	02 44	18	17 37	57	01 46	52
14	11 40	−10	24 55	17	11 24	60	02 39	60	15 19	0	03 07	+6	18 34	62	02 22	59
15	12 06	22	00 55	17	12 27	58	03 38	59	16 29	+13	03 29	−6	19 24	62	03 04	62
16	12 35	−34	02 11	+30	13 37	−51	04 27	+54	17 37	+25	03 51	−18	20 07	+59	03 53	−62
17	13 11	46	03 28	42	14 52	41	05 08	45	18 44	36	04 14	29	20 44	53	04 49	58
18	13 55	55	04 45	52	16 08	29	05 41	34	19 50	47	04 40	40	21 15	45	05 49	51
19	14 49	59	05 59	58	17 23	16	06 09	21	20 52	55	05 09	50	21 42	35	06 53	41
20	15 54	58	07 03	59	18 36	−3	06 34	+9	21 50	60	05 44	57	22 06	24	07 58	31
21	17 08	−52	07 57	+54	19 48	+10	06 58	−3	22 42	+62	06 25	−61	22 28	+12	09 05	−19
22	18 25	41	08 41	45	20 57	22	07 21	15	23 28	60	07 12	62	22 49	0	10 13	−7
23	19 42	29	09 16	34	22 05	34	07 45	27	24 07	55	08 05	59	23 11	−12	11 23	+6
24	20 57	16	09 45	22	23 10	44	08 11	38	00 07	55	09 04	54	23 35	24	12 34	19
25	22 09	−4	10 11	+10	24 13	52	08 40	47	00 39	47	10 07	44	24 03	37	13 49	32
26	23 19	+9	10 34	−2	00 13	+52	09 14	−54	01 08	+38	11 13	−34	00 03	−37	15 05	+45
27	24 25	20	10 56	14	01 11	58	09 53	59	01 33	27	12 21	22	00 37	48	16 21	55
28	00 25	20	11 19	25	02 04	61	10 39	61	01 56	15	13 31	−9	01 20	57	17 34	61
29	01 31	31	11 44	35	02 51	59	11 32	59	02 18	+3	14 43	+4	02 14	62	18 39	62
30	02 34	41	12 12	44	03 31	55	12 30	53	02 42	−10	15 59	18	03 21	61	19 33	56
31	03 35	+50	12 44	−52	04 06	+48	13 34	−45	03 07	−23	17 18	+31	04 36	−54	20 16	+46

Day	FEBRUARY Rise	v	Set	v	APRIL Rise	v	Set	v	JUNE Rise	v	Set	v	AUGUST Rise	v	Set	v
1	04 34	+56	13 22	−57	04 36	+38	14 41	−34	03 36	−36	18 39	+44	05 57	−42	20 50	+34
2	05 28	59	14 07	60	05 03	27	15 51	22	04 12	48	19 58	55	07 18	29	21 19	21
3	06 16	59	14 58	58	05 28	15	17 03	−10	04 57	58	21 13	61	08 37	15	21 44	+8
4	06 58	55	15 56	53	05 52	+3	18 17	+4	05 52	62	22 17	62	09 52	−1	22 07	−5
5	07 35	48	16 59	46	06 16	−10	19 33	17	06 59	61	23 09	56	11 04	+12	22 29	18
6	08 06	+39	18 05	−36	06 42	−23	20 50	+31	08 12	−53	23 50	+47	12 14	+25	22 53	−29
7	08 34	29	19 13	25	07 11	35	22 08	43	09 29	43	24 23	35	13 22	36	23 18	40
8	08 58	18	20 22	−12	07 45	47	23 24	53	10 45	30	00 23	35	14 28	47	23 47	49
9	09 22	+6	21 33	0	08 27	56	24 34	60	11 59	17	00 50	23	15 30	55	24 21	57
10	09 45	−6	22 45	+13	09 18	60	00 34	60	13 10	−4	01 14	+10	16 28	61	00 21	57
11	10 10	−18	23 59	+26	10 18	−60	01 36	+61	14 20	+9	01 36	−2	17 20	+63	01 02	−61
12	10 37	30	25 13	38	11 26	55	02 27	57	15 28	21	01 57	14	18 06	61	01 49	62
13	11 09	42	01 13	38	12 39	45	03 09	49	16 35	33	02 20	26	18 45	56	02 42	60
14	11 48	51	02 28	49	13 53	34	03 44	38	17 41	43	02 44	37	19 18	48	03 41	54
15	12 36	58	03 41	56	15 07	21	04 13	26	18 44	52	03 12	46	19 46	38	04 44	45
16	13 34	−59	04 47	+60	16 19	−8	04 38	+14	19 44	+59	04 22	−55	20 11	+27	05 50	−34
17	14 42	56	05 44	57	17 31	+5	05 01	+2	20 38	62	04 22	60	20 33	16	06 57	22
18	15 56	47	06 32	50	18 41	17	05 23	−11	21 26	62	05 07	63	20 55	+4	08 05	−10
19	17 14	36	07 10	40	19 49	29	05 46	22	22 07	58	05 58	61	21 16	−8	09 14	+2
20	18 31	23	07 42	28	20 56	40	06 11	33	22 42	51	06 56	56	21 39	21	10 24	15
21	19 46	−10	08 10	+16	22 01	+50	06 38	−44	23 12	+42	07 57	−48	22 05	−33	11 37	+28
22	20 58	+3	08 34	+3	23 01	57	07 10	52	23 37	31	09 01	38	22 35	45	12 51	41
23	22 08	15	08 57	−9	23 57	61	07 47	58	24 00	20	10 07	27	23 13	54	14 05	52
24	23 15	27	09 21	20	24 47	61	08 30	61	00 00	20	11 15	15	24 01	61	15 17	60
25	24 21	38	09 45	31	00 47	61	09 20	61	00 22	+8	12 24	−2	00 01	61	16 24	63
26	00 21	+38	10 12	−41	01 29	+58	10 16	−57	00 44	−4	13 37	+11	01 00	−62	17 21	+60
27	01 24	+47	10 43	−50	02 06	52	11 17	49	01 08	17	14 52	24	02 10	58	18 08	52
28	02 24	+54	11 18	−56	02 37	43	12 22	40	01 34	30	16 10	38	03 28	48	18 45	40
29	03 20	+59	12 00	−59	03 05	33	13 30	28	02 05	42	17 29	50	04 49	36	19 17	27
30					03 30	+21	14 40	−16	02 44	−53	18 47	+59	06 09	22	19 43	14
31													07 28	−8	20 07	+1

2000 – MOONRISE and MOONSET

SEPTEMBER / NOVEMBER

Day	SEPTEMBER Rise	v	Set	v	NOVEMBER Rise	v	Set	v
	h m		h m		h m		h m	
1	08 43	+ 6	20 30	− 12	11 52	+ 65	20 13	− 65
2	09 57	20	20 54	25	12 39	64	21 06	63
3	11 07	32	21 19	36	13 19	59	22 04	57
4	12 15	43	21 47	47	13 52	51	23 07	48
5	13 20	53	22 19	55	14 20	41	24 12	37
6	14 20	+ 59	22 57	63	14 45	+ 30	00 12	− 37
7	15 15	63	23 42	63	15 07	18	01 19	26
8	16 03	62	24 34	62	15 28	+ 6	02 28	− 13
9	16 44	58	00 34	62	15 49	− 7	03 39	0
10	17 19	51	01 31	56	16 12	20	04 52	+ 14
11	17 49	+ 42	02 33	− 48	16 38	− 33	06 08	+ 28
12	18 15	31	03 38	38	17 09	46	07 26	41
13	18 38	20	04 46	27	17 47	56	08 45	53
14	19 00	+ 8	05 54	14	18 35	63	10 00	62
15	19 21	− 1	07 04	− 1	19 34	65	11 07	65
16	19 44	− 17	08 15	+ 12	20 43	− 60	12 03	+ 62
17	20 08	30	09 28	25	21 57	51	12 47	54
18	20 37	42	10 42	38	23 14	39	13 23	43
19	21 12	52	11 56	49	24 31	25	13 52	30
20	21 55	60	13 08	58	00 31	25	14 17	17
21	22 49	− 63	14 15	+ 63	01 46	− 11	14 39	+ 4
22	23 53	61	15 14	62	03 00	+ 2	15 00	− 9
23	25 06	53	16 03	56	04 12	16	15 22	22
24	01 06	53	16 43	46	05 24	29	15 46	34
25	02 24	42	17 15	34	06 34	41	16 12	45
26	03 44	− 28	17 43	+ 20	07 42	+ 52	16 43	− 55
27	05 02	− 14	18 07	+ 7	08 46	60	17 20	62
28	06 19	0	18 31	− 6	09 44	65	18 04	65
29	07 34	+ 14	18 54	19	10 35	65	18 55	65
30	08 47	27	19 18	32	11 18	62	19 52	60

OCTOBER / DECEMBER

Day	OCTOBER Rise	v	Set	v	DECEMBER Rise	v	Set	v
1	09 58	+ 39	19 45	− 43	11 53	+ 55	20 52	− 52
2	11 06	50	20 16	52	12 23	46	21 56	43
3	12 10	58	20 52	60	12 48	35	23 01	31
4	13 08	63	21 34	63	13 11	24	24 08	19
5	13 59	64	22 23	63	13 31	+ 12	00 08	19
6	14 43	+ 61	23 18	− 60	13 52	0	01 17	− 6
7	15 20	55	24 19	52	14 13	− 13	02 27	+ 7
8	15 51	46	00 19	52	14 36	26	03 41	21
9	16 18	36	01 23	43	15 04	39	04 58	34
10	16 42	25	02 30	32	15 38	51	06 17	48
11	17 04	+ 12	03 38	− 19	16 22	− 61	07 36	+ 59
12	17 25	0	04 48	− 7	17 18	65	08 49	65
13	17 47	− 13	06 00	+ 7	18 25	63	09 53	65
14	18 11	26	07 14	20	19 41	55	10 44	58
15	18 38	38	08 30	34	21 00	44	11 25	48
16	19 11	− 50	09 46	+ 46	22 19	− 30	11 57	+ 35
17	19 52	59	11 01	57	23 36	16	12 23	22
18	20 43	64	12 11	63	24 50	2	12 46	+ 8
19	21 44	63	13 12	64	00 50	− 2	13 07	− 5
20	22 53	57	14 03	59	02 02	+ 12	13 29	17
21	24 09	− 47	14 44	+ 50	03 13	+ 25	13 51	− 30
22	00 09	47	15 18	39	04 23	37	14 16	41
23	01 26	34	15 46	26	05 31	48	14 45	51
24	02 43	20	16 10	+ 13	06 36	57	15 19	60
25	03 59	− 6	16 33	− 1	07 36	64	16 00	65
26	05 14	+ 8	6 55	− 14	08 30	+ 66	16 48	− 66
27	06 27	21	17 18	26	09 16	64	17 42	62
28	07 39	34	17 44	38	09 54	58	18 42	56
29	08 49	46	18 12	49	10 26	50	19 45	47
30	09 56	55	1846	58	10 52	40	20 49	36
31	10 57	+ 62	19 26	− 63	11 15	+ 29	21 54	− 24

Corrections to Moonrise and Moonset

N Lat (v)	30°	35°	40°	45°	50°	52°	54°	56°	58°	60°
	m	m	m	m	m	m	m	m	m	m
0	0	0	0	0	0	0	0	0	0	0
2	− 2	− 2	− 1	− 1	0	0	+ 1	+ 1	+ 1	+ 2
4	4	3	2	1	0	+ 1	1	2	3	4
6	6	5	3	2	0	1	2	3	4	5
8	8	6	5	3	0	1	2	4	5	7
10	− 10	− 8	− 6	− 3	0	+ 1	+ 3	+ 5	+ 7	+ 9
12	12	10	7	4	0	2	4	6	8	11
14	14	11	8	4	0	2	4	7	9	12
16	16	13	9	5	0	2	5	8	11	14
18	18	14	10	6	0	3	5	9	12	16
0	− 20	− 16	− 12	− 6	0	+ 3	+ 6	+ 10	+ 14	+ 18
22	22	18	13	7	0	3	7	11	15	20
24	24	19	14	8	0	3	7	12	16	22
26	26	21	15	8	0	4	8	13	18	23
28	28	22	16	9	0	4	9	14	19	25
30	− 30	− 24	− 17	− 9	0	+ 4	+ 9	+ 15	+ 21	+ 27
32	32	26	18	10	0	5	10	16	22	29
34	34	27	20	11	0	5	10	17	23	31
36	36	29	21	11	0	5	11	18	25	33
38	38	31	22	12	0	6	12	19	26	35
40	− 40	− 32	− 23	− 13	0	+ 6	+ 12	+ 20	+ 28	+ 37
42	42	34	24	13	0	6	13	21	30	39
44	44	35	26	14	0	7	14	22	31	42
46	46	37	27	15	0	7	15	23	33	44
48	48	39	28	15	0	7	15	24	34	46
50	− 50	− 40	− 29	− 16	0	+ 8	+ 16	+ 25	+ 36	+ 48
52	52	42	30	17	0	8	17	26	38	51
54	54	44	32	17	0	8	17	28	39	53
56	56	45	33	18	0	9	18	29	41	56
58	58	47	34	19	0	9	19	30	43	58
60	− 60	− 48	− 35	− 19	0	+ 9	+ 20	+ 31	+ 45	+ 61
62	62	50	36	20	0	10	20	33	47	64
64	64	52	38	21	0	10	21	34	49	67
66	66	53	39	22	0	10	22	35	51	70
68	68	55	40	22	0	11	23	37	53	73
70	− 70	− 57	− 41	− 23	0	+ 11	+ 24	+ 38	+ 55	+ 76
72	72	58	43	24	0	11	24	40	58	80
74	74	60	44	24	0	12	25	41	60	83
76	76	62	45	25	0	12	26	43	62	87
78	78	63	46	26	0	13	27	44	65	91
80	− 80	− 65	− 48	− 27	0	+ 13	+ 28	+ 46	+ 68	+ 96
82	82	67	49	27	0	13	29	48	70	101
84	84	68	50	28	0	14	30	49	73	106
86	86	70	51	29	0	14	31	51	77	112
88	88	72	53	30	0	15	32	53	80	119
90	− 90	− 73	− 54	− 30	0	+ 15	+ 33	+ 55	+ 84	+ 127

If v is minus reverse the sign of the correction

The daily times of moonrise and moonset given above are the local mean times (LMT) of the phenomena for latitude 50°N, together with their variations v. The variations are the differences in minutes between the time of the phenomenon for latitudes 50N° and 30°N. The LMT of the phenomenon for latitudes between 30°N and 60°N is found as follows:

Take out the tabulated time and v corresponding to the required date. Using v and latitude as arguments in the table above of "Corrections to Moonrise and Moonset", extract the correction. This table is for positive v. If v is minus, reverse the sign of the correction.

Add a small extra correction of 1m for every 7° of longitude if west. Subtract if east.

Convert LMT to UT by adding the longitude in time if west, or subtracting if east.

Examples of the use of these tables are given on p. 276.

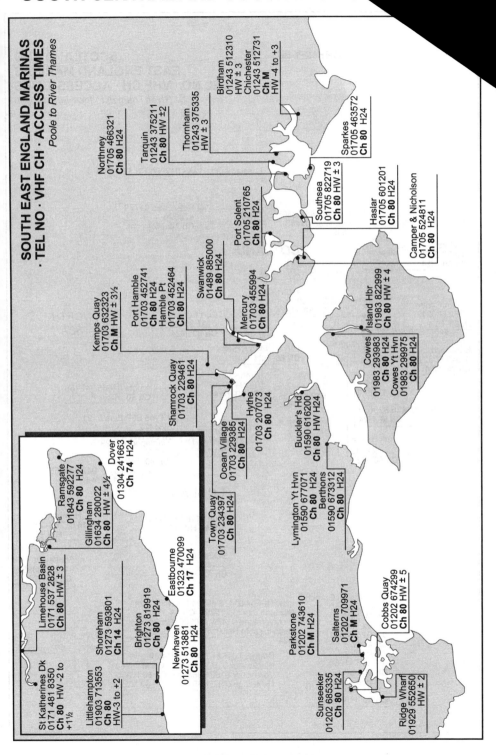

SOUTH EAST ENGLAND MARINAS
· TEL NO · VHF CH · ACCESS TIMES
Poole to River Thames

Birdham
01243 512310
HW ± 3
Chichester
01243 512731
Ch M
HW -4 to +3

Thorham
01243 375335
HW ± 3

Tarquin
01243 375211
Ch 80 HW ±2

Northney
01705 466321
Ch 80 H24

Sparkes
01705 463572
Ch 80 H24

Southsea
01705 822719
Ch 80 HW ± 3

Haslar
01705 601201
Ch 80 H24

Camper & Nicholson
01705 524811
Ch 80 H24

Port Solent
01705 210765
Ch 80 H24

Swanwick
01489 885000
Ch 80 H24

Mercury
01703 455994
Ch 80 H24

Port Hamble
01703 452741
Ch 80 H24
Hamble Pt
01703 452464
Ch 80 H24

Kemps Quay
01703 632323
Ch M HW ± 3½

Island Hbr
01983 822999
Ch 80 HW ± 4

Cowes
01983 293983
Ch 80 H24
Cowes Yt Hvn
01983 299975
Ch 80 H24

Shamrock Quay
01703 229461
Ch 80 H24

Hythe
01703 207073
Ch 80 H24

Ocean Village
01703 229385
Ch 80 H24

Buckler's Hd
01590 616200
Ch 80 HW H24

Town Quay
01703 234397
Ch 80 H24

Lymington Yt Hvn
01590 677071
Ch 80 H24
Berthons
01590 673312
Ch 80 H24

Parkstone
01202 743610
Ch M H24

Salterns
01202 709971
Ch M H24

Cobbs Quay
01202 674299
Ch 80 HW ± 5

Sunseeker
01202 685335
Ch 80 H24

Ridge Wharf
01929 552650
HW ± 2

St Katherines Dk
0171 481 8350
Ch 80 HW -2 to
+1½

Limehouse Basin
0171 537 2828
Ch 80 HW ± 3

Ramsgate
01843 592277
Ch 80 H24

Gillingham
01634 280022
Ch 80 HW ± 4½

Dover
01304 241663
Ch 74 H24

Littlehampton
01903 713553
Ch 80
HW-3 to+2

Shoreham
01273 593801
Ch 14 H24

Brighton
01273 819919
Ch 80 H24

Eastbourne
01323 470099
Ch 17 H24

Newhaven
01273 513881
Ch 80 H24

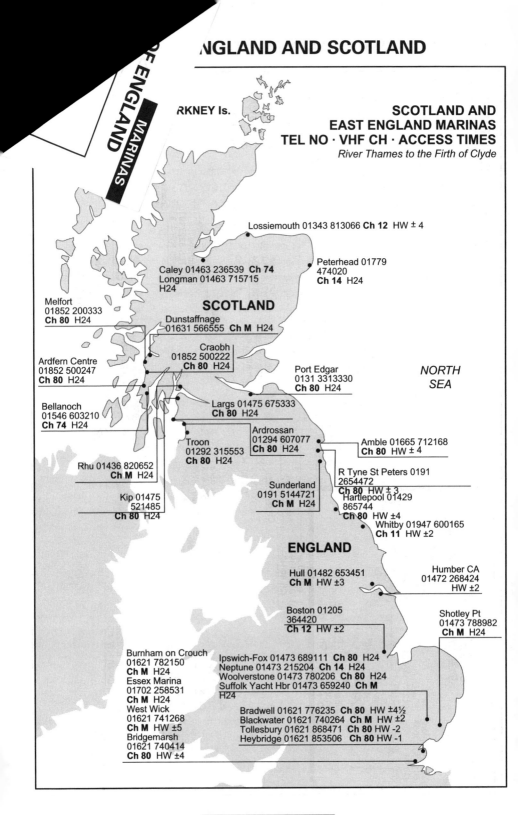

MARINAS **OF ENGLAND**

NGLAND AND SCOTLAND

RKNEY Is.

SCOTLAND AND EAST ENGLAND MARINAS
TEL NO · VHF CH · ACCESS TIMES
River Thames to the Firth of Clyde

Lossiemouth 01343 813066 **Ch 12** HW ± 4

Caley 01463 236539 **Ch 74**
Longman 01463 715715
H24

Peterhead 01779 474020
Ch 14 H24

Melfort 01852 200333
Ch 80 H24

SCOTLAND

Dunstaffnage 01631 566555 **Ch M** H24

Craobh 01852 500222
Ch 80 H24

Ardfern Centre 01852 500247
Ch 80 H24

Port Edgar 0131 3313330
Ch 80 H24

NORTH SEA

Bellanoch 01546 603210
Ch 74 H24

Largs 01475 675333
Ch 80 H24

Ardrossan 01294 607077
Ch 80 H24

Amble 01665 712168
Ch 80 HW ± 4

Rhu 01436 820652
Ch M H24

Troon 01292 315553
Ch 80 H24

R Tyne St Peters 0191 2654472
Ch 80 HW ± 3

Kip 01475 521485
Ch 80 H24

Sunderland 0191 5144721
Ch M H24

Hartlepool 01429 865744
Ch 80 HW ±4

Whitby 01947 600165
Ch 11 HW ±2

ENGLAND

Hull 01482 653451
Ch M HW ±3

Humber CA 01472 268424
HW ±2

Boston 01205 364420
Ch 12 HW ±2

Shotley Pt 01473 788982
Ch M H24

Burnham on Crouch 01621 782150
Ch M H24
Essex Marina 01702 258531
Ch M H24
West Wick 01621 741268
Ch M HW ±5
Bridgemarsh 01621 740414
Ch 80 HW ±4

Ipswich-Fox 01473 689111 **Ch 80** H24
Neptune 01473 215204 **Ch 14** H24
Woolverstone 01473 780206 **Ch 80** H24
Suffolk Yacht Hbr 01473 659240 **Ch M** H24

Bradwell 01621 776235 **Ch 80** HW ±4½
Blackwater 01621 740264 **Ch M** HW ±2
Tollesbury 01621 868471 **Ch 80** HW -2
Heybridge 01621 853506 **Ch 80** HW -1

WEST OF ENGLAND, WALES AND IRELAND

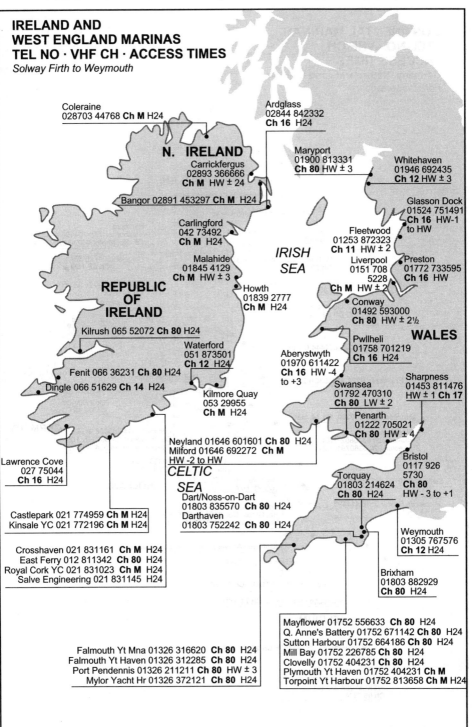

**IRELAND AND
WEST ENGLAND MARINAS
TEL NO · VHF CH · ACCESS TIMES**
Solway Firth to Weymouth

Coleraine
028703 44768 **Ch M** H24

Ardglass
02844 842332
Ch 16 H24

N. IRELAND

Carrickfergus
02893 366666
Ch M HW ± 24

Maryport
01900 813331
Ch 80 HW ± 3

Whitehaven
01946 692435
Ch 12 HW ± 3

Bangor 02891 453297 **Ch M** H24

Glasson Dock
01524 751491
Ch 16 HW-1
to HW

Carlingford
042 73492
Ch M H24

Fleetwood
01253 872323
Ch 11 HW ± 2

Malahide
01845 4129
Ch M HW ± 3

*IRISH
SEA*

Liverpool
0151 708
5228
Ch M HW ± 2

Preston
01772 733595
Ch 16 HW

**REPUBLIC
OF
IRELAND**

Howth
01839 2777
Ch M H24

Conway
01492 593000
Ch 80 HW ± 2½

Kilrush 065 52072 **Ch 80** H24

Pwllheli
01758 701219
Ch 16 H24

WALES

Waterford
051 873501
Ch 12 H24

Aberystwyth
01970 611422
Ch 16 HW -4
to +3

Fenit 066 36231 **Ch 80** H24

Swansea
01792 470310
Ch 80 LW ± 2

Sharpness
01453 811476
HW ± 1 **Ch 17**

Dingle 066 51629 **Ch 14** H24

Kilmore Quay
053 29955
Ch M H24

Penarth
01222 705021
Ch 80 HW ± 4

Lawrence Cove
027 75044
Ch 16 H24

Neyland 01646 601601 **Ch 80** H24
Milford 01646 692272 **Ch M**
HW -2 to HW

*CELTIC
SEA*

Bristol
0117 926
5730
Ch 80
HW - 3 to +1

Dart/Noss-on-Dart
01803 835570 **Ch 80** H24
Darthaven
01803 752242 **Ch 80** H24

Torquay
01803 214624
Ch 80 H24

Castlepark 021 774959 **Ch M** H24
Kinsale YC 021 772196 **Ch M** H24

Weymouth
01305 767576
Ch 12 H24

Crosshaven 021 831161 **Ch M** H24
East Ferry 012 811342 **Ch 80** H24
Royal Cork YC 021 831023 **Ch M** H24
Salve Engineering 021 831145 H24

Brixham
01803 882929
Ch 80 H24

Falmouth Yt Mna 01326 316620 **Ch 80** H24
Falmouth Yt Haven 01326 312285 **Ch 80** H24
Port Pendennis 01326 211211 **Ch 80** HW ± 3
Mylor Yacht Hr 01326 372121 **Ch 80** H24

Mayflower 01752 556633 **Ch 80** H24
Q. Anne's Battery 01752 671142 **Ch 80** H24
Sutton Harbour 01752 664186 **Ch 80** H24
Mill Bay 01752 226785 **Ch 80** H24
Clovelly 01752 404231 **Ch 80** H24
Plymouth Yt Haven 01752 404231 **Ch M**
Torpoint Yt Harbour 01752 813658 **Ch M** H24

GERMANY, NETHERLANDS AND BELGIUM

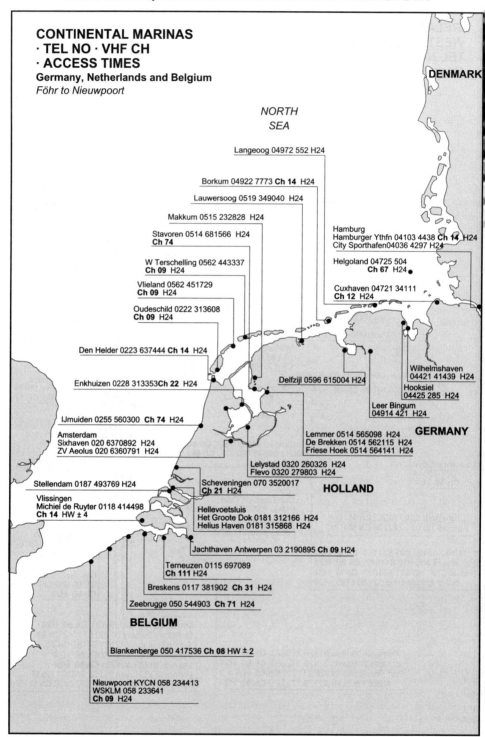

CONTINENTAL MARINAS
· TEL NO · VHF CH
· ACCESS TIMES
Germany, Netherlands and Belgium
Föhr to Nieuwpoort

DENMARK

NORTH
SEA

Langeoog 04972 552 H24

Borkum 04922 7773 **Ch 14** H24
Lauwersoog 0519 349040 H24
Makkum 0515 232828 H24
Stavoren 0514 681566 H24
Ch 74
W Terschelling 0562 443337
Ch 09 H24
Vlieland 0562 451729
Ch 09 H24
Oudeschild 0222 313608
Ch 09 H24

Hamburg
Hamburger Ythfn 04103 4438 **Ch 14** H24
City Sporthafen04036 4297 H24
Helgoland 04725 504
Ch 67 H24
Cuxhaven 04721 34111
Ch 12 H24

Den Helder 0223 637444 **Ch 14** H24

Enkhuizen 0228 313353 **Ch 22** H24

Delfzijl 0596 615004 H24

Wilhelmshaven
04421 41439 H24
Hooksiel
04425 285 H24
Leer Bingum
04914 421 H24

IJmuiden 0255 560300 **Ch 74** H24

Amsterdam
Sixhaven 020 6370892 H24
ZV Aeolus 020 6360791 H24

Lemmer 0514 565098 H24
De Brekken 0514 562115 H24
Friese Hoek 0514 564141 H24

GERMANY

Lelystad 0320 260326 H24
Flevo 0320 279803 H24

Stellendam 0187 493769 H24

Scheveningen 070 3520017
Ch 21 H24

HOLLAND

Vlissingen
Michiel de Ruyter 0118 414498
Ch 14 HW ± 4

Hellevoetsluis
Het Groote Dok 0181 312166 H24
Helius Haven 0181 315868 H24

Jachthaven Antwerpen 03 2190895 **Ch 09** H24

Terneuzen 0115 697089
Ch 111 H24

Breskens 0117 381902 **Ch 31** H24

Zeebrugge 050 544903 **Ch 71** H24

BELGIUM

Blankenberge 050 417536 **Ch 08** HW ± 2

Nieuwpoort KYCN 058 234413
WSKLM 058 233641
Ch 09 H24

FRANCE

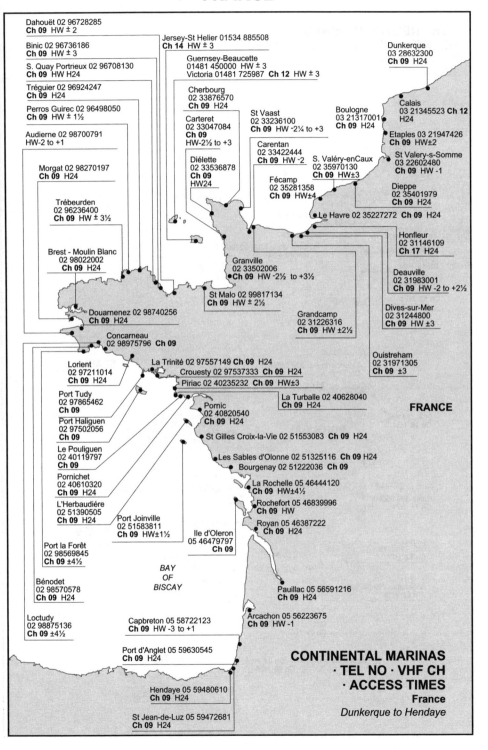

Dahouët 02 96728285
Ch 09 HW ± 2

Binic 02 96736186
Ch 09 HW ± 3

S. Quay Portrieux 02 96708130
Ch 09 HW H24

Tréguier 02 96924247
Ch 09 H24

Perros Guirec 02 96498050
Ch 09 HW ± 1½

Audierne 02 98700791
HW-2 to +1

Morgat 02 98270197
Ch 09 H24

Trébeurden
02 96236400
Ch 09 HW ± 3½

Brest - Moulin Blanc
02 98022002
Ch 09 H24

Douarnenez 02 98740256
Ch 09 H24

Concarneau
02 98975796 **Ch 09**

Lorient
02 97211014
Ch 09 H24

Port Tudy
02 97865462
Ch 09

Port Haliguen
02 97502056
Ch 09

Le Pouliguen
02 40119797
Ch 09

Pornichet
02 40610320
Ch 09 H24

L'Herbaudiére
02 51390505
Ch 09 H24

Port la Forêt
02 98569845
Ch 09 ±4½

Bénodet
02 98570578
Ch 09 H24

Loctudy
02 98875136
Ch 09 ±4½

Jersey-St Helier 01534 885508
Ch 14 HW ± 3

Guernsey-Beaucette
01481 450000 HW ± 3
Victoria 01481 725987 **Ch 12** HW ± 3

Cherbourg
02 33876570
Ch 09 H24

Carteret
02 33047084
Ch 09
HW-2½ to +3

Diélette
02 33536878
Ch 09
HW24

St Vaast
02 33236100
Ch 09 HW -2¼ to +3

Carentan
02 33422444
Ch 09 HW -2

Fécamp
02 35281358
Ch 09 HW±4

Le Havre 02 35227272 **Ch 09** H24

Granville
02 33502006
Ch 09 HW -2½ to +3½

St Malo 02 99817134
Ch 09 HW ± 2½

Grandcamp
02 31226316
Ch 09 HW ±2½

La Trinité 02 97557149 **Ch 09** H24
Crouesty 02 97537333 **Ch 09** H24
Piriac 02 40235232 **Ch 09** HW±3

La Turballe 02 40628040
Ch 09 H24

Pornic
02 40820540
Ch 09 H24

St Gilles Croix-la-Vie 02 51553083 **Ch 09** H24

Les Sables d'Olonne 02 51325116 **Ch 09** H24
Bourgenay 02 51222036 **Ch 09**

La Rochelle 05 46444120
Ch 09 HW±4½

Rochefort 05 46839996
Ch 09 HW

Royan 05 46387222
Ch 09 H24

Port Joinville
02 51583811
Ch 09 HW±1½

Ile d'Oleron
05 46479797
Ch 09

*BAY
OF
BISCAY*

Capbreton 05 58722123
Ch 09 HW -3 to +1

Arcachon 05 56223675
Ch 09 HW -1

Pauillac 05 56591216
Ch 09 H24

Port d'Anglet 05 59630545
Ch 09 H24

Hendaye 05 59480610
Ch 09 H24

St Jean-de-Luz 05 59472681
Ch 09 H24

Dunkerque
03 28632300
Ch 09 H24

Calais
03 21345523 **Ch 12**
H24

Boulogne
03 21317001
Ch 09 H24

Etaples 03 21947426
Ch 09 HW±2

St Valery-s-Somme
03 22602480
Ch 09 HW -1

S. Valéry-enCaux
02 35970130
Ch 09 HW±3

Dieppe
02 35401979
Ch 09 H24

Honfleur
02 31146109
Ch 17 H24

Deauville
02 31983001
Ch 09 HW -2 to +2½

Dives-sur-Mer
02 31244800
Ch 09 HW ±3

Ouistreham
02 31971305
Ch 09 ±3

FRANCE

CONTINENTAL MARINAS
· TEL NO · VHF CH
· ACCESS TIMES
France
Dunkerque to Hendaye

SPAIN AND PORTUGAL

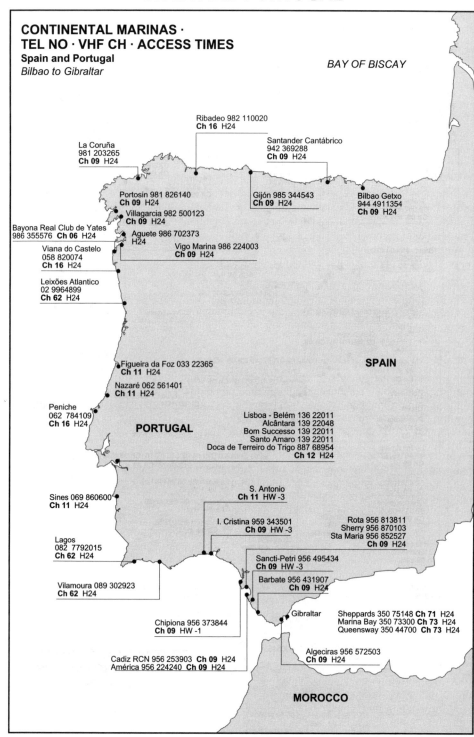

CONTINENTAL MARINAS ·
TEL NO · VHF CH · ACCESS TIMES
Spain and Portugal
Bilbao to Gibraltar

BAY OF BISCAY

Ribadeo 982 110020
Ch 16 H24

Santander Cantábrico
942 369288
Ch 09 H24

La Coruña
981 203265
Ch 09 H24

Portosin 981 826140
Ch 09 H24

Gijón 985 344543
Ch 09 H24

Bilbao Getxo
944 4911354
Ch 09 H24

Villagarcia 982 500123
Ch 09 H24

Bayona Real Club de Yates
986 355576 **Ch 06** H24

Aguete 986 702373
H24

Viana do Castelo
058 820074
Ch 16 H24

Vigo Marina 986 224003
Ch 09 H24

Leixões Atlantico
02 9964899
Ch 62 H24

Figueira da Foz 033 22365
Ch 11 H24

SPAIN

Nazaré 062 561401
Ch 11 H24

Peniche
062 784109
Ch 16 H24

PORTUGAL

Lisboa - Belém 136 22011
Alcântara 139 22048
Bom Successo 139 22011
Santo Amaro 139 22011
Doca de Terreiro do Trigo 887 68954
Ch 12 H24

S. Antonio
Ch 11 HW -3

Sines 069 860600
Ch 11 H24

I. Cristina 959 343501
Ch 09 HW -3

Rota 956 813811
Sherry 956 870103
Sta Maria 956 852527
Ch 09 H24

Lagos
082 7792015
Ch 62 H24

Sancti-Petri 956 495434
Ch 09 HW -3

Vilamoura 089 302923
Ch 62 H24

Barbate 956 431907
Ch 09 H24

Gibraltar

Sheppards 350 75148 **Ch 71** H24
Marina Bay 350 73300 **Ch 73** H24
Queensway 350 44700 **Ch 73** H24

Chipiona 956 373844
Ch 09 HW -1

Algeciras 956 572503
Ch 09 H24

Cadiz RCN 956 253903 **Ch 09** H24
América 956 224240 **Ch 09** H24

MOROCCO

POSITION SECTION

CONTENTS

PRINCIPAL LIGHTS

Range 15M and over
Abbreviations used in List of Lights:
Al Alternating
Bu Blue
Dir Direction light
F Fixed
Fl Flashing
Fl( ) Group flashing
G Green
(hor) Horizontal
intens Intensified sector
Iso Isophase
Lanby Large Automatic Navigational Buoy
Ldg Lts Leading lights
LFl Long flash
Lt F Light-float
Lt V Light-vessel
M Sea miles
m Metres
Mo Morse code ligth or fog signal
Oc Occulting
Occas Occasional
(P) Provisional, preliminary
Q Quick flashing
R Red
Ra Coast radar station
Racon Radar responder beacon
Radio Coast radio station
RG Radio direction finding station
s Seconds
(T) Temporary
TE Light temporarily extinguished
unintens Unintensified sector
(vert) Vertical
Vi Violet
Vis Visible
VQ Very quick flashing
W White
Y Yellow, amber or orange

SOUTH COAST OF ENGLAND

A0002 **Bishop Rock** 49°52'·3N 06°26'·7W
Fl(2)W 15s 44m 24M
Partially obscured 204°-211°(7°), obscured 211°-233°(22°), 236°-259°(23°). Racon (T)

A0006 **St Mary's**
Peninnis Head 49°54'·2N 06°18'·2W
Fl W 20s 36m 17M
vis: 231°-117°(246°), partially obscured 048°-083°(35°) within 5M

A0018 **Round Island**
N side of group 49°58'·7N 06°19'·3W
Fl W 10s 55m 24M
vis: 021°-288°(267°)

A0020 **Seven Stones Lt F** 50°03'·6N 06°04'·3W
Fl(3)W 30s 12m 25M *Racon (O)*

A0028 **Longships** 50°04'·0N 05°44'·8W
Iso WR 10s 35m 19/15/14M
vis: R189°-208°(19°), R(unintens)208°-307°(99°), R307°-327°(20°), W327°-189°(222°)

A0030 **Wolf Rock** 49°56'·7N 05°48'·5W
Fl W 15s 34m 23M *Racon (T)*

A0032 **Tater-du** 50°03'·1N 05°34'·6W
Fl(3)W 15s 34m 23M
vis: 241°-074°(193°)

A0046 **Penzance Harbour**
South Pier. Head 50°07'·0N 05°31'·6W
Fl WR 5s 11m 17/12 M
vis: R(unintens)159°-224°(65°), R224°-268°(44°), W268°-344·5°(76·5°), R344·5°- shore

A0060 **Lizard** 49°57'·6N 05°12·1'·W
Fl W 3s 70m 25M
vis: 250°-120°(230°), partly vis: 235°-250°(15°).

A0062 **St Anthony Head** 50°08'·4N 05°00'·9W
Oc WR 15s 22m 22/20/20M
vis: W295°- 004°(69°), R004°- 022°(18°) over Manacle rocks, W(unintens) 022°-100°(78°) W100°- 172° (72°)

A0094 **Looe Harbour**
Banjo Pier. Head 50°21'·0N 04°27'·0'W
Oc WR 3s 8m 15/12M
vis: W013°-207° (194°), R207°- 267°(60°), W267°-313°(46°), R313°-332°(19°)

A0098 **Eddystone** 50°10'·8N 04°15'·9W
Fl(2)W 10s 41m 20M *Racon (T)*

A0228 **Start Point** 50°13'·3N 03°38'·5W
Fl(3)W 10s 62m 25M
vis: 184°-068°(244°)

A0294 **Portland Bill** 50°30'·8N 2°27'·3W
Fl(4)W 20s 43m 25M
Gradually changes from 1fl to 4fl 221°-244°(23°), 4fl 244°-117°(233°), gradually changes from 4fl to 1fl 117°-141°(24°).

A0314 **Portland Harbour** NE Breakwater SE end, A head 50°35'·1N 02°25'·0W
Fl W 10s 22m 20M

A0496 **Anvil Pt** 50°35'·5N 01°57'·5W
Fl W 10s 45m 24M
vis: 237°-076°(199°)

A0528 **Needles** 50°39'·7N 01°35'·4W
Oc(2)WRG 20s 24m 17/14/13M
vis: R shore-300°, W300°-083°(143°), R(unintens) 083°- 212°(129°), W212°-217°(5°), G217°-224°(7°)

A0538-1 **Hurst Point** 50°42'·5N 01°32'·9W
Iso WRG 4s 19m 21/18/17M, G038·6°-040·6°(2°), W040·6°-041·6°(1°), (2°)R041·6°-043·6°

A0774 **St Catherine's Point** 50°34'·5N 01°17'·8W
Fl W 5s 41m 26M
vis: 257°-117°(220°).

A0780 **Nab** 50°40'·0N 00°57'·1W
Fl W 10s 27m 16M
vis: 300°-120° (180°). Racon (T)

A0814-1 **Shoreham Harbour** Leading light 355°
Rear 192m from front 50°49'·8N 00°14'·8W
Fl W 10s 13m 15M
vis: 283°-103°(180°)

A0839 **Greenwich Lt F** 50°24'·5N 00°00'·0E **Fl 5s** 12m 21M *Racon (M)*

A0840 **Beachy Head** 50°44'·0N 00°14'·6E
Fl(2)W 20s 31m 20M
vis: 248°-101°(213°)

A0876 **Dungeness** 50°54'·8N 00°58'·7E
Fl W 10s 40m 27M

Partially obsc 078°-shore.

A0892 Folkestone
Breakwater head 51°04'·5N 01°11'·8E
Fl(2)W 10s 14m 22M

A0900 Dover Hbr Admiralty pier 51°06'·6N 01°19'·8E
FIW 8s 21m 20M
vis: 096°-090°(354°), Obscured in The Downs
by S Foreland inshore of 226°

A0924 Dover Harbour - South Breakwater
West head 51°06'·8N 01°19'·9E
OcR 30s 21m 18M

A0926 Dover Harbour
Knuckle 51°07'·0N 01°20'·6E
Fl(4)WR 10s 15m 15/13M
vis: R059°-239°(180°), W239°-059°(180°)

A0966 North Foreland 51°22'·5N 01°26'·8E
Fl(5)WR 20s 57m 19/16/15M
vis: W shore - 150°, R 150°-181°(31°),
R181°-200°(19°), W200°-011°(171°).

A0970 Varne Lt F 51°01'·2N 01°24'·0E
FIR 20s 12m 19M Racon (T)

A0980 South Goodwin Lt F 51°07'·9N 01°28'·6E Fl(2)W
20s 12m 15M

A0984 East Goodwin Lt F 51°13'·2N 01°36'·5E FIW
15s 12m 21M Racon (T)

A0992 F3 Lt F 51°23'·8N 02°00'·6E
FIW 10s 12m 22M Racon (T)

EAST COAST OF ENGLAND

A2096 Shornmead 51°27'·0N 00°26'·6E
Fl(2)WRG 10s 12m 17/13/13M
vis: G054°- 081·5°(27·5°), R081·5°-086·2°
(4·7°), W086·2°- 088·7°(2·5°),
G088·7°- 141°(52·3°), W141°-205°(64°),
R205°-213°(8°)

A2118 Tilbury
Northfleet Lower 51°26'·9N 00°20'·4E OcWR 5s
15m 17/14M
vis: W164°- 271°(107°),
R271°-S shore in Gravesend reach

A2119 Tilbury
Northfleet Upper 51°26'·9N 00°20'·2E OcWRG
10s 30m 16/12/12M
vis: R126°-149°(23°), W149°-159°(10°),
G159°-268°(109°), W268°-279°(11°)

A2170 Sunk Lt F 51°51'·0N 01°35'·0E
Fl(2)W 20s 12m 24M Racon (T)

A2258 Orford Ness 52°05'·0N 01°34'·6E
FIW 5s 28m 25M Racon (T)
also F RG 14m 15/14M.
vis: R shore-210°, R038°-047°(9°), G047°-
shore

A2272 Southwold 52°19'·6N 01°41'·0E
Fl(4)WR 20s 37m 17/15/14M
vis: R(intens) 204°-220°(16°),
W220°-001°(141°), R001°-032·3°(31·3°)

A2280 Lowestoft 52°29'·2N 01°45'·5E
FIW 15s 37m 28M
Partially obsc 347°-shore

A2332 Newarp Lt F 52°48'·3N 01°55'·8E
FIW 10s 12m 21M Racon (O)

A2342 Cromer 52°55'·5N 01°19'·1E
FIW 5s 84m 23M
vis: 102°-307°(205°). Racon (O)

A2351 Inner Dowsing Lt F 53°19'·5N 00°34'·0E
FIW 10s 12m 15M Racon (T)

A2420 B 1D Dowsing 53°33'·7N 00°52'·7E
Fl(2)W 10s 28m 22M Racon (T)

A2582 Flamborough Head 54°07'·0N 00°04'·8W
Fl(4)W 15s 65m 24M

A2596 Whitby High 54°28'·6N 00°34'·0W
IsoWR 10s 73m 18/16M
vis: R128°-143°(15°), W143°-319°(176°)

A2626 South Gare 54°38'·8N 01°08'·1W
FIWR 12s 16m 20/17M
vis: W020°-274°(254°). R274°-357°(83°).
Shown from a structure 84m S, obscured on a
bearing 197·5°(T) 1997

A2627·1 River Tees. Ldg Lts. 210°04'.
Rear. 560m from front 54°37'·0N 01°10'·3E FR
20m 16M

A2663 The Heugh
Hartlepool 54°41'·8N 01°10'·5W
Fl(2)W 10s 19m 19M

A2681 Port of Sunderland Roker Pier Head.
54°55'·3N 01°21'·0W
FIW 5s 25m 23M
vis: 211°-357°(146°)

A2700 Tynemouth Entrance N pier-head.
55°00'·9N 01°24'·1W
Fl(3)W 10s 26m 26M

A2702.5 Herd Groyne 55°00'·5N 01°25'·3W
DirOcW 10s 14m 19M vis: 246·5°-251·5°(5°)

A2754 Blyth Harbour East Pier
East Pier-head 55°07'·0N 01°29'·1W
Fl(4)W 10s 19m 21M

A2780 Coquet 55°20'·0N 01°32'·2W
Fl(3)WR 30s 25m 21/16M
vis: R330°-140°(170°), W140°- 163°(23°),
R163°-180°(17°), W180°-330°(150°)

A2810 Bamburgh
Black Rocks Point 55°37'·0N 01°43'·3W
Oc(2)WRG 15s 12m 17/13/13M
vis: G122°-165°(43°), W165°- 175° (10°),
R175°-191°(16°), W191°-238°(47°), R238°-
275°(37°), W275-289°(14°), G289°-300°(11°)

A2814 Farne Island Longstone.
West Side 55°38'·6N 01°36'·5W
FIW 20s 23m 24M

SCOTLAND

A2850 St Abb's Head 55°55'·0N 02°08'·3W
FIW 10s 68m 26M Racon (T)

A2868 Fidra 56°04'·4N 02°47'·0W
Fl(4)W 30s 34m 24M
Obscured by Bass Rock, Craig Leith & Lamb Is

A2912 Inchkeith Summit 56°02'·0N 03°08'·1W
FIW 15s 67m 22M

A2915·4 Braefoot Bay Terminal West Jetty.
Leading Lights 247°15'.
Front 56°02'·2N 03°18'·6W
FIW 3s 6m 15M
vis: 237·2°-257·2°(20°)

A2915·41 Braefoot Bay Terminal
Rear 88m from front 56°02'·2N 03°18'·7W
FIW 3s 12m 15M
vis: 237·2°-257·2°(20°). Synchronised with
front

A3060	**Elie Ness** 56°11'·0N 02°48'·6W
	FlW 6s 15m 18M
A3090	**Isle of May** Summit 56°11'·2N 02°33'·3W
	Fl(2)W 15s 73m 22M
A3102	**Fife Ness** 56°16'·7N 02°35'·1W
	IsoWR 10s 12m 21/20M
	vis: W143°-197°(54°). R197°-217°(20°). W217°-023°(166°).
A3108	**Bell Rock** 56°26'·1N 02°23'·1W
	FlW 5s 28m 18M *Racon (M)*
A3142	**Tayport** High Lighthouse.
	Dir Lt 269° 56°27'·2N 02°53'·8W
	Dir IsoWRG 3s 24m 22/17/16M
	vis: G267°- 268°(1°), W268°-270°(2°), R270°-271°(1°)
A3220	**Scurdie Ness** 56°42'·1N 02°26'·1W
	Fl(3)W 20s 38m 23M *Racon* (T)
A3234	**Todhead** 56°53'·0N 02°12'·8W
	Fl(4)W 30s 41m 18M
A3246	**Girdle Ness** 57°08'·3N 02°02'·8W
	Fl(2)W 20s 56m 22M *Obscured by Greg Ness when brg more than about 020°. Racon (G)*
A3280	**Buchan Ness** 57°28'·2N 01°46'·4W
	FlW 5s 40m 28M *Racon (O)*
A3304	**Rattray Head** Ron Rock 57°36'·6N 01°48'·9W
	Fl(3)W 30s 28m 24M *Racon*
A3332	**Kinnaird Head** 57°41'·9N 02°00'·1W
	FlW 5s 25m 22M *vis: 092°-297°(205°).*
A3394	**Buckie Harbour** 60m from NW pier head
	57°40'·9N 2°57'·5W **OcR 10s** 15m 15M
A3394·1	**Buckie Harbour**
	Cliff Terrace 57°40'·7N 02°57'·2W
	IsoWG 2s 20m 16/12M
	vis: G090°-110°(20°), W110°-225°(115°)
A3414	**Covesea Skerries** 57°43'·5N 03°20'·2W
	FlWR 20s 49m 24/20M
	vis: W076°-267°(191°). R267°-282°(15°)
A3440	**Chanonry** 57°34'·5N 04°05'·4W
	OcW 6s 12m 15M *vis: 148°-073°(285°)*
A3490	**Cromarty** The Ness 57°41'·0N 04°02'·1W
	OcWR 10s 18m 15/11M
	vis: R079°-088°(9°), W088°-275°(187°). Obscured by North Sutor when bearing less than 253°.
A3506	**Tarbat Ness** 57°51'·9N 03°46'·5W
	Fl(4)W 30s 53m 24M *Racon (T)*
A3524	**Clythness** 58°18'·7N 03°12'·6W
	Fl(2)W 30s 45m 16M
A3544	**Noss Head** 58°28'·8N 03°03'·0W
	FlWR 20s 53m 25/21M
	vis: R shore-191°, W191°-shore
A3558	**Duncansby Head** 58°38'·6N 03°01'·4W
	FlW 12s 67m 22M *Racon (T)*
A3562	**Pentland Skerries** 58°41'·4N 02°55'·4W
	Fl(3)W 30s 52m 23M
A3568	**Swilkie Point** Stroma 58°41'·8N 03°07'·0W
	Fl(2)W 20s 32m 26M
A3574	**Dunnet Head** 58°40'·3N 03°22'·4W
	Fl(4)W 30s 105m 23M
A3578	**Holborn Head** Little Head.
	Thurso Bay 58°36'·9N 03°32'·4W

	FlWR 10s 23m 15/11M
	vis: W198°-358°(160°), R358°-shore
A3590	**Strathy Point**
	Thurso Bay 58°36'·1N 04°00'·9W
	FlW 20s 45m 26M
A3602	**Cantick Head** 58°47'·2N 03°07'·8W
	FlW 20s 35m 18M
A3644	**Graemsay Island** Hoy Sound.
	Front Leading Light. 104°
	58°56'·5N 03°18'·4W
	IsoW 3s 17m 15M
	vis: 070°-255°(185°)
A3644·1	**Graemsay Island Rear** Hoy Sound.
	Rear Ldg Lt.1·2M from front
	58°56'·2N 03°16'·3W
	OcWR 8s 35m 20/16M
	vis: R097°-112°(15°), W112°- 163° (51°), R163°-178°(15°), W178°-332°(154°). Obscured on leading line within 0·5M
A3676	**Copinsay** 58°53'·8N 02°40'·2W
	Fl(5)W 30s 79m 21M
A3680	**Auskerry** 59°01'·6N 02°34'·2W
	FlW 20s 34m 18M *Range reduced to 9M (T) 1999*
A3688	**Kirkwall** Pier.
	North end 58°59'·3N 02°57'·6W
	IsoWRG 5s 13m 15/13/13M
	G153°-183°(30°), W183°-192°(9°), R192°-210°(18°)
A3700	**Brough of Birsay** 59°08'·2N 03°20'·3W
	Fl(3)W 25s 52m 18M
A3718	**Sanday Island** Start Point 59°16'·7N 02°22'·5W
	Fl(2)W 20s 24m 19M *Range reduced to 9M (T) 1999*
A3722	**North Ronaldsay**
	Near NE end 59°23'·4N 02°22'·8W
	FlW 10s 43m 24M *Racon* (T)
A3736	**Westray** Noup Head 59°19'·9N 03°04'·0W
	FlW 30s 79m 22M
	vis: about 335°-242°(267°), 248-282°(34°). Obscured by cliffs on easterly bearings within 0·8M, partially obscured 240°- 275°(35°) Range reduced to 9M (T) 1999
A3750	**Skadan** Fair Isle - South 59°30'·9N 01°39'·0W
	Fl(4)W 30s 32m 22M
	vis: 260°- 146°(246°), but obscured close inshore from 260°-282°(22°).
A3756	**Skroo** Fair Isle - North. 59°33'·2N 01°36'·5W
	Fl(2)W 30s 80m 22M
	vis: 086·7°-358°(271·3°)
A3766	**Sumburgh Head** 59°51'·3N 01°16'·3W
	Fl(3)W 30s 91m 23M
A3776	**Kirkabister Ness** Bressay
	60°07'·2N 01°07'·2W
	Fl(2)W 20s 32m 23M
A3807	**Out Skerries**
	Bound Skerry 60°25'·5N 00°43'·5W
	FlW 20s 44m 20M
A3812	**Yell Sound** Firths Voe.
	North shore 60°27'·2N 01°10'·6W
	OcWRG 8s 9m 15/10/10M
	vis: W189°-194°(5°), G194°-257°(63°), W257°-261°(4°), R261°-339°(78°), W339°-066°(87°)

A3817·5 **Yell Sound**
Point of Fethaland 60°38'·1N 01°18'·6W
Fl(3)WR 15s 65m 24/20M
vis: R080°-103°(23°),W103°-160°(57°),
R160°-206°(46°), W206°-340°(134°)

A3822 **Sullom Voe** Gluss Isle
Leading Lights 194°44'.
Front 60°29'·8N 01°19'·3W
FW 39m 19M

A3822·1 **Sullom Voe**
Rear 0·75M from front
60°29'·1N 01°19'·5W
FW 69m 19M

A3832 **Muckle Flugga**
60°51'·3N 00°53'·0W
Fl(2)W 20s 66m 22M

A3838 **Esha Ness** 60°29'·3N 01°37'·6W
FIW 12s 61m 25M

A3845·5 **West Burra Firth**
Inner Lt 60°17'·8N 01°32'·0W
FWRG 9m 15/9/9M
vis: G095°-098°(3°), W098°-102°(4°),
R102°- 105°(3°)

A3860 **Foula** 60°06'·8N 02°03'·7W
Fl(3)W 15s 36m 18M
Obscured 123°-221°(98°) Range reduced to 9M
(T) 1999

A3868 **Sule Skerry** 59°05'·0N 04°24'·3W
Fl(2)W 15s 34m 21M *Racon (T)*

A3869 **Rona**
North Rona 59°07'·3N 05°48'·8W
Fl(3)W 20s 114m 24M

A3880 **Cape Wrath** 58°37'·5N 04°59'·9W
Fl(4)W 30s 122m 24M

A3881 **Kinlochbervie** 58°27'·5N 05°03'·0W
Dir WRG 15m 16M
vis: FG326°-325·5°(0·5°),
AlGW326·5°-326·75°(0·25°),
FW326·75°-327·25°(0·5·),
AlRW 327°·25°-327·5°(0·25°),
FR327·5°-328°(0·5°). Floodlit.

A3882 **Stoer Head**
Cluas Deas 58°14'·4N 05°24'·0W
FIW 15s 59m 24M

A3900 **Rubha Reidh** 57°51'·4N 05°48'·6W
Fl(4)W 15s 37m 24M

A3904 **Rona** - South Rona.
NE Pt 57°34'·7N 05°57'·5W
FIW 12s 69m 19M
vis: 050°-358°(308°) Replaced by 2 synch
FIW12s 69m 9M (T) 1999

A3944 **Sound of Sleat** Ornsay.
South East End. Islet 57°08'·6N 05°46'·4W
OcW 8s 18m 15M
vis: 157°-030°(233°)

A3968 **Butt of Lewis**
58°31'·0N 06°15'·7W
FIW 5s 52m 25M
vis:056°-320°(264°).

A3972 **Tiumpan Head**
58°15'·6N 06°08'·3W
Fl(2)W 15s 55m 25M

A3976 **Stornoway Harbour**
Arnish Point 58°11'·5N 06°22'·2W
FIWR 10s 17m 19/15M
vis: W088°- 198° (110°), R198°-302°(104°),
W302°-013°(71°)

A3990 **East Loch Tarbert** Scalpay.
Eilean Glas 57°51'·4N 06°38'·5W
Fl(3)W 20s 43m 23M *Racon*

A4004 **South Uist** Ushenish 57°17'·9N 07°11'· 5W
FIWR 20s 54m 19/15M
vis: W193°-356°(163°). R356°-013°(17°)
Fl.W.20s 54m 9M (T) 1999

A4020 **Berneray**
West side. Barra Head 56°47'·1N 07°39'·2W
FIW 15s 208m 18M
Obscured by the islands to NE

A4020·3 **Haskeir Island** 57°42'·0N 07°41'·3W
Fl W 20s 44m 23M

A4028 **Flannan Isles**
Eilean Mór 58°17'·3N 07°35'·4W
Fl(2)W 30s 101m 20M
Obscured in places by islands W of Eilean
Mór

A4064 **Skye**
Neist Point 57°25'·4N 06°47'·2W
FIW 5s 43m 16M

A4076 **Òigh Sgeir** Near South end.
Hyskeir 56°58'·2N 06°40'·9W
Fl(3)W 30s 41m 24M *Racon (T)*

A4082 **Ardnamurchan** 56°43'·6N 6°13'·4W
Fl(2)W 20s 55m 24M
vis:002°-217°(215°)

A4092 **Scarinish**
South side of entrance 56°30'·0N 06°48'·2W
FIW 3s 11m 16M
vis:210°-030°(180°)

A4096 **Skerryvore** 56°19'·4N 07°06'·9W
FIW 10s 46m 23M *Racon (M)*

A4098 **Dubh Artach** 56°08'·0N 06°37'·9W
Fl(2)W 30s 44m 20M

A4112 **Sound of Mull**
Rubha nan Gall 56°38'·3N 06°03'·9W
FIW 3s 17m 15M

A4170 **Lismore** Eilean Musdile.
SW end 56°27'·4N 05°36'·4W
FIW 10s 31m 19M
vis:237°-208°(331°)

A4236 **Sound of Islay**
Rubh'a' Mháil. Ruvaal 55°56'·2N 06°07'·3W
Fl(3)WR 15s 45m 24/21M
vis:R075°-180°(105°), W180°-075°(255°)

A4256 **Orsay I.**
Rhinns of Islay 55°40'·4N 06°30'·8W
FIW 5s 46m 24M
vis:256°-184°(288°)

A4272 **Mull of Kintyre** 55°18'·6N 05°48'·1W
Fl(2)W 20s 91m 24M
vis:347°-178°(191°)

A4274 **Sanda Island**
South side 55°16'·5N 05°34'·9W
FIW 10s 50m 15M *Racon (T)*

A4276   Campbeltown Loch Island Davaar.
N Point 55°25'·7N 05°32'·4W
Fl(2)W 10s 37m 23M *vis: 073°-330°(257°)*

A4293   Skipness
Calibration range 55°46'·7N 05°19'·0W
Oc(2)Y 10s 24M *Shown when range in use*

A4326   Arran Island Pladda 55°25'·5N 05°07'·3W
Fl(3)W 30s 40m 17M

A4330   Holy Island
Pillar Rock Point 55°31'·0N 05°03'·6W
Fl(2)W 20s 38m 25M

A4362   Toward Point 55°51'·7N 04°58'·7W
FIW 10s 21m 22M

A4421   Beacon No 8 N
Gareloch. Dir Lt 080° 55°59'·1N 04°44'·1W
DirWRG 4m 16/13/13M
vis: FG075°-077·5°(2·5°),
AlWG077·5°-079·5°(2°),
FW079·5°-080·5°(1°),
AlWR080·5°-082·5°(2°), FR082·5°-085°(2·5°)

A4421   Gareloch Beacon No 8N.
Dir Lt 138° 55°59'·1N 04°44'·1W
DirWRG 4m 16/13/13M
vis: FG132°-134°(2°), AlWG134°-137°(3°),
FW137°-139°(2°), AlWR139°-142°(3°). Sectors
unreliable (T) 1997

A4422   Beacon No 7N Gareloch. 356°.
Front. 56°00'·1N 04°45'·3W
DirWRG 5m 16/13/13M
vis: AlWG353°-355°(2°), FW355°-357°(2°),
AlWR357°-000°(3°), FR000°-002°(2°)

A4422·5 Rhu Point Dir Lt 318°
56°00'·9N 04°47'·1W
DirWRG 9m 16/13/13M
vis: AlWG315°-317°(2°), FW317°-319°(2°),
AlWR319°-321°(2°), FR321°-325°(4°)

A4423   Beacon No 2N
Rhu Narrows Limekiln Pt. Bn No 2N.
Dir Lt 295° 56°00'·7N 04°47'·6W
DirWRG 5m 16/13/13M
vis: AlWG291°-294°(3°), FW294°-296°(2°),
AlWR296°-299°(3°), FR299°-301°(2°).

A4423·5 Roseneath Bay Beacon No 3N
Dir Lt 149° 56°00'·1N 04°46'·6W
DirWRG 9m 16/13/13M
vis: FG144°-145°(1°), AlWG145°-148°(3°),
FW148°-150°(2°), AlWR150°-153°(3°),
FR153°-154°(1°). Sectors unreliable (T) 1998

A4580   Turnberry Point
Near castle ruins 55°19'·6N 04°50'·6W
FIW 15s 29m 24M

A4582   Ailsa Craig 55°15'·1N 05°06'·4W
FIW 4s 18m 17M
vis: 145°-028°(243°)

A4604   Corsewall Point 55°00'·5N 05°09'·5W
Fl(5)W 30s 34m 22M
vis: 027°-257°(230°)

A4606   Killantringan
Black Head 54°51'·7N 05°08'·7W
Fl(2)W 15s 49m 25M

A4608   Crammag Head 54°39'·9N 04°57'·8W
FIW 10s 35m 18M

A4610   Mull of Galloway
South East end 54°38'·1N 04°51'·4W
FIW 20s 99m 28M *vis: 182°-105°(283°)*

WEST COAST OF ENGLAND

A4710   Saint Bees Head 54°30'·8N 03°38'·1W
Fl(2)W 20s 102m 21M
Obscured shore-340°

ISLE OF MAN

A4720   Point of Ayre
54°24'·9N 04°22'·1W
Fl(4)W 20s 32m 19M *Racon (M)*

A4746   Calf of Man
West Point 54°03'·2N 04°49'·6W
FIW 15s 93m 26M
vis: 274°-190°(276°)

A4770   Douglas Head   54°08'·6N 04°27'·9W
FIW 10s 32m 24M
Reduced range shore-220°. Obscured when
bearing more than 037°

A4786   Maughold Head 54°17'·7N 04°18'·4W
Fl(3)W 30s 65m 21M

WEST COAST OF ENGLAND

A4820   Isle of Walney 54°02'·9N 03°10'·6W
FIW 15s 21m 23M
Obscured 122°-127°(5°) within 3M of the
shore.

WALES

A5160   Point Lynas 53°25'·0N 04°17'·3W
OcW 10s 39m 20M
vis: 109°-315°(206°).

A5168   The Skerries 53°25'·3N 04°36'·4W
Fl(2)W 10s 36m 22M *Racon (T).*
Also FR 26m 16M vis: 231°-254°(23°)

A5204   South Stack 53°18'·4N 04°41'·9W
FIW 10s 60m 27M
Obscured to the northward by North Stack,
and may also be obscured in Penrhos Bay by
the high land of Penrhyn Mawr, but is visible
over the land from the southward when in line
with Rhoscolyn Beacon

A5234   Bardsey Island 52°45'·0N 04°47'·9W
Fl(5)W 15s 39m 26M
Obscured by Bardsey Island 198°-250°(52°)
and in Tremadoc Bay when bearing less than
260°

A5274   Strumble Head
Ynysmeicel 52°01'·8N 05°04'·3W
Fl(4)W 15s 45m 26M *vis: 038°-257°(219°)*

A5276   South Bishop 51°51'·2N 05°24'·7W
FIW 5s 44m 19M

A5278   The Smalls 51°43'·2N 05°40'·1W
Fl(3)W 15s 36m 25M *Racon (T)*

A5282   Skokholm Island 51°41'·6N 05°17'·2W
FIWR 10s 54m 18/15M
vis: W301°-154°(213°) R154°-301°(147°) partially
obscured 226°-258°(32°)

A5284   St Ann's Head   51°40'·9N 05°10'·4W
FIWR 5s 48m 18/17/14M
vis: W233°-247°(14°), R247°-285°(38°),
R(intens) 285°-314°(29°), R314°-332°(18°),
W332°-131°(159°), partially obscured
between 124°-129°(5°). Ra

A5286·3 **Watwick Point** Leading light. Common rear.
0·5M from front 51°41'·8N 05°09'·2W
FW 80m 15M
vis: 013·5°-031·5°(18°)

A5287 **Great Castle Head**
Leading Lights 039°45'.
Front 51°42'·6N 05°07'·0W
OcW 4s 27m 15M
*vis: 031·2°-048·2°(17°) On request through
Milford Haven Port radio.*

A5287·1 **Great Castle Head - Little Castle Head**
Rear. 890m from front 51°43'·0N 05°06'·6W
OcW 8s 53m 15M
*vis: 031·2°-048·2°(17°) On request through
Milford Haven Port radio*

A5356 **Burry Port** 51°40'·6N 04°15'·0W
FIW 5s 7m 15M

A5358 **Mumbles** 51°34'·0N 03°58'·2W
Fl(4)W 20s 35m 15M

A5406 **Nash Pt** 51°24'·0N 03°33'·1W
Fl(2)WR 15s 56m 21/16M
*vis: R280°-290°(10°), W290°-100°(167°),
R100°- 120°(20°), W120°- 128°(8°)*

A5426 **Flat Holm** SE point 51°22'·5N 03°07'·0W
Fl(3)WR 10s 50m 15/12M
*vis: R106°-140°(34°), W140°- 151°(11°)
R151°-203°(52°), W203°- 106°(263°)*

A5433 **Cardiff** Leading Lights 349°.
Front 51°27'·7N 03°09'·9W **FW** 4m 17M ·

A5433·1 **Cardiff - Rear**
520m from front 51°27'·9N 03°10'·0W
FW 24m 17M

A5454 **River Usk** East Usk 51°32'·4N 02°57'·9W
Fl(2)WRG 10s 11m 15/11/11M
*vis: W284°- 290°(6°), R290°-017°(87°), W017°-
037°(20°), G037°- 115°(78°),
W115°-120°(5°)*

WEST COAST OF ENGLAND

A5482 **Black Nore Point** 51°29'·1N 02°48'·0W
Fl(2)W 10s 11m 15M
*vis: 044°-243°(199°), Obscured by Sand Pt
when bearing less than 049°*

A5484 **Portishead Point** 51°29'·6N 02°46'·4W
Q(3)W 10s 9m 16M
vis: 060°-262°(202°)

A5590 **Lynmouth Foreland** 51°14'·7N 03°47'·1W
Fl(4)W 15s 67m 18M *vis: 083°-275°(192°)*

A5600 **Bull Point** 51°12'·0N 04°12'·0W
Fl(3)W 10s 54m 24M
Obscured by high ground from shore -056°

A5610 **Bideford** Instow. Leading Lights 118°.
Front 51°03'·6N 04°10'·6W
OcW 6s 22m 15M *vis: 104·5°-131·5°(27°)*

A5610·1 **Bideford**
Rear 427m from front 51°03'·5N 04°10'·3W
OcW 10s 38m 15M
vis: 103°-133°(30°)

A5616 **Lundy** - Near N point 51°12'·1N 04°40'·6W
FIW 15s 48m 17M
vis: 009°-285°(276°)

A5618 **Lundy - SE point** 51°09'·7N 04°39'·3W
FIW 5s 53m 15M
vis: 170°-073°(263°)

A5622 **Hartland Point** 51°01'·3N 04°31'·4W
Fl(6)W 15s 37m 25M

A5638 **Trevose Head** NW end 50°32'·9N 05°02'·1W
FIW 8s 62m 21M

A5670 **Pendeen**
Near Watch House 50°09'·8N 05°40'·2W
Fl(4)W 15s 59m 16M
*vis: 042°-240°(198°); in the bay between
Gurnard Head and Pendeen, it shows to the
coast*

IRELAND

A5702 **Fastnet** W end 51°23'·3N 09°36'·1W
FLW 5s 49m 27M *Racon (G)*

A5708 **Galley Head** Summit 51°31'·7N 08°57'·1W
Fl(5)W 20s 53m 23M
vis: 256°-065°(169°)

A5710 **Old Head of Kinsale**
S point 51°36'·3N 08°31'·9W
Fl(2)W 10s 72m 25M

A5718 **Roche's Point** 51°47'·6N 08°15'·3W
FIWR 3s 30m 20/16M
*vis: R shore-292°, W292°- 016°(84°),
R016°-033°(17°), W(unintens) 033°-159°(126°),
R159°-shore*

A5728 **Cork Hr**
Fort Davis Dir Lt 354° 05'. 51°48'·8N
08°15'·8W
DirWRG 29m 17M
*FG 351·5-352·25°(0·75), AIWG 352·25°-
353°(0·75°), FW 353°-355°(2°), AIWR 355°-
355·75°(0·75°), FR 355·75°-356·5°(0·75°) (P)
1999*

A5774 **Ballycotton** 51°49'·5N 07°59'·1W
FIWR 10s 59m 21/17M *W238°-048°(170°),
R048°-238°(190°)*

A5776 **Youghal**
West side of entrance 51°56'·5N 07°50'·5W
FIWR 2s 24m 17/13M
*vis: W183°-273°(90°), R273°- 295°(22°),
W295°-307°(12°), R307°-351°(44°), W351°-
003°(12°)*

A5778 **Mine Head** 51°59'·6N 07°35'·2W
Fl(4)W 20s 87m 28M
vis: 228°-052°(184°)

A5798 **Hook Head** 52°07'·3N 06°55'·7W
FIW 3s 46m 23M *Racon (K)*

A5800 **Dunmore East**
East Pier Head
52°08'·9N 06°59'·3W
FIWR 8s 13m 17/13M
vis: W225°-310°(85°), R310°-004°(54°)

A5832 **Coningbeg Lt F**
52°02'·4N 06°39'·4W
Fl(3)W 30s 12m 24M *Racon (M)*

A5838 **Tuskar** 52°12'·2N 06°12'·4W
Q(2)W 7·5s 33m 24M *Racon (T)*

A5845 **Arklow Lanby** 52°39'·5N 05°58'·1W
Fl(2)W 12s 12m 15M *Racon (O)*

A5850 **Wicklow Head** 52°57'·9N 05°59'·8W
Fl(3)W 15s 37m 23M

A5861 **Codling Lanby** 53°03'·0N 05°40'·7W
FIW 4s 12m 15M *Racon (G)*

A5865 **Kish Bank** 53°18'·7N 05°55'·3W
Fl(2)W 20s 29m 22M *Racon (T)*

A5872 **Dun Laoghaire**
East Breakwater Head 53°18'·10N 06°07'·60W
Fl(2)R 10s 16m 17M

A5882 **Port of Dublin - Poolbeg** Great S Wall. Head.
Poolbeg 53°20'·5N 06°09'·0W
Oc(2)R 20s 20m 15M

A5884 **Port of Dublin**
North Bull Wall 53°20'·7N 6°08'·9W
Fl(3)G 10s 15m 15M

A5886 **Port of Dublin - N Bank** 53°20'·7N 06°10'·5W
OcG 8s 10m 16M

A5898 **Ben of Howth** Baily 53°21'·7N 06°03'·1W
FIW 15s 41m 26M

A5904 **Rockabill** 53°35'·8N 06°00'·3W
FIWR 12s 45m 22/18M
vis: W178°-329°(151°), R329°-178°(209°)

A5910 **Drogheda Harbour** Entrance Lights in line
about 248°. Front 53°43'·1N 06°14'·9W
OcW 12s 8m 15M
vis: 203°-293°(90°)

A5910·1 **Drogheda Harbour**
Rear 85m from front 53°43'·1N 06°14'·9W
OcW 12s 12m 17M
vis: 246°-252°(6°)

A5911 **Drogheda Harbour**
North Light 53°43'·4N 06°15'·2W
FIR 4s 7m 15M *vis: 282°-288°(6°)*

A5920 **Dundalk Harbour** North training wall.
Head 53°58'·5N 06°17'·6W
FIWR 15s 10m 21/18M
*vis: W124°- 151°(27°), R151°-284°(133°),
W284°-313°(29°), R313°-124°(171°)*

A5928 **Haulbowline** 54°01'·2N 06°04'·7W
Fl(3)W 10s 32m 17M

A5958 **St John's Point** 54°13'·6N 05°39'·5W
Q(2)W 8s 37m 25M
Fl WR 3s 14m 15/11M
vis: W064°-078°(14°), R078°-shore

A5966 **South Rock Lt F**
Strangford Lough 54°24'·5N 05°21'·9W
Fl(3)R 30s 12m 20M *Racon (T)*

A5974 **Donaghadee**
South pier. Head 54°38'·7N 05°31'·8W
IsoWR 4s 17m 18/14M
vis: W shore-326°, R326°-shore

A5976 **Mew Island**
North East end 54°41'·9N 05°30'·7W
Fl(4)W 30s 37m 24M *Racon (O)*

A6028 **Black Head** 54°46'·0N 05°41'·3W
FIW 3s 45m 27M

A6031 **Chaine Tower** 54°51'·3N 05°47'·8W
IsoWR 5s 23m 16M
vis: W230°-240°(10°), R240°-shore

A6042 **Maidens** 54°55'·7N 05°43'·6W
Fl(3)W 20s 29m 24M *Racon (M)*

A6062 **Rathlin Island** Altacarry Hd.
Rathlin East 55°18'·1N 06°10'·2W
Fl(4)W 20s 74m 26M
*vis: 110°-006°(256°) and 036°-058°(22°). Racon
(G)*

A6064 **Rathlin Island - Rathlin West**
0·5M North East of Bull Point
55°18'·1N 06°16'·7W

FIR 5s 62m 22M
vis: 015°-225°(210°)

A6084 **Inishowen** W tower
55°13'·6N 06°55'·7W
Fl(2)WRG 10s 28m 18/14/14M
*vis: G197°-211°(14°), W211°- 249°(38°),
R249°-000°(111°)*

A6164 **Inishtrahull** 55°25'·8N 07°14'·6W
Fl(3)W 15s 59m 25M *Racon (T)*

A6168 **Fanad Head** 55°16'·6N 07°37'·9W
Fl(5)WR 20s 39m 18/14M
*vis: R100°-110°(10°), W110°-313° (203°),
R313°-345°(32°), W345°-100°(115°)*

A6200 **Tory Island** NW point 55°16'·4N 08°14'·9W
Fl(4)W 30s 40m 27M *Racon (M)*
Obscured by land about 277°-302°(25°).

A6208 **Aranmore**
Rinrawros Point 55°00'·9N 08°33'·6W
Fl(2)W 20s 71m 29M
*Obscured by land about 234°- 007°(133°) and
when bearing about 013°*

A6216 **Rathlin O'Birne**
W side 54°39'·8N 08°49'·9W
FIWR 15s 35m 18/14M. *Racon (O)*
vis: R195°-307°(112°), W307°-195°(248°).

A6224 **Rotten Island** 54°36'·9N 08°26'·3W
FIWR 4s 20m 15/11M
*vis: W255°-008°(113°), R008°-039°(31°),
W039°-208°(169°)*

A6268 **Eagle Island** W end 54°17'·0N 10°05'·5W
Fl(3)W 10s 67m 23M

A6270 **Black Rk** 54°04'·0N 10°19'·2W
FIWR 12s 86m 22/16M
vis: W276°-212°(296°), R212°-276°(64°)

A6276 **Achillbeg Island**
S point 53°51'·5N 09°56'·8W
FIWR 5s 56m 18/18/15M
*vis: R262°-281°(19°), W281°- 342°(61°),
R342°-060°(78°), W060°-092°(32°),
R(intens) 092°-099°(7°), W099°-118°(19°)*

A6288 **Slyne Head** N tower
53°24'·0N 10°14'·0W
Fl(2)W 15s 35m 24M, Racon (T)

A6296 **Galway Bay - Eeragh.**
Rock Island 53°08'·9N 09°51'·4W
FIW 15s 35m 23M
vis: 297°-262°(325°)

A6298 **Galway Bay - Straw Island**
53°07'·0N 09°37'·9W
Fl(2)W 5s 11m 17M

A6334 **Galway Bay - Inisheer** 53°02'·8N 09°31'·5W
IsoWR 12s 34m 20/16M. *Racon (K)*
*vis: W (partially vis beyond 7M) 225°-
231°(6°), W231°- 245°(14°), R245°-269°(24°),
W269°- 115°(206°).*

A6338 **Loop Head** 52°33'·7N 09°55'·9W
Fl(4)W 20s 84m 23M
vis: 280°-218°(298°).

A6392 **Little Samphire Island** 52°16'·2N 09°52'·9W
FIWRG 5s 17m 16/13/13M
*vis: R262°-275°(13°). R280°-090°(170°),
G090°-140°(50°), W140°- 152°(12°),
R152°-172°(20°)*

A6408 **Inishtearaght** Westernmost of The Blasket
Islands 52°04'·5N 10°39'·7W
Fl(2)W 20s 84m 27M
vis: 318°-221°(263°). Racon (O)

A6416 **Valentia Hbr - Fort (Cromwell) Point**
Fort (Cromwell) Pt 51°56'·0N 10°19'·3W
FlWR 2s 16m 17/15M
*vis: R304°-351°(47°), W104°-
304°(200°). Obscured from seaward by Doulus
Hd when bearing over 180°*

A6422 **Skelligs Rock** 51°46'·2N 10°32'·5W
Fl(3)W 10s 53m 27M
*vis: 262°-115°(213°). Partially obscured by
land within 6M 110°-115°(5°)*

A6430 **Bull Rock** 51°35'·5N 10°18'·1W
FlW 15s 83m 21M, Racon (N)
vis: 220°-186°(326°)

A6432 **Sheep's Hd** 51°32'·5N 09°50'·8W
Fl(3)WR 15s 83m 18/15M
vis: R007°-017°(10°), W017°-212°(195°)

A6434 **Bearhaven. W entrance** Ardnakinna Point
51°37'·1N 09°55'·0W
Fl(2)WR 10s 62m 17/14M
*vis: R319°-348°(29°), W348°-066°(78°),
R066°-shore*

A6442 **Roancarrigmore** 51°39'·1N 09°44'·8W
FlWR 3s 18m 18/14M
*vis: W312°-050°(98°). R050°-122°(72°),
R(unintens) 122°-242°(120°), R242°-312°(70°)*

A6448 **Mizen Head** 51°26'·9N 09°49'·2W
IsoW 4s 55m 15M. *Racon (T)
313°-133°(180°).*

BELGIUM

B0074 **Nieuwpoort - E Pier** 51°09'·3N 02°43'·8E
Fl(2)R 14s 28m 16M

B0092 **Oostende** 51°14'·2N 02°55'·9E
Fl(3)W 10s 65m 27M
Obscured 069·5°-071°(1·5°)

B0112 **Blankenberge** Comte Jean Jetty
51°18'·8N 03°06'·9E
Fl(2)W 8s 30m 20M
vis: 065°-245°(80°)

B0122 **Zeebrugge**
Heist. Mole. Head 51°20'·9N 03°12'·1E
OcWR 15s 22m 20/18M
*vis: W068°- 145°(77°), R145°-201°(56°),
W201°-296°(95°)*

NETHERLANDS

B0174 **Walcheren** Westkapelle. Common rear.
51°31'·8N 03°26'·9E
FlW 3s 50m 28M
Obscured by the land on certain bearings

B0500 **Zeegat van Brouwershaven**
West Schouwen 51°42'·6N 03°41'·6E
Fl(2+1)W 15s 58m 30M

B0518 **Westhoofd** 51°48'·8N 3°51'·9E
Fl(3)W 15s 56m 30M

B0593·39 **Dordsche Kil - De Wacht**
Ldg Lts Rear 164°
190m from front 51°44'·6N 04°38'·2E
IsoW 2s 18m 15M *Synchronised with front*

B0593·4 **Dordsche Kil**
Common front 51°44'·7N 04°38'·1E
IsoW 2s 14m 15M
IsoW 4s 14m 16M

B0593·41 **Dordsche Kil** Ldg Lts Rear 015°.
500m from front 51°45'·0N 04°38'·2E
IsoW 4s 20m 16M *Synchronised with front*

B0593·5 **Dordsche Kil - S-Gravendeel** - Ldg Lts
Front 344°. 51°46'·1N 04°37'·5E
IsoW 2s 12m 15M

B0593·51 **Dordsche Kil**
Rear 125m from front 51°46'·1N 04°37'·5E
IsoW 2s 15m 15M *Synchronised with front*

B0593·7 **Dordsche Kil - De Wacht**
Ldg Lts 183°. Front 183°. 51°45'·4N 04°37'·6E
IsoW 8s 12m 15M

B0593·71 **Dordsche Kil**
Rear 490m from front 51°45'·1N 04°37'·6E
IsoW 8s 19m 15M *Synchronised with front*

B0593·8 **Dordsche Kil - N entrance**
Ldg Lts Front 346°30'.
51°48'·2N 04°37'·3E
IsoW 4s 14m 15M

B0593·81 **Dordsche Kil**
Rear 217m from front 51°48'·3N 04°37'·2E
IsoW 4s 16m 15M *Synchronised with front*

B0593·9 **Dordsche Kil - Wieldrecht**
Ldg Lts - Front 166°30'. 51°46'·6N 04°37'·9E
IsoW 4s 12m 15M

B0593·91 **Dordsche Kil**
Rear 225m from front 51°46'·5N 04°37'·9E
IsoW 4s 16m 15M *Synchronised with front*

B0630 **Goeree** 51°55'·5N 03°40'·2E
Fl(4)W 20s 32m 28M. *Racon (T)*

B0633 **Maasvlakte**
Hook of Holland 51°58'·2N 04°00'·9E
Fl(5)W 20s 67m 28M
vis 340°-267°(287°)

B0637 **Hook of Holland - Maasmond** Ldg Lts 112°.
Front 51°58'·9N 04°04'·9E
IsoW 4s 30m 21M
*vis 101°- 123°(22°), for use of very deep draught
vessels*

B0637·1 **Hook of Holland - Maasmond** Ldg Lts 112°
Rear 0·6M from front 51°58'·7N 04°05'·9E
IsoW 4s 47m 21M
Synchronised with front. vis 101°-123°(22°)

B0638 **Hook of Holland**
Ldg Lts 107°. Front 51°58'·6N 04°07'·6E
IsoR 6s 29m 18M
*vis 099·5°- 114 ·5°(15°). For vessels other
than those of very deep draught*

B0638·1 **Hook of Holland**
Rear 450m from front 51°58'·5N 04°08'·0E
IsoR 6s 43m 18M
*Synchronised with front. vis: 099·5°-
114·5°(15°)*

B0642 **Europoort - Calandkanal** Ldg Lts 116°.
Front Calandkanaal entrance.
51°57'·6N 04°08'·8E
OcG 6s 29m 16M
vis 108·5°-123·5°(15°)

B0642·1 **Europoort - Calandkanal**
Rear 550m from front 51°57'·5N 04°09'·2E
OcG 6s 43m 16M
*vis 108·5°-123·5°(15°). Synchronised with
front.*

B0648·31 **Europoort - Mississippihaven**
Ldg Lts Rear E side Ldg Lts 249°30'.
584m from front 51°56'·0N 04°02'·3E

IsoW 3s 23m 15M
vis 242°-257°(15°).
Synchronised with front

B0712 Oude Maas
Huis Te Engeland Ldg Lts 157°30'
Front 51°52'·9N 04°19'·8E
IsoW 8s 12m 15M
vis 150°-165°(15°)

B0712·1 Oude Maas - Rear 115m from front
51°52.80'N 4°19.80'E
IsoW 8s 14m 15M
Vis 150°-165°(15°). *Synchronised with front*

B0713·5 Oude Maas - Botlekbrug - Ldg Lts - Front
161°30'. 51°51.70'N 4°20.30'E
IsoW 2s 13m 15M
Vis 154°-169°(15°)

B0713·51 Oude Maas - Rear 232m from front
51°51.50'N 4°20.30'E
IsoW 2s 16m 15M
Vis 154°-169°(15°). *Synchronised with front*

B0717·1 Oude Maas - Allemanshaven Ldg Lts Front
No6 143°. No 6 51°50.80'N 4°21.50'E
IsoW 4s 12m 15M *Vis 135.5°-150.5°(15°)*

B0717·11 Oude Maas - Allemanshaven - Rear 186m from
front 51°50.70'N 4°21.60'E
IsoW 4s 15m 15M *Vis 135.5°-150.5°(15°)*.
Synchronised with front

B0719·2 Oude Maas - Johannapolder- Oost Ldg Lts -
Front 082°30'. 51°50.70'N 4°24.90'E
IsoW 2s 12m 15M *Vis 075°-090°(15°)*

B0719·21 Oude Maas - Johannapolder - Rear 190m from
front
51°50.70'N 4°25.00'E **IsoW 2s** 15m 15M
Vis 075°-090°(15°). *Synchronised with front*

B0721·5 Oude Maas - Johannapolder - West Ldg Lts -
Front 300°30'. 51°50.70'N 4°24.80'E
IsoW 8s 12m 15M
Vis 293°-308°(15°)

B0721·51 Oude Maas - Johannapolder - West Rear 534m
from front 51°50.90'N 4°24.40'E
IsoW 8s 17m 15M *Vis 293°-308°(15°)*.
Synchronised with front

B0721·6 Oude Maas - Goidschalxpolder-Oost Ldg Lts -
Front 120°30'. 51°49.80'N 4°27.10'E
IsoW 4s 12m 15M *Vis 113°-128°(15°)*

B0721·61 Oude Maas - Rear 389m from front 51°49.70'N
4°27.40'E
IsoW 4s 16m 15M *Vis 113°-128°(15°)*.
Synchronised with front

B0722·4 Oude Maas - Goidschalxpolder-West Ldg Lts -
Front 257°. 51°49.90'N 4°26.90'E
IsoW 4s 12m 15M *Vis 249.5°-264.5°(15°)*

B0722·41 Oude Maas - Rear 484m from front 51°49.80'N
4°26.50'E
IsoW 4s 17m 15M *Vis 249.5°-264.5°(15°)*.
Synchronised with front

B0722·8 Oude Maas - Koedood-Oost Ldg Lts - Front
077°. 51°50.40'N 4°30.50'E
IsoW 4s 12m 15M *Vis 069.5°-084.5°(15°)*

B0722·81 Oude Maas - Rear 510m from front
51°50.40'N 4°30.90'E
IsoW 4s 17m 15M *Vis 069.5°-084.5°(15°)*.
Synchronised with front

B0723 Oude Maas - Ldg Lts - Front 291°. No 12
51°50.30'N 4°29.80'E
IsoW 6s 15M *Vis 283.5°-298.5°(15°)*

B0723·1 Oude Maas - Rear 130m from front 51°50.30'N
4°29.70'E
IsoW 6s 15M *Vis 283.5°-298.5°(15°)*.
Synchronised with front

B0726 Oude Maas - Ldg Lts - Front 347°.
Front 51°49.80'N 4°33.50'E
IsoW 6s 15M *Vis 339.5°-354.5°(15°)*

B0726·1 Oude Maas - Rear 50m from front 51°49.90'N
4°33.50'E
FW 15M *Vis 339.5°-354.5°(15°)*.

B0728·3 Oude Maas - Puttershoek-West Ldg Lts -
Front 275°30'. 51°48.50'N 4°34.50'E
IsoW 4s 12m 15M *Vis 267.5°-282.5°(15°)*

B0728·31 Oude Maas - Rear 120m from front 51°48.50'N
4°34.40'E
IsoW 4s 14m 15M *Vis 267.5°-282.5°(15°)*.
Synchronised with front

B0730 Oude Maas - Krabbepolder Ldg Lts - Front 112°.
51°48.00'N 4°37.70'E
IsoW 6s 15M

B0730·1 Oude Maas - Rear 190m from front
51°47.90'N 4°37.90'E
IsoW 6s 15M *Synchronised with front*

B0750 Scheveningen 52°06.30'N 4°16.20'E
Fl(2)W 10s 49m 29M *Vis 014°-244°(230°)*

B0760 Noordwijk-aan-Zee 52°14.90'N 4°26.10'E
Oc(3)W 20s 32m 18M

B0766 Haven Van Ijmuiden Ldg Lts - Front 100°30'.
52°27.80'N 4°34.50'E
FWR 30m 16/13M *W050°- 122°(72°), R122°-*
145°(23°), W145°-160°(15°). RC

B0766·1 Haven Van Ijmuiden - Rear 570m from front
52°27.70'N 4°35.00'E
Fl W 5s 52m 29M *Vis 019°-199°(180°)*

B0842 Egmond-aan-Zee 52°37.20'N 4°37.60'E
IsoWR 10s 36m 18/14M *W010°-175°(165°),*
R175°-188°(13°)

B0852 Zeegat van Texel Schulpengat. Ldg Lts 026°30'.
Front 53°00.90'N 4°44.50'E
IsoW 4s 18M *Vis 024.5°-028.5°(4°)*

B0852·1 Zeegat van Texel - Den Hoorn Rear. 0.83M
from front 53°01.60'N 4°45.10'E
OcW 8s 18M *Vis 024°-028.5°(4°)*

B0858 Zeegat van Texel - Kijkduin
Rear 52°57.40'N 4°43.70'E
Fl(4)W 20s 56m 30M *Vis except where*
obscured by dunes on Texel. Ldg Lt 253°30'
with B0865

B0859 Zeegat van Texel
Schilbolsnol 53°00'·6N 04°45'·8E
FWRG 27m 15/12/11M
vis: W338°-002°(24°), G002°- 035°(33°),
W035°-038°(3°)
Ldg sector for Schulpengat, R038°-
051°(13°), W051°-068.5°(17.5°)

B0886 Texel N Point. Eierland 53°11'·0N 04°51'·4E
Fl(2)W 10s 52m 29M

B0894 Zeggat van Terschelling
Vlieland. 53°17'·8N 05°03'·6E
IsoW 4s 53m 20M

B0904 Zeggat van Terschelling - Terschelling
Brandaris Tower 53°21'·7N 05°12'·9E
Fl W 5s 55m 29M
Visible except when obscured by dunes on
Vlieland & Terschelling

B0920　**Zeegat van Ameland**
W end 53°27'·0N 05°37'·6E
Fl(3)W 15s 57m 30M

B0938　**Friesche Zeegat**
Schiermonnikoog. 53°29'·2N 06°09'·0E
Fl(4)W 20s 43m 28M. Also **FWR** 29m 15/12M
W210°-221°(11°), R221°-230°(9°)

GERMANY

B0970　**Borkum Grosser**
53°35'·4N 06°39'·8E
Fl(2)W 12s 63m 24M
F WRG 46m 19/15/15M *vis: G107·4°-109°
(1·6°), W109°-111·2°(2·2°), R111·2°-
112·6°(1·4°)*

B0972　**Borkum Kleiner**
53°34'·8N 06°40'·1E
FW 32m 30M
vis: 089·9°-090·9°(1°) Ldg sector for Hubertgat.
RC
FIW3s 16M *vis: 088°-089·9°(1·9°)*
Q(4)W10s 16M *vis: 090·9°-093° (2·1°)*

B0976　**Fischerbalje**
Borkum 53°33'·2N 06°43'·0E
Oc(2)WRG 16s 15m 16/12/11M
*vis: R260°-313° (53°), G313°-014° (61°),
W014°-068°(54°)
Ldg sector for Fischerbalje, R068°-123°(55°)*

B0983　**Campen** Borkum 53°24'·4N 07°01'·0E
FW 62m 30M
vis: 126·8°-127·1°(0·3°)

B1051　**GW/EMS Lt F** 54°10'·0N 06°20'·8E
IsoW 8s 12m 17M. *Racon (T)*

B1052　**German Bight Lt F** 54°10'·8N 07°27'·6E **IsoW
8s 12m** 17M *Racon (T)*

B1054　**Norderney** 53°42'·6N 07°13'·8E
Fl(3)W 12s 59m 23M
*vis: Unintens 067°-077°(10°) and 270°-
280°(10°)*

B1112　**Wangerooge**
W end 53°47'·4N 07°51'·5E
Fl R 5s 60m 23M
F WR 24m 15/11M *vis 055°-060·5° (5·5°), 060·5°-
065·5° (5°), 065·5°-071° (5·5°)*
Dir F WRG 24m 22/18/17M vis G119·4°-138·8°
(19·4°), W138·8°-152·2° (13·4°) Ldg Sector,
R152·2°-159·9° (7·7°)

B1122　**Mellumplate** 53°46'·3N 08°05'·6E
FW 28m 24M
*vis: 116·1°-116·4°(0·3°) Ldg sector for outer
part of Wangerooger Fahrwasser*
F IW 4s 23M *vis 114°-115·2° (1·2°)*
F l(4)W 15s *vis 117·2°-118·4° (1·2°)*
Mo(A)W 7·5s *vis 115·2°-116·1° (0·9°) Ldg
sector*
Mo(N)W 7·5s *vis 116·4°-117·2° (0·8°) Ldg
sector*

B1134　**Tossens**
Ldg Lts 146°.
Front 53°34'·5N 08°12'·4E
OcW 6s 15m 20M

B1134·1　**Tossens**
Rear 2M from front 53°32'·8N 08°14'·4E
OcW 6s 51m 20M

B1138　**Voslapp** Ldg Lts 164°30'.
Front 53°37'·3N 08°06'·8E

IsoW 6s 15m 24M
Intens on leading line

B1138·1　**Voslapp**
Rear 2·35M from front 53°34'·9N 08°07'·9E
IsoW 6s 60m 27M
Synchronised with front. Intens on leading line

B1141　**Eckwarden**
Front Ldg Lts 154°.
Solthörner Watt. Front 53°32'·5N 08°13'·1E
IsoWRG 3s 15m 19/12/9/8M
*vis: R346°-348°(2°), W348°-028°(40°),
R028°-052°(24°), W(intens)052°-054°(2°)
Ldg sector. G054°-067·5°(13·5°),
vis: W067·5°-110°(42·5°),G110°-152·6°(42·6°),
W(intens) 152·6°-across fairway, with
undefined limit on E side of Ldg line*

B1141·1　**Eckwarden**
Rear 1·27M from front 53°31'·3N 08°14'·0E
IsoW 3s 41m 21M *Synchronised with front*

B1152　**Arngast** 53°28'·9N 08°11'·0E
FWRG 30m 21/16/17M
*vis W135°-142°(7°), G142°-150°(8°),
W150°-152°(2°), G152°-174·6°(22·6°),
R180·5°-191°(10·5°), W191°-213°(22°),
R213°-225°(12°), W(10M)286°-303°(17°),
G(7M)303°-314°(11°),
Oc W 6s 20M vis 176·4°-177·4°(1°) Ldg sector*

B1188　**Alte Weser** 53°51'·9N 08°07'·6E
FWRG 33m 23/19/18M
*vis W288°-352°(64°), R352°-003°(11°),
W003°-017°(14°)
Ldg sector for Alte Weser, G017°-045°(28°),
W045°-074°(29°),G074°-118°(44°),
W118°-123°(5°)
Ldg sector for Alter Weser, R123°-140°(17°),
G140°-175°(35°), W175°-183°(8°),
R183°-196°(13°), W196°-238°(42°).*

B1196　**Tegeler Plate**
N end 53°47'·9N 08°11'·5E
Oc(3)WRG 12s 21m 21/17/16M
*vis W329°-340°(11°), R340°-014°(34°),
W014°-100°(86°), G100°-116° (16°),
W116°-119°(3°)
Ldg sector for Neue Weser, R119°-123°(4°),
G123°-144°(21°), W144°-147°(3°)
Ldg sector for Alte Weser, R147°-264°(117°).*

B1198　**Hohe Weg**
NE part 53°42'·9N 08°14'·7E
FWRG 29m 19/16/15M
*vis: W102°-138·5°(36·5°), G138·5°-14·5°(4°),
W142·5°-145·5°(3°), R145·5°-184°(38·5°),
W184°-278·5°(94·5°).*

B1214　**Robbenplate** Ldg Lts 122°18'.
Front 53°40'·9N 08°23'·0E
OcW 6s 15m 17M *Intens on leading line*

B1214·1　**Robbenplate**
Rear 0·54M from front 53°40'·6N 08°23'·8E
OcW 6s 37m 18M
*vis: 116°-125·5°(9·5°). Synchronised with
front*

B1225　**Dwarsgat**
Front Ldg Lts 320°06'. Front 53°43'·2N
08°18'·5E **IsoW 6s** 16m 15M

B1225·1　**Dwarsgat**
Rear 0·75M from front 53°43'·7N 08°17'·8E
IsoW 6s 35m 17M *Synchronised with front*

B1230·1 **Imsum Rear**
Ldg Lts 125°12'
1·02M from front 53°35'·8N 08°32'·0E
OcW 6s 39m 16M *Synchronised with front*

B1239·1 **Solthorn - Rear** Ldg Lts 320°36'.
Rear. 700m from front 53°38'·6N 08°27'·0E
IsoW 4s 31m 17M *Synchronised with front*

B1240 **Hofe - Front** Ldg Lts 330°48'.
Front 53°37'·1N 08°29'·8E
OcW 6s 15m 18M

B1240·1 **Hofe**
Rear 0·7M from front 53°37'·7N 08°29'·2E
OcW 6s 35m 18M *Synchronised with front*

B1256·9 **Fischeriehafen**
Rear Ldg Lts 150°48'.
0·68M from front 53°31'·3N 08°35'·2E
OcW 6s 45m 18M *Synchronised with front*

B1257 **Fischeriehafen**
Common front 53°31'·9N 08°34'·6E
OcW 6s 17m 18/11M

B1279·9 **Reitsand**
Ldg Lts 233°54'.
Front. 480m from rear 53°30'·0N 08°30'·3E
OcW 6s 18m 15M

B1280 **Reitsand**
Common Rear 53°29'·9N 08°29'·9E
OcW 6s 36m 17M

B1280·1 **Flagbalgersiel** Ldg Lt 005°18'.
Front 580m from rear 53°29'·6N 08°29'·9E
OcW 6s 18m 15M

B1286 **Nordenham**
Front Ldg Lts 355°54'.
53°27'·9N 8°29'·4E
IsoW 4s 15m 16M

B1286·1 **Nordenham**
Rear 1M from front 53°28'·9N 08°29'·2E
IsoW 4s 41m 19M *Synchronised with front*

B1288 **Grosserpater**
Front Ldg Lts 175°54'.
53°19'·8N 08°30'·4E
IsoW 4s 15m 19M *Intens on leading line*

B1288·1 **Grosserpater**
Rear 0·71M from front 53°19'·1N 08°30'·4E
IsoW 4s 34m 22M *Synchronised with front.*
Intens on leading line

B1294 **Reiherplate** Ldg Lts 185°18'.
Front 53°25'·6N 08°29'·2E
OcW 6s 14m 15M

B1294·1 **Reiherplate**
Rear 850m from front 53°25'·1N 08°29'·2E
OcW 6s 27m 16M *Synchronised with front*

B1297 **Sandstedt** Ldg Lts 021°.
Front 53°21'·7N 08°30'·7E
OcW 6s 15m 15M *Intens on leading line*

B1297·1 **Sandstedt**
Rear 420m from front 53°21'·9N 08°30'·8E
OcW 6s 23m 15M
Intens on leading line. Synchronised with front

B1299·21 **Osterpater** Ldg Lts 173°42'.
Rear. 250m from front 53°17'·2N 08°29'·8E
IsoW 4s 21m 15M
Intens on leading line. Synchronised with front

B1299·41 **Harriersand**
Rear Ldg Lts 007°36'.
0·5M from front 53°19'·5N 08°29'·9E
OcW 6s 22m 15M *Intens on leading line*

B1302·39 **Berne - Rear** Ldg Lts 147°54'.
220m from front 53°11'·7N 08°31'·2E
OcW 6s 22m 15M *Intens on leading line*

B1302·4 **Berne**
Common front 53°11'·8N 08°31'·1E
OcW 6s 15m 15M
Synchronised with rear lights. Intens on leading line

B1302·41 **Juliusplate** Rear Ldg Lts 299°36'.
490m from front 53°11'·9N 08°30'·7E
IsoW 4s 29m 15M *Intens on leading line*

B1303 **Lemwerder - Front** Ldg Lts 119°36'.
Front 53°10'·3N 08°35'·4E
IsoW 4s 15m 15M

B1303·1 **Lemwerder**
Rear 430m from front 53°10'·2N 08°35'·7E
IsoW 4s 26m 15M *Synchronised with front*

B1312 **Helgoland** 54°11'·0N 07°53'·0E
FIW 5s 82m 28M

B1332 **Elbe Lt F** 54°00'·0N 08°06'·6E
IsoW 10s 12m 17M *Racon (T)*
vis 085·1°-087·1°(2°).

B1344 **Neuwerk**
S side 53°55'·0N 08°29'·8E
LFl(3)WRG 20s 38m 16/12/11M
vis G 165·3°-215·3°(50°), W 215·3°- 238·8°
(23·5°), R 238·8°-321°(82·2°), R 343°- 100°(117°)

B1360·9 **Baumronne**
Front Ldg Lts 151°12' 1·55M from rear
53°51'·2N 08°44'·2E
FIW 3s 25m 17M
vis 143·8°-149·2°(5·4°) Iso W 4s 17M vis:
149·2°-154·2°(5°) Fl(2)W 9s 17M vis: 154·2°-
156·7°(2·5°)

B1361 **Altenbruch**
Common Rear 53°49'·9N 08°45'·5E
IsoW 4s 58m 21M *Intens on leading line.*
Synchronised with front
Iso W 8s 51m 22M *Synchronised with front*

B1361·1 **Cuxhaven - Ldg Lts**
Common Front 53°50'·1N 08°47'·8E
IsoW 8s 19m 19M

B1395·9 **Belum**
Rear Ldg Lts 092°48'.
0·83M from front 53°50'·1N 08°57'·4E
IsoW 4s 45m 18M .
vis on leading line only. Synchronised with
front

B1396 **Belum**
Common front 53°50'·2N 08°56'·2E
IsoW 4s 23m 18M *vis: on leading line only*

B1396·1 **Otterndorf** Ldg Lts 245°30'.
Rear 53°49'·6N 08°54'·1E
IsoW 4s 52m 21M *vis on leading line only.*
Synchronised with front

B1412 **Balje** Ldg Lts 081°. Front 53°51'·4N 09°02'·7E
IsoW 8s 24m 17M *Intens on leading line*

B1412·1 **Balje**
Rear 1·35M from front 53°51'·5N 09°04'·9E
IsoW 8s 54m 21M
Intens on leading line. Synchronised with
front

B1416 **Brunsbüttel der Nord Ostee Kanal**
Ldg Lts 065°30'. Schleuseninsel.
Front 53°53'·4N 09°08'·5E
IsoW 3s 24m 16M *vis N of 063·3°*

B1416·1 **Brunsbüttel-Industriegebiet**
Rear. 0·9M from front 53°53'·7N 09°09'·9E
IsoW 3s 46m 21M *Synchronised with front*

B1453·9 **St Margarethen** Ldg Lts 311°48'.
Rear. 0·58M from front 53°53'·3N 09°15'·0E
IsoW 8s 36m 19M
Intens on leading line. Synchronised with front

B1454 **Scheelenkuhlen**
Common front 53°52'·9N 09°15'·7E
IsoW 8s 20m 18M *Intens on leading line*

B1454·1 **Scheelenkuhlen - Ldg Lts 089°12'.**
Rear. 1M from front 53°52'·9N 09°17'·4E
IsoW 8s 44m 22M *Synchronised with front*

B1456 **Glückstadt** Leading Lights 131°48'.
Front 53°48'·4N 09°24'·3E
IsoW 8s 15m 19M *Intens on leading line*

B1456·1 **Glückstadt**
Rear 0·68M from front 53°47'·9N 09°25'·2E
IsoW 8s 30m 21M *Intens on leading line*

B1457·51 **Osterende** Ldg Lts 115°48'.
Rear. 0·6M from front 53°50'·8N 09°21'·3E
IsoW 4s 36m 15M *Synchronised with front*

B1458 **Hollerwettern**
Ldg Lts 340°30'.
Front 53°50'·5N 09°21'·2E
IsoW 4s 21m 19M *Intens on leading line*

B1460 **Hollerwettern** Ldg Lts
Rear. 0·9M from front 53°51'·2N 09°20'·9E
IsoW 4s 44m 22M
Synchronised with front. Intens on leading line

B1474 **Ruthensand** Ldg Lts 161°36'.
Front 53°43'·3N 09°25'·5E
OcWRG 6s 15m 15/12/11M
*vis G170°- 176·1°(6·1°),
W176·1°-177·6°(1·5°),R177·6°-182°(4·4°)*

B1501 **Pagensand** Ldg Lts 345°18'.
Front 53°43'·0N 09°29'·4E
IsoW 8s 20m 15M *Intens on leading line*

B1501·1 **Pagensand - Kollmar**
Rear. 0·7M from front 53°43'·6N 09°29'·1E
IsoW 8s 40m 16M *Synchronised with front*

B1522·1 **Stadersand** Ldg Lts 165°18'.
Rear. 785m from front 53°37'·3N 09°31'·9E
IsoW 8s 40m 16M

B1540 **Lühe** Ldg Lts 278°18'.
Front 53°34'·3N 09°38'·0E
IsoW 4s 16m 17M

B1540·1 **Lühe** Ldg Lts - **Grünendeich**
Rear. 0·82M from front 53°34'·5N 09°36'·6E
IsoW 4s 36m 21M *Synchronised with front*

B1568·1 **Wittenbergen.**
Ldg Lts 286°42'. Tinsdal.
Rear. 800m from front 53°34'·0N 09°44'·5E
IsoW 8s 56m 16M
Synchronised with front. Intens on leading line

B1568·7 **Blankenese** Ldg Lts 098°18'.
Front 53°33'·5N 9°47'·8E
IsoW 4s 41m 16M

B1568·71 **Blankenese**
Rear 0·8M from front 53°33'·4N 9°49'·0E
IsoW 4s 84m 20M

B1581·7 **Hamburg** Budendey-Ufer.
Ldg Lts 106°42'. Front 53°32'·4N 09°53'·2E
IsoW 8s 20m 16M

B1581·71 **Hamburg**
Rear 0·6M from front 53°32'·3N 09°54'·1E
IsoW 8s 38m 18M

B1606 **Büsum**
W side of fishing harbour 54°07'·7N
08°51'·6E **IsoWRG 6s** 22m 17/14/13M
*vis W248°-317°(69°),R317°-024°(67°),
W024°-084°(60°),G084°-092·5°(8·5°),
W092·5°-094·5°(2°)
Ldg sector for Süder Piep, R094·5°-097°(2·5°),
W097°-148°(51°)*

B1624 **St Peter** 54°17'·3N 08°39'·2E
LFl(2)WR 15s 23m 15/13M
*vis: R271°-294°(23°), W294°- 325°(31°),
R325°-344°(19°),W344°-035°(51°),
R035°-055°(20°), W055°-068°(13°),
R068°- 091°(23°), W091°-120°(29°)*

B1652 **Westerheversand** 54°22'·5N 08°38'·5E
Oc(3)WRG 15s 18m 21/17/16M
*vis: W012·2°- 069°(56·8°),
G069°-079·5°(10·5°), W079·5°- 080·5°(1°)
Ldg sector for Hever. R080·5°- 107°(26·5°),
W107°-157°(50°), R157°- 169°(12°),
W169°- 206·5°(37·5°), R206·5°- 218·5°(12°),
W218·5°- 233°(14·5°), R233°-248°(15°)*

B1672 **Süderoogsand** Cross light 54°25'·5N
08°28.'·7E **IsoWRG 6s** 18m 15/12/11M
*vis: R240°-244°(4), W244°- 246°(2°),
G246°-263°(17°), W263°- 320°(57°),
R320°-338°(18°), W338°-013°(35°),
R013°- 048°(35°), W048°-082·5°(34·5°),
R082·5°- 122·5°(40°), W122·5°-150°(27·5°)*

B1676 **Pellworm** S side. Ldg Lts 041°.
Front 54°29'·3N 08°39'·1E
OcWR 5s 14m 20/11/8M
vis: W(intens) on leading line. W303·5°-313·5°(10°), R313·5°-316·5°(3°)

B1676·1 **Pellworm**
Rear 0·8M from front 54°29'·8N 08°40'·0E
OcW 5s 38m 20M *Synchronised with front*

B1685·1 **Amrum Hafen. Ldg Lts 272°**
Rear. 0·9M from front 54°37'·9N 08°21'·3E
IsoR 4s 33m 15M *TE 1997*

B1686 **Amrum** 54°37·9'N 08°21·3'E
FIW 8s 63m 23M

B1691 **Nebel** 54°38·8'N 08°21·7'E
OcWRG 5s 16m 20/15/15M
*vis: R255·5°-258·5°(3°), W258·5°-260·5°(2°),
G260·5°-263·5°(3°)*

B1702 **Nieblum** 54°41'·1N 08°29'·2E
Oc(2)WRG 10s 11m 19/15/15M
*vis: G028°-031°(3°), W031°- 032·5°(1·5°),
R032·5°-035·5°(3°)*

B1718 **Dagebüll** 54°43'·8N 08°41'·4E
IsoWRG 8s 23m 18/15/15M
*vis: G042°-043°(1°), W043°-044·5°(1·5°),
R044·5°-047°(2·5°)*

B1728 **Amrum** W side. Norddorf 54°40'·3N
08°18'·6E **OcWRG 6s** 22m 15/12/11M
vis: W009°-036·8°(27·8°), R036·8°-099°(62·2°),

W099°-146°(47°), R146°-176·5°(30·5°),
W176·5°-178·5°(2°), G178·5°- 188°(9·5°),
G(unintens)188°-202°(14°),W(partially
obsc)202°-230°(28°)

B1735 **Sylt - Hörnum** 54°45'·3N 08°17'·5E
Fl(2)W 9s 48m 20M

B1740 **Sylt - Kampen** Rote Kliff 54°56'·8N 08°20'·5E
LFlWR 10s 62m 20/16M
vis: W193°-260°(67°), W(unintens)
260°-339°(79°), W339°-165°(186°),
R165°-193°(28°)

DENMARK

B1772 **Sædding Strand Ldg lt.**
Front 053°48' 55°29'·8N 08°24'·0E
IsoW 2s 12m 21M
vis: 051·8°-055·8° (4°)

B1772·1 **Middle** 630m from front 55°30'·0N 08°24'·4E
IsoW 4s 26m 21M
vis: 051°-057°(6°)

B1772·2 **Rear** 0·75M from front 55°30'·2N 08°25'·0E
FW 36m 18M
vis: 052°-056° (4°)

B1778 **South Ldg Lt 067°.**
Front 55°28'·7N 08°24'·7E
FG 10m 16M

B1778·1 **Rear** 55°29'·1N 08°26'·1E
FG 25m 16M

B1779 **North Ldg Lt 049°.**
Front 55°29'·9N 08°23'·8E
FR 16m 16M

B1779·1 **Rear** 550m from front 55°30'·1N 08°24'·1E
FR 27m 16M

B1848 **Blåvandshuk** 55°33'·5N 8°05'·1E
Fl(3)W 20s 54m 23M

B1849 **Oksbøl Firing Range** 55°33'·6N 08°04'·7E
AlFlWR 4s 35m 16/13M
By day Q W 10M. Shown when firing in
progress

B1849·4 **Oksbøl Firing Range** 55°37'·3N 08°07'·E
A1F1WR 4s 35m 16/13M
By day Q W 10M. Shown when firing in
progress

B1868 **Lyngvig** Holmlands Klit
56°03'·0N 08°06'·3E
FlW 5s 53m 22M

B1886 **Bovbjerg** 56°30'·8N 08°07'·3E
LFl(2)W 15s 62m 16M

B1890 **Thyborøn Kanal**
Approach 56°42'·5N 08°13'·0E
Fl (3)W 10s 24m 16M
Intens 023·5°-203·5°(180°).

B2050·1 **Løgstør Grundge Ldg Lt** 079°.
Rear. 1·25M from front. 56°58'·4N 09°17'·4E
IsoW 4s 38m 18M
vis: 077·25°-080·75°(3·5°). The near lt is
midway between the two front lts. The rear
lt in line with the G front lt indicates the S
side of the ch and in line with the R front lt
the N side. FW (T) 1996

B2070 **Lodbjerg** 56°49'·4N 8°15'·8E
Fl (2)W 20s 48m 23M

B2084 **Hanstholm** 57°06'·8N 08°36'·0E
Fl (3)W 20s 65m 26M

B2101 **Tranum** Signal mast. No 157°10'·8N 09°26'·7E
AlWR 4s 20m 16/13M
Shown when firing in progress

B2106 **Hirtshals** 57°35'·1N 09°56'·6E
FFIW 30s 57m F18/Fl25M
Works in Progress (T) 1996

FRANCE

A0994 **Sandettié Lt F** 51°09'·4N 01°47'·2E
FlW 5s 12m 24M Racon (T)

A1114 **Dunkerque** 51°03'·0N 02°21'·9E
Fl(2)W 10s 59m 26M

A1116 **Dunkerque - Jetée Est** Head
51°03'·6N 02°21'·2E
Fl(2)R 10s 12m 16M

A1126 **Dunkerque Port Ouest** Ldg Lights 120°.
Front 51°01'·7N 02°12'·0E
Dir FG 16m 19M
Intens 119°-121°(2°) Irregular (T) 1997

A1126·1 **Dunkerque**
Rear 600m from front 51°01'·6N 02°12'·5E
Dir FG 30m 19M
Intens 119°-121°(2°). Irregular (T) 1997

A1144 **Calais** Main Light. 50°57'·7N 01°51'·2E
Fl(4)W 15s 59m 22M
vis: 073°-260°(187°).

A1146 **Calais - Jetée Est** Head 50°58'·4N 01°50'·5E
Fl(2)R 6s 12m 17M

A1166 **Cap Gris-Nez** 50°52'·2N 01°35'·0E
FlW 5s 72m 29M
vis: 005°-232°(227°).

A1170 **Boulogne - Digue Carnot**
Digue Carnot. 50°44'·5N 01°34'·1E
Fl(2+1)W 15s 25m 19M

A1190 **Cap d'Alprech** 50°42'·0N 01°33'·8E
Fl(3)W 15s 62m 23M

A1196 **Le Touquet** (La Canche) 50°31'·4N 01°35'·6E
Fl(2)W 10s 54m 25M

A1202 **Pointe du Haut-Blanc**
Berck-Plage 50°23'·9N 01°33'·7E
FlW 5s 44m 23M

A1208 **Baie du Somme - Cayeux sur Mer**
Cayeux-sur-Mer 50°11'·7N 01°30'·7E
FlR 5s 32m 22M

A1220 **Ault** 50°06'·3N 01°27'·2E
Oc(3)WR 12s 95m 18/14M
vis: W040°-175°(135°), R175°-220°(45°)

A1222 **Le Tréport**
Jetée Ouest. Head 50°03'·9N 01°22'·2E
Fl(2)G 10s 15m 20M

A1234 **Pointe d'Ailly** 49°55'·0N 00°57'·6E
Fl(3)W 20s 95m 31M

A1244 **Fécamp - Jetée Nord** 49°46'·0N 00°21'·9E
Fl(2)W 10s 15m 16M

A1250 **Cap d'Antifer** 49°41'·1N 00°10'·0E
FlW 20s 128m 29M
vis: 021°-222°(201°)

A1250·2 **Port d'Antifer** Entrance Ldg Lts 127°30'.
Front 49°38'·3N 00°09'·2E
Dir OcW 4s 113m 22M
vis: 127°-128°(1°)

A1250·21 **Port d'Antifer**
Rear 430m from front 49°38'·2N 00°09'·4E
Dir OcW 4s 135m 22M
vis: 127°-128°(1°)

A1250·8 Port d'Antifer - 49°39'·5N 00°09'·2E
Dir OcWRG 4s 24m 15/13/13M
vis: G068·5°- 078·5°(10°), W078·5°-
088·5°(10°), R088·5°-098·5°(10°)

A1251·2 Port d'Antifer - Bassin de Caux
Mole Ouest - Elbow Dir Lt 018°30'
49°39'·3N 00°09'·0E
Dir OcWRG 4s 11m 15/11/11M
vis: G006·5°-017·5°(11°), W017·5°- 019·5°(2°),
R019·5°-036·5°(17°)

A1251·7 Port d'Antifer - Digue M Thieullent
Post 2 49°40'·3N 00°08'·1E
Dir Oc(2)WRG 6s 24m 15/13/13M
vis: G334·5°- 346·5°(12°), W346·5°-
358·5°(12°), R358·5°-004·5°(6·5°)

A1251·8 Port d'Antifer - Digue M Thieullent
Post 3 49°40'·3N 00°07'·7E
Dir OcWRG 4s 21m 15/13/13M
vis: R352·5°-358°·5(6°), W358·5°- 010·5°(12°),
G010·5°-022·5°(12°)

A1256 Cap de la Hève 49°30'·8N 00°04'·2E
FIW 5s 123m 24M vis: 225°-196°(331°)

A1260 Le Havre Leading Lights 106°48'.
Quai Roger Meunier, Front 49°29·0N 00°06'·5E
Dir FW 36m 25M Intens 106°-108°(2°)

A1260·1 Le Havre - Quai J Couvert
Rear 0·73M from front 49°28'·8N 00°07'·6E
Dir FW 78m 25M Intens 106°-108°(2°)

A1261 Le Havre - Leading Lights 090°
Front 49°29'·6N 00°05'·9E
Dir FR 21m 19M Intens 089°-091°(2°). Occas

A1261·1 Le Havre
Rear 680m from front 49°29'·6N 00°06'·4E
Dir FR 43m 19M Intens 089°-091°(2°). Occas

A1262 Le Havre - Digue Nord
Head 49°29'·2N 0°05'·5E FIR 5s 15m 21M

A1269 Le Havre - Quai R Meunier
W corner 49°29'·0N 00°06'·4E
FI(3)W 5s 4m 23M Occas

A1290 Honfleur - Falaise des Fonds
49°25'·5N 00°12'·9E
FI(3)WRG 12s 15m 17/13/13M
vis: G040°-080°(40°), R080°-084°(4°),
G084°-100°(16°), W100°-109°(9°),
R109°-162°(53°), G162°-260°(98°)

A1377 Ouistreham - Mian Light
Main Light 49°16'·8N 0°14'·9W
OcWR 4s 37m 17/13M
vis: R115°-151°(36°), W151°- 115°(324°)

A1381 Ouistreham - Leading Lights 184°30'
Jetée Est. Head. Front 49°17'·2N 00°14'·7W
Dir Oc(3+1)R 12s 10m 17M
Intens 183·5°-186·5°(3°)

A1381·1 Ouistreham
Rear 610m from front 49°16'·9N 00°14'·8W
Dir Oc(3+1)R 12s 30m 17M
Synchronised with front. Intens 183·5°-
186·5°(3°)

A1396 Ver 49°20'·5N 00°31'·1W
FI(3)W 15s 42m 26M
Obscured by St Aubin cliffs when more than
275°. RC

A1411 La Maresquerie Leading Lights 146°.
Front 49°23'·4N 01°02'·8W
Dir QW 9m 15M vis: 144·5°- 147·5°(3°)

A1411·1 La Maresquerie
Rear 102m from front 49°23'·4N 01°02'·8W
Dir QW 12m 15M
vis: 144·5°-147·5°(3°)

A1412 Isigny-Sur-Mer Leading Lights 172°30'
Front 49°19'·6N 1°06'·7W
Dir Oc(2+1)W 12s 7m 18M
Intens 170·5°-174·5°(4°)

A1412·1 Isigny-Sur-Mer
Rear 625m from front 49°19'·3N 01°06'·8W
Dir Oc(2+1)W 12s 19m 18M
Synchronised with front. Intens 170·5°-
174·5°(4°)

A1418 Carentan Leading Lights 209°30'
Front 49°20'·5N 01°11'·1W
Dir Oc(3)R 12s 6m 18M
Intens 208·2°-210·7°(2·5°)

A1454 Pointe de Barfleur
Gatteville 49°41'·8N 01°15'·9W
FI(2)W 10s 72m 29M
Obscured when bearing less than 088°.

A1462 Cap Lévi 49°41'·8N 01°28'·4W
FIR 5s 36m 22M

A1480 Cherbourg Fort de L'Ouest
49°40'·5N 01°38'·8W
FI(3)WR 15s 19m 24/20M
vis: W122°-355°(233°), R355°-122°(127°).

A1484 Cherbourg - Lts in Line - Front
49°39'·6N 01°37'·9W 140°18' and 142°12'
Dir 2Q(hor)W5s 17M
63m apart. Intens 137·3°- 143·3°(6°) and
139·2°-145·2°(6°). Marks SW/NE limit of
dredged channel.

A1484·1 Cherbourg - Gare Maritime
Rear. 0·99M from front 49°38'·8N 01°37'·0W
Dir QW 35m 19M Intens 140°-142·5°(2·5°)

A1488·1 Cherbourg Lts in Line 192°
Rear. 652m from front 49°39'·3N 01°38'·6W
Dir QG 26m 15M Intens 189°-195°(6°)

A1512 Cap de la Hague 49°43'·4N 01°57'·3W
FIW 5s 48m 23M

ENGLISH CHANNEL
A1518 Lanby South West 48°31'·7N 05°49'·1W
FIW 4s 10m 20M

A1520 Channel Lt Float 49°54'·4N 02°53'·7W
FIW 15s 12m 25M Racon (O)

CHANNEL ISLANDS
A1532 Casquets 49°43'·4N 02°22'·7W
FI(5)W 30s 37m 24M Racon (T)

A1536 Alderney 49°43'·8N 02°09'·8W
FI(4)W 15s 37m 23M
vis: 085°-027°(302°)

A1538 Alderney - Alderney Hbr Ldg Lts 215°.
Front 49°43'·4N 02°11'·8W
QW 8m 17M
vis: 210°-220°(10°)

A1538·1 Alderney
Rear 335m from front 49°43'·2N 02°12'·0W
QW 17m 18M
vis: 210°-220°(10°)

A1544 Sark Pt Robert 49°26'·2N 02°20'·7W
FIW 15s 65m 20M
vis: 138°-353°(215°)

LIGHTS

A1548 **Guernsey**
PlatteFougère 49°30'·9N 02°29'·0W
FIWR 10s 15m 16M *Racon (P)*
vis: W155°-085°(290°), R085°-155°(70°).

A1560 **Guernsey**
St Peter Port Leading Lights 220°.
Front 49°27'·4N 02°31'·4W
AIWR 10s 14m 16M
vis: 187°-007°(180°).

A1580 **Guernsey**
Les Hanois 49°26'·2N 02°42'·1W
FI(2)W 13s 33m 20M
vis: 294°-237°(303°)

A1584 **Jersey**
Sorel Point 49°15'·7N 02°09'·4W
LFIWR 8s 50m 15M
vis: W095°-112°(17°), R112°-173° (61°),
W173°-230°(57°)R230°-269°(39°), W269°-273°(4°)

A1620 **Jersey**
La Corbière 49°10'·8N 02°14'·9W
IsoWR 10s 36m 18/16M
vis: *W shore-294°, R294°-328° (34°),*
W328°-148°(180°), R148°-shore.

A1622 **Jersey**
Grosnez Point 49°15'·5N 02°14'·7W
FI(2)WR 15s 50m 19/17M
vis: W081°-188°(107°), R188°-241°(53°)

FRANCE

A1638 **Cap de Carteret** 49°22'·4N 01°48'·4W
FI(2+1)W 15s 81m 26M

A1654 **Îles Chausey** 48°52'·2N 01°49'·3W
FIW 5s 39m 23M

A1660 **Port de Granville**
Pte du Roc 48°50'·1N 01°36'·8W
FI(4)W 15s 49m 23M

A1670 **La Pierre-de-Herpin** 48°43'·8N 01°48'·9W
Oc(2)W 6s 20m 17M

A1676 **Saint Malo** Leading Lights 089°06'.
Le Grand Jardin, Front 48°40'·2N 02°05'·0W
FI(2)R 10s 24m 15M *In line 129·7° with A
1686·1 leads through the channel of Petite
Port. Obscured by Cap Fréhel when bearing
less than 097°, by Île de Cézembre 220°-
233°(13°), by Grande Conchée 241°-243°(2°)
by Grande Chevreun & Pointe du Meinga when
bearing more than 251°.*

A1676·1 **Saint Malo - Rochebonne**
Rear. 4·2M from front 48°40'·3N 01°58'·7W
Dir FR 40m 24M
Intens 088·2°-089·7°(1.5°)

A1686 **Saint Malo Leading Lights** 128°42'.
Les Bas-Sablons. Front 48°38'·2N 02°01'·2W
Dir FG 20m 22M *Intens 127·5°-130·5°(3°)*

A1686·1 **Saint Malo La Balue**
Rear. 0·9M from front 48°37'·7N 02°00'·2W
Dir FG 69m 25M *Intens 128·2°-129·7 (1·5°)*

A1698 **Cap Fréhel** 48°41'·1N 02°19'·2W
FI(2)W 10s 85m 29M

A1713·55 **Portrieux**
NE Môle. Elbow 48°39'·0N 02°49'·1W
Dir IsoWRG 4s 16m 15/11/11M
vis: *W159°-179° (20°), G179°-316°(137°),
W316°-320·5°(4·5°), R320·5°-159°(198·5°)*

A1716 **Le Grand-Léjon**
48°44'·9N 02°39'·9W

FI(5)WR 20s 17m 18/14M
*vis: R015°-058°(43°), W058°-283°(225°),
R283°-350°(67°), W350°-015°(25°)*

A1722 **Paimpol**
Pointe de Porz-Don 48°47'·5N 03°01'·6W
Oc(2)WR 6s 13m 15/11M
vis: W269°-272°(3°), R272°-279°(7°)

A1734 **Roches Douvres** 49°06'·5N 2°48'·8W
FIW 5s 60m 28M

A1738 **Les Héaux de Bréhat** 48°54'·5N 03°05'·2W
Oc(3)WRG 12s 48m 15/11/11M
*vis: R227°-247°(20°), W247°-270°(23°),
G270°-302°(32°), W302°-227°(285°)*

A1742 **Île de Bréhat** Rosédo 48°51'·5N 03°00'·3W
FIW 5s 29m 20M

A1748 **Le Trieux** Leading Lights 224°42'.
La Croix. Front 48°50'·3N 03°03'·3W
Dir OcW 4s 15m 19M
Intens 215°-235°(20°)

A1748·1 **Le Trieux - Bodic**
Rear. 2·1M from front 48°48'·8N 03°05'·4W
Dir QW 55m 22M *Intens 221°-229°(8°)*

A1762·1 **Rivière de Tréguier**
Sainte Antoine. Leading light 137°.
Rear. 0·75M from front 48°51'·1N 03°07'·0W
Dir OcR 4s 34m 15M *Intens 134°-140°(6°)*

A1770 **Perros-Guirec** Passe de l'Ouest.
Dir Lt 143°36' 48°47'·8N 03°23'·4W
Dir Oc(2+1)WRG 12s 78m 15/12/12M
*G133·7°-143·2°(9·5°), W143·2°- 144·8°(1·6°),
R144·8°-154·3°(9·5°)*

A1774 **Perros-Guirec - Passe de l'Est.**
Leading Lights 224°30'.
Le Colombier. Front 48°47'·9N 03°26'·7W
Dir Oc(4)W 12s 28m 15M
Intens 214·5°-234·5°(20°)

A1774·1 **Perros-Guirec - Kerprigent**
Rear 1·5M from front 48°46'·9N 03°28'·2W
Dir QW 79m 21M *Intens 221°-228°(7°)*

A1786 **Les Sept-Îles**
Île-aux-Moines 48°52'·8N 03°29'·5W
FI(3)W 15s 59m 24M
*Obscured by Îliot Rouzic and E end of Île de Bono
237°-241°(4°) and in Baie de Lannion when
bearing less than 039°*

A1800 **Baie de Morlaix** La Lande.
Common rear Leading light 190°30' & 176°24'
48°38'·2N 03°53'·1W **FIW 5s** 85m 23M
*Obscured by Pointe Annelouesten when
bearing more than 204°*

A1800·1 **Baie de Morlaix - Leading Lights** 176°24'.
Île Louet. Front 48°40'·5N 03°53'·4W
Oc(3)WG 12s 17m 15/10M
*vis: W305°- 244°(299°), G244°-305°(61°),
vis: 139°-223°(84°) from offshore, except
where obscured by islands*

A1812·1 **Roscoff Leading Lights** 209°.
Rear 430m from front 48°43'·4N 03°58'·7W
Oc(2+1)W 12s 24m 15M *vis: 062°-242°(180°)*

A1816 **Île de Batz** 48°44'·8N 04°01'·6W
FI(4)W 25s 69m 23M

A1822 **Île-Vierge** 48°38'·4N 04°34'·1W
FIW 5s 77m 27M *vis: 337°-325°(348°).*

A1842 **Ouessant (Ushant)**
Le Stiff 48°28'·5N 05°03'·4W
FI(2)R 20s 85m 24M

A1844 Ouessant - Créac'h 48°27'·6N 05°07'·8W
FI(2)W 10s 70m 32M
Obscured 247°-255°(8°). Racon (C)
A1848 Ouessant
La Jument 48°25'·4N 05°08'·1W
FI(3)R 15s 36m 22M *vis: 241°-199°(318°)*
A1850 Ouessant - Kéréon (Men-Tensel)
48°26'·3N 05°01'·6W
Oc(2+1)WR 24s 38m 17/7M
vis: W019°-248°(229°), R248°-019°(131°)
A1854 Chenal du Four (North Part)
Le Four 48°31'·4N 04°48'·3W
FI(5)W 15s 28m 18M
A1856 Chenal du Four
L'Aber-Ildut 48°28'·3N 04°45'·6W
Dir Oc(2)WR 6s 12m 25/20M
vis: W081°-085°(4°), R085°-087°(2°)
A1873·9 Chenal du Four (South Part) Ldg Lts 007°.
Trézien. Rear 48°25'·4N 04°46'·8W
Dir Oc(2)W 6s 84m 20M
Intens 003°-011°(8°)
A1874 Chenal du Four - Kermorvan
Front Leading Light 137·9° for Chenal de la
Helle with A1880 48°21'·7N 04°47'·4W
FIW 5s 20m 22M
*Obscured by Pointe de Saint Mathieu when
bearing less than 341°. Front Leading light
137·9° for Chenal de la Helle with 1880*
A1874·1 Chenal du Four Leading Lights 158°30'.
St Mathieu. Rear 48°19'·8N 04°46'·3W
FIW 15s 56m 29M
A1874·1 Chenal du Four Leading Lights 158°30'.
St Mathieu. Rear 48°19'·8N 04°46'·3W
Dir F W 54m 28M
Intens F W 157·5°-159·5°(2°)
A1880 Lochrist 48°20'·6N 04°45'·7W
Dir Oc(3)W 12s 49m 22M
*Intens 135°-140°(5°) Rear Leading light 137·9°
for Chenal de la Helle with 1874*
A1886 Les Pierres Noires 48°18'·7N 04°54'·9W
FIR 5s 27m 19M
D0790 Pointe du Petit-Minou 48°20'·2N 04°36'·9W
FI(2)WR 6s 32m 19/15M
*vis: R Shore- 252°, W252°- 260°(8°),
R260°-307°(47°) W(unintens) 307°-015°(68°),
W015°-065·5°(50·5°), W070·5°-shore.
Leading Lights 068°.
Front Dir Q W 30m 23M
Intens 067·3°-068·8°(1·5°)*
D0790·1 Pointe du Petit-Minou -
Pointe due Portzic 48°21'·6N 04°32'·0W
Oc(2)WR 12s 56m 19/15M
*vis: R219°-259°(40°), W259°-338°(79°),
R338°-000°(22°), W000°-065·5°(65·5°),
W070·5°-219°(148·5°). vis: 041°- 069 (28°)
when W of Goulet.
Rear Dir Q W 54m 22M Intens 065°-071°(6°)*
D0790.2 Pointe du Petit-Minou
48°21'·6N 04°32'·0W
Dir Q(6) + LFIW 15s 54m 24M
Intens 045°-050(5°)
D0818 Pointe du Toulinguet
48°16'·8N 04°37'·8W
Oc(3)WR 12s 49m 15/11M
*vis: W shore-028°, R028°- 090°(62°),
W090°-shore.*

D0826 Pointe de Morgat 48°13'·2N 04°29'·9W
Oc(4)WRG 12s 77m 15/11/10M
*vis: W shore-281°. G281°-301°(20°).
W301°-021°(80°), R021°- 043°(22°)*
D0836 Douarnene
Pointe du Millier 48°05'·9N 04°27'·9W
Oc(2)WRG 6s 34m 16/12/11M
*vis: G080°- 087°(7°), W087°-113°(26°),
R113°- 120°(7°), W120°-129°(9°),
G129°-148°(19°), W148°-251°(103°),
R251°-258°(7°)*
D0852 Chaussée de Sein
Ar-men 48°03'·0N 04°59'·9W
FI(3)W 20s 29m 23M
D0856 Chaussée de Sein
Main light. Île de Sein 48°02'·6N 04°52'·1W
FI(4)W 25s 49m 29M
D0870 Raz de Sein - La Vieille 48°02'·5N 04°45'·4W
Oc(2+1)WRG 12s 33m 18/13/14M
*vis W290°- 298°(8°), R298°-325°(27°),
W325°-355°(30°), G355°-017°(22°),
W017°-035°(18°), G035°- 105°(70°),
W105°-123°(18°), R123°- 158°(35°),
W158°-205°(47°).*
D0890 Pointe de Penmarc'h
Eckmühl 47°47'·9N 04°22'·4W
FIW 5s 60m 23M
D0906 Loctudy
Point de Langoz 47°49'·9N 04°09'·6W
FI(4)WRG 12s 12m 15/11/11M
*vis W115°-257°(142°), G257°-284°(27°),
W284°-295°(11°), R295°-318°(23°),
W318°-328°(10°), R238°-025°(57°)*
D0913·9 Bénodet Rivière Odet Ldg Lts 345°30'.
Pointe du Coq. Front. 47°52'·4N 04°06'·6W
Dir Oc(2+1)G 12s 11m 17M
Intens 345°-347°(2°)
D0918 Îles de Glénan
Île-aux-Moutons 47°46'·5N 04°01'·7W
Oc(2)WRG 6s 18m 15/11/11M
*vis W035°-050°(15°), G050°-063°(13°),
W063°- 081°(18°), R081°-141°(60°),
W141°-292°(151°), R292°-035°(103°)*
D0918 Îles de Glénan
Auxiliary Light 47°46'·5N 04°01'·7W
Dir Oc(2)W 6s 17m 24M
*Sychronised with main light. Intens 278·5°-
283·5°(5°)*
D0922 Îles de Glénan
Penfret 47°43'·3N 03°57'·2W
FIR 5s 36m 21M
D0930 Concarneau Beuzec. Ldg Lt 028°30'
Rear. 1·34M from front 47°53'·4N 03°54'·0W
Dir QW 87m 23M
Intens 026·5°-030·5°(4°)
D0962 Île de Groix
Pen-Men 47°38'·9N 03°30'·5W
FI(4)W 25s 59m 29M
vis: 309°-275°(326°).
D0970 Tudy Pointe des Chats 47°37'·3N 03°25·3W
FIR 5s 16m 19M
D0971·1 Lorient Port Louis. Ldg Lt 057°
Rear 740m from front 47°42'·4N 03°21'·3W
Dir QW 22m 18M

D0976 **Lorient - Passe Sud**
Ldg Lts 008°30'.
Fish Market. Front 47°43'·8N 03°21'·7W
Dir QR 16m 17M
Intens 006°-011°(5°)

D0976·1 **Lorient - Kergroise-La Perrière**
Rear. 515m from front 47°44'·1N 03°21'·6W
Dir QR 34m 17M
Synchronised with front. Intens 006°-011°(5°)

D0978 **Lorient - Île Saint-Michel**
Ldg Lts 016°30'. Front 47°43'·5N 03°21'·6W
Dir Oc(3)G 12s 8m 16M
Intens 014·5°-017·5°(3°)

D0978·1 **Lorient**
Rear 306m from front 47°43'·7N 03°21'·5W
Dir Oc(3)G 12s 14m 16M
Synchronised with front. Intens 014·5°-017·5°(3°)

D0990 **Lorient - Kéroman** Submarine Base.
Ldg Lts 350°. Front 47°43'·7N 03°21'·9W
Dir Oc(2)R 6s 25m 15M *Intens 349°-351°(2°)*

D0990·1 **Lorient - Kéroman Ldg Lts**
Rear 91m from front 47°43'·7N 03°21'·9W
Dir Oc(2)R 6s 31m 15M
Synchronised with front. Intens 349°-351°(2°)

D0996 **Kernével Ldg Lts** 217°
Front 47°43'·1N 03°22'·3W
Dir QR 10m 15M *Intens 215°-219°(4°)*

D0996·1 **Rear** 290m from front 47°42'·9N 03°22'·4W
Dir QR 18m 15M *Intens 215°-219°(4°)*

D1022 **Passage de la Teignouse**
47°27'·5N 03°02'·8W
FIWR 4s 20m 15/11M
vis W033°-039°(6°), R039°-033°(354°)

D1030 **Belle Île**
Pointe des Poulains 47°23'·3N 3°15'·1W
FIW 5s 34m 23M
vis 023°-291°(268°)

D1032 **Belle Île**
Goulphar 47°18'·7N 03°13'·6W
FI(2)W 10s 87m 26M

D1036 **Belle Île**
Pte de Kerdonis 47°18'·6N 03°03'·6W
FI(3)R 15s 35m 15M
Obscured by Pointes d'Arzic and de Taillefer 025°-129°(104°)

D1050·1 **R.de Crac'h Ldg Lt** 347°
Rear 47°34'·4N 03°00'·4W
Dir QW 21m 15M
Synch with front. Intens 337°-357°(20°)

D1054 **Port-Navalo**
47°32'·9N 02°55'·1W
Oc(3)WRG 12s 32m 15/11/11M
W155°-220°(65°), G317°-359°(42°), W359°-015°(16°), R015°-105°(90°)

D1055 **Port du Crouesty Ldg Lts** 058°.
Front 47°32'·6N 02°53'·8W
Dir QW 10m 19M *Intens 056·5°-059·5°(3°)*

D1055·1 **Port du Crouesty**
Rear 315m from front 47°32'·7N 02°53'·6W
Dir QW 27m 19M
Intens 056·5°-059·5°(3°)

D1064 **La Vilaine Entrance**
Penlan 47°31'·0N 02°30'·2W
Oc(2)WRG 6s 26m 15/11/11M

vis: R292·5°-025°(92·5°), G025°-052°(27°), W052°-060°(8°), R060°-138°(78°), G138°-180°(42°)

D1080 **Le Four**
47°17'·9N 02°38'·1W
FIW 5s 23m 18M

D1090 **Le Croisic Ldg Lts** 156°.
Front 47°18'·0N 02°31'·0W
Dir Oc(2+1)W 12s 10m 19M
Intens 154°-158°(4°)

D1090·1 **Le Croisic**
Rear 116m from front 47°18'·0N 02°30'·9W
Dir Oc(2+1)W 12s 14m 19M
Intens 154°-158°(4°). Synchronised with front

D1096 **Estuaire de la Loire**
La Banche 47°10'·6N 02°28'·1W
FI(2+1)WR 15s 22m 15/11M
vis: R266°-280°(14°), W280°-266°(346°)

D1106 **Estuaire de la Loire - Portcé Ldg Lts** 025°30'.
Front 47°14'·6N 02°15'·4W
Dir QW 6m 22M *Intens 024·7°- 026·2°(1·5°)*

D1106·1 **Estuaire de la Loire**
Rear 0·75M from front 47°15'·3N 02°14'·9W
Dir QW 36m 24M
Intens 024°-027°(3°). Synchronised with front

D1152 **Baie de Bourgneuf**
Île du Pilier 47°02'·6N 02°21'·6W
FI(3)W 20s 33m 29M

D1162 **Île de Noirmoutier**
Pointe des Dames 47°00'·7N 02°13'·3W
Oc(3)WRG 12s 34m 19/15/15M
vis: G016·5°-057°(40·5°), R057°-124°(67°), G124°-165°(41°), W165°-191°(26°), R191°- 267°(76°), W267°-357°(90°), R357°-016·5°(19·5°)

D1174 **Fromentine Bridge**
46°53'·5N 02°09'·0W **IsoW 4s** 32m 18M

D1176 **Île d'Yeu**
Petite Foule 46°43'·1N 02°22'·9W
FIW 5s 56m 24M

D1186 **Île d'Yeu**
Pointe des Corbeaux 46°41'·4N 02°17'·1W
FI(2+1)R 15s 25m 20M
Obscured by the high land of Île d'Yeu 083°-143°(60°)

D1189.6 **Saint Gilles-Sur-Vie**
Pointe de Grosse Terre
46°41'·6N 01°57'·8W
FI(4)WR 12s 25m 17/13M
vis: W290°-125°(195°), R125°-145°(20°)

D1196 **Les Sables d'Olonne**
L'Armandèche 46°29'·4N 01°48'·3W
FI(2+1)W 15s 42m 24M
vis: 295°-130°(195°)

D1207 **Les Sables d'Olonne - Passe du SW**
Ldg Lts 033°. Front 46°29'·5N 01°46'·3W
IsoR 4s 14m 16M *Iso W 4s(T) 1994*

D1207·1 **Les Sables d'Olonne - Rear** La Potence.
330m from front 46°29'·6N 01°46'·1W
IsoR 4s 33m 16M *Iso W 4s (T) 1994*

D1214 **Pointe du Grouin-du-Cou**
46°20'·7N 1°27'·8W
FIWRG 5s 29m 20/16/16M *R034°-061°(27°), W061°- 117°(56°), G117°-138°(21°), W138°- 034°(256°)*

D1218 **Île de Ré** Les Baleines 46°14'·7N 01°33'·7W
Fl(4)W 15s 53m 27M
D1220·1 **Île de Ré - Le Fier d'Ars** Ldg Lts 265°.
Rear. 370m from front 46°14'·1N 01°28'·8W
Dir IsoG 4s 13m 15M
Synchronised with front. Intens 264°-266°(2°)
D1238 **Île de Ré - Chauveau** 46°08'·1N 01°16'·3W
Oc(2+1)WR 12s 27m 15/11M
*vis: W057°-094°(37°), R094°- 104°(10°),
W104°-342°(238°), R342°-057°(75°)*
D1256 **La Charente - Ile d'Aix**
46°00'·6N 01°10'·7W
FlWR 5s 24m 24/20M
vis: R103°-118°(15°), W118°-103°(345°)
D1257 **La Charente - Ldg Lts** 115°.
Fort de la Pointe. Front 45°58'·0N 01°04'·3W
Dir QR 8m 19M *Intens 113°-117°(4°)*
D1257·1 **La Charente**
Rear 600m from front 45°57'·9N 01°03'·8W
Dir QR 21m 20M *Intens 113°-117°(4°)*
D1270 **Île D'Oléron**
Chassiron 46°02'·9N 01°24'·5W
FlW 10s 50m 28M
Part obscured 297°-351°(54°)
D1290 **La Gironde**
La Coubre 45°41'·8N 01°14'·0W
Fl(2)W 10s 64m 28M
D1293·9 **La Gironde - Ldg Lts** 081°30'.
Front. 1·1M from rear 45°39'·6N 01°08'·7W
Dir IsoW 4s 21m 20M
Intens 080·5°-082·5°(2°)
D1294 **La Gironde**
Common rear 45°39'·8N 01°07'·2W
Dir QW 57m 27M *Intens 080·5°-082·5°(2°). Ra.
Dir FR* 57m 17M *intens 325·5°-328·5°(3°)*
D1294·1 **La Gironde - Ldg Lts** 327°. Terre-Nègre.
Front. 1·1M from rear 45°38'·8N 01°06'·3W
Oc(3)WRG 12s 39m 18/14/14M
*vis: R304°-319°(15°), W319°-327°(8°),
G327°-000°(33°), W000°-004°(4°),
G004°- 097°(93°), W097°-104°(7°),
R104°-116°(12°)*
D1300 **La Gironde - Cordouan** 45°35'·2N 01°10'·4W
Oc(2+1)WRG 12s 60m 22/18/18M
*vis: W014°-126°(112°), G126°-178·5°(52·5°),
W178·5°-250°(71·5°), W(unintens) 250°-267°(17°),
R(unintens) 267°- 294·5°(27·5°),
R294·5°-014°(79·5°). Obscured in estuary
when bearing more than 285°*
D1310 **La Gironde - 1st Ldg Lts** 063°.
St Nicolas. Front 45°33'·8N 01°04'·9W
Dir QG 22m 16M *Intens 061·5°-064·5°(3°)*
D1310·1 **La Gironde - Pointe de Grave**
Rear. 0·84M from front 45°34'·2N 01°03'·9W
OcWRG 4s 26m 19/15/15M
*vis: W(unintens) 033°-054°(21°),
W054°233·5°(179·5°), R233·5°-303°(69.5°),
W303°-312°(9°), G312°-330°(18°),
W330°-341°(11°), W(unintens) 341°-025°(44°)*
D1312 **La Gironde - Ldg Lts** 041°.
Le Chay. Front 45°37'·3N 01°02'·4W
Dir QR 33m 18M *Intens 039·5°-042·5°(3°)*
D1312·1 **La Gironde - Saint-Pierre**
Rear. 0.97M from front 45°38'·1N 01°01'·4W
Dir·QR 61m 18M *Intens 039°-043°(4°)*

D1372 **Hourtin** 45°08'·5N 01°09'·7W
FlW 5s 55m 23M
D1378 **Cap Ferret** 44°38'·7N 01°15'·0W
FlR 5s 53m 27M
D1382 **Contis** 44°05'·7N 01°19'·2W
Fl(4)W 25s 50m 23M
D1387·2 **L'Adour** Boucau.
Ldg Lts 090°. Front 43°31'·9N 01°31'·2W
Dir QW 9m 19M *Intens 086·5°-093·5°(7°)*
D1387·21 **L'Adour**
Rear 250m from front 43°31'·9N 01°31'·0W
Dir QW 15m 19M *Intens 086·5°-093·5°(7°)*
D1396 **L'Adour - La Forme de Radoub**
Ldg Lts 205°. Front 43°30'·6N 01°29'·7W
Dir FG 17m 16M *Intens 203·5°-206·5°(3°)*
D1396·1 **L'Adour**
Rear 147m from front 43°30'·5N 01°29'·8W
Dir FG 24m 16M
Intens 203·5°-206·5°(3°)
D1410 **Pointe Saint-Martin** 43°29'·6N 01°33'·3W
Fl(2)W 10s 73m 29M
D1414 **Baie de Saint-Jean-de-Luz** Sainte-Barbe.
Ldg Lts 101°. Front 43°24'·0N 01°39'·8W
Dir Oc(4) R 12s 30m 18M *Intens 095°-
107°(12°)*
D1416 **Baie de Saint-Jean-de-Luz**
Rear 340m from front 43°24'·0N 01°39'·5W
Dir Oc(4) R 12s 47m 18M
Synchronised with front. Intens 095°-107°(12°)
D1418 **Baie de Saint-Jean-de-Luz**
Entrance Ldg Lts 150°42'.
Front. Jetée Est 43°23'·3N 01°40'·1W
Dir QG 18m 16M *Intens 149·5°-152°(2·5°)*
D1420 **Baie de Saint-Jean-de-Luz -**
Rear 410m from front 43°23'·1N 01°39'·9W
Dir QG 27m 16M *Intens 149·7°-152·2°(2·5°)*
D1424·1 **Baie de Saint-Jean-de-Luz - Passe D'illarguita**
Ldg Lts 138°30' Bordagain.
Rear. 0·77M from front 43°23'·2N 01°40'·4W
Dir QW 67m 20M *Intens 134·5°141·5°(7°)*

SPAIN

D1452 **Cabo Higuer** 43°23'·6N 01°47'·4W
Fl(2)W 10s 63m 23M
vis: 072°-340°(268°) Aero marine
D1459 **Puerto de Pasajes. Senocozulúa**
Ldg Lts 154°49'. Front 43°20'·0N 01°55'·5W
QW 67m 18M
D1459·1 **Puerto de Pasajes**
Rear 45m from front 43°20'·0N 01°55'·5W
OcW 3s 86m 18M
D1483 **Igueldo or San Sebastian**
43°19'·3N 02°00'·7W
Fl (2+1)W 15s 132m 26M
D1489 **Puerto de Guetaria**
Isla de San Antón, 43°18'·6N 02°12'·1W
Fl (4)W 15s 91m 21M
D1502 **Cabo de Santa Catalina**
43°22'·6N 02°30'·6W
Fl (1+3)W 20s 44m 17M
D1520 **Cabo Machichaco** 43°27'·2N 02°45'·2W
FlW 7s 120m 24M
D1523 **Gorliz** 43°26'·0N 02°56'·6W
Fl (1+2)W 16s 163m 22M
D1524 **Puerto de Bilbao**

Punta Galea 43°22'·4N 03°02'·0W
Fl (3)W 8s 82m 19M
vis: 011°-227°(216°)

D1536 **Puerto de Castro - Urdiales**
Castillo de Santa Ana 43°23'·1N 03°12'·9W
Fl (4)W 24s 46m 20M

D1552 **Cabo Ajo** 43°30'·8N 03°35'·3W
Oc (3)W 16s 69m 17M

D1561 **Cabo Mayor** 43°29'·5N 03°47'·4W
Fl (2)W 10s 89m 21M

D1562 **Ría de Suances**
Punta del Torco de Fuera 43°26'·5N 04°02'·6W
Fl (1+2)W 24s 33m 22M
Obscured close inshore by higher land 091°-
113°(22°)

D1580 **Punta San Emeterio** 43°23'·9N 04°32'·1W
FlW 5s 66m 20M

D1582 **Llanes**
Punta de San Antón 43°25'·2N 04°44'·9W
Oc (4)W 15s 16m 15M

D1586 **Puerto de Ribadesella**
Somos 43°28'·4N 05°05'·0W
Fl(1+2)W 12s 113m 25M

D1591 **Cabo Lastres** 43°32'·1N 05°18'·0W
FlW 12s 116m 23M

D1592 **Tazones** 43°32'·9N 05°24'·0W
Oc (3)W 15s 125m 20M

D1596 **Puerto de Gijon**
Cabo de Torres 43°34'·4N 05°41'·9W
Fl(2)W 10s 80m 20M

D1614 **Puerto de Candás**
Punta del Cuerno 43°35'·7N 05°45'·7W
Oc(2)W 10s 38m 15M

D1628 **Cabo Peñas** 43°39'·4N 05°50'·8W
Fl(3)W 15s 115m 35M

D1630 **Ría de Avilés** Punta del Castillo.
Avilés 43°35'·8N 05°56'·6W
OcWR 5s 38m 20/17M R091·5°-113°(21·5°)
over Bajo El Petón. W113°- 091·5°(338·5°)

D1634 **Puerto de San Esteban de Pravia**
W Breakwater, Elbow 43°34'·0N 06°04'·7W
Fl(2)W 12s 19m 15M

D1634·2 **San Esteban de Pravia**
W Breakwater. Head 43°34'·3N 06°04'·6W
Fl(2)W 12s 19m 15M

D1640 **Puerto de Cudillero**
Punta Rebollera 43°33'·9N 06°08'·6'W
Oc(4)W 16s 42m 16M

D1641 **Cabo Vidio** 43°35'·6N 06°14'·7W
FlW 5s 99m 25M Aeromarine

D1642 **Cabo Busto** 43°34'·1N 06°28'·2W
Fl(4)W 20s 84m 25M Aeromarine

D1657 **Ría de Navía**
Cabo de San Augustín 43°33'·8N 06°44'·1W
Oc(2)W 12s 70m 25M

D1658 **Isla Tapia** Summit 43°34'·4N 06°56'·8W
Fl(1+2)W 19s 22m 18M

D1660 **Ría de Ribadeo**
Isla Pancha 43°33'·4N 07°02'·50W
Fl(3+1)W 20s 26m 21M

D1676 **Puerto de San Ciprián**
Punta Atalaya 43°42'·1N 07°26'·1W
Fl(5)W 20s 39m 20M

D1678·8 **Punta Roncadoira** 43°44'·1N 7°31'·5W
FlW 8s 92m 21M

D1686 **Punta Estaca de Bares** 43°47'·3N 07°41'·0W
Fl (2)W 8s 99m 25M Aeromarine
Obscured when bearing more than 291°.

D1686·3 **Cabo Ortegal** 43°46'·3N 07°52'·2W
OcW 8s 122m 18M

D1687 **Punta Candelaria** 43°42'·7N 08°02'·8W
Fl(3+1)W 24s 87m 21M

D1690 **Punta de la Frouxeira** 43°37'·1N 08°11'·3W
Fl(5)W 15s 73m 20M

D1692 **Cabo Prior** 43°34'·1N 08°18'·9W
Fl(1+2)W 15s 105m 22M
vis: 055·5°-310° (254·5°)

D1694 **Cabo Prioriño Chico** 43°27'·5N 08°20'·3W
FlW 5s 34m 23M

D1704 **Torre de Hércules** 43°23'·2N 08°24'·3W
Fl(4)W 20s 104m 23M
Obscured in entrance to Ensenada del Orzán

D1728 **Islas Sisargas** 43°21'·6N 08°50'·7W
Fl(3)W 15s 108m 23M

D1729 **Punta Nariga** 43°19'·2N 08°54'·6W
Fl(3+1)W 20s 53m 22M

D1732 **Punta Lage** 43°13'·9N 09°00'·7W
Fl(5)W 20s 64m 20M

D1736 **Cabo Villano** 43°09'·7N 09°12'·6W
Fl(2)W 15s 102m 28M
vis: 031·5°-228·5°(197°). Racon (M)

D1740 **Cabo Toriñana** 43°03'·2N 09°17'·9W
Fl(2+1)W 15s 63m 24M
vis: 340·5°-235·5°(255°)

D1742 **Cabo Finisterre** 42°52'·9N 09°16'·3W
FlW 5s 141m 23M
Obscured when bearing more than 149°.
Racon (O)

D1782 **Punta Insúa** 42°46'·3N 09°07'·6W
FWR 26m 15/14M FW vis: 093°-172·5°(79·5)
but obscured by high land 145°-172·5°(27·5°).
FR vis 308°-012·5°(64·5°)

D1794 **Cabo Corrubedo** 42°34'·6N 09°05'·4W
Fl(3+2)R 20s 30m 15M
Clear sector Fl (3+2) 089·4°- about
200°(110·6°). Fl(3)R 20s Dangerous sector
Fl(3) about 332°- (325° within Ensenada de
Corrubedo)-089·4°(117·4°)

D1796 **Isla Sálvora** 42°27'·9N 09°00'·8W
Fl(3+1)W 20s 38m 21M
Clear sector Fl(3+1)217°- 126° (269°),
dangerous sector Fl(3) 126°- 160°(34°)

D1846 **Isla Ons** 42°22'·9N 08°56'·2W
Fl(4)W 24s 125m 25M

D1884 **Monte Faro** 42°12'·8N 08°54'·9W
Fl(2)W 8s 185m 22M
Obscured 315°-016·5°(61·5°) over Bajos de
Los Castros and Forcados

D1890 **Cabo Estay**
Ldg Lts 069°20'. Front 42°11'·1N 08°48'·9W
IsoW 2s 16m 18M
vis: 066·3°-072·3(6°). Racon (B)

D1890·1 **Cabo Estay**
Rear 660m from front 42°11'·3N 08°48'·3W
OcW 4s 48m 18M vis: 066·3°-072·3°(6°)

D1904 **Punta Areiño**
La Guia 42°15'·6N 08°42'·1W
Oc(2+1)W 20s 35m 15M

D1916 **Cabo Silleiro** 42°06'·2N 08°53'·8W
Fl(2+1)W 15s 83m 24M

PORTUGAL

D2008 **Promontório de Montedor**
41°44'·9N 08°52'·4W
Fl(2)W 9·5s 102m 22M

D2012 **Viana do Castelo** Rio Lima.
Barra Sul Ldg Lts 012°30'. Castelo de
Santiago.
SW battery. Front 41°41'·4N 08°50'·3W
IsoR 4s 14m 23M
vis 241°-151°(270°)

D2012·1 **Viana do Castelo - Senhora da Agonia**
Rear. 500m from front 41°41'·7N 08°50'·2W
OcR 6s 32m 23M
vis 005°-020°(15°)

D2016 **Forte da Barra do Rio Cávado**
41°32'·5N 08°47'·4W
FIW 5s 20m 21M

D2020 **Póvoa de Varzim**
Regufe 41°22'·4N 08°45'·2W
IsoW 6s 29m 15M

D2032 **Leça** 41°12'·1N 08°42'·6W
Fl(3)W 14s 57m 28M

D2056 **Aveiro** 40°38'·6N 08°44'·8W
Fl(4)W 13s 65m 23M

D2060 **Cabo Mondego** 40°11'·4N 08°54'·2W
FIW 5s 101m 28M

D2072 **Penedo da Saudade** 39°45'·8N 09°01'·8W
Fl(2)W 15s 54m 30M

D2086 **Ilha Berlenga** 39°24'·8N 09°30'·5W
Fl(3)W 20s 120m 27M

D2088 **Cabo Carvoeiro** 39°21'·5N 09°24'·4W
Fl(3)R 15s 58m 15M

D2108 **Cabo da Roca** 38°46'·8N 09°29'·8W
Fl(4)W 18s 164m 26M

D2110 **Forte de São Brás** 38°42'·6N 09°29'·1W
Fl(3)W 15s 22m 20M
vis: 324°-189°(225°)

D2114 **Cascais** Barra do Norte.
Ldg Lts 284·7°. Nossa Senhora de Guia.
Rear 38°41'·6N 09°26'·7W
IsoWR 2s 57m 19/16M
vis: W326°-092°(126°), R278°-292°(14°)

D2118 **Cascais - Forte de Santa Marta**
Front 38°41'·3N 09°25'·2W
OcWR 6s 24m 18/14M
vis: R223°-334°(101°), W334°-098°(124°)

D2126 **Forte Bugio** 38°39'·5N 09°17'·9W
FIG 5s 27m 21M

D2127 **Barra do Sul** Ldg Lts 047°.
Gibalta. Front 38°41'·8N 09°15'·9W
OcR 3s 30m 21M
vis 039·5°-054·5°(15°)

D2127·1 **Barra do Sul - Esteiro**
Rear. 760m from front 38°42'·1N 09°15'·6W
OcR 6s 81m 21M
vis: 039·5°-054·5°(15°). Racon (Q)

D2127·15 **Mama Sul** 38°43'·7N 09°13'·6W
IsoW 6s 154m 21M

D2138 **Chibata** 38°38'·5N 09°13'·0W
FR 15M Occas

D2139 **Cabo Espichel** 38°24'·8N 09°12'·9W
FIW 4s 167m 26M

D2151-1 **Porto de Setúbal** Ldg Lts 039°48'. Azêda.
Rear 1·7M from front 38°32'·4N 08°52'·6W
IsoR 6s 61m 20M vis: 038·3°-041·3° (3°)

D2160 **Cabo de Sines** 37°57'·5N 08°52'·7W
Fl(2)W 15s 55m 26M
Obscured 001°- 003°(2°), 004°-007°(3°)
within 17M.

D2164 **Cabo Sardão**
Ponto do Cavaleiro 37°35'·8N 08°48'·9W
Fl(3)W 15s 66m 23M

D2168 **Cabo de São Vicente** 37°01'·3N 08°59'·7W
FIW 5s 84m 32M

D2174 **Ponta da Piedade** 37°04'·8N 08°40'·1W
FIW 7s 49m 20M

D2192 **Alfanzina** 37°05'·1N 08°26'·5W
Fl(2)W 15s 62m 29M

D2197·2 **Vilamoura** 37°04'·4N 08°07'·3W
FIW 10s 17m 19M

D2206 **Cabo de Santa Maria** 36°58'·4N 07°51'·8W
Fl (4)W 17s 49m 25M

D2246 **Vila Real de Santo António**
37°11'·1N 07°24'·9W
FIW 6s 51m 26M

SPAIN

D2312 **Rompido de Cartaya**
37°12'·9N 07°07'·6W
Fl(2)W 10s 41m 24M

D2320 **Picacho** 37°08'·2N 06°49'·5W
Fl(2+4)W 30s 51m 25M

D2345 **Higuera** 37°00'·6N 06°34'·1W
Fl(3)W 20s 46m 20M

D2351 **Chipiona**
Punta del Perro 36°44'·3N 06°26'·4W
FIW 10s 68m 25M

D2355 **Rota** 36°38'·2N 06°20'·8W
Aero AlFIWG 9s 79m 17M

D2362 **Puerto de Cádiz**
Castilla de San Sebastián
36°31'·8N 06°18.'·9W
Fl(2)W 10s 38m 25M
Unintens 085°-121°(36°) Obscured over the
port by the houses in the town.

D2405 **Cabo Roche** 36°17'·8N 06°08'·3W
Fl(4)W 24s 44m 20M

D2406 **Cabo Trafalgar** 36°11'·0N 06°02'·0W
Fl(2+1)W 15s 50m 22M

D2414 **Tarifa**
S end of peninsula 36°00'·1N 05°36'·5W
Fl(3)WR 10s 40m 26/18M
vis: W113°-089°(336°) R089°-113°(24°).
Racon (C)

D2420 **Punta Carnero** 36°04'·7N 5°25'·5W
Fl(4)WR 20s 42m 18/9M
vis: W018°-325°(307°), R 325°- 018°(53°)

GIBRALTAR

D2438 **Gibraltar. Europa Point**
Victoria Tower 36°06'·7N 05°20'·6W
IsoW 10s 49m 19M
vis: 197°-042°(205°), intens 067°- 125°(58°).
Oc R 10s and F R both 44m 15M.
vis: 042°-067°(25°)

D2442 **Gibraltar. South Mole**
A head 36°08'·1N 05°21'·8W
FIW 2s 18m 15M

D2456 **Gibraltar. Aero light** 36°08'·7N 05°20'·5W
Aero Mo (GB)R 10s 405m 30M
Obscured on westerly bearings within 2M

Electronic navigation systems

Two position fixing systems are available to yachtsmen. These are: the satellite **Global Positioning System (GPS)**, and the terrestrial hyperbolic area navigation system **Loran-C**.

A differential GPS system, providing overlapping coverage around the coast of UK and Republic of Ireland is now operational and offers increased GPS accuracy within coverage from the reference stations.

The UK Decca system is due to shut down on 31 Mar 2000. Most of the European Decca chains are expected to close on 31 Dec 1999. Decca will be replaced by the four NW European Loran-C System chains (NELS).

GPS

GPS provides highly accurate, worldwide, continuous three dimensional position fixing (latitude, longitude and altitude) together with velocity and time data in all weather conditions.

The GPS constellation consists of 27 satellites in six orbital planes inclined to the Equator at 55°. Satellites circle the earth in approximately 12 hour orbits at heights of 10,900 miles. Three of the satellites are active spares.

The spacing of satellites is so arranged that a minimum of four to five satellites are in view to users worldwide. The Standard Positioning Service (SPS) available to civilian users provides fix accuracies of the order of 100 metres for 95% of the time. Accuracy will be ± 300 metres for 99·99% of the time. This means that errors > 300 metres can occasionally occur for 0·01% of the time.

Fixes are obtained by measuring the ranges from several, satellites to a receiver. This is achieved by accurately knowing the times of transmission and reception of precisely timed signals together with information on the satellites' position in space. In effect this means that each satellite transmits a code saying "this is my position and this is the time". Multiply the signal transit time by the speed of light and you get the range to the satellite. If measurements are made on a minimum of three satellites, three intersecting range circles are obtained each centred on the satellites position at the time of transmission.

Differential GPS

Differential GPS is a method of improving the basic accuracy of GPS within a localised area of about 50-100M of a user's receiver.

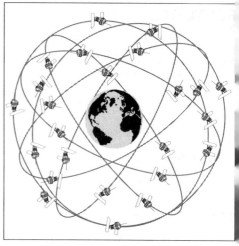

The GPS constellation consists of 27 satellites (24 operational plus 3 active spares) located in six planes to form a birdcage around the Earth. Satellite spacing is arranged to ensure that at least 4 satellites are in view from anywhere on Earth.

The principle of dGPS is to compare the position given by a user's receiver with position obtained by a receiver located at a accurately surveyed reference point, called the reference station.

This is achieved by pseudorange measurement. A correction message is then broadcast on a radiobeacon frequency.

In order to make use of broadcast GPS corrections, users will require an MSK (Minimum Shift Keying) radiobeacon receiver *plus* a GPS receiver capable of incorporating the dGPS correction data in the RTCM SC 105 format. The accuracy of the dGPS service is expected to be better than ±10 metres.

GPS integrity monitoring

Urgent GPS status information, excluding satellite almanac data, is issued in Coastguard navigational warning broadcasts on VHF and MF SSB when necessary, or from any Navtex station under message category "J".

The US Coast Guard is the US Government interface for all civil users of GPS. Information is available from the US Coast Guard GPS Navigation Centre (NAVCEN) located in Alexandria, Virginia. The Navigation Information Service (NIS). is there to meet the needs of the civil user. The information available includes present or future satellite outages, constellation changes, and other information related to GPS.

NIS services available from the US Coast Guard are listed below:

US Coastguard GPS Information Centre (GPSIC) ☎ 00 1 703 313 5907 (H24) which gives a pre-recorded daily status message

GPSIC duty personnel can be contacted on ☎ 00 1 703 313 5900 (H24),

or by 🖷 00 1 703 313 5931/5932

Internet:

HTTP: www.navcen.uscg.mil

FTP://ftp.navcen.uscg.mil

The USA. also transmits recorded time information through **Fort Collins (WWV)** and **Kekaha (Honolulu) (WWVH)** on frequencies 2500, 5000, 10,000, 15,000 and 20,000 kHz. GPS status and outage information is broadcast during the 40 second interval between time clicks by WWV at H+14 and H+15 and WWVH at H+43 and H+44.

Loran-C

Loran-C is a pulsed, long range hyperbolic radionavigation system operating in the 90 to 110 kHz frequency band suitable for coastal and offshore navigation within chain coverage. The system is based upon the measurement of the difference in time of arrival of pulses sent out by synchronised transmitters which are separated by hundreds of miles.

The NW European Loran-C System (NELS) consists of four new Loran-C chains. They provide extensive coverage over NW Europe and the British Isles.

A Loran-C chain consists of three to five powerful transmitting stations spaced several hundred miles apart and geometrically located so that signals from the master and at least two secondary stations may be received throughout the required coverage area. One transmitter is designated as the master station (M), and the other transmitters as secondary or slave stations (W, X, Y and Z).

Signals transmitted from the secondaries are synchronised with the master signal. The groundwave can normally be received at ranges of 800-1200M but skywaves can be received at a much greater range, albeit with less accuracy. Within groundwave coverage, accuracy varies from about 100m at a range of 200M from transmitters, to 250m to 1M or more at 500M range.

The principle of operation is based on the accurate measurement of the difference in the time of arrival of signals transmitted from a chain of synchronised transmitters. The Master transmits first and the signal is

received both at the Secondary station and the user's receiver. The Secondary station waits a precise amount of time before transmitting its own signal. The transmissions from both stations travel at 186,000mps and the difference in arrival time, called the **Time Difference (TD)**, is very accurately measured by the receiver.

All Loran stations transmit on the same carrier frequency (100 kHz) and there is a need to identify chains. This is achieved by each station transmitting groups of pulses at a specified **Group Repetition Interval (GRI)** which identifies the chain.

In order to get the best out of the system it is necessary to have an understanding of two commonly used terms. These are:

(a) **Absolute accuracy** is a measure of your ability to determine actual or true geographic position – latitude and longitude from a navigation system such as Loran-C. You would use absolute accuracy to keep track of your true position if you were crossing an ocean or visiting a new location.

(b) **Repeatable accuracy** is a measurement of the ability to go back to a specified location on the basis of previously obtained Loran readings. Repeatable accuracy helps you to return to exactly the same spot, time after time, by using the Loran-C readings for that spot as a reference.

NELS Chains

Lessay chain (GRI 6731)

Master:	Lessay (M) (France)
Secondaries:	Soustons (X) (France)
	Loop Head (Y)* (Ireland)
	Sylt (Z) (Germany)

Sylt chain (GRI 7499)

Master:	Sylt (M) (Germany)
Secondaries:	Lessay (X) (France)
	Vælandet (Y) (Norway)

Ejde chain (GRI 9007)

Master:	Ejde (M) (Færoe Islands)
Secondaries:	Jan Mayen (W) (Norway)
	Bø (X) (Norway)
	Vælandet (Y) (Norway)
	Loop Head (Z)*

Bø chain (GRI 7001)

Master:	Bø (M) (Norway)
Secondaries:	Jan Mayen (X) (Norway)
	Berlevåg (Y) (Norway)

Note: * The Irish transmitter at Loop Head is not expected to be operational before the end of 2000.

NORTH WEST EUROPE – LORAN-C CHAINS

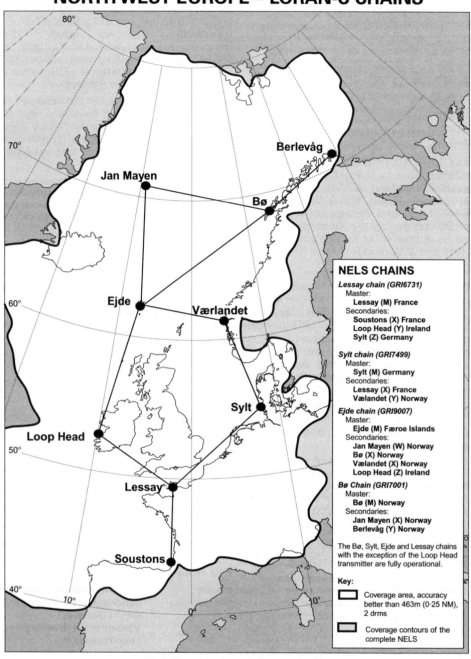

NELS CHAINS

Lessay chain (GRI6731)
Master:
  Lessay (M) France
Secondaries:
  Soustons (X) France
  Loop Head (Y) Ireland
  Sylt (Z) Germany

Sylt chain (GRI7499)
Master:
  Sylt (M) Germany
Secondaries:
  Lessay (X) France
  Vælandet (Y) Norway

Ejde chain (GRI9007)
Master:
  Ejde (M) Færoe Islands
Secondaries:
  Jan Mayen (W) Norway
  Bø (X) Norway
  Vælandet (X) Norway
  Loop Head (Z) Ireland

Bø Chain (GRI7001)
Master:
  Bø (M) Norway
Secondaries:
  Jan Mayen (X) Norway
  Berlevåg (Y) Norway

The Bø, Sylt, Ejde and Lessay chains with the exception of the Loop Head transmitter are fully operational.

Key:

☐ Coverage area, accuracy better than 463m (0·25 NM), 2 drms

☐ Coverage contours of the complete NELS

DISTANCE FROM DIPPING LIGHT IN NAUTICAL MILES

Height of eye in feet

Height of light in metres	2	3	4	5	6	7	8	9	10	20	30	40	50
2	4·6	4·9	5·2	5·5	5·7	6·0	6·2	6·4	6·6	8·1	9·2	10·2	11·0
3	5·2	5·6	5·9	6·2	6·4	6·6	6·8	7·0	7·2	8·7	9·9	10·8	11·7
4	5·8	6·1	6·4	6·7	6·9	7·2	7·4	7·6	7·8	9·3	10·4	11·4	12·2
5	6·3	6·6	6·9	7·2	7·4	7·7	7·9	8·1	8·3	9·8	10·9	11·9	12·7
6	6·7	7·1	7·4	7·6	7·9	8·1	8·3	8·5	8·7	10·2	11·3	12·3	13·2
7	7·1	7·5	7·8	8·0	8·3	8·5	8·7	8·9	9·1	10·6	11·8	12·7	13·6
8	7·5	7·8	8·2	8·4	8·7	8·9	9·1	9·3	9·5	11·0	12·1	13·1	14·0
9	7·8	8·2	8·5	8·8	9·0	9·2	9·5	9·7	9·8	11·3	12·5	13·5	14·3
10	8·2	8·5	8·8	9·1	9·4	9·6	9·8	10·0	10·2	11·7	12·8	13·8	14·6
11	8·5	8·9	9·2	9·4	9·7	9·9	10·1	10·3	10·5	12·0	13·1	14·1	15·0
12	8·8	9·2	9·5	9·7	10·0	10·2	10·4	10·6	10·8	12·3	13·4	14·4	15·3
13	9·1	9·5	9·8	10·0	10·3	10·5	10·7	10·9	11·1	12·6	13·7	14·7	15·6
14	9·4	9·7	10·0	10·3	10·6	10·8	11·0	11·2	11·4	12·9	14·0	15·0	15·8
15	9·6	10·0	10·3	10·6	10·8	11·1	11·3	11·5	11·6	13·1	14·3	15·3	16·1
16	9·9	10·3	10·6	10·8	11·1	11·3	11·5	11·7	11·9	13·4	14·6	15·5	16·4
17	10·2	10·5	10·8	11·1	11·3	11·6	11·8	12·0	12·2	13·7	14·8	15·8	16·6
18	10·4	10·8	11·1	11·4	11·6	11·8	12·0	12·2	12·4	13·9	15·1	16·0	16·9
19	10·7	11·0	11·3	11·6	11·8	12·1	12·3	12·5	12·7	14·2	15·3	16·3	17·1
20	10·9	11·3	11·6	11·8	12·1	12·3	12·5	12·7	12·9	14·4	15·5	16·5	17·3
25	12·0	12·3	12·6	12·9	13·2	13·4	13·6	13·8	14·0	15·5	16·6	17·6	18·4
30	13·0	13·3	13·6	13·9	14·1	14·4	14·6	14·8	15·0	16·5	17·6	18·6	19·4
40	14·7	15·1	15·4	15·7	15·9	16·1	16·3	16·5	16·7	18·2	19·4	20·3	21·2
50	16·3	16·6	16·9	17·2	17·4	17·7	17·9	18·1	18·3	19·8	20·9	21·9	22·7
60	17·7	18·0	18·3	18·6	18·8	19·1	19·3	19·5	19·7	21·2	22·3	23·3	24·1

SPEED, TIME AND DISTANCE IN NAUTICAL MILES

Speed in knots

Time in minutes	1	2	3	4	5	6	7	8	9	10	15	20
1	0·0	0·0	0·1	0·1	0·1	0·1	0·1	0·1	0·2	0·2	0·3	0·3
2	0·0	0·1	0·1	0·1	0·2	0·2	0·2	0·3	0·3	0·3	0·5	0·7
3	0·1	0·1	0·2	0·2	0·3	0·3	0·4	0·4	0·5	0·5	0·8	1·0
4	0·1	0·1	0·2	0·3	0·3	0·4	0·5	0·5	0·6	0·7	1·0	1·3
5	0·1	0·2	0·3	0·3	0·4	0·5	0·6	0·7	0·8	0·8	1·3	1·7
6	0·1	0·2	0·3	0·4	0·5	0·6	0·7	0·8	0·9	1·0	1·5	2·0
7	0·1	0·2	0·4	0·5	0·6	0·7	0·8	0·9	1·1	1·2	1·8	2·3
8	0·1	0·3	0·4	0·5	0·7	0·8	0·9	1·1	1·2	1·3	2·0	2·7
9	0·2	0·3	0·5	0·6	0·8	0·9	1·1	1·2	1·4	1·5	2·3	3·0
10	0·2	0·3	0·5	0·7	0·8	1·0	1·2	1·3	1·5	1·7	2·5	3·3
11	0·2	0·4	0·6	0·7	0·9	1·1	1·3	1·5	1·7	1·8	2·8	3·7
12	0·2	0·4	0·6	0·8	1·0	1·2	1·4	1·6	1·8	2·0	3·0	4·0
13	0·2	0·4	0·7	0·9	1·1	1·3	1·5	1·7	2·0	2·2	3·3	4·3
14	0·2	0·5	0·7	0·9	1·2	1·4	1·6	1·9	2·1	2·3	3·5	4·7
15	0·3	0·5	0·8	1·0	1·3	1·5	1·8	2·0	2·3	2·5	3·8	5·0
16	0·3	0·5	0·8	1·1	1·3	1·6	1·9	2·1	2·4	2·7	4·0	5·3
17	0·3	0·6	0·9	1·1	1·4	1·7	2·0	2·3	2·6	2·8	4·3	5·7
18	0·3	0·6	0·9	1·2	1·5	1·8	2·1	2·4	2·7	3·0	4·5	6·0
19	0·3	0·6	1·0	1·3	1·6	1·9	2·2	2·5	2·9	3·2	4·8	6·3
20	0·3	0·7	1·0	1·3	1·7	2·0	2·3	2·7	3·0	3·3	5·0	6·7
21	0·4	0·7	1·1	1·4	1·8	2·1	2·5	2·8	3·2	3·5	5·3	7·0
22	0·4	0·7	1·1	1·5	1·8	2·2	2·6	2·9	3·3	3·7	5·5	7·3
23	0·4	0·8	1·2	1·5	1·9	2·3	2·7	3·1	3·5	3·8	5·8	7·7
24	0·4	0·8	1·2	1·6	2·0	2·4	2·8	3·2	3·6	4·0	6·0	8·0
25	0·4	0·8	1·3	1·7	2·1	2·5	2·9	3·3	3·8	4·2	6·3	8·3
30	0·5	1·0	1·5	2·0	2·5	3·0	3·5	4·0	4·5	5·0	7·5	10·0
35	0·6	1·2	1·8	2·3	2·9	3·5	4·1	4·7	5·3	5·8	8·8	11·7
40	0·7	1·3	2·0	2·7	3·3	4·0	4·7	5·3	6·0	6·7	10·0	13·3
45	0·8	1·5	2·3	3·0	3·8	4·5	5·3	6·0	6·8	7·5	11·3	15·0
50	0·8	1·7	2·5	3·3	4·2	5·0	5·8	6·7	7·5	8·3	12·5	16·7

COMMUNICATIONS SECTION

CONTENTS

HM COASTGUARD CHART

SHETLAND MRSC
The Knab, Knab Road,
Lerwick, Shetland ZE1 0AX
Tel: 01595 692976

PENTLAND MRSC
Cromwell Road, Kirkwall, Orkney
KW15 1LN. Tel: 01856 873268

STORNOWAY MRSC
Battery Point, Stornoway
Isle of Lewis HS1 2RT
Tel: 01851 702013

*NORTH & EAST
SCOTLAND REGION*

ABERDEEN MRCC
Marine House, Blaikies Quay
Aberdeen AB1 2PB.
Tel: 01224 592334

*WEST OF SCOTLAND
& NORTHERN
IRELAND
REGION*

OBAN MRSC
Boswell House, Argyll Square
Oban PA34 4BD.
Tel: 01631 563720

STIRLING

FORTH MRSC
Fifeness, Crail, Fife, KY10 3XN
Tel: 01333 450666

**CLYDE
MRCC**
Navy Buildings
Eldon Street
Greenock PA16 7QY.
Tel: 01475 729988

TYNE TEES MRSC
Priory Grounds, Tynemouth, Tyne & Wear
NE30 4DA. Tel: 0191 2572691

**BELFAST
MRSC**
Bregenz House
Quay Street, Bangor
Co Down BT20 5ED
Tel: 01247 463933

EASTERN REGION

HUMBER MRSC
Lime Kiln Lane,
Bridlington
North Humberside
YO15 2LX
Tel: 01262 672317

HOLYHEAD MRSC
Prince of Wales Road
Holyhead
Anglesey
Gwynedd
LL65 1ET
Tel: 01407
762051

LIVERPOOL
MRSC
Hall Road West
Crosby, Liverpool L23 8SY
Tel: 0151 931 3341

*WESTERN
REGION*

YARMOUTH MRCC
Havenbridge House, 5th Floor
Great Yarmouth NR30 1HA
Tel: 01493 851338

MILFORD HAVEN MRSC
Gorsewood Drive, Hakin
Milford Haven, Dyfed SA73 3ER
Tel: 01646
690909

SWANSEA MRCC
Tutt Head, Mumbles
Swansea SA3 4EX
Tel: 01792 366534

**SOUTHAMPTON
COASTGUARD
HEADQUARTERS**

**THAMES
MRSC**
East terrace
Walton-on-Naze
Essex CO14 8PY
Tel: 01255 675518

*SOUTH
WESTERN
REGION*

**DOVER
MRCC**
Langdon Battery
Swingate, Dover
Kent CT15 5NA
Tel: 01304 210008

PORTLAND
MRSC
Custom House Quay
Weymouth
Dorset, DT4 8BE
Tel: 01305 760439

SOLENT
MRSC
44a Marine Parade West
Lee on Solent, Hants PO13 9NR
Tel: 01705 552100

FALMOUTH MRCC
Pendennis Point, Castle Drive
Falmouth, Cornwall TR11 4WZ
Tel: 01326 317575

BRIXHAM
MRSC
Kings Quay,
Brixham
Devon TQ5 9TW
Tel: 01803 882704

SOUTH EASTERN REGION

■ MARITIME RESCUE COORDINATION CENTRE (REGIONAL) MRCC   ▲ MARITIME RESCUE SUB CENTRE (DISTRICT) MRSC
—— REGIONAL BOUNDARY   ---- DISTRICT BOUNDARY   □ MPCU EQUIPMENT STOCKPILE

RADIO OPERATION

Avoiding interference

Before transmitting, first listen on the VHF channel. If occupied, wait for a break before transmitting, or choose another. If you cause interference you must comply immediately with any request from a Coastal Radio Station (CRS) to stop transmitting. The request will indicate how long to desist.

Control of communications

Ship-to-Shore: Except in the case of distress, urgency or safety, communications between ship and CRS are controlled by the latter.

Intership: The ship *called* controls communication. If you call another ship, then it has control. If you are called by a ship, you assume control. If a CRS breaks in, both ships must comply with instructions given. A CRS has better aerials and equipment and thus its transmission and reception areas are greater.

Radio confidentiality

Inevitably you will overhear people's private conversations on VHF. These must not be reproduced, passed on or used for any purpose.

Voice technique There are two considerations when operating:
What to say – *i.e. voice procedure*
How to say it – *i.e. voice technique*

Clear R/T speech is vital. If a message cannot be understood by the receiving operator it is useless. Anyone can become a good operator by following a few rules: The voice should be pitched at a higher level than for normal conversation. Avoid dropping the voice pitch at the end of a word or phrase. Hold the microphone a few inches in front of the mouth and speak directly into it at a normal level. Speak clearly so that there can be no confusion. Emphasise words with weak syllables; 'Tower', if badly pronounced, could sound like 'tar'. People with strong accents must try to use as understandable a pronunciation as possible. Messages which have to be written down at the receiving station should be sent slowly. This gives time for it to be written down by the receiving operator. Remember, the average reading speed is 250 words a minute, whilst average writing speed is only 20. If the transmitting operator himself writes it down all should be well.

The phonetic alphabet

The syllables to emphasise are underlined

letter	morse	phonetic	spoken as
A	• –	Alfa	AL-fah
B	– • • •	Bravo	BRAH-voh
C	– • – •	Charlie	CHAR-lee
D	– • •	Delta	DELL-tah
E	•	Echo	ECK-oh
F	• • – •	Foxtrot	FOKS-trot
G	– – •	Golf	GOLF
H	• • • •	Hotel	hoh-TELL
I	• •	India	IN-dee-ah
J	• – – –	Juliett	JEW-lee-ett
K	– • –	Kilo	KEY-loh
L	• – • •	Lima	LEE-mah
M	– –	Mike	MIKE
N	– •	November	no-VEM-ber
O	– – –	Oscar	OSS-car
P	• – – •	Papa	pa-PAH
Q	– – • –	Quebec	keh-BECK
R	• – •	Romeo	ROW-me-oh
S	• • •	Sierra	see-AIR-rah
T	–	Tango	TANG-go
U	• • –	Uniform	YOU-nee-form or OO-nee-form
V	• • • –	Victor	VIK-tah
W	• – –	Whiskey	WISS-key
X	– • • –	X-Ray	ECKS-ray
Y	– • – –	Yankee	YANG-key
Z	– – • •	Zulu	ZOO-loo

Difficult words may be spelled phonetically. Operators precede this with 'I spell'. If the word is pronounceable include it before and after it has been spelt. If an operator sends the message 'I will moor alongside the yacht Coila' he would transmit: 'I will moor alongside the yacht Coila – I spell – Charlie Oscar India Lima Alfa – Coila'. When asked for your international callsign – say it is MGLA4 – transmit: 'My callsign is Mike Golf Lima Alfa Four.'

Phonetic numerals

When numerals are transmitted, the following pronunciations make them easier to understand.

no morse	spoken as	no morse	spoken as
1 • – – – –	WUN	2 • • – – –	TOO
3 • • • – –	TREE	4 • • • • –	FOW-ER
5 • • • • •	FIFE	6 – • • • •	SIX
7 – – • • •	SEV-EN	8 – – – • •	AIT
9 – – – – •	NIN-ER	0 – – – – –	ZERO

Numerals are transmitted digit by digit except that multiples of thousands may be spoken as follows.

numeral	spoken as
44	FOW-ER FOW-ER
90	NIN-ER ZERO
136	WUN TREE SIX
500	FIFE ZERO ZERO
1478	WUN FOW-ER SEV-EN AIT
7000	SEV-EN THOU-SAND

Punctuation

Punctuation marks should be used only where their omission would cause confusion.

mark	word	spoken as
.	Decimal	DAY-SEE-MAL
,	Comma	COMMA
.	Stop	STOP

Procedure words or 'prowords'

These are used to shorten transmissions

All after: Used after proword *'say again'* to request repetition of a portion of a message

All before: Used after proword *say again'* to request repetition of a portion of message

Correct: Reply to repetition of message that was preceded by prowords *'read back for check'* when it has been correctly repeated. Often said twice

Correction: Spoken during the transmission of a message means an error has been made in this transmission. Cancel the last word or group of words. The correct word or group follows.

In figures: Following numeral or group of numerals to be written as figures

In letters: Following numeral or group of numerals to be written as figures as spoken

I say again: I am repeating transmission or portion indicated

I spell: I shall spell the next word or group of letters phonetically

Out: This is the end of working to you

Over: Invitation to reply

Read back: If receiving station is doubtful about accuracy of whole or part of message it may repeat it back to the sending station, preceding the repetition with prowords *'I read back'*.

Say again: Repeat your message or portion referred to ie *'Say again all after', 'Say again address'*, etc.

Station calling: Used when a station is uncertain of the calling station's identification

This is: This transmission is from the station. whose callsign or name immediately follows.

Wait: If a called station is unable to accept traffic immediately, it will reply 'WAIT.......MINUTES'. If probable delay exceeds 10 minutes the reason will be given

Word after or Word before: Used after the proword *'say again'* to request repetition.

Wrong: Reply to repetition of message preceded by prowords *'read back'* when it has been incorrectly repeated.

Calls, calling and callsigns
CRSs normally identify themselves by using their geographical name followed by the word Radio, e.g. Niton Radio, Humber Radio, etc. Vessels normally identify themselves by the name on their licence but the International callsign assigned to the ship may be used in certain cases. If two yachts bear the same name or where some confusion may result, you should give your International callsign when starting communications, and thereafter use your ship's name as callsign.

'All ships' broadcast
Information to be received or used by all who intercept it, eg Gale warnings, navigational warnings, weather forecasts etc, is generally broadcast by CRSs and addressed 'All stations'. No reply is needed.

Establishing communication with CRS
The initial call is always made on a working channel.
- Switch to one of CRS's working channels, pause to ensure no station is transmitting
- Are you close enough to try low power *(1 watt)* first? Possible at ranges up to 10 miles. Otherwise use high power *(25 watts)* with more

battery drain. Then give the callsign of the station called *(up to three times only)* and prowords 'This is'
- The callsign of calling station up to three times only
- Indication of number of R/T calls you have to make
- Proword 'Over.'

If yacht *Vasco* wishes to ring a telephone number in the UK this is the procedure
- 'Niton radio, this is Vasco, Vasco. One link call please. Over.' If your call is loud enough to register at Niton, you will hear a regular 'pip' signal which will continue until operator has time to talk. Then he will say
- 'Station calling Niton radio, this is Niton radio. Repeat your call. Over. '

Vasco replies
- 'Niton radio, this is Vasco, Vasco. Callsign MIKE GOLF HOTEL VICTOR FOUR. One link call please. Over.'

Niton radio will reply when ready
- 'Vasco, this is Niton radio. What number do you want? Over.'

Vasco would reply with the number, preceded by arrangements for payment, either by quoting accounting code *'Golf Bravo One Four',* which together with the callsign allows a British or foreign CRS to send the bill to the owner of the boat's radio licence. Alternatively boat's operator could use phrase *'Yankee Tango Delta'* which stands for *'Yacht Telephone Debit.'* In this case the charge is made to the number called.

- 'Niton, this is Vasco, YANKEE TANGO DELTA ZERO ONE TWO FOUR THREE THREE SEVEN THREE SEVEN EIGHT FIVE THREE NINE. Over.'

Niton radio would reply
- 'Vasco, This is Niton radio. Roger, Stand by.'

Niton radio will then establish connection with the telephone network and call *Vasco* when ready. Beginners repeat callsigns and names unnecessarily. Once communication is established there is no need for repetition.

If you don't hear the pips
Even if before calling, you could hear Niton clearly you might still be out of transmission range, or your VHF might not be transmitting well.

The battery/ies may need charging or the aerial cable has a poor connection. Small faults can drastically reduce your transmitting range. Possibly the aerial for the channel chosen has been optimised for areas east of the CRS and you are to the west. If approaching the CRS wait 15 minutes and call again. If the range is opening, either try again in hope, or try another CRS within range.

Every time you call at high power, you are decreasing battery state and the range your VHF will achieve.

UK COASTGUARD RADIO STATIONS

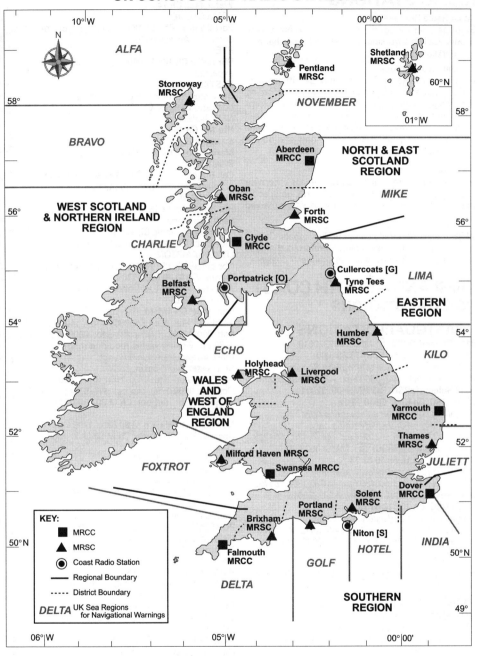

10°W   05°W   00°00'

ALFA

Shetland
MRSC
60°N
58°
01°W

Stornoway
MRSC
58°

NOVEMBER

BRAVO

Aberdeen
MRCC

NORTH & EAST
SCOTLAND
REGION

Oban
MRSC

MIKE

56°
WEST SCOTLAND
& NORTHERN IRELAND
REGION

Forth
MRSC

56°

CHARLIE

Clyde
MRCC

Cullercoats [G]

Belfast
MRSC

Portpatrick [O]

Tyne Tees
MRSC

LIMA

EASTERN
REGION

54°

ECHO

Humber
MRSC

54°

KILO

Holyhead
MRSC

Liverpool
MRSC

WALES
AND
WEST OF
ENGLAND
REGION

Yarmouth
MRCC

52°

Thames
MRSC

52°

Milford Haven MRSC

FOXTROT

Swansea MRCC

JULIETT

Dover
MRCC

Solent
MRSC

Portland
MRSC

INDIA

Brixham
MRSC

Niton [S]

50°N

Falmouth
MRCC

HOTEL

50°N

GOLF

DELTA

SOUTHERN
REGION

49°

KEY:

■ MRCC

▲ MRSC

◉ Coast Radio Station

— Regional Boundary

---- District Boundary

DELTA UK Sea Regions
for Navigational Warnings

06°W   05°W   00°00'

RADIO STATIONS

Coast Radio Stations 🄡
Stations operate continuously H24 except where shown. Call on a working channel: preferred channels are marked *

Coastal radio stations
Listed Coastal Radio Stations may be either Coast Radio Stations 🄡 or Coastguard stations 🄖 according to the country concerned. Stations operate H24 except where shown. Call on a working channel: preferred channels are marked *. Coastguard stations handle Distress, Urgency and Safety traffic only and do not handle public correspondence link calls.

Port radio stations
Hours of watch are continuous **H24** unless otherwise shown, **HJ** indicate day service only, **HX** no specific hours. Times given are local time except where marked **UT**.

ALRS means Admiralty List of Radio Signals. Calling channels precede a semi colon ;, preferred channels are marked *. *Call on a working channel if possible.*

ENGLAND – SOUTH COAST
COASTAL STATIONS

COASTGUARD STATIONS
0111 Dover (MRCC) 🄖 MMSI 002320010
Ch 70 DSC. Ch 16 10 11 67 73 80 69(a)
(a) Channel Navigation Information Service
Phone: +44 (0)1304 210008 Fax: +44 (0)1304 202137
0038 Solent (MRSC) 🄖 MMSI 002320011
Ch 70 DSC. Ch 67(a) 06 10 73 16
(a) Calling channel for safety traffic only.
Distress, urgent and safety traffic only.
Phone: +44 (0)1705 552100 Fax: +44 (0)1705 551763
0041·1 Portland (MRSC) 🄖 MMSI 002320010
Ch 70 DSC. Ch 16 69 10 67 73
Distress, urgent and safety traffic only.
Phone: +44 (0)1305 760439 Fax: +44 (0)1305 760452
0042 Brixham (MRSC) 🄖 MMSI 002320013
Ch 70 DSC. Ch 16* 10 67 73
Distress, urgent and safety traffic only.
Phone: +44 (0)1803 882704 Fax +44 (0)1803 882780
0045 Falmouth (MRCC) 🄖 MMSI 002320014
Ch 70 DSC. Ch 16 10 67 73
Distress, urgent and safety traffic only.
Phone: +44 (0)1326 317575 Fax +44 (0)1326 318342

PORT STATIONS
RAMSGATE:
VTS: Call Port Control **Ch 14**
Marina: Ch 14 80 Contact Hr Mr. Access HW±2
DOVER STRAIT:
Channel Navigation Information Service CNIS:
Call Dover Coastguard **Ch 69* 16 67 80**
Ch 11 Info bcsts every H+40 plus extra bcst when visibility less than 2M and
Ch 79 Gris Nez Traffic every H+10 plus additional bcst every H+25 when visibility less than 2M
DOVER:
VTS: Call Port Control **Ch 74 12 16**
Marina: Call Port Control **Ch 80** Access: HW±1½

Diesel Fuel: Call Dover Boat Co **Ch 74**
Water Taxi: Ch 74
FOLKESTONE:
Port Control: Ch 15* 16 Contact Port Control before entering. Access HW±2½
RYE:
Hbr radio: Ch 16 ; 14 0900-1700 LT or when vessel expected
EASTBOURNE:
Sovereign Yacht Harbour: Ch 15* 16
Lock and Bridges: Ch 17
NEWHAVEN:
Hbr Mr: Ch 16 ; 12
Swing bridge: Ch 12
Marina: Ch M 80 0800-1700. Access HW±4
BRIGHTON:
Call Brighton Control **Ch 16 M 80 ; 11 M 68 80** Access 0800-1800 through the lock
SHOREHAM:
Hbr office: Ch 14 16
Lady Bee Marina:
Call Harbour Radio **Ch 14* 16**
Mon-Sat: 0800-1830, Sun: 0900-1300
LITTLEHAMPTON:
Hbr office: Ch 16 ; 71 When vessel expected
Marina: Ch M 80 0800-1700
Arun Yacht Club: Call Lisboa **Ch M** Access HW±3
CHICHESTER:
Hbr office: Ch 14* 16
1 Oct - 31 Mar: Mon-Fri: 0900-1300, 1400-1730 LT. Sat: 0900-1300 LT. 1 Apr-31 Sep: 0900-1300, 1400-1730 LT. Visiting yachts requiring moorings should make arrangements in advance.
Chichester Yacht Basin: Ch M
Apr-Sep: Mon-Thu: 0700-2100, Fri-Sun: 0700-0000, Oct-Mar: 0800-1700. Access HW±5 through lock
Tarquin Yacht Harbour: Ch M 80 0800-1700. Access HW±2½
Northney Marina: Ch M 80 0800-1700
Sparkes Yacht Harbour: Ch M 80 0900-1800
LANGSTONE:
Hbr office: Ch 12 16 ; 12
Apr-Sep: 0730-1700, Oct-Mar Mon-Fri: 0730-1700 Sat Sun: 0730-1300
Southsea Marina: Ch M* 80 Access HW±3
PORTSMOUTH:
VTS: Call QHM **Ch 11**
PORTSMOUTH COMMERCIAL HARBOUR:
Listening watch: Ch 11 14
Commercial Port: Call Hbr Radio **Ch 11 14**
Gosport Marina: Call Camper Base **Ch M 80**
Haslar Marina: Ch 11 M 80
Port Solent Marina: Ch M 80 At the entrance the lock should only be approached if 3 green lights show.
Fareham Marina: Ch M 80 0900-1730
Wicor Marina: Ch 80 Mon-Sat: 0900-1730
SOUTHAMPTON:
VTS: Port operations Ch 12* 14
Distress, Safety and Calling: Ch 16
Traffic Information: Ch 14
Every hour 0600-2200 LT Fri-Sun and Bank Holiday Mon, Easter – 30 Sep
Keep Listening Watch: Ch 12
SOUTHAMPTON WATER:
Hythe Marina: Ch M 80
Ocean Village Marina: Ch M 80, fuel: Call Wyefuel or **Mr Diesel: Ch 08**
Town Quay Marina: Ch 80 Apr-Oct

Shamrock Quay: Ch M 80 0830-2130
Itchen Marina: Ch 12 When vessel expected
HAMBLE:
Hbr office: Ch 68
Mon-Fri: 0830-1700, Sat Sun: 0830-1930
Water Taxi: Call Blue Star Boats **Ch 77**
Hamble Point Marina: Ch M 80
Port Hamble Marina: Ch M 80 33
Mercury Yacht Harbour: Ch M 80
Swanwick Marina: Ch M 80
Hamble Yacht Services: Call HYS **Ch 80** 0900-1700
Universal Shipyards, Sarisbury Green: Ch M 80
0900-1700
Foulkes & Son Riverside Boatyard: Ch 08 Launch
BEAULIEU RIVER:
Ch M 80 Report to the HM within 24h
BEMBRIDGE:
Call Harbour Office BHL **Ch 16 ; 80**
Marina: Ch M 80 Access $-3HW+2\frac{1}{2}$
RYDE:
Hbr office: Ch 80
Summer 0900-2000 Winter HX. Access HW±2
COWES:
Hbr Office Ch 69
Mon-Fri: 0830-1700 LT and by arrangement
Chain Ferry: Ch 69
Water Taxi: Ch 08
Water Taxi: Call 'Thumper' **Ch 77**
West Cowes Yacht Haven: Ch 80
East Cowes Marina: Ch 80 0800-1600
Island Hbr Marina: Ch 80 0830-1730. Access HW±4
NEWPORT:
Hr Mr: 69 16
Marina: M 80
LYMINGTON:
Yacht Haven: Ch M 80
Summer: 0800-2100, Winter 0800-1800
Marina: Ch M 80
Summer 0800-2200, Winter 0800-2000
RIBS Marina, Little Avon Marina: Ch M 80
0800-1700. Access HW±2
YARMOUTH:
Hbr office: Ch 68
POOLE:
VTS: Call Harbour Control **Ch 14**
Bridge: Ch 14
Salterns Marina: Ch M 80 0800-2400
Yacht Club Haven: Ch M 80 May-Sep: 0800-2200
Cobbs Quay Marina: Ch M 80
0730-1930. Access HW±4
Poole Bay Fuels: Ch M
Mon-Fri: 0900-1730, weekends in season 0830-1800
Dorset Yacht Co Ltd: Ch M 0900-1730
Sandbanks Yacht Co: Call SYC **Ch M**
0900-1700. Access not LW
WEYMOUTH:
VTS: Ch 74
Mon-Thurs: 0800-1700 Fri: 0800-1630
Marina: Ch 80
Fuel: Ch 06
Town Bridge: Ch 12
PORTLAND:
Call Harbour Radio Ch 74 09 (H24)
Port Ops: Ch 74 14 20 28 71
BRIDPORT:
Ch 11 16 Summer: 0730-1700
LYME REGIS:
Ch 14 16

Summer: 0800-2000, Winter: 1000-1500. Access HW±2$\frac{1}{2}$
EXETER:
Ch 16 ; 06 12
Mon-Fri: 0730-1630 LT and when vessel expected
Retreat Boatyard: Ch M HW±3$\frac{1}{2}$
TEIGNMOUTH:
Ch 12 16 ; 12
Mon-Fri 0800-1700, Sat 0900-1200 and when vessel
expected
TORBAY HARBOURS:
Call Brixham Port or Torquay Port **Ch 12 16**
Ch 16 ; 14 May-Sep: 0800-1700,
Oct-Apr: Mon-Fri: 0900-1800
Torquay Marina: Ch M 80
Brixham Marina: Ch M 80
DARTMOUTH:
Ch 11 16 Mon-Fri: 0900-1700 LT, Sat: 0900-1200 LT
Britannia Royal Naval College: Ch 71
Dart Marina, Sandquay: Ch M 80 0730-2000
Dartside Quay: Ch M 80 Access HW±3
Noss Marina: Ch M 0730-1800
Darthaven Marina, Kingswear: Ch M 80 0830-1730
SALCOMBE:
Port: Ch 14
Mon-Thu: 0900-1645 Fri: 0900-1615,
May-Sep Sat Sun: 0900-1300 1400-1615
Harbour Master Launches: Ch 14
Summer: 0600-2200
Water Taxi: Call Salcombe Harbour Taxi **Ch 12**
Fuel Barge: Ch 06
Winters Marine: Call Lincolme Yard **Ch 72**
Access HW±5
HMS CAMBRIDGE:
Call Wembury Range **Ch 11* 10 16**
When range operating
PLYMOUTH:
Naval: Call Longroom Control **Ch 16 ; 08 11 12 13**
Commercial: Call Longroom Control **Ch 16 ; 14**
Millbay Docks: Ch 16 ; 12 14 Ferry hours only
Sutton Harbour Marina: Ch M 80
Lock: Ch 16 ; 12
Cattewater Harbour: Ch 16 ; 14 Mon-Fri: 0900-1700
Mayflower marina: Ch M 80
Millbay Marina Village: Ch M 80 0800-1700
Queen Anne's Battery Marina: Ch M 80
Clovelly Bay Marina: Ch M 80
Southdown Marina: Ch M 80
0900-1700. Access HW±6
LOOE: Ch 16 HX
FOWEY:
Ch 12*; 11 16 0900-1700
Harbour Launch: Call Port Radio **Ch 09** Apr-Oct
Refueller: Ch 16 10
Summer: 0900-1800, Winter: Mon-Fri: 0900-1800
PAR:
Hbr office: Ch 16 ; 12 Access HW±2
CHARLESTOWN:
Hbr office: Ch 16 ; 14
Access $-2HW+1$ only when vessel expected
MEVAGISSEY:
Hbr office: Ch 16 ; 14
Summer: 0900-2100, Winter: 0900-1700
FALMOUTH:
Falmouth Docks: Ch 16
Harbour Working: Ch 12
Port Operations Working: Ch 11
Alternative Working: Ch 14
Pollution: Ch 10

Harbour Launch 'Killigrew': Ch 12
Mon-Fri: 0800-1700
Port Pendennis Marina: Ch M 80
No visitors. Lock gate opens HW±3. Traffic Lights
Mylor Yacht Harbour: Ch M 80 0830-1730
Malpas Marine: Ch M
Mon-Sat 0900-1700. Access HW±3
PENZANCE:
Hbr office: Ch 16 ; 09 12
Mon-Fri: 0800-1630 Sat: 0830-1230. Access −2HW+1
NEWLYN:
Hbr office: Ch 16 ; 09 12
Mon-Fri: 0800-1700, Sat: 0800-1200
OFF LAND'S END TSS:
Call Falmouth Coastguard Ch 16 ; 67
St Mary's, Isles of Scilly: Ch 16 ; 14
Summer 0800-1700, Winter Mon-Fri 0800-1700 Sat
0800-1200

ENGLAND – EAST COAST
COASTAL STATIONS

COASTGUARD STATIONS
0089 Tyne Tees (MRSC) (CG) MMSI 002320006
Ch 70 DSC. Ch 16 10 67 73
Distress, urgent and safety traffic only.
Phone: +44 (0)191 257 2691 Fax: +44 (0)191 258 0373
0093-1 Humber (MRSC) (CG) MMSI 002320007
Ch 70 DSC. Ch 16 10 67 73
Distress, urgent and safety traffic only.
Phone: +44 (0)1262 672317 Fax: +44 (0)1262 606915
0099 Yarmouth (MRSC) (CG) MMSI 002320008
Ch 70 DSC. Ch 16 10 67 73
Distress, urgent and safety traffic only.
Phone: +44 (0)1493 851338 Fax: +44 (0)1493 852307
0107 Thames (MRSC) (CG) MMSI 002320009
Ch 70 DSC. Ch 16 10 67 73
Distress, urgent and safety traffic only.
Phone: +44 (0)1255 675518 Fax: +44 (0)1255 675249

PORT STATIONS
BERWICK-UPON-TWEED:
Hbr office: Ch 16 ; 12 Mon-Fri: 0800-1700
WARKWORTH HARBOUR:
Hbr office: Ch 16 ; 14
BLYTH:
Hbr office: Ch 12 16 11 12
PORT OF TYNE:
VTS: Ch 12 16 ; 11 14
Harbour Launch: Ch 16 ; 06 08 11 12 14
St Peter's Marina: Ch M 80* 0800-0000. Access −5HW+4
SUNDERLAND:
Port: Ch 16 ; 14
Marina: Ch M
SEAHAM:
Hbr office: Ch 12*; 16 06
Hr Mr Office −2½HW+1½,
Operations Office Mon-Fri: Office hours
TEES:
Port operations: Ch 16 ; 12 14 22 08
Barrage: Ch M
HARTLEPOOL:
Call Tees Ports Control Ch 14* 22* 08 11 12
Marina: Ch M 80 Access HW±4½
Yacht Club: Ch M HX

WHITBY:
Hbr office: Ch 11* 16 ; 12
Bridge: Ch 11* 16 ; 06
Access HW±2
SCARBOROUGH:
Call Scarborough Lighthouse Ch 16 ; 12 16
Access HW±3
BRIDLINGTON:
Hbr office: Ch 16 ; 12* 67 HX. Access HW±3
HUMBER:
VTS Area 1: Ch 14 (Seawards to Clee Ness Lt F)
VTS Area 2: Ch 12
Port: Ch 12 14 16
Navigation and Safety Information: Ch 12
Weather, tides and nav: Ch 12 Every odd H+03
Listening watch - R Humber & approaches: Ch 12
Listening watch - R Ouse: Ch 14
Listening watch - R Trent (Ouse to Keadby Br): Ch 08
Listening watch - R Trent (Keadby Br to
Gainsborough): Ch 06
Marina: Ch M* 80 0900-1700. Access HW±3
South Ferriby: Ch 74 80
Mon-Fri: 0930-1700, Sat Sun & Holidays: 1030-1700.
Access HW±3
Grimsby: Ch 74 ; 18 74 79
Docks Marina: Call Fish Dock Island Ch 74 Access
HW±2
Marina: Ch 09 18 Access −3HW+2½
Immingham Docks: Ch 19 68 ; 17 19 68 69 71 73 74
69 71 73 74
SOUTH KILLINGHOLME: Ch 19 69 71
NORTH KILLINGHOLME: Ch 19 74
King George Dock: Ch 11 ; 09 11 22
Alexandra Dock: Ch 11 ; 09 11 22
Mobile Marina: Ch 79
Port Operations: Ch 22 ; 11 22
Mon-Fri −2HW Hull+1.
Sat 0900-1100 (irrespective of tide)
Albert Dock: Ch 09 ; 09 11 22
New Holland: Ch 11 22
Blackt Docks: Ch 14 ; 09 14 19
Railway Bridge: Ch 09
Howdendyke: Ch 09
Boothferry bridge: Ch 09
Selby lock: Ch 16 74
Selby railway bridge: Ch 09
Toll Bridge: Ch 09
Outward vessels contact 10 min in advance.
NABURN:
Lock: Ch 16 74 HJ
Burton-upon-Stather: Ch 17
Flixborough: Ch 17
Grove: Ch 17
Keadby: Ch 17
Keadby Lock: Ch 16 74
Gunness: Ch 17
West Stockwith, Torksey and Cromwell locks:
Ch 16 74
Gainsborough: Ch 17
BOSTON:
VTS: Ch 12*
Dock: Ch 11 12 16
Marina: Ch 06 M ; M 0900-1700. Access HW±2
Grand Sluice: Ch 16 74 Only when lock is operating
Denver Sluice: Ch 73 When vessel expected
WISBECH:
Port: Ch 16 ; 14* 09
Sutton Bridge: Ch 16; 09

KING'S LYNN:
Call KLCB **Ch 14*; 16 11 12**
Mon-Fri: 0800-1730 and –4HW+1
Docks: Call Docks Radio ABP **Ch 14* 16; 11**
Access –2½HW+1
WISBECH:
Ch 14* 09 16 –3HW when vessel expected
WELLS-NEXT-THE-SEA:
Hbr office: Ch 12 16
HJ and 3h before HW when vessel expected
GREAT YARMOUTH:
VTS: Ch 12 16
Port: Ch 12 16 ; 09 12
Haven Bridge: Ch 12
Norwich Bridges: Ch 12
LOWESTOFT:
Hbr office: Ch 14* 16
Yachts may use bridge openings for commercial
ships by arrangement with Hbr Control on Ch 14
Royal Norfolk & Suffolk YC: Ch 14 M Access HW±4
Mutford Lock and Road Bridge: Ch 09 14
SOUTHWOLD:
Hr Mr: Ch 12* 16 ; 12 0800-1800 LT
RIVER DEBEN:
Hbr office: Ch 08
Felixstowe Ferry Boatyard: Ch 08 16 ; 08
Access HW±4
Tide Mill Harbour: Ch M 80 Access –2HW+3
HARWICH HARBOUR:
VTS: Ch 71* 14
Calling and Safety: Ch 16
Hbr services: Ch 11
Parkstone Quay: Ch 16 ; 18
RIVER ORWELL:
Shotley Marina: Ch M* 16 71 80 ; M 80
Suffolk Yacht Harbour: Ch M* 80 0730-2130
Woolverstone Marina: Ch M 80
Mon-Fri: 0800-1900, Sat-Sun: 0800-2100
Ipswich: Ch 14* 16 ; 14* 12
Fox's Marina: Ch M 80 0800-1700
Neptune Marina: Call Ipswich Port Radio
Ch 14 M 80 0730- 2230. Access –2HW+½
WALTON BACKWATERS:
Ch M 80
Summer only 0800-1700. Access HW±5
COLCHESTER:
Hbr office: Ch 68* 16 ; 68* 11 14
Mon-Fri: 0900-1700 LT and –3HW+1
Listening Watch: Ch 68
BRIGHTLINGSEA:
Port: Ch 68 0800-2000. Access not LWS
RIVER BLACKWATER:
River Bailiff: Ch 16 0900-1700 Access HW±2
Bradwell Marina: Ch M 80 Mon-Fri: 0830-1700
Sat/Sun: 0830-2000. Access NOT LW±1½
West Mersea Marine: Ch M
Tollesbury Saltings Ltd: Ch M 80
Mon-Sa:t 0800-1800. Access HW±3
Tollesbury Marina: Ch M 80
Mon-Fri: 0900-1700 Sat: 0930-1230 1430-1600
Sun: 1000-1230 1430-1600. Access HW±2
Blackwater Marina: Ch M
0900-1700. Access HW±2½
RIVER CROUCH:
Burnham Yacht Hbr: Ch M 80 0700-1800
North Fambridge Yacht Centre: Ch M 80 0900-1730
West Wick Marina: Ch M 80 Access NOT LW±2
Rice & Cole, Burnham on Crouch: Ch M

Essex Marina: Ch M 80
Season H24, out of season 0900-1800
Halcon Marine Ltd: Ch M
0800-1700. Access HW±2
Holehaven Marine: Ch 12 ; 12 M
Mon-Fri: 0800-1600
Havengore Bridge: Ch 16 ; 72 Office hours
PORT OF LONDON:
Port Control: Ch 12
(seaward approaches to Sea Reach No 4 Lt buoy)
Port Control: Ch 13
Sea Reach No 4 Lt buoy to Crayford Ness
Port Control: 68 18 20
Below Crayford Ness **Woolwich Radio: Ch 14* 16 22**
Above Crayford Ness **Port Control London: Ch 12***
16 18 20
Patrol Launches: Call Thames Patrol **Ch 06 12 13 14 16**
RIVER THAMES:
Tilbury Docks Lock: Ch 04
Thames Barrier: Ch 14* 16 22
All vessels equipped with VHF intending to navigate
in the Thames Barrier Control Zone must report to
Woolwich Radio on Ch 14
King George V Dock Lock: Call KG Control **Ch 68**
West India Dock Lock: Ch 13
Gallions Point Marina: Ch 68 Access HW±5
Bow Lock: Ch 16 74 0500-2200
Greenwich Yacht Club: Ch M
South Dock Marina: Ch M 80 Access HW±2
Limehouse Marina: Ch 80
Summer: 0800-1800, Winter: 0800-1630. Access HW±1
Thames Lock (Brentford): Ch 74
Summer 0800-1800 Winter 0800-1630
S Katharine Haven: Ch M 80
Summer –2HW+1½ between 0600 and 2030,
Winter –2HW+1½ between 0800 and 1800
Chelsea Harbour Ltd: Ch 80
0900-1700. Access HW±1½
Cadogan Pier: Ch 14 0900-1700
Brentford Dock Marina: Ch M
1000-1800. Access HW±2½
Chiswick Quay Marina: Ch 14 Access HW±2
MEDWAY: Ch 74* 16 ; 09 11 22 73
BP Kent, Isle of Grain: Ch 16; 73
While vessels are berthing
Kingsferry Bridge: Ch 10
Gillingham Marina: Ch M 80 0830-1700
Access West Basin HW±2, East Basin HW±4½
Medway Pier Marina: Ch M 80
0700-2230. Access HW±2
Medway Bridge Marina: Ch M 80
0900-1800. Access NOT LWS±2
Port Medway Marina: Ch M 80 0800-1800
Hoo Marina: Ch M 80 Access HW±3½
Elmhaven Marina: Ch M Access HW±4
Conyer Marina: Ch 16 M 80 Access HW±1
Whitstable: Ch 09* 12 16
Mon-Fri: 0800-1700 and –3HW+1

SCOTLAND
COASTAL STATIONS

COASTGUARD STATIONS
0072 Clyde ⑥ (MRSC) MMSI 002320022
Ch 70 DSC. Ch 16 10 67 73
Distress, urgent and safety traffic only.
Phone: +44 (0)1475 729988 Fax +44 (0)1475 786955

0075 Oban (MRSC) (CG) MMSI 002320023
Ch 70 DSC. Ch 16 10 67 73
Distress, urgent and safety traffic only.
Phone: +44 (0)1631 583720 Fax +44 (0)1631 564917
0079 Stornoway (MRSC) (CG) MMSI 002320024
Ch 70 DSC. Ch 16 10 67 73
Distress, urgent and safety traffic only.
Phone: +44 (0)1851 702013 Fax: +44 (0)1851 704387
0081 Pentland (MRSC) (CG) MMSI 002320002
Ch 16 10 67 73
Distress, urgent and safety traffic only.
Phone: +44 (0)1856 873268 Fax +44 (0)1856 874202
0083 Shetland (MRSC) (CG) MMSI 002320001
Ch 70 DSC. Ch 16 10 67 73
Distress, urgent and safety traffic only.
Phone: +44 (0) 1595 692976 Fax: +44 (0)1595 694810
0086-1 Aberdeen (MRSC) (CG) MMSI 002320004
Ch 70 DSC. Ch 16 06 10 67 73
Distress, urgent and safety traffic only.
Phone: +44 (0)1224 592334 Fax: +44 (0)1224 575920
0086-2 Forth (MRSC) (CG) MMSI 002320005
Ch 70 DSC. Ch 16 10 67 73
Distress, urgent and safety traffic only.
Phone: +44 (0)1333 450666 Fax: +44 (0)1333 450725

PORT STATIONS

KIRKCUDBRIGHT: Ch 16 ; 12 HW±2½
STRANREAR: Ch 16 ; 14
GIRVAN: Ch 16 ; 12
Mon-Fri: 0900-1700 LT
AYR: Ch 16 ; 14
TROON: Ch 16 ; 14
Mon-Thu: 0800-2400 LT, Fri: 0800-230 LT, other times on request
Marina: Ch 80* M
IRVINE: Ch 16 ; 12
Mon-Fri: 0800-1600
CLYDEPORT:
VTS: 12
Port Control: Ch 16 ; 12
QHM Faslane: Ch 13
Greenock Control: Ch 73
Conservancy vessels: Ch 16 ; 11
ARDROSSAN:
Hbr office: Ch 16 ; 12 14
Marina: Ch 16 80
Tarbert, Loch Fyne: Ch 16 14
ROTHESAY, Bute: Ch 16 ; 12
May-Sep: 0600-2100 LT, Oct-Apr: 0600-1900 LT
DUNOON:
Pier: Ch 31 ; 31* 12 16
Mon-Sat 0700-2035 LT, Sun: 0900-2015 LT
LOCH LONG: Ch 16 ; 10 12 19
FIRTH OF CLYDE:
Largs Yacht Haven: Ch M 80
Rhu Marina: Ch M 80 0800-0000
Silvers Marine: Ch M 0800-1630
Kip Marina: Ch M 80 16
Ardfern Yacht Centre: Ch M 80 0830-1730
Craobh Marina - Loch Shona: Ch M 80
Oct-Apr: 0830-1700, May Jun Sep: 0830-1800, Jul Aug: 0830-1900
CRINAN: Ch 16 74
May-Sep: 0800-1200 1230-1600 1620-1800, Oct: Mon-Sat: 0800-1200 1230-1600, Nov-Apr: Mon-Fri: 0900-

1530. Access summer 0800-1800 Spring/Autumn: Mon-Sat: 0800-1630 Winter: Mon-Fri: 0900-1530
Crinan Boats: Ch 16 ; 12 M
Loch Melfort: Ch 16 ; 12
Kilmelford Yacht Haven: Ch M* 80
Mon-Sat: 0830-1700
CAMPBELTOWN: Ch 16 12 14
Mon-Thu: 0845-1645, Fri: 0845-1600
Glensanda Harbour: Ch 14 When vessel expected
OBAN: Ch 16 ; 12
0900-1700. No moorings or alongside berths
Information - HMCG Oban: Ch 67 Submarine exercise warning
Ardoran Marine: Ch 16 Access NOT LW±2
Oban Yachts & Marine Services: Ch 16 80 0800-1700
Tobermory: Ch 16 12 Office Hours, listens only
Dunstafffnage Yacht Haven: Ch M 0900-1700
Craignure Pier, Island of Mull: Ch 31 HX
Gott Bay Pier, Tiree: Ch 31
Arinagour Pier, Isle of Coll: Ch 31
Corpach: Ch 16 74
Summer: 0800-1800, Spring/Autumn: 0800-1700, Winter: 0945-1600
Salen Jetty: Ch 16 M
0900-1900. Access –3HW+2
Mallaig: Ch 16 09 Office hours. No visitors moorings
KYLE OF LOCHALSH:
VTS: Call Oban Coastguard **Ch 16 67**
Skye Bridge Crossing: Ch 12
Uig: Ch 16 HX
Portree Harbour, Isle of Skye: Ch 16 12 HX
Gairloch Harbour: Ch 16 HX
ULLAPOOL:
Ch 14 16 12 H24 fishing season, else office hours
Lochinver: Ch 09 16 HX
Kinlochbervie: Ch 14 16 HX
LITTLE MINCH & NORTH MINCH:
VTS: Call Stornoway Coastguard **Ch 67**
STORNOWAY:
Hbr office: Ch 16 12
Loch Maddy, N Uist: Ch 16 12
S Kilda: Call Kilda Radio **Ch 16** HJ
Scrabster, Thurso: Ch 16 12 H24
PENTLAND FIRTH:
Call Pentland Coastguard **Ch 16**
ORKNEY HARBOURS:
Call Orkney Harbour Radio **Ch 16 20 09 11**
Scapa Flow: Ch 16 ; 69
Kirkwall: Ch 16 12
Mon-Fri: 0800-1700 and when vessel expected
Stromness Harbour: Ch 16 ; 12 Mon-Fri: 0900-1700
Orkney: Ch 16
Westray: Ch 16 14 When vessel expected
FAIR ISLE:
VTS: Call Shetland Coastguard **Ch 16**
Lerwick, Shetland: Ch 12* 11 16
Scalloway, Shetland: Ch 16 12* 09
Mon-Fri: 0600-1800, Sat: 0600-1230
SULLOM VOE HARBOUR, Shetland:
Distress and Safety: Ch 16
Port Control: Ch 14* 12 20
Traffic information on request: Ch 14 16
Balta Sound Harbour: Ch 16 20
Office hours or as required
Wick: Ch 16 ; 14 When vessel expected
Helmsdale: Ch 12 16

CROMARTY FIRTH, INVERGORDON: Ch 11* 16 13
INVERNESS:
Port: Ch 16 06 12
Mon-Fri: 0900-1700 LT and when vessel expected
Clachnaharry Lock: call Clachnaharry Sea Lock Ch 16
74 HW±4h
Burghead: Ch 16 ; 12 14
Working Hours and when vessel expected
HOPEMAN:
Call Burghead Radio Ch 14 Hours by arrangement
LOSSIEMOUTH: Ch 12 16 ; 12
0700-1700 LT and 1h before vessel expected
BUCKIE: Ch 12 16 ; 12 H24 on Ch 16
WHITEHILLS: Ch 16 ; 09 08
MACDUFF: Ch 16 ; 12
BANFF: Ch 14 By arrangement
FRASERBROUGH: Call Pilots MCUW4 **Ch 16 ; 12**
PETERHEAD:
VTS: Ch 14 (VTS is a voluntary system)
ABERDEEN:
Call Aberdeen Port Control Ch 16 12* 06 13
MONTROSE:
Call Port Control Ch 16 ; 12
DUNDEE:
Call Dundee Harbour Radio Ch 16 12
Royal Tay Yacht Club: Ch M
Anstruther: Ch 11 16
PERTH:
Call Perth Harbour Ch 16 09
FORTH PORTS:
Call Forth Navigation Ch 71* ; 12 20
Methil Docks: Ch 16 ; 14 Access –3HW+1
Leith: Ch 16 ; 12
Hound Point: Ch 09
N Queensferry: Ch 16 71 ; 74
Rosyth: Call QHM Ch 16 74 ; 13 73
Mon-Fri 0730-1700
Grangemouth Docks: Ch 16 ; 14
Amble Marina: Ch M* 80 Access HW±4
R. Forth Yacht Club: Call Boswall Ch M 80 Access HW±4
FIRTH OF FORTH:
Port Edgar Marina: Ch 80* M
Apr-Sep: 0900-1930, Oct-Mar: 0900-1630
Eyemouth: Ch 16 ; 12 office hours

ENGLAND – WEST COAST
COASTAL STATIONS

COASTGUARD STATIONS
0056 Swansea ⑯ **(MRCC)** MMSI 002320016
Ch 70 DSC. Ch 16 10 67 73
Distress, urgent and safety traffic only.
Phone: +44 (0)1792 366534 Fax: +44 (0)1792 369005
0057 Milford Haven ⑯ **(MRSC)** MMSI 002320017
Ch 70 DSC. Ch 16 10 67 73
Distress, urgent and safety traffic only.
Phone: +44 (0)1646 690909 Fax: +44 (0)1646 692176
0059·1 Holyhead ⑯ **(MRSC)** MMSI 002320018
Ch 70 DSC. Ch 16 10 67 73
Distress, urgent and safety traffic only.
Phone: +44 (0)1407 762051 Fax +44 (0)1407 764373
0061 Liverpool ⑯ **(MRSC)** MMSI 002320019
Ch 70 DSC. Ch 16 10 67 73
Distress, urgent and safety traffic only.
Phone: +44 (0)151 931 3341 Fax: +44 (0)151 931 3347

PORT STATIONS
ST IVES: Ch 14 HX
Hayle Harbour: Ch 18* ; 16 14 0900-1700
NEWQUAY: Ch 14 16
PADSTOW:
Hbr office: Ch 16 ; 12
Mon-Fri: 0800-1700 and HW±3
BUDE:
Hbr office: Ch 16 ; 12 When vessel expected
APPLEDORE-BIDEFORD:
Call PV 'Two Rivers' Ch 16 ; 12 Access –2HW
ILFRACOMBE:
Hbr office: Ch 16; 12
Apr-Oct: 0815-1700, when manned, Nov-Mar: HX.
Access HW±2
Watermouth Harbour: Ch 08 16 ; 08 12 Access HW±3
MINEHEAD:
Hbr office: Ch 16 ; 12 14 HX
WATCHET:
Hbr office: Ch 16 ; 09 12 14 Access from –2HW
BRIDGEWATER:
Hbr office: Ch 16 ; 08
Access –3HW when vessel expected
WESTON-SUPER-MARE:
Hbr office: Ch 16
Mon-Sat: 0930-1730. HW±2
PORT OF BRISTOL:
Avonmouth Signal Station:
Call Avonmouth Radio Ch 16
VTS: Ch 12
Port operations: Ch 14
Alternative working: Ch 09 11
BRISTOL:
Hbr office: Ch 16 ; 14* 12 Access –4HW+3½
Portishead Dock: Ch 16 ; 14* 12 Access –2½HW+1
Royal Edward Dock: Ch 16 ; 14* 12
City Docks: Ch 14 ; 14* 11 Access –3HW+1
Prince Street Bridge: Ch 73
Floating Harbour: Ch 16 73; 73
Mon-Thu: 0800- 1700, Fri: 0800-1630, other times
0800-sunset. Access –3HW+1
Netham Lock: Ch 73
Marina: Ch M 80 Office Hours. Access –3HW
SHARPNESS:
Call Sharpness Radio Ch 17
Distress & safety: Ch 16
Canal operations: Ch 74 Access –6HW+2
NEWPORT:
VTS: Call Newport Radio Ch 16 ; 71* 09 69 Access
HW±4
Port: Ch 16 ; 09 11 Access HW±4
CARDIFF:
Ch 14* 16 ; 11 Access –4HW+3
Barrage control: Ch 72
Penarth Marina: Ch 80 Access HW±4
Barry Docks: Ch 11* 16 ; 10 Access –4HW+3
Porthcawl: Ch 80 0900-2100. Access HW±3
Port Talbot: Ch 12 16 ; 12
Neath: Ch 16 ; 77
SWANSEA:
Docks: Ch 14 HJ
Tawe Lock: Ch 18
Swansea Marina: Ch 18 80
Barrage Summer: 0700-2200 Winter: Mon-Fri: 0700-
1900 Sat Sun: 0700-22. Access 0700-2200.
Access NOT LW±1 Springs
Barrage: Ch 80 See Yacht Haven

Saundersfoot: Ch 16 ; 11
Summer: 0800-2100, Winter: Mon-Fri: 0800-1800.
Access HW±2½
Monkstone Sailing Club: Ch M Access HW±2½
Tenby: Ch 16 80 Access HW±2½
MILFORD HAVEN:
Navigation Service: Ch 12* 09 10 11 14 15 16 67
Weather Forecasts: Ch 12 14
At 0300 0900 1500 2100 approx.
Patrol Launches: Call Milford Haven Patrol Ch 06 08
09 11 12 14 16 67 Ch 11 12 H24
Neyland Yacht Haven: Ch M 80
Lawrenny Yacht Station: Ch M 0800-2000
Milford Docks: Call Pierhead Ch 09 12 14 16
Locking approx HW±3
Milford Marina: Ch 12 M Access –2HW
Pembroke Dock: Ch 13
Port of Pembroke: Call 'Port of Pembroke'
Ch 12; 68 H24
FISHGUARD: Hbr office: Ch 16 ; 14
ABERAERON: Ch 14* 16 Served by New Quay
Harbourmaster. 0900-1700. Access HW±3
ABERYSTWYTH: Ch 16 ; 14 Access HW±3
ABERDOVEY:
Call Aberdovey Hbr Ch 12 16 ; 12
0900-1700 LT Access HW±3
BARMOUTH:
Ch 12* 16 ; 12 Apr-Sep: 0900-2200 LT,
Oct-Mar: 0900-1600 LT Access HW±2
Pwllheli: Call Hafen Pwllheli Ch M 80 Access HW±5
Cyngor Dosbarth Dwytor: call Pwllheli Harbour
Master Ch 16 ; 08 0900-1715. Access –2HW+1½
Abersoch Land & Sea: Ch M 0800-1700
PORTHMADOG:
Call Portmadog Hbr Ch 16 ; 12 14
0900-1700, and when vessel expected.
Access HW±1½
Caernarvon:
Call Caernarvon Hbr Ch 14 16; 14
Mon-Fri: 0900-1700 Sat: 0900-1200. Access HW±3
Marina: Ch 80 Summer: 0700-2300, winter: HJ.
Access HW±3
Port Dinorwic Yacht Harbour: Ch M
Office Hours. Access –2HW–3½
HOLYHEAD:
Ch 14 ; 16
Holyhead Sailing Club: Ch M
Beaumaris & Menai Bridge: Ch 16 ; 69
Mon-Fri: 0800-1700
Conwy: Ch 14 16 ; 12* 06 08 14 71 80
Apr-Sep: 0900-1700, Oct-Mar: Mon-Fri: 0900-1700.
Access –3HW+2.
Marina: Ch 80 Access –3HW–4h
Raynes Jetty: Ch 16 ; 14
–4HW only when vessel expected
Llanddulas: Ch 16 ; 14
Access –4HW only when vessel expected
Mostyn Dock & River Dee Pilots:
Ch 14* 16 ; 14 –2HW or by arrangement
LIVERPOOL PORT OPERATIONS AND
INFORMATION:
VTS: Call Mersey Radio Ch 12* 16
Information broadcasts: Ch 09 at 3h and 2h
before HW
Liverpool Marina: Ch M Access HW±2½
Fiddlers Ferry Yacht Haven: Ch M
0900-1700. Access HW±1

Canning Dock: Ch M
0900-1700. Access -2HW
Alfred Dock: Ch 22
Langton Dock: Ch 21
Gladstone Dock: Ch 05
MANCHESTER SHIP CANAL
VTS: Call Eastham VTS: Ch 14
Garston Dock: Ch 20
Eastham Locks: Ch 07 14
Stanlow Oil Docks: Ch 14 20
Weaver Navigation: Ch 73* 14 ; 71
H24 except 1800-1900 LT
Latchford Locks: Ch 14 (Ch 18 Emergency use only)
Irlam Locks: Ch 14 (Ch 18 Emergency use only)
Barton Locks: Ch 14 (Ch 18 Emergency use only)
Modewheel Locks: Ch 14 (Ch 18 Emergency use only)
Blundellsands Sailing Club: Ch M Access HW±2
PRESTON:
Marina: Call Riversway Control Ch 16 ; 14
0900-1700. Access HW Liverpool ±1½
Douglas Boatyard: Ch 16 Mon-Fri 0830-1800 Sat &
Sun 1400-1800. Access HW Liverpool ±2
FLEETWOOD:
0400-1100 1600-2300 and when vessel expected
Docks: Ch 12 Access HW±2
Harbour Village: Ch 11 12 16 ; 11 12
0900-1700. HW±2
Glasson Dock: Ch 16 ; 69 Access –2HW+1
Glasson Basin Yacht Ltd: Ch 80 Access –1HW
Heysham: Ch 16 ; 14 74
Barrow Docks: Ch 16 ; 12
Ramsden Dock: Ch 16 Access –2½HW
DOUGLAS, Isle of Man:
VTS: Ch 12
Calling and Port Ops: Ch 12
Castletown, Isle of Man: Ch 16 ; 12 0830-1700
Port St Mary, Isle of Man: Ch 16 ; 12 HJ and when
vessel expected. At other times contact Douglas
Peel, Isle of Man: Ch 16 ; 12
HJ and when vessel expected. At other times contact
Douglas
Ramsey, Isle of Man: Ch 16 ; 12 0830-1700 and when
vessel expected. At other times contact Douglas
WHITEHAVEN:
Call PV 'J T Pears' MZVA Ch 16 ; 12
Access HW±3h
WORKINGTON:
Hbr Radio: Ch 16 ; 11 14 Access –2½HW+2
Maryport Marina: Ch 16 M 80 Access HW±3½
Silloth Docks: Ch 16 ; 12 Access –2½HW+1

CHANNEL ISLANDS
COASTAL STATIONS

COAST RADIO STATIONS
0115 St Peter Port (CRS) Ch 16 20* 62*(a) 67
(a) Available for link calls
*Phone: +44 (0)1481 720672 or 710277 (Shore-Ship
Link Call) Fax +44 (0)1481 714177 (HM)*
Traffic lists: **Ch 20** 0133 0533 0933 1333 1733 2133
0120 Jersey (CRS) Ch 25*(b) 16 67(a) 82
*(a) Small craft distress and safety - call on Ch 16
(b) Link calls*
Phone: +44 (0)1534 41121 Fax: +44 (0)1534 499089
Traffic lists: **Ch 25 82** 0645 0745 1245 1845 2245

PORT STATIONS

BRAYE, Alderney:
Port: Ch 16 ; 12 74
Apr-Sep: 0800-1800 Oct: 0800-1700 Nov-Mar: Mon-Fri: 0800-1700. Outside these hours, call St Peter Port
GUERNSEY:
St Peter Port: Ch 12
St Sampson: Ch 12 Via St Peter Port Port Control
Beaucette Marina: Ch M 80
0830-2030. Access HW±3
JERSEY:
St Helier: Ch 14
Pierheads: Ch 18 Access HW±3
(Note: Do not use Ch M in St Helier)
Gorey: Ch 74 HW±3

IRELAND

COASTAL STATIONS

COAST RADIO STATIONS

0124 Dublin (CRS) **Ch 83* 16 67(a)**
(a) For safety messages only.
Traffic lists: Ch 83 0103 0503 0903 1103 1303 1503 1703 1903 2103 2303 UT
0125 Wicklow Head (CRS) **Ch 16 87 67(a)**
(a) For safety messages only Remotely controlled from Dublin.
Traffic lists: Ch 87 0103 0503 0903 1103 1303 1503 1703 1903 2103 2303 UT
0126 Rosslare (CRS) **Ch 23* 16 67(a)**
(a) For safety messages only Remotely controlled from Dublin. Traffic lists: Ch 23 0103 0503 0903 1103 1303 1503 1703 1903 2103 2303 UT
0127 Mine Head (CRS) **Ch 83 16 67(a)**
(a) For safety messages only Remotely controlled from Dublin. Traffic lists: Ch 83 0103 0503 0903 1103 1303 1503 1703 1903 2103 2303 UT
0128 Bantry (CRS) **Ch 23* 16 85 67(a)**
(a) Safety messages only. Remotely controlled from Valentia. Traffic lists: Ch 23 0333 0733 0933 1133 1333 1533 1733 1933 2133 2333 UT
0129 Cork (CRS) **Ch 26 16 67(a)**
(a) Safety messages only. Remotely controlled from Valentia.Traffic lists: Ch 26 0333 0733 0933 1133 1333 1533 1733 1933 2133 2333 UT
0130 Valentia (CRS) **Ch 16 24 28 67(a)**
(a) Safety information for small craft.
Phone: +353 (0) 667 6109 Fax: +353 (0) 667 6289.
Traffic lists: Ch 24 0333 0733 0933 1133 1333 1533 1733 1933 2133 2333 UT
0134 Shannon (CRS) **Ch 28* 16 24 67(a)**
(a) Safety messages only Remotely controlled from Valentia. Traffic lists: Ch 28 0333 0733 0933 1133 1333 1533 1733 1933 2133 2333 UT
0135 Clifden (CRS) **Ch 26* 16 67(a)**
(a) For safety messages only Remotely controlled from Malin Head.
0136 Belmullet (CRS) **Ch 83* 16 67(a)**
(a) Safety messages only Remotely controlled from Malin Head. Traffic lists: Ch 83 0103 0503 0903 1103 1303 1503 1703 1903 2103 2303 UT
0137 Glen Head (CRS) **Ch 16 24 67(a)**
(a) For safety messages only Remotely controlled from Malin Head.
Traffic lists: Ch 24 0103 0503 0903 1103 1303 1503 1703 UT

0140 Malin Head (CRS) **Ch 16 23 85 67(a)**
(a) For safety messages only Phone +353 (0)77 70103
Fax: +353 (0)77 70221 Traffic lists: Ch 23 0103 0503 0903 1103 1303 1503 1703 1903 2103 2303 1903 2103 2303 UT
Donegal Bay (CRS) New station planned 2000
Greenore (CRS) New station planned 2000
Crookhaven (CRS) New station planned 2000
Galway Bay (CRS) New station planned 2000
Dublin (CG) **(MRSC)** MMSI (To be Notified later)
Valentia (CG) **(MRSC)** MMSI 002500200 (To be Notified later)
Malin Head (CG) **(MRSC)** MMSI 002500100 (To be Notified later)

COASTGUARD STATIONS

0121 Belfast (MRSC) (CG) MMSI 002320021
Ch 70 DSC. Ch 16 10 67 73
Distress, urgent and safety traffic only.
Phone: +44 (0)1247 463933 Fax: +44 (0)1247 465886

PORT STATIONS

LONDONDERRY:
Hbr radio: Ch 14* 12
COLERAINE:
Ch 16 ; 12 Mon-Fri: 0900-1700
Marina: Ch M Office hours
Portrush: Ch 16 ; 12 Mon-Fri: 0900-1700, extended Jun-Sep, Sat Sun: 0900-1700, Jun-Sep only
LARNE:
Hr Mr: Ch 16 ; 14
Cloghan Point: Ch 16 ; 10
Carrickfergus: Hbr office: Ch 16 ; 12 14 Access±3
BELFAST:
VTS: Ch 12* 16
Marina: Ch M
BANGOR:
Marina: Ch 80 M 11 16
Portavogie: Ch 16 ; 12 14 Mon-Fri: 0900-1700
STRANGFORD HARBOUR:
Call Strangford Terminal: Ch 16 ; 12 14 M
Ardglass Harbour: Ch 16 ; 14 12
Carlingford Marina: Ch 16
Malahide Marina: Ch M 80
Killyleagh: Ch 16 ; 12 HX
Kilkeel: Ch 16 ; 12* 14 Mon-Fri: 0900-2000
Warrenport: Ch 16 ; 12
Greenore: Ch 16 HJ
Dundalk: Ch 14 Mon-Fri: 0900-1700
Drogheda: Ch 11 Mon-Fri: 0900-1700. HX
HOWTH:
Hr Mr: Ch 16 ; 08 Mon-Fri: 0700-2300 LT Sat/Sun: HX
Marina: Ch M 16
DUBLIN:
Port: Ch 12* 13
Distress and Safety: Ch 16
Lifting Bridge: Call Eastlink Ch 12 13
DUN LAOGHAIRE:
Hbr office: Ch 14 16 ; 14
Small craft: Ch M
WICKLOW:
Port: Ch 14*; 16 12
ARKLOW:
Port: Ch 16 HJ
ROSSLARE:
Hbr office: Ch 12* 14 16
Kilmore Quay Marina: Ch 09 16 M

IRISH COAST RADIO STATIONS

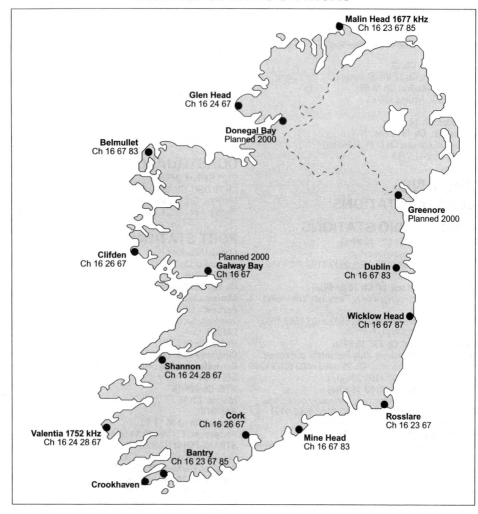

Malin Head 1677 kHz
Ch 16 23 67 85

Glen Head
Ch 16 24 67

Donegal Bay
Planned 2000

Belmullet
Ch 16 67 83

Greenore
Planned 2000

Clifden
Ch 16 26 67

Planned 2000
Galway Bay
Ch 16 67

Dublin
Ch 16 67 83

Wicklow Head
Ch 16 67 87

Shannon
Ch 16 24 28 67

Cork
Ch 16 26 67

Rosslare
Ch 16 23 67

Valentia 1752 kHz
Ch 16 24 28 67

Mine Head
Ch 16 67 83

Bantry
Ch 16 23 67 85

Crookhaven

Waterford: Ch 16 ; 12 14 HJ and when vessel expected
New Ross: Ch 16 ; 12 14
Youghal: Ch 16 ; 14 Access HW±3
CORK:
VTS: Ch 12 14 16 ; 12 14
East Ferry Marina: Ch M
Crosshaven Boatyard Marina: Ch M
Mon-Fri: 0830-1700
Salve Marina: Ch M
Royal Cork Yacht Club Marina: Ch M 0900-2300
Kinsale: Ch 14* 16 ; 06
Office hours and when vessel expected
Kinsale YC Marina: Ch M
Castle Park Marina: Ch M 06 16
BALTIMORE:
Ch 16; 09 06
Bantry: Ch 16 ; 06 11 14

Castletown Bearhaven: Ch 14 16 ; 14
Dingle: Ch M* 11
Fenit: Ch 16 ; 14 HX
Limerick: Ch 16 ; 12 13
Office hours & when vessel expected
Foynes Harbour: Ch 16 ; 12 13 Office Hours
Aughinish Marine Terminal: Ch 16 ; 12 13
Kilrush Creek Marina: Ch 80
Fenit: Ch M
Galway: Ch 16 ; 12
Access $-2\frac{1}{2}$HW+1
Rossaveel: Ch 16 ; 12 14 Office Hours
SLIGO:
Hr Mr: Ch 16 ; 12* 14
0900-1700 and when vessel expected
Killybegs: Ch 16 ; 14
Burton Port: Ch 16 ; 14* 06 12

BELGIUM
COASTAL STATIONS
COAST RADIO STATIONS
0155 Oostende (CRS) MMSI 002050480
Ch 70 DSC. Ch 28 27 63 78 85 87(a) 16
(a) Ch 27 for vessels in vicinity of Zeebrugge and
Oostende, Chs 28 and 78 for vessels in vicinity of
Zeebrugge and Oostende and Ch 28 and 78 for
vessels in vicinity of La Panne.
Phone: +32 59 706565 Fax: +32 59 701339
Traffic lists: Ch 27 every H+20
0160 Antwerpen (CRS) MMSI 002050485
Ch 70 DSC. Ch 24* 07 16 27 87
Traffic lists: Ch 24 every H+05
0160-01 Antwerpen-Kortrijk (CRS) Ch 24
0160-02 Antwerpen-Gent (CRS) Ch 24 16 81
0160-03 Antwerpen-Vilvoorde (CRS) Ch 24
0160-04 Antwerpen-Ronquiéres (CRS) Ch 24
0160-05 Antwerpen-Mol (CRS) Ch 24
0160-06 Antwerpen-Liége (CRS) Ch 24

BELGIUM & NETHERLANDS
PORT STATIONS
NIEUWPOORT:
Hbr office: Ch 09 16
KYCN Marina: Ch 08
WSKLuM Marina: Ch 72
VVW Marina: Ch 09 77
OOSTENDE:
Hbr office: Ch 10
Lock and Mercator Marina: Ch 14
Canal moorings: Ch 10
BLANKENBERGE:
VVW Marina: Ch 08
SYCB Marina: Ch 08
VNZ Marina: Ch 08
ZEEBRUGGE:
Port Entrance: Ch 71
Port Control: Ch 71
Emergencies: Ch 67
Locks: Ch 68
Visserhaven Marina: Ch 71
WESTERSCHELDE:
VTS: See VTS Chart No 3. Reporting, in English or
Dutch, is compulsory within the VTS Schelde and
Estuaries area for all Inward-Bound and Outward-
Bound vessels. Vessels must maintain a continuous
listening watch on the VHF channel for the appropriate
Traffic Area including vessels at anchor. Each Traffic
Area is marked by buoys and the appropriate Traffic
Centre must be called on the relevant channel when a
vessel enters the area
WANDELAAR TRAFFIC AREA:
VTS Tfc Centre: Ch 65
Outward bound vessels report when between buoys
A1 bis and Scheur 2.
Radar: Ch 04
Emergency: Ch 67
ZEEBRUGGE TRAFFIC AREA:
VTS Tfc Centre: Ch 69
Report when inward/outward bound and within
Zeebrugge Hr.
Radar: Ch 04

Harbour: Ch 19
Emergency: Ch 67
Radar Control Zeebrugge: Ch 19
STEENBANK TRAFFIC AREA:
VTS Tfc Centre: Ch 64
Emergency: Ch 67
VTS Tfc Centre: Ch 14
Radar: Ch 21
Emergency: Ch 67
TERNEUZEN TRAFFIC AREA:
VTS Tfc Centre: Ch 03
Emergency: Ch 67
GENT/TERNEUZEN TRAFFIC AREA:
VTS Tfc Centre: Ch 11
Emergency: Ch 67
HANSWEERT TRAFFIC AREA:
VTS Tfc Centre: Ch 65
Emergency Reporting In and Out: Ch 67
Centrale Hansweert, In: Ch 65
Centrale Zandvliet, Out: Ch 12
Centrale Vlissingen: Ch 14
ANTWERPEN TRAFFIC AREA:
VTS: Tfc Centre: Ch 12
Radar Waarde: Ch 19
Radar Saeftinge: Ch 21
Radar Zandvliet: Ch 04
Radar Kruischans: Ch 66
Emergency Reporting: In and Out: Ch 67
Information by Vlissingen: Ch 14
In Dutch and English every H+50
Information by Terneuzen: Ch 03 11
In Dutch and English every H+05 on Ch 03 and every
H+55 on Ch 11
Information by Zandvliet: Ch 12
In Dutch and English every H+00
Information by Antwerpen: Ch 16
Traffic lists and navigation warnings between H+05
and H+10
VLISSINGEN:
Call Flushing Port Control Ch 09
Locks: Ch 22
Bridge: Ch 22
Breskens Marina: Ch 31
Braakmanhaven: Call DOW Chemical Terneuzen
Ch 06 13 34 ; 06 08 11 13 34 Ch 06 13 - H24
TERNEUZEN:
Hr office: Ch 11 14
Locks: Ch 69
Westsluis and Middensuis: Ch 06
Oostsluis: Ch 18
Information: Ch 11 Every H+00
Gent: Ch 05 11
Hansweert Locks: Ch 22
ANTWERPEN:
Calling and safety: Ch 74
VTS Centre: Ch 18
Bridges: Ch 13
Dock Mr: Ch 63
Radar: Ch 02 60
Boudewijnsluis & Van Cauwelaertsluis: Ch 08 11
Royerssluis & Kattendijksluis: Ch 22
Kallosluis: Ch 03 08
Zandvlietsluis and Barendrechtsluis: Ch 06 79
Winthamsluis: Ch 68
Marina: Call MIC Marina Ch 09
Harbour gates HW±1

NETHERLANDS COASTGUARD RADIO STATIONS

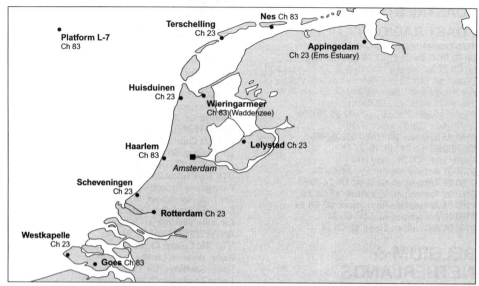

GERMAN COASTGUARD RADIO STATIONS

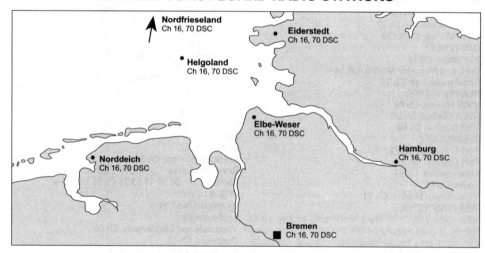

NETHERLANDS
COASTGUARD STATIONS
IJMUIDEN RADIO
Monitors Ch 16 and 2182 kHz for Distress, Urgency and Safety traffic only. Operates DSC on 2187·5 kHz and Ch 70. (MMSI 002442000).

Westkapelle (CG)	Ch 23
Haarlem (CG)	Ch 83
Terschelling (CG)	Ch 23
Goes (CG)	Ch 83
Huisduinen (CG)	Ch 23
Nes (CG)	Ch 83
Rotterdam (CG)	Ch 23
Wieringermeer (CG)	Ch 83
Appingeda(CG)	Ch 23
Scheveningen (CG)	Ch 23
Platform L-7 (CG)	Ch 83
Lelystad (CG)	Ch 23

PORT STATIONS
OOSTERSCHELDE:
Call Roompotsluis **Ch 18** Lock operating times: Mon and Thu: 0000-2200 LT, Tue and Sun: 0600-0000 LT, Wed: H24, Fri and Sat: 0600-2200 LT. Vessels should report to the locks as follows: S bound: after passing Tholen Hr: N bound: after passing Bath Br.
Roompot: Ch 31
Ouddorp Coastguard: Ch 74
Wemeldinge: Ch 68
Zeelandbrug: Ch 18
Krammer: Ch 22 68
Kreekraksluizen: Ch 20 Vessels should report to the locks as follows: S bound: after Tholen Hr; N bound: after Bath bridge
Harlingvliet-Sluizen: Ch 20 Operating times Mon/Thu: H24 Fri: 0000-2200 Sat/Sun & hols: 0800-2000
HOEK VAN HOLLAND ROADSTEAD:
VTS: Call Maasmond Entrance **Ch 03** See VTS chart No 4. Yachts should follow a track close W of a line joining buoys MV, MVN and Indusbank N. Before crossing, report vessel's name, position and course. Whilst crossing, maintain continuous listening watch
NIEUWE WATERWEG:
HCC Central Traffic Control **Ch 11 14** See VTS Charts Nos 4 and 5. Report to and keep a continuous listening watch on the appropriate Traffic Centres
OUDE MAAS: Ch 13 19
Bridges and Locks: Ch 18
Brienenoordbrug: Ch 20
Sluis W eurt: Ch 18
Prins Bernhardsluis: Ch 18
Sluis S. Andries: Ch 20
DORDRECHT:
Port: Ch 19 Keep a continuous listening watch
Sector Heerjansdam: Ch 04
Information: Call Post Dordrecht **Ch 71**
Brugen: Ch 19
Alblasserdamse brug: Ch 22
Papendrechtse brug: Ch 19
Merwedesluis en Verkeersbrug: Ch 18
Algera sluis en Stuw: Ch 22
Julianasluis: Ch 18
Grote Sluis Vianen and Andel Wilhelminasluis: Ch 22
Volkeraksluizen: Ch 18 69

SCHEVENINGEN:
Traffic Centre: Ch 14
Radar: Ch 21
IJMUIDEN:
Traffic Centre: Ch 88 West of IJmuiden Light buoy
Port Control: Ch 61 From IJmuiden Lt by to the North Sea Locks
Seaport Marina: Call SPM **Ch 74**
NORDZEEKANAAL:
VTS: Ch 61
See VTS Chart No 6. From IJmuiden Lt By to the IJmuiden Sluices
Noordzeesluizen: Call Sluis IJmuiden **Ch 22**
Noordzeekanaal: Ch 03 From Ijmuiden Sluices to km 11·2
Zijkanaal C Sluice: Call Sluis IJmuiden **Ch 68**
AMSTERDAM:
Port Control: Ch 04
Port Information: Ch 14
Beverwijk: Ch 71 HX
Wilhelminasluis: Ch 20 HX
Westerkeersluis: Ch 22
Haarlem: Ch 18
Oranjesluisen: Ch 18
Enkhuizen or Krabbersgat: Ch 22
Lock operates weekdays 0300-2300, Sun and holidays 0800-2000
DEN HELDER: Ch 12
VTS: See VTS chart No 7. All vessels equipped with VHF to report when entering/leaving the area, berthing/unberthing, anchoring/weighing or entering/leaving Koopvaardersschutsluis stating vessel's name, type, position, destination and special details
Port Control: Ch 14
Moormanbrug Bridge: Ch 18
Koopvaarders Lock: Ch 22
Den Oever: Ch 20
Kornwerderzand: Ch 18
Eierland Coastguard: Ch 05 0800-2330
Harlingen: Ch 11 Mon 0000-Sat 2200
Terschelling: Call Brandaris VTS **Ch 02**
See VTS No 8. All vessels must report when entering/leaving the area and thereafter keep a continuous listening watch
Waddenzee Central Reporting - Incidents: Ch 04
Waddenzee Central Reporting - SAR Rescue: Ch 16
AMELAND:
Coastguard: Ch 05 0800-2330 LT
SCHIERMONNIKOOG:
Lauwersoog: Ch 09
Mon: 0000-1700,Tue-Wed: 0800-1700, Thur-Sat: 0700-1500
Locks: Ch 22 May-Sep Mon-Fri: 0700-2000 Sat: 0700-1900 Sun: 0900-1200 1400-1830, Oct-Apr Mon-Fri: 0700-1800 Sat: 0700-1700
Lauwersmeer Firing Range: Ch 71
Keep listening watch for information on firing times
EEMSHAVEN:
Hbr office: Ch 14
Radar: Ch 19
DELFZIJL:
Hbr office: Ch 14 Special Regulations apply when visibility falls below 500m
Information: Ch 14 Every H+10
Locks: Ch 11 Mon-Sat: H24, Sun & holidays on request
Weiwerder Bridge: Ch 11
Heemskes and Handelshaven Bridges: Ch 14
Mon-Sat: 0600-1400
Farmsumerhaven: Ch 14

GERMANY
COASTAL STATIONS

COAST RADIO STATIONS
The Coast Radio Stations provided by SMD-Schiffsmeldedienst are:

Hamburg (CRS)	Ch 27 83 16	DSC Ch 70
Finkenwerder (CRS)	Ch 23 16	DSC Ch 70
Cuxhaven (CRS)	Ch 83 16	DSC Ch 70
Elbe Weser (CRS)	Ch 01 24 16	DSC Ch 70
Helgoland (CRS)	Ch 27 88 16	DSC Ch 70

COASTGUARD STATIONS
North Sea Coastguard MRCC radio stations are remotely controlled from Bremen MRCC (MMSI 00211240). All monitor Ch 16 H24. Initial call is made on Ch 16 using the name of the local station as callsign. All stations opwerate DSC on VHF Ch 70 (H24). No MRCC stations accept public correspondence calls.

Bremen MRCC (CG)	Ch 16	DSC Ch 70
Norddeich Radio (CG)	Ch 16	DSC Ch 70
Helgoland Radio (CG)	Ch 16	DSC Ch 70
Elbe-Weser Radio (CG)	Ch 16	DSC Ch 70
Hamburg Radio (CG)	Ch 16	DSC Ch 70
Eiderstadt Radio (CG)	Ch 16	DSC Ch 70
Nordfriesland Radio (CG)	Ch 16	DSC Ch 70

PORT STATIONS
IMPORTANT: *Before navigating German waterways, all vessels must report to waterway authorities.*

DIE EMS VTS: Call Ems Traffic **Ch 18*** 15 16 20 21 Ems Traffic broadcasts every H+50 on Ch 15 18 20 and 21 in German. All vessels must report to waterway authorities, and keep a continuous watch on the appropriate channel
Emden Locks: Ch 13 16
Oldersum Lock: Ch 13 May-Sep Mon-Fri 0700-2000 Sat & Sun 0800-2000, Oct-Apr Mon-Thur 0700-1530 Fri 0700-1400
Leer Road Bridge: Ch 15
Leer Lock: Ch 13 16
Weener Bridge: Ch 15
Weener Lock: Ch 13 16 1 Apr- 31 Oct only: Mon-Thu 0700-1600 Fri: 0700-sunset Sat & Sun: sunrise-sunset
Papenburg Lock: Ch 13 16
Leysiel Lock: Ch 17
BORKUM:
Port: Ch 14 17 All year Mon-Fri: 0700-2200, Sep-Apr Sat & Sun: 0700-1700, May-Aug Sat: 0800-1200 1500-2100 Sun: 0700-1100 1400-2000. All vessels report arrival/departure.
Norddeich: Ch 28* 16 61
Mon: 0730-1900, Tue-Fri: 0700-1300 1330-1900, Sat & Sun: 0800-1200 1230-1730
Traffic lists: Ch 28 every H+45
Traffic Lists: Ch 28 Every H+45
Nordeney: Ch 17 Mon: 0700-1200 1230-1730, Tues: 0900-1200 1230-1900, Wed-Sun: 0700-1200 1230-1900
Langeoog: Ch 17 0700-1700

Benersiel: Ch 17 Oct-Mar Mon-Fri: 0700-1230 1330-1700, Apr-Sep Mon-Fri: 0700-1900 Sat & Sun: 0700-1100 1300-1700
Harlesiel: Ch 17 0700-2100
Wangerooge: Ch 17 0700-1700
INNER DEUTSCHE BUCHT (GERMAN BIGHT):
VTS: Eastern part: Ch 80 16
VTS: Western part: Ch 79 16
DIE JADE:
VTS: Ch 20 63 16
Information bcsts: Ch 20 63 every H+10
WILHEMSHAVEN:
Port: Ch 11 16
Naval Port: Ch 11 16
Lock: Ch 13 16
Bridges: Ch 11
Varel Lock: Ch 13 HW±2
DIE WESER AND DIE HUNTE:
Bremerhaven Weser Tfc: Ch 02 04 05 07 16 21 22 82
Bremen Weser Traffic: Ch 16 19 78 81
Hunte Traffic:
VTS: Ch 16 63
Information in German: Ch 02 04 05 07 21 22 82 every H+20 by Bremerhaven Weser Traffic
Information in German: Ch 19 78 81 H+30 by Bremen Weser Traffic
Information in German: Ch 63 H+30 by Hunte Traffic
BREMERHAVEN:
Port: Ch 12 16
Locks: Ch 12
Bremerhaven Weser:
Port: Ch 14 16
Brake Lock: Ch 10
Elsfleth-Ohrt Railway Bridge: Ch 73
Hunte Lock: Ch 73
Hunte lifting bridge: Ch 69
Oldenburg:
Railway Bridge: Ch 73
H24 except Sun and public holidays 0030-0630
Lock: Ch 20 Mon-Sat: 0500-2100 Sun: 0900-1200
Cäcilien Bridge: Ch 73
Oslebshausen Lock: Ch 12
BREMEN:
Port: Ch 03 14 16
Lock: Ch 20 Mon-Sat: 0600-2200, Sun: Oct-Apr 0800-1100 May-Sep: 0800-1100 1730-1930
DIE ELBE:
VTS: Ch 71* 16
Brunsbüttel Elbe Traffic: Ch 68* 16
CUXHAVEN ELBE:
Cuxhaven Elbe Port: Ch 12* 16
Cuxhaven Port and Lock: Ch 69
BRUNSBÜTTEL ELBE PORT:
Port: Ch 12* 16
Oste Bridge: Ch 16 69
Apr-Sep the bridge is opened on request Ch 69. Oct-Mar request through Ch 03 or 16 Belum Radar or Ch 21 Cuxhaven Radar
Geversdorf Bridge: Ch 69 ; The bridge opens on request for small craft Apr-Sep: 1930-0730 and every H+00 and H+30
Obendorf Bridge: Ch 69 Oct-Mar H24, Apr-Sep 1930-0730. The bridge is opened on request by telephone 04752 5 21
Stör Llock: Ch 09 16 The bridge is opened on request
Glückstadt Lock: Ch 11 0700-1600 and during HW

Stadersand Elbe Port: Ch 12* 16
Este Lock: Ch 10 16
Este Bridge: Ch 11 Opened on request
HAMBURG:
VTS: Ch 74* 13 14 16
Port Traffic: Ch 73* 13 14 16
Elbe Port: Ch 12* 16
Rethe Bridge: Ch 13* 16
Kattwyk Bridge: Ch 13* 16
Harburg Lock: Ch 13* 16
Tiefstack Lock: Ch 11
NORD-OSTSEE KANAL:
KIEL KANAL: Ch 02
Every H+15 and H+45. See VTS Chart(s)
Information by Kiel Kanal 3:
Ch 03 Every H+20 and H+50
Brieholz: Ch 73
Ostermoor: Ch 73
Friedrichskoog: Ch 10 Access HW±2h
Büsum Port: Ch 11 16
Eider Lock: Ch 14 16
Husum Port: Ch 11 16
Information bcsts: Ch 11 every H+00, Access –4HW+2
Pellworm Port: Ch 11 0700-1700
Wyk Port: Ch 11 16
List Port: Ch 11 0800-1200 1600-1800
HELGOLAND:
Port: Ch 16 67
1 May-31 Aug Mon-Thu: 0700-1200 1300-2000 Fri
Sat: 0700-2000 Sun: 0700-1200 1 Sep-30 Apr: Mon-
Thurs: 0700-1200 1300-1600 Fri: 0700-1200
TÓRSHAVN: Ch 16; 09 12
Runavik: Ch 16; 09 12 13
STRENDUR (STÆNDER): Ch 16 ; 09 12
SKAALA (SKÁLI): Ch 16 ; 09 12 13
Kollefjord: Ch 16 ; 09 12 13
Midvaag/Sandevaag: Ch 16 ; 09 12 13
Lervikar (Leirvik): Ch 16 ; 09 12 13
FUGLAFJ'RDUR: Ch 16 ; 09 12 13
Klaksvik: Ch 16 ; 06 12
Svinoy: Ch 16 ; 09 12
HVANNASUND (KVANNESUND):
Ch 16 ; 09 12 13
Hattarvik (Hattervig): Ch 16 ; 09 12
Kirkja: Ch 16 ; 09 12

DENMARK
COASTAL STATIONS
All Danish Coast Radio Stations are remotely
controlled from Lyngby Radio (MMSI
002191000). All MF stations, except Skagen,
maintain an H24 watch on 2182 kHz. The stations
listed below monitor Ch 16 H24 and Ch 70 DSC.
Users should call on working frequencies to
assist in keeping Ch 16 clear. Routine traffic lists
are broadcast on all VHF frequencies every odd
H+05.

Lyngby ⒸⓇⓈ	Ch 07 85
Blåvand ⒸⓇⓈ	Ch 23
Bovbjerg ⒸⓇⓈ	Ch 02
Hanstholm ⒸⓇⓈ	Ch 66
Skagen ⒸⓇⓈ	Ch 04
Frejlev ⒸⓇⓈ	Ch 03
Silkeborg ⒸⓇⓈ	Ch 27
Als ⒸⓇⓈ	Ch 07 85

PORT STATIONS
Rømø Havn: Ch 16 ; 10 12 13 HX
Esbjerg: Ch 16 ; 12 13 14
Hvide Sande: Ch 16 ; 12 13 HX
Torsminde: Ch 16 ; 12 13 0300-1300, 1400-2400
LIMFJORD:
Port: Ch 16 ; 12 13 HX
Lemvig: Ch 16 ; 13 HX
Oddesund Bridge: Ch 16 ; 12 13 HX
Holstebro-Struer: Ch 16 ; 12 13 HX
Vilsund Bridge: Ch 16 ; 12 Opens sunrise to 30 mins
after sunset
Thisted: Ch 16 ; 12 13 HX
Nykøbing: Ch 16 ; 12 HX
Fur Havn Ferry: Ch 16 77
Skive: Ch 16 ; 09 12 HX
Hjarbaek Bridge and Lock: Ch 12 16
Aggersund Bridge: Ch 16 ; 12 13
Opens sunrise to 30 mins after sunset
ÅLBORG:
Port: Ch 16 ; 12 13
Bridge: Ch 16 ; 12 13 HX
Rørdal: Ch 16 ; 12 13 HX
Hanstholm Havn: Ch 16 ; 12 13 HX
Torup Strand: Ch 16 ; 12 13 HX
Hirtshals Havn: Ch 16 ; 14 HX
Skagen: Ch 16 12 13

FRANCE
COASTAL STATIONS

COAST RADIO STATIONS
VHF Ch 16 is monitored H24. Make initial call on
working channel, H24. VHF channels of Coast
Radio Stations do not broadcast traffic lists. All
times are UT but broadcasts are made 1 hour
earlier when DST is in force.

0840 Boulogne-sur-Mer ⒸⓇⓈ	Ch 23* 25* 16	
Phone +33 (0) 3 21 33 25 26 Fax +33 (0) 3 21 91 99 71		
0830 Dunkerque ⒸⓇⓈ	Ch 24* 61* 16	
0835 Calais ⒸⓇⓈ	Ch 01* 87* 16	
0845 Dieppe ⒸⓇⓈ	Ch 02* 24* 16	
0848 Fécamp ⒸⓇⓈ	Ch 16	
0850 Le Havre ⒸⓇⓈ	Ch 26* 28* 16 23	
0855 Rouen ⒸⓇⓈ	Ch 25* 16 27	
0856 Port-en-Bessin ⒸⓇⓈ	Ch 03* 16	
0857 Cherbourg ⒸⓇⓈ	Ch 27* 16	
0858 Jobourg ⒸⓇⓈ	Ch 21	

COASTGUARD STATIONS
Coastguard MRCC radio stations are remotely
controlled from Bremen MRCC (MMSI 00211240). All
monitor Ch 16 H24. Initial call is made on Ch 16 using
the name of the local station as callsign. All stations
opwerate DSC on VHF Ch 70 (H24). No MRCC stations
accept public correspondence calls.

0842 Gris-Nez (CROSS) (MRCC) ⒸⒼ
MMSI 002275100
Ch 70 DSC. Ch 16 15 67 68 73
Distress, urgent and safety traffic only.
Phone: +33 (0)3 21 87 21 87 Fax: +33 (0)3 21 87 78 55

PORT STATIONS

DUNKERQUE
Port: Ch 73
Marina (Private): Ch 09
Season: Mon-Sat: 0800-1200 1400-2000.
Out of season: Mon-Sat: 0900-1200 1400-1830.
Sun: 1000-1200 1600-1800
Marina (Public): Ch 09 H24
GRAVELINES:
Marina: Ch 09
Mon-Fri: 0800-1200 1330-1730
CALAIS:
Port: Call Calais Port Traffic Ch 16 ; 12
Marina: Ch 12 0800-1200 1400-1800
Hoverport: Ch 20 HX
Ecluse Carnot: Ch 12 16 HX
CROSS GRIS NEZ:
VTS: Ch 13* 79 16
Distress and Safety: Ch 13 79 Calling and working
Information: Call Gris Nez Traffic Ch 13 79 H+10.
Occasional when visibility less than 2M H+25
SAR Coordination: Ch 68* 15 67 73
SAR Coordination:
BOULOGNE:
Call Control Tower, Boulogne Port Ch 12
Marina: Ch 09 HW±3
Hoverport: Ch 20 HX
Le Touquet: Ch 09 ; 77 Access −2HW+1
Étaples-Sur-Mer: Ch 09 Access HW±2
Le Treport: Ch 16 ; 12 72 Access HW±3
DIEPPE:
Port: Ch 12 16 ; 12*
(Ch 12 Office Hours, Ch 16 H24)
S VALÉRY-EN-CAUX: Ch 09
Lock operates: Day: HW±2, Night: HW±$\frac{1}{2}$
Fécamp: Ch 16 ; 10 12 Access −3HW+1
Gayant Lock (Bassin Freycinet):
Call Bureau du Port Ch 16
Bérigny Lock: Call Ecluse Bérigny Ch 09
Marina: Ch 09
Season: 0800-1200 1400-2000
Out of season: Mon-Sat: 0830-1200
LE HAVRE:
VTS: Ch 12 20
Marina: Ch 09
Season 0800-1200 1400-1800, Out of season Mon-Fri
as season, Sat 0800-1200, Sun & holidays closed
Antifer Port: Ch 22* 14
LA SEINE:
VTS: Ch 73 15 16
Call Radar Honfleur when entering and then Rouen
control Centre while on passage
Honfleur: Port: Ch 17 73 16
Access −2HW Le Havre+4
Locks and Bridges: Ch 16 17 H24.
Access −2HW Le Havre+4
Tancarville: Ch 16 HX
Lock: Ch 18 HX
Port Jérome: Call PR Ch 16 ; 73
ROUEN:
Port: Ch 73* 16 68
ROUEN TO PARIS LOCKS: Ch 18
Send ETA by VHF to next lock 30 mins in advance
throughout the passage
Notre-Dame-de-la-Garenne: Ch 22

Mericourt: Ch 18
Andrésy: Ch 22
Bougival: Ch 22
Chatou: Ch 18
Suresnes: Ch 22
Paris-Arsenal: Ch 09
Deauville-Trouville: Ch 09 0800-1730 LT
Marina Bassin Morny: Ch 09 0900-1200 1400-1800 LT
Marina Port-Deauville: Ch 09
Mon-Fri (except closed Wed): 0900-1200 1400-1800,
Sat: 0900-1200 1500-1800, Sun & holidays: 1000-
1200 1500-1800
Port Guillaume, Dives-sur-Mer: Ch 09
Access Neaps HW±2, Springs HW±2$\frac{1}{2}$
CAEN-OUISTREHAM:
Port: Ch 68* 16
Lock: Ch 12 68 Access −2HW+3
Marina (Public): Ch 09 0815-1200 1400-1800 LT
Canal de Caen: Ch 68 Keep listening watch
Marina: Ch 68 HX
Courseulles-sur-Mer: Ch 09 0900-1200 and HW±3
Port-en-Bessin: Ch 18 HW±2
Grandcamp-Maisy: Ch 09
Season 0600-2200, out of season office hours
Isigny-sur-Mer: Ch 09 0900-1200 1400-1800
Carentan: Ch 09 0800-1800
ST VAAST-LA HOUGUE:
Marina: Ch 09
Season: −2HW+3, Out of season: as season 0800-
1800 only
CHERBOURG: Call Le Homet Ch 16; 12 H24.
Advise ETA on entering the Grande Rade
Lock: Ch 06 Access HW±$\frac{3}{4}$
Marina: Call Chantereyne Ch 09 0800-2300

FRANCE
COASTAL STATIONS

COAST RADIO STATIONS

0859 Carteret (CRS)	Ch 64* 16
0861 Saint-Malo (CRS)	Ch 01* 02* 16
0862 Paimpol (CRS)	Ch 84* 16
0863 Plougasnou (CRS)	Ch 81* 16
0864 Ouessant (CRS)	Ch 24* 82* 16
0865 Brest-Le Conquet (CRS)	Ch 26* 28* 16

Phone +33 (0) 2 98 43 63 63 Fax: +33 (0) 2 98 89 06 11

0867 Pont l'Abbe (CRS)	Ch 86* 16
0869 Belle-Île (CRS)	Ch 05* 25* 16
0871 St-Nazaire (CRS)	Ch 23* 24* 16
0872 Saint-Herblain (CRS)	Ch 28* 16
0874 Saint-Hilaire-de-Riez (CRS)	Ch 27* 16
0876 Île de Ré (CRS)	Ch 21* 26* 16

Phone +33 (0)5 56 83 40 50

0877 Royan (CRS)	Ch 23* 25* 16
0878 Bordeaux (CRS)	Ch 27* 16
0880 Bordeaux-Arcachon (CRS)	Ch 28* 82* 16
0885 Bayonne (CRS)	Ch 24* 16

COASTGUARD STATIONS
0860 Jobourg (CROSS) (MRCC) (CG) MMSI 002275200
Ch 70 DSC. Ch 16 67 68
Distress, safety and urgent traffic only.
Call CROSS Jobourg.
Phone: +33 (0) 2 33 52 72 13, Fax: +33 (0) 2 33 52 71 72

FRENCH COAST RADIO STATIONS

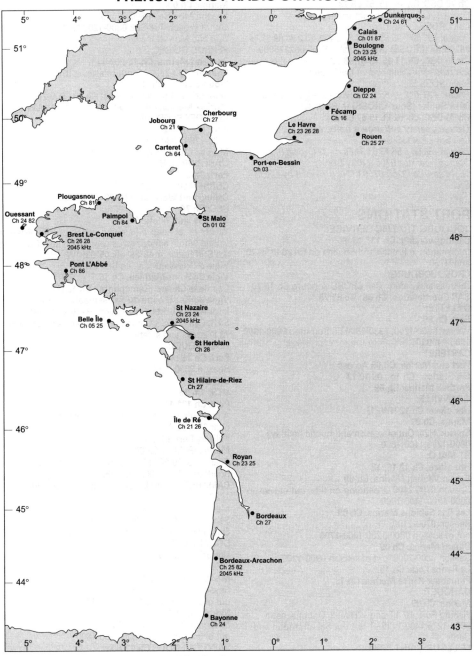

Dunkerque
Ch 24 61

Calais
Ch 01 87

Boulogne
Ch 23 25
2045 kHz

Dieppe
Ch 02 24

Fécamp
Ch 16

Cherbourg
Ch 27

Jobourg
Ch 21

Le Havre
Ch 23 26 28

Rouen
Ch 25 27

Carteret
Ch 64

Port-en-Bessin
Ch 03

Plougasnou
Ch 81

Ouessant
Ch 24 82

Paimpol
Ch 84

St Malo
Ch 01 02

Brest Le-Conquet
Ch 26 28
2045 kHz

Pont L'Abbé
Ch 86

St Nazaire
Ch 23 24
2045 kHz

Belle Île
Ch 05 25

St Herblain
Ch 28

St Hilaire-de-Riez
Ch 27

Île de Ré
Ch 21 26

Royan
Ch 23 25

Bordeaux
Ch 27

Bordeaux-Arcachon
Ch 25 82
2045 kHz

Bayonne
Ch 24

0866 Corsen (CROSS) (MRCC) ⒼⒷ MMSI 002275300
Ch 70 DSC. Ch 16 15 67 68 73
Distress, safety and urgent traffic only.
Call CROSS Corsen.
Phone: +33 (0) 2 98 89 31 31 Fax: +33 (0) 2 98 89 65 75
0870 Étel (CROSS) (MRCC) ⒼⒷ MMSI 002275000
Ch 70 DSC. Ch 11 15 16 67 68 73
Distress safety and urgent traffic only.
Call CROSS Étel.
Phone: +33 (0) 2 97 55 35 35 Fax: +33 (0) 2 97 55 49 34
0879 Soulac (Sous-CROSS) (MRSC) ⒼⒷ
Ch 70 DSC. Ch 16 11 15 67 68 73
Distress, safety and urgent traffic only.
Call Sous CROSS Soulac.
Phone: +33 (0) 5 56 73 31 31 Fax: +33 (0) 5 56 09 79 73
Station operates 0700-2200 LT only.
Night service (2200-0700 LT) is provided by CROSS Étel.

PORT STATIONS

JOBOURG TRAFFIC SERVICE:
Calling/working: **Ch 13* 16 80**
Information in French and English on **Ch 80** at H+20 and H+50
CROSS JOBOURG:
Distress and Safety: Call CROSS Jobourg **Ch 16 70**
SAR Coordination: **Ch 68* 15 67 73**
DIÉLETTE:
Port: **Ch 09**
Winter: 0900-1200, 1330-1800 LT. Summer: 0800-1300, 1400-1400 LT
CARTERET:
Port and Marina: **Ch 09** Access HW±2½
Sig Station: **Ch 16 ; 09 10 13**
Portbail Marina: **Ch 09**
GRANVILLE:
Hbr office: **Ch 12** HW±1½
Marina: **Ch 09**
Season H24, Out of season and public holidays 0800-1200 1400-1800
ST MALO:
Hbr office: **Ch 12 16; 12**
Bassin Vauban Marina: **Ch 09**
Season 0700-2400 depending on tide, out of season 0800-1200 1400-1800
Les Bas Sablons Marina: **Ch 09**
Season 0700-2100,
out of season 0800-1200 1400-1700
Dinard Marina: **Ch 09**
Season 0800-2000, out of season 0900-1200
La Rance Lock: **Ch 13**
Plouer-sur-Rance Marina: **Ch 13**
DAHOUËT:
Marina: **Ch 09**
Fishing Port: **16** LT and −2HW+1. Out of season 0830-1215 1400-1715 LT (except Sat afternoon and Sun)
LE LÉGUÉ, SAINT BRIEUC:
Call Légué Port **Ch 16 ; 12**
−2HW+1½ and −1HW+1½ depending on height of tide
Binic: **Ch 09** Office hours
SAINT-QUAY PORTRIEUX:
Port and Marina: **Ch 09**
Paimpol-Pontrieux: **Ch 09** Access HW±2
LÉZARDRIEUX:
Marina: **Ch 09**
Pontrieux Lock: **Ch 12** Access −2HW+1

TRÉGUIER:
Marina: **Ch 09**
Season Mon-Sat: 0800-120 LT.
Out of season Tue-Sat: 0800-1200 1330-1700,
Sun and Mon: closed
PERROS-GUIREC:
Port and Marina: **Ch 16 ; 09**
Season 0730-2100 LT, out of season 0730-1730 LT
Ploumanac'h: Ch 09
Trébeurden: Port and Marina: Ch 09 0600-2400
Morlaix Marina: Ch 16 ; 09 HW±2, lock −1½HW+1
ROSCOFF-BLOSCON:
Port: **Ch 16 ; 12**
0830-1200 1330-1800 LT
Marina: **Ch 09** 0800-1200 1330-1730 LT
L'ABERWRAC'H
Port: **Ch 09 16**
CORSEN-OUESSANT:
Calling and Working: **13* 79**
DSC: **Ch 70**
Distress and Safety: **Ch 16**
Yachts must keep a listening watch on **Ch 16** when sailing within a 35M radius centred on Ile d'Ouessant (Le Stiff Radar Tr 48°28'·6N 05°03'·1W)
Vigie d'Ouessant: Call Le Stiff **Ch 16**
Vigie de Saint-Mathieu: Ch 16
Cap de la Chevre (Semaphore): **Ch 16** HJ
Vigie du Raz (Pointe du Raz semaphore): **Ch 16**
Information bcsts: **Ch 79** Every H+10 and H+40
SAR: Call CROSS Corsen or Ouessant **Ch 68* 15 67 73** Distress and safety
LE CONQUET:
Port: **Ch 16 ; 08**
Season 0830-1200 1330-1800 LT, out of season HX
BREST:
VTS: **Ch 16**
Port: **Ch 12* 16**
A compulsory reporting system exists for vessels over 25m LOA
Military Port: **Ch 74**
Marina (Public): **Ch 09**
Season: 0800-2000 LT, Out of season: 0830-1800 LT, holidays: 0900-1200 1400-1900 LT
CAMARET-SUR-M LT, out of season: 0830-1200 1330-1730 LT
Morgat: **Ch 09**
Season: 0800-1200 1400-2000 LT.
Out of season: 0800-1200 1400-1800 LT
DOUARNENEZ:
Hbr office: **Ch 16 ; 12**
0800-1200 1330-1730 LT
Marina (Public): **Ch 09**
Season: 0700-1200 1330-2100 LT,
out of season: 0800-1200 1300-1700 LT
Morgat: **Ch 09**
Season: 0800-1200 1400-2000,
out of season: 0800-1200 1400-1800
SAINT GUÉNOLE: Ch 12 HJ
LE GUILVINEC:
Port: **Ch 12** HX
LOCTUDY:
Hbr office: **Ch 12** (Portable VHF)
Mon-Fri: 0630-1200 1400-1900 LT. Sat: 0800-1200 LT
Marina (Public): **Ch 09**
Season: 0730-2100 LT, out of season Mon-Sat: 0830-1200 1330-1800 LT, Sun and holidays closed
Bénodet Marina: Ch 09

Season: 0800-2000 LT. Out of season: 0800-1200
1400-1800 LT
Port-La-Forêt: Ch 09
Season 0800-2000 LT, out of season Mon-Sat: 0830-
1200 1330-1830 LT Sun and holidays: 0900-1200
1330-1830 LT
CONCARNEAU:
Port: Ch 16 ; 12
Marina: Ch 09
Season: 0700-2100 LT, out of season: 0900-1200
1330-1730 LT
SAINTE-MARINE: Ch 09
Season 0800-1200 1500-2000 LT, out of season 0800-
1200 1400-1800 LT
LORIENT:
Hbr office: Call Vigie Port Louis **Ch 16 ; 12**
Marina (Private): Ch 09 (Hours as for Kernevel below)
Kernevel: Ch 09
Season 0800-1230 1330-2000 LT, out of season Mon-
Sat 0830-1230 1400-1800 LT, Sun and holidays 0900-
1230 LT
Marina (Public): Ch 09
Season 0830-1900 LT, out of season 0830-1230 1400-
1800 LT
ÉTEL CROSS:
Distress and Safety: Ch 11 15 16 68 73
Information: Ch 16 ; 80
Urgent navigational messages bcst on receipt and
then every 2h. Non-urgent navigational messages
bcst 0433 and 2133 after weather forecasts.
Marina: Ch 16 ; 13
Season 15 Jun-1 Sep –3HW+2. Out of season HX
Le Palais: Ch 09
Season: 0800-1200 1500-2000, out of season: 0830-
1200 1400-1800, closed Sun
Port-Haliguen Marina: Ch 09
Season: 0800-1230 1400-2000 LT, out of season:
0900-1200 1400-1800 LT
La Trinité-sur-Mer Marina: Ch 09
Season: 0830-1900 LT, out of season: 0830-1230
1400-1800 LT
Le Crouesty Marina: Ch 09
Season 0800-2000 LT, out of season 0900-1230 1330-
1800 LT
Vannes Marina: Ch 09
Season: 0830-2100 LT, out of season HW±2½,
morning 0900-1230 LT
Arzal-Camoel Marina: Ch 09
Season: 0830-1230 1400-2000 LT,
out of season: 0830-1230 1330-1730 LT
Lock: Ch 18 HX
Port and Marina: Ch 09
Season: 0700-1100 1500-2100 LT, out of season 0800-
1000 1600-1800 LT
Le CroisicPort and Marina: Ch 09
Season: 0800-2000 LT, out of season 0800-1700 LT
except holidays
Pornichet Marina: Ch 09
Season 0800-2100 LT, out of season 0800-2000 LT
La Loire Signal Station: Call Chemoulin **Ch 16**
Reporting System: Ch 12* 16 ; 12* 06 14 67 69
Compulsory for all commercial vessels
SAINT-NAZAIRE:
VTS: Ch 12* 16 06 14 67 69
Tidal Information: Ch 73 Tidal information between
Saint-Nazaire and Nantes automatically broadcast
at H+00, H+15, H+30 and H+45

DONGES:
Port: Ch 12 16
Nantes Port: Ch 12* 16 ; 12* 06 14 67 69
Pornic Marina: Ch 09
L'HERBAUDIÈRE, (Île de Noirmoutier)
Port and Marina: Ch 09
Season 0830-1200 1530-2000 LT except July-Aug
0730-2230 LT, out of season 0830-1200 1400-1800 LT
Port-Joinville Marina (Île d'Yeu): Ch 09
Contact Hr Mr before arrival.
Entry to wet basin HW±2, mooring by arrangement
with Hr Mr
SAINT-GILLES-CROIX-DE-VIE:
Port and Marina: Ch 09
Season: 0600-2200 LT, out of season 0800-1200 1400-
1800 LT
Les Sables d'Olonne:
Port: Ch 12
Harbour Master Mon-Fri: 0800-1800 LT, lock HW±2 or
HW±1½ depending on tide
Marina: Ch 09 (H24)
PORT DE BOURGENAY
Port: Ch 12* 16 ; 12
Marina (Public): Ch 09
ROCHEFORT:
Hr office: Ch 16 ; 12
0800-1200 1400-1800LT
Marina: Ch 09 HW±1
Tonnay-Charente: Ch 16 ; 12 HX
BORDEAUX RIVER:
VTS: Ch 12
Compulsory for all vessels in the area from BXA Lt
buoy to Bordeaux
Radar: Ch 12 ; 16
Tidal Information: Ch 17
Height of water between Le Verdon and Bordeaux
bcst automatically every 5 min
Royan: Ch 16 ; 09
Season 0800-2000 LT, out of season 0900-1800 LT
except Sat afternoons and Sun
Le Verdon:
Port: Ch 16 ; 11 12 14
PAUILLIC:
Hbr office: Ch 12
Marina: Ch 09
BLAYE:
Port: : Ch 12
Ambès: Ch 12
BORDEAUX:
Hbr office: Ch 16 ; 12
Marina: Ch 09 Office hours during season
SOULAC CROSS:
Distress and Safety: Ch 16 70
Calling and Working: Ch 13* 79
SAR Coordination: Ch 68* 15 67 73
Information: Ch 79
Urgent navigational information is bcst on receipt
and then every 2h. Non-urgent navigational
information is bcst at 0433 and 2133 LT after the
weather forecast.
ARCACHON:
Marina: Ch 09
CAPBRETON:
Marina: Ch 09
Season: 0800-1900. Out of season: 0800-1200 1330-
1830 (Sats and holidays 1730)
Anglet: Ch 12 Office hours
Bayonne: Ch 12

SAINT-JEAN-DE-LUZ:
Port and Marina: **Ch 16 ; 09**
Season 0630-1300 1330-2000 LT, out of season 0730-
1230 1330-1830 LT
HENDAYE:
Marina: **Ch 09 H24**

SPAIN
COASTAL STATIONS

COAST RADIO STATIONS
The Spanish Coast Radio Stations listed below are
remotely controlled from CCR Bilbao or Coruña. No
Traffic Lists are broadcast on VHF. All vessels should
call initially on Ch 16.

0901 Pasajes ⒸⓇⓈ	**Ch 27* 16**
0905 Bilbao ⒸⓇⓈ	**Ch 26* 16**
0910 Santander ⒸⓇⓈ	**Ch 24* 16**
0916 Cabo Peñas ⒸⓇⓈ	**Ch 26* 16**
0918 Navia ⒸⓇⓈ	**Ch 27* 16**
0919 Cabo Ortegal ⒸⓇⓈ	**Ch 02* 16**
0925 Coruña ⒸⓇⓈ	**Ch 26* 16**
0927 Finisterre ⒸⓇⓈ	**Ch 01* 22* 16**
0929 Vigo ⒸⓇⓈ	**Ch 20* 16**
0930 La Guardia ⒸⓇⓈ	**Ch 82* 16**

COASTGUARD STATIONS
Coastguard radio stations do not accept public
correspondence calls.

0906 Bilbao (MRCC) ⒸⒼ MMSI 002240996
Ch 70 DSC Ch 10 16
Distress, safety and urgent traffic only
*Phone: +34 (9) 4 483 9411 (Emergency) +34 (9) 4 483
9286 / 483 7053 Fax: +33 (9) 4 483 9161*
0911 Santander (MRSC) ⒸⒼ MMSI 002241009
Ch 70 DSC Ch 16 11
Distress, safety and urgent traffic only
Phone: +34 (9) 42 213030 Fax: +34 (9) 942 213638
0914 Gijón (MRCC) ⒸⒼ MMSI 002240997
Ch 70 DSC Ch 16 10 15 17
Distress, safety and urgent traffic only.
Call Gijón Traffic.
Phone: +34 (9) 85 326 050/373 Fax: +34 (9) 85 320 908
0924 Coruña (MRSC) ⒸⒼ
Ch 70 DSC Ch 13 67 16
Distress, safety and urgent traffic only.
Call La Coruña Port Control
Phone: +34 81 209 548 Fax: +34 81 209 518
0928 Finisterre (MRCC) ⒸⒼ MMSI 002240993
Ch 70 DSC Ch 11 16
Distress, safety and urgent traffic only.
Call Finisterre Traffic.
Phone: +34 (9) 81 767 320/738/500
Fax +34 (9) 81 767 740
0929·1 Vigo (MRSC) ⒸⒼ MMSI 002240998
Ch 70 DSC Ch 10 74 16
Distress, safety and urgent traffic only.
Call Vigo Traffic
Phone: +34 (9) 86 297 403/299 719
Fax +34 (9) 86 290 455

PORT STATIONS
PASAJES:
Call Pasajes Prácticos **Ch 16 ; 14* 11 12 13**
BILBAO:
VTS: **Ch 12* 16 05**
Signal Station: **Ch 16 ; 12 13 HX**
SANTANDER:
Port: **Ch 16 ; 06 12 14**
Pilot Office: **Ch 16 ; 12* 09 14**
REQUEJADA, SUANCES:
Pilots: **Ch 12 16** When vessel expected
Gijón: **Ch 16 ; 14* 11 12**
Avilés: **Ch 12 ; 06 09 14 16**
Pilot Office: **Ch 16 ; 14* 11 12**
Ribadeo Pilots: **Ch 16**
PUERTO DE SAN CIPRIÄN:
Pilots and Port: **Ch 14 16**
EL FERROL DEL CAUDILLO:
Ch 14* 16 ; 10 11 12 13 14
Ch 14 H24
LA CORUÑA:
Port: **Ch 16 12 HX**
CORCUBIÓN:
Pilots: **Ch 16**
FINISTERRE:
VTS: **Ch 11 74 16**
Ch 11 16 (H24)
Voluntary reporting for non-Spanish vessels
VILLAGARCIA DE AROSA:
Port: **Ch 16 ; 12**
Marin: Call Marin Pilots **Ch 16 ; 12** When vessel
expected
VIGO:
VTS: Call Vigo Traffic (H24) **Ch 16 10**
Port: Call Vigo Prácticos **Ch 16 ; 14** HX

PORTUGAL
COASTAL STATIONS

COAST RADIO STATIONS

0935 Arga ⒸⓇⓈ	**Ch 16 25 28 83**
0949 Arestal ⒸⓇⓈ	**Ch 16 24 26 85**
0950 Montejunto ⒸⓇⓈ	**Ch 16 23 27 87**
0952 Lisboa ⒸⓇⓈ	**Ch 16 23 25 26 27 28**
0958 Atalaia ⒸⓇⓈ	**Ch 16 24 26 85**
0959 Picos ⒸⓇⓈ	**Ch 16 23 27 85**
0963 Estoi ⒸⓇⓈ	**Ch 16 24 28 86**

RADIONAVAL STATIONS
The radionaval stations listed below do not accept
public correspondence.

0955 Algés (Radionaval): Ch 11 16
0960 Sagres (Radionaval): Ch 11 16

SPANISH AND PORTUGUESE COAST RADIO STATIONS

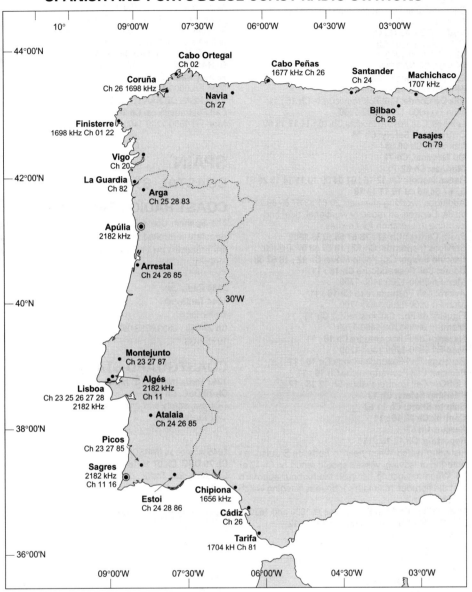

10°   09°00'W   07°30'W   06°00'W   04°30'W   03°00'W

44°00'N

Cabo Ortegal
Ch 02

Cabo Peñas
1677 kHz Ch 26

Santander
Ch 24

Machichaco
1707 kHz

Coruña
Ch 26 1698 kHz

Navia
Ch 27

Bilbao
Ch 26

Finisterre
1698 kHz Ch 01 22

Pasajes
Ch 79

Vigo
Ch 20

42°00'N

La Guardia
Ch 82

Arga
Ch 25 28 83

Apúlia
2182 kHz

Arrestal
Ch 24 26 85

40°N

30'W

Montejunto
Ch 23 27 87

Algés
2182 kHz
Ch 11

Lisboa
Ch 23 25 26 27 28
2182 kHz

Atalaia
Ch 24 26 85

38°00'N

Picos
Ch 23 27 85

Sagres
2182 kHz
Ch 11 16

Estoi
Ch 24 28 86

Chipiona
1656 kHz

Cádiz
Ch 26

Tarifa
1704 kH Ch 81

36°00'N

09°00'W   07°30'W   06°00'W   04°30'W   03°0'W

PORT STATIONS

Caminha: Call Postradcaminha **Ch 16 ; 11**
Mon-Fri 0900-1200 1400-1700
VIANA DO CASTELO:
Call Postradviana **Ch 16 ; 11**
Mon-Fri 0900-1200 1400-1700
PÓVOA DE VARZIM:
Call Postradvarzim **Ch 16 ; 11**
Mon-Fri 0900-1200 1400-1700
Vila Do Conde: Call Postradviconde **Ch 16 ; 11**
Mon-Fri 0900-1200 1400-1700
Leixões: Call Postradleixões **Ch 16 ; 11 13 19 60**
Distress and Safety: Ch 16
Intership: Ch 06 08
Oil Terminal: Ch 74
Marinas: Ch 62
**Radar Station: Ch 12 16 ; 01 04 09 10 11 14 18 20 61
63 67 68 06 09 10 11 14 18**
Additional working channels 20 61 63 67 68 69 71 79
80 84. Controls all radar, navigational, tidal and
berthing information for Leixões
Posto Central: Ch 12 ; 18 67 68 0730-1900
Serviços Maritimos: Ch 12 ; 18 67 68 0700-2400
Bascule Bridge: Call Pónte Movel **Ch 12 ; 18 67 68**
Douro: Call Postraddouro **Ch 16 ; 11**
Mon-Fri 0900-1200 1400-1700
Aveiro: Call Postradaveiro **Ch 16 ; 11**
Mon-Fri 0900-1200 1400-1700
Figueira da Foz: Call Postradfoz **Ch 16 ; 11**
Mon-Fri 0900-1200 1400-1700
Nazaré: Call Postradnazare **Ch 16 ; 11**
Mon-Fri 0900-1200 1400-1700
Berlenga: Call Postradberlenga **Ch 16 ; 11**
Peniche: Call Postradpeniche **Ch 16 ; 11**
LISBOA: Call Contrololisboa **Ch 12 16 ; 12**
Intership Safety: Ch 13
Ship to Shore: Ch 11 63
Control: Ch 12 16 ; 11
Rescue: Ch 67
Reporting: Ch 12 16 ; 11
Listening watch When near to Forte de S Julao, on
entering or leaving, vessels should report on Ch 12 or
16. When navigating between the harbour approach
and the harbour, maintain continuous listening watch
on Ch 13
Information: Ch 11 In Portuguese at 1030 and 1630
LISBOA DOCKS: Call Docopesca **Ch 03 12**
0100 Mon-0100 Sat
Doca de Alcântara Lock: Ch 12 ; 05
0700 0815 0915 1015 1115 1315 1500 1630 1800
Rocha Drydocks: Ch 14 74
Lisnave Drydocks: Ch 14
Alfeite Signal Station:
Call Radiosinaisfaleite **Ch 16 ; 11**
Sesimbra: Call Postradsesimbra **Ch 16 ; 11**
Mon-Fri 0900-1200 1400-1700
Setúbal: Call Postradsetúbal **Ch 16 ; 11 13**
Sines: Call Postradsines **Ch 16 ; 11 13**
Serviços Maritimos: Ch 12 16; 01 04 09 10 11 18 20
Additional working channels 63 67 68 69 81 84
Lagos: Call Postradlagos **Ch 16; 11**
Mon-Fri 0900-1200 1400-1700
Marina: Ch 16 ; 62
1 June-15 Sep 0900-2200, else 0900-1230 1400-1900

Portimão: Call Postradportimão **Ch 16; 11**
Mon-Fri 0900-1200 1400-1700
Fishery Radio Station: Ch 03 Mon-Fri 0630-2130
Vilamoura: Call Vilamouraradio **Ch 16 20 62**
0830-1830 (2130 in summer)
Faro: Call Postradfaro **Ch 16 ; 11**
OLHÃO: Call Postradiolhão **Ch 16 ; 11**
Fishery Radio Station: Ch 03 ; 16
Mon-Fri 0900-1200
VILA REAL DE SANTO ANTÓNIO:
Call Postradvilareal **Ch 16 ; 11**
Mon-Fri 0900-1200 1400-1700

SPAIN
COASTAL STATIONS

COAST RADIO STATIONS

The Spanish Coast Radio Stations listed below are
remotely controlled from CCR Malaga. No Traffic Lists
are broadcast on VHF. All vessels should call initially
on Ch 16.

1034 Cádiz (CRS)	**Ch 26* 16**
1044 Tarifa (CRS)	**Ch 81* 16**

Traffic lists:
Ch 27 0333 0533 0733 0933 1133 1333 1533 1733
1933 2333

COASTGUARD STATIONS

1043 Tarifa (MRCC) (CG) MMSI 002240994
Ch 70 DSC. Ch 16
Distress, safety and urgent traffic only.
Call Tarifa Traffic.
Phone +34 956 684 740 Fax +34 956 680 606

1045 Algeciras (MRSC)
Ch 70 DSC. Ch 07 15 16
Call Algeciras Traffic. Distress, safety and urgent
traffic only

PORT STATIONS

EL ROMPIDO:
Marina: Ch 09 16 HX
PUNTA UMBRÍA:
Marina: Ch 09 16 HX
Bridge: Call Huelva Pilots **Ch 16 ; 14* 06 11 12**
HUELVA:
Port: Call Huelva Barra Prácticos for Bar or Huelva
Puerto Prácticos for Harbour **Ch 14 16 06 11 12**
Marina: Ch 09 16 HX
RÍO GUADALQUIVIR:
Call Obras Puerto Sevilla **Ch 12**
Marina: Ch 09 16 HX
Puerto Sherry Marina: Ch 09 16 HX
Real Club Nautico de Santa Marina: Ch 09 16 HX
CÁDIZ:
Call Cádiz Prácticos
Ch 14 16* 11 12
Real Club Nautico de Cadiz Marina: Ch 09 16 HX

STRAIT OF GIBRALTAR
TARIFA:
VTS: Call Tarifa Traffic **Ch 10 16**
(also Ch 67 by mutual arrangement)
DSC Ch 70
Information: Ch 10 16
Urgent messages will be bcst at any time on Ch 10
and Ch 16. Routine messages will be bcst every even
H+15 on Ch 10
ALGECIRAS:
Port: Call Algeciros Prácticos **Ch 16 ; 09 12 13** HX
Marina: Ch 09 16 HX
Real Club Nautico de Algeciras: Ch 09 16 HX
Algeciras Iberia: Call Sea Land Iberia **Ch 16 ; 09** HX

GIBRALTAR
COASTAL STATIONS
COAST RADIO STATION
1047 Gibraltar (RS) **Ch 01 02 03 04 16 23 24 25 27 28
86 87**
Ch 04 *is exclusively used for Autolink RT.*
Ch 24 & 28 *can be used as second and third choices
respectively for Autolink RT services on a shared basis
with the operator during hours of service only. Phone:
+350 77464/74767 Fax +350 78851*

PORT STATIONS
GIBRALTAR: Ch 06* 12* 13 14 16
Ch 12 is the Gibraltar Bay Working Channel
Information: Ch 10 16
Urgent messages will be broadcast at any time on
Ch 10 and Ch 16. Routine messages will be broadcast
every even H+15 on Ch 10.
Lloyds Gibraltar Radio: Ch 12* 08 16 14
Queen's Harbour Master: Ch 08
Mon-Thu: 0800-1630 LT Fri: 0800-1600 LT
Queensway Quay Marina: Ch 73
Summer: 0830-2145 LT, Winter: 0830-2015 LT
Shepherds Marina: Ch 71
Mon-Fri: 0900-1300, 1430-1800, Sat: 0900-1300.
Duty staff until 1900
Marina Bay: Ch 73
Summer: 0830-2230 LT, Winter: 0830-2030 LT

DIFFERENTIAL GPS STATIONS

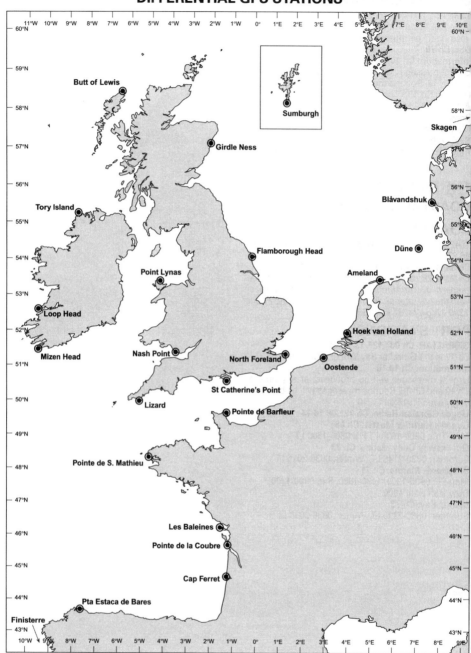

Differential GPS beacons

UNITED KINGDOM

S. Catherine's Point Lt   50°34'·52N 05°12'·07W
293·50 kHz   100M   Transmitting station 440 441
Reference station(s) 680 690

Lizard Lt   49°57'·58N 05°12'·07W
284·00 kHz   100M   Transmitting station 44
Reference station(s) 681 691

Nash Point Lt   51°24'·03N 03°33'·06W
299·00 kHz   100M   Transmitting station 449
Reference station(s) 689 699

Point Lynas Lt   53°24'·97N 04°17'·30W
305·00 kHz   100M   Transmitting station 442
Reference station(s) 682 692

Butt of Lewis Lt   58°30'·93N 06°15'·72W
294·00 kHz   150M   Transmitting station 444
Reference station(s) 684 694

Sumburgh   59°52'·08N 01°16'·35W
304·00 kHz   150M   Transmitting station 445
Reference station(s) 685 695

Girdle Ness Lt   57°08'·32N 02°02'·83W
311·00kHz   150M   Transmitting station 446
Reference station(s) 686 69

Flamborough Hd Lt   54°06'·95N 00°04'·87W
302·50kHz   100M   Transmitting station 447
Reference station(s) 687 697

North Foreland   51°22'·49N 01°26'·85E
310·50 kHz   100M   Transmitting station 448
Reference station(s) 688 698

IRELAND

Tory Island Lt   55°16'·35N 08°14'·92W
313·50 kHz   150M   Transmitting station 435
Reference station(s) 670 694

Loop Head Lt   52°33'·65N 09°55'·90W
312·00 kHz   50M   Transmitting station 432
Reference station(s) 665 666

Mizen Head   51°27'·05N 09°48'·80W
300·50 kHz   100M   Transmitting station 430
Reference station(s) 660 661

FRANCE

Pointe de Barfleur   49°41'·87N 01°15'·87E
297·50 kHz   (TBN)   Transmitting station 330
Reference station(s) 460

Pointe S. Mathieu   48°19'·85N 04°46'·17W
291·50 kHz   40M   Transmitting station 332
Reference station(s) 462

Les Baleines Lt, Île de Ré   46°14'·70N 01°33'·60W
299·50 kHz   40M   Transmitting station 334
Reference station(s) 464

Pointe de la Coubre Lt   45°41'·87N 01°13'·93W
1655 & 3328·8 kHz   330M
Note: Specialist equipment needed to use this aid.

Cap Ferret Lt   44°38'·77N 01°14'·81W
287·00 kHz   40M   Transmitting station 336
Reference station(s) 466

SPAIN (North and North-West Coast)

Punta Estaca de Bares Lt   43°47'·17N 07°41'·07W
310·00 kHz (TBN)   Transmitting station (TBN)
Reference station(s) (TBN)

Cabo Finisterre Lt   43°27'·45N 02°45'·08W
289·00 kHz   60M   Transmitting station 353
Reference station(s) 506 507

PORTUGAL

Cabo Carvoeiro Lt   39°21'·53N 09°24'·40W
301·00 kHz (TBN)   Transmitting station 62

Cabo Espichel Lt   38°24'·83N 09°12'·90W
306·00 kHz (TBN)   Transmitting station 351

BELGIUM

Oostende   51°14'·36N 02°55'·94E
311·50 kHz   38M   Transmitting station 420
Reference station(s) 640 641

NETHERLANDS

Ameland Lt   53°27'·02N 05°37'·60E
299·50 kHz   120M   Transmitting station 428
Reference station(s) 655 656

Hoek van Holland   51°58'·90N 04°06'·83E
287·90 kHz   120M   Transmitting station 425
Reference station(s) 650 651

GERMANY

Düne   54°11'·20N 07°54'·38E
313·00 kHz   70M   Transmitting station 491
Reference station(s) 822 823

DENMARK

Blåvandshuk Lt   55°33'·52N 08°05'·07E
296·50 kHz   120M   Transmitting station 452
Reference station(s) 705 706

Skagen W Lt   57°44'·98N 10°35'·78E
298·50 kHz   100M   Transmitting station 453
Reference station(s) 710 711

Hammerodde Lt, Bornholm 55°17'·97N 14°46'·43E
289·00 kHz   120M   Transmitting station 451
Reference station(s) 700 701

RADAR BEACONS

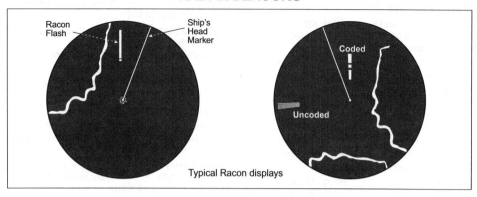

Typical Racon displays

RACONS (RADAR BEACONS)

Description

A Racon is a transponder beacon which, when triggered by a transmission from a vessel's radar, sends back a distinctive signal which appears on the vessel's radar display. Racons are often fitted to major light-vessels, lighthouses and buoys. They are shown on charts by a magenta circle and the word Racon.

In most cases the Racon flash on the radar display is a line extending radially outward from a point slightly beyond the actual position of the Racon, due to the slight delay in the response of the Racon apparatus. Thus the distance to the spot of the Racon flash is a little more than the vessels real distance from the Racon. Some Racons give a flash composed of a Morse identification signal, often with a tail to it, the length of the tail depending on the number of Morse characters.

The typical maximum range of a Racon is 10M, but may be as much as 25M. In practice, picking up a Racon at greater ranges depends on the power and elevation of both the Racon and the boat's radar. With abnormal radio propagation, a spurious Racon flash may be seen at much greater distances than the beacon's normal range, appearing at any random position along the correct bearing on the display. Only rely on a Racon flash if it appears to be consistent, and the boat is believed to be within its quoted range. At short range a Racon sometimes causes unwanted interference on the radar display, and this may be reduced by adjusting the rain clutter control on the set.

Radar beacon Listing

Radar beacons within the coverage area of this Almanac are shown in the following listing.

Details given in the listing are:

a. The name of the beacon.

b. Latitude and longitude.

c. Approximate range in nautical miles. This to some extent depends on the effective range of the yacht's radar set.

c. The morse identification signal. Racons coded 'D' are used to mark new dangers such as wrecks.

d. The sector within which signals may be received, if not 360° (all-round).

Most Racons respond throughout 360°. A few respond only within an angular sector, bearings quoted always being towards the beacon, clockwise from 000° to 359°. 360° indicates all round operation.

The majority of Racons sweep the frequency range of marine 3cm (X-band) radar emissions. The older type of Racon (swept frequency) take 30 to 90 seconds to sweep the band.

The newer type of Racon (frequency agile) responds immediately . to both 3cm and 10cm (S-band) emissions. In order that the Racon response should not obscure wanted echoes, the agile response is switched 'on' and 'off' at a predetermined rate to suit the installation.

RACONS – EUROPE

Name	Position		Range	Ident	Sector
ENGLAND – SOUTH COAST					
Bishop Rock Lt	49°52'·33N	06°26'·68W	15M	T	254°-2
Seven Stones Lt F	50°03'·58N	06°04'·28W	15M	O	360
Wolf Rock Lt	49°56'·67N	05°48'·48W	10M	T	360°
Eddystone Lt	50°10'·81N	04°15'·87W	10M	T	360°
Bridge Lt By	50°39'·59N	01°36'·80W	10M	T	
West Bramble Lt By	50°47'·17N	01°18'·57W	3M	T	360°
Nab Lt	50°40'·05N	00°57'·07W	10M	T	360°
Owers Lt By	50°37'·27N	00°40'·60W	10M	O	360°
MID CHANNEL					
Channel Lt F	49°54'·42N	02°53'·67W	15M	O	360°
East Channel	49°58'·67N	02°28'·87W	10M	T	360°
EC1 Lt By	50°05'·90N	01°48'·35W	10M	T	360°
EC2 Lt By	50°12'·10N	01°12'·40W	10M	T	360°
EC3 Lt By	50°18'·30N	00°36'·10W	10M	T	360°
Greenwich Lt V	50°24'·50N	00°00'·00	10M	M	360°
CHANNEL ISLANDS					
East Goodwin Lt F	51°13'·05N	01°36'·32E	10M	T	360°
Sandettié Lt F	51°09'·40N	01°47'·20E	10M	T	360°
Varne Lt V	51°01'·26N	01°24'·01E	10M	T	360°
East Channel Lt By	49°58'·67N	02°28'·87W	10M	T	360°
Channel Lt F	49°54'·42N	02°53'·67W	15M	O	360°
Casquets Lt	49°43'·38N	02°22'·55W	25M	T	360°
Platte Fougère Lt	49°30'·88N	02°29'·05W		P	
St Helier Demi de Pas Lt	49°09'·07N	02°06'·05W	10M	T	360°
ENGLAND – EAST COAST					
Inter Bank Lt By	51°16'·45N	01°52'·33E	10M	M	
North East Goodwin Lt By	51°20'·28N	01°34'·27E	10M	M	360°
Dover Strait TSS F3 Lt V	51°23'·82N	02°00'·62E	10M	T	360
Thames Reach Lt By No. 1	51°29'·42N	00°52'·67E	10M	T	360
Thames Reach Lt By No. 7	51°30'·08N	00°37'·15E	10M	T	360°
Outer Tongue Lt By	51°30'·69N	01°26'·50E	10M	T	360°
Barrow Lt By No. 3	51°41'·99N	01°20'·35E	10M	T	360°
South Galloper Lt By	51°43'·95N	01°56'·50E	10M	T	360
Sunk Lt F	51°51'·00N	01°35'·00E	10M	T	360°
Harwich Channel No 1 Lt By	51°56'·11N	01°27'·30E	10M	T	360°
Outer Gabbard Lt By	51°57'·80N	02°04'·30E	10M	O	360
North Shipwash Lt By	52°01'·70N	01°38'·38E	10M	M	360°
Orfordness Lt	52°05'·01N	01°34'·56E	18M	T	360°
Cross Sand Lt By	52°37'·00N	01°59'·25E	10M	T	360°
Winterton Old Lt	52°42'·75N	01°41'·82E	10M	T	360°
Smiths Knoll Lt By	52°43'·50N	02°18'·00E	10M	T	360
Newarp Lt V	52°48'·35N	01°55'·80E	10M	O	360°
Cromer Lt	52°55'·45N	01°19'·10E	25M	O	360°
North Haisbro Lt By	53°00'·20N	01°32'·40E	10M	T	360°
North Well Lt By	53°03'·00N	00°28'·00E	10M	T	360°
Dudgeon Lt By	53°16'·60N	01°17'·00E	10M	O	360°
Anglia Field Platform A48/19-B	53°22'·03N	01°39'·21E	15M	Q	360
Inner Dowsing Lt V	53°19'·50N	00°33'·96E	10M	T	360°
Dowsing Platform B1D	53°33'·65N	00°52'·75E	10M	T	360°
Spurn Lt F	53°33'·53N	00°14'·33E	5M	M	360°
Humber Lt By	53°36'·72N	00°21'·60E	7M	T	360°
Tees Fairway By	54°40'·93N	01°06'·37W		B	360°

Name	Position		Range	Ident	Sector
SCOTLAND – EAST AND NORTH COAST					
St Abb's Head Lt	55°54'·97N	02°08'·20W	18M	T	360°
Inchkeith Fairway By	56°03'·50N	03°00'·00W	5M	T	360°
Firth of Forth N Channel Lt By	56°02'·80N	03°10'·87W	5M	T	360°
Bell Rock Lt	56°26'·05N	02°23'·07W	18M	M	360
Abertay Lt By	56°27'·41N	02°40'·52W	8M	T	360°
Scurdie Ness Lt	56°42'·12N	02°26'·15W	14-16M	T	360
Girdle Ness Lt	57°08'·35N	02°02'·82W	25M	G	360°
Aberdeen Fairway By	57°09'·33N	02°01'·85W	7M	T	360°
Buchan Ness Lt	57°28'·23N	01°46'·37W	14-16M	O	360°
Rattray Head Lt	57°36'·62N	01°48'·83W	15M	M	360°
Kessock Bridge Centre Mark	57°29'·99N	04°13'·71W	6M	K	
Cromarty Firth Fairway By	57°39'·98N	03°54'·10W	5M	M	360°
Tarbat Ness Lt	57°51'·92N	03°46'·52W	14-16M	T	360
Saltire Oil Field Platform Saltire Alpha	58°25'·05N	00°19'·85E		Z	360°
Piper Oilfield, Platform PB	58°27'·68N	00°15'·07E		N	360°
Duncansby Head Lt	58°38'·67N	03°01'·42W	16M	T	360°
Lother Rock Lt	58°43'·82N	02°58'·59W	10M	M	360°
North Ronaldsay Lt	59°23'·40N	02°22'·80W	14-17M	T	360°
Rumble Rock Bn	60°28'·22N	01°07'·13W	8-10M	O	360°
Gruney Issland Lt	60°39'·20N	01°18'·03W	14M	T	360
Ve Skerries Lt	60°22'·40N	01°48'·67W	15M	T	360°
Foinaven Oil Field 204/24	60°18'·95N	04°16'·40W		X	360°
Sule Skerry Lt	59°05'·10N	04°24'·30W	20M	T	360°
SCOTLAND – WEST COAST					
Eilean Glas Lt	57°51'·43N	06°38'·45W	16-18M	T	360°
Ardivachar Pt	57°22'·90N	07°25'·45W	16M	T	360°
Carrach Rocks Lt By	57°17'·20N	05°45'·29W	5M	T	360°
Hyskeir Lt	56°58'·15N	06°40'·80W	14-17M	T	360°
Castlebay South By	56°56'·10N	07°27'·17W	7M	T	360°
Bo Vich Chuan Lt By	56°56'·17N	07°23'·25W	5M	M	360°
Skerryvore Lt	56°19'·40N	07°06'·90W	18M	M	360°
Dubh Sgeir Lt	56°14'·78N	05°40'·12W	5M	M	360
Sanda Lt	55°16'·50N	05°34'·90W	20M	T	360°
ENGLAND – WEST COAST					
Point of Ayre Lt	54°24'·95N	04°22'·03W	13-15M	M	360°
Halfway Shoal Lt Bn	54°01'·46N	03°11'·79W	10M	T	360°
Lune Deep Lt By	53°55'·80N	03°11'·00W	10M	T	360°
Bar Lt F	53°32'·00N	03°20'·90W	10M	T	360°
The Skerries Lt	53°25'·27N	04°36'·44W	25M	T	360°
The Smalls Lt	51°43'·23N	05°40'·10W	25M	T	360°
S. Gowan Lt By	51°31'·90N	04°59'·70W	10M	T	360°
West Helwick Lt By W.HWK	51°31'·37N	04°23'·58W	10M	T	360°
Swansea Bar Lt By W. Scar	51°28'·28N	03°55'·50W	10M	T	360°
Cabenda Lt By	51°33'·33N	03°52'·16W		Q	
English & Welsh Grounds Lt By	51°26'·90N	03°00'·10W	7M	T	360°
Second Severn Crossing Centre Lt SW	51°34'·42N	02°41'·94W		O	
Breaksea Lt F	51°19'·85N	03°18'·98W	10M	T	360°
NORTHERN IRELAND					
Hellyhunter Lt By	54°00'·34N	06°01'·99W	5-14M	K	
South Rock Lt F	54°24'·47N	05°21'·92W	13M	T	360°
Mew Island Lt	54°41'·91N	05°30'·75W	14M	O	360°
East Maiden Lt	54°55'·73N	05°43'·61W	11-21M	M	360°
Rathlin East Lt	55°18'·10N	06°10'·20W	15-27M	G	089°-003°

Name	Position		Range	Ident	Sector
IRELAND					
Mizen Head Lt	51°26'·97N	09°49'·18W	24M	T	360°
Fastnet Lt	51°23'·33N	09°36'·14W	18M	G	360°
Cork Lt By	51°42'·90N	08°15'·50W	7M	T	360°
Hook Head Lt	52°07'·40N	06°55'·72W	10M	K	237°-177°
Coningbeg Lt F	52°02'·38N	06°39'·45W	13M	M	360°
Tuskar Rock Lt	52°12'·15N	06°12'·38W	18M	T	360°
Arklow Lanby	52°39'·50N	05°58'·10W	10M	0	360°
Codling Lanby	53°03'·02N	05°40'·70W	10M	G	360°
Dublin Bay Lt By	53°19'·90N	06°04'·58W		M	
Kish Bank Lt	53°18'·68N	05°55'·38W	15M	T	360°
FRANCE					
Dyck (Dunkerque Approach) Lt By	51°02'·96N	01°51'·86E			360°
Vergoyer Lt By N	50°39'·70N	01°22'·30E	5-8M	C	360°
Bassurelle Lt By	50°32'·70N	00°57'·80E	5-8M	B	360°
Antifer Approach Lt By A5	49°45'·89N	00°17'·40W		K	360°
Le Havre LHA Lanby	49°31'·44N	00°09'·78W	8-10M		360°
Ouessant NE Lt By	48°45'·90N	05°11'·60W	20M	B	360°
Ouessant SW Lanby	48°31'·20N	05°49'·10W	20M	M	360°
Pointe de Créac'h Lt (Ile Ouessant)	48°27'·62N	05°07'·65W	20M	C	030°-248°
Chausée de Sein Lt By	48°03'·80N	05°07'·70W	10M	O	360°
S. Nazaire Lt By SN1	47°00'·12N	02°39'·75W	3-8M	Z	360°
S. Nazaire La Couronnée	47°07'·67N	02°20'·00W	3-5M		360°
BXA Lanby	45°37'·60N	01°28'·60W		B	360°
NORTH SPAIN					
Puerto de Pasajes Pilot Look-out	43°20'·17N	01°55'·39W	20M	K	
Punta Barracomuturra Lt Ondarroa	43°19'·60N	02°24'·86W	20M	X	360°
Bilbao Digue de Punta de Lucero Lt	42°22'·73N	03°04'·96W	20M	X	360°
Punta Rabiosa Front Ldg Lt	43°27'·58N	03°46'·35W	10M	K	360°
Punta Mera Front Lt	43°23'·08N	08°21'·17W	18M	M	020°-196°
Cabo Villano Lt	43°09'·68N	09°12'·60W	35M	M	360°
Toriñana Monte Xastas	43°01'·82N	09°16'·43W	35M	T	360°
Cabo Finisterre Lt	42°53'·00N	09°16'·23W	35M	O	360°
Cabo Estay Front Leg Lt	42°11'·20N	08°48'·73W	22M	B	
PORTUGAL					
Esteiro Lt	38°42'·14N	09°15'·51W	15M	Q	
Canal do Barreiro Lt By No. 13B IS	38°39'·21N	09°05'·74W	15M	Q	360°
Tejo Lt By	38°36'·23N	09°23'·60W	15M	C	
Porto de Setúbal Bn No. 2	38°27'·29N	08°58'·37W	15M	B	360°
SOUTH-WEST SPAIN					
Huelva (Dique)	37°06'·56N	06°49'·85W	12M	K	360°
Bajo Salmedina Lt	36°44'·36N	06°28'·55W	10M	M	
Tarifa Lt	36°00'·13N	05°36'·47W	20M	C	360°
BELGIUM					
West Hinder Lt	51°23'·36N	02°26'·35E		W	
West Hinder Route Lt By	51°20'·95N	02°43'·00E		K	
Wandelaar Lt MOW 0	51°23'·70N	03°02'·80E	10M	S	360°
Bol Van Heist MOW 3	51°23'·43N	03°11'·98E	10M	H	360°
NETHERLANDS					
Kweeten Lt By	51°36'·40N	03°58'·12E		K	360°
Zuid Vlije Lt By ZV11/SRK 4	51°38'·23N	04°14'·56E		K	360°
Noord Hinder Lt By NHR-SE	51°45'·50N	02°40'·00E	10M	N	360°
Noord Hinder Lt By	52°00'·15N	02°51'·20E		T	

Name	Position		Range	Ident	Sector
Noord Hinder Noord Lt By	52°10'·95N	03°04'·85E		K	
Schouwenbank Lt By	51°45'·00N	03°14'·40E	10M	O	360°
Goeree Lt	51°55'·53N	03°40'·18E	12-15M	T	360°
Maas Centre Lt By MC	52°01'·18N	03°53'·57E	10M	M	360°
Scheveningen Approach R&W Lt By	52°09'·00N	04°05'·50E		Z	On trial
Scheveningen Approach Red Lt By	52°10'·80N	04°07'·15E		Q	On trial
Rijn Field Platform P15B	52°18'·48N	03°46'·72E	12-15M	B	030°-270°
IJmuiden Lt By	52°28'·70N	04°23'·93E	10M	Y	360°
Horizon P9-6 Platform	52°33'·20N	03°44'·54E		Q	
Helm Veld A Platform	52°52'·39N	04°08'·58E		T	360°
Schulpengat Fairway Lt By SG	52°52'·95N	04°38'·00E		Z	
DW Route Lt By BR/S	52°54'·95N	03°18'·15E		G	
Logger Platform	53°00'·90N	04°13'·05E	12-15M	X	060°-270°
NAM Field Platform K14-FA	53°16'·17N	03°37'·66E		7	360°
Vlieland Lanby VL-CENTER	53°27'·00N	04°40'·00E	12-15M	C	360°
Wintershall Platform L8-G	53°34'·92N	04°36'·32E	12-15M	G	000°-340°
Botney Ground BG/S Lt By	53°35'·78N	03°00'·98E		T	
Placid Field Platform PL-K9C-PA	53°39'·20N	03°52'·45E		8	360°
Markham Field Platform J6-A	53°49'·39N	02°56'·75E		M	000°-180°
West Frisesland Platform L2-FA-1	53°57'·65N	04°29'·85E		9	
DW Route Lt By	54°00'·35N	04°21'·41E		M	360°
Elf Petroland Platform F15-A	54°12'·98N	04°49'·71E		U	360°
DW Route Lt By EF	54°03'·30N	04°59'·80E		T	
DW Route Lt By EF/B	54°06'·65N	05°40'·00E		M	
NAM Field Platform F3-OLT	54°51'·30N	04°43'·60E		D	360°

GERMANY

Name	Position		Range	Ident	Sector
Westerems Lt By	53°36'·97N	06°19'·48E	8M	T	360°
Borkumriff Lt By	53°47'·50N	06°22'·13E	8M	T	360°
GW/EMS Lt F	54°10'·00N	06°20'·80E	8M	T	360°
German Bight Lt V	54°10'·80N	07°27'·60E	8M	T	360°
Jade/Weser Lt By	53°58'·33N	07°38'·83E	8M	T	360
Tonne 3/Jade 2 Lt By	53°52'·12N	07°47'·33E	8M	T	360
Elbe Lt F	54°00'·00N	08°06'·58E	8M	T	360°

DENMARK

Name	Position		Range	Ident	Sector
Skagens Rev, Route 'T' Lt By No.1	57°47'·15N	10°46'·10E	10M	T	360°
Skagen Lt	57°44'·20N	10°37'·90E	20M	G	360°
Thyboron Approach Lt By	56°42'·60N	08°08'·80E	10M	T	360°
Dan Oil Field Platform DUC-DF-C	55°28'·73N	05°06'·43E		U	
Gorm Oil Field, Platform 'C'	55°34'·85N	04°45'·60E	10M	U	360°
Dagmar Oil Field Platform 'A'	55°34'·63N	04°37'·18E		U	360°
Rolf Oil Field Platform 'A'	55°36'·40N	04°29'·57E		U	
Valdema Oil Field Platform 'A'	55°50'·10N	04°33'·77E		U	
Svend Gas Plaform 'A'	56°10'·76N	04°10'·89E		U	
Harald Gas Field Platform West 'B'	56°20'·75N	04°16'·40E		U	
Gradyb Approach Lt By	55°24'·67N	08°11'·69E	10M	G	360°

EMERGENCY VHF DF STATIONS

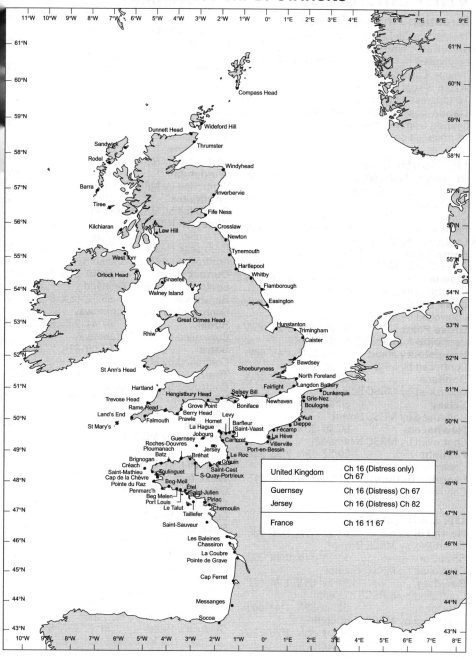

| 11°W | 10°W | 9°W | 8°W | 7°W | 6°W | 5°W | 4°W | 3°W | 2°W | 1°W | 0° | 1°E | 2°E | 3°E | 4°E | 5°E | 6°E | 7°E | 8°E | 9°E |

61°N — 61°N
60°N — 60°N

Compass Head

59°N — 59°N

Dunnett Head Wideford Hill

Sandwick Thrumster
Rodel

Windyhead

58°N — 58°N

Barra Inverbervie
Tiree
Fife Ness

57°N — 57°N

Kilchiaran Crosslaw
Law Hill Newton

56°N — 56°N

Tynemouth

West Torr Hartlepool
Whitby
Orlock Head Snaefell Flamborough
Walney Island Easington

55°N — 55°N
54°N — 54°N

Great Ormes Head Hunstanton
Rhiw Trimingham
Caister

53°N — 53°N

Bawdsey

St Ann's Head Shoeburyness
North Foreland

52°N — 52°N

Hartland Fairlight Langdon Battery
Trevose Head Hengistbury Head Selsey Bill Dunkerque
Rame Head Grove Point Boniface Gris-Nez
Land's End Berry Head Newhaven Boulogne
Falmouth Prawle Levy Ault
St Mary's Homet Barfleur Dieppe
La Hague Saint-Vaast Fécamp
Jobourg Carteret La Hève
Guernsey Villerville
Roches-Douvres Jersey Port-en-Bessin
Ploumanach Le Roc
Batz Bréhat Grouin
Brignogan Saint-Cast
Créach S-Quay-Portrieux
Saint-Mathieu Aulinguet
Cap de la Chèvre Beg-Meil
Pointe du Raz Étel
Penmarc'h Saint-Julien
Beg Melen Piriac
Port Louis Chemoulin
Le Talut
Taillefer
Saint-Sauveur

51°N — 51°N
50°N — 50°N
49°N — 49°N
48°N — 48°N

Les Baleines
Chassiron
La Coubre
Pointe de Grave

47°N — 47°N
46°N — 46°N

Cap Ferret

45°N — 45°N

Messanges

44°N — 44°N

Socoa

43°N — 43°N

United Kingdom	Ch 16 (Distress only) Ch 67
Guernsey	Ch 16 (Distress) Ch 67
Jersey	Ch 16 (Distress) Ch 82
France	Ch 16 11 67

VHF - Emergency

Direction Finding Service

This service is for emergency use only. Each direction- finding station is remotely controlled by an HM Coastguard Maritime Rescue Co-ordination Centre or Sub-Centre. Watch is kept on Ch 16. Ship transmits on Ch 16 (distress only) or Ch 67 in order that the station can determine its bearing. Ship's bearing from the station is transmitted on Ch 16 (distress only) or Ch 67.

UK South Coast

St Mary's, Scilly Isles	49°55'·70N	6°18'·17W

Controlled by MRCC Falmouth
| Land's End | 50°08'·13N | 5°38'·19W |

Controlled by MRCC Falmouth
| Falmouth | 50°08'·68N | 5°02'·69W |

Controlled by MRCC Falmouth
| Rame Head | 50°18'·99N | 4°13'·10W |

Controlled by MRSC Brixham
| Prawle | 50°13'·10N | 3°42'·48W |

Controlled from MRSC Brixham
| Berry Head | 50°23'·94N | 3°28'·97W |

Controlled by MRSC Brixham
| Grove Point | 50°32'·90N | 2°25'·13W |

Controlled from MRSC Portland
| Hengistbury Head | 50°42'·92N | 1°45'·56W |

Controlled by MRSC Portland
| Boniface | 50°36'·20N | 1°11'·95W |

Controlled by MRSC Solent
| Selsey | 50°43'·80N | 0°48'·15W |

Controlled by MRSC Solent
| Newhaven | 50°46'·90N | 0°03'·13E |

Controlled by MRSC Newhaven
| Fairlight | 50°52'·19N | 0°38'·83E |

Controlled from MRCC Dover
| Langdon Battery | 51°07'·91N | 1°20'·21E |

Controlled by MRCC Dover

UK East Coast

| North Foreland | 51°22'·50N | 1°26'·82E |

Controlled by MRCC Dover
| Shoeburyness | 51°31'·34N | 0°46'·69E |

Controlled by MRSC Thames
| Bawdsey | 51°59'·55N | 1°24'·59E |

Controlled by MRSC Thames
| Caister | 52°39'·59N | 1°43'·00E |

Controlled by MRCC Yarmouth
| Trimingham | 52°54'·55N | 1°20'·73E |

Controlled by MRCC Yarmouth
| Hunstanton | 52°56'·93N | 0°29'·70E |

Controlled by MRCC Yarmouth
| Easington | 53°39'·13N | 0°05'·95E |

Controlled by MRSC Humber
| Flamborough | 54°07'·08N | 0°05'·12W |

Controlled by MRSC Humber
| Whitby | 54°29'·40N | 0°36'·25W |

Controlled by MRSC Humber

Hartlepool 54°41'·79N 1°10'·47W
Controlled by MRSC Tyne/Tees
Tynemouth 55°01'·08N 1°24'·90W
Controlled by MRSC Tyne/Tees
Newton 55°31'·01N 1°37'·10W
Controlled by MRSC Tyne/Tees
Crosslaw 55°54'·50N 2°12'·20W
Controlled by MRSC Forth

Scotland

Fife Ness 56°16'·78N 2°35'·25W
Controlled by MRSC Forth
Inverbervie 56°51'·10N 2°15'·65W
Controlled by MRCC Aberdeen
Windyhead 57°38'·90N 2°14'·50W
Controlled by MRSC Aberdeen
Thrumster 58°23'·55N 3°07'·25W
Controlled by MRSC Pentland
Wideford Hill 58°59'·29N 3°01'·40W
Controlled by MRSC Pentland
Compass Head 59°52'·05N 1°16'·30W
Controlled by MRSC Shetland
Dunnet Head 58°40'·31N 3°22'·52W
Controlled by MRSC Pentland
Sandwick 58°12'·65N 6°21'·27W
Controlled by MRSC Stornoway
Rodel 57°44'·90N 6°57'·41W
Controlled by MRSC Stornoway
Barra 57°00'·81N 7°30'·42W
Controlled by MRSC Stornoway
Tiree 56°30'·62N 6°57'·68W
Controlled by MRSC Oban
Kilchiaran 55°45'·90N 6°27'·19W
Controlled by MRCC Clyde
Law Hill 55°41'·76N 4°50'·46W
Controlled by MRCC Clyde

UK West Coast

West Torr 55°11'·91N 6°05'·60W
Controlled by MRSC Belfast
Orlock Head 54°40'·41N 5°34'·97W
Controlled by MRSC Belfast
Snaefell 54°15'·82N 4°27'·59W
Controlled by MRSC Liverpool
Walney Island 54°06'·59N 3°15'·88W
Controlled by MRSC Liverpool
Great Ormes Head 53°19'·98N 3°51'·11W
Controlled by MRSC Holyhead
Rhiw 52°49'·98N 4°37'·69W
Controlled by MRSC Holyhead
St· Ann's Head 51°40'·97N 5°10'·52W
Controlled by MRSC Milford Haven
Hartland 51°01'·20N 4°31'·32W
Controlled by MRCC Swansea
Trevose Head 50°32'·91N 5°01'·89W
Controlled by MRCC Falmouth

Channel Islands

Guernsey 49°26'·27N 2°35'·77W
Jersey 49°10'·85N 2°14'·30W

FRANCE

Emergency use only Each station is remotely controlled either by CROSS or a Naval Lookout Station. Stations watch on Ch 16,11; 67. Ship transmits on Ch 16 (distress only) or Ch 11 in order that the station can determine its bearing. Ship's bearing from the station is transmitted on Ch 16 (distress only) or Ch 11

Dunkerque H24   51°03'·40N   2°20'·40E
Controlled by Signal Station
Gris-Nez H24   50°52'·20N   1°35'·00E
Controlled by CROSS
Boulogne HJ   50°44'·00N   1°36'·00E
Controlled by Signal Station
Ault   HJ   50°06'·50N   1°27'·50E
Controlled by Signal Station
Dieppe   HJ   49°56'·00N   1°05'·20E
Controlled by Signal Stn
Fécamp H24   49°46'·10N   0°22'·20E
Controlled by Signal Station
La Hève H24   49°30'·60N   0°04'·20E
Controlled by Signal Station
Villerville HJ   49°23'·20N   0°06'·50E
Controlled by Signal Station
Port-en-Bessin H24   49°21'·10N   0°46'·30W
Controlled by Signal Station
Saint-Vaast HJ   49°34'·50N   1°16'·50W
Controlled by Signal Station
Barfleur H24   49°41'·90N   1°15'·90W
Controlled by Signal Station
Levy   HJ   49°41'·70N   1°28'·20W
Controlled by Signal Station
Homet H24   49°39'·50N   1°37'·90W
Controlled by Lookout Station
Jobourg H24   49°41'·10N   1°54'·60W
Controlled by CROSS
La Hague HJ   49°43'·60N   1°56'·30W
Controlled by Signal Station
Carteret HJ   49°22'·40N   1°48'·30W
Controlled by Signal Station
Le Roc   HJ   48°50'·10N   1°36'·90W
Controlled by Signal Station
Grouin Cancale HJ   48°42'·60N   1°50'·60W
Controlled by Signal Station
Saint-Cast HJ   48°38'·60N   2°14'·70W
Controlled by Signal Station
S--Quay-Portrieux H24 48°39'·30N   2°49'·50W
Controlled by Signal Station
Roches-Douvres H24 49°06'·50N   2°48'·80W
Controlled by CROSS-Jobourg
Bréhat   HJ   48°51'·30N   3°00'·10W
Controlled by Signal Station
Ploumanach H24   48°49'·50N   3°28'·20W
Controlled by Signal Station

Batz   HJ   48°44'·80N   4°00'·60W
Controlled by Signal Station
Brignogan H24   48°40'·60N   4°19'·70W
Controlled by Signal Station
Créach Ouessant H24 48°27'·60N   5°07'·80W
Controlled by CROSS Corsen
Créach Ouessant HJ 48°27'·60N   5°07'·70W
Controlled by Signal Station
Saint-Mathieu H24   48°19'·80N   4°46'·20W
Controlled by Lookout Station
Toulinguet Camaret HJ 48°16'·80N   4°37'·50W
Controlled by Signal Station
Cap de La Chèvre HJ 48°10'·20N   4°33'·00W
Controlled by Signal Station
Pointe du Raz H24   48°02'·30N   4°43'·80W
Controlled by Signal Station
Penmarc'h H24   47°47'·90N   4°22'·40W
Controlled by Signal Station
Beg-Meil HJ   47°51'·30N   3°58'·40W
Controlled by Signal Station
Étel RG   H24   47°39'·80N   3°12'·00W
Controlled by CROSS
Beg Melen HJ   47°39'·20N   3°30'·10W
Controlled by Signal Stn
Port-Louis H24   47°42'·60N   3°21'·80W
Controlled by Lookout Station
Saint-Julien HJ   47°29'·70N   3°07'·50W
Controlled by Signal Station
Taillefer HJ   47°21'·80N   3°09'·00W
Controlled by Signal Station
Le Talut HJ   47°17'·70N   3°13'·00W
Controlled by Signal Station
Piriac   HJ   47°22'·50N   2°33'·40W
Controlled by Signal Station
Chemoulin H24   47°14'·10N   2°17'·80W
Controlled by Signal Station
Saint-Sauveur HJ   46°41'·70N   2°18'·80W
Controlled by Signal Station
Les Baleines HJ   46°14'·60N   1°33'·70W
Controlled by Signal Station
Chassiron HJ   46°02'·80N   1°24'·50W
Controlled by Signal Station
La Coubre H24   45°41'·90N   1°13'·40W
Controlled by Signal Station
Pointe de Grave HJ   45°34'·30N   1°03'·90W
Controlled by Signal Station
Cap Ferret HJ   44°37'·50N   1°15'·00W
Controlled by Signal Station
Messanges HJ   43°48'·80N   1°23'·90W
Controlled by Signal Station
Socoa   H24   43°23'·30N   1°41'·10W
Controlled by Signal Station

GMDSS

The Global Maritime Distress and Safety System (GMDSS) is a communications system introduced by the IMO in 1997, with a two year implementation period. All commercial vessels must now fully comply with the GMDSS requirements.

In essence the system makes use of improved digital communications and satellite systems to enable faster receipt and transmission of distress and safety communications between ships and/or shore stations. GMDSS is automated and does not involve Morse code nor the need to monitor calling channels.

However, the yachtsman, as a leisure user, is not required to fit a GMDSS VHF DSC or other GMDSS equipment, but it will be in his best interests to do so in the longer term. For inshore and coastal use around the UK a VHF set and a Navtex receiver will suffice for the present time. UK Coastguard intend to monitor Ch 16 for the foreseeable future (possibly up to the year 2005), and other yachts will still have their VHF sets. After February 1999, you may need GMDSS DSC to call other ships or ground stations unable to listen on VHF Ch 16.

How it works

GMDSS utilizes digital technology through Digital Selective Calling (DSC). New radios have this built in to specification MPT1279. This enables the yachtsman to call Coastguard, Coast Radio Stations and other vessels provided he has a Maritime Mobile Service Identity (MMSI). These are available on initial application or renewal of a radio licence.

The first three digits are the country code, which for the UK are 232 & 233. Shore stations all begin with 00.

Under GMDSS all vessels and shore stations maintain a DSC watch on VHF Ch70. This is the digital calling frequency and after calling station normal voice communication is then effected as normal.

Distress

In the event of a distress situation a dedicated button on the set is pressed which automatically transmits a distress message on Ch 70. If a GPS set is interfaced with the DSC unit position will also be transmitted. The distress alert will automatically be re-transmitted until acknowledged by the nearest Coastguard station.

Upon acknowledgment the GMDSS set retunes to Ch16 and the normal distress radio procedures are then followed.

Satellite EPIRBS and Search and Rescue Transponders (SART) are a part of the GMDSS. A SART responds to another vessel's radar up to 5 miles away.

Safety

Marine Safety Information (MSI) broadcasts are also transmitted automatically on GMDSS. Inshore and coastal waters utilise the Navtex system. For offshore areas beyond 300M from the coast you will require Inmarsat 'C' or MF/HF SSB.

VHF FREQUENCIES

In the UK certain frequencies are used by marinas, yacht clubs, rescue services etc:

VHF Ch	MHz	Use
0	156·000	UK Coastguard for SAR
M or M1	157·850	Marinas, yacht clubs, etc.
00	160·600	UK Coastguard for SAR
M2	161·425	Private: Yacht clubs, etc.

Distress, safety & calling

Ch	MHz	MHz	Note
75	156·7625	156·7875	Guard-band - do not use
16	156·800	156·800	Distress, safety & calling
76	156·8125	156·8375	Guard-band - do not use
67	156·375	156·375	Small ships safety chan
70	156·525	156·525	Digital selective calling

Intership

Channels listed in order of preference of use

Channels: 06, 08, 10, 13, 09, 72, 73, 69, 67, 77, 15, 17

Port operations - single frequency

Channels listed in order of preference of use

Channels: 12, 14, 11, 13, 09, 68, 71, 74, 10, 67, 69, 73, 17, 15

Port operations - two frequency

Channels listed in order of preference of use

Channels: 20, 22, 18, 19, 21, 05, 07, 02, 03, 01, 04, 78, 82, 79, 81, 80, 60, 63, 66, 62, 65, 64, 61, 84

Ship movements - single frequency

Channels listed in order of preference of use

Channels: 11, 68, 12, 69, 13, 71, 14, 74, 67, 10, 73, 09, 17, 15

Ship movements - two frequency

Channels listed in order of preference of use

Channels: 79, 80, 61, 64, 65, 62, 66, 63, 60, 81, 82, 84, 78, 04, 01, 03, 02, 07, 05, 21, 19, 18, 20, 22

Public correspondence

Channels listed in order of preference of use

Channels: 26, 27, 25, 24, 23, 28, 04, 01, 03, 02, 07, 05, 84, 87, 86, 83, 85, 88, 61, 64, 65, 62, 66, 63, 60, 82, 78, 81

Note - A Ship Radio Licence is required by anyone proposing to install or use a radio transmitter on board his vessel. To obtain a licence you must have a relevant qualification. Most pleasure boat users opt for the minimum (VHF only) qualification. Tuition and examination is organised by the RYA in most areas of the UK. A Callsign is issued together with a licence disc which must be displayed on your vessel's port side. A licence may also be obtained for a portable VHF handset allowing the operator to transmit from any vessel, but no Callsign is issued. Contact the Radiocommunications Agency and the RYA for further information.

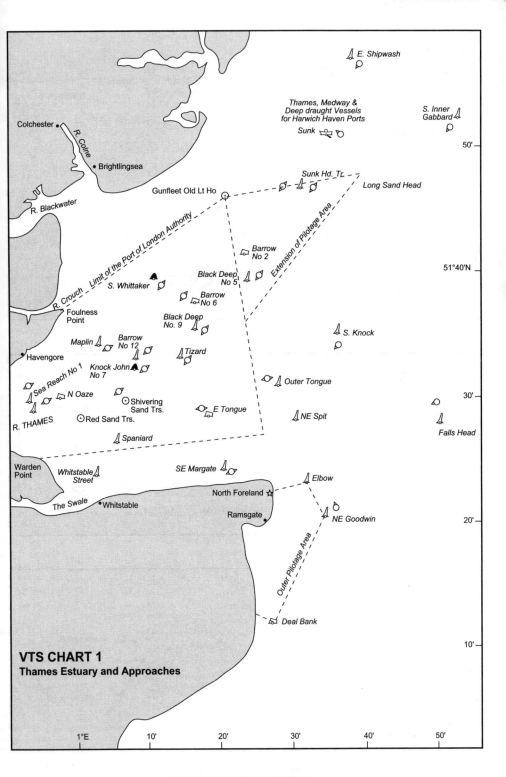

E. Shipwash

Thames, Medway &
Deep draught Vessels
for Harwich Haven Ports

Sunk

S. Inner
Gabbard

50'

Colchester

R. Colne

Brightlingsea

Sunk Hd. Tr.

Long Sand Head

R. Blackwater

Gunfleet Old Lt Ho

Limit of the Port of London Authority

R. Crouch

S. Whittaker

Barrow
No 2

Black Deep
No 5

Barrow
No 6

Extension of Pilotage Area

51°40'N

Foulness
Point

Black Deep
No. 9

S. Knock

Maplin

Barrow
No 12

Tizard

Havengore

Knock John
No 7

Sea Reach No 1

Outer Tongue

N Oaze

Shivering
Sand Trs.

30'

R. THAMES

Red Sand Trs.

E Tongue

NE Spit

Spaniard

Falls Head

Warden
Point

Whitstable
Street

SE Margate

Elbow

North Foreland

NE Goodwin

The Swale

Whitstable

Ramsgate

Outer Pilotage Area

20'

Deal Bank

10'

VTS CHART 1
Thames Estuary and Approaches

1°E   10'   20'   30'   40'   50'

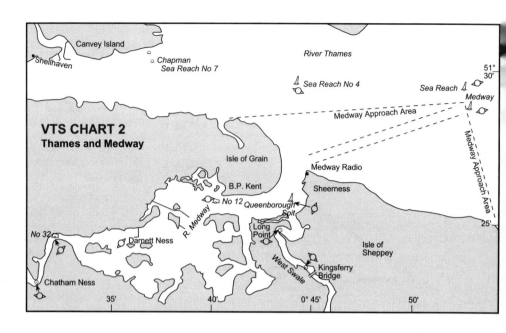

VTS CHART 2
Thames and Medway

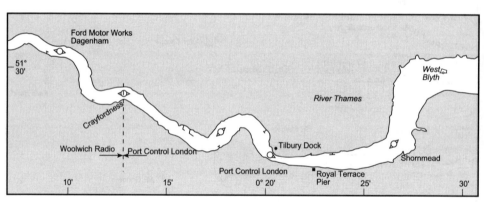

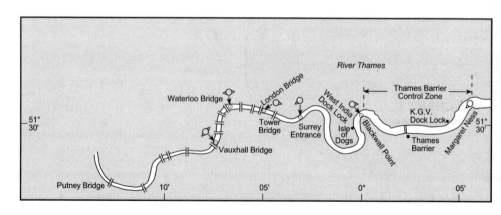

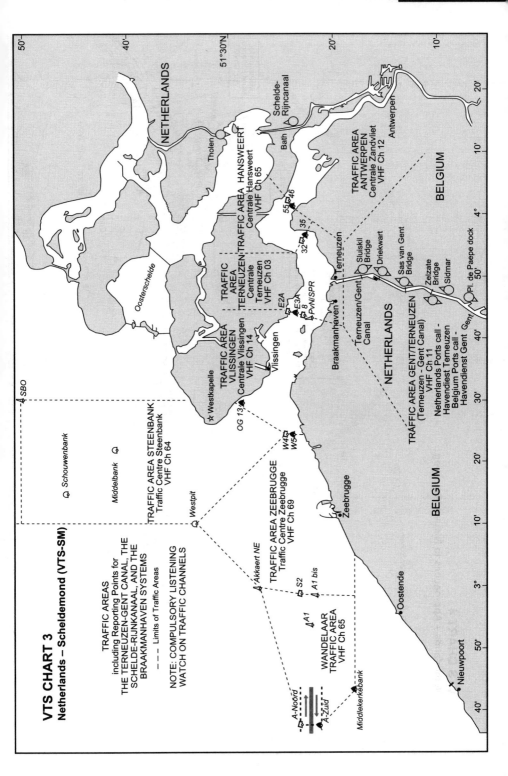

VTS CHART 3
Netherlands – Scheldemond (VTS-SM)

TRAFFIC AREAS
including Reporting Points for
THE TERNEUZEN-GENT CANAL, THE
SCHELDE-RIJNKANAAL, AND THE
BRAAKMANHAVEN SYSTEMS

– – – Limits of Traffic Areas

NOTE: COMPULSORY LISTENING
WATCH ON TRAFFIC CHANNELS

⚓ Schouwenbank

Middelbank ⚓

TRAFFIC AREA STEENBANK
Traffic Centre Steenbank
VHF Ch 64

⚓ SBO

★ Westkapelle

TRAFFIC AREA
VLISSINGEN
Centrale Vlissingen
VHF Ch 14

Vlissingen

OG 13

TRAFFIC AREA
TERNEUZEN
Centrale
Terneuzen
VHF Ch 03

E2A
E3A
8
PVN/SPR

Braakmanhaven

Terneuzen/Gent
Canal

TRAFFIC AREA GENT/TERNEUZEN
(Terneuzen - Gent Canal)
VHF Ch 11
Netherlands Ports call -
Havendienst Terneuzen
Belgium Ports call -
Havendienst Gent

NETHERLANDS

Sluiskil
Bridge
Driekwart
Sas van Gent
Bridge
Zelzate
Bridge
Sidmar
Pl. de Paepe dock

Gent

TERNEUZEN TRAFFIC AREA HANSWEERT
Centrale Hansweert
VHF Ch 65

32
35
55 46

TRAFFIC AREA
ANTWERPEN
Centrale Zandvliet
VHF Ch 12

Bath

Schelde-
Rijncanaal

Tholen

NETHERLANDS

Antwerpen

BELGIUM

Oosterschelde

Westpit

W4
W5

TRAFFIC AREA ZEEBRUGGE
Traffic Centre Zeebrugge
VHF Ch 69

Akkaert NE

S2
A1 bis

TRAFFIC AREA ZEEBRUGGE
Traffic Centre Zeebrugge
VHF Ch 69

Zeebrugge

A1

WANDELAAR
TRAFFIC AREA
VHF Ch 65

Middelkerkebank

BELGIUM

Oostende

Nieuwpoort

A-Noord
A-Zuid

51°30'N

50'
40'
40'
30'
20'
10'
4°
3°
50'
40'
10'
20'
10'
20'

VTS CHART 4
Netherlands – Approaches to Nieuwe Waterweg

- - - - Traffic Separation Scheme

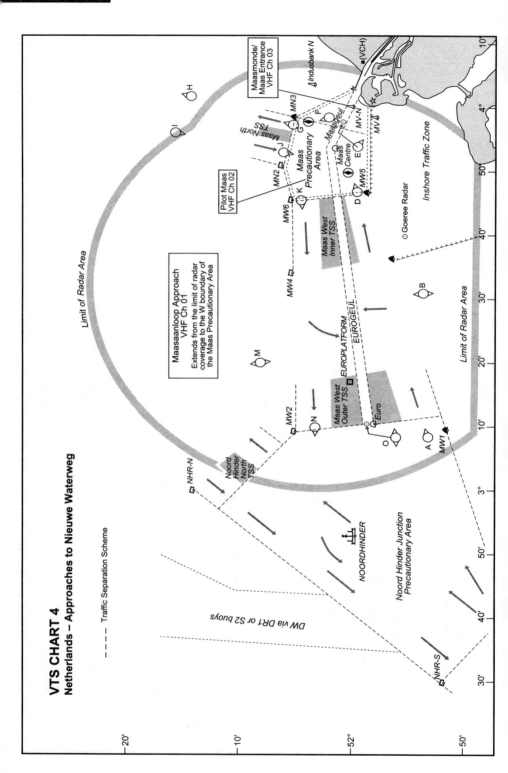

Limit of Radar Area

Maasmonde/
Maas Entrance
VHF Ch 03

Maas North TSS

Pilot Maas
VHF Ch 02

Maas Precautionary Area

Maas Centre

Maasgeul

MN3

MN2

MW6

MW5

MW4

MW2

MW1

Goeree Radar

Inshore Traffic Zone

Maas West Inner TSS

Maas West Outer TSS

EUROPLATFORM

EUROGEUL

Euro

Noord Hinder North TSS

NHR-N

Maasaanloop Approach
VHF Ch 01
Extends from the limit of radar
coverage to the W boundary of
the Maas Precautionary Area

NOORDHINDER

Noord Hinder Junction
Precautionary Area

DW via DR1 or S2 buoys

NHR-S

Limit of Radar Area

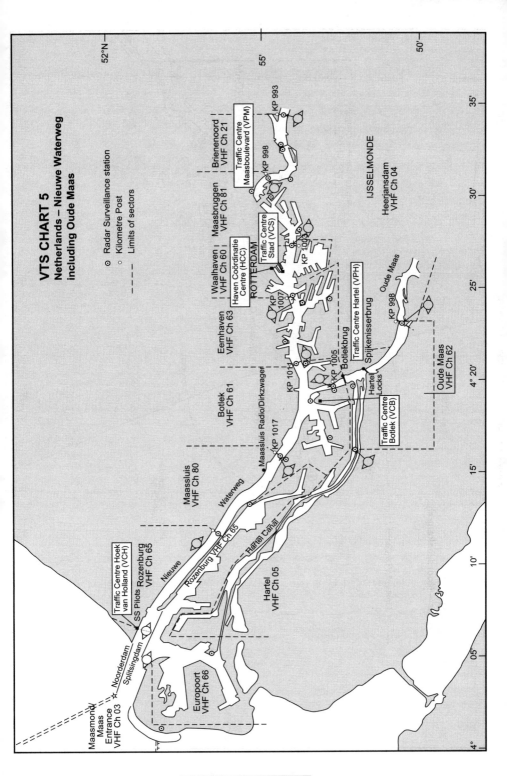

VTS CHART 5
Netherlands – Nieuwe Waterweg including Oude Maas

⊚ Radar Surveillance station
○ Kilometre Post
- - - Limits of sectors

ROTTERDAM

IJSSELMONDE

Traffic Centre Maasboulevard (VPM)
VHF Ch 21
KP 993
KP 998

Brienenoord
VHF Ch 21

Maasbruggen
VHF Ch 81

Waalhaven
VHF Ch 60

Traffic Centre Stad (VCS)
Haven Coördinatie Centre (HCC)
VHF Ch 60

KP 1003

Heerjansdam
VHF Ch 04

Eemhaven
VHF Ch 63

KP 1007

Oude Maas

Traffic Centre Hartel (VPH)

Spijkenisserbrug

KP 998

Botlek
VHF Ch 61

KP 1011

KP 1005
Botlekbrug

Hartel Locks

Oude Maas
VHF Ch 62

Maassluis Radio/Dirkzwager

KP 1017

Traffic Centre Botlek (VCB)

Maassluis
VHF Ch 80

Waterweg

Hartel Canal

Traffic Centre Hoek van Holland (VCH)
SS Pilots Rozenburg
VHF Ch 65

Nieuwe

Rozenburg VHF Ch 65

Hartel
VHF Ch 05

Noorderdam
Splitsingdam

Europoort
VHF Ch 66

Maasmond/
Maas
Entrance
VHF Ch 03

52°N
55'
50'
35'
30'
25'
4° 20'
15'
10'
05'
4°

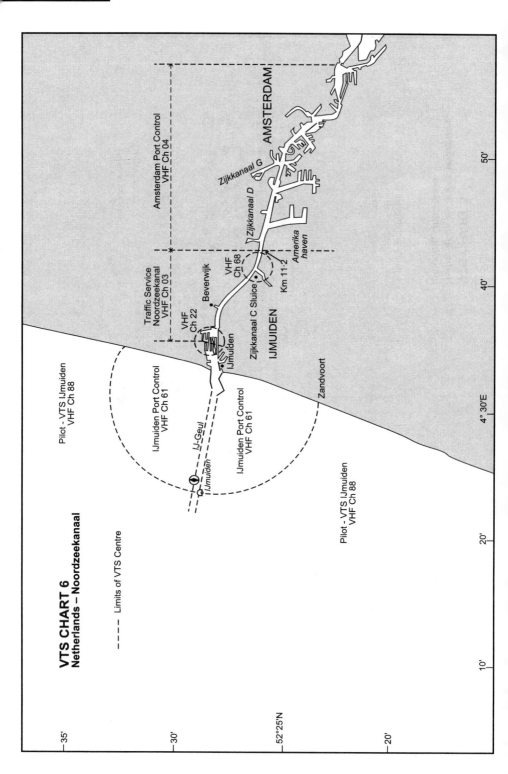

VTS CHART 6
Netherlands – Noordzeekanaal

– – – – Limits of VTS Centre

Pilot - VTS IJmuiden
VHF Ch 88

IJmuiden Port Control
VHF Ch 61

IJmuiden Port Control
VHF Ch 61

Pilot - VTS IJmuiden
VHF Ch 88

IJ-Geul

IJmuiden

Zandvoort

IJMUIDEN

IJmuiden

VHF Ch 22

Zijkkanaal C Sluice

VHF Ch 68

Km 11·2

Amerika haven

Beverwijk

Traffic Service
Noordzeekanaal
VHF Ch 03

Zijkkanaal D

Zijkkanaal G

Amsterdam Port Control
VHF Ch 04

AMSTERDAM

35'

30'

52°25'N

20'

10'   20'   4° 30'E   40'   50'

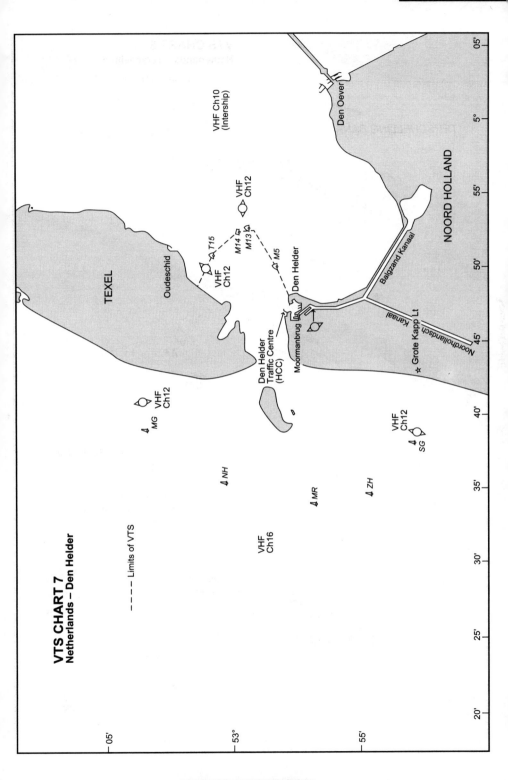

VTS CHART 7
Netherlands – Den Helder

– – – – Limits of VTS

TEXEL

Oudeschid

VHF Ch10
(Intership)

VHF
Ch12

T15

M14
M13

M5

VHF
Ch12

Den Helder

Den Helder
Traffic Centre
(HCC)

Moormanbrug

MG
VHF Ch12

NH

MR

ZH

VHF
Ch16

SG
VHF
Ch12

NOORD HOLLAND

Balgzand Kanaal

Noordhollandsch Kanaal

Grote Kapp Lt

Den Oever

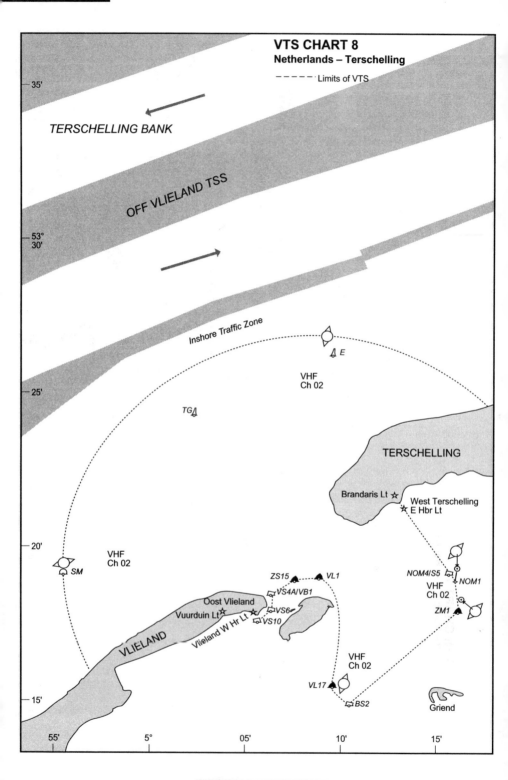

VTS CHART 8
Netherlands – Terschelling

– – – – Limits of VTS

35'

TERSCHELLING BANK

OFF VLIELAND TSS

53°
30'

Inshore Traffic Zone

E

VHF
Ch 02

25'

TG

TERSCHELLING

Brandaris Lt ☆

West Terschelling
☆ E Hbr Lt

20'

VHF
Ch 02

SM

ZS15   VL1

VS4A/VB1

NOM4/S5   NOM1

Oost Vlieland   VS6

Vuurduin Lt ☆   ☆

VHF
Ch 02

ZM1

Vlieland W Hr Lt   VS10

VLIELAND

VHF
Ch 02

VL17

BS2   Griend

15'

55'   5°   05'   10'   15'

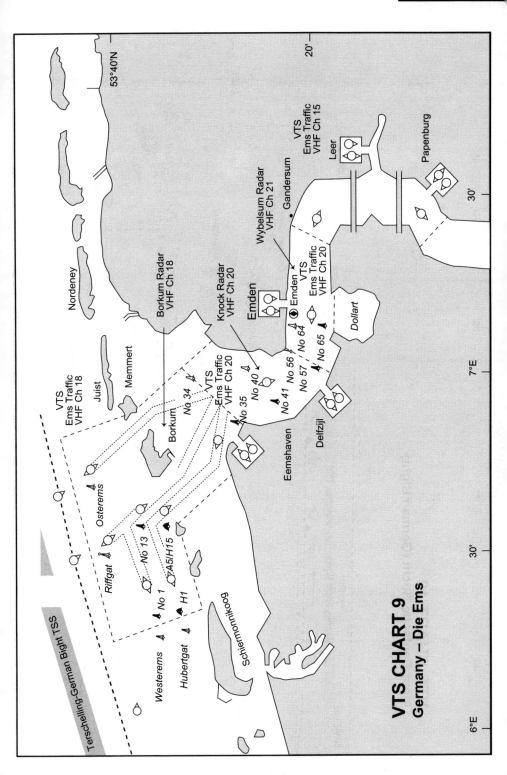

VTS CHART 9
Germany – Die Ems

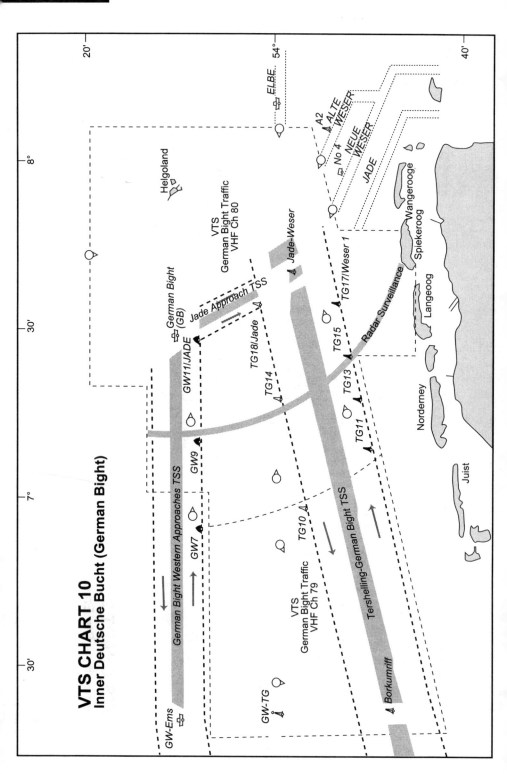

VTS CHART 10
Inner Deutsche Bucht (German Bight)

GW-Ems

GW-TG

German Bight Western Approaches TSS

GW7

GW9

GW11/JADE

German Bight (GB)

Helgoland

VTS German Bight Traffic VHF Ch 80

Jade Approach TSS

TG18/Jade

TG14

TG10

VTS German Bight Traffic VHF Ch 79

Tershelling-German Bight TSS

Borkumriff

TG11

TG13

TG15

TG17/Weser 1

Radar Surveillance

Jade-Weser

ELBE.

A2

No 4

ALTE WESER

NEUE WESER

JADE

Wangerooge

Spiekeroog

Langeoog

Norderney

Juist

20'

8°

30'

7°

30'

54°

40'

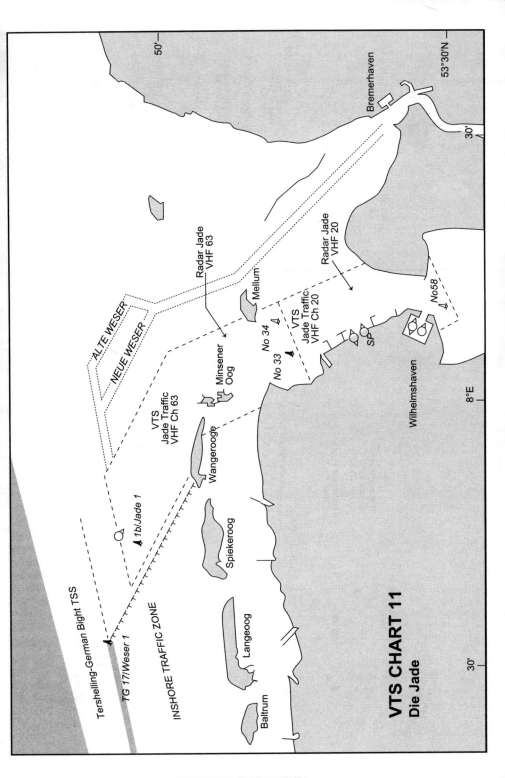

VTS CHART 11
Die Jade

Bremerhaven

53°30'N

30'

Radar Jade
VHF 63

Radar Jade
VHF 20

Mellum

No58

50'

No 34

VTS
Jade Traffic
VHF Ch 20

No 33

Minsener
Oog

SP

Wilhelmshaven

8°E

ALTE WESER

NEUE WESER

VTS
Jade Traffic
VHF Ch 63

Wangerooge

Spiekeroog

Langeoog

Baltrum

30'

1bI/Jade 1

Tershelling-German Bight TSS

TG 17/Weser 1

INSHORE TRAFFIC ZONE

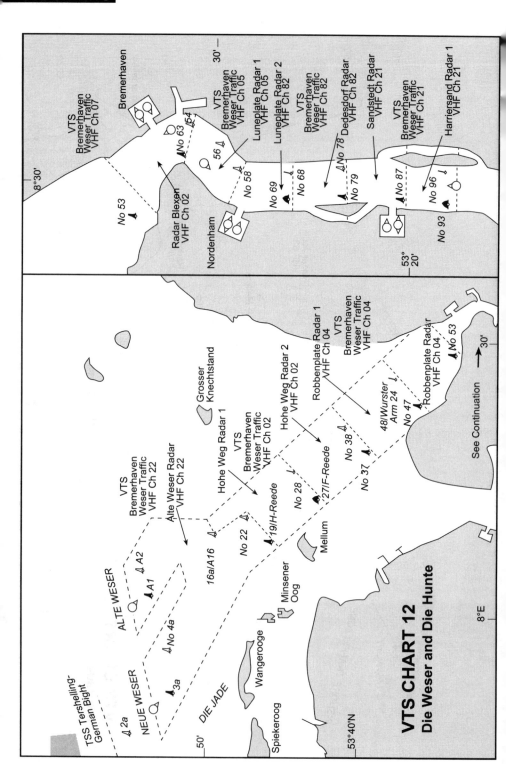

VTS CHART 12
Die Weser and Die Hunte

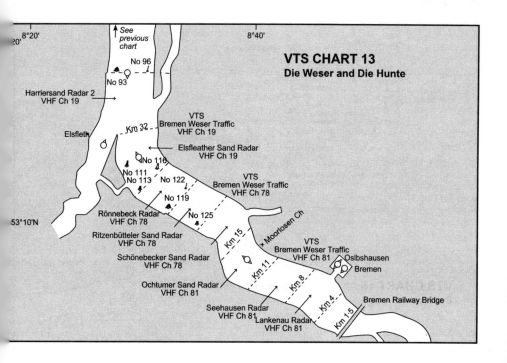

VTS CHART 13
Die Weser and Die Hunte

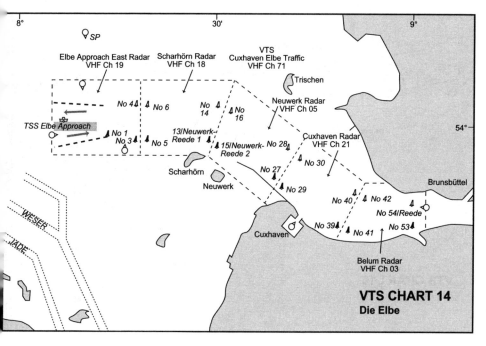

VTS CHART 14
Die Elbe

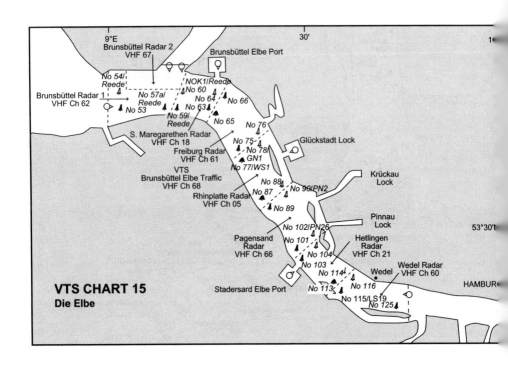

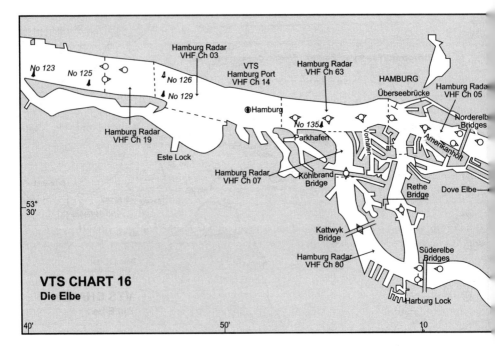

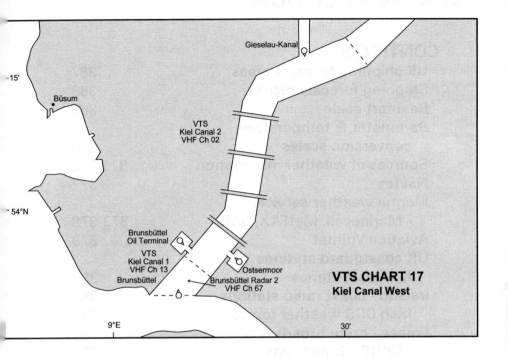

Gieselau-Kanal

Büsum

VTS
Kiel Canal 2
VHF Ch 02

-15'

-54°N

Brunsbüttel
Oil Terminal

VTS
Kiel Canal 1
VHF Ch 13

Brunsbüttel

Ostsermoor

Brunsbüttel Radar 2
VHF Ch 67

VTS CHART 17
Kiel Canal West

9°E

30'

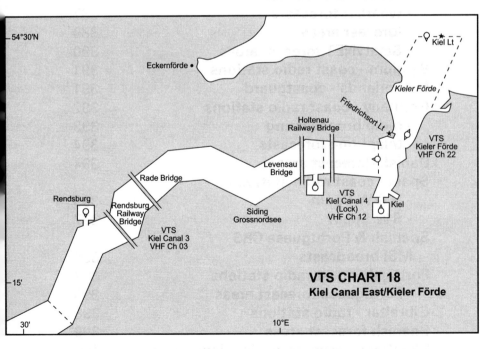

Kiel Lt

-54°30'N

Eckernförde

Kieler Förde

Friedrichsort Lt

Holtenau
Railway Bridge

VTS
Kieler Förde
VHF Ch 22

Levensau
Bridge

Rade Bridge

Rendsburg

Rendsburg
Railway
Bridge

VTS
Kiel Canal 3
VHF Ch 03

Siding
Grossnordsee

VTS
Kiel Canal 4
(Lock)
VHF Ch 12

Kiel

VTS CHART 18
Kiel Canal East/Kieler Förde

-15'

30'

10°E

WEATHER SECTION

CONTENTS

GENERAL WEATHER INFORMATION

Map of UK shipping forecast areas

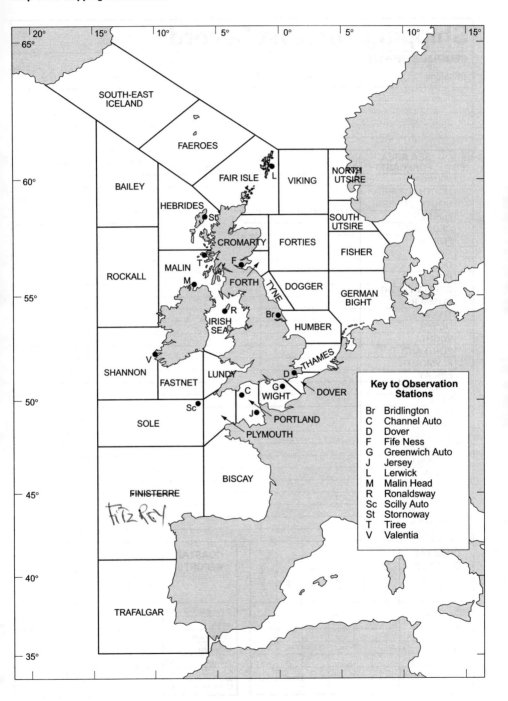

Key to Observation Stations

Br	Bridlington
C	Channel Auto
D	Dover
F	Fife Ness
G	Greenwich Auto
J	Jersey
L	Lerwick
M	Malin Head
R	Ronaldsway
Sc	Scilly Auto
St	Stornoway
T	Tiree
V	Valentia

Shipping Forecast Record

Shipping Forecast Record Time/Day/Date ....

GENERAL SYNOPSIS   at .... UT/BST

System	Present position	Movement	Forecast position	at

Gales	SEA AREA FORECAST	Wind (At first)	(Later)	Weather	Visibility
	VIKING				
	NORTH UTSIRE				
	SOUTH UTSIRE				
	FORTIES				
	CROMARTY				
	FORTH				
	TYNE				
	DOGGER				
	FISHER				
	GERMAN BIGHT				
	HUMBER				
	THAMES				
	DOVER				
	WIGHT				
	PORTLAND				
	PLYMOUTH				
	BISCAY				
	FINISTERRE				
	SOLE				
	LUNDY				
	FASTNET				
	IRISH SEA				
	SHANNON				
	ROCKALL				
	MALIN				
	HEBRIDES				
	BAILEY				
	FAIR ISLE				
	FAEROES				
	S E ICELAND				

COASTAL REPORTS at .... BST UT	Wind Direction	Force	Weather	Visibility	Pressure	Change
Tiree (T)						
Stornoway (St)						
Lerwick (L)						
Fife Ness (F)						
Bridlington (Br)						
Sandettie auto (S)						

COASTAL REPORTS	Wind Direction	Force	Weather	Visibility	Pressure	Change
Greenwich Lt V (G)						
Jersey (J)						
Channel auto (C)						
Scilly auto (Sc)						
Valentia (V)						
Ronaldsway (R)						
Malin Head (M)						

Beaufort scale

Force	Wind speed (knots)	(km/h)	(m/sec)	Description	State of sea	Probable wave ht(m)
0	0–1	0–2	0–0·5	Calm	Like a mirror	0
1	1–3	2–6	0·5–1·5	Light air	Ripples like scales are formed	0
2	4–6	7–11	2–3	Light breeze	Small wavelets, still short but more pronounced, not breaking	0·1
3	7–10	13–19	4–5	Gentle breeze	Large wavelets, crests begin to break; a few white horses	0·4
4	11–16	20–30	6–8	Moderate breeze	Small waves growing longer; fairly frequent white horses	1
5	17–21	31–39	8–11	Fresh breeze	Moderate waves, taking more pronounced form; many white horses, perhaps some spray	2
6	22–27	41–50	11–14	Strong breeze	Large waves forming; white foam crests more extensive; probably some spray	3
7	28–33	52–61	14–17	Near gale	Sea heaps up; white foam from breaking waves begins to blow in streaks	4
8	34–40	63–74	17–21	Gale	Moderately high waves of greater length; edge of crests break into spindrift; foam blown in well-marked streaks	5·5
9	41–47	76–87	21–24	Severe gale	High waves with tumbling crests; dense streaks of foam; spray may affect visibility	7
10	48–55	89–102	25–28	Storm	Very high waves with long overhanging crests; dense streams of foam make surface of sea white. Heavy tumbling sea; visibility affected	9
11	56–63	104–117	29–33	Violent storm	Exceptionally high waves; sea completely covered with long white patches of foam; edges of wave crests blown into froth. Visibility affected	11
12	64 plus	118 plus	33 plus	Hurricane	Air filled with foam and spray; sea completely white with driving spray; visibility very seriously affected	14

Notes: (1) The state of sea and probable wave heights are a guide to what may be expected in the open sea, away from land. In enclosed waters, or near land with an offshore wind, wave heights will be less but possibly steeper – particularly with wind against tide.

(2) It should be remembered that the height of sea for a given wind strength depends upon the fetch and length of time for which the wind has been blowing.

Barometer and temperature conversion scales

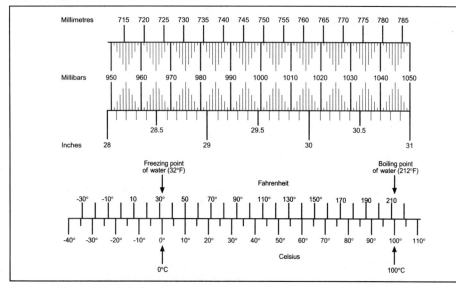

Terms used in weather bulletins

a. Speed of movement of pressure systems

Slowly:	Moving at less than 15 knots
Steadily:	Moving at 15 to 25 knots
Rather quickly:	Moving at 25 to 35 knots
Rapidly:	Moving at 35 to 45 knots
Very rapidly:	Moving at more than 45 knots

b. Visibility

Good:	More than 5 miles
Moderate:	2 – 5 miles
Poor:	1000 metres – 2 miles
Fog:	Less than 1000 metres

c. Barometric pressure changes (tendency)

Rising or falling slowly: Pressure change of 0·1 to 1·5 millibars in the preceding 3 hours.

Rising or falling: Pressure change of 1·6 to 3·5 millibars in the preceding 3 hours.

Rising or falling quickly: Pressure change of 3·6 to 6 millibars in the preceding 3 hours.

Rising or falling very rapidly: Pressure change of more than 6 millibars in the preceding 3 hours.

Now rising (or falling): Pressure has been falling (rising) or steady in the preceding 3 hours, but at the time of observation was definitely rising (falling).

d. Gale warnings

A *'Gale'* warning means that winds of at least force 8 (34-40 knots) or gusts reaching 43-51 knots are expected somewhere within the area, but not necessarily over the whole area. *'Severe Gale'* means winds of at least force 9 (41-47 knots) or gusts reaching 52-60 knots. *'Storm'* means winds of force 10 (48-55 knots) or gusts of 61-68 knots. *'Violent Storm'* means winds of force 11 (56-63 kn) or gusts of 69 kn or more, and *'Hurricane Force'* means winds of force 12 (64 knots or more).

Gale warnings remain in force until amended or cancelled ('gales now ceased'). If a gale persists for more than 24 hours the warning is re-issued.

e. Timing of gale warnings

Imminent	Within 6 hrs of time of issue
Soon	Within 6 – 12 hrs of time of issue
Later	More than 12 hrs from time of issue

f. Strong wind warnings

Issued, if possible 6 hrs in advance, when winds F6 or more are expected up to 5M offshore; valid for 12 hrs.

g. Wind

Wind direction: Indicates the direction from which the wind is blowing.

Winds becoming cyclonic: Indicates that there will be considerable changes in wind direction across the path of a depression within the forecast area.

Veering: The changing of the wind in a clockwise direction, i.e. SW to W.

Backing: The changing of the wind in an anti-clockwise direction, i.e. W to SW.

SOURCES OF WEATHER INFORMATION

RADIO BROADCASTING

BBC Radio 4 Shipping forecast

Shipping forecasts are broadcast by BBC Radio 4 at:

```
0048
0535
0542 Sun
0556 Sat
1201
1754
```

on the following frequencies:

LW   198 kHz

FM England:	92·4-94·6 MHz:	
Scotland:	92·4-96·1 MHz	
Scotland and Wales:	92·4-96·1 MHz and 103·5-104·9 MHz	
N Ireland and Wales:	103·5-104·9 MHz	
Channel Islands:	97·1 MHz	
MW Tyneside:	603 kHz;	
London and N Ireland:	720 kHz;	
Redruth:	756 kHz;	
Enniskillen and Plymouth:	774 kHz;	
Aberdeen:	1449 kHz;	
Carlisle:	1485 kHz.	

Contents of shipping forecast

The bulletin contains a summary of gale warnings in force; a general synopsis of weather patterns for the next 24 hours with changes expected during that period; and a forecast for each sea area for the next 24 hours, giving wind direction and speed, weather and visibility. Sea area Trafalgar is included only in the 0048 forecast. Gale warnings are also broadcast at the earliest juncture in Radio 4 programmes after receipt, as well as after the next news bulletin.

The forecast is followed by weather reports from coastal stations, as marked by their initial letters on the UK shipping forecast area chart. These reports of actual weather include wind direction and Beaufort force, present weather, visibility, and (if available) sea-level pressure and tendency.

The 1201 and 1754 forecasts do not contain reports from coastal stations.

On Sundays only, at 0542, a seven day planning outlook is broadcast which includes weather patterns likely to affect UK waters. On Saturdays only, at 0556, a three minutes "topical leisure" forecast is broadcast.

Shipping forecasts cover large sea areas, and rarely include the detailed variations that may occur near land. The Inshore waters forecast (see below) can be more helpful to yachtsmen on coastal passages.

Inshore waters forecast, BBC Radio 4

A forecast for inshore waters (up to 12M offshore) around the UK and N Ireland, valid until 1800, is broadcast after the 0535 and 0048 forecasts. It includes a general synopsis, forecasts of wind direction and force, visibility and weather for stretches of inshore waters referenced to well-known places and headlands, clockwise from Berwick-upon-Tweed.

Reports of actual weather at the following stations are broadcast only after the 0048 forecast: Boulmer, Bridlington, Sheerness, St Catherine's Point, Scilly auto, Milford Haven, Aberporth, Valley, Liverpool (Crosby), Ronaldsway, Machrihanish, Greenock MRCC, Stornoway, Lerwick, Wick auto, Aberdeen and Leuchars.

BBC general (land) forecasts

Land area forecasts may include an outlook period up to 48 hours beyond the shipping forecast, more details of frontal systems and weather along the coasts. The most comprehensive land area forecasts are broadcast by BBC Radio 4 .

Land area forecasts – Wind strength

Wind descriptions used in land forecasts, with their Beaufort scale equivalents, are:

Calm:	0	Fresh:	5
Light:	1–3	Strong:	6 – 7
Moderate:	4	Gale:	8

Land area forecasts – Visibility

The following definitions apply to land forecasts:

Mist:	Visibility between 2000m and 1000m
Fog:	Visibility less than 1000m
Dense fog:	Less than 50m

Weather systems

To obtain the best value from weather forecasts and reports, it is desirable to have some basic understanding of the characteristics and behaviour of different weather which can be expected from the passage of any particular type of weather system.

The following books provide further reading:

"This is Practical Weather Forecasting", by Dieter Karnetzki, published by Adlard Coles Nautical.

"The Weather Handbook" by Alan Watts, published by Waterline.

"Weather at Sea", by David Houghton, published by Fernhurst.

UK Local Radio Stations

Local radio stations (both BBC and commercial) sometimes broadcast marine weather forecasts and small craft warnings. The scope and quality of these forecasts vary considerably and broadcast times change constantly. Many of these stations provide only land forecasts.

Gale warnings and Strong Wind warnings (winds of Force 6 or more expected within the next 12 hrs, up to 5M offshore) are broadcast at the first programme juncture or after the first news bulletin following receipt.

NAVTEX

Introduction

Navtex prints or displays navigational warnings, weather forecasts and other safety information by means of a dedicated aerial and receiver with built-in printer or screen. It is a component of GMDSS.

All messages are in English on a single frequency of 518 kHz, with excellent coverage of Europe. A few stations, e.g. La Coruña (Spain), also transmit in the national language as well as English. Interference between stations is avoided by time sharing and by limiting the range of transmitters to about 300M. Thus three stations cover the UK.

The user programmes the receiver for the station(s) and message category(s) required. Nav warnings (A), Gale warnings (B) and SAR (D) are always printed.

Messages

Each message is prefixed by a four-character group. The first character is the code letter of the transmitting station (e.g: S for Niton). The second character is the message category, see next column. The third and fourth are message serial numbers, from 01 to 99. The serial number 00 denotes urgent messages which are always printed. Messages which are corrupt or have already been printed are rejected.

Navtex information applies only to the area for which the transmitting station is responsible, Fig 5 (1).

Weather information accounts for about 75% of all messages and is particularly valuable when out of range of other sources or if there is a language problem. The areas covered by the 3 UK stations are:

Cullercoats (G)	Faeroes clockwise to Wight
Niton (S)	Thames clockwise to Malin
Niton (K)	The French coast from Cap Gris Nez to Île Brehat
Portpatrick (O)	Lundy clockwise to Fair Isle

Message categories

A	Navigational warnings
B	Gale warnings
C	Ice reports (unlikely to apply in UK)
D	SAR information and pirate attack warnings
E	Weather forecasts
F	Pilot service messages
H	Loran-C messages
K	Other electronic navaid messages
L	Subfacts and Gunfacts for the UK
V	Amplifying details of nav warnings initially sent under A; plus the weekly oil rig list.
Z	No messages on hand at scheduled time

Stations

The table below shows Navtex stations in Navarea I to III with their identity codes and transmission time (UT). Times of weather messages are in bold.

Notes:

Oostende (M) transmits nav warnings for the are bounded by North Foreland and Lowestoft on the UK coast, longitude 03°E and the Belgian/French coast to Calais. **Oostende (T)** provides nav info for the Belgian coast and weather for sea areas Thames and Dover.

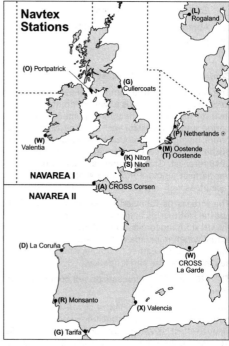

Navtex Stations

Fig. 5 (1)   Navtex areas – UK and NW Europe

NAVAREA I (Co-ordinator – UK)						
	Transmission times (UT)					
O – **Portpatrick**, UK	0220	0620	**1020**	1420	**1820**	2220
G – **Cullercoats**, UK	0100	0500	**0900**	1300	1700	**2100**
S – **Niton**, UK	0300	**0700**	1100	1500	**1900**	2300
K – **Niton**, UK (Note i above)	0140	0540	**0940**	1340	1740	**2140**
W – **Valentia**, Eire (on trial 1998)	No times published					
P – **Netherlands CG**, IJmuiden	0348	0748	1148	1548	1948	2348
M – **Oostende**, Belgium (Note ii)	0200	**0600**	1000	1400	1800	2200
T – **Oostende**, Belgium (Note ii)	0248	0648	1048	1448	1848	2248
L – **Rogaland**, Norway	0148	0548	**0948**	1348	1748	**2148**
NAVAREA II (Co-ordinator – France)						
A – **Corsen**, Le Stiff, France	0000	0400	0800	1200	1600	2000
D – **Coruña**, Spain	**0030**	0430	**0830**	**1230**	1630	**2030**
R – **Monsanto**, (Lisbon) Portugal	0250	0650	1050	1450	1850	2250
G – **Tarifa**, Spain	0050	0450	0850	1250	1650	2050
I – **Las Palmas**, Islas Canarias	0120	0520	**0920**	**1320**	**1720**	2120
NAVAREA III (Co-ordinator – Spain)						
X – **Valencia**, Spain	0350	0750	1150	1550	1950	2350
W – **La Garde**, (Toulon), France	0340	0740	1140	1540	1940	2340

TELEPHONE & FAX

Marinecall

Provides recorded telephone forecasts for 16 inshore areas around the UK. Dial **09068-500 + Area number** shown on the Marinecall map (see Fig. 5 (2). Calls cost 50p per minute at all times.

Forecasts cover the inshore waters out to 12M offshore for up to 48 hrs and include: General situation, any strong wind or gale warnings in force, wind, weather, visibility, sea state, maximum air temperature and sea temperature. The two-day forecasts are followed by forecasts for days three to five. Forecasts are updated at 0700 and 1900 daily. Area 432 (Channel Islands), is updated at 0700, 1300 and 1900 daily.

The local inshore forecast for Shetland is not given by Marinecall, but is available from Lerwick CG on ☎ 01595 692976. Or dial ☎ 09068 500 426 for a Weathercall general land forecast for Caithness, Orkney and Shetland.

Planning forecasts for the following areas are updated at 0800 daily.

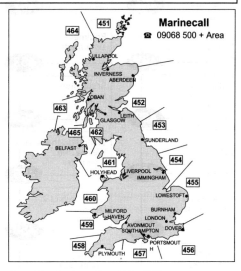

Fig 5 (2)   Marinecall and MetFAX areas

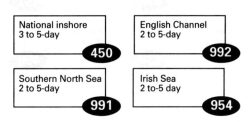

Coastal reports (Marinecall Select)

For latest weather reports and forecasts from 47 coastal stations dial ☎ 09068 110 010 and follow instructions, keying in the three-digit area number shown in Fig 5 (2), when requested.

Each of the 16 Marinecall areas contains two to four actual weather reports, which are updated hourly.

The reports include details of wind/gusts, visibility, weather, cloud, temperature, pressure and tendency. After these reports a two day or three – five day forecast for that area is available.

Weather by FAX (MetFAX marine)

MetFAX Marine provides printed weather forecasts and charts by dialling 09060 100 + the area number shown in Figs 5(3) and 5(4). Calls cost £1 per minute and the length of call is about 3 minutes. Do not forget to press the 'Start' button on you fax machine when a connection is made.

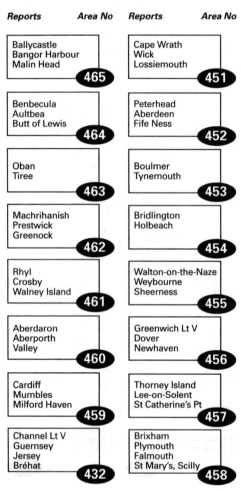

Reports	Area No	Reports	Area No
Ballycastle Bangor Harbour Malin Head	465	Cape Wrath Wick Lossiemouth	451
Benbecula Aultbea Butt of Lewis	464	Peterhead Aberdeen Fife Ness	452
Oban Tiree	463	Boulmer Tynemouth	453
Machrihanish Prestwick Greenock	462	Bridlington Holbeach	454
Rhyl Crosby Walney Island	461	Walton-on-the-Naze Weybourne Sheerness	455
Aberdaron Aberporth Valley	460	Greenwich Lt V Dover Newhaven	456
Cardiff Mumbles Milford Haven	459	Thorney Island Lee-on-Solent St Catherine's Pt	457
Channel Lt V Guernsey Jersey Bréhat	432	Brixham Plymouth Falmouth St Mary's, Scilly	458

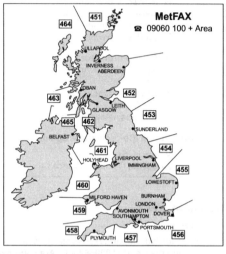

MetFAX
☎ 09060 100 + Area

Fig. 5 (3)   MetFAX planning forecast areas

For two day forecasts and charts for inshore waters covering the Areas shown in Fig. 5 (3), dial **09060 100 + Area No** required

For two to five day forecasts and 48/72 hour forecast charts for the Areas shown in Fig. 5 (4) dial **09060-100 + Area No** of the area required.

English Channel	09060-100 471
Channel Islands	09060-100 466
Southern North Sea	09060-100 472
Irish Sea	09060-100 473
North Sea	09060-100 469
North West Scotland	09060-100 468
Biscay	09060-100 470
National inshore 3-5 day	09060-100 450

For additional fax services dial 09060 100 plus:

24 hr shipping forecast	441
Guide to surface charts	446
Surface analysis chart	444
24 hr surface forecast chart	445
Chart of latest UK weather reports	447
Index to chart of UK weather reports	448
3-5 day UK inshore forecast and charts	450
Users guide to satellite image	498
Satellite image	499

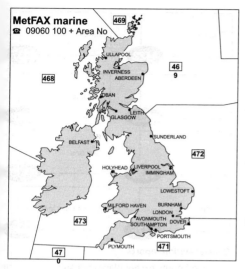

Fig. 5 (4)   MetFAX area planners

Mediterranean plotted weather reports	474
South Coast tide tables	497
Marine index	401

Note: MetFAX, MetCALL, MetWEB, Marinecall Select and MetFAX Marine are registered trademarks of the Meteorological Office.

Short Message Service (SMS) – introduction

By means of the SMS, the following weather information can be obtained from the Met Office via digital mobile telephones which utilise the Vodofone network:

a.   Coastal station weather reports

b.   Shipping forecasts for sea areas

c.   Inshore waters forecasts for seven new areas along the South coast of the UK.

It is likely that the service will be extended to cover other geographical areas in due course.

How to use SMS

Dial 0374 555 838 and follow the recorded main menu. It will prompt you to press:

Key 1	for service information
Key 2	to receive index of products on fax
Key 3	to order a product
Key 4	to connect to customer helpline
Key 0	to return to the main menu

After pressing Key 3, press key 1 for a one-off order or key 2 for a regular order. A regular order ensures that a product, e.g. shipping forecast for sea area around Tyne, is automatically sent to your mobile as it is updated four times during the day.

Then order the product by keying in the appropriate 4 digit code from the list below. The information will duly appear on the screen of your mobile. It can then be read, stored in memory or deleted.

Fig. 5 (5)   SMS areas

5.4.6   SMS forecast areas

Updated at 0530 for the period 0600 to 1200, 1130 for the period 1200 to 1800 and 1630 for the period 1700 to 2300.

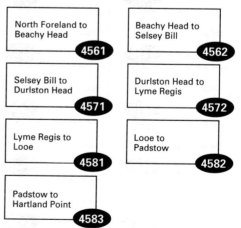

Shipping forecast Sea Areas

Updated at 0001, 0500, 100 and 1700 LT; valid for the same period as the BBC Radio 4 broadcasts.

Viking **4411**	Plymouth **4426**
North Utsira **4412**	Biscay **4427**
South Utsira **4413**	Finisterre **4428**
Forties **4414**	Sole **4429**
Cromarty **4415**	Lundy **4430**
Forth **4416**	Fastnet **4431**
Tyne **4417**	Irish Sea **4432**
Dogger **4418**	Shannon **4433**
Fisher **4419**	Rockall **4434**
German Bight **4420**	Malin **4435**
Humber **4421**	Hebrides **4436**

Thames **4422**	Bailey **4437**
Dover **4423**	Fair Isle **4438**
Wight **4424**	Faeroes **4439**
Portland **4425**	South East Iceland **4440**

Coastal station reports

Updated hourly, except places marked * which are updated every 3 hours i.e. 0000, 0300, 0600, etc...

Ballycastle, Bangor Harbour **4301**	Channel L/V, Guernsey **4313**
Oban, Greenock **4302**	Jersey, Brehat **4314**
South Uist, Tiree **4303**	Thorney Island, Lee-on-Solent **4315**
Aultbea, Stornoway **4304**	St Catherine's Point, Greenwich L/V **4316**
Machrihanish, Prestwick **4305**	Dover, Newhaven **4317**
Walney Island, St Bees Head **4306**	Walton-on-the-Naze, Sheerness **4318**
Rhyl, Crosby **4307**	Weybourne Holbeach **4319**

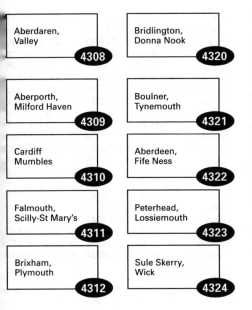

Aberdaren, Valley **4308**	Bridlington, Donna Nook **4320**
Aberporth, Milford Haven **4309**	Boulner, Tynemouth **4321**
Cardiff Mumbles **4310**	Aberdeen, Fife Ness **4322**
Falmouth, Scilly-St Mary's **4311**	Peterhead, Lossiemouth **4323**
Brixham, Plymouth **4312**	Sule Skerry, Wick **4324**

Charging information and Notes

Coastal reports (2 stations) and Shipping forecast sea areas are charged at 30p/message. The UK South coast forecasts are charged at 50p/message. Charges are only made for those messages received.

FORECASTERS

Weather Centres

Forecasts for port areas can be obtained at a charge from the Weather Centres listed below:

United Kingdom

Southampton	023 8022 8844
London	020 7696 0573 or 020 7405 4356
Birmingham	0121 717 0570
Norwich	01603 660779
Leeds	0113 245 1990
Newcastle	0191 232 6453
Aberdeen Airport	01224 210574
Kirkwall Airport, Orkney	01856 873802
Sella Ness, Shetland	01806 242069
Glasgow	0141 248 3489
Manchester	0161 477 1060
Cardiff	029 2039 7020
Bristol	0117 927 9298
Belfast International Airport	028 9094 2339
Jersey	01534 46111 Ext 2229

Republic of Ireland

Central Forecast Office, Dublin (H24)	(01) 424655
Dublin Airport Met	(01) 379900 ext 4531
Cork Airport Met (0900–2000)	(021) 965974
Shannon Airport Met (H24)	(061) 61333

Forecaster direct (MetCALL Direct)

A Met Office forecaster can be consulted by direct telephone line H24 for detailed discussion of, for example, the synoptic situation, specific weather windows or the longer term outlook. The consultancy would normally include a briefing and answers to any questions. A Fax forecast service is also available

To talk to a forecaster in the UK call ☎ 08074 767 888; from the Continent call ☎ + 44 8700 767 888. To talk to a forecaster in Gibraltar about weather in the Mediterranean or Canary Islands call ☎ 08700 767 818: from the Continent call + 44 8700 767 818. Payment of £15·00 is by credit card; there is no specified time limit, but 5-10 minutes is average. A Helpline is available on ☎ 08700 750 075.

Note: MetCALL is a trade mark of the Met Office.

HF RADIO FACSIMILE BROADCASTS

5.6.1 Introduction

Facsimile recorders that receive pictorial images such as weatherfax charts are now available for use in yachts and at marinas. Not all the meteorological information provided is relevant to the average yachtsman, but among items of direct interest are:

> Isobaric charts (actual and forecast)
> Sea and swell charts
> Satellite cloud images
> Sea temperature charts
> Wind charts.

Map areas and comprehensive schedules are published in the *Admiralty List of Radio Signals, Vol 3* (NP 283).

UK HF Fax stations

Internationally exchanged data is processed and transmitted from various centres. In the UK these are:

Bracknell (GFA) (England)

> 2618·5* 4610 8040 14436 18261** kHz
>
> * 1800-0600 UT only
>
> ** 0600-1800 UT only

Northwood (GYA) (GYZ) (GZZ) (England)

> 3652 4307 6452·5 8331·8 kHz

Schedule of selected UK Fax broadcasts

0230	Northwood	Schedule
0320	Northwood	General Met
0341	Bracknell	Surface analysis
0400	Northwood	Surface analysis
0431	Bracknell	24h surface analysis
0600	Northwood	Gale summary
0650	Northwood	General Met
0806	Bracknell	48h & 72h surface analysis
0935	Bracknell	24h sea state prog
0941	Bracknell	Surface analysis
0950	Northwood	General Met
1031	Bracknell	24h surface analysis
1040	Northwood	Routeing,significant winds
1045	Bracknell	48h & 72h surface analysis
1130	Northwood	Gale summary
1210	Northwood	General Met
1230	Northwood	Sea and swell, wave height
1500	Northwood	General Met
1530	Northwood	Schedule
1541	Bracknell	Surface analysis
1545	Northwood	Surface analysis
1631	Bracknell	24h surface analysis
1640	Northwood	Gale summary
1730	Northwood	Sea and swell, wave height
1800	Northwood	General Met
1950	Northwood	Gale summary
2018	Bracknell	24h sea state prog
2050	Northwood	Routeing, significant winds
2120	Northwood	General Met
2141	Bracknell	Surface analysis
2222	Bracknell	48h & 72h surface analysis
2231	Bracknell	24h surface analysis
2320	Northwood	General Met
2327	Bracknell	24h surface analysis

The quality of reception depends on the frequency used and the terrain between transmitter and receiver.

Additional frequencies to those above are also available for limited periods during any 24-hour period. Transmission frequencies and schedules are published in the Admiralty List of Radio Signals, Vol 3 (NP 283).

MISCELLANEOUS SOURCES

HM Coastguard

If requested the following MRCC/MRSCs may be prepared to supply reports of the present weather in their immediate vicinity. Such information only applies to reports of the present weather and do not include forecasts or information concerning other regions.

Falmouth:	☎ 01326 317575	🖪 01326 31834
Brixham:	☎ 01803 882704	🖪 01803 88278
Portland:	☎ 01305 760439	🖪 01305 76045
Solent:	☎ 023 9255 2100	🖪 023 9255 176
Dover:	☎ 01304 210008	🖪 01304 21030
Thames:	☎ 01255 675518	🖪 01255 67524
Yarmouth:	☎ 01493 851338	🖪 01493 85230
Humber:	☎ 01262 672317	🖪 01262 60691
Tyne Tees:	☎ 0191 2572691	🖪 0191 258037
Forth:	☎ 01333 450666	🖪 01333 45072
Aberdeen:	☎ 01224 592334	🖪 01224 57592
Pentland:	☎ 01856 873268	🖪 01856 87420
Shetland:	☎ 01595 692976	🖪 01595 69481
Stornoway:	☎ 01851 702013	🖪 01851 70438
Oban:	☎ 01631 563720	🖪 01631 56491
Clyde:	☎ 01475 729988	🖪 01475 78698
Belfast:	☎ 028 9056 3933	🖪 028 9056 588
Liverpool:	☎ 0151 931 3341	🖪 0151 931 334
Holyhead:	☎ 01407 762051	🖪 01497 76437
Milford Haven:	☎ 01646 690909	🖪 01646 69217
Swansea:	☎ 01792 366534	🖪 01792 36900

Internet (MetWEB)

A full range on meteorological information is now available over the Internet. This includes MetFAX marine services, two day and 3 to 5 day inshore forecasts, shipping forecasts, gale warnings; coastal reports charts and satellite images. Visit the Meteorological Office MetWEB site at:

www.met-office.gov uk

More information is available from the MetWEB Helpline ☎ 08700 750 077 or e-mail:

metweb@meto.gov.uk

Note: MetWEB is a trade mark of the Met Office.

Press forecasts

The interval between the time of issue and the time at which they are available next day make press forecasts of only limited value to yachtsmen. However, the better papers include a synoptic chart which, in the absence of any other chart, can help to interpret the shipping forecast.

Television forecasts

Some TV forecasts show a synoptic chart which, with the satellite pictures, can be a useful guide to the weather situation.

In the UK Ceefax (BBC) gives the forecast for inshore waters on page 409. Teletext (ITV) gives the shipping forecast on page 107 and the inshore waters and tide times on page 108.

Antiope is the equivalent French system. In some remote areas abroad a TV forecast in a bar, cafe or even shop window may be the best or only source of weather information.

Volmet

Volmet is a meteorological service provided for aviation which continuously transmits reports of actual weather conditions and/or weather forecasts for selected airfields on HF SSB and/or VHF.

It is possible to receive HF SSB Volmet broadcasts using a suitable portable radio (such as the Sony 7600), provided it is fitted with a SSB function. Reception can often be improved by using a short wire aerial instead of the built-in extendable whip aerial.

Yachtsman wishing to monitor closely the weather situation may find the Volmet reports useful as they are now the only available source of continual weather broadcasts. The continuously updated reports of actual weather conditions can be particularly valuable when drawing your own weather map see Fig. 5 (7) for airfield locations.

Reports contain: airport name, wind direction and speed, visibility, cloud amount and height, temperature and dew point, sea level pressure (QNH) and any significant weather.

The RAF Volmet continuously broadcasts actual weather reports for military and civil airports on:

5450 kHz   H24

11253 kHz   H24.

Broadcasts of airfields are made twice per hour in the slot times (in minutes past the hour) allocated below:

Slot 1   H+00/30 Aldergrove;Manchester;Prestwick; Stansted; Bardufoss (Norway); Bodo (Norway); Oslo (Norway); Gibraltar; Porto (Portugal).

Slot 2   H+06/36 Benson; Brize Norton; Bruggen; Geilenkirchen; Hannover; Laarbruch; Lyneham; Northolt; Odiham; Lyneham.

Slot 3   H+12/42 Coltishall; Cranwell, Leeming; Leuchars; Lossiemouth; Marham; St Mawgan; Waddington; Kinloss

Slot 4   H+18/48 Ascension; Bahrain; Brize Norton; Dakar (Senegal); Keflavik (Iceland); Nairobi (Kenya; Mombasa (Kenya); Montevideo; Rio de Janeiro (Brazil).

Slot 5   H+24/54 Adana (Turkey), Akrotiri (Cyprus), Ancona (Italy), Aviano (Italy); Gioia (Italy), Rimini (Italy), Rome (Italy) (Portugal); Skopje (Macedonia); Split (Croatia); Waddington (UK); Brindisi (Italy).

Shannon Volmet broadcasts on 3413 kHz (HN) and H24 on 5505 kHz, 8957 kHz and 13264 kHz (HJ). Groups of airports are broadcast every 5 mins. Coastal airports covered by this Almanac include: Shannon, Prestwick, Dublin, Amsterdam and Hamburg.

Fig. 5 (6)   Coastguard inshore waters areas

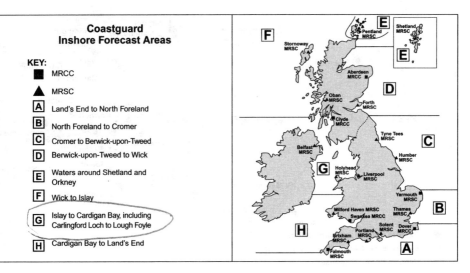

Note: The Inshore Waters forecast area boundaries above may be substituted for the MetFAX area boundaries shown in Fig. 5 (8).

Fig. 5 (7) Reports of present weather

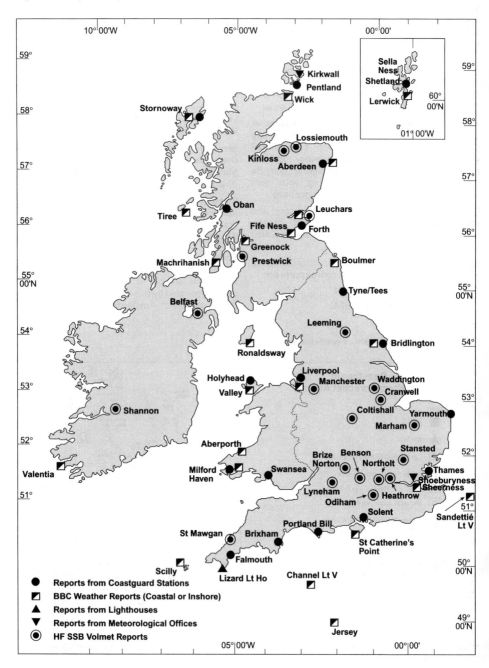

● Reports from Coastguard Stations
◪ BBC Weather Reports (Coastal or Inshore)
▲ Reports from Lighthouses
▼ Reports from Meteorological Offices
◉ HF SSB Volmet Reports

UK COASTGUARD STATIONS

Weather messages

Gale or strong wind warnings, weather messages and shipping forecasts will be broadcast on VHF Ch 10 and/
or Ch 73 and, where indicated below, on MF SSB after an initial announcement on VHF Ch 16, and 2182 kHz.

INSHORE WATERS FORECASTS

South Coast	Inshore area No			Times			
Falmouth	Area 458	0140	0540	0940	1340	1740	2140 UT
Brixham	Area 458	0050	0450	0850	1250	1650	2050 UT
Portland	Area 457	0220	0620	1020	1420	1820	2220 UT
Solent	Area 457	0040	0440	0840	1240	1640	2040 UT
Dover	Area 456	0105	0505	0905	1305	1707	2105 UT
East Coast							
Thames	Area 455	0010	0410	0810	1210	1610	2010 UT
Yarmouth	Area 455	0040	0440	0840	1240	1640	2040 UT
Humber	Area 454	0340	0740	1140	1540	1940	2340 UT
Tyne Tees	Area 453	0150	0550	0950	1350	1750	2150 UT
Forth	Area 452	0205	0605	1005	1405	1805	2205 UT
Aberdeen	Areas 451 & 452	0320	0720	1120	1520	1920	2320 UT
Pentland	Area 451	0135	0535	0935	1335	1735	2135 UT
Shetland	Local Shetland waters	0105	0505	0905	1305	1705	2105 UT
West Coast							
Stornoway	Area 464	0110	0510	0910	1310	1710	2110 UT
Oban	Area 463	0240	0640	1040	1440	1840	2240 UT
Clyde	Area 462	0020	0420	0820	1220	1620	2020 UT
Belfast	Area 465	0305	0705	1105	1505	1905	2305 UT
Liverpool	Area 461	0210	0610	1010	1410	1810	2210 UT
Holyhead	Areas 460 & 461	0235	0635	1035	1435	1835	2235 UT
Milford Haven	Areas 459 & 460	0335	0735	1135	1535	1935	2335 UT
Swansea	Area 459	0005	0405	0805	1205	1605	2005 UT

SHIPPING FORECASTS

South Coast		Shipping forecast areas	Times
Falmouth	VHF & MF 2226 kHz	Plymouth, Lundy, Fastnet and Sole	0940 and 2140 UT
Brixham	VHF	Plymouth, Portland and Wight	1020 and 2220 UT
Solent	VHF & MF 1641 kHz	Portland and Wight	0840 and 2040 UT
Dover	VHF	Thames, Dover and Wight	0905 and 2105 UT
East Coast			
Thames	VHF	Thames and Dover	0810 and 2010 UT
Yarmouth	VHF & MF 1869 kHz	Humber and Thames	0840 and 2040 UT
Humber	VHF & MF 2226 kHz	Tyne, Dogger and Humber	0740 and 1940 UT
Tyne Tees	VHF & MF 2719 kHz	Forth, Tyne, Dogger and Humber	0950 and 2150 UT
Forth	VHF	Forth, Tyne, Dogger and Forties	1005 and 2205 UT
Aberdeen	VHF & MF 2226 kHz	Fair I, Cromarty, Forth and Forties	0720 and 1920 UT
Pentland	VHF	Fair I, Cromarty and Viking	0935 and 2135 UT
Shetland	VHF & MF 1770 kHz	Faeroes, Fair I and Viking	0905 and 2105 UT
West Coast			
Stornoway	VHF & MF 1743 kHz	Fair I, Faeroes, Bailey, Malin and Hebrides	0910 and 2110 UT
Oban	VHF	Malin and Hebrides	0640 and 1840 UT
Clyde	VHF & MF 1883 kHz	Bailey, Hebrides, Rockall and Malin	0820 and 2020 UT
Belfast	VHF	Irish Sea and Malin	0705 and 1905 UT
Liverpool	VHF	Irish Sea and Malin	1010 and 2210 UT
Holyhead	VHF & MF 1880 kHz	Irish Sea	0635 and 1835 UT
Milford Haven	VHF & MF 1767 kHz	Lundy, Irish Sea and Fastnet	0735 and 1935 UT
Swansea	VHF	Lundy, Irish Sea and Fastnet	0805 and 2005 UT

Fig. 5 (8)   Coastguard weather forecasts

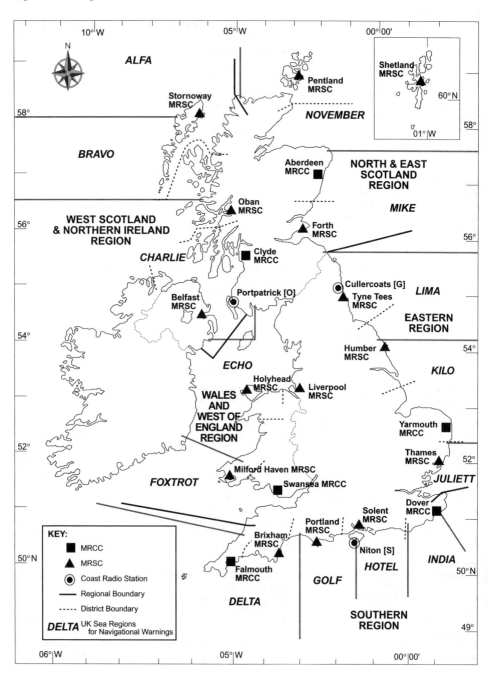

IRELAND

Coast Radio Stations

Weather bulletins for the Irish Sea and waters up to 30M off the Irish coast are broadcast on VHF at 0103 0403 0703 1003 1303 1603 1903 2203 (LT) after an initial announcement on Ch 16. Bulletins include gale warnings, synopsis and a 24-hour forecast. The stations and channels are:

Malin Head (DS)	Ch 23	**Glen Head** (DS)	Ch 24	**Belmullet** (DS)	Ch 83	**Clifden** (DS)	Ch 26
Shannon (DS)	Ch 28	**Valentia** (DS)	Ch 24	**Bantry** (DS)	Ch 23	**Cork** (DS)	Ch 26
Mine Head (DS)	Ch 83	**Rosslare** (DS)	Ch 23	**Wicklow Head** (DS)	Ch 87	**Dublin** (DS)	Ch 83
Greenore (DS)	TBN	**Crookhaven** (DS)	TBN	**Donegal Bay** (DS)	TBN		

Valentia Radio broadcasts on MF 1752 kHz forecasts for sea areas Shannon and Fastnet at 0833, 2033UT and on request.

Gale warnings are broadcast on above VHF channels on receipt and repeated at 0033 0633 1233 1833 (LT), after an initial announcement on Ch 16. They are also broadcast by Valentia Radio on 1752 kHz at the end of the next silence period after receipt and at 0303 0903 1503 2103 (UT) after an initial announcement on 2182 kHz.

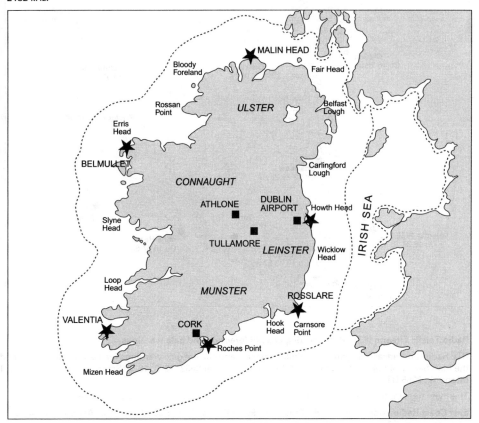

Fig. 5 (9) shows Provinces, coastal stations, ☆ and headlands referred to in forecasts; also RTE 1 and 2 transmitters ■

Fig 5 (10)   Irish CRS weather forecasts

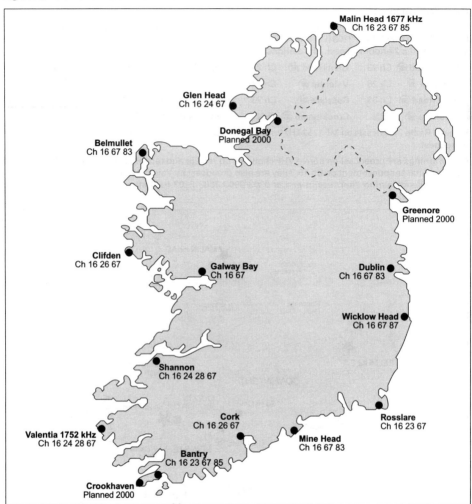

Malin Head 1677 kHz
Ch 16 23 67 85

Glen Head
Ch 16 24 67

Donegal Bay
Planned 2000

Belmullet
Ch 16 67 83

Greenore
Planned 2000

Clifden
Ch 16 26 67

Galway Bay
Ch 16 67

Dublin
Ch 16 67 83

Wicklow Head
Ch 16 67 87

Shannon
Ch 16 24 28 67

Cork
Ch 16 26 67

Rosslare
Ch 16 23 67

Valentia 1752 kHz
Ch 16 24 28 67

Mine Head
Ch 16 67 83

Bantry
Ch 16 23 67 85

Crookhaven
Planned 2000

Radio Telefis Eireann (RTE) Broadcasting coastal forecasts and gale warnings

RTE Radio 1 broadcasts a synopsis, detailed forecast and current gale warnings for Irish coastal waters and the Irish Sea, a 24 hrs outlook and coastal station reports at 0602, 1253, 1823 (Sat, Sun, Public Hols), 1824 (Mon-Fri), 2355 UT.

The main transmitters and FM frequencies are:

East Coast Radio: Kippure 89·1 MHz, Bray Head 96·2 MHz, Wicklow Head 102·9 MHz, Arklow 101·4 MHz.
At: Every H+06 (0700-1800 LT) after news bulletin

SE Radio: Mount Leinster 89·6 MHz, Gorey 96·2 MHz, Wexford 96·4 MHz.
At: 0712 LT (Mon-Fri) and every H+30 (0700-1800 LT) after commercial break.

LR FM: Faha Ring 95·1 MHz, Carrickpherish 97·5 MHz.
every H+03 and 1315 1815 LT broadcasts a general forecast, gale warnings, wind strength for area
om Youghal to Kilmore Quay. Tidal information included from Jun-Sep.

adio Kerry: Mullaghanish 90 MHz, Knockanure 97·6 MHz, Kilkieveragh 96·2MHz, Tralee 96·2 MHz.
:: 0004 0104 0704 0804 0835 0910 1004 1107 1204 1330 1404 1507 1607 1704 1740 1904 2204 2104 2304.
oadcasts a general forecast, synopsis, gale warnings and wind strength for the coastal area from
ork to Shannon.
:: 0755 and 1155 LT a fcst is broadcast including synopsis, visibility, sea state and wind strength for sea areas
astnet and Shannon. Three Rock 88·5 MHz, Maghera 88·8 MHz, Truskmore 88·2 MHz, Holywell Hill 89·2 MHz,
ermont Carn 95·2 MHz. MW – Tullamore 567 kHz.

torm warnings

ale warnings are broadcast by RTE Radio 1 at the first programme juncture after receipt and with news
ulletins; also by RTE 2FM from Athlone 612 kHz, Dublin 1278 kHz and Cork 1278 kHz.

ocal Radio stations which broadcast forecasts are shown, with frequencies, in the relevant part of Areas 12
nd 13.

elephone and Fax

he latest Sea area forecast and gale warnings can be obtained through Weatherdial ☎ 1550 123 855.
he same information, plus isobaric, swell and wave charts are available from Weatherdial Fax 🖹 on 1570
31 838 (H24).

RANCE

adio broadcasting

RANCE INTER (LW)
or all areas: storm warnings, synopsis, 24h fcst and outlook, broadcast in French at 2005 daily on 162 kHz.
n Sat/Sun at 0654, 2003 LT.

ADIO INTERNATIONALE (RFI)
FI broadcasts weather messages in French on HF at 1140 UT daily. Frequencies are: 6175 kHz for North Sea,
nglish Channel and Bay of Biscay; 11700 kHz, 15530 kHz and 17575 kHz for the North Atlantic, E of 50°W.

ADIO BLEUE (MW)
ssentially a music programme, but with Forecasts in French at 0655 LT covering:

nglish Channel and North Sea	–	**Paris**	864 kHz	**Lille**	1377 kHz
nglish Channel and East Atlantic	–	**Rennes**	711 kHz	**Brest**	1404 kHz
ay of Biscay and East Atlantic	–	**Bordeaux**	1206 kHz	**Bayonne**	1494 kHz

OCAL RADIO (FM)

Radio France Cherbourg 100·7

oastal forecast, storm warnings, visibility, wind strength, tidal information, small craft warnings, in French,
or the Cherbourg peninsula, broadcast at 0829 LT by:

Cherbourg	100·7 MHz	**St Vaast-la-Hougue**	85·0 MHz;
La Hague	99·8 MHz	**Barneville Carteret**	99·9 MHz.

Recorded forecasts by telephone

. MÉTÉO (Weather). The BQR (Bulletin Quotidien des Renseignements) is a very informative daily bulletin
isplayed in Hr Mr offices and YC's. For each French port, under TELEPHONE, Météo is the ☎ of a local Met
)ffice. Auto gives the ☎ for recorded inshore and Coastal forecasts; dial 08·36·68·08·dd (dd is the Départment
Io, shown under each port). To select the inshore (rivage) or Coastal (Côte; out to 20M offshore) bulletin, say
STOP" as your choice is spoken. Inshore bulletins contain 5 day forecasts, local tides, signals, sea temperature,
urf conditions, etc. strong wind/gale warnings, general synopsis, 24hrs forecast and outlook.

. For Offshore bulletins (zones du large) for Channel and North Sea, Atlantic or Mediterranean, dial
☎ 08·36·68·08·08. To select desired offshore area say "STOP" as it is named. Offshore bulletins contain
trong wind/gale warnings, the general synopsis and forecast, and the 5 day outlook.

CROSS VHF broadcasts

CROSS broadcasts in French, after an announcement on Ch 16: Gale warnings, synopsis, a 12 hrs foreca
48 hrs outlook for coastal waters. VHF channels, coastal areas covered and local times are shown below.
the English Channel broadcasts can also be given in English, on request Ch 16. Gale warnings are broadca
in French and **English** by all stations on VHF channels listed below at H+03 and at other times as shown.

CROSS GRIS-NEZ   Ch 79   **Belgian border to Baie de Somme**

Dunkerque	0720, 1603, 1920 LT
Gris-Nez	0710, 1545, 1910 LT
Ailly	0703, 1533, 1903 LT

Gale warnings on receipt, on request and at H+03 and H+10, in French and **English**.

CROSS JOBOURG   Ch 80   **Baie de Somme to Cap de la Hague**

Antifer	0803, 1633, 2003 LT	
Port-en-Bessin	0745, 1615, 1945 LT	
Jobourg	0733, 1603, 1933 LT	
Jobourg Traffic	H+20 and H+50	Cap de la Hague to Pte de Penmarc'h
Jobourg	0715, 1545, 1915 LT	
Granville	0703, 1533, 1903 LT	

Gale warnings in French and **English** on receipt, on request and at H+03. Also by Jobourg at H+20 & +50.

CROSS CORSEN   Ch 79   **Cap de la Hague to Pte de Penmarc'h** Times in **bold** = 1 May to 30 Sep.

Pte du Raz	0445, 0703, **1103**, 1533, 1903 LT
Le Stiff	0503, 0715, **1115**, 1545, 1915 LT
Ile de Batz	0515, 0733, **1133**, 1603, 1933 LT
Bodic	0533, 0745, **1145**, 1615, 1945 LT
Cap Fréhel	0545, 0803, **1203**, 1633, 2003 LT

Gale warnings in French and **English** on receipt, on request and at H+03.
Le Stiff broadcasts gale warnings at H+10 and H+40; also weather bulletins in French and **English** every
3 hrs from 0150 UT. All stations broadcast fog warnings in French and **English** when visibility requires.

CROSS ÉTEL   Ch 80   **Pte de Penmarc'h to L'Anse de l'Aiguillon (46°17'N 01°10'W)**

Penmarc'h	0703, 1533, 1903 LT
Groix	0715, 1545, 1915 LT
Belle Ile	0733, 1603, 1933 LT
St Nazaire	0745, 1615, 1945 LT
Ile d'Yeu	0803, 1633, 2003 LT
Les Sables d'Olonne	0815, 1645, 2015 LT

Gale warnings on receipt, on request and at H+03; in French, plus **English** in summer.

Sous-CROSS SOULAC   Ch 79   **L'Anse de l'Aiguillon to Spanish border**

Chassiron	0703, 1533, 1903 LT
Soulac	0715, 1545, 1915 LT
Cap Ferret	0733, 1603, 1933 LT
Contis	0745, 1615, 1945 LT
Biarritz	0803, 1633, 2003 LT

Gale warnings on receipt, on request and at H+03; in French, plus **English** in summer.
Station operates 0700 to 2200 LT. Night service is provided by CROSS Étel.

CROSS MF broadcasts

CROSS Gris Nez and CROSS Corsen both broadcast routine weather bulletins and gale warnings on 1650 kH
and 2677kHz in French, as follows:

CROSS	Routine bulletins	Areas covered (see Fig. 5(13))	Gale warnings
Gris Nez	0833, 2033 LT	Humber, Thames, French areas 12-14	On receipt, and at every odd H+03.
Corsen	0815, 2045LT	French areas 12-24	On receipt, and at every even H+03.

Fig. 5 (11)   French weather forecasts

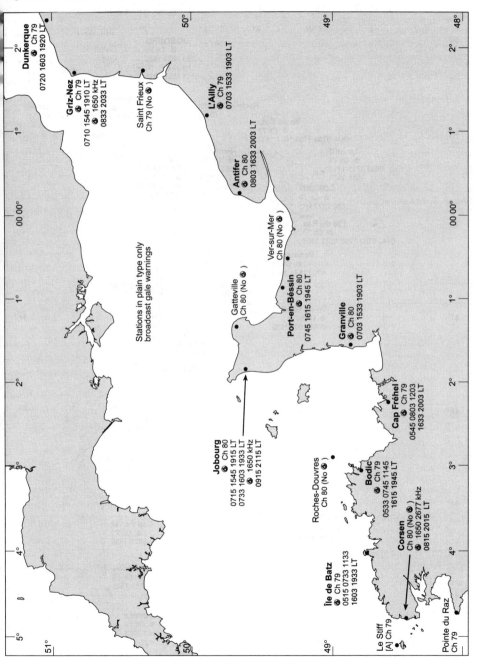

Stations in plain type only broadcast gale warnings

Dunkerque
Ch 79
0720 1603 1920 LT

Griz-Nez
Ch 79
0710 1545 1910 LT
1650 kHz
0833 2033 LT

Saint Frieux
Ch 79 (No ●)

L'Ailly
Ch 79
0703 1533 1903 LT

Antifer
Ch 80
0803 1633 2003 LT

Ver-sur-Mer
Ch 80 (No ●)

Gatteville
Ch 80 (No ●)

Port-en-Béssin
Ch 80
0745 1615 1945 LT

Granville
Ch 80
0703 1533 1903 LT

Jobourg
Ch 80
0715 1545 1915 LT
0733 1603 1933 LT
1650 kHz
0915 2115 LT

Roches-Douvres
Ch 80 (No ●)

Bodic
Ch 79
0533 0745 1145
1615 1945 LT

Cap Fréhel
Ch 79
0545 0803 1203
1633 2003 LT

Corsen
Ch 80 (No ●)
1650 2677 kHz
0815 2015 LT

Île de Batz
Ch 79
0515 0733 1133
1603 1933 LT

Le Stiff
[A] Ch 79

Pointe du Raz
Ch 79

Fig. 5 (12)   French weather forecasts

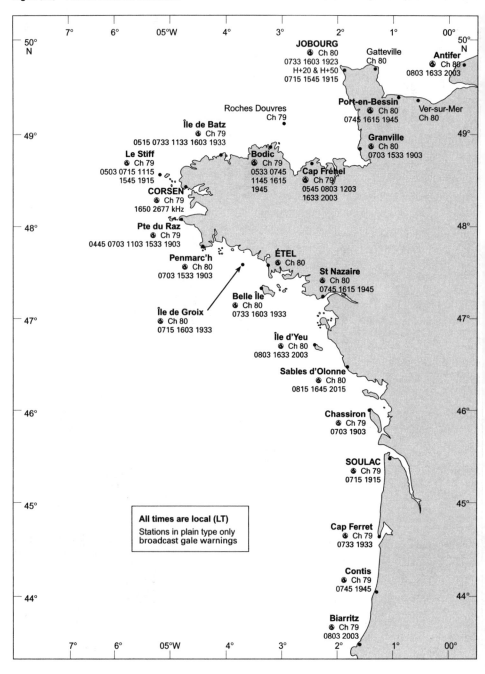

JOBOURG
④ Ch 80
0733 1603 1923
H+20 & H+50
0715 1545 1915

Gatteville
Ch 80

Antifer
④ Ch 80
0803 1633 2003

Roches Douvres
Ch 79

Port-en-Bessin
④ Ch 80
0745 1615 1945

Ver-sur-Mer
Ch 80

Île de Batz
④ Ch 79
0515 0733 1133 1603 1933

Granville
④ Ch 80
0703 1533 1903

Le Stiff
④ Ch 79
0503 0715 1115
1545 1915

Bodic
④ Ch 79
0533 0745
1145 1615
1945

Cap Fréhel
④ Ch 79
0545 0803 1203
1633 2003

CORSEN
④ Ch 79
1650 2677 kHz

Pte du Raz
④ Ch 79
0445 0703 1103 1533 1903

ÉTEL
④ Ch 80

Penmarc'h
④ Ch 80
0703 1533 1903

St Nazaire
④ Ch 80
0745 1615 1945

Belle Île
④ Ch 80
0733 1603 1933

Île de Groix
④ Ch 80
0715 1603 1933

Île d'Yeu
④ Ch 80
0803 1633 2003

Sables d'Olonne
④ Ch 80
0815 1645 2015

Chassiron
④ Ch 79
0703 1903

SOULAC
④ Ch 79
0715 1915

All times are local (LT)
Stations in plain type only
broadcast gale warnings

Cap Ferret
④ Ch 79
0733 1933

Contis
④ Ch 79
0745 1945

Biarritz
④ Ch 79
0803 2003

Fig. 5 (13)   France – Forecast areas

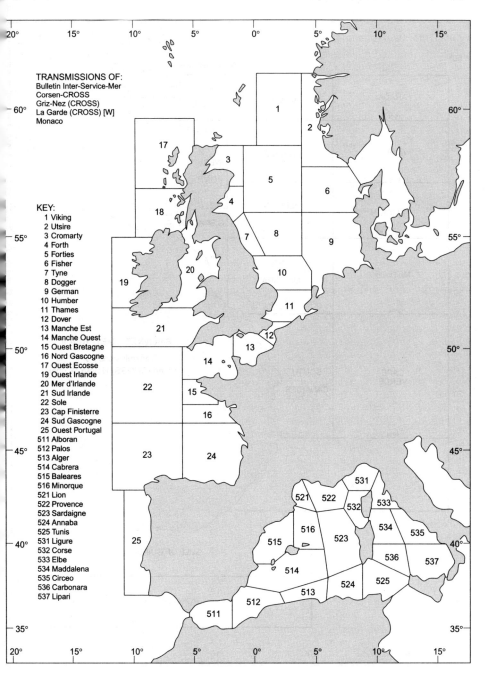

TRANSMISSIONS OF:
Bulletin Inter-Service-Mer
Corsen-CROSS
Griz-Nez (CROSS)
La Garde (CROSS) [W]
Monaco

KEY:
 1 Viking
 2 Utsire
 3 Cromarty
 4 Forth
 5 Forties
 6 Fisher
 7 Tyne
 8 Dogger
 9 German
10 Humber
11 Thames
12 Dover
13 Manche Est
14 Manche Ouest
15 Ouest Bretagne
16 Nord Gascogne
17 Ouest Ecosse
19 Ouest Irlande
20 Mer d'Irlande
21 Sud Irlande
22 Sole
23 Cap Finisterre
24 Sud Gascogne
25 Ouest Portugal
511 Alboran
512 Palos
513 Alger
514 Cabrera
515 Baleares
516 Minorque
521 Lion
522 Provence
523 Sardaigne
524 Annaba
525 Tunis
531 Ligure
532 Corse
533 Elbe
534 Maddalena
535 Circeo
536 Carbonara
537 Lipari

Fig. 5 (14)   France – SafetyNET forecast areas Metarea II

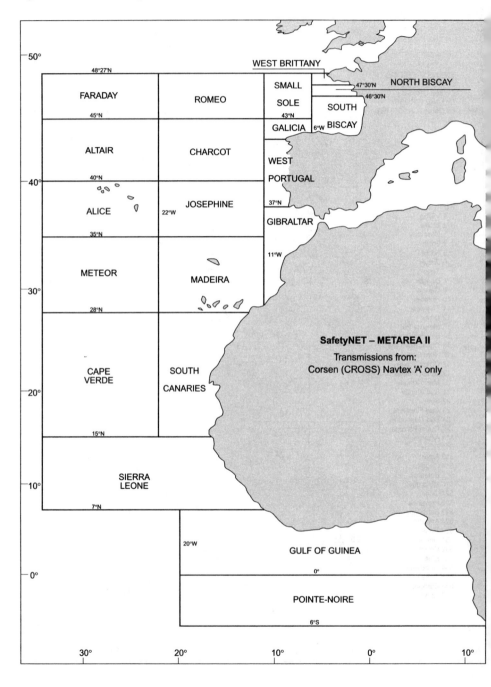

BELGIUM

Coast Radio Stations

Oostende Radio 🔘 broadcasts in English and Dutch strong breeze warnings and a forecast on 2761 kHz and VHF Ch 27 at 0820 and 1720 UT, valid for sea areas Thames and Dover. Gale warnings are issued in English and Dutch on receipt and after the next two silent periods.

Antwerpen Radio 🔘, on VHF Ch 24, broadcasts gale warnings on receipt and after the next two silent periods. Also strong wind warnings (F6+) on receipt and at every H+03 and H+48. All valid for the Schelde estuary.

Radio broadcasting

BRTN Radio 1 (Belgische Radio en Televisie) broadcasts weather messages in Dutch after the news at 0445, 0530, 0630, 0730, 0830, 1130, 1545, 1645, 1845, and 2245 LT. The frequencies are 927 kHz, 91·7 MHz, 94·2 MHz, 95·7 MHz and 98·5 MHz. The weather messages include the present situation, forecast for 24 hrs, outlook for the next few days and windspeed; valid for sea areas Humber, Thames, Dover, Wight and Portland.

NETHERLANDS

Netherlands Coastguard (IJmuiden) 🔘

a. VHF weather broadcasts

Weather messages are broadcast in Dutch at 0805, 1305, and 2305 LT by the remote stations on the VHF channels shown below. The messages include strong breeze and gale warnings, a synopsis, wind forecasts for up to 24 hrs. They are valid for Dutch coastal waters up to 30M offshore and the IJsselmeer.

Westkapelle 🔘	Ch 23	**Goes** 🔘	Ch 23	**Rotterdam** 🔘	Ch 87
Scheveningen 🔘🔘	Ch 83	**Haarlem** 🔘	Ch 25	**Lelystad** 🔘	Ch 23
Wieringermeer 🔘	Ch 27	**Huisduinen** 🔘	Ch 23	**Platform L7** 🔘	Ch 84
Terschelling 🔘	Ch 78	**Nes** 🔘	Ch 23	**Appingedam** 🔘	Ch 27

b. MF weather broadcasts

Netherlands Coastguard (IJmuiden) Radio 🔘 broadcasts weather messages in **English** and Dutch daily at 0940 and 2140 UT on 3673 kHz. The messages include: Near gale warnings, synopsis, 12hrs forecast, outlook for further 24hrs, and reports from coastal stations. The areas covered are the southern North Sea, Dutch coastal waters up to 30M offshore and the IJsselmeer.

Gale warnings are broadcast by Netherlands Coastguard on receipt, and at 0333, 0733, 1133, 1533, 1933 and 2333 UT.

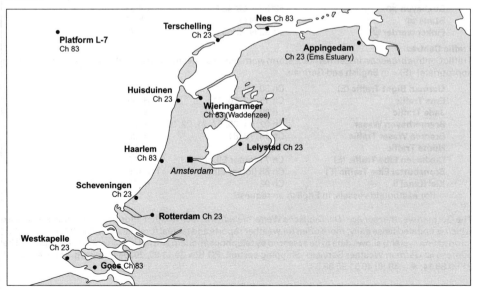

Fig. 5 (16)   German MSI broadcasts

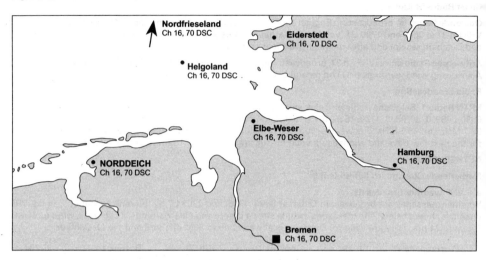

GERMANY

oast Radio stations – Hamburg/Cuxhaven (SMD – Schiffsmeldedienst)
SMD broadcast a weather report, synopsis, 12h forecast and outlook for a further 12h, in German, for Areas B10, B11, B12, N9, N10 and Eastern Boddenwässer at 0730 and 1530 UT. Broadcasts are first announced on Ch 16 before being broadcast on the channel below:

Nordsee ⑳	54°11'N 07°53'E	Ch 23
Cuxhaven ⑳	53°52'N 08°43'E	Ch 83
Stade ⑳	53°32'N 09°38'E	Ch 26
Finkenwerder ⑳	53°32'N 09°53'E	Ch 23

Traffic Centres
Traffic Centres broadcast in German local storm warnings, weather messages, visibility and ice reports (when appropriate). (E) = in **English** and German.

German Bight Traffic (E)	Ch 80	H+00
Ems Traffic	Ch 15, 18, 20, 21	H+50
Jade Traffic	Ch 20, 63	H+10
Bremerhaven Weser	Ch 02, 04, 05, 07, 21, 22, 82	H+20
Bremen Weser Traffic	Ch 19, 78, 81	H+30
Hunte Traffic	Ch 63	H+30
Cuxhaven Elbe Traffic (E)	Ch 71 (outer Elbe)	H+55
Brunsbüttel Elbe Traffic (E)	Ch 68 (lower Elbe)	H+05
Kiel Kanal II	Ch 02	H+15 and H+45
(for eastbound vessels, in English on request)		

The German weather service (*Der Deutsche Wetterdienst*) provides weather information through a databank which is updated twice daily; more often for weather reports and textual forecasts. SEEWIS (Marine weather information system) allows data to be accessed by telephone/modem and fed into an onboard computer. The address is: German Weather Service – Shipping section, PO Box 30 11 90, 20304 Hamburg. ☎ + 49 (0) 40 31 90 88 14; 🖷 + 49 (0) 40 31 90 88 03.

Radio broadcasting

Norddeutscher Rundfunk (NDR)

a.   NDR 1 Welle Nord (FM)
Weather messages in German, comprising synopsis, 12hrs forecast and 24 hrs outlook, are broadcast at 0830 LT (1 May – 30 Sept) for Helgoland, Elbe and North Frisian coast, by the following stations:
Helgoland 88·9 MHz; **Hamburg** 89·5 MHz; **Flensburg** 89·6 MHz; **Heide** 90·5 MHz; **Sylt** 90·9 MHz.

b.   NDR 4 Hamburg (MW)
Weather messages in German, comprising synopsis, 12hrs forecast and 24 hrs outlook, are broadcast at 0005, 0830 and 2220 LT on 702 & 972 kHz for Areas N9–N12.

Radio Bremen (RB1) (MW and FM)
Weather messages in German, comprising synopsis, 12hrs forecast and 24 hrs outlook, are broadcast at 0930 and 2305LT for Areas N9-N12, by the following stations:
Hansawelle 936, 6190 kHz; **Bremerhaven** 89·3 MHz; **Bremen** 93·8 MHz.
Also, about 0930LT, wind forecast for Weser-Ems area; and synopsis and forecast for next 12hrs in German Bight.

Deutschlandfunk (Köln) (MW)
Weather messages in German, comprising synopsis, 12hrs forecast and 24 hrs outlook, are broadcast at 0105, 0640 and 1105 LT for Areas N9-N12, on 1269 kHz.

Deutschland Radio (Berlin) (LW)
Weather messages in German, comprising synopsis, 12hrs forecast and 24 hrs outlook, are broadcast at 0105, 0640 and 1105LT for Areas N9-N12, on 177 kHz. Gale warnings in German follow the news.

Offenbach (Main) (HF)
The following **English** language broadcasts are made on 4583 kHz, 7646 kHz and 10100·8 kHz:

0505 UT	Synopsis, 12 hrs forecast, 24 hrs outlook for Fisher, German Bight and English Channel
1034 UT	Synopsis and 2 day forecast for the North Sea and Baltic
1059 UT	Synopsis and 2 day forecast for the North Sea and Baltic, with outlook for the next few days
1202 UT	Synopsis and 5 day forecast for the North Sea and Baltic
1740 UT	Synopsis, 12 hrs forecast, 24 hrs outlook for Viking, Forties, Dogger, Fisher and German Bight including station reports for the North Sea and Baltic
2113 UT	Weather report, synopsis and 2 day forecast for the North Sea

DENMARK
The following CRS broadcast in Danish and English gale warnings, synopsis and forecasts on th VHF and MF frequencies shown below.

	1734 kHz	On request
Bovbjerg ⊛	Ch 02	On request
Hanstholm ⊛	Ch 01	On request
Hirtshals ⊛	Ch 66	On request
Skagen ⊛	Ch 04	On request
	1758 kHz	On request

Radio broadcasts – Denmarks Radio (National Radio)
Broadcasts in Danish storm warnings, synopsis and 12h or 18h forecasts for all Danish Areas (Areas 16 to 20 from 1 Jan to 30 Apr only) and Jylland, Øerne and Bornholm, plus reports from coastal stations at 1100, 0445, 0745 1045 1645 and 2145 UT. Stations and frequencies are:

Kalundborg	243 kHz	**Kalundborg**	1062 kHz	**North Jutland**	96·6 MHz
West Jutland	92·9 MHz	**SW Jutland**	92·3 MHz	**South Jutland**	97·2 MHz

Fig. 5 (17)   Danish forecast areas

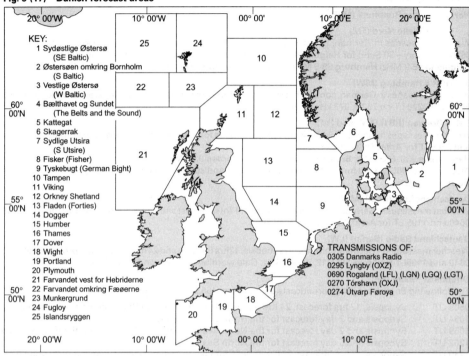

KEY:
1 Sydøstlige Østersø (SE Baltic)
2 Østersøen omkring Bornholm (S Baltic)
3 Vestlige Østersø (W Baltic)
4 Bælthavet og Sundet (The Belts and the Sound)
5 Kattegat
6 Skagerrak
7 Sydlige Utsira (S Utsire)
8 Fisker (Fisher)
9 Tyskebugt (German Bight)
10 Tampen
11 Viking
12 Orkney Shetland
13 Fladen (Forties)
14 Dogger
15 Humber
16 Thames
17 Dover
18 Wight
19 Portland
20 Plymouth
21 Farvandet vest for Hebriderne
22 Farvandet omkring Fæøerne
23 Munkergrund
24 Fugloy
25 Islandsryggen

TRANSMISSIONS OF:
0305 Danmarks Radio
0295 Lyngby (OXZ)
0690 Rogaland (LFL) (LGN) (LGQ) (LGT)
0270 Tórshavn (OXJ)
0274 Útvarp Føroya

German Telephone Forecasts

Similar to the British Marinecall; from 1 April – 30 Sept, forecast and outlook are available by dialling 0190 1160 plus two digits for the following areas:
 – 40 = Inland pleasure craft;
 – 45 = North Frisian Islands and Helgoland;
 – 46 = R Elbe from Elbe 1/Cuxhaven to Hamburg;
 – 47 = Weser Estuary and Jade Bay;
 – 48 = East Frisian Islands and Ems Estuary;
 – 53 = For foreign pleasure craft;
 – 54 = Denmark;
 – 55 = Netherlands.

For year round weather synopsis, forecast and outlook, dial 0190 1169 plus two digits as follows:
 – 20 = General information;
 – 21 = North Sea and Baltic;
 – 22 = German Bight and SW North Sea;
 – 31 = 5 day bulletin for North Sea and Baltic.
(Containing an outlook and forecasts of wind, sea state, air and water temperature, plus warnings of fog, thunderstorms etc.)

Strong wind (>F6) and storm warnings for the German North Sea coast may be obtained from ☎0403 196628 (H24); if no warnings are in force, a wind forecast is given.

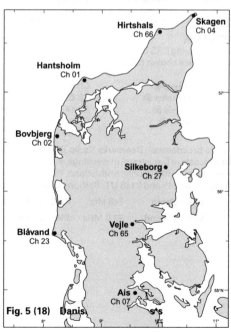

Fig. 5 (18)   Danish

SPAIN

NORTH AND NORTH WEST SPAIN

Coast Radio Stations
The following CRS broadcast in Spanish gale warnings, synopsis and forecasts for Areas 1-5 at the times and on the MF frequencies shown (there are no VHF weather broadcasts by CRS):

Machichaco ⓐ	1707 kHz	at 0903 1733 UT
Cabo Peñas ⓐ	1677 kHz	at 0803 1703 UT
La Coruña ⓐ	1698 kHz	at 0833 1733 UT
Finisterre ⓐ	1764 kHz	at 0803 1703 UT

Coastguard MRCC/MRSC
Broadcast in Spanish and English gale warnings on receipt, plus synopsis and forecasts for the Areas, times (UT) and VHF channels listed below:

Bilbao MRCC ⓖ	VHF Ch 10	every 4h from 0033 for Areas 2-4.
Santander MRSC ⓖ	VHF Ch 11	every 4h from 0245 for Areas 2-4.
Gijón MRCC ⓖ	VHF Ch 10 16	every even H+15 from 0015 to 2215 for Areas 3 & 4.
Coruña MRSC ⓖ	VHF Ch 12 13 14	every 4h from 0005 for Areas 1-5.
Finisterre MRCC ⓖ	VHF Ch 11	every 4h from 0233 for Areas 1-5.
Vigo MRSC ⓖ	VHF Ch 10	every 4h from 0015 for Areas 3-6.

Radio broadcasts – Radio Nacional de España (National Radio)
Broadcasts in Spanish storm warnings, synopsis and 12h or 18h forecasts for Spanish Areas 3 & 4 at 1100, 1400, 1800 and 2200 LT. Stations and frequencies are:

San Sebastián	774 kHz	Bilbao	639 kHz	Santander	855 kHz
Oviedo	729 kHz	La Coruña	639 kHz		

Recorded telephone forecasts
A recorded telephone marine weather information service in Spanish is available for the Spanish forecast areas 1 to 4, i.e. Gran Sol, Vizcaya (North Biscay), Cantábrico and Finisterre. The service also provides forecasts for Coastal waters from the French to Portuguese borders i.e. Guipuzcoa, Vizcaya, Cantabria, Austurias, Lugo, Coruña and Pontevedra. This service is only available within Spain or for Autolink equipped vessels. Dial ☎ 906 365 372.

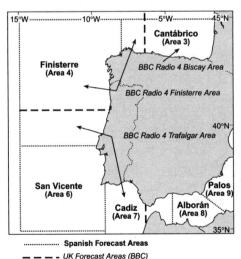

Fig. 5 (19) Spanish forecast areas

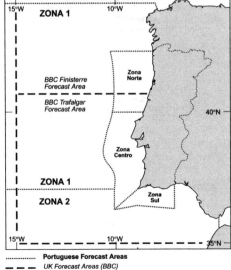

Fig. 5 (20) Portuguese forecast areas

Fig. 5 (21)   Spanish and Portuguese CRS MSI broadcasts

10°30'W   09°00'W   07°30'W   06°00'W   04°30'W   03°00'W

44°00'N

Cabo Ortegal
Ch 02

Cabo Peñas
1677 kHz Ch 26

Santander
Ch 24

Machichaco
1707 kHz

Coruña
Ch 26 1698 kHz

Navia
Ch 27

Bilbao
Ch 26

Finisterre
1698 kHz Ch 01 22

Pasajes
Ch 79

Vigo
Ch 20

42°00'N

La Guardia
Ch 82

Apúlia
2657 kHz
0735 2335 UT

Leixões
Ch 11
1030 1630 UT

40°N

Monsanto
2657 kHz
0805 2005 UT
Ch 11 1000 1630 UT

Setúbal
Ch 11 1030 1630 UT

Lisboa
Ch 11 1030 1700 UT

38°00'N

Sagres
2657 kHz 0835 2035 UT
Ch 11 1030 1630 UT

Chipiona
1656 kHz

Cádiz
Ch 26

Tarifa
1704 kH Ch 81

36°00'N

09°00'W   07°30'W   06°00'W   04°30'W   03°0'W

PORTUGAL

Coast Radio Stations

The following CRS broadcast in Portuguese gale warnings, synopsis and coastal waters forecasts for Portugal, up to 50M offshore for Zona Norte, Zona Centro and Zona Sul.

Leixões ⑱	Ch 11	at 1030 1630 UT	For Porto de Leixões
Lisboa ⑱	Ch 11	at 1030 1730 UT	For Porto de Lisboa
Setúbal ⑱	Ch 11	at 1030 1630 UT	For Porto Setúbal
Finisterre ⑱	1764 kHz	at 0803 1703 UT	

Naval Radio weather broadcasts

Broadcast in Spanish and English gale warnings on receipt, plus synopsis and forecasts for the Areas, times (UT) and VHF channels listed below:

Apúlia	MF 2657 kHz	0735 2335 UT	Zonas Norte, Centra and Sul
Monsanto	VHF Ch 11	1000 1630 UT	Gale warnings & fcst for Alges
	MF 2657 kHz	0805 2005 UT	
Sagres	VHF Ch 11	0835 2035 UT	For Porto de Sages
	2567 kHz	1030 1630 UT	Zonas Norte, Centra and Sul

Radio broadcasts – Radiofusão Portuguesa (National Radio) – Programa 1

Broadcasts 24h forecasts for North, Central and South Zones in Portuguese at 1100 UT. Transmitters and frequencies are:

Porto	720 kHz	**Coimbra**	630 kHz	**Lisboa 1**	666 kHz, 95·7 MHz
Miranda do Douro	630 kHz	**Elvas**	720 kHz	**Faro**	720 kHz, 97·6 MHz

Recorded telephone forecasts

Within **Portugal** call ☎ 0601 123, plus 3 digits below:

	Offshore	Inshore
N border-Lisboa	140	123
Lisboa-C St Vincent	141	124
C St Vincent-E border	142	125

For a 9 day general forecast ☎ 0601 123 131. All forecasts are in Portuguese.

SOUTH WEST SPAIN

Coast Radio Stations

The following CRS broadcast in Spanish gale warnings, synopsis and forecasts for Areas 5 to 8 at the times and on the MF frequencies shown (there are no VHF weather broadcasts by CRS):

Chipiona ⑱	1656 kHz	at 0833 1733 UT
Tarifa ⑱	1704 kHz	at 0803 1703 UT

Coastguard MRCC/MRSC

Broadcast in Spanish and English gale warnings on receipt, plus synopsis and forecasts for the Areas, times (UT) and VHF channels listed below:

Tarifa MRCC ⑱	VHF Ch 10 74	every even H+15 for Gibraltar, Cádiz Bay and Alborán
Algeciras MRSC ⑱	VHF Ch 15,74	every 4h from 0315

Recorded telephone forecasts

In SW Spain ☎ 906 365 373 for offshore bulletins for forecast areas San Vicente, Cádiz, Alborán, Azores and Canaries; also coastal bulletins from Portugal to Gibraltar, and Canaries. All forecasts are in Spanish. The service is only available within Spain and to Autolink-equipped vessels.

Fig. 5 (22)   Portuguese forecast areas

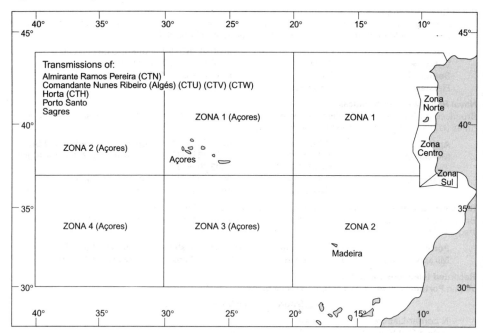

GIBRALTAR

Gibraltar Radio ⓑ   Ch 01 02 03 23 24
                                 25 27 28 86 87 16

a. **Radio Gibraltar** (Gibraltar Broadcasting Corporation) broadcasts in English General synopsis, wind direction and strength, visibility and sea state for area 50M radius from Gibraltar. Frequencies are 1458 kHz, 91·3 MHz, 92·6 MHz and 100·5 MHz. Times (UT) are Mon-Fri: 0610 0930 1030 1230 1300 (in Spanish) 1530 1715; Sat: 0930 1030 1230 1300 (in Spanish); Sun: 1030 1230.

b. **British Forces Broadcasting Service Gibraltar** broadcasts in **English** General synopsis, wind direction and strength, visibility and sea state for area 50M radius from Gibraltar, plus times of HW/LW. Frequencies are 93·5 MHz and 97·8 MHz. Times (LT) are Mon-Fri: 0745 0845 1130 1715 2345, and every H+06 (0700-2400); Sat-Sun: 0845 0945 1230 and every H+06 (0700-1000 & 1200-1400).

c. **Gibraltar CRS** ⓑ broadcasts in English on request: Gale warnings, 12 hrs Fcst and outlook for a further 12 hrs, from 0000, 0600, 1200 or 1800, for area radius 50M from Gibraltar. Broadcasts are on VHF Ch 01 04 23 25 27 86 and 87.

Fig. 5 (23) Spanish forecast areas

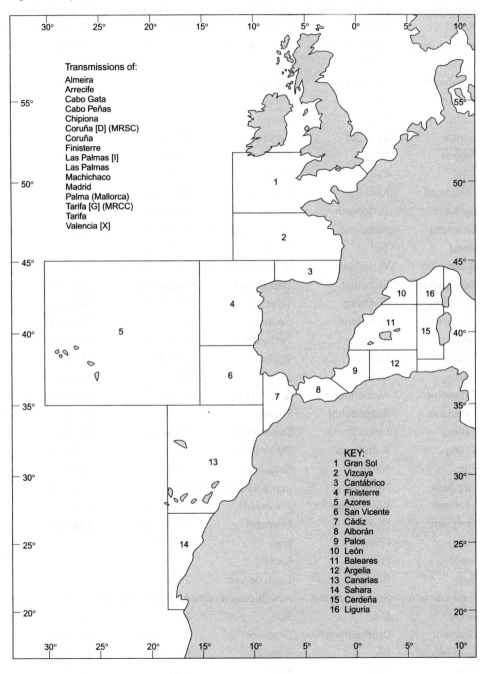

Transmissions of:
Almeira
Arrecife
Cabo Gata
Cabo Peñas
Chipiona
Coruña [D] (MRSC)
Coruña
Finisterre
Las Palmas [I]
Las Palmas
Machichaco
Madrid
Palma (Mallorca)
Tarifa [G] (MRCC)
Tarifa
Valencia [X]

KEY:
1 Gran Sol
2 Vizcaya
3 Cantábrico
4 Finisterre
5 Azores
6 San Vicente
7 Cádiz
8 Alborán
9 Palos
10 León
11 Baleares
12 Argelia
13 Canarias
14 Sahara
15 Cerdeña
16 Liguria

FOREIGN WEATHER TERMS

English	German	French	Spanish	Dutch
Air mass	Luftmasse	Masse d'air	Massa de aire	Luchtmassa
Anticyclone	Antizyklonisch	Anticyclone	Anticiclón	Hogedrukgebied
Area	Gebiet	Zone	Zona	Gebied
Backing wind	Rückdrehender Wind	Vent reculant	Rolar el viento	Krimpende wind
Barometer	Barometer	Baromètre	Barómetro	Barometer
Breeze	Brise	Brise	Brisa	Bries
Calm	Flaute	Calme	Calma	Kalmte
Centre	Zentrum	Centre	Centro	Centum
Clouds	Wolken	Nuages	Nube	Wolken
Cold	Kalt	Froid	Frio	Koud
Cold front	Kaltfront	Front froid	Frente frio	Kou front
Cyclonic	Zyklonisch	Cyclonique	Ciclonica	Cycloonachtig
Decrease	Abnahme	Affaiblissement	Disminución	Afnemen
Deep	Tief	Profond	Profundo	Diep
Deepening	Vertiefend	Approfondissant	Ahondamiento	Verdiepend
Depression	Sturmtief	Dépression	Depresión	Depressie
Direction	Richtung	Direction	Direción	Richting
Dispersing	Auflösend	Se dispersant	Disipación	Oplossend
Disturbance	Störung	Perturbation	Perturbación	Verstoving
Drizzle	Niesel	Bruine	Lioviena	Motregen
East	Ost	Est	Este	Oosten
Extending	Ausdehnung	S'étendant	Extension	Uitstrekkend
Extensive	Ausgedehnt	Etendu	General	Uitgebreid
Falling	Fallend	Descendant	Bajando	Dalen
Filling	Auffüllend	Secomblant	Relleno	Vullend
Fog	Nebel	Brouillard	Niebla	Nevel
Fog bank	Nebelbank	Ligne de brouillard	Banco de niebla	Mist bank
Forecast	Vorhersage	Prévision	Previsión	Vooruitzicht
Frequent	Häufig	Fréquent	Frecuenta	Veelvuldig
Fresh	Frisch	Frais	Fresco	Fris
Front	Front	Front	Frente	Front
Gale	Sturm	Coup de vent	Temporal	Storm
Gale warning	Sturmwarnung	Avis de coup de vent	Aviso de temporal	Stormwaarschuwing
Good	Gut	Bon	Bueno	Goed
Gradient	Druckunterschied	Gradient	Gradiente	Gradiatie
Gust, squall	Bö	Rafalle	Ráfaga	Windvlaag
Hail	Hagel	Grêle	Granizo	Hagel
Haze	Diesig	Brume	Calina	Nevel
Heavy	Schwer	Abondant	Abunante	Zwaar

English	German	French	Spanish	Dutch
High	Hoch	Anticyclone	Alta presión	Hoog
Increasing	Zunehmend	Augmentant	Aumentar	Toenemend
Isobar	Isobar	Isobare	Isobara	Isobar
Isolated	Vereinzelt	Isolé	Aislado	Verspreid
Lightning	Blitze	Eclair de foudre	Relampago	Bliksem
Local	Örtlich	Locale	Local	Plaatselijk
Low	Tief	Dépression	Baja presión	Laag
Mist	Dunst	Brume légere	Nablina	Mist
Moderate	Mäßig	Modéré	Moderado	Matig
Moderating	Abnehmend	Se modérant	Medianente	Matigend
Moving	Bewegend	Se déplacant	Movimiento	Bewegend
North	Nord	Nord	Septentrional	Noorden
Occluded	Okklusion	Couvert	Okklusie	Bewolkt
Poor	Schlecht	Mauvais	Mal	Slecht
Precipitation	Niederschlag	Précipitation	Precipitación	Neerslag
Pressure	Druck	Pression	Presión	Druk
Rain	Regen	Pluie	lluvia	Regen
Ridge	Hochdruckbrücke	Crête	Cresta	Rug
Rising	Ansteigend	Montant	Subiendo	Stijgen
Rough	Rauh	Agitée	Bravo o alborotado	Ruw
Sea	See	Mer	Mar	Zee
Seaway	Seegang	Haute mer	Alta mar	Zee
Scattered	Vereinzelt	Sporadiques	Difuso	Verspreid
Shower	Schauer	Averse	Aguacero	Bui
Slight	Leicht	Un peu	Leicht	Licht
Slow	Langsam	Lent	Lent	Langzaam
Snow	Schnee	Neige	Nieve	Sneeuw
South	Süd	Sud	Sur	Zuiden
Storm	Sturm	Tempête	Temporal	Storm
Sun	Sonne	Soleil	Sol	Zon
Swell	Schwell	Houle	Mar de fondo	Deining
Thunder	Donner	Tonnerre	Tormenta	Donder
Thunderstorm	Gewitter	Orage	Tronada	Onweer
Trough	Trog, Tiefausläufer	Creux	Seno	Trog
Variable	Umlaufend	Variable	Variable	Veranderlijk
Veering	Rechtdrehend	Virement de vent	Dextrogiro	Ruimende wind
Warm front	Warmfront	Front chaud	Frente calido	Warm front
Weather	Wetter	Temps	Tiempo	Weer
Wind	Wind	Vent	Viento	Wind
Weather report	Wetterbericht	Météo	Previsión meteorologica	Weer bericht

REFERENCE SECTION

CONTENTS

Nautical miles to Kilometres		Kilometres to Nautical miles	
multiply by 1·8520		multiply by 0·5400	
N Miles	km	km	N Miles
0.25	0.46	0.25	0.14
0.5	0.93	0.5	0.27
0.75	1.39	0.75	0.41
1	1.85	1	0.54
2	3.70	2	1.08
3	5.56	3	1.62
4	7.41	4	2.16
5	9.26	5	2.70
10	18.52	10	5.40
15	27.78	15	8.10
20	37.04	20	10.80
30	55.56	30	16.20
40	74.08	40	21.60
50	92.60	50	27.00
100	185.20	100	54.00

Feet to Metres		Metres to Feet	
multiply by 0·3048		multiply by 3·.2810	
feet	metres	metres	feet
0.25	0.08	0.25	0.82
0.5	0.15	0.5	1.64
0.75	0.23	0.75	2.46
1	0.30	1	3.28
2	0.61	2	6.56
3	0.91	3	9.84
4	1.22	4	13.12
5	1.52	5	16.41
10	3.05	10	32.81
15	4.57	15	49.22
20	6.10	20	65.62
30	9.14	30	98.43
40	12.19	40	131.24
50	15.24	50	164.05
100	30.48	100	328.10

GLOSSARY OF FOREIGN TERMS

English	German	French	Spanish	Dutch
Ashore				
Ashore	An Land	A terre	A tierra	Aan land
Airport	Flughafen	Aéroport	Aeropuerto	Vliegveld
Bank	Bank	Banque	Banco	Bank
Boathoist	Bootskran	Travelift	Travelift	Botenlift
Boatyard	Bootswerft	Chantier naval	Astilleros	Jachtwerf
Bureau de change	Wechselstelle	Bureau de change	Cambio	Geldwisselkantoor
Bus	Bus	Autobus	Autobús	Bus
Chandlery	Yachtausrüster	Shipchandler	Efectos navales	Scheepswinkel
Chemist	Apotheke	Pharmacie	Farmacia	Apotheek
Dentist	Zahnarzt	Dentiste	Dentista	Tandarts
Doctor	Arzt	Médecin	Médico	Dokter
Engineer	Motorenservice	Ingénieur/mécanique	Mecánico	Ingenieur
Ferry	Fähre	Ferry/transbordeur	Ferry	Veer/Pont
Garage	Autowerkstatt	Station service	Garage	Garage
Harbour	Hafen	Port	Puerto	Haven
Hospital	Krankenhaus	Hôpital	Hospital	Ziekenhuis
Mast crane	Mastenkran	Grue	Grúa	Masten kraan
Post office	Postamt	Bureau de poste/PTT	Correos	Postkantoor
Railway station	Bahnhof	Gare de chemin de fer	Estación de ferrocanil	Station
Sailmaker	Segelmacher	Voilier	Velero	Zeilmaker
Shops	Geschäfte	Boutiques	Tiendas	Winkels
Slip	Slip	Cale	Varadero	Helling
Supermarket	Supermarkt	Supermarché	Supermercado	Supermarkt
Taxi	Taxi	Taxi	Taxis	Taxi
Village	Ort	Village	Pueblo	Dorp
Yacht club	Yachtclub	Club nautique	Club náutico	Jacht club

English	German	French	Spanish	Dutch
Engine and machinery				
Air filter	Luftfilter	Filtre à air	Filtro a aire	Lucht filter
Battery	Batterie	Batterie/accumulateur	Baterías	Accu
Bilge pump	Bilgepumpe	Pompe de cale	Bomba de achique	Bilge pomp
Carburettor	Vergaser	Carburateur	Carburador	Carburateur
Charging	Laden	Charger	Cargador	Opladen
Compression	Kompression	Compression	Compresión	Compressie
Cooling water	Kühlwasser	Eau de refroidissement	Agua refrigerado	Koelwater
Diesel	Diesel	Diésel/gas-oil	Gas-oil	Dieselolie
Diesel engine	Dieselmotor	Moteur diésel	Motor a gas-oil	Dieselmotor
Dynamo	Lichtmaschine	Alternateur	Alternador	Dynamo
Electrical wiring	Elektrik	Réseau électrique	Circuito eléctrico	Elektrische bedrading
Engine mount	Motorenfundament	Support moteur	Bancada del motor	Motorsteun
Engine oil	Maschinenöl	Huile de moteur	Aceite motor	Motorolie
Exhaust pipe	Auspuff	Tuyau d'échappement	Tubos de escape	Uitlaat
Fuel filter	Kraftstofffilter	Filtre de fuel	Filtro de combustible	Brandstoffilter
Fuel tank	Tank, Kraftstofftank	Réservoir à fuel	Tanque de Combustible	Brandstof tank
Fuse	Sicherung	Fusible	Fusible	Zekering
Gearbox	Getriebe	Transmission	Transmisión	Keerkoppeling

FOREIGN GLOSSARY

English	German	French	Spanish	Dutch
Generator	Generator	Groupe électrogène	Generador	Generator
Grease	Fett	Graisse	Grasa	Vet
Head gasket	Zylinderkopfdichtung	Joint de culasse	Junta de culata	Koppakking
Holding tank	Schmutzwassertank	Réservoir à eaux usées	Tanque aguas negras	Vuil-watertank
Inboard engine	Einbaumotor	Moteur in-bord	Motor intraborda	Binnen boord motor
Injectors	Einspritzdüsen	Injecteurs	Inyectores	Injectoren
Main engine	Hauptmaschine	Moteur principal	Motor	Hoofdmotor
Outboard engine	Außenborder	Moteur hors-bord	Motor fuera borda	Buitenboord motor
Petrol	Benzin	Essence	Gasolina	Benzine
Petrol engine	Benzinmotor	Moteur à essence	Motor a gasolina	Benzine motor
Propeller	Propeller	Hélice	Hélice	Schroef
Propeller bracket	Propeller-Halterung	Chaise	Arbotante	Schroefsteun
Regulator	Regler	Régulateur de charge	Regulador	Regulateur
Shaft	Welle	Arbre d'hélice	Eje	As
Spark plug	Zündkerze	Bougie	Bujia	Bougie
Starter	Starter	Démarreur	Arranque	Start motor
Stern gland	Stopfbuchse	Presse étoupe	Bocina	Schroefasdoorvoer
Throttle	Gas	Accélérateur	Acelerador	Gashendel
Water tank	Wassertank	Réservoir à eau	Tanque de agua	Water tank
Water pump	Wasserpumpe	Pompe à eau	Bomba de agua	Water pomp

General yachting terms

English	German	French	Spanish	Dutch
One	Eins	Un	Uno	Een
Two	Zwei	Deux	Duo	Twee
Three	Drei	Trois	Tres	Drie
Four	Vier	Quatre	Cuatro	Vier
Five	Fünf	Cinq	Cinco	Vijf
Six	Sechs	Six	Seis	Zes
Seven	Sieben	Sept	Siete	Zeven
Eight	Acht	Huit	Ocho	Acht
Nine	Neun	Neuf	Nueve	Negen
Ten	Zehn	Dix	Diez	Tien
Aft	Achtern, achteraus	En arriere	Atrás	Achter
Ahead	Voraus	En avant	Avante	Vooruit
Anchor	Anker	Ancre	Ancia	Anker
Anchor chain	Ankerkette	Chaîne d'ancre	Cadena	Ankerketting
Anchor warp	Ankerleine	Orin	Cabo	Ankerlijn
Anchor winch	Ankerwinsch	Guindeau	Molinete	Anker lier
Babystay	Babystag	Babystay	Babystay	Baby stag
Backstay	Achterstag	Pataras	Estay de popa	Achterstag
Beating	Kreuzen	Au près	Ciñendo a rabier	Kruisen
Bilge	Bilge	Galbord	Sentina	Bilge
Bilge keel	Kimmkiel	Bi-quilles	Quillas de balance	Door lopende kiel
Block	Block	Poulie	Motón	Blok
Boat	Boot	Bateau	Barco	Boot
Boom	Baum	Bôme	Botavara	Giek
Bow	Bug	Etrave	Proa	Boeg
Bridgedeck	Brückendeck	Bridgedeck	Bridgedeck	Brug dek
Cabin	Kajüte	Cabine	Cabina	Kajuit

English	German	French	Spanish	Dutch
Cap shrouds	Oberwanten	Gal haubans	Obenques altos	Zalingkap
Centreboard	Schwert	Dérive	Orza	Midzwaard
Cockpit	Cockpit	Cockpit	Bañera	Cockpit
Companionway	Niedergang	Descente	Entrada cámera	Gangboord
Cruising chute	Cruising chute	Spi asymétrique	MPS	Cruising chute
Cutter stay	Kutterstag	Etai intermédiaire	Estay de tringqueta	Kotter stag
Deck	Deck	Pont	Cubierta	Dek
Dinghy	Jolle	You-you	Chinchorro	Bijboot
Fender	Fender	Défense	Defensa	Stootwil
Ferry	Fähre	Ferry	Ferry	Veerboot
Fin keel	Kurzkiel	Quille courte	Quilla de aleta	Fin kiel
Foresail	Vorsegel	Voile avant/foc	Foque	Fok
Forestay	Vorstag	Etai	Estay	Voorstag
Genoa	Genua	Génois	Génova	Genua
Halyard	Fall	Drisse	Driza	Val
Hull	Rumpf	Carène	Carena	Romp
Inflatable	Schlauchboot	Gonflable	Bote Hinchable	Opblaasbare boot
Jumper	Jumpstag	Guignol	Violín	Trui
Keel	Kiel	Quille	Quilla	Kiel
Long keel	Langkiel	Quille longue	Quilla corrida	Doorlopende kiel
Lower shrouds	Unterwanten	Bas haubans	Obenques bajos	Beneden zaling
Mainsail	Großsegel	Grand' voile	Mayor	Grootzeil
Mast	Mast	Mât	Mast	Mast
Mizzen	Besan	Artimon	Mesana	Bezaan
Motoring	Motoren	Naviguer au moteur	Navegar a motor	Met motor aan
Navigate	Navigieren	Naviguer	Navegar	Navigeren
Port	Backbord	Bâbord	Babor	Bakboord
Pulpit	Bugkorb	Balcon arrière	Púlpito	Preekstoel
Pushpit	Heckkorb	Balcon avant	Balcón de popa	Hekrailing
Railing	Reling	Rambarde	Guardamencebos	Railing
Reaching	Raumschodts	Au portant	Viento a través	Ruime wind
Rigging	Rigg	Gréement	Jarcia	Verstaging
Rope	Tauwerk	Cordage	Cabo	Touw
Rudder	Ruder	Safran/gouvernail	Pala de Timón	Roer
Running	Vorm Wind	Vent arrière	Viento a favor	Voor de wind
Running backstay	Backstag	Bastaque	Burde volanto	Bakstag
Sail batten	Segellatte	Latte	Sables	Zeillat
Sailing	Segeln	Naviguer à la voile	Navegar a velas	Zeilen
Shackle	Schäkel	Manille	Grillete	Harp
Sheet	Schoot	Ecoute	Escota	Schoot
Ship	Schiff	Navire	Buque	Schip
Shrouds	Wanten	Haubans	Obenques	Zaling
Spinnaker	Spinnaker	Spi	Spi	Spinnaker
Spinnaker boom	Spinnakerbaum	Tangon de spi	Tangon	Spinnaker boom
Stanchion	Seerelingsstütze	Chandelier	Candelero	Scepter
Starboard	Steuerbord	Tribord	Estribor	Stuurboord
Staysail	Stagsegel	Trinquette	Trinquete	Stagzeil
Steamer	Dampfer	Vapeur	Buque de vapor	Vrachtschip
Stern	Heck	Arrière	Popa	Spiegel

English	German	French	Spanish	Dutch
Storm jib	Sturmfock	Tourmentin	Tormentin	Storm fok
Storm trysail	Trysegel	Voile de cap	Vela de capa	Trysail
Superstructure	Aufbau	Superstructure	Superestructura	Bovenbouw
Tender	Beiboot	Annexe	Anexo (bote)	Bijboot
Tiller	Pinne	Barre franche	Caña	Helmstok
Toe rail	Fußleiste	Rail de fargue	Regala	Voetrail
Topsides	Rumpfseiten	Oeuvres mortes	Obra muerta	Romp
Underwater hull	Unterwasserschiff	Oeuvres vives	Obra viva	Onderwaterschip
Upwind	Am Wind	Au vent	Vienta en contra	Aan de wind
Wheel	Rad	Barre à roue	Rueda	Stuurwiel
Winch	Winsch	Winch	Winche	Lier
Working jib	Arbeitsfock	Foc de route	Foque	Werk fok
Yacht	Yacht	Yacht	Yate	Jacht

Navigation

English	German	French	Spanish	Dutch
Abeam	Querab	A côté	Por el través	Naast
Ahead	Voraus	Avant	Avante	Voor
Astern	Achteraus	Arrière	Atrás	Achter
Bearing	Peilung	Cap	Maración	Peiling
Buoy	Tonne	Bouée	Boya	Boei
Binoculars	Fernglas	Jumelles	Prismáticos	Verrekijker
Channel	Kanal	Chenal	Canal	Kanaal
Chart	Seekarte	Carte	Carta náutica	Zeekaart
Compass	Kompass	Compas	Compás	Kompas
Compass course	Kompass Kurs	Cap du compas	Rumbo de aguja	Kompas koers
Current	Strömung	Courant	Coriente	Stroom
Dead reckoning	Koppelnavigation	Estime	Estimación	Gegist bestek
Degree	Grad	Degré	Grado	Graden
Deviation	Deviation	Déviation	Desvio	Deviatie
Distance	Entfernung	Distance	Distancia	Afstand
Downstream	Flußabwärts	En aval	Río abajo	Stroom afwaards
East	Ost	Est	Este	Oost
Ebb	Ebbe	Jusant	Marea menguante	Eb
Echosounder	Echolot	Sondeur	Sonda	Dieptemeter
Estimated position	Gegißte Position	Point estimé	Posición estimado	Gegiste positie
Fathom	Faden	Une brasse	Braza	Vadem
Feet	Fuß	Pieds	Pie	Voet
Flood	Flut	Flot	Flujo de marea	Vloed
GPS	GPS	GPS	GPS	GPS
Handbearing compass	Handpeilkompass	Compas de relèvement	Compás de marcaciones	Handpeil kompas
Harbour guide	Hafenhandbuch	Guide du port	Guia del Puerto	Havengids
High water	Hochwasser	Peine mer	Altamer	Hoog water
Latitude	Geographische Breite	Latitude	Latitud	Breedte
Leading lights	Feuer in Linie	Alignement	Luz de enfilación	Geleide lichten
Leeway	Abdrift	Dérive	Hacia sotavento	Drift
Lighthouse	Leuchtturm	Phare	Faro	Vuurtoren
List of lights	Leuchtfeuer Verzeichnis	Liste des feux	Listude de Luces	Lichtenlijst
Log	Logge	Loch	Corredera	Log

English	German	French	Spanish	Dutch
Longitude	Geographische Länge	Longitude	Longitud	Lengte
Low water	Niedrigwasser	Basse mer	Bajamar	Laag water
Metre	Meter	Mètre	Metro	Meter
Minute	Minute	Minute	Minuto	Minuut
Nautical almanac	Nautischer Almanach	Almanach nautique	Almanaque náutico	Almanak
Nautical mile	Seemeile	Mille nautique	Milla marina	Zeemijl
Neap tide	Nipptide	Morte-eau	Marea muerta	Dood tij
North	Nord	Nord	Norte	Noord
Pilot	Lotse	Pilote	Práctico	Loods/Gids
Pilotage book	Handbuch	Instructions nautiques	Derrotero	Vaarwijzer
RDF	Funkpeiler	Radio gonio	Radio-gonió	Radio richtingzoeker
Radar	Radar	Radar	Radar	Radar
Radio receiver	Radio, Empfänger	Réceptor radio	Receptor de radio	Radio ontvanger
Radio transmitter	Sender	Emetteur radio	Radio-transmisor	Radio zender
River outlet	Flußmündung	Embouchure	Embocadura	Riviermond
South	Süd	Sud	Sud, Sur	Zuid
Spring tide	Springtide	Vive-eau	Marea viva	Springtij/springvloed
Tide	Tide, Gezeit	Marée	Marea	Getijde
Tide tables	Tidenkalender	Annuaire des marées	Anuario de mareas	Getijdetafel
True course	Wahrer Kurs	Vrai cap	Rumbo	Ware Koers
Upstream	Flußaufwärts	En amont	Río arriba	Stroom opwaards
VHF	UKW	VHF	VHF	Marifoon
Variation	Mißweisung	Variation	Variación	Variatie
Waypoint	Wegpunkt	Point de rapport	Waypoint	Waypoint/Route punt
West	West	Ouest	Oeste	West

Officialdom

English	German	French	Spanish	Dutch
Certificate of registry	Schiffszertifikat	Acte de franchisation	Documentos de matrícuia	Zeebrief
Check in	Einklarieren	Enregistrement	Registrar	Check-in
Customs	Zoll	Douanes	Aduana	Douane
Declare	Verzollen	Déclarer	Declarar	Aangeven
Harbour master	Hafenmeister	Capitaine du port	Capitán del puerto	Havenmeester
Insurance	Versicherung	Assurance	Seguro	Verzekering
Insurance certificate	Versicherungspolice	Certificat d'assurance	Certificado deseguro	Verzekeringsbewijs
Passport	Paß	Passeport	Pasaporte	Paspoort
Police	Polizei	Police	Policía	Politie
Pratique	Verkehrserlaubnis	Pratique	Prático	Verlof tot ontscheping
Register	Register	Liste de passagers	Lista de tripulantes/rol	Register
Ship's log	Logbuch	Livre de bord	Cuaderno de bitácora	Logboek
Ship's papers	Schiffspapiere	Papiers de bateau	Documentos del barco	Scheepspapieren
Surveyor	Gutachter	Expert maritime	Inspector	Opzichter

Safety/Distress

English	German	French	Spanish	Dutch
Assistance	Hilfeleistung	Assistance	Asistencia	Assistentie
Bandage	Verband	Pansement	Vendas	Verband
Burns	Verbrennung	Brûlures	Quemadura	Brand wond
Capsize	Kentern	Chavirage	Volcó	Omslaan
Coastguard	Küstenwache	Garde de côte	Guarda costas	Kust wacht
Dismasted	Mastbruch	Démâtè	Desarbolar	Mastbreuk
Distress	Seenot	Détresse	Pena	Nood

English	German	French	Spanish	Dutch
Distress flares	Signalraketen	Fusées de détresse	Bengalas	Nood signaal
Doctor	Doktor	Médecin	Médico	Doktor/Arts
EPIRB	EPIRB	Balise	Baliza	EPIRB
Emergency	Notfall	Urgence	Emergencias	Noodgeval
Exhaustion	Erschöpfung	Epuisement	Agotamiento	Uitputting
Fever	Fieber	Fièvre	Fiebre	Koorts
Fire extinguisher	Feuerlöscher	Extincteur	Extintor	Brand blusser
First aid	Erste Hilfe	Premier secours	Primeros auxillos	Eerste hulp
Fracture	Fraktur	Cassure	Fractura	Breuk
Grounded	Aufgelaufen	Echoué	Encallado	Vastgelopen
Harness	Lifebelt	Harnais	Arnés de seguridad	Harnas/Tuig
Headache	Kopfschmerz	Mal à la tête	Dolor de cabeza	Hoofdpijn
Heart attack	Herzanfall	Crise cardiaque	Ataque corazón	Hartaanval
Helicopter	Hubschrauber	Hélicoptère	Helicóptero	Helikopter
Hospital	Krankenhaus	Hôpital	Hospital	Ziekenhuis
Illness	Krankheit, Übelkeit	Maladie	Enfermo	Ziekte
Injury	Verletzung	Blessure	Lesión	Verwonding
Jackstay	Strecktau	Contre-étai	Violín	Veiligheidstag
Lifeboat	Rettungsboot	Canot de sauvetage	Lancha de salvamento	Reddingsboot
Liferaft	Rettungsinsel	Radeau de sauvetage	Balsa salvavidas	Reddingsvlot
Lifejacket	Schwimmweste	Gilet de sauvetage	Chaleco salvavidas	Reddingsvest
Man overboard	Mann über Bord	Homme à la mer	Hombre al agua	Man over boord
Pulse	Puls	Poux	Pulso	Hartslag
Rest	Ruhen	Repos	Reposo	Rust
Seacock	Seeventil	Vanne	Grifos de fondo	Afsluiter
Seasickness	Seekrankheit	Mal de mer	Mareo	Zeeziekte
Seaworthy	Seetüchtig	Marin	Marinero	Zeewaardig
Shock	Schock	Choc	Choque	Shock
Sinking	Sinken	En train de couler	Hundiendo	Zinken
Sleep	Schlaf	Sommeil	Sueño	Slaap
Tow line	Schleppleine	Filin de remorque	Cabo	Sleeplijn
Unconscious	Bewußtlos	Inconscient	Inconsciente	Buiten bewustzijn
Wound	Wunde	Blessure	Herida	Wond

Signs and warnings

English	German	French	Spanish	Dutch
Anchoring	Ankern	Mouiller l'ancre	Fondear	Ankeren
Breakwater	Außenmole	Brise-lame	Escolera	Pier
Cable	Kabel	Encablure	Cadena	Kabel
Catwalk	Schlengel	Passerelle	Pasarela	Loopplank
Commercial port	Handelshafen	Port de commerce	Puerto comercial	Commerciele haven
Customs office	Zollamt	Bureau de douane	Aduanas	Douanekantoor
Depth	Wassertiefe	Profondeur	Profundidad	Diepte
Dries	Trockenfallend	Découvrant	Descubierto	Droogvallen
Drying port	Trockenfallender Hafen	Port d'échouage	Puerto secarse	Droogvallende haven
Ferry terminal	Fährterminal	Gare maritime	Terminal marítmo	Veerboot steiger
Firing range	Schießgebiet	Zone de tir	Zona de tiro	Schietbaan
Fishing harbour	Fischereihafen	Port de pêche	Puerto de pesca	Vissershaven
Foul ground	unreiner Grund	Fond maisain	Fondo sucio	Slechte grond
Guest berths	Gastliegeplätze	Place visiteurs	Amarradero visitantes	Gasten plaatsen
Harbour entrance	Hafeneinfahrt	Entrée du port	Entradas	Haveningang

English	German	French	Spanish	Dutch
Harbourmaster's office	Hafenmeisterei	Capitainerie	Capitania	Havenmeesters Kantoor
Hazard	Hindernis	Danger	Peligro	Gevaar
Height	Höhe	Hauteur	Alturas	Hoogte
Jetty	Steg	Jetée	Malecón	Steiger
Landing place	Anlegeplatz	Point d'accostage	Embarcadero	Plaats om aan l and te gaan
Lock	Schleuse	Ecluse	Esclusa	Sluis
Marina	Marina	Marina	Marina	Marina
Mooring	Anlegen	Mouillage	Fondeadero	Meerplaats
Permitted	Erlaubt	Permis	Permitido	Toegestaan
Pier	Pier, Mole	Appontement/quai	Muelle	Pier
Prohibited	Verboten	Interdit	Prohibido	Verboden
Prohibited area	Sperrgebiet	Zone interdite	Zona de phrohibida	Verboden gebied
Swell	Schwell	Houle	Mar de fondo	Golfslag
Swing bridge	Klappbrücke	Pont tournant	Puente giratorio	Klapbrug
Underwater	Unterwasser	Sous-marin	Debajo del agua	Onderwater
Wreck	Wrack	Epave	Naufrago	Wrak
Yacht club	Yachtclub	Club nautique	Club náutico	Jachtclub
Yacht harbour	Yachthafen	Port de plaisance	Puerto deportive	Jachthaven

Useful phrases

English	German	French
Can I moor here please	Kann ich hier festmachen?	Puis-je accoster ici s'il vous plait?
How far is it to....?	Wie weit ist es nach ..... ?	Est -ce loin jusqu'à...?
How much does that cost?	Was kostet es?	Combien est-il?
Is there enough water?	Ist dort genug Wassertiefe?	Y a-t-il du fond?
Let go aft	Achtern loswerfen.	Larguer à l'arrière
Let go foreward	Vorne loswerfen.	Larguer à l'avant
Make fast aft	Können Sie bitte achtern festmachen?	Amarrer à l'arrière
Make fast foreward	Können Sie bitte vorne festmachen?	Amarrer à l'avant
Please direct me to......?	Bitte zeigen Sie mir den Weg nach	S'il vous plait, vevillez m'indiquer le chemin à...?
Please take my line	Können Sie bitte die Leine annehmen?	Prenez mon amarre, s'il vous plait
Where can I get...?	Wo kann ich ..... bekommen?	Où puis-je obtenir...?
Where can I moor?	Wo kann ich festmachen?	Où puis-je accoster?

English	Spanish	Dutch
Can I moor here please	Puedo atracar aqui por favor?	Mag ik hier aanleggen?
How far is it to....?	A que distancia esta ...?	Hoe ver is het naar...?
How much does that cost?	Cudnto cuesta ...?	Hoeveel kost het?
Is there enough water?	Hay bastante agua?	Is er genoeg water?
Let go aft	Suelta los cabos del amarre de popa	Achter losgooien
Let go foreward	Suelta los cabos del amarre de proa	Voor losgooien
Make fast aft	Asegurar los amarres de popa	Achter vastleggen
Make fast foreward	Asegurar los amarres de proa	Voor vastleggen
Please direct me to......?	Por favor, digame a ...?	Kunt u my de weg naar .. wÿzen
Please take my line	Por favor cojan mi cabo	Kunt u mijn landvast aanpakken?
Where can I get...?	Donde puedo conseguir ...?	Waar kan ik...verkrijgen?
Where can I moor?	Dondo puedo atracar?	Waar kan ik vastmaken?

Conversion Tables

Sq inches to sq millimetres	645.2	1	0.002	**Sq millimetres to sq inches**
multiply by **645.20**				multiply by **0.0016**
Inches to millimetres	25.40	1	0.04	**Millimetres to inches**
multiply by **25.40**				multiply by **0.0394**
Sq feet to square metres	0.09	1	10.76	**Sq metres to sq feet**
multiply by **0.093**				multiply by **10.7640**
Inches to centimetres	2.54	1	0.39	**Centimetres to inches**
multiply by **2.54**				multiply by **0.3937**
Feet to metres	0.31	1	3.28	**Metres to feet**
multiply by **0.305**				multiply by **3.2810**
Nautical miles to kilometres	1.85	1	0.54	**Kilometres to nautical miles**
multiply by **1.852**				multiply by **0.5400**
Miles to kilometres	1.61	1	0.62	**Kilometres to miles**
multiply by **1.609**				multiply by **0.6214**
Miles to nautical miles	0.87	1	1.15	**Nautical miles to miles**
multiply by **0.8684**				multiply by **1.1515**
HP to metric HP	1.01	1	0.99	**Metric HP to HP**
multiply by **1.014**				multiply by **0.9862**
Pounds per sq inch to kg per sq centimetre	0.07	1	4.22	**Kg per sq centimetre to pounds per sq inch**
multiply by **0.0703**				multiply by **14.2200**
HP to kilowatts	0.75	1	1.34	**Kilowatts to HP**
multiply by **0.746**				multiply by **1.341**
Cu inches to cu centimetres	16.39	1	0.06	**Cu centimetres to cu inches**
multiply by **16.39**				multiply by **0.0610**
Gallons to litres	4.54	1	0.22	**Litres to gallons**
multiply by **4.540**				multiply by **0.2200**
Pints to litres	0.57	1	1.76	**Litres to pints**
multiply by **0.5680**				multiply by **1.7600**
Pounds to kilogrammes	0.45	1	2.21	**Kilogrammes to pounds**
multiply by **0.4536**				multiply by **2.2050**

ABBREVIATIONS

AAAAAAAA

A1A .... Continuous wave telegraphy, morse code
A2A .... Telegraphy by the on-off keying of a tone modulated carrier, morse code: double sideband
A3E .... Telephony using amplitude modulation: double sideband
ALRS .... Admiralty list of radio signals
approx .... Approximate

BBBBBBBB

BBC .... British Broadcasting Corporation
Bcst .... Broadcast
Bn(s) .... Beacon(s)
brg .... Bearing

CCCCCCCC

CG .... Coastguard
Ch .... Channel
CNIS .... Channel navigation information service
COLREGS .... Convention on the international regulations for preventing collisions at sea
Conspic .... Conspicuos
Cont .... Continuous
CROSS .... Centres regionaux operationnels de surveillance et de sauvetage
CRS .... Coast radio station

DDDDDDDD

DF .... Direction-finding
DGPS .... Differential global positioning system
DGNSS .... Differential global navigation satellite systems
DSB .... Double sideband
DSC .... Digital selective calling
DST .... Daylight saving time

EEEEEEEEE

EPIRB .... Emergency position-indicating radio beacon
ETA .... Estimated time of arrival
ETD .... Estimated time of departure

FFFFFFFFFFF

Fcst .... Forecast
FM .... Frequency modulation
Fri .... Friday
Fx .... Frequency

GGGGGGGG

GMT .... Greenwich mean time
GPS .... Global positioning system

HHHHHH

H .... Hours
H+ .... Commencing at...minutes past the hour
H24 .... Continuous
HF .... High frequency (3-30 MHz)
HJ .... Day service only
Hr .... Harbour
Hr Mr .... Harbour master
HW .... High water
HX .... No specific hours or fixed intermittent hours
Hz .... Hertz

IIIIIIIIIIII

IMO .... International maritime organisation
INMARSAT .... International mobile satellite organisation
Inop......................... Inoperative

KKKKKKKKKK

kHz	Kilohertz
km	Kilometre(s)
kW	Kilowatt(s)

LLLLLLLLLLL

Lanby	Large navigational buoy
Ldg	Leading
Lt(s)	Light(s)
Lt F	Lt F
Lt Ho	Light house
Lt V	Light vessel
LT	Local time
LW	Low water

M M M M M M

M(s)	Mile(s)
m	Metre(s); Minute(s)
MF	Medium frequency (300-3000 kHz)
MHz	Megahertz
MRCC	Maritime rescue co-ordination centre
MRSC	Maritime rescue co-ordination sub-centre
ms	Millisecond(s)

NNNNNNN

NM	Notice to mariners
n mile	International nautical mile

OOOOOOO

Occas	Occasional

PPPPPPPPPP

PA	Position approximate
Pt	Point
PV	Pilot vessel

RRRRRRRRRR

RC	Non-directional radiobeacon
RD	Directional radiobeacon
Rep	Reported
RCC	Rescue co-ordinatlon centre
RG	Radio direction-finding station
RT	Radio telephony
Rt	Radio transmitter
Rx	Receiver

SSSSSSSSSS

SAR	Search and rescue
Sept	September
Seq	Sequence
Sous-CROSS	Sous-centres regionaux operationnels de surveillance et de sauvetage
SSB	Single side band

TTTTTTTTT

Tel	Telephone
temp	Temporarily
Tx	Transmitter; transmission

UUUUUUUUU

UHF	Ultra high frequency (300-3000MHz)
UT	Universal time

VVVVVVVVVV

VHF	Very high frequency (30-300 MHz)
VTS	Vessel traffic service

WWWWWW

WT	Wireless telegraphy
Wx	Weather

INDEX

SOUNDS

VESSELS IN SIGHT OF ONE ANOTHER

Short blast ◖◀ - about I second, Long blast ●◀◀ - about 5 seconds

◖◀	I am turning to **Starboard**
◖◀ ◖◀	I am turning to **Port**
◖◀ ◖◀ ◖◀	My engines are going **Astern**
◖◀ ◖◀ ◖◀ ◖◀ ◖◀ - *at least*	**Look Out**

In a narrow channel

●◀◀ ●◀◀ ◖◀	I intend to overtake you on your **Starboard** side
●◀◀ ●◀◀ ◖◀ ◖◀	I intend to overtake you on your **Port** side
●◀◀ ◖◀ ●◀◀ ◖◀	In response to the above two signals - **Agreed** (Morse C - affirmative)

Approaching a bend in the channel or a harbour wall which restricts visibility

●◀◀	Look out - I am coming
●◀◀	Reply to above - so am I

VESSELS IN FOG

●◀◀	Power vessel under way (every 2 mins)
●◀◀ ●◀◀	Power vessel stopped (every 2 mins)
●◀◀ ◖◀ ◖◀	All the lame ducks - not under command, restricted, sailing, fishing or towing - (every 2 mins)(Morse D - I am manoeuvring with difficulty)
●◀◀ ◖◀ ◖◀ ◖◀	Last vessel in tow (immediately after tug signal)
🔔 5 seconds	At ⚓ (bell, every minute)
🔔 5 seconds +	At anchor over 100m
🔔 5 seconds	(bell forward, gong aft, every minute)
◖◀ ●◀◀ ◖◀	At ⚓, in addition to above, to warn approaching vessel

Yachts under 12m are not obliged to sound the fog signals listed above, but if they do not, they *must* make some efficient noise every two minutes

SHAPES

Shape	Description	Shape	Description
◆	Towing vessel - length of tow over 200m	▼	Sailing vessel under sail *and* power
● ◆ ●	Restricted vessel	●	Vessel at anchor
● ●	Vessel not under command	⧗	Fishing vessel
▮	Vessel constrained by her draught	⧓	Fishing vessel below 20m

SYMBOLS

⏣	Yacht harbour, Marina	⊕	Underwater rock over which depth is unknown and is considered dangerous to surface navigation
⏣	Yacht berths without facilities		
Ⓥ	Visitor's berth		
⏣	Visitor's mooring		
ⓒⓇⓈ	Coast Radio Station	⊞	Wreck, depth unknown, which is considered dangerous to surface navigation
ⓒⓖ	Coastguard Radio		
ⓟⓡ	Port or Marina Radio		
Ⓥⓣⓢ	Vessel Traffic Service Radio	✳	Rock which covers and uncovers
ⓣⓢⓢ	Traffic Separation Scheme Radio		
CG ⚠	Coastguard MRCC/MRSC	⊚))	Fog signal
⚲	Weather information	#	Foul area no longer dangerous to surface navigation
ⓡⓒ	Marine Radiobeacon		
ⓡⓒ Aero	Aeronautical Radiobeacon	⌘	Church
⊕	Harbour Masters Office	⚊	Radio tower/mast
✳	Anchoring prohibited	☉	Radio or Radar aid
⚓	Recommended anchorage	▶	Yacht Club, Sailing Club
Ⓗ	Hospital	▦	Customs
ⓘ	Visitor's information	△	Precautionary area
⊙	Laundrette	⌘	Church, chapel
⊠	Post Office	⌐	Public slipway
✈	Airport	⌐	Public landing, Steps, Ladder
⊥	Water tap	▯	Fuel station (Petrol, Diesel)
WC	Public toilets	▯	Refuse bin
⌁	Search & Rescue helicopter	♁⚏	Holding tank pumpout
⎍	Railway station	△	Precautionary area
⊕	Waypoint	▦	Customs
☆	Major light	◆	Lifeboat station
⊛	Rock awash at chart datum	⊖	Fishing harbour

BUOYS

▲ ▲ ◢ ◣	Starboard Hand Mark (SHM) (lit & unlit)
◹ ◺	Port Hand Mark (PHM) (lit & unlit)
⚐ ⚑	North Cardinal Mark (NCM) (lit & unlit)
⚐ ⚑	East Cardinal Mark (ECM) (lit & unlit)
⚐ ⚑	South Cardinal Mark (SCM) (lit & unlit)
⚐ ⚑	West Cardinal Mark (WCM) (lit & unlit)
⚐ ⚑ ⚬ ⚬ ⚐ ⚑	Safe Water Mark (SWM) (lit & unlit)
⚑ ⚑ ⚑ ⚑	Isolated Danger Mark (IDM) (lit & unlit)
⚐ ⚑ ⚬ ⚬ ⚑ ⚑	Special Marks (lit & unlit)
⊏⊐	Light Vessel, Light Float, Lanby
◬ ◬ ◺ ◹	Single colour other than green or black
◣ ◢ ◿ ◺ ◣ ◢	Single colour other than red or black
◣ ◢	Mooring buoy (lit & unlit)

THE PINK PAGE DIRECTORY

This useful guide is the *"Yellow Pages"* for boat owners.

SECTION 1 lists more than ninety services which all owners will require from time to time. It provides a quick and easy reference to manufacturers and retailers of equipment, services and supplies both nationally and locally at coastal locations around the British Isles, together with harbours, marinas and emergency services. Each entry carries concise information for guidance.

SECTION 2 lists waterside accommodation - hotels and restaurants which in many instances have their own berths and moorings and cater for travelling yachtsmen and their families.

SECTION 3 lists service and product providers by coastal area and will be especially useful for in transit maintenance, emergencies or simply planning ahead from port to port.

If you are unable to find the service you require, visit the PINK PAGE DIRECTORY website: www.nauticaldata.com or call us on **01494 782376.**

CONTENTS

AIR CONDITIONING

CRUISAIR UK LTD - TAYLOR MADE ENVIRONMENTAL SYSTEMS
26 Old Wareham Road, Poole,
Dorset BH12 4QR.
Tel (01202) 716469 Fax (01202) 716478
e-mail: sales@cruisair.co.uk
Marine air conditioning.

ANENOMETERS/ AUTOPILOTS

SIMRAD LTD
Woolmer Way, Bordon,
Hampshire GU35 9QE.
Tel (01420) 483200 Fax (01420) 489073
For full entry see under:
ELECTRONIC DEVICES & EQUIPMENT

THOMAS WALKER GROUP LTD
37-41 Bissell Street,
Birmingham B5 7HR.
Tel 0121-622 4475 Fax 0121-622 4478
Manufacturer of marine instruments including, Neco Autopilots, Walker Logs and Towing Logs, Walker Anemometers, Chernikeeff Logs.

ASSOCIATIONS

CHART & NAUTICAL INSTRUMENT TRADE ASSOCIATION (CNITA)
The Secretaries, Dalmore House,
310 St Vincent Street, Glasgow G2 5QR.
Tel 0141-226 8000 Fax 0141-228 8310
Members of the Association are able to place their experience and service at the disposal of the shipping industry and all navigators.

ROYAL INSTITUTE OF NAVIGATION
1 Kensington Gore, London SW7 2AT.
Tel 020 7591 3130 Fax 020 7591 3131
Forum for all interested in navigation - Air: Sea: Land: Space.

THE TRIDENT FORUM
c/o Posford Duvivier, Eastchester House,
Harlands Road, Haywards Heath,
East Sussex RH16 1PG.
Tel (01444) 458551 Fax (01444) 440665
e-mail: proach@posford-hh.co.uk
The Trident Forum provides knowledge, experience and commitment in marine-related work. Our members are professional firms, skilled in a multitude of marine fields. The Forum's purpose is to make these skills easily accessible through a single point of reference.

ASTRO NAVIGATION

REED'S NAUTICAL BOOKS
The Barn, Ford Farm, Bradford Leigh,
Bradford on Avon, Wiltshire BA15 2RP.
Tel (01225) 868821 Fax (01225) 868831
e-mail: tugsrus@abreed.demon.co.uk
REED'S HEAVENLY BODIES - Annual astro-navigation tables for yachtsmen edited by Lt Cdr H J Baker. Price £13.95 incl p&p. Showing monthly pages for Sun, Moon, Planets and Stars accompanied by examples and all necessary tables. Complete SIGHT REDUCTION PACKAGE with programmed calculator also available together with book and chart catalogues, for worldwide mail order.
Website: www.reedsnautical.com

BATTERIES & BATTERY EQUIPMENT

G B ATTFIELD & COMPANY
29 Woodmancote, Dursley,
Gloucestershire GL11 4AF.
Tel/Fax +44 (0) 1453 547185
VOLTWATCH battery monitor, the 'Fuel Gauge for your Battery'. See our display advertisement below.

BERTHS & MOORINGS

BALTIC WHARF WATER LEISURE CENTRE
Bristol Harbour, Underfall Yard,
Bristol BS1 6XG.
Tel 0117-929 7608 Fax 0117-929 4454
Tuition: 0117-952 5202
Sailing school and centre, with qualified instruction in most watersports. Also moorings available throughout the Bristol harbour for all types of leisurecraft.

W BATES & SON BOATBUILDERS LTD
Bridge Wharf, Chertsey, Surrey KT16 8LG.
Tel (01932) 562255 Fax (01932) 565600
110-berth marina in quiet picturesque area

and additional riverside moorings. Fu facilities including electricity to most berths toilets and showers. 12-ton crane and har standing for winter storage. Always welcome to visitors from our friendly staf Sales office open seven days a week.

BRIGHTON MARINA
Marine Trade Centre, Brighton Marina,
Brighton, East Sussex BN2 5UG.
Tel (01273) 819919 Fax (01273) 675082
The UK's No 1 marina village with 130 pontoon berths. 24-hour manned receptio and CCTV. Five-Gold Anchors for faciltie and service with excellent new toilet an showers. Full boatyard and shore facilitie with Marine Trade Centre offering a associated trades and leisure area with 1 pub/restaurants, ASDA superstore, Virgi cinema, David Lloyd Health Centre an Bowlplex. Entrance dredged to 2 metres with 24-hour access to the sea withou locking. Five minutes from Brighton tow centre.

BURGH CASTLE MARINA
Butt Lane, Burgh Castle,
Norfolk, Norwich NR31 9PZ.
Tel (01493) 780331 Fax (01493) 780163
e-mail: rdw_chesham@compuserve.con
100 serviced pontoons and quay moorings accessible at all tides. Secure car and boa parking. Adjoining boatyard services, access to holiday park showers, laundry and heatec pool. Riverside pub and shop. Complex open all year.

CARRICKFERGUS WATERFRONT
The Marina' Rodger's Quay,
Carrickfergus, Co Antrim,
Northern Ireland BT38 8BE.
Tel +44 (0) 28 93366666
Fax +44 (0) 28 93350505
e-mail: carrick.marina@virgin.net
300 fully serviced pontoon berths with excellent full on-shore facilities. Steeped in a wealth of historical legend. Carrickfergus has excellent restaurants, hotels, pubs, shops and a host of recreational leisure facilities.

CHELSEA HARBOUR LTD
108 The Chambers, Chelsea Harbour,
London SW10 0XF.
Tel 020 7761 8600 Fax 020 7352 7868
A tranquil and intimate marina of 55 berths close to the heart of the west end of London. 5-Star hotel, restaurants and bars. Overnight pontoon and amenities. 24-hour security patrols and CCTV.

THE CREGGANS INN
Strachur, Argyll PA27 8BX.
Tel (01369) 860279 Fax (01369) 860637
e-mail: info@creggans-inn.co.uk
The Creggans Inn makes a useful stop for lunch, dinner or overnight respite! Five moorings available. Bar meals from 12 noon - 2.30pm and 6pm to 9pm (Saturday and Sunday 12 noon - 8pm). Excellent restaurant serving from 7pm to 9.30pm. Shower and changing facilities for our travelling yachtsmen.

CRINAN BOATS LTD
Crinan, Lochgilphead, Argyll PA31 8SP.
Tel (01546) 830232 Fax (01546) 830281
Boatbuilders, chandlers, engineers, slipping, repairs, charts, electricians, pontoon, moorings, showers, laundry and basic stores.

DART MARINA
Sandquay, Dartmouth, Devon TQ6 9PH.
Tel (01803) 833351 Fax (01803) 832307
High quality 110-berth marina on the fabulous river Dart, opposite the Dart Marina hotel. A superb situation with all amenities, 24-hour security, hotel and restaurant, showers, baths and laundry, fuel berth, holding tank pump-out facility and a warm welcome to all visitors.

DEAN & REDDYHOFF LTD
- EAST COWES MARINA
Clarence Road, East Cowes,
Isle of Wight PO32 6HA.
Tel (01983) 293983 Fax (01983) 299276
This existing marina (but new to Dean and Reddyhoff) is undergoing a facelift which will include dredging, new pontoons, toilets and showers and possibly a clubhouse. Regular yachtsmen, visitors and rallies will be welcome as before.

DEAN & REDDYHOFF LTD
- HASLAR MARINA
Haslar Road, Gosport,
Hampshire PO12 1NU.
Tel 023 9260 1201 Fax 023 9260 2201
Haslar Marina is just inside the entrance of Portsmouth harbour on the Gosport side. Included in the 600 berths is a visitors' area which is adjacent to a converted lightship with bar facilities and excellent toilets and showers.

DEAN & REDDYHOFF LTD
- WEYMOUTH MARINA
70 Commercial Road, Weymouth,
Dorset DT4 8NA.
Tel (01305) 767576 Fax (01305) 767575
This new marina in the inner harbour of Weymouth provides facilities for visitors which are proving very popular. The marina is right next to Weymouth's high street, and the area has a multitude of pubs and restaurants.

DUCHY OF CORNWALL
Harbour Office, St Mary's,
Isles of Scilly, Cornwall TR21 0HU.
Tel/Fax (01720) 422768
Harbour of St Mary's, Isles of Scilly - 38 visitor moorings. Visitor centre, hot showers, toilets, launching facilities, winter storage, security lockers, fuel and fresh water. Five minutes from town centre. Ferry terminal and airport close by. Contact Harbour Master for more information.

ELKINS BOATYARD
Tidesreach, 18 Convent Meadow,
The Quay, Christchurch,
Dorset BH23 1BD.
Tel (01202) 483141
All boatyard facilities. Moorings alongside, water and electricity, storage ashore, repairs. Boats up to 45', 10 tons maximum, haul-out.

EMSWORTH YACHT HARBOUR LTD
Thorney Road, Emsworth,
Hampshire PO10 8BP.
Tel (01243) 377727 Fax (01243) 373432
Friendly marina in Chichester harbour. Water, electricity, diesel, Calor gas, 25-tonne mobile crane, slipways, hard-standing and storage areas. Showers and toilets, car parking, chandlery, engineers and boat repairs.

FIDDLERS FERRY YACHT HAVEN
Off Station Road, Penketh, Warrington,
Cheshire WA5 2UJ.
Tel (01925) 727519
Sheltered moorings up to 6'6" draught, 50' long. Access through lock from river Mersey 1½ hours either side of high tide. Signed from A652. Boatyard and lift-out facilities. Annual rate per foot £8.25.

THE GUNFIELD Hotel & Restaurant
Castle Road, Dartmouth, Devon TQ6 0JN.
Tel (01803) 834843 Fax (01803) 834772
e-mail: enquiry@gunfield.co.uk
VHF ChM2 or Ch37 Waterfront position with 10 impressive en suite bedrooms, central heating etc, all command fantastic river views. Restaurant offers modestly priced, delicious Mediterranean cuisine. Continental bar and lounge open to non-residents. Large terraces and gardens, BBQs during summer. Pontoon and deep water moorings.
Website: www.gunfield.co.uk

HAFAN PWLLHELI
Glan Don, Pwllheli, Gwynedd LL53 5YT.
Tel (01758) 701219 Fax (01758) 701443
VHF Ch80
Hafan Pwllheli has over 400 pontoon berths and offers access at virtually all states of the tide. Ashore,its modern purpose-built facilities include luxury toilets, showers, landerette, a secure boat park for winterstorage, 40-ton travel hoist, mobile crane and plenty of space for car parking. Open 24-hours a day, 7 days a week.

HALCON MARINE LTD
The Point, Canvey Island, Essex SS8 7TL.
Tel (01268) 511611 Fax (01268) 510044
Marine engineers, repairs and full boatyard services in this quiet and picturesque area. Berths, moorings, slipping facilities. Summer and winter storage. Dry dock (70t max), diesel 1 to 2 hours ±. Water, electric, toilets and showers. A friendly welcome awaits you.

HARTLEPOOL MARINA
Lock Office, Slake Terrace,
Hartlepool, Cleveland TS24 0RU.
Tel (01429) 865744 Fax (01429) 865947
The north's premier marina. The year 2000 sees the completion of a massive redevelopment to include 700 berths, a new 300 ton boat hoist along with luxury leisure, residential and retail facilities on-site. Please call 01429 865744 for more information 24 hours.

THE HAVEN ARMS PUB & RESTAURANT
Henry Street, Kilrush, Co Clare, Ireland.
Tel +353 65 51267 Fax +353 65 51213
'The Haven Arms' - Kilrush - *Sail* into this pub and restaurant which has become a landmark to generations of local people and visitor alike. The 'Ship' restaurant offers appetising meals complemented by good service from our friendly staff. **MOORINGS ARE FREE.**

ISLE OF ANGLESEY COUNTY COUNCIL
Highways & Technical Services
Department, Council Offices, Llangefni,
Anglesey LL77 7TW
Tel (01248) 752331 Fax (01248) 724839
Berths and moorings available at Menai bridge, Amlwch harbour and north east Menai Straits (Beaumaris). Winter storage at competitive rates available at Beaumaris and Amlwch. Contact Maritime Officer 01248 752331 for details.

JERSEY HARBOURS
Maritime House, La Route du Port
Elizabeth, St Helier, Jersey JE1 1HB.
Tel (01534) 885588 Fax (01534) 885599
e-mail: jsyhbr@itl.net
A warm welcome to visiting yachts! St Helier Marina has 50 more finger berths for visitors. 5-Gold Anchor facilities. 3 hours ±HW. Berths available to lease from one month to 10 years in our *NEW ELIZABETH MARINA.*

KAMES HOTEL
Kames, By Tighnabruaich,
Argyll PA21 2AF.
Tel (01700) 811489 Fax (01700) 811 283
On the Kyles of Bute with 15 free moorings. Good food, real ales, fine malts. Showers available for visitors. 10 en-suite bedrooms. Regular music nights. Fresh local seafood in season.

KINSALE YACHT CLUB MARINA
Kinsale, Co Cork, Ireland.
Tel +353 21 772196 Fax +353 21 774455
e-mail: kyc@iol.ie
Magnificent deep water yacht club marina offering Kinsale hospitality to visiting yachtsmen. Full facilities include berths up to 20 metres, fresh water, electricity, diesel on pier. Club bar and wealth of pubs and restaurants in Kinsale. Enter Kinsale Harbour - lit at night - no restrictions.

LIVERPOOL MARINA
Coburg Dock, Sefton Street,
Liverpool L3 4BP.
Tel 0151-709 0578 (2683 after 5pm)
Fax 0151-709 8731
300-berth yacht harbour. All serviced pontoons. Tidal access HW + or - 2½ hours approximately, depending on draught. 60-ton hoist, workshops, bar and restaurant, toilets and showers. City centre one mile. Open all year. Active yacht club and yacht brokerage.

MARITIME TOURISM LTD
- CASTLEPARK MARINA
Kinsale, Co Cork, Ireland.
Tel +353 21 774959 Fax +353 21 774958
100-berth fully serviced marina with restaurant, laundry, showers and toilets.

Waterside hotel-type accommodation available. New restaurant catering for both breakfast and evening meals. Access at all stages of the tide.

THE MAYFLOWER INTERNATIONAL MARINA
Ocean Quay, Richmond Walk, Plymouth, Devon PL1 4LS.
Tel (01752) 556633 Fax (01752) 606896
Plymouth's only Five-Gold Anchor marina. Known for its extensive facilities, courtesy and security. Owned by berth holders and run to a very high standard.

MILFORD MARINA
The Docks, Milford Haven, Pembrokeshire, West Wales SA73 3AE.
Tel (01646) 696312 Fax (01646) 696314
Safe sheltered haven, 250 berths, 5 minutes from shopping, rail and bus services. Water and electricity to all berths. Staff available 24 hours. Restaurant, chandlery, electronics, boat repair, lifting and storage available on-site.

NOSS-ON-DART MARINA
Noss Quay, Dartmouth, Devon TQ6 0EA.
Tel (01803) 833351 Fax (01803) 832307
Peacefully located on the east shore of the river Dart, this relaxing marina is the perfect base for cruising yachtsmen. Extensive parking, chandlery, repair and lift-out facilities, easy access from London and the Midlands. Boat taxi to Dartmouth.

THE OYSTERCATCHER RESTAURANT
Otter Ferry, Argyll PA21 2DH.
Tel (01700) 821229 Fax (01700) 821300
Situated on Loch Fyne, just north of the Otter Spit, about one hour's sailing from the Crinan canal. Moorings (insured to 12t) free to patrons. French chef and superb food, seafood our speciality. 1996 Tourist Board winner 'BEST PLACE TO EAT'. Children's play area.

PADSTOW HARBOUR COMMISSIONERS
Harbour Office, Padstow, Cornwall PL28 8AQ.
Tel (01841) 532239 Fax (01841) 533346
e-mail: padstowharbour@compuserve.com
Inner harbour controlled by tidal gate - opens HW ±2 hours. Minimum depth 3 metres at all times. Yachtsmen must be friendly as vessels raft together. Services include showers, toilets, diesel, water and ice. Security by CCTV.

THE PANDORA INN
Restronguet Creek, Mylor, Falmouth, Cornwall TR11 5ST.
Tel/Fax (01326) 372678
Thatched creek-side inn with floating pontoon. Morning coffee, delicious bar meals, cream teas and fine dining in the superb Andrew Miller restaurant (entitles yachtsmen to free mooring). Telephone, showers and water available. Open all day in the summer.

PARKSTONE YACHT CLUB
Pearce Avenue, Parkstone, Poole, Dorset BH14 8EH.
Tel (01202) 743610 Fax (01202) 716394
e-mail: office@parkstoneyc.co.uk
Deep water club haven facilities in Poole harbour. Access at all states of the tide. Berths for yachts up to 15 metres. Facilities include electricity, fresh water, toilets and showers. Visitors welcome by appointment. Club bar and restaurant.

PORT FLAIR LTD
Bradwell Marina, Waterside, Bradwell-on-Sea, Essex CM0 7RB.
Tel (01621) 776235/776391
300 pontoon berths with water and electricity, petrol and diesel, chandlery, marine slip/hoistage to 20 tons. Repairs, winter lay-ups, licensed club, yacht brokerage.

PORT OF TRURO
Harbour Office, Town Quay, Truro, Cornwall TR1 2HJ.
Tel (01872) 272130 Fax (01872) 225346
VHF Ch12
Facilities for the yachtsman include visitor pontoons located at Turnaware Bar, Ruan Creek and Boscawen Park. Visitor moorings at Woodbury. Quay facilities at Truro with free showers and toilets. Chemical toilet disposal, fresh water, electricity and garbage disposal.

RAMSGATE ROYAL HARBOUR MARINA
Harbour Office, Military Road, Ramsgate, Kent CT11 9LQ.
Tel (01843) 592277 Fax (01843) 590941
Ramsgate Royal Harbour is situated on the south east coast, making an ideal base for crossing to the Continent. 24-hour access to finger pontoons. Comprehensive security systems. Amenities: Launderette, repairs, slipways, boatpark. Competitive rates for permanent berths and discounts for visitors' group bookings.

RHU MARINA LTD
Helensburgh, Dunbartonshire G84 8LH.
Tel (01436) 820238 Fax (01436) 821039
e-mail: any@rhumarina.force9.co.uk
Berths accessible at all times and moorings available on the Clyde at the entrance to the Gareloch and 30 minutes from Glasgow. Hotels, shops and yacht clubs all adjacent.

RUDDERS BOATYARD & MOORINGS
Church Road, Burton, Milford Haven, Pembrokeshire SA73 1NU.
Tel (01646) 600288
Moorings, pontoon, storage. All repairs.

SOUTH DOCK MARINA
South Lock Office, Rope Street, Plough Way, London SE16 1TX.
Tel 020 7252 2244 Fax 020 7237 3806
London's largest marina. 200+ berths. Spacious, tranquil setting. Manned 24 hours. Lift-out for 20 tonnes. Competitve mooring rates.

SWANSEA MARINA
Lockside, Maritime Quarter, Swansea, West Glamorgan SA1 1WG.
Tel (01792) 470310 Fax (01792) 463948
Access all states of the tide except LWST. City centre marina, restaurants, theatres etc. Call us on Ch 18 or 80 to check locking times. Visitors always welcome - a good destination for your annual trip.

WEIR QUAY BOATYARD
Heron's Reach, Bere Alston, Devon PL20 7BT.
Tel (01822) 840474 Fax (01822) 840948
Deepwater swinging moorings, shore storage, full boatyard facilities and services, cranage to 12 tons, repairs, maintenance, slipway. A traditional boatyard at affordable rates *in a superb setting* on the Tamar, with excellent security.

WHITEHAVEN HARBOUR MARINA
Harbour Commissioners, Pears House, 1 Duke Street, Whitehaven, Cumbria CA28 7HW.
Tel (01946) 692435 Fax (01946) 691135
VHF Ch12
Long and short-term berths available at newly created 100 capacity marina, maximum length 12m. Eleven hectare permanent locked harbour with 45 tonne boat hoist, access at least HW ±3hours. Sheltered historic location adjacent to town centre.

WORCESTER YACHT CHANDLERS LTD
Unit 7, 75 Waterworks Road, Barbourne, Worcester WR1 3EZ.
Tel (01905) 22522 & 27949
Chandlery, paints, ropes, cables, chain, clothing, footwear, shackles, books, bottled gas, anti-foul, fastenings, oakam, fenders. Hard storage, crane, haulage, engine service, oils, navigation aids, buoyancy aids, life jackets, distress flares, *small boat hire*.

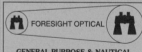
USE THESE PAGES FOR ALL YOUR MARINE SERVICES AND SUPPLIES

FORESIGHT OPTICAL
13 New Road, Banbury,
Oxfordshire OX16 9PN.
Tel (01295) 264365
Suppliers of general purpose and nautical
binoculars, spotting scopes, astronomical
telescopes, night vision equipment, microscopes, magnifiers, spotlights, tripods and
accessories. National mail order service.

BOAT BUILDERS & REPAIRS

ARDFERN YACHT CENTRE
Ardfern By Lochgilphead,
Argyll PA31 8QN.
*Tel (01852) 500247/636 Fax (01852) 500624
and 07000 ARDFERN*
Boatyard with full repair and maintenance
facilities. Timber and GRP repairs, painting
and engineering. Sheltered moorings and
pontoon berthing. Winter storage,
chandlery, showers, fuel, Calor, brokerage,
20-ton boat hoist, rigging. Hotel, bars and
restaurant.

BOATWORKS + LTD
Castle Emplacement, St Peter Port,
Guernsey, Channel Islands GY1 1AU.
Tel (01481) 726071 Fax (01481) 714224
Boatworks+ provides a comprehensive
range of services including boatbuilding
and repairs, chandlery, clothing and fuel
supplies.

CRINAN BOATS LTD
Crinan, Lochgilphead, Argyll PA31 8SP.
Tel (01546) 830232 Fax (01546) 830281
Boatbuilders, chandlers, engineers, slipping, repairs, charts, electricians, pontoon,
moorings, showers, laundry and basic
stores.

DARTHAVEN MARINA LTD
Brixham Road, Kingswear,
Dartmouth, Devon TQ6 0SG.
*Tel (01803) 752242 Fax (01803) 752722
Marina Office: (01803) 752545
Chandlery: (01803) 752733
Fax (01803) 752790 VHF Ch80.*
All types of repair facilities available. Fully
trained staff. 30-ton mobile hoist available
all states of tide. Extensive chandlery open
7 days. Agents for all major suppliers
including B&G, Raytheon, Yanmar (Main
Dealers),Volvo Penta agents, Simpson
Lawrence, Sowester installer dealer,
International Coatings and many others.
Emergency engineer call out - Mobile: 0411
404259. Electrician - Mobile: 0467 250787.
Visitors welcome. All marina facilities
available.

ELKINS BOATYARD
Tidesreach, 18 Convent Meadow,
The Quay, Christchurch,
Dorset BH23 1BD.
Tel (01202) 483141
All boatyard facilities. Moorings alongside,
water and electricity, storage ashore,
repairs. Boats up to 45', 10 tons maximum,
haul-out.

HAINES BOATYARD
Itchenor, Chichester,
West Sussex PO20 7AN.
Tel (01243) 512228 Fax (01243) 513900
Racing keelboat specialists. Boat building
and repairs with top quality joinery in teak
and other hardwoods. Controlled fibreglass
and epoxy work facilities. Moorings and
winter boat and dinghy storage, masts spars
and rigging service.

HULL MARINA LTD
Warehouse 13, Kingston Street,
Hull HU1 2DQ.
Tel (01482) 613451 Fax (01482) 224148
Four-Anchor marina. Situated 5 minutes
from the centre of Hull and all national and
international transport systems. First class
leisure, boatyard and brokerage facilities.
4-Star hotel and quayside restaurants. Professional and caring staff. Competitive rates.

LANGNEY MARINE SERVICES LTD
Sovereign Harbour Marina,
Pevensey Bay Road,
Eastbourne, East Sussex BN23 6JH.
Tel (01323) 470244 Fax (01323) 470255
We offer a complete service to the boat
owner offering repairs on all types of eng-
ines, GRP, steel, wood, electronics, rigging,
cleaning, etc. We are also contractors to the
RNLI.

MILFORD MARINA
The Docks, Milford Haven,
Pembrokeshire, West Wales SA73 3AE.
Tel (01646) 696312 Fax (01646) 696314
Safe sheltered haven, 250 berths, 5 min-
utes from shopping, rail and bus services.
Water and electricity to all berths. Staff
available 24 hours. Restaurant, chandlery,
electronics, boat repair, lifting and storage
available on-site.

ROSDEN GLASS FIBRE
La Rue Durell, La Collette, St Helier,
Jersey JE2 3NB.
Tel (01534) 625418 Fax (01534) 625419
Specialists in all types of glass fibre marine
works, structural repairs, alterations, re-
flow coating, GEL coat work. Blakes and
International approved osmosis treatment
centre. Spray painting. Manufacturer of fuel
tanks, bathing platforms and boat builders.
General refurbishment and polishing. A
division of Precision Plastics (Jersey) Ltd.

SLEAT MARINE SERVICES
Ardvasar, Isle of Skye IV45 8RS.
*Tel (01471) 844216 Fax (01471) 844387
e-mail: enquiries
@sleatmarineservices.co.uk*
Yacht charter (bareboat and skippered) from
Armadale Bay, Isle of Skye.Six yachts 34' to
40' LOA. All medium to heavy displacement
blue water cruisers. Fuel, water and emergency services for passing yachts with problems.
Website: www.sleatmarineservices.co.uk

SOUTHDOWN MARINA
Southdown Quay, Millbrook,
Cornwall PL10 1HG.
Tel/Fax (01752) 823084
32-berth marina on edge of river Tamar in
quiet location behind Rame Peninsula.

Plymouth is just across the river. Quayside
berths available for large vessels. Dry
Berthing. 24-hour security. DIY facilities
available.

WINTERS MARINE LTD
(Lincombe Boatyard)
Lincombe, Salcombe, Devon TQ8 8NQ.
*Tel (01548) 843580
e-mail: lincombeboatyard@eclipse.co.uk*
Deep water pontoon moorings. Winter storage for 150 boats. All maintenance and
repair facilities. Slipway capacity 30 tonnes.
Inflatable raft sales and service. Liferaft
surveys and repairs. Short and long-term
liferaft hire.

BOAT JUMBLES

SCOTTISH BOAT JUMBLE
Steelbank Cottage, Dalgarven,
Nr Kilwinning, Ayrshire KA13 6PL.
Fax (01294) 552417 Mobile: 0421 888789
New and used nautical bargains galore.
Everything from radios, safety equipment,
clothing and deck equipment. Jumbles held
in Scotland twice a year - Ireland and New-
castle once a year. See main advertisement.

BOAT NAMING SYSTEMS

GRAPHIC INNOVATION
35 Chequers Hill, Amersham,
Buckinghamshire HP7 9DQ.
*Tel/Fax (01494) 431500
e-mail: info@graphicinnovation.com*
Leading specialist manufacturer of self-
adhesive graphics for the marine industry.
Original equipment volume production for
boatbuilders, or individual one-off names
etc for boat owners.
Website: www.graphicinnovation.com

WET & WILD GRAPHICS
Falcon House, Hamble Point Marina,
Hamble, Southampton,
Hampshire SO31 4NB.
*Tel 023 8045 8332 Fax 023 8045 6830
e-mail: sales@wild-graphics.co.uk*
Supply and application of vinyl graphics,
signboards, banners and flags. Specialist
materials for sails and spinnakers. Brochure
available for mail order boat names. Dead-
lines never a problem!!!
Website: www.wild-graphics.co.uk

BOAT STORAGE

CALEY MARINA
Canal Road, Inverness IV3 6NF.
*Tel +44 (0) 1463 236539
Fax +44 (0) 1463 238323
e-mail: info@caleymarina.com*
Open 08.30 - 17.30. Berths: 50 Pontoons
(visitors available). Facilities: Fuel, water,
pump-out facilities, provisions (nearby
shops), repair, cranage, secure storage
afloat and ashore. Comprehensive chandlery, showers, workshop. Situated at eastern
end of Caledonian canal above Muirtown
locks. Access via sea locks 4 hours either
side of high water.
Website: www.caleymarina.com

ELKINS BOATYARD
Tidesreach, 18 Convent Meadow,
The Quay, Christchurch,
Dorset BH23 1BD.
Tel (01202) 483141
All boatyard facilities. Moorings alongside, water and electricity, storage ashore, repairs. Boats up to 45', 10 tons maximum, haul-out.

EMSWORTH YACHT HARBOUR LTD
Thorney Road, Emsworth,
Hampshire PO10 8BP.
Tel (01243) 377727 Fax (01243) 373432
Friendly marina in Chichester harbour. Water, electricity, diesel, Calor gas, 25-tonne mobile crane, slipways, hard-standing and storage areas. Showers and toilets, car parking, chandlery, engineers and boat repairs.

HALCON MARINE LTD
The Point, Canvey Island, Essex SS8 7TL.
Tel (01268) 511611 Fax (01268) 510044
Marine engineers, repairs and full boatyard services in this quiet and picturesque area. Berths, moorings, slipping facilities. Summer and winter storage. Dry dock (70t max), diesel 1 to 2 hours ±. Water, electric, toilets and showers. A friendly welcome awaits you.

ISLE OF ANGLESEY COUNTY COUNCIL
Highways & Technical Services
Department, Council Offices,
Llangefni, Anglesey LL77 7TW
Tel (01248) 752331 Fax (01248) 724839
Berths and moorings available at Menai bridge, Amlwch harbour and north east Menai Straits (Beaumaris). Winter storage at competitive rates available at Beaumaris and Amlwch. Contact Maritime Officer 01248 752331 for details.

SOUTHDOWN MARINA
Southdown Quay, Millbrook,
Cornwall PL10 1HG.
Tel/Fax (01752) 823084
32-berth marina on edge of river Tamar in quiet location behind Rame Peninsula. Plymouth is just across the river. Quayside berths available for large vessels. Dry Berthing. 24-hour security. DIY facilities available.

SPARKES YACHT HARBOUR LTD
38 Wittering Road, Hayling Island,
Hampshire PO11 9SR.
Tel 023 9246 3572 Fax 023 9246 5741
e-mail:
enquiries@sparkesmarina.freeserve.co.uk
Sparkes Marina - a small friendly, family run business offering all the facilities you require including access at all states of the tide to a depth of 2 metres at lowest low water springs. In addition to marina berths, accessible through a security gate, we also offer dry boat sailing, moorings, storage ashore plus full maintenance facilities, new boat sales and brokerage, chandlery and restaurant.

BOATYARD SERVICES & SUPPLIES

ARDORAN MARINE
Lerags, Oban, Argyll PA34 4SE.
Tel (01631) 566123 Fax (01631) 566611
All marine services. Moorings and self-catering chalets.

BURGH CASTLE MARINA
Butt Lane, Burgh Castle, Norfolk,
Norwich NR31 9PZ.
Tel (01493) 780331 Fax (01493) 780163
e-mail: *rdw_chesham@compuserve.com*
100 serviced pontoons and quay moorings accessible at all tides. Secure car and boat parking. Adjoining boatyard services, access to holiday park showers, laundry and heated pool. Riverside pub and shop. Complex open all year.

CHALLENGER MARINE
Freeman's Wharf, Falmouth Road,
Penryn, Cornwall TR10 8AS.
Tel (01326) 377222 Fax (01326) 377800
Marine engineers, chandlery, boatyard. Main Volvo Penta dealer, marina berths, brokerage, Bombard and Zodiac inflatables' dealer.

CRAOBH MARINA
By Lochgilphead, Argyll PA31 8UD.
Tel (01852) 500222 Fax (01852) 500252
VHF Ch37 and 80 (M).
250-berth marina on Loch Shuna. Water, electricity, diesel and gas. Full boatyard services.Chandlery. Brokerage. Insurance. Shops, bar. 24-hour access.

DALE SAILING COMPANY
Brunel Quay, Neyland, Milford Haven,
Pembrokeshire SA73 1PY.
Tel (01646) 601636 Fax (01646) 601061
Engine service and repair, hull repair, chandlery. Boatyard, lifting, boat building, sea school and new and used boat sales.

DART MARINA
Sandquay, Dartmouth, Devon TQ6 9PH.
Tel (01803) 833351 Fax (01803) 832307
High quality 110-berth marina on the fabulous river Dart, opposite the Dart Marina hotel. A superb situation with all amenities, 24-hour security, hotel and restaurant, showers, baths and laundry, fuel berth, holding tank pump-out facility and a warm welcome to all visitors.

DEACONS BOATYARD LTD
Bursledon Bridge, Southampton,
Hampshire SO31 8AZ.
Tel 023 8040 2253 Fax 023 8040 5665
This yard has all major services for yachts-men. Moorings, hardstanding, repairs, marine engineers, riggers, chandlery and brokerage - new yacht sales. Deacons are UK importers for Feeling yachts.

FIDDLERS FERRY YACHT HAVEN
Off Station Road, Penketh, Warrington,
Cheshire WA5 2UJ.
Tel (01925) 727519
Sheltered moorings up to 6'6" draught, 50' long. Access through lock from river Mersey 1½ hours either side of high tide. Signed

from A652. Boatyard and lift-out facilities. Annual rate per foot £8.25.

HALCON MARINE LTD
The Point, Canvey Island, Essex SS8 7TL.
Tel (01268) 511611 Fax (01268) 510044
Marine engineers, repairs and full boatyard services in this quiet and picturesque area. Berths, moorings, slipping facilities. Summer and winter storage. Dry dock (70t max), diesel 1 to 2 hours ±. Water, electric, toilets and showers. A friendly welcome awaits you.

HARBOUR MARINE
Marrowbone Slip, Sutton Road,
Plymouth, Devon PL4 0HX.
Tel (01752) 204690/1
Parts Dept: (01752) 204696
Fax (01752) 204693
A complete boatyard and engineering service situated on one side, facilities from haulout, full engineering workshop, osmosis treatment. Specialising in leisure or commercial boat building and repairs.

JACKSON YACHT SERVICES
Le Boulevard, St Aubin, Jersey,
Channel Islands JE3 8AB.
Tel (01534) 743819 Fax (01534) 745952
Boatyard, chandler, sailoft, liferaft service, yacht management and brokerage.

KIP MARINA
The Yacht Harbour, Inverkip,
Renfrewshire PA16 0AS.
Tel (01475) 521485 Fax (01475) 521298
Marina berths for vessels up to 65' LOA. Full boatyard facilities including travel hoist, crane, on-site engineers, GRP repairs etc. Bar, restaurant, saunas, launderette and chandlery. Distributors for Moody yachts, Northshore and Searanger motor yachts.

LOCH NESS CHARTERS
The Boatyard, Dochgarroch,
Inverness IV3 6JY.
Tel (01463) 861303 Fax (01463) 861353
Yacht and cruiser charter. Boat services and repairs. Hardstanding and slipway. Diesel supply. Boat finishing.

THE MAYFLOWER INTERNATIONAL MARINA
Ocean Quay, Richmond Walk,
Plymouth, Devon PL1 4LS.
Tel (01752) 556633 Fax (01752) 606896
Plymouth's only Five-Gold Anchor marina. Known for its extensive facilities, courtesy and security. Owned by berth holders and run to a very high standard.

NOSS-ON-DART MARINA
Noss Quay, Dartmouth, Devon TQ6 0EA.
Tel (01803) 833351 Fax (01803) 832307
Peacefully located on the east shore of the river Dart, this relaxing marina is the perfect base for cruising yachtsmen. Extensive parking, chandlery, repair and lift-out facilities, easy access from London and the Midlands. Boat taxi to Dartmouth.

PAUL JOHNSON LTD
Marine Vessel Management
Unit 6, 24 Station Square,
Inverness IV1 1LD.
Tel 07074 370 470 Fax 07074 370 570
e-mail: info@pauljohnson.co.uk
We manage all aspects of the day to day and
long-term running of your vessel. Giving
store support to you or your captain. Leaving
you the pleasure of owning a boat.
Independent insurance and finance,
brokerage, crews, registration and maintain,
but NO HEADACHES!
Website: www.pauljohnson.co.uk

PORT FALMOUTH BOATYARD
North Parade, Falmouth,
Cornwall TR11 2TB.
Tel (01326) 313248 Fax (01326) 319395
Powered hoist and slipway. Cradle with 100
tons capacity. Shipwrights, marine
engineering, hard standing and friendly
efficient service.

RETREAT BOATYARD (TOPSHAM) LTD
Retreat Drive, Topsham, Exeter,
Devon EX3 OLS.
Tel (01392) 874720 & 875934
Fax (01392) 876182
Five minutes off M5 (Junction 30) the
traditional service yard. International centre
for Gelshield and Interspray. Agent for Volvo
Penta, Yamaha and Bukh. Dealer for Avon,
Autohelm, Seldén and Whitlock. Boat
repairs, rigging, mooring, storage, com-
prehensive chandlery. Brokerage and
insurance department.

SHOTLEY MARINA LTD
Shotley Gate, Ipswich, Suffolk IP9 1QJ.
Tel (01473) 788982 Fax (01473) 788868
Fully equipped yard and repair service.
Heated workshop (up to 90' LOA). Experts
in wood, GRP and steel fabricated vessels
from small repairs to full refits. Registered
Blakes osmosis centre. Commissioning of
new vessels. Please call for further
information for a free quotation.

SOUTHSEA MARINA
Fort Cumberland Road, Southsea,
Hampshire PO4 9RJ.
Tel 023 9282 2719 Fax 023 9282 2220
e-mail: southseamarina@ibm.net
Marina operators, yard services, chandlery,
brokerage. Sea school. Bar and restaurant.
Visitor berthing, dry boating, winter
hardstanding, on-site contractors, glass
fibre repairs, osmosis treatment, engineers,
riggers, sail repairs, sail alterations and
upholstery.
Website: www.southsea-marina.com

SPARKES YACHT HARBOUR LTD
38 Wittering Road, Hayling Island,
Hampshire PO11 9SR.
Tel 023 9246 3572 Fax 023 9246 5741
e-mail: enquiries@sparkesmarina.frees
erve.co.uk
Sparkes Marina - a small friendly, family
run business offering all the facilities you
require including access at all states of the
tide to a depth of 2 metres at lowest low
water springs. In addition to marina berths,
accessible through a security gate, we also
offer dry boat sailing, moorings, storage

ashore plus full maintenance facilities, new
boat sales and brokerage, chandlery and
restaurant.

TITCHMARSH MARINA
Coles Lane, Walton-on-the-Naze,
Essex CO14 8SL.
Tel (01255) 672185 Fax (01255) 851901
Friendly service in the peaceful backwaters.
Visiting yachtsmen welcome. Sheltered
marina berths. Full marina facilities: Travel-
lift, cranage, 16 amp electricity, diesel.
Winter storage. Restaurant and bar open
every day. (See Harbour Lights Restaurant.)

TOLLESBURY MARINA
The Yacht Harbour, Tollesbury,
Maldon, Essex CM9 8SE.
Tel (01621) 869202 Fax (01621) 868489
e-mail: marina@woodrolfe.demon.uk
VHF Ch37 and 80
Dedicated to customer service, this family-
run marina can offer 240 marina berths
with water and electricity on all pontoons.
Cruising club with bar, restaurant,
swimming pool and tennis courts. Repair
workshop, osmosis treatment centre. Full
brokerage service listing over 200 boats.

WEIR QUAY BOATYARD
Heron's Reach, Bere Alston,
Devon PL20 7BT.
Tel (01822) 840474 Fax (01822) 840948
Deepwater swinging moorings, shore
storage, full boatyard facilities and services,
cranage to 12 tons, repairs, maintenance,
slipway. A traditional boatyard at affordable
rates *in a superb setting* on the Tamar, with
excellent security.

BOOKS & CHARTS/ PUBLISHERS

BOGERD NAVTEC NV
Oude Leeuwenrui 37, Antwerp 2000,
Belgium.
Books and charts.

BOOK CABIN
Unit 20, Canutes Pavilion, Ocean Village,
Southampton, Hampshire SO14 3JS.
Tel 023 8021 1199 Fax 023 8033 8488
Nautical and general booksellers.

BROWN SON & FERGUSON LTD
4-10 Darnley Street, Glasgow G41 2SD.
Tel 0141-429 1234
Books and charts.

W & H CHINA
Howley Properties Ltd., PO Box 149,
Warrington WA1 2DW.
Fax (01925) 418009
Manufacturer of China chart dividers.

B COOKE & SON LTD
Kingston Observatory,
58-59 Market Place, Hull HU1 1RH.
Tel (01482) 223454
Books and Charts. DoT Certified Compass
Adjusters - available day or night.

DUBOIS, PHILLIPS & McCALLUM LTD
Mersey Chambers, Covent Garden,
Liverpool L2 8UF.
Tel 0151-236 2776
Books and charts.

IMRAY LAURIE NORIE AND WILSON LTD
Wych House, The Broadway, St Ives,
Huntingdon, Cambridgeshire PE17 4BT.
Tel (01480) 462114 Fax (01480) 496109
e-mail: ilnw@imray.com
Publishers of nautical charts and books.
Imray's chart list is the most comprehensive
available for yachtsmen. Imray pilots are
available for home waters, the Mediterr-
anean and distant waters. Also Admiralty
specialised chart distributor.
Website: www.imray.com

IVER C WEILBACH & CO., A/S
35 Toldbodgade, Postbox 1560, DK-1253
Copenhagen K, Denmark.
Books and charts.

JOHN LILLEY & GILLIE LTD
Clive Street, North Shields,
Tyne & Wear NE29 6LF.
Tel 0191-257 2217
Books and Charts. DoT Certified Compass
Adjusters - available day or night.

J GARRAIO & CO LTD
Avenida 24 de Julho, 2-1°, D-1200,
Lisbon, Portugal.
Books and Charts.

KELVIN HUGHES
Glasgow: 26 Holland Street,
Glasgow G2 4LR.
Tel 0141-221 5452 Fax 0141-221 4688
e-mail: glasgow@kelvinhughes.co.uk
The world's largest chart agency. The
world's finest nautical bookshops, plus
software, navigation instruments, for all
your chart table requirements.

KELVIN HUGHES
Southampton: Kilgraston House,
Southampton Street,
Southampton SO15 2ED.
Tel 023 8063 4911 Fax 023 8033 0014
e-mail: southampton@kelvinhughes.co.uk

KELVIN HUGHES
City of London: 142 Minories,
London EC3N 1NH.
Tel 020 7709 9076 Fax 020 7481 1298
e-mail: minories@kelvinhughes.co.uk

KELVIN HUGHES
CHARTS & MARITIME SUPPLIES
New North Road, Hainault,
Ilford, Essex IG6 2UR.
Tel 020 8500 1020
Books and charts. DoT Certified Compass
Adjusters - available day or night.

KELVIN HUGHES OBSERVATOR BV
Nieuwe Langeweg 41, 3194 DC Hoogvliet
(Rt), Rotterdam, The Netherlands.
Book and charts. DoT Certified Compass
Adjusters - available day or night.

**Please mention
The Pink Page Directory
when making enquiries**

LONDON YACHT CENTRE LTD - LYC
13 Artillery Lane, London E1 7LP.
Tel 020 7247 2047 Fax 020 7377 5680
Newly refitted book and chart department
with over 2000 titles covering subjects
including navigation, astro' and meteor-
ology, RYA endorsed publications, boat
preparation and maintenance, design and
construction, racing, cruising guides, pilots
and almanacs, fiction and biographies,
computer software and videos. Imray,
Stamford's and Admiralty SC charts - plus
four floors of chandlery.

MARINE INSTRUMENTS
The Bosun's Locker, Upton Slip,
Falmouth, Cornwall TR11 3DQ.
Tel (01326) 312414
Books and charts. DoT Certified Compass
Adjusters - available day or night.

MARTIN & CO
Oude Leewenrui 37, Antwerp 2000,
Belgium.
Books and charts. DoT Certified Compass
Adjusters - available day or night.

R J MUIR
22 Seymour Close, Chandlers Ford,
Eastleigh, Southampton SO5 2JE.
Tel 023 8026 1042
Books and charts. DoT Certified Compass
Adjusters - available day or night.

OCEAN LEISURE LTD
11-14 Northumberland Avenue,
London WC2N 5AQ.
Tel 020 7930 5050 Fax 020 7930 3032
e-mail: info@oceanleisure.co.uk
Complete range of sailing clothing, swim
and beachwear stocked all year round.
Chandlery includes marine electronic
equipment, marine antiques, books and
charts. Also canoeing, underwater photography, diving and waterskiing specialists.
Learn to scuba dive.
Website: www.oceanleisure.co.uk

W F PRICE & CO LTD
Northpoint House, Wapping Wharf,
Bristol BS1 6UD.
Tel 0117-929 2229
Books and charts. DoT Certified Compass
Adjusters - available day or night.

REED'S NAUTICAL BOOKS
The Barn, Ford Farm, Bradford Leigh,
Bradford on Avon, Wiltshire BA15 2RP.
Tel (01225) 868821 Fax (01225) 868831
e-mail: tugsrus@abreed.demon.co.uk
REED'S HEAVENLY BODIES - Annual astro-
navigation tables for yachtsmen edited by
Lt Cdr H J Baker. Price £13.95 incl p&p.
Showing monthly pages for Sun, Moon,
Planets and Stars accompanied by examples
and all necessary tables. Complete SIGHT
REDUCTION PACKAGE with programmed
calculator also available together with book
and chart catalogues, for worldwide mail
order.
Website: www.reedsnautical.com

S I R S NAVIGATION LTD
186a Milton Road, Swanscombe,
Kent DA10 0LX.
Tel (01322) 383672
Books and Charts. DoT Certified Compass
Adjusters - available day or night.

**THE SEA CHEST
NAUTICAL BOOKS & CHARTS**
Queen Anne's Battery Marina,
Plymouth, Devon PL4 0LP.
Tel (01752) 222012 Fax (01752) 252679
Admiralty Chart Agent. Worldwide mail
order service.

SEATH INSTRUMENTS (1992) LTD
Unit 30, Colville Road Works, Colville
Road, Lowestoft NR33 9QS.
Tel (01502) 573811
Books and charts. DoT Certified Compass
Adjusters - available day or night.

SHAMROCK CHANDLERY
Shamrock Quay, William Street,
Northam, Southampton,
Hampshire SO14 5QL.
Tel 023 8063 2725 Fax 023 8022 5611
e-mail: sales@shamrock.co.uk
Situated on Shamrock Quay, a busy working
yard with a pub, restaurant and boutiques.
Shamrock Chandlery is renowned for
extensive quality stocks and service, and is
widely used by both the trade and boat
owners. Excellent mail order facilities - Order
Hotline 023 8022 5746.
Website: www.shamrock.co.uk

A M SMITH (MARINE) LTD
33 Epping Way, Chingford,
London E4 7PB.
Tel 020 8529 6988
Books and charts.

SOFTWAVE
Riverside, Mill Lane, Taplow,
Maidenhead SL6 0AA.
Tel 01628 637777 Fax 01628 773030
Provider of PC based navigation *Seavision*
hardware and *Nobeltec* and *Transas*
software. Using charts drawn from
Admiralty sources the quality navigation
software that we provide can be easily
installed to customers own laptops or
computers. For on-board installations we
manufacture hardware that include sun-
readable, waterproof screens linked to high
performance, ruggedised compact PCs.
Website: www.softwave.co.uk

STANFORDS CHARTS
Editorial Office, PO Box 2747,
Tollesbury, Maldon, Essex CM9 8XE.
Sales Office: 9-10 Southern Court,
South Street, Reading RG1 4QS.
Tel 01621 868580 Fax 0118-959 8283
e-mail:sales@allweathercharts.co.uk
Stanford Charts - the best in coastal and
harbour charts. Publishers of waterproof
tear-resistant yachtsmen's charts. Full chart
information can be found on our website,
and further help can be had from our editorial
office.
www.allweathercharts.co.uk

THOMAS GUNN NAVIGATION SERVICES
Anchor House, 62 Regents Quay,
Aberdeen AB11 5AR.
Tel (01224) 595045
Books and charts. DoT Certified Compass
Adjusters - available day or night.

TODD CHART AGENCY LTD
4 Seacliff Road, The Harbour,
Bangor, County Down,
Northern Ireland BT20 5EY.
Tel 028 9146 6640 Fax 028 9147 1070
e-mail: admiralty@toddchart.co.uk
International Admiralty Chart Agent, char
correction service and nautical booksellers
Stockist of Imray charts and books
navigation and chartroom instruments
binoculars, clocks etc. UK agent for Icelandic
Hydrographic Service. Mail order - Visa
Mastercard, American Express and Switch
Delta accepted.

G UNDERY & SONS
PO Box 235, Unit 31, The New Harbours,
Gibraltar.
Books and Charts. DoT Certified Compass
Adjusters - available day or night.

**THE UNITED KINGDOM
HYDROGRAPHIC OFFICE**
Admiralty Way, Taunton,
Somerset TA1 2DN.
Tel (01823) 337900 Fax (01823) 284077
The UKHO publishes a worldwide series of
navigational charts and publications,
distributed through chart agents. Small craft
folios and editions are derived from standard
charts, but are tailored to be ideal for
yachtsmen.
Website: www.ukho.gov.uk

WARSASH NAUTICAL BOOKSHOP
6 Dibles Road, Warsash, Southampton,
Hampshire SO31 9HZ.
Tel (01489) 572384 Fax (01489) 885756
e-mail: alan@nauticalbooks.co.uk
Nautical bookseller and chart agent. Callers
and mail order. Free new and secondhand
book lists. Credit cards taken. Publishers of
the Bibliography of Nautical books.
Website: www.nauticalbooks.co.uk

WESSEX MARINE EQUIPMENT LTD
Logistics House, 2nd Avenue Business
Park, Millbrook Road East,
Southampton, Hampshire SO1 0LP.
Tel 023 8051 0570
Books and charts.

BREAKDOWN

SEA START
Unit 13, Hamble Point Marina,
Southampton, Hampshire SO31 4JD.
Tel 0800 88 55 00 or 023 8045 8000
Fax 023 8045 2666
Sea Start is the 24-hour marine breakdown
service on both sides of the English Channel
and the Channel Islands. Membership cost
from as little as £9 per month. Join now
using your credit card on 0800 88 55 00 or
ring for our colour brochure.

CHANDLERS

ARDFERN YACHT CENTRE
Ardfern By Lochgilphead,
Argyll PA31 8QN.
*Tel (01852) 500247/636 Fax (01852) 500624
and 07000 ARDFERN*
Boatyard with full repair and maintenance
facilities. Timber and GRP repairs, painting
and engineering. Sheltered moorings and
pontoon berthing. Winter storage, chandlery, showers, fuel, Calor, brokerage, 20-
ton boat hoist, rigging. Hotel, bars and
restaurant.

BOATWORKS + LTD
Castle Emplacement, St Peter Port,
Guernsey, Channel Islands GY1 1AU.
Tel (01481) 726071 Fax (01481) 714224
Boatworks+ provides a comprehensive
range of services including boatbuilding
and repairs, chandlery, clothing and fuel
supplies.

BOSUNS LOCKER - RAMSGATE
10 Military Road, Royal Harbour,
Ramsgate, Kent CT11 9LG.
Tel/Fax (01843) 597158
The Bosun's Locker - a friendly family owned
business, caters for a wide range of boat
owners and is staffed by experienced
yachtsmen. The stock is extensive, including
paints, ropes, quality clothing for foul
weather and fashion, electronics, inflatables
and charts.

**BOSUNS LOCKER CHANDLERY -
MILFORD HAVEN**
Cleddau House, Milford Marina,
Milford Haven,
Pembrokeshire SA73 3AF.
Tel (01646) 697834 Fax (01646) 698009
Chandlery and cafe - Books, charts, engine
spares, clothing, electronics, Blakes, Jotrun,
International paints, clothing. Special
orders and mail order service. Weekly
deliveries to Aberystwyth Marina.
Website: www.bosunslocker.co.uk

BRIXHAM YACHT SUPPLIES LTD
72 Middle Street, Brixham,
Devon TQ5 8EJ.
Tel (01803) 882290
We stock a complete range of sailing and
leisure clothing. English and Continental
pure wool traditional knitwear. Camping
accessories.

CALEY MARINA
Canal Road, Inverness IV3 6NF.
*Tel +44 (0) 1463 236539
Fax +44 (0) 1463 238323
e-mail: info@caleymarina.com*
Open 08.30 - 17.30. Berths: 50 Pontoons
(visitors available). Facilities: Fuel, water,
pump-out facilities, provisions (nearby
shops), repair, cranage, secure storage
afloat and ashore. Comprehensive
chandlery, showers, workshop. Situated at
eastern end of Caledonian canal above
Muirtown locks. Access via sea locks 4
hours either side of high water.
Website: www.caleymarina.com

CHALLENGER MARINE
Freeman's Wharf, Falmouth Road,
Penryn, Cornwall TR10 8AS.
Tel (01326) 377222 Fax (01326) 377800
Marine engineers, chandlery, boatyard.
Main Volvo Penta dealer, marina berths,
brokerage, Bombard and Zodiac inflatables'
dealer.

CRINAN BOATS LTD
Crinan, Lochgilphead, Argyll PA31 8SP.
Tel (01546) 830232 Fax (01546) 830281
Boatbuilders, chandlers, engineers,
slipping, repairs, charts, electricians, pontoon, moorings, showers, laundry and basic
stores.

DARTHAVEN MARINA LTD
Brixham Road, Kingswear, Dartmouth,
Devon TQ6 0SG.
*Tel (01803) 752242 Fax (01803) 752722
Marina Office: (01803) 752545
Chandlery: (01803) 752733
Fax (01803) 752790   VHF Ch80.*
All types of repair facilities available. Fully
trained staff. 30-ton mobile hoist available
all states of tide. Extensive chandlery open 7
days. Agents for all major suppliers
including B&G, Raytheon, Yanmar (Main
Dealers),Volvo Penta agents, Simpson
Lawrence, Sowester installer dealer,
International Coatings and many others.
Emergency engineer call out - Mobile: 0411
404259. Electrician - Mobile: 0467 250787.
Visitors welcome. All marina facilities
available.

FOX'S MARINA IPSWICH LTD
The Strand, Wherstead, Ipswich,
Suffolk IP2 8SA.
Tel (01473) 689111 Fax (01473) 601737
The most comprehensive boatyard facility
on the east coast. Extensive chandlery.
Marina access 24-hours. Diesel dock, two
travel hoists to 70 tons, 10 ton crane. Full
electronics, rigging, engineering, stainless
steel services. Specialists in osmosis and
spray painting.

JOSEPH P LAMB & SONS
Maritime Building
(opposite Albert Dock),
Wapping, Liverpool L1 8DQ.
Tel 0151-709 4861 Fax 0151-709 2786
Situated in the centre of Liverpool, J P
Lamb have provided a service to world
shipping for over 200 years. All chandlery
supplies, clothing, rope, paint and flags are
available. Full sailmaking and repairs. Kemp
Retail Outlet for spars and rigging. Open
Mon to Fri 8am to 5.30pm - Sat 9am to
12.30pm.

LONDON YACHT CENTRE LTD - LYC
13 Artillery Lane, London E1 7LP.
Tel 020 7247 2047 Fax 020 7377 5680
Two minutes from Liverpool Street railway
station. Four floors with 10000 top name
product lines including Musto, Henri Lloyd
and Douglas Gill. Extensive range of
chandlery, inflatables, outboards, liferafts,
electronics, software, books, charts, optics,
rope and chain. All at discount prices.

MANX MARINE
35 North Quay, Douglas,
Isle of Man IM1 4LB.
Tel/Fax (01624) 674842
The Island's leading and most established
yacht chandlery. Stockists of quality foul-
weather clothing and thermal wear. Large
stock holdings of stainless steel fixtures
and fittings and a comprehensive range of
general chandlery including rigging
facilities.

MARQUAND BROS LTD
- Yacht Chandlers
North Quay, St Peter Port, Guernsey,
Channel Islands.
Tel (01481) 720962 Fax (01481) 713974
Yacht chandlers, stockists of a compr-
ehensive range of marine products.
Guernsey distributor for International
Coatings. Extensive leisure and marine
clothing department including Barbour,
Driza-Bone, Dubarry and Quayside.

NORTH QUAY MARINE
North Side, St Sampson's Harbour,
Guernsey, Channel Islands.
Tel (01481) 246561 Fax (01481) 243488
The complete boating centre. Full range of
chandlery, rope, chain, lubricants, paint,
boatwear and shoes. Fishing tackle for on-
shore and on-board. Inflatables and safety
equipment. Electronics and small outboard
engines.

OCEAN LEISURE LTD
11-14 Northumberland Avenue,
London WC2N 5AQ.
*Tel 020 7930 5050 Fax 020 7930 3032
e-mail: info@oceanleisure.co.uk*
Complete range of sailing clothing, swim
and beachwear stocked all year round.
Chandlery includes marine electronic
equipment, marine antiques, books and
charts. Also canoeing, underwater
photography, diving and waterskiing
specialists. Learn to scuba dive.
Website: www.oceanleisure.co.uk

SHAMROCK CHANDLERY
Shamrock Quay, William Street,
Northam, Southampton,
Hampshire SO14 5QL.
*Tel 023 8063 2725 Fax 023 8022 5611
e-mail: sales@shamrock.co.uk*
Situated on Shamrock Quay, a busy working
yard with a pub, restaurant and boutiques.
Shamrock Chandlery is renowned for
extensive quality stocks and service, and is
widely used by both the trade and boat
owners. Excellent mail order facilities - Order
Hotline 023 8022 5746.
Website: www.shamrock.co.uk

SPORT NAUTIQUE CHANDLERS
2 Newcomen Road,
Dartmouth, Devon TQ6 9AF.
Tel (01803) 832532 Fax (01803) 832538
Extensive range of chandlery from rope,
paint, deck equipment, books and charts,
electronic equipment and stockists of a
comprehensive choice of foul-weather gear,
marine and leisure clothing and footwear.
**Personal delivery to your boat - just call
for service.**

9

UPPER DECK MARINE/OUTRIGGERS
Albert Quay, Fowey, Cornwall PL23 1AQ.
Tel (01726) 832287 Fax (01726) 833265
Chandlery, fastenings, paints, cords, fenders, anchors, compasses, lifejackets, Gaz. Leading names in waterproofs and warm wear.

WEYMOUTH OLD HARBOUR
Weymouth & Portland Borough Council, Environmental Services Department, Council Offices, North Quay, Weymouth, Dorset DT4 8TA.
Tel (01305) 206423/206363
Fax (01305) 206422
e-mail: harbour@weymouth.co.uk
Access at all stages of tide. Visitor berths in centre of prime tourist resort with shops, restaurants and night life at hand. Diesel fuelling from pontoon or tanker. Chandlery and repair facilities available.
Website:www.weymouth.gov.uk/marine.htm

WORCESTER YACHT CHANDLERS LTD
Unit 7, 75 Waterworks Road, Barbourne, Worcester WR1 3EZ.
Tel (01905) 22522 & 27949
Chandlery, paints, ropes, cables, chain, clothing, footwear, shackles, books, bottled gas, anti-foul, fastenings, oakam, fenders. Hard storage, crane, haulage, engine service, oils, navigation aids, buoyancy aids, life jackets, distress flares, *small boat hire.*

YACHT PARTS PLYMOUTH
Victoria Building,
Queen Anne's Battery Marina,
Plymouth, Devon PL4 0LP.
Tel (01752) 252489 Fax (01752) 225899
e-mail: sales@yachtparts.co.uk
From anchors to zinc anodes - probably the best stocked chandler in the country. Open seven days with free easy parking. Open large clothing department caters for everyone from the dinghy sailor to the ocean going yachtsman.
Website: www.yachtparts.co.uk

CLOTHING

BOATWORKS + LTD
Castle Emplacement, St Peter Port, Guernsey, Channel Islands GY1 1AU.
Tel (01481) 726071 Fax (01481) 714224
Boatworks+ provides a comprehensive range of services including boatbuilding and repairs, chandlery, clothing and fuel supplies.

OCEAN LEISURE LTD
11-14 Northumberland Avenue,
London WC2N 5AQ.
Tel 020 7930 5050 Fax 020 7930 3032
e-mail: info@oceanleisure.co.uk
Complete range of sailing clothing, swim and beachwear stocked all year round. Chandlery includes marine electronic equipment, marine antiques, books and charts. Also canoeing, underwater photography, diving and waterskiing specialists. Learn to scuba dive.
Website: www.oceanleisure.co.uk

OUTRIGGERS/UPPER DECK MARINE
Albert Quay, Fowey, Cornwall PL23 1AQ.
Tel (01726) 833233 Fax (01726) 833265
'Outriggers' casual and marine clothing, footwear, nautical gifts, Admiralty chart agent and marine books.

SHAMROCK CHANDLERY
Shamrock Quay, William Street,
Northam, Southampton,
Hampshire SO14 5QL.
Tel 023 8063 2725 Fax 023 8022 5611
e-mail: sales@shamrock.co.uk
Situated on Shamrock Quay, a busy working yard with a pub, restaurant and boutiques. Shamrock Chandlery is renowned for extensive quality stocks and service, and is widely used by both the trade and boat owners. Excellent mail order facilities - Order Hotline 023 8022 5746.
Website: www.shamrock.co.uk

SIMPSON-LAWRENCE
218 Edmiston Drive, Glasgow G51 2YT.
Tel 0141-300 9100 Fax 0141-427 5419
e-mail: info@simpson-lawrence.co.uk
SL CLOTHING - The SL Clothing collection features some of the most advanced technical garments available today. From the SLX Ocean suit to our fully breathable offshore and leisure jackets. The range features very high quality together with value for money.
Website: www.simpson-lawrence.com

YACHT PARTS PLYMOUTH
Victoria Building,
Queen Anne's Battery Marina,
Plymouth, Devon PL4 0LP.
Tel 01752 252489 Fax 01752 225899
e-mail: sales@yachtparts.co.uk
From anchors to zinc anodes - probably the best stocked chandler in the country. Open seven days with free easy parking. Our large clothing department caters for everyone from the dinghy sailor to the ocean going yachtsman.
Website: www.yachtparts.co.uk

CODE OF PRACTICE EXAMINERS

ANDREW JAGGERS -
MARINE SURVEYOR & CONSULTANT
75 Clifton Road, Bangor,
Co Down BT20 5HY.
Tel 028 9145 5677 Fax 028 9146 5252
At Bangor Marina: 028 9145 3297
Fax 028 9145 3450 Mobile: 0385 768474
Claims investigations for all major insurers. Code of Compliance examiner. Expert Witness reports. Flag State Inspections. Consultant to solicitors, brokers, loss adjusters on marine and marina matters. Ireland, Isle of Man and West of Scotland.

ANDREW POTTER MA AMYDSA
- YACHT SURVEYOR
Penrallt Cottage, Cichle Hill, Llandegfan, Anglesey LL59 5TD.
Tel/Fax (01248) 712358
Mobile: 0374 4411681
Prompt and professional surveys prior to purchase and for insurance purposes throughout Wales, the north west and Midlands. Services also include valuations,

osmosis inspections and consultancy. Surveyor for MCA Code of Practice.

DAVID M CANNELL & ASSOCIATES
River House, Quay Street,
Wivenhoe, Essex CO7 9DD.
Tel +44 (0) 1206 823 337
Fax +44 (0) 1206 825 939
e-mail: post@dmcnavarch.demon.co.uk
Design of yachts and commercial craft to 80m. Newbuilding and refit overseeing. Condition surveys, valuations, MCA Code of Practice Compliance and Stability, Expert Witness. Members: Royal Institute of Naval Architects, Yacht Designers and Surveyors Association.

FOX ASSOCIATES
Cambria, Rhos y Coed, Bethesda,
Bangor, Gywnedd LL57 3NW.
Tel/Fax (01248) 601079
Marine surveyors and consultants. Claims investigation and damage reports. Code of Practice examiners. Valuations and condition surveys.

GEORGE REOHORN YBDSA SURVEYOR
Chancery Cottage, Gors Road, Burry Port, Carmarthenshire SA16 0EL.
Tel/Fax (01554) 833281
Full condition and insurance surveys on pleasure and working vessels. Also Code of Pratice examiner. Approved British registration measurer. 36 years practical experience on GRP, timber, steel and ferro construction.

GRAHAM BOOTH MARINE SURVEYS
4 Epple, Birchington-on-Sea,
Kent CT7 9AY.
Tel (01843) 843793 Fax (01843) 846860
e-mail: gbms@clara.net
Authorised for MCA Codes of Practice, most frequently on French and Italian Riviera - also for certification of Sail Training vessels and other commercial craft. Call UK office for further information. Other expert marine consultancy services also available.

LIVERPOOL & GLASGOW
SALVAGE ASSOCIATION
St Andrews House, 385 Hillington Road, Glasgow G52 4BL.
Tel 0141-303 4573 Fax 0141-303 4513
e-mail: lgsaglasgow@compuserve.com
Marine surveyors and consultants: Prepurchase, damage, insurance (risk and liabilities) surveys on all vessels including yachts, fishing vessels and commercial ships. Offices also at Liverpool, Hull, Leicester and Grangemouth. Overseas work also undertaken.

MARINTEC
Silverton House, Kings Hyde,
Mount Pleasant Lane, Lymington,
Hampshire SO41 8LT.
Tel (01590) 683414 Fax (01590) 683719
MARINTEC was established at the beginning of 1983 and undertake comprehensive surveys, including mechanical and electrical, both at home and overseas. Refit management including the drawing up of specifications and the tender document by YDSA surveyor.

V A MacGREGOR & CO
- MARINE SURVEYORS
Dooley Terminal Building, The Dock,
Felixstowe, Suffolk IP11 8SW.
Tel (01394) 676034 Fax (01394) 675515
Mobile: (0860) 361279
Yacht and small craft surveys for all
purposes and in all materials. Specialist in
wood and restoration of classic craft,
continually involved with steel, aluminium,
GRP. Charter and workboat codes YDSA
surveyor.

PETER HALLAM MARINE SURVEYOR
83 Millisle Road, Donaghadee, Co Down,
Northern Ireland BT21 0HZ.
Tel/Fax 028 9188 3484
Surveys for yachts, fishing and commercial
craft. Supervision of new buildings, repairs
and specification writing for the same.
Insurance assessments/inspections and
completed repairs. Tonnage measurement.
Accident assessment/reports for solicitors.
MSA Code of Practice surveys.

RICHARD AYERS
- YACHT SURVEYOR & CONSULTANT
5A Church Street, Modbury,
Devon PL21 0QW.
Tel (01548) 830496 Fax (01548) 830917
e-mail: ayers_survey@hotmail.com
YDSA member - Yacht and powerboat
survey, MCA Code of Practice for small
commercial vessels. Survey for registration,
marine insurance and claim inspections.
Legal work. Plymouth - Salcombe -
Dartmouth - Fowey - Falmouth - Totnes all
local. No mileage charges.

RODNEY CLAPSON MARINE SURVEYS
16 Whitecross Street,
Barton-on-Humber DN18 5EU.
Tel (01652) 632108 & 635620
Fax (01652) 660517
e-mail: surveys@clapsons.co.uk
Surveys for purchase and insurance.
Damage repair and osmosis supervision.
East coast from the Wash to North-
umberland including inland waterways.
Surveys in the Netherlands. We are YDSA
members.

E K WALLACE & SON LTD
Whittinghame House,
1099 Great Western Road,
Glasgow G12 0AA.
Tel 0141-334 7222 Fax 0141-334 7700
Pre-purchase, insurance and valuation
surveys on sail and power vessels, private
and commercial, UK and abroad. Approved
for Code of Practice, registration and
tonnage meaurements. Members YDSA,
SCMS. Offices in Glasgow, Edinburgh and
Argyll.

WARD & McKENZIE (Dorset) LTD
69 Alexander Road, Parkstone,
Poole, Dorset BH14 9EL.
Tel (01202) 718440
National and International marine surveyors.
Technical and legal consultants. Contact:
Tony McGrail - Mobile: 0411 329314.
Website: www.ward-mckenzie.co.uk

WARD & McKENZIE (North East) LTD
11 Sherbuttgate Drive, Pocklington,
York YO4 2ED.
Tel (01759) 304322 Fax (01759) 303194
e-mail: nev.styles@dial.pipex.com
National and International marine surveyors.
Technical and legal consultants. Contact:
Neville Styles - Mobile: 0831 335943.
Website: www.ward-mckenzie.co.uk

WARD & McKENZIE (North West) LTD
2 Healey Court, Burnley,
Lancashire BB11 2QJ.
Tel/Fax (01282) 420102
e-mail: marinesurvey@wmnw.freeserve.
co.uk
National and International marine surveyors.
Technical and legal consultants. Contact:
Bob Sheffield - Mobile: 0370 667457.
Website: www.ward-mckenzie.co.uk

WARD & McKENZIE (South Wales) LTD
58 The Meadows, Marshfield,
Cardiff CF3 8AY.
Tel (01633) 680280
National and International marine surveyors.
Technical and legal consultants. Contact:
Kevin Ashworth - Mobile: 07775 938666.
Website: www.ward-mckenzie.co.uk

WARD & McKENZIE (South West) LTD
Little Brook Cottage, East Portlemouth,
Salcombe, Devon TQ8 8PW.
Tel (01803) 833500 Fax (01803) 833350
National and International marine surveyors.
Technical and legal consultants. Contact:
Chris Olsen - Mobile: 07971 250105.
Website: www.ward-mckenzie.co.uk

WARD & McKENZIE LTD
3 Wherry Lane, Ipswich, Suffolk IP4 1LG.
Tel (01473) 255200 Fax (01473) 255044
e-mail: collett@wardmck.keme.co.uk
National and International marine surveyors.
Technical and legal consultants - offering a
comprehensive service to boat owners and
those seeking to acquire pleasure yachts.
All aspects of title/lien check, registration.
Survey, purchase and ownership under-
taken, including insurance surveys, finance
and disputes.
Contact: Clive Brown - Mobile: 0585 190357
Mike Williamson - Mobile: 0498 578312
and Ian Collett - Mobile: 0370 655306.
River Ouse Office: 01462 701461.
Website: www.ward-mckenzie.co.uk
See regional offices in Area Directory.

COMMUNICATIONS EQUIPMENT

NORTH QUAY MARINE
North Side, St Sampson's Harbour,
Guernsey, Channel Islands.
Tel (01481) 246561 Fax (01481) 243488
The complete boating centre. Full range of
chandlery, rope, chain, lubricants, paint,
boatwear and shoes. Fishing tackle for on-
shore and on-board. Inflatables and safety
equipment. Electronics and small outboard
engines.

RADIO & ELECTRONIC SERVICES LTD
Les Chênes, Rohais,
St Peter Port, Guernsey,
Channel Islands GY1 1FB.
Tel (01481) 728837 Fax (01481) 714379
Chart Plotters, GPS, Radars. Fixed and
portable VHF, Autopilots. Programming
dealer for C-Map NT and Jotron EPIRBS.
Sales and service dealers for Furuno,
Humminbird, Icom, KVH, Lowrance,
Magellan, Raytheon, Sailor and Shipmate.

ROWLANDS MARINE ELECTRONICS LTD
Pwllheli Marina Centre,
Glan Don, Pwllheli,
Gwynedd LL53 5YT.
Tel (01758) 613193 Fax (01758) 613617
BEMA and BMIF members, dealer for
Autohelm, B&G, Cetrek, ICOM, Kelvin
Hughes, Marconi, Nasa, Navico, Navstar,
Neco, Seafarer, Shipmate, Stowe, Racal-
Decca, V-Tronix, Ampro and Walker.
Equipment supplied, installed and serviced.

SIMRAD LTD
Woolmer Way, Bordon,
Hampshire GU35 9QE.
Tel (01420) 483200 Fax (01420) 489073
For full entry see under:
ELECTRONIC DEVICES & EQUIPMENT

COMPASS ADJUSTERS/ MANUFACTURERS

B P S C MARINE SERVICES
Unit 4 Park Business Centre,
1 Park Road, Freemantle,
Southampton, Hampshire SO15 5US.
Tel 023 8051 0561
BPSC offer a fast efficient repair service on
a wide range of nautical and survey instruments. Free estimates and advice. A comprehensive range of spares are carried, most of
which can be despatched same day.
Instruments commissioned. Compass
adjusting service.

B.P.S.C. MARINE SERVICES
Offer a fast, efficient repair service
for ALL compasses, binoculars
etc. A range of spares carried.
Estimate and advice given.
Tel: 023 8051 0561
Unit 4 Park Business Centre
1 Park Road, Freemantle, Southampton
Hampshire SO15 3US
e-mail: bgphillips@msn.com

B COOKE & SON LTD
Kingston Observatory,
58-59 Market Place, Hull HU1 1RH.
Tel (01482) 223454
Books and Charts. DoT Certified Compass
Adjusters - available day or night.

USE THESE PAGES FOR ALL YOUR MARINE SERVICES AND SUPPLIES

JOHN LILLEY & GILLIE LTD
Clive Street, North Shields,
Tyne & Wear NE29 6LF.
Tel 0191-257 2217
Books and Charts. DoT Certified Compass
Adjusters - available day or night.

KELVIN HUGHES
CHARTS & MARITIME SUPPLIES
New North Road, Hainault, Ilford,
Essex IG6 2UR.
Tel 020 8500 1020
Books and charts. DoT Certified Compass
Adjusters - available day or night.

KELVIN HUGHES OBSERVATOR BV
Nieuwe Langeweg 41,
3194 DC Hoogvliet (Rt), Rotterdam,
The Netherlands.
Book and charts. DoT Certified Compass
Adjusters - available day or night.

MARINE INSTRUMENTS
The Bosun's Locker, Upton Slip,
Falmouth, Cornwall TR11 3DQ.
Tel (01326) 312414
Books and charts. DoT Certified Compass
Adjusters - available day or night.

MARTIN & CO
Oude Leewenrui 37, Antwerp 2000,
Belgium.
Books and charts. DoT Certified Compass
Adjusters - available day or night.

R J MUIR
22 Seymour Close, Chandlers Ford,
Eastleigh, Southampton SO5 2JE.
Tel 023 8026 1042
Books and Charts. DoT Certified Compass
Adjusters - available day or night.

W F PRICE & CO LTD
Northpoint House, Wapping Wharf,
Bristol BS1 6UD.
Tel 0117-929 2229
Books and charts. DoT Certified Compass
Adjusters - available day or night.

S I R S NAVIGATION LTD
186a Milton Road, Swanscombe,
Kent DA10 0LX.
Tel (01322) 383672
Books and Charts. DoT Certified Compass
Adjusters - available day or night.

SEATH INSTRUMENTS (1992) LTD
Unit 30, Colville Road Works,
Colville Road, Lowestoft NR33 9QS.
Tel (01502) 573811
Books and charts. DoT Certified Compass
Adjusters - available day or night.

THOMAS GUNN NAVIGATION SERVICES
Anchor House, 62 Regents Quay,
Aberdeen AB11 5AR.
Tel (01224) 595045
Books and charts. DoT Certified Compass
Adjusters - available day or night.

G UNDERY & SONS
PO Box 235, Unit 31, The New Harbours,
Gibraltar.
Books and Charts. DoT Certified Compass
Adjusters - available day or night.

COMPUTERS & SOFTWARE

DOLPHIN MARITIME SOFTWARE LTD
713 Cameron House, White Cross,
Lancaster LA1 4XQ.
Tel/Fax (01524) 841946
e-mail: 100417.744@compuserve.com
Marine computer programs for IBM PC,
Psion and Sharp pocket computers.
Specialists in navigation, tidal prediction
and other programs for both yachting and
commercial uses.
Website: www.ourworld.compuserve.com/
homepages/dolphin_software

EURONAV NAVIGATION
20 The Slipway, Port Solent,
Portsmouth, Hampshire PO6 4TR.
Tel 023 9237 3855 Fax 023 9232 5800
Electronic charting specialists, offering the
sea Pro 2000 range of PC-based chart plotting systems, ARCS, Livechart 'B' and BSB
top quality electronic charts. Products are
available from good chandlers or direct
from Euronav.
Website: www.euronav.co.uk

NEPTUNE NAVIGATION SOFTWARE
P O Box 5106, Riseley,
Berkshire RG7 1FD.
Tel 0118-988 5309
Route Passage Planning, Tides and Tidal
Stream Predictions, Waypoint Manager -
software for your PC or CE machines. A
range of intuitively easy to use navigation
programs at affordable prices.
Website: www.neptunenav.demon.co.uk

SOFTWAVE
Riverside, Mill Lane, Taplow,
Maidenhead SL6 0AA.
Tel 01628 637777 Fax 01628 773030
Provider of PC based navigation *Seavision*
hardware and *Nobeltec* and *Transas*
software. Using charts drawn from
Admiralty sources the quality navigation
software that we provide can be easily
installed to customers own laptops or
computers. For on-board installations we
manufacture hardware that include sun-
readable, waterproof screens linked to high
performance, ruggedised compact PCs.
Website: www.softwave.co.uk

CORPORATE PROMOTIONS

SEA VENTURES YACHT CHARTER
Lymington Yacht Haven, Lymington,
Hampshire SO41 3QD.
Tel (01590) 672472 Fax (01590) 671924
Based in Lymington and Plymouth, our

large modern fleet offers both skippered
and bareboat charters. A large selection of
yachts from 29' to 52' and most less than 3
years old. Corporate and team building and
yacht management also available.
Website: www.sea-ventures.co.uk

CORPORATE YACHT OWNERSHIP

BACHMANN MARINE SERVICES LTD
Frances House, Sir William Place,
St Peter Port, Guernsey,
Channel Islands GY1 4HQ.
Tel (01481) 723573 Fax (01481) 711353
British yacht registration, corporate
yacht ownership and management,
marine insurance, crew placement and
management. Bachmann Marine Services aims to provide a personal and
individual service to its clients.

CORRESPONDENCE COURSES

GLOBAL MARITIME TRAINING
Hoo Marina, Vicarage Lane, Hoo,
Kent ME3 9TW.
Tel (01634) 256288 Fax (01634) 256284
e-mail: info@seaschool.co.uk
RYA theory courses by correspondence.
Start your course anywhere in the world at
any time. Also practical courses from our
north Kent base. Worldwide yacht deliveries
with free RYA tutition for owners 'en-route'.
Website: www.seaschool.co.uk

DECK EQUIPMENT

LEWMAR MARINE LTD
Southmoor Lane, Havant,
Hampshire PO9 1JJ.
Tel 023 9247 1841 Fax 023 9248 5720
Manufacturers of winches, windlasses,
hatches, hardware, hydraulics and marine
thrusters for boats ranging in size from 25'
to 300' LOA.

DIESEL MARINE FUEL ADDITIVES

CHICK'S MARINE LTD/VOLVO PENTA
Collings Road, St Peter Port, Guernsey,
Channel Islands GY1 1FL.
Tel (01481) 723716 Fax (01481) 713632
Distributor of diesel fuel biocide used to
treat and protect contamination in fuel tanks
where an algae (bug) is present. Most
owners do not realise what the problem is,
loss of power, blocked fuel filter, exhaust
smoking, resulting in expensive repairs to
injectors - fuel pump - or complete engine
overhaul. Marine engineers, engines,
spares, service - VAT free. Honda outboards,
pumps and generators. Volvo Penta
specialists.

FUELCARE LIMITED
Sanders Road, Bromsgrove,
Worcestershire B61 7DG.
Tel (01527) 879600 Fax (01527) 879666
e-mail: fuelcare@rtconnect.com
Use FUELCARE fuel biocides to cure and
prevent microbiological growth or the
'Diesel Bug'. Engine and filter problems
eliminated and preventing the formation of
black sludge and slime caused by bacteria
and fungal growth. Use FUELCARE to stop
poor engine performance and fuel system
corrosion caused by microbiological
growth.

ELECTRICAL & ELECTRONIC ENGINEERS

LANGNEY MARINE SERVICES LTD
Sovereign Harbour Marina,
Pevensey Bay Road, Eastbourne,
East Sussex BN23 6JH.
Tel (01323) 470244 Fax (01323) 470255
We offer a complete service to the boat
owner offering repairs on all types of
engines, GRP, steel, wood, electronics,
rigging, cleaning, etc. We are also
contractors to the RNLI.

MARINE RADIO SERVICES LTD
50 Merton Way, East Molesley,
Surrey KT8 1PQ.
Tel 020 8979 7979 Fax 020 8783 1032
Maritime Electronics: Service, sales and
repair of marine radio, radar, autopilots and
electronic equipment.

REGIS ELECTRONICS LTD
Regis House, Quay Hill, Lymington,
Hampshire SO41 3AR.
Tel (01590) 679251 & 679176
Fax (01590) 679910
(Also at Cowes, Southampton & Chichester).
Sales, service and installation of marine
electronic equipment. Leading south coast
agents for AUTOHELM, FURUNO,
RAYTHEON, CETREK, A.P. NAVIGATOR,
GARMIN, SIMRAD, SAILOR and other
manufacturers of quality marine electronic
equipment. Competitively priced quotations
(including owner familiarisation and sea
trials) forwarded by return of post.

ROWLANDS MARINE ELECTRONICS LTD
Pwllheli Marina Centre, Glan Don,
Pwllheli, Gwynedd LL53 5YT.
Tel (01758) 613193 Fax (01758) 613617
BEMA and BMIF members, dealer for
Autohelm, B&G, Cetrek, ICOM, Kelvin
Hughes, Marconi, Nasa, Navico, Navstar,
Neco, Seafarer, Shipmate, Stowe, Racal-
Decca, V-Tronix, Ampro and Walker.
Equipment supplied, installed and serviced.

SWALE MARINE (ELECTRICAL)
The Old Stable, North Road,
Queenborough, Kent ME11 5EH.
Tel (01795) 580930 Fax (01795) 580238
For all your electrical and electronic needs.
Authorised agents for: Furuno, Autohelm,
Raytheon and most major manufacturers.
Fight crime with Harbourguard monitored
security: Medway and Swale coverage -
Boatmark registration centre.

ELECTRONIC DEVICES & EQUIPMENT

G B ATTFIELD & COMPANY
29 Woodmancote, Dursley,
Gloucestershire GL11 4AF.
Tel/Fax +44 (0) 1453 547185
VOLTWATCH battery monitor, the 'Fuel
Gauge for your Battery'. See our display
advertisement in the Guide under Batteries
and Battery Equipment.

BOSUNS LOCKER - RAMSGATE
10 Military Road, Royal Harbour,
Ramsgate, Kent CT11 9LG.
Tel/Fax (01843) 597158
The Bosun's Locker - a friendly family owned
business, caters for a wide range of boat
owners and is staffed by experienced
yachtsmen. The stock is extensive, including
paints, ropes, quality clothing for foul
weather and fashion, electronics, inflatables
and charts.

DIVERSE YACHT SERVICES
Unit 12, Hamble Yacht Services,
Port Hamble, Hamble,
Hampshire SO31 4NN.
Tel 023 8045 3399 Fax 023 8045 5288
Marine electronics and electrics. Supplied
and installed. Specialists in racing yachts.
Suppliers of 'Loadsense' Loadcells for
marine applications.

GREENHAM MARINE
King's Saltern Road, Lymington,
Hampshire SO41 9QD.
Tel (01590) 671144 Fax (01590) 679517
Greenham Marine can offer yachtsmen one
of the most comprehensive selections of
marine electronic equipment currently
available. Also at Poole/Weymouth 01202
676363 and Emsworth/Chichester 01243
378314.

LONDON YACHT CENTRE LTD - LYC
13 Artillery Lane, London E1 7LP.
Tel 020 7247 2047 Fax 020 7377 5680
Two minutes from Liverpool Street railway
station. Four floors with 10000 top name
product lines including Musto, Henri Lloyd
and Douglas Gill. Extensive range of
chandlery, inflatables, outboards, liferafts,
electronics, software, books, charts, optics,
rope and chain. All at discount prices.

RADIO & ELECTRONIC SERVICES LTD
Les Chênes, Rohais, St Peter Port,
Guernsey, Channel Islands GY1 1FB.
Tel (01481) 728837 Fax (01481) 714379
Chart Plotters, GPS, Radars. Fixed and
portable VHF, Autopilots. Programming
dealer for C-Map NT and Jotron EPIRBS.
Sales and service dealers for Furuno,
Humminbird, Icom, KVH, Lowrance,
Magellan, Raytheon, Sailor and Shipmate.

REGIS ELECTRONICS LTD
Regis House, Quay Hill, Lymington,
Hampshire SO41 3AR.
Tel (01590) 679251 & 679176
Fax (01590) 679910
(Also at Cowes, Southampton & Chichester).
Sales, service and installation of marine
electronic equipment. Leading south coast

agents for AUTOHELM, FURUNO,
RAYTHEON, CETREK, A.P. NAVIGATOR,
GARMIN, SIMRAD, SAILOR and other
manufacturers of quality marine electronic
equipment. Competitively priced quotations
(including owner familiarisation and sea
trials) forwarded by return of post.

ROWLANDS MARINE ELECTRONICS LTD
Pwllheli Marina Centre, Glan Don,
Pwllheli, Gwynedd LL53 5YT.
Tel (01758) 613193 Fax (01758) 613617
BEMA and BMIF members, dealer for
Autohelm, B&G, Cetrek, ICOM, Kelvin
Hughes, Marconi, Nasa, Navico, Navstar,
Neco, Seafarer, Shipmate, Stowe, Racal-
Decca, V-Tronix, Ampro and Walker.
Equipment supplied, installed and serviced.

SIMPSON-LAWRENCE
218 Edmiston Drive, Glasgow G51 2YT.
Tel 0141-300 9100 Fax 0141-427 5419
e-mail: info@simpson-lawrence.co.uk
LOWRANCE - Simpson-Lawrence distribute
the comprehensive range of LOWRANCE.
Fish Finders and GPS products. All units
feature superior displays and are packed
with user-friendly option. All backed by a
comprehensive warranty.
Website: www.simpson-lawrence.com

SIMRAD LTD
Woolmer Way, Bordon,
Hampshire GU35 9QE.
Tel (01420) 483200 Fax (01420) 489073
e-mail: sales@simrad.co.uk
World-leading manufacturer of marine
electronics and professional technology
designed and built to operate in all conditions. Autopilots, instruments for sail and
power, chartplotters, GPS, GMDSS VHF
radios, advanced radars, professional
echosounders and sophisticated combined
instruments.
www.simrad.com

SOFTWAVE
Riverside, Mill Lane, Taplow,
Maidenhead SL6 0AA.
Tel 01628 637777 Fax 01628 773030
Provider of PC based navigation *Seavision*
hardware and *Nobeltec* and *Transas*
software. Using charts drawn from Admiralty survey navigation software
that we provide can be easily installed to
customers own laptops or computers. For
on-board installations we manufacture
hardware that include sun-readable,
waterproof screens linked to high
performance, ruggedised compact PCs.
Website: www.softwave.co.uk

TOLLEY MARINE LTD
Unit 7, Blackhill Road West,
Holton Heath Trading Park, Poole,
Dorset BH16 6LS.
Tel (01202) 632644 Fax (01202) 632622
Branches at Salterns Marina (01202)
706040 and Plymouth (01752) 222530.
Agents for all major marine electronics man-
ufacturers. Autohelm, B&G, Cetrek, Furuno,
Garmin, Icom, Koden, Lo-Kata, MLR,
Magnavox, Navico, Panasonic, Raytheon,
Robertson, Sailor, Shipmate, Trimble.

ENGINES & ACCESSORIES

CHICK'S MARINE LTD/VOLVO PENTA
Collings Road, St Peter Port, Guernsey,
Channel Islands GY1 1FL.
Tel (01481) 723716 Fax (01481) 713632
Distributor of diesel fuel biocide used to
treat and protect contamination in fuel tanks
where an algae (bug) is present. Most
owners do not realise what the problem is,
loss of power, blocked fuel filter, exhaust
smoking, resulting in expensive repairs to
injectors - fuel pump - or complete engine
overhaul. Marine engineers, engines,
spares, service - VAT free. Honda outboards,
pumps and generators. Volvo Penta
specialists.

FUELCARE LIMITED
Sanders Road, Bromsgrove,
Worcestershire B61 7DG.
Tel (01527) 879600 Fax (01527) 879666
e-mail: fuelcare@rtconnect.com
Use FUELCARE fuel biocides to cure and
prevent microbiological growth or the
'Diesel Bug'. Engine and filter problems
eliminated and preventing the formation of
black sludge and slime caused by bacteria
and fungal growth. Use FUELCARE to stop
poor engine performance and fuel system
corrosion caused by microbiological
growth.

LANGNEY MARINE SERVICES LTD
Sovereign Harbour Marina, Pevensey
Bay Road, Eastbourne,
East Sussex BN23 6JH.
Tel (01323) 470244 Fax (01323) 470255
We offer a complete service to the boat
owner offering repairs on all types of
engines, GRP, steel, wood, electronics,
rigging, cleaning, etc. We are also
contractors to the RNLI.

SILLETTE SONIC LTD
182 Church Hill Road, North Cheam,
Sutton, Surrey SM3 8NF.
Tel 020 8715 0100 Fax 020 8288 0742
Mobile: 077 10270107
Sillette manufactures a range of propulsion
systems - stern drive, saildrives etc and
sterngear. Markets Radice & Gori fixed and
folding propellers. Acts as agents for Morse
Controls, Yanmar and Lombardini marine
engines, and Fuji Robin generators. See
distribution depot Poole, Dorset - Area 2.

SIMPSON-LAWRENCE
218-228 Edmiston Drive,
Glasgow G51 2YT.
Tel 0141-300 9100 Fax 0141-427 5419
e-mail: info@simpson-lawrence.co.uk
JOHNSON - Simpson-Lawrence distributes
the comprehensive range of JOHNSON
outboards, which offers excellent quality
and superior durability - from the original
manufacturer of the outboard motor.
Website: www.simpson-lawrence.com

VETUS DEN OUDEN LTD
39 South Hants Industrial Park, Totton,
Southampton, Hampshire SO40 3SA.
Tel 023 8086 1033 Fax 023 8066 3142
Suppliers of marine diesel equipment,
exhaust systems, steering systems, bow
propellers, propellers and shafts, hatches,

portlights, windows, electronic instruments,
batteries, ventilators, windlasses, water and
fuel tanks, chandlery items and much much
more.

VOLVO PENTA LTD
Otterspool Way, Watford,
Hertfordshire WD2 8HW.
Tel (01923) 28544
Volvo Penta's leading marine power-petrol
and diesel for leisurecraft and workboats -
is supported by an extensive network of
parts and service dealers.

FIRE EXTINGUISHERS

FIREMASTER EXTINGUISHER LTD
Firex House, 174/176 Hither Green Lane,
London SE13 6QB.
Tel 020 8852 8585 Fax 020 8297 8020
e-mail: sales@firemaster.co.uk
Third party accredited fire extinguishers
manufactured to meet both RYA and Boat
Safety Scheme requirements. Also auto-
matic detection and extinguishing systems.
Website: www.firemaster.co.uk

FIRST AID

K T Y YACHTS
Unit 12, Universal Marina,
Crableck Lane, Sarisbury Green,
Southampton, Hampshire SO31 7ZN.
Tel (0385) 335189 Fax (01489) 570302
MCA First Aid and Medical Care aboard
ship. Qualified, practical instruction from a
sailor and paramedic.

FLAGS, FLAGSTAFFS & PENNANTS

JOSEPH P LAMB & SONS
Maritime Building (opposite Albert
Dock), Wapping, Liverpool L1 8DQ.
Tel 0151-709 4861 Fax 0151-709 2786
Situated in the centre of Liverpool, J P
Lamb have provided a service to world
shipping for over 200 years. All chandlery
supplies, clothing, rope, paint and flags are
available. Full sailmaking and repairs. Kemp
Retail Outlet for spars and rigging. Open
Mon to Fri 8am to 5.30pm - Sat 9am to
12.30pm.

SARNIA FLAGS
8 Belmont Road, St Peter Port, Guernsey,
Channel Islands GY1 1PY.
Tel (01481) 725995 Fax (01481) 729335
Flags and pennants made to order. National
flags, house, club and battle flags, and
burgees made to order. Any size, shape or
design. Prices on request.

FLOTILLA HOLIDAYS

GREEK SAILS YACHT CHARTER
21 The Mount, Kippax, Leeds LS25 7NG.
Tel/Fax 0113-232 0926
Freephone 0800 731 8580
e-mail: greek_sails_uk@msn.com
Bareboat yacht charter throughout Greece
and the islands. Flotilla based in Corfu and
the Ionian Islands. Family dinghy sailing
holidays in Corfu. Skippered charter and
sail training.

FOUL WEATHER GEAR

BOSUNS LOCKER - RAMSGATE
10 Military Road, Royal Harbour,
Ramsgate, Kent CT11 9LG.
Tel/Fax (01843) 597158
The Bosun's Locker - a friendly family owned
business, caters for a wide range of boat
owners and is staffed by experienced
yachtsmen. The stock is extensive, including
paints, ropes, quality clothing for foul
weather and fashion, electronics, inflatables
and charts.

MARQUAND BROS LTD
- Yacht Chandlers
North Quay, St Peter Port,
Guernsey, Channel Islands.
Tel (01481) 720962 Fax (01481) 713974
Yacht chandlers, stockists of marine
products. Guernsey distributor for
International Coatings. Extensive leisure and
marine clothing department including
Barbour, Driza-Bone, Dubarry and Quayside.

SIMPSON-LAWRENCE
218 Edmiston Drive, Glasgow G51 2YT.
Tel 0141-300 9100 Fax 0141-427 5419
e-mail: info@simpson-lawrence.co.uk
- The SL Clothing collection features some
of the most advancedtechnical garments
available today. From the SLX Ocean suit to
our fully breathable offshore and leisure
jackets. The range features very high quality
together with value for money.
Website: www.simpson-lawrence.com

SPORT NAUTIQUE CHANDLERS
2 Newcomen Road, Dartmouth,
Devon TQ6 9AF.
Tel (01803) 832532 Fax (01803) 832538
Extensive range of chandlery from rope,
paint, deck equipment, books and charts,
electronic equipment and stockists of a
comprehensive choice of foul-weather gear,
marine and leisure clothing and footwear.
*Personal delivery to your boat - just call for
service.*

GENERAL MARINE EQUIPMENT & SPARES

A B MARINE LTD
Castle Walk, St Peter Port, Guernsey,
Channel Islands GY1 1AU.
Tel (01481) 722378 Fax (01481) 711080
We specialise in safety and survival
equipment and are a DoT approved service
station for liferafts including R.F.D., Beau-
fort/Dunlop, Zodiac, Avon, Plastimo and
Lifeguard. We also carry a full range of new
liferafts, dinghies and lifejackets, and are
agents for Bukh marine engines.

G B ATTFIELD & COMPANY
29 Woodmancote, Dursley,
Gloucestershire GL11 4AF.
Tel/Fax +44 (0) 1453 547185
VOLTWATCH battery monitor, the 'Fuel
Gauge for your Battery'. See our display
advertisement in the Guide under Batteries
and Battery Equipment.

IMRAY LAURIE NORIE AND WILSON LTD
Wych House, The Broadway, St Ives,
Huntingdon, Cambridgeshire PE17 4BT.
Tel (01480) 462114 Fax (01480) 496109
e-mail: ilnw@imray.com
Publishers of nautical charts and books.
Imray's chart list is the most comprehensive
available for yachtsmen. Imray pilots are
available for home waters, the Medit-
erranean and distant waters. Also Admiralty
specialised chart distributor.
Website: www.imray.com

LEWMAR MARINE LTD
Southmoor Lane, Havant,
Hampshire PO9 1JJ.
Tel 023 9247 1841 Fax 023 9248 5720
Manufacturers of winches, windlasses,
hatches, hardware, hydraulics and marine
thrusters for boats ranging in size from 25'
to 300' LOA.

SCOTTISH BOAT JUMBLE
Steelbank Cottage, Dalgarven,
Nr Kilwinning, Ayrshire KA13 6PL.
Fax (01294) 552417 Mobile: 0421 888789
New and used nautical bargains galore.
Everything from radios, safety equipment,
clothing and deck equipment. Jumbles held
in Scotland twice a year - Ireland and New-
castle once a year. See main advertisement.

VETUS DEN OUDEN LTD
39 South Hants Industrial Park, Totton,
Southampton, Hampshire SO40 3SA.
Tel 023 8086 1033 Fax 023 8066 3142
Suppliers of marine diesel equipment,
exhaust systems, steering systems, bow
propellers, propellers and shafts, hatches,
portlights, windows, electronic instruments,
batteries, ventilators, windlasses, water and
fuel tanks, chandlery items and much much
more.

WORCESTER YACHT CHANDLERS LTD
Unit 7, 75 Waterworks Road, Barbourne,
Worcester WR1 3EZ.
Tel (01905) 22522 & 27949
Chandlery, paints, ropes, cables, chain,
clothing, footwear, shackles, books, bottled gas, anti-foul, fastenings, oakam, fenders. Hard storage, crane, haulage, engine
service, oils, navigation aids, buoyancy aids,
life jackets, distress flares, *small boat hire.*

YACHT PARTS PLYMOUTH
Victoria Building,
Queen Anne's Battery Marina,
Plymouth, Devon PL4 0LP.
Tel (01752) 252489 Fax (01752) 225899
e-mail: sales@yachtparts.co.uk
From anchors to zinc anodes - probably the
best stocked chandler in the country. Open
seven days with free easy parking. Our
large clothing department caters for
everyone from the dinghy sailor to the ocean
going yachtsman.
Website: www.yachtparts.co.uk

GENERATORS

GenACis
Power House, Gordon Road,
Winchester, Hampshire SO23 7DD.
Tel (01962) 841828 Fax (01962) 841834
Dolphin water cooled diesel generators,
3 - 16 KVA.

GLASS FIBRE MARINE SPECIALISTS

ROSDEN GLASS FIBRE
La Rue Durell, La Collette, St Helier,
Jersey JE2 3NB.
Tel (01534) 625418 Fax (01534) 625419
Specialists in all types of glass fibre marine
works, structural repairs, alterations, re-
flow coating, GEL coat work. Blakes and
International approved osmosis treatment
centre. Spray painting. Manufacturer of fuel
tanks, bathing platforms and boat builders.
General refurbishment and polishing. A
division of Precision Plastics (Jersey) Ltd.

GRAPHICS

GRAPHIC INNOVATION
35 Chequers Hill, Amersham,
Buckinghamshire HP7 9DQ.
Tel/Fax (01494) 431500
e-mail: info@graphicinnovation.com
Leading specialist manufacturer of self-
adhesive graphics for the marine industry.
Original equipment volume production for
boatbuilders, or individual one-off names
etc for boat owners.
Website: www.graphicinnovation.com

WET & WILD GRAPHICS
Falcon House, Hamble Point Marina,
Hamble, Southampton,
Hampshire SO31 4NB.
Tel 023 8045 8332 Fax 023 8045 6830
e-mail: sales@wild-graphics.co.uk
Supply and application of vinyl graphics,
signboards, banners and flags. Specialist
materials for sails and spinnakers. Brochure
available for mail order boat names.
Deadlines never a problem!!!
Website: www.wild-graphics.co.uk

HARBOURS

BALTIC WHARF
WATER LEISURE CENTRE
Bristol Harbour, Underfall Yard,
Bristol BS1 6XG.
Tel 0117-929 7608 Fax 0117-929 4454
Tuition: 0117-952 5202
Sailing school and centre, with qualified
instruction in most watersports. Also moor-
ings available throughout the Bristol harbour
for all types of leisurecraft.

BEAULIEU RIVER MANAGEMENT LTD
Harbour Master's Office,
Bucklers Hard Yacht Harbour, Beaulieu,
Hampshire SO42 7XB.
Tel (01590) 616200 Fax (01590) 616211
110-berth yacht harbour (pontoon berths),
fully serviced with back-up facilities of
historic Bucklers Hard village. Agamemnon
boatyard - 290 swinging moorings let on
annual basis. Visiting craft welcome.
Capacity 100+ pile/pontoon.

CHELSEA HARBOUR LTD
108 The Chambers, Chelsea Harbour,
London SW10 0XF.
Tel 020 7761 8600 Fax 020 7352 7868
A tranquil and intimate marina of 55 berths
close to the heart of the west end of London.
5-Star hotel, restaurants and bars. Overnight pontoon and amenities. 24-hour
security patrols and CCTV.

CLYDE MARINA - ARDROSSAN
The Harbour, Ardrossan,
Ayrshire KA22 8DB.
Tel (01294) 607077 Fax (01294) 607076
e-mail: clydmarina@aol.com
Located on the north Ayrshire coast within
easy cruising reach of Arran, the Cumbrae
Islands, Bute and the Kintyre Peninsula.
Deep draught harbour with 200 pontoon
berths and quayside for vessels up to 120'.
20-ton hoist, undercover storage and most
services and facilities. Ancasta Scotland
brokerage, also Beneteau, Nimbus-Maxi,
Westerly yachts, SeaRay and Marlin RIBs.

DUCHY OF CORNWALL
Harbour Office, St Mary's, Isles of Scilly,
Cornwall TR21 0HU.
Tel/Fax (01720) 422768
Harbour of St Mary's, Isles of Scilly - 38
visitor moorings. Visitor centre, hot
showers, toilets, launching facilities, winter
storage, security lockers, fuel and fresh
water. Five minutes from town centre. Ferry
terminal and airport close by. Contact
Harbour Master for more information.

HAFAN PWLLHELI
Glan Don, Pwllheli, Gwynedd LL53 5YT.
Tel (01758) 701219 Fax (01758) 701443
VHF Ch80
Hafan Pwllheli has over 400 pontoon berths
and offers access at virtually all states of
the tide. Ashore, its modern purpose-built
facilities include luxury toilets, showers,
launderette, a secure boat park for winter
storage, 40-ton travel hoist, mobile crane
and plenty of space for car parking. Open
24-hours a day, 7 days a week.

JERSEY HARBOURS
Maritime House,
La Route du Port Elizabeth, St Helier,
Jersey JE1 1HB.
Tel (01534) 885588 Fax (01534) 885599
e-mail: jsyhbr@itl.net
A warm welcome to visiting yachts! St
Helier Marina has 50 more finger berths for
visitors. 5-Gold Anchor facilities. 3 hours
±HW. Berths available to lease from one
month to 10 years in our **NEW ELIZABETH
MARINA**.

PADSTOW HARBOUR COMMISSIONERS
Harbour Office, Padstow,
Cornwall PL28 8AQ.
Tel (01841) 532239 Fax (01841) 533346
e-mail: padstowharbour@compuserve.
com
Inner harbour controlled by tidal gate -
opens HW ±2hours. Minimum depth 3
metres at all times. Yachtsmen must be
friendly as vessels raft together. Services
include showers, toilets, diesel, water and
ice. Security by CCTV.

PETERHEAD BAY AUTHORITY
Bath House, Bath Street,
Peterhead AB42 1DX.
Tel (01779) 474020 Fax (01779) 475712
Contact: Stephen Paterson. Peterhead Bay
Marina offers fully serviced pontoon berth-
ing for local and visiting boat owners. Local
companies provide a comprehensive range
of supporting services. Ideal stopover for
vessels heading to/from Scandinavia or the
Caledonian canal.
Website: www.peterhead-bay.co.uk

PORT OF TRURO
Harbour Office, Town Quay, Truro,
Cornwall TR1 2HJ.
Tel (01872) 272130 Fax (01872) 225346
VHF Ch12
Facilities for the yachtsman include visitor
pontoons located at Turnaware Bar, Ruan
Creek and Boscawen Park. Visitor moorings
at Woodbury. Quay facilities at Truro with
free showers and toilets. Chemical toilet
disposal, fresh water, electricity and garbage
disposal.

QUEENBOROUGH HARBOUR
Town Quay, South Street,
Queenborough, Isle of Sheppey,
Kent ME11 5AF.
Tel/Fax (01795) 662051
Moorings available in sought after position
close to Thames and Medway estuaries.

RAMSGATE ROYAL HARBOUR MARINA
Harbour Office, Military Road,
Ramsgate, Kent CT11 9LQ.
Tel (01843) 592277 Fax (01843) 590941
Ramsgate Royal Harbour is situated on the
south east coast, making an ideal base for
crossing to the Continent. 24-hour access
to finger pontoons. Comprehensive security
systems. Amenities: Launderette, repairs,
slipways, boatpark. Competitive rates for
permanent berths and discounts for visitors'
group bookings.

SUFFOLK YACHT HARBOUR LTD
Levington, Ipswich, Suffolk IP10 0LN.
Tel (01473) 659240 Fax (01473) 659632
500-berths - access at all states of tide
(dredged to 2.5 meters at LW Springs).
Boat hoist facilities up to 60 tons. Full boatyard services, chandlery, gas, diesel, petrol,
engineering, sailmaking, electronics. Club
house and restaurant.

SUTTON HARBOUR MARINA
Sutton Harbour, Plymouth,
Devon PL4 0RA.
Tel (01752) 204186 Fax (01752) 205403
A superb sheltered marina with 24-hour
access and fully serviced visitor berths with
full on-shore facilities in the city's historic
Elizabethan quarter. Just a few minutes
stroll from the shops, restaurants and
entertainment in the city centre.

WEYMOUTH OLD HARBOUR
Weymouth & Portland Borough Council,
Environmental Services Department,
Council Offices, North Quay,
Weymouth, Dorset DT4 8TA.
Tel (01305) 206423/206363
Fax (01305) 206422
e-mail: harbour@weymouth.co.uk
Access at all stages of tide. Visitor berths in
centre of prime tourist resort with shops,
restaurants and night life at hand. Diesel
fuelling from pontoon or tanker. Chandlery
and repair facilities available.
Website: www.weymouth.gov.uk/marine.htm

WHITEHAVEN HARBOUR MARINA
Harbour Commissioners, Pears House,
1 Duke Street, Whitehaven,
Cumbria CA28 7HW.
Tel (01946) 692435 Fax (01946) 691135
VHF Ch12
Long and short-term berths available at
newly created 100 capacity marina,
maximum length 12m. Eleven hectare
permanent locked harbour with 45 tonne
boat hoist, access at least HW ± 3hours.
Sheltered historic location adjacent to town
centre.

W & H CHINA
Howley Properties Ltd,
PO Box 149, Warrington WA1 2DW.
Fax (01925) 418009
Manufacturer of China chart dividers.

DIVERSE YACHT SERVICES
Unit 12, Hamble Yacht Services, Port
Hamble, Hamble, Hampshire SO31 4NN.
Tel 023 8045 3399 Fax 023 8045 5288
Marine electronics and electrics. Supplied
and installed. Specialists in racing yachts.
Suppliers of 'Loadsense' Loadcells for
marine applications.

GREENHAM MARINE
King's Saltern Road, Lymington,
Hampshire SO41 9QD.
Tel (01590) 671144 Fax (01590) 679517
Greenham Marine can offer yachtsmen one
of the most comprehensive selections of
marine electronic equipment currently

available. Also at Poole/Weymouth 01202
676363 and Emsworth/Chichester 01243
378314.

SIMRAD LTD
Woolmer Way, Bordon,
Hampshire GU35 9QE.
Tel (01420) 483200 Fax (01420) 489073
For full entry see under:
ELECTRONIC DEVICES & EQUIPMENT

SOFTWAVE
Riverside, Mill Lane, Taplow,
Maidenhead SL6 0AA.
Tel 01628 637777 Fax 01628 773030
Provider of PC based navigation *Seavision*
hardware and *Nobeltec* and *Transas*
software. Using charts drawn from Admiralty sources the quality navigation software
that we provide can be easily installed to
customers own laptops or computers. For
on-board installations we manufacture
hardware that include sun-readable,
waterproof screens linked to high
performance, ruggedised compact PCs.
Website: www.softwave.co.uk

SWALE MARINE (ELECTRICAL)
The Old Stable, North Road,
Queenborough, Kent ME11 5EH.
Tel (01795) 580930 Fax (01795) 580238
For all your electrical and electronic needs.
Authorised agents for: Furuno, Autohelm,
Raytheon and most major manufacturers.
Fight crime with Harbourguard monitored
security: Medway and Swale coverage -
Boatmark registration centre.

BACHMANN MARINE SERVICES LTD
Frances House, Sir William Place,
St Peter Port, Guernsey,
Channel Islands GY1 4HQ.
Tel (01481) 723573 Fax (01481) 711353
British yacht registration, corporate
yacht ownership and management,
marine insurance, crew placement and
management. Bachmann Marine Services aims to provide a personal and
individual service to its clients.

**BISHOP SKINNER INTERNATIONAL
INSURANCE BROKERS**
Oakley Crescent, City Road,
London EC1V 1NU.
Tel 020 7566 5800 Fax 020 7608 2171
Dinghy Insurance - As insurance brokers to
the RYA we offer cover for accidental
damage, racing risks, 30-days European
extension, discounts for dinghy instructors,
third party indemnity of £2,000,000, no
claim bonus (transferable) and first class
security. Immediate quotation and instant
cover all at competitive rates.

C CLAIMS Loss Adjusters
PO Box 8, Romford, Essex RM4 1AL.
Tel Helpline: 020 8502 6999
Fax 020 8500 1005
e-mail: cclaims@compuserve.com
C Claims are specialist marine and small craft claims adjusters with a central record of stolen vessels and equipment. They have provided a unique service to marine insurers since 1979 and welcome trade and private enquiries. They are represented throughout the world.

CRAVEN HODGSON ASSOCIATES
Suite 15, 30-38 Dock Street,
Leeds LS10 1JF.
Tel 0113-243 8443
As an independent insurance adviser and intermediary, we provide comprehensive, individual and impartial assistance, acting as your agent.

FOWEY CRUISING SCHOOL & SERVICES
Fore Street, Fowey, Cornwall PL23 1AQ.
Tel (01726) 832129 Fax (01726) 832000
e-mail: fcs@dial.pipex.com
The best cruising in Britain, with matue instructors. Practical shore-based RYA courses. Family cruising a speciality. Yachtmster/Coastal exams. Diesel, First Aid, VHF etc. Our quarter century experience shows. *ALSO Marine and travel insurance with top companies.*

PLEASE MENTION THE PINK PAGE DIRECTORY WHEN MAKING YOUR ENQUIRIES

LOMBARD GENERAL INSURANCE CO LTD
Lombard House, 182 High Street,
Tonbridge, Kent TN9 1BY.
Tel (01732) 376317 Fax (01732) 773117
One of the UK's largest specialist yacht underwriters and risk carriers. For full details of the range of insurance products available for all types of pleasurecraft, please contact your local marine insurance broker or intermediary.

MARSH YACHT DIVISION
Havelock Chambers, Queens Terrace,
Southampton, Hampshire SO14 3PP.
Tel 023 8031 8300 Fax 023 8031 8391
A member of the largest insurance broking firm in the world with associated offices in Antibes and Fort Lauderdale. Specialists in yacht insurance for craft cruising UK, Mediterranean, Caribbean and US waters.

NORTHERN STAR INSURANCE CO LTD
London Road, Gloucester GL1 3NS.
Tel (01452) 393000
Yacht Department Direct Line: 01452 393109. Founded over four decades ago and now part of the Fortis Group, Northern Star underwrites most classes of insurance but specialises in insurances for homeworkers, pleasurecraft, holiday and travel, property owners and householders.

ST MARGARETS INSURANCES LTD
153-155 High Street, Penge,
London SE20 7DL.
Tel 020 8778 6161 Fax 020 8659 1968
e-mail: yachts@stminsurance.co.uk
Over 30 years dedicated to insuring yachts and pleasurecraft. Many unique policies available only through St Margarets. Immediate quotations available.
Website: www.stminsurance.co.uk

INTERIOR LIGHTS

TOOMER & HAYTER LTD
74 Green Road, Winton,
Bournemouth, Dorset BH9 1EB.
Tel (01202) 515789 Fax (01202) 538771
Marine upholstery manufacturers. Cabin and cockpit upholstery made to any shape or size. Sprung interior mattresses made to measure. Foam backed cabin lining always in stock, also carpet side lining. Visit our factory and showroom.

LEGAL SERVICES

LEGAL SUPPORT SERVICES
Virides, Victoria Road, Bishops
Waltham, Hampshire SO32 1DJ.
Tel/Fax (01489) 890961
Mobile: 0966 389367
Support services for marine companies for legal and quasi-legal activities, eg liaison with local authorities and government departments, and discrete research projects. **Also Marine Job-Spot** low cost recruitment services for the UK marine industry.

LIFERAFT/INFLATABLES & REPAIRS

A B MARINE LTD
Castle Walk, St Peter Port, Guernsey,
Channel Islands GY1 1AU.
Tel (01481) 722378 Fax (01481) 711080
We specialise in safety and survival equipment and are a DoT approved service station for liferafts including R.F.D., Beaufort/Dunlop, Zodiac, Avon, Plastimo and Lifeguard. We also carry a full range of new liferafts, dinghies and lifejackets, and are agents for Bukh marine engines.

ADEC MARINE LTD
4 Masons Avenue, Croydon,
Surrey CR0 9XS.
Tel 020 8686 9717 Fax 020 8680 9912
e-mail: adecmarine@lineone.net
Approved liferaft service station for south east UK. Additionally we hire and sell new rafts and sell a complete range of safety equipment for yachts including pyrotechnics, fire extinguishers, lifejackets, buoys and a buoyancy bag system.

**BOSUNS LOCKER CHANDLERY -
MILFORD HAVEN**
Cleddau House, Milford Marina,
Milford Haven,
Pembrokeshire SA73 3AF.
Tel (01646) 697834 Fax (01646) 698009
Chandlery and cafe - Books, charts, engine spares, clothing, electronics, Blakes, Jotrun, International paints, inflatables. Special orders and mail order service. Weekly deliveries to Aberystwyth Marina.
Website: www.bosunslocker.co.uk

PREMIUM LIFERAFT SERVICES
Liferaft House, Burnham Business Park,
Burnham-on-Crouch, Essex CM0 8TE.
Tel (01621) 784858 Fax (01621) 785934
Freephone 0800 243673
e-mail:liferaftuk@aol.com
Hire and sales of DoT and RORC approved liferafts. Long and short-term hire from 18 depots nationwide. Servicing and other safety equipment available.

**SOUTH EASTERN
MARINE SERVICES LTD**
Units 13 & 25, Olympic Business Centre,
Paycocke Road, Basildon,
Essex SS14 3EX.
Tel (01268) 534427 Fax (01268) 281009
e-mail: sems@bt.internet.com
Liferaft service, sales and hire, 1-65 persons. Approved by major manufacturers and MSA. Callers welcome. View your own raft. Family owned and operated. Inflatable boat repairs and spares. WE WANT YOU TO COME BACK.
Website: www.sems.com

X M YACHTING LTD
The Mill, Berwick, Polegate,
East Sussex BN26 8SL.
Tel (01323) 870092 Fax (01323) 870909
For the 21st Century. Extensive range of
marine quality equipment including clothing, footwear, inflatables, safety equipment,
liferafts and the XM Quickfit range of lifejackets manufactured to CE standard, and
the TH-5 offshore breathable suit. Performance technology - designed to be worn.
Please call 01323 870092 for further details
and catalogue or visit your local stockist.

MAIL ORDER

A S A P SUPPLIES - DIRECT ORDER
Beccles, Suffolk NR34 7TD.
Tel (01502) 716993 Fax (01502) 711680
e-mail: infomma@asap-supplies.com
Worldwide supply of equipment and spares.
Anodes, cables, contrads, coolers, exhausts,
fenders, fuel systems, gear boxes, impellers,
insulation, lights, marinisation, panels,
propellers and shafts, pumps, seacocks,
silencers, sound proofing, steering, toilets,
trimtabs, water heaters, wipers and much
much more....
Website: www.asap-supplies.com

B P S C MARINE SERVICES
Unit 4 Park Business Centre,
1 Park Road, Freemantle, Southampton,
Hampshire SO15 3US.
Tel 023 8051 0561
BPSC offer a fast efficient repair service on
a wide range of nautical and survey
instruments. Free estimates and advice. A
comprehensive range of spares are carried,
most of which can be despatched same
day. Instruments commissioned. Compass
adjusting service.

THE CARTOON GALLERY
(Wavelength Design)
37 Lower Street, Dartmouth,
Devon TQ6 9AN.
Tel/Fax (01803) 834466
Tel (01803) 834425 Evenings
Rick, the International cartoonist specialises
in hand coloured and personalised sailing
cartoon prints (eg A3 £10). Commissions
are carried out in Rick's Dartmouth gallery
and studio. Prints available by mail order.
Telephone or fax for details.

EURONAV NAVIGATION
20 The Slipway, Port Solent, Portsmouth,
Hampshire PO6 4TR.
Tel 023 9237 3855 Fax 023 9232 5800
Electronic charting specialists, offering the
seaPro 2000 range of PC-based chart
plotting systems, ARCS, Livechart 'B' and
BSB top quality electronic charts. Products
are available from good chandlers or direct
from Euronav.
Website: www.euronav.co.uk

FORESIGHT OPTICAL
13 New Road, Banbury,
Oxfordshire OX16 9PN.
Tel (01295) 264365
Suppliers of general purpose and nautical
binoculars, spotting scopes, astronomical
telescopes, night vision equipment, micro-

scopes, magnifiers, spotlights, tripods and
accessories. National mail order service.

REED'S NAUTICAL BOOKS
The Barn, Ford Farm, Bradford Leigh,
Bradford on Avon, Wiltshire BA15 2RP.
Tel (01225) 868821 Fax (01225) 868831
e-mail: tugsrus@abreed.demon.co.uk
REED'S HEAVENLY BODIES - Annual astro-
navigation tables for yachtsmen edited by
Lt Cdr H J Baker. Price £13.95 incl p&p.
Showing monthly pages for Sun, Moon,
Planets and Stars accompanied by examples
and all necessary tables. Complete SIGHT
REDUCTION PACKAGE with programmed
calculator also available together with book
and chart catalogues, for worldwide mail
order.
Website: www.reedsnautical.com

SARNIA FLAGS
8 Belmont Road, St Peter Port, Guernsey,
Channel Islands GY1 1PY.
Tel (01481) 725995 Fax (01481) 729335
Flags and pennants made to order. National
flags, house, club and battle flags, and
burgees made to order. Any size, shape or
design. Prices on request.

SHAMROCK CHANDLERY
Shamrock Quay, William Street,
Northam, Southampton,
Hampshire SO14 5QL.
Tel 023 8063 2725 Fax 023 8022 5611
e-mail: sales@shamrock.co.uk
Situated on Shamrock Quay, a busy working
yard with a pub, restaurant and boutiques.
Shamrock Chandlery is renowned for
extensive quality stocks and service, and is
widely used by both the trade and boat
owners. Excellent mail order facilities - Order
Hotline 023 8022 5746.
Website: www.shamrock.co.uk

TODD CHART AGENCY LTD
4 Seacliff Road, The Harbour,
Bangor, County Down,
Northern Ireland BT20 5EY.
Tel 028 9146 6640 Fax 028 9147 1070
e-mail: admiralty@toddchart.co.uk
International Admiralty Chart Agent, chart
correction service and nautical booksellers.
Stockist of Imray charts and books,
navigation and chartroom instruments,
binoculars, clocks etc. UK agent for Icelandic
Hydrographic Service. Mail order - Visa,
Mastercard, American Express and Switch/
Delta accepted.

TOOMER & HAYTER LTD
74 Green Road, Winton, Bournemouth,
Dorset BH9 1EB.
Tel (01202) 515789 Fax (01202) 538771
Marine upholstery manufacturers. Cabin
and cockpit upholstery made to any shape
or size. Sprung interior mattresses made to
measure. Foam backed cabin lining always
in stock, also carpet side lining. Visit our
factory and showroom.

WARSASH NAUTICAL BOOKSHOP
6 Dibles Road, Warsash, Southampton,
Hampshire SO31 9HZ.
Tel (01489) 572384 Fax (01489) 885756
e-mail: alan@nauticalbooks.co.uk
Nautical bookseller and chart agent. Callers
and mail order. Free new and secondhand
book lists. Credit cards taken. Publishers of
the Bibliography of Nautical books.
Website: www.nauticalbooks.co.uk

WET & WILD GRAPHICS
Falcon House, Hamble Point Marina,
Hamble, Southampton,
Hampshire SO31 4NB.
Tel 023 8045 8332 Fax 023 8045 6830
e-mail: sales@wild-graphics.co.uk
Supply and application of vinyl graphics,
signboards, banners and flags. Specialist
materials for sails and spinnakers. Brochure
available for mail order boat names.
Deadlines never a problem!!!

MARINA DEVELOPMENT CONSULTANTS

CREST NICHOLSON MARINAS LTD
- BRISTOL
Parklands, Stoke Gifford,
Bristol BS34 8QU.
Tel 0117-923 6466 Fax 0117-923 6508
Marina development management and
consultancy.
Website: www.aboard.co.uk/c.n.marinas

MARINAS

ABERYSTWYTH MARINA
- IMP DEVELOPMENTS
Ylanfa-Aberystwyth Marina, Trefechan,
Aberyswyth, Dyfed SY23 1AS.
Tel (01970) 611422 Fax (01970) 624122
e-mail: abermarina@aol.com
NEW fully serviced marina. Diesel, gas,
water, toilets and hot showers.

ARDFERN YACHT CENTRE
Ardfern By Lochgilphead,
Argyll PA31 8QN.
Tel (01852) 500247/636 Fax (01852) 500624
and 07000 ARDFERN
Boatyard with full repair and maintenance
facilities. Timber and GRP repairs, painting
and engineering. Sheltered moorings and
pontoon berthing. Winter storage, chandlery, showers, fuel, Calor, brokerage, 20-
ton boat hoist, rigging. Hotel, bars and
restaurant.

W BATES & SON BOATBUILDERS LTD
Bridge Wharf, Chertsey,
Surrey KT16 8LG.
Tel (01932) 562255 Fax (01932) 565600
110-berth marina in quiet picturesque area
and additional riverside moorings. Full
facilities including electricity to most berths,
toilets and showers. 12-ton crane and hard
standing for winter storage. Always a
welcome to visitors from our friendly staff.
Sales office open seven days a week.

 **Macmillan Reeds Nautical Almanac
- the yachtsman's Bible**

BEAUCETTE MARINA
Vale, Guernsey,
Channel Islands GY3 5BQ.
Tel (01481) 45000 Fax (01481) 47071
e-mail:
beaucette@premier-marinas.co.uk
Situated on the north east coast, Beaucette is one of Europe's most charming deep water marinas. With 140 berths, the marina offers all the services and facilities you would expect. Beaucette is a PREMIER marina.

BEAULIEU RIVER MANAGEMENT LTD
Harbour Master's Office,
Bucklers Hard Yacht Harbour, Beaulieu,
Hampshire SO42 7XB.
Tel (01590) 616200 Fax (01590) 616211
110-berth yacht harbour (pontoon berths), fully serviced with back-up facilities of historic Bucklers Hard village. Agamemnon boatyard - 290 swinging moorings let on annual basis. Visiting craft welcome. Capacity 100+ pile/pontoon.

BRIGHTON MARINA
Marine Trade Centre, Brighton Marina,
Brighton, East Sussex BN2 5UG.
Tel (01273) 819919 Fax (01273) 675082
The UK's No 1 marina village with 1300 pontoon berths. 24-hour manned reception and CCTV. Five-Gold Anchors for facilties and service with excellent new toilet and showers. Full boatyard and shore facilities with Marine Trade Centre offering all associated trades and leisure area with 11 pub/restaurants, ASDA superstore, Virgin cinema, David Lloyd Health Centre and Bowlplex. Entrance dredged to 2 metres with 24-hour access to the sea without locking. Five minutes from Brighton town centre.

BURGH CASTLE MARINA
Butt Lane, Burgh Castle, Norfolk,
Norwich NR31 9PZ.
Tel (01493) 780331 Fax (01493) 780163
e-mail: rdw_chesham@compuserve.com
100 serviced pontoons and quay moorings accessible at all tides. Secure car and boat parking. Adjoining boatyard services, access to holiday park showers, laundry and heated pool. Riverside pub and shop. Complex open all year.

BURNHAM YACHT HARBOUR MARINA LTD
Burnham Yacht Harbour,
Burnham-on-Crouch, Essex CM0 8BL.
Tel (01621) 782150 Fax (01621) 785848
VHF Ch80
The only Five-Gold Anchor marina in Essex. 350 fully serviced pontoon berths and 120 deep water swing moorings. Marina access at all states of tide with minimum 2.5m depth at low water.

CALEY MARINA
Canal Road, Inverness IV3 6NF.
Tel +44 (0) 1463 236539
Fax +44 (0) 1463 238323
e-mail: info@caleymarina.com
Open 08.30 - 17.30. Berths: 50 Pontoons (visitors available). Facilities: Fuel, water, pump-out facilities, provisions (nearby shops), repair, cranage, secure storage afloat and ashore. Comprehensive chandlery, showers, workshop. Situated at eastern end of Caledonian canal above Muirtown locks. Access via sea locks 4 hours either side of high water.
Website: www.caleymarina.com

CARLINGFORD MARINA - IRELAND
Carlingford, Co Louth, Ireland.
Tel/Fax +353 42 73492
VHF Ch16 and 37 (M)
Superb location in beautiful setting close to historic village of Carlingford, our friendly marina provides a top class service for all boat users. Moorings, chandlery, slipway, 16-ton cranage, power, diesel, water, laundry, showers and coffee shop. Visitors always welcome. New restaurant and bar complex now open and welcoming. *Sailing Holidays in Ireland - Only the Best.*

CARRICKFERGUS WATERFRONT
The Marina' Rodger's Quay,
Carrickfergus, Co Antrim, Northern
Ireland BT38 8BE.
Tel +44 (0) 28 93366666
Fax +44 (0) 28 93350505
e-mail: carrick.marina@virgin.net
300 fully serviced pontoon berths with excellent full on-shore facilities. Steeped in a wealth of historical legend. Carrickfergus has excellent restaurants, hotels, pubs, shops and a host of recreational leisure facilities.

CASTLEPARK MARINA - IRELAND
Kinsale, Co Cork, Ireland.
Tel +353 21 774959 Fax +353 21 774958
100-berth fully serviced marina with restaurant, laundry, showers and toilets. Waterside hostel-type accommodation available. New restaurant catering for both breakfast and evening meals. Access at all stages of the tide. *Sailing Holidays in Ireland - Only the Best.*

CHELSEA HARBOUR LTD
108 The Chambers, Chelsea Harbour,
London SW10 0XF.
Tel 020 7761 8600 Fax 020 7352 7868
A tranquil and intimate marina of 55 berths close to the heart of the west end of London. 5-Star hotel, restaurants and bars. Overnight pontoon and amenities. 24-hour security patrols and CCTV.

CHICHESTER MARINA
Birdham, Chichester,
West Sussex PO20 7EJ.
Tel (01243) 512731 Fax (01243) 513472
e-mail:
chichester@premier-marinas.co.uk
Situated in the north east corner of Chichester harbour, Chichester Marina enjoys one of the most attractive locations in the country. With 1100 berths, Chichester offers a unique combination of service, facilities, security and friendliness, unparalleled in UK marinas. Chichester Marina is a PREMIER Marina.

CHISWICK QUAY MARINA LTD
Marina Office, Chiswick Quay,
London W4 3UR.
Tel 020 8994 8743
Small, secluded, peaceful marina on tidal Thames at Chiswick. Slipway, marine engineers and electricians, power, water, toilets and sluice. Some residential moorings.

CLYDE MARINA - ARDROSSAN
The Harbour, Ardrossan,
Ayrshire KA22 8DB.
Tel (01294) 607077 Fax (01294) 607076
e-mail: clydmarina@aol.com
Located on the north Ayrshire coast within easy cruising reach of Arran, the Cumbrae Islands, Bute and the Kintyre Peninsula. Deep draught harbour with 200 pontoon berths and quayside for vessels up to 120'. 20-ton hoist, undercover storage and most services and facilities. Ancasta Scotland brokerage, also Beneteau, Nimbus-Maxi, Westerly yachts, SeaRay and Marlin RIBs.

COLERAINE MARINA
64 Portstewart Road, Coleraine,
Co Londonderry,
Northern Ireland BT52 1RS.
Tel 028 7034 4768
Wide range of facilities.

COWES YACHT HAVEN
Vectis Yard, High Street, Cowes,
Isle of Wight PO31 7BD.
Tel (01983) 299975 Fax (01983) 200332
VHF Ch80
Cowes Yacht Haven is the Solent's premier sailing event centre offering 200 fully serviced berths right in the heart of Cowes. Our improved facilities, capability and location ensures the perfect venue and profile for every kind of boating event.

CRAOBH MARINA
By Lochgilphead, Argyll PA31 8UD.
Tel (01852) 500222 Fax (01852) 500252
VHF Ch37 and 80 (M).
250-berth marina on Loch Shuna. Water, electricity, diesel and gas. Full boatyard services. Chandlery. Brokerage. Insurance. Shops, bar. 24-hour access.

CREST NICHOLSON MARINAS LTD - BANGOR
Bangor Marina, Bangor, Co Down,
Northern Ireland BT20 5ED.
Tel 028 9145 3297 Fax 028 9145 3450
Situated on the south shore of Belfast Lough, Bangor, is Ireland's largest and most comprehensive yachting facility. The marina is within convenient walking distance of all the town's amenities and may be accessed at any time of day or state of the tide (minimum depth 2.9 metres.)

CREST NICHOLSON MARINAS LTD - CONWY
Conwy Marina, Conwy Morfa, Conwy,
Gwynedd LL32 8EP.
Tel (01492) 593000 Fax (01492) 572111
Conwy Marina is ideally placed on the south shore of the Conwy estuary. The marina is set within idyllic surroundings and has comprehensive facilities. Road access is extremely convenient, with the A55 dual carriageway passing close by.

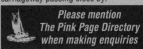

Please mention
The Pink Page Directory
when making enquiries

CREST NICHOLSON MARINAS LTD - MALAHIDE

(Marketing Agents) Malahide Marina, Malahide, Co Dublin, Ireland.
+353 1 845 4129 Fax +353 1 845 4255
Situated within Malahide's estuary north of Dublin Bay. Full range of marina facilities available.

CREST NICHOLSON MARINAS LTD - NORTH SHIELDS

Royal Quays Marina, Coble Dene Road, North Shields NE29 6DU.
Tel 0191-272 8282 Fax 0191-272 8288
Situated 2 miles from the entrance of the river Tyne. 24-hour lock access. Extensive range of facilities.

CREST NICHOLSON MARINAS LTD - PENARTH

Portway Village, Penarth, South Glamorgan CF64 1TQ.
Tel 029 2070 5021 Fax 029 2071 2170
Situated within the sheltered waters of Cardiff Bay the marina provides fully serviced, secure berths and wide ranging ancillary services. Open 24-hours, year round. We can assure visitors of a warm welcome. Please apply for details.

CROSSHAVEN BOATYARD MARINA - IRELAND

Crosshaven, Co Cork, Ireland.
Tel +353 21 831161 Fax +353 21 831603
All facilities at this 100-berth marina situated 12 miles from Cork City and close to ferryport and airport. Travel lift, full repair and maintenance services, spray painting and approved International Gelshield centre. Storage undercover and outside for 250 boats. Brokerage. RNLI and Defence contractors. *Sailing Holidays in Ireland - Only the Best.*

DART MARINA

Sandquay, Dartmouth, Devon TQ6 9PH.
Tel (01803) 833351 Fax (01803) 832307
High quality 110-berth marina on the fabulous river Dart, opposite the Dart Marina hotel. A superb situation with all amenities, 24-hour security, hotel and restaurant, showers, baths and laundry, fuel berth, holding tank pump-out facility and a warm welcome to all visitors.

DARTHAVEN MARINA LTD

Brixham Road, Kingswear, Dartmouth, Devon TQ6 0SG.
Tel (01803) 752242
Fax (01803) 752722
Marina Office: (01803) 752545
Chandlery: (01803) 752733
Fax (01803) 752790 VHF Ch80.
All types of repair facilities available. Fully trained staff. 30-ton mobile hoist available all states of tide. Extensive chandlery open 7 days. Agents for all major suppliers including B&G, Raytheon, Yanmar (Main Dealers),Volvo Penta agents, Simpson Lawrence, Sowester installer dealer, International Coatings and many others. Emergency engineer call out - Mobile: 0411 404259. Electrician - Mobile: 0467 250787. Visitors welcome. All marina facilities available.
www.darthaven.co.uk

DEAN & REDDYHOFF LTD - EAST COWES MARINA

Clarence Road, East Cowes, Isle of Wight PO32 6HA.
Tel (01983) 293983 Fax (01983) 299276
This existing marina (but new to Dean and Reddyhoff) is undergoing a facelift which will include dredging, new pontoons, toilets and showers and possibly a clubhouse. Regular yachtsmen, visitors and rallies will be welcome as before.

DEAN & REDDYHOFF LTD - HASLAR MARINA

Haslar Road, Gosport, Hampshire PO12 1NU.
Tel 023 9260 1201 Fax 023 9260 2201
Haslar Marina is just inside the entrance of Portsmouth harbour on the Gosport side. Included in the 600 berths is a visitors' area which is adjacent to a converted lightship with bar facilities and excellent toilets and showers.

DEAN & REDDYHOFF LTD - WEYMOUTH MARINA

70 Commercial Road, Weymouth, Dorset DT4 8NA.
Tel (01305) 767576 Fax (01305) 767575
This new marina in the inner harbour of Weymouth provides facilities for visitors which are proving very popular. The marina is right next to Weymouth's high street, and the area has a multitude of pubs and restaurants.

DINGLE MARINA - IRELAND

Harbour Master, Strand Street, Dingle, Co Kerry, Ireland.
Tel +353 66 9151629 Fax +353 66 9152629
e-mail: dinglemarina@tinet.ie
Europe's most westerly marina on the beautiful south west coast of Ireland in the heart of the old sheltered fishing port of Dingle. Visitor berths, fuel and water. Shops, 52 pubs and many restaurants with traditional music and hospitality. Harbour easily navigable day or night. *Sailing Holidays in Ireland - Only the Best.*

EMSWORTH YACHT HARBOUR LTD

Thorney Road, Emsworth, Hampshire PO10 8BP.
Tel (01243) 377727 Fax (01243) 373432
Friendly marina in Chichester harbour. Water, electricity, diesel, Calor gas, 25-tonne mobile crane, slipways, hard-standing and storage areas. Showers and toilets, car parking, chandlery, engineers and boat repairs.

FALMOUTH MARINA

North Parade, Falmouth, Cornwall TR11 2TD.
Tel (01326) 316620 Fax (01326) 313939
e-mail: falmouth@premier-marinas.co.uk
The most westerly marina in England, Falmouth is an ideal starting point for a cruise to the Channel Islands, Brittany or the Scilly Isles. The marina offers fully serviced permanent and visitor berths with a professional and friendly service you would expect from a PREMIER marina.

FENIT HARBOUR MARINA - IRELAND

Fenit, Co Kerry, Ireland.
Tel/Fax +353 66 36231
A new marina opened in July 1997 with 104 berths for all sizes of boat up to 15m x 3m draught, with one berth available for larger vessels up to 30m. Access at all tides. Minimum approach depth 5m. Facilities include smartcard access, toilets, showers, laundry and harbour office. Visitors are welcome to use the superb clubhouse facilities of the Tralee Sailing Club and participate in races Tuesdays. *Sailing Holidays in Ireland - Only the Best.*

USE THESE PAGES FOR ALL YOUR MARINE SERVICES AND SUPPLIES

FIDDLERS FERRY YACHT HAVEN
Off Station Road, Penketh,
Warrington, Cheshire WA5 2UJ.
Tel (01925) 727519
Sheltered moorings up to 6'6" draught, 50'
long. Access through lock from river Mersey
1½ hours either side of high tide. Signed
from A652. Boatyard and lift-out facilities.
Annual rate per foot £8.25.

FOX'S MARINA IPSWICH LTD
The Strand, Wherstead,
Ipswich, Suffolk IP2 8SA.
Tel (01473) 689111 Fax (01473) 601737
The most comprehensive boatyard facility
on the east coast. Extensive chandlery.
Marina access 24-hours. Diesel dock, two
travel hoists to 70 tons, 10 ton crane. Full
electronics, rigging, engineering, stainless
steel services. Specialists in osmosis and
spray painting.

HAFAN PWLLHELI
Glan Don, Pwllheli,
Gwynedd LL53 5YT.
Tel (01758) 701219 Fax (01758) 701443
VHF Ch80
Hafan Pwllheli has over 400 pontoon berths
and offers access at virtually all states of
the tide. Ashore,its modern purpose-built
facilities include luxury toilets, showers,
landerette, a secure boat park for winter
storage, 40-ton travel hoist, mobile crane
and plenty of space for car parking. Open
24-hours a day, 7 days a week.

HARTLEPOOL MARINA
Lock Office, Slake Terrace, Hartlepool,
Cleveland TS24 0RU.
Tel (01429) 865744 Fax (01429) 865947
The north's premier marina. The year 2000
sees the completion of a massive
redevelopment to include 700 berths, a
new 300 ton boat hoist along with luxury
leisure, residential and retail facilities on-
site. Please call 01429 865744 for more
information 24hours.

HOWTH MARINA - IRELAND
Howth, Co Dublin, Ireland.
Tel +353 1 8392777 Fax +353 1 8392430
Modern marina in beautiful sheltered
location. Fully serviced berths with every
facility and 24-hour security. Very popular
marina for traffic in the Irish Sea. Is available
at all states of the tide with extremely easy
access. *Sailing Holidays in Ireland - Only
the Best.*
Website: www.hss.ac.uk

HULL MARINA LTD
Warehouse 13,
Kingston Street,
Hull HU1 2DQ.
Tel (01482) 613451 Fax (01482) 224148
Four-Anchor marina. Situated 5 minutes
from the centre of Hull and all national and
international transport systems. First class
leisure, boatyard and brokerage facilities.
4-Star hotel and quayside restaurants. Professional and caring staff. Competitive rates.

JERSEY HARBOURS
Maritime House, La Route du Port
Elizabeth, St Helier, Jersey JE1 1HB.
Tel (01534) 885588 Fax (01534) 885599
e-mail: jsyhbr@itl.net
A warm welcome to visiting yachts! St
Helier Marina has 50 more finger berths for
visitors. 5-Gold Anchor facilities. 3 hours
±HW. Berths available to lease from one
month to 10 years in our **NEW ELIZABETH
MARINA.**

KILMORE QUAY MARINA - IRELAND
Kilmore Quay, Co Wexford, Ireland.
Tel/Fax +353 53 29955
Kilmore Quay in the south east of Ireland
has a new Blue Flag marina with 20 pontoon
visitor berths. This friendly fishing port has
pleasant hotel facilities, pubs and
restaurants offering a traditional Irish
welcome. Rosslare ferryport is only 15 miles
away. *Sailing Holidays in Ireland - Only the
Best.*

KILRUSH MARINA - IRELAND
Kilrush, Co Clare, Ireland.
Tel +353 65 9052072 Fax +353 65 9051692
e-mail: kem@shannon.dev.ie
Mobile: +353 87 2313870 VHF Ch80
Kilrush Marina on Ireland's beautiful west
coast, is a new marina with 120 fully serviced
berths. The marina has all shore facilities
including a modern boatyard with 45-ton
hoist. It adjoins the busy market town of
Kilrush which has every facility required by
the visiting yachtsman. *Sailing Holidays in
Ireland - Only the Best.*
Website: www.shannon-dev.ie/kcm

KIP MARINA
The Yacht Harbour, Inverkip,
Renfrewshire PA16 0AS.
Tel (01475) 521485 Fax (01475) 521298
Marina berths for vessels up to 65' LOA.
Full boatyard facilities including travel hoist,
crane, on-site engineers, GRP repairs etc.
Bar, restaurant, saunas, launderette and
chandlery. Distributors for Moody yachts,
Northshore and Searanger motor yachts.

LARGS YACHT HAVEN
Irvine Road, Largs, Ayrshire KA30 8EZ.
Tel (01475) 675333 Fax (01475) 672245
Perfectly located 600-berth marina with full
services afloat and ashore. 45-ton travel
hoist operational 7 days; fuel (diesel and
petrol); gas and ice on sale 24-hours. Bar,
coffee shop, dive shop plus usual marine
services.

LAWRENCE COVE MARINA - IRELAND
Bere Island, Bantry Bay,
Co Cork, Ireland.
Tel/Fax +353 27 75044
Lawrence Cove Marina is situated in Bantry
Bay in the south west corner of Ireland in
the heart of the best cruising ground in
Europe. It is a new marina, family run with
full facilities and a very safe haven to leave
a boat. It is two hours from Cork airport
with good connections. *Sailing Holidays in
Ireland - Only the Best.*

LIVERPOOL MARINA
Coburg Dock, Sefton Street,
Liverpool L3 4BP.
Tel 0151-709 0578 (2683 after 5pm)
Fax 0151-709 8731
300-berth yacht harbour. All serviced
pontoons. Tidal access HW + or - 2½ hours
approximately, depending on draught. 60-
ton hoist, workshops, bar and restaurant,
toilets and showers. City centre one mile.
Open all year. Active yacht club and yacht
brokerage.

LYMINGTON YACHT HAVEN
King's Saltern Road, Lymington,
Hampshire SO41 3QD.
Tel (01590) 677071 Fax (01590) 678186
Perfectly situated at the mouth of the
Lymington river giving instant access to the
Western Solent. Full marina services,
boatyard, brokerage, diesel, petrol, gas,
restaurant and bar.

MALAHIDE MARINA - IRELAND
Malahide, Co Dublin, Ireland.
Tel +353 1 8454129 Fax +353 1 8454255
Located next to the picturesque village of
Malahide our marina village is the ideal spot
to enjoy and relax. There are 350 fully
serviced berths, petrol and diesel available,
30-ton hoist with full boatyard facilities
with winter storage ashore or afloat. A fine
selection of shops, and friendly pubs and
restaurants serving good food are close by.
Sailing Holidays in Ireland - Only the Best.

**MARITIME TOURISM LTD
- CASTLEPARK MARINA**
Kinsale, Co Cork, Ireland.
Tel +353 21 774959 Fax +353 21 774958
100-berth fully serviced marina with
restaurant, laundry, showers and toilets.
Waterside hotel-type accommodation
available. New restaurant catering for both
breakfast and evening meals. Access at all
stages of the tide.

**THE MAYFLOWER
INTERNATIONAL MARINA**
Ocean Quay, Richmond Walk,
Plymouth, Devon PL1 4LS.
Tel (01752) 556633 Fax (01752) 606896
Plymouth's only Five-Gold Anchor marina.
Known for its extensive facilities, courtesy
and security. Owned by berth holders and
run to a very high standard.

MILFORD MARINA
The Docks, Milford Haven,
Pembrokeshire, West Wales SA73 3AE.
Tel (01646) 696312 Fax (01646) 696314
Safe sheltered haven, 250 berths, 5 minutes
from shopping, rail and bus services. Water
and electricity to all berths. Staff available
24 hours. Restaurant, chandlery, electronics, boat repair, lifting and storage
available on-site.

NEYLAND YACHT HAVEN LTD
Brunel Quay, Neyland,
Pembrokeshire SA73 1PY.
Tel (01646) 601601 Fax (01646) 600713
Marina operators with all facilities. 360 fully
serviced pontoon berths in a sheltered, tree
lined marina. On-site services include
boatyard, sailmaker, sailing school,

chandlery, cafe, lounge/bar, launderette, showers and toilets. 30 visitor berths. 24-hour access and security.

NOSS-ON-DART MARINA
Noss Quay, Dartmouth, Devon TQ6 0EA.
Tel (01803) 833351 Fax (01803) 832307
Peacefully located on the east shore of the river Dart, this relaxing marina is the perfect base for cruising yachtsmen. Extensive parking, chandlery, repair and lift-out facilities, easy access from London and the Midlands. Boat taxi to Dartmouth.

PADSTOW HARBOUR COMMISSIONERS
Harbour Office, Padstow,
Cornwall PL28 8AQ.
Tel (01841) 532239 Fax (01841) 533346
e-mail:
padstowharbour@compuserve.com
Inner harbour controlled by tidal gate - opens HW ±2hours. Minimum depth 3 metres at all times. Yachtsmen must be friendly as vessels raft together. Services include showers, toilets, diesel, water and ice. Security by CCTV.

PETERHEAD BAY AUTHORITY
Bath House, Bath Street,
Peterhead AB42 1DX.
Tel (01779) 474020 Fax (01779) 475712
Contact: Stephen Paterson. Peterhead Bay Marina offers fully serviced pontoon berthing for local and visiting boat owners. Local companies provide a comprehensive range of supporting services. Ideal stopover for vessels heading to/from Scandinavia or the Caledonian canal.
Website: www.peterhead-bay.co.uk

PLYMOUTH YACHT HAVEN
Shaw Way, Mount Batten,
Plymouth, Devon PL9 9XH.
Tel (01752) 404231 Fax (01752) 484177
VHF Ch37 and 80
Position: Southern side of cattewater, sheltered from prevailing winds by Mountbatten Peninsula. **Open:** All year, 24 hours. **Callsign:** Clovelly Bay. **Berths:** 180 berths, vessels up to 150', some fore and afts. Visitors welcome. **Facilities:** electricity, water, 24-hour security, workshop, chandlery, brokerage, showers, laundry, diesel. Calor gas. **NEW MARINA NOW OPEN.**

PORT FLAIR LTD
Bradwell Marina, Waterside,
Bradwell-on-Sea, Essex CM0 7RB.
Tel (01621) 776235/776391
300 pontoon berths with water and electricity, petrol and diesel, chandlery, marine slip/hoistage to 20 tons. Repairs, winter lay-ups, licensed club, yacht brokerage.

PORT OF TRURO
Harbour Office, Town Quay,
Truro, Cornwall TR1 2HJ.
Tel (01872) 272130 Fax (01872) 225346
VHF Ch12
Facilities for the yachtsman include visitor pontoons located at Turnaware Bar, Ruan Creek and Boscawen Park. Visitor moorings at Woodbury. Quay facilities at Truro with free showers and toilets. Chemical toilet disposal, fresh water, electricity and garbage disposal.

PORT SOLENT
South Lockside, Port Solent,
Portsmouth, Hampshire PO6 4TJ.
Tel 023 9221 0765 Fax 023 9232 4241
e-mail:
portsolent@premier-marinas.co.uk
From a marine superstore and outstanding slipway services to restaurants, bars and multiscreen cinema, Port Solent offers visitors and berth holders superb facilities, unsurpassed by any other UK marina. Port Solent is a PREMIER Marina.

PREMIER MARINAS LTD
South Lockside, Port Solent,
Portsmouth, Hampshire PO6 4TJ.
Tel 023 9221 4145 Fax 023 9222 1876
e-mail: office@premier-marinas.co.uk
At our marinas we're always on hand to help you. PREMIER GROUP MARINAS - Beaucette - Chichester - Falmouth - Port Solent.
Website: www.premier-marinas.co.uk

RAMSGATE ROYAL HARBOUR MARINA
Harbour Office, Military Road,
Ramsgate, Kent CT11 9LQ.
Tel (01843) 592277 Fax (01843) 590941
Ramsgate Royal Harbour is situated on the south east coast, making an ideal base for crossing to the Continent. 24-hour access to finger pontoons. Comprehensive security systems. Amenities: Launderette, repairs, slipways, boatpark. Competitive rates for permanent berths and discounts for visitors' group bookings.

RHU MARINA LTD
Helensburgh, Dunbartonshire G84 8LH.
Tel (01436) 820238 Fax (01436) 821039
e-mail: any@rhumarina.force9.co.uk
Berths accessible at all times and moorings available on the Clyde at the entrance to the Gareloch and 30 minutes from Glasgow. Hotels, shops and yacht clubs all adjacent.

RIDGE WHARF YACHT CENTRE
Ridge, Wareham, Dorset BH20 5BG.
Tel (01929) 552650 Fax (01929) 554434
Marina with full boatyard facilities. Winter lay-up and fuels etc.

SALVE MARINE LTD - IRELAND
Crosshaven, Co Cork, Ireland.
Tel +353 21 831145 Fax +353 21 831747
The marina is situated just 20 minutes from Cork City, Cork airport and Ringaskiddy ferry port. Located yards from Royal Cork yacht club and Crosshaven village centre. Facilities for yachts up to 140' x 14' draught including mains electricity 240/380 volts, telephone, fax, toilets and showers. Welding and machining in stainless steel, aluminium and bronze. Repairs and maintenance to hulls and rigging. Routine and detailed engine maintenance. Slip. *Sailing holidays in Ireland - Only the best.*

SHOTLEY MARINA LTD
Shotley Gate, Ipswich, Suffolk IP9 1QJ.
Tel (01473) 788982 Fax (01473) 788868
A modern state of the art marina with 350 berths offering all the services expected. Open 24-hours with full security. Access all states of tide, ideal cruising base. Well stocked chandlery and general store, repair

facilities, laundry and ironing centre, showers/baths and toilets. Restaurants, bar, children's room, TV/video and function rooms with dance floor and bar. Disabled facilities.

SOUTH DOCK MARINA
South Lock Office, Rope Street,
Plough Way, London SE16 1TX.
Tel 020 7252 2244 Fax 020 7237 3806
London's largest marina. 200+ berths. Spacious, tranquil setting. Manned 24 hours. Lift-out for 20 tonnes. Competitve mooring rates.

SOUTHDOWN MARINA
Southdown Quay, Millbrook,
Cornwall PL10 1HG.
Tel/Fax (01752) 823084
32-berth marina on edge of river Tamar in quiet location behind Rame Peninsula. Plymouth is just across the river. Quayside berths available for large vessels. Dry Berthing. 24-hour security. DIY facilities available.

SOUTHSEA MARINA
Fort Cumberland Road, Southsea,
Hampshire PO4 9RJ.
Tel 023 9282 2719 Fax 023 9282 2220
e-mail: southseamarina@ibm.net
Marina operators, yard services, chandlery, brokerage. Sea school. Bar and restaurant. Visitor berthing, dry boating, winter hardstanding, on-site contractors, glass fibre repairs, osmosis treatment, engineers, riggers, sail repairs, sail alterations and upholstery.
Website: www.southsea-marina.com

SPARKES YACHT HARBOUR LTD
38 Wittering Road, Hayling Island,
Hampshire PO11 9SR.
Tel 023 9246 3572 Fax 023 9246 5741
e-mail:
enquiries@sparkesmarina.freeserve.co.uk
Sparkes Marina - a small friendly, family run business offering all the facilities you require including access at all states of the tide to a depth of 2 metres at lowest low water springs. In addition to marina berths, accessible through a security gate, we also offer dry boat sailing, moorings, storage ashore plus full maintenance facilities, new boat sales and brokerage, chandlery and restaurant.

ST KATHARINE HAVEN
50 St Katharine's Way, London E1 9LB.
Tel 020 7264 5312 Fax 020 7702 2252
In the heart of London, St Katharine's 200-berth Haven offers facilities for 100'+ vessels, access to the West End and City, its own shops, restaurants, health club and yacht club, plus water, electric, showers and sewerage disposal. Entry via a lock. Operational HW - 2hrs to HW + 1½ hours London Bridge. October-March 0800-1800. April-August 0600-2030 or by arrangement.

SUFFOLK YACHT HARBOUR LTD
Levington, Ipswich, Suffolk IP10 0LN.
Tel (01473) 659240 Fax (01473) 659632
500-berths - access at all states of tide (dredged to 2.5 meters at LW Springs). Boat hoist facilities up to 60 tons. Full boatyard services, chandlery, gas, diesel, petrol, engineering, sailmaking, electronics. Club house and restaurant.

SUTTON HARBOUR MARINA
Sutton Harbour, Plymouth, Devon PL4 0RA.
Tel (01752) 204186 Fax (01752) 205403
A superb sheltered marina with 24-hour access and fully serviced visitor berths with full on-shore facilities in the city's historic Elizabethan quarter. Just a few minutes stroll from the shops, restaurants and entertainment of the city centre.

SWANSEA MARINA
Lockside, Maritime Quarter, Swansea, West Glamorgan SA1 1WG.
Tel (01792) 470310 Fax (01792) 463948
Access all states of the tide except LWST. City centre marina, restaurants, theatres etc. Call us on Ch 18 or 80 to check locking times. Visitors always welcome - a good destination for your annual trip.

TITCHMARSH MARINA
Coles Lane, Walton-on-the-Naze, Essex CO14 8SL.
Tel (01255) 672185 Fax (01255) 851901
Friendly service in the peaceful backwaters. Visiting yachtsmen welcome. Sheltered marina berths. Full marina facilities: Travel-lift, cranage, 16 amp electricity, diesel. Winter storage. Restaurant and bar open every day. (See Harbour Lights Restaurant.)

TOLLESBURY MARINA
The Yacht Harbour, Tollesbury, Maldon, Essex CM9 8SE.
Tel (01621) 869202 Fax (01621) 868489
e-mail: marina@woodrolfe.demon.uk
VHF Ch37 and 80
Dedicated to customer service, this family-run marina can offer 240 marina berths with water and electricity on all pontoons. Cruising club with bar, restaurant, swimming pool and tennis courts. Repair workshop, osmosis treatment centre. Full brokerage service listing over 200 boats.

TROON YACHT HAVEN
The Harbour, Troon, Ayrshire KA10 6DJ.
Tel (01292) 315553 Fax (01292) 312836
Sheltered harbour of 350 berths. Well placed for those on passage to and from the Clyde. Bar, restaurant, marine services. Attractive seafront town with good beaches and championship golf.

WATERFORD CITY MARINA - IRELAND
Waterford City, Ireland.
Tel +353 51 309900 Fax +353 51 870813
Located right in the heart of the historic city centre. There are 80 fully serviced berths available. The marina has full security, with CCTV in operation. Showers available on shore in adjoining hostel. Wide range of shops, restaurants, pubs and other amenities available on the doorstep of the marina because of its unique city-centre

location. Open all year with both winter and summer season rates available. *Sailing holidays in Ireland - Only the best.*

WEYMOUTH OLD HARBOUR
Weymouth & Portland Borough Council, Environmental Services Department, Council Offices, North Quay, Weymouth, Dorset DT4 8TA.
Tel (01305) 206423/206363
Fax (01305) 206422
e-mail: harbour@weymouth.co.uk
Access at all stages of tide. Visitor berths in centre of prime tourist resort with shops, restaurants and night life at hand. Diesel fuelling from pontoon or tanker. Chandlery and repair facilities available.
Website: www.weymouth.gov.uk/marine.htm

WHITEHAVEN HARBOUR MARINA
Harbour Commissioners, Pears House, 1 Duke Street, Whitehaven, Cumbria CA28 7HW.
Tel (01946) 692435 Fax (01946) 691135
VHF Ch12
Long and short-term berths available at newly created 100 capacity marina, maximum length 12m. Eleven hectare permanent locked harbour with 45 tonne boat hoist, access at least HW ± 3hours. Sheltered historic location adjacent to town centre.

MARINE ACCOUNTANTS

ERNST & YOUNG - THE TRIDENT FORUM
Wessex House, 19 Threefield Lane, Southampton, Hampshire SO14 3QB.
Tel 023 8038 2000 Fax 023 8038 382001
The Trident Forum aims to provide the maritime business community with first class professional services backed by substantial experience of working in the marine industry. Contact John Liddell

MARINE ACTIVITY CENTRES

BALTIC WHARF WATER LEISURE CENTRE
Bristol Harbour, Underfall Yard, Bristol BS1 6XG.
Tel 0117-929 7608 Fax 0117-929 4454
Tuition: 0117-952 5202
Sailing school and centre, with qualified instruction in most watersports. Also moorings available throughout the Bristol harbour for all types of leisurecraft.

TOLLESBURY MARINA
The Yacht Harbour, Tollesbury, Maldon, Essex CM9 8SE.
Tel (01621) 869202 Fax (01621) 868489
e-mail: marina@woodrolfe.demon.uk
VHF Ch37 and 80
Dedicated to customer service, this family-run marina can offer 240 marina berths with water and electricity on all pontoons. Cruising club with bar, restaurant, swimming pool and tennis courts. Repair workshop, osmosis treatment centre. Full brokerage service listing over 200 boats.

MARINE ARTISTS/ CARTOONISTS

THE CARTOON GALLERY
(Wavelength Design)
37 Lower Street, Dartmouth, Devon TQ6 9AN.
Tel/Fax (01803) 834466
Tel (01803) 834425 Evenings
Rick, the International cartoonist specialises in hand coloured and personalised sailing cartoon prints (eg A3 £10). Commissions are carried out in Rick's Dartmouth gallery and studio. Prints available by mail order. Telephone or fax for details.

MARINE CONSULTANTS & SURVEYORS

ANDREW JAGGERS - MARINE SURVEYOR & CONSULTANT
75 Clifton Road, Bangor, Co Down BT20 5HY.
Tel 028 9145 5677 Fax 028 9146 5252
At Bangor Marina: 028 9145 3297
Fax 028 9145 3450 Mobile: 0385 768474
Claims investigations for all major insurers. Code of Compliance examiner. Expert Witness reports. Flag State Inspections. Consultant to solicitors, brokers, loss adjusters on marine and marina matters. Ireland, Isle of Man and West of Scotland.

BOSE
7 Carse Road, Rowan Gate, Chichester, West Sussex PO19 4YG.
Tel/Fax (01243) 538300
Marine surveying and design specialition: ocean cruising, specialist fittings, project supervision.

COMPASS MARINE SURVEYS
22 Montague Road, Midhurst, West Sussex GU29 9BJ.
Tel/Fax (01730) 816268
e-mail: compassmarine@freeuk.com
25 years' experience in multihull, monohull sailing vessels and power craft. Condition, Insurance, full/partial, pre-purchase, project management, client/builder liaison. UK - Europe - Worldwide. Quotation/Brochure telephone +44 (0) 1730 816268.

DAVID M CANNELL & ASSOCIATES
River House, Quay Street, Wivenhoe, Essex CO7 9DD.
Tel +44 (0) 1206 823 337
Fax +44 (0) 1206 825 939
e-mail: post@dmcnavarch.demon.co.uk
Design of yachts and commercial craft to 80m. Newbuilding and refit overseeing. Condition surveys, valuations, MCA Code of Practice Compliance and Stability, Expert Witness. Members: Royal Institute of Naval Architects, Yacht Designers and Surveyors Association.

FOX ASSOCIATES
Cambria, Rhos y Coed, Bethesda, Bangor, Gwynedd LL57 3NW.
Tel/Fax (01248) 601079
Marine surveyors and consultants. Claims investigation and damage reports. Code of Practice examiners. Valuations and condition surveys.

FRANK VERRILL & PARTNERS
6 Old Bridge House Road, Bursledon,
Hampshire SO31 8AJ.
Tel 023 8040 2881 Fax 023 8040 4698
Mobile: 0880 321155
Consulting engineers, marine surveyors,
loss adjusters, insurance investigators, legal
Expert Witnesses.

GEORGE REOHORN YBDSA SURVEYOR
Chancery Cottage, Gors Road, Burry
Port, Carmarthenshire SA16 0EL.
Tel/Fax (01554) 833281
Full condition and insurance surveys on
pleasure and working vessels. Also Code of
Pratice examiner. Approved British
registration measurer. 36 years practical
experience on GRP, timber, steel and ferro
construction.

GRAHAM BOOTH MARINE SURVEYS
4 Epple, Birchington-on-Sea,
Kent CT7 9AY.
Tel (01843) 843793 Fax (01843) 846860
e-mail: gbms@clara.net
Authorised for MCA Codes of Practice, most
frequently on French and Italian Riviera -
also for certification of Sail Training vessels
and other commercial craft. Call UK office
for further information. Other expert marine
consultancy services also available.

J & J MARINE MANAGEMENT
PO Box 1696, Fordingbridge,
Hampshire SP6 2RR.
Tel (01425) 650201 Fax (01425) 657740
e-mail: jjmarine@dial.pipex.com
Marine surveyors and consultants. Pre-
purchase, insurance, valuation and damage
surveys. Supervision of refit, new
construction and design projects. MCA
compliance surveys, stability booklets and
yacht registration.

LIONSTAR YACHT & MOTORBOAT SURVEYS
The Lawn, Ashbrooke Road, Sunderland,
Tyne & Wear SR2 7HQ.
Tel 0191-528 6422
Lionstar Yacht Services, Sunderland -
Surveys of sailing and motor yachts by
chartered marine engineers and naval
architects with full PI and PL insurance.
Northern England and southern Scotland.
Telephone Derek May on 0191-528 6422
for quote.

MARINTEC
Silverton House, Kings Hyde,
Mount Pleasant Lane, Lymington,
Hampshire SO41 8LT.
Tel (01590) 683414 Fax (01590) 683719
MARINTEC was established at the beginning
of 1983 and undertake comprehensive
surveys, including mechanical and
electrical, both at home and overseas. Refit
management including the drawing up of
specifications and the tender document by
YDSA surveyor.

Please mention
The Pink Page Directory
when making your
enquiries

W A MacGREGOR & CO - MARINE SURVEYORS
Dooley Terminal Building, The Dock,
Felixstowe, Suffolk IP11 8SW.
Tel (01394) 676034 Fax (01394) 675515
Mobile: (0860) 361279
Yacht and small craft surveys for all
purposes and in all materials. Specialist in
wood and restoration of classic craft,
continually involved with steel, aluminium,
GRP. Charter and workboat codes YDSA
surveyor.

NORWOOD MARINE
65 Royal Esplanade, Margate,
Kent CT9 5ET.
Tel/Fax (01843) 835711
e-mail: ggreenfield1@compuserve.com
Marine consultant and advisers. Specialists
in collisions, groundings, pilotage. Yachting
and RYA examinations. Fellow of Nautical
Institute and RIN.

PETER HALLAM MARINE SURVEYOR
83 Millisle Road, Donaghadee,
Co Down, Northern Ireland BT21 0HZ.
Tel/Fax 028 9188 3484
Surveys for yachts, fishing and commercial
craft. Supervision of newbuildings, repairs
and specification writing for the same.
Insurance assessments/inspections and
completed repairs. Tonnage measurement.
Accident assessment/reports for solicitors.
MSA Code of Practice surveys.

RICHARD AYERS
- YACHT SURVEYOR & CONSULTANT
5A Church Street, Modbury,
Devon PL21 0QW.
Tel (01548) 830496 Fax (01548) 830917
e-mail: ayers_survey@hotmail.com
YDSA member - Yacht and powerboat
survey, MCA Code of Practice for small
commercial vessels. Survey for registration,
marine insurance and claim inspections.
Legal work. Plymouth - Salcombe -
Dartmouth - Fowey - Falmouth - Totnes all
local. No mileage charges.

RODNEY CLAPSON MARINE SURVEYS
16 Whitecross Street,
Barton-on-Humber DN18 5EU.
Tel (01652) 632108 & 635620
Fax (01652) 660517
e-mail: surveys@clapsons.co.uk
Surveys for purchase and insurance.
Damage repair and osmosis supervision.
East coast from the Wash to North-
umberland including inland water-ways.
Surveys in the Netherlands. We are YDSA
members.

MARINE ENGINEERS

CHALLENGER MARINE
Freeman's Wharf, Falmouth Road,
Penryn, Cornwall TR10 8AS.
Tel (01326) 377222 Fax (01326) 377800
Marine engineers, chandlery, boatyard.
Main Volvo Penta dealer, marina berths,
brokerage, Bombard and Zodiac inflatables'
dealer.

CHICK'S MARINE LTD/VOLVO PENTA
Collings Road, St Peter Port, Guernsey,
Channel Islands GY1 1FL.
Tel (01481) 723716 Fax (01481) 713632
Distributor of diesel fuel biocide used to
treat and protect contamination in fuel tanks
where an algae (bug) is present. Most owners do not realise what the problem is, loss
of power, blocked fuel filter, exhaust smoking, resulting in expensive repairs to injectors - fuel pump - or complete engine overhaul. Marine engineers, engines, spares,
service - VAT free. Honda outboards, pumps
and generators. Volvo Penta specialists.

CHISWICK QUAY MARINA LTD
Marina Office, Chiswick Quay,
London W4 3UR.
Tel 020 8994 8743
Small, secluded, peaceful marina on tidal
Thames at Chiswick. Slipway, marine engi-
neers and electricians, power, water, toilets
and sluice. Some residential moorings.

FOX'S MARINA IPSWICH LTD
The Strand, Wherstead, Ipswich,
Suffolk IP2 8SA.
Tel (01473) 689111 Fax (01473) 601737
The most comprehensive boatyard facility
on the east coast. Extensive chandlery.
Marina access 24-hours. Diesel dock, two
travel hoists to 70 tons, 10 ton crane. Full
electronics, rigging, engineering, stainless
steel services. Specialists in osmosis and
spray painting.

JEFFREY WOOD MARINE LTD
53a North Street, Romford,
Essex RM1 1BA.
Tel +44 (0) 1708 733454 Fax +44 (0) 1708
747431 Freephone 0800 0832530
e-mail: woodship@ukonline.com.u
Consultant forensic marine engineers, boat
designers and surveyors, naval architects.
Osmosis and ferro cement specialists -
wood or steel boats of all types.

NORWOOD MARINE
65 Royal Esplanade, Margate,
Kent CT9 5ET.
Tel/Fax (01843) 835711
e-mail: ggreenfield1@compuserve.com
Marine consultant and advisers. Specialists
in collisions, groundings, pilotage. Yachting
and RYA examinations. Fellow of Nautical
Institute and RIN.

POSFORD DUVIVIER
- THE TRIDENT FORUM
Eastchester House, Harlands Road,
Haywards Heath, Sussex RH16 1PG.
Tel (01444) 458551 Fax (01444) 440665
The Trident Forum aims to provide the
maritime business community with first
class professional services backed by sub-
stantial experience of working in the marine
industry. Contact Peter Roach.

R K MARINE LTD
Hamble River Boatyard, Bridge Road,
Swanwick, Southampton,
Hampshire SO31 7EB.
Tel (01489) 583572 Fax (01489) 583172
Volvo Penta main dealer with full boatyard
facilities.

RETREAT BOATYARD (TOPSHAM) LTD
Retreat Drive, Topsham, Exeter,
Devon EX3 OLS.
Tel (01392) 874720 & 875934
Fax (01392) 876182
Five minutes off M5 (Junction 30) the
traditional service yard. International centre
for Gelshield and Interspray. Agent for Volvo
Penta, Yamaha and Bukh. Dealer for Avon,
Autohelm, Seldén and Whitlock. Boat
repairs, rigging, mooring, storage,
comprehensive chandlery. Brokerage and
insurance department.

ROB PERRY MARINE
Monmouth Beach, Lyme Regis,
Dorset TQ7 3LE.
Tel (01297) 445816 Fax (01297) 445886
Outboard and inboard sales and service.
Wetsuits, lifejackets. Some chandlery. Fast
efficient service. Marine surveys and
insurance.

MARINE LAW

SHOOSMITHS - THE TRIDENT FORUM
Russell House, Solent Business Park,
Fareham, Hampshire PO15 7AG.
Tel (01489) 881010 Fax (01489) 616942
The Trident Forum aims to provide the
maritime business community with first
class professional services backed by
substantial experience of working in the
marine industry. Contact Heather Nichols.

MARINE PHOTOGRAPHERS/ LIBRARIES

PETER CUMBERLIDGE PHOTO LIBRARY
Sunways, Slapton, Kingsbridge,
Devon TQ7 2PR.
Tel (01548) 580461 Fax (01548) 580588
Large selection of nautical, travel and coastal
colour transparencies. Specialities boats,
harbours, lighthouses, marinas and inland
waterways in Britain, Northern Europe, the
Mediterranean and the Baltic. Commissions
undertaken.

MARINE PROPERTY

VAIL WILLIAMS - THE TRIDENT FORUM
Meridians House, 7 Ocean Way,
Ocean Village, Southampton,
Hampshire SO14 3TJ.
Tel 023 8063 1973 Fax 023 8063 223884
The Trident Forum aims to provide the
maritime business community with first
class professional services backed by
substantial experience of working in the
marine industry. Contact Simon Ward.

MASTS/SPARS & RIGGING

ATLANTIC SPARS (KEMP WEST) LTD
Hatton House, Bridge Road, Churston
Ferrers, Brixham, Devon TQ5 0JL.
Tel (01803) 843322 Fax (01803) 845550
e-mail: atlantic@spars.co.uk
Regional centre for SELDÉN and KEMP
integrated sailing systems. Services include

standing and running rigging, repairs, custom spars and furling systems. Aluminium
design and fabrications for industry. Official suppliers to the BT Global Challenge.
Website: www.spars.co.uk

CALIBRA MARINE INTERNATIONAL
26 Foss Street, Dartmouth,
Devon TQ6 9DR.
Tel (01803) 833094 Fax (01803) 833615
e-mail: calibra1@aol.com
A complete boating centre. Marine and
architectural rigging service. Sail makers,
repairs and valeting. All types of canvas
work. Boat brokerage, new and used. Yacht
management services. Agents for Nemo, Z-
Spar, Whitlock, Lewmar, Norseman and
many others.

CARBOSPARS LTD
Hamble Point, School Lane, Hamble,
Southampton, Hampshire SO31 4JD.
Tel 023 8045 6736 Fax 023 8045 5361
e-mail: carbospars@compuserve.com
Design and manufacture of carbon spars
for racing and cruising and the award-
winning AeroRig®.

HOLMAN RIGGING
Chichester Yacht Basin,
Chichester, West Sussex PO20 7EJ.
Tel/Fax (01243) 514000
Agent for major suppliers in this field we
offer a specialist mast and rigging service.
Purpose designed mast trailer for quick and
safe transportation. Installation for roller
headsail and mainsail reefing systems.
Insurance reports and quotations.

JOSEPH P LAMB & SONS
Maritime Building
(opposite Albert Dock),
Wapping, Liverpool L1 8DQ.
Tel 0151-709 4861 Fax 0151-709 2786
Situated in the centre of Liverpool, J P
Lamb have provided a service to world
shipping for over 200 years. All chandlery
supplies, clothing, rope, paint and flags are
available. Full sailmaking and repairs. Kemp
Retail Outlet for spars and rigging. Open
Mon to Fri 8am to 5.30pm - Sat 9am to
12.30pm.

MANX MARINE
35 North Quay, Douglas,
Isle of Man IM1 4LB.
Tel/Fax (01624) 674842
The Island's leading and most established
yacht chandlery. Stockists of quality foul-
weather clothing and thermal wear. Large
stock holdings of stainless steel fixtures
and fittings and a comprehensive range of
general chandlery including rigging
facilities.

SOUTHERN MASTS & RIGGING
(SELDÉN SOUTH EAST)
Marina Trade Centre, Brighton Marina,
Brighton, East Sussex BN2 5UG.
Tel (01273) 818189 Fax (01273) 818188
Mobile: 07803 086860
e-mail sales@smr-uk.com
Regional centre for SELDÉN and KEMP
integrated sailing systems. Builders of
masts and spars, standing and running
rigging. Rig surveyors. Suppliers of rope,

wire, mast and deck hardware, booms,
kickers and reefing systems. Mobile service
available.
Website: www.smr-uk.com

SOUTHERN SPAR SERVICES
(KEMP SOUTH)
Shamrock Quay, William Street,
Northam, Southampton,
Hampshire SO14 5QL.
Tel 023 8033 1714 Fax 023 8023 0559
Mobile: 0850 736540
Regional centre for SELDÉN and KEMP
integrated sailing systems. Convectional
and furling spars for UK and abroad. Also
headsail and mainsail reefing, deck
equipment, toe rails and stanchion bases.
All forms of repairs and modifications
undertaken.

MOISTURE METRES

TRAMEX LTD
Shankill Business Centre, Shankill,
Co Dublin, Ireland.
Tel+353 1 282 3688 Fax +353 1 282 7880
e-mail: tramex@iol.ie
Manufacturers of Moisture Metre and
osmosis detection instruments for boats.
Website: www.tramexltd.com

NAUTICAL TABLEWARE

NEWHALL CHINA COMPANY
Grange House, 102 Grindley Lane,
Meir Heath, Stoke on Trent,
Staffordshire ST3 7LP.
Tel (01782) 396220 Fax: (01782) 396230
Mobile: 0370 952 146
Suppliers of bone china tableware and
hotelware with nautical theme. Whether it
be your own boat name on beakers, plates,
cups/saucers or crested and personalised
ware for yacht clubs, large yachts, hotels
and restaurants.

NAVIGATION EQUIPMENT - GENERAL

DOLPHIN MARITIME SOFTWARE LTD
713 Cameron House, White Cross,
Lancaster LA1 4XQ.
Tel/Fax (01524) 841946
e-mail: 100417.744@compuserve.com
Marine computer programs for IBM PC,
Psion and Sharp pocket computers.
Specialists in navigation, tidal prediction
and other programs for both yachting and
commercial uses.
Website: www.ourworld.compuserve.com/
homepages/dolphin_software

EURONAV NAVIGATION
20 The Slipway, Port Solent, Portsmouth,
Hampshire PO6 4TR.
Tel 023 9237 3855 Fax 023 9232 5800
Electronic charting specialists, offering the
seaPro 2000 range of PC-based chart
plotting systems, ARCS, Livechart 'B' and
BSB top quality electronic charts. Products
are available from good chandlers or direct
from Euronav.
Website: www.euronav.co.uk

KELVIN HUGHES
Glasgow: 26 Holland Street,
Glasgow G2 4LR.
Tel 0141-221 5452 Fax 0141-221 4688
e-mail: glasgow@kelvinhughes.co.uk
The world's largest chart agency. The
world's finest nautical bookshops, plus
software, navigation instruments, for all
your chart table requirements.

KELVIN HUGHES
City of London: 142 Minories,
London EC3N 1NH.
Tel 020 7709 9076 Fax 020 7481 1298
e-mail: minories@kelvinhughes.co.uk.

KELVIN HUGHES
Southampton: Kilgraston House,
Southampton Street,
Southampton SO15 2ED.
Tel 023 8063 4911 Fax 023 8033 0014
e-mail:southampton@kelvinhughes.co.uk

NEPTUNE NAVIGATION SOFTWARE
P O Box 5106, Riseley,
Berkshire RG7 1FD.
Tel 0118-988 5309
Route Passage Planning, Tides and Tidal
Stream Predictions, Waypoint Manager -
software for your PC or CE machines. A
range of intuitively easy to use navigation
programs at affordable prices.
Website: www.neptunenav.demon.co.uk

RADIO & ELECTRONIC SERVICES LTD
Les Chênes, Rohais, St Peter Port,
Guernsey, Channel Islands GY1 1FB.
Tel (01481) 728837 Fax (01481) 714379
Chart Plotters, GPS, Radars. Fixed and
portable VHF, Autopilots. Programming
dealer for C-Map NT and Jotron EPIRBS.
Sales and service dealers for Furuno,
Humminbird, Icom, KVH, Lowrance,
Magellan, Raytheon, Sailor and Shipmate.

ROYAL INSTITUTE OF NAVIGATION
1 Kensington Gore, London SW7 2AT.
Tel 020 7591 3130 Fax 020 7591 3131
Forum for all interested in navigation - Air:
Sea: Land: Space.

SIMPSON-LAWRENCE
218 Edmiston Drive, Glasgow G51 2YT.
Tel 0141-300 9100 Fax 0141-427 5419
e-mail: info@simpson-lawrence.co.uk
LOWRANCE - Simpson-Lawrence distribute
the comprehensive range of LOWRANCE.
Fish Finders and GPS products. All units
feature superior displays and are packed
with user-friendly option. All backed by a
comprehensive warranty.
Website: www.simpson-lawrence.com

SIMRAD LTD
Woolmer Way, Bordon,
Hampshire GU35 9QE.
Tel (01420) 483200 Fax (01420) 489073
For full entry see under:
ELECTRONIC DEVICES & EQUIPMENT

STANFORDS CHARTS
Editorial Office, PO Box 2747,
Tollesbury, Maldon, Essex CM9 8XE.
Sales Office: 9-10 Southern Court,
South Street, Reading RG1 4QS.
Tel 01621 868580 Fax 0118-959 8283
For full entry see under:
BOOKS & CHARTS/PUBLISHERS

SWALE MARINE (ELECTRICAL)
The Old Stable, North Road,
Queenborough, Kent ME11 5EH.
Tel (01795) 580930 Fax (01795) 580238
For all your electrical and electronic needs.
Authorised agents for: Furuno, Autohelm,
Raytheon and most major manufacturers.
Fight crime with Harbourguard monitored
security: Medway and Swale coverage -
Boatmark registration centre.

NAVIGATION LIGHT SWITCHES & MONITORS

MECTRONICS MARINE
PO Box 8, Newton Abbot,
Devon TQ12 1FF.
Tel (01626) 334453
LIGHT ACTIVATED SWITCHES, rugged solid
state devices to automatically switch anchor
lights at sunset and sunrise. NAVLIGHT
SELECTORS, protected enclosed rotary
switches internally connected to ensure
approved navigation light combination on
auxiliary sailing vessels. NAVLIGHT STATUS
MONITORS, diagnostic displays on which
the appropriate indicator flashes quickly or
slowly in the event of a short or open circuit
fault. Also drives an optional, audible
warning device.

OUTBOARD MOTORS

HARBOUR MARINE LEISURE
Marrowbone Slip, Sutton Road,
Plymouth, Devon PL4 0HX.
Tel (01752) 204694 Parts Dept:(01752)
204696 Fax (01752) 204695
Plymouth marine engine and watersports
centre. Main dealers for Seadoo watercraft,
Mercury outboard, Fletcher sports boats,
combined with a comprehensive parts
service.

SIMPSON-LAWRENCE
218-228 Edmiston Drive,
Glasgow G51 2YT.
Tel 0141-300 9100 Fax 0141-427 5419
e-mail: info@simpson-lawrence.co.uk
JOHNSON - Simpson-Lawrence distributes
the comprehensive range of JOHNSON
outboards, which offers excellent quality
and superior durability - from the original
manufacturer of the outboard motor.
Website: www.simpson-lawrence.com

TORBAY BOATING CENTRE
South Quay, The Harbour, Paignton,
Devon TQ4 6TD.
Tel (01803) 558760 Fax (01803) 663230
For all your boating requirements from
Seadoo watercraft, inflatables, Fletcher
sports boats to Mercury outboard and
Yamaha sterndrive. A complete sales and
engineering workshop. Retail sales and
engineering.

PAINT & OSMOSIS

INTERNATIONAL COATINGS LTD
24-30 Canute Road, Southampton,
Hampshire SO14 3PB.
Tel 023 8022 6722 Fax 023 8033 5975
International Coatings Ltd is the leading
supplier of quality paints, epoxies, varnishes
and anti-foulings to the marine industry.
Over half the world's pleasure craft are
protected by International products.

JEFFREY WOOD MARINE LTD
53a North Street, Romford,
Essex RM1 1BA.
Tel +44 (0) 1708 733454 Fax +44 (0) 1708
747431 Freephone 0800 0832530
e-mail: woodship@ukonline.com.uk
Consultant forensic marine engineers, boat
designers and surveyors, naval architects.
Osmosis and ferro cement specialists -
wood or steel boats of all types.

NORTH QUAY MARINE
North Side, St Sampson's Harbour,
Guernsey, Channel Islands.
Tel (01481) 246561 Fax (01481) 243488
The complete boating centre. Full range of
chandlery, rope, chain, lubricants, paint,
boatwear and shoes. Fishing tackle for on-
shore and on-board. Inflatables and safety
equipment. Electronics and small outboard
engines.

ROSDEN GLASS FIBRE
La Rue Durell, La Collette, St Helier,
Jersey JE2 3NB.
Tel (01534) 625418 Fax (01534) 625419
Specialists in all types of glass fibre marine
works, structural repairs, alterations, re-
flow coating, GEL coat work. Blakes and
International approved osmosis treatment
centre. Spray painting. Manufacturers of
fuel tanks, bathing platforms and boat
builders. General refurbishment and
polishing. A division of Precision Plastics
(Jersey) Ltd.

SP EPOXY SYSTEMS
St Cross Business Park, Newport,
Isle of Wight PO30 5WU.
Tel (01983) 828000 Fax (01983) 828100
Epoxy resins for laminating, bonding,
coating and filling. Usable with wood, GRP,
concrete. GRP/FRP materials including
glass, carbon and Kevlar fibres. Structural
engineering of GRP and composite
materials. Technical advice service.

TRAMEX LTD
Shankill Business Centre, Shankill,
Co Dublin, Ireland.
Tel+353 1 282 3688 Fax +353 1 282 7880
e-mail: tramex@iol.ie
Manufacturers of Moisture Metre and
osmosis detection instruments for boats.
Website: www.tramexltd.com

VOLVO PENTA

PERSONALISED CHINA

NEWHALL CHINA COMPANY
Grange House, 102 Grindley Lane,
Meir Heath, Stoke on Trent,
Staffordshire ST3 7LP.
Tel (01782) 396220 Fax: (01782) 396230
Mobile: 0370 952 146
Suppliers of bone china tableware and
hotelware with nautical theme. Whether it
be your own boat name on beakers, plates,
cups/saucers or crested and personalised
ware for yacht clubs, large yachts, hotels
and restaurants.

PROPELLERS & STERNGEAR/REPAIRS

PROPROTECTOR LTD
74 Abingdon Road,
Maidstone,
Kent ME16 9EE.
Tel (01622) 728738 Fax (01622) 727973
e-mail: prop_protector@compuserve.com
Prevention is better than cure when it comes
to fouled propellers. ProProtectors are now
welcome and used worldwide as the most
economical and simplest way to combat
stray rope, netting, weed and plastic bags.
Fit one before it is too late.
Website: www.prop-protector.co.uk

SILLETTE SONIC LTD
Unit 5 Stepnell Reach,
541 Blandford Road, Hamworthy,
Poole, Dorset BH16 5BW.
Tel (01202) 621631 Fax (01202) 625877
Mobile: 077 10270107
Distribution Depot: Sillette manufactures a
range of propulsion systems - stern drive,
saildrives etc and sterngear. Markets Radice
and Gori fixed and folding propellers. Acts
as agents for Morse Controls, Yanmar and
Lombardini marine engines, and Fuji Robin
generators. See Area 3.

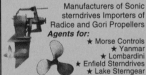

SILLETTE - SONIC LTD
182 CHURCH HILL ROAD
NORTH CHEAM SUTTON SURREY SM3 8NF
TEL: 020-8715 0100 FAX: 020-8288 0742
MOBILE: 077 10270107
Manufacturers of Sonic
sterndrives Importers of
Radice and Gori Propellers
Agents for:
★ Morse Controls
★ Yanmar
★ Lombardini
★ Enfield Sterndrives
★ Lake Sterngear
Manufacturing depot based at Poole.

SILLETTE SONIC LTD
182 Church Hill Road, North Cheam,
Sutton, Surrey SM3 8NF.
Tel 020 8715 0100 Fax 020 8288 0742
Mobile: 077 10270107
Sillette manufactures a range of propulsion
systems - stern drive, saildrives etc and
sterngear. Markets Radice & Gori fixed and
folding propellers. Acts as agents for Morse
Controls, Yanmar and Lombardini marine
engines, and Fuji Robin generators. See
distribution depot Poole, Dorset - Area 2.

STREAMLINED PROPELLER REPAIRS

Unit 17 Cavendish Mews,
off Grosvenor Road,
Aldershot, Hampshire GU11 3EH.
Tel (01252) 316412
Established in 1978 specialising in all types
of propeller repairs up to 6' diameter. Recommended by all leading outboard concessionaires. Largest stock of propeller
bushes and parts in the UK.

QUAY SERVICES

CHISWICK QUAY MARINA LTD
Marina Office, Chiswick Quay,
London W4 3UR.
Tel 020 8994 8743
Small, secluded, peaceful marina on tidal
Thames at Chiswick. Slipway, marine
engineers and electricians, power, water,
toilets and sluice. Some residential
moorings.

RACING KEELBOAT SPECIALISTS

HAINES BOATYARD
Itchenor, Chichester,
West Sussex PO20 7AN.
Tel (01243) 512228 Fax (01243) 513900
Racing keelboat specialists. Boat building
and repairs with top quality joinery in teak
and other hardwoods. Controlled fibreglass
and epoxy work facilities. Moorings and
winter boat and dinghy storage, masts spars
and rigging service.

RADIO COURSES/SCHOOLS

HOYLAKE SAILING SCHOOL
43a Market Street, Hoylake,
Wirral L47 2BG.
Tel 0151-632 4664 Fax 0151-632 4776
e-mail: purser@hss.ac.uk
RYA recognised shorebased teaching
establishment offering a wide range of
courses including Day Skipper to
Yachtmaster Ocean, VHF, Radar and First
Aid. Day, evening or intensive classes.
Pratical courses by arrangement. Books,
charts and gifts available by mail order.
Website: www.hss.ac.uk

Visit our website
www.nauticaldata.com

RECRUITMENT

LEGAL SUPPORT SERVICES
Virides, Victoria Road, Bishops
Waltham, Hampshire SO32 1DJ.
Tel/Fax (01489) 890961
Mobile: 0966 389367
Support services for marine companies for
legal and quasi-legal activities, eg liaison
with local authorities and government
departments, and discrete research
projects. Also **Marine Job-Spot** low cost
recruitment services for the UK marine
industry.

REEFING SYSTEMS

HOLMAN RIGGING
Chichester Yacht Basin, Chichester,
West Sussex PO20 7EJ.
Tel/Fax (01243) 514000
Agent for major suppliers in this field we
offer a specialist mast and rigging service.
Purpose designed mast trailer for quick and
safe transportation. Installation for roller
headsail and mainsail reefing systems.
Insurance reports and quotations.

REFITS & FITTING OUT

A S A P SUPPLIES - DIRECT ORDER
Beccles, Suffolk NR34 7TD.
Tel (01502) 716993 Fax (01502) 711680
e-mail: infomma@asap-supplies.com
Worldwide supply of equipment and spares.
Anodes, cables, contrads, coolers, exhausts,
fenders, fuel systems, gear boxes, impellers,
insulation, lights, marinisation, panels,
propellers and shafts, pumps, seacocks,
silencers, sound proofing, steering, toilets,
trimtabs, water heaters, wipers and much
much more....
Website: www.asap-supplies.com

REPAIR MATERIALS & ACCESSORIES

C C MARINE SERVICES LTD
PO Box 155, Chichester,
West Sussex PO20 8TS.
Tel +44 (0) 1243 672606
Fax +44 (0) 1243 673703
Innovators of marine tape technology.
Included in the range *Rubbaweld*, the
original self-amalgamating marine tape and
a complete range of specialised products
for every yachtsman's needs. Available from
all good chandlers.

ROSDEN GLASS FIBRE
La Rue Durell, La Collette,
St Helier, Jersey JE2 3NB.
Tel (01534) 625418 Fax (01534) 625419
Specialists in all types of glass fibre marine
works, structural repairs, alterations, re-
flow coating, GEL coat work. Blakes and
International approved osmosis treatment
centre. Spray painting. Manufacturers of
fuel tanks, bathing platforms and boat
builders. General refurbishment and
polishing. A division of Precision Plastics
(Jersey) Ltd.

SP EPOXY SYSTEMS
St Cross Business Park, Newport,
Isle of Wight PO30 5WU.
Tel (01983) 828000 Fax (01983) 828100
Epoxy resins for laminating, bonding,
coating and filling. Usable with wood, GRP,
concrete. GRP/FRP materials including
glass, carbon and Kevlar fibres. Structural
engineering of GRP and composite
materials. Technical advice service.

ROPE & WIRE SUPPLIES

**SOUTHERN MASTS & RIGGING
(SELDÉN SOUTH EAST)**
Marina Trade Centre, Brighton Marina,
Brighton, East Sussex BN2 5UG.
Tel (01273) 818189 Fax (01273) 818188
Mobile: 07803 086860
e-mail: sales@smr-uk.com
Regional centre for SELDÉN and KEMP
integrated sailing systems. Builders of
masts and spars, standing and running
rigging. Rig surveyors. Suppliers of rope,
wire, mast and deck hardware, booms,
kickers and reefing systems. Mobile service
available.
Website: www.smr-uk.com

SAFETY EQUIPMENT

A B MARINE LTD
Castle Walk, St Peter Port, Guernsey,
Channel Islands GY1 1AU.
Tel (01481) 722378 Fax (01481) 711080
We specialise in safety and survival
equipment and are a DoT approved service
station for liferafts including R.F.D.,
Beaufort/Dunlop, Zodiac, Avon, Plastimo
and Lifeguard. We also carry a full range of
new liferafts, dinghies and lifejackets, and
are agents for Bukh marine engines.

ADEC MARINE LTD
4 Masons Avenue, Croydon,
Surrey CR0 9XS.
Tel 020 8686 9717 Fax 020 8680 9912
e-mail: adecmarine@lineone.net
Approved liferaft service station for south
east UK. Additionally we hire and sell new
rafts and sell a complete range of safety
equipment for yachts including pyrotechnics, fire extinguishers, lifejackets,
buoys and a buoyancy bag system.

CREWSAVER LTD
Crewsaver House, Mumby Road,
Gosport, Hampshire PO12 1AQ.
Tel 023 9252 8621
MARLIN - Leading manufacturer of stylish,
comfortable, hardwearing wetsuits, lifejack-
ets, buoyancy aids and accessories for all
seasons and all-surface watersports. YAK -
Catering for all canoeing needs from cags
and decks to long johns and buoyancy aids.

FIREMASTER EXTINGUISHER LTD
Firex House, 174/176 Hither Green Lane,
London SE13 6QB.
Tel 020 8852 8585 Fax 020 8297 8020
e-mail: sales@firemaster.co.uk
Third party accredited fire extinguishers
manufactured to meet both RYA and Boat
Safety Scheme requirements. Also auto-

matic detection and extinguishing systems.
Website: www.firemaster.co.uk

OCEAN SAFETY
Centurian Industrial Park,
Bitterne Road West, Southampton,
Hampshire SO18 1UB.
Tel 023 8033 3334 Fax 023 8033 3360
e-mail: enquiries@oceansafety.com
Your Life Saving Supplier: Liferafts,
lifejackets, MOB, flares, fire fighting,
medical, EPIRBS. In addition to our
extensive product range we also boast two
of the largest liferaft, lifejacket and inflatable
service stations in Europe with the
introduction of our facility in Palma de
Mallorca, Spain. A product advice service is
available for customers who need to comply
with ORC or Code of Practice Charter
regulations.

PREMIUM LIFERAFT SERVICES
Liferaft House,
Burnham Business
Park, Burnham-on-Crouch,
Essex CM0 8TE.
Tel (01621) 784858 Fax (01621) 785934
Freephone 0800 243673
e-mail:liferaftuk@aol.com
Hire and sales of DoT and RORC approved
liferafts. Long and short-term hire from 18
depots nationwide. Servicing and other
safety equipment available.

SHAMROCK CHANDLERY
Shamrock Quay, William Street,
Northam, Southampton,
Hampshire SO14 5QL.
Tel 023 8063 2725 Fax 023 8022 5611
e-mail: sales@shamrock.co.uk
Situated on Shamrock Quay, a busy working
yard with a pub, restaurant and boutiques.
Shamrock Chandlery is renowned for
extensive quality stocks and service, and is
widely used by both the trade and boat
owners. Excellent mail order facilities - Order
Hotline 023 8022 5746.
Website: www.shamrock.co.uk

**SOUTH EASTERN
MARINE SERVICES LTD**
Units 13 & 25, Olympic Business Centre,
Paycocke Road, Basildon,
Essex SS14 3EX.
Tel (01268) 534427 Fax (01268) 281009
e-mail: sems@bt.internet.com
Liferaft service, sales and hire, 1-65 persons.
Approved by major manufacturers and MSA.
Callers welcome. View your own raft. Family
owned and operated. Inflatable boat repairs
and spares. WE WANT YOU TO COME BACK.
Website: www.sems.com

WINTERS MARINE LTD
(Lincombe Boatyard)
Lincombe, Salcombe,
Devon TQ8 8NQ.
Tel (01548) 843580
e-mail: lincombeboatyard@eclipse.co.uk
Deep water pontoon moorings. Winter
storage for 150 boats. All maintenance and
repair facilities. Slipway capacity 30 tonnes.
Inflatable raft sales and service. Liferaft
surveys and repairs. Short and long-term
liferaft hire.

X M YACHTING LTD
The Mill, Berwick, Polegate,
East Sussex BN26 8SL.
Tel (01323) 870092 Fax (01323) 870909
For the 21st Century. Extensive range of
marine quality equipment including
clothing, footwear, inflatables, safety
equipment, liferafts and the XM Quickfit
range of lifejackets manufactured to CE
standard, and the TH-5 offshore breathable
suit. Performance technology - designed to
be worn. Please call 01323 870092 for
further details and catalogue or visit your
local stockist.

SAILMAKERS & REPAIRS

CALIBRA MARINE INTERNATIONAL
26 Foss Street, Dartmouth,
Devon TQ6 9DR.
Tel (01803) 833094 Fax (01803) 833615
e-mail: calibra1@aol.com
A complete boating centre. Marine and
architectural rigging service. Sail makers,
repairs and valeting. All types of canvas
work. Boat brokerage, new and used. Yacht
management services. Agents for Nemo, Z-
Spar, Whitlock, Lewmar, Norseman and
many others.

KEMP SAILS LTD
The Sail Loft,
2 Sandford Lane Industrial Estate,
Wareham, Dorset BH20 4DY.
Tel (01929) 554308 & 554378
Fax (01929) 554350
e-mail: kempltd@globalnet.co.uk
Sailmakers: New sails and repairs. Hardware
and reefing systems. Sprayhoods, sail
covers and canvas products.
Website: www.scoot.co.uk/kemp_sails

PARKER & KAY SAILMAKERS - EAST
Suffolk Yacht Harbour, Levington,
Ipswich, Suffolk IP10 0LN.
Tel (01473) 659878 Fax (01473) 659197
e-mail: pandkeast@aol.com
A complete sailmaking service, from small
repairs to the construction of custom
designed sails for racing or cruising yachts.
Covers constructed for sail and powercraft,
plus the supply of all forms of sail handling
hardware.

PARKER & KAY SAILMAKERS - SOUTH
Hamble Point Marina, School Lane,
Hamble, Southampton,
Hampshire SO31 4JD.
Tel 023 8045 8213 Fax 023 8045 8228
e-mail: pandksouth@aol.com
A complete sailmaking service, from small
repairs to the construction of custom
designed sails for racing or cruising yachts.
Covers constructed for sail and powercraft,
plus the supply of all forms of sail handling
hardware.

UK/McWILLIAM SAILMAKERS
Crosshaven, Co Cork, Ireland.
Tel +353 21 831505 Fax +353 21 831700
e-mail: ukireland@uksailmakers.com
Ireland's premier sailmaker, prompt repairs
and service.

SEA DELIVERIES

GLOBAL MARITIME TRAINING
Hoo Marina, Vicarage Lane, Hoo,
Kent ME3 9TW.
Tel (01634) 256288 Fax (01634) 256284
e-mail: info@seaschool.co.uk
RYA theory courses by correspondence.
Start your course anywhere in the world at
any time. Also practical courses from our
north Kent base. Worldwide yacht deliveries
with free RYA tutition for owners 'en-route'.
Website: www.seaschool.co.uk

MAX WALKER YACHT DELIVERIES
Zinderneuf Sailing, PO Box 105,
Macclesfield, Cheshire SK10 2EY.
Tel (01625) 431712 Fax (01625) 619704
e-mail: mwyd.@clara.net
Fixed price deliveries. Sailing yachts
delivered with care in north west European,
UK and Eire waters by RYA/DoT yachtmaster
and crew - 30 years' experience. Owners
welcome. Tuition if required. References
available. Your enquiries welcome 24 hours.

PETERS & MAY LTD
18 Canute Road, Ocean Village,
Southampton, Hampshire SO14 3FJ.
Tel 023 8048 0480 Fax 023 8048 0400
The 'Round the World' specialists in
shipping, transporting, cradling yachts and
powerboats. Weekly service to USA, Far
East, Mediterranean, Middle East and
Caribbean.

RELIANCE YACHT MANAGEMENT LTD
International Maritime Services
Tel +44 (0) 1252 378239
Fax +44 (0) 1252 521736
e-mail: info@reliance-yachts.com
With over 10 years' experience we offer a
professional management and delivery
service. Your yacht can be safely and
expertly delivered anywhere in the world by
highly experienced skippers and crews. We
are also able to offer 'Total solution
Management Packages' designed to suit
your needs. Offices in the Caribbean, Pacific,
Asia and France.
Website: www.reliance-yachts.com

SEALAND BOAT DELIVERIES LTD
Tower, Liverpool Marina,
Coburg Wharf, Liverpool L3 4BP.
Tel (01254) 705225 Fax (01254) 776582
e-mail: ros@mcr1.poptel.org.uk
Nationwide and European road transporters
of all craft. No weight limit. We never close.
Irish service. Worldwide shipping agents.
Extrication of yachts from workshops and
building yards. Salvage contractors.
Established 27 years.
Website: www.btx.co.uk

TREVOR VINCETT DELIVERIES
Coombe Cottage, 9 Swannaton Road,
Dartmouth, Devon TQ6 9RL.
Tel/Fax (01803) 833757
Mobile: 07970 208799
Worldwide delivery of yachts and
commercial vessels undertaken at short
notice by RYA/DoT Yachtmaster Ocean (with
commercial endorsement). Over 28 years'
experience including three masted
schooners, tugs, motor yachts and hi-tec

racers. For instant quotes call/fax 01803
833757.

SKIPPERED CHARTERS/ CRUISING

DINGLE SEA VENTURES
YACHT CHARTER
Dingle, Co Kerry, Ireland.
Tel +353 66 52244 Fax +353 66 52313
e-mail: jgreany@iol.ie
Bareboat charter, skippered charter, sailing
tuition on south west coast of Ireland: One
way charter Dingle-Kinsale-Dingle - 1997
and 1998 fleet of eight boats 31' - 44'. Close
to all ferries and airports. Personal, friendly
service. PINTS OF PEACE.

ISLANDER YACHT CHARTERS
& ISLANDER SAILING SCHOOL
7 Torinturk, Argyll PA29 6YE.
Tel (01880) 820012 Fax (01880) 821143
e-mail: r.fleck@virgin.net
Sail the spectacular and uncrowded waters
of the Scottish west coast and Hebrides
from our base at Ardfern Yacht Centre,
Argyll. Bareboat or skippered yachts from
33' to 44', all DoT certificated. RYA recognised sailing school, YM, CS, DS and CC
courses from March to October.

PLYMOUTH SAILING SCHOOL
Queen Anne's Battery Marina,
Plymouth, Devon PL4 0LP.
Tel (01752) 667170 Fax (01752) 257162
e-mail: school@plymsail.demon.co.uk
Established in the 1950s the school offers
year-round training (sail and power). RYA
and MCA approved courses and private
tuition ashore and afloat. A friendly reception
and honest advice will always be found
here.
Website: www.plymsail.demon.co.uk

SEALINE SEA SCHOOL & CHARTER
Hamble River Boatyard, Bridge Road,
Swanwick, Southampton,
Hampshire SO31 7EB.
Tel (01489) 579898 Fax (01489) 582123
Mobile: 0370 613788
Sealine Sea School & Charter - Training to
RYA standards in the superb location of the
Solent, or take your guests out for an unfor-
gettable day cruising Solent ports. Family/
friends and corporate events all catered for.

SLIPWAYS

RIVERSFORD HOTEL
Limers Lane, Bideford, Devon EX39 2RG.
Tel (01237) 474239
Peace and tranquility in gardens beside the
river Torridge. A relaxing retreat with
convenient slipway close by. Excellent
restaurant with efficient, friendly service
with a choice of imaginative food and wine
from our extensive menu and wine list.
Comfortable, flexible lounge bar.

ST MAWES SAILING CLUB
No 1 The Quay, St Mawes,
Cornwall TR2 5DG.
Tel (01326) 270686 Fax (01326) 270040
Quayside sailing club in centre of village.
Visitor moorings in harbour. Private slip,
launching and recovery facilities. Dinghy
park, post box, showers. Visitors encour-
aged. Chandlery and sail repairs to order.
No marina but a warm welcome awaits.

WEIR QUAY BOATYARD
Heron's Reach, Bere Alston,
Devon PL20 7BT.
Tel (01822) 840474 Fax (01822) 840948
Deepwater swinging moorings, shore
storage, full boatyard facilities and services,
cranage to 12 tons, repairs, maintenance,
slipway. A traditional boatyard at affordable
rates *in a superb setting* on the Tamar, with
excellent security.

WINTERS MARINE LTD
(Lincombe Boatyard)
Lincombe, Salcombe, Devon TQ8 8NQ.
Tel (01548) 843580
e-mail: lincombeboatyard@eclipse.co.uk
Deep water pontoon moorings. Winter storage for 150 boats. All maintenance and
repair facilities. Slipway capacity 30 tonnes.
Inflatable raft sales and service. Liferaft
surveys and repairs. Short and long-term
liferaft hire.

SOLAR POWER

MARLEC ENGINEERING CO LTD
Rutland House, Trevithick Road, Corby,
Northamptonshire NN17 5XY.
Tel (01536) 201588 Fax (01536) 400211
For wind and solar powered battery charging
on board talk to Marlec. We manufacture
the Rutland Marine range of wind wind-
chargers, and import and distribute Solarex
photovoltaic modules. Manufacturer of
Leisurelights - IOW energy high efficiency
12v lamps.

SPEED LOGS

THOMAS WALKER GROUP LTD
37-41 Bissell Street,
Birmingham B5 7HR.
Tel 0121-622 4475 Fax 0121-622 4478
Manufacturer of marine instruments
including, Neco Autopilots, Walker Logs
and Towing Logs, Walker Anemometers,
Chernikeeff Logs.

SPRAYHOODS & DODGERS

MARTELLO YACHT SERVICES
Mulberry House, Mulberry Road,
Canvey Island, Essex SS8 0PR.
Tel/Fax (01268) 681970
Manufacturers and suppliers of made-to-
measure upholstery, covers, hoods,
dodgers, sailcovers, curtains and cushions
etc. Repairs undertaken. DIY materials,
chandlery and fitting-out supplies.

SEAFILE ELECTRONIC - Don't go to sea without it!

STAINLESS STEEL FITTINGS

MANX MARINE
35 North Quay, Douglas,
Isle of Man IM1 4LB.
Tel/Fax (01624) 674842
The Island's leading and most established yacht chandlery. Stockists of quality foul-weather clothing and thermal wear. Large stock holdings of stainless steel fixtures and fittings and a comprehensive range of general chandlery including rigging facilities.

SURVEYORS & NAVAL ARCHITECTS

ANDREW JAGGERS - MARINE SURVEYOR & CONSULTANT
75 Clifton Road, Bangor,
Co Down BT20 5HY.
Tel 028 9145 5677 Fax 028 9146 5252
At Bangor Marina: 028 9145 3297
Fax 028 9145 3450 Mobile: 0385 768474
Claims investigations for all major insurers. Code of Compliance examiner. Expert Witness reports. Flag State Inspections. Consultant to solicitors, brokers, loss adjusters on marine and marina matters. Ireland, Isle of Man and West of Scotland.

ANDREW POTTER MA AMYDSA - YACHT SURVEYOR
Penrallt Cottage, Cichle Hill,
Llandegfan, Anglesey LL59 5TD.
Tel/Fax (01248) 712358
Mobile: 0374 411681
Prompt and professional surveys prior to purchase and for insurance purposes throughout Wales, the north west and Midlands. Services also include valuations, osmosis inspections and consultancy. Surveyor for MCA Code of Practice.

BOSE
7 Carse Road, Rowan Gate, Chichester,
West Sussex PO19 4YG.
Tel/Fax (01243) 538300
Marine surveying and design specialition: ocean cruising, specialist fittings, project supervision.

COMPASS MARINE SURVEYS
22 Montague Road, Midhurst,
West Sussex GU29 9BJ.
Tel/Fax (01730) 816268
e-mail: compassmarine@freeuk.com
25 years' experience in multihull, monohull sailing vessels and power craft. Condition, insurance, full/partial, pre-purchase, project management, client/builder liaison. UK - Europe - Worldwide. Quotation/Brochure telephone +44 (0) 1730 816268.

DAVID M CANNELL & ASSOCIATES
River House, Quay Street,
Wivenhoe, Essex CO7 9DD.
Tel +44 (0) 1206 823 337
Fax +44 (0) 1206 825 939
e-mail: post@dmcnavarch.demon.co.uk
Design of yachts and commercial craft to 80m. Newbuilding and refit overseeing. Condition surveys, valuations, MCA Code of Practice Compliance and Stability, Expert

JEFFREY WOOD MARINE LIMITED
Tel: +44(0) 1708 733454
Fax: +44(0) 1708 747431
Mobile: 0385 335110
Freephone: 0800 0832530
53A North Street, Romford, Essex RM1 1BA
e-mail: woodship@ukonline.co.uk
Full condition, damage or other surveys of all types of boats in GRP, wood, steel or ferro by fully qualified marine surveyors with over fifty years of experience.
Members of: American Boat and Yacht Council CORGI registered.
Approved surveyors to the Marine Safety Agency, the Metropolitan Police, British Waterways, The Environment Agency and the Admiralty Marshal
Eur.Ing. Jeffrey Casciani-Wood
Chartered Engineer, Fellow RINA, Member ASNAME, Member AE.
Fellow of the Society of Consulting Marine Engineers and Ship Surveyors.
President of the International Institute of Marine Surveyors.

Witness. Members: Royal Institute of Naval Architects, Yacht Designers and Surveyors Association.

FOX ASSOCIATES
Cambria, Rhos y Coed, Bethesda,
Bangor, Gywnedd LL57 3NW.
Tel/Fax (01248) 601079
Marine surveyors and consultants. Claims investigation and damage reports. Code of Practice examiners. Valuations and condition surveys.

FRANK VERRILL & PARTNERS
45 years' experience in yachting and commercial shipping
Consulting Engineers • Marine Surveyors • Loss Adjusters • Insurance Investigators • Legal Expert Witness
6 Old Bridge House Road,
Bursledon, Southampton,
Hampshire SO31 8AJ.
Tel: 023 8040 2881 Fax: 023 8040 4698
Mobile: 0880 321155

FRANK VERRILL & PARTNERS
6 Old Bridge House Road, Bursledon,
Hampshire SO31 8AJ.
Tel 023 8040 2881 Fax 023 8040 4698
Mobile: 0880 321155
Consulting engineers, marine surveyors, loss adjusters, insurance investigators, legal Expert Witnesses.

GEORGE REOHORN YBDSA SURVEYOR
Chancery Cottage, Gors Road,
Burry Port, Carmarthenshire SA16 0EL.
Tel/Fax (01554) 833281
Full condition and insurance surveys on pleasure and working vessels. Also Code of Pratice examiner. Approved British registration measurer. 36 years practical experience on GRP, timber, steel and ferro construction.

GRAHAM BOOTH MARINE SURVEYS
4 Epple, Birchington-on-Sea,
Kent CT7 9AY.
Tel (01843) 843793 Fax (01843) 846860
e-mail: gbms@clara.net
Authorised for MCA Codes of Practice, most frequently on French and Italian Riviera - also for certification of Sail Training Vessels and other commercial craft. Call UK office for further information. Other expert marine consultancy services also available.

J & J MARINE MANAGEMENT
PO Box 1696, Fordingbridge,
Hampshire SP6 2RR.
Tel (01425) 650201 Fax (01425) 657740
e-mail: jjmarine@dial.pipex.com
Marine surveyors and consultants. Pre-purchase, insurance, valuation and damage surveys. Supervision of refit, new construction and design projects. MCA compliance surveys, stability booklets and yacht registration.

JEFFREY WOOD MARINE LTD
53a North Street, Romford,
Essex RM1 1BA.
Tel +44 (0) 1708 733454 Fax +44 (0) 1708 747431 Freephone 0800 0832530
e-mail: woodship@ukonline.co.u
Consultant forensic marine engineers, boat designers and surveyors, naval architects. Osmosis and ferro cement specialists - wood or steel boats of all types.

LIONSTAR YACHT & MOTORBOAT SURVEYS
The Lawn, Ashbrooke Road, Sunderland,
Tyne & Wear SR2 7HQ.
Tel 0191-528 6422
Lionstar Yacht Services, Sunderland - Surveys of sailing and motor yachts by chartered marine engineers and naval architects with full PI and PL insurance. North of England and southern Scotland. Telephone Derek May for quote.

LIVERPOOL & GLASGOW SALVAGE ASSOCIATION
St Andrews House, 385 Hillington Road,
Glasgow G52 4BL.
Tel 0141-303 4573 Fax 0141-303 4513
e-mail: lgsaglasgow@compuserve.com
Marine surveyors and consultants. Pre-purchase, damage, insurance (risk and liabilities) surveys on all vessels including yachts, fishing vessels and commercial ships. Offices also at Liverpool, Hull, Leicester and Grangemouth. Overseas work also undertaken.

MARINTEC
Silverton House, Kings Hyde,
Mount Pleasant Lane, Lymington,
Hampshire SO41 8LT.
Tel (01590) 683414 Fax (01590) 683719
MARINTEC was established at the beginning of 1983 and undertake comprehensive surveys, including mechanical and electrical, both at home and overseas. Refit management including the drawing up of specifications and the tender document by YDSA surveyor.

30

PETER HALLAM MARINE SURVEYOR
83 Millisle Road, Donaghadee, Co Down,
Northern Ireland BT21 0HZ.
Tel/Fax 028 9188 3484
Surveys for yachts, fishing and commercial
craft. Supervision of newbuildings, repairs
and specification writing for the same.
Insurance assessments/inspections and
completed repairs. Tonnage measurement.
Accident assessment/reports for solicitors.
MSA Code of Practice surveys.

RICHARD AYERS
- YACHT SURVEYOR & CONSULTANT
5A Church Street, Modbury,
Devon PL21 0QW.
Tel (01548) 830496 Fax (01548) 830917
e-mail: ayers_survey@hotmail.com
YDSA member - Yacht and powerboat
survey, MCA Code of Practice for small
commercial vessels. Survey for registration,
marine insurance and claim inspections.
Legal work. Plymouth - Salcombe -
Dartmouth - Fowey - Falmouth - Totnes all
local. No mileage charges.

ROB PERRY MARINE
Monmouth Beach, Lyme Regis,
Dorset DT7 3LE.
Tel (01297) 445816 Fax (01297) 445886
Outboard and inboard sales and service.
Wetsuits, lifejackets. Some chandlery. Fast
efficient service. Marine surveys and
insurance.

RODNEY CLAPSON MARINE SURVEYS
16 Whitecross Street,
Barton-on-Humber DN18 5EU.
Tel (01652) 632108 & 635620
Fax (01652) 660517
e-mail: surveys@clapsons.co.uk
Surveys for purchase and insurance.
Damage repair and osmosis supervision.
East coast from the Wash to Northumberland including inland waterways.
Surveys in the Netherlands. We are YDSA
members.

E K WALLACE & SON LTD
Whittinghame House,
1099 Great Western Road,
Glasgow G12 0AA.
Tel 0141-334 7222 Fax 0141-334 7700
Pre-purchase, insurance and valuation
surveys on sail and power vessels, private
and commercial, UK and abroad. Approved
for Code of Practice, registration and
tonnage meaurements. Members YDSA,
SCMS. Offices in Glasgow, Edinburgh and
Argyll.

WARD & McKENZIE (Balearics)
C/Gral Antonio Barcelo No 2 Esc A lo 2a,
E-07015, Palma de Mallorca, Spain.
Tel/Fax +34 971 701148
e-mail: yacht_surveyor@compuserve.com
National and International marine surveyors.
Technical and legal consultants. Contact:
Peter Green - Mobile: +34 61 992 6053.
Website: www.ward-mckenzie.co.uk

WARD & McKENZIE (Dorset) LTD
69 Alexander Road, Parkstone, Poole,
Dorset BH14 9EL.
Tel (01202) 718440
National and International marine surveyors.
Technical and legal consultants. Contact:
Tony McGrail - Mobile: 0411 329314.
Website: www.ward-mckenzie.co.uk

WARD & McKENZIE (Holland)
West End, Veendijk 22k, 1231 PD
Loosdrecht, Holland.
Tel +31 35 5827195 Fax +31 35 5828811
e-mail: technoserv@wxs.nl
National and International marine surveyors.
Technical and Legal Consultants.
Website: www.ward-mckenzie.co.uk

WARD & McKENZIE (North East) LTD
11 Sherbuttgate Drive, Pocklington,
York YO4 2ED.
Tel (01759) 304322 Fax (01759) 303194
e-mail: nev.styles@dial.pipex.com
National and International marine surveyors. Technical and legal consultants. Contact: Neville Styles - Mobile: 0831 335943.
Website: www.ward-mckenzie.co.uk

WARD & McKENZIE (North West) LTD
2 Healey Court, Burnley,
Lancashire BB11 2QJ.
Tel/Fax (01282) 420102
e-mail: marinesurvey@wmnw.freeserve.co.uk
National and International marine surveyors. Technical and legal consultants. Contact: Bob Sheffield - Mobile: 0370 667457.
Website: www.ward-mckenzie.co.uk

WARD & McKENZIE (South Wales) LTD
58 The Meadows, Marshfield,
Cardiff CF3 8AY.
Tel (01633) 680280
National and International marine surveyors. Technical and legal consultants. Contact: Kevin Ashworth - Mobile: 07775 938666.
Website: www.ward-mckenzie.co.uk

WARD & McKENZIE (South West) LTD
Little Brook Cottage, East Portlemouth,
Salcombe, Devon TQ8 8PW.
Tel (01803) 833500 Fax (01803) 833350
National and International marine surveyors. Technical and legal consultants. Contact: Chris Olsen - Mobile: 07971 250105.
Website: www.ward-mckenzie.co.uk

WARD & McKENZIE LTD
3 Wherry Lane, Ipswich, Suffolk IP4 1LG.
Tel (01473) 255200 Fax (01473) 255044
e-mail: collett@wardmck.keme.co.uk
National and International marine surveyors.
Technical and legal consultants - offering a
comprehensive service to boat owners and
those seeking to acquire pleasure yachts.

All aspects of title/lien check, registration.
Survey, purchase and ownership
undertaken, including insurance surveys,
finance and disputes. Contact:
Clive Brown - Mobile: 0585 190357
Mike Williamson - Mobile: 0498 578312
and Ian Collett - Mobile: 0370 655306.
River Ouse Office: 01462 701461.
Website: www.ward-mckenzie.co.uk
See regional offices in Area Directory.

TANKS

TEK-TANKS
Units 5A - 5B Station Approach,
Four Marks, Nr Alton,
Hampshire GU34 5HN.
Tel (01420) 564359 Fax (01420) 561605
e-mail: enquiries@tek-tanks.com
Manufacturers and suppliers of made-to-measure and standard polypropylene water,
waste and HDPE diesel tanks.
Website: www.tek-tanks.com

TAPE TECHNOLOGY

C C MARINE SERVICES LTD
PO Box 155, Chichester,
West Sussex PO20 8TS.
Tel +44 (0) 1243 672606
Fax +44 (0) 1243 673703
Innovators of marine tape technology.
Included in the range *Rubbaweld*, the
original self-amalgamating marine tape and
a complete range of specialised products
for every yachtsman's needs. Available from
all good chandlers.

TRANSPORT/ YACHT DELIVERIES

CONVOI EXCEPTIONNEL LTD
Castleton House, High Street, Hamble,
Southampton, Hampshire SO31 4HA.
Tel 023 8045 3045 Fax 023 8045 4551
e-mail: info@convoi.co.uk
International marine haulage and abnormal
load consultants. European abnormal load
permits obtained and escort car service.
Capacity for loads up to 100 tons.

EXONIA EUROPEAN MARINE
TRANSPORT
The Sidings, Heathfield,
Newton Abbot, Devon TQ12 6RG.
Tel (01626) 836688 Fax (01626) 836831
Europe's premier overland marine transport
company, 25 years' experience, expertise
cross border formalities, documentation,

notifications, escorts, permits and schedules. Highly experienced well briefed drivers with a fully qualified back-up team. *Indubitably the best.*

MAX WALKER YACHT DELIVERIES
Zinderneuf Sailing, PO Box 105,
Macclesfield, Cheshire SK10 2EY.
Tel (01625) 431712 Fax (01625) 619704
e-mail: mwyd.@clara.net
Fixed price deliveries. Sailing yachts delivered with care in north west European, UK and Eire waters by RYA/DoT yachtmaster and crew - 30 years' experience. Owners welcome. Tuition if required. References available. Your enquiries welcome 24 hours.

MOONFLEET SAILING
4 Arun Path, Uckfield,
East Sussex TN22 1NL.
Tel/Fax (01825) 760604
Moonfleet Sailing offers all RYA recognised practical and theory courses from Competent Crew to Yachtmaster Offshore, VHF Radio, First Aid and Diesel Engine. Also available own boat tuition and yacht delivery.

PETERS & MAY LTD
18 Canute Road, Ocean Village,
Southampton, Hampshire SO14 3FJ.
Tel 023 8048 0480 Fax 023 8048 0400
The 'Round the World' specialists in shipping, transporting, cradling yachts and powerboats. Weekly service to USA, Far East, Mediterranean, Middle East and Caribbean.

SEALAND BOAT DELIVERIES LTD
Tower, Liverpool Marina,
Coburg Wharf, Liverpool L3 4BP.
Tel (01254) 705225 Fax (01254) 776582
e-mail: ros@mcr1.poptel.org.uk
Nationwide and European road transporters of all craft. No weight limit. We never close. Irish service. Worldwide shipping agents. Extrication of yachts from workshops and building yards. Salvage contractors. Established 27 years.
Website: www.btx.co.uk

TREVOR VINCETT DELIVERIES
Coombe Cottage, 9 Swannaton Road,
Dartmouth, Devon TQ6 9RL.
Tel/Fax (01803) 833757
Mobile: 07970 208799
Worldwide delivery of yachts and commercial vessels undertaken at short notice by RYA/DoT Yachtmaster Ocean (with commercial endorsement). Over 28 years' experience including three masted schooners, tugs, motor yachts and hi-tec racers. For instant quotes call/fax 01803 833757.

if you can't find what you're looking for here, visit our website.
www.nauticaldata.com

TUITION/SAILING SCHOOLS

DINGLE SEA VENTURES YACHT CHARTER
Dingle, Co Kerry, Ireland.
Tel +353 66 52244 Fax +353 66 52313
e-mail: jgreany@iol.ie
Bareboat charter, skippered charter, sailing tuition on south west coast of Ireland: One way charter Dingle-Kinsale-Dingle - 1997 and 1998 fleet of eight boats 31' - 44'. Close to all ferries and airports. Personal, friendly service. PINTS OF PEACE.

FOWEY CRUISING SCHOOL & SERVICES
Fore Street, Fowey, Cornwall PL23 1AQ.
Tel (01726) 832129 Fax (01726) 832000
e-mail: fcs@dial.pipex.com
The best cruising in Britain, with matue instructors. Practical shore-based RYA courses. Family cruising a speciality. Yachtmster/Coastal exams. Diesel, First Aid, VHF etc. Our quarter century experience shows. *ALSO Marine and travel insurance with top companies.*

GLOBAL MARITIME TRAINING
Hoo Marina, Vicarage Lane,
Hoo, Kent ME3 9TW.
Tel (01634) 256288 Fax (01634) 256284
e-mail: info@seaschool.co.uk
RYA theory courses by correspondence. Start your course anywhere in the world at any time. Also practical courses from our north Kent base. Worldwide yacht deliveries with free RYA tutition for owners 'en-route'.
Website: www.seaschool.co.uk

HOYLAKE SAILING SCHOOL
43a Market Street, Hoylake,
Wirral L47 2BG.
Tel 0151-632 4664 Fax 0151-632 4776
e-mail: purser@hss.ac.uk
RYA recognised shorebased teaching establishment offering a wide range of courses including Day Skipper to Yachtmaster Ocean, VHF, Radar and First Aid. Day, evening or intensive classes. Pratical courses by arrangement. Books, charts and gifts available by mail order.
Website: www.hss.ac.uk

ISLANDER YACHT CHARTERS & ISLANDER SAILING SCHOOL
7 Torinturk, Argyll PA29 6YE.
Tel (01880) 820012 Fax (01880) 821143
e-mail: r.fleck@virgin.net
Sail the spectacular and uncrowded waters of the Scottish west coast and Hebrides from our base at Ardfern Yacht Centre, Argyll. Bareboat or skippered yachts from 33' to 44', all DoT certificated. RYA recognised sailing school, YM, CS, DS and CC courses from March to October.

MOONFLEET SAILING
4 Arun Path, Uckfield, Sussex TN22 1NL.
Tel/Fax (01825) 760604
Moonfleet Sailing offers all RYA recognised practical and theory courses from Competent Crew to Yachtmaster Offshore, VHF Radio, First Aid and Diesel Engine. Also available own boat tuition and yacht delivery.

PLYMOUTH SAILING SCHOOL
Queen Anne's Battery Marina,
Plymouth, Devon PL4 0LP.
Tel (01752) 667170 Fax (01752) 257162
e-mail: school@plymsail.demon.co.uk
Established in the 1950s the school offers year-round training (sail and power). RYA and MCA approved courses and private tuition ashore and afloat. A friendly reception and honest advice will always be found here.
Website: www.plymsail.demon.co.uk

Motor cruising courses, beginner to yachtmaster, school boat or own boat. Powerboat level I & II I.C.C. for cruising abroad
Have fun learning with
SEALINE SEA SCHOOL
RYA recognised teaching establishment
Quay House, Hamble River Boatyard, Swanwick, Southampton SO31 7EB
Tel: 01489 885115
Fax: 01489 582123
Mobile: 0370 613788

SEALINE SEA SCHOOL & CHARTER
Hamble River Boatyard, Bridge Road,
Swanwick, Southampton,
Hampshire SO31 7EB.
Tel (01489) 579898 Fax (01489) 582123
Mobile: 0370 613788
Sealine Sea School & Charter - Training to RYA standards in the superb location of the Solent, or take your guests out for an unforgettable day cruising Solent ports. Family/friends and corporate events all catered for.

UPHOLSTERY & COVERS

MARTELLO YACHT SERVICES
Mulberry House, Mulberry Road,
Canvey Island, Essex SS8 0PR.
Tel/Fax (01268) 681970
Manufacturers and suppliers of made-to-measure upholstery, covers, hoods, dodgers, sailcovers, curtains and cushions etc. Repairs undertaken. DIY materials, chandlery and fitting-out supplies.

TOOMER & HAYTER LTD
74 Green Road, Winton,
Bournemouth, Dorset BH9 1EB.
Tel (01202) 515789 Fax (01202) 538771
Marine upholstery manufacturers. Cabin and cockpit upholstery made to any shape or size. Sprung interior mattresses made to measure. Foam backed cabin lining always in stock, also carpet side lining. Visit our factory and showroom.

WEATHER INFORMATION

MARINECALL - TELEPHONE INFORMATION SERVICES
Avalon House, London EC2A 4PJ.
Tel 020 7631 6000
Marinecall provides detailed coastal weather forecasts for 17 different regions up to 5 days ahead from the Met Office. For a full fax list of services dial 0891 24 66 80. Telephone forecasts are updated daily, morning and afternoon.

WIND POWER

ARIES VANE GEAR SPARES
8 St Thomas Street, Penryn,
Cornwall TR10 6JW.
Tel (01326) 377467 Fax (01326) 378117
e-mail: ariespares@compuserve.com
Spare parts, re-build kit for all existing
Aries gears.

MARLEC ENGINEERING CO LTD
Rutland House, Trevithick Road, Corby,
Northamptonshire NN17 5XY.
Tel (01536) 201588 Fax (01536) 400211
For wind and solar powered battery charging
on board talk to Marlec. We manufacture
the Rutland Marine range of wind wind-
chargers, and import and distribute Solarex
photovoltaic modules. Manufacturer of
Leisurelights - IOW energy high efficiency
12v lamps.

WOOD FITTINGS

SHERATON MARINE CABINET
White Oak Green, Hailey, Witney,
Oxfordshire OX8 5XP.
Tel/Fax (01993) 868275
Manufacturers of quality teak and mahogany
marine fittings, louvre doors, gratings and
tables. Special fitting-out items to customer
specification. Colour catalogue available on
request.

WORLWIDE SPARES & EQUIPMENT DELIVERY

A S A P SUPPLIES - DIRECT ORDER
Beccles, Suffolk NR34 7TD.
Tel (01502) 716993 Fax (01502) 711680
e-mail: infomma@asap-supplies.com
Worldwide supply of equipment and spares.
Anodes, cables, contrads, coolers, exhausts,
fenders, fuel systems, gear boxes, impellers,
insulation, lights, marinisation, panels,
propellers and shafts, pumps, seacocks,
silencers, sound proofing, steering, toilets,
trimtabs, water heaters, wipers and much
much more....
Website: www.asap-supplies.com

YACHT BROKERS

ARDFERN YACHT CENTRE
Ardfern By Lochgilphead,
Argyll PA31 8QN.
Tel (01852) 500247/636
Fax (01852) 500624 and 07000 ARDFERN
Boatyard with full repair and maintenance
facilities. Timber and GRP repairs, painting
and engineering. Sheltered moorings and
pontoon berthing. Winter storage,
chandlery, showers, fuel, Calor, brokerage,
20-ton boat hoist, rigging. Hotel, bars and
restaurant.

CALIBRA MARINE INTERNATIONAL
26 Foss Street, Dartmouth,
Devon TQ6 9DR.
Tel (01803) 833094 Fax (01803) 833615
e-mail: calibra1@aol.com
A complete boating centre. Marine and
architectural rigging service. Sail makers,
repairs and valeting. All types of canvas
work. Boat brokerage, new and used. Yacht
management services. Agents for Nemo, Z-
Spar, Whitlock, Lewmar, Norseman and
many others.

CRAOBH MARINA
By Lochgilphead, Argyll PA31 8UD.
Tel (01852) 500222 Fax (01852) 500252
VHF Ch37 and 80 (M).
250-berth marina on Loch Shuna. Water,
electricity, diesel and gas. Full boatyard
services. Chandlery. Brokerage. Insurance.
Shops, bar. 24-hour access.

DEACONS BOATYARD LTD
Bursledon Bridge, Southampton,
Hampshire SO31 8AZ.
Tel 023 8040 2253 Fax 023 8040 5665
This yard has all major services for
yachtsmen. Moorings, hardstanding,
repairs, marine engineers, riggers, chand-
lery and brokerage - new yacht sales.
Deacons are UK importers for Feeling
yachts.

RETREAT BOATYARD (TOPSHAM) LTD
Retreat Drive, Topsham, Exeter,
Devon EX3 0LS.
Tel (01392) 874720 & 875934
Fax (01392) 876182
Five minutes off M5 (Junction 30) the
traditional service yard. International centre
for Gelshield and Interspray. Agent for Volvo
Penta, Yamaha and Bukh. Dealer for Avon,
Autohelm, Seldén and Whitlock. Boat
repairs, rigging, mooring, storage,
comprehensive chandlery. Brokerage and
insurance department.

YACHT CHARTERS & HOLIDAYS

DINGLE SEA VENTURES
YACHT CHARTER
Dingle, Co Kerry, Ireland.
Tel +353 66 52244 Fax +353 66 52313
e-mail: jgreany@iol.ie
Bareboat charter, skippered charter, sailing
tuition on south west coast of Ireland: One
way charter Dingle-Kinsale-Dingle - 1997
and 1998 fleet of eight boats 31' - 44'. Close
to all ferries and airports. Personal, friendly
service. PINTS OF PEACE.

FOWEY CRUISING SCHOOL & SERVICES
Fore Street, Fowey, Cornwall PL23 1AQ.
Tel (01726) 832129 Fax (01726) 832000
e-mail: fcs@dial.pipex.com
The best cruising in Britain, with matue
instructors. Practical shore-based RYA
courses. Family cruising a speciality.
Yachtmster/Coastal exams. Diesel, First Aid,
VHF etc. Our quarter century experience
shows. *ALSO Marine and travel insurance
with top companies.*

GREEK SAILS YACHT CHARTER
21 The Mount, Kippax, Leeds LS25 7NG.
Tel/Fax 0113-232 0926
Freephone 0800 731 8580
e-mail: greek_sails_uk@msn.com
Bareboat yacht charter throughout Greece
and the islands. Flottila based in Corfu and
the Ionian Islands. Family dinghy sailing
holidays in Corfu. Skippered charter and
sail training.

ISLANDER YACHT CHARTERS
& ISLANDER SAILING SCHOOL
7 Torinturk, Argyll PA29 6YE.
Tel (01880) 820012 Fax (01880) 821143
e-mail: r.fleck@virgin.net
Sail the spectacular and uncrowded waters
of the Scottish west coast and Hebrides
from our base at Ardfern Yacht Centre,
Argyll. Bareboat or skippered yachts from
33' to 44', all DoT certificated. RYA
recognised sailing school, YM, CS, DS and
CC courses from March to October.

LOCH NESS CHARTERS
The Boatyard, Dochgarroch,
Inverness IV3 6JY.
Tel (01463) 861303 Fax (01463) 861353
Yacht and cruiser charter. Boat services
and repairs. Hardstanding and slipway.
Diesel supply. Boat finishing.

ODYSSEUS YACHTING HOLIDAYS
33 Grand Parade, Brighton,
East Sussex BN2 2QA.
Tel (01273) 695094 Fax (01273) 688855
Templecraft Yacht Charters are bonded tour
operators specialising in independent yacht
charter holidays in the Mediterranean and
in the Caribbean, and as Odysseus Yachting
Holidays in flotilla sailing holidays in Corfu
and the Ionian islands.

RELIANCE YACHT MANAGEMENT LTD
International Maritime Services
Tel +44 (0) 1252 378239
Fax +44 (0) 1252 521736
e-mail: info@reliance-yachts.com
With over 10 years' experience we offer a professional management and delivery service. Your yacht can be safely and expertly delivered anywhere in the world by highly experienced skippers and crews. We are also able to offer 'Total solution Management Packages' designed to suit your needs. Offices in the Caribbean, Pacific, Asia and France.
Website: www.reliance-yachts.com

SEA VENTURES YACHT CHARTER
Lymington Yacht Haven, Lymington, Hampshire SO41 3QD.
Tel (01590) 672472 Fax (01590) 671924
Based in Lymington and Plymouth, our large modern fleet offers both skippered and bareboat charters. A large selection of yachts from 29' to 52' and most less than 3 years old. Corporate and team building and yacht management also available.
Website: www.sea-ventures.co.uk

SLEAT MARINE SERVICES
Ardvasar, Isle of Skye IV45 8RS.
Tel (01471) 844216 Fax (01471) 844387
e-mail: enquiries
@sleatmarineservices.co.uk
Yacht charter (bareboat and skippered) from Armadale Bay, Isle of Skye. Six yachts 34' to 40' LOA. All medium to heavy displacement blue water cruisers. Fuel, water and emergency services for passing yachts with problems.
Website: www.sleatmarineservices.co.uk

TEMPLECRAFT YACHT CHARTERS
33 Grand Parade, Brighton,
East Sussex BN2 2QA.
Tel (01273) 695094 Fax (01273) 688855
Templecraft Yacht Charters are bonded tour operators specialising in independent yacht charter holidays in the Mediterranean and in the Caribbean, and as Odysseus Yachting Holidays in flotilla sailing holidays in Corfu and the Ionian islands.

YACHT CLUB FACILITIES

KINSALE YACHT CLUB MARINA
Kinsale, Co Cork, Ireland.
Tel +353 21 772196 Fax +353 21 774455
e-mail: kyc@iol.ie
Magnificent deep water yacht club marina offering Kinsale hospitality to visiting yachtsmen. Full facilities include berths up to 20 metres, fresh water, electricity, diesel on pier. Club bar and wealth of pubs and restaurants in Kinsale. Enter Kinsale Harbour - lit at night - no restrictions.

PARKSTONE YACHT CLUB
Pearce Avenue, Parkstone, Poole,
Dorset BH14 8EH.
Tel (01202) 743610 Fax (01202) 716394
e-mail: office@parkstoneyc.co.uk
Deep water club haven facilities in Poole

harbour. Access at all states of the tide. Berths for yachts up to 15 metres. Facilities include electricity, fresh water, toilets and showers. Visitors welcome by appointment. Club bar and restaurant.

ROYAL WESTERN YACHT CLUB
Queen Anne's Battery, Plymouth,
Devon PL4 0TW.
Tel (01752) 660077 Fax (01752) 224299
e-mail: admin@rwyc.org
Home of shorthanded sailing. Visiting yachtsmen welcome. Mooring facilities available.

ST MAWES SAILING CLUB
No 1 The Quay, St Mawes,
Cornwall TR2 5DG.
Tel (01326) 270686 Fax (01326) 270040
Quayside sailing club in centre of village. Visitor moorings in harbour. Private slip, launching and recovery facilities. Dinghy park, post box, showers. Visitors encouraged. Chandlery and sail repairs to order. No marina but a warm welcome awaits.

YACHT DESIGNERS

BOSE
7 Carse Road, Rowan Gate,
Chichester, West Sussex PO19 4YG.
Tel/Fax (01243) 538300
Marine surveying and design specialition: ocean cruising, specialist fittings, project supervision.

DAVID M CANNELL & ASSOCIATES
River House, Quay Street,
Wivenhoe, Essex CO7 9DD.
Tel +44 (0) 1206 823 337
Fax +44 (0) 1206 825 939
e-mail: post@dmcnavarch.demon.co.uk
Design of yachts and commercial craft to 80m. Newbuilding and refit overseeing. Condition surveys, valuations, MCA Code of Practice Compliance and Stability, Expert Witness. Members: Royal Institute of Naval Architects, Yacht Designers and Surveyors Association.

YACHT MANAGEMENT

BACHMANN MARINE SERVICES LTD
Frances House, Sir William Place,
St Peter Port, Guernsey,
Channel Islands GY1 4HQ.
Tel (01481) 723573 Fax (01481) 711353
British yacht registration, corporate yacht ownership and management, marine insurance, crew placement and management. Bachmann Marine Services aims to provide a personal and individual service to its clients.

LOCH NESS CHARTERS
The Boatyard, Dochgarroch,
Inverness IV3 6JY.
Tel (01463) 861303 Fax (01463) 861353
Yacht and cruiser charter. Boat services and repairs. Hardstanding and slipway. Diesel supply. Boat finishing.

PAUL JOHNSON LTD
Marine Vessel Management
Unit 6, 24 Station Square,
Inverness IV1 1LD.
Tel 07074 370 470 Fax 07074 370 570
e-mail: info@pauljohnson.co.uk
We manage all aspects of the day to day and long-term running of your vessel. Giving store support to you or your captain. Leaving you the pleasure of owning a boat. Independent insurance and finance brokerage, crews, registration and maintain but NO HEADACHES!
Website: www.pauljohnson.co.uk

RELIANCE YACHT MANAGEMENT LTD
International Maritime Services
Tel +44 (0) 1252 378239
Fax +44 (0) 1252 521736
e-mail: info@reliance-yachts.com
With over 10 years' experience we offer a professional management and delivery service. Your yacht can be safely and expertly delivered anywhere in the world by highly experienced skippers and crews. We are also able to offer 'Total solution Management Packages' designed to suit your needs. Offices in the Caribbean, Pacific, Asia and France.
Website: www.reliance-yachts.com

SEA VENTURES YACHT CHARTER
Lymington Yacht Haven, Lymington, Hampshire SO41 3QD.
Tel (01590) 672472 Fax (01590) 671924
Based in Lymington and Plymouth, our large modern fleet offers both skippered and bareboat charters. A large selection of yachts from 29' to 52' and most less than 3 years old. Corporate and team building and yacht management also available.
Website: www.sea-ventures.co.uk

YACHT REGISTRATION

BACHMANN MARINE SERVICES LTD
Frances House, Sir William Place,
St Peter Port, Guernsey,
Channel Islands GY1 4HQ.
Tel (01481) 723573 Fax (01481) 711353
British yacht registration, corporate yacht ownership and management, marine insurance, crew placement and management. Bachmann Marine Services aims to provide a personal and individual service to its clients.

Waterside Accommodation & Restaurants

Sometimes after a long haul, or at the end of an arduous day carrying out necessary maintenance on you boat, or indeed as part of your holiday you may wish to enjoy the luxury of haute cuisine or simply a good meal cooked by somebody else, followed maybe, by a comfortable bed for the night. The following list guides you to hotels, restaurants and accommodation with their own private berths or mooring close by.

THE GUNFIELD HOTEL & RESTAURANT
Castle Road, Dartmouth, Devon TQ6 0JN.
Tel (01803) 834843 Fax (01803) 834772
e-mail: enquiry@gunfield.co.uk   VHF ChM2 or Ch37
Waterfront position with 10 impressive en suite bedrooms, central heating etc, all command fantastic river views. Restaurant offers modestly priced, delicious Mediterranean cuisine. Continental bar and lounge open to non-residents. Large terraces and gardens, BBQs during summer. Pontoon and deep water moorings.
Website: www.gunfield.co.uk

AREA 1

THE PANDORA INN
Restronguet Creek, Mylor Bridge, Falmouth, Cornwall TR11 5ST.
TelFax (01326) 372678
Thatched creek-side inn with floating pontoon. Morning coffee, delicious bar meals, cream teas and fine dining in the superb Andrew Miller restaurant (entitles yachtsmen to free mooring). Telephone, showers and water available. Open all day in the summer.

RIVERSFORD HOTEL
Limers Lane, Bideford, Devon EX39 2RG.
Tel (01237) 474239
Peace and tranquility in gardens beside the river Torridge. A relaxing retreat with convenient slipway close by. Excellent restaurant with efficient, friendly service with a choice of imaginative food and wine from our extensive menu and wine list. Comfortable, flexible lounge bar.

LYMINGTON YACHT HAVEN
King's Saltern Road, Lymington, Hampshire SO41 3QD.
Tel (01590) 677071 Fax (01590) 678186
Perfectly situated at the mouth of the Lymington river giving instant access to the Western Solent. Full marina services, boatyard, brokerage, diesel, petrol, gas, restaurant and bar.

AREA 2

THE MILLPOND
1 Main Road, Emsworth, West Sussex PO10 8AP.
Tel (01243) 372089
Cosy bed and breakfast pub. Six letting rooms en suite with TV and tea/coffee-making facilities. Boules, terrine/garden overlooking the Millpond. Snacks and light food available Thursdays and Saturdays. Goodwood - Chichester - Portsmouth approximately 20 minutes away.

JARVIS MARINA HOTEL - RAMSGATE
Harbour Parade, Ramsgate, Kent CT11 8LZ.
Tel (01843) 588276 Fax (01843) 586866
Situated on the edge of Ramsgate's Marina, the ideal accommodation venue for the travelling yachtsman. Club bar open all day serving drinks and snacks. Hobson's restaurant offers an extensive menu. Leisure club open to non-residents.

AREA 3

THE HARBOUR LIGHTS RESTAURANT
Titchmarsh marina, Coles Lane, Walton-on-the-Naze, Essex CO14 8SL.
Tel (01255) 851887 Fax (01255) 677300
Open 7 days a week the Harbour Lights offers a welcome to yachtsmen and land-lubbers alike. Fine views over the marina and Walton Backwaters. Hearty breakfasts are served 8am - 10am, and extensive bar meals are available all day. Sizzling summer weekend barbecues, weather permitting. Silver service restaurant with traditional English fare.

AREA 4

HULL MARINA LTD
Warehouse 13, Kingston Street, Hull HU1 2DQ.
Tel (01482) 613451 Fax (01482) 224148
Four-Anchor marina. Situated 5 minutes from the centre of Hull and all national and international transport systems. First class leisure, boatyard and brokerage facilities. 4-Star hotel and quayside restaurants. Professional and caring staff. Competitive rates.

AREA 5

BRIDGE HOUSE HOTEL
St Clair Road, Ardrishaig, Argyll PA30 8EW.
Tel (01546) 606379 Fax (01546) 606593

AREA 8

4-Crown Highly Commended. Close to the Crinan canal sea lock with views down to Loch Fyne to Arran and Gower. We offer a warm welcome to all visitors. Comfortable en suit bedrooms, good food and friendly bar. Open all year.

THE CREGGANS INN
Strachur, Argyll PA27 8BX.
Tel (01369) 860279 Fax (01369) 860637 e-mail: info@creggans-inn.co.uk
The Creggans Inn makes a useful stop for lunch, dinner or overnight respite! Five moorings available. Bar meals from 12 noon - 2.30pm and 6pm to 9pm (Saturday and Sunday 12 noon - 8pm). Excellent restaurant serving from 7pm to 9.30pm. Shower and changing facilities for our travelling yachtsmen.

THE GALLEY OF LORNE INN
Ardfern, By Lochgilphead, Argyll PA31 8QN.
Tel (01852) 500284
A warm welcome for yachtsmen and women at The Galley. Only two minutes from Ardfern yacht centre. Excellent food. Bar meals available all year. Restaurant open Easter to November. Friendly pub with log fires.

KAMES HOTEL
Kames, By Tighnabruaich, Argyll PA21 2AF.
Tel (01700) 811489 Fax (01700) 811283
On the Kyles of Bute, with 15 free moorings. Good food, real ales, fine malts. Showers available for visitors. 10 en-suite bedrooms. Regular music nights. Fresh local seafood in season.

TIGH AN EILEAN HOTEL
Shieldaig by Strathcaron, Ross-shire IV54 8XN.
Tel (01520) 755251 Fax (01520) 755321
On the edge of the sea amongst some of the most dramatic landscapes in the Highlands, this friendly 12-bedroom hotel is run under the personal supervision of the proprietors. Our restaurant serves local produce cooked with flair and complemented with good wine. Excellent drying room for those wet clothes!!

THE TOBERMORAY HOTEL - STB 3-Star
53 Main Street, Tobermoray, Isle of Mull, Argyll PA75 6NT.
Tel (01688) 302091 Fax (01688) 302254
Situated on the beautiful Tobermoray Bay on the lovely Isle of Mull the Tobermoray Hotel offers a traditional Scottish welcome to all visiting yachtsmen. Come and eat at our excellent restaurant serving delicious fish and steak with good wines and spirits.

THE OYSTERCATCHER RESTAURANT
Otter Ferry, Argyll PA21 2DH.
Tel (01700) 821229 Fax (01700) 821300

AREA 9

Situated on Loch Fyne, just north of the Otter Spit, about one hour's sailing from the Crinan canal. Moorings (insured to 12t) free to patrons. French chef and superb food, seafood our speciality. 1996 Tourist Board winner 'BEST PLACE TO EAT'. Children's play area.

THE HAVEN ARMS PUB & RESTAURANT
Henry Street, Kilrush, Co Clare, Ireland.
Tel +353 65 51267 Fax +353 65 51213

AREA 12

'The Haven Arms' - Kilrush - *Sail* into this pub and restaurant which has become a landmark to generations of local people and visitor alike. The 'Ship' restaurant offers appetising meals complemented by good service from our friendly staff. **MOORINGS ARE FREE.**

KING SITRIC FISH RESTAURANT & ACCOMMODATION
East Pier, Howth, Co Dublin, Ireland.
Tel +353 1 832 5235 & 6729 Fax +353 1 839 2442
Lovely location on the harbour front. Marina and Howth Yacht Club 3 minutes walk. Established 1971, Aidan and Joan MacManus have earned an international reputation for superb, fresh seafood, service and hospitality. Wine connoisseurs take note! Quality accommodation now available. Informal summer lunch -dinner all year.

MARITIME TOURISM LTD - CASTLEPARK MARINA
Kinsale, Co Cork, Ireland.
Tel +353 21 774959 Fax +353 21 774958
100-berth fully serviced marina with restaurant, laundry, showers and toilets. Waterside hotel-type accommodation available. New restaurant catering for both breakfast and evening meals. Access at all stages of the tide.

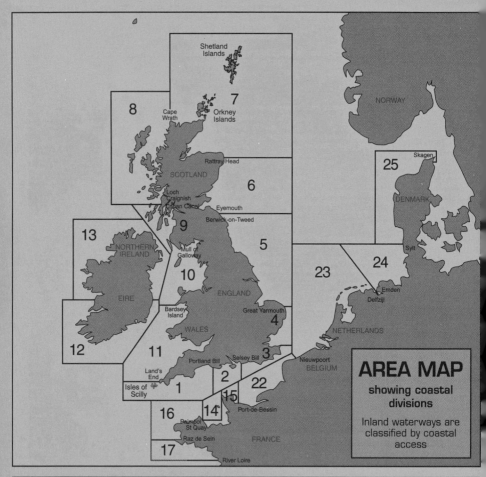

AREA MAP

showing coastal divisions

Inland waterways are classified by coastal access

SOUTH WEST ENGLAND	(AREA 1)	Scilly Isles to Portland Bill
CENTRAL SOUTHERN ENGLAND	(AREA 2)	Portland Bill to Selsey Bill
SOUTH EAST ENGLAND	(AREA 3)	Selsey Bill to North Foreland
THAMES ESTUARY	(AREA 4)	North Foreland to Great Yarmouth
EAST ENGLAND	(AREA 5)	Blakeney to Berwick-on-Tweed
SOUTH EAST SCOTLAND	(AREA 6)	Eyemouth to Rattray Head
NORTH EAST SCOTLAND	(AREA 7)	Rattray Head to Cape Wrath including Orkney and Shetland
NORTH WEST/CENTRAL WEST SCOTLAND	(AREA 8)	Cape Wrath to Crinan Canal
SOUTH WEST SCOTLAND	(AREA 9)	Crinan Canal to Mull of Galloway
NORTH WEST ENGLAND	(AREA 10)	Isle of Man and North Wales, Mull of Galloway to Bardsey Island
W. WALES, S. WALES & BRISTOL CHANNEL	(AREA 11)	Bardsey Island to Lands End
SOUTHERN IRELAND	(AREA 12)	Malahide , south to Liscanor Bay
NORTHERN IRELAND	(AREA 13)	Lambay Island, north to Liscanor Bay
CHANNEL ISLANDS	(AREA 14)	Guernsey, Jersey, Alderney.
BELGIUM AND THE NETHERLANDS	(AREA 23)	Nieuwpoort to Delfzijl
GERMANY	(AREA 24)	Emden to the Danish border
DENMARK	(AREA 25)	Sylt to Skagen

Coastal and Waterways Services Directory - Area by Area

SOUTH WEST ENGLAND   (AREA 1)
Scilly Isles to Portland Bill

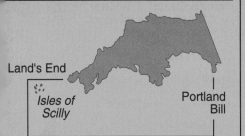

Land's End

Isles of Scilly

Portland Bill

ARIES VANE GEAR SPARES
48 St Thomas Street, Penryn, Cornwall TR10 6JW. Tel (01326) 377467 Fax (01326) 378117 e-mail: ariespares@compuserve.com Spare parts, re-build kit for all existing Aries gears.

ATLANTIC SPARS (KEMP WEST) LTD
Hatton House, Bridge Road, Churston Ferrers, Brixham, Devon TQ5 0JL. Tel (01803) 843322 Fax (01803) 845550 e-mail: atlantic@spars.co.uk Regional centre for SELDÉN and KEMP integrated sailing systems. Services include standing and running rigging, repairs, custom spars and furling systems. Aluminium design and fabrications for industry. Official suppliers to the BT Global Challenge. **Website: www.spars.co.uk**

BRIXHAM YACHT SUPPLIES LTD
72 Middle Street, Brixham, Devon TQ5 8EJ. Tel (01803) 882290 We stock a complete range of sailing and leisure clothing. English and Continental pure wool traditional knitwear. Camping accessories.

CALIBRA MARINE INTERNATIONAL
26 Foss Street, Dartmouth, Devon TQ6 9DR. Tel (01803) 833094 Fax (01803) 833615 e-mail: calibra1@aol.com A complete boating centre. Marine and architectural rigging service. Sail makers, repairs and valeting. All types of canvas work. Boat brokerage, new and used. Yacht management services. Agents for Nemo, Z-Spar, Whitlock, Lewmar, Norseman and many others.

THE CARTOON GALLERY (Wavelength Design)
37 Lower Street, Dartmouth, Devon TQ6 9AN. Tel/Fax (01803) 834466 Tel (01803) 834425 Evenings Rick, the International cartoonist specialises in hand coloured and personalised sailing cartoon prints (eg A3 £10). Commissions are carried out in Rick's Dartmouth gallery and studio. Prints available by mail order. Telephone or fax for details.

CHALLENGER MARINE
Freeman's Wharf, Falmouth Road, Penryn, Cornwall TR10 8AS. Tel (01326) 377222 Fax (01326) 377800 Marine engineers, chandlery, boatyard. Main Volvo Penta dealer, marina berths, brokerage, Bombard and Zodiac inflatables' dealer.

DART MARINA
Sandquay, Dartmouth, Devon TQ6 9PH. Tel (01803) 833351 Fax (01803) 832307 High quality 110-berth marina on the fabulous river Dart, opposite the Dart Marina hotel. A superb situation with all amenities, 24-hour security, hotel and restaurant, showers, baths and laundry, fuel berth, holding tank pump-out facility and a warm welcome to all visitors.

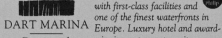
DARTHAVEN MARINA LTD
Brixham Road, Kingswear, Dartmouth, Devon TQ6 0SG. Tel (01803) 752242 Fax (01803) 752722 Marina Office: (01803) 752545 Chandlery: (01803) 752733 Fax (01803) 752790 VHF Ch80. All types of repair facilities available. Fully trained staff. 30-ton mobile hoist available all states of tide. Extensive chandlery open 7 days. Agents for all major suppliers including B&G, Raytheon, Yanmar (Main Dealers),Volvo Penta agents, Simpson Lawrence, Sowester installer dealer, International Coatings and many others. Emergency engineer callout - Mobile: 0411 404259. Electrician - Mobile: 0467 250787. Visitors welcome. All marina facilities available.

DUCHY OF CORNWALL
Harbour Office, St Mary's, Isles of Scilly, Cornwall TR21 0HU.
Tel/Fax (01720) 422768 Harbour of St Mary's, Isles of Scilly - 38 visitor moorings. Visitor centre, hot showers, toilets, launching facilities, winter storage, security lockers, fuel and fresh water. Five minutes from town centre. Ferry terminal and airport close by. Contact Harbour Master for more information.

EXONIA EUROPEAN MARINE TRANSPORT
The Sidings, Heathfield, Newton Abbot, Devon TQ12 6RG.
Tel (01626) 836688 Fax (01626) 836831 Europe's premier overland marine transport company, 25 years' experience, expertise cross border formalities, documentation, notifications, escorts, permits and schedules. Highly experienced well briefed drivers with a fully qualified back-up team. *Indubitably the best.*

FALMOUTH MARINA
North Parade, Falmouth, Cornwall TR11 2TD. Tel (01326) 316620 Fax (01326) 313939 e-mail: falmouth@premier-marinas.co.uk
The most westerly marina in England, Falmouth is an ideal starting point for a cruise to the Channel Islands, Brittany or the Scilly Isles. The marina offers fully serviced permanent and visitor berths with a professional and friendly service you would expect from a PREMIER marina.

FOWEY CRUISING SCHOOL & SERVICES
Fore Street, Fowey, Cornwall PL23 1AQ. Tel (01726) 832129 Fax (01726) 832000 e-mail: fcs@dial.pipex.com The best cruising in Britain, with matue instructors. Practical shore-based RYA courses. Family cruising a speciality. Yachtmster/Coastal exams. Diesel, First Aid, VHF etc. Our quarter century experience shows. *ALSO Marine and travel insurance with top companies.*

THE GUNFIELD HOTEL & RESTAURANT
Castle Road, Dartmouth, Devon TQ6 0JN. Tel (01803) 834843 Fax (01803) 834772 e-mail: enquiry@gunfield.co.uk VHF ChM2 or Ch37 Waterfront position with 10 impressive en suite bedrooms, central heating etc, all command fantastic river views. Restaurant offers modestly priced, delicious Mediterranean cuisine. Continental bar and lounge open to non-residents. Large terraces and gardens, BBQs during summer. Pontoon and deep water moorings. **Website: www.gunfield.co.uk**

HARBOUR MARINE
Marrowbone Slip, Sutton Road, Plymouth, Devon PL4 0HX. Tel (01752) 204690/1 Parts Dept:(01752) 204696 Fax (01752) 204693 A complete boatyard and engineering service situated on one side, facilities from haulout, full engineering workshop, osmosis treatment. Specialising in leisure or commercial boat building and repairs.

HARBOUR MARINE LEISURE
Marrowbone Slip, Sutton Road, Plymouth, Devon PL4 0HX. Tel (01752) 204694 Parts Dept: (01752) 204696 Fax (01752) 204695 Plymouth marine engine and watersports centre. Main

dealers for Seadoo watercraft, Mercury outboard, Fletcher sports boats, combined with a comprehensive parts service.

MARINE INSTRUMENTS
The Bosun's Locker, Upton Slip, Falmouth, Cornwall TR11 3DQ. Tel (01326) 312414 Books and charts. DoT Certified Compass Adjusters - available day or night.

THE MAYFLOWER INTERNATIONAL MARINA
Ocean Quay, Richmond Walk, Plymouth, Devon PL1 4LS. Tel (01752) 556633 Fax (01752) 606896 Plymouth's only Five-Gold Anchor marina. Known for its extensive facilities, courtesy and security. Owned by berth holders and run to a very high standard.

MECTRONICS MARINE
PO Box 8, Newton Abbot, Devon TQ12 1FF. Tel (01626) 334453 LIGHT ACTIVATED SWITCHES, rugged solid state devices to automatically switch anchor lights at sunset and sunrise. NAVLIGHT SELECTORS, protected enclosed rotary switches internally connected to ensure approved navigation light combination on auxiliary sailing vessels. NAVLIGHT STATUS MONITORS, diagnostic displays on which the appropriate indicator flashes quickly or slowly in the event of a short or open circuit fault. Also drives an optional, audible warning device.

NOSS-ON-DART MARINA
Noss Quay, Dartmouth, Devon TQ6 0EA. Tel (01803) 833351 Fax (01803) 832307 Peacefully located on the east shore of the river Dart, this relaxing marina is the perfect base for cruising yachtsmen. Extensive parking, chandlery, repair and lift-out facilities, easy access from London and the Midlands. Boat taxi to Dartmouth.

OUTRIGGERS/UPPER DECK MARINE
Albert Quay, Fowey, Cornwall PL23 1AQ. Tel (01726) 833233 Fax (01726) 833265 'Outriggers' casual and marine clothing, footwear, nautical gifts, Admiralty chart agent and marine books.

PADSTOW HARBOUR COMMISSIONERS
Harbour Office, Padstow, Cornwall PL28 8AQ. Tel (01841) 532239 Fax (01841) 533346 e-mail: padstowharbour@comp userve.com Inner harbour controlled by tidal gate - opens HW ±2hours. Minimum depth 3 metres at all times. Yachtsmen must be friendly as vessels raft together. Services include showers, diesel, water and ice. Security by CCTV.

THE PANDORA INN
Restronguet Creek, Mylor Bridge, Falmouth, Cornwall TR11 5ST. Tel/Fax (01326) 372678 Thatched creek-side inn with floating pontoon. Morning coffee, delicious bar meals, cream teas and fine dining in the superb Andrew Miller restaurant (entitles yachtsmen to free mooring). Telephone, showers and water available. Open all day in the summer.

PETER CUMBERLIDGE PHOTO LIBRARY
Sunways, Slapton, Kingsbridge, Devon TQ7 2PR. Tel (01548) 580461 Fax (01548) 580588 Large selection of nautical, travel and coastal colour transparencies. Specialities boats, harbours, lighthouses, marinas and inland waterways in Britain, Northern Europe, the Mediterranean and the Baltic. Commissions undertaken.

PLYMOUTH SAILING SCHOOL
Queen Anne's Battery Marina, Plymouth, Devon PL4 0LP. Tel (01752) 667170 Fax (01752) 257162 e-mail: school @plymsail.demon.co.uk Established in the 1950s the school offers year-round training (sail and power). RYA and MCA approved courses and private tuition ashore and afloat. A friendly reception and honest advice will always be found here. **Website:** www.plymsail.demon.co.uk

PLYMOUTH YACHT HAVEN
Shaw Way, Mount Batten, Plymouth, Devon PL9 9XH. Tel (01752) 404231 Fax (01752) 484177 VHF Ch37 and 80 **Position:** Southern side of cattewater, sheltered from prevailing winds by Mountbatten Peninsula. **Open:** All year, 24 hours. Callsign: Clovelly Bay. **Berths:** 180 berths, vessels up to 150', some fore and afts. Visitors welcome. **Facilities:** electricity, water, 24-hour security, workshop, chandlery, brokerage, showers, laundry, diesel. Calor gas. **NEW MARINA NOW OPEN.**

PORT FALMOUTH BOATYARD
North Parade, Falmouth, Cornwall TR11 2TB. Tel (01326) 313248 Fax (01326) 319395 Powered hoist and slipway. Cradle with 100 tons capacity. Shipwrights, marine engineering, hard standing and friendly efficient service.

PORT OF TRURO
Harbour Office, Town Quay, Truro, Cornwall TR1 2HJ. Tel (01872) 272130 Fax (01872) 225346 VHF Ch12 Facilities for the yachtsman include visitor pontoons located at Turnaware Bar, Ruan Creek and Boscawen Park. Visitor moorings at Woodbury. Quay facilities at Truro with free showers and toilets. Chemical toilet disposal, fresh water, electricity and garbage disposal.

RETREAT BOATYARD (TOPSHAM) LTD
Retreat Drive, Topsham, Exeter, Devon EX3 0LS. Tel (01392) 874720 & 875934 Fax (01392) 876182 Five minutes off M5 (Junction 30) the traditional service yard. International centre for Gelshield and Interspray. Agent for Volvo Penta, Yamaha and Bukh. Dealer for Avon, Autohelm, Seldén and Whitlock. Boat repairs, rigging, mooring, storage, comprehensive chandlery. Brokerage and insurance department.

RICHARD AYERS - YACHT SURVEYOR & CONSULTANT
5A Church Street, Modbury, Devon PL21 0QW. Tel (01548) 830496 Fax (01548) 830917 e-mail: ayers_survey@hotmail.com YDSA member - Yacht and powerboat survey, MCA Code of Practice for small commercial vessels. Survey for registration, marine insurance and claim inspections. Legal work. Plymouth - Salcombe - Dartmouth - Fowey - Falmouth - Totnes all local. No mileage charges.

RIVERSFORD HOTEL
Limers Lane, Bideford, Devon EX39 2RG. Tel (01237) 474239 Peace and tranquility in gardens beside the river Torridge. A relaxing retreat with convenient slipway close by. Excellent restaurant with efficient, friendly service with a choice of imaginative food and wine from our extensive menu and wine list. Comfortable, flexible lounge bar.

ROYAL WESTERN YACHT CLUB
Queen Anne's Battery, Plymouth, Devon PL4 0TW. Tel (01752) 660077 Fax (01752) 224299 e-mail: admin@rwyc.org Home of shorthanded sailing. Visiting yachtsmen welcome. Mooring facilities available.

THE SEA CHEST NAUTICAL BOOKS & CHARTS
Queen Anne's Battery Marina, Plymouth, Devon PL4 0LP. Tel (01752) 222012 Fax (01752) 252679 Admiralty Chart Agent. Worldwide mail order service.

SIMPSON-LAWRENCE GROUP LIMITED
National Contact Line: 0870 9000 597 Website: www.simpson-lawrence.com

SOUTHDOWN MARINA
Southdown Quay, Millbrook, Cornwall PL10 1HG. Tel/Fax (01752) 823084 32-berth marina on edge of river Tamar in quiet location behind Rame Peninsula. Plymouth is just across the river. Quayside berths available for large vessels. Dry Berthing. 24-hour security. DIY facilities available.

SPORT NAUTIQUE CHANDLERS
2 Newcomen Road, Dartmouth, Devon TQ6 9AF. Tel (01803) 832532 Fax (01803) 832538 Extensive range of chandlery from rope, paint, deck equipment, books and charts, electronic equipment and stockists of a comprehensive choice of foul-weather gear, marine and leisure clothing and footwear. **Personal delivery to your boat - just call for service.**

ST MAWES SAILING CLUB
No 1 The Quay, St Mawes, Cornwall TR2 5DG. Tel (01326) 270686 Fax (01326) 270040 Quayside sailing club in centre of village. Visitor moorings in harbour. Private slip, launching and recovery facilities. Dinghy park, post box, showers. Visitors encouraged. Chandlery and sail repairs to order. No marina but a warm welcome awaits.

SUTTON HARBOUR MARINA
Sutton Harbour, Plymouth, Devon PL4 0RA. Tel (01752) 204186 Fax (01752) 205403 A superb sheltered marina with 24-hour access and fully serviced visitor berths with full on-shore facilities in the city's historic Elizabethan quarter. Just a few minutes stroll from the shops, restaurants and entertainment at the city centre.

TORBAY BOATING CENTRE
South Quay, The Harbour, Paignton, Devon TQ4 6TD. Tel (01803) 558760 Fax (01803) 663230 For all your boating requirements from Seadoo watercraft, inflatables, Fletcher sports boats to Mercury outboard and Yamaha sterndrive. A complete sales and engineering workshop. Retail sales and engineering.

TREVOR VINCETT DELIVERIES
Coombe Cottage, 9 Swannaton Road, Dartmouth, Devon TQ6 9RL. Tel/Fax (01803) 833757 Mobile: 07970 208799 Worldwide delivery of yachts and commercial vessels undertaken at short notice by RYA/DoT Yachtmaster Ocean (with commercial endorsement). Over 28 years' experience including three masted schooners, tugs, motor yachts and hi-tec racers. For instant quotes call/fax 01803 833757.

UPPER DECK MARINE/OUTRIGGERS
Albert Quay, Fowey, Cornwall PL23 1AQ. Tel (01726) 832287 Fax (01726) 833265 Chandlery, fastenings, paints, cords, fenders, anchors, compasses, lifejackets, Gaz. Leading names in waterproofs and warm wear.

WARD & McKENZIE (South West) LTD
Little Brook Cottage, East Portlemouth, Salcombe, Devon TQ8 8PW. **Tel** (01803) 833500 **Fax** (01803) 833350 National and International marine surveyors. Technical and legal consultants. Contact: Chris Olsen - Mobile: 07971 250105. **Website: www.ward-mckenzie.co.uk**

WEIR QUAY BOATYARD
ON THE TAMAR
Deepwater : Moorings : Shore Storage
Cranage : Repairs : Maintenance
Water Electricity Diesel Butane Visitors' Moorings DIY Launching
A traditional yard in a superb setting with moorings at very affordable rates
01822 - 840474

WEIR QUAY BOATYARD
Heron's Reach, Bere Alston, Devon PL20 7BT. **Tel** (01822) 840474 **Fax** (01822) 840948 Deepwater swinging moorings, shore storage, full boatyard facilities and services, cranage to 12 tons, repairs, maintenance, slipway. A traditional boatyard at affordable rates *in a superb setting* on the Tamar, with excellent security.

WINTERS MARINE LIMITED
Salcombe (01548) 843580
Slipway & Moorings
Repairs & Storage
Inflatable Dinghy & Raft service & hire.
E-mail: lincombeboatyard@eclipse.co.uk

WINTERS MARINE LTD (Lincombe Boatyard)
Lincombe, Salcombe, Devon TQ8 8NQ. **Tel** (01548) 843580 **e-mail:** lincombeboatyard@eclipse.co.uk Deep water pontoon moorings. Winter storage for 150 boats. All maintenance and repair facilities. Slipway capacity 30 tonnes. Inflatable raft sales and service. Liferaft surveys and repairs. Short and long-term liferaft hire.

Yacht Parts Plymouth
Biggest & Best Stocked Chandler in the West
Tel: 01752 252489 Fax: 01752 225899
Victoria Building, Queen Anne's Battery, Plymouth PL4 0LP.
E-mail: sales@yachtparts.co.uk Website: www.yachtparts.co.uk

YACHT PARTS PLYMOUTH
Victoria Building, Queen Anne's Battery Marina, Plymouth, Devon PL4 0LP. **Tel** (01752) 252489 **Fax** (01752) 225899 **e-mail:** sales@yachtparts.co.uk From anchors to zinc anodes - probably the best stocked chandler in the country. Open seven days with free easy parking. Our large clothing department caters for everyone from the dinghy sailor to the ocean going yachtsman. **Website: www.yachtparts.co.uk**

CENTRAL SOUTHERN ENGLAND
(AREA 2)
Portland Bill to Selsey Bill

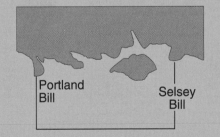

B P S C MARINE SERVICES
Unit 4 Park Business Centre, 1 Park Road, Freemantle, Southampton, Hampshire SO15 3US. **Tel** 023 8051 0561 BPSC offer a fast efficient repair service on a wide range of nautical and survey instruments. Free estimates and advice. A comprehensive range of spares are carried, most of which can be despatched same day. Instruments commissioned. Compass adjusting service.

BEAULIEU RIVER MANAGEMENT LTD
Harbour Master's Office, Bucklers Hard Yacht Harbour, Beaulieu, Hampshire SO42 7XB. **Tel** (01590) 616200 **Fax** (01590) 616211 110-berth yacht harbour (pontoon berths), fully serviced with back-up facilities of historic Bucklers Hard village. Agamemnon boatyard - 290 swinging moorings let on annual basis. Visiting craft welcome. Capacity 100+ pile/pontoon.

BOOK CABIN
Unit 20, Canutes Pavilion, Ocean Village, Southampton, Hampshire SO14 3JS. **Tel** 023 8021 1199 **Fax** 023 8033 8488 Nautical and general booksellers.

You're ready to go offshore..... But is your yacht?
BOSE MARINE DESIGN & SURVEYS
Tel/Fax +44 (0) 1243 538300
Condition, Damage, Valuation & Purchase Surveys.
New Project and Repair Supervision.
We advise on specialist installations and the Design of Cruising Yachts.
CHICHESTER, WEST SUSSEX

BOSE
7 Carse Road, Rowan Gate, Chichester, West Sussex PO19 4YG. Tel/Fax (01243) 538300 Marine surveying and design specialition: ocean cruising, specialist fittings, project supervision.

C C MARINE SERVICES LTD
PO Box 155, Chichester, West Sussex PO20 8TS. **Tel** +44 (0) 1243 672606 **Fax** +44 (0) 1243 673703 Innovators of marine tape technology. Included in the range *Rubbaweld*, the original self-amalgamating marine tape and a complete range of specialised products for every yachtsman's needs. Available from all good chandlers.

CARBOSPARS LTD
Hamble Point, School Lane, Hamble, Southampton, Hampshire SO31 4JD. **Tel** 023 8045 6736 **Fax** 023 8045 5361 **e-mail:** carbospars@compuserve.com Design and manufacture of carbon spars for racing and cruising and the award-winning AeroRig®.

CHICHESTER MARINA
Birdham, Chichester, West Sussex PO20 7EJ. **Tel** (01243) 512731 **Fax** (01243) 513472 **e-mail: chichester@premier-marinas.co.uk** Situated in the north east corner of Chichester harbour, Chichester Marina enjoys one of the most attractive locations in the country. With 1100 berths, Chichester offers a unique combination of service, facilities, security and friendliness, unparalleled in UK marinas. Chichester Marina is a PREMIER Marina.

COMPASS MARINE SURVEYS
25 years' experience multihill monohull
sailing vessels and power craft
Insurance • Full/Partial • Condition • Pre-purchase
Pre-delivery • Project Management
22 Montague Road, Midhurst, West Sussex GU29 9BJ.
Tel/Fax:+44 (0) 1730 816268 E-mail: compass marine@freeuk.com
UK - EUROPE - WORLDWIDE

COMPASS MARINE SURVEYS
22 Montague Road, Midhurst, West Sussex GU29 9BJ. **Tel/Fax** (01730) 816268 **e-mail: compassmarine@freeuk.com** 25 years' experience in multihull, monohull sailing vessels and power craft. Condition, Insurance, full/partial, pre-purchase, project management, client/builder liaison. UK - Europe - Worldwide. Quotation/Brochure telephone +44 (0) 1730 816268.

CONVOI EXCEPTIONNEL LTD
Castleton House, High Street, Hamble, Southampton, Hampshire SO31 4HA. **Tel** 023 8045 3045 **Fax** 023 8045 4551 **e-mail: info@convoi.co.uk** International marine haulage and abnormal load consultants. European abnormal load permits obtained and escort car service. Capacity for loads up to 100 tons.

COWES YACHT HAVEN
Vectis Yard, High Street, Cowes, Isle of Wight PO31 7BD. Tel (01983) 299975 Fax (01983) 200332 VHF Ch80 Cowes Yacht Haven is the Solent's premier sailing event centre offering 200 fully serviced berths right in the heart of Cowes. Our improved facilities, capability and location ensures the perfect venue and profile for every kind of boating event.

CREWSAVER LTD
Crewsaver House, Mumby Road, Gosport, Hampshire PO12 1AQ. Tel 023 9252 8621 MARLIN - Leading manufacturer of stylish, comfortable, hardwearing wetsuits, lifejackets, buoyancy aids and accessories for all seasons and all-surface watersports. YAK - Catering for all canoeing needs from cags and decks to long johns and buoyancy aids.

CRUISAIR UK LTD
- TAYLOR MADE ENVIRONMENTAL SYSTEMS
26 Old Wareham Road, Poole, Dorset BH12 4QR. Tel (01202) 716469 Fax (01202) 716478 e-mail: sales@cruisair.co.uk Marine air conditioning.

DEACONS BOATYARD LTD
Bursledon Bridge, Southampton, Hampshire SO31 8AZ. Tel 023 8040 2253 Fax 023 8040 5665 This yard has all major services for yachtsmen. Moorings, hardstanding, repairs, marine engineers, riggers, chandlery and brokerage - new yacht sales. Deacons are UK importers for Feeling yachts.

DEAN & REDDYHOFF LTD - EAST COWES MARINA
Clarence Road, East Cowes, Isle of Wight PO32 6HA. Tel (01983) 293983 Fax (01983) 299276 This existing marina (but new to Dean and Reddyhoff) is undergoing a facelift which will include dredging, new pontoons, toilets and showers and possibly a clubhouse. Regular yachtsmen, visitors and rallies will be welcome as before.

DEAN & REDDYHOFF LTD - HASLAR MARINA
Haslar Road, Gosport, Hampshire PO12 1NU. Tel 023 9260 1201 Fax 023 9260 2201 Haslar Marina is just inside the entrance of Portsmouth harbour on the Gosport side. Included in the 600 berths is a visitors' area which is adjacent to a converted lightship with bar facilities and excellent toilets and showers.

HASLAR MARINA
Superb marina berths in Portsmouth Harbour, at £230 per metre per annum plus VAT.
Tel: 023 9260 1201

WEYMOUTH MARINA
Opened in 1996, this marina is proving to be popular with visitors. Annual berthing at £205 per metre per annum plus VAT.
Tel: 01305 767576

EAST COWES MARINA
Sheltered pontoon moorings on the Isle of Wight, with annual berths costing £180 per metre per annum plus VAT.
Tel: 01983 293983

DEAN & REDDYHOFF LTD - WEYMOUTH MARINA
70 Commercial Road, Weymouth, Dorset DT4 8NA. Tel (01305) 767576 Fax (01305) 767575 This new marina in the inner harbour of Weymouth provides facilities for visitors which are proving very popular. The marina is right next to Weymouth's high street, and the area has a multitude of pubs and restaurants.

DIVERSE YACHT SERVICES
Unit 12, Hamble Yacht Services, Port Hamble, Hamble, Hampshire SO31 4NN. Tel 023 8045 3399 Fax 023 8045 5288 Marine electronics and electrics. Supplied and installed. Specialists in racing yachts. Suppliers of 'Loadsense' Loadcells for marine applications.

ELKINS BOATYARD
Tidesreach, 18 Convent Meadow, The Quay, Christchurch, Dorset BH23 1BD. Tel (01202) 483141 All boatyard facilities. Moorings alongside, water and electricity, storage ashore, repairs. Boats up to 45', 10 tons maximum, haul-out.

EMSWORTH YACHT HARBOUR LTD
Thorney Road, Emsworth, Hampshire PO10 8BP. Tel (01243) 377727 Fax (01243) 373432 Friendly marina in Chichester harbour. Water, electricity, diesel, Calor gas, 25-tonne mobile crane, slipways, hard-standing and storage areas. Showers and toilets, car parking, chandlery, engineers and boat repairs.

ERNST & YOUNG - THE TRIDENT FORUM
Wessex House, 19 Threefield Lane, Southampton, Hampshire SO14 3QB. Tel 023 8038 2000 Fax 023 8038 382001 The Trident Forum aims to provide the maritime business community with first class professional services backed by substantial experience of working in the marine industry. Contact John Liddell

EURONAV NAVIGATION
20 The Slipway, Port Solent, Portsmouth, Hampshire PO6 4TR. Tel 023 9237 3855 Fax 023 9232 5800 Electronic charting specialists, offering the seaPro 2000 range of PC-based chart plotting systems, ARCS, Livechart 'B' and BSB top quality electronic charts. Products are available from good chandlers or direct from Euronav. **Website:** www.euronav.co.uk

FRANK VERRILL & PARTNERS
6 Old Bridge House Road, Bursledon, Hampshire SO31 8AJ. Tel 023 8040 2881 Fax 023 8040 4698 Mobile: 0880 321155 Consulting engineers, marine surveyors, loss adjusters, insurance investigators, legal Expert Witnesses.

GREENHAM MARINE
King's Saltern Road, Lymington, Hampshire SO41 9QD. Tel (01590) 671144 Fax (01590) 679517 Greenham Marine can offer yachtsmen one of the most comprehensive selections of marine electronic equipment currently available. Also at Poole/Weymouth 01202 676363 and Emsworth/Chichester 01243 378314.

GenACis
Power House, Gordon Road, Winchester, Hampshire SO23 7DD. Tel (01962) 841828 Fax (01962) 841834 Dolphin water cooled diesel generators, 3 - 16 KVA.

HAINES BOATYARD
Itchenor, Chichester, West Sussex PO20 7AN. Tel (01243) 512228 Fax (01243) 513900 Racing keelboat specialists. Boat building and repairs with top quality joinery in teak and other hardwoods. Controlled fibreglass and epoxy work facilities. Moorings and winter boat and dinghy storage, masts spars and rigging service.

HOLMAN RIGGING
Chichester Yacht Basin, Chichester, West Sussex PO20 7EJ. Tel/Fax (01243) 514000 Agents for major suppliers in this field we offer a specialist mast and rigging service. Purpose designed mast trailer for quick and safe transportation. Installation for roller headsail and mainsail reefing systems. Insurance reports and quotations.

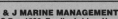
INTERNATIONAL COATINGS LTD
24-30 Canute Road, Southampton, Hampshire SO14 3PB. Tel 023 8022 6722 Fax 023 8033 5975 International *Coatings Ltd* is the leading supplier of quality paints, epoxies, varnishes and anti-foulings to the marine industry. Over half the world's pleasure craft are protected by International products.

J & J MARINE MANAGEMENT
PO Box 1696, Fordingbridge, Hampshire SP6 2RR. Tel (01425) 650201 Fax (01425) 657740 e-mail: jjmarine@dial.pipex.com Marine surveyors and consultants. Pre-purchase, insurance, valuation and damage surveys. Supervision of refit, new construction and design projects. MCA compliance surveys, stability booklets and yacht registration.

K T Y YACHTS
Unit 12, Universal Marina, Crableck Lane, Sarisbury Green, Southampton, Hampshire SO31 7ZN. Tel (0385) 335189 Fax (01489) 570302 MCA First Aid and Medical Care aboard ship. Qualified, practical instruction from a sailor and paramedic.

KELVIN HUGHES
Southampton: Kilgraston House, Southampton Street, Southampton SO15 2ED. Tel 023 8063 4911 Fax 023 8033 0014 e-mail: southampton@kelvinhughes.co.uk The world's largest chart agency. The world's finest nautical bookshops, plus software, navigation instruments. For all your chart table requirements.

KEMP SAILS LTD
The Sail Loft, 2 Sandford Lane Industrial Estate, Wareham, Dorset BH20 4DY. Tel (01929) 554308 & 554378 Fax (01929) 554350 e-mail: kempltd@globalnet.co.uk Sailmakers: New sails and repairs. Hardware and reefing systems. Sprayhoods, sail covers and canvas products. **Website: www.scoot.co.uk/kemp_sails**

LEGAL SUPPORT SERVICES
Virides, Victoria Road, Bishops Waltham, Hampshire SO32 1DJ. Tel/Fax (01489) 890961 Mobile: 0966 389367 Support services for marine companies for legal and quasi-legal activities, eg liaison with local authorities and government departments, and discrete research projects. Also **Marine Job-Spot** low cost recruitment services for the UK marine industry.

LEWMAR MARINE LTD
Southmoor Lane, Havant, Hampshire PO9 1JJ. Tel 023 9247 1841 Fax 023 9248 5720 Manufacturers of winches, windlasses, hatches, hardware, hydraulics and marine thrusters for boats ranging in size from 25' to 300' LOA.

LYMINGTON YACHT HAVEN
King's Saltern Road, Lymington, Hampshire SO41 3QD. Tel (01590) 677071 Fax (01590) 678186 Perfectly situated at the mouth of the Lymington river giving instant access to the Western Solent. Full marina services, boatyard, brokerage, diesel, petrol, gas, restaurant and bar.

MARINTEC
Silverton House, Kings Hyde, Mount Pleasant Lane, Lymington, Hampshire SO41 8LT. Tel (01590) 683414 Fax (01590) 683719 MARINTEC was established at the beginning of 1983 and undertake comprehensive surveys, including mechanical and electrical, both at home and overseas. Refit management including the drawing up of specifications and the tender document by YDSA surveyor.

MARSH YACHT DIVISION
Havelock Chambers, Queens Terrace, Southampton, Hampshire SO14 3PP. Tel 023 8031 8300 Fax 023 8031 8391 A member of the largest insurance broking firm in the world with associated offices in Antibes and Fort Lauderdale. Specialists in yacht insurance for craft cruising UK, Mediterranean, Caribbean and US waters.

THE MILLPOND
1 Main Road, Emsworth, West Sussex PO10 8AP. Tel (01243) 372089 Cosy bed and breakfast pub. Six letting rooms en suite with TV and tea/coffee-making facilities. Boules, terrine/garden overlooking the Millpond. Snacks and light food available Thursdays and Saturdays. Goodwood - Chichester - Portsmouth approximately 20 minutes away.

R J MUIR
22 Seymour Close, Chandlers Ford, Eastleigh, Southampton SO5 2JE. Tel 023 8026 1042 Books and Charts. DoT Certified Compass Adjusters - available day or night.

PARKER & KAY SAILMAKERS - SOUTH
Hamble Point Marina, School Lane, Hamble, Southampton,
Hampshire SO31 4JD. Tel 023 8045 8213 Fax 023 8045 8228
e-mail: pandksouth@aol.com A complete sailmaking service, from
small repairs to the construction of custom designed sails for racing
or cruising yachts. Covers constructed for sail and powercraft, plus
the supply of all forms of sail handling hardware.

PARKSTONE YACHT CLUB
Pearce Avenue, Parkstone, Poole, Dorset BH14 8EH. Tel (01202)
743610 Fax (01202) 716394 e-mail: office@parkstoneyc.co.uk
Deep water club haven facilities in Poole harbour. Access at all
states of the tide. Berths for yachts up to 15 metres. Facilities include
electricity, fresh water, toilets and showers. Visitors welcome by
appointment. Club bar and restaurant.

PETERS & MAY LTD
18 Canute Road, Ocean Village, Southampton, Hampshire SO14
3FJ. Tel 023 8048 0480 Fax 023 8048 0400 The 'Round the World'
specialists in shipping, transporting, cradling yachts and
powerboats. Weekly service to USA, Far East, Mediterranean,
Middle East and Caribbean.

PORT SOLENT
South Lockside, Port Solent, Portsmouth, Hampshire PO6 4TJ.
Tel 023 9221 0765 Fax 023 9232 4241 e-mail: portsolent@
premier-marinas.co.uk From a marine superstore and outstanding
slipway services to restaurants, bars and multiscreen cinema, Port
Solent offers visitors and berth holders superb facilities,
unsurpassed by any other UK marina. Port Solent is a PREMIER
Marina.

PREMIER MARINAS LTD
South Lockside, Port Solent, Portsmouth, Hampshire PO6 4TJ.
Tel 023 9221 4145 Fax 023 9222 1876 e-mail: office@premier-
marinas.co.uk At our marinas we're always on hand to help you.
PREMIER GROUP MARINAS - Beaucette - Chichester - Falmouth -
Port Solent. Website: www.premier-marinas.co.uk

R K MARINE LTD
Hamble River Boatyard, Bridge Road, Swanwick, Southampton,
Hampshire SO31 7EB. Tel (01489) 583572 Fax (01489) 583172
Volvo Penta main dealer with full boatyard facilities.

REGIS ELECTRONICS LTD
Regis House, Quay Hill, Lymington, Hampshire SO41 3AR.
Tel (01590) 679251 & 679176 Fax (01590) 679910 (Also at Cowes,
Southampton & Chichester). Sales, service and installation of marine
electronic equipment. Leading south coast agents for AUTOHELM,
FURUNO, RAYTHEON, CETREK, A.P. NAVIGATOR, GARMIN,
SIMRAD, SAILOR and other manufacturers of quality marine
electronic equipment. Competitively priced quotations (including
owner familiarisation and sea trials) forwarded by return of post.

RELIANCE YACHT MANAGEMENT LTD
International Maritime Services Tel +44 (0) 1252 378239
Fax +44 (0) 1252 521736 e-mail: info@reliance-yachts.com With
over 10 years' experience we offer a professional management and
delivery service. Your yacht can be safely and expertly delivered
anywhere in the world by highly experienced skippers and crews.
We are also able to offer 'Total solution Management Packages'
designed to suit your needs. Offices in the Caribbean, Pacific, Asia
and France. Website: www.reliance-yachts.com

RIDGE WHARF YACHT CENTRE
Ridge, Wareham, Dorset BH20 5BG. Tel (01929) 552650
Fax (01929) 554434 Marina with full boatyard facilities. Winter lay-
up and fuels etc.

ROB PERRY MARINE
Monmouth Beach, Lyme Regis, Dorset DT7 3LE. Tel (01297)
445816 Fax (01297) 445886 Outboard and inboard sales and
service. Wetsuits, lifejackets. Some chandlery. Fast efficient service.
Marine surveys and insurance.

SEA START
Unit 13, Hamble Point Marina, Southampton, Hampshire SO31
4JD. Tel 0800 88 55 00 or 023 8045 8000 Fax 023 8045 2666 Sea
Start is the 24-hour marine breakdown service on both sides of the
English Channel and the Channel Islands. Membership cost from
as little as £9 per month. Join now using your credit card on 0800
88 55 00 or ring for our colour brochure.

SEA VENTURES YACHT CHARTER
Lymington Yacht Haven, Lymington, Hampshire SO41 3QD. Tel
(01590) 672472 Fax (01590) 671924 Based in Lymington and
Plymouth, our large modern fleet offers both skippered and
bareboat charters. A large selection of yachts from 29' to 52' and
most less than 3 years old. Corporate and team building and yacht
management also available. Website: www.sea-ventures.co.uk

SEALINE SEA SCHOOL & CHARTER
Hamble River Boatyard, Bridge Road, Swanwick, Southampton,
Hampshire SO31 7EB. Tel (01489) 579898 Fax (01489) 582123
Mobile: 0370 613788 Sealine Sea School & Charter - Training to
RYA standards in the superb location of the Solent, or take your
guests out for an unforgettable day cruising Solent ports. Family/
friends and corporate events all catered for.

SHAMROCK CHANDLERY
Shamrock Quay, William Street, Northam, Southampton,
Hampshire SO14 5QL. Tel 023 8063 2725 Fax 023 8022 5611 e-
mail: sales@shamrock.co.uk Situated on Shamrock Quay, a busy
working yard with a pub, restaurant and boutiques. Shamrock
Chandlery is renowned for extensive quality stocks and service,
and is widely used by both the trade and boat owners. Excellent
mail order facilities - Order Hotline 023 8022 5746. Website:
www.shamrock.co.uk

SHERATON MARINE CABINET
White Oak Green, Hailey, Witney, Oxfordshire OX8 5XP. Tel/Fax (01993) 868275 Manufacturers of quality teak and mahogany marine fittings, louvre doors, gratings and tables. Special fitting-out items to customer specification. Colour catalogue available on request.

SHOOSMITHS - THE TRIDENT FORUM
Russell House, Solent Business Park, Fareham, Hampshire PO15 7AG. Tel (01489) 881010 Fax (01489) 616942 The Trident Forum aims to provide the maritime business community with first class professional services backed by substantial experience of working in the marine industry. Contact Heather Nichols.

SILLETTE SONIC LTD
Unit 5 Stepnell Reach, 541 Blandford Road, Hamworthy, Poole, Dorset BH16 5BW. Tel (01202) 621631 Fax (01202) 625877 Mobile: 077 10270107 Distribution Depot: Sillette manufactures a range of propulsion systems - stern drive, saildrives etc and sterngear. Markets Radice and Gori fixed and folding propellers. Acts as agents for Morse Controls, Yanmar and Lombardini marine engines, and Fuji Robin generators. See Area 3.

SIMPSON-LAWRENCE GROUP LIMITED
National Contact Line: 0870 9000 597 Website: www.simpson-lawrence.com

SIMRAD LTD
Woolmer Way, Bordon, Hampshire GU35 9QE. Tel (01420) 483200 Fax (01420) 489073 e-mail: sales@simrad.co.uk World-leading manufacturer of marine electronics and professional technology designed and built to operate in all conditions. Autopilots, instruments for sail and power, chartplotters, GPS, GMDSS VHF radios, advanced radars, professional echosounders and sophisticated combined instruments. www.simrad.com

SOUTHERN SPAR SERVICES (KEMP SOUTH)
Shamrock Quay, William Street, Northam, Southampton, Hampshire SO14 5QL. Tel 023 8033 1714 Fax 023 8023 0559 Mobile: 0850 736540 Regional centre for SELDEN and KEMP integrated sailing systems. Convectional and furling spars for UK and abroad. Also headsail and mainsail reefing, deck equipment, toe rails and stanchion bases. All forms of repairs and modifications undertaken.

SOUTHSEA MARINA
Fort Cumberland Road, Southsea, Hampshire PO4 9RJ. Tel 023 9282 2719 Fax 023 9282 2220 e-mail: southseamarina@ibm.net Marina operators, yard services, chandlery, brokerage. Sea school. Bar and restaurant. Visitor berthing, dry boating, winter hardstanding, on-site contractors, glass fibre repairs, osmosis treatment, engineers, riggers, sail repairs, sail alterations and upholstery. Website: www.southsea-marina.com

SP EPOXY SYSTEMS
St Cross Business Park, Newport, Isle of Wight PO30 5WU. Tel (01983) 828000 Fax (01983) 828100 Epoxy resins for laminating, bonding, coating and filling. Usable with wood, GRP, concrete. GRP/FRP materials including glass, carbon and Kevlar fibres. Structural engineering of GRP and composite materials. Technical advice service.

SPARKES YACHT HARBOUR LTD
38 Wittering Road, Hayling Island, Hampshire PO11 9SR. Tel 023 9246 3572 Fax 023 9246 5741 e-mail: enquiries@sparkesmarina.freeserve.co.uk Sparkes Marina - a small friendly, family run business offering all the facilities you require including access at all states of the tide to a depth of 2 metres at lowest low water springs. In addition to marina berths, accessible through a security gate, we also offer dry boat sailing, moorings, storage ashore plus full maintenance facilities, new boat sales and brokerage, chandlery and restaurant.

STREAMLINED PROPELLER REPAIRS
Unit 17 Cavendish Mews, off Grosvenor Road, Aldershot, Hampshire GU11 3EH. Tel (01252) 316412 Established in 1978 specialising in all types of propeller repairs up to 6' diameter. Recommended by all leading outboard concessionaires. Largest stock of propeller bushes and parts in the UK.

TEK-TANKS
Units 5A - 5B Station Approach, Four Marks, Nr Alton, Hampshire GU34 5HN. Tel (01420) 564359 Fax (01420) 561605 e-mail: enquiries@tek-tanks.com Manufacturers and suppliers of made-to-measure and standard polypropylene water, waste and HDPE diesel tanks. Website: www.tek-tanks.com

TOLLEY MARINE LTD
Unit 7, Blackhill Road West, Holton Heath Trading Park, Poole, Dorset BH16 6LS. Tel (01202) 632644 Fax (01202) 632622 Branches at Salterns Marina (01202) 706040 and Plymouth (01752) 222530. Agents for all major marine electronics manufacturers. Autohelm, B&G, Cetrek, Furuno, Garmin, Icom, Koden, Lo-Kata, MLR, Magnavox, Navico, Panasonic, Raytheon, Robertson, Sailor, Shipmate, Trimble.

TOOMER & HAYTER LTD
74 Green Road, Winton, Bournemouth, Dorset BH9 1EB. Tel (01202) 515789 Fax (01202) 538771 Marine upholstery manufacturers. Cabin and cockpit upholstery made to any shape or size. Sprung interior mattresses made to measure. Foam backed cabin lining always in stock, also carpet side lining. Visit our factory and showroom.

VAIL WILLIAMS - THE TRIDENT FORUM
Meridians House, 7 Ocean Way, Ocean Village, Southampton, Hampshire SO14 3TJ. Tel 023 8063 1973 Fax 023 8063 223884 The Trident Forum aims to provide the maritime business community with first class professional services backed by substantial experience of working in the marine industry. Contact Simon Ward.

VETUS DEN OUDEN LTD
39 South Hants Industrial Park, Totton, Southampton, Hampshire SO40 3SA. Tel 023 8086 1033 Fax 023 8066 3142 Suppliers of marine diesel equipment, exhaust systems, steering systems, bow propellers, propellers and shafts, hatches, portlights, windows, electronic instruments, batteries, ventilators, windlasses, water and fuel tanks, chandlery items and much much more.

WARD & McKENZIE (Dorset) LTD
69 Alexander Road, Parkstone, Poole, Dorset BH14 9EL.
Tel (01202) 718440 National and International marine surveyors.
Technical and legal consultants. Contact: Tony McGrail - Mobile:
0411 329314. **Website: www.ward-mckenzie.co.uk**

WARSASH NAUTICAL BOOKSHOP
6 Dibles Road, Warsash, Southampton, Hampshire SO31 9HZ.
Tel (01489) 572384 Fax (01489) 885756 e-mail: alan@nautical
books.co.uk Nautical bookseller and chart agent. Callers and mail
order. Free new and secondhand book lists. Credit cards taken.
Publishers of the Bibliography of Nautical books. **Website:**
www.nauticalbooks.co.uk

WESSEX MARINE EQUIPMENT LTD
Logistics House, 2nd Avenue Business Park, Millbrook Road East,
Southampton, Hampshire SO1 0LP. Tel 023 8051 0570 Books and
charts.

WET & WILD GRAPHICS
Falcon House, Hamble Point Marina, Hamble, Southampton,
Hampshire SO31 4NB. Tel 023 8045 8332 Fax 023 8045 6830
e-mail: sales@wild-graphics.co.uk Supply and application of vinyl
graphics, signboards, banners and flags. Specialist materials for
sails and spinnakers. Brochure available for mail order boat names.
Deadlines never a problem!!! **Website: www.wild-graphics.co.uk**

WEYMOUTH OLD HARBOUR
Weymouth & Portland Borough Council, Environmental
Services Department, Council Offices, North Quay, Weymouth,
Dorset DT4 8TA. Tel (01305) 206423/206363 Fax (01305) 206422
e-mail: harbour@weymouth.co.uk Access at all stages of tide.
Visitor berths in centre of prime tourist resort with shops, restaurants
and night life at hand. Diesel fuelling from pontoon or
tanker. Chandlery and repair facilities available. **Website:**
www.weymouth.gov.uk/marine.htm

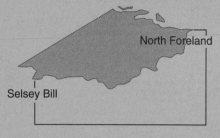
ADEC MARINE LTD
4 Masons Avenue, Croydon, Surrey CR0 9XS. Tel 020 8686 9717
Fax 020 8680 9912 e-mail: adecmarine@lineone.net Approved
liferaft service station for south east UK. Additionally we hire and
sell new rafts and sell a complete range of safety equipment for
yachts including pyrotechnics, fire extinguishers, lifejackets, buoys
and a buoyancy bag system.

BOSUNS LOCKER - RAMSGATE
10 Military Road, Royal Harbour, Ramsgate, Kent CT11 9LG.
Tel/Fax (01843) 597158 The Bosun's Locker - a friendly family
owned business, caters for a wide range of boat owners and is
staffed by experienced yachtsmen. The stock is extensive, including
paints, ropes, quality clothing for foul weather and fashion,
electronics, inflatables and charts.

BRIGHTON MARINA
Marine Trade Centre, Brighton Marina, Brighton, East Sussex
BN2 5UG. Tel (01273) 819919 Fax (01273) 675082 The UK's No 1
marina village with 1300 pontoon berths. 24-hour manned reception
and CCTV. Five-Gold Anchors for facilities and service with excellent
new toilet and showers. Full boatyard and shore facilities with Marine
Trade Centre offering all associated trades and leisure area with
11 pub/restaurants, ASDA superstore, Virgin cinema, David Lloyd
Health Centre and Bowlplex. Entrance dredged to 2 metres with
24-hour access to the sea without locking. Five minutes from
Brighton town centre.

BURNHAM YACHT HARBOUR MARINA LTD
Burnham Yacht Harbour, Burnham-on-Crouch, Essex CM0 8BL.
Tel (01621) 782150 Fax (01621) 785848 VHF Ch80 The only Five-
Gold Anchor marina in Essex. 350 fully serviced pontoon berths
and 120 deep water swing moorings. Marina access at all states of
tide with minimum 2.5m depth at low water.

GLOBAL MARITIME TRAINING
Hoo Marina, Vicarage Lane, Hoo, Kent ME3 9TW. Tel (01634)
256288 Fax (01634) 256284 e-mail: info@seaschool.co.uk RYA
theory courses by correspondence. Start your course anywhere in
the world at any time. Also practical courses from our north Kent
base. Worldwide yacht deliveries with free RYA tutition for owners
'en-route'. **Website: www.seaschool.co.uk**

GRAHAM BOOTH MARINE SURVEYS
4 Epple, Birchington-on-Sea, Kent CT7 9AY. Tel (01843) 843793 Fax (01843) 846860 e-mail: gbms@clara.net Authorised for MCA Codes of Practice, most frequently on French and Italian Riviera - also for certification of Sail Training vessels and other commercial craft. Call UK office for further information. Other expert marine consultancy services also available.

JARVIS MARINA HOTEL - RAMSGATE
Harbour Parade, Ramsgate, Kent CT11 8LZ. Tel (01843) 588276 Fax (01843) 586866 Situated on the edge of Ramsgate's Marina, the ideal accommodation venue for the travelling yachtsman. Club bar open all day serving drinks and snacks. Hobson's restaurant offers an extensive menu. Leisure club open to non-residents.

LANGNEY MARINE SERVICES LTD
Sovereign Harbour Marina, Pevensey Bay Road, Eastbourne, East Sussex BN23 6JH. Tel (01323) 470244 Fax (01323) 470255 We offer a complete service to the boat owner offering repairs on all types of engines, GRP, steel, wood, electronics, rigging, cleaning, etc. We are also contractors to the RNLI.

LOMBARD HOUSE, 182 HIGH STREET, TONBRIDGE, KENT TN9 1BY

Tel: 01732 376317   Fax: 01732 773117

One of the UK's largest specialist yacht underwriters and risk carriers. Range of insurance products for all types of pleasurecraft.

GENERAL INSURANCE COMPANY LTD

CONTACT YOUR LOCAL MARINE INSURANCE BROKER OR INTERMEDIARY.

LOMBARD GENERAL INSURANCE CO LTD
Lombard House, 182 High Street, Tonbridge, Kent TN9 1BY. Tel (01732) 376317 Fax (01732) 773117 One of the UK's largest specialist yacht underwriters and risk carriers. For full details of the range of insurance products available for all types of pleasurecraft, please contact your local marine insurance broker or intermediary.

PRACTICAL:		THEORY:
COMPETENT CREW		DAY SKIPPER
DAY/COASTAL SKIPPER		COASTAL SKIPPER
YACHTMASTER PREP		YACHTMASTER OFFSHORE
OWN BOAT TUITION	Moonfleet	VHF • FIRST AID
YACHT DELIVERIES	SAILING	DIESEL ENGINE

BASED IN BEAUTIFUL POOLE HARBOUR
4 Arun Path, Uckfield, East Sussex TN22 1NL. Tel/Fax: 01825 760604

MOONFLEET SAILING
4 Arun Path, Uckfield, East Sussex TN22 1NL. Tel/Fax (01825) 760604 Moonfleet Sailing offers all RYA recognised practical and theory courses from Competent Crew to Yachtmaster Offshore, VHF Radio, First Aid and Diesel Engine. Also available own boat tuition and yacht delivery.

NORWOOD MARINE
65 Royal Esplanade, Margate, Kent CT9 5ET. Tel/Fax (01843) 835711 e-mail: ggreenfield1@compuserve.com Marine consultant and advisers. Specialists in collisions, groundings,pilotage. Yachting and RYA examinations. Fellow of Nautical Institute and RIN.

ODYSSEUS YACHTING HOLIDAYS
33 Grand Parade, Brighton, East Sussex BN2 2QA. Tel (01273) 695094 Fax (01273) 688855 Templecraft Yacht Charters are bonded tour operators specialising in independent yacht charter holidays in the Mediterranean and in the Caribbean, and as Odysseus Yachting Holidays in flotilla sailing holidays in Corfu and the Ionian islands.

POSFORD DUVIVIER - THE TRIDENT FORUM
Eastchester House, Harlands Road, Haywards Heath, Sussex RH16 1PG. Tel (01444) 458551 Fax (01444) 440665 The Trident Forum aims to provide the maritime business community with first class professional services backed by substantial experience of working in the marine industry. Contact Peter Roach.

ProProtector LTD
74 Abingdon Road, Maidstone, Kent ME16 9EE. Tel (01622) 728738 Fax (01622) 727973 e-mail: prop_protector@compu serve.com Prevention is better than cure when it comes to fouled propelleRS. ProProtectors are now welcome and used worldwide as the most economical and simplest way to combat stray rope, netting, weed and plastic bags. Fit one before it is too late. Website: www.prop-protector.co.uk

QUEENBOROUGH HARBOUR
Town Quay, South Street, Queenborough, Isle of Sheppey, Kent ME11 5AF. Tel/Fax (01795) 662051 Moorings available in sought after position close to Thames and Medway estuaries.

RAMSGATE ROYAL HARBOUR MARINA
Harbour Office, Military Road, Ramsgate, Kent CT11 9LQ. Tel (01843) 592277 Fax (01843) 590941 Ramsgate Royal Harbour is situated on the south east coast, making an ideal base for crossing to the Continent. 24-hour access to finger pontoons. Comprehensive security systems. Amenities: Launederette, repairs, slipways, boatpark. Competitive rates for permanent berths and discounts for visitors' group bookings.

SILLETTE SONIC LTD
182 Church Hill Road, North Cheam, Sutton, Surrey SM3 8NF. Tel 020 8715 0100 Fax 020 8288 0742 Mobile: 077 10270107 Sillette manufactures a range of propulsion systems - stern drive, saildrives etc and sterngear. Markets Radice & Gori fixed and folding propellers. Acts as agents for Morse Controls, Yanmar and Lombardini marine engines, and Fuji Robin generators. See distribution depot Poole, Dorset - Area 2.

SIMPSON-LAWRENCE GROUP LIMITED
National Contact Line: 0870 9000 597 Website: www.simpson-lawrence.com

SOUTHERN MASTS & RIGGING (SELDÉN SOUTH EAST)
Marina Trade Centre, Brighton Marina, Brighton, East Sussex BN2 5UG. Tel (01273) 818189 Fax (01273) 818188 e-mail: sales@ smr-uk.com Mobile: 07803 086860 Regional centre for SELDÉN and KEMP integrated sailing systems. Builders of masts and spars, standing and running rigging. Rig surveyors. Suppliers of rope, wire, mast and deck hardware, booms, kickers and reefing systems. Mobile service available. Website: www.smr-uk.com

SWALE MARINE (ELECTRICAL)

The Old Stable, North Road
Queenborough, Kent ME11 5EH.

Tel: 01795 580930

FOR ALL YOUR ELECTRICAL AND ELECTRONIC NEEDS

Agents for Furuno, Autohelm, Raytheon and other major manufacturers. Registration Centre for BOATMARK Security, Medway & Swale HARBOURGUARD security cover

Fax: 01795 580238

SWALE MARINE (ELECTRICAL)
The Old Stable, North Road, Queenborough, Kent ME11 5EH. Tel (01795) 580930 Fax (01795) 580238 For all your electrical and electronic needs. Authorised agents for: Furuno, Autohelm, Raytheon and most major manufacturers. Fight crime with Harbourguard monitored security: Medway and Swale coverage - Boatmark registration centre.

TEMPLECRAFT YACHT CHARTERS
33 Grand Parade, Brighton, East Sussex BN2 2QA. Tel (01273) 695094 Fax (01273) 688855 Templecraft Yacht Charters are bonded tour operators specialising in independent yacht charter holidays in the Mediterranean and in the Caribbean, and as Odysseus Yachting Holidays in flotilla sailing holidays in Corfu and the Ionian islands.

THE TRIDENT FORUM
c/o Posford Duvivier, Eastchester House, Harlands Road, Haywards Heath, East Sussex RH16 1PG. Tel (01444) 458551 Fax (01444) 440665 e-mail: proach@posford-hh.co.uk The Trident Forum provides knowledge, experience and commitment in marine-related work. Our members are professional firms, skilled in a multitude of marine fields. The Forum's purpose is to make these skills easily accessible through a single point of reference.

X M YACHTING LTD
The Mill, Berwick, Polegate, East Sussex BN26 8SL. Tel (01323) 870092 Fax (01323) 870909 For the 21st Century. Extensive range of marine quality equipment including clothing, footwear, inflatables, safety equipment, liferafts and the XM Quickfit range of lifejackets manufactured to CE standard, and the TH-5 offshore breathable suit. Performance technology - designed to be worn. Please call 01323 870092 for further details and catalogue or visit your local stockist.

THAMES ESTUARY   (AREA 4)
North Foreland to Great Yarmouth

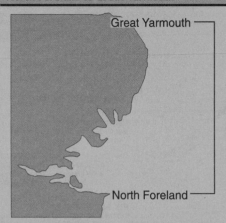

Great Yarmouth

North Foreland

A S A P SUPPLIES - DIRECT ORDER
Beccles, Suffolk NR34 7TD. Tel (01502) 716993 Fax (01502) 711680 e-mail: infomma@asap-supplies.com Worldwide supply of equipment and spares. Anodes, cables, contrads, coolers, exhausts, fenders, fuel systems, gear boxes, impellers, insulation, lights, marinisation, panels, propellers and shafts, pumps, seacocks, silencers, sound proofing, steering, toilets, trimtabs, water heaters, wipers and much much more.... **Website:** www.asap-supplies.com

C CLAIMS Loss Adjusters
PO Box 8, Romford, Essex RM4 1AL. Tel Helpline: 020 8502 6999 Fax 020 8500 1005 Personal: 020 8502 6644 e-mail: cclaims@compuserve.com C Claims are specialist marine and small craft claims adjusters with a central record of stolen vessels and equipment. They have provided a unique service to marine insurers since 1979 and welcome trade and private enquiries. They are represented throughout the world.

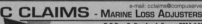
CHELSEA HARBOUR LTD
108 The Chambers, Chelsea Harbour, London SW10 0XF. Tel 020 7761 8600 Fax 020 7352 7868 A tranquil and intimate marina of 55 berths close to the heart of the west end of London. 5-Star hotel, restaurants and bars. Overnight pontoon and amenities. 24-hour security patrols and CCTV.

FOX'S MARINA IPSWICH LTD
The Strand, Wherstead, Ipswich, Suffolk IP2 8SA. Tel (01473) 689111 Fax (01473) 601737 The most comprehensive boatyard facility on the east coast. Extensive chandlery. Marina access 24-hours. Diesel dock, two travel hoists to 70 tons, 10 ton crane. Full electronics, rigging, engineering, stainless steel services. Specialists in osmosis and spray painting.

HALCON MARINE LTD
The Point, Canvey Island, Essex SS8 7TL. Tel (01268) 511611 Fax (01268) 510044 Marine engineers, repairs and full boatyard services in this quiet and picturesque area. Berths, moorings, slipping facilities. Summer and winter storage. Dry dock (70t max), diesel 1 to 2 hours ±. Water, electric, toilets and showers. A friendly welcome awaits you.

THE HARBOUR LIGHTS RESTAURANT
(Walton-on-the-Naze)
Titchmarsh Marina, Coles Lane, Walton-on-the-Naze, Essex CO14 8SL. Tel (01255) 851887 Fax (01255) 677300 Open 7 days a week the Harbour Lights offers a welcome to yachtsmen and land-lubbers alike. Fine views over the marina and Walton Backwaters. Hearty breakfasts are served 8am - 10am, and extensive bar meals are available all day. Sizzling summer weekend barbecues, weather permitting. Silver service restaurant with traditional English fare.

JEFFREY WOOD MARINE LTD
53a North Street, Romford, Essex RM1 1BA. Tel +44 (0) 1708 733454 Fax +44 (0) 1708 747431 Freephone 0800 0832530 e-mail: woodship@ukonline.com.u Consultant forensic marine engineers, boat designers and surveyors, naval architects. Osmosis and ferro cement specialists - wood or steel boats of all types.

KELVIN HUGHES CHARTS & MARITIME SUPPLIES
New North Road, Hainault, Ilford, Essex IG6 2UR. Tel 020 8500 1020 Books and charts. DoT Certified Compass Adjusters - available day or night.

LONDON YACHT CENTRE LTD - LYC
13 Artillery Lane, London E1 7LP. Tel 020 7247 2047 Fax 020 7377 5680 Two minutes from Liverpool Street railway station. Four floors with 10000 top name product lines including Musto, Henri Lloyd and Douglas Gill. Extensive range of chandlery, inflatables, outboards, liferafts, electronics, software, books, charts, optics, rope and chain. All at discount prices.

MARINECALL - TELEPHONE INFORMATION SERVICES
Avalon House, London EC2A 4PJ. Tel 020 7631 6000 Marinecall provides detailed coastal weather forecasts for 17 different regions up to 5 days ahead from the Met Office. For a full fax list of services dial 0891 24 66 80. Telephone forecasts are updated daily, morning and afternoon.

MARTELLO YACHT SERVICES
Mulberry House, Mulberry Road, Canvey Island, Essex SS8 0PR. Tel/Fax (01268) 681970 Manufacturers and suppliers of made-to-measure upholstery, covers, hoods, dodgers, sailcovers, curtains and cushions etc. Repairs undertaken. DIY materials, chandlery and fitting-out supplies.

W A MacGREGOR & CO - MARINE SURVEYORS
Dooley Terminal Building, The Dock, Felixstowe, Suffolk IP11 8SW. Tel (01394) 676034 Fax (01394) 675515 Mobile: (0860) 361279 Yacht and small craft surveys for all purposes and in all materials. Specialist in wood and restoration of classic craft, continually involved with steel, aluminium, GRP. Charter and workboat codes YDSA surveyor.

PARKER & KAY SAILMAKERS - EAST
Suffolk Yacht Harbour, Levington, Ipswich, Suffolk IP10 0LN. Tel (01473) 659878 Fax (01473) 659197 e-mail: pandkeast @aol.com A complete sailmaking service, from small repairs to the construction of custom designed sails for racing or cruising yachts. Covers constructed for sail and powercraft, plus the supply of all forms of sail handling hardware.

PORT FLAIR LTD
Bradwell Marina, Waterside, Bradwell-on-Sea, Essex CM0 7RB. Tel (01621) 776235/776391 300 pontoon berths with water and electricity, petrol and diesel, chandlery, marine slip/hoistage to 20 tons. Repairs, winter lay-ups, licensed club, yacht brokerage.

PREMIUM LIFERAFT SERVICES
Liferaft House, Burnham Business Park, Burnham-on-Crouch, Essex CM0 8TE. Tel (01621) 784858 Fax (01621) 785934 Freephone 0800 243673 e-mail:liferaftuk@aol.com Hire and sales of DoT and RORC approved liferafts. Long and short-term hire from 18 depots nationwide. Servicing and other safety equipment available.

S I R S NAVIGATION LTD
186a Milton Road, Swanscombe, Kent DA10 0LX. Tel (01322) 383672 Books and Charts. DoT Certified Compass Adjusters - available day or night.

SEATH INSTRUMENTS (1992) LTD
Unit 30, Colville Road Works, Colville Road, Lowestoft NR33 9QS. Tel (01502) 573811 Books and charts. DoT Certified Compass Adjusters - available day or night.

SHOTLEY MARINA LTD
Shotley Gate, Ipswich, Suffolk IP9 1QJ. Tel (01473) 788982 Fax (01473) 788868 A modern state of the art marina with 350 berths offering all the services expected. Open 24-hours with full security. Access all states of tide, ideal cruising base. Well stocked chandlery and general store, repair facilities, laundry and ironing centre, showers/baths and toilets. Restaurants, bar, children's room, TV/video and function rooms with dance floor and bar. Disabled facilities.

SIMPSON-LAWRENCE GROUP LIMITED
National Contact Line: 0870 9000 597 Website: www.simpson-lawrence.com

A M SMITH (MARINE) LTD
33 Epping Way, Chingford, London E4 7PB. Tel 020 8529 6988 Books and charts.

SIMPSON-LAWRENCE GROUP LIMITED
National Contact Line: 0870 9000 597 Website: www.simpson-lawrence.com

SOUTH DOCK MARINA
South Lock Office, Rope Street, Plough Way, London SE16 1TX. Tel 020 7252 2244 Fax 020 7237 3806 London's largest marina. 200+ berths. Spacious, tranquil setting. Manned 24 hours. Lift-out for 20 tonnes. Competitve mooring rates.

SOUTH EASTERN MARINE SERVICES LTD
Units 13 & 25, Olympic Business Centre, Paycocke Road, Basildon, Essex SS14 3EX. Tel (01268) 534427 Fax (01268) 281009 e-mail: sems@bt.internet.com Liferaft service, sales and hire, 1-65 persons. Approved by major manufacturers and MSA. Callers welcome. View your own raft. Family owned and operated. Inflatable boat repairs and spares. WE WANT YOU TO COME BACK. Website: www.sems.com

ST KATHARINE HAVEN
50 St Katharine's Way, London E1 9LB. Tel 020 7264 5312 Fax 020 7702 2252 In the heart of London, St Katharine's 200-berth Haven offers facilities for 100'+ vessels, access to the West End and City, its own shops, restaurants, health club and yacht club, plus water, electric, showers and sewerage disposal. Entry via a lock. Operational HW - 2hrs to HW +1½hrs London Bridge. October-March 0800-1800. April-August 0600-2030 or by arrangement.

ST MARGARETS INSURANCES LTD
153-155 High Street, Penge, London SE20 7DL. Tel 020 8778 6161 Fax 020 8659 1968 e-mail: yachts@stminsurance.co.uk Over 30 years dedicated to insuring yachts and pleasurecraft. Many unique policies available only through St Margarets. Immediate quotations available. Website: www.stminsurance.co.uk

SUFFOLK YACHT HARBOUR LTD
Levington, Ipswich, Suffolk IP10 0LN. Tel (01473) 659240 Fax (01473) 659632 500-berths - access at all states of tide (dredged to 2.5 meters at LW Springs). Boat hoist facilities up to 60 tons. Full boatyard services, chandlery, gas, diesel, petrol, engineering, sailmaking, electronics. Club house and restaurant.

TITCHMARSH MARINA
Coles Lane, Walton-on-the-Naze, Essex CO14 8SL. Tel (01255) 672185 Fax (01255) 851901 Friendly service in the peaceful backwaters. Visiting yachtsmen welcome. Sheltered marina berths. Full marina facilities: Travel-lift, cranage, 16 amp electricity, diesel. Winter storage. Restaurant and bar open every day. (See Harbour Lights Restaurant.)

TOLLESBURY MARINA
The Yacht Harbour, Tollesbury, Maldon, Essex CM9 8SE. Tel (01621) 869202 Fax (01621) 868489 e-mail: marina@wood rolfe.demon.uk VHF Ch37 and 80 Dedicated to customer service, this family-run marina can offer 240 marina berths with water and electricity on all pontoons. Cruising club with bar, restaurant, swimming pool and tennis courts. Repair workshop, osmosis treatment centre. Full brokerage service listing over 200 boats.

WARD & McKENZIE (East Anglia) LTD - Head office
3 Wherry Lane, Ipswich, Suffolk IP4 1LG. Tel (01473) 255200
Fax (01473) 255044 e-mail: collett@wardmck.keme.co.uk
National and International marine surveyors. Technical and legal
consultants. Contact: Clive Brown - Mobile: 0585 190357, Mike
Williamson - Mobile: 0498 578312 and Ian Collett - Mobile: 0370
655306. River Ouse Office: 01462 701461. **Website: www.ward-mckenzie.co.uk**

UPPER THAMES   **(AREA 4)**
Navigable west of Westminster Bridge

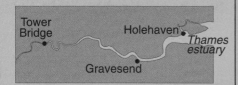

W BATES & SON BOATBUILDERS LTD
Bridge Wharf, Chertsey, Surrey KT16 8LG. Tel (01932) 562255
Fax (01932) 565600 110-berth marina in quiet picturesque area
and additional riverside moorings. Full facilities including electricity
to most berths, toilets and showers. 12-ton crane and hard standing
for winter storage. Always a welcome to visitors from our friendly
staff. Sales office open seven days a week.

**BISHOP SKINNER
INTERNATIONAL INSURANCE BROKERS**
Oakley Crescent, City Road, London EC1V 1NU. Tel 020 7566
5800 Fax 020 7608 2171 Dinghy Insurance - As insurance brokers
to the RYA we offer cover for accidental damage, racing risks, 30-
days European extension, discounts for dinghy instructors, third
party indemnity of £2,000,000, no claim bonus (transferable) and
first class security. Immediate quotation and instant cover all at
competitive rates.

CHISWICK QUAY MARINA LTD
Marina Office, Chiswick Quay, London W4 3UR. Tel 020 8994
8743 Small, secluded, peaceful marina on tidal Thames at Chiswick.
Slipway, marine engineers and electricians, power, water, toilets
and sluice. Some residential moorings.

DAVID M CANNELL & ASSOCIATES
River House, Quay Street, Wivenhoe, Essex CO9 9DD.

FORESIGHT OPTICAL
13 New Road, Banbury, Oxfordshire OX16 9PN. Tel (01295)
264365 Suppliers of general purpose and nautical binoculars,
spotting scopes, astronomical telescopes, night vision equipment,
microscopes, magnifiers, spotlights, tripods and accessories.
National mail order service.

KELVIN HUGHES
City of London: 142 Minories, London EC3N 1NH. Tel 020 7709
9076 Fax 020 7481 1298 e-mail: minories@kelvinhughes.co.uk
The world's largest chart agency. The world's finest nautical
bookshops, plus software, navigation instruments, for all your chart
table requirements.

MARINE RADIO SERVICES LTD
50 Merton Way, East Molesley, Surrey KT8 1PQ. Tel 020 8979
7979 Fax 020 8783 1032 Maritime Electronics: Service, sales and
repair of marine radio, radar, autopilots and electronic equipment.

NEPTUNE NAVIGATION SOFTWARE
P O Box 5106, Riseley, Berkshire RG7 1FD. Tel 0118-988 5309
Route Passage Planning, Tides and Tidal Stream Predictions,
Waypoint Manager - software for your PC or CE machines. A range
of intuitively easy to use navigation programs at affordable prices.
Website: www.neptunenav.demon.co.uk

OCEAN LEISURE LTD
11-14 Northumberland Avenue, London WC2N 5AQ. Tel 020 7930
5050 Fax 020 7930 3032 e-mail: info@oceanleisure.co.uk
Complete range of sailing clothing, swim and beachwear stocked
all year round. Chandlery includes marine electronic equipment,
marine antiques, books and charts. Also canoeing, underwater
photography, diving and waterskiing specialists. Learn to scuba
dive. Website: www.oceanleisure.co.uk

ROYAL INSTITUTE OF NAVIGATION
1 Kensington Gore, London SW7 2AT. Tel 020 7591 3130
Fax 020 7591 3131 Forum for all interested in navigation - Air: Sea:
Land: Space.

SIMPSON-LAWRENCE GROUP LIMITED
National Contact Line: 0870 9000 597 Website: www.simpson-lawrence.com

SOFTWAVE
Riverside, Mill Lane, Taplow, Maidenhead SL6 0AA. Tel 01628
637777 Fax 01628 773030 Provider of PC based navigation
Seavision hardware and *Nobeltec* and *Transas* software. Using
charts drawn from Admiralty sources the quality navigation software
that we provide can be easily installed to customers own laptops
or computers. For on-board installations we manufacture hardware
that include sun-readable, waterproof screens linked to high
performance, ruggedised compact PCs.
Website: www.softwave.co.uk

STANFORDS CHARTS
Editorial Office, PO Box 2747, Tollesbury, Maldon, Essex CM9
8XE. Sales Office: 9-10 Southern Court, South Street, Reading,
Berkshire RG1 4QS. Tel 01621 868580 Fax 0118-959 8283
e-mail:sales@allweathercharts.co.uk Stanford Charts - the best
in coastal and harbour charts. Publishers of waterproof tear-resistant
yachtsmen's charts. Full chart information can be found on our
website, and further help can be had from our editorial office.
www.allweathercharts.co.uk

EAST ENGLAND (AREA 5)
Blakeney to Berwick-on-Tweed

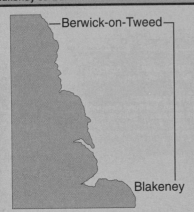

—Berwick-on-Tweed—

Blakeney

BURGH CASTLE MARINA
Butt Lane, Burgh Castle, Norfolk, Norwich NR31 9PZ. Tel (01493) 780331 Fax (01493) 780163 e-mail: rdw_chesham@ compuserve.com 100 serviced pontoons and quay moorings accessible at all tides. Secure car and boat parking. Adjoining boatyard services, access to holiday park showers, laundry and heated pool. Riverside pub and shop. Complex open all year.

Breathtakingly Beautiful Burgh
Cruise centre for Broadland and the Norfolk Coast
Our peaceful location at the confluence of the Yare and Waveney Rivers and the Head of Breydon Water is ideal for day cruising inland or at sea.

BURGH CASTLE MARINA *& CARAVAN PARK*

Tel: 01493 780331 Fax: 01493 780163
E-mail: rdw_chesham@compuserve.com

B COOKE & SON LTD
Kingston Observatory, 58-59 Market Place, Hull HU1 1RH. Tel (01482) 223454 Books and Charts. DoT Certified Compass Adjusters - available day or night.

CREST NICHOLSON MARINAS LTD - NORTH SHIELDS

Royal Quays Marina, Coble Dene Road, North Shields NE29 6DU. Tel 0191-272 8282 Fax 0191-272 8288 Situated 2 miles from the entrance of the river Tyne. 24-hour lock access. Extensive range of facilities.

HARTLEPOOL MARINA
Tel: 01429 865744

THE PREMIER MARINA OF THE NORTH SEES THE COMPLETION OF THE MASSIVE REDEVELOPMENT FOR THE YEAR 2000.

A MARINA AND MUCH MORE

700 BERTHS • 300 TON BOAT HOIST AND STORAGE.
24-HOUR SECURITY • FULL SERVICES • 24-HOUR LOCK ACCESS
PUBS • RESTAURANTS • CINEMA
LUXURY LEISURE • RESIDENTIAL AND RETAIL FACILITIES.

PLEASE CALL 01429 865744 FOR MORE INFORMATION
24 HOURS

LOCK OFFICE, SLAKE TERRACE, HARTLEPOOL, CLEVELAND TS24 0RU

HARTLEPOOL MARINA
Lock Office, Slake Terrace, Hartlepool, Cleveland TS24 0RU. Tel (01429) 865744 Fax (01429) 865947 The north's premier marina. The year 2000 sees the completion of a massive redevelopment to include 700 berths, a new 300 ton boat hoist along with luxury leisure, residential and retail facilities on-site. Please call 01429 865744 for more information 24 hours.

HULL MARINA LTD
Warehouse 13, Kingston Street, Hull HU1 2DQ. Tel (01482) 613451 Fax (01482) 224148 Four-Anchor marina. Situated 5 minutes from the centre of Hull and all national and international transport systems. First class leisure, boatyard and brokerage facilities. 4-Star hotel and quayside restaurants. Professional and caring staff. Competitive rates.

JOHN LILLEY & GILLIE LTD
Clive Street, North Shields, Tyne & Wear NE29 6LF. Tel 0191-257 2217 Books and Charts. DoT Certified Compass Adjusters - available day or night.

LIONSTAR YACHT & MOTORBOAT SURVEYS
The Lawn, Ashbrooke Road, Sunderland, Tyne & Wear SR2 7HQ. Tel 0191-528 6422 Lionstar Yacht Services, Sunderland - Surveys of sailing and motor yachts by chartered marine engineers and naval architects with full PI and PL insurance. Northern England and southern Scotland. Telephone Derek May on 0191-528 6422 for quote.

Rodney Clapson Marine Surveys
16 Whitecross Street,   Member of the YDSA
Barton-on-Humber DN18 5EU
Tel: 01652 632108 & 635620   Fax: 01652 660517   E-mail: surveys@clapsons.co.uk

East coast from the Wash to Northumberland and the Netherlands.
Purchase and insurance surveys, damage repair and osmosis supervision Including Inland Waterways

---

RODNEY CLAPSON MARINE SURVEYS
16 Whitecross Street, Barton-on-Humber DN18 5EU. Tel (01652) 632108 & 635620 Fax (01652) 660517 e-mail: surveys@ clapsons.co.uk Surveys for purchase and insurance. Damage repair and osmosis supervision. East coast from the Wash to Northumberland including inland waterways. Surveys in the Netherlands. We are YDSA members.

SIMPSON-LAWRENCE GROUP LIMITED
National Contact Line: 0870 9000 597 Website: www.simpson-lawrence.com

WARD & McKENZIE (North East) LTD
11 Sherbuttgate Drive, Pocklington, York YO4 2ED. Tel (01759) 304322 Fax (01759) 303194 e-mail: nev.styles@dial.pipex.com National and International marine surveyors. Technical and legal consultants. Contact: Neville Styles - Mobile: 0831 335943. Website: www.ward-mckenzie.co.uk

---

SOUTH EAST SCOTLAND   (AREA 6)
Eyemouth to Rattray Head

Rattray Head

Eyemouth

PETERHEAD BAY AUTHORITY
Bath House, Bath Street, Peterhead AB42 1DX. Tel (01779) 474020 Fax (01779) 475712 Contact: Stephen Paterson. Peterhead Bay Marina offers fully serviced pontoon berthing for local and visiting boat owners. Local companies provide a comprehensive range of supporting services. Ideal stopover for vessels heading to/from Scandinavia or the Caledonian canal. **Website: www.peterhead-bay.co.uk**

SIMPSON-LAWRENCE GROUP LIMITED
National Contact Line: 0870 9000 597 Website: www.simpson-lawrence.com

THOMAS GUNN NAVIGATION SERVICES
Anchor House, 62 Regents Quay, Aberdeen AB11 5AR.
Tel (01224) 595045 Books and charts. DoT Certified Compass Adjusters - available day or night.

NORTH EAST SCOTLAND   (AREA 7)
Rattray Head to Cape Wrath including Orkney and Shetland

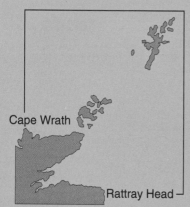

CALEY MARINA
Canal Road, Inverness IV3 6NF. Tel +44 (0) 1463 236539 Fax +44 (0) 1463 238323 e-mail: info@caleymarina.com Open 08.30 - 17.30. Berths: 50 Pontoons (visitors available). Facilities: Fuel, water, pump-out facilities, provisions (nearby shops), repair, cranage, secure storage afloat and ashore. Comprehensive chandlery, showers, workshop. Situated at eastern end of Caledonian canal above Muirtown locks. Access via sea locks 4 hours either side of high water. **Website: www.caleymarina.com**

Caley Marina & Chandlery
Canal Road, Inverness IV3 8NF, Scotland
Tel (01463) 236539 Fax (01463) 238323
Comprehensive chandlery, showers, workshop.
Situated at the eastern end of Caledonian canal above Muirtown locks. Access via sea locks four hours either side of high water.

Open 08.30 - 17.30. Berths: 50 Pontoon (visitors available) Facilities: Fuel, water, pump out facilities, provisions (nearby shops), repair, cranage, secure storage afloat and ashore.

LOCH NESS CHARTERS
The Boatyard, Dochgarroch, Inverness IV3 6JY. Tel (01463) 861303 Fax (01463) 861353 Yacht and cruiser charter. Boat services and repairs. Hardstanding and slipway. Diesel supply. Boat finishing.

SCOTTISH LOCH & CANALS
Cruise or sail the Caledonian Canal - through the beautiful, Great Glen - with Loch Ness Charters. Tuition available for both yachts and cruisers. Contact us now for the 2000 season.
LOCH NESS CHARTERS The Boatyard, Dochgarroch, Inverness IV3 6JY. Tel: 01463 861303 Fax: 01463 861353

PAUL JOHNSON LTD Marine Vessel Management
Unit 6, 24 Station Square, Inverness IV1 1LD. Tel 07074 370 470 Fax 07074 370 570 e-mail: info@pauljohnson.co.uk We manage all aspects of the day to day and long-term running of your vessel. Giving store support to you or your captain. Leaving you the pleasure of owning a boat. Independent insurance and finance, brokerage, crews, registration and maintain, but NO HEADACHES! **Website: www.pauljohnson.co.uk**

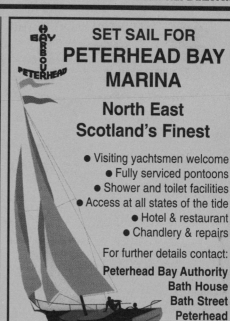

SET SAIL FOR
PETERHEAD BAY MARINA
North East Scotland's Finest

- Visiting yachtsmen welcome
- Fully serviced pontoons
- Shower and toilet facilities
- Access at all states of the tide
- Hotel & restaurant
- Chandlery & repairs

For further details contact:
**Peterhead Bay Authority
Bath House
Bath Street
Peterhead
AB42 1DX**

*Tel: (01779) 474020 Fax: (01779) 475712
Website: www.Peterhead-Bay.co.uk*

SIMPSON-LAWRENCE GROUP LIMITED
National Contact Line: 0870 9000 597 Website: www.simpson-lawrence.com

NORTH WEST/CENTRAL WEST SCOTLAND   (AREA 8)
Cape Wrath to Crinan Canal

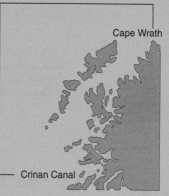

ARDFERN YACHT CENTRE
Ardfern By Lochgilphead, Argyll PA31 8QN. Tel (01852) 500247/636 Fax (01852) 500624 and 07000 ARDFERN Boatyard with full repair and maintenance facilities. Timber and GRP repairs, painting and engineering. Sheltered moorings and pontoon berthing. Winter storage, chandlery, showers, fuel, Calor, brokerage, 20-ton boat hoist, rigging. Hotel, bars and restaurant.

ARDORAN MARINE
Lerags, Oban, Argyll PA34 4SE. Tel (01631) 566123 Fax (01631) 566611 All marine services. Moorings and self-catering chalets.

BRIDGE HOUSE HOTEL
St Clair Road, Ardrishaig, Argyll PA30 8EW. Tel (01546) 606379 Fax (01546) 606593 4-Crown Highly Commended. Close to the Crinan canal sea lock with views down to Loch Fyne to Arran and Gower. We offer a warm welcome to all visitors. Comfortable en suit bedrooms, good food and friendly bar. Open all year.

CRAOBH MARINA
By Lochgilphead, Argyll PA31 8UD. Tel (01852) 500222 Fax (01852) 500252 VHF Ch37 and 80 (M). 250-berth marina on Loch Shuna. Water, electricity, diesel and gas. Full boatyard services.Chandlery. Brokerage. Insurance. Shops, bar. 24-hour access.

THE CREGGANS INN
Strachur, Argyll PA27 8BX. Tel (01369) 860279 Fax (01369) 860637 e-mail: info@creggans-inn.co.uk The Creggans Inn makes a useful stop for lunch, dinner or overnight respite!Five moorings available. Bar meals from 12 noon - 2.30pm and 6pm to 9pm (Saturday and Sunday 12 noon - 8pm). Excellent restaurant serving from 7pm to 9.30pm. Shower and changing facilities for our travelling yachtsmen.

CRINAN BOATS LTD
Crinan, Lochgilphead, Argyll PA31 8SP. Tel (01546) 830232 Fax (01546) 830281 Boatbuilders, chandlers, engineers, slipping, repairs, charts, electricians, pontoon, moorings, showers, laundry and basic stores.

THE GALLEY OF LORNE INN
Ardfern, By Lochgilphead, Argyll PA31 8QN. Tel (01852) 500284 A warm welcome for yachtsmen and women at The Galley. Only two minutes from Ardfern yacht centre. Excellent food. Bar meals available all year. Restaurant open Easter to November. Friendly pub with log fires.

ISLANDER YACHT CHARTERS & ISLANDER SAILING SCHOOL
7 Torinturk, Argyll PA29 6YE. Tel (01880) 820012 Fax (01880) 821143 e-mail: r.fleck@virgin.net Sail the spectacular and uncrowded waters of the Scottish west coast and Hebrides from our base at Ardfern Yacht Centre, Argyll. Bareboat or skippered yachts from 33' to 44', all DoT certificated. RYA recognised sailing school, YM, CS, DS and CC courses from March to October.

KAMES HOTEL
Kames, By Tighnabruaich, Argyll PA21 2AF. Tel (01700) 811489 Fax (01700) 811 283 On the Kyles of Bute with 15 free moorings. Good food, real ales, fine malts. Showers available for visitors. 10 en-suite bedrooms. Regular music nights. Fresh local seafood in season.

SIMPSON-LAWRENCE GROUP LIMITED
National Contact Line: 0870 9000 597 Website: www.simpson-lawrence.com

SLEAT MARINE SERVICES
Ardvasar, Isle of Skye IV45 8RS. Tel (01471) 844216 Fax (01471) 844387 e-mail: enquiries @sleatmarineservices.co.uk Yacht charter (bareboat and skippered) from Armadale Bay, Isle of Skye.Six yachts 34' to 40' LOA. All medium to heavy displacement blue water cruisers. Fuel, water and emergency services for passing yachts with problems. Website: www.sleatmarineservices.co.uk

TIGH AN EILEAN HOTEL
Shieldaig by Strathcaron, Ross-shire IV54 8XN. Tel (01520) 755251 Fax (01520) 755321 On the edge of the sea amongst some of the most dramatic landscapes in the Highlands, this friendly 12-bedroom hotel is run under the personal supervision of the proprietors. Our restaurant serves local produce cooked with flair and complemented with good wine. Excellent drying room for those wet clothes!!

THE TOBERMORAY HOTEL - STB 3-Star
53 Main Street, Tobermoray, Isle of Mull, Argyll PA75 6NT. Tel (01688) 302091 Fax (01688) 302254 Situated on the beautiful Tobermoray Bay on the lovely Isle of Mull the Tobermoray hotel offers a traditional Scottish welcome to all visiting yachtsmen. Come and eat at our excellent restaurant serving delicious fish and steak with good wines and spirits.

SOUTH WEST SCOTLAND   (AREA 9)
Crinan Canal to Mull of Galloway

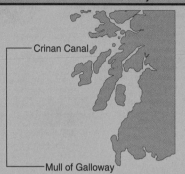

Crinan Canal

Mull of Galloway

BROWN SON & FERGUSON LTD
4-10 Darnley Street, Glasgow G41 2SD. Tel 0141-429 1234
Books and charts.

CLYDE MARINA - ARDROSSAN
The Harbour, Ardrossan, Ayrshire KA22 8DB. Tel (01294) 607077 Fax (01294) 607076 e-mail: clydmarina@aol.com Located on the north Ayrshire coast within easy cruising reach of Arran, the Cumbrae Islands, Bute and the Kintyre Peninsula. Deep draught harbour with 200 pontoon berths and quayside for vessels up to 120'. 20-ton hoist, undercover storage and most services and facilities. Ancasta Scotland brokerage, also Beneteau, Nimbus-Maxi, Westerly yachts, SeaRay and Marlin RIBs.

KELVIN HUGHES
Glasgow: 26 Holland Street, Glasgow G2 4LR. Tel 0141-221 5452 Fax 0141-221 4688 e-mail: glasgow@kelvinhughes.co.uk The world's largest chart agency. The world's finest nautical bookshops, plus software, navigation instruments, for all your chart table requirements.

KIP MARINA
The Yacht Harbour, Inverkip, Renfrewshire PA16 0AS. Tel (01475) 521485 Fax (01475) 521298 Marina berths for vessels up to 65' LOA. Full boatyard facilities including travel hoist, crane, on-site engineers, GRP repairs etc. Bar, restaurant, saunas, launderette and chandlery. Distributors for Moody yachts, Northshore and Searanger motor yachts.

LARGS YACHT HAVEN
Irvine Road, Largs, Ayrshire KA30 8EZ. Tel (01475) 675333 Fax (01475) 672245 Perfectly located 600-berth marina with full services afloat and ashore. 45-ton travel hoist operational 7 days; fuel (diesel and petrol); gas and ice on sale 24-hours. Bar, coffee shop, dive shop plus usual marine services.

LIVERPOOL & GLASGOW SALVAGE ASSOCIATION
St Andrews House, 385 Hillington Road, Glasgow G52 4BL. Tel 0141-303 4573 Fax 0141-303 4513 e-mail: lgsaglasgow@compuserve.com Marine surveyors and consultants: Pre-purchase, damage, insurance (risk and liabilities) surveys on all vessels including yachts, fishing vessels and commercial ships. Offices also at Liverpool, Hull, Leicester and Grangemouth. Overseas work also undertaken.

THE OYSTERCATCHER RESTAURANT
Otter Ferry, Argyll PA21 2DH. Tel (01700) 821229 Fax (01700) 821300 Situated on Loch Fyne, just north of the Otter Spit, about one hour's sailing from the Crinan canal. Moorings (insured to 12t) free to patrons. French chef and superb food, seafood our speciality. 1996 Tourist Board winner 'BEST PLACE TO EAT'. Children's play area.

RHU MARINA LTD
Helensburgh, Dunbartonshire G84 8LH. Tel (01436) 820238 Fax (01436) 821039 e-mail: any@rhumarina.force9.co.uk Berths accessible at all times and moorings available on the Clyde at the entrance to the Gareloch and 30 minutes from Glasgow. Hotels, shops and yacht clubs all adjacent.

SCOTTISH BOAT JUMBLE
Steelbank Cottage, Dalgarven, Nr Kilwinning, Ayrshire KA13 6PL. Fax (01294) 552417 Mobile: 0421 888789 New and used nautical bargains galore. Everything from radios, safety equipment, clothing and deck equipment. Jumbles held in Scotland twice a year - Ireland and Newcastle once a year. See main advertisement.

SIMPSON-LAWRENCE GROUP LIMITED
National Contact Line: 0870 9000 597 Website: www.simpson-lawrence.com

TROON YACHT HAVEN
The Harbour, Troon, Ayrshire KA10 6DJ. Tel (01292) 315553 Fax (01292) 312836 Sheltered harbour of 350 berths. Well placed for those on passage to and from the Clyde. Bar, restaurant, marine services. Attractive seafront town with good beaches and championship golf.

E K WALLACE & SON LTD
Whittinghame House, 1099 Great Western Road, Glasgow G12 0AA. Tel 0141-334 7222 Fax 0141-334 7700 Pre-purchase, insurance and valuation surveys on sail and power vessels, private and commercial, UK and abroad. Approved for Code of Practice, registration and tonnage meaurements. Members YDSA, SCMS. Offices in Glasgow, Edinburgh and Argyll.

NORTH WEST ENGLAND   (AREA 10)
Isle of Man and North Wales,
Mull of Galloway to Bardsey Island

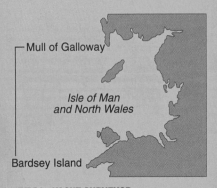

Mull of Galloway

Isle of Man
and North Wales

Bardsey Island

AMYDSA - YACHT SURVEYOR
Penrallt Cottage, Cichle Hill, Llandegfan, Anglesey LL59 5TD. Tel/Fax (01248) 712358 Mobile: 0374 4411681 Prompt and professional surveys prior to purchase and for insurance purposes throughout Wales, the north west and Midlands. Services also include valuations, osmosis inspections and consultancy. Surveyor for MCA Code of Practice.

CREST NICHOLSON MARINAS LTD - CONWY
Conwy Marina, Conwy Morfa, Conwy, Gwynedd LL32 8EP. Tel (01492) 593000 Fax (01492) 572111 Conwy Marina is ideally placed on the south shore of the Conwy estuary. The marina is set within idyllic surroundings and has comprehensive facilities. Road access is extremely convenient, with the A55 dual carriageway passing close by.

DOLPHIN MARITIME SOFTWARE LTD
713 Cameron House, White Cross, Lancaster LA1 4XQ. Tel/Fax (01524) 841946 e-mail: 100417.744@compuserve.com Marine computer programs for IBM PC, Psion and Sharp pocket computers. Specialists in navigation, tidal prediction and other programs for both yachting and commercial uses. Website: www.ourworld.compuserve.com/homepages/dolphin_software

DUBOIS, PHILLIPS & McCALLUM LTD
Mersey Chambers, Covent Garden, Liverpool L2 8UF. Tel 0151-236 2776 Books and charts.

FIDDLERS FERRY YACHT HAVEN
Off Station Road, Penketh, Warrington, Cheshire WA5 2UJ. Tel (01925) 727519 Sheltered moorings upto 6'6" draught, 50' long. Access through lock from river Mersey 1½ hours either side of high tide. Signed from A652. Boatyard and lift-out facilities. Annual rate per foot £8.25.

FOX ASSOCIATES
Cambria, Rhos y Coed, Bethesda, Bangor, Gywnedd LL57 3NW. Tel/Fax (01248) 601079 Marine surveyors and consultants. Claims investigation and damage reports. Code of Practice examiners. Valuations and condition surveys.

HOYLAKE SAILING SCHOOL
43a Market Street, Hoylake, Wirral L47 2BG. Tel 0151-632 4664 Fax 0151-632 4776 e-mail: purser@hss.ac.uk RYA recognised shorebased teaching establishment offering a wide range of courses including Day Skipper to Yachtmaster Ocean, VHF, Radar and First Aid. Day, evening or intensive classes. Pratical courses by arrangement. Books, charts and gifts available by mail order. Website: www.hss.ac.uk

ISLE OF ANGLESEY COUNTY COUNCIL
Highways & Technical Services Department, Council Offices, Llangefni, Anglesey LL77 7TW Tel (01248) 752331 Fax (01248) 724839 Berths and moorings available at Menai bridge, Amlwch harbour and north east Menai Straits (Beaumaris). Winter storage at competitive rates available at Beaumaris and Amlwch. Contact Maritime Officer 01248 752331 for details.

JOSEPH P LAMB & SONS
Maritime Building (opposite Albert Dock), Wapping, Liverpool L1 8DQ. Tel 0151-709 4861 Fax 0151-709 2786 Situated in the centre of Liverpool, J P Lamb have provided a service to world shipping for over 200 years. All chandlery supplies, clothing, rope, paint and flags are available. Full sailmaking and repairs. Kemp Retail Outlet for spars and rigging. Open Mon to Fri 8am to 5.30pm - Sat 9am to 12.30pm.

LIVERPOOL MARINA
Coburg Dock, Sefton Street, Liverpool L3 4BP. Tel 0151-709 0578 (2683 after 5pm) Fax 0151-709 8731 300-berth yacht harbour. All serviced pontoons. Tidal access HW + or - 2½ hours approximately, depending on draught. 60-ton hoist, workshops, bar and restaurant, toilets and showers. City centre one mile. Open all year. Active yacht club and yacht brokerage.

MANX MARINE
35 North Quay, Douglas, Isle of Man IM1 4LB. Tel/Fax (01624) 674842 The Island's leading and most established yacht chandlery. Stockists of quality foul-weather clothing and thermal wear. Large stock holdings of stainless steel fixtures and fittings and a comprehensive range of general chandlery including rigging facilities.

MAX WALKER YACHT DELIVERIES
Zinderneuf Sailing, PO Box 105, Macclesfield, Cheshire SK10 2EY. Tel (01625) 431742 Fax (01625) 619704 e-mail: mwyd.@clara.net Fixed price deliveries. Sailing yachts delivered with care in north west European, UK and Eire waters by RYA/DoT yachtmaster and crew - 30 years' experience. Owners welcome. Tuition if required. References available. Your enquiries welcome 24 hours.

SEALAND BOAT DELIVERIES LTD
Tower, Liverpool Marina, Coburg Wharf, Liverpool L3 4BP. Tel (01254) 705225 Fax (01254) 776582 e-mail: ros@mcr1.pop tel.org.uk Nationwide and European road transporters of all craft. No weight limit. We never close. Irish service. Worldwide shipping agents. Extrication of yachts from workshops and building yards. Salvage contractors. Established 27 years. Website: www.btx.co.uk

SIMPSON-LAWRENCE GROUP LIMITED
National Contact Line: 0870 9000 597 Website: www.simpson-lawrence.com

WARD & McKENZIE (North West) LTD
2 Healey Court, Burnley, Lancashire BB11 2QJ. Tel/Fax (01282) 420102 e-mail: marinesurvey@wmnw.freeserve.co.uk National and International marine surveyors. Technical and legal consultants. Contact: Bob Sheffield - Mobile: 0370 667457. Website: www.ward-mckenzie.co.uk

WHITEHAVEN HARBOUR MARINA
Harbour Commissioners, Pears House, 1 Duke Street, Whitehaven, Cumbria CA28 7HW. Tel (01946) 692435 Fax (01946) 691135 VHF Ch12 Long and short-term berths available at newly created 100 capacity marina, maximum length 12m. Eleven hectare permanent locked harbour with 45 tonne boat hoist, access at least HW ±3hours. Sheltered historic location adjacent to town centre.

WEST WALES, SOUTH WALES AND BRISTOL CHANNEL   (AREA 11)
Bardsey Island to Lands End

ABERYSTWYTH MARINA - IMP DEVELOPMENTS
Ylanfa-Aberystwyth Marina, Trefechan, Aberyswyth, Dyfed SY23 1AS. Tel (01970) 611422 Fax (01970) 624122 e-mail: abermarina@aol.com NEW fully serviced marina. Diesel, gas, water, toilets and hot showers.

BALTIC WHARF WATER LEISURE CENTRE
Bristol Harbour, Underfall Yard, Bristol BS1 6XG. Tel 0117-929 7608 Fax 0117-929 4454 Tuition: 0117-952 5202 Sailing school and centre, with qualified instruction in most watersports. Also moorings available throughout the Bristol harbour for all types of leisurecraft.

BOSUNS LOCKER CHANDLERY - MILFORD HAVEN
Cleddau House, Milford Marina, Milford Haven, Pembrokeshire SA73 3AF. Tel (01646) 697834 Fax (01646) 698009 Chandlery and cafe - Books, charts, engine spares, clothing, electronics, Blakes, Jotrun, International paints, inflatables. Special orders and mail order service. Weekly deliveries to Aberystwyth Marina. Website: www.bosunslocker.co.uk

 ## CREST NICHOLSON MARINAS LTD - BRISTOL
Parklands, Stoke Gifford, Bristol BS34 8QU. Tel 0117-923 6466 Fax 0117-923 6508 Marina development management and consultancy.Website:www.aboard.co.uk/c.n.marinas

 ## CREST NICHOLSON MARINAS LTD - PENARTH
Portway Village, Penarth, South Glamorgan CF64 1TQ. Tel 029 2070 5021 Fax 029 2071 2170 Situated within the sheltered waters of Cardiff Bay the marina provides fully serviced, secure berths and wide ranging ancilliary services. Open 24-hours, year round. We can assure visitors of a warm welcome. Please apply for details.

DALE SAILING COMPANY
Brunel Quay, Neyland, Milford Haven, Pembrokeshire SA73 1PY. Tel (01646) 601636 Fax (01646) 601061 Engine service and repair, hull repair, chandlery. Boatyard, lifting, boat building, sea school and new and used boat sales.

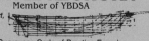

GEORGE REOHORN YBDSA SURVEYOR
Chancery Cottage, Gors Road, Burry Port, Carmarthenshire SA16 0EL. Tel/Fax (01554) 833281 Full condition and insurance surveys on pleasure and working vessels. Also Code of Pratice examiner. Approved British registration measurer. 36 years practical experience on GRP, timber, steel and ferro construction.

HAFAN PWLLHELI
Glan Don, Pwllheli, Gwynedd LL53 5YT. Tel (01758) 701219 Fax (01758) 701443 VHF Ch80 Hafan Pwllheli has over 400 pontoon berths and offers access at virtually all states of the tide. Ashore,its modern purpose-built facilities include luxury toilets, showers, landerette, a secure boat park for winter storage, 40-ton travel hoist, mobile crane and plenty of space for car parking. Open 24-hours a day, 7 days a week.

MILFORD MARINA
The Docks, Milford Haven, Pembrokeshire, West Wales SA73 3AE. Tel (01646) 696312 Fax (01646) 696314 Safe sheltered haven, 250 berths, 5 minutes from shopping, rail and bus services. Water and electricity to all berths. Staff available 24 hours. Restaurant, chandlery, electronics, boat repair, lifting and storage available on-site.

NEYLAND YACHT HAVEN LTD
Brunel Quay, Neyland, Pembrokeshire SA73 1PY. Tel (01646) 601601 Fax (01646) 600713 Marina operators with all facilities. 360 fully serviced pontoon berths in a sheltered, tree lined marina. On-site services include boatyard, sailmaker, sailing school, chandlery, cafe, lounge/bar, launderette, showers and toilets. 30 visitor berths. 24-hour access and security.

W F PRICE & CO LTD
Northpoint House, Wapping Wharf, Bristol BS1 6UD. Tel 0117-929 2229 Books and charts. DoT Certified Compass Adjusters - available day or night.

ROWLANDS MARINE ELECTRONICS LTD
Pwllheli Marina Centre, Glan Don, Pwllheli, Gwynedd LL53 5YT. Tel (01758) 613193 Fax (01758) 613617 BEMA and BMIF members, dealer for Autohelm, B&G, Cetrek, ICOM, Kelvin Hughes, Marconi, Nasa, Navico, Navstar, Neco, Seafarer, Shipmate, Stowe, Racal-Decca, V-Tronix, Ampro and Walker. Equipment supplied, installed and serviced.

RUDDERS BOATYARD & MOORINGS
Church Road, Burton, Milford Haven, Pembrokeshire SA73 1NU. Tel (01646) 600288 Moorings, pontoon, storage. All repairs.

SIMPSON-LAWRENCE GROUP LIMITED
National Contact Line: 0870 9000 597 Website: www.simpson-lawrence.com

First class service at value for money prices, plus the beautiful Gower coastline equals Swansea Marina!

Telephone 01792 470310 for further information.
Lockside, Maritime Quarter, Swansea, West Glamorgan SA1 1WG.

SWANSEA MARINA
Lockside, Maritime Quarter, Swansea, West Glamorgan SA1 1WG. Tel (01792) 470310 Fax (01792) 463948 Access all states of the tide except LWST. City centre marina, restaurants, theatres etc. Call us on Ch 18 or 80 to check locking times. Visitors always welcome - a good destination for your annual trip.

THE UNITED KINGDOM HYDROGRAPHIC OFFICE
Admiralty Way, Taunton, Somerset TA1 2DN. Tel (01823) 337900 Fax (01823) 284077 The UKHO publishes a worldwide series of navigational charts and publications, distributed through chart agents. Small craft folios and editions are derived from standard charts, but are tailored to be ideal for yachtsmen. **Website:** www.ukho.gov.uk

WARD & McKENZIE (South Wales) LTD
58 The Meadows, Marshfield, Cardiff CF3 8AY. Tel (01633) 680280 National and International marine surveyors. Technical and legal consultants. Contact: Kevin Ashworth - Mobile: 07775 938666. **Website:**   www.ward-

WORCESTER YACHT CHANDLERS LTD
Unit 7, 75 Waterworks Road, Barbourne, Worcester WR1 3EZ

We stock paints, ropes, clothing, footwear, bottled gas, navigation and buoyancy aids. Engine service, oils, crane, haulage.
Motor boats and rowing boats available.
Travel upstream on the river Severn and discover idyllic picnic spots.
Tel: 01905 22522/27949

WORCESTER YACHT CHANDLERS LTD
Unit 7, 75 Waterworks Road, Barbourne, Worcester WR1 3EZ. Tel (01905) 22522 & 27949 Chandlery, paints, ropes, cables, chain, clothing, footwear, shackles, books, bottled gas, anti-foul, fastenings, oakam, fenders. Hard storage, crane, haulage, engine service, oils, navigation aids, buoyancy aids, life jackets, distress flares, *small boat hire.*

SOUTHERN IRELAND   (AREA 12)
Malahide , south to Liscanor Bay

Liscanor Bay — Malahide

CARLINGFORD MARINA - IRELAND
Carlingford, Co Louth, Ireland. Tel/Fax +353 42 73492 VHF Ch16 and 37 (M) Superb location in beautiful setting close to historic village of Carlingford, our friendly marina provides a top class service for all boat users. Moorings, chandlery, slipway, 16-ton cranage, power, diesel, water, laundry, showers and coffee shop. Visitors always welcome. New restaurant and bar complex now open and welcoming. *Sailing Holidays in Ireland - Only the Best.*

CASTLEPARK MARINA - IRELAND
Kinsale, Co Cork, Ireland. Tel +353 21 774959 Fax +353 21 774958 100-berth fully serviced marina with restaurant, laundry, showers and toilets. Waterside hostel-type accommodation available. New restaurant catering for both breakfast and evening meals. Access at all stages of the tide. *Sailing Holidays in Ireland - Only the Best.*

CREST NICHOLSON MARINAS LTD - MALAHIDE (Marketing Agents) Malahide Marina, Malahide, Co Dublin, Ireland. +353 1 845 4129 Fax +353 1 845 4255 Situated within Malahide's estuary north of Dublin Bay. Full range of marina facilities available.

CROSSHAVEN BOATYARD MARINA - IRELAND
Crosshaven, Co Cork, Ireland. Tel +353 21 831161 Fax +353 21 831603 All facilities at this 100-berth marina situated 12 miles from Cork City and close to ferryport and airport. Travel lift, full repair and maintenance services, spray painting and approved International Gelshield centre. Storage undercover and outside for 250 boats. Brokerage. RNLI and Defence contractors. *Sailing Holidays in Ireland - Only the Best.*

DINGLE MARINA - IRELAND
Harbour Master, Strand Street, Dingle, Co Kerry, Ireland. Tel +353 66 9151629 Fax +353 66 9152629 e-mail: dingle marina@tinet.ie Europe's most westerly marina on the beautiful south west coast of Ireland in the heart of the old sheltered fishing port of Dingle. Visitor berths, fuel and water. Shops, 52 pubs and many restaurants with traditional music and hospitality. Harbour easily navigable day or night. *Sailing Holidays in Ireland - Only the Best.*

DINGLE SEA VENTURES YACHT CHARTER
Dingle, Co Kerry, Ireland. Tel +353 66 52244 Fax +353 66 52313 e-mail: jgreany@iol.ie Bareboat charter, skippered charter, sailing tuition on south west coast of Ireland: One way charter. Dingle-Kinsale-Dingle - 1997 and 1998 fleet of eight boats 31' - 44'. Close to all ferries and airports. Personal, friendly service. PINTS OF PEACE.

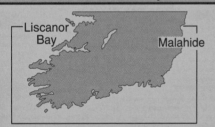

★ BAREBOAT CHARTER ★ SKIPPERED CHARTER ★ SAILING TUITION
IRELAND
SOUTH WEST COAST
One-way charter: Dingle-Kinsale-Dingle   Personal friendly service
1998 Fleet of Boats   YCA Bond No. 95019
Close to all ferries and airports   Pints of Peace!
Dingle Sea Ventures, Dingle, County Kerry, Ireland.
Tel: +353 66 52244 Fax: +353 66 52313 e-mail:jgreany@iol.ie

FENIT HARBOUR MARINA - IRELAND
Fenit, Co Kerry, Ireland. Tel/Fax +353 66 36231 A new marina opened in July 1997 with 104 berths for all sizes of boat up to 15m x 3m draught, with one berth available for larger vessels up to 30m. Access at all tides. Minimum approach depth 5m. Facilities include smartcard access, toilets, showers, laundry and harbour office. Visitors are welcome to use the superb clubhouse facilities of the Tralee Sailing Club and participate in races Tuesdays. *Sailing Holidays in Ireland - only the best*

SAIL into The Haven Arms Pub and Restaurant
Landmark to generations of local people and visitors alike. Awarded several Bar Food Awards over the years. A traditional Irish welcome from your hosts Gerry and Gretta Malone. Henry Street, Kilrush, Co Clare, Ireland.
Tel: 00 353 65 51267 Fax: 00 353 65 51213   Kilrush

THE HAVEN ARMS PUB & RESTAURANT
Henry Street, Kilrush, Co Clare, Ireland. Tel +353 65 51267 Fax +353 65 51213 'The Haven Arms' - Kilrush - *Sail* into this pub and restaurant which has become a landmark to generations of local people and visitor alike. The 'Ship' restaurant offers appetising meals complemented by good service from our friendly staff. MOORINGS ARE FREE.

HOWTH MARINA - IRELAND
Howth, Co Dublin, Ireland. Tel +353 1 8392777 Fax +353 1 8392430 Modern marina in beautiful sheltered location. Fully serviced berths with every facility and 24-hour security. Very popular marina for traffic in the Irish Sea. Is available at all states of the tide with extremely easy access. *Sailing Holidays in Ireland - Only the Best.* **Website: www.hss.ac.uk**

KILMORE QUAY MARINA - IRELAND
Kilmore Quay, Co Wexford, Ireland. Tel/Fax +353 53 29955 Kilmore Quay in the south east of Ireland has a new Blue Flag marina

with 20 pontoon visitor berths. This friendly fishing port has pleasant hotel facilities, pubs and restaurants offering a traditional Irish welcome. Rosslare ferryport is only 15 miles away. *Sailing Holidays in Ireland - Only the Best.*

KILRUSH MARINA - IRELAND
Kilrush, Co Clare, Ireland. Tel +353 65 9052072 Fax +353 65 9051692 e-mail: kem@shannon.dev.ie Mobile: +353 87 2313870 VHF Ch80 Kilrush Marina on Ireland's beautiful west coast, is a new marina with 120 fully serviced berths. The marina has all shore facilities including a modern boatyard with 45-ton hoist. It adjoins the busy market town of Kilrush which has every facility required by the visiting yachtsman. *Sailing Holidays in Ireland - Only the Best.* Website: www.shannon-dev.ie/kcm

king sitRic FISH RESTAURANT & ACCOMMODATION
East Pier,　Howth, Dublin, Established 1971
Ireland. *Tel: +353 1 832 5235 & 6729 Fax: +353 1 839 2442*
Situated on the harbour front - your hosts Aidan and Joan MacManus offer a traditional Irish welcome. Superb, fresh seafood. Summer lunch, dinner all year. Quality accommodation now available

KING SITRIC FISH RESTAURANT & ACCOMMODATION
East Pier, Howth, Co Dublin, Ireland. Tel +353 1 832 5235 & 6729 Fax +353 1 839 2442 Lovely location on the harbour front. Marina and Howth Yacht Club 3 minutes walk. Established 1971, Aidan and Joan MacManus have earned an international reputation for superb, fresh seafood, service and hospitality. Wine connoisseurs take note! Quality accommodation now available. Informal summer lunch -dinner all year.

KINSALE YACHT CLUB MARINA
Kinsale, Co Cork, Ireland. Tel +353 21 772196 Fax +353 21 774455 e-mail: kyc@iol.ie Magnificent deep water yacht club marina offering Kinsale hospitality to visiting yachtsmen. Full facilities include berths up to 20 metres, fresh water, electricity, diesel on pier. Club bar and wealth of pubs and restaurants in Kinsale. Enter Kinsale Harbour - lit at night - no restrictions.

Kinsale Yacht Club Marina
Kinsale, Co Cork, Ireland. Tel: +353 21 772196
Fax: +353 21 774455 e-mail: kyc@iol.ie
BLUE FLAG MARINA IN THE HEART OF KINSALE
Facilities: Deep water marina - fresh water - electricity
yacht club bar - restaurant - showers - W.C.
1 minute's walk to Kinsale town - The "Gourmet Capital" of Ireland with a wealth of bars, restaurants, shops and entertainment.

LAWRENCE COVE MARINA - IRELAND
Bere Island, Bantry Bay, Co Cork, Ireland. Tel/Fax +353 27 75044 Lawrence Cove Marina is situated in Bantry Bay in the south west corner of Ireland in the heart of the best cruising ground in Europe. It is a new marina, family run with full facilities and a very safe haven to leave a boat. It is two hours from Cork airport with good connections. *Sailing Holidays in Ireland - Only the Best.*

MALAHIDE MARINA - IRELAND
Malahide, Co Dublin, Ireland. Tel +353 1 8454129 Fax +353 1 8454255 Located next to the picturesque village of Malahide our marina village is the ideal spot to enjoy and relax. There are 350 fully serviced berths, petrol and diesel available, 30-ton hoist with full boatyard facilities with winter storage ashore or afloat. A fine selection of shops, and friendly pubs and restaurants serving good food are close by. *Sailing Holidays in Ireland - Only the Best.*

CASTLEPARK MARINA
Kinsale, Co Cork, Eire. *Tel: +353 21 774959*
Fax: +353 21 774958
100 berth fully serviced marina. Access at all stages of tide. Located within picturesque Kinsale Harbour with ferry service to town. New marina centre located next to Dock pub. Facilities include hot showers, toilets, laundry, waterside hostel accommodation and restaurant open all day. MARITIME TOURISM LIMITED

MARITIME TOURISM LTD - CASTLEPARK MARINA
Kinsale, Co Cork, Ireland. Tel +353 21 774959 Fax +353 21 774958 100-berth fully serviced marina with restaurant, laundry, showers and toilets. Waterside hotel-type accommodation available. New restaurant catering for both breakfast and evening meals. Access at all stages of the tide.

SALVE MARINE LTD - IRELAND
Crosshaven, Co Cork, Ireland. Tel +353 21 831145 Fax +353 21 831747 The marina is situated just 20 minutes from Cork City, Cork airport and Ringaskiddy ferry port. Located yards from Royal Cork yacht club and Crosshaven village centre. Facilities for yachts up to 140' x 14' draught including mains electricity 240/380 volts, telephone, fax, toilets and showers. Welding and machining in stainless steel, aluminium and bronze. Repairs and maintenance to hulls and rigging. Routine and detailed engine maintenance. Slip. *Sailing holidays in Ireland - only the best.*

SIMPSON-LAWRENCE GROUP LIMITED
National Contact Line: 0870 9000 597 Website: www.simpson-lawrence.com

TRAMEX LTD
Shankill Business Centre, Shankill, Co Dublin, Ireland. Tel+353 1 282 3688 Fax +353 1 282 7880 e-mail: tramex@iol.ie Manufacturers of Moisture Metre and osmosis detection instruments for boats. Website: www.tramexltd.com

UK/McWILLIAM SAILMAKERS
Crosshaven, Co Cork, Ireland. Tel +353 21 831505 Fax +353 21 831700 e-mail: ukireland@uksailmakers.com Ireland's premier sailmaker, prompt repairs and service.

WATERFORD CITY MARINA - IRELAND
Waterford City, Ireland. Tel +353 51 309900 Fax +353 51 870813 Located right in the heart of the historic city centre. There are 80 fully serviced berths available. The marina has full security, with CCTV in operation. Showers available on shore in adjoining hostel. Wide range of shops, restaurants, pubs and other amenities available on the doorstep of the marina because of its unique city-centre location. Open all year with both winter and summer season rates available. *Sailing Holidays in Ireland - Only the Best.*

NORTHERN IRELAND　　　(AREA 13)
Lambay Island, north to Liscanor Bay

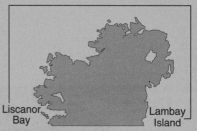

Liscanor Bay　　　　　Lambay Island

ANDREW JAGGERS - MARINE SURVEYOR & CONSULTANT
75 Clifton Road, Bangor, Co Down BT20 5HY. Tel 028 9145 5677 Fax 028 9146 5252 At Bangor Marina: 028 9145 3297 Fax 028 9145 3450 Mobile: 0385 768474 Claims investigations for all major insurers. Code of Compliance examiner. Expert Witness reports. Flag State Inspections. Consultant to solicitors, brokers, loss adjusters on marine and marina matters. Ireland, Isle of Man and West of Scotland.

CARRICKFERGUS WATERFRONT
The Marina' Rodger's Quay, Carrickfergus, Co Antrim, Northern Ireland BT38 8BE. Tel +44 (0) 28 93366666 Fax +44 (0) 28 93350505 e-mail: carrick.marina@virgin.net 300 fully serviced pontoon berths with excellent full on-shore facilities. Steeped in a wealth of historical legend. Carrickfergus has excellent restaurants, hotels, pubs, shops and a host of recreational leisure facilities.

COLERAINE MARINA
64 Portstewart Road, Coleraine, Co Londonderry, Northern Ireland BT52 1RS. Tel 028 7034 4768 Wide range of facilities.

 CREST NICHOLSON MARINAS LTD - BANGOR
Bangor Marina, Bangor, Co Down, N. Ireland BT20 5ED. Tel 028 9145 3297 Fax 028 9145 3450 Situated on the south shore of Belfast Lough, Bangor, is Ireland's largest and most comprehensive yachting facility. The marina is within convenient walking distance of all the town's amenities and may be accessed at any time of day or state of the tide (minimum depth 2.9 metres.)

PETER HALLAM MARINE SURVEYOR
83 Millisle Road, Donaghadee, Co Down, Northern Ireland BT21 0HZ. Tel/Fax 028 9188 3484 Surveys for yachts, fishing and commercial craft. Supervision of new buildings, repairs and specification writing for the same. Insurance assessments/ inspections and completed repairs. Tonnage measurement. Accident assessment/reports for solicitors. MSA Code of Practice surveys.

SIMPSON-LAWRENCE GROUP LIMITED
National Contact Line: 0870 9000 597 Website: www.simpson-lawrence.com

TODD CHART AGENCY LTD
4 Seacliff Road, The Harbour, Bangor, County Down, Northern Ireland BT20 5EY. Tel 028 9146 6640 Fax 028 9147 1070 e-mail: admiralty@toddchart.co.uk International Admiralty Chart Agent, chart correction service and nautical booksellers. Stockist of Imray charts and books, navigation and chartroom instruments, binoculars, clocks etc. UK agent for Icelandic Hydrographic Service. Mail order - Visa, Mastercard, American Express and Switch/Delta accepted.

CHANNEL ISLANDS   [AREA 14]
Guernsey, Jersey, Alderney.

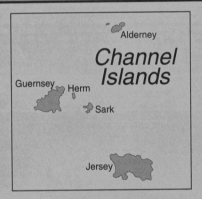

A B MARINE LTD
Castle Walk, St Peter Port, Guernsey, Channel Islands GY1 1AU. Tel (01481) 722378 Fax (01481) 711080 We specialise in safety and survival equipment and are a DoT approved service station for liferafts including R.F.D., Beaufort/Dunlop, Zodiac, Avon, Plastimo and Lifeguard. We also carry a full range of new liferafts, dinghies and lifejackets, and are agents for Bukh Marine engines.

BACHMANN MARINE SERVICES LTD
Frances House, Sir William Place, St Peter Port, Guernsey, Channel Islands GY1 4HQ.
Tel: 01481 723573 Fax: 01481 711353
E-mail: jamesa@bachmanngroup.com
Providing a personal and individual service to our clients.
Registration • corporate ownership • insurance management • crew placement

Please mention the Pink Page Directory when making enquiries

BACHMANN MARINE SERVICES LTD
Frances House, Sir William Place, St Peter Port, Guernsey, Channel Islands GY1 4HQ. Tel (01481) 723573 Fax (01481) 711353 British yacht registration, corporate yacht ownership and management, marine insurance, crew placement and management. Bachmann Marine Services aims to provide a personal and individual service to its clients.

BEAUCETTE MARINA
Vale, Guernsey, Channel Islands GY3 5BQ. Tel (01481) 45000 Fax (01481) 47071 e-mail: beaucette@premier-marinas.co.uk Situated on the north east coast, Beaucette is one of Europe's mostcharming deep water marinas. With 140 berths, the marina offers all the services and facilities you would expect. Beaucette is a PREMIER marina.

BOATWORKS +
Comprehensive range of services including chandlery with a good range of clothing, boatbuilders and repairs, boatyard facilities, fuel.
Castle Emplacement, St Peter Port, Guernsey GY1 1AU, Channel Islands. Tel (01481) 726071 Fax (01481) 714224

BOATWORKS + LTD
Castle Emplacement, St Peter Port, Guernsey, Channel Islands GY1 1AU. Tel (01481) 726071 Fax (01481) 714224 Boatworks+ provides a comprehensive range of services including boatbuilding and repairs, chandlery, clothing and fuel supplies.

A 'BUG' LURKS DEEP IN THE DIESEL TANK RECESSES
Avoid the risk of breakdown at sea or costly engine troubles caused by diesel fuel contamination (algae), by treating and protecting the fuel in your tank
CHICK'S MARINE LTD
is the sole distributor for
CM 89-1 DIESEL FUEL BIOCIDE
100ml bottle will treat up to 300 gallons
Price per bottle - £8 plus £1.25 p&p
500ml bottle - £35.00 plus £2.50 p&p
Collings Road, St Peter Port, Guernsey, Channel Islands.
Tel: (01481) 723716/(0860) 741305 Fax: (01481 713 632

CHICK'S MARINE LTD/VOLVO PENTA
Collings Road, St Peter Port, Guernsey, Channel Islands GY1 1FL. Tel (01481) 723716 Fax (01481) 713632 Distributor of diesel fuel biocide used to treat and protect contamination in fuel tanks where an algae (bug) is present. Most owners do not realise what the problem is, loss of power, blocked fuel filter, exhaust smoking, resulting in expensive repairs to injectors - fuel pump - or complete engine overhaul. Marine engineers, engines, spares, service - VAT free. Honda outboards, pumps and generators. Volvo Penta specialists.

JACKSON YACHT SERVICES
Le Boulevard, St Aubin, Jersey, Channel Islands JE3 8AB. Tel (01534) 743819 Fax (01534) 745952 Boatyard, chandler, sailoft, liferaft service, yacht management and brokerage.

Jersey Harbours
A warm welcome to visiting yachts!
St Helier Marina has 50 more finger berths for visitors, 5 Gold Anchor facilities. 3 hours ±HW. Berths available to lease from one month to 10 years in our new Elizabeth Marina
Maritime House, La Route du Port Elizabeth, St Helier, Jersey JE1 1HB.
Tel 01534 885588 Fax 01534 885599 e-mail: jsyhbr@itl.net

JERSEY HARBOURS
Maritime House, La Route du Port Elizabeth, St Helier, Jersey JE1 1HB. Tel (01534) 885588 Fax (01534) 885599 e-mail: jsyhbr@itl.net A warm welcome to visiting yachts! St Helier Marina has 50 more finger berths for visitors. 5-Gold Anchor facilities. 3 hours ±HW. Berths available to lease from one month to 10 years in our NEW ELIZABETH MARINA.

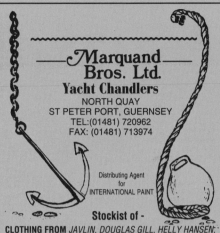

MARQUAND BROS LTD - Yacht Chandlers
North Quay, St Peter Port, Guernsey, Channel Islands.
Tel (01481) 720962 Fax (01481) 713974 Yacht chandlers, stockists
of a comprehensive range of marine products. Guernsey distributor
for International Coatings. Extensive leisure and marine clothing
department including Barbour, Driza-Bone, Dubarry and Quayside.

NORTH QUAY MARINE
North Side, St Sampson's Harbour, Guernsey, Channel Islands.
Tel (01481) 246561 Fax (01481) 243488 The complete boating
centre. Full range of chandlery, rope, chain, lubricants, paint,
boatwear and shoes. Fishing tackle for on-shore and on-board.
Inflatables and safety equipment. Electronics and small outboard
engines.

RADIO & ELECTRONIC SERVICES LTD
Les Chênes, Rohais, St Peter Port, Guernsey, Channel Islands
GY1 1FB. Tel (01481) 728837 Fax (01481) 714379 Chart Plotters,
GPS, Radars. Fixed and portable VHF, Autopilots. Programming
dealer for C-Map NT and Jotron EPIRBS. Sales and service dealers
for Furuno, Humminbird, Icom, KVH, Lowrance, Magellan,
Raytheon, Sailor and Shipmate.

ROSDEN GLASS FIBRE
La Rue Durell, La Collette, St Helier, Jersey JE2 3NB. Tel (01534)
625418 Fax (01534) 625419 Specialists in all types of glass fibre
marine works, structural repairs, alterations, re-flow coating, GEL
coat work. Blakes and International approved osmosis treatment
centre. Spray painting. Manufacturers of fuel tanks, bathing
platforms and boat builders. General refurbishment and polishing.
A division of Precision Plastics (Jersey) Ltd.

SARNIA FLAGS
8 Belmont Road, St Peter Port, Guernsey, Channel Islands GY1
1PY. Tel (01481) 725995 Fax (01481) 729335 Flags and pennants
made to order. National flags, house, club and battle flags, and
burgees made to order. Any size, shape or design. Prices on
request.

SIMPSON-LAWRENCE GROUP LIMITED
National Contact Line: 0870 9000 597 Website: www.simpson-
lawrence.com

PORTUGAL   (AREA 20)
Hendaye to Rio Miño

J GARRAIO & CO LTD
Avenida 24 de Julho, 2-1°, D-1200, Lisbon, Portugal.
Books and Charts.

GIBRALTER   (AREA 21)

Rio Guardiana to Gibraltar

G UNDERY & SONS
PO Box 235, Unit 31, The New Harbours, Gibraltar. Books and Charts. DoT Certified Compass Adjusters - available day or night.

BELGIUM & THE NETHERLANDS
                              (AREA 23)

Nieuwpoort to Delfzijl

BOGERD NAVTEC NV
Oude Leeuwenrui 37, Antwerp 2000, Belgium. Books and charts.

KELVIN HUGHES OBSERVATOR BV
Nieuwe Langeweg 41, 3194 DC Hoogvliet (Rt), Rotterdam, The Netherlands. Book and charts. DoT Certified Compass Adjusters - available day or night.

MARTIN & CO
Oude Leewenrui 37, Antwerp 2000, Belgium. Books and charts. DoT Certified Compass Adjusters - available day or night.

WARD & McKENZIE (Holland)
West End, Veendijk 22k, 1231 PD Loosdrecht, Holland. Tel +31 35 5827195 Fax +31 35 5828811 e-mail: technoserv@wxs.nl National and International marine surveyors. Technical and Legal Consultants. **Website: www.ward-mckenzie.co.uk**

DENMARK   (AREA 25)

Sylt to Skagen

IVER C WEILBACH & CO., A/S
35 Toldbodgade, Postbox 1560, DK-1253 Copenhagen K, Denmark. Books and charts.

MEDITERRANEAN

References outside the navigational scope of this volume

GRAHAM BOOTH MARINE SURVEYS
4 Epple, Birchington-on-Sea, Kent CT7 9AY. Tel (01843) 843793 Fax (01843) 846860 e-mail: gbms@clara.net Authorised for MCA Codes of Practice, most frequently on French and Italian Riviera - also for certification of Sail Training vessels and other commercial craft. Call UK office for further information. Other expert marine consultancy services also available.

GREEK SAILS YACHT CHARTER
21 The Mount, Kippax, Leeds LS25 7NG. Tel/Fax 0113-232 0926 Freephone 0800 731 8580 e-mail: greek_sails_uk@msn.com Bareboat yacht charter throughout Greece and the islands. Flotilla based in Corfu and the Ionian Islands. Family dinghy sailing holidays in Corfu. Skippered charter and sail training.

OCEAN SAFETY
Centurian Industrial Park, Bitterne Road West, Southampton, Hampshire SO18 1UB. Tel 023 8033 3334 Fax 023 8033 3360 e-mail: enquiries@oceansafety.com Your Life Saving Supplier: Liferafts, lifejackets, MOB, flares, fire fighting, medical, EPIRBS. In addition to our extensive product range we also boast two of the largest liferaft, lifejacket and inflatable service stations in Europe with the introduction of our facility in Palma de Mallorca, Spain. A product advice service is available for customers who need to comply with ORC or Code of Practice Charter regulations.

WARD & McKENZIE (Balearics)
C/Gral Antonio Barcelo No 2 Esc A lo 2a, E-07015, Palma de Mallorca, Spain. Tel/Fax +34 971 701148 e-mail: yacht_surveyor @compuserve.com National and International marine surveyors. Technical and legal consultants. Contact: Peter Green - Mobile: +34 61 992 6053. **Website: www.ward-mckenzie.co.uk**